12001285

The Dartnell

PERSONNEL
ADMINISTRATION
HANDBOOK

DARTNELL is a publisher serving the world of business with business books, business manuals, business newsletters and bulletins, training materials for business executives, managers, supervisors, salesmen, financial officials, personnel executives and office employees. In addition, Dartnell produces management and sales training films and cassettes, publishes many useful business forms, conducts scores of management seminars for business men and women and has many of its materials and films available in languages other than English. Dartnell, established in 1917, serves the world's whole business community. For details, catalogs, and product information, address: DARTNELL, 4660 N. Ravenswood Avenue, Chicago, Illinois 60640, USA—or phone (312) 561-4000.

OTHER DARTNELL HANDBOOKS

Advertising Manager's Handbook
Direct Mail and Mail Order Handbook
Office Administration Handbook
Marketing Manager's Handbook
Public Relations Handbook
Sales Manager's Handbook
Sales Promotion Handbook

The Dartnell

PERSONNEL ADMINISTRATION
Handbook

by
Wilbert E. Scheer

THIRD EDITION

THIRD EDITION
First Printing

Copyright © 1985
in the United States, Canada and Great Britain by
THE DARTNELL CORPORATION
All rights reserved

FIRST EDITION 1969

SECOND EDITION 1979

Library of Congress Catalog Card
Number 76-77249

ISBN 0-85013-148-0

Printed in the United States of America by
DARTNELL PRESS, CHICAGO, ILLINOIS 60640

DEDICATION

First and always, to the memory of my dear wife Erna, who all her
life had to contend with my peregrinations into the field of writing;
Second, to the many people and their companies who have contributed so much in the way of ideas, illustrations and case histories;
Finally, to the people who use this personnel handbook, in search of
guidance in specific situations;
I respectfully dedicate this book.

INTRODUCTION:

THE PERSONNEL ADMINISTRATION HANDBOOK: IT CAN DOUBLE YOUR PRODUCTIVITY

by EDWIN B. GILROY

General Manager

Los Angeles Office

Selection Research, Inc.

Lincoln, Nebraska

What follows these introductory pages is a marvelous source of personnel know-how written for current application by a leading personnel practitioner. The basic design of the book is both simple and wonderful: To help you be a more effective personnel administrator.

I recommend the contents of the book, and recommend its use. Knowledge is its purpose, your success is its objective.

You will find the Personnel Administration Handbook comprehensive. The 14 sections embrace the whole gamut of personnel topics. In fact, over 500 subjects are covered. Alphabetically, the subjects begin with absenteeism, accidents and automation; and range through vision, wills and zero defects.

While topically wide-ranging, the book is also timely. The Second Edition of the Personnel Administration Handbook updates knowledge for the late 1970's and 1980's. The facts are fresh. The concepts recognize much has changed in commerce and industry since the First Edition (which ran into its third printing) was published in 1969. Examples of newer subjects are Assessment Centers, Business Social Climate, Multiphasic Screening and Personnel Data Systems. Yet, classic and germane subjects are not ignored. Quite to the contrary. Employment, compensation, employee relations, training and union negotiations are subjects rewritten with contemporary foundations and futuristic ideas.

The author belongs to the school of philosophy that recognizes techniques are important and must be learned. But it is their human implications that make them effective and you successful. The author has tried to reach for examples which have utility and ideas that work: ideas generated in the caldron of competition and which have been tested for results in the arena of action. Applications for the ideas are possible in banking, finance and insurance; retail and wholesale business; light and heavy manufacturing; and government. Such a wide range of application requires a book easily read; hence, easy to use. The book's utility is one of its charms.

Ease of use is, of course, one of the keys to the book's value. But then, I would expect such a standard. After all, the author and publisher are noted for their pragmatism and superior quality. So, help yourself! Keep the Personnel Administration Handbook handy. Feel free to use it generously and know at all times you are on the right track.

THE FUTURE IS NOW

Linking People and Business

The success of any company is merely the sum total of the success of its people. The Personnel Administration Handbook can tell you "what"; that's the knowledge part. It can tell you "how"; that's the systematic side. But, it cannot tell you "when" or "where"; that's the artistic oil that lubricates the technical applications. Only your professional acumen can tell you "when" and "where" to take timely and effective action. Action which results in better performance, a satisfied employee, a problem resolved, a grievance settled or whatever is needed to handle the situation.

In my judgment, the greatest need in our vocation today is to link our personnel actions with the objectives of our organizations, the values of our employees and the needs of both. Indeed, I consider this linkage to be mandatory. Gone are the days of "keeping up with the Jones Company," picking-off the ideas of the corporate "winners," or doing a survey to determine what is "safe" and "trendy." We need to anticipate and respond to the basic needs of our own organizations. Not the needs, practices or policies of someone else. We are managing in a time of great social, political and economic re-evaluation.

The objectives of an organization flow from its underlying economic and social legitimacy and its utility. The market place is the arena where this legitimacy and utility are determined. Our satisfied customers and productive employees are a large part of the evidence of the legitimacy.

To contribute to an organization's objectives, a Personnel Director must be able to identify such crucial factors as its market position, capital structure and basic strengths. Then, to support these strengths and add to them.

Simultaneously, we must be able to identify limitations of our economic resources and organization's abilities. These limitations are very real. We must neutralize them or minimize them. To ignore them may mean we contribute to corporate failure.

The values of our employees flow from their early life experiences and environment. They can only be understood by listening or learning about them through our first-line supervisors, employee opinion or attitude surveys, and value studies.

Probably, the greatest danger for a Personnel Director is to believe he or she has the know-how without the test of learning first-hand about the real values and needs of employees. The key to the future for Personnel lies with concern about asking the right questions; not whether we possess the right answers.

It may seem easier "to follow a leader" or "keep up with the Joneses," but our responsibilities require careful thought about our actions. Linking them with business needs in real-life situations is the way of the future.

THE FUTURE IS NOW

Living Leadership

The way of the future may be difficult to envision in sharp detail, with clear exposition for all to comprehend. Yet, there are distinctive trends. They can be detected. Even more, they can be used as guides to apply our actions.

The industrial and commercial world of western civilization is in transition from a nationalistic, independent capital base to an inter-dependent, economic-social capital base. The causes are many, with origins rooted into our evolving from agrarianism to commercialism to industrialism. Technology, education, communication, affluence, in-dustrial efficiency, natural resources, military defense and political un-rest all are components which weigh on the forces moving to the future. The effect, at present, is economic, political and social turbulence. The outlook over the next 10 to 20 years is more of the same.

At our level of perspective and action, people are now as important as profits. Social legislation across the world points to a growing con-cern for human life and quality of living. Occupational safety and health laws are not confined to the North American continent. Nor are em-ployee rights relative to job opportunity, job value and retirement income. These subjects all reflect a shift to a new order of social priori-ties.

Yet, profits are needed to fuel the future investments in technology and social legislation and change. Such profits can be generated only by people, working with a sustained level of productivity and satisfac-tion at or near their level of capability and interest. For although there is a reordering of social priorities, no one has reordered poverty to replace affluence or economic well-being with a depression. We appear to be moving toward a broader base of economic wealth coupled with an awareness of social purpose. Social capitalism is gaining momentum.

The transition to a more clearly defined economic, political and social structure may well take two, three, possibly four decades. Who knows? During this transitional period, Personnel Directors can catalyze the efforts of managers and employees to satisfy customers, owners and themselves, simultaneously generating profits for distribution and reinvestment.

THE FUTURE IS NOW

We are Living it.

The seers of academia, industry, commerce, and government concur on the meaning of the shift to emphasis on improving the quality of life. They believe the character and the living processes of the late 20th and early 21st centuries are visible. Clearly, the trends emphasize that people are as important as profits, quality transcends quantity, and living well is replacing existing. These distinctive and visible trends provide personnel administrators with a great opportunity to contribute to productivity and better living.

We can become part of the excitement of shaping new institutions and reshaping older ones. The Personnel Administration Handbook provides us with a resource to be participants in the reordering of our economies rather than just spectators. It is time to contribute to the success of our employers, not trail the efforts of our marketing, engineering, and producing colleagues. The Handbook will be an ally on these necessary attempts to contribute to productivity. Use it frequently and treat it well.

ACKNOWLEDGMENTS

Author and publisher are grateful to the following for their valuable contributions to this handbook:

INDIVIDUALS

FRED T. ALLEN
JOHN W. ANNAS
WALTER E. BAER
ROLF G. BRUHL,
    Buenos Aires, Argentina
JOHN KING BRUUN
PHILIP B. CROSBY
ARNOLD R. DEUTSCH
HAROLD W. DICKHUT
EDWIN B. GILROY
WINNIE GRAY
W. F. HACHMEISTER
SYDNEY J. HARRIS
AMY K. HARTMAN
WILLIAM H. HILL
C. L. HOKONSON
HARRY LEVINSON, PH.D.

LUCILLE S. LUCAS
KIM MCLYNN
LEWIS A. MELTZER
KARL H. METTKE
GEORGE S. ODIORNE, PH.D.
KEITH L. OESTREICH
JUANITA RILEY
PAUL H. SHEATS, DEAN
JACK C. STAEHLE
GEORGE R. TERRY, PH.D.
MICHAEL J. THARP
GEORGE R. THOMPSON
WILLIAM H. VAUGHT, JR.
WILLIAM M. WALSH
ROY W. WALTERS
ERIC WEBSTER (THE LATE)
EDWIN R. WERNER

CORPORATIONS AND ASSOCIATIONS

ACTION FOR INDEPENDENT MATURITY (AIM)
ADMINISTRATIVE MANAGEMENT SOCIETY
AMAX, INC.
AMERICAN HOSPITAL SUPPLY
AMERICAN PREPAID LEGAL SERVICES INSTITUTE
AMERICAN SOCIETY FOR PERSONNEL ADMINISTRATION
AMSTERDAM PRINTING AND LITHO CORPORATION
BADGE-A-MINIT, LTD.
BENEFICIAL MANAGEMENT CORPORATION
BLUE CROSS AND BLUE SHIELD ASSOCIATIONS
BLUE CROSS-BLUE SHIELD OF GEORGIA/COLUMBUS, INC.
BUREAU OF INDUSTRIAL RELATIONS,
    Graduate School of Business, University of Michigan
BURGESS-NORTON MANUFACTURING COMPANY
CADDYLAK SYSTEMS, INC.
CANNON MILLS COMPANY
CANTEEN CORPORATION
CARPENTER TECHNOLOGY CORPORATION
CHAMBER OF COMMERCE OF THE UNITED STATES
CHICAGO LIGHTHOUSE FOR THE BLIND
CHICAGO TRIBUNE
CHINA CLAY ASSOCIATION, Cornwall, England
CINCINNATI TIME RECORDER COMPANY
COOK COUNTY SCHOOL OF NURSING
CREDIT UNION NATIONAL ASSOCIATION, INC.
DOMINION FOUNDRIES AND STEEL, Hamilton, Ontario, Canada

DOW CHEMICAL COMPANY
ECONOMICS PRESS, INC.
EQUITABLE LIFE ASSURANCE SOCIETY
EXXON COMPANY, USA
FLICK-REEDY CORPORATION
FRITO-LAY, INC.
GAMBLERS ANONYMOUS
GREATER BOSTON HOSPITAL COUNCIL
GRUMMAN AEROSPACE CORPORATION
GTE AUTOMATIC ELECTRIC, INC.
HOSPITAL CARE CORPORATION
ILLINOIS STATE CHAMBER OF COMMERCE
INFORMATION SCIENCE, INC.
INLAND STEEL COMPANY
INTERNATIONAL BUSINESS MACHINES CORPORATION (IBM)
INTERNATIONAL MINERALS & CHEMICAL CORPORATION
INTERNATIONAL SALT COMPANY
JOHNSON, S. C., & SON, INC.
KIMBERLY-CLARK CORPORATION
LEAR SIEGLER, INC.
LEVI STRAUSS & COMPANY
MCMURRY COMPANY
MICHIGAN MILLERS MUTUAL INSURANCE COMPANY
MIDAMERICA COMMODITY EXCHANGE
MIDLOCK COMPANY
MIDWEST INDUSTRIAL MANAGEMENT ASSOCIATION
MONTGOMERY WARD & COMPANY
MOTOWN RECORD CORPORATION
NATIONAL ASSOCIATION OF SUGGESTION SYSTEMS
NATIONAL INDUSTRIAL RECREATION ASSOCIATION
NATIONAL INSTITUTE FOR OCCUPATIONAL HEALTH
NATIONAL LABOR RELATIONS BOARD
NATIONAL RESEARCH BUREAU, INC.
NATIONAL RIGHT TO WORK COMMITTEE
NATIONAL SAFETY COUNCIL
NATIONAL SECRETARIES ASSOCIATION (International)
NATIONWIDE INSURANCE COMPANIES
NEWCOMB & SAMMONS
NORTHERN TRUST COMPANY, THE
OFFICE & PROFESSIONAL EMPLOYEES INTERNATIONAL UNION (OPEIU)
PARSONS PINE PRODUCTS, INC.
PENNSYLVANIA STATE UNIVERSITY
PENNSYLVANIA TIRE AND RUBBER COMPANY OF MISSISSIPPI, INC.
PERFORMANCE INCENTIVES CORPORATION
PERSONAL CENSUS SERVICE BRANCH, BUREAU OF THE CENSUS
PRAIRIE STATE SCREW AND BOLT CORPORATION
PRATT & WHITNEY AIRCRAFT GROUP
PROCTER & GAMBLE COMPANY, THE
PROFIT SHARING RESEARCH FOUNDATION
PUBLIC UTILITY DISTRICT NO. 1 OF KLICKITAT COUNTY,
     Goldendale, California
REID, JOHN E., AND ASSOCIATES
ROYAL BANK OF CANADA, Montreal, Quebec, Canada
SCIENCE RESEARCH ASSOCIATES, INC.
SOCIAL SECURITY ADMINISTRATION

ACKNOWLEDGMENTS

SZABO FOOD SERVICE
TELEX COMMUNICATIONS, INC.
THILLENS CHECASHERS
3M COMPANY
TOASTMASTERS INTERNATIONAL
UNITED PARCEL SERVICE
UNITED STATES DEPARTMENT OF LABOR
WESTERN ELECTRIC
WOODWARD GOVERNOR COMPANY
ZENITH RADIO CORPORATION

ABOUT WILBERT E. SCHEER

WILBERT E. SCHEER'S varied experience in all aspects of personnel administration qualified him to write and compile this definitive handbook. Since the first edition was published in 1969 there have been all sorts of developments, changes, improvements in laws and attitudes in this dynamic field. In this completely-revised edition, he has taken cognizance of all of these and also enlisted the experience and practices of many individuals and corporations.

For many years he was Director of Personnel of Blue Cross-Blue Shield, Chicago. Before that he was Personnel Director for The Illinois Agricultural Association and its 19 affiliated companies. He also has taught on the faculties of Maine Township High School, Central YMCA, University of Chicago and Northwestern University.

His education embraces Northwestern University, Medill School of Journalism, University of Illinois, University of Chicago, Washington & Jefferson College and the University of Michigan.

Wil Scheer has been a guest lecturer at many universities including Wisconsin, Marquette, Northern Illinois, Southern Illinois, Toledo, Notre Dame and many others. Companies and associations have utilized his services as a seminar leader in various aspects of office administration and personnel management.

He has authored the following books:

"You Can Improve Your Communication," published by *Personnel Journal.*

"The Art of Successful Self-Expression and Communication," published by *Motivation, Inc.*

"Corporate Growth Through Internal Management Development," published by *The Dartnell Corporation*.

"How to Develop an Effective Company Growth Plan," published by *The Dartnell Corporation*.

He has authored more than 300 articles in national and trade magazines in the United States, as well as in Canada, Argentina and Belgium.

He is a member of MENSA and among his many awards are the International Speaker's Award for 1957 and 1958 (both by Administrative Management Society) and the Diamond Merit Award Key—1961; for three successive years he won the Award for Merit of the Research Institute of America.

CONTENTS

Introduction by Edwin B. Gilroy

Functions of personnel . . . personnel responsibilities and relationships . . . personnel director . . . philosophy of management
. . . human assets . . . B-U-S-I-N-E-S-S . . .
ethics . . . workaholics . . . personnel administration . . . personnel research . . . fringe
benefits . . . turnover research . . . major
laws affecting personnel . . . periodicals.

Table of organization . . . manpower inventory and forecasting . . . manpower planning
. . . assessing the labor market . . . acquisition cost . . . recruitment . . . college recruiting . . . management trainees . . . executive
search . . . help-wanted ads . . . The Public
Employment Service . . . hiring the handicapped . . . temporary help . . . part-time
workers . . . job resumes.

Interviewing . . . Dartnell forms . . . selection . . . testing . . . test validation . . . reference checks . . . moving policy . . .

employment contract . . . transfers . . . promotions . . . demotions . . . terminations . . .
severance pay . . . how good are firing practices? . . . layoffs . . . outplacement . . . exit
interviews . . . why employees quit . . . affirmative action . . . sex equality . . . two-
career families . . . two-shift families . . . age
discrimination . . . compliances.

Induction . . . indoctrination . . . sponsors
. . . bulletin boards . . . company meetings
. . . orientation . . . employee communications . . . employee handbook . . . employee
publications . . . zero defects . . . motivation
. . . attitude . . . stress . . . job enrichment.

On-the-job instruction . . . telephone courtesy . . . telemarketing . . . creative business
writing . . . secretary . . . employee education . . . training films . . . adult education
. . . retraining . . . supervision . . . supervisory training . . . assessment center . . . executive development . . . second careers . . .
PERT . . . time management . . . human factors in management . . . temporary task force
. . . outside consultants . . . management
meetings . . . leadership styles.

Employment physical examinations . . . company doctor/clinic . . . health services and

education . . . cancer detection . . . alcoholism . . . drug use and abuse . . . ongoing
physical examinations . . . safety programs
and education . . . occupational health . . .
OSHA.

Company-sponsored employee activities . . .
service recognition . . . credit union . . . suggestion system . . . employee lounge . . .
employee cafeterias . . . purchase discounts
. . . recreation programs . . . office collections . . . employee complaints and grievances . . . counseling . . . problem employees
. . . wage assignments . . . transportation
. . . parking . . . music . . . check cashing
. . . payroll automation.

Employee compensation . . . methods of pay
. . . incentive pay . . . deferred compensation
. . . cost-of-hiring increases . . . payroll deductions . . . guaranteed wage . . . overtime
. . . shift differential . . . job evaluation . . .
job analysis . . . job descriptions . . . wage
administration . . . salary surveys . . . performance rating . . . exempt positions . . .
Equal Pay Act.

Fringe benefit programs . . . group insurance
. . . employee health insurance programs . . .
health care or illness care . . . group insurance trends . . . sick pay . . . group disability

income insurance . . . medical-surgical insurance . . . Blue Cross and Blue Shield . . . HMO's . . . new approach to control health care insurance costs . . . dental insurance . . . Medicare (A and B) . . . Workers Compensation . . . pensions . . . early retirement buyout . . . Individual Retirement Account . . . The Keogh plan . . . ERISA . . . preretirement counseling . . . Social Security . . . Railroad Retirement . . . profit sharing.

Labor unions . . . collective bargaining . . . third party bargaining . . . white-collar unions . . . organizing efforts . . . recognizing the union . . . how to keep the union out . . . bargaining . . . givebacks . . . strikes . . . union trends . . . National Labor Relations Act . . . labor laws.

Personnel records . . . privacy protection . . . compliance records . . . personnel reports . . . reference replies . . . budgets . . . industrial espionage . . . lie detector use . . . personnel data system . . . computerization of records and reports.

Corporate policies . . . employment policy . . . antidiscrimination policy . . . rules and regulations . . . moonlighting . . . work at home . . . flextime . . . how to reduce absen-

teeism . . . robot mail delivery . . . housekeeping.

CHAPTER I

PERSONNEL MANAGEMENT

THE FUNCTIONS OF PERSONNEL

TO GUIDE them in their planning and operating, many companies have organization charts. Similarly, divisions within a company often have sections of an overall chart developed into greater detail to help them in planning.

Personnel, too, could utilize such a chart. Personnel activities within an organization ought to be clearly set forth. But the personnel chart should show functions, not staff. Functions are usually permanent; interests and abilities of individuals tend to change with time.

There are two methods by which the personnel chart may be developed. The popular way is to list all the separate items that are being performed and arrange these into natural groupings. This type of chart shows what *is* done; there is no indication of what *should be* done.

Too often, personnel programs grow without any real plan of organization. Sometimes they include items that do not belong. Some phases of a personnel program are often done by other departments, or possibly not done at all.

How to Begin

Therefore a better way to design a personnel chart is to forget for the moment the program as it is presently in practice. Consider what a comprehensive personnel program ought to include. Start with a purely academic approach to find this answer.

Such standard version of an organization chart for the personnel program will classify all activities into logical subdivisions. The number of such subdivisions is not important so long as it is reasonable—not too few nor too many. For this discussion let us suggest these breakdowns:

1. Research and Standards
2. Employment
3. Education and Training

1

4. Safety and Health
5. Employee Activities
6. Wages and Salaries
7. Benefit Administration.

Labor Relations could be a separate category if this is a serious and troublesome area; otherwise its involvements should rightfully be included in the above groupings since it is usually concerned with wages and benefits.

Starting with these separate section headings, the chart is then expanded into greater detail by arranging the individual personnel practices appropriately until all activities of a comprehensive program are properly listed.

This standard, or one similar to it, is applicable to all industry. It fits a two-man butcher shop, small business establishment, large corporation, and far-flung international conglomerate. The difference between personnel programs in various companies is not in basic functions but in the degree to which these functions are formalized, and the size of the staff necessary to carry them out.

Dividing a total program into a specific number of logical areas does not mean that in an average-size firm the personnel officer needs that same number of staff assistants. In a small company, two or more functions could well be handled by the same employee. In large industrial establishments each one of these areas could be a large section requiring many employees possibly in different locations.

Applying the Standard Locally

After this chart has been understood it can be applied to any company by adapting it to the particular needs. This is accomplished by making a comparison between the standard chart and the present or existing chart. At a glance it will point up two areas of disagreement. First, it will reveal items presently performed that probably should be transferred elsewhere or possibly discontinued. Second, it will disclose phases of a comprehensive personnel program that should be initiated or, if performed elsewhere, should perhaps be absorbed.

This tailor-made personnel chart incorporates all the characteristics that are necessary and desirable. It is obtained by philosophizing as to what the relationship of the many separate personnel functions should be to the company's overall objectives.

It must be remembered that there can never be any "pure" personnel program regardless of how attractive it may be made to appear on paper. In actual practice the ideal is seldom, if ever, attained. The personal influence of top executives, financial situation, nature of the

2

PERSONNEL FUNCTIONS

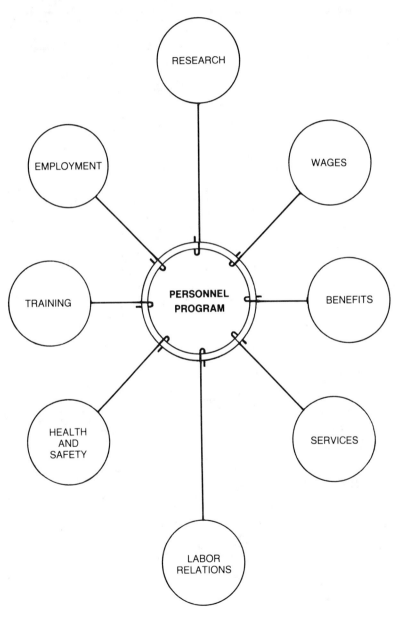

PERSONNEL ADMINISTRATION HANDBOOK

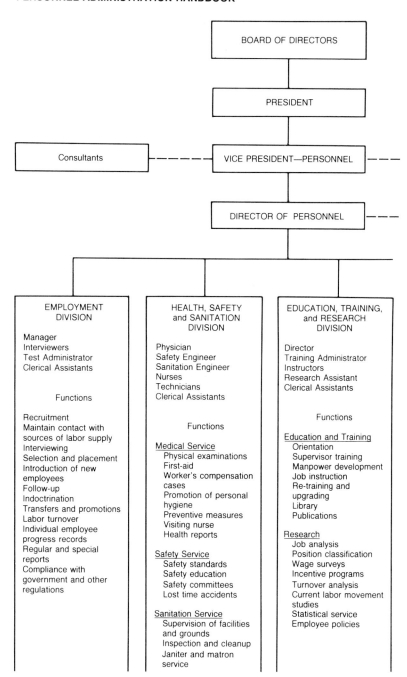

BOARD OF DIRECTORS

PRESIDENT

Consultants

VICE PRESIDENT—PERSONNEL

DIRECTOR OF PERSONNEL

EMPLOYMENT DIVISION

Manager
Interviewers
Test Administrator
Clerical Assistants

Functions

Recruitment
Maintain contact with sources of labor supply
Interviewing
Selection and placement
Introduction of new employees
Follow-up
Indoctrination
Transfers and promotions
Labor turnover
Individual employee progress records
Regular and special reports
Compliance with government and other regulations

HEALTH, SAFETY and SANITATION DIVISION

Physician
Safety Engineer
Sanitation Engineer
Nurses
Technicians
Clerical Assistants

Functions

Medical Service
  Physical examinations
  First-aid
  Worker's compensation cases
  Promotion of personal hygiene
  Preventive measures
  Visiting nurse
  Health reports

Safety Service
  Safety standards
  Safety education
  Safety committees
  Lost time accidents

Sanitation Service
  Supervision of facilities and grounds
  Inspection and cleanup
  Janiter and matron service

EDUCATION, TRAINING, and RESEARCH DIVISION

Director
Training Administrator
Instructors
Research Assistant
Clerical Assistants

Functions

Education and Training
  Orientation
  Supervisor training
  Manpower development
  Job instruction
  Re-training and upgrading
  Library
  Publications

Research
  Job analysis
  Position classification
  Wage surveys
  Incentive programs
  Turnover analysis
  Current labor movement studies
  Statistical service
  Employee policies

4

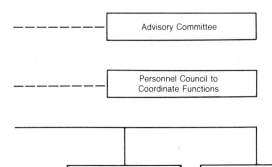

Advisory Committee

Personnel Council to
Coordinate Functions

WELFARE SERVICE DIVISION

Supervisor
Benefits Administrator
Counselor
Assistant Supervisors
Clerical Assistants

Functions

Administration of
Sick pay
Health and accident
insurance
Salary continuation
Disability insurance
Group life insurance
Retirement program
Credit Union
Thrift program
Wage assignments
Legal aid
Financial advice
Personal guidance
Cafeteria
Meetings
Employee activities
Athletic teams
Social events
United Fund
Reports and employee
feedback

JOINT REPRESENTATION DIVISION

Manager
Secretary
Clerical Assistants

Functions

Hearing complaints
Grievance adjustments
Working conditions
Promotion of efficiency
Control of discipline
Cooperation in benefits
Cooperation in
educational, publicity, and
public relations activities
Community affairs
Special reports

industry, competition, location, bargaining agreement, and the *status quo* will have their effect. In many respects this effect can be wholesome, not necessarily detrimental.

No matter how much time and energy are expended developing and refining the personnel chart, the real effort comes in maintaining it. Like any other organization chart it cannot be static. It must be dynamic to keep pace with change which is inevitable. Even the standard should be restudied constantly, since a standard is defined as: The best known today, which is to be improved tomorrow.

A good organization chart does not ensure a good organization, nor does it insure good management. It does reflect good planning. This, however, is at best only a beginning. The implementation of a good personnel program depends upon many factors, the most important of which is the leadership provided by the personnel executive who directs it.

CAREERS IN PERSONNEL

There are excellent opportunities for men and women with educational backgrounds or equivalent work experience that provide the foundation for careers in the personnel and industrial relations field.

Employee relations assignments hold greater responsibilities today than ever before. No profession has been more widely affected by recent federal legislation than the personnel field. Social pressures and expectations of more meaningful work make job design and training crucial to the success of all organizations. Productivity, showing signs of stagnating, and the maze of employee benefits have both contributed to the need for more skilled personnel practitioners.

To manage these problems organizations must rely ever more heavily on personnel staffs. Today's human resources manager is expected to be both a philosopher and a specialized technician guiding the organization to sound, up-to-date policies. He or she must formulate appropriate action to implement these policies and have the skill to explain and interpret them to other managers.

In its brochure, "Careers in personnel and industrial relations," the American Society for Personnel Administration, 19 Church Street, Berea, Ohio 44107, speaks directly to candidates who are considering careers in personnel.

The Personnel Function

It is often said that people are an organization's greatest asset, and you, as a personnel administrator, will be charged with the judicious management of those resources. In this position you must understand why people behave as they do in a multitude of situations and anticipate how they will react in specific ones.

Your primarily responsibility will be to provide expert assistance to the other members of the management team in making the best possible use of the organization's human resources. Personnel administrators advise management of the requirements for achieving the maximum utilization of the talents of the individual employees.

You will "wear many hats," being called upon to interview and hire new employees, evaluate their progress and potential, train them for greater efficiency, instill pride in their product or service, explain and enforce management policies and procedures, recognize achievement, arbitrate differences, forecast manpower requirements, plan wage and salary schedules, supervise benefit programs, ensure compliance with labor laws, represent the organization in a community relations capacity, and so forth. Your specific duties will depend on the nature and size of the business or industry where you work.

Personnel administrators are employed in virtually every business enterprise and government agency. The total number is estimated at more than 335,000. Well over half of all personnel workers are employed by private firms. The next largest number are employed by federal, state and local government agencies.

The personnel function in federal, state and local government agencies is similar to that in large business firms. Government personnel staffs, however, spend considerably more time in activities related to classifying jobs and devising, administering and scoring the competitive examinations given to job applicants.

The Personnel Office

The personnel staff varies in size and composition with the organization. In a small company, the administrative function may be performed by an individual—while in a large corporation employing thousands, the staff may number over a hundred, with specialists in the areas of employment, training, wage and salary administration, health and safety, compensation and labor relations.

Personnel office surroundings are usually very comfortable and pleasant. Hours are fairly regular, but the personnel staff members must be flexible enough to cope with occasional overtime—for instance, during an employment buildup or work stoppage which can make the personnel executive's hours highly irregular.

In a dynamic profession such as personnel administration, it is necessary for practitioners to keep themselves constantly informed of developments in the field. The American Society for Personnel Administra-

7

tion was formed to perform this function, while furthering the aims of the profession. ASPA has over 275 professional chapters throughout the United States which provide the opportunity for members to exchange information and ideas. Several universities have ASPA-sponsored student chapters which provide future personnel administrators with supplemental educational information and interaction with practitioners.

ASPA publishes a professional journal, *The Personnel Administrator,* and several news digests and topical research materials to assist the personnel administrator on the job. ASPA also sponsors a number of conferences, seminars and workshops to aid in the professional development of members.

The Personnel Specialists

Employment and placement: Consults with top management in setting employment policies of the firm and in planning programs. Recommends revisions in the organizational structure of the company and maintains manning tables, replacement schedules and personnel inventories. Recruits personnel for factory, office, sales, technical, professional, supervisory and managerial positions. Analyzes jobs, prepares job descriptions and job specifications. Administers tests, interviews applicants and refers selected applicants to specific job openings. Develops appraisal procedures for employees and executives. Processes transfers, promotions, terminations, layoffs, claims and conducts exit interviews.

Training: Sets training policies in consultation with top management, and organizes training activities to carry out these policies. Coordinates the training activities of the company which may include the following types: on-the-job, apprentice, supervisory, sales and management. Consults with other managers to determine training needs. Prepares manuals and other materials for use in training sessions. Arranges and conducts training sessions. Counsels employees concerning training opportunities. Advises other managers concerning revisions of the organizational structure of the company.

Labor relations: Represents company at collective bargaining negotiations, arbitration hearings and grievance meetings. Participates with top management in formulating labor relations policies. Plans programs and activities to implement the policies. Checks company compliance with federal and state labor laws. Interprets contract provisions to all levels of management. Deals with union representatives on matters of contract interpretation and administration.

Wage and salary administration: Plans and administers the wage and salary program. In consultation with other managers determines wage

PERSONNEL RESPONSIBILITIES

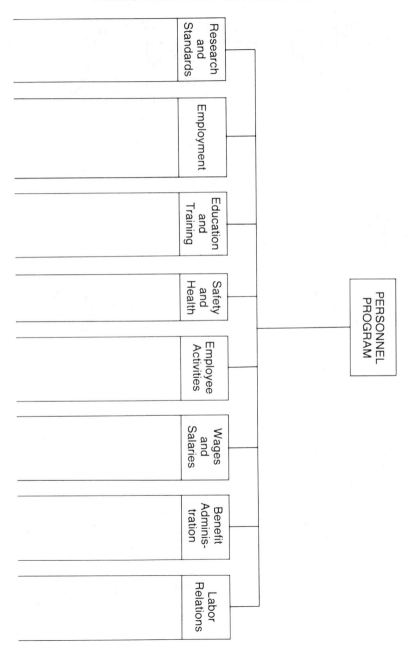

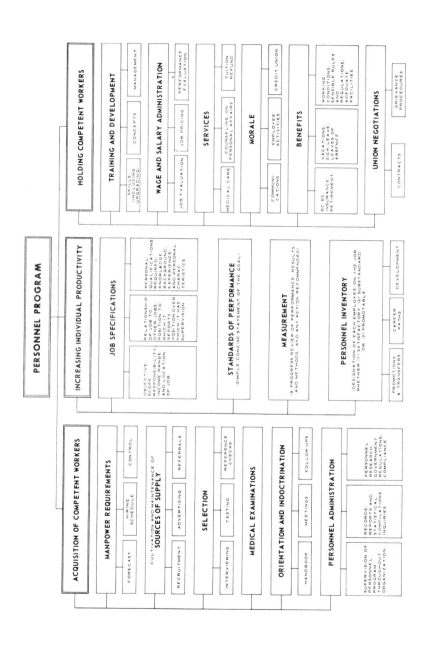

and salary policies. Checks company compensation policies and practices for compliance with laws and regulations. Analyzes jobs, prepares job descriptions and job specifications. Maintains records and prepares periodic reports of wage and salary information. Coordinates the evaluation of jobs for compensation purposes. Establishes and maintains wage and salary structures. Conducts wage and salary surveys. May recommend and administer plans for incentive wage systems or supplementary compensation.

Benefits and services: Administers company insurance, disability, pension and retirement programs and a variety of other employee benefits and services. Reviews requests for leaves, vacations, claims for workers' compensation, unemployment insurance and severance pay. May represent the company at hearings related to these claims. Responsible for employee communications, which may include preparation and distribution of employee newspapers, magazines, handbooks or manuals, and maintenance of bulletin boards. Directs recreational and social programs for employees. May direct the operation of an employee food service. Counsels employees on vocational and personal problems. Sometimes directs health and safety activities.

Outlook for the Future

The expansion of the personnel field is evident in the newspaper classified sections; however, competition for beginning professional positions is likely to be keen throughout the country. Employment prospects will probably be best for college graduates who have specialized training in personnel administration.

Employment in some specialized areas of personnel will rise faster than others. The need for experts to oversee compliance with government regulations will probably continue to increase; and the growth of employee services, safety programs, training, pension and other benefit plans, and personnel research is also likely to continue.

Employment in personnel work is expected to expand rapidly as employers recognize the impact of employee relations on bottom-line profits and depend more heavily on the services of trained personnel professionals to achieve maximum utilization of human resources.

PERSONNEL RESPONSIBILITIES

The editors of *The Personnel Administrator* took a poll of the membership of the American Society for Personnel Administration asking about the areas of responsibility for the personnel staff. They got the following replies from the poll:

Employment	98%
Employee Relations	94%
Personnel Records	94%
Recruiting	92%
Compensation	89%
Training and Development	88%
Insurance	84%
Performance Evaluation	84%
Safety	74%
Manpower Planning and Forecasting	74%
Medical and First Aid	74%
Retirement Program	69%
Labor Relations	66%
Organizational Development	66%
Communications	60%
Community Relations	56%
Recreation	55%
Legislative Awareness	51%
Pension Planning	47%
Plant Protection and Security	47%
Leisure Activities	43%
In-Plant Feeding	42%
Public Relations	40%

Organization of the Personnel Activity

Depending upon the size of the company, the many, varied personnel activities should be organized into logical groupings. The following basic chart, showing breakdowns and the additional list of duties for each unit, may be helpful in organizing the total, comprehensive personnel program.

Research and Standards

Internal and external personnel research

Organization planning and charting

Table of organization

Policy manual

Government compliance

Legal conformance

Personnel costs and budgets

Personnel inventory

Manpower forecasting

Exempt position classification

Analysis of forms, procedures, reports

Test development and validation

Reports and statistics

Research on ads and ad writing
Fringe benefit studies
Wage surveys
Miscellaneous surveys and audits

Morale readings
Consultants
Mechanization of personnel data
Periodicals

Employment

Recruitment
Liaison with outside applicant referral sources
Campus visits
Executive search
Ad writing, placement, billing
Job posting
Reception of applicants
Interviewing
Selection (preliminary)
Temporary help
Test administration
Reference checking
Communications with prospects and new hires
Relocation expense reimbursement
Bench interviews
Fidelity bonds
Conflict of interest

Payroll form processing
Employment records and files
Employee progress records
Fair employment practices and claims
Compliance records, statistics, reports
Transfers
Promotions
Demotions
Layoffs
Dismissals
Terminations, voluntary
Exit interviews
Acquisition cost
Inquiries about former employees
Unemployment compensation, claims, hearings

Education and Training

Indoctrination
Sponsors (for new employees)
Orientation
In-house (group) training
Off-the-job courses
Tuition refund
Supervisory training
Executive development
Individual career path charting
Retraining
Federal assistance
Outside seminars, meetings, conferences
Training manuals

Programmed learning
Instructional films
Communications
House organ
Employee handbook
Bulletin boards
Posters
Productivity improvement pamphlets
Library
Reading racks
Employee meetings
Management councils

13

Safety and Health

First-aid
Clinic
Emergency off-hour protection
Employment physicals
Ongoing physical checkups
Occupational health
Health education
Flu shots
Blood banks
Working conditions
Sanitation
Cafeteria inspection

Safety education
Accidents
Disability reports
Workman's compensation
Emergency evacuation and safety drills
Attendance
Lost time
Leaves of absence
Sick leave
Maternity furloughs
Medical records

Employee Activities

Company-sponsored social events
Anniversary service awards
Service recognition dinner
Employee-conducted activities
Picnic
Parties
Sports events
Bowling
Softball
Golf tournament
Recreation
Employee clubs

Flower or gift fund
Cafeteria
Vending machines
Employee lounge
Lunch-hour films
Credit union
Suggestion system
Music
Purchase discounts
United fund and other charity drives

Wages and Salaries

Employee compensation
Wage administration
Overtime
Shift differentials
Incentives
Sick pay
Salary continuation plan
General increase
Severance pay
Bonus
Thrift plan
Stock options
Profit sharing
Supplemental pay programs
Salary controls

Job analysis
Job classification
Job grading
Job pricing
Salary studies
Salary scatterdiagrams
Performance rating
Work measurement
Production records
Check cashing
Status changes
Salary records
Savings bond purchases
Wage assignments and levies
Credit verification

Benefit Administration

Fringe benefit administration
Self-insurance plans
Group insurance enrollments
Group insurance claims handling
Group insurance billing
Hospitalization insurance
Medical-surgical insurance
Major medical coverage
Health and accident insurance
Travel insurance
Group automobile insurance
Disability insurance
Life insurance

Key man insurance plans
Retirement income program
Preretirement planning
Social security
Medicare
Retiree counselling
Employee counselling on personal, legal, financial matters
Inquiries about employees
Welfare and pension Disclosure Act
Benefit handbook

Labor Relations

Organization attempts
Union election
Negotiations
Union contracts
Contract interpretation meetings
Labor-management internal relations

Grievances
Arbitration
N L R B
Labor laws
Liaison with the labor community

ORGANIZING

Organizing is the process of putting everything together properly. It involves the integrating of related activities required for the successful achievement of company objectives into a coordinated structure, staffing this structure with qualified, competent personnel, and equipping them with the physical factors necessary to perform their tasks.

Through organization management guides the activities in the right direction toward desired goals. Organization is the framework within which company purposes are served.

The three factors in organizing are:

1. Structure: crystallized into a graphic chart.
2. Staffing: right people in right places.
3. Physical support: facilities, systems and resources.

A formal organization is almost always a hierarchy—levels of command, one above the other, reach a president (or other chief executive) at the top. The hierarchy form of management is used in business, in

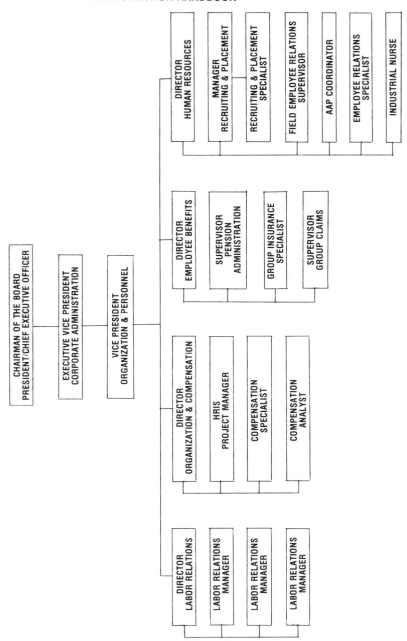

Personnel Organization Chart of International Minerals & Chemical Corporation, Mundelein, Illinois

government, in the military and in the church. It is an ancient yet persistent form of social organization. In modern times, hierarchy has been analyzed under the name "bureaucracy."

The advantage of having a hierarchy is that it can bring together great numbers of diverse people to accomplish a task. The familiar chain of command provides a means for pinpointing responsibility and authority. People are assigned certain parts of the general task by being required to perform specific duties. According to the weight and significance of their particular roles, people occupy logical places in the hierarchical structure.

Line and Staff

The line and staff concept adapted by the business world had its origin in the military organization. The line consisted of officers and men who stood in the line of combat. They are often referred to as being "in the line of fire." Staff referred to those who advised and formulated policy, as well as those who supplied supportive services.

The history of staff began with Gaius Julius Caesar. As general and statesman, he used a personal staff to aid him in building the Roman Empire. Titus Labrinus acted as his military chief of staff, while Mark Anthony assisted in governmental affairs. Caesar's staff allowed him to conquer countries and maintain power in government while vacationing in Egypt. Some of the earliest recorded conflicts between line and staff were a result of the Roman senators having to consult Caesar's staff to ascertain his wishes. This is still a problem in government.

Modern business avoids costly and delaying conflicts by having its corporate policies clearly spelled out. Coupled with operating procedures, these policies become guidelines for both line and staff personnel.

Staff people serve the company by working through the line organization. Staff people cannot participate directly in deciding, doing or controlling in finance, production or sales. Nor can staff people issue orders to line people through setting policy, devising standards or prescribing methods.

The manager in the office or the foreman in the factory must always remain the "total boss" of the area of the business for which he is held accountable. Staff assistants, in the performance of their duties; may exercise a measure of functional authority.

The existence of four types of staff functions is generally acknowledged. These are:

1. Advisory (Example: legal, planning, consultants).
2. Functional (Example: personnel, medical).

17

3. Service (Example: purchasing, switchboard, cafeteria).
4. Control (Example: budget, auditing, inspection).

In its original concept the line organization produced income and staff functions were condoned as support. The accounting schools considered manufacturing and sales as revenue producing work and referred to the office as burden or overhead.

This is no longer true. Who sells the canned soup to the consumer —a salesman (line) or the package designer (staff)?

A more realistic distinction today would be that line managers make the operating decisions and staff personnel supply the line managers with better information and more specialized assistance which results in better decisions.

Organization Chart

An organization chart is a map that shows in graphic form the operational units and formal lines of authority. A company organization chart depicts:

1. Functions
2. Incumbents
3. Relationships
4. Levels
5. Lines of authority.

Most charts are conventionally drawn boxes and lines in a pyramidal arrangement with the large box at the top designating the boss.

The scalar, or line, form is fixed, clear, simple, and makes for easy decisions; but it can be autocratic. The line and staff form provides for team effort and permits specialization; but it can be unclear and lead to conflicts.

A well-designed chart is impressive. It should be noted, however, that the importance of the organization chart is not in the way it is drawn but in the way it is used. There are some things an organization chart does not show:

1. Status: location on chart can be misleading.
2. Authority and responsibility: the degree can vary between "like" positions.
3. Relationships: line and staff decisions are often unclear.
4. Communications: channels do not follow lines.
5. Informality: interpersonal and intergroup relations seem to develop their own "least resistance" paths.

The informal organization defies charting. Work-oriented relationships can be structured but people-oriented relationships cannot.

18

Typical corporate organization charts showing the relationship of personnel to other management functions.

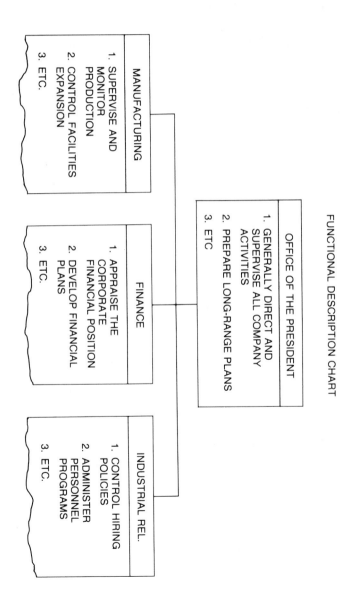

FUNCTIONAL DESCRIPTION CHART

OFFICE OF THE PRESIDENT
1. GENERALLY DIRECT AND SUPERVISE ALL COMPANY ACTIVITIES
2. PREPARE LONG-RANGE PLANS
3. ETC

MANUFACTURING
1. SUPERVISE AND MONITOR PRODUCTION
2. CONTROL FACILITIES EXPANSION
3. ETC.

FINANCE
1. APPRAISE THE CORPORATE FINANCIAL POSITION
2. DEVELOP FINANCIAL PLANS
3. ETC.

INDUSTRIAL REL.
1. CONTROL HIRING POLICIES
2. ADMINISTER PERSONNEL PROGRAMS
3. ETC.

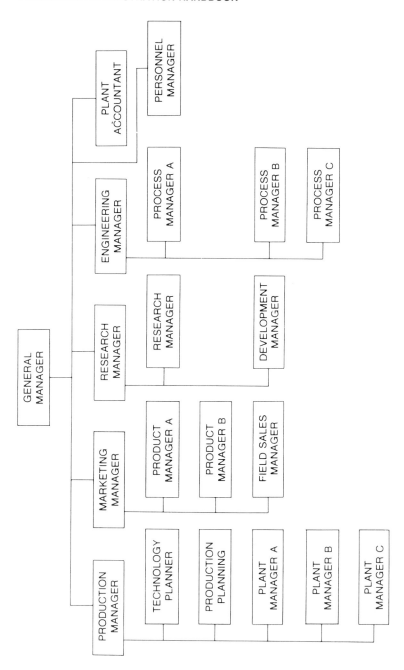

PERSONNEL MANAGEMENT

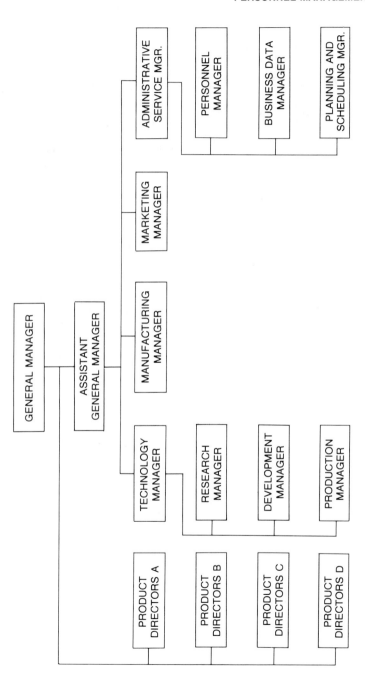

21

BASIC EXECUTIVE CHARACTERISTICS

Composed by Wilbert E. Scheer, author of The Dartnell Personnel Director's Handbook

POSITIONS	THEY WEAR	THEY EAT	THEY BELIEVE	THEY HOPE	THEY KNOW	THEY WANT	THEY'LL SETTLE FOR
BOARD CHAIRMEN	double-breasted blue suits	yogurt	they're industrial statesmen	other people believe it, too	everything	a cabinet position	writing a book
PRESIDENTS	$200 suits	banquet chicken and peas	they make all the decisions	they're indispensable	they aren't	to be industrial statesmen	making a speech at the Rotary Club
EXECUTIVE VICE-PRESIDENTS	$400 suits	steak	they're running the company	the president will retire	the president won't	power and prestige	power
COMPTROLLERS	vests	pot roast	people don't know the value of money	they can teach them	they can't	to cut costs 20 percent	cutting costs 2 percent
SALES MANAGERS	sports clothes	on expense accounts	they can sell everything they can produce	the company will build up inventory	the production department is dragging its feet	a bigger sales force	a bonus
PRODUCTION MANAGERS	shirtsleeves	salami sandwiches	they can produce everything they can sell	they can reduce inventory	the sales forecast is ridiculous	new machinery	a bonus
ADVERTISING MANAGERS	custom-tailored suits	on the agency's expense account	advertising sells the company's products	they're right	the Nielsen ratings	a bigger budget	a bigger office
R&D DIRECTORS	sweaters	when they think of it	they're Einsteins	they can prove it	$E\ mc^2$	professional recognition	patent rights
PURCHASING DIRECTORS	off-the-rack suits	on the suppliers expense accounts	purchasing is a profession	other people think so, too	other people don't	top value for low prices	low prices
PUBLIC RELATIONS DIRECTORS	casual outfits	with financial reporters	they should report to the president	the president knows they're alive	the president doesn't	to place an article in Fortune	a paragraph in local paper
PERSONNEL DIRECTORS	bifocals	in the company cafeteria	they like people	people like them	people don't	the best person for every job	anyone the agency sends

The formal organization chart is stiff and must be redrawn to accommodate the slightest change. It is also lifeless; it cannot reflect morale, character, climate, leadership, styles, innovation, creativity or philosophy.

Notwithstanding its inherent weaknesses, the organization chart is necessary and useful to the efficient operation of modern business. The business corporation, as we know it, is about 100 years old. Its development left an imprint on society as it moved through stages of robber barons, the faceless trust, the soulless enterprise, the impersonal bureaucracy, the mindless mechanism and the vicious power struggle.

The corporate organization has changed from a monolithic hierarchy to an increasingly democratic free form team. The organization chart explains how it is structured, shows how it operates and helps to keep things orderly.

THE PERSONNEL DIRECTOR

The personnel director is generally regarded as a specialist in the field. But in the eyes of Amy K. Hartman, former director of personnel at St. Vincent's Hospital, Jacksonville, Florida, the personnel executive may be looked upon as a general practitioner because he must possess many of the specialties associated with the medical profession.

He must be:

A *radiologist:* to be able to read people's minds like a fluoroscope, to deduce who the "introverts" and the "extroverts" are.

A *psychologist:* to be able to understand not only what the employee said, and what he meant, but what he should have said, and what's more important, what he did not say.

An *orthopedist:* to be able to understand and cope with those employees who have "chips" on their shoulders, look upon change as a fractured way of life, and refuse to be anything but "hard-headed."

An *allergist:* to be able to handle all types of allergies and to stimulate self-improvement for those employees who suddenly are allergic to work and to almost everything else, except payday.

A *dermatologist:* to be able to handle the "thin-skinned" ones.

A *rhinologist:* to straighten out the ones who get their "noses out of joint."

A *dietitian:* to be able· to "cook up" appetizing policies, rules and regulations that can be easily digested and well-flavored with enthusiasm.

An *otologist:* to be an expert in the "art of listening"—to complaints, to personal problems, to "lonely conversations."

PERSONNEL INFLUENCES

Forces that influence the personnel director but which the personnel director also can influence.

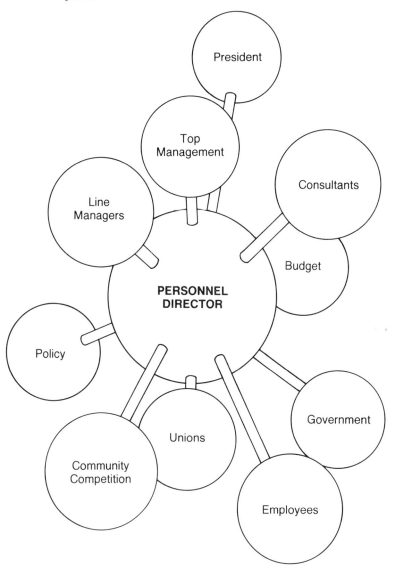

PERSONNEL RELATIONSHIPS

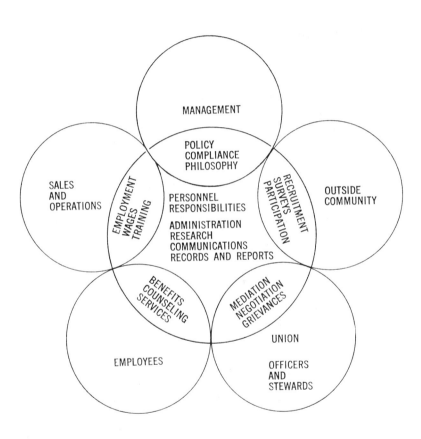

A *diagnostician:* not only to listen to problems but also to make suggestions, to advise, to inform.

The personnel director must be alert to all the "ills" that can affect the job satisfaction of the individual, the efficiency of a department or the general attitude within the company.

The Personnel Executive as
THE PHILOSOPHER OF MANAGEMENT

There is much more to personnel management than the necessary day-to-day administrative duties involving people. Applying scientific, or at least systematic, procedures to the area of human relations calls for a different understanding from that used in the materialistic realm. Here we are dealing with human values, blood-bought souls, divinely created and eternally destined beings. We are not dealing with human machines.

If men and women were animals it would be efficient to use them, depreciate them, consume them and discard them; but people are human beings. When we think of the human element in our business we must think in terms and values that are different from those we apply to the technical side of our jobs.

In our employee relations programs we need more than methods and devices, no matter how good they are. We need also the leaven of compassion and the understanding of human relations. What the soul is to the body, that is what human relations is to personnel administration. Employee programs that are made up of techniques but not understanding have a shell for a body and an ache for a soul.

Anyone, by whatever title he may be known, who is entrusted with anything as vital as the human relations activities in his company, must be a unique person. On the one hand he cannot be dictatorial, for the success of his endeavors is not determined by prestige nor by his position on the official organization chart. No matter where or how he ranks he cannot be effective by imposing his will upon people.

On the other hand he has to be more than the instrument of management. He must recognize that he has a responsibility to people, not just to top officials who seek to maintain control over his activities. To fulfill his obligation he cannot be just the administrator of everybody else's ideas, some sound, soem untried. He must also be an influence in the human relations functions of company operations.

Let's use one of his many duties to explain this. Let's talk about his involvement in writing policies to make this point. Our policies are merely the outgrowth of practice; they are an expression of our management philosophy. For a personnel man to write policies he should be careful that he does not copy from a book. His written policy statements must reflect the philosophy of the company and serve the interests of the people. While he cannot dictate, he has a twofold obligation: (1) he has to be certain that these official policies are not based on prejudice, tradition, sentiment or personal whims; and (2) they must fit the work force or they are useless.

It's More Than a Job

This puts the personnel executive in the singular position of becoming the philosopher of management. While other officials are preoccupied with specific functions he must, in addition to his day-to-day duties, also theorize on what is happening. He becomes concerned about the immediate decision but he cannot stop there. He must look at the current action in terms of its long-range implications. Besides being practical he should also be studying, probing, thinking, talking, listening, asking penetrating questions—all the while testing his theories as I am doing here.

At any rate, he doesn't have a job; personnel administration should never be thought of as a job. This is not an occupation that young people are encouraged to enter for a good livelihood. The man who wants to get into personnel work because it is better than driving a truck belongs on a truck.

For this reason I have mixed feelings about those companies that use the position of personnel director as a training ground for other management work. The danger lies in performing the day-to-day functions of personnel administration intelligently, perhaps, but with cold efficiency, the way a tradesman "lays bricks instead of building a cathedral." A church organist who plays flawlessly with his head and his hands may be a polished musician, but if he expects to inspire the congregation into spirited singing he must play from the heart.

Conscience of the Company

Remember, personnel administration is never a job; it is a vocation. No one has a right to be in the explosive area of human relations who has only the brain for the occupation and not the conscience of the vocationalist. For a vocation is truly a "calling," and this classic definition carries with it divine overtones.

Any job in the field of human relations is at once the most precious and the most dangerous duty entrusted by mankind to man. In the final analysis, the personnel executive who performs his own administrative work well is still doing only half of his job. As the philosopher of management he must also make certain that in the area of human relations the entire company performs well. This is his opportunity and his obligation.

PUBLIC PERSONNEL ADMINISTRATION

by GEORGE S. THOMPSON
Executive Director
Virginia Governmental Employees Association, Inc.

It is an amazing accomplishment that public employees (State) have as good employee benefit programs as they do.

Most routine employee benefits provided by a private corporation when sought for state employees must travel a most discouraging path through legislation and any number of regulatory agencies.

Public employee personnel administrators, no doubt, look with great envy at their counterparts in the private sector who can develop and implement programs with a minimum of interference.

From fringe benefit surveys, meetings with personnel executives, and other contacts with the private sector, they see public employees being left behind in health care, retirement, vacations, insurance and any number of similar benefits that employees of private firms enjoy.

The effort to correct just a minor inequity suffered by public employees discourages even a strong-hearted state personnel executive when he contemplates the long road from idea to implementation.

A state director of personnel must be a politician, student of campaign promises, adroit fence straddler, yes man, adamant and gifted interpreter of some piece of weird legislation pushed through the State Legislature by a well-meaning but impractical legislator who feels he is doing right by public employees.

Secretly, state personnel directors observe the apparently unwanted efforts of employee groups as they seek employee benefit improvements that he himself desires and would not dare propose but would welcome and enjoy if enacted.

Public employee benefits are good, but not as good as they could be if State Legislators would stop thinking of themselves as personnel management experts and leave such programs to the professionals whom they employ but do not let perform.

ORGANIZATION PLANNING
as Related to Personnel

The personnel officer plays an increasingly important role in organization planning. In most of today's organization charts the personnel officer reports to a top executive, quite often the president. This puts him in a responsible position of becoming involved in overall planning provided, of course, he is qualified in this area.

The day of the "personnel department"—similar to other operating departments—concerned mainly with "doing" is over. In addition to day-to-day administrative duties, the personnel officer must also plan for the future, not just the future of the personnel program but how this relates to and serves corporate planning. This makes the personnel officer a part of the corporate "think" team.

In fact, in medium and large companies, where the personnel contribution has been recognized, the planning and doing functions of personnel administration are often separated. One may not even be accountable to the other. The "planning" aspect, known as "Human Resources" or "Manpower Utilization" or "Corporate Personnel" is accountable to the President. The "doing" function, known as "Manager of Personnel" or "Personnel Director" may report to the Works Manager or the Vice-President of Manufacturing or the Vice-President of Administration—executives responsible for day-to-day operations.

In all these cases, the planning job rates higher than the doing job. Its duties include manpower resources, management development, labor and employment policy, and compensation. Its main responsibility is to assist top management in overall corporate planning, especially as related to human resources.

This development places a unique responsibility upon the personnel officer. It moves his opportunity from the periphery of company operations to the very center of management activities where the hard decisions are made.

PHILOSOPHY OF MANAGEMENT

An example of employees who need technical skills and those who need the human skills of management, or how these skills shift as jobs go up, is illustrated in this diagram.

PHILOSOPHY OF MANAGEMENT

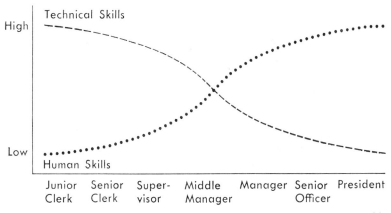

Note that technical skills are high at the clerical level and drop slowly but definitely until the officers, although they may have technical skills, no longer use them as much. On the other hand, the human skills are low at the clerical level and rise steadily until the officers must have a real degree of skill in this area.

As one man expressed it: The higher a man goes in his company the less he is the technician and the more he becomes the politician. Or put another way: as an executive advances in his company, his perspective changes. It is like looking at a painting; as he steps back he sees less detail but is more aware of the total picture.

HUMAN ASSETS

Business does not exist merely to produce more goods or broader services, though that is no small part of its task. Business, also, especially in today's enlightened era, affords the principal means whereby individuals may gain the satisfaction of accomplishing something more than merely sustaining their own lives.

A company program built around procedures, even though each separate instrument is a technical masterpiece, is lifeless. Programs made up of techniques but not understanding have a shell for a body and an ache for a soul.

To make the point, I go back to Blue Cross and Blue Shield where for 23 years I enjoyed the pleasure and benefits of rewarding employment.

The Blue Cross and Blue Shield movement is a powerful force for good. It has left its imprint on the way we live. The emphasis on national health and, in large measure, the improvement in health care, are due to the missionary zeal of a few visionary patriarchs back in the 1930's.

The evolution of leadership in the Blue Cross and Blue Shield Plans is that they were first run by do-gooders, welfare types, who were not necessarily good business heads. As the idea caught on, the peddlers took charge and began promoting a very salable product. Once volume was generated, administrative management moved up and stabilized the operation with controlled procedures. With billions of dollars taken in and paid out, it was inevitable that the financial people were able to assume direction. But in my opinion, the ultimate in keeping Blue Cross and Blue Shield a viable instrument in the health care industry

PHILOSOPHY OF MANAGEMENT

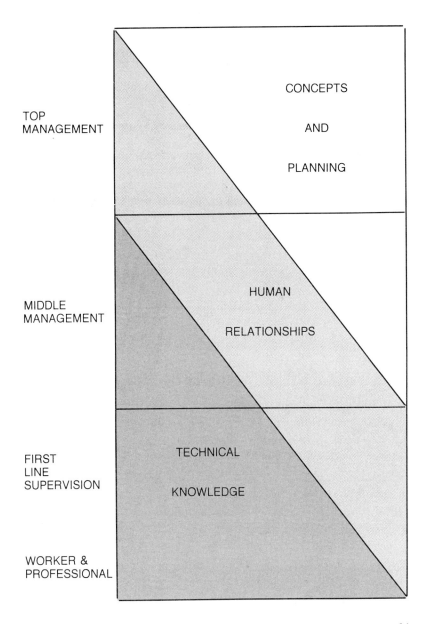

is not any type of sophisticated specialization at all. Its future is wrapped up in an appreciation of the human element in business.

Blue Cross and Blue Shield have no product, no display room of new models. Nor do they sell any services; the providers of care do that. Blue Cross and Blue Shield take in and pay out money, exerting some influence in the process. And computerization notwithstanding, the transactions with subscribers, providers, professionals, government, suppliers and the public are handled by people.

Blue Cross and Blue Shield need physical assets—buildings, machines, methods and the like. But these are only the structure of the business and, of themselves, accomplish nothing. They need financial assets, of course, and the judicious use of money entrusted to their care is paramount. But these are merely the paraphernalia of the business. Blue Cross and Blue Shield are, in the final analysis, a people business and their strength, effectiveness and usefulness depend upon the utilization of their human assets.

Many Plans have come around to understand the logic of this fundamental truth. These are the Plans that enjoy a good reputation in the communities they serve, that provide courteous, prompt and impressive service to subscribers, and which have no need to abdicate their responsibilities in employee relations to any third-party union representation.

I asked presidents of two large Plans to express their personal philosophies about the human element in business and the part this plays in the successful operations of their respective Plans. Their statements follow.

THE VALUE OF HUMAN RESOURCES IN BUSINESS

by EDWIN R. WERNER
President and Chief Executive Officer
Blue Cross and Blue Shield of Greater New York
New York, New York 10017

The business with which I am most familiar—health care insurance —more specifically the Blue Cross and Blue Shield Plans across the country—has undergone such a profound change that I'm often not sure I'm part of the same industry in which I started my career some 38 years ago. In fact, the company of which I am President and Chief Executive Office, Blue Cross and Blue Shield of Greater New York, bears only some resemblance to the company it was 10 years ago.

We're a service industry. We try to provide the greatest number of people with the best possible health care at the lowest cost. That has always been our policy. In the not too distant past the achievement of our corporate goals was relatively straightforward and uncomplicated. Today it is complex beyond recognition. To say it is comparable to the difference between driving the average family sedan and piloting a Boeing 747 may be underestimating the case.

Our experience is probably typical of American business. As a growth company we have experienced the joys and pains of expansion, we have multiplied our product lines and services, we represent the consolidation of two companies, we have acquired new plant and equipment, we have and are continuing to automate as many functions as are feasible.

To accommodate all the changes we are in a continuing process of organizational restructuring. Finally, government at the federal and state levels impacts heavily and in untold ways on our business.

We have always valued our human resources both as a matter of humane principle and in recognition of their contribution to the company's well-being. But we could not run our business today with yesterday's staff. Our staff today is infinitely more talented, competent and better educated.

We have had to develop entirely new internal capabilities to deal with the increased complexity of our business. For instance, the number of data processing personnel alone has more than doubled over the past five years.

We work closely with hospitals, physicians and governmental agencies in order to contain costs and provide high quality medical services. Because the results of these transactions spell the difference between strength and weakness, we need highly-skilled, well-educated and experienced employees. Those categorized as professionals on our staff, e.g., lawyers, accountants, systems analysts, institutional efficiency experts and economists, writers, nurses, etc. have doubled in number in the past four years alone.

The entire category of "knowledge workers" now represents about 30% of the staff whereas 30 years ago, it represented no more than five percent of the staff at most.

Quite apart from the increased utilization of specialists, overall there has been an upward shift in the contribution to the common business effort. It is safe to say that most of the functions that required relatively simple clerical skills—which occupied a large part of the time of most of our staff in the past—have been replaced by the computer. What is left and what the computer has created are more complicated work that requires knowledge, a capacity for logical thinking and good judgment.

The need today is for creative and innovative problem solvers who know what to do with the information that comes off the computer.

The complexity which has descended upon American business has also changed the roles of the Chief Executive Officer and his managers. On a day-to-day and on an immediate emotional level, my position as President and Chief Executive Officer makes me aware of still another way in which the value of our human resources has increased. In the past it was not uncommon for a CEO to have a commanding grasp of the details of the business. What he lacked could be filled in by the few top managers who reported to him directly. As a matter of course, the CEO along with his immediate staff made policy, and they made most of the big decisions. People below had little input and made few or no important decisions. The CEO in effect could literally "run the business."

Today, you have the ironic situation of the CEO having responsibility over infinitely more complex operations but less control. The CEO simply no longer can make all the big decisions nor should he be expected to. Decisions today are based on highly-sophisticated and specialized knowledge, on the seasoned judgment of the innumerable experts in the company. Other top officers are often unable to grasp enough of the complexity to make decisions. Thus, almost routinely in today's complicated business world, heavy decisions are "rooted" several levels down the line. Decisions, of course, can be and are rigorously reviewed at the top, individually and in committee, their feasibility studied and approved or disapproved in light of the total corporate position. But, in truth, decisions committing the company to large amounts of money and to courses of action the consequences of which will not become manifest for five to 10 years are now being made several levels below top management.

What this demonstrates is that more than ever the CEO has to select top managers he can trust, whose expertise and judgment he can rely upon. His role has changed from one of controlling and commanding to one of offering leadership by offering support and guidance and making effective the strengths of his top managers.

This form of leadership must represent a model for all managers in the company and extend as far down the line as possible.

It is important to point out several other ways in which we think about human resources. The contribution of human resources and their value to the company varies under different conditions. Thus, we are constantly concerned about finding those organizational forms and those conditions of work which are most conducive to optimal performance.

Human resources, moreover, are corporate assets whose value can increase over time. Management's task is not only to select with great care but also to develop and make available programs for all levels of employees that nurture their talents, ambitions and energies.

HUMAN RELATIONS

> You as the boss should know your people personally, we're told. Do you? Of course you do, you say . . . and you demonstrate it by walking around and talking with them. You ask the employee how he is, what problems he has, about his wife and children, and so on. In all those man-hours of contact, asking the employee about his problems, how many times has the employee asked about your wife and your problems? If you talk to your employee and he does not feel free to ask you about your problems, as you feel free to ask him about his, you are increasing rather than decreasing the distance that already exists between you as employer and employee.

B-U-S-I-N-E-S-S

Managers, supervisors, administrators on all levels of jobs, who are responsible for results, will attain those results better if they also recognize their responsibility to the people who help them accomplish their mission. When we think of our personal success we must remember that there are many people, all kinds of people, in the act with us. Our own effectiveness is in direct relation to our ability to get along with these other people. Give me a blackboard and I can show you how easy this can be.

In this demonstration, the key word is "Business." When we look over any group in an office, factory, or other work unit, we see all kinds of people and we wonder what molds them into an efficient team. Represented are both sexes, different ages, backgrounds, education, religions, national origin, and family environment. But we all have one thing in common. We are together in business.

When we look at this word B-U-S-I-N-E-S-S, what do we learn? We find that "U" and "I" are in business. In fact, if "U" and "I" were not in the business then what is left is an assortment of desks and chairs, equipment, facilities, methods . . . none of which gets anything done of itself. These inanimate components of business are there also when we're gone—and nothing happens. It is only when "U" and "I" come back into business that business becomes alive again. The key ingredient in business, you see, is people.

Let's examine this further. Who comes first in business? "U" do. "I" come second. In this meeting you are more important than I am. For if I can develop one helpful thought then it goes out of here multiplied, through you, twenty-five times . . . and I, alone, fall into proper perspective, that of relative insignificance. In any interpersonal relationship we should think of the other person first. Yet how often do we do this?

The boss says "Good Morning" every morning, except today, and we feel neglected and our normal reaction is to complain, "What's wrong with the old grouch?" Perhaps there is a logical explanation but we would rather gripe about the situation than have it clarified. Whenever something displeases us we snap, "He (or she) can't do that to me." Are we ever touchy! Why not something like, "I wonder what I might have done that would cause him (or her) to act this way toward me."

If only we could think of each such problem in terms of the other person, or look at it from that person's point of view, how much easier all this would be for us. By giving the other person the benefit of the doubt, how many heartaches, headaches, ulcers, and other occupational diseases could be avoided.

And finally, in business the "I" is silent. Let's realize that in the total business picture each one of us is little more than a silent partner. Let's take our jobs seriously but let's not take ourselves too seriously. The business existed before we came aboard, and it will continue after we are forgotten.

And since in business the "I" is silent, that's my cue to shut up.

THE BLIND SPOT IN THE CRYSTAL BALL

by SYDNEY J. HARRIS*
Chicago Sun Times

Whenever people say, "I wonder what life will be like 30 years from now?" or whenever some journalistic visionary draws a portrait of life in 1990, it is always the material conditions of mankind that intrigue them.

We listen to speculations about our buildings, our highways, our merchandising, our scientific and technological changes. The portraits are attractive, if a little frightening—but none of them considers the most important thing.

Nobody asks, "What will people be like 30 years from now?" or "How will we behave with one another and toward one another in 1990?" We fail to ask this because most of us believe (mistakenly) that human conduct remains substantially the same, that "human nature doesn't change."

But while the basic nature doesn't change, different social orders bring out different traits and patterns of conduct in people. We do not behave like the ancient Romans or the medieval French or the Elizabethan English or even the nineteenth-century New Englanders. For

*Sydney J. Harris, as millions of newspaper readers know, is the author of "Strictly Personal," a daily column that originated on the editorial page of the Chicago *Sun Times* and syndicated to a hundred newspapers throughout the United States, Canada, and South America. The above essay is reprinted, with the author's permission, from his book, *On the Contrary.*

better and for worse, our attitudes and relations are vastly different today.

It seems plain to me that the essential question we must ask about the future is: "What sort of people is this society bound to produce?"

As our society becomes more urbanized, more mechanized, more militarized, more specialized, there can be no doubt that what is called the *ethos* of the American people will change along with our ways of physical living. Certain traits will be encouraged, and others will be repressed; certain kinds of knowledge will be highly rewarded, and others will be ignored or even frowned upon.

And this is why most speculation about the future strikes me as trivial and marginal. At the root of all our problems is always the *human personality;* and this is the last field of inquiry we seem interested in. Or, at most, we want to "adjust" the personality to fit the technical and social changes, rather than shape the culture to fit what we think a full human being ought to be.

We don't even think in terms of a full human being, as the old Greek philosophers understood it. We think of "economic man" and "psychological man" and "man the citizen" and "man the maker." Our pragmatic society is concerned with *functions,* not with *goals,* with "Will it work?" not with "Is it worth the human effort?"

What kind of children are we turning out? What attitudes and ideals and sentiments are we encouraging and discouraging? These are the proper questions for the future, and not space travel or electronic kitchens.

THE DANGER IS NOT IN MACHINES THINKING LIKE MEN BUT IN MEN THINKING LIKE MACHINES

Personnel administration, to be effective, should be personal. But the trend seems to be the other way. In a mechanistic age we substitute impersonal procedures for personal considerations. We worry about automation, then try to apply automation principles to human values. We in industry have too much automation, not in machines and methods but in the minds of men.

Too many managers want everything spelled out for them. A supervisor's manual contains an assortment of administrative policies to guide him. A policy is a standard solution to a constantly recurring problem. Nothing lends itself so readily to a standard solution to a constantly recurring problem as the electronic computer. This may be the ideal solution for operations but the application of binary logic to human affairs creates a whole new set of problems.

For some reason it is difficult to be personal and still remain objective. This difficulty, however, is in keeping with a weakness inherent in all aspects of management. It is impossible, under our method of doing business, to measure success, progress, sales or profit in anything but numbers.

We show improved reports to stockholders, better statements to boards of directors, impressive charts to top management—all expressed in figures, generally dollars, which is all that we seem to be able to comprehend. We've had no way of measuring results in intangibles which, in the final analysis, are the important factors since they govern the figures we put down on paper.

Until such time as our presidents and comptrollers can grasp the singificance of human resources as readily as they can understand trends and summaries in figure comparisons, we'll have to continue to coat our personnel activities with an artificial frosting of numbers.

Everything in business seems to be measurable in numbers. This is also true of personnel management. When we invent a job evaluation method we let the influence of the industrial engineer, who is mathematically trained, govern the system. In merit rating, or performance rating, we reduce factors and degrees to rating scales and end up considering scores, not performance at all. In testing procedures we establish a norm or percentage, and less than a passing grade eliminates an applicant. This happens, you see, because the line managers we're trying to assist get the message of a personnel technique easier when we reduce it to numbers.

It's too bad that personnel management, in its efforts to appear scientific, has fallen into this pit of conformity. For in the area of human relations it is well to remember that "the things that count most cannot be counted."

BUSINESS IN A SOCIAL CLIMATE

It is impossible to separate the industrial society from the rest of the world in which we live. There are forces in our social and spiritual lives that affect the way in which we behave in business.

In what we call our modern society are many factors that appear to be out of tune with purely business objectives. To say, for instance, that there is no sentiment in business is nonsense. Yet how can kindness, consideration and understanding be reconciled with the competitive demands of our impersonal business operations? Can the business executive be ethical and still be prosperous?

There are many different strands of tradition and belief that are woven into the fabric of modern living. Imbedded in the culture that conditions us for life are influences which are handed down from generation to generation. Their roots can be traced back to a form of existence quite different from what we enjoy in our industrial existence today. We cling to these values since they give meaning and substance to living in a world which would otherwise be cruel and confusing.

Many of these influences are moral principles that have stood the test of time. Without relaxing them in precept we try to adapt them to changing conditions. But do they, collectively, become an impossible ideal which meets head-on with practical business requirements? In that case, which standards should be adjusted or abandoned?

Must the Golden Rule be bent a bit to keep from interfering with the normal course of business? Is the old, distinct difference between good and bad now warped into shadings of good and shadings of bad? Does trust in ethics become altruistic in a materialistic world? Compromising principles in business, as in other walks of life, is neither good nor necessary.

The spread of scientific application to business operations need not precipitate a conflict with the higher values which play such an important part in individual and business lives. It is quite possible that the doctrine of moral right and the principles of industrial might can be coalesced into a power of unknown potency for the greater benefit of mankind.

How to Avoid Conflict

To do this the social influences in our lives must be recognized in business. Actually they have become so thoroughly ingrained in our pattern of everyday living that they can hardly be ignored without serious consequences. They exert a powerful force on the way we, as individuals, conduct ourselves in business. In fact, the whole structure of our business prosperity is built upon the foundation of a great national and religious heritage that oftentimes runs counter to the materialistic ambitions of a profit-minded industrial society.

Managements are wise who do not let these social mores develop into a problem. Instead of fighting them, which could create an untenable situation, it would be better to stand up to them, admit their existence, and put them to use.

How? The basic desires of human beings are a tremendous motivating force. They account for all our actions. Business should not resist these personal and social motivations. Common sense tells us that the better business activity can be dovetailed into the natural drives of its people the smoother will be its operation. In today's concept of living, business is the focal point around which we build our personal and family lives. In strengthening the fiber of our industrial society we must take into account all the many varied and seemingly unrelated contributions made by the social climate within which business functions.

Relationships in business are of three orders: (1) to things, which we must dominate; (2) to people, whom we must respect as equals; and (3) to a higher authority, to whom we must be willing to submit. These are the materialistic, humanistic and divinistic relationships that exist in our day-to-day operation of business. These three forces exist; we cannot hope to be successful by ignoring any one of them.

It is quite obvious that no one of us succeeds alone. We are all interdependent upon each other. It was Tennyson who said, "I am a part of all I have met." While this is truly a potent observation, there is more to success than that. Let me remind you that in life all of us have met more than each other.

Throughout our lives there is an invisible means of support which guides and directs our individual and national destinies. That this influence is a factor in our personal success is evidenced by the fact that many problem situations in life, which may not conform to the obvious laws of nature or man, often find easy solution in the spiritual laws, which also exert an impelling force in the universe.

The lesson is a simple one, but by its simplicity it leaves a profound message. If we want to be successful in business we must first come to a full and final realization that business does not operate in a vacuum. The fact remains that our cold, competitive, calculating business operates in many situations in what is anything but a businesslike climate.

ETHICS

It is strange that here in the United States where average wages are the highest in the world, vast number of people display a cynical attitude toward their daily work. In our expanding service industries, for instance, surliness and irresponsibility among workers who deal with the public have become almost legendary.

The purchaser of a high-priced automobile finally traced the persistent rattle in his new car to an empty Coke bottle inside the right front door assembly and found a note addressed to "You Capitalist!" This typifies the resentment and hostility of many overly-pampered production workers. The indifferent quality of the workmanship in some American factories has caused the manufacture of certain technical equipment to be lost to European and Asiatic facilities.

Among people employed in offices and factories we can discern two basic types: The intensely-involved minority and an extremely-bored majority. The minority is made up of senior executives with a substantial personal stake in the enterprise; junior executives hoping for promotion; salesmen on commission; new employees who are not yet disillusioned; and a few exceptions to every rule, sometimes called "wheelhorses," who do a good job in spite of management's abject disinterest in them as human beings. The wheelhorses seem to be regarded by the bored majority with a sort of pity, as neurotics who bury themselves in work to escape from personal frustrations.

A quote from Winston Churchill's book, *Amid These Storms:* "Rational, industrious, useful human beings are divided into two classes; first, those whose work is work and whose pleasure is pleasure; and secondly, those whose work and pleasure are one. Of these the former are the majority."

Clearly, many Americans are far from enthusiastic about their jobs —at a time when wages are at an all-time high, fringe benefits run an average of one-third of payroll, and the coddling of workers includes such nonjob-related gimmicks as paid time off for shopping, no docking for coming in late, tuition refunds, picnics, haircuts on company time, free coffee—you name it!

Why is all this? Why don't decent wages reduce costly turnover? Why don't fringe benefits motivate more than they do? Why don't employees appreciate all we do *for* them? I'll tell you why.

Because in the administration of our personnel programs we've become impersonal. In the process of developing personnel programs we've appealed to the worker's pocketbook and not to his heart. In our efforts to simplify and standardize work, to reduce training time, we have destroyed the very soul of personal job satisfaction and pride of accomplishment. We have made human machines out of people.

Anything Goes

Somehow, in our modern materialistic world we've got to figure out how to improve the worker, not the machine or the method. We've got to appeal to the better instincts of man so he will produce more and produce better because he wants to, not because he is expected to.

This personnel attitude merely mirrors the whole philosophy of business. In supermarkets, for example, food processors produce foods that are designed to be sold, not eaten. Every dietitian can attest to that.

Like so many other industries, business needs a code of ethics. Many employers criticize the attitude of their workers which, in reality, is little different from that of the company. The father who flagrantly violates the speed laws is hardly in a position to preach personal integrity to his son.

Many employers are not averse to a little hanky-panky, corner-cutting, playing fast and loose with the trust reposed in them, engaging in shady but not illegal deals, taking unfair advantage of situations, treating people shabbily. Because of pressure they bend a little, go with the tide. And their employees see this.

But this seems to be the pattern of life. Whenever there is an embarrassing investigation in the House of Representatives of Senate a hue and cry goes up for a new code of ethics for members. But once the clamor subsides, Congress moves with less-than-deliberate speed in devising the code. Most of the time the reform movement is lost in hearings confined to generalities. After a flurry of activity to impress the general public, everybody goes home.

Movie and television people have established their own code; but judging from some of the trash that is permitted to escape the censors, nobody pays much attention to the self-imposed restrictions. The code is little more than window dressing to placate the public while fattening the pocketbook.

There are other examples: The price-fixing scandals make news headlines every once in a while. Graft and bribes are accepted as everyday practices in many places. We could mention ticket-fixing, payola and other payoffs, loan rackets, phony insurance schemes, investment pyramiding. It is only wrong, apparently, if a person gets caught; until then, anything goes.

Yet, a moral person can be successful in business. There are many respectable companies where ethical behavior influences the conduct. Many executives, managers and supervisors are able to reconcile personal beliefs with commercial interests. They can preserve their devotion to fundamentals and not compromise with truth.

After the U.S. Supreme Court ruled prayer and religion out of the classroom, a friend wiser than I said, "We can accomplish the same purposes by putting religion into the teachers. That way it becomes personal rather than academic and is much more effective."

Morality Does Pay

We are a Judeo-Christian-oriented society and religion plays a part. Whether or not a person is a participant, i.e., a churchgoer, he cannot escape the influence. He should not rationalize that the principles of right or wrong, which he accepts in his personal and family life, are not applicable in the cold, calculating, dog-eat-dog business existence. The laws of morality are as implacable as the laws of nature.

Just as parents are usually held accountable for the delinquency of their children (and lately, the vandalism), so may our society, including the industrial society, be breeding the kind of work attitude that business abhors and thus will be held accountable.

It is not what the boss says or does that counts, but what he believes. People will trust us if we first trust them. Workers will willingly help management reach its goals if in the process management helps them realize their own hopes and ambitions. Employees will give an honest performance when they recognize that the company's every policy and manner of operating are motivated by honesty and integrity for fair dealing and a respect for the dignity of man.

Business ethics and moral principles are not the same in precept. Business ethics is not something that is preached by people who are not in business. Businessmen have to be their own ethicians. Ethics has to do with what is right and what is wrong. Decisions should not conflict with the laws of God, of nature and of the land.

There is a difference between making a profit and profiteering. Charging a fair price is not the same as charging as much as the traffic will bear.

The unscrupulous businessman can "get away with it" because he operates in a scrupulous society. If every other businessman would be similarly unscrupulous, then he would lose his ill-gotten advantage.

We're all familiar with the ancient history story of a public wedding to which many families were invited. Each householder was asked to bring a jug of his best wine and pour it into the main vat. One man brought water, figuring he could outsmart the others. When the festivities began and the groom sampled the first dipper, it was discovered that it was all water.

Unrestricted greediness in business ultimately leads to control, usually by governmental agencies. Industries often establish a "code of correct conduct" to avoid outside restrictions. Otherwise when a company or an industry fails to recognize its responsibility to the community it serves, and subverts the public interest in favor of "gain at any price," it follows that civic, church, consumer groups and possibly national reaction will exert a pull in the other direction.

WORKAHOLICS

Business in today's competitive economy is a severe taskmaster. Many executives may be unaware of the toll their dedication to work exacts. Oftentimes they do not find out until it is too late.

"Workaholics" is an ugly word, but useful in describing men and women who focus their time and energies on their work first and on their personal and social lives second. They place a greater value on achievement goals than on domesticity.

There are men and women who are unhappy in the situations in which they find themselves who try to compensate for failure in one

43

area by striving for success in another direction. For some people engaging in the race for money, power, and prestige is the best way to correct the imbalance in their lives.

There are others who are genuinely happy only in the workshop, who delight in creating or producing the product of their own design, who reap tremendous satisfaction from their involvement and accomplishments. It is easy for them to get carried away when circumstances at home permit and tolerate this dedication to work.

Workaholism is either a stimulant or a narcotic. It is a stimulant for those who love their work and derive genuine satisfaction from it. It is a narcotic for those who use it to deaden the pain of an insupportable family burden. One person's meat could be another person's poison.

How many men do we know who are literally married to their jobs. With some men, the company often takes the place of the other woman. And business is a demanding mistress. This is an industrial version of the eternal triangle.

In our modern liberated society, more women are abandoning careers in the home—where long hours and seven-day work weeks somehow seem acceptable—for careers in business and the professions—where overtime and dedication lead to neglect of other obligations.

Companies absorb too much time, energy, and devotion, as industry squeezes all the mileage possible out of workers, particularly managers and executives. The heavy corporate demands, coupled with an individual's driving ambition, are affecting the lives of business people and their families. Important jobs may be exciting and fulfilling but they can devour the people in them. In the process we are developing a breed of business widows, widowers, and orphans.

The lopsided balance between work and home, for both men and women, is sometimes difficult to correct, and if not corrected, more difficult to adjust to. Many families cannot accommodate the demands of business life. Pressures are a major contributing factor. The jet age has increased the time away from home. Frequent transfers keep families from rooting down.

All the while preoccupied executives may be unaware of what is happening to their marriage and family lives. Frustrated spouses, with feelings of insecurity and inadequacy, may become tipplers or gamblers as they seek surcease from loneliness. The marriage erosion often leads to marital infidelity. Neglected children become troubled and confused, and more than a few have been known to resort to narcotics or alcohol without their parents even suspecting.

Business even dictates our mode of living. Families are going from private homes to public high-rise apartments. These buildings are dehumanizing forms of dwelling. They reduce human beings to ciphers. They are a manifestation of the regimentation of business life.

The workaholic is as much a victim as a culprit of the system. A cartoon depicted business as a rat race and showed the president's office identified as "No. 1 Rat." This is, of course, an exaggeration, but it does remind us of how wretched our lives could become. Maybe we should step off the dizzy merry-go-round long enough to reflect on the trend. Like the richest man in the cemetery, we might discover one day that we are going down in the graveyard of history as executives with full business success and empty lives.

PERSONNEL ADMINISTRATION IS THE RESPONSIBILITY OF ALL

Ours is an era of specialization. Throughout our personal and family lives we encounter professional and business people who devote their full time to one activity. The lawyer, schoolteacher, merchant and tradesman are illustrations. Even the good old family doctor has given way to medical specialists—the pediatrician, eye-ear-nose-and-throat specialist and the like.

In business, too, this holds true. Everywhere in our factories and offices are staff experts who handle one specific type of duty, generally off to the side away from the main stream of production. They are in all divisions of the company working on legal matters, budgets, real estate, market analysis and so on. Usually the operating supervisor has no clear picture of exactly what they do or how they fit into the organization.

To most line operators the personnel function is also an activity of staff specialists. It is located up front in a central office, conveniently tied to the top executives. It is a friendly office, a place where the manager or foreman can take his problem. There a so-called expert refers to a policy manual for the answer. The line operator then goes back and tries to put into effect what he considers is someone else's solution, not his. This is the picture in most companies.

Where such a condition exists the personnel officer is probably to blame. When the personnel chief succumbs to the temptation to take over management responsibilities that should remain within the line manager's scope of control, it is difficult to help line managers on a consultative basis.

Managers and supervisors often feel that the personnel director thinks he knows all about handling employees; actually, many foremen and supervisors know much about their workers, how to get along with them and how to get them to produce. Sometimes they feel that personnel people overrate the value of meetings that only take time away from more important duties. Again they may feel that the personnel director accepts every complaint from an employee as fact, that he is too quick to sympathize with the employee; to the line supervisor the personnel office is an escape, a place of last resort which the employee is encouraged to use to go over the manager's head. Finally, the manager or supervisor often feels that personnel interferes too much with the way he runs his department. When the personnel director offers panaceas without thoroughly understanding the situation, managers tend to wash their hands of problem employees, saying, in effect, "You're the expert —you straighten them out!"

The Better Arrangement

This type of relationship between the line organization and personnel office is not conducive to mutual trust and cooperation, both of which are paramount to the success of a company's employee relations program. This is not the way the picture should look, nor is it the way the dedicated personnel executive wants it to be.

In an ideal situation the staff personnel director endeavors to build his employee program by building the supervisor, not himself. For all practical purposes he prefers to stay out of the act. He tries to make the line supervisor the personnel practitioner in his particular area. He does not do thing *for* the supervisor but *through* the supervisor.

And this is for a reason, a selfish reason: The front-line supervisor is the key person in management. He alone can relate workers' needs accurately for top-management decisions. He alone can interpret management's needs to the workers for the personal good of employees and the overall good of the firm. He alone stands between a good performance and a mediocre performance.

It stands to reason, therefore, that a company's employee relations program is more effective when as much of it as possible is handled by front-line supervisors and managers. Personnel problems should be met at the operational level. These problems cannot be isolated and transplanted to a central staff which is removed from the scene of action.

Personnel administration is not the responsibility of a few specialists, but of all people in management. It is just as effective as the trained personnel staff guides and directs it; and as line supervisors understand, accept and apply it. The central personnel staff members are expected to be experienced and competent, but they should not be visionaries who have lost the common touch.

On the other hand, the supervisor responsible for results will attain those results better if he also recognizes his responsibility to the workers through whom he accomplishes his mission. It is important that the supervisor recognizes this, for he is involved in every phase of the employee relations program. It is the supervisor in his day-today activities who deals directly with the workers. Members of the central personnel office concern themselves with the factors affecting people.

This dual relationship in a common program is confusing to many people. To clarify it the following outline of the complete personnel procedure has been prepared. It covers the program from the time the new worker is hired until he leaves. Each separate step is listed. The work of the line organization is indicated by an (L) and the work of the personnel staff is marked with a (P).

THE LINE MANAGER'S ROLE IN THE PERSONNEL PROCEDURE

1. (L) In regular day-to-day conduct of work, help create reputation that will attract applicants.

2. (P) Develop sources of qualified applicants from local labor market. This requires carefully planned community relations, advertisements, employee referrals, and active high school, college and technical school recruiting, including participation in career programs.

3. (L) When vacancy occurs, or new job opens, prepare requisition outlining specific qualifications necessary to fill particular position.

4. (P) Conduct skilled interviews, give appropriate tests, and make thorough reference checks, etc., using requisition and job description as guides. Screening must meet company standards and conform with employment laws.

5. (P) Refer best candidates to manager, after physical examinations and qualifications for the position available have been carefully evaluated.

6. (L) Interview and select from candidates screened by Personnel. Make specific job placement that will utilize new employee's highest skills to promote maximum production and job satisfaction.

7. (P) Give new employee preliminary indoctrination about the company, its policies, benefits and necessary regulations.

8. (L) Give new employee local indoctrination with specific details regarding assigned job, explain "our customs," and introduce to associates.

9. (L) Instruct and train on the job according to procedure which has proved effective.

10. (P) Schedule orientation classes for new employees in order to impart company information, such as history, background and philosophy.

11. (L) Follow up, develop and rate employee job performance; decide on raises, promotion, transfer, layoff or discharge.

12. (P) Maintain record of current performance and future potential of each employee.

13. (P) Administer and counsel on separate aspects of employee benefit program.

14. (L) Hold separation interview when employee leaves—determine causes. Make internal department adjustments to minimize turnover.

15. (P) Conduct exit interview with terminating employee, to verify reason given or to uncover underlying cause. Explain checkout package: rights under benefit program, unemployment compensation, etc.

16. (P) Diagnose information given in separation interviews, analyze causes, and take positive steps to correct.

17. (P) Maintain for some period the files of terminated employees for purpose of answering reference inquiries, unemployment claims, etc.

PERSONNEL GENERALITIES vs. SPECIFICS

One of the functions of personnel research is to discover new and better ways of doing things. The old, comfortable paths could easily become deep ruts. The personnel executive should pause occasionally to reflect on what is happening. He must be able to depart from the traditional, be willing to experiment with a different approach.

For the personnel director who is satisfied with his procedures but unhappy with the results, here are a few ideas. They are presented not as a comprehensive list of problem areas but as "teasers" or "thought starters."

Recruiting

We are still using the old standbys of recruiting methods that were originated years ago to meet emergency situations. These methods are rapidly reaching the point of no return as, for example, the uselessness of help-wanted ads for typists, stenos and secretaries. In one Sunday newspaper I counted 152 ads calling for shorthand; I wondered how any likely applicant would ever find our company ad calling attention to what (we must have felt) was the best offer in the bunch. Ads no longer give the public a notion of expansion but rather, of desperation. We are in a recruiting stalemate; we need new and better recruiting approaches.

Shortage of Skills

With machines taking over increasing amounts of clerical as well as factory work, a careful inventory of human resources needs to be made. We may have plenty of people—loyal, dedicated workers at that. But do we still have plenty of necessary skills? The shortage is not in hands, the shortage is in skills; and this becomes more acute as the demand for talent and ability increases. Typists are scarcer than file clerks, secretaries harder to hire than typists, and so on. The shortage, however, doesn't stop "along the line" but goes right on up. The real shortage, the one companies ought to worry about, is the executive shortage.

Testing

Many companies use tests for employment and promotion to determine learning ability, aptitudes, interests and personality traits. But how many realize that these tests, most of which were developed decades ago and validated under conditions existing then, don't hold up when challenged today? Compliance investigators insist test use and their norms must be applicable to the specific job under consideration. But even more important than any positive predictability is their negative weakness. Tests can measure what a person *can* do but not what he *will* do. They cannot predict attitude, a very significant ingredient of success. Using present-day testing devices, Horatio Alger would not have had a chance; Benjamin Franklin would have flunked; Leonardo da Vinci would not have made it past the reception desk; Nellie Fox would not have been signed by the Chicago White Sox, but he went on to be named the American League's Most Valuable Player in 1959 because of two traits that tests cannot measure—desire and determination. The questions are: Have tests lost their usefulness? and, What new tests are being created?

Selection

We use the word "selection," but are we really selecting from a list of applicants? Or has the selection process become a series of eliminations? The number of candidates for a job is reduced by tests, physical exams, references, interviews and such devices, until there is no selection; we merely hire the one who is left. A very well-known group of

12 applicants would have been turned away, for by our standards they would have been declared unfit because of age, lack of education, inexperience; 11 of the 12 were unmarried, all were unqualified for saleswork; yet these are the 12 Apostles who became the best sales force the world has ever known.

Employment Requirements

At a time when skilled office workers are in short supply, we turn down qualified applicants simply because we are unwilling or unable to bend our rigid nine-to-five, five-days-a-week, 50-weeks-a-year routine, which is geared more to cherished past practices than to modern business needs. There are thousands of secretaries, stenos, typists, bookkeepers and other experienced white-collar workers who are "out of reach" because we don't know how to fit these odd-hour, on-again off-again workers in with the regimented regular staff. Consequently we tell them to take their job needs to some of the temporary-help agencies from whom we then hire them anyway.

Policies

This reminds us that policies in general are made in terms of the total work force and not the individuals. Is this good, or does it create more problems than it solves? Work hours, for instance, are different for computer personnel than for clerical workers. Employees who work by the job should not be required to fit the mold of employees who work by the clock. Imposing sameness upon people who are different leads to difficulties. Policies should relate to the classes, not the masses.

Vacations

The usual policy is to schedule a worker's vacation on the basis of: (1) seniority and (2) convenience to the company. This idea goes back to early days and was designed for primary wage earners—the chief worker, more than likely the only worker, in a household. Today our offices are full of secondary wage earners whose vacation choice is dictated by the spouse's requirements, not by company convenience. In such conflicting circumstances how flexible can we afford to be?

Holidays

We will probably never see fewer holidays. Even now when Christmas or Independence Day fall on a Saturday we have been pressured into closing the preceding Friday. If you are considering increasing the number of holidays from the standard six, how far do you dare to innovate? Can you add a "floating" holiday or two? How about a "personal" holiday, observed at the discretion of the employee? Today's restless workers like to vary the pattern.

Training

We have always accepted training as part of the personnel activity and as necessary for increasing the productivity and efficiency of the work force. But training is not enough anymore. This is the first generation in which a person's earlier training is no longer sufficient to carry him through life. So the new problem is retraining, which few companies are doing much about. The government has picked up the challenge and has agencies and funds ready for this purpose. Are we going to accept retraining as the responsibility of industry or are we going to leave the door of opportunity wide open for unwanted government intervention?

Retirement

Retirement is many things to many people. To some it is freedom from a lifetime of work; to others a dreaded point of no return, a "ringing down of the curtain." Like it or not, many who work for someone else are routinely forced into retirement at an arbitrary age. The age of 65 was originally chosen because for government and industry it makes for uniform and easy administration. While it may be true that "all people are created equal" it soon becomes obvious that by the time they reach age 65 or 70 they are anything but equal. Should we try to devise a retirement system that suits the individual's age and abilities instead of taking the easy way out and using one that fits the convenience of the company? Would not the company benefit in most instances?

Promotion

There are two main routes to business promotion: (1) the passive route and (2) the active route. It is entirely possible to get to the top in business by being passive. It is possible to rise to eminence from humble beginnings by doing practically nothing, but looking good while doing it. Given a well-developed instinct for survival, it is possible in some businesses to get ahead simply be being available—by being the handiest person to fall heir to the promotion as smarter people move up or out, or otherwise clear the way. The logical way, however, calls for careful selection of successor prospects. And this task of selecting the one right person need not be difficult as long as we are honest with ourselves, our companies and our candidates. We confound the issue by interjecting seniority, loyalty or sentimental personal qualities, thereby making the problem complicated.

Discrimination

Maybe you think you follow all the guidelines and don't discriminate, but you do. To check, just look at your board of directors, your management group or even your supervisors and administrators, and see how many members of minority groups are in influential positions. Firms which do not discriminate against race, color or creed might be guilty of discriminating against age which, incidentally, is far more serious. And industry continues to discriminate against women, despite some of the best efforts to the contrary. Discrimination in any form is a luxury that is too expensive to tolerate.

SUGGESTIONS FOR BETTER EMPLOYEE RELATIONS

In addition to asking questions, as we have done in the foregoing article, let's make a few suggestions. Here are 10 thoughts which we hope will make your employee relations programs better and more effective.

1. Can we treat applicants as guests instead of strangers? How about simplifying the processing procedure with less cumbersome application forms, more respect for the applicant's time, more interest in each one as a person. How about following up with replies to all responses, not just the selected few? And how about reducing the indecision annoyances of unsure interviewers?

2. In hiring workers, let's not try only to fill a vacancy in one of our departments. Let's try at the same time to help an applicant solve one of his own problems by finding a job to his liking. Ideally, every placement should be a happy job marriage in which *both* sides are satisfied.

3. When we want to transfer or promote a worker we should not think only of solving our problem. People should not be looked upon as a load of cinders moved around to fill a hole. We should be big enough to respect the worker's feelings about the new job for which he is being considered.

4. Can we arrange to give our people through training, a chance to increase their skills or add new ones to help them qualify for better job opportunities? This would enhance their earning power for themselves and their value to the company.

5. If we are going to establish a recognition program for something like length of service, let's honor each worker individually on his anniversary date, the day which means something to him, rather than lumping them all together once a year, for the easy planning of a group dinner or party.

6. Let's develop a better hearing aid for business. You say you practice the "open door" policy, but who walks in? Why don't you walk around among the workers, preferably in shirt sleeves. You'll be surprised at what you will learn.

7. Why wait until you have to announce something before you write a "memo to all employees?" Why not write when nothing is at stake and tell your associates what a good job they're doing?

8. Instead of distributing your expensive but dull annual statements, accompanied by a mass-produced cover note full of lifeless statistics, what would be wrong with a "personal letter from the president" telling each worker, at home where the family may also read it, that the company is making good progress and his job is secure.

9. Should there be a Golden Rule in business? Man is a sacred personality made in the image of God. If man were a machine, then it would be appropriate to use him, depreciate him, consume him and discard him. But man is not a machine. No one, no company, no employer, no supervisor can trample with impunity upon the human personality.

10. If respecting the dignity of man in our fellow, blood-bought souls sounds altruistic, then for selfish reasons let's recognize how important other people are to us in the accomplishment of our own goals. Our employees are the people through whom we do our work and through whom we attain our purpose. They are the ones who, in reality, make us look good. Let's make our personnel programs "people programs."

PERSONNEL RESEARCH

All personnel offices engage in some form of research activities. It is impossible to run a personnel program without some preplanning and postreviewing.

Unfortunately, most of this is done out of necessity, not out of foresight. Once the minimum results have been accomplished, the study is over. Much more could be contributed to a sound personnel program if "research and standards" were made an integral part of the personnel activity, as are other aspects, such as employment, wages and benefits.

In a good research approach the object is to get facts and information about personnel specifics in order to develop and to maintain a program that works. Don't just hire applicants, as is so often the case, but explore the market, use the best aids, to reach the goal of hiring not the first but the best available applicants. Who knows what the ideal combination might be unless he does a bit of research?

Every salary survey is, in a sense, research. Most of the time this consists of gathering outside data to support a recommendation for an upward revision of existing wage scales. Perhaps there are other possibilities to consider. What are the trends in the community or in the industry, what is best for the particular makeup of the company's workforce? Who knows without doing some research?

For that matter, any survey on any personnel policy or practice is good research. How many companies analyze their turnover? It has long been recognized that turnover is an excellent barometer of wages, benefits and other aspects of an employee program. When wages fall below the community average, turnover will increase to reflect this.

How about classifying terminations? Most terminations occur in the first year of employment. Why merely accept this as a fact of personnel life? Why not try to do something about it? Are the terminations among men or women, married or single, young or old, lower-rated jobs or higher classifications? Once the source of the problem can be pinpointed, perhaps employment patterns can be altered to alleviate the expensive problem of turnover.

Research certainly applies to employment. Before any new worker can be hired the job must be analyzed, described, specifications spelled out, an evaluation made, the job classified and a rate set. This is obvious, and to some extent these steps are taken. How much better would the placement be if this helpful information were arrived at by objective means.

Are Acquisition Costs Taken for Granted?

What about the sources of applicants? And the costs of acquisition? Where are the *most* applicants coming from? Where are the *best* applicants coming from? Which of the referrals are the more skilled, stay the longest, become promotable and work out the best? Research here can provide answers which in turn can reduce employment costs.

Research is also required in the building of an adequate testing program, and certainly in its validation within a specific company. The universities and other agencies create these tests on the basis of their research findings. But a local research application should be made before any tests, developed in outside locations, are used to aid in solving company problems. What tests to use, what combination of tests to put together into a test battery, what different tests or batteries to consider for different jobs, what norms to be guided by, how to challenge these norms in a tightening employment market, and how to apply the whole concept of tests in a climate of nondiscrimination, are questions that must be answered long after the printed test is completed and made ready for industry use.

In a tight labor market while business is expanding, the need to forecast employment requirements is almost a matter of corporate life and death. This begins with an inventory of existing jobs and people, their qualifications and potential, and a planned effort to recruit, train and build people at all levels to maintain the lifeblood of the organization. A personnel audit should be made periodically as a basis upon which to plan, and the amount and depth of research to accomplish all this will determine the effectiveness of the employment effort for years to come.

Speaking of training, how much is planned and how much is hit-and-miss? A bit of research will help identify those areas where training would be useful. In too many instances people are sent off to meetings or seminars for no justifiable reason. In-house courses are sometimes offered to employees not because the need has expressed itself but simply because a promoter sold the boss on the idea. Education and training are too important to be left to chance and research of the need, the program and the results will aid a company in getting more value for the time, money and effort expended.

Few Companies Really Know

The whole area of welfare benefits lends itself to research. What elements should be included in a comprehensive program, how extensive should the coverages be, which of several available insurance contracts would best fit the particular work group, how should the entire program be administered, how much red tape is involved, and what are the trends in this field—all these aspects need constant study.

A delicate attempt at research is a morale reading. Through a well-designed attitude survey, employee opinions are asked on wages, promotions, working conditions, opportunities, job security, leadership, management and the like. It is easy enough to ask questions of employees; it is more difficult to take the actions their answers suggest, and downright dangerous to ignore their well-intentioned advice.

Policies should not be put into effect without being researched. Practices should be checked out and never based solely on whim or personal prejudice.

The same logic applies to personnel reports which are often requested for incidental use, only to be perpetuated long afterwards. Research should test the practical value of such reports, as well as other statistical data, many of which may be compiled for no better reason than an almost automatic machine printout. Publishing periodic reports on tardiness or absences is worthless if nothing is done to try to correct the problems.

The forms used in personnel to gather information or to dispense information ought to be researched to determine how well they may be fulfilling the original purpose for which they were designed. Conditions change and personnel paperwork should keep in step.

There are many other opportunities for research in personnel administration. One important concern is that of the organization structure and organization planning. And there are always requests for special studies. By and large, research is no one-time duty. Like safety education, it must be continuous, not sporadic.

In most companies research is the most neglected area because the personnel people are too busy putting out fires. Research is not done to put out fires but to prevent them. It could well be the most meaningful aspect of personnel management, worth so much more than it costs, so that neglecting it becomes an extravagance too expensive to tolerate.

ANALYSIS OF FORMS, PROCEDURES, PRACTICES, REPORTS

As time goes by, and personnel administration becomes more complex and involved, it seems that personnel people are so busy "doing" that they cannot find time for "thinking," which should also be done. As the familiar accusation puts it, they spend so much time putting out fires that they cannot work on fire prevention.

What began as a simple form is now more detailed. What was a routine procedure is today more cumbersome. Reports are getting wider distribution and evoking more comments, some of which lead to localized or interim reports. All sorts of influences are exerting a pull on personnel practices.

All of this seems understandable at the time it happens. The extra involvement comes in small doses, insignificant in each request, and hardly worth resisting at the time. Yet the cumulative effect over a period of time throws the best-designed personnel program out of kilter.

The line of least resistance calls for adding more people to the personnel staff. The number of people in the personnel office should increase as the total workforce grows or as new functions are added. But it is unprofitable to add people because of red tape. Maybe some of the red tape that has been sneaking in is no longer necessary.

It is better to analyze forms, procedures, practices and reports periodically if not regularly. Put each on trial to determine whether it can be simplified, combined, mechanized or possibly even eliminated. The results may well be surprising.

FRINGE BENEFIT SURVEY

Fringe benefit growth, during the past several decades, has substantially improved employee well-being, and has also increased the cost of doing business.

Payments for vacations, holidays, rest periods, etc., constitute almost half of total fringe benefits. These payments are included in government wage reports as a portion of employee wages. Such payments give employees increased compensation. Thus, they also increase the employer's cost for productive labor.

Pension, social security and other employer payments for employee benefits are not part of the payroll, and are not reflected in current income or wages of employees. Such benefits, however, greatly improve employee security and well-being, and also increase the cost of doing business.

The Chamber of Commerce of the United States, noting the scarcity of statistical information regarding the scope and nature of fringe benefits, conducted in 1947 the first comprehensive fringe benefit study for a cross section of American industry. This study was widely and favorably received and at the request of employers it has been repeated biennially with extended coverage and in greater detail.

The survey is conducted in the Chamber's Economic Policy Group. Its questionnaire, which follows, is available from the Chamber of Commerce of the United States, 1615 H Street, N.W., Washington, D.C. 20062.

The survey report developed from the last questionnaire can be obtained for a price from the same address.

TURNOVER RESEARCH

A turnover report is a good barometer of what is happening in the employment picture. A rise in the turnover rate is a signal that something is changing. It could also be a warning of danger ahead.

An increase in the turnover percentage is often an indication that the salary level has fallen below the community average. Benefits may be inadequate and consequently a company might be losing employees to competitors whose programs are more attractive. A bad turnover report might also point up poor supervision.

It is unwise to ignore the message which a good turnover study delivers. But in addition to soft spots in a company's employee program, a turnover report also reflects the times. Even when salaries, benefits and working conditions check out well, the turnover rate might

ECONOMIC POLICY/CHAMBER OF COMMERCE OF THE UNITED STATES/WASHINGTON, D.C. 20062

CONFIDENTIAL

EMPLOYEE BENEFITS SURVEY-1977

(Fringe Benefits)

For Office
Coding—
Leave Blank

| 1 | — — — — — |

— — — — —
— — — — —
— — — — —

Name of Firm _____ Date_____

Street_____ City _____ State _____ Zip Code _____

Name of Company Official _____ Title _____

| Show actual data or best estimate for employees covered in survey. | | Total amount for 1977 |

A. GROSS PAYROLL FOR EMPLOYEES IN SURVEY: (See Instructions No. 4)

1. Straight-time for employees in survey .... $ _____
2. Overtime premium pay .... $ _____
3. Holiday premium pay .... $ _____
4. Shift differential .... $ _____
5. Earned incentive or production bonus .... $ _____
6. Other (Specify: _____) .... $ _____
7. Total gross payroll .... $ _____

Include **BONUS AND PREMIUM PAY ONLY** on lines 2-6. Report straight-time pay on line 1.

B. LEGALLY REQUIRED PAYMENTS (employer's share only):

1. Old-Age, Survivors, Disability and Health Insurance .... $ _____
2. Unemployment Compensation (Federal and state taxes) .... $ _____
3. Workmen's Compensation (estimate cost of self-insured) .... $ _____
4. Railroad Retirement Tax .... $ _____
5. Railroad Unemployment and Cash Sickness Insurance .... $ _____
6. State sickness benefits insurance .... $ _____
7. Other (Specify: _____) .... $ _____
8. Total .... $ _____

C. VOLUNTARY OR AGREED-UPON PAYMENTS (employer's share only):

1. Pension plan premiums under insurance and annuity contracts (net) (See Instructions No. 5) .... $ _____
2. Payments to uninsured trusteed pension plans .... $ _____
3. Pension payments under unfunded pension programs .... $ _____
4. Life insurance premiums (net) (See Instructions Nos. 5 and 6) .. $ _____
5. Death benefits not covered by insurance .... $ _____
6. Hospital, surgical, medical and major medical insurance premiums (net) (See Instructions No. 7) .... $ _____
7. Hospital, accident, surgical and medical care payments self insured ... $ _____
8. Salary continuation or long term disability (insured, self-administered or trust) .... $ _____
9. Dental insurance premiums .... $ _____
10. Discounts on goods and services purchased from company by employees ... $ _____
11. Employee meals furnished by company .... $ _____
12. Other (Specify: _____) .... $ _____
13. Total .... $ _____

Coding numbers in right margin: 27, 33, 34, 40, 46, 53, 59, 65, 71, 6, 12, 18, 21

Please return the filled-out questionnaire to:
ECONOMIC POLICY/CHAMBER OF COMMERCE OF THE UNITED STATES/WASHINGTON, D.C. 20062

CONFIDENTIAL

	Total amount for 1977	For Office Coding— Leave Blank

D. PAID REST PERIODS, LUNCH PERIODS, WASH-UP TIME, TRAVEL TIME, CLOTHES-CHANGE TIME, GET-READY TIME, ETC. $ _____ 24 ___ ___ ___

E. PAYMENTS FOR TIME NOT WORKED:
1. Payments for or in lieu of vacations $ _____ 27 ___ ___ ___
2. Payments for holidays not worked $ _____
3. Sick leave pay $ _____ 33 ___ ___ ___
4. Payments required under guaranteed workweek or workyear $ _____
5. Jury, witness and voting pay allowances $ _____
6. National Defense, State or National Guard duty $ _____
7. Payment for time lost due to death in family or other personal reasons $ _____
8. Other (Specify: _____) $ _____ 36 ___ ___ ___
9. Total $ _____

F. OTHER ITEMS:
1. Profit sharing payments (See Instructions No. 8)
   (a) Current cash payments $ _____ 39 ___ ___ ___
   (b) Payments to deferred profit sharing trusts $ _____
2. Contributions to employee thrift plans (See Instructions No. 9) $ _____ 45 ___ ___ ___
3. Christmas or other special bonuses (not tied to profits), service awards, suggestion awards, etc. $ _____
4. Employee education expenditures (tuition refunds, seminar attendance, etc.) $ _____ 51 ___ ___ ___
5. Payments to union stewards or officials for time spent in settling grievances or in negotiating agreements $ _____
6. Special wage payments ordered by courts, wage adjustment boards, etc. $ _____
7. Other (Specify: _____) $ _____ 54 ___ ___ ___
8. Total $ _____

G. EMPLOYEE PAYROLL DEDUCTIONS: (See Instructions No. 10)
1. Old-age, Survivors, Disability and Health Insurance $ _____ 57 ___ ___ ___
2. Railroad Retirement Tax $ _____
3. State sickness benefits insurance tax $ _____
4. Pension plan premiums or contributions $ _____ 63 ___ ___ ___
5. Life insurance premiums $ _____
6. Hospital, accident, surgical and medical care insurance premiums or contributions (including Blue Cross-Blue Shield) $ _____ 66 ___ ___ ___
7. Total $ _____

H. MAN HOURS (man hours worked or paid for, including time actually worked, plus holidays, vacation, sick leave and other time paid for but not worked) (See Instructions No. 11) 69 ___ ___ ___
1. Total for all employees in survey _____ hours
2. For typical full-time employee _____ hours 73 ___ ___ ___

I. TYPE OF BUSINESS and principal lines or products manufactured or handled: _____

Please return the filled-out questionnaire to:
ECONOMIC POLICY/CHAMBER OF COMMERCE OF THE UNITED STATES/WASHINGTON, D.C. 20062

still climb simply because the employment market is unstable, making employees restless.

In that event, a study of turnover may reveal hiring practices that need to be reviewed. The employment situation may have become desperate, through a shortage of qualified applicants or a rapid expansion of company business, to force the personnel office in its referrals and the managers in their acceptance to relax the standards somewhat. If this leads to higher turnover, an analysis of terminations will point up those areas where changes may be needed.

Generally, turnover occurs during the first six or 12 months of employment. If this is the problem, then steps need to be taken to stay closer to new employees, to make them feel welcome, to help them over problems—in short, to give them that feeling of belonging so they will not quit so readily.

But a turnover analysis will come up with more than generalities. In such a study all terminations for a given period of time—say, six to 12 months back—are tallied. They are broken into those categories which should be examined. These could well be: age, sex, job classification, salary, length of service, referral source, etc. This way the source of the problem could be pin-pointed better.

At any rate, the turnover analysis will reveal the weak spots in either the employee program or in hiring practices. These then become the problem over which management should be concerned.

TURNOVER IN MANAGEMENT

The head of one of the nation's largest executive and technical placement firms listed these reasons for managerial turnover:

1. More money.
2. Opportunity for greater responsibility.
3. Geographical relocation (worry about the quality of life in some cities).
4. Inability to discuss problems.
5. Management's resistance to new ideas.
6. Corporate promotion policies.
7. Dual standards.
8. Management's unwillingness to give proper credit.

Many men and women look around in their chosen field when they realize they're stuck in wrong jobs and are finally able to do something about it. Once the burden of financial obligations gets under control, they can afford the risk of changing careers.

TYPICAL TURNOVER REPORT

DIVISION	TABLE OF ORGANIZATION				TERMINATIONS		PERCENT TURNOVER		
	June 1 Previous Year	May 1 This Year	June 1 This Year	Year Average	Month	Last 12 Months	Month	Year	Year Ago
Executive	27	26	25	26	-	4	-	15	8
Sales	166	168	168	167	6	23	4	14	6
Research	12	12	13	12	-	3	-	25	25
Financial	71	89	91	83	5	38	5	46	21
Manufacturing—A	276	334	338	313	8	112	2	36	26
Manufacturing—B	207	227	229	217	6	117	3	54	38
Manufacturing—C	177	361	367	306	16	154	4	50	3
Companywide	936	1217	1231	1124	41	451	3	40	24

RESEARCH ON ADS AND AD WRITING

Most help wanted advertisements are rather matter of fact. They tell the story of a job opportunity in convincing terms. Since there is really very little difference in basic salaries, fringe benefits and working conditions, all ads begin to sound alike.

The help wanted pages of the big metropolitan newspapers look more like a directory of corporations in trouble than a list of career opportunities.

The big screaming ads actually sound more like desperation than job openings. In an effort to evoke a response, some ads attempt to be different. When ads do not pull, new approaches are tried.

One man told why his secretarial position was open. His secretary couldn't put up with his temper and unreasonableness. He was honest and said he was a tough boss. He filled his job while other sterile ads which boasted about "convenient location, excellent benefits, good opportunity for the right person" (whatever all that means) went unanswered.

Another ad asked for "an applicant smart enough to be worth $150 a week but dumb enough to start for less." It brought in sufficient replies to give the employer a choice of candidates.

Why? Why do some ads appeal to job hunters while others fall on deaf ears? There are many reasons, some of which, such as a tight labor market, we have no control over.

Ads should be studied to see how well they serve their purpose. A good check is to keep a record of telephone, mail or walk-in responses, how many who inquire are invited in for interviews, how many show up, how many are considered at all, how many listen to the job offer, how many accept and how many are hired.

There is no rule of thumb which tells when an advertisement is effective. A newspaper ad for middle-aged homemakers to do unskilled office or factory work will pull better than an ad for secretaries. But any ad which does not bring in a fair response should be reviewed and revised before it is rerun.

Maybe the medium is wrong. A newspaper that brings in responses for clerical jobs may not be the place to use an ad for actuaries or engineers. The time of the year makes a difference. High school students may be reached in June but not at other times.

Most of the time help wanted advertisements are placed because a problem exists. If the job opening is filled, the problem is forgotten and the employment interviewers concentrate on a new problem. If the job opening is not filled, the strategy is repeated, possibly changed. Somehow, through trial and error, results are attained.

Help wanted advertising, like other recruiting efforts, is costly. How can we know if we are getting our money's worth or whether we are wasteful? How can we know if the results we get are the best possible under existing circumstances?

Research helps. A simple record of results, as indicated earlier, will be helpful as a guide for future ads. Costing out acquisition expense per new worker hired may serve as an eye-opener. Follow-up on applicants hired, to see how well they worked out, how long they stayed, may indicate the type of applicant attracted through one medium as against another.

It is not recommended that endless paperwork should be undertaken. The effort must be on getting the jobs filled. But a studied effort will produce a better result.

MAJOR LAWS AFFECTING PERSONNEL

The *Norris-La Guardia Anti-Injunction Act of 1932* defines the conditions under which injunctions can be issued, thereby drastically limiting the federal courts. This Act also forbids the use of "yellow-dog contracts" which required, as a condition of employment, the employee to enter into an agreement with the employer not to join a union.

The *Walsh-Healey Public Contracts Act* sets labor standards on U.S. government contracts. It covers minimum wage and overtime, prohibits hiring minors under 16 years of age, prohibits convict labor and contains safety and health provisions.

The *Fair Labor Standards Act*—also known as the Wage and Hour Law—was passed in 1938 and amended several times. It establishes minimum wage, overtime pay, equal pay and child labor standards. It is applicable to all firms engaged in interstate commerce.

The *Civil Rights Act of 1964 in Title VII* prohibits discrimination on the basis of race, color, religion, sex or national origin, in any term, condition or privilege of employment.

The *Equal Employment Opportunity Act of 1972* is a series of amendments to Title VII of the Civil Rights Act of 1964. It empowers an independent agency, the Equal Employment Opportunity Commission, to prohibit all kinds of employment discrimination based on race, religion, color, sex or national origin.

The *Equal Pay Act of 1963,* an amendment to the Fair Labor Standards Act, forbids unequal pay policies or fringe benefits based on sex.

The *Age Discrimination in Employment Act of 1967,* as amended, prohibits discrimination against persons 40 to 65 years of age, in hiring, discharge, leave, compensation, promotion and other areas of employment.

The *Federal Employees' Compensation Act,* as amended, provides for payment of worker's compensation benefits to civil officers and employees of all branches of the federal government.

Executive Orders are issued by the President of the United States to employers having contracts for government work. Executive Order *11246* covers race, creed, color and national origin; *11375* covers sex; *11141* covers age. All require that equal opportunity be provided to all persons employed or seeking employment within government, with government contractors, or with contractors performing under federally-assisted construction. Title VII of the Civil Rights Act of 1964 requires employers to *refrain* from discriminating, but Executive Orders impose *positive* obligations. They require that companies take *affirmative action.* This means doing whatever is necessary to provide additional job opportunities to those people who have been denied these opportunities before.

The *Rehabilitation Act of 1973,* as amended, requires in Section 503, government contractors and subcontractors to take affirmative action to employ and to advance in employment qualified handicapped individuals.

The *Veterans' Reemployment Rights* provides that any employee enlisting in or inducted into the Armed Services of the United States who leaves a position in order to perform military service, receives a certificate of satisfactory service, and makes application for reemployment within 90 days of leaving the service, shall be restored to the position that he otherwise would have achieved but for his military service, with attendant seniority status and pay if still qualified to perform.

The *Consumer Credit Protection Act*—also known as the Federal Wage Garnishment Law—under Title III limits the amount of an employee's disposable earnings that may be withheld to satisfy creditors.

The *Wagner Act* is also known as the National Labor Relations Act of 1935. It is one of two federal laws (the other is the Railway Labor Act of 1926) that outline employees' rights with regard to union activities. It outlawed only *employer* unfair labor practices.

The *Taft-Hartley Act*—also known as the Labor-Management Relations Act—was passed in 1947 and amended the Wagner Act to recognize the right of employees to refrain from union activity, to broaden the employer's right of speech, and to modify the procedures for election and for determining bargaining units. It encourages collective bargaining and protects workers' rights to organize. It added prohibitions against certain types of *union* conduct. It permits union shop agreements; however, section 14(b) negates union shops in states where they are forbidden by law.

The *Landrum-Griffin Act*—also known as the Labor-Management Reporting and Disclosure Act of 1959—amends the Taft-Hartley Act. It is designed to safeguard union members against possible abuse by their union.

The *Employee Retirement Income Security Act of 1974* (ERISA) provides protection of the interests of participants and beneficiaries in private pension and welfare plans by requiring reporting and disclosure of plan and financial information to the U.S. Department of Labor and to employees.

Worker's Compensation Laws. Every state has legislation concerned with paying injured employees with private insurance funds, company funds or state funds. Some of the benefits include medical expense, indemnity payments when disabled, death benefits and burial expenses.

Unemployment Compensation Laws. When Congress passed Social Security legislation in 1935, it required each state to establish basic unemployment compensation laws. Originally designed as a cushion against a cessation of spending when factories cut back work forces, benefits were intended for legitimate wage earners who had lost jobs thrugh no fault of theirs, to tide them over until they could find work. As a rule, covered workers receive enough money to pay for food, shelter, clothing and medical care.

The *Williams-Steiger Occupational Safety and Health Act of 1970* (OSHA) requires employers to furnish a safe and healthful work place and conditions free of recognized hazards. It sets standards and requires records be maintained of work-related injuries, illnesses and deaths.

PERSONNEL PERIODICALS

Members of the personnel staff may wish to subscribe to publications to aid them in their work. Listed below are magazines in the field of personnel administration as well as others of a specialized or technical nature.

Administrative Management
51 Madison Avenue
New York, New York 10010

Association Management
2011 Eye Street, N.W.
Washington, D.C. 20036

Canadian Personnel and Industrial Relations Journal
2221 Yonge Street
Toronto, Ontario, Canada M4S 2B4

Data Processing
134 North 13th Street
Philadelphia, Pennsylvania 19107

Dun's Review
666 Fifth Avenue
New York, New York 10019

Editor & Publisher
575 Lexington Avenue
New York, New York 10022

Federal Personnel Manual
Superintendent of Documents
Washington, D.C. 10402

Harvard Business Review
Harvard University
Boston, Massachusetts 02163

PERSONNEL ADMINISTRATION HANDBOOK

Human Behavior
12031 Wilshire Boulevard
Los Angeles, California 90025

Management of Personnel Quarterly
Bureau of Industrial Relations
Graduate School of Business
Administration
University of Michigan
703 Haven Street
Ann Arbor, Michigan 48104

Management Review
135 West 50th Street
New York, New York 10020

Modern Office Procedures
614 Superior Ave. West
Cleveland, Ohio 44113

National Business Woman
2012 Massachusetts Avenue, N.W.
Washington, D.C. 20036

The Office
1200 Summer Street
Stamford, Connecticut 06904

Office Administration
1450 Don Mills Road
Toronto, Ontario, Canada M3B 2X7

Personnel
135 West 50th Street
New York, New York 10020

The Personnel Administrator
10 Beech Street
Berea, Ohio 44017

Personnel and Guidance Journal
1607 New Hampshire Avenue, N.W.
Washington, D.C. 20009

Personnel Journal
1131 Olympic Boulevard
Santa Monica, California 90404

Personnel Management
1231-25th Street, N.W.
Washington, D.C. 20037

Personnel Management Abstracts
703 Haven Street
Ann Arbor, Michigan 48104

Personnel Policies and Practices
Bank Administration Institute
303 South Northwest Highway
Park Ridge, Illinois 60068

Personnel Psychology
P.O. Box 6965
College Station
Durham, North Carolina 27708

Personnel Service
National Retail Merchants Association
100 West 31st Street
New York, New York 10001

Public Personnel Management
1313 East 60th Street
Chicago, Illinois 60637

Recruiting Trends
20 North Wacker Drive
Chicago, Illinois 60606

Studies in Personnel Policy
845 Third Avenue
New York, New York 10022

Supervision
104 South Michigan Avenue
Chicago, Illinois 60603

Supervisory Management
135 West 50th Street
New York, New York 10020

Systems Management, Journal of
24587 Bagley Road
Cleveland, Ohio 44138

Today's Secretary
1221 Avenue of the Americas
New York, New York 10020

Training
731 Hennepin Avenue
Minneapolis, Minnesota 55403

Training and Development Journal
P.O. Box 5307
Madison, Wisconsin 53705

Women in Business
9100 Ward Parkway
Kansas City, Missouri 64114

Working Woman   plus   **Publications of the United States**
600 Madison Avenue   **Department of Labor**
New York, New York 10022   Washington, D.C. 20402

PERSONNEL UPDATE

To keep abreast of current trends and developments in the dynamic field of personnel administration, busy personnel executives subscribe to PERSONNEL UPDATE, a concise four-page newsletter published twice a month by Dartnell.

The subscription rate is surprisingly low. This is not intended as a money-making promotion on the part of the publisher. Rather it is a sincere effort to be of service to modern personnel executives who know how important it is to be well-informed in the vital area of human resources management with all its social and legislative implications. Despite all the pressures and influences, personnel management, today more than ever, must be efficient and effective to contribute its share to the profitability and growth of the company.

Inquiries and requests for a sample copy may be directed to PER-SONNEL UPDATE, Dartnell, 4660 Ravenswood Avenue, Chicago, Illinois 60640.

PERSONNEL UPDATE

The Newsletter that emphasizes Government and other third-party involvements

PERSONNEL ASSOCIATIONS

by WILLIAM H. HILL

When I first began working in the field of personnel, I did not know about organizations or groups that were established to help the personnel people perform a better job. Most companies have small personnel staffs, when compared to accounting, marketing or administration. The personnel administrator is pretty much alone, must make decisions that affect the entire company's policy, and must back up these decisions.

Where does one go for advice and counsel? Personnel associations were founded for such a purpose. Since then many advantages have come out of these groups.

In belonging to a national association, a member is immediately put on the membership list. The roster identifies the company, the personnel practitioner's title, and many times the number of employees. This helps a member relate to the problems that exist in comparable companies.

Other services from a national association are:

1. Research reports: the surveys conducted cover all phases of personnel activities. These studies enable the members to evaluate the strong and weak points of their own programs, and to keep informed on new trends.

2. Periodicals: magazines or periodicals are published all year long. These bring the members interesting feature articles and news of the latest developments in business and industry, with case histories, research studies and exclusive coverage of personnel activities.

3. Consultation service: whatever one needs, whether it is the planning of a personnel activity from scratch or technical advice on an unfamiliar activity, the national association's staff are on call to help. Most of the staff are available for speaking engagements.

4. Membership directory: listing of personnel directors, managers, officers and associate members is published annually. Membership certificates are issued to all members.

5. Conferences, workshops and monthly meetings: national annual conference and exhibits are open to all members where educational sessions and seminars are conducted for personnel executives. Monthly meetings of the local chapter can be very worthwhile. Here members meet their peers and are able to exchange information and resolve problems that one might be experiencing. The lasting acquaintances in the personnel field are very important.

6. Employment services: special assistance is offered members in finding career opportunities and to companies in finding qualified staff personnel. Recruiting and search service offers screening and referral of candidates for personnel positions.

Finally, an important aspect of the association is for an individual to become active in the governing of the group. This cooperative participation is good training and the involvement brings a great measure of self-satisfaction. A member may volunteer for committees or run for office. The experience will be very rewarding and the benefits can last a long time.

CHAPTER II

RECRUITMENT

TABLE OF ORGANIZATION

HOW MANY employees does a company need? How should they be divided among the several organizational units? How can the number be kept from increasing unnecessarily?

One effective control is a "Table of Organization." This is a device to aid in the efficient operation of a company through establishing and controlling manpower requirements.

The Table of Organization as used in industry (T/O) is an adaptation of the Table of Organization and Equipment of army days (TO/E) which is a table prescribing a standard unit composition with its organic personnel and equipment. Categories of personnel, from the highest level commissioned officer to enlisted personnel, are designated. Military occupational specialty (MOS) codes and grades are prescribed. Provisions are made for reduced strength and contingencies. Its purpose is to conserve military manpower.

The business use of T/O is a simple statement of the total manpower needs of a company. It is a listing, arranged along structural or functional lines, of the number and classification of positions in a total organization, broken down into divisions, departments or other operational units.

The tabulation shows each separate job title, the salary grade or position classification, and the number of such jobs in the unit. It would not list all 10 secretarial jobs in the firm in one place but rather show one such position in each department where it belongs. The order follows that of the budget, using the same code numbers. If, for instance, the Executive Division has its departments in budget series 10, it will be listed ahead of the Marketing Division whose budget series is in the 20's; Finance Division, budget 30, would precede Manufacturing if its budgets were in the 40's.

To illustrate: that portion of a company's total T/O which covers the Personnel and Public Relations functions, each with its separate budget, might look like this:

Budget	Job Title	Grade	Number
50	Personnel Director	X	1
	Secretary I	8	1
	Asst. Personnel Director	VIII	1
	Secretary II	6	1
51	Employment Manager	VI	1
	Interviewer	10	2
	Employment Clerk	5	1
	Compliance Clerk	6	1
	Receptionist	3	1
52	Wage Administrator	VI	1
	Job Analyst	IV	1
	Clerk, etc.	4	1
60	Public Relations Director	X	1
	Secretary I	8	1
61	Artist	IX	1
62	Copywriter	VII	2
	Typist, etc.	5	3

In the above hypothetical example, the jobs are further differentiated in that the salary grade of exempt positions (using one job evaluation system) is shown in Roman numerals, while wage-and-hour jobs (evaluated under another system) are designated in arabic numeral classifications.

The orderly listing of all jobs in a company by title, grade and number would of itself make the T/O a convenient instrument for management. But that is not its purpose. It serves as a control if a proper procedure for maintaining it is followed. This could be something like the following typical policy.

Jobs Protected, Dropped or Added

As soon as any job is vacated, either because the employee terminates or transfers, Personnel is given a requisition for a replacement. This protects the job. The requisition is signed by the Manager and approved by his immediate superior, who may have his own opinion whether the job should be continued, changed or dropped.

A job may be abolished at any time simply by written notice from the Manager to the Personnel office, or whoever is in charge of the T/O, asking that it be removed from his list. Some companies go so far as to automatically delete any job which remains unfilled for a reasonable period of time (maybe 90 days or six months) on the theory that if the Manager was able to get along without someone in that job maybe the job isn't necessary.

By observing the foregoing procedure the T/O will remain intact or possibly be reduced. If management's objective is to be satisfied with the status quo, no further control may be necessary. If the work volume or operating cost fluctuate, it may be advisable to have the Comptroller or Budget Administrator countersign all replacement requisitions.

In all cases, it is recommended that a tighter control be installed for additions to the T/O. These could be either new jobs or extra personnel for existing jobs. This control can be accomplished by having the President approve all requests for additions to the T/O. Usually the Manager completes a requisition for an additional job or person, has his superior concur with his request, and then, supported with substantial documentation, pleads his case before the Chief Executive.

In companies where more sophisticated planning is attempted, the special approval for additional personnel is not a formality as long as the planning program or project that requires additional personnel has been approved. Such planning is coordinated with annual budgets and if the money to pay for the additional personnel has been allocated, the personnel needed to carry out the plan may be added to the payroll at the time specified in the budget.

Any additional job once approved becomes a permanent addition to the T/O. A similar procedure may be followed for temporary jobs except that it is suggested these be authorized for a short duration, possibly 30 days, so that the need can be reviewed periodically.

A Table of Organization, if properly drawn up and carefully administered, can indeed be an effective control mechanism over the manpower requirements, not only of an entire company but also for each of its separate operating units.

MANPOWER INVENTORY

The first step in manpower planning is to take an inventory of the human resources that already exist in the company. How can a company do an honest job unless it knows what it already has on board—and most companies do not know?

What is critical to manpower planning is that present and future job needs be systematically reviewed against all employees who may be qualified or qualifiable for these new opportunities. To do this a company needs to take inventory.

The inventory provides documentation of biographical and historical data on each employee for use in official and personal decisions. It consists of a complete job history, compensation record, current and past performance, strengths, development needs and an estimate of potential for each individual. It updates the information supplied years ago on the application blank, and taken annually it keeps this information current.

In companies with relatively small numbers of employees, each employee's experience and background may be well known. In these cases earmarking certain individuals for special consideration does not require any sophisticated technique.

The danger, however, is that as companies grow larger, top management may mistakenly believe they still know all about their employees. They may know about some employees, particularly old-timers, but it is doubtful that they know everything about everybody. The tragic consequence is that some talent is innocently overlooked. To avoid such mistakes an objective procedure should be followed.

An impersonal method should be designed to assure equitable consideration for all. Some employees, because of their duties or personalities, are not as visible as others and their good qualities are likely to go unrecognized. Inadvertently overlooking anyone is unfair to the individual and costly to the company.

Taking Stock

Taking an inventory periodically is merely a mechanical procedure. Its purpose is to:

1. Identify employees who can possibly fill critical positions included in the forecast.
2. Assure that deserving employees are not overlooked.
3. Establish what skill requirements can be met by training and development—and which cannot.
4. Determine what shortages of skills exist that make it necessary to recruit on the outside to fill certain positions.
5. Avoid any needless recruitment expense.
6. Decide to what extent the forecast has to be altered because the number and types of employees required may not be available either internally or through an economically-feasible, outside effort.

Jobs must be filled now and in the future with employees who are already qualified, with employees who are developable and can be made ready, or else with outsiders. When an outsider is considered, his qualifications, background, experience and interests are reviewed. Is not a candidate from within entitled to the same treatment?

There is also a significant side benefit that should not go unnoticed. A manpower inventory will uncover and bring to the surface the "shelf sitters," a rapidly-proliferating species dispersed throughout every organization. These are the men and women who have turned-off, dead-ended or otherwise suffered career arrest. Often through no fault of their own they have been sidetracked onto comfortable parking places along the road to success. Not all productivity dropouts can be salvaged, of course, but there may be a few whose credentials are still good, who can be redirected, thereby reducing this tragic carnage of damaged lives.

MANPOWER FORECASTING

All over the industrial scene "planning" is in vogue. There is corporate planning, marketing planning, product planning, financial planning and now manpower planning.

Planning about money and material is very nice but useless unless companies give equal time to their people planning. To meet other planning objectives, how many and what kind of people will be needed? When? What skills or academic disciplines? Where will they come from? How many are in the company? What can the company do to attract the right candidates from the outside, where this is the only solution?

Forecasting and manpower planning are inseparable. By way of definition, forecasting is a process which translates corporate objectives to present operational requirements and future plans in terms of the number and types of jobs. It consists of estimating the number and kinds of employees required to acquire, deliver and retain the ongoing and also the changing business at a predetermined date in the future.

There are many different factors to be considered in making a workforce forecast including:

1. Looking at the composition of jobs in the present organization.
2. Listing the vacant positions.
3. Estimating losses through normal attrition.
4. Noting possible surpluses of skills or people.
5. Expressing any extension of productivity in terms of jobs.
6. Taking into account new projects and their requirements.
7. Making allowance for anticipated changes in systems.

Underlying the methodology is the contention that information about the past workforce and its productivity provides a springboard from which to project future workforce needs.

Much Like Money Budgeting

The procedure for conducting a workforce forecast varies with the size and type of business but generally includes the following steps:

1. Prepare data base (past productivity and present structure).
2. Estimate future needs (ongoing and new).
3. Adjust for assumed changes in work.
4. Translate work loads into specific jobs.
5. Consolidate the forecasts, if done fractionally.
6. Cost out the total forecast.
7. Review with top management.
8. Approve as submitted or modified.
9. Prepare the timetables and schedules.
10. Proceed to develop the manpower plan.

For this purpose, simple manpower forecasting methods are widely used. The more advanced techniques such as computer modeling are rarely employed, while interest in them is high.

Forecasting is not educated guessing. It is a combination of direct estimates and projections—mathematical extensions of past and present data. Forecasting is deliberate and calculated planning based on a pattern of performance, basic assumptions, evaluations of prospects, and a thorough understanding of the industrial, economic, social and political environment.

Once the overall forecast is completed, it can be separated into the applicable divisions and departments. A bottoms-up procedure may be easier, with each functional division making its own analysis. Approaching the forecast from both directions (as is often done in budgeting) offers a checks-and-balances way of making the forecast more accurate and practical.

Workforce forecasting is useful because it is not visionary. It looks ahead, not back, but keeps its feet firmly on the solid ground of facts. Manpower planning, therefore, based on these forecasts, becomes a very usable management tool.

MANPOWER PLANNING

If material resources can be systematically programmed, why can't the same approach be applied to human resources? That's what manpower planning attempts to do. In a more formal sense, manpower planning is a process to assure that essential manpower will be available and ready, in both numbers and disciplines, as needed.

Manpower planning is necessary for every company that expects

THE MANPOWER PLANNING PROCESS

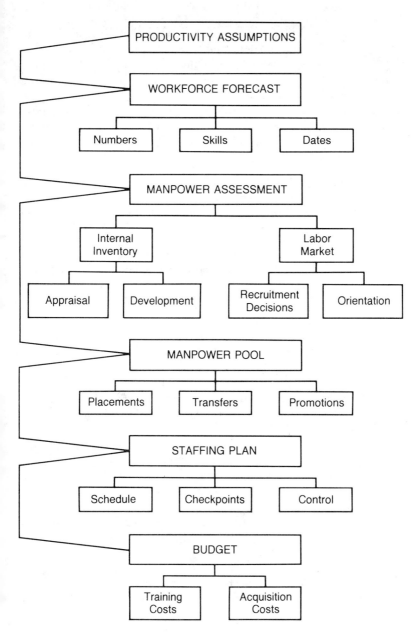

normal growth, gradual expansion, diversification of product lines, even cutbacks.

The primary purpose of manpower planning, as with any other aspect of planning, is to prepare for the future by reducing its uncertainty. It has as a basic goal the reduction of the uncertainty as related to the acquisition, placement and development of employees for future needs.

How much more sensible to attack the problem before it gets out of bounds than to simply continue to react as needs arise! When future needs are not "felt" in advance, the results are hiring delays, desperation placements, inadequately-trained workers, and the filling of positions without proper consideration of qualifications and preparation.

Manpower planning, on the other hand, is a systematic effort that comprises three key elements:

1. *Workforce forecast:* what kind and how many employees will be needed—and when?
2. *Manpower assessment* or workforce inventory: what talents and abilities are already "on board" to fill many of the critical forecasted needs?
3. *Staffing program:* what outside recruiting schedule or inside assistance for promising and promotable employees is called for to have people ready?

Workforce forecasting consists of estimating the numbers and kinds of employees required to acquire, deliver and retain the ongoing and also the changing business at a predetermined date in the future.

After the forecast has been made and the assortment of jobs listed, employees should be evaluated to establish who are ready or could be made ready for assignments. What is critical to manpower planning is that job needs, as specified through the forecast, be systematically reviewed against all employees who may be qualified or qualifiable for these new opportunities.

The purpose of the assessment is to permit management to make rational choices between filling jobs from internal or external sources. In any case, programs should be developed for meeting future manpower needs.

Manpower planning means more than matching estimated number needs with corresponding recruitment drives. For better results it is advisable to develop talent ahead of the need, particularly for upper-level positions.

To make manpower planning effective it would indeed be helpful if top management would indicate its interest and express its support. This can be done with a corporate policy statement such as the one that follows:

**CORPORATE
POLICY**

NO.

DATE

TITLE

EMPLOYMENT

It is corporate policy to fill every vacant position, existing and anticipated, with the best available candidate.

Toward this end management will establish and pursue a workable and practical program of internal training and development to recognize and reward deserving men and women on their way up.

At the same time an effective outside recruitment effort should be implemented and maintained for those occasions when the internal system may not produce qualified or qualifiable employees in the numbers and skills required at any given time.

DYNAMICS OF MANAGEMENT DEVELOPMENT SYSTEM

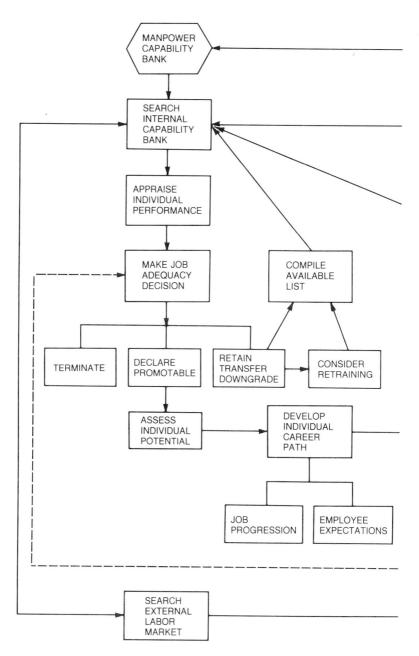

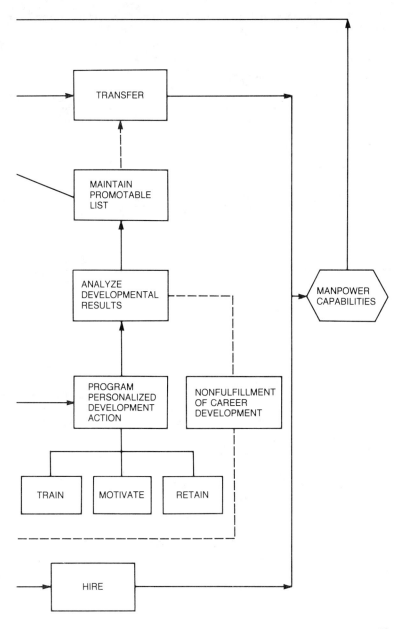

79

The Need is Now

Admittedly, manpower planning is a paperwork exercise. But it is unfortunate when it is looked upon as little more than "busy work," a kind of numbers game, for the personnel staff. The need for a serious application is here and it is now.

Intuitive maneuvering of human beings on the management chessboard is giving way to more sophisticated systematization. Airplane pilots had pride and self-confidence in their reliance on their own instrument landing equipment; they have now come to accept and appreciate ground control approach systems. A person may still go out in an automobile or airplane for a joyride without maps, but to land an astronaut on the moon requires a very precise scientific system.

Companies can no longer fly by the seats of their pants, either. They must rely on instruments under all sorts of economic weather. In personnel management the importance of an objective, systematic approach with its resultant impartiality cannot be overemphasized.

For too long, companies have watched problems of employment surface and have been satisfied to try to meet them with emergency measures. It is only recently that companies are accepting the fact that their problems are in front of them. The idea is no longer how to repair the past but how to adjust the future to prevent the same or similar troubles recurring in the future.

This new enlightenment calls for management to anticipate and to plan. For example, looking ahead to have a candidate ready for a future assignment, that is yet unknown, or at best ill-defined, is far more difficult than filling a replacement requisition for a job that has been standardized for years.

The comptroller does financial planning; the sales manager does marketing and product planning; the personnel executive must do manpower planning. If he shirks his responsibility he is not a member of the management team.

ASSESSING THE LABOR MARKET

Whenever a job vacancy, especially a critical one, is to be filled, an in-house search should be undertaken. It is always desirable to reward deserving employees with preferential consideration before going on the outside. But this should be the policy only when present employees qualify or can be made to qualify.

It is axiomatic that for best results every position should be filled by the best qualified candidate who is available, no matter where he comes from. This means that the employment office must at all times know what the labor market has to offer.

To meet this responsibility, the interviewers should be surveying the market on the availability and cost of acquiring the number and types of people necessary to fill the positions. In its continuing study attempts should be made to obtain information for each position as it relates to:

1. The best applicant source.
2. The prevailing starting salary.
3. The availability of qualified candidates.
4. The lead time needed to acquire acceptable applicants.
5. The cost of acquisition.

It is usually necessary to go outside to fill jobs calling for special skills or where the "get ready" time is too short to prepare someone. The decision in each case is whether to train an individual internally for the job or recruit an individual already possessing the necessary skills. Training time for individuals will vary because some jobs are more difficult than others and some employees may be closer to being ready than others.

An assessment of the workforce and an assessment of the labor market will determine what route to follow to fill certain jobs by a given time—from internal transfer or external recruitment.

HELP WANTED REQUISITIONS

Some type of control, for keeping track of all jobs, filled and unfilled, is recommended. This need be little more than a listing of all authorized jobs by title, type, division or department, and classification. Postings are made to the list as jobs are added, dropped, vacated or filled.

Under even a simple system the number of jobs filled and unfilled is known at all times. Jobs that remain open for a while should be investigated for possibly they are not needed. Additional jobs should carry the approval of a top officer, preferably the president or comptroller. This precaution requires divisions or departments to justify creating jobs and assures that necessary budgetary support has been provided for.

The mechanics of control should rest with Personnel, where the responsibility for keeping jobs filled rests. In auditing an action, Personnel can make certain that jobs are filled by new hires, transfers or promotions in accordance with policy.

The control device is a Help Wanted Requisition. A requisition is filled out, signed and authenticated whenever a job is open—either by being added or when it is vacated by a termination. This requisition lists

A help-wanted requisition form suitable for a manual personnel records system.

PERMANENT HELP REQUISITION

To: Personnel

JOB CLASSIFICATION _____ DATE _____

Recommended Salary to start — from $ _____ to $ _____ DEPARTMENT _____

Duties (including machines to be operated) _____

Replacement for _____

Education _____ Experience _____

Requested by _____ Approved _____ Approved _____
              Manager   Vice-President   President

TO BE COMPLETED BY PERSONNEL

Job filled by _____ From _____

the job title, location, classification, starting salary, qualifications, description of duties, date to be filled and other information needed to fill the job.

It is advisable to have a different requisition, or the regular one in a different color, for jobs that are temporary, emergency, summer vacation or otherwise short term. Filling one of these short-term jobs does not cancel out a regular requisition.

ACQUISITION COST

The employment function is a continuing one in every company, regardless of whether or not the procedure is formalized. The selection and retention of efficient workers is one of the most important operations of any company. In a tightening labor market this is also one of the greatest problems.

The reason this becomes a problem of dimensions is not simply to keep jobs in the company filled. The problem is concerned with cost. The cost of hiring applicants has been variously estimated in different companies and in different parts of the country. For female clerical workers, for instance, the employment agency fee itself, often paid by the employer, is sizable. For this fee the agency does little more than refer applicants; there is no testing and very little screening.

For certain types of jobs newspaper advertising is effective; for other jobs it is of little value today. For instance, an advertisement in a local newspaper for housewives to do typing for a few hours each day will bring in an avalanche of inquiries. On the other hand, an advertisement in a big city daily for a secretary will bring in little response, especially when such notice is included among hundreds of other similar ads for stenos and secretaries. In such case the few referrals and the limited selection resulting from the advertisement make newspaper classified or display ads quite expensive. It is not sufficient to think of the cost of the ad itself; the number of ads and the amount of work in connection with replies must be considered in relation to results obtained.

Many companies have found it profitable to reward employees who refer their friends or relatives for employment. This payment may take any of many forms, such as cash, government bonds, time off and the like. This practice has two distinct advantages. First, it is the cheapest form in use, for surely a government bond or two is less in cost than an advertisement and all the screening work this entails, or an agency fee. Second, it tends to bring in the same type of person who has already been found acceptable to the company. There is another intangible benefit that many companies recognize as valuable: The employee who recommends his company to another person not only sells the company

ACQUISITION COST ANALYSIS

Newspaper	Telephone Responses					Total	Mail Responses					Total	Personal Interviews					Total	Acceptances					Total
	M	T	W	Th	F		M	T	W	Th	F		M	T	W	Th	F		M	T	W	Th	F	
1.																								
2.																								
3.																								
4.																								
5.																								

Newspaper	Cost of Ad	Total Leads	Cost per Lead	Total Acceptances	Cost per Acceptance
1.					
2.					
3.					
4.					
5.					

84

and its favorable working conditions to the friend but in so doing also resells this to himself.

Whatever method is used, we can be almost certain that the cost of each new worker is high, much higher than we realize. Add to this the expense of interviewing, low production during the beginning or training period, the time of the person who does the training, and all the many other obvious as well as hidden costs, and we get some idea of the cost of employment.

It is, therefore, advisable to analyze the cost against results. The following acquisition cost analysis chart should be helpful.

EMPLOYMENT COSTS OUTLINE

1. **Acquisition**
   1.1 Advertisements
      1.11 Preparation of advertisement (writing it)
      1.12 Blind advertisement
         1.121 Writing the advertisement
         1.122 Screening replies
         1.123 Contact applicant by telephone or letter
   1.2 Agency (free or fee)
      1.21 Preparation of job orders
      1.22 Time and cost of phone orders
      1.23 Those interviewed who are rejected at once
   1.3 Bonus payment for employee referral
   1.4 Recruitment
      1.41 Membership in organizations for applicant contact
      1.42 Visiting high schools and colleges
      1.43 Participation in career days
      1.44 Expenses of entertaining
      1.45 Work study or work experience program costs
2. **Employee Processing**
   2.1 Receptionist
      2.11 Supplies
         2.111 Application blanks
         2.112 Other forms
      2.12 Interviewer
         2.121 Time of interviewing
         2.122 Education to improve oneself
         2.123 Cost of tests
            2.1231 Supplies themselves
            2.1232 Administration and interpretation
            2.1233 Training on improved methods
            2.1234 Reports kept to establish company norms

85

SOURCES OF APPLICANTS

Throughout history there always seemed to be an inexhaustible supply of workers. There was no shortage of applicants for jobs until World War II. Then the tremendous defense effort, combined with the transfer of millions of able-bodied young men and women to the armed services, caused a severe crisis. The problem was eased somewhat after 1945, when the war ended, but the help situation remained critical.

A review of industrial history shows that whenever the supply of labor became a problem, there was a solution nearby. For years the boatloads of immigrants brought a continuing supply of skilled and unskilled workers to American companies. When this source became inadequate, another developed.

Farm labor moved from rural areas to the big factories in the urban communities. Small towns saw their workers attracted to the cities. Schools graduated an endless supply of trained and educated workers until finally this source was no longer sufficient to meet industries' growing demands.

What saved the war effort was the widespread acceptance of women into the nation's work force. Remember "Rosie the riveter"? After the war the women stayed on because they liked the life they'd found. It wasn't long until this source was exhausted. There are today comparatively few women left who can be hired.

Still the labor shortage remained critical. So business turned to the minorities, people who were previously hopelessly out of consideration. These are the Blacks, Puerto Ricans, Asians, Appalachian whites and migrants. Now they've been used up. There are no qualified minority group members overlooked anymore.

During all this time some relief was provided by the moonlighters, workers who accept a second job in another firm. But their number is shrinking as these people are able to increase their earnings through overtime on their primary jobs. Nor is there any hope left trying to recruit workers away from other geographical areas since the problem there is usually no less acute.

The only untapped source is that of the unskilled workers. Government, trade associations and social agencies are making serious efforts to interest business in these people. As long as there are thousands of men and women unemployed, there are potential workers available if only they can be made employable.

It appears that companies have a choice—either to continue indefinitely short-handed or cooperate in programs to utilize these people who, on their own, are unqualified and unprepared to enter the labor force on our present terms.

UTILIZING THE "UNPREPARED"

Some of the old concepts of personnel administration do not hold true anymore. There are forces at work in our society which are rearranging conditions. For the first time we're getting third-party influence sufficiently strong to affect everything we learned and held sacred before.

As a preface, a brief review might help set the stage. During the industrial revolution the emphasis was on technological progress. Human resources did not get into the consideration; it was not in the thinking of the time. There were dire consequences to this neglect, which managements realized too late. One example was the widespread unionization of defenseless workers who responded to the leadership from outside when their own companies failed them.

The past three decades have produced unprecedented progress in the fields of automation and electronics. But again the advances have been all one way; no corresponding improvement has been made in human relations. People, as usual, have been taken for granted, and are once again beginning to assert themselves. There are many signs that the pendulum is swinging back to people. Only this time they're getting their encouragement and support from government. This, then, is the environment in which companies today recruit and hire applicants.

Government intervention in the affairs of business is, of course, not new. We've long had government regulating hours, working conditions, overtime rates, minimum pay, bargaining rights and the like. Business has come to accept these controls against exploitation of employees by employers. In addition, pensions, insurance, and welfare payments are established and administered by government and industry has no choice but to fall in step. Business, largely, is in sympathy with the motives.

Compulsory Partnership

The new intrusion on the part of government, which we are witnessing today, is, however, something entirely different. The socialistic trend so evident in government planning during the past 40 years has produced a geometric patchwork of social programs designed to extirpate all social ills from poverty to rheumatism. These schemes have been so varied and so all-encompassing that government is finding it necessary to form "government-industry partnerships" to carry them out.

In short, business is expected to implement government social legislation. And government is no longer subtle in its efforts to saddle business with this responsibility. The forced cooperation that results does nothing to help business operate more effectively; in fact, it impedes operating efficiency much as a millstone around the neck hampers the swimmer.

Government has all sorts of ways to "influence" business to come around to its way of thinking. It holds all the trumps. There is hardly a business enterprise, no matter how small, that is not involved in some way with government business, if not as a prime contractor then at least as a subcontractor. The contract says in effect that the contractor agrees to do business with government on government's terms. This can mean anything from corporate subservience to the laws to willing compliance with executive orders. As the nation's largest direct and indirect employer, government is now setting the standards.

Industry has already been directed to revalidate employment tests, even discontinue the use of some tests, since they work a hardship upon applicants who have little or no chance of passing them. Compliance investigators have had the audacity to "suggest" that nothing detrimental should be included in an employee's file, that negative responses to reference inquiries, prison records, unemployment claims, wage assignments and the like serve only to prejudice a manager against an individual who may be under consideration for employment or promotion.

Terms Spelled Out

Already new words are coming into the industrial vocabulary. First we heard of the *disadvantaged,* then the *unemployed* and *underemployed,* and now we're getting pressure to help the *unprepared.* Industry is told to put them on the payroll, with some measure of reimbursement toward the costs of recruiting, counseling, on-the-job training, remedial education and supportive services such as minor medical care and possibly transportation. The idea seems to be "employ 'em or support 'em" with employment the preferred choice since this supposedly will reduce the skyrocketing tax burden. Whether industry gets its fair share of productivity from these substandard workers, or some compensation for all the red tape that is necessary, seems to be of little concern to the social planners.

And red tape there will be. It is not sufficient to submit obediently to the laws and carry out the provisions of the contract, but a company is always suspect to the burgeoning, faceless army of government auditors and investigators. Charges against a firm are easily made, and even a routine inspection can call for endless and detailed records and reports just to prove a company is innocent of any alleged or implied wrongdoing.

The penalties for passivity in meeting the government's terms, instead of enthusiasm for embracing a positive program of "affirmative action," are in such devices as prolonged investigations of complaints, public hearings and always the threat of contract cancellation. Lately there has come the hint of "negative" penalties in the form of assurances that firms which meet the government's terms willingly with an announced program of cooperation may be rewarded with extra consideration in the awarding of government contracts and more definite profit guarantees. Talk about having the whip hand!

Turn Challenge into Opportunity

What all this means is that personnel administration as we learned and practiced it is a thing of the past. One Washington official told an audience of 300 prime contractors to "throw away the book and start over."

The gradual encroachment of government upon the industrial scene has bent the established and proven concepts out of shape. As a result, we will revise forms, records, reports, tests and test norms, recruiting sources, hiring standards, promotion sequences, training qualifications, grievance procedures, dismissal practices and other personnel techniques which have served business so well. From now on their primary purpose will be to promote the government's social legislation aims.

It is in this climate that business is expected to employ people who were heretofore considered unemployable. Maybe in a more favorable employment market companies were guilty of depriving some people of their right to work. But can we in good conscience lower hiring standards in order to bring some of these unfortunate but deserving individuals into our workforce? Will we be content with their subpar performance while at the same time expecting our regular employees to hold up their end? Or have we found a way of making these "unprepared" persons productive? That would be the ideal solution.

Personally I believe this social problem can be solved if industry develops an enthusiasm for it and if government keeps its meddling hands off. This would work if business embraced the idea, not from a public relations point of view, but sincerely in the interests of the community which supports the business. But that does not seem to be the prospect. Industry, following its usual pattern, has neglected much of its social responsibility, making it necessary for government to move in and take the initiative. It is not a compliment to American business that the federal government had to initiate an interest in the person, with some penalties implied, before much thought was given to underprivileged or minority workers.

My own feeling is that every American has the right to earn a living commensurate with his ability and ambition. But in order to do this he must have the will to work. I also believe that the person who can't get a job would, if properly handled, accept a chance for training so that he can qualify for work that has some permanency to it—a job that will permit him to improve his lot in life. A decent job means dignity to an individual; it means resources to a family; it means a place in the community. Every American needs that—and our society will benefit from whatever efforts are expended to accomplish this.

JOB POSTING

Job posting, or open posting, is a method of publicizing to employees, possibly on bulletin boards, the jobs that are open in the company. The purpose is to fill as many jobs as possible from within the company and also to aid in the promotion of employees who are ready to be rewarded.

This can be a time-consuming procedure since many workers could apply for the same job and all have to be dealt with. Everyone who responds must be interviewed. During the interview the duties are explained and the requirements outlined. The applicant's training and experience are reviewed. Every qualified employee who expresses interest must then be considered to be "in the running" for the job. When the final selection is made the decision must be reported individually to each remaining candidate in such a way as to get his understanding and also to maintain his willingness to apply again when another job appeals to him.

When job vacancies are made known to the workforce, good and bad results may follow.

Good:

1. Keeps employees informed.
2. Present employees bring in applicants.
3. They apply themselves, thereby making their interests known.
4. They reveal feelings in present placement.
5. Lets jobs and salary grades for jobs be known.

Bad:

1. May encourage job hoppers.
2. May let disgruntled employee "run away" instead of meeting problem in present job.
3. May attract applicants who are more interested in money than in using their skills.
4. Results in a long chain reaction at times, with bumping involved.
5. Sometimes hard to select if ability is the criterion; usually it becomes seniority, especially where a union contract is involved.
6. It is easier to turn away an outsider than a co-worker.

Rules:

1. Use a definite posting period and close it, after which accept no more bids.
2. Announce in a definite place, openly, to avoid suspicion.
3. Must be controlled by some neutral agency, like Personnel, not by a line department.

RECRUITMENT

The employment of workers begins with the act of recruiting. Recruitment, as this is called, is like the outstretched arms in the employment picture. Ideally it should gather in enough applicants from whom the final selection can then be made.

The problem of recruiting varies by type of job, industry, location and current labor market. The company must: (1) establish and maintain the most productive sources of supply, and (2) devise the most effective and efficient means of reaching applicants. Then it must succeed in encouraging them to inquire about the job opportunities offered.

There are two sources of applicants to fill vacant positions: internal and external. The internal source is inside the company for lateral transfer and promotion. This rewards faithful and loyal workers with more remunerative positions or with work that is more to their liking. But it could have the disadvantage of inbreeding.

For some jobs it might be better to go outside. Most job vacancies, especially beginner positions, are filled from the external source. This consists of many aspects. Sources of external applicants are among the following:

1. Employment agencies
   a. Private—or fee
   b. Government—or free
2. Advertisements
   a. Metropolitan newspapers
   b. Neighborhood weeklies
   c. Trade publications
3. Schools
   a. High schools
      (1) City public
      (2) Suburban
      (3) Parochial
   b. Junior colleges
   c. Universities
   d. Business colleges
   e. Trade schools
4. Employee referrals
5. Miscellaneous sources
   a. Churches
   b. Clubs

c. Fraternal organizations
d. Minority group headquarters
e. Handicapped
f. Business associations
6. Unsolicited applications
   a. Walk-ins
   b. Write-ins
   c. Job-shoppers

COLLEGE RECRUITING

The techniques used in college recruiting vary from one company to another, but the basic mechanics remain fairly standardized. On-campus and in-plant activities follow well-established paths. Since the approaches are similar, if not identical, then the success of the program depends on innovations, the peculiar differences that reflect organizational idiosyncracies and management philosophy.

First off, the competitive search for college graduates will meet with lukewarm success if it is treated as another recruiting function of the personnel office, as is the case throughout much of industry. Every member of management shares in the responsibility of attracting new talent. The most effective recruiters are the alumni who return to their *alma maters* where they are familiar with the administration and personally acquainted with members of the faculty. More important, they are not only qualified to tell the story of their company and the opportunities it offers, but they are also living proof of successful placements.

The alumni do not become involved in the interviewing process and all this entails. Their job is to maintain year-round relationships with their schools, to ensure that faculty and staff understand the company, what it does, and what it offers. This means school visits and possibly participation or support of school programs to keep themselves and the company fresh in the minds of school administrators.

Companies where college recruiting is considered the serious business it should be, go so far as to have the alumni volunteer their time, and the time of specialized executives, to serve as guest lecturers or speakers at professional meetings. They may extend an invitation to make company time and facilities available for student visits and faculty research. They may organize visits to the plant for instructors and guided tours for student groups.

Not all members of management are utilized. Some are not in any

---

LOOKING FOR THAT FIRST JOB ?

**Consider these
benefits. . .**

- full-time permanent employment

- 37½ hour week

- congenial atmosphere

- regular salary review

- cost of living program

- opportunity for advancement

- convenient bus transportation

- equal opportunity for everyone

and these. . .

- college tuition refund program

- paid vacation (two weeks after one year)

- 10 paid holidays (including your birthday)

- free corporation parking lot

- cafeteria meals at reduced cost

- free medical programs (blood bank, flu shots, TB skin tests)

- complete health care protection (at no cost to you)

- dental program

- life insurance program

- pension program (for career employees)

- social activities

---

*Part of the recruitment brochure used by Hospital Care Corporation, Cincinnati, Ohio
to attract applicants.*

REFERRAL CARD

This will introduce . . . .

Name _____

Address _____

Phone _____

to the personnel office.

Referred by_____

Relationship_____

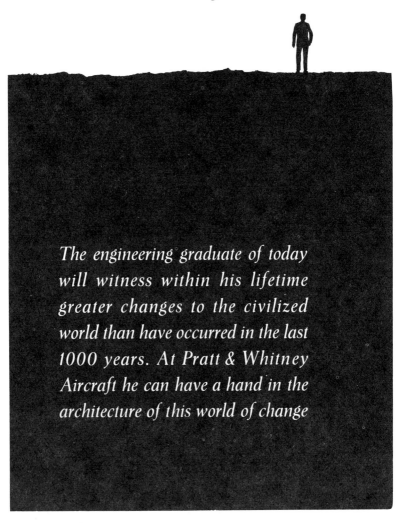

Pratt & Whitney Aircraft

The engineering graduate of today will witness within his lifetime greater changes to the civilized world than have occurred in the last 1000 years. At Pratt & Whitney Aircraft he can have a hand in the architecture of this world of change

Cover of a typical college recruiting brochure.

position to cooperate, others may be too far removed in years to properly identify with current college administration, and still others may not be effective or respond well to the opportunity. Only those who embrace the challenge with enthusiasm are considered and they are then extensively trained for the assignments.

Ideally every such company representative should be young enough to be in tune with college life, experienced enough to know the company and its opportunities, and impressive and likeable to get ready acceptance.

Come Fully Prepared

Obviously, the formation of a team is only the first step. What are they trying to promote? Is their mission clearly outlined and fully supported with time and budget? Or is this treated as a sideline effort, to be carried out haphazardly?

Are they expected to produce results while equipped only with generalities? Or do they have specific jobs to try to fill based on the long-range manpower plan? What kind of talent and how many of each academic discipline are they looking for?

Upon acceptance of a job offer, what can the graduate expect? Will he or she merely be "absorbed" or is there a well-developed career path geared to the individual?

The surest way to disillusion a prospect is to have a personable recruiter sell "a bill of goods" only to find in the face of reality that overworked line management is already too busy to bother with a "hot shot" off the campus.

To avoid this unpleasantness, these newly-hatched technicians are often mistakenly hidden away in a training group, isolated from the operations, and given "make work" projects. After years of study, this is precisely what the graduates do not want—more lectures and study halls.

Assure them that they will be assigned to clearly-defined and accepted positions in their specialty, given their own challenges, and encouraged to put their theoretical understanding to the test. Make no false promises but don't throttle their ambition.

It is unfair to ask them (especially MBAs) to be satisfied with "watch and learn" clerical jobs that dull their incisive thinking. Also, some salaried positions are not suited for college graduates and these should be avoided. Generally, they should be promised one of two types of jobs:

1. Specialty positions requiring analytical skills.
2. Supervisory positions over people or functions.

Trained interviewers from the personnel office develop the interview schedules with the college placement directors, conduct the individual interviews, and evaluate the prospects. They should be equipped with descriptive company booklets and qualified to give direct answers to questions.

They must also be familiar with company policies and able to interpret these policies and practices in the light of each candidate's circumstances. They must know moving and relocation procedures and explain about expense reimbursement.

Naturally, they must know every detail of the routine set up to greet the accepted candidates, whether they arrive singly or as a group. Their induction and orientation is more than necessary paperwork processing.

Assimilation is a continuous process. These promising newcomers must be accepted, assisted and counselled. Their work must be monitored and their progress appraised. Their problems must be attended to promptly. They must be allowed to distinguish themselves at their appropriate levels and at the same time submerge this distinction and "fit in" with the rest of the work force—their peers, superiors and subordinates.

Postscript

Big business goes to the campuses courting for brainpower. But the experience may not always be courtly. This annual matchmaking is often frenetic and coy ritual.

The students concede that artifice is a proven method for building first contacts into coveted job offers. And the executives concede just as freely that they regularly circumvent business-school restrictions on recruiting to hire the best students as early as they can.

It's an expensive arrangement. They conduct a remarkable high number of interviews for a comparatively small number of jobs. Job offers go to about one in 10 students interviewed.

COLLEGE RECRUITING—TRAINING MANAGERS FOR THE FUTURE

Long-term planning is essential to the minerals industry. It takes years to develop a mine. At AMAX, Inc., Greenwich, Connecticut, plans are also made far in advance for the future of the company's management.

Where will new leadership talent come from? The Corporate Human Resources Department at AMAX has great confidence in what it calls

COMPANY POLICY AND EMPLOYEE BENEFITS

It is the policy of the Pratt & Whitney Aircraft Group of United Technologies Corporation to recruit, hire, train, and promote persons in all job classifications without regard to race, color, age, religion, sex, or national origin, except where sex is a bona fide occupational qualification.

Company Pays Relocation Expenses

Pratt & Whitney Aircraft reimburses new employees relocating from distances of greater than 50 miles for reasonable expenses incurred reporting for work. Reimbursements include transportation costs, a substantial enroute allowance for all immediate family members, as well as a liberal allowance for moving household effects.

Employees relocating from within 50 miles will receive an allowance for the shipment of household effects if the provisions of the company's short-distance moving policy are met.

Insurance Program Is Extensive

The protection of life insurance, disability income, hospital, dental, and surgical and major medical coverage is available to eligible employees under the group insurance program. Much of this broad coverage is extended to the employee's family. The total premium for both employee and dependent insurance is paid by the company. Additional life insurance is optional.

A patent compensation plan is available to all employees to encourage new and useful inventions for the development of products and manufacturing processes. P&WA also provides assistance in evaluating and processing of patents.

Suggestion Awards up to $7500

Management welcomes suggestions which will save time or materials, reduce overhead, or improve the product. Accepted suggestions entitle employees to awards up to $7500.

Part of the section explaining company policy and employee benefits.

99

	Financial	Information Systems	Purchasing	Product Support	Materials Planning	Personnel
Liberal Arts			●			●
Business Administration		●	●	●	●	●
Accounting	●	●	●			
Finance	●		●			
Computer Science		●				
Industrial Management			●	●	●	●
Personnel Management						●
Mathematics		●			●	
Economics			●	●		

A listing of the fields in which job opportunities exist and the academic majors sought.

its M.B.A. Program. The initials refer to the college degree, Master of Business Administration. AMAX's recruiting staff began scouting for outstanding M.B.A. recruits back in 1965. However, in 1972 it inaugurated the new program.

The program has a number of unique features. Each AMAX group and its divisions, including the corporate staff departments, compete for such talents in a special way. Each year, before the recruiting season begins, Corporate Human Resources requests a formal proposal from each unit desiring an M.B.A. The proposal must be project oriented, bringing into play much of the multifaceted business education acquired by the M.B.A.

The project must offer exposure to several functional areas and exposure to a cross section of key executives and management personnel. One of the central criteria in judging these proposals is the degree to which it will challenge the ingenuity, analysis and problem-solving skills of the M.B.A. in handling a project. And finally, the project must have a business purpose. It may involve the development of a new distribution system, the evaluation of a sales leaseback versus buy decision, the development of an improved marketing program, or a variety of other projects which represent cost savings, efficiencies and improvements which affect profits. The degree to which the project proposal will and can affect profit improvement is the final and most important criterion in Corporate Human Resources' evaluation.

Those proposals which meet these criteria best are approved, and the appropriate AMAX units are notified that recruiting for their M.B.A. will begin.

Progress is Watched

During the first year of their employment, Corporate Human Resources' recruiting section requests and receives a quarterly evaluation from each unit concerning each M.B.A.'s progress and performance.

The M.B.A. is on Corporate Human Resources' payroll during the first year with AMAX. Providing the M.B.A. has met the high standards of the program, the intern will be offered a permanent position with the AMAX unit which initially requested his or her services. However, if the M.B.A. has not met the high standards, he will not be offered a permanent post with AMAX.

According to Frank F. Mangus, Director of Human Resources who developed this program, "These M.B.A.'s represent an investment in the future of AMAX. They are looked upon as potential future management talent."

What goes into the making of a Master of Business Administration? Candidates for the degree are already college graduates, with a Bachelor's Degree in a technical or nontechnical field. In pursuit of a Master's degree, they spend two years in postgraduate work in a university business school. Here they gain a broad, overall view of the business world plus special knowledge in a particular field of concentration such as finance, marketing or production.

Corporate Human Resources' M.B.A. program begins each year with the planning of a recruitment campaign designed to attract the most capable students. Then campus recruiters visit selected business schools to look for and screen the kind of M.B.A.'s who will fit AMAX's tough selection criteria and the proposals which have been approved.

As Mr. Mangus explains it, "We look for a number of things in selecting the M.B.A.: clearly-defined interests, job objectives and career goals. The M.B.A. should possess strong ambition, drive, self-confidence and an incisive, analytical mind. Above all, we look for an individual with a very practical business bent."

In recent years, a number of M.B.A.'s from this program have progressed up the executive ladder to positions such as: Vice-President—Planning, Director—Market Planning, Director of Budgeting, Controller, Marketing Director—Europe, Director—Business Planning, and many others.

No more than six to 12 M.B.A.'s are recruited each year for this program. Each of them is a potential executive. It is up to all of them to reach their goals and objectives. As pointed out, "The company's growth in the past decade indicates that there is no shortage of opportunity for a meaningful professional career for the right person."

MANAGEMENT TRAINEES

Management trainees for replacement and expansion are recruited and developed for the future. Locating them, convincing them they should accept your opportunity, and fitting them into the company are real problems. But the biggest problem is keeping them.

Anyone good enough to qualify for special management training consideration is certainly going to be attractive to a competitive employer. All it takes in some cases is an offer of more money or a better opportunity.

No qne keeps tab nationally on turnover among people in this group, but there are surveys made on college graduates, from whose ranks most of the trainees come. There is a rapidly-growing group of recent college graduates who are finding it more profitable and easier than ever to switch jobs.

Hanging on to management trainees poses a mounting problem at many firms. Studies indicate that more than 50% of college graduates change jobs at least once during their first five years.

For one thing there seems to be a lot of unrest in these young people. They are eager and impatient. They don't know what they want; they know only that what they find is often not what they'd hoped to make a career of. Once young people are ready to settle down, they expect to move up fast.

Money is a big concern, but money alone won't solve the problem. These people need to be challenged. Many companies try to keep their recent college graduates satisfied by assigning them more difficult and meaningful work.

Faced with the threat of losing promising potentials, in technical fields as well as in management, companies are coming up with new ways to keep these people happy. Conventional attractions such as tuition reimbursement are expanded to cover post-graduate study. Time off with pay for special study and exams is granted liberally. The eligibility requirements for profit-sharing are lowered so that they may participate immediately. Research projects are encouraged. Training programs are shortened drastically to give them earlier on-the-job responsibilities. Chances for travel are increased.

But the biggest single item in keeping and developing trainees is frequent evaluation and review sessions where they can air their complaints to supervisors and vice-presidents.

EXECUTIVE SEARCH

In certain types of recruiting, especially for top level or executive positions, it may be advisable to engage a professional search firm. For many corporations the professional search is literally the executive market place. Such executive search organizations are not only better equipped as recruiting specialists for management talent but also more uniquely qualified than the customary employment efforts.

By using experienced search consultants, a company is relieved of the time-consuming tasks of recruiting, screening and interviewing all candidates who make themselves available, most of whom turn out to be underqualified or otherwise unacceptable. Besides, there is no way of knowing whether the right candidates have been reached by the company offer.

A search outfit, by concentrating on this type of executive recruitment, has access to many applicants and also to fields of specialization in which the proper kind of candidate may be located. In addition, the search consultants are impartial and neutral and are not handicapped by the built-in bias that many companies may have toward an individual or his former employer.

Once the search firm is engaged, the consultants assigned to the task familiarize themselves with the company and the position to be filled. They review the qualifications asked for, the experience needed, and the personality desired as they endeavor to find someone who comes closest to meeting the precise requirements.

The search outfit scans its files of registered applicants, discusses the need with companies, trade associations and other acquaintances in the hopes of getting referrals.

Their methods of locating likely prospects by telephone, mail or in person vary but are still similar:

1. "One name leads to another."
2. Industry sources known from previous contacts.
3. Industry directories.
4. Local files of articles about successful individuals (promotions, leadership, civic duty, etc.) who might be approached in the future.
5. In-house inventory of impressive resumés collected or submitted.
6. Trends such as cutbacks, geographic relocations, prospects by-passed in favor of others, personal growth of individuals through academic achievement, professional standing, official certification, etc.

Confidentiality Respected

On the initial approach, once clearance to contact a likely prospect is obtained, the client company's name is held confidential by the search consultants. They identify and contact candidates without jeopardizing the client's position (where the search may not be "out in the open"). They present each applicant's resumé or abstract of qualifications. The company screens a paper instead of a person as the first step toward selection.

The first report to the client company is a list of screened candidates and a preliminary appraisal of one or more possibilities secured from these outside references and investigations. Candidates in which the company expresses interest are then approached confidentially on a personal basis. On the results of their depth interviews, they make recommendations of those candidates who should be considered further.

The recruiters' job isn't over once they get a candidate in touch with company officials. They stay on as a sounding board or a buffer if negotiations get sticky. The recruiters will tell a company when its compensation offer seems low, and will also caution a candidate whose demands appear excessive.

Throughout the negotiations the search consultants stay close to candidates and client company. The objective is to present to the client company one or more of the best prospects, considering qualifications, interest and availability.

Service Commands Fee

Naturally, the search consultants charge for their service. They are paid by companies, not applicants. Their charge can be a fixed amount or other contract. One arrangement calls for a fee of 25% of the annual starting salary. As the search progresses they bill per diem time charges monthly. These per diem charges are automatically credited to the placement fee billing at the completion of the project.

To this they add normal and reasonable out-of-pocket expenses, such as telephoning, travel, field interviewing, promoting and other incidentals incurred during the conduct of the search.

The company may cancel the search and entire agreement at any time, with the liability limited to the original advance payment or per diem time charges plus out-of-pocket expenses accumulated to that time.

There is no guarantee of completing a successful placement. The search firm can reasonably assure a client company of qualified referrals, otherwise they should not accept the assignment. But the final decision to select or reject any of their referrals is with the client company, and over this they have no authority or control and possibly little influence.

The executive recruiting industry has doubled in recent years because it is no longer considered expensive and justified only for upper echelon positions. Its biggest increase is in middle management jobs which now account for half of their assignments.

Employment agencies are often referred to as flesh peddlers; recruiters are often known as headhunters. The biggest distinction between these two employment services is that employment agencies find jobs for applicants; search firms find candidates for companies.

The secret to success for search firms is in trying to find likely candidates who are happily employed and not actively seeking other employment but who are not adverse to being approached discreetly about a possible job change that would be an improvement in earnings, status, location or other factors.

Function, services, value and cost of

EXECUTIVE SEARCH

by HAROLD W. DICKHUT
Author of "PROFESSIONAL RESUMÉ/JOB SEARCH GUIDE"*

Executive search is a widely-accepted means of recruiting higher level executives and managers, used primarily by larger corporations and organizations. Executive search firms or executive recruiters, as they are often called, are retained and paid by their corporate clients, and not by the applicants they select.

What a recruiter does, after accepting an assignment to locate applicants for corporate consideration, is to search the marketplace for highly-qualified individuals who come as close as possible to the client's precise position requirements. Great strides have been made during the past 25 years toward professionalizing the industry and improving the image of the work.

Three rather distinct types of organizations make up the field. First, the firms acting in an executive search capacity only. In staff size, they may range from one man (or woman) owner-consultants, to international multi-office firms, with many professional consultants specializing in particular fields of business, industry, education, nonprofit organizations and government. However, "big" does not necessarily equate with "better" in all situations.

A second group is the management consulting firms, which maintain executive search divisions. Since management consultants offer a wide range of services to clients, the establishment of executive recruiting was a natural outgrowth of their other work of assisting management with problem solving.

Third, the leading CPA firms became executive recruiters in effect, as a steady flow of their own employees found themselves on corporate client payrolls. This condition, long prevalent in CPA-client relationship, led to separate executive recruiting functions, especially among the "Big 8" CPA firms.

The use of executive recruiters can solve many problems arising because of a corporate need for an executive. The search firm is expected to have a knowledge of the personnel marketplace. It can search in a confidential manner which the corporate client simply can't do. Corporate time and money are saved by avoiding the otherwise necessary steps of advertising, screening and preliminary interviewing.

Corporations consider that a great advantage in using recruiters lies

---

*Published by Management Counselors, Inc., Chicago, Illinois.

in the objectivity which an outsider can offer. A recruiter does maintain the confidential nature of the search, so that executive changes in a corporation can be made without their becoming common knowledge in advance. In cases of replacement and expansion, this advantage is obviously valuable. A corporate client can rely on a recruiter to search among competitive firms for outstanding executive talent. Finally, the recruiter can be expected to do a better job than the in-house personnel staff, because it's all he does, all the time.

How They Operate

Executive recruiting firms, upon receiving an assignment, begin by studying closely the client company itself. Not from a distance, or just on paper, but with personal contact. The consultant endeavors to get the pulse of a client, so he can match not just the requirements of the position, but present an applicant whose personality will mesh easily with his potential new employer, and the human beings who make up the organization. The consultant assigned to the search now determines the exact requirements of the job to be filled, the client specifications of desirable attributes and experience needed. A new corporate client is told how the recruiter works, the time probably required, the estimated cost range, and what the recruiter expects from the client.

A recruiter will identify possible candidates. Methods vary, but a final net result is the selection by the recruiter of one or two best individuals. At a point, maintaining client name confidentiality, contact is made with approved applicants. In-depth interviews follow, and a candidate's interest determined. Recommendations are made to the client, who makes a final decision to offer. Recruiter consultants work with both the client and the candidate during negotiations.

The executive search firm may charge 20% to 30% of the first year's compensation, plus all out-of-pocket expenses such as telephone, travel and miscellaneous. Clients are billed monthly as the search progresses. Fees are expected to be paid, even though a search may not be successful, or concluded within the allotted time span. In such an event, however, the search firm may be expected to renew the search without additional compensation. While this figure will vary from recruiter to recruiter, a common minimum annual executive salary, excluding fringes, with which a search firm will work is $25,000 to $30,000. Below this, the recruiter will not usually accept the assignment.

There is no set standard for the time required to bring a search to a successful conclusion. From three to six months might be a fairly accurate range. Variable factors are many: tightness of the market, uniqueness of the corporate specifications, experience and ability of the consultant all affect the outcome. Not every selected executive accepts an offer, even after the most careful selection and negotiations.

CPA firms and management consulting firms may charge for executive search assignments as they do for any other type of work. That is, on a per diem basis plus out-of-pocket costs.

Finding the Right Consultant

A corporation, seeking executive search for the first time or in changing search firms, faces the key question: of the hundreds of search firms, which one? The one best way probably is through word of mouth in the industry or a reference from a search firm's client who is satisfied. Corporate management executives can call their contacts in trade and professional associations for leads. Once an investigation is underway, various firms' names come into the picture.

An executive search firm will cooperate with a potential corporate client by discussing an assignment, by presenting its qualifications, and by supplying references from satisfied clients. Normally, a visit to a search firm's office facility can be beneficial, and will be welcomed. A search firm will describe its recruiting procedures, its reporting procedures, and give time and cost estimates. A potential client can and should request a written proposal covering all basic points.

A Directory of Executive Recruiters is published by Consultants News, Templeton Road, Fitzwilliam, New Hampshire 03447. Be sure to get the latest edition. The 168-page paperback book was in its 9th edition in 1978, priced at $11.00 ($10.00 if prepaid). It lists over 1,400 recruiter offices in the United States, Canada and Mexico, and carries a cross index by industry, management function and geography.

As examples of top-rated executive search firms, mention can be made of Ward Howell Associates, Inc., Boyden Associates, Inc., and Thorndike Deland Associates, all of New York City. In Chicago, two large firms with outstanding reputations are Heidrick & Struggles, Inc. and Billington, Fox & Ellis, Inc. Among excellent small firms in Chicago are Tully and Hobart and Spriggs & Company. Many other fine firms exist all across the United States and Canada, located mostly but not necessarily in larger metropolitan centers.

A word of suggestion for corporate users of executive search firms: back up the search firm selected, establish good working relations with the consultant, and help him to get the job done well.

Corporations planning to make use of executive search will want to consider possible choices from among those firms which deal only in executive search, or who are recognized management consulting firms, or who are leading public accounting firms with search divisions or consultants. Various other firms which use similar sounding names may not truly be executive search organizations at all. Such firms as executive career counselors, executive guidance or placement agencies may not fit into the true search pattern.

Executive search offers a number of advantages in the recruitment of executives or management personnel. A possible disadvantage may be the cash outlay necessary. But, few guarantees of solid corporate satisfaction or long tenure of key people exist, regardless of the method of recruiting. Executive search does deserve serious consideration, and may very well be the one best way in a particular situation. If a decision is made to use executive search, then the consultant on the assignment needs, and should get, full corporate client support.

HELP WANTED ADVERTISING

How do you build in response to a help wanted ad? The answer to this question lies in relating the right kind of information to the right kind of classified reader.

The following helpful ideas and suggestions are taken from a booklet, "A Guide to Writing Productive Help Wanted Advertising," published by *The Chicago Tribune* and reprinted here with special permission.

You're the one who's advertising, so tell 'em right off about the good things you've got to offer. Let's face it, cold, dull, plain or stereotyped ads aren't going to attract the higher end of the employment market. They're not going to attract the more qualified job-seeker who is looking for something better, something special. One or several factors can motivate the job-seeker; among them are: better pay, prestige, location, opportunity for advancement, working conditions, and interesting or pleasant work. So tell the reader the strong points or unique features that set your company and the job you're offering apart from the rest of the field.

A headline catches the eye and sets the tone of your ad. It can immediately announce an outstanding benefit or feature of the job. Providing you can back up your statement, headlines such as "You'll Love Your Boss" or "Challenging Work in Cybernetics" are infinitely more arresting than "Secretary Wanted" or "Programmer Wanted." Take another example: "Work With The Beautiful People" and "Fastest Growing Firm in the Field" beat the heck out of "Typist" and "Sales Opportunity."

The idea is to project a human quality, a warmth that says here's something special, here's a company that offers more than just another job, here's a real opportunity.

Another tip on professional copywriting technique: your ad is directed to people and one of the most important aspects of their lives —their job. Remember that the liberal use of the simple word "you" in your ads provides the personalization that will produce the response you want.

7 Basic Points

After first-glance attention is gained, follow through with specific information about the job.

If you've got a good story to tell, don't be stingy with words, but remember that certain information is essential to the job-seeker. He is most concerned with these seven basic points:

1. Hours.
   Sample statements: 37½ hour week.
   Choose your shift.
   No Saturday work necessary.
   Set your own hours.
   Get off early enough to shop after work.

2. Remuneration.
   Sample statements: Show us what you can do and we'll pay off.
   Two ways to earn—salary and commission.
   We like to pay money for merit.
   Our people are making the highest wages in the industry.
   Higher pay for experienced people.

3. Distinguishing Features of Work or Product.
   Sample statements: We promote from the ranks.
   Ask someone who is working here.
   You've seen our product advertised nationally.
   Work for my boss. He has a high powder-room rating.
   We want good people because we work for the best people.

4. Benefits.
   Sample statements: Not seasonal employment.
   Free dental service.
   Liberal bonus every Christmas.
   Three-week vacation after the first year.
   Our nursery will watch your children while you work.

5. Location and Transportation.
   Sample statements: Suburban location saves time and expense.
   Big 3 transportation—train, "L" and bus.
   In the heart of the shopping district.
   We'll pay your cab fare.
   You won't get wet when it rains.

6. Qualifications.
   Sample statements: A head for figures.
   Will train mechanically-inclined personnel.

Must be familiar with medical terms.
Applicant should be free to travel.
Chef skilled in the preparation of fancy foods.

7. How to Apply.
   Sample statements: Come in today and see Mike (or Mary).
   Please apply in person.
   Phone—and reverse the charges.
   Write us a letter telling about your experience.
   All replies considered strictly confidential.

As with the headline, attention should always be shown to presenting each piece of information naturally and in a way that invites response.

HELP WANTED DISPLAY ADVERTISING

The use of display can be one of the most effective means of successful help wanted advertising. Some of the advantages of using display, taken from the Chicago Tribune booklet, are:

1. Attracts Attention. The mere fact that a display ad is different from most of the other ads on the page makes it stand out. It is likely the first ad to be looked at. Also the use of graphics and different type styles and sizes makes the ad more attractive and easier to read.

2. Establishes Company Identity. Use of the company logo can allow the reader to identify with other company advertising. A good graphic can also identify the type of job that is being offered.

3. Adds Professionalism. The use of display ads will make the job offering seem more important and thus attract the more qualified applicant.

4. Increases Emphasis. By using different type styles and sizes that are available only in display ads, the advertiser can emphasize whatever points are most important in the ad, whether it be job description or benefit package.

Like any other ad, a display ad must follow certain guidelines in order to be effective. When writing a display ad, six basic parts should be included.

1. Keyline. This assures you that your ad will be placed in the proper job classification. This is the first step in the screening of your reader.

2. Headline. Once the reader has turned to the proper job classification it's now up to the headline to attract him to your ad. The heading should be larger than the rest of the copy and say some-

Typical Help Wanted Ads.

thing that will arouse the reader's interest, something that will make him want to read the rest of the ad.

3. Paragraph About Your Company. Now that the reader has decided to read your ad, you should answer his first question, "What kind of company is this?" Tell him the good points of your company, the ones that are unique to you. Location is of prime importance to most people.

4. Job Specifications. Now is the time to get down to the actual job itself. Make the position seem as interesting as possible, but don't forget to include all the qualifications. Aim your message at the ideal applicant.

5. How to Apply. Now that the reader has decided that the job sounds worth pursuing, make it easy for him to apply. Simple instructions telling him exactly what to do are all that is needed.

6. Logo. This will give the applicant the name of the company and other pertinent information. If your company name and logo are well known, this will be as important an attention getter as your headline.

By following these few guidelines your display advertising dollars will perform like never before, bringing more and better qualified responses.

Blind Ads

Should you use a box number or would an open signature be best? As with any option there are some basic considerations and decisions to be made.

Obviously, if the fact that you are hiring is confidential, a box number is necessary and advantageous. On the other hand, ads containing a blind box number for applicant reply generally will not produce the same volume of response as an open addressed ad.

Here are some of the functions which a box number can serve:

1. Provides an opportunity to screen applicants' background prior to interview.

2. Provides better flow control of applicants when personnel staff is inadequate for mass interviewing.

3. Provides insight into ability of applicant to write, spell properly, organize material, etc.

4. If telephone voice or manner of applicant is important, requesting inclusion of applicant's phone number in the reply will provide a chance for evaluation.

Using display help wanted advertising

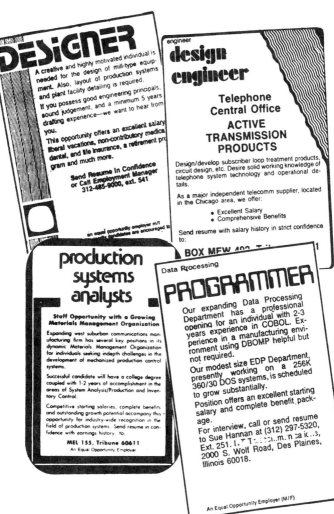

DESIGNER

A creative and highly motivated individual is needed for the design of mill-type equipment. Also, layout of production systems and plant facility detailing is required.

If you possess good engineering principals, sound judgement, and a minimum 5 years drafting experience—we want to hear from you.

This opportunity offers an excellent salary, liberal vacations, non-contributory medical, dental, and life insurance, a retirement program and much more.

Send Resume In Confidence or Call Employment Manager 312-485-9000, ext. 541

an equal opportunity employer m/f

---

engineer

design engineer

Telephone Central Office
ACTIVE TRANSMISSION PRODUCTS

Design/develop subscriber loop treatment products, circuit design, etc. Desire solid working knowledge of telephone system technology and operational details.

As a major independent telecomm supplier, located in the Chicago area, we offer:

- Excellent Salary
- Comprehensive Benefits

Send resume with salary history in strict confidence to:

BOX MEW 400

---

production systems analysts

Staff Opportunity with a Growing Materials Management Organization

Expanding west suburban communications manufacturing firm has several key positions in its dynamic Materials Management Organization for individuals seeking indepth challenges in the development of mechanized production control systems.

Successful candidate will have a college degree coupled with 1-2 years of accomplishment in the areas of System Analysis/Production and Inventory Control.

Competitive starting salaries, complete benefits and outstanding growth potential accompany this opportunity for industry-wide recognition in the field of production systems. Send resume in confidence with earnings history, to:

MEL 155, Tribune 60611
An Equal Opportunity Employer

Data Rrocessing

PROGRAMMER

Our expanding Data Processing Department has a professional opening for an individual with 2-3 years experience in COBOL. Experience in a manufacturing environment using DBOMP helpful but not required.

Our modest size EDP Department, presently working on a 256K 360/30 DOS systems, is scheduled to grow substantially.

Position offers an excellent starting salary and complete benefit package.

For interview, call or send resume to Sue Hannan at (312) 297-5320, Ext. 251. I, T T: :.:.m. n a k .3, 2000 S. Wolf Road, Des Plaines, Illinois 60018.

An Equal Opportunity Employer (M/F)

When a blind box number is used, consideration should be given to the advertiser's responsibility to the applicant. When an applicant takes the time to prepare a written reply to an ad, it indicates that he is seriously interested in the job and therefore should receive thoughtful treatment. An acknowledgement of all responses is both courteous and good business, even if only a postcard signed with the box number, if you wish to keep identity confidential. Remember, as an advertiser you want readership of your help wanted ads. When respondents receive no response to their replies, it reduces believability and thereby readership.

THE PUBLIC EMPLOYMENT SERVICE

The public employment service was established in 1933 under the authority of the Wagner-Peyser Act. It was created as a nationwide Federal-State system of no-fee, local employment offices to assist workers to obtain employment. It is administered by the U.S. Employment Service (USES) of the Employment and Training Administration (ETA), Department of Labor, which formulates programs and policies, issues regulations, apportions funds to state employment security agencies for employment service operations, provides technical assistance and monitors program progress.

Nearly all state employment security agencies are now using "Job Service" to more accurately reflect their primary role as a labor exchange agency. The Job Service consists of nearly 2,500 local offices and about 30,000 staff members who serve people seeking employment and employers needing qualified workers. General services include applicant registration, interviewing, testing, counseling, job development, recruitment and other services for employers, referrals to jobs and referrals to training or other services concerned with preparing people for employment.

Services for Applicants

Local Job Service offices provide job placement services to all job-seekers. Job Service staff solicit information on job openings from employers. Applications from job seekers are screened regularly against available job openings. Applicants are referred to job opportunities for which they are qualified. Computers are now being used in many offices to speed up selection and referral and to give job seekers a wider exposure to job opportunities available.

The men and women served by the Job Service have a wide variety of backgrounds and needs. Of every five applicants, three are high school graduates, and one of these three has had some college. Applicants include veterans, minorities, youth, older workers, the handicapped, women, migrants and poor people with limited skills. Many have more than one of these characteristics. Others are persons in the prime working ages (22 to 44) with diverse skills and experience, who are temporarily unemployed.

In one recent year, nearly 16.5% of all applicants were veterans, who get priority in job referrals and a full range of services to help them obtain civilian jobs. Nearly 29% of the jobseekers were minority group members, and about 32% were youths under 22 years of age. As needed, and to the extent that resources are available, these and other applicants can get job counseling and testing, career guidance, and help in entering training and in finding a job. About 14% were older workers, aged 45 or older.

Of all applicants, about 6% are people with mental or physical handicaps, who can often excel if placed in the right job by skilled selective placement interviewers. More than 44.7% are women—many seeking to enter or reenter the labor force. Others are professionals. About one out of three is a poor person with limited education and few job skills. Assistance for such a worker ranges from outreach to make him aware of available services through follow-up to help him stay on the job.

Services to Employers

Job Service staff maintain contact with employers to assist them in recruiting new workers and in achieving or improving stability of current workforces. Employers with Federal contracts who are required to list job openings with Job Service local offices are assisted in meeting their veterans affirmative action obligations and in obtaining qualified workers.

A recent approach to improving the responsiveness of the Job Service to employers is the Job Service Improvement and Employer Committee Expansion efforts which have yielded improvements in local office operations and increased job listings. This effort establishes employer committees or councils which study and recommend improvements in operations and services, and has resulted in closer-working relationships between the Job Service and the employer community. Currently, more than 400 employer committees are functioning, involving about 10,000 employers.

Program Emphasis

The Job Service is moving to strengthen its services to help reduce unemployment; a productivity increase of 10% for individuals placed has been set as one of its goals. Emphasis is being given to increasing placement services for migrant and seasonal farmworkers. Special efforts are being made to help more veterans find jobs or training leading to jobs. As youth unemployment is still far too high, the Job Service is also focusing on helping young people make the transition from school to work and on improving the summer job program.

For further information employers are advised to contact a local office of any State Job Service (see State government listing in the telephone directory); the U.S. Employment Service, Employment and Training Administration, U.S. Department of Labor, Room 8000, 601 D Street, N.W., Washington, D.C. 20213; or the Office of Information, Room 10406 at the same address, telephone (202) 376 6905. Or call any of the 10 regional offices of the Department (Boston, New York, Philadelphia, Atlanta, Chicago, Dallas, Kansas City, Denver, San Francisco and Seattle), referring to local telephone directory for address and telephone number.

HIRING THE HANDICAPPED

In hiring the handicapped, keep in mind that companies, as a cardinal rule of survival, hire no one who for any reason is incapable of doing the work. When the incapability is the result of physical impairment or mental limitations, the first bugaboo to remove from our minds is one that implies we are seriously considering employing someone who cannot do the work.

The decision to hire should be based on ability, not disability. But this does not mean we should unthinkingly close the door to any and all applicants who have obvious limitations. A physically-handicapped person may not be industrially handicapped. He regularly performs many services for himself; he might be able to do certain types of work if given a chance, training and encouragement.

For many jobs, poor eyesight is a definite liability. By the use of corrective lenses, however, many individuals are quite capable of performing most jobs, including tasks which would otherwise be dangerous. Driving an automobile is a good illustration. Even professional athletes remain competitive by wearing glasses or contact lenses.

A hard-of-hearing person could be disqualified for many jobs, but a hearing aid may be all he needs to restore him to full usefulness.

These are obvious examples of handicapped persons becoming employable. Other workers with some degree of physical limitation include men and women recovering from recent illnesses, some who have a "controlled" condition, and others with minor deformities. Perhaps the day will come when a crutch or artificial limb will be fully acceptable in offices and factories.

117

Sometimes the corrective measures are as simple as a cushion on a chair or a raised platform. A person who cannot bend his arms enough to reach back to comb his own hair may, nonetheless, be able to do telephone work if the receiver can be mounted on the wall or desk; a speaker phone would eliminate any problem completely.

The key is to understand the content of the job and the skills required to perform it. A man crippled in his legs may be able to do desk work, and a man crippled in his arms may be able to do messenger work.

Blind workers can be trained for many occupations. Blind typists have been known to be successful, and blind musicians are familiar to all of us. One company had a very good experience with deaf-and-dumb keypunch operators; once the supervisor learned to communicate with them, they became proficient because they were not distracted. Some supervisors believe that because of their need for sign language they develop higher manual dexterity.

Managers in one company learned to talk with their hands in a 10-week course designed to teach people how to communicate by fingerspelling and sign language. The purpose of the course was not only to inform managers how to communicate with deaf employees but also how to understand some of the problems they experience.

Rehabilitation agencies cooperate with employers who are willing to consider hiring the handicapped for work for which they are suited. These workers receive counseling and are referred to a school or medical service for guidance and help, therapy and psychotherapy.

State and federal funds are available with no economic need requirement for tuition. These services are available for deaf, blind or otherwise visually handicapped, and others with cardiac, arthritic and rheumatic conditions.

All They Ask Is a Chance

The handicapped want no more than an opportunity to work. They don't expect favored treatment or special privileges. They have learned to lead productive lives, and usually ask for no concession. They are appreciative of their jobs and are therefore loyal and dedicated in return. Employers of handicapped persons claim that once they are properly placed there is less turnover, less absenteeism, less tardiness.

Many handicapped people develop remarkable powers that compensate for their impairments. The handicapped employee:

1. Stays on the job; is not a job rover.
2. Is safety conscious; this helps cut down employer's insurance rates.
3. Tries hard to do well; may out-produce others.
4. Is seldom absent.
5. Displays a sense of gratitude.

Companies should realize that many people who are physically handicapped may not be vocationally handicapped. Given a job within their limitations, in a company with an understanding climate, these people can indeed be good employees.

Many companies hire the handicapped moved by a humanitarian spirit. Many companies hire them from a selfish motive because they make good employees. The government has entered upon the scene by making it illegal not to hire them. Government contractors holding contracts worth $50,000 or more must develop affirmative action plans for hiring the handicapped. The guidelines cover an individual who is "capable of performing a particular job with reasonable accommodation to his handicap."

Section 503 of the Vocational Rehabilitation Act of 1973 requires that this "reasonable accommodation" be made for a disabled worker. Installing ramps, lowering water fountains, widening restroom stalls, using raised leters on hallway signs, and adding warning lights on machines are some of the measures companies are expected to take.

The law defines the handicapped as individuals who have a disabling mental or physical condition, or a history of such a condition, or are "regarded" as impaired. The list includes the blind, deaf and crippled, epileptics and people with shortened life expectancy. Under this broad definition, one estimate asserts that half of the Americans of working age could claim protection under the law.

PROVISIONS FOR THE PHYSICALLY HANDICAPPED

The international symbol of access for the handicapped means, "No barriers." The familiar symbol reassures and marks the way.

Companies now build gradual ramps and automatic, powered doors. Restroom facilities include assistance railings and special towel dispensers. Additional features are low-mounted telephones with touch-tone dialing and amplifiers to increase the hearing volume.

Eating places have height-adjustable tables and tables without aprons. Cafeteria serving areas have wider entrances and trays that rest on the arms of wheel chairs.

Physically Handicapped

HIRING THE MENTALLY HANDICAPPED

As the slogan says, hiring the handicapped is good business. This is true as long as their employment serves to make business better.

Sympathy is a strong motivator, and hiring the handicapped may well be looked upon as an act of kindness. But from a selfish company point of view, altruism should not be the reason for offering jobs to handicapped men and women.

Managers are not without compassion for people who work for them. But they must also keep an eye on performance; after all, performance can make the difference between a business surviving and not surviving. As a cardinal rule of survival, no applicant should ever be hired who is incapable of doing the work.

But this does not mean that employers should unthinkingly close the door to any and all applicants who have obvious limitations. This shortsighted view may cause a company to be shortchanging itself.

The question is not whether individuals are physically or mentally handicapped but whether they are industrially handicapped. They regularly perform many services for themselves; hence, they might be able to do certain types of work if given a chance, training and encouragement.

Mental Retardates Can Work

In discussions about hiring the handicapped, most employers think first of those who are physically disabled—amputees, crippled, blind, deaf mutes, people with deformities, and people with some degree of physical impairments, including those recovering from recent illnesses or accidents. Of late, however, consideration is extended to mentally handicapped individuals. It is estimated there are three million mentally retarded persons who are capable of full employment.

The mentally retarded often have skills that business is constantly seeking. They are overlooked while lower-skilled jobs remain unfilled. They should be given a chance to prove themselves. Those who are employable enjoy a satisfaction that no amount of dependent care or institutional therapy can-ever hope to equal.

Work gives people the feeling of being part of the society in which they live. Work builds respect. Work fulfills. Sigmund Freud called work "man's strongest tie to reality." Mentally retarded people who have the capabilities ought not to be deprived of opportunities to work. They too are entitled to the right to be useful.

All jobs are worthwhile or they would not exist. Matching each worker's capabilities and limitations to the requirements of each job results in better placements for the employer and greater job satisfaction for the employee.

Jobs filled by the mentally handicapped should not be created or rearranged to fit special circumstances. They should be regular established jobs that happen to fall within the capabilities of retarded individuals. These people are not looking for pity; they are looking for opportunity.

The Proof is There

Animal caretakers, laundry workers, building maintenance workers, library assistants, card punch operators, mail clerks, carpenters, medical technicians, store clerks, nursery workers, messengers, cooks, dishwashers, office machine operators.

Elevator operators, painters, engineering aides, printers, factory workers, farm laborers, photocopy operators, furniture refurbishers, radio repair helpers, grocery clerks, janitors, ground maintenance workers, sales personnel, stock clerks.

General laborers, construction workers, hospital attendants, warehouse workers, car wash attendants, nurse aides, cashiers, bakery workers, carpet layers, waiters, maids, housekeepers, meatcutters, ushers, ambulance attendants.

The above list represents some of the types of jobs in which mentally retarded workers have already proven their abilities to be successful in competitive employment. These job titles are from records of the National Association for Retarded Citizens' On-The-Job Training Project and a study by the U.S. Civil Service Commission. With the help of imaginative employers, the list of jobs being capably filled by mentally retarded workers is gradually erasing the stereotypes that have so restricted job opportunities in the past.

Evaluations Should Be Made

Before any mentally retarded person is hired he should be evaluated to determine the kind of work for which he is best suited.

The *psychological evaluation* finds the person's intellectual level, personality characteristics, aptitudes and interests, hobbies, levels of achievement in reading, spelling, and arithmetic—anything to help others understand him and to understand himself.

The *social evaluation* goes into family background, the type of neighborhood he was raised in, what kind of acceptance he gets, how well he mingles with others, and how he handles himself in situations involving other people.

The *medical evaluation* determines the extent of limitations, both mental and physical, that must be taken into account, what medical care may be required, and whether the condition gives clues to where the person should or should not work.

The *vocational evaluation* probes into employment potentials by reviewing school records, prior jobs held, interests demonstrated, attitudes and aspirations, and tries to fit these findings into available jobs.

The goal of society is not to place mentally retarded persons in sheltered workshops—although this may be the most desirable solution in some cases. The hope is to place them properly in the regular work force, under regular employment conditions.

They Make Good Workers

The mentally retarded men and women want to be useful in society and they appreciate the opportunity to work. This appreciation is reflected in their attitude toward their jobs.

Surveys show that the mentally handicapped worker is reliable, loyal and diligent. He wants to make good, and wants to stay on the job. He is not a job-hopper. Additionally, because he is so eager to work, and willing to remain at routine tasks, his attendance record is ordinarily above the average.

While there are clearly limitations as to how much the mentally retarded can learn, the fact is that in many types of routine, repetitive

122

work, he has proven to be far better suited than the "quick thinker," who easily becomes bored, impatient and ambitious for higher level work.

High turnover rates in nonstatus jobs have always been a problem in business and industry. The mentally retarded worker turns the negative aspects of such jobs into pluses; the repetitive, monotonous character of these jobs is precisely what makes them comfortable and secure to the mentally retarded person. He wants this kind of work because he is good at it.

The key is "proper placement." This means understanding the content of the jobs and the skills necessary to perform them, and then matching these requirements against the qualifications of the applicant.

Hiring Pays Off

The Lutheran Home for the Aged, in Arlington Heights, Illinois, has been employing mentally retarded persons for some time.

They employ them throughout the home in housekeeping, laundry and food service departments. The same individual who works on the dishwashing machine can also be used to serve in the dining room. One is a pots-and-pans washer. Others work on the tray line making simple placements, such as cups and saucers. Even those who can read a little cannot read fast enough to individualize tray items, as indicated on the tickets. They do better on routine, repetitive tasks.

"When they learn a routine, they master it and changing it upsets them," says Dick Soukup, the food service director. "Give them one job at a time. Don't switch them around too much. Don't let other employees pamper them," are things he has learned. In fact, it takes a little doing to learn how to handle them, but the payoff makes it all worthwhile.

No two mentally handicapped persons are alike, of course. Some are happy-go-lucky while others are morose and sullen. They have distinctly different personalities, attitudes and outlooks, just as other people do. But in general, it takes only a little longer to train retarded workers for routine tasks than it does persons of more normal intelligence. And once they learn what has to be done, they develop speed. Their slower mental processes do not affect their manual dexterity.

A problem is that sometimes they work too fast. This may come about because of their complete concentration. It takes all their mental ability to perform even simple tasks; hence, they are forced to keep their minds on their work.

Employers of the mental retardates have noticed the unusual pride they take in their work. They are dependable; they insist on coming to work regardless of how they feel. Problems that beset the ordinary workers in terms of colds, headaches, and the like do not deter them from appearing at their work places.

Employees Should Be Prepared

The first step is to establish a corporate commitment and then develop a positive plan. The owner or manager must let it be known that the company has taken an official position to hire one or more mentally handicapped persons for certain types of jobs provided they are available and ready for work.

The present employees must also know of the company decision, hopefully in advance. It might be necessary to prepare them on a positive note to counter built-in prejudices, no matter how ill-founded these personal impressions may be.

There are a couple of common myths that should be dispelled before any meaningful hiring of mentally retarded persons can be undertaken:

> *Myth:* The mentally retarded are mentally ill or mentally deranged.
>
> *Fact:* The mentally retarded are not mentally ill. They are persons who are lower intellectually—their I.Q. is below normal.
>
> *Myth:* Mentally retarded persons are totally dependent and need institutional care.
>
> *Fact:* People often fail to distinguish between degrees of retardation. They think in terms of the most severely retarded who look and act "different." Actually, the great majority of the mentally retarded are mildly affected—with no obvious "symptoms" of retardation.

A misconception of some managers about mentally retarded people is that the odds of success are not too favorable. Just the opposite is true, for the odds are in favor of the mentally retarded individual long before he seeks a competitive job. This is accomplished through vocational evaluation, which matches the individual to suitable jobs, and through various forms of pre-employment training.

This job preparation may begin at a very young age. It continues through years of schooling as the mentally retarded persons are helped to develop vocational abilities. Occupational training centers further expand the training opportunities used as a bridge to competitive employment. This training, coupled with vocational evaluation, is a significant reason behind the increasing acceptance of mentally retarded workers by employers.

Employment Barriers Must Be Removed

Not all the barriers in America are in the form of fences and road-blocks and "keep out" signs. Some are traditional rules, regulations and practices that serve to keep mentally retarded people out of jobs just as effectively as barbed wire. Here are examples of some of the more common barriers:

Entrance tests. Some employers still demand written tests for all kinds of jobs, whether the jobs warrant such tests or not. Where does this leave mentally retarded people who could do the jobs but who could not pass the tests?

Supervisors. Some supervisors never have gotten the knack of supervising mentally retarded employees. They mumble a few instructions, point in a vague direction, and walk away. Where does this leave new retarded employees who are trying so hard to understand what they're supposed to do?

Orientation. Some businesses expect new employees, mentally retarded included, to find their own way around: first aid stations, payroll departments, cafeterias, etc. Where does this leave mentally retarded people who keep hoping that someone will show them?

Acceptance. Some employers aren't quite sure what to expect when a mentally retarded person comes to work, so they display all sorts of give-aways of their apprehensions. They may talk louder than usual to the mentally retarded employee; they may overwhelm him with paternalism. Where does this leave mentally retarded people who want nothing more than to be shown the same kind of acceptance that other workers are shown?

Tokenism. Some employers hire one mentally retarded person and feel they have fulfilled an obligation. "We've done our duty," proclaim these employers. Where does this leave qualified retarded job applicants who never get inside the front door?

Unselective Rejection vs. Selective Placement. Modern personnel practices call for selective placement: putting the right person in the right job, regardless of his handicap. Yet some employers still practice old-fashioned unselective rejection: automatically saying "No" to any mentally retarded job applicant, simply because he's mentally handicapped. Where does this leave the person who is able to do the job and do it well?

Ironically, the rigid practices and procedures that leave mentally retarded workers out in the cold also leave well-intentioned prospective employers without access to a group of highly-motivated, dedicated workers, a situation easily remedied by managerial skill and understanding, to the benefit of all.

MENTALLY RETARDED DOES NOT MEAN
MENTALLY ILL

It is a mistake to lump together the mentally retarded and the mentally ill. The mentally retarded are men and women of limited intellectual ability. Generally they enjoy performing routine, repetitive tasks—the kind of work that a normal worker would consider boring.

Mental illness, on the other hand, does not affect basic intellectual ability. When recovered from their illness, former mental patients are capable of holding virtually any job for which their training and experience has qualified them.

Supervisory Management (American Management Association).

HIRING THE BLIND

A handicap is any mental, physical or social condition that limits an individual from living a normal, productive, independent life in our society without extreme effort both on his part and through special services to help him overcome that handicap.

The philosophy of rehabilitation services for the visually handicapped focuses on men, women and children who are blind or partially blind to aid them in reaching their highest potential as independent, productive members of the community.

On the theory that to work productively is a basic need every person has in life, much of the emphasis is in assisting blind people in gaining meaningful work that is a true challenge to their potential and that rewards them financially to the extent of their ability to be productive.

One private agency, the Chicago Lighthouse for the Blind, has since 1906 been serving blind, visually impaired and multihandicapped persons who cannot make it on their own. The main thrust is vocational. In addition to skills training it includes work-route orientation to and from the place of employment.

1. Office skills. This program provides training in four areas: transcription typing, word processing, medical terminology (8,000 terms), and legal terminology. A blind typist learns special techniques for correcting errors, setting margins and spacing, and organizing files. Classroom instruction is supplemented by field trips to offices.

2. Industrial program. This consists of two phases: individualized work adjustment followed by on-the-job training in a realistic environment. Industry placement follows.

3. Vocational center. Blind workers capable of job placements in competitive industry may instead work in the rehabilitation workshop for further adjustment or high skills training on complex equipment. Here they work only on jobs obtained through competitive subcontract bids.

The placement service aims at dispelling fears that employers have about hiring visually-impaired workers. Through education, facts and references they show that blind persons are capable, conscientious, low-risk and high-efficiency employees. They also point out that the practice of denying qualified persons employment is not only unfair but actually illegal.

HIRING THE HEALTHY

An organization called GASP has launched a campaign called, "Hire a Non-Smoker," because:

1. Nonsmokers have less absenteeism than smokers. The U.S. Public Health Service studies show that smokers are absent from work because of illness 30% more often than nonsmokers.
2. Nonsmokers have fewer illnesses. Smokers are particularly susceptible to invading viruses and bacteria. They catch the common cold 1½ times more often than nonsmokers.
3. Nonsmokers have fewer chronic diseases leading to early disability. Smoker's diseases often turn workers into permanent invalids, necessitating early retirement and costly disability payments.
4. Nonsmokers have fewer work accidents. Smoking is often a distraction and can lead to accidents. (Ex: Many car accidents occur because the driver was searching for, lighting or disposing of a cigaret and his attention was diverted.)
5. Nonsmokers tend to be more productive. They don't take time out for "smoking breaks," trips to the cigaret machine, nor do they fumble with matches, lighters and ashtrays.
6. Nonsmokers make a better impression with the general public. Receptionists, salespeople and executives present a better image if they don't smoke. They smell better, look better, and don't risk offending nonsmokers who don't like smoke.
7. Nonsmokers are less destructive of company property. Fire damage caused by careless smokers represents huge financial losses. A conservative estimate by the National Fire Protective Association is that one-quarter of all fires resulting in property losses are caused by smoking materials. In fires where lives are lost, more than one-half are smoking-related. Destruction, such as cigaret burns in

rugs, on desks, trash-can fires, and damaged merchandise, adds up to plenty.

8. Nonsmokers do not offend fellow workers. No need to elaborate on this. Any nonsmoker who has had to work with smokers will tell what it's like.

9. Nonsmokers are less subject to many occupational health hazards. When there already exists an industrial condition such as airborne contaminants, nonsmokers do not further endanger their health with tobacco smoke.

10. Nonsmokers can work around sensitive machinery. Smokers may foul instruments, making them inaccurate or, at best, necessitate frequent cleaning.

At a time when there is intense competition for jobs, being a non-smoker can be a distinct advantage.

EX-OFFENDERS

Most big companies have ex-convicts on their payrolls. Some of the employers know it; but many of them aren't aware of their presence.

That's because some ex-offenders, as they prefer to be called, hide the fact they served time when they applied for jobs. As far as job qualifications go, the people with prison records feel they are no different from other applicants except that they have been branded—they got caught breaking the law.

Companies that knowingly hire ex-offenders claim that many have shown they are reliable and good workers. Parolees, for example, have a lot to lose if they foul up.

For selfish reasons, it is expected that business will turn increasingly to employing ex-offenders as an extension of the low-income labor pool just as it did when it made a conscious effort to hire members of minority groups.

The pattern of success in hiring ex-offenders is essentially the same as employing disadvantaged workers because so many of both groups come from the same poor environment. They are not likely to be the most preferred employees in terms of attitudes, education or skills. Spending years behind bars tends to destroy confidence and warps the sense of responsibility. Besides, the prison system generally fails to rehabilitate inmates. Education and skill training too often are nonexistent or ineffective.

As a consequence, ex-offenders have special problems in finding and holding jobs.

The main trouble is that the newly-freed prisoner expects to fail. He

128

is socially and vocationally crippled from his prison experience. The employer must go to great lengths to build his confidence.

Prison graduates no longer are used to the workaday world. They imagine all kinds of innuendoes in the most ordinary shop talk. That makes them touchy and withdrawn.

This raises the question: who should know about the prison record? If employees know they might become hostile and even try to blackball them.

Problems are compounded when ex-offenders, in their eagerness to get hired, are dumped into hard-to-fill boring jobs. They are not all educationally disadvantaged. Many are smart, quick to learn. They could have positive attitudes.

Firms that failed with the former prisoners they hired did so because they did not give them active help. Companies are more likely to succeed if they deal with them on a personal basis.

If society can accept that released prisoners, having served their sentences, have paid their dues, then it follows that they are entitled to reestablish themselves in the community. By providing jobs and sympathetic understanding, business could develop and train ex-offenders upon their release and help immeasurably in making them good workers and good citizens.

TEMPORARY HELP

The temporary-help industry, which started when Sam Workman began offering temporary service in Chicago in 1935, has mushroomed into a quarter of a billion dollars per year business. It currently employs a million wage earners. Under its arrangements workers are hired by the temporary help agency (which does not charge them any fee), then leased to industrial and professional firms on a short-term basis.

The company pays a flat hourly rate, based on the skill. The employee is on the payroll of the agency, not the company where the work is performed. The agency assumes the obligations for Social Security taxes and records, insurance, vacation and other benefits. The big item, of course, is that the agency recruits, interviews, tests, selects and hires the employees and either finds them qualified in a specialty skill or trains them. The employing company gets a fully-trained worker.

Temporary workers are mostly women, especially married women. These are often well-trained and skilled workers who for reasons of their own are unable or unwilling to accept full-time employment.

The temporary-help industry is a blessing for wives who want extra money. But it may also be the answer for career women who like to travel, students working their way through college, actresses between engagements, athletes during the off season, and older people who need new jobs.

Job arrangements can be tailored to the worker, who can work those weeks when he or she is available, certain days of the week, and occasionally even limited hours of the day. Mothers can take the summer months off to be home with school-age children simply by making themselves unavailable during that period.

Travel for single women is more than saving money while working for a vacation trip. Companies which have offices in different cities have been known to certify employees in their home city and then assign them out of offices in other cities. An example is the British secretaries recruited and hired in London for six or 12 months' work, then assigned to companies in various cities in the United States.

Many workers like the variety which this kind of service offers. Creative types may find working for the same company somewhat stifling. As temporary workers they can move about, actually pick and choose the kind of work they prefer.

Temporary workers are mostly typists and secretaries. But there are also many other types of office skills—calculating machine operators, clerks, bookkeepers, file clerks, key punch operators. Some are trained as computer programmers, receptionists, demonstrators, convention registrars, ushers, pollsters, survey interviewers, etc.

A few agencies are now specializing in men for temporary jobs. Some of these supply laborers, freight handlers, watchmen—hired and paid by the day. Others are office and factory workers, product demonstrators, booth attendants, sample distributors, and so on.

Benefits Both Ways

While there are many advantages from the employee point of view, there are equally as many benefits accruing to employers.

Temporary workers are used for work overloads caused by:

1. Peak loads.
2. Cyclical conditions.
3. Inventories.
4. Vacations.
5. Sickness.
6. Unfilled job openings.

For companies there is:

1. No red tape.
2. No recruiting.
3. No interviewing.

4. No selection.
5. No union rules.
6. No payroll deductions.
7. No fringe benefits.
8. No training.
9. No supervision.
10. No age limit.

Companies save since:
1. They pay only for the number of hours worked.
2. They do not have the costs of employment.
3. They have no fringe benefit costs.
4. They pay on weekly invoice in place of the usual amount of payroll work and recordkeeping.

Temporary personnel is a new industrial cost-savings tool. Apart from the savings in record keeping, payroll taxes, worker's compensation, and fringe benefits, the big item is direct labor cost savings. Temporary workers are used only when there is work for them. Whereas regular employees remain on the payroll even when the volume of work decreases, the temporary workers are released. No work, no direct labor cost.

The use of temporary personnel has introduced a new cost-control concept of flexible planning. Companies retain a minimum core permanent staff, and supplement this with temporary workers who are used only as needed.

There are hundreds of temporary help offices in all major cities in the United States and Canada. Some of the largest are well known, but there are others that are strictly local with possibly a few neighborhood branches. A company interested in using temporary help will most likely go where it gets the best service and satisfaction.

HOW TO PREPARE FOR TEMPORARY HELP

When temporary help is needed, either in the office or the plant, there are certain steps that can be taken to facilitate matters for both the company and the temporary worker and use this "extra hand" to best advantage.

1. *Improvise a work station manual.* This can be simple—samples of the kind of work to be done, something about the company, the department where the work is to be done. This should be readied before the temporary worker arrives.

2. *Check the equipment.* Have the supervisor to whom the temporary worker will report check in advance to see that the machine or equipment is working properly, that supplies are adequate and

handy, that the temporary worker will be ready to go upon reporting in.

3. *Welcome the temporary.* Upon arrival, the temporary worker should be shown around quickly and introduced to co-workers in the unit. The temporary worker should be made to feel at home, free to ask questions, and should easily join in with the group.

4. *Provide good supervision.* Make it clear to whom the temporary worker reports. Explain the problem which necessitated the temporary help and outline thoroughly the significance of the work. Understanding leads to better productivity and efficiency.

5. *Discuss the local routines.* The temporary worker will feel more at ease if the customs, such as coffee breaks, lunch hours and any other rules and regulations of the firm are explained.

6. *Explain the company style.* Every firm has its own peculiarities. These may be a distinctive letter form, a unique way of packaging, stylized telephone answering, etc. The temporary worker should be adequately instructed in these matters.

7. *Arrange for a contact.* Assign a regular employee to act as sponsor to the temporary worker. This will make the temporary worker more comfortable since the fellow worker will be a source of immediate information and help should problems arise.

8. *Be friendly.* Make the temporary worker feel needed and wanted. Try to create a favorable rapport with permanent employees. Don't make the temporary worker feel like an outsider.

9. *Explain the situation to the permanent staff.* Discuss the need for temporary help with the regular employees who will be involved. Make it clear that this is a special case, that the temporary worker is in no way competing with them, and not a threat to their job security.

10. *Keep in touch with the referral source.* Let the agency know that the temporary worker arrived, report on progress whether good or bad, keep the lines open in case a replacement or addition may be needed, and upon completion of the assignment, give a fair and honest report of the performance.

PART-TIME WORKERS

Latest figures show 18.3 million people work part-time. This is almost one-fifth of the country's employed workers. In one decade, the number of employed rose 26.5% to 99.5 million from 78.6 million while at the same time the number of part-time workers rose 57.9% to 18.3 million from 11.5 million.

Some people work part-time by choice because this arrangement fits their personal circumstances. They work but still have time to pay attention to taking care of their families, education, or leisure pursuits. Short hours and short weeks open money doors to students, homemakers, and senior citizens who ordinarily are not in the regular labor force.

Other people work part-time out of necessity because they cannot find full-time employment and need modest income to tide them over. They take whatever is available while their careers are on hold. Less-than-full-time employment allows them time to conduct a job search and report for interviews.

Part-time work is offered by banks, drug stores, retailers, supermarkets, insurance companies, fast-food establishments, hospitals, government agencies, libraries, universities, and similar employers. In one year recently, 32% of employees in the wholesale and retail trade worked part-time, and 24.3% of service workers, 11.6% of finance, and 8.4% of manufacturing were part-timers.

Employers like the increasing use of part-time workers because it reduces labor costs. The work force is more fluid, thus the hours worked and paid for are more flexible and fit work load fluctuations. In addition to paying only for hours worked, these employees receive no fringe benefits such as sick pay, vacations, health and hospitalization insurance.

Organized labor charges that companies are turning to part-time workers to thwart unionization. These employees are transient and almost impossible to organize. Their main concern is to turn available time into money. They are not attracted to whatever it is the union offers to provide.

Most part-time jobs are in production or service categories. The numbers include few managerial or professional people although some might moonlight as university lecturers, public speakers, writers, or consultants. Colleges and universities in particular prefer part-time instructors because they can draw on people with broad and practical real-life business experience. One survey showed 24% of the faculty of four-year liberal arts colleges were part-timers, as were 20% at research universities, and 51% at two-year community colleges.

Many employers contend that part-time employees are more productive than full-time workers since their work is concentrated. Usually there are plenty of part-time workers in the job market so that employers can select the better ones with little screening, and they can also easily replace those workers who are not measuring up. The part-time market favors the employer.

The use of part-time help is a phenomenon of American business. For the employees: it opens doors for people who would otherwise not be employable. For the employers: it provides a steady source of workers who fit irregular schedules, off hours, and short terms. Part-time workers round out the basic full-time staff. The trend will not only continue but will also grow.

FULL-TIME OPERATION with PART-TIME EMPLOYEES
A practical example

Control Data Corporation, a world-wide business employing 27,800, headquartered in Minneapolis, Minnesota, has the only plant in the country known to employ part-time workers for nearly all its work force. Ten full-time employees supervise the operation.

This innovation is in keeping with the strategy of the corporation whose philosophy is "to approach inner city and other societal problems with the objective that solutions can be turned into profitable business opportunities."

Let William C. Norris, chairman, tell how this came about:

"While the child development center helped solve the problems of employment for some working mothers, we learned that there were many job seekers who could not meet working hour requirements. These included mothers and female heads of households with school-age children as well as high school, vocational and college students in need of income to stay in school or to supplement family income.

"We decided in 1974 to construct a bindery plant employing part-time workers in the economically-depressed Selby area of St. Paul. The employment level is at 160 persons on three shifts. The morning shift (8:30 A.M. to 2:00 P.M.) is mostly made up of mothers of school-age children. The three-hour afternoon shift (2:00 P.M. to 5:00 P.M.) is students. The evening shift (5:30 P.M. to 9:30 P.M.) is men and women hired on the basis of economic need.

The operation has been so successful that it is being expanded and, with an addition to the plant now in progress, will go up to 275 employees.

JOB SHOP

A job shop, or contract manufacturing service, offers benefits similar to those of temporary help or a service bureau. But there are differences: (1) a temporary help agency sends out workers to a company to help out during emergencies or vacancies; (2) in a service bureau the client company farms out its work overloads to the bureau which completes the work in its own office with its regular staff; (3) a job shop takes over a portion of the production process for the client company on subcontract terms.

One electronics manufacturing and service operation, for example, provides a variety of engineering, manufacturing, and technical services to clients. Activities include the fabrication of printed circuit boards and electronic assemblies for government organizations and commercial product manufacturers on a contract basis. Another activity is their service in supplying engineers, technicians, and other skilled personnel to perform their function at the customers' facilities.

In an office application, a typical example would be the payroll service provided by a bank's computer for the small business firm. The company prepares the data up to a point, then lets the bank complete the transaction, print the individual paychecks, and compile necessary statements and reports. An insurance claims administration company in San Francisco sent its daily information to a data processing firm in Ireland. The turnaround time was 36 hours. The success of the endeavor depended upon the precise courier delivery and pickup in airports at both ends.

One company offers data processing services nationwide consisting of computer time, electronic laser printing, data entry, and full service. One-time or continuous services can be provided in their own offices for clients or in the customer's location by local or remote hookup. This arrangement brings a full staff of experienced systems and programming specialists within the range of all sized companies. Particularly in the computer area, one big reason for the shift from a service bureau to a job shop is processing costs. With the proliferation and sophistication of computer hardware and programs, the unit cost can be reduced whereas labor costs keep rising.

In using the job shop, the customer has an opportunity to:

1. *Pay only for acceptable products.* Otherwise, the customer pays up-front for direct labor and fringe benefits and direct material and support costs before anything is produced.
2. *Balance the internal work force.* There are some peaks and valleys in any manufacturing business caused by delays in getting materials, changes in design, etc. The customer staffs for expected needs, and is strapped with fixed costs when delays occur.
3. *Get a fix on manufacturing costs.* This allows for improved planning and reduces exposure to peaks and valleys.
4. *Improve cash flow.* With payment to the contractor not due until receipt of acceptable product, the customer avoids up-

front cash outlays. The customer also has better control of inventory and as the cost of money goes up, this becomes more important.

5. *Make better utilization of management.* This advantage may be more significant than the others. The dilution of a company's most valuable asset, its people, can cause long-term problems as well as near-term frustrations.

In many companies the strengths are not in manufacturing but rather in marketing, or in new product development, or in financial dealings, or in knowledge of the marketplace they serve. Jobbing out those portions of the production process for which they are least equipped could indeed be a wise management decision. At least, it might be worth looking into.

The potential advantages of contracting out some of the production varies, depending on the customer's own capabilities. The philosophy of a company wanting to do everything connotes expertise beyond the facts and can lead to diversion of talents away from real strengths. The specialized job shop becomes a natural extension of the enterprise and can contribute to a better product or service and at the same time improve the profit potential.

JOB RESUMÉS

There are people who feel the job resumé is an overrated paper tool and "worse than useless." Recruiters use the resumé in judging whether a particular applicant is worth interviewing. Beyond that it is impossible to predict potential success or failure, they contend.

Its use is justified in that it becomes an easy elimination device when many candidates make themselves available for few jobs. In this context, applicants eliminate themselves by submitting unimpressive resumés.

Common mistakes are: too long (it is not an autobiography), too sketchy or vague (listing job titles instead of duties), too negative in tone, or overplaying personally-flattering details unrelated to the job under consideration.

The essentials of a good resumé are: (1) personal data (name, address, family status, etc.), (2) work experience (chronologically in inverse order), (3) education (subjects and activities), and (4) possibly references (although these are meaningless they are often expected). If education is recent and work background limited, these two elements may be interchanged in the order of importance.

Brevity is the key; it should be concise. It should be neatly typed with spelling and grammar perfect. It must be well organized, with emphasis on work experience, academic qualifications, specialized training, skills and abilities. A photograph is unnecessary and physical characteristics are extraneous. Minority group members need not indicate their ethnic or other backgrounds.

An applicant is advised to accompany his preprinted, mass-produced resumé with a personalized cover letter, indicating the reason for interest in the company. A little research on the company helps to learn the name of the individual to whom to address the letter; otherwise direct it to the personnel or employment chief, not the president of the firm.

An employer is also interested in the aspirations of an applicant as well as the qualifications. The employer is more concerned with estimating future performance with him than reviewing the past record elsewhere.

APPLICATION BLANK

The "Application for Employment" form is used to obtain information. By the use of a standard form the information is always in the same place and the interviewer is spared the time and annoyance of having to hunt for the specifics he needs to know. The form may be professionally prepared (store-bought) and widely used, or individually developed by any one company through its own experience.

The information asked for depends upon company requirements and job demands. In all cases certain necessary data, such as name and address, are essential. But questions to a sales applicant will vary considerably from those of a shop worker.

The sections of an application blank are usually these:

1. Personal data: name, home address, telephone number, social security number.
2. Helpful information: type of work sought, salary desired, when available to start work, reason for wanting to change jobs, and from what source the applicant was referred.
3. Education: chronological education history, highest level attained with everything leading to it detailed out by names and locations of grammar school, high school, trade or business college, correspondence school, college or university, night school: years attended, whether graduated, courses specialized in.
4. Work experience: work history in inverse order, names and addresses of companies worked for (listing most recent one

137

first and working back), dates of employment, earnings, types of work done, progress made, reason for leaving, and name of supervisor who may be contacted for reference.

Other information requested may pertain to machine skills learned in schools or on previous jobs, military experience, if any, and specialized training received, and talents or hobbies that could be useful in employment. Job reference may be asked for but references from personal acquaintances are not used much anymore because they have little value.

Provision should be made for the applicant to supply additional data which he feels would be pertinent to his qualifications. Usually, the bigger the job, the more information is asked.

It is advisable to have the applicant sign the form. Above the space for the signature enter a "clearance" statement which guarantees all information to be accurate and gives the prospective employer the right to investigate any of it. Quite often, however, the interviewer will be asked not to check with the present employer, and this request, of course, should be respected.

Questions Should be Pertinent

Different application blanks may be used for:

1. Office personnel
2. Factory workers
3. Salesmen
4. Technicians
5. Supervisors and managers
6. Executives

Since different information is often needed for higher positions, the appropriate application blanks are more detailed. They provide for information about the applicant's background and stability, extracurricular activities, scholastic honors, leadership positions, military accomplishments, civic responsibilities, interests and the like.

On the general subject of application blanks there are two schools of thought. Some people feel the blank should ask only those questions that are pertinent to employment in the company. Their application form lists only minimum questions. Others believe there is value to interspersing necessary questions with general and possibly irrelevant ones on the theory that everybody likes to talk about himself. While the applicant is concentrating on harmless questions, he is unaware of the importance attached to some of the less obvious but more meaningful statements he makes.

Because of the usually tight labor market as well as the pressure to hire marginal applicants, some companies are purposely expanding their application blanks to ask for more personal data. As protection for the company that wants to cooperate but does not want to hire bad risks, and also to protect the applicants from being hired for work for which they are unsuited, these firms now ask more in-depth questions about an applicant's preparation and readiness to become a trouble-free employee. This is a delicate matter and care must be exercised in not asking for data which conflicts with legislation.

It is unlawful to ask questions about:

1. Name: original name if name has been changed.
   if he ever worked under another name.
   however, a married woman may be asked to tell her maiden name.

2. Birth: birthplace of applicant.
   birthplace of applicant's parents, spouse or other relatives.
   birth certificate, baptismal record, or naturalization or first papers.

3. Citizenship: citizen of what country.
   where applicant was naturalized.
   whether parents or spouse were naturalized.

4. National origin: lineage, ancestry, descent, parentage, nationality.
   what is the mother tongue.
   language commonly used at home or with parents.
   how applicant learned to read, write or speak foreign language.

5. Race: complexion or color of skin.
   require applicant to affix photograph.

6. Religion: religious affiliation.
   religious holidays observed.

7. Age: unless to satisfy minimum age statutes (Ex: under 18?) or to determine if applicant is over 70.

8. Sex and marital status: sex of applicant.
   marital situation past and present.
   dependents.

9. Physical characteristics: height.
   weight.
   hair length and style.
   handicap, unless this is a bona fide occupational limitation.

10. Organizations: membership in what clubs, societies or lodges to which applicant belongs.

APPLICATION FOR POSITION

EEOC & FCCC Approved Form

Position Applied For	Permanent ☐ Temporary ☐	Part Time ☐ Seasonal ☐	Date Available

PERSONAL INFORMATION

Mr. ☐ Mrs. ☐ **Last Name** Ms. ☐	**First Name**	**Social Security Number**

Present Permanent Address	City	County	State	Zip Code

Home Phone No.	Date of Birth	

Any physical limitations? Yes ☐ No ☐	If so, please explain

Active duty in U.S. armed forces?* Yes ☐ No ☐	Dates of Duty From To	Branch

EDUCATIONAL INFORMATION

Circle highest grade completed	Grade School 1 2 3 4 5 6 7 8	High School 9 10 11 12	College 13 14 15 16	Post Graduate BS/BA MA PHD

Name and Address of last High School	Date of Graduation	Have you passed GED Test? Yes ☐ No ☐

Type School	Name and address of School	From	To	No. Qtr. Credits	No. Sem. Credits	Degree	Major
College/ University							
College/ University							
Graduate							
Technical							
Technical							
Military							

List any correspondence courses, special courses, seminars, workshops, training sessions, etc., that might relate to this position. Also list any licenses or certificates relating to position.

_____

_____

_____

_____

_____

_____

_____

_____

*(Not to be asked in New Jersey)

Form No. OA-201

EMPLOYMENT HISTORY (Begin With the Most Recent)

Employer's Name		Mailing Address		Zip Code	Phone No.
Position Held		Duties Performed			Immed. Supervisor
Employment Dates	Last Salary	Full Time ▢ Part Time ▢	Reason For Leaving		

Employer's Name		Mailing Address		Zip Code	Phone No.
Position Held		Duties Performed			Immed. Supervisor
Employment Dates	Last Salary	Full Time ▢ Part Time ▢	Reason For Leaving		

Employer's Name		Mailing Address		Zip Code	Phone No.
Position Held		Duties Performed			Immed. Supervisor
Employment Dates	Last Salary	Full Time ▢ Part Time ▢	Reason For Leaving		

Employer's Name		Mailing Address		Zip Code	Phone No.
Position Held		Duties Performed			Immed. Supervisor
Employment Dates	Last Salary	Full Time ▢ Part Time ▢	Reason For Leaving		

May we contact your present employer?   Yes ▢   No ▢   If NO, please explain.

UNSALARIED EXPERIENCE

Volunteer Organization		Mailing Address	Zip Code	Phone No.
Position Held		Duties Performed		Immed. Supervisor
Dates of Participation	Hrs. Per Wk.	Skills Learned		

List any other skills or experience which better qualifies you for position

CONVICTION INFORMATION

This Company <u>does not</u> automatically reject applicants who have been convicted.
Before any applicant is rejected because of convictions, he/she will be notified of his/her possible rejection. This notice will state the reasons for rejection. The applicant will be given one (1) week to appeal.

Have you ever been convicted as an adult for a criminal violation?   Yes ▢   No ▢

If yes, date and place.	Nature of offense	Disposition
If yes, date and place.	Nature of offense	Disposition

141

Pre-Employment Information Form

(answer all questions - please print)

Qualified applicants are considered for employment, and employees are treated during employment, without regard to race, color, religion, sex, national origin, age, marital status, medical condition or handicap.

To help us comply with Federal/State equal employment opportunity record keeping, reporting and other legal requirements, please answer questions below.

This Pre-Employment Information Form will be kept in a <u>Confidential File</u> separate from the attached Application for Employment.

Date _____

Position(s) Applied For _____

Referred By: _____

Name (print) _____ Phone No._____
           LAST   FIRST   MIDDLE

Address _____
      STREET   CITY   STATE   ZIP

Birthdate_____ Age _____

Race/Ethnic Group: ☐ White   ☐ Black   ☐ Hispanic

              ☐ American Indian/Alaskan Native   ☐ Asian/Pacific Islander

Sex: ☐ Male   ☐ Female

Marital Status: ☐ Single   ☐ Married   ☐ Divorced   ☐ Widowed

Number of Children _____

Are You a Vietnam Era Veteran?   ☐ Yes   ☐ No

Are You a Disabled Veteran?   ☐ Yes   ☐ No

If Yes, What Is Your VA Disability Rating?_____%

Have You Ever Filed a Claim for Workmen's Compensation?

              ☐ Yes   ☐ No

Re-order Form #23960 From Amsterdam Printing and Litho Corp., Amsterdam, N. Y. 12010
©copyright 1978 Amsterdam Printing and Litho Corp., Amsterdam, N. Y. 12010

142

The "Application for Employment" blank is one of the chief tools in the selection procedure. It is important that it be properly designed and correctly interpreted.

APPLICATION BLANK DATA

Antidiscrimination laws do not prohibit "asking" questions about race, color, religion, sex, national origin, age, marital status, medical condition or handicap. They merely prohibit employers from discriminating against an applicant or employee on the basis of one of more of these factors. To be on the safe side, these questions are omitted from the application blank.

To comply with record keeping, reporting and other legal requirements, however, it is necessary for a company to obtain this information about employees. The caution is that this information may be gathered but cannot be used against employees. Some companies ask for this detailed information only after a decision to hire has been made based on other factors, such as qualifications and ability to perform the job.

EMPLOYMENT CHECKLIST

There are a few specific taboos regarding preemployment questions. The employer who asks for the types of information cautioned against must then stand ready to defend the need for that information as relevant to the hiring process.

The best guideline to follow is "If you don't need the information to make a hire or no-hire decision, don't ask it!"

The following checklist, prepared by the Illinois State Chamber of Commerce, should be helpful.

Where questions arise, employers should seek the advice of their attorneys in-house and those on retainer. The procedures used in employment decisions should be proper and lawful and should be documented so that those proper and lawful procedures would be reflected in an audit of the employment procedures. Finally, employment offices would be wise to subscribe to advisory services to keep up-to-date on interpretations of the laws and be acquainted with existing rules and regulations.

checklist

What can a prospective employer legally ask?

	Acceptable inquiry	Discriminatory inquiry
Name	Additional information relative to change of name, use of an assumed name or nickname necessary to enable a check on applicant's work records.	The fact of a change of name or the original name of an applicant whose name has been legally changed
Birthplace and residence	Applicant's place of residence Length of applicant's residence in Illinois and/or city where the employer is located	Birthplace of applicant Birthplace of applicant's parents Requirement that applicant submit birth certificate, naturalization or baptismal record
Creed and religion	None	Applicant's religious affiliation Church, parish, or religious holidays observed by applicant.
Race or color	General distinguishing physical characteristics such as scars, etc.	Applicant's race Color of applicant's skin, eyes, hair, etc.
Photographs	None	Photographs with application Photographs after interview, but before hiring
Age	If hired, can you furnish proof of age?	Date of birth or age of an applicant except when such information is needed for or to: 1. Maintain apprenticeship requirements based upon a reasonable minimum age. 2. Satisfy the provisions of either state or federal minimum age statures 3. Avoid interference with the operation of the terms and conditions and administration of any bona fide retirement, pension, employe benefit program 4. Verify that applicant is above the minimum legal age (21) but without asking for a birth certificate. Age specifications or limitations in newspaper advertisements which may bar workers under or over a certain age

	Acceptable inquiry	Discriminatory inquiry
Education	Academic, vocational or professional education, and the public and private schools attended	
Citizenship	Are you in the country on a visa which would not permit you to work here?	Any and all inquiries into whether applicant is now or intends to become a citizen of the U.S., or any other inquiry related to the aspect of citizenship
National origin and ancestry	None	Applicant's lineage, ancestry, national origin, or nationality. Nationality of applicant's parents or spouse
Language	Language applicant speaks and/or writes fluently	Applicant's mother tongue Language commonly used by applicant at applicant's home How the applicant acquired ability to read, write or speak a foreign language
Relatives	Names of relatives already employed by the company Name and address of person to be notified in case of accident or emergency Name and/or address of any relative of applicant	
Military experience	Military experience of applicant in the Armed Forces of the United States Whether applicant has received any notice to report for duty in the Armed Forces	Applicant's military experience in other than U.S. Armed Forces National Guard or Reserve Units of applicant Draft classification or other eligibility for military service Dates and conditions of discharge
Organizations	Applicant's membership in any union or professional or trade organization Names of any service organizations of which applicant is a member	All clubs, social fraternities, societies, lodges, or organizations to which the applicant belongs, other than professional, trade, or service organizations.
References	Names of persons willing to provide professional and/or character references for applicant. Names of persons who suggested applicant apply for a position with the employer	The name of applicant's pastor or religious leader

PERSONNEL ADMINISTRATION HANDBOOK

	Acceptable inquiry	Discriminatory inquiry
Sex and marital status	Maiden name of applicant	Sex of applicant Marital status of applicant Dependents of applicant
Arrest record	Number and kinds of convictions for felonies	The number and kinds of arrests of an applicant
Height	None	Any inquiry into height of applicant, except where it is a bona fide occupational requirement

Source: Illinois State Chamber of Commerce

CHAPTER III

EMPLOYMENT

INTERVIEWING IS "INNER VIEWING"

INTERVIEWING is a big part of every manager's or supervisor's job. His other involvements with the personnel program—such as recruiting, testing, selection, orientation, training—can easily be shared with the central personnel staff. But interviewing is his "tool of the trade" upon which he relies more than he realizes. He uses it in hiring new workers and in other functions of the employee relations program.

Since interviewing is usually associated with the hiring process, let's begin there. Let's start by classifying employment interviewers. Just as interviewers become adept, so do interviewees; we have all seen applicants who appeared to know all the angles.

Interviewers fall into certain types, as they try to outsmart their interviewees. An interesting commentary could be developed under the title, "Interviewers I Have Met." Included would be:

- The procedure-happy type; makes decisions "by the book."

- The big brother who can't say "no" but insists upon being helpful.

- The decision maker who tells the applicant what to do.

- The familiar type who gets chummy to the point of disarming the applicant.

- The up-from-the-ranks person who relates his personal progress.

- The fringe-benefit type who tells about pensions rather than opportunities.

When we get right down to it, few managers or supervisors know exactly what they want to discover or are looking for in an interview. Not one in a thousand has consciously prepared questions that will indicate those characteristics for which he might be looking. Consequently, the questions asked are the conventional ones that might or might not have much bearing on what the interviewer really needs to find out in order to make a decision.

"I'll Take the Blonde"

All of us are familiar with the hiring of secretaries, so let's use this as an example. Ask any group of managers for their personal comments about the kind of individual they are looking for when they want to hire a secretary, and we will get all the usual adjectives: neat, accurate, conscientious, good judgment, optimistic, natural, sincere, tolerant, honest, persistent, punctual, cooperative, conservative, fast, steady, energetic, vivacious, pleasant, logical, diligent, competent, emotionally stable, one with initiative, one who loves work. Now if the applicant met all these qualifications she could trade places with the interviewer. In the majority of cases the boss might as well take one look, eliminate the too-old, the too-young, see who recognizes a typewriter and steno notebook, flip a coin, and then announce in a decisive voice, "I'll take the blonde."

Most interviews are confused bluffing sessions; no one knows for sure who is trying to impress whom. Both interviewers and interviewees try so hard to cover up weaknesses that they don't get around to letting their good qualities show through. Is it any wonder that the interview becomes a conglomeration of disconnected questions and confused answers?

It's too bad that the interview is bungled so much. After all is said and done, the interview is the determining factor in the employment procedure. From the time the first worker was hired, the personal interview technique has been used. All of the later aids that have been developed have not minimized the importance of the interview. It is safe to say that more than 99% of all workers are hired as the result of interviews.

There are two specific types of employment interviews: the planned or patterned interview—aimed at getting directly to specific data; and the informal interview—aimed at getting indirectly at general impressions as well as necessary facts.

Both types of interviews have advantages and disadvantages. The common practice is to use the informal type; it is informal not because of training, but because of lack of training. It is too informal and too often misses the point; it consists of too much talking and too little listening.

In employment we generally recommend that the line manager also interview the applicant since he is the one responsible for the final decision to hire. But in some companies where this procedure is used

148

the sequence of interviews is somewhat like an obstacle course. What is designed as a multiple interview, a recommended approach if properly done, too often becomes a chain interview—a practice in which an applicant is passed along from the personnel manager to the department head and then down to the supervisor. And the supervisor is so busy and so far behind schedule he routinely accepts the applicant that the more skilled interviewers have been sparring with. No wonder our interviews are ineffective and costly.

The Art of Predicting

Interviewing is different from other management skills inasmuch as it involves the attitudes and behavior of people. No two interviews can be alike. The success of an interview depends upon the extent to which the interviewer can create a feeling of mutual confidence and cooperation between himself and the applicant.

The purpose of an employment interview is to collect information, combine and classify it, to help predict the likelihood of the applicant's being able to perform the job successfully. The personal interview provides the opportunity of meeting the applicant and observing his appearance, verbal ability, general personality and attitude toward life. While the applicant is on his best behavior—dressed in his best, polite and cooperative—the interviewer must cleverly disarm him so as to get a picture of the applicant's natural self, how he will appear later on the job.

In each case the objective is to appraise the individual's qualifications and personal traits in terms of his chances for success on a specific job. Sometimes the job to be filled can be adjusted to meet the qualifications of an applicant. Particularly in specialty types of positions, the kind of person on the job often influences the way the job shapes up and the various duties that are included.

The reason many interviews fail is that many people, when they get written or oral information, are unable to analyze their impressions objectively. Many interviews are affected by personal subjective traits that unconsciously result in some bias or prejudice which colors the decision. Companies are realizing that ability knows no restrictions, that unfounded prejudices create artificial barriers to success that are too costly to tolerate. Unfortunately some interviewers have not learned this lesson yet; they must be told how to be objective.

To improve the interview skilled and unskilled interviewers alike often resort to different types of aids. The use of prepared lists of questions can point up what is really being sought. Rating charts for the evaluation of answers are helpful. On a scale from low to high, opinions are recorded on such factors as experience, sincerity, general knowledge, personality, self-expression, enthusiasm, initiative and judgment. Some people use checklists on which items like appearance, character, attitude, physique and ability are rated from "very poor" to "excellent." Often a set of trade questions can serve as a guide. The written job description can be used to get better understanding of the nature of the job and the separate tasks that make up the job.

Interview Essentials

Some necessary essentials for all interviews include:

1. *Privacy.* A private office or booth is recommended in many situations, on the theory that both parties may speak without restraint. Sometimes clear-glass partitions give an impression that the candidate is being given the "once over" by the viewers outside. Therefore, just any area that lends itself to privacy may suffice. Many successful interviewers prefer to visit with applicants out in an open office, since no particularly confidential discussion takes place. The applicant is given a practical view of the environment instead of being sheltered in some ideal but unreal climate.

2. *Comfort.* Certainly the interviewee should be at ease, to permit a free exchange of information. On the other hand, letting him smoke in the waiting room or during the interview may lead to an erroneous impression of working conditions if this same privilege is not granted at the work station.

3. *Understanding.* The interview should not be attempted, nor should any decision be made, unless and until mutual understanding is reached. It often takes time, patience and some innovation to get through to the other person. A good practice is to turn the applicant —especially the beginner or one who is nervous—over to another employee with whom he or she may have something in common. A high school senior will be more comfortable in the hands of a recent graduate from the same school. The applicant will ask such a clerical worker many casual (though significant) questions that he would be afraid to broach with a more formidable interviewer. An applicant with a transportation problem will get more helpful answers from a worker living in the same locality.

4. *Attitude.* Much more important than the fine furniture, modern environment and other visible appurtenances is the attitude of the interviewer and the company toward the applicant. The best physical facilities will not offset insincerity, annoyance, or "going through the motions" which soon become apparent to the applicant. The interviewer's interest must be in both applicant and job, and it must be equally divided. The best applicant will not fit the job unless at the same time the job fits the applicant. The interviewer's concern over filling the

job for the company rather than filling the need of the applicant is one of the weaknesses of interviews.

A Few Simple Rules

Some do's and don'ts of interviewing are:

Do:
1. Use a quiet, comfortable place.
2. Put the interviewee at ease.
3. Be interested in the person as well as the job.
4. Outline clearly the requirements of the job.
5. Explain fully the conditions of employment.
6. Tell about benefits, promotions, opportunities.
7. Encourage the applicant to ask questions.
8. Guide the interview.
9. Listen; let him talk freely.
10. Be natural; use a conversational tone.
11. Know when and how to close the interview.
12. Announce your decision or explain your next step.

Don't:
1. Keep the applicant waiting.
2. Build false hopes.
3. Oversell the job.
4. Interrupt the applicant or the interview.
5. Rush through the interview.
6. Repeat questions already answered on the application form.
7. Develop a "canned" interview approach.
8. Give opinions; just answers.
9. Pry into his personal life needlessly.
10. Prejudge and reflect prejudices.
11. Use a phony excuse for turning him down.
12. Send him away with a bad taste in his mouth.

These are general suggestions, of course, and must be individualized to fit each particular situation.

Questions asked by the employer pertain to such items as the applicant's physical characteristics, health and record of illness, abilities and training, education qualifications, work experience, personal aspirations, and family and living conditions. Other questions cover dependents, handicaps and limitations, outside activities and hobbies, financial stability, habits (good and bad), social interests, citizenship, references and the like. His attitude toward many of these things is reflected in the reasons he gives for doing something or for not doing it. Debts, problems, time lapses or a bad record should be scrutinized critically.

The applicant must understand such things as:

- The job for which he is being considered.
- The reason the position is open.
- Why he would want to work for the company.
- Wages, hours, conditions of employment.
- Promotions and opportunity for growth.
- Benefits.
- Stability of employment in the company.
- The philosophy of the company toward its workers.

Finding the right person for any job is, however, only half the task. The applicant must feel that he too has found a job opportunity that meets or exceeds his expectations. Only when there is a happy job marriage, in which both sides are satisfied, does the placement stand a chance of being successful. In that case the company will provide the worker with the job satisfaction he needs in order to be happy; and he, in turn, will have that built-in motivation a company looks for in order to make his employment pay off.

Other Uses of the Interview

But the interview is more than an employment technique. It is widely used in business for seeking credit information, making loans, selling, adjusting complaints and diagnosing ailments. In the company's personnel program it is used in discipline cases, counseling, testing, transfer, promotion, layoff, salary adjustments and rejections, merit rating, appraisals, separations, as well as employment. It is used in every interpersonal relationship between manager and worker. It is in this broader context that I would like to offer a suggestion.

The suggestion concerns the word "interview" itself. We have become so accustomed to this word in the parlance of the trade that we don't realize that to many people, applicants and employees alike, it may be a foreboding word. If I were to visit with you in your home, you would ask me to sit beside you on the davenport or nearby in a comfortable chair. You would treat me as a guest and make me feel welcome. Yet when I come to your office to discuss our mutual business relationship (which may be much more significant to both of us than a friendly visit at your home) you unintentionally place a barrier between us. This barrier may be real in the form of a desk, an involved procedure or a cold, efficient approach. Or the barrier may be mental and imagined by the applicant. In any case it is there and has a direct bearing on the result.

In any situation, whether it be for employment, counseling or otherwise, if we would think of the word "interview" as "inner view" we would get through to the other person much easier. Let's try not to look at the situation, whatever it may be, from our own viewpoint; but instead let's try to see it from his side. Let's get his "inner view" and we will understand him much better.

I would like to suggest that we discard the word "interview" entirely. Then, for want of a better word, we would simply go back to holding "face-to-face conversations" with applicants and employees. How much better this would be for the other person, and how much easier for us, if we merely visited with each other—sat alongside him instead of across the desk. I'm sure you would find the experience more enjoyable and the results surprisingly better.

The purpose of any such face-to-face conversation, commonly referred to as the interview, is twofold:

1. To exchange information.
2. To make a friend.

So much depends upon the interview, so let's make it a good one. Let's not be concerned with the technique but rather with the purpose; not with the mechanics but with the results.

THE PATTERNED INTERVIEW

Many companies have established some sort of standards for the interview in selecting and placing personnel. But the interviewing technique of most executives has three great weaknesses:

1. The interviewer does not get complete or relevant information necessary to prevent errors in making a decision—in fact, many interviewers do not know what information should be sought.
2. Experienced interviewers may be able to determine from the information obtained what an applicant *can* do, but they lack a means for judging what he *will* do on the job.
3. Personal biases and prejudices enter into the interview, and the interviewer is influenced in making his decisions by promises and general rationalizations of the applicant, rather than the facts that show what the applicant *will do* based on what he *has done.*

The patterned interview has been designed to overcome the limitations and faults of ordinary interviewing. It has many advantages of which these are most important:

PATTERNED INTERVIEW
(Short Form)

Name _____   Date of Birth _____ Soc. Sec. No. _____

The age discrimination in the employment act and relevant FEP Acts prohibit discrimination with respect to individuals who are at least 40 but less than 65 years of age.

Address _____

SUMMARY

Rating: [1] [2] [3] [4]   Comments: _____
In making final rating, be sure to consider applicant's stability, industry, preserverance, loyalty, ability

to get along with others, self-reliance, leadership, maturity, motivation; also domestic situation and health.

Interviewer: _____   Job Considered for: _____   Date _____

If you were hired, how long would
it take you to get to work? _____   How would you get to work? _____
Is there anything undesirable here?

WORK EXPERIENCE. Cover all positions. This information is very important. Interviewer should record last position first. Every month since leaving school should be accounted for. Note military service in work record in continuity with jobs held since that time (In New Jersey exclude Military questions).

	LAST OR PRESENT POSITION		NEXT TO LAST POSITION		SECOND FROM LAST POSITION	
Name of Company						
Address						
Dates of employ.	From	To	From	To	From	To
			Do these dates check with application?			
Nature of work						
		Will applicant's previous experience be helpful on this job?				
Starting salary						
Salary at leaving						
What was especially liked about the job?	Has applicant made good work progress?			General or merit increases?		
		Has applicant been happy and contented in his/her work?				
What was especially disliked?						
	Were applicant's dislikes justified?			Is applicant chronically dissatisfied?		
Reasons for leaving						
		Are applicant's reasons for leaving reasonable and consistent?				

OTHER POSITIONS

Name of Company	Type of Work	Salary	Date Started	Date Left	Reasons for Leaving
	Has applicant stayed in one line of work for the most part?				
	Has applicant gotten along well on his/her jobs?				
	Are applicant's attitudes toward his/her employers loyal?				
	Was applicant interested in creative work?	In work requiring activity?			
	Has applicant improved self and position?				

Form No. OP-202

How many times did you draw
unemployment compensation? _____ When? _____ Why? _____
Does applicant depend on self?

How many weeks have you
been unemployed in the past five years? _____ How did you spend this time? _____
Did conditions in applicant's occupation justify this time? Did applicant use time profitably?

What accidents have you
had in recent years? _____
Is applicant "accident-prone"? Any disabilities which will interfere with work?

SCHOOLING

How far did you go in school? Grade: 1 2 3 4 5 6 7 8 High School: 1 2 3 4 College: 1 2 3 4 Date of leaving school _____
Is applicant's schooling adequate for the job?

If you did not graduate from
high school or college, why not? _____
Are applicant's reasons for not finishing sound?

What special training have you taken? _____
Will this be helpful? Indications of perseverance? Industry?

Extracurricular activities (Please omit any organizations
which reflect race, color, sex, national origin or religion.) _____
Did applicant get along well with others?

What offices did you hold in these groups? _____
Indications of leadership?

FAMILY BACKGROUND	PERSONAL SITUATION
Leisure time activities _____ Habits of industry?	When did you have last drink? _____ Sensible?
Summer vacations _____ Did applicant keep busy?	What types of people rub you the wrong way? _____ Bias?
Group activities _____ See note after Extracurricular activities.	Ever convicted of a felony? _____
Position of leadership _____ Leader?	Charges _____ Immaturity? (This does not constitute an automatic bar to employment)

HEALTH

What serious illnesses, operations,
or accidents did you have as a child? _____

What illnesses, operations, or
accidents have you had in recent years? _____
Has applicant retained any infantile personality traits due to childhood illnesses?
Are applicant's illnesses legitimate rather than indicating a desire to "enjoy ill health"?

How much time have you lost
from work because of illness during past year? _____
Will applicant be able to do the job?

How are your teeth? _____

Does anyone in your home suffer ill health? _____
Are spouse, children, or family relatively healthy?

Do you suffer from:
□ Poor Eyesight
□ Poor Hearing
□ Rupture
□ Rheumatism
□ Asthma
□ Heart Trouble
□ Diabetes
□ Ulcers
□ Hay Fever
□ Flat Feet
□ Nervousness

ADDITIONAL INFORMATION: _____
_____
_____
_____
_____
_____

155

1. It makes possible a systematic and complete coverage of all necessary information for predicting the applicant's probable success on the job.
2. It guides the interviewer in getting the facts and discovering valuable information about the applicant.
3. It provides a set of principles for use in interpreting the facts obtained for the purpose of judging what the applicant *will do* alongside of what he *can do.*
4. It provides a means for minimizing the interviewer's personal biases and prejudices.

The Dartnell Corporation has published several patterned interview forms, developed by The McMurry Company. Into these forms have been incorporated some of the latest techniques and devices found effective in personal selection plans of various companies.

One patterned interview form is designed especially for interviewing sales applicants (Form SP-102); another is designed for candidates for professional, executive and supervisory applicants (Form EP-312); a shorter form has been designed for interviewing office and factory personnel (Form OP-202); a very detailed form has been prepared for interviewing applicants for top executive and top management positions (Form EP-302).

A step toward improvement in present hiring methods can be made by the adoption of the patterned interview procedure in one department or section, eventually broadening its use to other departments.

MAKING THE INTERVIEW MORE EFFECTIVE

1. Decide carefully in advance just what you wish to and can determine by the interview. Review the application blank in advance as a guide.
2. Examine and discount your own prejudices.
3. Give personal appearance its proper weight, but no more.
4. Endeavor to talk to the applicant alone, preferably in a closed office or a desk away from ordinary distractions.
5. Open the interview by conversing briefly and informally about some subject of mutual interest. Be sure to introduce yourself and lead into the interview itself as soon as you feel applicant is at ease.
6. Ask questions which call for narrative statements, things done that have demonstrated the possession of certain qualities, rather than questions that call for an expression of opinions or a mere chronological statement of experience.
7. Avoid leading or suggestive questions.

INTERVIEWING PRIVACY

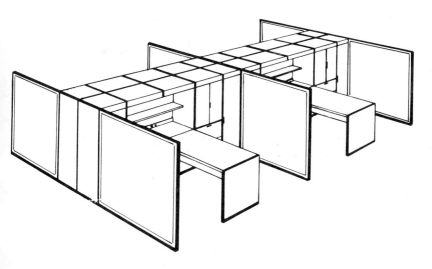

Interviewing generally calls for privacy. If space is limited, perhaps a modular arrangement such as this one will be practical.

8. Listen attentively and show evidence of being interested.

9. Talk only enough to keep the conversation informal and friendly; avoid expressing opinions or asking leading questions.

10. Encourage the applicant to ask questions about the work and working conditions.

11. Do not let the interview become mechanical; keep on the alert for unexpected evidence.

12. Guard against the "halo effect." Don't let a single favorable or unfavorable trait warp your judgment.

13. After the close of the formal interview, watch for additional evidence.

14. Be careful not to make too many notes during the interview.

15. Record impressions and reasons for them *immediately* after the person leaves, before starting the next interview.

16. Provide for a second interview whenever practicable.

17. Be especially careful as to what is said and how it is said when telling an applicant that he is not suited for the position for which he is applying.

Remember:

1. The chief problem is not getting the facts but interpreting them.

2. Pause occasionally, pretending to look the applicant over, giving the applicant the opportunity to talk.

3. Be objective.

4. The correct methods of interviewing can go a long way to reduce turnover.

5. The personal interview is the supervisor and the applicant sizing each other up well enough to judge whether they'll work together satisfactorily.

6. A competent interview takes the form of a conversation rather than a question and answer period.

7. An interviewer should be a good listener, impartial, a good judge, well acquainted with requirements of the job he is interviewing for.

8. What the applicant has done in the past in school and on the job is a good indication of what he will do in the future.

9. The following factors should be considered before a final decision:

   a. appearance
   b. education
   c. work background

   d. test scores

   e. references

10. Verify dates to make sure no period of time is overlooked which might be covering up a bad employment record.

SELECTION

The employment function is a continuing one in every company, regardless of whether or not the procedure is formalized or the job is centralized. The selection and retention of efficient workers is one of the most important operations of any company. In any kind of labor market the proper selection of applicants for jobs poses one of industry's greatest problems.

A big concern is that of cost. There are statistics available to tell us how many dollars were lost last year because of fires, termites, floods and hurricanes. Unfortunately, not even an estimate exists for the loss that is due to incompetent employees, the result of poor hiring practices and improper placement. But if such a survey could be made, the total would undoubtedly be in the billions of dollars. Add to this staggering cost the waste of human capacities and the countless cases of tragic frustration, and the significance of proper selection and placement becomes apparent.

This cost item is many things. Acquisition costs are more than agency fees, newspaper ads or employee referral bonds. The cost of interviewing and screening applicants, including the many who are rejected, must be taken into account. Medical examinations, if given for new employees, will add substantially to the cost. Whatever method is used, and whatever steps are taken, we can be certain that the cost of each new worker is higher, much higher, than we realize.

Add to this the expense of low production during the beginning or training period, the time of the other person during the training, and all the many other obvious as well as hidden costs, and we get some idea of the cost of employment, and the importance of good selection.

Poor selection, hurried placement, and such considerations add even more to the hidden cost of employment. The employment of incompetent, unstable and nonproductive workers can be a very costly item in terms of direct expense.

Costly Investment

Then think of the less desirable employees who get into the workforce who are not released for any of many reasons. Sometimes a contract complicates the firing of such employees. In other instances

SELECTION PROCESS

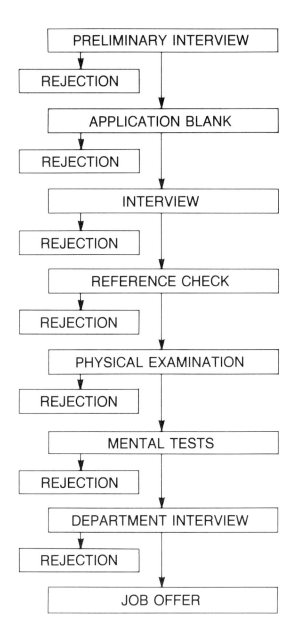

SELECTION AND EVALUATION SUMMARY

Applicant's Name_____ Date_____ 19____

Position Applied for_____ Job Class_____

	Check Each Factor	Above Requirements	Meets Requirements	Marginal	Unacceptable
CAN-DO FACTORS	Appearance, manner..				
	Availability...				
	Education...				
	Experience in this field (if applicable)......................				
	Knowledge of the product (if applicable)....................				
	Physical condition, health................................				

		A Lot	Some	Not Much	Almost None
WILL-DO FACTORS	**CHARACTER TRAITS (Basic Habits)**				
	STABILITY; maintaining same jobs and interests.............				
	INDUSTRY; willingness to work............................				
	PERSEVERANCE; finishing what applicant starts............				
	ABILITY TO GET ALONG WITH OTHERS.................				
	LOYALTY; identifying with employer.......................				
	SELF-RELIANCE; standing on own feet, making own decisions				
	LEADERSHIP..				
	JOB MOTIVATIONS (not already satisfied off the job)				
	NEED FOR INCOME or desire for money..................				
	NEED FOR SECURITY....................................				
	NEED FOR STATUS......................................				
	NEED FOR POWER.......................................				
	NEED TO INVESTIGATE..................................				
	NEED TO EXCEL (to compete)...........................				
	NEED FOR PERFECTION.................................				
	NEED TO SERVE..				
	BASIC ENERGY LEVEL (vigor, initiative, drive, enthusiasm)				
	DEGREE OF EMOTIONAL MATURITY				
	Dependence...				
	Regard for consequences.................................				
	Capacity for self-discipline...............................				
	Selfishness..				
	Show-off tendencies......................................				
	Pleasure-mindedness.....................................				
	Destructive tendencies...................................				
	Wishful thinking..				
	Willingness to accept responsibility.......................				

Important: Do not add or average these factors in making the Over-all Rating. Match the qualifications of the applicant against the requirements of the *particular position* for which applicant is being considered, and consider the importance of each mismatch.

Strong Points for This Position_____

Weak Points for This Position_____

Over-all Rating: [1] [2] [3] [4]   Recommendation to Employ: [ ] Yes [ ] No   Rating by_____

Form No. ES-404R-3

seniority or company policy keeps these people on the payroll. And don't think for a minute that there is no sentiment in business. Otherwise, how can we justify the retention of workers who obviously have lost their usefulness?

Add all these factors together and we begin to understand the investment companies have in their people. An investment decision of this magnitude in other departments would be given very close scrutiny and consideration. Yet, investments of this amount are made in newly-hired employees every day with very little caution. Employment is the one item that is governed by little objective decision. Everybody who hires new workers fashions himself to be somewhat of an amateur psychologist and a certain measure of subjective opinion influences the decision to hire or not to hire an applicant.

This kind of approach has some consequences. One of the consequences of ineffective selection of employees is a drag on efficiency, low production and poor morale. The notion that these people will somehow fit into the scheme of things is wishful thinking. Unsatisfactory work habits in people are usually the result of long-established habits and character traits that are very difficult, if not impossible, to change in the average work situation.

A Series of Rejections

The selection procedure covers the entire period from the initial contact with the applicant to his final acceptance or rejection. The screening out of unqualified applicants should be accomplished in the quickest time consistent with good community relations since this is costly and, of course, nonproductive.

Selection begins as soon as an applicant makes himself available for employment, either in person or by mail. Sight screening eliminates the obviously unqualified. Knock-out questions eliminate those who cannot meet specific job requirements. Interviewing is done to reduce the number of candidates. Defensible testing programs eliminate some applicants and serve as aids in interviewing the others. Reference inquiries, physical examinations and multiple interviews are additional devices used in the selection procedure.

Selection actually is a normal process of a series of rejections:

1. Preliminary interview   if not rejected, then . . .

2. Application blank   if not rejected, then . . .

3. Interview   if not rejected, then . . .

4. Check on references   if not rejected, then . . .

5. Physical examinations   if not rejected, then . . .

6. Mental tests   if not rejected, then . . .

7. Multiple interviews   if not rejected, then . . .

8. What is left   make final selection.

The sequence might be slightly rearranged in some companies or under some circumstances, but the idea of a series of rejection steps remains unchanged.

Six Appraisal Factors

For better selection, and a corresponding reduction in the size and cost of the problem of selection, it is well to know just what we are looking for. There are six appraisal factors involved in the selection and employment of applicants:

    1. Informational : abilities and personal data
    2. Motivational : drives and personal goals
    3. Emotional : maturity and business outlook
    4. Attitudinal : sense of values
    5. Behavioral : habit patterns and conduct
    6. Physical : health and peace of mind.

In selecting employees to work with us, these are the qualities we try to identify and evaluate. It is necessary, therefore, that the interviewer understand what is involved.

TESTING

Psychological testing of students, workers and others has been going on in one form or another for more than a half century. With some people it is almost an academic or industrial religion. Many large corporations process candidates for employment or promotion through a ritual of testing that must be passed satisfactorily in order to even be considered. Still there are others who are skeptical and, while they might not be openly against testing, they are far from enthusiastic.

In a broad sense, it is the purpose of testing to help predict future performance in various fields of endeavor, to diagnose personal characteristics, and to research for understanding of individual and group behavior. It is the purpose of personnel tests in business to assist in getting the best available person on the job, and the best available job for that person. The most effective test of a person's ability to handle a particular job is an actual trial of that person on the job. This, however, is costly. So various methods and tools are utilized to help in this process.

Testing is *one tool* used in determining the suitability of an individual for a particular position. Tests by themselves should not be thought of as giving all the answers to placement problems but, used in conjunction with the other tools, they can indicate a person's strengths and weaknesses. Test scores interpreted in terms of specific job requirements, combined with the personal interview, references and general work background, should provide a reliable guide to an applicant's or worker's potential.

Always keep in mind that tests are only another tool in the personnel director's kit. Personnel decisions can be made only by managers and supervisors. Analogy: tests have a "staff" function (provide information), not a "line" function (make decisions).

Progress Has Been Rapid

Testing has come a long way since Alfred Binet, working at the Sorbonne in Paris, began intelligence quizzing of school children in 1905. Spurred by World War II experience, businessmen and schools have come to embrace tests. This has created a new industry and spawned an army of psychologists who specialize in this area.

Tests are used in schools and colleges for admissions, ability groupings, scholarship awards, career planning. The military uses them to find specific aptitudes for skill training, such as radar operators. Business firms use tests to aid in the selection of people they hire or promote, probably in a negative sense by screening out the less competent and unqualified candidates. Tests are also used to uncover hidden talent among the "sleepers" in the workforce, to bring to the surface abilities which might otherwise go unnoticed.

About three out of five companies use tests of one kind or another in selecting office and factory employees. Tests are used more for white collar workers than blue collar workers. The responsibility for developing and administering the testing program is with the personnel staff. The personnel specialists explain the use of tests and interpret the individual results to line supervisors, foremen and managers with whom the responsibility for final selection rests.

Old-fashioned virtues of plodding, ambition and perseverance are giving way to measurable characteristics which now become the determining factors in employment, promotion and assignment.

There is some criticism against pigeonholing people into convenient slots by machine-manipulated cards. There is resentment against prying into the skulls of people, calibrating of capabilities, mechanized packaging of talents, shaping of humans' destinies.

Since tests as used today tend to become elimination devices, they have been accused of preventing deserving youngsters from entering certain professions. The bone of contention with the Equal Employment Opportunities Commission (EEOC) is that tests too often "rule out" rather than "rule in" minority applicants.

Yet the results seem to be better than the old ways of depending upon a boss' intuition and shrewd appraisal—possibly because these were not as good in the boss as he wanted to make himself and others believe they were. Testing is more objective, albeit limited. The old-time boss made more mistakes in judgment than he cared or dared to admit. As time went on these mistakes became more costly as employment, training, dismissal or retention proved to be costly.

Types of Tests

Purposes for which tests are used are twofold—diagnosis (what he knows and can do) and prediction (what he can be expected to do). These tests may be classified in five categories:

1. The *Learning Ability Test* is sometimes referred to as an Intelligence Test. This type of test measures the more fundamental factors of the mind. It gives a good indication of the approximate level at which a person can operate by establishing the extent of ability to learn in a variety of situations. A typical test of this design consists of three kinds of questions: arithmetical, vocabulary and block-counting.

2. The *Skill Test* measures the specific clerical or mechanical skills needed. These include the achievement exercises to see how much a person has learned. Among them are tests of arithmetic computation, error location, alphabetizing, coding, spelling, reading comprehension and grammar. Familiar are tests in typing and shorthand, and performance on standard office machines or shop equipment.

3. The *Aptitude Test* attempts to determine the inborn suitability, or the degree of natural endowment in a particular field. It measures the proclivity, or built-in readiness, for specified types of work. Generally, aptitude tests are simple for they take a narrow range of intellectual measurement.

4. The *Interest Inventory Test* measures the job preference of the employee by drawing out opinions about work, home and life. It should be noted here that a decided interest in a category does not mean an aptitude for it. These tests definitely aid in careful selection.

5. The *Personality Inventory Test* determines a person's reactions to different types of situations from which general conclusions can be drawn within the limits of measured personality characteristics. This type of test attempts to uncover drives and ambitions, or the lack of

them, plus traits of temperament such as stability, frankness, persistence, etc. Personality (nonintellectual) tests are subject to factor analysis and result interpretation.

A test battery is a group of carefully-chosen different tests, assembled to fit a situation. The choices and combinations of tests are varied according to the function: sales, clerical, trade, executive, secretarial, etc.

What Makes a Good Test

The criteria of a good test are: (1) reliability, (2) validity and (3) it must provide statistical norms for interpretation purposes. These terms should be defined.

Reliability is a measure of the test's consistency of performance over a group of people. Will the results be about the same if the tests are given to the same group later on, or to a similar group?

Validity refers to how well the test measures what it is supposed to measure. In the less complex work assignments, such as where typing skill or number checking or inspection for minor defects or mechanical assembly are the main duties, validity is more readily discoverable and attainable. Aptitude tests do not have as high validities as those known as intelligence tests. The tests of personality have even less validity. This validity is often expressed in the form of a coefficient of correlation between the test and a criterion of success.

Norms are the bases, usually expressed in terms of an average or median score, against which any individual's score is compared. How much better or worse is a person than the average or middle person, is the question to be answered. A test may have one or more sets of statistical norms derived from samplings of people of different backgrounds or levels of qualifications.

The test scores are meaningless out of context. These raw scores must be converted to the norms. It is the interpretation of these norms, the analysis of the composite test scores, and the resolution of confusing or even conflicting test evidence that is complied into a test profile. It is this finding, not the specifics of each test, that is reported to supervisors or management. Only generalized information should be revealed to the testee. There is a certain ethics in testing that requires careful safeguarding of confidential test data and results, as well as the material itself.

Tests serve best when kept secret. They reveal personal information which should be treated impersonally. Good testing procedures are effective because they are objective; unfortunately, some managers are not, and for that reason tests can fail.

Not a Cure-All

Psychological tests have limitations. They are good tools to assess certain abilities, traits and aptitudes. But they are much less accurate in judging motivation, creative capacity or other complexities of human nature. They cannot judge moral character or detect larceny in a person's heart.

Tests are not yet very successful in predicting such characteristics as initiative, imagination and loyalty because these are hard to measure. Too much depends upon environmental influences in the situation at the time. Tests do not measure two very necessary ingredients of success—the two D's—desire and determination.

Tests may tell what a person *can* do but not yet what he *will* do. The critical will-do factors are affected more by personality and social relations on and off the job. In selection and placement the problem is determining not what a worker can do but what he will do.

Occasionally testing is undertaken because it is regarded as fashionable or up-to-date. A company executive hears of a competitor's use of tests and instructs the employment office to "get on the ball" at once. Some companies use quickie tests because they are a relatively inexpensive adjunct to the employment procedure, easy to administer by a clerk, and simple to score by a receptionist—as though they have universal application. Testing is growing in popularity but in many cases it is getting a patent medicine approach.

Nor should tests be used to eliminate, or even reduce, the importance of interviews, reference checks, careful screening and thorough selection. Other factors must be weighed to estimate the potential development of an individual. Education opportunities, stimulation from home environment, societal background, appropriate habits of work, and attitudes toward self and life are all involved in any person's chances for success and satisfaction on a job.

Equal Opportunity Impact

The influx of minority group members into the labor force puts a strain on present employment and testing programs.

The following is taken from a publication of the Federal Equal Employment Opportunities Commission:

> Title VII of the Civil Rights Act of 1964 provides that an employer may give and act upon the results of "any professionally developed ability test provided that such test . . . is not designed, intended or used to discriminate because of race . . ." (Sec. 703(h)).

The language of this statute and its legislative history make it clear that tests may not be used as a device to exclude prospective employees on the basis of race.

This publication recognizes that many companies may be inadvertently discriminating because the tests used in employment programs do not measure equally well for all groups. Many things may influence a test score, quite apart from the attribute being measured.

As an immediate step in utilizing available standardized tests for evaluating persons from different cultural groups, or with limited educational experience, the EEOC and other writers have stressed the need for establishing different cultural validities and norms. This involves considerable research, but is nevertheless necessary. The potential of such persons for succeeding in training and on the job must be evaluated, and tests are probably the most adequate technique for doing so. For example, assumptions about ability that employers have traditionally made on the basis of formal educational achievement do not hold for these groups.

In addition to the development of local validity information and special normative standards for minority groups, professional test developers might be expected to provide more appropriate instruments over time.

Pros and Cons

The real danger in employment procedures is not only in relying too heavily upon tests. There are dangers inherent in the use of tests. One source of difficulty lies in inappropriate test choices, indifferent administration and inconclusive interpretation. Tests that measure the wrong abilities, that are too easy or too difficult, or that place a premium on certain types of experience and training will give inadequate results. Careless test administration leads to performance which is not typical of the applicant. Improper test interpretation permits incorrect standards and erroneous conclusions.

Another important thing to remember is that tests measure individuality. They relate to the applicant, not to his co-workers or supervisor. Nor do they take into account the company climate as an influence upon the applicant's development. These considerations can have more effect upon his chances for success in a job than any series of test results.

Finally, psychological tests are not infallible. They can occasionally be wrong. Yet, it would be unfair to condemn the whole notion of testing because of a few disappointing experiences with it. As with any other new procedure, the concern over testing should not be whether it achieves perfection, but whether it results in some improvement over earlier methods. It seems only fair to evaluate the testing program in

TEST PROFILE

NAME

		DATE	LOW	BELOW AVERAGE	AVERAGE	ABOVE AVERAGE	HIGH

L E A R N I N G   A B I L I T Y

TIFFIN ADAPTABILITY:
    A ....
    B ....
OTIS EMPLOYMENT: ....
THURSTONE PMA:
    Space ....
    Number ....
    Reasoning ....
    Word Fluency ....
    Verbal Meaning ....

A P T I T U D E S

GENERAL CLERICAL:
    Filing ....
    Grammatical ....
    Arithmetical ....
MINNESOTA CLERICAL:
    Names ....
    Numbers ....
HOW SUPERVISE:
    A ....
    B ....
    M ....
PRACTICAL JUDGMENT: ....

10 20 25 30 40 50 60 70 75 80 90 100

I N T E R E S T S

KUDER PREFERENCE:
    Mechanical ....
    Computational ....
    Scientific ....
    Persuasive ....
    Artistic ....
    Literary ....
    Musical ....
    Social Service ....
    Clerical ....

Personnel will analyze and interpret the test results and prepare a report to be discussed with the manager.

P E R S O N A L I T Y

PERSONAL AUDIT:
    Seriousness - Impulsiveness ....
    Firmness - Indecision ....
    Tranquility - Irritability ....
    Frankness - Evasion ....
    Stability - Instability ....
    Tolerance - Intolerance ....
    Steadiness - Emotionality ....
    Persistence - Fluctuality ....
    Contentment - Worry...........
THURSTONE TEMPERAMENT:
    Active ....
    Vigorous ....
    Impulsive ....
    Dominant ....
    Stable ....
    Sociable ....
    Reflective ....

Personnel will analyze and interpret the test results and prepare a report to be discussed with the manager.

SKILLS: Typing_____W.P.M.   Shorthand_____W.P.M.

terms of averages rather than in terms of specifics, either good or bad.

Proponents of testing can advance many convincing arguments and can point to all kinds of impressive results. But opponents of testing also want to be heard.

They maintain, for example, that there are many people who are successful in their chosen occupations who would not be able to pass the qualification tests. They believe it is one thing to test a prospective machine operator for manual dexterity but another to determine whether he will "make a go of it" once on the job. They point out that 90% of workers who lose or leave their jobs do so not because they are unqualified to perform the work but because of other reasons which are "out of reach" of tests.

At a time when top management is looking for leaders, the testing program scrupulously weeds out likely candidates by coming up with the standardized, supinely-adjusted, well-conformed personality that fits the norm. The biggest argument against tests is that testing in all forms has become too much of a cult and that the corporate world places too much reliance and blind faith on tests.

Testing is undoubtedly useful in getting people into jobs but opponents find comfort in the thought that farmers, housewives, bartenders and elected public officials are not asked to pass tests to get their jobs.

Well, where does this leave us? Maybe two observations would be in order.

1. Proponents of testing should understand that while tests can be helpful, they alone cannot be expected to predict success or satisfaction in a job. Testing is one tool in the selection procedure and used that way can be useful.
2. Opponents of testing might consider some of the advantages that are available to them. Certainly doing something ought to be better than doing nothing.

TEST VALIDATION

The Equal Employment Opportunity Commission and other government agencies have raised legitimate questions about the validity of selection procedures utilized in the employment process. They are requiring employers to show evidence that their tests and other standards for employment are valid. Since validity is specific to a particular job and applicant group, employers are now faced with the task of conducting local validation studies.

Company reactions to this requirement have been varied. Some organizations immediately initiated a personnel research activity and are proceeding in an orderly fashion. Others have chosen to sacrifice the benefits of testing programs in the erroneous belief that this act alone will bring them into compliance. It would seem that validation research has not been put into proper perspective—as an activity with potentially large returns for a modest investment, once it is organized.

The Validation Process

Many people think validity is an absolute characteristic that a test either has or does not have. Actually, a test has many validities, each specific to a given situation. For example, a test might be valid for selecting assemblers but not valid for selecting foremen for an assembly line. A test is valid in an occupational selection situation to the extent that it can provide both *differential* and *relevant* information about the applicants for the specific occupation involved.

Test information qualifies as *differential* if it reveals differences among the people tested. For example, a test measuring knowledge of simple mechanical principles would have little differential validity for an applicant group consisting of graduate mechanical engineers because all applicants would get nearly identical—in this case perfect—scores. Nor would such a test be valid for selecting office clerks, because the information yielded about mechanical ability would not be *relevant* to the question of whether the applicants could perform clerical tasks. Furthermore, a test could be valid (both relevant and differentiating) for applicants having the same background (such as education) but not valid for persons with different backgrounds.

Validation is usually discussed in relation to tests because test scores are quantitative and therefore lend themselves readily to statistical analysis. However, the steps in the validation process are equally applicable to determining the validity of other hiring standards, such as educational and experience requirements and interview and application form information. But whenever a company is required to validate materials of this kind, an additional and difficult step must be added to the research—the conversion of the biographical information and judgments into numerical form by means of a reliable, quantified scoring system.

The accompanying diagram shows the sequence of research steps to establish a valid applicant selection program for any occupation.

Tests Properly Used

A sound testing program is based on three critical steps:

1. *Analyzing the job.* Job analysis clarifies the composition of job activities and the circumstances under which they are carried out. First,

171

TEST VALIDATION

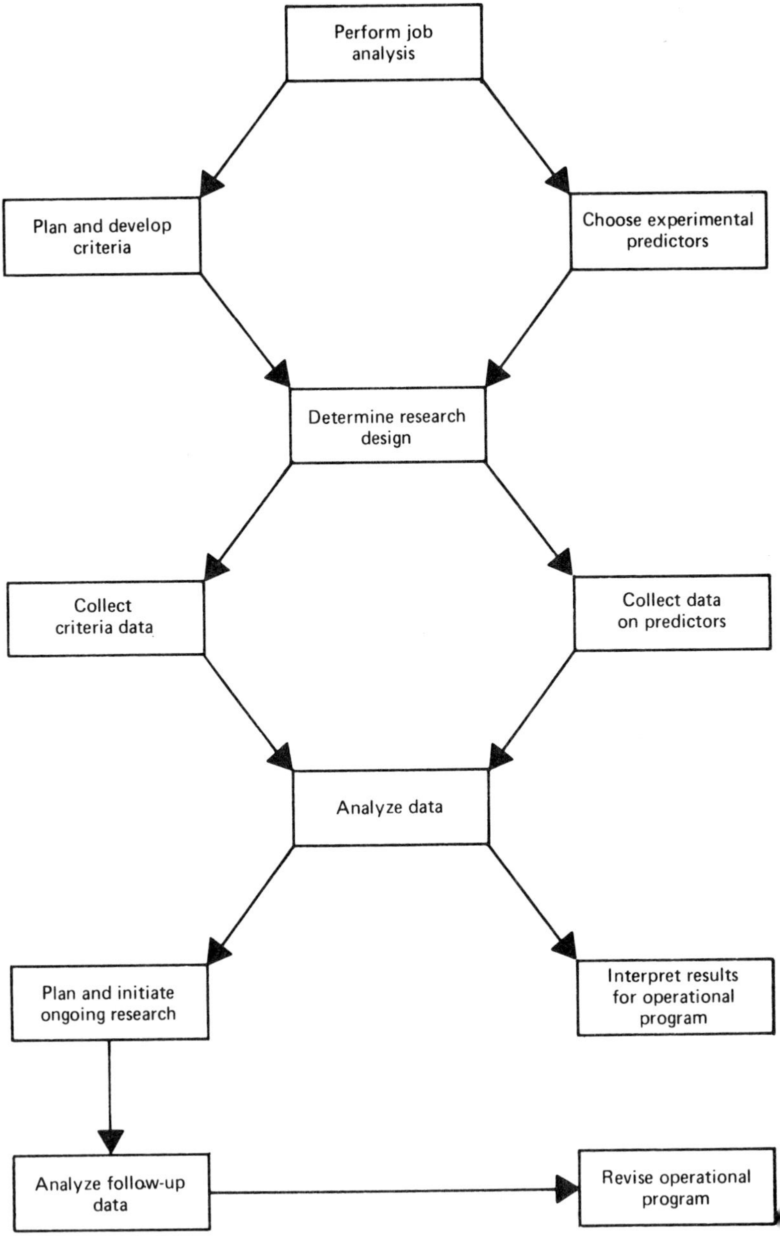

The steps in the validation process

a complete and systematic inventory of essential job activities should be undertaken and the resulting information organized into a written job description. The job description focuses on what an employee does—the tasks performed. Second, each task should be analyzed to determine all the behaviors or characteristics of a person that critically affect success in the various job tasks. These characteristics include knowledge, skills, aptitudes, interest, attitudes and temperament.

2. *Selecting the tests.* After the significant human requirements have been determined on the basis of the job analysis, it is then decided which of them might be measured reliably by tests and which by other techniques. The initial decisions concerning appropriate tests are of necessity hypotheses that must be substantiated or rejected through a validation study. The results of such a study are more likely to be positive if the tests for tryout have been selected with care.

3. *Testing the tests.* A test that has worked for one company in predicting success for a certain type of job will not necessarily work in another company, even though the job designation is similar. Jobs that seem the same often differ in subtle but important and measurable ways. What constitutes job success is also likely to vary from situation to situation. For these reasons companies should test their tests and other employment procedures through validation research at the local level.

Such validity studies are not always possible—often a company has too few employees in a given job classification to permit a statistical analysis of the relation between test scores and performance measures. Because government guidelines recognize these technical limitations, evidence from job analyses and from studies in other companies may provide justification for the selection program in some instances. Many companies, however, find themselves in the position of having to initiate a research activity that they have not undertaken before and with which they are unfamiliar. For them, professional assistance is available to help solve the problem.*

TESTING and the EEOC

Tests for employment and promotion are declining in use for reasons other than their accuracy. The biggest stumbling block is the Equal Employment Opportunities Commission (EEOC) and its inflexible rules. To many employers testing under their rigorous guidelines is impossible. It is simpler to chuck the testing program altogether.

---

*The above information was provided by Science Research Associates, Inc., 155 North Wacker Drive, Chicago, Illinois 60606.

In a spasm of anxiety about compliance requirements, employers are afraid they cannot support decisions based on test results. This may be a case of over-reacting but it is the easier way out.

Hiring and promoting cannot be justified solely on qualifications but must take into account local minority group percentages as determined by the EEOC. Companies cannot afford to become involved in statistical discrimination.

To continue to be influenced by test scores, a company must be able to show that the tests it gives for a specific job are necessary because they are related to what an employee actually has to do on the job. Most tests are developed outside the company and are too general in their application to serve the unique requirements of different jobs. The validations are, in most cases, impossible to prove; they just do not hold up in court.

Further, the validations of tests, which are customarily developed in the university laboratories, are not related to sex and race. As such, they are indefensible when challenged.

Established tests keyed to the qualifications of a given job are an efficient tool for a proper hiring decision. Once companies are scared off of testing they resort to less objective means and are influenced by pleasing or unpleasing appearance, references that are usually lackluster, performance in previous jobs that is difficult to assess, interviews that rub the interviewer the wrong way, and the untouched, built-in biases of managers.

Why such subjective involvement is supposed to be better than objective testing is not easily understood.

REFERENCE INQUIRIES

Reference inquiries, or checking references, is a very important part of the employment procedure. Inquiries are made about prior work experience, character, education and whatever else may be considered necessary to help arrive at a decision to hire or not to hire an applicant. Inquiries are chiefly addressed to former employers, schools and personal acquaintances of the applicant.

The names and addresses of the individuals, schools or firms are taken from the information supplied by the applicant on the application blank.

Former employers are queried about the applicant's dates of employment, the nature of his job, quality of performance, any strong or weak points that stand out and can be remembered, the reason for leaving, and so on. These are mechanical questions seeking factual answers. Whatever else is asked, the *key* question is "Would you rehire?"

Schools are asked about levels of academic achievement, such as completion of courses, graduation, degrees, and majors or concentration of study. They can also report on the former student's attendance record. One of the useful services schools can furnish is that of checking ages of people. School records are kept indefinitely and reveal the age of an individual accurately as a student, before the person might have been tempted to lie about the age and try to alter the year of birth.

As a suggestion, do not send schools a form letter listing a string of questions. Some details of a former student's record may no longer be accessible in the front office, and a clerk might have to spend hours in the archives hunting for an answer to a question that really does not deserve this much time and trouble. Usually the information that is readily available in the school office is more than sufficient.

Personal references are not used much anymore since their usefulness is questionable. Friends, relatives, acquaintances and clergymen are likely to give favorable reports. The only value might be to specific questions such as, "How long did the applicant work for his last company?" or "Where did he reside before you met him?"

Police records are worth checking for certain jobs. Local and national bureaus of information could come up with information not obtained in routine inquiries.

Military service records provide data that are useful. Discharge papers tell about the length of service, duty performed, advancement and type of release from service. It might be well to ask to see such papers, especially for a veteran whose military service is not too far in the past.

Types of Inquiries

Most references are checked by mail because this can be done in an easy routine manner. The signed replies form a permanent record, easily filed for possible future use. But written references also have disadvantages. Most people are reluctant to tell the truth if they think it will hurt someone. They tend to minimize adverse comments. Besides, once the former employee is gone and forgotten, and the sting of his termination no longer felt, a manager is inclined to brush off a written request with a response that has little substance. The tip-off comes when he answers "No" to your question, "Would you rehire?" He is trying to tell something without running the risk of putting his remarks on paper. In effect he is hinting, "Why don't you phone me and I'll tell you why."

REFERENCE INQUIRY FORM

Date: _____

May we verify the following information given to us by one of your former employees who has applied to us for a position?

_____
Name

_____
Position Held

_____
Employment Dates

_____
Earnings

_____
Reason given for leaving your firm

Is the above information correct?_____

Would you care to give us additional information on the following questions:

Were services satisfactory? _____

Would you rehire if you had an opening? _____

Do you know of any reason why we should not employ? _____

Is there anything outstanding about this employee that you would like to tell us? _____

Do you suggest we contact you by telephone? _____

Thank you for your cooperation.

_____   _____
Signature   Employment Manager

_____
Title

REFERENCE INQUIRY FORM

SALES APPLICATION VERIFICATION
(Confidential)

To

We are considering _____ Age _____ Social Security No. _____

for a position with us in the _____ Department. He/she has authorized our contacting you to verify the information given in his/her application. We are endeavoring properly to appraise and perhaps place the applicant so that he/she will have every opportunity for success. We shall appreciate your giving us the following information:

• • •

1. When was he/she in your employ? From _____ 19 ____ to _____ 19 _____

2. Was he/she under your supervision? _____ ; the supervision of someone reporting to you? _____ ; neither? _____

3. What was his/her title or position? _____

4. When he/she left what did his/her work consist of? _____

5. He/she stated that he/she was earning $ _____ per _____ when he/she left. Is this correct?   ☐ Yes,   ☐ No.

6. How much of this was commission? $ _____ Bonus? $ _____

7. How did his/her sales results compare with those of others in similar work? _____

8. Did he/she supervise anyone else? ☐ Yes,   ☐ No; How many? _____

9. How hard did he/she work? _____

10. How did he/she get along with other people? _____

11. Why did he/she leave? _____

12. In your opinion, under which of the following conditions would he/she be most successful? Please mark one in each category.

☐ Inside sales	☐ Established markets	☐ Close supervision	☐ Straight salary	☐ Lots of detail in his/her work
☐ Outside sales	☐ Pioneer markets	☐ Average supervision	☐ A little commission	☐ Normal detail
☐ Traveling sales		☐ Infrequent supervision	☐ Draw and commission	☐ Very little detail

☐ Selling materials to fabricators	☐ Selling one-time sales	☐ Selling intangibles	☐ Selling to women
☐ Selling to wholesalers or retailers	☐ Selling where there are some repeats	☐ Selling tangible service	☐ Selling to men
☐ Selling to consumers	☐ Selling regular customers	☐ Selling tangibles	☐ Selling to both men and women

☐ Selling principally to high income customers	☐ Selling a highly technical product	☐ Selling where he/she sets prices and determines profits
☐ Selling principally to low income customers	☐ Selling a somewhat technical product	☐ Selling where he/she can occasionally revise prices
☐ Selling to both high and low income customers	☐ Selling a nontechnical product	☐ Selling where prices are set and maintained

13. If your policies permitted, would you:

☐ Rehire for same position?   ☐ Rehire, but for different position?   ☐ Not rehire?

14. Remarks _____

Your co-operation is greatly appreciated.

Name _____

Title _____

Company _____

Address _____ Tel. No. _____

City _____ Zone _____ State _____

Form No. SV-104

The telephone is used because it is faster and more intimate. A direct two-way conversation can clear up questions. The telephone brings two people close together immediately, whereas it is usually total strangers who exchange letters in a routine mail inquiry. For the more important jobs telephone reference checking may be better. In these cases it is advisable to make a written report of the call, documenting the answers received.

The personal visit to a former employer or school is used infrequently since it is time consuming. It is done when the job is unusual or highly important, or when some questionable record needs to be looked into.

There are credit agencies that will check out an individual and report in writing their findings. Their detailed reports tell about the person's family, neighborhood, education, age, employment history, character, reputation, financial stability and anything else that may be requested. In the process of checking the individual they will uncover any lawsuits, bankruptcies or criminal background.

It takes time and talent to get useful answers to reference inquiries. It is safe to say that the value of any reference reply is worth very little unless the answer is negative. If it tells nothing new then it merely confirms what is already known. It verifies the information supplied by the applicant. This makes it safer to assume that other information may likewise be taken at face value.

A negative reply, on the other hand, alerts the employer to be on guard and suspect all the information given. If prior dates of employment, for example, are not correct as shown, perhaps the applicant is deliberately trying to gloss over an employment gap. Who knows but what he might be trying to conceal a prison term. A negative reply should be followed up immediately by a telephone call, possibly a personal visit, or a report from an outside agency.

Impress or Inform

Letter inquiries are usually done by form letter. The one standard letter for all applicants contains vacant spaces that are filled in from data taken off the application blank. The former employer is asked to verify this information. Usually this is followed by a few questions the new employer would like to have answered.

It is amazing how many form letters are designed to impress rather than inform the manager who is considering the applicant. Many ask too many questions which often are difficult or impossible to answer. My personal pet peeve is the letter that contains, among other things, something like this:

	Sup.	Exc.	Good	Fair	Poor
Integrity	☐	☐	☐	☐	☐
Honesty	☐	☐	☐	☐	☐
Personality	☐	☐	☐	☐	☐
Apperance	☐	☐	☐	☐	☐
Attendance	☐	☐	☐	☐	☐
Attitude	☐	☐	☐	☐	☐

Imagine trying to answer these questions conscientiously about a former employee who left five or 10 years ago. In the first place, companies do not keep such records. The supervisor may no longer be on the job and the successor is unfamiliar with the former employee. If the supervisor is still around, how good is his memory and is his recollection colored by the circumstance of the termination? Anyway, isn't it possible that the former employee might today be different from what his former employment record reveals? Additional education, work experience, military service, changed marital status, travel, maturity and the like could make him into a changed person and render the comparison almost useless.

Much to be preferred is a simple and direct request along these lines, as illustrated by the request form that follows.

TELEPHONE CHECK

The telephone check is the quickest means of getting outside information about an applicant. It saves time and often saves money as well.

It can be used to verify statements made by the applicant. It can also be used advantageously in advance of a second or follow-up interview to give the interviewer something to check against as he talks with the applicant.

A sample form, "Telephone Check on Sales Applicant," developed by The McMurry Company and published by Dartnell, follows.

REIMBURSEMENT for MOVING and RELOCATION EXPENSE

One characteristic of our modern industrial society may be described as "people on the move." It is not uncommon for executive, managerial, professional and sales personnel to transfer from one location to another.

179

A telephone reference check form for recording the information received in a reference inquiry.

TELEPHONE REFERENCE CHECK

Date: _____

Name of Applicant _____

Organization Name _____

Organization Address _____ Telephone _____

Person Contacted _____ Position _____

Verify:

Dates of Employment _____ Last Salary _____

Nature of his/her work assignment _____

_____

_____

Reason for leaving _____

Explore:

Skill level at which applicant is operating. Capacity to handle the position for which he/she is applying: _____

_____

Relationships with associates, clients, supervisors? Can he/she follow instructions, ask for and take help? _____

_____

What is applicant's record of illness? Is he/she punctual? _____

_____

How about dependability, cooperation, initiative, ambition? _____

_____

Are there areas where applicant could use additional training or supervision? _____

_____

Would they rehire? _____ If not, why _____

Comments _____

_____

(Use other side if necessary)

TELEPHONE CHECK

Name of Applicant	
Former Supervisor	Title
Company Where Applicant Worked	Telephone Number

1. (Applicant's name) has applied for employment with us. I would like to *verify* some of the information given us. When did he/she work for your company?

   From _____ 19 ____ To _____ 19 ____

2. What was his/her job when he/she started to work for you? _____

   When he/she left? _____

3. He/she says earnings were
   $ _____ per _____
   Is that correct?   □ Yes, □ No, $ _____

4. What did you think of him/her? (Quality and quantity of work, attendance, how he/she got along with others, etc.) _____

   4a. What accidents has he/she had? _____

5. Why did he/she leave your company? _____

6. Would you re-employ?   □ Yes, □ No, (If not, why not?) _____

Additional comments _____

Date of Check _____ 19 _____ Made by _____

Form No. OT-203

Copyright 1975, The Dartnell Corporation, Chicago, Ill. 60640. Printed in U.S.A.
Developed by The McMurry Company

At some stage of his life everyone must make a decision, either to remain bound to a geographical location or to stake his future with the corporation and move around as the opportunities for growth present themselves.

In this day of multiplant operations it is easy to shift a needed man or woman from one installation to another. The same situation obtains when a person finds he wants to change jobs and accepts employment with a new firm in a different state. Advertisements are placed in national magazines and in metropolitan newspapers in the large population centers, but the positions that are offered are often not in the vicinity of the applicant's place of residence.

What is the policy as it relates to easing the financial burden and personal inconvenience of an employee who is transferred or for an applicant who is hired from another area?

Usually if the action is initiated by the company, or is for the convenience of the company, the employee is reimbursed. In cases where an applicant decides, for reasons of his own, to move to another city and then to look for a job there, he is not reimbursed.

The common practice seems to be to pay the bill for moving a man and his family from their present location to their new one. This means door-to-door, moving of furniture and personal possessions, and includes crating and packing at one end, transporting by insured carrier, and delivery to the new address. If the family is moved by air or train, with luggage, the fare is paid for. If the family moves by private automobile, usually no travel allowance is made, although this could vary, depending upon circumstances and any agreement made.

When the man and his family relocate in another city additional expenses are encountered because of reestablishing their living in a different home or apartment. Carpets, drapes and other furnishings must be purchased anew. Many companies make an allowance or concession toward the additional expense incurred in a relocation. Here again much depends on individual circumstances.

There is at least one other item to consider. This is the maintenance of two places of residence if the moving and the start of employment in the new job do not coincide. Often a man starts the new job while his family remains behind to complete the sale of property, to dispose of personal or household belongings, to let children complete school terms, and the like. In such cases the man lives on expense account for a specified period of time, after which he is expected to have his family affairs in order. The company may also pay his fare traveling home periodically or on weekends until everything is settled.

Usually when a company wants a man it will make whatever arrangements are necessary. No man who takes a new job for the good of the company should be expected to pay a price for it. At the very least, he ought to break even.

TAX DEDUCTIBLE MOVING EXPENSE

Provisions of the 1976 Tax Reform Act changed deductible moving expenses in favor of the taxpayer. Even for people who do not itemize deductions, reasonable direct moving expenses are fully deductible and indirect moving expenses are allowable within specified limitations.

Who qualifies? A person must be moving to a new residence to work as an employee or as a self-employed individual at a new place of work. The new place of work must be at least 35 miles farther from the old residence than the old residence was from the old place of work.

What is deductible? The cost of packing, crating and transporting household goods and personal effects to a new residence is fully deductible. Other deductible expenses include the cost of shipping an automobile and the cost of transporting household pets. The final family trip to the new residence, including meals and lodging, is considered a direct moving expense and is fully deductible.

Indirect moving expenses, deductible within limits, include premove house-hunting trips, temporary quarters, selling the old residence and buying a new one, and obtaining settlement on a lease. The costs of selling one house and buying another take into account real estate commissions, attorney's fees, title appraisal and escrow fees, loan-placement charges, state transfer taxes and similar expenses.

MOVING POLICY

The following is the "Executive Moving Policy" of Beneficial Management Corporation, Wilmington, Delaware.

The Executive Committee has approved some amendments to the corporate moving policy for Field Executives who relocate at the request of the company either on a promotion or transfer basis. The two improvements are to include up to four points mortgage placement fees in selling the home and expansion of the maximum closing costs to $1,000.

The plan for Field Executives is summarized as follows:

1. Reimbursement for real estate brokerage fees and closing costs in connection with the sale of a residence; mortgage placement points will be included up to four points.
2. Interest-free bridge loans for 90 days will be provided to executives who buy at the new location before they dispose of their

present home. After 90 days, bridge loans revert to interest at 6% per annum.

3. Miscellaneous moving allowance equal to one-month's salary to a maximum of $1,500 will be permitted to cover such miscellaneous items as draperies, carpeting, phone installation, plumbing modifications, etc.

4. Closing costs on newly-purchased homes will be reimbursed to a maximum of $1,000 providing purchase occurs within one year of relocation.

For the present, this plan still covers Field Executives. Managers required to relocate are not included. However, if a manager is required to relocate and suffers a loss on real estate, the individual Operating Vice-President will continue to have the option of making a special recommendation based upon individual circumstances. Any recommendation for this type of extraordinary consideration should be made to the Executive Committee.

In addition, the Executive Committee may in unusual situations with extenuating circumstances provide an additional allowance above and beyond this basic coverage based upon individual recommendations.

FIDELITY BONDS

by KEITH L. OESTREICH
Shand, Morahan & Company

Embezzlement has reached the proportions of a national scandal with thievery by employees estimated as totaling between $1 billion and $1½ billion each year. A recent study by the Economic Unit of *U.S. News & World Report* revealed that crimes against business are increasing at a rate of about 10% a year. Embezzlement, once infrequent, has soared almost 70% since 1971.

No business is immune from theft by employees; acts of dishonesty can be found at every level from dock laborer to corporate management. To protect themselves from the rising threat of employee dishonesty, employers purchase fidelity bonds either as a separate coverage or as part of a broader crime insurance package.

All fidelity bonds indemnify an employer against loss that is due to dishonesty of employees. However, there are numerous variations in the coverage and provisions of these bonds. The earliest form was the Individual bond which indemnified the employer against loss from one named employee. The next step in the development of fidelity coverage was the Name Schedule bond which listed a number of employees on one instrument. Because the Name Schedule bond required numerous changes as employees came and went, the Position Schedule bond was designed to cover the occupants of certain specified positions. The final developments were the two blanket forms—Blanket Position and Commercial Blanket—which cover all employees without naming them or listing the positions they occupy. Either of these blanket forms can also be purchased as a part of the Comprehensive Dishonesty, Disappearance and Destruction policy which provides broader crime insurance coverage in addition to fidelity protection.

All fidelity bonds have the following important features:

1. The bonds are continuous instruments, that is, they do not expire and premiums are recomputed and billed every year or every three years as the case may be. The bond remains in force from the time it is written until it is terminated by either party or otherwise as provided in the bond.

2. The bonds contain a limit of liability. For Name Schedule or Position Schedule bonds, this limit may be varied as to different employees or different positions. The limit of liability is not cumulative from year to year.

3. The bond is terminated as soon as the employer learns of any loss committed by a bonded employee. In the case of an Individual bond, the whole bond is terminated. In the case of the schedule or blanket forms, coverage is at once terminated as to the defaulting employee. The employer is required to notify the bonding company immediately on learning of any loss involving a bonded employee. The provision that the coverage on that employee terminates at that time means that the employer cannot give the employee "another chance" and expect his coverage on that employee to continue.

4. Fidelity bonds are written on a loss-sustained basis. This means that a bond covers any loss sustained by the employer which is committed by an employee while the bond is in force. For example, an employer may discover that an employee has been guilty of several thefts from the employer, some before the effective date of the bond and some after. If so, the bond will cover, up to its limit of liability, only those thefts which can be shown to have occurred during the term of the bond.

5. Fidelity bonds allow for a discovery period. After a bond is terminated for any reason, the employer is given a certain time to discover losses which may have occurred while the bond was in force. This discovery period varies in different bonds from six months to three years.

Coverage Gap

Whenever it becomes necessary to rewrite a fidelity bond, whether because of a change of insurer or form of coverage, it is important to be sure there is no gap in the coverage. If there is a gap in coverage, the employer would be unprotected for losses occurring during the uninsured period even though his prior bond may have a discovery period which is still running. The discovery period applies only to a loss which occurred during the policy period even though it may be discovered after the policy has terminated.

If the replacing bond is one of the blanket forms, it will contain a provision wherein the coverage of the new bond is substituted for any prior bond where the prior bond is terminated, cancelled or allowed to expire as of the time of substitution. The three conditions of this provision are that the replacing bond must be a substitute for the previous bond, its coverage must be of the type which would respond to the particular loss had the loss occurred within the current bond period, and the loss must be one which would have been covered under the previous bond.

If a defalcation is found to have been committed totally during the period of a prior bond, and before the expiration of the discovery period of the prior bond, the employer must look to the insurer of his prior coverage. If, however, the discovery period of the prior bond has expired he can look to his present bond if it has this continuity provision. Individual, Name Schedule and Position Schedule bonds are not standardized and whether or not a similar provision is included depends upon the contract used by the particular insurer.

Blanket Bonds

The two Blanket Fidelity forms have become popular with both insurers and insureds and have displaced Individual, Name Schedule and Position Schedule forms to a large degree. The advantages of the Blanket forms are:

1. Blanket cover on all employees.
2. Automatic additions and deductions without notice to the insurer.
3. Recovery without identification of employee causing loss upon furnishing reasonable proof that loss was due to act or acts coming within the terms of the bonds.

It should be noted that a loss of an employer's physical property cannot be based on inventory or profit and loss computations. An employer must prove his loss through evidence wholly apart from such inventory computations. The reason for this is that inventory shortages may be due in part to employee dishonesty, shoplifters, breakage or over-measuring. A physical shortage may also be due to honest errors in inventory record-keeping or deliveries.

4. The cost for the broader coverage is sometimes less or equal to the cost of a more limited schedule form, since any risk developing an annual premium of over $150 is eligible for experience rating.

The two blanket forms already mentioned are the Commercial Blanket Bond and the Blanket Position Bond. The main difference between these two forms is that the Commercial Blanket Bond is blanket on all employees involved. The Blanket Position Bond covers all employees up to the limit of liability for each employee. The Blanket Position Bond is available to a maximum limit of $100,000. Because the bond amount of a Blanket Position Bond could theoretically be paid on every employee for a common loss, the premium rate is slightly higher than for the Commercial Blanket Bond.

CONFLICT OF INTEREST

It is customary in many companies to get signed "conflict of interest" statements from board members, officers, executives and others in positions of responsibility. This is to indicate that there is no direct or indirect involvement with the business of a competitor or client that could influence a decision or action.

Corporations try to impress upon these key people that their employment carries with it the expectation of undivided loyalty. They are required to agree not to engage in any outside activity that could result in personal gain at the expense of or embarrassment to the company.

Customarily such disclaimers also include an employee's blood relatives. Conflicts could arise when one member of a family has business or political dealings with another member's organization, in which case they might compare notes or disclose information.

Lately this conflict of interest declaration has been extended to include dual career couples who work at management or professional levels with competitors or clients. It is virtually impossible, companies feel, to keep from "talking shop" at home. When a conflicting job situation becomes known, it is not unlikely that one or the other will be expected to resign and thereby eliminate any danger of conflict.

Where higher-level managerial people are placed under contract, it is not unusual to include a clause forbidding the employee from taking a job with a competitor soon after his contract is terminated or expires.

To hold up in court such restrictions should be reasonable in geographic scope and time.

A request for a signed conflict of interest statement (renewed annually) does not violate a person's constitutional rights. Nor do specific policies for couples risk the fear of successful litigation as long as they are enforced equitably, irrespective of sex.

EMPLOYMENT CONTRACT

An employment contract, often a letter of agreement, contains a number of provisions. Some are standard, or "boiler plate," and others are tailored to the specific situation. They try to anticipate and cover every condition and possible contingency. The list would include such items as:

1. *Employment:* job title, duties, limitations, location, relationships, reporting accountability.
2. *Employment term:* length of employment, beginning and ending dates, extension, renewal considerations.
3. *Compensation:* base salary rate, method of payment, deferred arrangements, employee benefits, stock options, death and disability benefits, perquisites.
4. *Bonus:* guaranteed or contingent, formula basis, how calculated, when payable.
5. *Expenses:* incident to employment, incurred on behalf of the company, travel, entertainment, company car.
6. *Termination:* completion of term, separation rules, interruptions for any reason, settlement of obligations and covenants.
7. *Business properties:* protection of assets—financial and physical, and full-time devotion and dedication to both company and industry interests.
8. *Safeguarding "inside secrets":* maintaining total confidentiality of trade secrets, lists of suppliers and customers, guarding production processes, inventions, products.
9. *Non-competition:* during employment—avoiding conflict of interest; after employment—remaining out of field or territory for stated period of time.
10. *Incentives:* tied to performance or based on production improvement, reduction of liabilities, increased profits.
11. *Guarantees:* how binding in case of liquidation, merger, consolidation, or sale.
12. *Definitions:* clarification of terms used in contract.

As with everything else, there are advantages and disadvantages in the use of employment contracts:

Advantages:

1. Attracts experienced and skilled employees.
2. Guarantees continued employment to executives of acquired companies.
3. Adds security when it is necessary to ask someone to make a major relocation.
4. Offers stability by avoiding whims of members of family-owned firms.

Disadvantages:

1. Might be challenged in court and involve lengthy litigation.
2. Forces someone to stay who wants to leave; thus be counterproductive.
3. Could get stuck with a nonperformer.
4. Reduces ability to amend employment practices to changed conditions.
5. Restricts ability to adjust compensation to performance level.

Because typical employment contracts or letters of agreement contain many standard provisions, fill-in forms are available from office supply dealers. But whether a standard or special form is utilized, it is best to let a lawyer draw up or at least approve the contract. It is easy enough to enter into a contract with a new executive but the situation could become sticky later if a problem arises that was not clearly delineated and has to be thrashed out.

TRANSFERS

Transfers and promotions should not be confused. They are not the same and the two terms are not interchangeable.

A transfer is a lateral move within the same labor grade, or from one job to another job of like value and importance. A transfer is a movement from one job to another, with changes in duties, supervision, work conditions, but not necessarily salary. A promotion, on the other hand, is an upgrading from one job level to a higher one, and should carry with it an increase in salary.

Transfers are made for the convenience of the company, the convenience of the worker, or to increase the flexibility of the workforce.

Transfers are made for negative or positive reasons:

Negative

1. A worker is not suited for his present job.
2. His present job is eliminated.
3. Friction exists.
4. There is a physical handicap.

Positive

1. Improving environment.
2. Changing to more prestige duties.
3. Building morale.
4. Adding experience.

A transfer, while it does not carry with it any automatic consideration for more money, has other advantages. It could offer the employee any of the following:

1. A chance for broader experience.
2. More suitable work.
3. More interesting duties.
4. More congenial work group.
5. Better supervisor.
6. Better hours.
7. Location closer to home.

Quite often a manager or foreman is reluctant to suggest a transfer because he is unable to include a wage increase in the deal. This would be unfair to the employee who might eagerly accept the move for any of the above reasons, or others which are understandable to him.

Correcting Misplacements

A company may wish to transfer an employee who is worth keeping but who is obviously mis-assigned. A misfit in one type of work, provided his habits and attitude are good, might find his niche in another line of work. For example: a clerk who goes home tired every night might be better off on the next desk where less math is required.

Beware, however, of the person who seeks transfer as a means of running away from a situation he refuses to correct. Instead of admitting his shortcoming and agreeing with his supervisor to change a bad habit, such as excessive tardiness, he moves out taking his unsolved problem with him. Before anyone is transferred his performance should be carefully checked. Is his record clear? Is he worth transferring?

Temporary transfers are a stop-gap measure for an emergency situation. One or more employees may be transferred temporarily because another part of the company is shorthanded or overloaded and extra people are needed until the problem can be solved. In such cases, the employees may be moved bodily but not on paper; that is, no actual reassignment is effected. If their wages for this interim period are to be charged to the new department, this becomes an accounting transaction. Should the duration of the temporary transfer be more than just a short time, it might be advisable to keep the records straight by issuing the necessary transfer papers when the first move is made and again when the people return to their regular jobs. In all these cases, employees transferred for company convenience to a lower-rated job should not be penalized in the paycheck. Should they be working in their temporary duty in jobs which rate higher, some consideration might be given to paying them accordingly.

Transfers are part of the "bumping" process that goes on during a cut-back in the workforce. Rather than lay off a worker whose job has been eliminated, a company may permit an employee to bump another worker with less seniority or tenure.

Seniority generally accompanies a worker when he moves. This could be a deterrent since the new department, in addition to getting a loyal and experienced worker, also inherits all that goes with seniority —longer vacation with possibly an early choice, rate of pay possibly higher than others in the same job, etc. Seniority is company-wide and refers to length of service in the total organization. In those few cases where seniority is not plant-wide but departmental, or worse yet, job-line, the terms better be clearly spelled out and understood by all concerned.

PROMOTIONS

The best practice of filling any job vacancy is to select the best qualified candidate who is available, whether he comes from outside or inside the company. When he comes from within, he is moved into his new job by either transfer or promotion. There is a difference.

A horizontal promotion is really not a promotion but a lateral transfer. This results in a change of duties and opportunities but not in degree of responsibility, or job value, and therefore at no change in salary.

A true promotion is an upgrading of a worker's job from one level to a higher one with a correspondingly higher rate of pay.

A vertical promotion is an upgrading in the same area or type of work. Example: a stenographer to secretary.

A prestige promotion or transfer takes a worker to a less strenuous but more attractive job, sometimes at the same pay, but with certain more desirable features. Example: a typist clerk to receptionist.

A systematic promotion is one step in a sequence of jobs planned for workers to enlarge or broaden their understanding of overall operations. In management jobs this could be called "job rotation," when the movement is made more in the employee's interest and not only for company convenience. Systematic promotion is a device of getting workers out of blind-alley jobs.

Practically every employer boasts of having a promotion-from-within policy. But if a check were made, it could well be that the employees think otherwise.

Avoid Blanket Policy

A blanket statement of promotion-from-within in an employee handbook is not only erroneous but also foolish. No company today fills all its higher job openings from within. Some jobs require background and experience which cannot be found in the present workforce. As soon as the first outsider is hired for one of these jobs, the employees know the blase' promotion policy mentioned in the handbook is untrue, and they could be expected to distrust similar statements about other aspects of the employee program.

When an employee is ready for a bigger challenge, and an opportunity for promotion presents itself, it is well to consider the employee. This not only makes it easy for the company to fill the job, but it also offers more responsibility and a better earnings opportunity to a deserving worker. If he is by-passed, there is the likelihood of losing him as he acquires a "what's the use" attitude.

This does not mean that all or most jobs should be filled from within the organization. Promoting from within is good policy but should not be a rigid rule to close the door to qualified outsiders. Nor should better jobs be offered to outsiders and denied to present employees. Too much promotion from within results in inbreeding of ideas and experience, and does not take advantage of ideas from outside. An outsider's different viewpoint may be invaluable in some situations.

On the other hand, filling all or most of the job vacancies from the outside does not take advantage of valuable experience gained by employees. In many cases there is no substitute for on-the-job training and know-how. It should also be realized that too little promotion from within results in low morale and high turnover because of lack of opportunity.

Anyhow, jobs ought not to be filled by any company policy that says blindly that one course or the other must be followed. The most practical company policy is the one which says simply that jobs should be given to the best qualified and best suited applicant, whether from within the company or outside of it. Anything less, no matter how altruistic it may sound, shortchanges both the company and the workers.

Make Employees Promotable

What usually happens is that two types of jobs are filled from within: (1) those which are in the same field but are heavier or carry more responsibility, and (2) those which call for general training and not for a peculiar skill or special talent.

The better secretarial jobs can often be filled by up-and-coming stenographers who have improved their skill through practice and increased their knowledge of company operations through experience to the point where they are ready for something bigger. A company is fortunate when it has enough movement in its workforce to be able to offer bigger job opportunities to employees who have outgrown their present assignments.

Similarly, a job as order-checker in a jobbing warehouse can usually be filled by an experienced order-filler. Here knowledge of the company and its products is more important than a unique skill of checking. It is easier to teach a loyal company employee the new checking procedure than to acquaint a stranger with the thousands of products in the line.

It is for specialty jobs that companies have to go outside. A retail drug or food chain needing a real estate manager would be unlikely to find the necessary background among its regular workers. An advertising agency would be hard-pressed to promote even the best clerk into the position of commercial artist. A life insurance company would certainly have to bring in a physician from the medical community and not offer the position to any loyal and long-service nonprofessional employee.

There are two avenues which lead to a successful promotion-from-within program:

1. Training programs to help employees develop beyond present duties. Without this the better jobs will, of necessity, be filled from the outside.

2. A system for recognizing and rewarding growth in individuals. Without this, promotable employees will leave to take their chances elsewhere.

One value of promotion from within lies in its chain reaction. To fill one higher job, which in turn creates a vacancy lower down, at least two persons, and oftentimes more, are involved. Movement in jobs is generally desirable, especially when boredom may be a factor. It is not desirable in all cases as, for instance, a worker who is peculiarly adapted for a certain type of work, or a skilled worker who would have to abandon the one talent that sets him apart from co-workers.

Some jobs never change; some people do not change. But in those cases where jobs grow bigger, we can be grateful that some people grow bigger too, so that these jobs can be filled. One of the basic job satisfactions a worker requires is to enjoy his work and be interested in what he is doing. Work which challenged a worker at first but bores him once he has mastered it, does not provide this satisfaction. Ideally, every employee ought to have a job that is just a bit over his head. This would keep him on his toes. Promotion is the answer.

PROMOTION TO MANAGEMENT POSITIONS

There are two main routes to business success: (1) the passive route, and (2) the active route. It is entirely possible to get to the top in business by being passive.

A social climber can rise to eminence from humble beginnings by doing practically nothing, but looking good while doing it. Given a well-developed instinct for survival, it is possible in some businesses to get ahead simply by being available, and by being the handiest person to fall heir to the promotion as smarter men and women move up or out, or otherwise clear the way.

The logical way, however, calls for careful selection of successor prospects. And this task of selecting the one right person need not be difficult as long as we are honest with ourselves, our companies and our candidates. It is only when we confound the issue by interjecting seniority, loyalty or sentimental personal qualities that we make the problem complicated.

In the process of selection we should spell out the requirements of the position and then look for people who approximate, or show promise of approximating, the standards. An executive and an automobile may be compared. A man without judgment is like a car without brakes; a man without enthusiasm is like a car without a motor; a man without initiative is like a car without a starter; a man without vision is like a car without lights. We know what specifications we want when we get an automobile; why should it be any different when we get a man?

Selection Fallacies

The following list of "Selection Don'ts" indicates some of the fallacies in executive thinking that must be avoided if proper selection of candidates for management is to be achieved:

1. Don't arbitrarily pick the top producer in any area for a bigger job where the demands are quite different.
2. Don't rely too heavily on tests. They are useful in determining intelligence, certain skills or knowledge, even emotional stability or lack of it. But they cannot measure attitude or predict success in applying measurable skills or knowledge. You can't use test results as a crutch against a poor decision on your part.

3. Don't let seniority be a heavy influence lest you select a faithful veteran for a job he is simply not qualified to handle.

4. Don't kid yourself that training is the answer. A candidate who lacks courage, desire, judgment, intelligence or determination won't be helped by management training. Such training may fill his notebook but not his heart; it may move his pen but not his spirit. A man has to have it "inside" to be a leader.

5. Don't go overboard on intelligence. I once heard a Phi Beta Kappa described as a man with a key on his watch chain . . . but no watch. Leaders must be intelligent, certainly, but intelligence without stability of character, self-control or discretion is dangerous. A person's weaknesses must not be overlooked in favor of any outstanding strength.

6. Don't be overimpressed by any college degree. This country is mass-producing college graduates. Some are capable, some are not. Furthermore, today it is possible to get a degree in a wide variety of fields, some of which require very little in the way of hard disciplines such as Mathematics, Science and Languages. An honor student with a degree in "Supervised Recreation" probably doesn't qualify for management. So instead of looking for a degree, examine the credentials carefully.

7. Don't be misled by popularity. A man who goes out of his way to be liked, who is proud to be known as "one of the boys," may find it difficult, even impossible, to criticize or to reprimand because he doesn't want to run the risk of offending. A manager is often lonesome and by robbing a man of his biggest asset, that of popularity, we destroy the one trait which attracted us to him in the first place.

8. Don't close the door of opportunity to anyone. Selecting only the fair-haired boys is the best way to overlook or discourage some of the untapped talent which is just ripe for development. The crown prince theory would have closed the door to Abraham Lincoln, wouldn't it? Bright prospects should be encouraged but room must be allowed for the surprise candidate who is not in the spotlight.

The Positive Side

These are some of the "don'ts" that we should avoid. On the other side of the ledger are the positive aspects of selection for management positions. There are three broad groups of factors to consider for an objective, honest and reliable selection of a man for a management position:

1. The first is talent for the job ahead. A review of his background, skills, prior training and general knowledge will provide this kind

of information. In this area much can be learned from the use of appropriate tests.

2. The second is personality. Now he will be doing his work through others. A leader has to be someone others are "impelled" not "compelled" to follow.

3. The third factor is health, including emotional stability. Good health means more than physical fitness. It also includes peace of mind. Outside interests and relaxations are part of a balanced way of life. Lopsided living is a common cause of executive ill health.

In any selection process for promotion remember that the people singled out for management positions must "want" the job. Not everybody, you know, aspires to become an officer in the industrial army. Be happy, not annoyed, by the individual who dares to be contrary, who sees challenges instead of problems, who can discard tradition, who doesn't think in stereotypes. Watch for the person who is presently not sufficiently occupied by his job duties; if he has to find extra-curricular activities to round out his pattern of job satisfactions this is the signal that you are not channeling his abilities toward company objectives.

Beware of the person who is patient, willing to go along, satisfied that "the system" will take care of him. Loyal and unimaginative people do not make good managers, where creativity is an essential requirement.

The Marks of an Executive

When we make the final selection we will recognize it as the one right choice when we see in the individual these three executive traits:

1. Willingness to discipline himself: to manage himself, his time and his energies toward reaching realistic goals he has established as his objective.

2. Courage to seek change and face risks: with the right to success goes the right to failure. The man who is afraid to take risks does neither—fail or succeed.

3. Capacity for dedication: the extent of being able to be bigger than oneself, to lose himself in the cause he espouses.

This last point is worth another comment. Achieving the result, not the credit for doing it, should be the motivation. The salt loses its own identity in order to preserve; the oil is entirely consumed to give light; the yeast is completely absorbed in the dough it transforms. Each sacrifices itself so the function may be fulfilled.

Give me that outlook in a man or woman and I'll give you an executive.

DEMOTIONS

A promotion is easy to handle; it is always pleasant to give out good news. A transfer is usually not difficult; at least the employee who is moved is not hurt in earnings. But a demotion is more delicate, even when such a move is in the employee's best interest.

A demotion is made for one of two reasons:

1. The employee is unable to meet the performance requirements of his present assignment and is moved to another job which is more in keeping with his talent and ability.
2. An employee, whose job is eliminated, may be worth keeping and is "parked" on a lower job which is available until another opening comes up that is comparable in level to the one he had.

Demotions in industry should never be used as punishment or other disciplinary action. This practice is followed in the military service where, for example, a sergeant may be "busted" to private for misconduct or an infraction of the rules.

An employee who consistently receives a poor performance rating is obviously misassigned. Where counselling or training cannot bring about an improvement, the only choice may be to demote him to an easier job. In our eagerness to fill vacancies we may be guilty of hiring or promoting individuals who cannot meet the requirements of the job, even after a reasonable trial period. Such employee might actually be happier on a lower job for which he is better suited.

In those cases where an employee is out of his job through no fault of his own, it would be wise to save him on some lower job rather than release him outright. A follow-up should be kept to make certain he is not overlooked later when a higher position for which he qualifies becomes available.

In any event, demoting an employee is no easy matter and calls for tact and diplomacy in order to let him save face before co-workers. It is actually easier to dismiss a worker than to demote him, for while the hurt may be greater on impact, at least he doesn't have to hang around to wonder whether his fellow workers look upon him as a failure.

A demotion, in addition to hurting a person's pride, might also hurt his pocketbook. No one should be paid more than he is worth. If he has not been able to "cut the mustard" in his previous job, then possibly he was overpaid. This overpayment should not be carried to the lesser job. However, when the demotion is for company convenience, or if the company granted his raise more on seniority than performance, then he should not be penalized.

Most companies are reluctant to cut a worker's pay when he is downgraded in his job . . . unless this is absolutely necessary, or a union agreement spells out such terms. Usually, if his present earnings do not conflict with the wages of the employees in the job category to which he is being demoted, there is neither need nor desire to cut his pay. In a lower job classification, of course, he has a reduced earnings potential.

TERMINATIONS

A policy, preferably in written form and published for the guidance of managers, should be used for terminations. When an employee is separated from the payroll, for whatever reason, the specifics should not be left to chance, or worse yet, left to individual whim.

Voluntary (Resignation)

Most terminations are voluntary. The employee takes the initiative and quits. He may be unhappy with his job, or he may be quitting because of personal reasons or for circumstances beyond his control. It is customary to expect the courtesy of a notice, usually two weeks.

Involuntary

An employee may be separated from the payroll with the action initiated by the company. This action usually follows a warning or two to an unsatisfactory performer, possibly even a period of probation. When this release occurs it is considered proper, although legally not required, to give the employee a two-week notice or two weeks' pay in lieu of notice. Most of the time the company elects the latter option, preferring to pay off an undesirable employee rather than have him, unhappy and disgruntled, riding out his time without being very productive anyway.

A typical company policy is to pay two weeks' pay in lieu of notice to an employee with at least one year's service. The same policy might allow one week's pay for employees with less than one year of service; while this consideration may seem generous at times, especially if the employee has been working only a few weeks, it is nonetheless fair since the employee, at time of hire, quit his previous job, or at least surrendered any other job offers, and now needs paid time during which to start looking for a job all over again.

198

Discharge (Automatic Dismissal)

Apart from employees who are terminated involuntarily, there are also occasions where an employee must be fired. The reasons are many and are well known to employers. Here the action is generally more sudden, and separation from the payroll is immediate. It is still customary to give such fired employee two weeks' pay at time of discharge.

Retirement

At time of retirement an employee is paid up to retirement date, plus any unused earned vacation, severance pay if such program is in effect, and there may be special amenities such as official lunch, unofficial party, gifts, etc.

Death

In the event of the death of an employee, the company should request the beneficiary named by the employee to present a death certificate and, in a case involving accidental death, a coroner's report. The deceased employee's earnings, and possibly pay for unused vacation, are paid to the surviving spouse, children or parents of the deceased employee. The beneficiary is also asked to fill out necessary life insurance forms.

Pay for Unused Vacation

An employee who terminates his employment from a company, for any reason, ordinarily is paid for any vacation accrued under the company's vacation policy, which is still unused at time of termination.

Exit Interviews

Whenever possible, it is sound practice to exit interview employees who leave, especially those terminating of their own accord. This gives the employees an opportunity to express privately their real reasons for leaving the company, and it gives the company a last chance to learn from them any thoughts they may have about company practices or about supervision.

SEVERANCE PAY

At time of termination an employee is paid for all time worked since his last pay period until the date of separation. In case he is dismissed he may be given an additional two weeks' pay in lieu of notice. It is also customary to pay a terminating employee for any earned vacation still unused.

But many companies have a severance pay program which pays an employee extra money when he leaves. This severance pay plan may benefit all employees who leave for any reason, or it may be a program which applies only in cases of layoffs. There is a difference between the conditions under which an employee loses his job through no fault of his own (as a relocation of the plant or a cutback in production) and another separation in which a worker quits of his own accord. Many companies feel an obligation to longtime loyal employees who lose their jobs because of a change in circumstances initiated by the company.

Severance pay arrangements are clearly spelled out in many union contracts. One, for example, provides for 3½ days for each year of service, with a maximum amount equal to 70 days' pay. Every employee with five years of service or more is eligible for this consideration.

Another union agreement refers to severance pay as "Dismissal Indemnity." This is paid to any employee discharged, in addition to two weeks' notice of dismissal. A lump sum at the rate of two weeks' pay is paid for the first six months of service plus one week's pay for each subsequent six months of continuous service up to a maximum of 64 weeks' pay for 378 months or more.

Many nonunion companies also have provisions for severance pay. A typical layoff pay plan calls for:

> 2 weeks' pay ..... less than 5 years' service
> 4 weeks' pay ..... 5 years up to 10 years
> 6 weeks' pay ..... 10 years up to 15 years
> 8 weeks' pay ..... 15 or more years of service.

Programs such as these are ongoing plans which are applicable in the normal course of business. There are circumstances, of course, which are special for which arrangements peculiar to the situation are made. When a company moves to another state, for instance, those staff members who stay with the company can expect to be paid their moving expenses and may even get help in selling their present homes and buying new ones. However, those who cannot make the move (and this is by far the majority of rank-and-file workers) are usually "paid off" over a period of time in order to cushion the blow. The same is true when a firm goes out of business. Employees are given all the help possible to find new jobs but for those who are just "thrown out of work" some form of financial assistance is provided.

DISCHARGE

Discharge, or immediate dismissal, is an action taken only as a last resort after other measures, such as counseling, suspension, discipline or transfer have failed.

One company policy recognizes a number of situations when discharge is justified:

1. Refusal to perform an assigned job duty.
2. Stealing or damaging of corporate property or another employee's property.
3. Negligent use or abuse of corporate property in a willful manner.
4. Use of obscenities or defamatory remarks when communicating with the public.
5. Purchasing or selling of illegal drugs or alcoholic beverages while on corporate premises.
6. Being intoxicated or under the influence of illegal drugs during working hours.
7. Fighting with or inflicting physical harm on another employee.
8. Bringing firearms or other weapons onto corporate premises or having possession of them on corporate premises.
9. Absence of 15 days (not including extended sick leave) in a calendar year.
10. Tardiness of more than 20 times during a calendar year.

HOW GOOD ARE FIRING PRACTICES?

"Many companies that have well-established hiring procedures are very stupid when it comes to firing practices."

That's what the man said—this friend of mine who, after 30 years as an electrical engineer, was promoted in the twilight of his career to chief engineer. As one of his first responsibilities, he faced the unwelcome task of firing a young man. He couldn't bear to take a job away from a man who had a wife and family to support. He didn't know how to fire the man. What was worse, there was no place for him to go for direction.

(Incidentally, the epilogue to this true story reports sadly that this unpleasant duty, for which he was emotionally unprepared, so unnerved this engineer that he gradually fell apart and never made it to his normal retirement date two years away.)

To those of us who are making a lifetime career of personnel and industrial relations work, this experience sounded like a severe indictment. So I decided to investigate, and by gad, the man is right. There is nothing available on the subject of firing practices.

Therefore I made a little study of my own. I began by reviewing our own statistics for the past year. Approximately 11% of our terminations were involuntary. The most common reason was "poor attendance" and "unsatisfactory work" was second. All in all, however, it appeared that we were reasonably tolerant and could have fired more. Some employees were retained who, perhaps for their own good, should have been fired.

Justifying our patience with problem employees, we pointed to the labor market, arguing with ourselves that the replacements, in addition to being untrained, would most likely be no better. There was also the matter of acquisition costs and turnover which the comptroller was always complaining about. And who is the manager who can stand being second-guessed by his superiors on his initial selection procedures or his inability to develop available workers? Complications such as these served as deterrents to firing problem employees.

In other situations we were optimistic, eternally hopeful, that with continued understanding and kindness the problem employee might somehow be galvanized into a desirable and productive worker by having the supervisor press one of the magic buttons he learned about in the company training classes. Besides, those who anticipate being fired often make the decision difficult by being well-liked, exceptionally cooperative or otherwise generally acceptable in the eyes of fellow workers.

The truth is that in most instances the manager just disliked the unpleasantness that goes with firing a co-worker. This did not reflect so much his inadequate preparation for this task, but rather it revealed a soft heart behind a gruff exterior, which hesitated to inflict a hurt upon another sensitive human being.

After all, when an individual is banished from an organization against his will he is suddenly cut off from a source of contact with people, purpose and reality. Despite the progress being made toward systematizing operations, there is still a lot of sentiment in business.

This analysis of our own practices disclosed little of value except to show that in this respect we were behaving very much like other companies, as we discovered when we widened our research to other firms, local and national.

Who is Being Fired

Comparing notes with other companies it appears that workers are discharged for five main reasons:

1. For cause, such as dishonesty.
2. Continuous disobeyance of necessary orders.
3. Personality conflicts.
4. Inability to perform (didn't measure up).
5. What is even worse than lack of skill, that is, lack of will.

Dismissal seems to be the line of least resistance to apply to the employee who:

> lacks initiative or concentration.
> has outside interests which interfere.
> makes too many errors.
> becomes hopelessly confused with unfamiliar terminology.
> is slow.
> develops questionable behavior.
> has a poor memory.
> makes disparaging remarks against management.
> shows no capabilities.
> has inadequate skill for the job.
> is undependable.
> can no longer keep up with the work.
> borrows money.
> is a disturbing influence.
> has chronic tardiness.
> becomes involved in a personality conflict.

One mental health expert reported that "from 20% to 25% of all employees in every corporation or industrial unit are suffering from mental disorders. They range from psychoses to industrial maladjustment, manifested in absenteeism, accidents, dissatisfaction, alcoholism, turnover and poor job performance."

He added, "In dealing with these problems the essential factor is the understanding of the individual, rather than labeling his behavior with a diagnostic tag."

When certain employees become serious threats to production or morale, two courses of action are open. A supervisor can get rid of them by firing them, or he can attempt to provide or obtain sympathetic guidance which will help to reduce or possibly eliminate the difficulty.

What should companies do with employees who become problems? To many of them the answer apparently is to fire them. The friction builds up until finally the boss decides he has had enough. Even when this is the better choice, is their method of firing good?

How Firing is Being Done

Firing is always distasteful regardless how carefully done and how proper the motive. A professional baseball manager is fired. The sports world is stunned but nobody questions the owner's right to take such action. A national television personality is fired. His followers are disappointed, but nobody criticizes the network. Both cases were blazoned across the front pages of practically every newspaper in the country.

Both of these men continued to receive full pay since their unexpired contracts were honored. But this legal compliance doesn't impress the public, which reacts more to the unexpected suddenness than to any fair treatment. Continuing their salaries as a legal requirement took some of the onus off the owners. But getting fired hurts people's pride as much as it does their pocketbooks. No matter how the blow is cushioned, it leaves an indelible smear on their work record.

In some instances firing may actually be best for the worker—the old argument that a change of scenery will do him good. But even sympathetic firing leaves a scar; it hurts the ego.

Firing for cause is relatively easy—especially for the self-righteous manager. The causes fall into two broad categories: (1) discipline-related, and (2) production-related. The evidence is usually undeniable, the facts well-documented. The decision is arbitrary; the fired employee has little recourse except to disappear and lick his wounds. A variety of techniques, however, are used in the other situations.

Many supervisors use crude measures, believing better methods are not called for. They feel it is better to "get it over as fast as possible." Another trick is the "do it when I'm out of the office" routine.

Sometimes a boss "releases" a certain employee to reassert himself. It's either "him or me"—but as long as the boss has the power of life and death over the employee's job, it's obvious who gets the ax! In the process the boss loses face with other employees whose sympathies tend to lie with the underdog.

Oftentimes it is difficult for some supervisors to explain the real reason for firing an employee. Supervisors put up with an employee who has an undesirable habit or characteristic as, for example, carelessness; then when action is finally called for they hang their hats on some more convenient excuse, such as excessive absenteeism caused by poor health. This eases the employee out of the company, but it does not help him understand his own shortcomings, which were serious enough to cost him his job.

Many supervisors want to retain their right to the decision to fire, but expect to shift the act of firing—"giving him the bad news"—to some removed resource, such as the personnel office.

A heartless separation reflects a cruel company to the general public. A stupid firing reveals a poorly-trained management. A company's reputation in the community is often measured by such acts.

How to Do it Better

Since it was assumed at the outset that hiring procedures are better than firing practices, possibly a review of existing employment practices might contain a lesson or two.

Hiring procedures are quite formal in most companies. Even in companies where procedures are not generally considered to be formalized, they have nonetheless become well-established through time.

Firms have such practices as personal indoctrination, group orientation, organized tours, first day or first week checklists, bench interviews, big sisters or sponsors, and the like. Actually the initial interview has a threefold purpose: (1) to get information, (2) to give information, and (3) to make a friend.

The object, of course, is to have the new employee, as soon as he is hired, become a well-adjusted and productive citizen of the worker community in which he chose to place himself.

If by comparison firing techniques are not as good, perhaps it is because they have not been as well-planned. To be more effective these procedures should be clearly spelled out. The supervisor ought not to be left to his own devices, required to stumble through as best he can.

Possibly taking a cue from hiring practices, it might be in order to suggest that, like employment interviewing, it is most important who does the firing, and how it is done. This does not mean that one person should do it all, but it does suggest that all who do it should be properly trained.

The termination interview could also have three purposes: (1) to give reasons and in that way try to get understanding, (2) to inquire what the action may do to him, thereby learning how best to be helpful, and (3) to part as friends.

The fact remains that firing unwanted employees is one of the toughest tasks a manager has to face. In reality what he is doing is imposing the organizational death penalty upon an associate and possibly a friend. He should, first of all, try all sorts of means to avoid excessive firing. There are a number of things he might do for employees who are worth saving.

He could try to effect a transfer of the employee to another job elsewhere in the company where the employee would be better suited and happier. This salvages some of the investment the company has in the employee. He might recommend him for retraining to qualify him for other work. He might be able to assign him to a surplus manpower pool where he could "help out" until normal attrition opens up something for him. If his problem is personal, he might refer him to appropriate counseling services. The manager should be careful, however, not to evade his responsibility of firing through the devious use of

205

transfer, thereby merely transplanting a problem case and expecting someone else to eventually do his dirty work for him.

Maybe companies should not fire so many. After all, in so doing they merely send their problem to another employer—and take the chance of getting one from him in exchange. People earmarked for dismissal should be carefully reevaluated to determine whether the objection on the surface may conceal hidden worth beneath. A few rough edges worn down can change a stone into a gem.

When the employee is not entirely at fault, as is the case of personality conflicts or misassignments, perhaps a shift to other duties, other supervision or another work environment might solve the problem and spare him the hurt that always accompanies a firing, particularly one that he does not understand.

Lately a new word has been introduced into the industrial vocabulary. It is "dehiring" and is applied mostly to upper echelon personnel who are dismissed. As the term implies, it reverses the original hiring procedure. The company invests effort and money to help the terminated employee get relocated, even to the extent of referring him to a professional outside agency who will counsel and assist him, at company expense, in finding a job elsewhere.

Companies that demonstrate to the work force and to the community that they do not believe their responsibility to workers ends when they shove them out the back door, gain respect and loyalty of employees who then have less fear and cynicism. It is gratifying to employees to know they are not subject to the vagaries of whims and prejudices but that the company is actually on their side and has their interests at heart.

Try to Part on Friendly Terms

Whenever firing seems to be the only choice, managers should try to do it without hurting the individual. That way they stand a good chance of not hurting themselves or their companies. Even when a separation is made to appear as a resignation, or by mutual agreement, there is always the suspicion that the action was instigated by management—that the employee was fired.

Generally it is safer all around to be straightforward in each situation. A fair and honest appraisal of the conditions leading up to the firing of an individual leaves less to be disputed. A blunt approach is not necessarily recommended; it may be kinder to generalize and infer that management shares the fault in that it "might not have selected or used the employee properly." There is always the possibility that the employee "deemed a failure" could become successful elsewhere and management's one-sided decision could backfire.

Wherever possible, offer termination pay and other considerations.

The employee who resigns usually gets considerations, such as payment for unused vacation. The fired employee is out of work abruptly, as contrasted with the one who does so by choice, and he needs all the assistance he can get.

Just how to go about this may depend upon circumstances. Consider the effect of firing an employee on the community; in a small town this is far more critical than in a larger, impersonal city. Consider its effect on the product or service; will it disturb the confidence and trust customers have in the firm's good intentions? Consider also the nature of the business; obviously a firm with direct face-to-face dealings, as a department store, must treat firing differently from a factory where the employee has less opportunity to affect customer relations.

Everybody would gain if companies could learn to do this better. Any improvement would have a more salutary effect on the person involved, and on other employees whose feelings of security in their jobs and confidence in their future progress may otherwise be shaken.

What is the most satisfactory or effective way to fire people? There appears to be no authoritative source material to turn to for guidance. It is difficult to learn by example of others, as in other facets of employee relations. There is no pooling of ideas on the subject of firing, no publishing of experiences, as on other management problems. Apparently no one has yet come up with any "one best way" to do this.

Since the act of firing is of major importance to the individual involved, it is absolutely essential that it be done with tact, discretion and sincerity of purpose. Because there is always the possibility of untoward ramifications, it is vital that it be thoroughly contemplated and skillfully carried out.

LAYOFFS

In the American way of doing business it is inevitable that there will be periodic adjustments when production overtakes demand. From the standpoint of employment, this means layoffs. The alternative is to sacrifice the free enterprise system in favor of a planned economy with the government establishing controls. Both the industrialist and the worker feel this is a price they are unwilling to pay for the guarantee of constant employment.

Adjusting supply to demand would not be so difficult if it were the nature of people to put aside some of their earnings in good years for the possible rainy day. But in an era of credit buying and deficit spending, few people save to provide for their own financial security. As in so many other voids created by the people, government has moved in to help fill the gap. Unemployment insurance, paid for by a tax on employers, provides at least subsistence living for a period of time during which the worker waits to be recalled or looks elsewhere for other employment.

When cutbacks in employment are called for, the employer should think not only of his problem but also that of the employees being laid off. He cannot afford to be impersonal. If he deals only in number of workers and forgets that these workers are human beings, he is entitled to all the grief such a selfish viewpoint will surely bring him.

As a start he should try, as best he can, to explain the need for the retrenchment in the hope that through understanding he may gain the sympathy and support of his workers. If they know the problem they will better accept his action. Nothing is as cruel as abruptly cutting off a person from his job without a satisfactory explanation and some hope for rehire or some help for relocation.

Communicating Helps Understanding

There are many ways to communicate the layoff policy to workers. The house organ, bulletins, announcements or memos are all available. But these are merely substitutes for the best method, that of a straight and honest face-to-face talk. To the individual employee this is a more sincere approach than that of hiding behind an impersonal piece of paper. "Give 'em the bad news while I am out of the office" is the worst possible way of handling this delicate problem.

Instead of laying off half of the workforce it might be better to work all employees half time. This should, at least, be considered. Maybe a shortened work week will help spread the work. Every effort should be made to lay off as few workers as possible.

What about the employees who are let go? These are the same workers who until recently were lauded for their loyalty and value to the firm. Are they now simply cut loose? Or is there a serious attempt made to give them assurance, guidance and hope?

Do they understand the method of recall? How soon may they expect to be contacted? Do they understand their rights to their job? What benefits, such as unemployment insurance, are explained? What provision has been made for continuing their group insurance? Is some program put into action to keep in touch with these temporarily-laid-off employees so that their valuable training and experience does not go elsewhere?

What happens if they fail to return to work on the callback? Do they realize the stake they have in the company and the investment they had accrued through previous service? Are they aware of where they stand in the pension or profit-sharing plans?

Any layoff of employees is critical and even the most sympathetic approach does little to lessen the sting. Layoff and recall are difficult problems. They are further complicated when a union agreement is involved. Usually the terms are clearly spelled out and, to some degree, the union can take some of the pressure off management since it is involved, not in the decision for the layoff, but in the mechanics of handling it.

Relocation Means No Recall

But a curtailment of production or services is not the only cause of layoffs. The same problem, without the prospect of recall, obtains when a company moves to a new location afar off. Except for management, top staff personnel and some specialists, very few employees will move with the company. They will, by choice or necessity, stay behind when the company leaves.

In such case many things can be done to soften the blow. Among them are:

1. Early announcement of the move so that workers may plan accordingly.
2. Use of temporary workers to reduce the number of permanent employees who are affected.
3. Severance pay arrangement; example: so much for each year of service.
4. Job-seeking assistance and time off to look for jobs with other friendly and cooperative employers.

At best, any layoff is a nasty and unpleasant task. Handling it in the best interest of the workers, their families, the community and the company calls for management skills of the highest order.

RETRENCHMENT

There is a truism that anybody can manage when things are going well. In a continuing upcycle economy the untested prosperity makes it easy to tolerate inadequacies. But when the economy is depressed, managing takes on added dimensions as firms are forced to become "lean and mean" in order to stay afloat.

It isn't too difficult to weed out the unproductive workers who have been carried on the payroll. A manager faced with a budget cut can identify those workers who are not carrying their fair share of the total workload and whose absence would therefore hurt the least.

While a general tightening of operations will improve the profit picture, there may be occasions when cost-reduction and productivity-improvement plans might not be enough. When the recession is serious enough, if a major account is lost, a division relocated elsewhere, a system is mechanized, a company has to plan on retrenchment and the painful adjustment that is required calls for all sorts of sacrifices by the company and the workers. This is an experience that nobody anticipated and its traumatic impact drops like a bomb.

Here it is not only the marginal employees who are released but also many capable and conscientious workers. To soften the blow, a company will try to absorb some of these surplus workers in other jobs, help them in applying for jobs with other companies, strike a deal for early retirement, or offer other assistance. In addition, it may try to protect these employees temporarily by allowing them to remain in the employee group insurance program for a while.

One idea might be to set up a shared-jobs program. Instead of releasing one-half of the work force, it might be advisable to ask all employees to work half days. In some states the employees can collect partial unemployment compensation. Some will find full-time jobs elsewhere, and normal attrition will lessen the problem; in time the situation is handled with the least strain.

The advantages of shared-jobs are twofold: (1) all employees continue their fringe benefits, and (2) the employer retains the skills and experience of workers. There are disadvantages too. A veteran employee receives no more protection than the newcomer, and the skilled technician is treated the same as the unskilled laborer. Whatever is done will not please everybody.

Retrenchment, especially when it calls for the permanent release of workers, is traumatic. The employees who have to be cut loose are the same people who had always been lauded for their loyalty and dedication to the company and who had trustingly taken at face value the implied assurance of job security and the rewards of tenure.

The downward adjustment of any business is something no managers are prepared for. This is just a nasty and unpleasant task they never expected to be involved in. Handling it in the best interest of the workers, their families, the community and the company requires management skills of the highest order.

DE-HIRING

To ease the blow for executives on both sides of a termination interview, more companies have been seeking assistance from consulting firms that specialize in "de-hiring" or "outplacement" services. With client companies paying the costs, they help executives eased out of their jobs find comparable positions elsewhere.

Corporations cooperate with their terminated executives because they recognize there are such things as no-fault terminations. In many cases, closing down a plant, discontinuing a product line or reorganizing the staff require that capable individuals must be released. Such terminations are a fact of corporate life and managements feel an obligation to help these otherwise loyal and experienced personnel relocate without career harm.

Executive Assets Corporation, 1 East Wacker Drive, Chicago, Illinois 60601, is one such firm that has an outstanding success record. In its first three years it placed every one of the 200 executives it had taken on, typically within three or four months and without a cut in pay.

Their only clients are corporations. They do not work *for* individuals but *with* them. They teach the executive how to market himself realistically. A campaign can be designed that opens up the possibility of changing fields, industries or even careers. Professional guidance is provided and telephone and secretarial support services are available.

President Gerald P. Hanlon, Jr., says, "Engaging the services of an outplacement firm as a final company benefit promotes goodwill between the corporation and the released executive. Maintaining a good relationship at this level is important to the company's general image and future contact with him. Most important, it demonstrates a human concern for the former employee by providing much needed counsel at a crucial time."

OUTPLACEMENT

At first, instead of simply "firing" unwanted executives and sending them on their way with the customary handshake, companies with a conscience turned to "dehiring" them. This was an attempt to "let them down easy" by offering to provide in-house counseling and other assistance to help them in their efforts to find comparable employment elsewhere.

While this was a move in the right direction, it was nothing more than a token gesture and actually did little to ease the pain suffered by long-service executives who suddenly found themselves stranded in the cold world of unemployment. Some companies felt they should do more. What developed was a process of "outplacement" whereby the companies spend time and money to engage outside specialists to become involved in helping their former executives relocate.

Corporations cooperate with their terminated executives because they recognize there are such things as no-fault terminations. In many instances, closing down a plant, discontinuing a product line, or reorganizing the staff, requires that capable individuals must be released because there are no other suitable growth potential positions where they can be absorbed. Terminations such as these are a fact of corporate life and managements feel a humanitarian obligation to assist these otherwise loyal and experienced personnel reestablish themselves without career harm.

The practice has since been expanded beyond executive, managerial, and professional personnel to include technical, sales, clerical, secretarial and white-collar workers and, in some cases, foremen and factory hands. Management personnel receive individual help while wage-earners are counseled in groups. These outplacement services are appreciated by workers on all levels as well as companies as the best aid for employees experiencing layoffs resulting from a recession and economic turndown.

Firms specializing in outplacement services have only corporations as clients. They do not work *for* individuals but *with* them. They teach them how to evaluate their qualifications and market themselves realistically. They offer advice on job hunting, interviewing, resume writing, and the like. A customized campaign can be designed that opens up the possibility of changing fields, industries, or even careers. Professional guidance is provided and office space, telephone convenience, and secretarial support are available. The companies foot the bill for outplacement services.

Besides being a matter of conscience, it is also a good image builder and improves community relations. Applicants and employees alike feel more secure about working in a company "with a heart" that does not merely abandon workers when adversity strikes. Nor is it altogether altruistic. When a laid-off worker finds a new job, unemployment compensation stops and this reduces the employer's tax costs.

As one such specialist explained, "Engaging the services of an outplacement firm as a final company benefit promotes goodwill between the corporation and the released employees. Maintaining a good relationship is important to the company's general image and to future contacts with the individuals. Most important, it demonstrates a human concern for the former employees by providing much needed counsel at a crucial time."

SAFE AT THE TOP?

In the corporate suite, the façade may be neat and proper, but a conspiracy might be hatching that could erupt and topple the chief executive. Since 1975, presidents of major corporations have been ousted at an increasing rate.

There are two strategies used by subordinates:

1. Kitchen debates: top executives discuss the chief executive's weaknesses and discreetly leak to the board of directors the words that he no longer has their respect, confidence and support.

2. Palace revolt: this is open opposition, sides are chosen, and the revolting side makes a demand upon the board, "He goes or we go."

In the 1960's, there was greater respect for authority and an unwritten law among boards that a revolt would not be recognized. Boards today are made up differently and do not subscribe to the old ethic.

They meet oftener, there are more working committees, they have faster and more reliable information. There is no way a mediocre chief can hide his mistakes.

Studies show that most deposed presidents were vulnerable on three issues of effective leadership:

1. One demonstrated weakness was a tendency to patronize disgrunted people.
2. Another weakness was a reluctance to fire those who opposed them.
3. A third weakness was getting the feeling they were invincible or at least indispensable.

Summed up, he got fired not for making a decision that hurt profits, but for mismanaging people.

EXIT INTERVIEWS

When an employee leaves, do we just shake hands and wish the terminating employee good luck? A more formal procedure is the exit interview.

The exit interview is the final step in the employment procedure. It provides an opportunity to probe the employee's attitude toward the company, to listen to comments that might pinpoint strengths and weaknesses in employee relations. The purpose is to:

1. Try to uncover the real story behind the termination.
2. Locate trouble spots that contribute to turnover.
3. Advise the terminating employee of rights—conversion of life insurance or medical insurance, pension vesting, and other benefits.
4. Distribute the Unemployment Compensation brochure as required by law.
5. Go over final paycheck and other settlement compensation (pay for unused vacation, separation pay, pay in lieu of notice, etc.)

213

PATTERNED EXIT INTERVIEW

Date _____

Employee's
Name _____ Clock No. _____ Dept. _____ Shift _____ Supervisor _____

Job _____ Length of Service _____ Selection Rating 1 2 3 4

Final Disposition: □ Quit   □ Discharged   □ Laid Off   □ On Leave   □ Salvaged

Interviewer's evaluation of real reason for termination _____

Rating for rehire: 1 2 3 4 Why? _____

I. INTERVIEW WITH SUPERVISOR

I understand _____ is leaving. Did he/she work directly for you? □ No, □ Yes; How long? _____
Does supervisor know him/her well?

What was his/her job? _____ What was final pay rate? _____
Does this check with records? Does this check?

What did you think of the quality of his/her work? _____
A careful worker? Thoroughly trained?

What about the quantity? _____
Industrious? Properly trained?

Has there been any change in performance recently? □ No, □ Yes; What? _____ Why? _____
Correctable? Temporary?

How did he/she get along with others? _____
Well adjusted socially? Given proper orientation?

What supervisory problems did you have with him/her? _____
Is he/she a trouble maker? How well has supervisor handled him/her?

Why is employee leaving? _____
Is this the real reason? Can termination be avoided?

Why right now? _____
What is the full story? Can termination be avoided?

Is he/she worth trying to salvage? □ Yes, □ No; Why? _____
Does this affect suitability for all jobs?

(If yes) Would you like him/her back on his/her old job? □ Yes, □ No; Why? _____
Is this consistent?

Do you know of any other jobs he/she can handle? □ Yes, □ No; Specify _____
What is the best job for employee?

What is his/her home life like? _____
How has it affected his/her work? Does supervisor know him/her as well as he/she should?

Has there been any change in his/her home life recently? □ No, □ Yes; Specify _____
Temporary? Correctable?

What are employee's strongest points? _____
How does this affect job suitability?

Where is employee weakest? _____
How does this affect job suitability?

Exit Interviewer _____

214

II. INTERVIEW WITH EMPLOYEE

I understand that you're leaving. Before you do, I'd like to find out a little bit about your experience with the company. Let's see now . . .

Do you have another job? ☐ Yes ☐ No (If "Yes") Where? _____ What is new rate? _____

How long have you worked here? _____
Reasonable time? Evidence of improper selection?

What kind of work have you been doing? _____

What other kinds of work have you ever done? _____
Are these related to work here? Helpful in salvage?

What kind of work do you like best? _____ Why? _____
Evidence of poor selection?

When you first started here who introduced you to the people you worked with? _____
Proper orientation?

How fully was your job explained to you? _____ By whom? _____
Proper training?

How did you like your supervisor? _____
Good supervision? Enough supervision?

How well did he/she seem to know his/her job? _____
Good supervision? Adequate training?

What about his/her handling of gripes or complaints? _____
Good supervision?

Did he/she have "pets" or play favorites? _____
Good supervision?

What troubles have you had with supervisor? _____
A trouble maker? Good supervision?

What was your final pay rate? _____ When was your last increase? _____
In line?   Understandable?

How do you feel about your pay? _____
Reasonable attitude?

How do you feel about your progress with the company? _____
Reasonable? Has he/she been overlooked?

If you could tell the president of the company exactly how you feel about the way the company is run, what would you tell him? _____

_____

What have you liked best about your job here? _____
Are policies made clear? Legitimate gripes?

What have you disliked about it? _____
Healthy attitude?

Why are you leaving? _____
Is this the real reason? Can termination be avoided?

Why right now? _____
What is the full story? Can termination be avoided?

(If salvage seems possible) If a more satisfactory arrangement can be worked out, would you be willing to stay? ☐ No, ☐ Yes; Specify changes

_____
Reasonable?

Exit Interviewer _____

Form No. EX-501

215

EXIT INTERVIEW

Narne _____ Date _____

Comments _____

_____

_____

_____

_____

_____

Address if changed _____

Group Insurance paid to date _____

Literature Distributed re:

_____ Group Insurance conversion

_____ Life Insurance

_____ Unemployment Compensation brochure

_____
Exit interviewer

6. Explain final pay adjustments for any outstanding cash advances, refunds due, and the like.
7. Clear up housekeeping chores, to turn in keys, credit cards, building passes, identification cards, etc.
8. Make a necessary record of the circumstances surrounding the termination to satisfy government regulations and union agreements.
9. To turn ill will into goodwill by furnishing referrals, if possible, and giving assurance of a fair response to any reference inquiries.
10. To part as friends and hope the employee will leave, if not as a booster at least not as a knocker.

The exit interview procedure is intended to ensure fairness to the worker as well as protection for the company. The same approach applies to both voluntary and involuntary terminations.

The exit interview is conducted in the personnel office toward the close of the employee's last day on the job. In those cases where the employee is not in the office on the last day (at another location, absent, or unreported and removed from the payroll) the best substitute is to have someone in the personnel office write a letter and offer to be of service.

One company's policy manual reads:

An exit interview, like any other interview, is a "conversation with a purpose." During the exit interview the employee will be permitted to speak freely about the reason for leaving. Any misunderstanding that might have contributed to the reason for leaving will be cleared up. Insofar as it is possible to do so, each employee who leaves will be sent away with the feeling of having been given a sympathetic, full, and unbiased hearing; an understanding, or at least a knowledge, of the company's position; and satisfactory information about rights and benefits for personal use.

The report of the exit interview should be in writing. Eventually it will be placed in the employee's file to become part of the permanent record. In the meantime it may be discussed with the supervisor. If quits and/or firings are unusually high, it would be well to summarize and analyze the reasons to determine whether any corrective action may be called for.

A high turnover rate may indicate that:

1. Supervisory training is needed.
2. Hiring patterns should be reexamined.
3. Pay rates may have fallen below the community average.

Some companies have a practice of conducting exit interview follow-ups. They send out questionnaires to former employees one month or so after they have left. Firms that use this procedure believe the mail questionnaire brings franker comments once the termination has lost its sting and the trauma connected with it is more or less forgotten. On the last day of work the employee may be emotional about leaving the job if happy, or reluctant to give the real reason if unhappy about being released.

The information, of course, while interesting, is not worth the effort it costs to get it unless appropriate action, when called for, is taken. Some jobs might have to be redesigned, supervisors better instructed, and training instituted.

Note the two sample exit interview forms on the previous pages. One is very simple, the other more involved.

REDUCE TURNOVER—INCREASE PROFITS

Of all the problems in personnel management the one pertaining to labor turnover is one of the most perplexing—and unanswerable. Many companies are concerned with turnover. They are searching for some answer, some guidance, but finding nothing that is really helpful.

Comparisons of turnover rates between companies prove nothing. Apparently there is no standard formula for figuring turnover rates. Hence, percentage comparisons are meaningless.

In an effort to disperse the fog, a search was made through dozens of management textbooks to see what the academic approach might be. This effort resulted in the remarkable discovery that many of the recognized texts on office management and personnel administration hardly mention the subject at all. Makes one wonder what practical ideas the newly-hatched technicians from the campus are bringing into the business world.

And yet, although few companies agree upon the nature of turnover, they all admit that it is costly and therefore worth worrying about.

One author referred to turnover as "Management's Blind Spot," an area, he said, where management could cut costs sharply but many companies do little about it.

The term "labor turnover" is an adaptation from the field of merchandising. It is defined as the gross movement of people into and out of active employment status. The index of this movement is the measurement of labor turnover, known as the turnover rate.

Measures Instability

Turnover is one of the readily measurable aspects of industrial instability. It is one of the best tests of the relative value of employee relations policies and practices within a company.

The three standard methods of computing turnover are based on accessions, replacements or separations.

In any computation the rate is generally defined as the number of accessions, replacements or terminations per month or year per 100 of the working force.

The working force is the average number on the payroll during the period for which the computation is made. In the above methods the terms are defined as follows:

Accessions are the hiring of new workers or the rehiring of former employees.

Replacements are persons hired to fill vacancies caused by terminations.

Separations include all quits, layoffs and discharges.

Besides these three standard methods there are various other computations that are sometimes made. They are mentioned here but not necessarily recommended.

The stable force rate is the proportion of all employees not absent more than two periods per year.

The labor flux rate is the ratio of total accessions and separations to the fulltime working force.

The continuance rate is the proportion of employees hired at a specified date who are still on hand at the end of a given and fairly extensive period of time.

The net labor turnover rate is the number of replacements per 100 workers in the average work force.

In most companies there exists what is known as the "refined rate." This merely slants the computation to a figure that is less embarrassing than the bold facts. It is the "true" rate watered down to a more favorable percentage.

The "Quit Rate" Formula

Here again no uniform deviations are used; the modifications vary from one company to another depending upon what each one wants to prove. Eliminated from consideration are such items as unavoidable separations, as caused by illness, death, military service, moving from the area, following husband (or wife) who transfers, and the like. Many

219

companies do not include part-time or temporary workers. Others deduct pregnancies and retirement.

In these cases a more reliable figure would be the Quit Rate. This ignores the above separations as well as the involuntary terminations. It considers only employees who quit, whom the company lost to competitors or to more fertile fields. Actually this is the only group over which management is usually concerned.

For most purposes a simple arithmetical computation is satisfactory, and tells the truest story. A simple method is subject to limitations, however, since it does not take into account seasonal or cyclical fluctuations.

One simple and straightforward method presents a very practical picture. The average number of employees during the month (or the number at the end of the month if the force is stable) is divided into the total number of separations during that month. This gives the turnover rate for the month.

This formula is expressed as follows:

$$\text{labor turnover rate} = \frac{\text{number of separations}}{\text{average number on payroll}} \times 100$$

The same average or end-of-month number of employees divided into the total number of separations for the past 12 months gives the annual turnover rate. Each month the current month's figures are used and the 13th-month figures dropped so that a moving average turnover rate results.

Plotted on a graph, the year's high and low figures are easily recognized and trends from one period to another can be charted.

In calculating the turnover rate certain facts need to be known. To arrive at the average work force the number of employees on the payroll at the beginning and end of the period must be established. All terminations, whether voluntary or involuntary, must be accounted for, as well as all accessions, both hires and rehires.

Transfers between departments and divisions should not be included in a company's turnover rate since these shifts do not represent separations from the company.

Turnover is a Barometer

Some of the factors affecting turnover are changes in wage rates, working hours, working conditions and inconsistencies in policies. One of the most important factors is supervision.

Turnover is a direct barometer of wage levels. When turnover is high, wages should be examined for they might have fallen to substandard level. High turnover is also a sign of serious other problems. It signals the need for more careful selection procedures and more extensive training programs.

Some turnover is inevitable. Some turnover is desirable, to bring in new blood and new ideas. A certain amount of turnover is not unhealthy—it prevents an organization from stagnating. But excessive turnover is expensive, too expensive to ignore.

The cost of turnover is measurable in dollars. Included are such items as acquisition costs (advertisements, agency fees, interviews, tests, etc.), medical examinations, training time (both formal and informal are costly), and perhaps severance pay for the employee who left. Anyone who estimates these expenses soon learns that they add up to sizable amounts.

But turnover costs are more than money. Employees who quit because of dissatisfaction are a permanent source of ill-will that frequently counter-balances expensive public relations programs and prejudices potential employees against the management.

To improve the turnover picture these recommendations are presented:

- Make the initial employment contact pleasant.
- Give honest recruiting information.
- Utilize turnover analysis to improve selection techniques.
- Establish realistic hiring rates.
- Indoctrinate new employees thoroughly.
- Follow through after they are on the jobs.
- Counsel regularly.
- Provide training to permit growth.
- Develop better supervision.
- Always keep improving personnel planning and policies.

A company's turnover experience has considerable immediate significance. It should be computed honestly and studied carefully. But computing the turnover rate, no matter how, is only preliminary to analyzing it.

Analysis Can Be Revealing

Analysis of turnover seeks to find out when, where and why turnover occurs, in terms of any classification that will help in explaining it.

221

Turnover can be analyzed by type of employee, sex, age, marital status, education level, or any other criteria that may be meaningful.

Generally, unskilled workers show higher rates than skilled workers. Older workers have lower turnover rates than younger employees. Long service employees run lower than new hires. The bulk of terminations are among new workers; one company with 13% of workers with less than one year of service had over 50% of turnover in this less-than-one-year group.

Observations such as these, when properly documented, can be very useful in influencing policy and in effecting cost reduction.

Few supervisors concern themselves with the high cost of labor turnover. They must be made cost conscious and extend their appreciation of cost reduction beyond waste, scrap and similar apparent extravagant practices to the less obvious labor cost which is a much bigger item.

Unfortunately top management is often as indifferent toward the cost of labor turnover as are the supervisors. This opportunity to cut costs does not receive proper emphasis on top management's priority list of problems. Consultants have discovered and pointed out that annual cost of turnover in some cases was more than the profit for the year.

Anything done to improve the turnover situation automatically enhances the profit picture.

It would be convenient if some standardized approach or formula could be agreed upon so that true comparisons between companies could be made. Until such uniformity is accomplished it is almost impossible to evaluate how serious the problem really is.

Nevertheless, studies of turnover are not without value. Regardless of how they are computed, they do call attention to the problem, they help to pinpoint the causes, and they definitely suggest where and how improvements can be effected.

WHY EMPLOYEES QUIT

Much has been written about the reasons employees quit. Many good speeches have been delivered on the same subject. Yet all over the country workers are quitting jobs at an increasing rate. Turnover percentages are going up.

Perhaps very little can actually be done to stem the tide. The restlessness among workers may be a product of the full employment era, especially in offices, in which it is easy for workers to transfer. Part of it may come from living in a mobile economy in which workers and families move about.

If little can be done to control turnover, at least something might be done to control the literature on this subject. Most of the articles and speeches come under the heading of "talking to ourselves."

The same can be said for the assortment of curatives that these articles and talks advocate. Some are discussed in great detail, and in a most convincing manner. But the sad fact is that very few, if any, have any effect on turnover.

The only article that would make sense would be one written by the terminating employees—not by their bosses. Many companies, recognizing that the stated reason is often not the real one, attempt self-correction through exit interview procedures. Some companies use follow-up questionnaires 30 to 90 days later in an attempt to learn whether a study of their former employees' new jobs or later explanations might reveal hidden, significant data. While these devices serve a useful purpose they are not entirely factual, nor are they really necessary.

The Real Reason

Most supervisors know why their workers leave. The reasons given are usually quite close to the truth. Such statements as "husband transferred," and "illness in family," and "going back to school," are correct. And supervisors generally are close enough to their people to get explanations like these which are understandable and acceptable.

The only way to cut down terminations such as these is not to hire vulnerable employees in the first place. A quick analysis of a company's turnover report will indicate the weak spots in the hiring process. But in today's tight labor market it is imperative that many such applicants be accepted.

But it is the employees who quit to try their luck elsewhere that should concern management. In these cases, supervisors also know the reasons their workers leave. But because they hate to face facts, especially when these facts reflect unfavorably on their own abilities and personalities, they hide behind any available procedure that produces a more plausible excuse.

The typist who reports that she is taking a job closer to home for more money is telling the straight story—but not the whole story. In her job hunt she would not even consider another position where transportation was worse or the take-home pay less—would she? But the reason she went out looking in the first place is the one that the supervisor tries to avoid.

The underlying cause of excessive terminations has been, is and always will be salary. A climbing turnover rate is a direct barometer of what workers think about their earnings opportunities. Nothing in any employee relations program should be depended upon to offset inadequate rates of pay.

Impersonality and Pressure

In most companies, however, salary structures are satisfactory or are quickly adjusted simply as a matter of survival. Yet terminations persist. Why?

There are many reasons, perhaps, but the chief ones are: (1) impersonality and (2) pressure.

Both of these factors are behind controllable terminations. Both of these factors are getting worse in the present conduct of business.

Whatever labor unrest exists today can be blamed directly on the boss. American business has neglected its most important asset—its employees—causing more disquietude and restlessness than ever before in the history of the country.

This blunt accusation may sound harsh at first, especially in view of the social development of employee relations programs. "Look what we're all doing for our people," is the stock answer—which is usually followed by throwing up the hands in desperation. The reason the problem is more serious than ever is simply that employees are finally able to react to unfairness and lack of job satisfaction by asserting themselves. They are no longer at the mercy of heartless or blundering managers (one is as bad as the other) and they express their displeasure quietly by taking matters into their own hands—and quitting.

Much of this is caused by poor communications, which often deprives a well-intentioned management of credit for having employees' best interests at heart. Downward communications are bad enough; upward communications just do not exist to any effective degree anywhere.

Some of the best advice managers receive with open notebooks but closed minds, is the following:

1. Acquire the confidence of people. Don't proceed on any program unless and until you can do so in a climate of mutual trust and respect. Otherwise your employees will be apprehensive, suspicious and defensive against management.
2. Try to gain understanding of the workers. This means relating your planning, your program and your progress with it individually, not collectively, since no two workers are alike. Different people have different fears and require different considerations.

3. Keep people properly informed. Misinformation you may not be guilty of; but you will be guilty of something worse —lack of information. Remember, in the absence of information from management, workers will have a tendency to furnish the missing link of information themselves, as they see it. And you may not be happy with the consequences.

Still the problem of terminations continues—and worsens. Why? Because managers cannot reverse their habits to coincide with an about-face in the employment situation.

Regain Leadership

There is no easy cure, least of all wages, which have never been so favorable. Impersonal means cannot be used to solve personal problems. Human understanding is necessary.

The president of a national corporation suggested some obvious steps toward a solution:

1. Speed up the flow of ideas from employees.
2. Scrap "company policy or practice" and listen to the workers.
3. Make personnel management a top job.
4. Give more thought to picking supervisors.

He added that "businessmen lost their leadership because they failed to lead."

For the first time in history, ours is no longer an employer market. Today it is an employee market. Procedures and attitudes that were developed out of the pattern of the past won't work in today's changed situation.

We know why employees quit. Changing a method or procedure won't help much. Trying to change our people is futile. Improvement will come only when we are willing to change ourselves which, after all, is the only element over which we have control.

HOW MANY REALLY ARE UNEMPLOYED?

Unemployment figures coming out of Washington can be misleading. Without a doubt this is the most significant single figure given common currency in the country. The White House watches it, both political parties seize upon it, business and labor leaders argue over it, and economists try to interpret it.

But what does it really tell us? Who is included and who is not? The Bureau of Labor Statistics has its own interpretations of what "being unemployed" means. The arbitrary standard is 30 days. Anyone who has not worked within a 30-day period is officially unemployed even if he has signed a contract to go to work.

A teacher on summer vacation waiting to start teaching at a new school is considered unemployed. A teacher on summer vacation who is not changing schools is considered employed.

A baby sitter who has not received a call is unemployed. The definition takes in teen-agers down to the age of 14, but only when the 14-year-old has held a job or says he is looking for a job. At any given time, it is likely that at least one million boys and girls, aged 14 and 15, may be included in the official Washington figure on unemployment. This, despite the child labor laws and the minimum wage laws which bar full-time work for these same youths.

As many as a million persons—teen-agers, housewives, older persons —switch in and out of the labor market, and the lists of unemployed and employed, at any time. They work as little as one hour a week.

The irony is that there are more jobs unfilled than there are people unemployed. The challenge then, for government and industry, is to make the unemployed employable. This is presently the number one domestic problem both from the standpoint of humanitarianism and of economics.

AUTOMATION

A cow is a completely automated milk manufacturing machine. It is encased in untanned leather and mounted on four vertical, movable supports, one on each corner. The front end of the machine, or input, contains the cutting and grinding mechanism, utilizing a unique feedback device. Here also are the headlights, air inlet and exhaust, a bumper and a foghorn. At the rear, the machine carries the milk-dispensing equipment as well as a built-in flexible fly swatter and insect repeller.

The central portion houses a hydrochemical conversion unit. Briefly, this consists of four fermentation and storage tanks connected in series by an intricate network of flexible plumbing. This part also contains the central heating plant complete with automatic temperature controls, pumping station and main ventilating system. The waste disposal apparatus is located to the rear of this central section.

Cows are available, fully assembled, in an assortment of sizes and colors. Production output ranges from two to 20 tons of milk per year. In brief, the main externally visible features of the cow are: two lookers, two hookers, four stander-uppers, four hanger-downers and a swishy-wishy.

There is a similar machine known as the bull. It gives no milk but has other interesting uses.*

AUTOMATION AND TECHNOLOGICAL UNEMPLOYMENT

What is this thing called "Automation"?

Automation emerged as one of the magic words of the 1960's. It has taken on the coloration of glamour—and at times has been wrapped in the austere cloak of fear.

It is a word sometimes used to invoke visions of massive production systems wherein tireless and ingenious machinery takes over man's age-old burden of work, requiring only the most casual attention from a carefree human race given over to full-time leisure.

It is a word sometimes used to raise specters of a frustrated and idle population denied gainful employment, rendered obsolete and perhaps even hungry by robot machinery. It is feared as causing technological unemployment.

Neither of these extremes is remotely realistic. But the conflicting pictures reflect very real and contrary feelings about automation: as both good and evil, as both friend of man and foe. Some of the split vision stems from confusion about what automation is.

When the term was coined early in the 1950's, it had a very limited and specific application to one developing aspect of technology which promised easier and better means to get certain parts of man's work done. Engineers still prefer to use the word "automation" in this rather precise sense: the substitution of control devices (mechanical, hydraulic, pneumatic or electronic) for human organs of observation, decision and control. As such, these devices are the most recent and powerful extension of the industrial revolution which increased man's welfare by substituting powerful machines and energy sources for the very limited muscle power of man and animal.

The word is newer than the fact. Automated devices are neither recent nor revolutionary, as is demonstrated throughout industry. Nonetheless, these control devices and techniques have been so greatly improved in the past 10 or 20 years, and their use has spread so rapidly, that the glitter attached to the word, "automation," is well deserved.

This glamorous façade, however, has encouraged the loose employment of the term to describe or refer to developing technology in

---

*From a speech by the author which was titled, "We Can Always Invent a Better Milking Machine but We Will Still Need the Cow."

general. Indeed, postwar technological advances on the farm, in the factory and in the office have been so breathtaking that some new and striking word seemed necessary to define the age. "Automation" has been seized and used for this purpose even though a great part of recent technology makes no use, or very little use, of automation as the engineer thinks of it.

During this period of stunning technological advance society has also experienced some disappointments. In the United States, a principal frustration has been the failure of a booming economy to provide jobs for all members of its work force. Because one of the functions of technology is to get more work done with less human effort, there has been an unfortunate and inaccurate tendency to charge "automation" with the blame for continued pockets of recalcitrant unemployment.

Managing the Change

Automation has become a dynamic force in our changing economy. It is a phase of the technological progress that has made America great. The pace of our technological improvement has gradually quickened, rising in a geometric progression with each new development. Automation is the latest and the most dramatic example of this rising pace of advancement.

Automation may be defined as a means to a new level of productivity and a new era of industrial progress. It is a way of doing things faster, better and easier than before, and, in many cases of accomplishing tasks that previously could not be done at all.

Of all the factors that will determine the speed and direction of automation, the most important is its effect upon people. The installation of automation machines or electronic equipment will have a greater impact upon workers than it will upon methods.

The fantastic predictions of push-button factories and offices have in general been psychologically harmful to the attitudinal development of workers. This results in a blind fear of automation, the fear of unemployment, which persists in many circles. The fear is unfounded, of course, and in time the success of automation will dispel this fear.

The facts are already on our side. Machine-made unemployment as a consequence of labor-saving equipment in the office is a misconception. Surveys show that in 1940 some five million people in this country were employed in clerical work. Today the figure is more than double. All the while the use of office machines became more widespread. The long history of the arithmetic machine, from abacus to adding machine, cash register, calculator and punched cards, shows very clearly that the faster the machine process, the more jobs were created for the men and women who operate the machines.

Actually, automation should not cause any unemployment. What it may cause is some personnel displacements. There is no natural law which will routinely adjust the employment market to automation changes. This means confusion in the minds of businessmen and doubt in the minds of workers. In the long run this problem, following the pattern of history, should resolve itself. Society will gradually adjust to it. However, it is difficult to paint the broad picture, depicting a new abundance, to the individual who does not understand automation and who sees it only as a threat to his job security.

Handling this change skillfully and in everybody's best interest will require managerial ability of the highest order.

Better Jobs Ahead

Increased emphasis on automation in the meticulous advance planning for all company operations will be necessary to solve the two most pressing problems facing office executives today. Automation can slow the increasing pressure for office workers and it can increase per capita productivity.

Automation may someday be the only way of getting certain work done. Even now no one is left who "wants" to do the back-breaking labor jobs in factories. In 1850 muscle power performed 65% of all work; in 1950 only 1½%. It will become increasingly difficult to hire people to do routine and tedious work in offices, too. They will be demanding more challenging duties, which are more satisfying.

Machine development will be the emancipation of many workers from drudgery. This has already happened in the factory and is now taking place in the office as routinized jobs are transferred to automatic and electronic machines.

Manufacturing will lean more heavily upon automatic machinery to eliminate dull, monotonous, low-paid jobs. Repetitive office work, when in sufficient quantity as in department stores, insurance companies and utilities, will rely upon automation principles to get the work done.

Compared with the factory, the productivity of office workers is below par. At the present time there is n one phase of industrial activity that has more expendable fat than office systems and procedures.

The increase in the number of office workers in relation to the number of plant workers reflects a steady increase in the efficiency of plants. The development of automation has contributed to the narrowing of plant-office worker ratios.

The thing to do now is apply to the office the industrial engineering techniques and devices that have worked toward improving the efficiency of plants. The modern office can be the nerve center of cost control and operating efficiency it should be only if the office executive is alert to the new dimensions in his field—such as automation and electronics.

Automation in the office should not be greeted with skepticism, fear, apprehension or misgivings. It should be welcomed. For it is our best hope of providing the answer to many of the problems that are coming up, not the least of which is the need for increasing individual productivity.

The New Mix of Jobs

Machine development is not eliminating jobs; it is changing jobs. The automobile did not replace the horse and buggy; it replaced staying at home. The new family circle is the steering-wheel and this development opened up an entirely new industry.

As farming moves toward scientific and away from primitive methods, the result is more production per acre and more production per available man. One man today can do the jobs of a dozen and do them faster and better. We all know that people are migrating away from farm work. Thank goodness technology and machine development are coming to the rescue!

The telephone company moved into the early lead of the automation parade with the introduction of the dial system. This change did not cut employment of telephone operators. It made possible an increase in the value, efficiency and attractiveness of the service, which in turn brought on the great expansion in installation and use of phones. If we were still using manual telephones there would soon not be enough women 24 to 60 to be operators.

What's happening, you see, is that jobs are changing as our way of life changes. Domestic help is no longer available, but the housewife doesn't need a maid. In her completely modern kitchen and laundry what she needs is a mechanic.

Our big bakeries are run without bakers: in up-to-date plants bread is baked by machinists. And so it is also in our offices. Much of our accounting, billing and payroll work is done by technicians, many of whom don't have to know debits from credits.

Yes, the complexion of our workforce is changing. And automation is making it possible for industry to adjust to the changing satisfactions demanded by our workers.

Office Applications are Different

In applying automation principles to office operations there are many things to consider. All of the problems of automation are there. All of the benefits of automation are also possible. The application of principles may be the same, but these must be adapted specifically to office procedures and office needs.

In the factory the raw materials are usually the same in each type of operation. In the office the raw material fed into equipment is also of one kind—information. But the information is of a great variety of types and the end product is almost as varied, with as many different end products as there are varieties of incoming information.

The office is like a sorting device in which a mass of incoming material is sorted into various combinations at various stages in different processing lines. The raw information finally emerges from the various processing lines in the form of separate end products.

Since the design of a system to accomplish this is far more difficult than the design of a work flow system in a factory, the achievement of automation in the office must be built from the ground up. Throughout all stages, systems revision must be performed. The manual methods won't adapt themselves to most machine requirements.

In considering automation for the office, the areas to be studied are three:

1. Where production or clerical operation costs are high.
2. Where manual and interrupted operations predominate.
3. Where speed of reporting is inadequate for management needs.

The objectives of such study are three:

1. Lower costs.
2. Faster reporting.
3. Additional information.

Automation should not be thought of primarily as a labor-saving technique. One of the main functions of automation in practice has been to take the guesses out of top-level decisions by giving managers more complete answers soon enough to be of use.

Nor should the installation decision be based solely on direct dollar savings. Frequently office automation installations do not reduce total office costs. Progressive companies are content with improvements that are hard to evaluate in dollars and cents. These improvements may be:

1. More information.
2. Faster information.
3. More accurate information.

In the office the various business systems and machines have permitted a limited amount of automation in processing clerical data. The utilization of automatic machinery and electronic computer systems will unquestionably permit a very high degree of automation in the office, but more important still will permit the development of planning and control information of a kind never before possible.

Progress is Slow

This will be slow and gradual. A large number of individual operations, such as payroll, billing, stock control, etc., have been programmed and are now processed by various computers. However, not one company has yet turned over all of its major clerical functions to an electronic computer system.

When this happens, functional areas such as payroll, accounts payable, etc., will probably cease to exist as such, since a co-ordinated and consolidated system of processing data in one transaction will take place. It can be realized that piecemeal operations such as customers' orders, invoicing, stock control, production planning and all other related activities, will have to be integrated to make effective use of machines having the capacity to utilize the source document for simultaneous processing of subsequent requirements. Traditional line divisions will have to bend as total office operations become more functional.

The need for unskilled clerical workers will greatly decrease. However, there will be a demand for skilled people who will not be available unless this difficulty is overcome by individual companies through well-planned employee training programs. This is by far the most important undertaking and the greatest challenge to office management today. In fact, a planned program of employee education is a prerequisite to a change of this magnitude.

The problem of introducing automation principles to office operations can be simplified if management will remember three rules:

1. Acquire the confidence of people. Don't proceed on any program unless and until you can do so in a climate of mutual trust and respect. Otherwise your employees will be apprehensive, suspicious and defensive against management.
2. Try to gain understanding of the workers. This means relating your planning, your program and your progress with it individually, not collectively, since no two workers are alike. Different people have different fears and require different considerations.
3. Keep people properly informed. Misinformation you may not be guilty of; but you will be guilty of something worse

—lack of information. Remember, in the absence of information from management workers will have a tendency to furnish the missing link of information themselves, as they see it. And you may not be happy with the consequence.

The new management era will emphasize sympathetic understanding, sincerity and consideration of the human element in our businesses.

Summary

The forward march of automation will invigorate, not threaten, our economy. It will do for the businessman what the power-driven saw did for the carpenter.

It will take the work out of work. It will relieve workers, not replace them.

Automation will:

1. Result in more production at a time when increases in population are demanding more.
2. Upgrade workers who no longer are satisfied with menial tasks but are educated and trained for more challenging assignments.
3. Contribute to a higher standard of living for a nation that is looked upon as the example for al the rest of the world.
4. Lead to a reduction in hours of work for people who are rapidly learning to appreciate and utilize spare time.

Yes, automation is ready. The question is, "Are we?"

HUMAN OBSOLESCENCE

The growing use of robots in manufacturing will, like every other technological advancement in industry, have a profound impact on jobs. As these improvements are implemented, workers will be the leftover casualties.

Does society have an obligation to people who through no fault of their own suddenly face the prospect of technological unemployment? The federal government may have to take a more active role, not in expanding the dole, which is degrading and demeaning because it does not get to the root of the problem, but in supporting a variety of retraining programs. The unions can hardly be counted upon for assistance and understanding for they have demonstrated no leadership in grasping the opportunity of cooperating with corporate retraining efforts.

What is the company's responsibility to employees who are the victims of management's need to improve operations? Employees whose skills become technologically obsolete can not, in good conscience, be discarded the way unproductive systems are cast aside or the way outdated machines are relegated to the scrap heap.

What happens when an employee who has a good attendance record, a history of good performance, and a constructive attitude toward the company, finds that the job has disappeared? In most cases, the employee is reassigned to another job at a comparable level. With mutual understanding and appropriate guidance, the average employee makes an adjustment that turns out well for both the company and the employee.

In a few instances, unfortunately, the employee does not respond well to the switch to some other available job, cannot grasp the new duties, and does not perform satisfactorily compared with co-workers already established there. The employee simply cannot take advantage of the company's good intentions.

In such a case, rather than releasing the employee, every effort ought to be made to place that employee in a job of lesser skill and responsibility. In deference to years of loyal service and previous contribution, it is to be hoped that a reduction in wages can be avoided. The objective should be to relocate the employee in a job that is within reason. Before implementing the decision, each case should be reviewed to make sure the employee has received adequate training, proper counseling, and an opportunity to make good.

When it is decided that this is the appropriate step, it should be made clear to the employee the move is deserved because the company recognizes the employee's past record. In the judgment of the company, moving the employee into a job that can be handled is best for the employee who will thus remain on the payroll and continue to accrue employment benefits. At the very least, the employee should be given the choice of accepting or rejecting the company's offer.

Physical Impairments

But technological advancements, which dislodge faithful employees from their comfortable jobs, are not the only causes contributing to human obsolescence. Even when the jobs do not change, when new methods or equipment are not introduced, the problem could arise. Why? Because people can change.

In addition to growing older, which in itself might make it very hard for an otherwise good worker to continue to "keep up," there are many health problems that could befall a worker and make it difficult, or even impossible, for the worker to perform up to standard.

Most companies cover the employee's absence from work because of illness with comprehensive health insurance plans, which certainly eases the financial strain. They also have sick leave policies to protect the job for the worker and guarantee a continuation of employment benefits. This is all well and good for the employees who recover fully, return to their former jobs, and pick up where they previously left off.

But what about the men and women who suffer some form of temporary or permanent setback and do not recover fully? There are some who become totally and permanently disabled; this is defined simply as "no longer able to perform previous duties." Here again, most companies today have Disability Insurance which pays the disabled worker a monthly income for life under a formula based on earnings and years of service.

The majority of disabled workers, however, eventually do return to their jobs because of the necessity to support themselves in the style to which they have become accustomed. They are neither permanently disabled nor permanently recovered. Their illness has taken a toll, and while they may feel obligated or entitled to return to their former line of work, this decision might not be the best choice in the long run for either the employer or the employee.

Included in this category are the cases of illnesses, chronic diseases, surgical operations, strokes, heart attacks, and the like from which the patients recover but not without some degree of impairment. Many of these employees are unable to again perform their assigned duties at their earlier pace.

When a valuable worker becomes incapacitated, it is tough for an employer to avoid doing the wrong thing. The manager usually tries to be understanding and helpful but must be careful not to make decisions for the disabled worker. Instead, offer options to choose from. The worker should retain responsibility.

When it is determined that the disabled worker can no longer perform the job (a salesperson driving a car, or a lathe operator running a machine, etc.), it may be necessary to take firm action. The boss can not tell what a worker can do; decisions can only be made on what a worker "cannot do" when impaired.

A good way to handle the situation is to explain what skills are required in the job. This approach focuses the decision on the work instead of on the worker. The worst thing is to ignore the problem by pretending it doesn't exist.

ANTIDISCRIMINATION

As with so many other words in the English language, "discrimination" has two different meanings.

The original definition of discrimination is "the ability to distinguish differences." It means discernment, using good judgment in making distinctions. The ability to recognize differences assumes that differences exist.

Within the past twenty years, however, the word has taken on an opposite meaning and gone from a positive connotation to a negative one. An entire generation has grown up equating discrimination with racism. People in many walks of life, and particularly in government, are proclaiming that discrimination is bad and should be done away with.

The assumption that differences exist, as the original dictionary definition implies, is unsettling for a social movement obsessed with the notion of equality. But the contemporary interpretation of equality is based not on equality of opportunity as much as on equality of treatment. It tries to be a leveler with a uniform distribution of rights. The result of this development reverses the meaning of discrimination from a virtue, that is, distinguishing among qualities that are unlike, to a vice, that is, legislating to a condition of sameness for groups of diverse peoples who never asked for anything more than fairness.

Many people believe all men and women are descended from one couple. That would make us all brothers and sisters. Yet in life and in the business world we are not guided by a philosophy of brotherly love. In our culture we tend to discriminate *against* each other.

Nobody really wants to see a fellow human being discriminated against. But since this unfair circumstance, and the problems it generates, cannot be solved morally or spiritually, we have mandated the duty to the government. The government bureaucrats, defining the word "govern" to mean "to rule," apply their normal reaction and that is to set rules and try to solve the problem using a legal approach. Somehow, passing a law is supposed to settle everything.

But instead of uniting all men and women into one humankind, the government action divides people into categories. Now instead of being members of the same human race, people are members of arbitrary classifications depending upon such factors as skin pigmentation, facial structure, modes of dress, or alien speech.

The racial/ethnic grouping of citizens and workers provides convenient targeting for government programs. This also offers a simple method of tallying for endless reports, statistics, and quotas, and sets up an indisputable mathematical formula for meting out punitive responses for noncompliance with administrative edicts.

This numbers game might well be the best approach available, but its divisiveness could turn out to be the wrong way to achieve a harmonious unification because the mechanics of categorization can never be perfect. Simply pigeonholing people into convenient slots for record-keeping and reports cannot be 100% accurate. For example, an employee by the name of Jose has just moved in from Brazil. His native language is Portuguese. His skin color is light tan. How is he classified —white, black, caucasian, Latino, Iberian, Hispanic, or what?

A language professor cited the "insulting absurdity" of these mandatory classifications. He says, "Latins can be white. In Italy, there are no blacks; all Italians are white, and all are Latin. In France, some Latins are white and some are black (originating in the French colonies). In Argentina, there are no blacks and all Latins are white. In Cuba, some Latins are black (20%), some Mulattoes (35%), and the rest are white. It is an insult for a Latin or Hispanic to be called nonwhite, if he or she is white. A white Hispanic from Argentina or Spain is as caucasian as a white from England or Germany."

Bureaucratic instructions simply suggest that a student or a worker should be included in the group to which he or she appears to belong, identifies with, or is regarded by the community as belonging to. Hence, the designations are arrived at by opinion and judgment, not determined by statute.

The legalistic approach used by government is fraught with misgivings. There is not a man, woman, or child in America today who cannot identify with one or more minority groups, and for all of these groups to look to government for assistance is ludicrous. As it is, there is presently on the books protective legislation covering every worker except white males, and even they are included if they are under age 18 or between the ages of 40 and 65, veterans, or handicapped.

Government intervention is designed to keep past injustices from being perpetuated, and progress to date is testimony that this involvement is both useful and necessary. Yet it is not enough to solve the inherent problems of prejudice. Prejudice has been explained as "weighing all the facts with your thumb on the scale." Prejudice, which government wants to extirpate, is locked up in the hearts of people, where no law can penetrate.

The only permanent solution will come when we recognize that men and women are not biological accidents but are blood-bought souls, divinely created. Useless discrimination against one another, which poisons every aspect of the good life, will be eradicated not by continued policies of separatism but only by universal togetherness. God does not judge people until they are dead; who are we to judge our fellow human beings while they are yet alive!

ANTI-DISCRIMINATION LAWS

Discrimination in employment is legally obsolete. State and federal laws prohibit discrimination against job applicants or employees because of:

1. race
2. color
3. religion
4. national origin
5. sex
6. age

These laws prohibit discriminatory practices in:

1. hiring
2. discharging
3. promotion
4. layoff
5. pay

These policies extend to:

1. recruitment
2. selection
3. referral
4. training

Noble in concept, anti-discrimination laws, as they apply to personnel practices, have clearly been among the most visible and hard-to-comply-with regulations that companies must contend with.

Knotty problems of fairness have been raised, penalties can be severe, and there is a plethora of regulatory agencies overseeing these various laws.

AFFIRMATIVE ACTION

Title VII of the 1964 Civil Rights Act requires employers to *refrain* from discriminating. But Executive Orders, issued by the President to employers having contracts for government work, go a step further. They impose *positive* obligations. They require that companies take *affirmative action,* to better the score for neglected minority groups. This is defined in many ways, but it means, simply, doing whatever is necessary to provide additional job opportunities to those people who have not been given these opportunities before.

More precisely, it means doing everything necessary to move the company steadily toward the accomplishment of having minority group members and women represented throughout the organization at all levels.

For all practical purposes this means opening wide all doors leading to positions historically reserved for white males. All traditional and prejudicial barriers are down forever.

Affirmative action is not to be construed as a numbers game. Affirmative action is not a euphemism for quotas. Affirmative action obliges a company to set goals and timetables for the hiring and promoting of minority or female employees when an analysis of the company's workforce indicates an unjustified absence or underemployment of such individuals.

Affirmative action in concept, although sometimes not in practice, in no way requires the hiring or promoting of a minority member or female over a more qualified applicant who is nonminority or male. That would constitute a quota system which was never intended.

In setting up an affirmative action program, measurable progress is expected in:

1. Percentages: corresponding more closely to the community.
2. Balance: uniform distribution throughout the organization; not conveniently absorbed in traditional jobs.
3. Levels: dispersed upward as well as horizontally; not concentrated in menial jobs.

A company's total work force is expected to reflect as much as possible the same percentages of minorities as found in the population of the area it serves.

Compliance reviews or on-site inspections are results-oriented. The inspectors are not interested in words (grandiose policy statements), or devices (meetings and pep talks), or changed programs (organization restructuring) except as these produce results.

When companies are found to be out of compliance, they run the risk of losing their government contracts, or suffer harassment from feminist or civil rights groups. Violations often result in back pay and wage settlements.

Government bureaucrats make the affirmative action programs merely functional; to meet legal requirements. Civil rights activists strive to develop programs with a strong sense of social responsibilities; to meet moral obligations.

It's Results That Count

The most important way to measure the effectiveness of an affirmative action program is by results. Extensive efforts to develop procedures, analyses, data collection systems, report forms, and fine written policy statements are meaningless unless the end product will be measurable, yearly improvement in hiring, training, and promotion of minorities and females in all parts of the organization.

Just as the success of a company program to increase sales is judged in terms of the actual increases it produces, the only realistic basis for evaluating a program to increase opportunity for minorities and females is its actual impact upon these persons.

The essence of an affirmative action program, after all is said and done, should be:

1. Establish a strong company policy and commitment.
2. Assign responsibility and authority to a top company official.
3. Analyze present work force to identify jobs, departments and units where minorities and females are underutilized.
4. Set specific, measurable, attainable hiring and promotion goals, with target dates, in each area of underutilization.
5. Make every manager and supervisor responsible and accountable for helping to meet these goals.
6. Review job descriptions and hiring criteria to assure that they reflect actual job needs.
7. Revise employment procedures to assure they do not inadvertently have a discriminatory effect.
8. Find minorities and females who qualify or can become qualified for jobs previously inaccessible to them.
9. Focus on getting minorities and females into promotion pipelines with relevant training as support.
10. Develop systems to monitor and measure progress regularly, and make necessary adjustments if results are not satisfactory to meet goals.

Generally speaking, the obligation of an affirmative action program is accepted by industry as a cost and responsibility of operating a business in the modern environment of social reform. If there is any problem it is in mechanics more than in intent.

Reverse Discrimination

The affirmative action programs are forced upon business not by the law itself but by its interpretation by agencies enforcing the law. Quota integration is imposed not by legislation, not by court, not by vote, but by administrative fiat. To many people, this type of imposition bespeaks of dictatorship.

A challenge to the resilience of the U.S. Constitution comes with the accusation of reverse discrimination. This is the charge that affirmative action programs lean over backwards to right earlier wrongs.

Affirmative action programs have led to policies favoring candidates "from economically and educationally deprived backgrounds." The rationale is that for historical reasons these disadvantaged people deserve a better-than-even chance to catch up. There is a benign interest, an effort to ameliorate inequities of the past.

Noble as this attitude may be, non-minority applicants and employees often find themselves at a disadvantage when open or covert quotas take precedence over academic and personal qualifications. They argue that a policy, to be fair, should be applied equally and not give benefits or privileges to one group at the expense of other groups. Their appeal is that preferential treatment practiced by industry, government, and universities violates the 14th Amendment provision of equal protection for all under the law.

The courts will be hearing cases until the constitutionality issue is settled. Decades of progress in the cause of antidiscrimination is at stake.

No company can assume that its past policies and practices, no matter how effective they have been, will be sufficient to meet demands made upon them in the future. More than mechanics will change. Companies, like other institutions, will have to change many of their attitudes towards people in order to fulfill their role in this area of social revolution. Managements must become sensitive to the strain, stress, and even turmoil that will surely follow as personal prejudices, no matter how subdued, meet head-on with the practical realities of this movement.

What's Right in Civil Rights?

The Civil Rights Act of 1964 expressed the commitment to set right through legal means the social and moral injustices against black citizens. The mandate was to end denials to rights and aspirations.

To federal agencies, equal opportunity in employment means retribution based on raw statistical analysis. They ask redress by fixing quotas. The intent of the law was never that. It hoped for better industrial relations techniques to ensure fairer results, unfettered by bias, in hiring, promotion, and work assignments.

Chief Justice Warren E. Burger has said, "The Act does not command that any person be hired simply because he was formerly the subject of discrimination or because he is a member of a minority group."

Confusion, animosity, and litigation have resulted from giving the status of law to the interpretative opinions of federal officials. These opinions are presented as administrative fiat and enforcers expect blind obedience. In some cases the institutionalized conflicts that develop interfere with establishing the intended equality.

It would seem that the courts and the media would be serving a better purpose if they were to emphasize less the violations of rules resulting in implied guilt and concentrate instead on the noteworthy progress made in all sincerity by the vast majority of companies and managements who are trying—and succeeding—in willingly obeying the law of the land.

SEX EQUALITY

Business, some jokester once said, was invented by men to get away from women. Now women, aided by government, are asking men to accept them as business equals, and they are rapidly and deservedly approaching that status.

What has transpired during the transitionary period, known as the industrial revolution, tells the story. Let's summarize this progress briefly.

The industrial society as it is known today is hardly more than one century old. But industrial history goes back much further. It is divided into four eras.

1. The first was "domestic" production. This was production by members of one household, from raw materials furnished largely by the household itself.

2. This was followed by "handicraft" production in which the worker made a custom-built item which was sold locally by himself or exchanged for a different handicraft product of another worker.

3. With the development of capital and transportation the "cottage" period of production came into existence. Much of the work was done in cottages just outside the town. Handicraft workers still owned the tools of production, but the contact with consumers of their products was made for them by merchants. This practice still continues in many parts of the world and in some sections of the United States.

4. The "factory" system, wherein factory workers were brought together to perform their duties under one roof, had its start in England about the time of the American Revolution.

The Industrial Revolution had begun.

In all of this two factors stand out. First, work which was initially done in the home was gradually moved out. Second, production work was a man's responsibility.

Women Move In

Ever since they won the battle for suffrage, women have moved steadily forward into territory formerly considered sacred in man's domain. It was inevitable that women should invade the business world, which man had originally designed for himself.

There were many reasons, not the least of which was the shortage of trainable workers, especially during wartime. In World War II the nation's greatest manpower reserve was women. In the factory Rosie the Riveter did more than fill in for a man in uniform; she proved to be a crusader for her sex. Women's wartime contributions to industry helped push back the limitations and dispelled some of the prejudices. It is sad to reflect, but in any particular taboo it takes a stress to crack it.

In the office the introduction of the typewriter opened wide the door of opportunity. Over the past several decades, women have been successful in all types and levels of office work. In the process, women have also revolutionized the office. The contribution of women to offices has been more than chintz curtains and flowers. Many of the improvements which men take for granted are a direct result of the influence of increasing numbers of women into the workforce. Such things as rest periods, coffee breaks, modern work environment, fancy drapes, pastel wall colors, are the result of the woman's touch—which men enjoy as much as women.

Once women workers found their way into business and industry they signified their intention of not wanting to relinquish their gains. But not content to play passive roles, nor willing to stay within bounds on jobs which were ideally meant for them, they set out to acquire job equality. Instead of remaining satisfied with work as secretaries, nurses, hairdressers, manicurists, waitresses or teachers, women began spreading their talents all over the industrial map. The fact is that while shortages exist in the areas of work formerly performed by women, any number of women are sacrificing and struggling to gain recognition in occupations heretofore dominated by men. They are attempting, with measurable success, jobs as switchmen, brakemen, dockwallopers, stationary engineers, meat cutters, oilers and greasers, taxicab and bus drivers.

Fundamentally, the basic interests of most women are still centered in the home. Yet business has much to contribute to a woman's life. With its many uncertainties, life cannot always be directed as women would want it to be. In a changing social philosophy, business is also becoming a part of the personal life of many women. Gradually women are being attracted to a business career, either as a primary source of income or as supplementary earnings—in either case for a higher level of living. Besides the monetary incentive, many women, eager to exchange the monotony of domestic and personal service for more interesting vocations, are responding to the change of pace of office or factory employment.

Nondiscrimination Is Not Equality

Women workers have proved their point. They are here to stay, and men welcome their presence in the labor force. The question is: do men openly welcome sex equality?

This is where the complications come in. Many men are not ready to move over and let women share their lofty perch. Women, in the majority of cases, are not asking this. Besides, there is psychological resistance to women's getting complete economic equalization; despite legislation the progress does not match the plight of women in business. The prejudice against women in positions of authority appears to be even more deeply rooted in our culture than the concept of white supremacy.

But we have a law—Title VII of the Civil Rights Act—which says everything is equal between the sexes. But passing a law does not establish instant equality, anymore than passing a law against rheumatism would eliminate that scourge. Prejudice lies in the heart, which no law reaches.

Maybe women don't need legal protection against exploitation. Women lawyers, physicians and proprietors needed no law to help them in their ambitions. The tired argument that women's health would suffer if work hours were too long, is a laugh to the average housewife.

The egalitarian Equal Employment Opportunity Commission has a difficult, almost impossible, assignment. At best, all the EEOC can do is look after the legal rights of women. But in the long run, what is morally right, emotionally satisfying, psychologically proper, financially rewarding and socially acceptable may be of far greater significance.

As we said at the outset, the truth is that women are really competing in what has been, up to now, a man's world. Right or wrong, the simple fact is that man was there first.

Equality is Coming

Man for the field and woman for the hearth
Man for the sword and for the needle she
Man with the head and woman with the heart
Man to command and woman to obey
All else confusion.

—Tennyson

In the last 50 years, women in increasing numbers have left the hearth and needle, and confusion was the inevitable result as rearranged family relationships, business roles and social legislation made obsolete the above dogma.

In our Judeo-Christian heritage nobody, male or female, really objects to the principle of fairness and equality for everybody regardless of sex. Getting acceptance of the concept is not the issue; the problem is putting it into practice. With government solidly behind them, and rearranged social values endorsing them, women will in time push back the traditional barriers and move step by step closer to a realization of sex equality.

SEXUAL HARASSMENT

In the days before protective legislation it was popular to say, "Heaven help the working girl." Now the government has taken over that responsibility.

Sexual harassment by supervisors and fellow employees worries companies. Some firms may still wish to dismiss it as a nonissue. "You'll always have some boy propositioning a girl in one way or another," says one company president.

Many managements realize the possibilities for trouble exist and they are becoming concerned about the legal and psychological problems harassment can generate. "It's obvious that some people use their position to demand such things, and to think it doesn't happen is naive," says an airline executive.

Some nationwide corporations are adopting formal policies to deal with the problem. Revlon some years ago warned that harassers would be summarily fired. Dayton Power & Light dismissed an employee who made off-color remarks to female co-workers.

The difficulty is in defining harassment which may mean different things to different people in different circumstances. Governor James Thompson of Illinois defined it as "unsolicited, deliberate, or repeated sexually explicit derogatory statements, gestures, or physical contacts which are objectionable to the recipient or which cause discomfort or humiliation."

Following complaints, he ordered state agency heads to take steps to eliminate sexual harassment within their areas. "Sexual harassment undermines the integrity of the workplace and results in deleterious employment consequences to the victims," he said. The director of the Department of Human Rights set up training for department heads and they, in turn, were charged with disseminating information to employees.

As expected, it didn't take long for the federal government to get into the act. The Equal Employment Opportunity Commission has published new regulations concerning sexual harassment. Protection is guaranteed under Section 703 of the Civil Rights Act of 1964 and the EEOC has the muscle to back it up.

These guidelines define sexual harassment as unwelcome sexual advances or requests for sexual favors when:

1. Submission is even implied to be a job requirement.
2. Job decisions are based on submission or refusal.
3. The harassment interferes with job performance or creates "an intimidating, hostile, or offensive working environment."

Furthermore, it is now legally up to the employer to establish an environment where such harassment doesn't occur—by openly expressing strong disapproval, by sensitizing all concerned, by developing appropriate sanctions, and by telling employees how to complain under Title VII.

The Equal Employment Opportunity Commission is now playing office chaperone.

TWO-CAREER FAMILIES

With over half the married women working at jobs outside the home, there are many two-income families. In most of these cases, one spouse is the primary wage-earner and the other works for supplemental income, although there also are other reasons.

The *two-income family* has been around quite a while. What is becoming a phenomenon, and a growing one, is the *two-career family.* This is something entirely different. It creates a whole new set of conditions.

The difference is that the second wage-earner is not simply in a job but in a career. A career is defined as "any lifelong work characterized by strong commitment, personal growth, and increasing levels of responsibilities."

The two-career family has, necessarily, rearranged the traditional family roles, ingrained over generations in society and held to be untouchable by large segments of the population. The problems for two-career families are:

1. Allocation of time: the jobs always seem to come first.
2. Financial issues: double income but more than double bills.
3. Poor communication: going off in different directions.
4. Housekeeping chores: do both do shopping, cleaning, laundry, etc?

In a two-income family the secondary earner is much more willing to make the accommodation when something in the family interferes with work. The secondary wage-earner has less at stake and less to lose if the accommodation to non-job-related activities results in conflict. On the other hand, both members of the two-career family feel the constraints of corporate life, and neither can expect the other to always yield to contingencies and pressures.

It becomes more complicated to cope with problems when children are included. Child-care is expensive and it dilutes the advantage of combined incomes. But beyond money matters, there is also the need for sharing of parental responsibilities. The father is not as instinctively equipped and often reluctant to assume a fuller share of the children's upbringing. But now the father has to be more than a provider, which was acceptable in the past; he has to be a half-time mother.

The increase in the number of two-career families has possible advantages and disadvantages for business. But it offers a unique benefit to both the husband and the wife. It makes it possible for one to take time off to pursue a second career while the other holds the fort during the transition period.

In any event, this presents a new set of circumstances that employers have to contend with. In a given situation, there may be one job to consider but two employees (one inside the company and one outside) that may have to be taken into account. What does a company do, for example, when there is an opportunity to reward a deserving employee with promotion to a better job that calls for relocation to another geographical region? Does it not make the offer because of possible complications or does it also consider the other spouse and offer job-hunting assistance?

Many companies are unprepared to deal with problems like these.

TWO-SHIFT FAMILIES

We've talked about the *two-income* family and the *two-career* family, *both* of which introduce new employee relations problems for companies. Now let's talk about the *two-shift* family, which creates problems too.

In a two-income family, the primary wage-earner dominates and the secondary wage-earner, working for supplemental income, makes whatever accommodations are necessary. In a two-career family, the spouses follow independent paths in their work but tend to share responsibilities more equally on the home front.

The typical two-shift family is a married couple with children who, for a variety of reasons, cannot be left alone. One spouse (mother) has the daytime job and the other spouse (father) has the nighttime job. Or vice versa. More than one million American families with children under age 14 live this way.

The phenomenon of two-shift families is likely to spread. There are more mothers entering the outside work force. Latest figures show that in the United States 57% of married women with children under age 18 are employed or seeking jobs. Nighttime work is becoming more common, especially in the computer, health care, and other expanding service-sector industries. The choice of which spouse gets which shift may be more than convenience. The decision could come down to occupational preferences, lack of seniority, or premium pay offered.

In a family where father and mother both work, the spouses may seek separate shifts for reasons other than dual income. Both parents may want to get equally involved in raising their children and they might want to avoid reliance upon child care centers. There could be a little baby-sitting required if the two shifts overlap somewhat.

Family duties and responsibilities have to be dovetailed into the two separate work schedules. They must also be flexible to accommodate last minute adjustments. Depending upon work schedules, one spouse might drive the children to school and the other spouse might pick them up. The same goes for meals: the children might have breakfast with one spouse and supper with the other. Seldom will both parents be able to spend time together. Even on weekends when neither is working, one could be sleeping while the other is awake.

Despite the best intentions, routine housekeeping chores are seldom split down the middle because one spouse is more comfortable or natural with certain tasks than the other. Husbands try to do more housework but the wives may be more adept at it. Dividing necessary duties at home does not come easy. Where one spouse resents the extra burden and cooperates grudgingly the stage is set for strain and stress. A husband may expect the wife to do housework on her days off while he considers it quite proper to use his days off to go fishing. The inevitable tension at home spills over into the outside jobs of both workers.

The two-shift family is really two workers who are rarely home together. They are often like two ships passing in the night. They live parallel lives but not joint lives. When this puts a strain on their marriage, it could also put a strain on their jobs. Workers could be tired because of offbeat sleeping hours, or worried because of burdensome family problems. The arrangement can work out if the employees explain the circumstances to their employers and if the supervisors understand the situation and try to be sympathetic.

AGE DISCRIMINATION

Business, like life, is youth oriented. "We play up youth; we play down seniority."

Certainly youth should be encouraged wherever possible, but not at the expense of age, not to the extent of depreciating and diminishing the value of loyalty and long service and dependability and all the other ancient virtues.

A rigid and repressive society gives its young little change; a fluid and innovative society neglects its obligation to the old. That society is best which attains an equilibrium between the needs of youth and the rewards of age, which listens to the young, and honors the old.

People do their best work for honor and respect as much as for money. If these values are not forthcoming toward the end of a long tenure, then goals shift to the purely immediate and material and self-seeking, and no long-range company of venture can sustain itself on these terms.

A company wants a fresh, vital image; and the image is often more important to it than the substance. So substance, in terms of years of service, is often sacrificed to cosmetic rejuvenation. The firm wants a "mod" look to demonstrate that it is up-to-date, and it can get the mod look only by jettisoning its older employees.

Discrimination by color and sex is diminishing, but discrimination by age is beginning to take its place. This is not merely a personal injustice to the victim; it violently shifts the subsoil of the whole social structure, so that young people entering the labor market will no longer shape their career-lives on the basis of permanence and dependability but on the axiom of getting the most possible in the short time available to their "youth image."

AGE DISCRIMINATION LAWS

Laws that prohibit discrimination in employment because of age are based on the declaration that the practice of discriminating in employment is contrary to American principles of liberty and equality of opportunity. Further, a hiring bias against older workers deprives society of its most important resource of experienced employees, adds to the number of persons receiving public assistance, and denies older people the dignity and status of self-support.

The Age Discrimination in Employment Act of 1967 promotes the employment of the older worker based on ability rather than age; prohibits arbitrary age discrimination in employment; and helps employers and employees find ways to meet problems arising from the impact of age on employment.

The law protects individuals 40 to 65 years old from age discrimination by:

1. Private employers of 20 or more persons.
2. Public employers (federal, state or local governmental units) regardless of the number of employees.
3. Employment agencies serving such employers.
4. Labor organizations if they operate a hiring hall or procure workers for employers, or generally, if they have 25 or more members in an industry affecting interstate commerce.

It is against the law . . .

For an *employer:*

1. To fail or refuse to hire, or to discharge or otherwise discriminate against any individual as to compensation, terms, conditions or privileges of employment because of age;
2. To limit, segregate or classify his employees so as to deprive any individual of employment opportunities, or adversely affect his status as an employee because of age;
3. To reduce the wage rate of any employee in order to comply with the Act.

For an *employment agency:*

1. To fail or refuse to refer for employment, or otherwise discriminate against any individual because of age, or to classify or refer anyone for employment on the basis of age.

For a *labor organization:*

1. To discriminate against anyone because of age by excluding or expelling any individual from membership, or by limiting, segregating or classifying its membership on the basis of age, or by other means;
2. To fail or refuse to refer anyone for employment so as to result in a deprivation or limitation of employment opportunities or otherwise adversely affect the individual's status as an employee because of age;
3. To cause or attempt to cause an employer to discriminate against any individual because of age.

For *employers, employment agencies or labor organizations:*

1. To discriminate against a person for opposing a practice made unlawful by the Act, or for making a charge, assisting or participating in any investigation, proceeding or litigation under it;

2. To use printed or published notices or advertisements indicating any preference, limitation, specification or discrimination based on age.

Exceptions

The prohibitions against discrimination because of age do not apply:

1. When age is a bona fide occupational qualification reasonably necessary to the normal operations of the particular business;
2. When the differentiation is based on reasonable factors other than age;
3. When the differentiation is caused by observing the terms of a bona fide seniority system or any bona fide employee benefit plan. This applies to new and existing employee benefit plans, and to the establishment and maintenance of such plans. However, no employee benefit plan shall excuse the failure to hire any individual.
4. When the discharge or discipline of an individual is for good cause.

The Act is enforced by the Secretary of Labor, who can make investigations, issue rules and regulations for administration of the law, and enforce its provisions by legal proceedings when voluntary compliance cannot be obtained.

Age discrimination laws, federal and state, are careful not to affect the retirement system of any employer nor the varying of insurance coverages according to an employee's age.

GOVERNMENT COMPLIANCE AUDITS

by JOHN W. ANNAS
Vice President Management Counsel
Doherty Associates, Inc.

American business in one year paid approximately $150 million for its noncompliance with government laws and regulations. This penalty is a considerable cut off the bottom line and really not necessary.

The laws are readily available and well-defined. They include the

- Fair Labor Standards Act
- Equal Pay Act
- Age Discrimination and Employment Act

all of which are enforced by the U.S. Department of Labor.

Every investigative action is taken in the name of the Secretary of Labor to maintain complainant anonymity, even if the case goes to litigation. When an investigator visits an establishment, the Department of Labor has the enforcement power to extend the investigation over the preceding two years. In addition, there is a provision for willful violators for the extension of an additional year, to permit the further study of company personnel action.

Fair Labor Standards Act

The law most frequently violated by employers is the Fair Labor Standards Act and its minimum wage and record-keeping provisions. Many employers find it difficult to establish what jobs are bona fide executive, administrative or professional in nature. These classifications are spelled out in the Act, but like most laws there are gray areas.

The investigation of a company may stem from a routine audit or the officer may be following up a complaint. In either case, the officer will not specify the exact purpose of the visit, but will outline the scope of the investigation.

Following an introduction and company verification of the officer's credentials, the investigator may begin by reviewing both personnel and payroll records, all the while looking for the marginal case. If it is a complaint follow-up, the officer will normally zero in on the entire family of jobs surrounding the complainant's work.

Interviews are conducted in confidence. Questions pertain to duties and responsibilities and center on hours worked and compensation.

Should the officer determine an exempt employee is essentially nonexempt, the investigator will ask the employee to reconstruct the hours worked. Hopefully, the employer will have kept accurate records as the burden of complying with the Act rests with the company. Failing to keep such records, the officer with adequate corroboration will take the employee's record of hours worked as fact.

Equal Pay Act

This Act is a relatively narrow enforcement statute and less difficult to enforce. The Act permits the employer to set pay rates, but the compliance officer will determine if there is equity among differences and that rates of pay are not based solely on sex.

An investigation will normally focus on the hiring rates of selected job classes but the officer will also examine merit pay administration, vacation policy, sick pay allowances and other benefits.

During a compliance audit, the officer must first determine if the jobs in question require substantially similar skill, effort and responsibility. To establish a violation he must then prove, first, equal work; second, males and females are performing the work; and third, that varying pay rates are not related to merit, seniority, prior work history or education, but are based on sex.

The measure of damages can be substantial, as the company will be required to equalize the rates and payment may be retroactive for up to three years.

Age Discrimination and Employment Act

This law was designed to protect people between the ages of 40 and 65 from employment discrimination.

In conducting an investigation, the officer seeks to determine if the company is in full compliance with the Act by examining actual practices, not written policies, covering hiring, promotions, demotions and terminations. He is looking for any adverse action taken against an applicant or employee because of age.

The investigator will review records of applicants hired and not hired, qualifications listed in advertisements, questions asked on the application blank or posed by interviewers, and job specifications. In the case of a complaint follow-up, the officer will compare the credentials of the employee who was hired, promoted or retained against those of the complainant. In the case where someone in the "legally protected age group" has equal or better credentials than the person selected, the Labor Department has a *prima facie* case of discrimination and as such can transfer the burden of proving nondiscrimination to the compnay.

Avoiding Problems

There are ways to avoid violating these Acts. First, document all personnel actions as they occur and retain all such records at least three years. Second, train first-line supervisors on the various aspects of the laws so that noncompliance won't occur.

The supervisors and foremen are the company's first line of defense. They must have a working knowledge of the laws, be able to interpret the applicable provisions, understand the legal implications, and be aware of the consequences—all as part of administering their specific job responsibilities.

EQUAL EMPLOYMENT OPPORTUNITY EMPLOYER INFORMATION REPORT EEO-1

Under Public Law 88-352, Title VII of the Civil Rights Act of 1964, as amended by the Equal Employment Opportunity Act of 1972, employers are required to keep records and to make reports.

In the interests of consistency, uniformity and economy, Standard Form 100 has been jointly developed by the Equal Employment Opportunity Commission and the Office of Federal Contract Compliance Programs of the U.S. Department of Labor, as a single form which meets the statistical needs of both programs.

In addition, this form should be a valuable tool for companies to use in evaluating their own internal programs for ensuring equal employment opportunity. The consolidated report must include all employees by race, sex and job category.

Race/Ethnic Identification

The race/ethnic designations used by the EEOC do not denote scientific definitions of anthropological origins. For the purpose of the report, an employee may be included in the group to which he or she appears to belong, identifies with or is regarded in the community as belonging.

White: all persons having origins in any of the original peoples of Europe, North Africa, the Middle East or the Indian subcontinent.

Black: all persons having origins in any of the black racial groups.

Hispanic: all persons of Mexican, Puerto Rican, Cuban, Central or South American, or other Spanish culture or origin, regardless of race.

Asian or Pacific Islander: all persons having origins in any of the original peoples of the Far East, Southeast Asia or the Pacific Islands. This area includes, for example, China, Japan, Korea, the Philippine Islands and Samoa.

American Indian or Alaskan Native: all persons having origins in any of the original peoples of North America.

254

Job Categories

Employment data must be reported by job category. Jobs are considered as belonging in one of the broad occupations as defined in the Appendix.

Officials and managers: Occupations requiring administrative personnel who set broad policies, exercise overall responsibility for execution of these policies, and direct individual departments or special phases of a firm's operations. Include: officials, executives, middle management, plant managers, department managers, superintendents, salaried foremen who are members of management, purchasing agents and buyers, and kindred workers.

Professional: Occupations requiring either college graduation or experience of such kind and amount as to provide a comparable background. Include: accountants and auditors, airplane pilots, navigators, architects, artists, chemists, designers, dietitians, editors, engineers, lawyers, librarians, mathematicians, natural scientists, registered professional nurses, personnel and labor relations workers, physical scientists, physicians, social scientists, teachers and kindred workers.

Technicians: Occupations requiring a combination of basic scientific knowledge and manual skill which can be obtained through about two years of post high school education, such as is offered in many technical institutes and junior colleges, or through equivalent on-the-job training. Include: computer programmers and operators, drafters, engineering aides, junior engineers, mathematical aides, licensed, practical or vocational nurses, photographers, radio operators, scientific assistants, surveyors, technical illustrators, technicians (medical, dental, electronic, physical science) and kindred workers.

Sales: Occupations engaging wholly or primarily in direct selling. Include: advertising agents and sales-workers, insurance agents and brokers, real estate agents and brokers, stock and bond salesworkers, demonstrators, salesworkers and sales clerks, grocery clerks and cashier-checkers, and kindred workers.

Office and clerical: Include all clerical-type work regardless of level of difficulty, where the activities are predominantly nonmanual though some manual work not directly involved with altering or transporting the products is included. Include: bookkeepers, cashiers, collectors (bills and accounts), messengers and office helpers, office machine operators, shipping and receiving clerks, stenographers, typists and secretaries, telegraph and telephone operators, and kindred workers.

Craft worker (skilled): Manual workers of relatively high skill level having a thorough and comprehensive knowledge of the processes involved in their work. Exercise considerable independent judgment and usually receive an extensive period of training. Include: the build-

APPLICATION FOR OFFICE POSITION

Date_____

Name (print)_____ Home Tel. No._____ Soc. Sec. No._____

Present address_____

| No. | Street | City | State |

Position applied for?_____ Earnings expected $_____

Date of birth_____19____ Are you a U. S. citizen? ☐ Yes, ☐ No Alien Registration No.:_____

The age discrimination in the employment act and relevant FEP Acts prohibit discrimination with respect to individuals who are at least 40 but less than 65 years of age.

In case of emergency, notify_____

| Name | Address | Phone |

EDUCATION

Type of School	Name and Address of School	Courses Majored In	Check Last Year Completed				Graduate? Give Degrees		Last Year Attended
Elementary			5	6	7	8	☐ Yes,	☐ No	19
High School			1	2	3	4	☐ Yes,	☐ No	19
College			1	2	3	4			19
Business School	A.								19
	B.								19
Corresp. or Night School									19

(Indicate below specific experience which you have had)

Check Here	Type of Experience	Yrs.	Mos.	Check Here	Type of Experience	Yrs.	Mos.	Check Here	Type of Experience	Yrs.	Mos.
	Addressograph Operator				Confidential Secretary				Office Help		
	Blue Print Mach. Operator				Dictating Mach. Transcript'n				Office Supervisor		
	Clerical Supervisor				Key Punch Operator				Photostat Operator		
	Clerk				Mail Clerk				Receptionist		
	Correspondence				Duplicating Mach. Operator				Secretary		
	Cost				Ditto				Telephone Swbd. Operator		
	File				Mimeograph				Teletype Operator		
	General				Multigraph				Timekeeper		
	Statistical				Multilith						
	Stock				Other						

(Indicate below your office skills and check office machines you can operate efficiently)

☐ Typewriter	Speed in typing_____	☐ Billing Machine	Which ones_____
☐ Electric Typewriter	Speed in typing_____	☐ Bookkeeping Machines	Which ones_____
☐ Vari-type	Speed in typing_____	☐ Accounting Machine	Which ones_____
☐ Shorthand	Speed in taking dictation_____	☐ Calculating Machine	Which ones_____
☐ Stenotype	Speed in taking dictation_____	☐ Tabulating Machine	Which ones_____

What other languages do you speak?_____ Read?_____

Form No. OA-205

WORK HISTORY

(Record U. S. Military Service as a position)*

List below the names of all your former employers, beginning with the most recent:
a. Employer's Name
b. Address and telephone number

	Kind of Business	Time Employed				Nature of Work	Starting Salary	Salary at Leaving	Reasons for Leaving	Name of Immediate Supervisor
		From		To						
		Mo.	Yr.	Mo.	Yr.					
1. a. b.										Name Title
2. a. b.										Name Title
3. a. b.										Name Title
4. a. b.										Name Title
5. a. b.										Name Title
6. a. b.										Name Title
7. a. b.										Name Title
8. a. b.										Name Title

Indicate by number _____ any of the above employers whom you do not wish us to contact. Ever bonded? □ No, □ Yes; On what jobs? _____

What transportation would you use from home to office? _____
If your application is considered favorably, on what date will you be available for work? _____ 19___ Signature _____

References (Not former employers or relatives)

	Address	Phone Number
1.		
2.		

APPLICANT SHOULD NOT WRITE BELOW THIS LINE

1 2 3 4: Comments _____

*Not to be asked in New Jersey.
You are advised that an inquiry may now be made which will provide information concerning your character, general reputation and mode of living. Upon written request, we will provide information as to the scope of the inquiry, if you desire.

Interviewer _____

ing trades, hourly paid supervisors and lead operators who are not members of management, mechanics and repairers, skilled machining occupations, compositors and typesetters, electricians, engravers, job setters (metal), motion picture projectionists, pattern and model makers, stationary engineers, tailors and tailoresses, and kindred workers.

Operatives (semiskilled): Workers who operate machine or processing equipment or perform other factory-type duties of intermediate skill level which can be mastered in a few weeks and require only limited training. Include: apprentices (auto mechanics, plumbers, bricklayers, carpenters, electricians, machinists, mechanics, building trades, metalworking trades, printing trades, etc.), operatives, attendants (auto service and parking), blasters, chauffeurs, delivery workers, dressmakers and seamstresses (except factory), dryers, furnace workers, heaters (metal), laundry and dry cleaning operatives, milliners, mine operatives and laborers, motor operators, oilers and greasers (except auto), painters (except construction and maintenance), photographic process workers, stationary firefighters, truck and tractor drivers, weavers (textile), welders, flamecutters and kindred workers.

Laborers (unskilled): Workers in manual occupations which generally require no special training who perform elementary duties that may be learned in a few days. These duties require the application of little or no independent judgment. Include: garage laborers, car washers and greasers, gardeners (except farm) and groundskeepers, stevedores, woodchoppers, laborers performing lifting, digging, mixing, loading and pulling operations, and kindred workers.

Service workers: Workers in both protective and nonprotective service occupations. Include: attendants (hospital and other institutions, professional and personal service including nurses aides, and orderlies), barbers, charworkers and cleaners, cooks (except household), counter and fountain workers, elevator operators, firefighters and fire protection, guards, doorkeepers, stewards, janitors, police officers and detectives, porters, waiters and waitresses, and kindred workers.

On-the-job trainees:

Production: Persons engaged in formal training for craft worker— when not trained under apprentice programs—operative, laborers and service occupations.

White collar: Persons engaged in formal training, for official, managerial, professional, technical, sales, office and clerical occupations.

CHAPTER IV

INDOCTRINATION AND ORIENTATION

INDUCTION

" W ELCOME! You are now a member of Wards . . ." is the way Montgomery Ward's "Fact Book" for new employees begins. The booklet opens up with:

Your First Few Weeks

It will take a little time to learn the many activities of your job and your way around the department. Your duties will be explained step by step, and the elements will soon fall into place. Your trainer is interested in seeing that you get all the help you need and will:

- Introduce you to the people with whom you work.

- Train you for your schedule of activities and assist you in learning.

- Answer any questions you may have about your career.

- Check back periodically to see how you are getting along.

Training:

The nucleus of your training will be this booklet, audio cassettes, sound-slide films, and other materials explaining policies, procedures and standards. The purpose of this program is:

- To convey the maximum amount of information in the minimum amount of time.

- To give you significant information in a related way.

You will learn certain facts about your job that you can record in this Fact Book.

INDOCTRINATION

The newly-hired worker is, hopefully, qualified in the skill requirements of the job. But that is not enough. Now the employee needs to be educated in the business. This is generally known as training.

Employee training may be conveniently divided into four broad areas:

1. Indoctrination.
2. Orientation.
3. On-the-job instruction.
4. Education.

The entire gamut of training may be defined as "the process of aiding employees to gain effectiveness in their present or future work. This is accomplished through the development of appropriate habits of thought and action, skills, knowledge, and attitudes."

In any company, training goes on all the time. Somehow new workers learn their jobs; employees increase their skills; people learn to work together. This learning, however, may be hit or miss, slow or fast, right or wrong. It is better for management to give direction and assistance to this learning.

The first phase of employee education is that of indoctrination or induction. It is intended to get the new worker off to a good start. It occurs on the new worker's first day on the job.

Review of Basics

Much information is exchanged with an applicant during the employment interview. Many things are discussed, some in general terms, depending upon the person and the job under consideration. Other pertinent details, if they come up at all, may not be remembered since they did not contribute to the decision to accept or reject the job offer.

Therefore, when the new employee reports for work on the first day, the specifics about the work situation should be reviewed, preferably before beginning to work. It is best to do this individually, although there could be times or circumstances when this can be done effectively in groups. The indoctrination is usually done in the personnel office or central employment department before the worker is referred to the department where the job exists. Upon arrival in the department a local indoctrination also takes place.

In the personnel office items of *general* nature are presented. In the department the *specific* application is covered.

INDOCTRINATION AND ORIENTATION

In Personnel	*In Department*
Work week and work day	Work hours for particular job
Length of lunch period	Time of lunch period
Location of cafeteria or outside eating facilities	Usually assigns someone to go to lunch with first time
Rest periods	Time of scheduled rest periods
Pay day and method of payment	How to check in—time clocks or time sheets
Where to cash paychecks	Overtime arrangement
Starting job and starting pay	Job opportunities
Holidays	Absence reporting; tardiness
Vacation policy	How vacations are scheduled
Sick pay allowances	Location of cloakroom or locker, and washrooms
Location of clinic or first-aid	Location of nearest emergency exit
Group insurance with literature	Introduction to sponsor or other co-worker available for training or questions
Employee activities	
Availability of personnel services	

This "first-day-on-the-job" indoctrination in the personnel or employment office is the time to have the new worker sign the necessary papers for payroll processing:

- Form W-4—Employee's Withholding Exemption Certificate.
- Group Insurance Application blank.
- Employee gift fund participation.

Recognizing that a new worker is likely to sign anything associated with work, it is inadvisable to sign anyone up at this time for contributory Life Insurance, Credit Union membership, United Fund payroll deductions, and the like. Items such as these should be thoroughly explained at some later time.

Sponsors

Once the new worker is delivered to the department, ready to begin work, rolling out the welcome mat is of utmost importance. Since the manager has many duties and is often too busy to be concerned with every new employee, especially to the extent necessary, many companies have found the sponsor system effective.

261

The manager selects a trustworthy employee to serve as sponsor with the responsibility to make the new employee feel at home. The sponsor helps the newcomer get acquainted, introduces co-workers in the immediate area, answers questions about the company and the job, and makes starting on the new job as pleasant as possible. The sponsor usually accompanies the new employee on breaks and goes along to the cafeteria for a (free) lunch. The sponsor, with own work still to be performed, tries to stay close enough to the new worker until such time as the new employee develops the feeling of "belonging" and can get along alone.

Sponsors have to be chosen with care. In addition to knowing something about the business, they should have a working knowledge of the jobs. They must, of course, be sociable and friendly and want to help. They play an important role because a new employee's feelings and attitude are shaped by first impressions.

The purpose of the indoctrination procedure—both in personnel and in the work unit—is to welcome the new employee in a friendly manner and accept him or her as part of the employee group. It also provides the company with the initial opportunity of furnishing the new worker with useful and accurate information about the company and its products or services. It also advises the worker as to company requirements pertaining to working hours, safety regulations, and other rules and practices. This is a good time to distribute to the new worker a copy of the Employee Handbook, in which the employee program is completely covered.

BENCH INTERVIEWS

In connection with the indoctrination, some companies perform what is known as bench interviews. A bench interview is a conversation with the new worker at his work station on his first day on the job.

Someone from the employment office visits the new worker late in the day, at the worker's desk or machine. He makes it appear as though this were a casual "drop in" instead of a planned trip. It is amazing to discover how reassuring a familiar face is to the new employee after he has struggled along all day in unfamiliar surroundings with work that overwhelms him.

By the use of the bench interview the company has a chance to learn how the new worker is getting along, to answer questions, to determine that he is off on the right foot. This very personal action reminds him that the company is interested in seeing to it that he makes good by getting off to a good start.

EMERGENCY ARRANGEMENTS

Business as usual is the normal order of the day. But every once in a while the best laid plans go awry. Emergencies must therefore also be planned for. An emergency is defined as "any unexpected activity that disrupts the normal operation of the business."

Nature can easily upset the *status quo*. A blizzard can foul up public and private transportation making it virtually impossible for employees to get to work. A flood can call an overnight halt to industries along the river. An electrical brown-out can paralyze an entire city. Any time Mother Nature goes on a rampage she makes a mockery of man's puny efforts to maintain order.

But man himself can cause trouble. Strikes can throw a monkey wrench in the finest industrial machinery. The walkout doesn't even have to be in the company or in a related firm. When elevator operators go on strike, for example, all business in high-rise buildings is literally brought to a standstill. Daily operations must, of necessity, be rearranged. In some situations firms may shut down completely, operate on a curtailed schedule, or work with only a partial shift.

During the past decade a new danger has entered upon the scene to disturb the industrial calm. This is the threat of civil rights or other riots that take over a community and endanger the lives and property in a large sector of the city. When this flares up to riot proportions, police and military forces set the rules, and business is pushed aside.

In any of these unfortunate situations the results, as far as business is concerned, lead to confusion. How to get word to the employees, instructing them on what to do, is a big problem. Is the plant open? If not, when will it be reopened? What is happening in the meantime? The employee wonders how he can be helpful—what is expected of him. As a conscientious worker, should he make the effort, at great inconvenience and possibly danger, to get down to work? How does he feel when he shows up, only to find that no one else did?

Since the likelihood of these emergency situations appears to be increasing, companies are willing to consider the advisability of setting up "Operations Emergency" programs and committees.

The Telephone Tree

One plan calls for a telephone communications network whereby every employee is directly assigned to his immediate supervisor. This telephone relay system can be arranged beforehand and triggered into action when the signal is given. The chain of communications, both downward and upward, follows the organization chart. Once a decision is made by topside, the president reports it to his vice-presidents, they in turn to their assistant vice-presidents, who relay it to their managers. Each manager, possibly through supervisors, notifies those and only those who report directly to him. Every employee is accounted for.

The workers understand the procedure and know from whom to expect to "get the word." This would also make it clear to him how to reverse the procedure in the event he fails to get a message and wonders whom to call to inquire. It is wise to give each employee the telephone number of his boss. The problem here is to keep the names, telephone numbers and department rosters up-to-date at all times.

This arrangement, like a tree, requires that all leaves be attached to their respective branches and that all branches be attached to the trunk. Supervisors would have to be equipped with the telephone numbers of their subordinates, and these telephone lists would have to be kept current. As a precaution, alternates should be named (in case a key supervisor is out of reach) and this means duplicate lists. It might be a lot of work to set up and maintain this type of program but, like any other precautionary measure, it is probably better than the alternative of doing no planning in advance.

The bigger problem, however, is not so much in the mechanics of delivering the message as it is in getting the decision made. The man at the top is away and lesser executives hesitate to usurp his authority. Or even if he is accessible, he might prefer to consult with some other executives before he declares himself. While all this is going on questions come up, employees do not get answers, hasty makeshift actions are improvised, helpful outside agencies get no cooperation, and confusion runs rampant.

The Emergency Committee

It is imperative that the problems be considered before they happen and a committee, preferably a small one, be empowered to act. This committee might center around the personnel executive, who would take the initiative and move into action, the building superintendent, since building facilities must be considered, and a senior officer, to lend official sanction to any emergency decisions made. These three people should be quickly in touch with each other, arrive at a decision with a minimum of delay, and then trigger the emergency program.

Questions about telling the employee to report or stay home, to ask for police escorts, to shut down air conditioning, heating, motors, etc., to set up plant protection, to notify shippers and suppliers, to cooperate with radio and television media for free or paid announcements, to work with the press—all of these and other problems should get prompt attention. Unless some program is worked out in advance, and certain individuals authorized to proceed on their own, the procrastination, indecision, and illwill created by waiting for top management to get together by remote control will result in chaos.

Some employees, by virtue of convenient locations or transportation, or certain duty assignments, may get to the building. There are always a few who somehow can be depended upon to get through. These people could be the nucleus of a volunteer emergency crew. They could be trained to monitor the switchboard, relay messages to and from executives, attend operations that cannot be shut down and safeguard valuables.

Decisions not of an emergency nature may be made later. Whether to pay employees for the day or days the plant was closed could be decided after the plant is reopened and the officials are back on the job.

Programs of this type cannot be effective if they begin after the emergency has struck. Companies that have been hit by an emergency know from experience how important it is to prepare. The problems must be anticipated and the solutions worked out in advance. Preplanning is the answer.

MEMOS TO ALL PERSONNEL

There are frequent occasions for memos to be sent to all employees. General information must be disseminated, news distributed, announcements made. The easiest and most effective way to reach all employees promptly with the official message is to send a memo (blanket, not individually addressed) to all personnel.

The problem is not writing or sending out the memo. Many people are qualified to prepare, publish, and distribute it. The question is who should do it and under what circumstances.

A good policy is to clear all such memos through the personnel office. In many cases the personnel staff might be required to write the memo, although this is not always necessary. Usually the person closest to the information is in the best position to draft the memo unless, of course, the individual is not a capable writer in which case someone else, possibly in the personnel office, should be expected to polish it up.

The personnel people have a right to check and approve every memo that goes to employees just as the public relations staff would expect to see anything sent to the newspapers. In approving each such memo, the personnel people do not second-guess the message or the content but they look for conformity to policy, standards of preparation, schedule of distribution, etc. Clearing all employee memos through the personnel office keeps everybody and every department from sending messages indiscriminately throughout the house.

Some discretion must be exercised, otherwise if employees are bombarded with a steady flow of ordinary or inconsequential memos from different people and departments, they may not take proper note of a message from top management when it arrives.

"From the Top"

A good rule to follow is to use an executive letterhead, instead of blank paper, to differentiate official memos from routine notices. A message from the president should by its appearance immediately impress the recipient with its importance. It is too bad when a reminder of a bowling league meeting gets more attention than an announcement authorizing extra time off for voting.

Another suggestion might be to limit executives or managers in sending messages only to their own people, with informational copies to their peers or counterparts in other divisions who may then decide whether or not to relay the information to all or some of their own people. Not every memo needs to be sent routinely across the board and some check should be established to stop this practice.

For that matter not all memos should be broadcast to all employees. Some are intended only for limited or specific distribution. The army used a good system in World War II known as the "message center." All outgoing messages were coded and distributed accordingly. In business we tend to address them to the group they're aimed at, such as "All Personnel," "Sales Staff," "Management," "Exempt Employees," and so on.

General memos are addressed to groups and not individually identified. A memo "To All Employees" is given total or company-wide distribution. There are, however, occasions when letters might be individually addressed and mailed to the employees at home, or individually marked by name and hand delivered in the office or plant. The nature of the message should determine the treatment it receives. Certainly a year-end report of progress from the president should get personalized attention whereas a routine announcement of Mother's Day candy for sale at a discount may not merit any special consideration by employees.

A good suggestion would be to limit the number of memos and concentrate on the important ones. Too many notices tend to dilute the significance of all of them. Writing up the story in the company house organ, while not as fast, still gets the message to all employees. Or posting notices on the bulletin boards may suffice. Surely it isn't necessary, or advisable, to send out a memo for every bit of general interest information.

266

At any rate, let somebody or some office look over the written messages for content, wording, grammar and composition, importance, and distribution. At least this will keep these "Memos to All Personnel" under better control.

OPEN DOOR

As a way of encouraging free communications, some companies maintain an open door policy. The open door policy is a reflection of corporate belief in the dignity of the individual and respect for the right of workers to seek or proffer answers to questions.

It is expected that visits will be controlled, on appointment when this is necessary, and follow prescribed procedures where the steps have been clearly spelled out and properly publicized, as in the case of grievances.

The important point is that no door should be closed to any individual. Communication between management and employees is one of the best continuing surveys of company health.

An executive who subscribes to the open door policy and believes in supporting it, must wonder when nobody "drops in." That executive should be reminded that the door to any office works both ways—in and out. The same purpose could be served by going out of the office occasionally to mingle with the troops.

POSTING OF NOTICES

In addition to memos for general distribution, and other forms of communication, there often arise occasions to post notices publicly.

Some system should be established. Otherwise all sorts of authorized and unauthorized notices will go up. Somebody has kittens to give away and a handwritten note may be placed next to an official announcement of a new advertising campaign.

Just as an editor screens material used in the house organ, so should someone or some policy decide what may be posted, where, by whom and for how long.

If there is a convenient clearing house for personals, possibly in the cafeteria or lounge, that's where a "Flat for rent" sign may be placed. On the other hand, United Fund posters may be plastered all over the plant as a way of letting management get this message before all the workers.

The best method is to have one person in each area post or approve the posting of notices. This could be the manager or foreman of a department or the personnel manager for company-designated locations. In this way the employee who has a message to post will have to clear it with someone, which means getting his concurrence.

BULLETIN BOARDS

In the area of employee communications, the company bulletin board, conceived and administered internally, is by far the oldest mechanism for conveying information. It was in existence long before the first so-called "house organ" was produced. Its growth has been slowed because of management's failure to view the medium's potentials, but it is moving ahead more recently as a member of the oral and written communication team.

A bulletin board program, to be useful, needs to be meshed officially into a company's total communications effort, not left to drift by itself. Otherwise it could deteriorate into a junkyard for shop-level trivia. Nor should it become a catch basin for syndicated morale stuff that management buys to save itself the trouble of speaking for itself. It is, in reality, a tool of communication and used properly it is a powerhouse of persuasion. At bargaining time it is management's more reliable friend.

Benefits and Pitfalls

According to Newcomb & Sammons, 3200 North Lake Shore Drive, Chicago, Illinois 60657, publishers of *The Score,* a monthly report to management on developments and trends in employer-employee communications, the advantages of a good bulletin board program are:

1. It is generally the fastest and most accurate medium of communication. Even in plants where public address systems are dependable, or where the telephone recording device is used, the bulletin board lets the employees *see* all day what they *heard* earlier possibly only one time.
2. It is gaining fast recognition as a medium of information on labor-management developments. It is a dependable medium for presenting the company's story promptly.
3. In the multiple-plant company, it has an "umbrella" effect. Headquarters can supply solid, interesting, pictorial information on matters of company concern simultaneously to plants in different locations, thus putting a friendly arm around all the people.

4. It is the classic rumor silencer. The one-two-punch effect of a bulletin board program can put a rumor in its place in a few minutes.
5. The board becomes a meeting place. It has its own captive audience. It gets their attention at least once a day, maybe oftener, and this gives the company an opportunity to be as persuasive as the talents of the communicator permit.

What are the roadblocks in the way of effective communication by bulletin board? Here are pitfalls to watch for:

1. Shortage of manpower needed to implement the program. At the plant level the personnel assistant often assigned to this task may have his hands well occupied with other chores. Remedy: Straighten this out first with the plant manager, sell him on the importance of the medium as a tool for his communication, emphasize the fact that bulletin board preparation doesn't take too long.
2. Training the local-level personnel in bulleting board preparation. These people are usually inexperienced. Remedy: Set up a briefing session, probably on a regional basis in a company of any size, to coach the people. Also issue a manual in order to keep these plant representatives on the beam.
3. Employee lack of interest. Some communicators complain that employees will not read bulletin boards, no matter how good. The answer obviously is that they're not good enough. Remedy: Determine by personal check or simple survey the subjects that interest employees most.
4. No real interest at top management level. This can be serious. If the top executive is lukewarm, subordinates will be the same. Therefore it is essential that the sales job be undertaken again. Remedy: Link the bulletin board program directly into the total communications program; sell it as an arm of total communications, not as an independent agency. Stress low cost; minimum manpower requirements, value of the medium in talking up productivity, quality, competition.
5. Boards offer little subject variety. To the unimaginative, they don't. Remedy: Let the communicator solicit subject themes from employees themselves (see No. 3 above), add to it the topics he knows management would like covered.

In connection with item No. 5 above, one of the biggest headaches involved in bulletin board handling is getting the local level representative to spot "the news." One communicator, cudgeled by this problem, compiled for his field staffers some "typical subjects"—personnel shifts; production, expansion plans; building specifics; product quality; elements of cost; taxes, both corporate and personal; labor negotiations and developments; research projects; business economics; special employee events; retirements; service club news; plant people in community affairs, etc.

News sources are: Top management, this is the key source; public relations, for corporate news; personnel, for news about people; club officers, for social activities, games, scores; community, for news in the area; advertising, for public announcements; and similar places.

Change of Pace

The office bulletin board program calls for an understandable change of pace here and there. Here are some recommendations:

1. Single approval. One department should be responsible for posting notices, and everything cleared through the department head.
2. Irregular change. Avoid the once-a-week routine, or readers will soon notice the pattern and read the boards only once a week.
3. Signed notices. For authority, make certain all notices are signed with the name of the originator or the originating department. Indicate removal date for each notice.
4. Make boards attractive. Avoid the appearance of sameness and don't overuse plain white paper for typing notices; try a felt-tip pen for printing attention-getting headlines; use colored paper and change colors often; use sketches or comic strip cutouts to illustrate notices.
5. Eye-catching titles. Stop the reader with live headlines. For that matter, give the boards themselves live titles. Suggestions: Message Center, Hitching Post, Cracker Barrel, On Target, The Word, Now Hear This, Action Board, Postings, The Notebook.
6. Good location. Across from the elevators is an ideal location, if space and other conditions permit. Consider the cafeteria or coffee lounge. Bulletin boards near time clocks could jam up traffic when good-reading items are posted.

In general, avoid posting notices on other than clean paper and replace if the paper becomes soiled through handling. Don't use notices that "flop over" the board edges. Stay away from too many "don't" notices from management; keep track of the "negatives" that are posted and bring this information to management's attention. In short, accentuate the positive.

The consensus of companies boils down to this: "If you're not using your bulletin boards to the fullest extent—in single-and multiple-plant operations, in small shops as well as large—you're passing up a real opportunity to communicate."

OFFICIAL EMPLOYEE GROUP MEETINGS

There are occasions when it is necessary that the employees be brought together for a meeting. "The boss wants to discuss something with them."

This happens when an official report needs to be delivered or a special announcement is to be made. Telling the workers directly is preferred over the rumor mill. There is information the employees are entitled to know and they should get it straight.

There are many times when employees are asked to a meeting. The subject might be the annual United Fund campaign, U.S. Bond drive or other program that affects employees and has the endorsement of the company. Of course, new products, next year's models, relocation of plant, organization changes, revision of benefits, business trends, cost-cutting, mergers or acquisition are all subjects for discussions with employees. It is good, also, for the chief executive to simply reassure employees that business is good and their jobs are secure.

Official meetings of this type are usually presided over, informally or otherwise, by the executive who has the message, but the details are handled by the personnel office. Someone in personnel writes the memo announcing the time and place of the gathering and, hopefully, explains the reason. The personnel staff arranges for the facilities. They also make certain the employees show up, on time, and are adequately accommodated. They may be expected to arrange the agenda and possibly even write a speech for someone else to deliver. In short, when employee meetings are held, the personnel office takes the responsibility for them.

There are other meetings of employees that are not officially conducted but still have company support. Examples are Credit Union elections, bowling league, gift fund, and the like. While the personnel people are not in charge, in fact, may not even be present on the occasion, they should nevertheless be consulted to make certain that these employee get-togethers are conducted within company policy. Their foreknowledge of the meeting and their cooperation with the group leaders will assure that nothing goes wrong inadvertently.

In all employee group meetings, official and nonofficial, the personnel office is the link between the employees and the company.

INDUCTION AND ORIENTATION

The first day on a new job can be a frightening and unpleasant experience, especially if there's neither a formal orientation program nor a co-worker or supervisor to soothe those first day jitters.

A survey by the Dartnell Institute of Business Research of 350 companies throughout the United States and Canada found that 85% offer an orientation program.

Of all the companies surveyed, 61% have put their orientation policies in writing, while 39% have yet to formalize their break-in programs.

Length of the initiation period can vary depending upon the program structure, number of speakers, and products or processes to be demonstrated and introduced.

More than 87% of all businesses distribute an orientation manual or handbook to new employees that provides information and reference assistance.

ORIENTATION

In the training of newly-hired workers, induction or indoctrination is done on an individual or one-on-one basis, customarily on the first day at work. After the new workers have been on the job a short time, usually within the first month, they are brought together for a group orientation session.

Orientation is an organized effort on the part of the company to get the new employees acclimated to their jobs, their co-workers, and the company. It is an attempt to have the new workers learn quickly and accurately what they would otherwise pick up over a longer period of time, and perhaps somewhat incorrectly, through osmosis.

Its purpose is to inform workers about rules, regulations, and policies

Companies and orientation steps

Orientation step	Personnel department	Department head	Co-worker
Welcome	87%	51%	8%
Explaining daily routine	17%	89%	26%
Procedures & regulations	70%	67%	9%
Job introduction	15%	92%	27%

Source: Dartnell Institute of Business Research

in an effort to have them gain understanding and give willing compliance. Further than that, orientation programs instruct employees as to the company history, personality, products, and philosophy. This is important to workers since it explains a company's reputation, character, and future—all of which are vital factors in their personal job ambitions.

An orientation program gives the company an excellent opportunity to show how much it depends upon the workers. Workers are made to feel they "belong" and that they are needed—otherwise they would not have been hired. It also provides a channel for presenting information to employees and influencing their reaction to it.

Sufficient care should be taken in planning and designing an orientation program so that the material is prepared for the benefit of the new workers and not simply to glorify the company. Unless it is made meaningful to the employees it is a waste of time.

Don't assume that just because you are impressed your people will also be impressed, and by the same things. Plan your program carefully because it will represent a big investment in time, money, and talent of both those who participate in its presentation and those who attend.

In larger firms particularly, orientation programs may be developed and conducted by staff officers, possibly from the personnel office, who arrange classes for groups of workers. It is generally conceded that the best orientation program consists basically of two parts and could be handled by two different sets of people. The first part, the necessary rules, regulations, and policies, should be explained by someone experienced in line operations. The second part, that of outlining the history and background of the company, can perhaps be presented by a staff officer in a lecture format.

While orientation programs are generally conducted for new employees, the value of holding refresher courses for older employees should not be discounted. Sometimes older employees can attend the classes for new hires; often a happy blending of workers results which aids in the discussion. In other situations it might be advisable to design special programs, to avoid unnecessary time-consuming repetition and to keep the discussion on an advanced level.

EMPLOYEE COMMUNICATION

If "creativity" is the most overworked word in advertising, then "communication" is just as misused in employee relations.

When a problem arises, the blame is often laid to poor communication. Improve the communication and the situation gets better. That seems to be the theory.

Good communication is vital to good employee relations. But it should not be assumed that communication, any kind of communication, is a cure-all for personnel ills. Do we really understand what is useful communication?

Too much mere information is being passed off as communication. The business world, according to one authority, is "suffering from an epidemic of worditis."

He continued, "We are being buried under mountains of memos, letters, carbon copies, duplicated copies, bulletins, directives, house organs, newsletters, copies of speeches that never should have been made in the first place, and press releases that are absolutely of no interest to anyone except the sender."

All of this goes by the mythical name of "communication" and we assume that it is good, necessary and serving our purpose.

Much Communication Wasted

One of the difficulties is overstimulus of response. Employees hear the sound or read the words but fail to get the message. Much of what we call employee communication is wasted simply because the human sensory apparatus reacts negatively to the sheer volume and constant flow of information.

Much information is designed to fill a vacuum, not a need. Genuine communication creates a bridge between minds; mere information takes up time, energy and paper—makes the sender seem busy and the receiver seem important.

Overcommunication creates more problems than it solves. But it must be pointed out that many companies are guilty of something worse, that is, undercommunication. Saying something is generally better than saying nothing. In the absence of information from management, employees will arrive at their own conclusions. Rumors and the grapevine, the only tools employees can use under these conditions, can produce strange results and easily destroy good intentions. In such cases, companies should blame only themselves if they don't like what they get.

Occasional but meaningful communication instead of endless messages, planned presentations instead of a hit-and-miss assortment of verbal barrages, employee-centered information instead of pronouncements which impress the company—this is being on the right track and traveling in the right direction.

Employees like to know and be kept informed about things in the company which affect them. Communication in any form, to be effective, should be simple, direct, straightforward and sincere.

274

Employee Communication Media

Bulletin boards— company or departmental, prominently located and well maintained

Employee magazine (house organ)— for personals, news, social activities

Company magazine— for products and services, history, plans

Newsletter— digest of news and current events relating to company business

Employee handbook— rules and regulations, working conditions

Benefit book (companion handbook)— welfare programs, insurance

Policy manual— helpful guide on official company position

Indoctrination— individual consultations to get new worker off to a good start

Orientation— group meetings of both new and old employees to influence attitude of employees toward company objectives

Individual counselling— on job-related and personal problems

Performance rating interviews— to tell the employee how he is doing and where he may improve

Suggestion system— to give formal recognition to good ideas

Grievance procedure— to resolve problems in troublesome areas

Group meetings— to announce or explain organization changes, new products, financial stability, results, progress, programs

Public address system— for quick messages and late news

Annual report— to reassure employees of company growth and personal job security

THE GRAPEVINE

During the Civil War military telegraph lines were strung from tree to tree, as a vine might grow. Messages often were garbled, so a rumor was said to come from the grapevine.

Today every company has a grapevine. Most managements believe they should quash the grapevine, that it works against them. Recent studies, however, indicate that quite the opposite is true. The unofficial grapevine is an important element of employee communications and useful to the company.

Keith Davis, a professor of management at Arizona State University, has for years observed the operation of the grapevine and has written extensively on the subject. His research shows that in normal business situations, between 75% and 95% of grapevine information is correct, although often incomplete.

"Organizations would perish if they did not have a grapevine to fill the gaps existing in the formal communication system," he notes. His studies show "men are just as active on the grapevine as women."

He recommends that during periods of uncertainty, companies feed the grapevine "as much factual information as possible to keep it from getting out of hand."

But the grapevine is not to be confused with the dreaded rumor mill. Rumor is the injudicious use of communication, much like gossip, and is without factual evidence to back it up. Every story on the grapevine, however wild and fanciful, has its root cause. The grapevine is the concerned employees' advance reaction to a planned move before it is announced. Management would do well to listen.

Much is written, and consultants get rich, advising how to combat and squelch rumors. The problem could be serious, but it can't be solved with more paid verbiage. The best way to avoid damage from fires is to prevent them, not fight them after they get started. The best way to keep employees and their conversations on the side of the company is to understand that what employees want to know, and need to know, can be summed up in two easily-remembered questions:

1. How sound is the business?
2. How secure is my job?

Every organization functions under two structures, one formal and one informal. To serve this informal organization, an informal communication system arises that is variable and fickle. It is able to penetrate the most rigid corporate security and cannot be held accountable for its errors. The very existence of the informal grapevine reflects the inadequacies and weaknesses in the formal communication system. Together they become a complete communications apparatus serving the interests of the company and the employees.

The weed killer that can stunt the growth of the grapevine has not yet been formulated. In those cases where a peddler disguised as a consultant offers a well-packaged nostrum to unsuspecting managements, it should be required to carry a label that the cure-all may be dangerous to industrial health. The best advice is simply: feed the grapevine, don't fight it!

EMPLOYEE COMMUNICATIONS
and FREEDOM OF DISCUSSION

A good approach to better employee relations, called "Consultative Supervision," is used by Public Utility District No. 1 of Klickitat County, Goldendale, Washington. This policy, as well as the District's emphasis on communications and freedom of discussion, is outlined below:

Consultative Supervision

Because it emphasizes respect for the individuality and dignity of each employee and encourages his development, the District believes that the most satisfactory and enduring personnel relations will be attained by means of consultation and explanation. This means:

1. That employees should be encouraged to express their views on matters affecting their jobs and interests;
2. That consideration should be given to their views before reaching decisions materially affecting their jobs and interests;
3. That any criticism to an employee of his work, activities or expressions should be made privately, and in no case should an employee be criticized in the presence of employees of equal or subordinate position;
4. All who direct the work of others should see to it that in the daily operation of our business, no one is ignored on those matters about which he thinks he has or ought to have a right to be consulted;
5. That promotions, individual wages or salary changes, and disciplinary actions should be communicated to an employee, after proper approvals, only by his immediate supervisor; and
6. That all matters affecting employee relations should be fully explained.

Communications

It is the policy of the District to give the employee prompt and full information on matters affecting his job, either directly or indirectly. This includes background information on social, political and economic events and problems about which the employee needs adequate information if he is to make good decisions and promote the District.

Freedom of Discussion

One of the principal objectives of the District is to encourage and maintain freedom of contact between the employees and management.

Employees should feel free to seek the counsel of their supervisors and to learn about District policies and operational problems, to offer suggestions or to ask advice on any matter which is troubling them. No employee need hesitate to do this.

EMPLOYEE HANDBOOK

Nothing takes the place of face-to-face conversations with employees to answer questions and to impart information. But this isn't always possible. So that nothing an employee should know is left unsaid, many companies, especially the larger ones, have their policies, regulations and employee benefits written out in an Employee Handbook. A copy is given to each employee.

The purpose is to acquaint new employees and remind old employees of their benefits and opportunities.

Such a booklet describing the employee program may become the basis for discussion during the initial indoctrination which takes place on the new worker's first day on the job. It may be distributed at that time or at the orientation program some few days later.

The contents of the book cover company organization, established policies, personnel practices and operating rules. Specifically, the following types of items are included:

- A greeting of welcome to the new employee
- Brief story about the company and its products or services
- Organization of company (chart)
- Location, including branches
- Employment policy including part-time, rehirees, minorities, etc.
- Job posting
- Promotion policy
- Training programs
- Exempt employees defined and how rules apply to them
- Work day—regular hours and exceptions
- Time records or time clocks
- Overtime
- Rest periods

- Lunch period
- Eating facilities available; cafeteria
- Lounge
- Records and the importance of keeping them up-to-date
- Clinic and health
- Job security
- Promptness (not tardiness)
- Attendance (not absence)
- Dependability
- Personal appearance
- Personal telephone calls and mail
- Smoking—where permitted
- Performance rating
- Job evaluation, a fair system for setting wage ranges
- Payday and where to cash checks
- Shift premiums
- Social Security; company matches employee deduction
- Withholding tax deductions
- Savings bonds—how to buy them through payroll deduction
- Credit Union
- Wage assignments—how these are handled
- Employment referrals
- Holidays, national and religious; personal and floating
- Vacations
- Death, time off for funerals
- Marriage leave
- Jury duty and witness summons
- Voting—time off in national elections
- Hospitalization insurance

- Medical-surgical insurance
- Health and accident insurance
- Income continuation program
- Disability insurance
- Life insurance
- Retirement income
- Sick pay
- Illness absence
- Personal leave of absence
- Furlough
- Pregnancy and child care leave
- Military leave including National Guard duty
- Extended military service
- Reporting accidents
- Workers' compensation
- Safety and accident prevention
- Fire drills
- Care of equipment and machines
- Company sponsored employee parties, picnics, dances
- Service recognition dinner
- Service awards
- Suggestion system
- Employee sponsored activities
- Recreational programs
- Parking
- House organ
- Communications
- Orientation program
- Gift or flower fund

- Canvassing and soliciting
- Fund raising drives endorsed by company
- Bulletin boards
- Lost and found
- Notary public
- Counselling on personal problems
- Grievance procedure
- Exit interview
- Unemployment compensation
- Compliance with government laws and regulations

plus possibly some of these where applicable:

- Profit sharing
- Incentive pay
- Bonus
- Savings plan
- Company discount purchases
- Tuition reimbursement
- Layoffs and recalls
- Probation or suspension
- Policy on gambling
- Attitude toward outside activities
- Moonlighting
- Civic responsibilities

It is impossible to describe the one best format for an Employee Handbook. It might be advisable to use the assistance of others, such as public relations or advertising people, who will introduce imagination into its creation. The use of color, photographs, drawings or graphs will help get the message across. But it must be written, or at least influenced, 'by the personnel executive who retains the responsibility for its accuracy, compliance with policy and effectiveness. In addition to detailing the specifics of the employee program, it should reflect the personality of the company.

Companies that plan to prepare or revise their Employee Handbook are cautioned to avoid publishing an obvious *rule book* and should also be careful not to overdo the sickening "you" approach. A straightforward and sincere presentation will be more acceptable, and an interesting style, possibly narrative form, will make it readable.

A good place to start is by gathering as many handbooks as possible from other companies in the community or industry. You will pick up ideas from the books that impress you. Be careful, however, not to copy blindly for in so doing you will borrow bad habits as well as good ones.

COMPANY HISTORY

Typically, an employee handbook begins with a brief history of the company and its business. The following is taken from *The Dofasco Way,* the employee handbook of Dominion Foundries and Steel, Limited, Hamilton, Ontario, Canada.

Dominion Foundries and Steel has expanded and diversified its steel production in Hamilton since its beginnings in 1912. Clifton W. Sherman founded the Company that year, which was called Dominion Steel Casting Company, because it produced the steel castings required by locomotive and freight car builders.

During the first year, the Company had an 80-ton daily capacity and employed 150 people. Today, Dofasco has approximately 8,000 on its payroll and produces well over 7,500 tons of steel per day. The figures continue to expand. For instance, Dofasco began operations on four acres of land, but now with the purchase of property along Lake Erie, Dofasco owns approximately 6,000 acres. (National Steel Car, a wholly-owned subsidiary of Dofasco, has approximately 115 acres.)

The early years were rough and as did most industries in the 20's and 30's, Dofasco struggled along. However, new developments in products, production and employee relations were not uncommon at Dofasco. Dofasco became the first Canadian source for such important products as steel plate, floor plate, tin plate, continuously galvanized steel and electrical steels. In 1938, profit sharing was introduced to allow employees to share in the profits they helped to create.

In the early 50's, Dofasco became a fully-integrated steel producer with the building of its first blast furnace. There are four blast furnaces operating at present; the latest beginning production in 1971.

Oxygen steelmaking was a revolutionary process introduced in 1954 by Dofasco in North America. It produces a batch of steel in less than one hour.

The Company's expanding role in the economy is not limited to the production of steel. Dofasco has expanded its base by acquiring Canadian sources of iron ore located in Temagami and Kirkland Lake, Ontario, and at Wabash Lake, Labrador. In 1962, the Company acquired National Steel Car, one of Canada's leading manufacturers of railway equipment.

Expansion continued into the 60's and early 70's. Approximately $32.5 million has been directed toward pollution abatement installations from 1960 to 1972, aimed at protecting our environment. This program is continuing. A new, 2-high slabbing mill in the hot rolling division, soaking pits, additional annealing facilities, a 56" cold mill, along with a new, electrolytic tinning line, were completed in the early 70's. Presently, Dofasco is completing a $100 million expansion program. The future looks promising.

HOUSE ORGAN or EMPLOYEE MAGAZINE

The editor of an employee magazine who thinks only of giving the news is missing half of his opportunity. He is thinking of himself as a reporter instead of as an editor.

A reporter tells who did what, when and where, and possibly why. The editor—and this may come as a surprise—editorializes. He seeks to shape opinions. The reporter presents a word picture; the editor uses the word picture to educate and influence.

Some employee publications are so shallow they are little more than useless. Telling about one employee who visited grandma on a farm in Iowa is of little interest except possibly to the one employee. Close friends already know this and others really don't care.

Then there are employee publications that go to the other extreme —they are company "mouthpieces." An employee magazine is for employees and even official stories should be presented to show how they benefit employees.

Instead of a bullhorn announcement of what a great pension plan management provides, a news story about the recent retiree can carry a quiet note about benefits. That way the viewpoint is that of the employee rather than of management.

The objectives of the employee publication should be to:

1. Promote a feeling among employees that management is fair, reasonable and human.
2. Show that management respects employees as individuals with rights and aspirations and leaves them with the feeling that they are needed, wanted and appreciated.

3. Convince employees that their working conditions are good, their benefits adequate, that their company is one of the best, and their future is secure.

The difference between an employee magazine and a house organ is subtle, but definite. One suggests it is truly written with the employees primarily in mind; the other sounds as if the company and its management can't resist the temptation of talking about themselves.

BENEFIT BOOK

An employee handbook, to be complete, should include a summary description of every item in the insurance or welfare program. Here we offer a suggestion.

There are two problems. First, to describe each type of insurance adequately, with benefit schedules, rates and examples, takes more space than most other items in the handbook. Try to describe the retirement program in a few paragraphs!

Second, insurance programs are subject to revisions as coverages are expanded and benefits increased. The rates the employees pay may be revised every year. This causes the handbook to become out-of-date.

The easiest solution is to publish a set of two matching handbooks. The first one can contain everything but insurance benefits—company history, management line-up, products, policies, procedures, conditions of employment and the like. This is the part of the book that remains fairly stable.

The insurance coverage could then be described in a companion book. This separate book would include insurances for hospitalization, medical-surgical, major medical, dental, disability, group life and retirement, together with eligibility requirements and other provisions of the policies.

Some companies even go so far as to publish a series of separate pamphlets for each item of insurance. Then as something changes it is not necessary to discard the original handbook or do an entire reprint simply because one part of it is obsolete.

READING RACKS

Employees think about many things. Interests vary according to the individual, but in general they cover vacations, buying a car or home, hobbies, gardening, crafts and the like. Women think about recipes, clothes, home furnishings, families and entertaining friends. Men think about sports, guns, money and such matters. Both men and women, fathers and mothers, think about taxes and government, war and voting.

Since what people think about determines what they do off the job, some companies give consideration to activities or projects to guide the thinking of their workers into constructive channels. Distributing useful literature should never be used as an excuse for selfish propaganda, but rather to clear up fuzzy ideas employees may have about things in life that concern them and their well-being. At the same time, companies make available to their workers helpful hints on a variety of subjects.

These companies subscribe to one of the several, reputable booklet rack services. This keeps the material neutral as well as easy to obtain. The distributor furnishes display racks which are then conveniently located in the office and around the plant.

The suppliers often offer a purchaser a choice of material. A new set of pamphlets is sent out periodically, usually monthly. Companies may, in some cases, get a preview and can make a selection. The companies purchase the booklets at a nominal quantity rate and make them available free of charge to employees who are encouraged to take whatever is of interest.

In addition to booklets, some publishers supply newspapers, posters and other items which contain articles or messages that are in keeping with the booklet theme.

An analysis of subjects breaks down as follows:

1. Sports and pastimes
2. Home crafts
3. Leisure hobbies
4. Skill development
5. Economics and government
7. Health

The objectives, according to the National Research Bureau, Inc., of Burlington, Iowa, a distributor of the material, are:

1. To aid the development of employee goodwill.
2. To create better employee understanding of our American business system and good government.
3. To give employees self-help information about health, sports, hobbies, money and a variety of similar topics.

Their program is being used by more than 2,000 companies, large and small, throughout the United States and Canada, reaching more than three and one-half million employees.

THE MODERN METHOD OF EMPLOYEE COMMUNICATION

6 No. 6 RACK. Will stand on its own easel or hang on wall – (NO POSTER FRAME)

19" High—17" Wide—6" Deep, with three 2" tiers
(Will hold about 225 Booklets)

An Informed Employee... Is a More Efficient One

The employee information rack program serves as a medium of communication between management and employees, to create an improved realtionship.

The contributing factors making the program successful are:

1. Voluntary use. Literature is placed in a rack for voluntary pickup by employees.
2. Diversification of material. A variety of topics with different titles is available at regular intervals.
3. Brevity of articles. Educational messages covering good government, economics, human relations, success stories, health and employee welfare are condensed into short articles for quick reading.
4. Source of material. Articles are obtained from original manuscripts by writers who are recognized authorities in their fields.

EMPLOYEE ECONOMIC INFORMATION PROGRAM

There is a notion abroad in the land that many Americans feel a hostility toward American business. They perceive business to be greedy, selfish, and self-serving. They forget that the entrepreneurs built this great country and that today's employers are providing the vitality necessary to sustain as well as expand the economy upon which the citizens depend for their livelihood.

The misinterpretation about the role of business in the lives of everyone results from misinformation, of course. Unions, activists, revisionists, and pressure groups have been actively spreading their gospels, while business has failed to counteract their propaganda by telling its side of the story.

Few people understand how the free enterprise system works. They do not consider the impact of business upon the community it serves. When a business fails or moves away, and an irreparable void is left in its wake, only then do they finally comprehend how much their personal and family lives were entwined with that of the businesses which through jobs provide security and stability.

Many companies are beginning to realize that their neglect in this area has allowed an adverse reflection on their image, reputation and standing to develop. They are finally doing something about this situation by instituting "Employee Economic Information" programs.

Employees are the best place to start in restoring confidence in the firm and pride in the products and services it offers. But before employees can be expected to change their attitudes, they must: (1) know more about their company, and (2) learn about the role of business in the economy.

Employees have to be sold on their own companies before they can be sold on business in general. They must be satisfied that the products and services sold are useful, that working conditions are proper, wages competitive, safety assured, benefits adequate, and the company's reputation is above reproach.

In an employee economic information program, the topics presented include: business in general and the company's place; social responsibility of business; profit as a motivating influence; productivity and the impelling necessity for improvement; the role of government, regulations, compliance; effect of many-level taxes; inflation and its cost on corporate financial health.

Any employee economic information program is no one-shot distribution of canned literature that companies are inclined to buy. Like safety education, it must be continuous. It needs more than company support; it requires active participation by qualified higher-ups. Questions from employees should be invited and these questions must be answered. Questionnaires can be utilized to survey the employees about the plausibility of the program.

The employee economic information program costs time, money, and effort. But it is one corporate endeavor that promises to yield a rewarding payoff.

LIBRARY

Just as it is normal to expect children to attend school, so it is becoming accepted for adults to keep on studying. Instead of putting a period at the end of school days, we use a comma, as we do not stop but branch out into a more spacious version of life. A new concept of education is emerging.

The accelerating pace of social change makes education a lifelong, not a terminal, process. The social, economic and cultural climate in which adults live is no longer the same as that for which they trained in early life. Continued learning enables us to understand broadening responsibilities, to detect opportunities, and to build a philosophy in the art of living in a changing world.

One way to cooperate with employees in their ambitions to keep on growing is through a company library. A central library will serve employees of a large office, or of a company with both office and factory workers housed in the same or nearby buildings. In multiple building plants, convenient branch libraries, or "reading centers," may be opened in the plant, utilizing cafeterias, recreation rooms or other handy areas.

The purpose is to widen the reading habits of employees. Company libraries contain good books and quality magazines, as well as the weekly news magazines and a file of back issues of newspapers. Homecraft and hobby books are included. Technical textbooks and trade publications are available for specific interests. There are also books and articles on management, supervision, human relations, and on economics, government and politics. The company library often contains books relating to the business and the industry which are not usually found at public libraries.

Promotion Helps

The benefits of continuous education are, however, not universally accepted. Some people are enmeshed in a mood which worships leisure time as idleness. They know of no pleasure other than the gratification of the senses and the delights of society, leaving their minds unenlightened and their faculties unchallenged. They indulge themselves in the conceit that they are making good use of free time when they are only engaged in the humbler occupation of killing time.

Tennyson said, "Come, my friends, 'tis not too late to seek a newer world." We can find happiness by understanding and directing the current of progress. This requires continuous study. The human nervous system has great adaptive capacity if we keep it vibrant and working. Each person can choose to keep an active open mind or elect to become inactive, forgetful and depend upon emotional patterns fixed from early experiences. The latter is the sign leading to unhappiness, old age and discontent.

A company library should be under the supervision of an experienced librarian, possibly part time. This person is responsible, of course, for loaning books and for their on-time return in good condition. In large cities arrangements may be made with the public library for the lending of books.

But a good librarian does more than handle in-and-out books. The library should be promoted and its regular and frequent use encouraged. A sign of a good library is to have its books "out," not neatly stacked in rows on fancy shelves.

How many books should a company library contain? One rule of thumb is one book per employee; at least this is as good a starting point as any. An appropriation may be set up to purchase a certain number of new books each month in order to keep the library up-to-date. The new books can be reviewed in the employee publication (house organ); such review also reminds employees of the library service.

In companies where a regular library may not be feasible, the beginnings of an employee library may be established with the use of popular paperback books. Not only are these books cheaper to purchase, but employees are likely to donate their personal paperback books instead of throwing them away.

In any case a company library, as a form of adult education, offers everybody the chance for self-betterment, to keep in step with our jobs and our place in the world.

LIBRARY DISPLAY

A wall file offers a convenient and space-saving way to display current library material, such as magazines, bulletins, catalog sheets, travel literature, and the like.

The 13" × 36" wall file illustrated here is available from Caddylak Systems, Inc., 201 Montrose Road, Westbury, New York 11590.

LUNCH-HOUR FILM SHOWINGS

Apart from movies or filmstrips used during training sessions or official meetings, some companies, particularly large factories, often show motion pictures to employees as entertainment or recreation.

Such films are usually shown in a large open area on the employees' own time. One popular arrangement is to run short movies once or twice a week in the cafeteria. Employees may sit in that section where the screen is placed and watch while they eat.

Or films may be shown on a scheduled or continuous basis in a room nearby. Employees eat in a hurry, then move to the movie room. There they may occupy chairs or benches or stand as they watch the movies.

Films for lunch-hour showing fall into four categories:

1. *Entertainment*— comedies or skits by professional actors, or animated cartoons.
2. *Recreational*— travel, spectator sports, fishing, races. The annual World Series film is a good example.
3. *Educational*— economic information, health, community relations, investments.
4. *Promotional*— new company products or services, advertising commercials, employee services.

Films may be borrowed or rented. There are regular film lending libraries that are glad to supply films on a rotating basis. Films may also be obtained from other companies and agencies which make them available as a public service.

It is best to schedule films in advance and to post the list. Employees may then plan to watch those films which appeal to them.

EFFICIENCY*

Any attempt to help the supervisor increase his personal efficiency logically begins with a definition of efficiency. The dictionary defines efficiency as, "effective operation as measured by a comparison of production with cost in energy, time, money." Yet, a definition by itself is useless. It is much like a theory that is different on paper from what it is in practice. It is easy to state but difficult to apply.

"Each duty should be given to the lowest-paid worker qualified to perform it. Anything else is a waste of company money."

This statement is a beautiful theory on efficiency. As a theory we defy anyone to challenge it. But it is only a theory. In the practical operation of our offices and plants we are satisfied to settle for less—much less than the perfection implied in this theory.

So it is with efficiency. The truth is that we cannot expect 100% efficiency. But we can and should expect to improve our efficiency and

---

*The above article, written by the author and originally titled, "Let's Talk About Efficiency," was used as the Introduction to the book *Leadership In the Office*, published by the American Management Association.

that of our workers. In a practical sense, efficiency may be defined as the best utilization of whatever we have available to us. This includes our talents, money, methods and people.

When we look for improvement we think in terms of procedures and machines, and try to make them better. Work simplification and methods improvement are substantial contributions to more efficient operations. But even the application of electronic principles and the introduction of computer equipment, fantastic and revolutionary as these may turn out to be, pale into insignificance compared with the potential that is locked up in the human will to work.

It is generally accepted that people seldom, if ever, work at full capacity. Under ordinary conditions workers coast along at a much lesser rate which employers have come to accept as satisfactory. Workers are not expected to perform regularly and consistently at capacity. But even a small improvement would produce phenomenal results.

Our present productivity rate, which is good enough to provide the highest standard of living on earth, still reflects a tragic extravagance in the utilization of our human resources. With skilled labor in short supply, a growing emphasis on cost cutting, and competition getting tougher, one must wonder how much longer we can afford the expensive luxury of squandering this greatest of all natural resources. While we can point with pride to the headway we make along technological lines, we cannot make similar claims for our accomplishments in the human area.

The True Nature of Waste

Some managers may try to dismiss this part of their responsibilities in the belief that a certain amount of inefficiency in business is not necessarily bad. They argue that our entire standard of living is built upon waste. They may even contend that there is a divine implication in this concept of waste.

In many respects nature is just as wasteful as man. If all the seeds that fall to the ground were to grow, within a year there would be no room for man. So, many persons conclude that if biological waste is acceptable, possibly even good, perhaps our economic waste may also have its useful purpose.

We must remind ourselves, however, that even biological waste is constantly being challenged. For example: We probably consider weeds as worthless. But Emerson described a weed as "a plant whose virtues we have not yet discovered." Each time a botanical specimen is moved from the weed category to that of a useful medicinal plant, we reduce the area of biological waste.

That's what we must do with the economic waste through better utilization of the human element in business. We must recognize that some waste is inevitable, possibly justified. But we must never become resigned to the acceptance of this waste. We must probe continuously for ways to minimize it.

No one can tell the supervisor how to do this. He alone knows his people and the conditions under which they work. However, we can suggest that the best way to motivate workers to more and better production is through helping them derive greater personal satisfaction from the work they do.

In his efforts to install cost-cutting methods or labor-saving techniques, the supervisor should not overlook the impact these changes may have on people. Scientifically sound procedures will do more harm than good unless there is also understanding. For without understanding there cannot be acceptance, and without acceptance how can there be any benefit?

When we hire workers in our offices and plants we are not buying people. It may be true that what we are buying is a certain amount of their time. Actually, we are buying results. But since these results are realized through people, we must focus our attention on people and not on things.

A good supervisor believes in people. He genuinely likes people, and by his words, actions and beliefs lets them know this. Finally, he likes his own job, he lives it, and gets excited about it. This enthusiasm rubs off on workers and stimulates them to a similar appreciation of their jobs. Can anyone suggest a more effective motivation device?

Whatever we do, as we strive to increase the productivity of our work force by improving ourselves and our people, we should not try for 100% efficiency. This is not possible nor perhaps desirable. Just a percentage of increase in efficiency is all that is needed to show progress. And in the final analysis progress, not perfection, should be our goal.

Z IS FOR ZERO DEFECTS

by PHILIP B. CROSBY
Director, Quality Control
International Telephone and Telegraph Corporation

The idea is to prevent errors, not just detect them. It takes real cooperation all down the line, plus some real horse sense, but this program for perfection pays off.

Let us begin by citing three present-day Parables of Human Frailty and Foible:

1. The garage attendant wiped his hand on a rag. "There you are Mr. Thompkins, as good as new. Don't know how they could have gotten the blinker wires switched on your new car, but from now on when you signal for a right turn no one will think you're turning left. By the way, that's a nasty bump on your head, did you have it looked at?"

2. A florist received a call from a worried young swain. Seems the corsage he had ordered for his girl hadn't arrived, and they were off to a dance in a few minutes. "Let's see," said the florist, "that order was delivered to 1324 East Sampson Street early this afternoon." "But she lives at 1324 West Sampson Street," the young man said. "Hmmm, must remember to speak to the delivery boy," said the florist.

3. Seven hundred miles away, the sky burst into a wild display of burning fuel and exploding dynamite. A huge intercontinental ballistic missile had swerved off course and the range safety officer had pressed the destruct button. Millions of manhours sputtered into the sea. Three days later, the operations chief was told the disaster had been caused by failure to remove the caging pin in the autopilot. "Well," shrugged the chief, "guess nothing will ever be perfect as long as people are involved in it."

The common denominator in all three of these parables is human error—and contrary to most opinion it is *not* inevitable.

The tragedy of modern business is that it is plagued with just such mistakes every day. No great incidents in themselves, they can cause an operation to fail, a customer to be disappointed, or costly rework of an end product.

From the football field to the launching pad, these are the little unpredictables that result in big disasters—"tremendous trifles."

The cost of these errors is immeasurable, and the reason they cannot and have not been measured is that we are inclined to accept them as inevitable. Yet each and every mistake made in the world today has two things in common: It is performed by somebody, and it could have been prevented.

Preventing, Not Detecting

We are going to talk about preventing errors. *Preventing,* not detecting. Detecting costs a lot of money and only saves you future grief. It can't do a thing to solve the problems with which you've already been blessed.

And detecting is only as successful as the detector, the inspector or the checker happens to be at that very moment.

Prevention means getting people and systems to do the job right the first time. There are several techniques involved, but the goal is the same: do it once and do it right.

In order to go wholeheartedly into the study of prevention, it is first necessary to examine the attitude of prevention. The positive attitude is the constant companion of success. What mountain climber ever inspired himself by chanting, "I can't do it. I can't do it"? Prevention is as much a state of mind as it is an understanding of management techniques.

People are carefully conditioned throughout their lives to accept the fact that they are human and humans make mistakes; "To err is human, to forgive, divine."

By the time they enter a business career, this thought is so firmly fixed in their minds that it no longer bothers them to make errors, within reason of course. Acting on the principle that one must not be perfect in order to be human, they will permit themselves a defect level. "I am 95% accurate, which is about all you can expect."

The Philosophy of 95%

Thus they drill holes correctly 95% of the time, deliver packages correctly 95% of the time, design a circuit right 95% of the time, and so forth. They have established a defect level of 5%. The exact figure varies with people, but there is a limit in each one of us at which we become upset over our errors. We do not become upset within our 5% level.

So, if this defect level is standard within us, it should become apparent that we will be shortchanged 5% of the time when we cash our pay checks. We should go home to the wrong house 5% of the time, by mistake. We should go through the back of the garage 5% of the time.

However, these things do not happen. Is it possible that people have developed one standard for the things they do for themselves and one for their business tasks? Does a dual attitude exist? Yes.

We set a higher requirement on the tasks we perform for ourselves than on the ones we do at work. Why? Because the family will tolerate less error than the company.

Mistakes are caused by two things: lack of knowledge or lack of attention. You can measure lack of knowledge and fix it by tried and true means. But lack of attention is an attitude problem and must be repaired by the person himself. He must develop a constant conscious desire to perform the job right the first time. He does this when cashing his pay check, for he knows that there is one chance and one only to obtain the correct return. Once he steps away from the teller's window, he has had it. He is very conscious of what must occur.

The Dual Standard

So people have accepted a dual standard. In cases involving work, they are not bothered by a few errors, but in personal requirements the standard must be zero defects.

Zero Defects is the name given to a motivation and improvement program developed at Martin-Orlando that has achieved a great deal of success in the weapons industry. Some commercial firms have tried it and feel that it provides real gains for them, too.

The whole program is based on explaining to people that it is not necessary for them to prove their humanity by fulfilling their requirements for error. Rather, they can accept as a challenge the task of making a constant, conscious effort to do the job right the first time. You will find that most of them have never been told that.

The usual improvement programs are based on the principle that "Quality is everybody's job. We must do better." No one will disagree, yet if it is everyone's job, then it is nobody's especially.

The challenge of Zero Defects is that it requires the individual to pledge himself to improve. He is given a pin or card in return to seal the bargain. There is one stipulation, however; the worker must sign up for the program as an individual, pledging himself to the cause, "Z-D means prevention, not detection."

There are three phases to Martin's Zero Defects program:

1. Show workers why they should join the program.
2. Review specifications and requirements to eliminate the unattainable or the overly strict.
3. Develop error-proof processes and/or instructions so that anyone who wants to do a good job can do so.

The most dedicated, conscientious "Zero-Defect-minded" person in the world couldn't be expected to deliver a package from Peoria, Illinois to Paris, France, in 20 minutes and return. That requirement is unattainable today.

Automobile gasoline tanks made out of paper are going to leak after a while, no matter how dedicated the workers that make them. Cutting a sheet of aluminum to a tolerance of 0.0001 inch with tin snips would tax the patience (and talents) of a saint.

Thus there has to be give and take on the part of management and the worker if perfection is to be attained. Management must not set ridiculous and unattainable goals for its workers, and it must eliminate those that already exist. In instances where the ridiculous and unattainable cannot be eliminated (such things do exist in the precision industries), something must be done to bring them within the range of human skills. You can, for example, order a man to lift 10,000 pounds. He can't do it by himself, but he can do it with the help of a crane.

Down From Cloud Nine

Thus a proper combination of management skill and employee willingness can pull just about any requirement down from Cloud Nine and into the realm of attainment. One by-product of this is drastic cost reduction.

The next step is to develop processes and instructions that will make any task defect proof. First off, it's a matter of attitude. You can't, for example, find a way to drill a perfect hole in just the right spot every time if you don't think it can be done.

Now, assuming that you do think it can be done, let's take a look at how a Zero Defects program can be accomplished.

A Z-D program can be carried out by a one-man shop, or it can be carried out in a shop that employs 35,000 people.

Thus Z-D begins with making employees aware of quality. Build them up slowly to make them more conscious of the need for better product quality. This can be done effectively with signs, pamphlets and little personal talks about how important it is in this day and age to turn out a good product in the face of stiffening competition.

Anyone can make a fly swatter, but the successful fly swatter is the one that will stand up to its job time after time yet be inexpensive and attractive. (Come to think of it, who ever heard of an attractive fly swatter? But be that as it may, that's the principle of a successful product).

If you take defect level measurements within your operation—that is, if you have an inspection function that examines work in process or at the end, and records defects—hang a defect level chart over each area so monitored. This chart should show the percent of units found to be defective as submitted to inspection. These charts show trends in performance, and people like to be measured.

Here is what you need to launch the program formally:

1. A kickoff date for Zero Defects Day—this should be recognized as a big deal. Top management of the company should be available on that day (on the floor and in the office areas) to show by their presence that they take it seriously.

2. Posters, pamphlets and other giveaway material that describes the logic of the program should be ready.
3. Pledge cards should be prepared. These should be in two parts. The first should be an IBM-sized card that carries the pledge, "I freely pledge myself to make a constant, conscientious effort to do my job right the first time, recognizing that I am an important part of the company's effort to move toward the Zero Defects goal." (Once this card is signed, it should be taken with great formality to the vault and locked up).

   The second card should be wallet-size and should restate the pledge, plus some of the program logic. The employee keeps it.
4. Zero Defect pins, simple but dignified, should be presented to the employee when he signs up.

Try some special attention getters. If you have a cafeteria, have a Z-D luncheon bargain. Place tent cards around the building saying, "It means prevention, not detection."

Next, it must be emphasized that no disciplinary action will result from employees making an error. The idea is to help them get better, not become perfect over night. If the wrong impression is given, they start hiding mistakes.

Total Participation

And, *everybody* must participate. Don't make the mistake of concentrating on the assembly line or manual workers. They can do very little to improve the quality of the hardware. All they can do is not make it worse than the design and material. Put a lot of effort into the engineering and business side of the house. This is the fruitful area.

The motivation phase of the program must be followed up periodically—some rededication effort every four months helps.

It is fair to ask why such a program should be required. Or, rather, why don't people automatically do their job right? Why don't they want to?

Well, people do want to do a good job. They want to have the proper attitude. But they receive their attitude and standards from their supervisors, and the supervisors work on the things that they think the company wants. Thus everytime management has a schedule emphasis period they may find quality or cost suffers.

It is not enough to depend upon the eyeballs and the skill of the detection personnel, they are at best 85% accurate in their trade. The only way to produce detect-free products or services is to not have the error occur in the first place. The only way to have that happen is to convince people that that is the company's standard.

Now let's examine the second phase of Z-D: requirements.

The most difficult part about starting a realistic requirements program is getting people to understand that it doesn't mean just getting rid of tough jobs—only the unnecessary.

Let's suppose that you were making parts to 125 mu-in. rms finish —which is pretty good. But if you looked at the assembly you'd find that the part came in contact with nothing on that surface and you could go to 250. Thus the job is easier, cheaper, and just as useful. Well, you say, that's not very exciting. Smacks of common sense.

But each organization is filled with sincere people who are interested in protecting their judgments and prerogatives. They do not want to be found wrong. Thus they issue specifications, requirements and regulations that contain a margin of safety.

When these people are indoctrinated in the Zero Defects concept, they can have the feeling of confidence that people will then respect the real requirement and they won't have to fudge it.

Now how do you go about formalizing this requirements evaluation business?

Task Force and Plan

First, a steering task team must be established. This team should represent four functions: manufacturing, quality, engineering and finance. If the operation is small all of these might be one man. But he must consider each viewpoint individually to make sure that he is not biasing the program.

Second, a plan of attack must be defined. The order of priority for investigation: (1) the most troublesome area, (2) which areas are the most expensive? (3) which things seem unreasonable or unnecessary?

Once the group investigates and gets into its first problem, the order of execution will have defined itself. The success of the task will be proportional to the enthusiasm of the participants.

It is a good idea to conduct classes for personnel, so that they can see the results of the first few efforts. The understanding they obtain, plus the opportunity to have another crack at the difficult areas, will more than pay for the time spent.

In the final analysis, you are not after the clarification of individual requirements here and there. The goal is to ingrain into every person in the operation the feeling that rules should always be followed, but if the rule is not compatible with common sense, it should be modified. The channel for modification needs to be short, and the judgments sincere. But once people find out that you will listen to them, the ideas will flow and blossom.

Directions and Instructions

The processes for conducting a business are one of any company's most significant possessions. Call them instructions, or directions, or recipes (there are all kinds of names) but essentially they are a detailed documentation of the way to do a job.

In electronics, the processes are quite complex; the chemical industry is very heavy with these directions. And what bleary-eyed father has not tried on Christmas Eve to "place bolt K in hole #4 making sure that Fin V is perpendicular to the red side of the main body."

Most instructions are written with the thought that the people who are going to do the job already know how and thus need just reminders. When I purchased a swimming pool, I received much literature on the art of placing chemicals in the pool to assure safe swimming water. However, all of it talked about the refinements of the art—nowhere did the basics appear for someone who was not quite clear on what H_2O was. Sort of like reading an instruction booklet for airplane flying that begins "Once up in the air . . ."

Each step of the operation should be examined in detail, each tool or instrument used must stand the test of why it has been selected. And most important of all, the process must be written in language that the worker will understand, so the minimum amount of interpretation will be required.

Review of Difficulties

As the operation progresses any difficulties encountered should be reviewed with the task team and specific correction obtained. In a brief period, repeatability will set in; then the cycle can start anew with an eye to improvement. If this repeat cycle is not encouraged and demanded, the new process will become as troublesome as the old within the course of time. Problem magnitude will be lower, but your organization will be much more sensitive to potential discrepancies and less easy to satisfy.

What does all of this concentration on attitude bring you? A new way of life—both professionally and personally. A desire to eliminate the error potential becomes part of your thoughts. It is not possible to sit down and say, "Now for this 45-minute period, I am going to concentrate on preventing defects. Then I shall return to normal operations." The mind does not work like that unless the basic orientation has been accomplished.

Although I have been out of the Navy many years, the words, "deck, ladder, bulkhead," still creep into my conversations. They were deeply ingrained there by an organization that was determined that all sailors would talk like sailors. It's the same with the thought of Zero Defects.

How does management set the tone of Z-D in daily operations in order to assure that this occurs? Let's take the example of "breadboard." As everyone knows, a breadboard (and each business has its own word for it) is a device where you build up a potential product strictly for feasibility, just to see if it'll work. The name comes from the practice in electronics of pinning parts to a big board and making a circuit out of them. It is a fine, useful technique.

However, it is much misused, to the detriment of the eventual product. Research and development have been confused with breadboarding. If management permits the engineering and research (or sales types) people to develop the basic product on strictly a functional basis then the production of it will be up to its you-know-what in troubles.

It is essential that the processes, controls, documentation, etc., be developed in parallel with the new product. This is not a big effort. But, oh! How many units perform perfectly until they are taken from the laboratory and given to the production line to build. Every error, every misinterpretation, must be learned all over again. You can tell by looking at your rejection rate when your suppliers have made the switch from lab to production.

The manufacturing man is in the position of one who hears a knock on his door and opens it to find a black box nestled in a wicker basket. An accompanying note says, "make a thousand a month." He has had little or no input to the packaging of the unit, or to the material used. Companies that think this way are going to have an interesting problem.

The mind set must be carried into personal dealings with subordinates and associates. "I won't be able to give you that report Friday afternoon as I promised, but you'll get it first thing Monday morning." Now there's a familiar statement. If you accept it, then the Z-D mind is cracking. If you request that the man keep his promise and look like you mean it, you'll never hear the request again. People will do what you put up with.

Is the difference between Friday afternoon and Monday morning that important? Usually not. However, the difference between keeping promise dates and not is life and death to your business. Many companies with good quality and competitive costs have failed because they couldn't deliver on time—consistently.

The attitude of defect prevention—Zero Defects—is all that stands between mediocrity and a great performance.

MOTIVATION*

Companies no longer have any natural advantage over each other. What then distinguishes one firm from another? The company that enjoys a more profitable position in today's competitive economy is the one which makes the best utilization of its resources.

There are six elements of an enterprise. These are the six M's:

- Material
- Machines
- Methods
- Money
- Markets
- Manpower

Since other elements in business are relatively fixed, the opportunity for improvement lies in the only variable element, the available manpower. All companies have access to the same material, machines, methods, money and markets. They even have access to the same manpower. It is the utilization of the only variable element, the workforce, that determines whether one firm operates better or poorer than another.

The most promising source of increased productivity is not in machine development or methods improvement; it is locked up in the human will to work. This is also the most neglected area of management since most of the emphasis has traditionally been on the material side of business.

A veritable goldmine awaits managements who succeed in moving workers to greater productive activity and greater efficiency. We know that people do not work at 100% efficiency. Nor are they expected to. Andrew Carnegie said that the average person puts only 25% of his energy and ability into his work. Psychologists have estimates that run all the way from 17% to 50%. You may make your own guess. But the fact remains that people do not work up to 100% capacity except in a few isolated instances.

One such example might be the Czechs who worked around the clock and reached back for unknown strength to thwart off the Communist despot who threatened their homeland. Another illustration is that of the drowning man who managed to save himself despite the fact that he did not know how to swim. In the ordinary conduct of business,

---

*The above article on "Motivation" is an updated version of the one that appeared in the first edition. It is included again because the late Edward Throm, Dartnell Senior Editor, was so impressed at the time. He commented, "I've never seen the case for humanistic motivation put better."

however, we do not get or expect such dedication. Whatever the percentage, one economist estimated that just a one percent improvement factor in the United States workforce would result in enough additional manhours of work to run United States Steel, General Electric and International Harvester for one year.

The Last Frontier

This then is the frontier that managers are encouraged to explore. The fundamentals and procedures that are used, the necessary scientific techniques that have been developed, and their human application comprise what is generally termed "motivation."

Motivation is an abstract term. It imparts an incentive that requires a response on the part of someone else to achieve a defined goal. The salesman does not sell; by persuasion he motivates the customer to buy.

In business, motivation is not synonymous with wages. Money is a means for accommodating the economic needs of workers. Motivation means an inner wholesome desire to exert effort without the external stimulus of money. To motivate the employee, the employee must be reached; to reach the employ there must be a complete understanding of the complexity of his make-up.

Motivation efforts must be directed toward improving company operations. That much is basic. To be effective, however, they must also be designed to show benefits to the employee. In fact, motivation can best be accomplished when workers are able to merge their personal ambitions with those of the company.

In initial employment, for example, finding the right person for any job is only half of the task. The applicant must feel that he, too, has found a job opportunity which meets or exceeds his expectations. Only when there is a happy job marriage, in which both sides are satisfied, does the placement stand a chance of being successful. In such cases the company will provide the worker with the job satisfaction he needs to be happy; and he, in turn, will have that built-in motivation companies look for in order to make his employment profitable.

Motivating is the ability of indoctrinating the personnel with a unity of purpose and maintaining a continuing, harmonious relationship among all the people. It is a force which encourages and promotes a willingness of every employee to cooperate with every other member of the team.

Basic to good motivation on the part of managers is the maintenance of conditions conducive to cooperate effort. To motivate is to create and perpetuate the climate which brings harmony and equilibrium into the entire work group for the benefit of all who are involved—the company as a whole and the employees as individuals.

Motivation Through Individuality

To utilize the human element in business effectively, it is well to devote adequate attention to the fundamentals of motivation. Unlike machines and other material matters, people have personalities, can think, have beliefs and exercise some control over their work both in how well it is done and how much is done. Leadership, communications and good attitude play very important roles. Creating conditions that provide interest, job satisfaction and personal reward are vital.

Managements do well to emphasize this aspect of the line manager's responsibility. The four functions of a manager or supervisor are:

1. Planning
2. Organizing
3. Motivating
4. Controlling

Plans and organized efforts are of no value until they are put into action. It is necessary to actuate these efforts by motivating members of the workforce to start and continue to work along the lines determined best by managers.

Since management is accomplishing a predetermined objective through the efforts of other people, it is evident that motivation is extremely important. Stated simply, without manpower the machines would be idle, material would remain unused, and so on. Conversely, a well-staffed, carefully-selected and well-motivated workforce enhances the value of the machines, methods and other elements of business.

The degree of success in motivating employees is in direct relation to the manager's ability to help employees realize personal ambitions and aspirations. The basic wants of workers are:

1. Economic
2. Psychological
3. Social

Man does not live by bread alone. While money is necessary, it is not the only form of wealth, nor in the final analysis the most important. In addition to material wealth, employees need to increase their cultural wealth, social wealth and spiritual wealth.

Group Approaches Ineffective

In trying to understand employees it is well to learn about individual and group behavior. Individuals often react differently when in groups. But always, whether alone or in league with co-workers, employees are individuals. Attempts to motivate workers are more successful when related to individuals and not groups.

It takes some doing on our part to comprehend this. In business we've become so accustomed to using mass techniques—in manufacturing, advertising, marketing, bargaining agreements—that we also try to apply these methods to individuals.

This is what psychologists call the "fetish of symmetrical development." It is not recommended as a motivation technique for the simple reason that no two people are alike. Different people have different fears, different problems, different desires and hopes, and different ways of reacting to similar situations. They require different treatment.

A realistic approach leads to a recognition of individual strengths and weaknesses and then giving consideration accordingly. Only as people are different do they become noticed in a world of conformity. Only as we as managers and supervisors play up to the individuality, rather than the sameness, do we succeed in getting through to people with our message.

We must never forget that the people whom chance has brought our way, who spend a good portion of their waking hours in our trust, are not only trying to make a living . . . they are also trying to make a life!

Motivation of rank-and-file workers is becoming more of a challenge because the workforce is changing, the value system is being rearranged, and attitudes of people generally are unpredictable. Therefore the former approach to employee motivation has to be changed, too.

There is a new breed of employee on the scene. He wants the rewards of hard work but not the trouble, strain and effort of hard work. He not only responds differently to tried-and-tested methods of motivation, but his outlook has a contaminating effect on co-workers.

Workers are also more educated and this makes them impatient and dissatisfied with drudgery jobs that consist of monotonous tasks. Inspirational pep talks don't improve job content. Employees are no longer self-motivated simply out of economic necessity. It isn't easy to overcome negative attitudes toward business, free enterprise and work itself.

The opportunity is to infuse jobs with enough spice, variety and excitement to offset the inevitable drudgery that cannot be avoided. Any manager who can make headway in this direction will get more out of the worker and out of the job.

What People Expect From Work

Sometimes it appears that the reasons people like to work are better known to workers than to management. A poll to decide what motivates employees brought interesting results.

Bosses gave these reasons, in this order:
> good wages
> job security
> promotion and growth in company
> good working conditions
> interesting work
> boss' loyalty to workers
> tactful disciplining
> full appreciation of work done
> help on personal problems
> feeling of being "in" on things.

Employees, on the other hand, listed much these same reasons, but in a different order of priority. They said:
> full appreciation of work done
> feeling of being "in" on things
> help on personal problems
> job security
> good wages
> interesting work
> promotion and growth
> loyalty from boss
> good working conditions
> tactful disciplining

It is significant to note that three factors considered least important by management seemed most important to employees. Maybe managements don't know as much about their employees' needs and wants as they imagine they do.

Workers require certain satisfactions from their jobs. Managements which identify these basic needs and attempt to satisfy them are on solid ground. Managements which are preoccupied with other matters will continue to muddle along, wondering "what's the matter with people today?" The opportunity to minimize problems is there for all. The landscape is the same; the difference is in beholders.

The worker must see that his contribution flows into the common ocean of human effort. The telephone lineman is not merely tying together two strands of wire; he is linking patient to doctor, and so forth. Similarly, the manager or supervisor is more than a skilled technician; he is engaged in a form of human engineering.

The executive who thinks his people are working only for a paycheck is deluded. Only when he tries to understand that his workers are flesh and blood human beings with individuality expressed in the way they act and respond, is he on the right track and going in the right direction —toward success for his workers, his company and himself.

Basic Job Satisfactions People Need

To get workers to respond, company programs should understand what job satisfactions people require of their jobs. Each worker wants:

1. Recognition as an individual: known by name and respected.
2. A meaningful task: its purpose and prestige understood by him.
3. An opportunity to do something worthwhile: and recognition for his contribution.
4. Job security: for himself and his family.
5. Good wages: fair in community and fairly administered.
6. Adequate benefits: protection against the unexpected.
7. Opportunity to advance: chance to earn a better living.
8. Information about what is going on: especially what concerns him.
9. Freedom from arbitrary action: a voice in matters affecting him.
10. Satisfactory working conditions: considerate of his safety, comfort, convenience and health.
11. Congenial associates: best part of day, week and life is spent at work and it should be pleasant.
12. Competent leadership: bosses whom he can admire and respect as persons and as bosses.

Motivation in Training Programs

Motivation has always been a likely topic for training, particularly in supervisory development courses. Most of the training lies in the academic approach to motivation. This stresses basic human needs and tries to associate them to employee on-the-job behavior. Consequently the discussions are theoretical and not always useful. They look good on the agenda, and they often sound good to conference leaders and observers. But how much impact do they have on actual office or factory operations?

Too many are designed to provide the supervisor with a magic formula, or convenient push button, which when pressed into use will galvanize every subordinate into action and immediately increase his productivity. In real business life this just does not happen.

A more down-to-earth type of training would suggest less textbook problem solving and more practical discussions in the laboratory of day-to-day business activity. A supervisor brings in an actual problem and places it before the other members of the training group. This focuses attention and invites constructive thinking on a familiar, or easily understood, problem situation. Members of the group discuss the problem in terms of their own experience. In so doing they reveal how they would react to a similar situation and what possible approaches toward meeting it they would consider using.

The discussion is realistic, the problem understandable and the conclusions meaningful. The practical value is apparent. They are on their way to becoming successful managers and supervisors once they realize that problems of this sort do not lend themselves to any pat back-of-the-book answers.

The History of Motivation

Learning the techniques is not as important as knowing the reasons people react as they do. Perhaps a quick resumé of the history of motivation will be helpful in understanding it.

In the early history of the laboring man there was no real thought or concern on the meaning of motivation. Until the latter part of the 20th century, the workingman was not recognized as a human being endowed with motivation energies that could be raised to his personal summit. Indeed, he was treated as a puppet and manipulated as such by the employer.

Motivation in business and industry is identified with three distinct phases:

1. Years ago it was *Fear.* The danger of losing a job, or even worse, the threat of having it taken away, was all the motivation hard-fisted bosses had to use. This type of motivation has long ago been discarded simply because it is not in harmony with managements' new concept of dealing with people.

Any supervisor who still thinks he can motivate workers by threatening them had better "wise up" to the facts of life. Fear actually never was a good motivator. Examples: fear of lung cancer has not decreased cigarette smoking; fear of imprisonment has not lowered the crime rate; fear of highway deaths has not diminished traffic accidents; fear of the hydrogen bomb has not lessened preparations for war.

2. If not fear, which was used in early days, what do we use for motivation now? Today it seems to be *Fringe Benefits.* Companies are smothering employees with benefits and welfare services, almost trying to buy their loyalty and dedication. "Look what we're doing for our people," we say. But we all know that increasing the company-paid group life insurance, for instance, from $1,000 to $2,000 has no noticeable effect on a worker's daily output. As important as fringe benefits are, they are no longer effective as motivation forces; they are conditions of employment. Fringe benefits are productivity's contribution to social development.

3. Tomorrow it will be *Leadership.* A concept is emerging. It recognizes that employees are human entities and must derive satisfaction

both physically and psychologically. The manager of tomorrow will be the kind of person others want to follow. He must set a good example. He must be competent, of course, but he must also be considerate, fair and understanding. His success in motivating others will be dependent not upon what he says, or what he does, but what he believes.

Conclusion

The three basic wants of American citizens which find expression in management's employee relations are:

1. Economic security
2. Personal freedom
3. A rising standard of living

What then do we suggest companies do to motivate their workers to more and better production, to help them reach personal goals and at the same time meet company objectives?

1. Establish the kind of climate wherein people will give of themselves without giving up themselves.
2. Give workers optimum communications, not maximum. Neglecting to keep workers informed is dangerous; in the absence of authoritative information the rumor mill will fill in. But overcommunicating is even worse. This is like over-clogging the channels with noise. One word of trust and respect will carry more impact than a thousand words of double-talk.
3. Don't imagine you can develop others. No one can develop anyone else except himself. The door to development is locked from the inside. We can keep knocking at the door but the other person must respond and open it for himself.
4. Try not to change behavior. This is a head-against-the-wall futility. Make the worker aware of his strong points and capitalize on them. Keep the weaknesses out of sight and under control.
5. Do not try to teach the worker how to behave or what to think. Teach him instead how to learn and think for himself.

THEORIES OF MOTIVATION

"Satisfying a want is the key to motivation achievement," according to George R. Terry, in his popular textbook, *Office Management and Control.* Success lies in finding out what the employees' wants are and making it possible for those wants to be satisfied from their work effort.

It sounds simple, but it isn't. Individual and group wants vary among workers. Furthermore, the wants do not remain constant; they change from day to day. The reasons include both employee behavior and the influence of the work and work environment.

The Maslow Theory

Abraham Maslow's theory says it is possible to rank basic needs in a hierarchical ladder from low to high. Until one level is satisfied, the individual does not become concerned with the next level.

The "average person"
in our society might
have these percentages
satisfied:

Self-fulfillment Needs	10%
Egoistic Needs	40%
Social Needs	50%
Safety Needs	70%
Physiological Needs	85%

The hierarchy of needs consists of:

1. *Physiological* needs

- the need for food

- the need for air

- the need for rest

- the need for exercise

- the need for shelter

2. *Safety* needs

- the need for protection against danger

- the need for protection against threat

- the need for protection against arbitrary deprivation

3. *Social* needs

- the need for belonging
- the need for association
- the need for acceptance by one's fellows
- the need for giving and receiving friendship and love

4. *Egoistic* needs

a. Those related to one's self-esteem

- the need for self-respect
- the need for self-confidence
- the need for autonomy
- the need for achievement
- the need for competence
- the need for knowledge

b. Those related to one's reputation

- the need for status
- the need for recognition
- the need for appreciation
- the need for the deserved respect of one's fellows

5. *Self-fulfillment* needs

- the need for realizing one's own potentialities
- the need for continued self-development
- the need for being creative in the broadest sense of that term

Just as the Constitution of the United States guarantees the *pursuit* of happiness, not happiness itself, it is the need to satisfy these basic wants, not the successful accomplishment of them, that motivates people. A satisfied need is no longer a motivator of behavior.

The Herzberg Theory

Frederick Herzberg's theory divides motivation factors into two categories—job content and job context.

Job *content* provides the potential motivators. These are achievement,

311

recognition, responsibility, growth and advancement, and are built into the job. These are the positive factors.

Job *context* considers pay, supplemental benefits, company policy and administration, behavior of supervisor and working conditions. These are negative factors because high motivation does not result from their improvement, but dissatisfaction does result from their deterioration.

Job satisfaction and high production are connected with the positive motivators, while disappointment and ineffectiveness are usually connected with the negative factors (dissatisfiers).

The McGregor Theory

Douglas McGregor developed theories X and Y.

Assumptions of Theory X:

1. The average human being has an inherent dislike of work and will avoid it if he can.
2. Because of this human characteristic of dislike of work, most people must be coerced, controlled, directed, threatened with punishment to get them to put forth adequate effort toward the achievement of organizational objectives.
3. The average human being prefers to be directed, wishes to avoid responsibility, has relatively little ambition, wants security above all.

Assumptions of Theory Y:

1. The expenditure of physical and mental effort in work is as natural as play or rest.
2. External control and the threat of punishment are not the only means for bringing about effort toward organizational objectives. Man will exercise self-direction and self-control in the service of objectives to which he is committed.
3. Commitment to objectives is a function of the rewards associated with their achievement.
4. The average human being learns, under proper conditions, not only to accept but to seek responsibility. Avoidance of responsibility, lack of ambition and emphasis on security are generally consequences of experience, not inherent human characteristics.
5. The capacity to exercise a relatively high degree of imagination, ingenuity and creativity in the solution of organizational problems is widely, not narrowly, distributed in the population.
6. Under the conditions of modern industrial life, the intellectual potentialities of the average human being are only partially utilized.

Theory X and Theory Y probably represent the two extremes of a management continuum approach. Neither is followed in its pure form. Most managers operate somewhere in the in-between area, reflecting the mores of the culture in which they serve.

MOTIVATIONAL NEEDS

It is the needs and wants of individuals that motivate them. These needs are not the same for all people because desires and circumstances vary. But they can be categorized. There is the need for:

1. Security: comfortable well-being today and tomorrow.
2. Prestige: looked up to as an influence.
3. Status: an obvious standing or rank.
4. Responsibility: a sense of importance in job obligations.
5. Recognition: well-deserved attention.
6. Approval: the desire to be liked.
7. Belonging: sharing with others pleasures and experiences.
8. Accomplishment: exercising capacities to the fullest.
9. Independence: expression and assertion in one's own right.
10. Possession: the satisfactions of ownership.

As the needs begin to be satisfied, the basic need diminishes in its motivational impact and another need begins to emerge as a force.

JOB SATISFACTION

In the early days people didn't expect that they ought to enjoy their work. A job was a job and people were grateful for employment.

As time went on people began to look for some measure of personal satisfaction from their jobs. True, the job might not be the major source of happiness, but at least it should be compatible with a person's total life pattern, all of which should be as pleasant as circumstances permitted.

As the employment market changed and the pendulum started to swing over toward the employee, a person tried to select the job where he stood the best chance of being content. If this didn't work out as anticipated, a worker would leave the job and try for a different kind of company or a different type of work.

In a world of rapidly changing social values, many workers today are putting job satisfaction ahead of job performance. They want to work at something they believe in. They respond more to their own inner feelings than to the requirements of the job. The work ethic is being overhauled.

Therein lies the crux of worker dissatisfaction which is plaguing industrialized countries all over the world. The whole thrust of industry is to make jobs more simple and perfunctory while workers have been making themselves more qualified. Today's better educated worker is bored with putting two bolts on a bumper every 65 seconds, but managements feel he should be loyal and dependable in return for a steady paycheck.

Employers are still mainly concerned with the problems of the business—more productivity, greater efficiency and increased profits. Management, which sets the policies and makes the decisions, thinks in terms of the company; employees think in terms of themselves and their families. In this day and age when workers are more assertive, this contradiction creates a conflict that has all sorts of ramifications.

Business is still interested more in the people who buy its products or services and less in the people who buy (i.e., perform) its jobs. Managements use all sorts of devices to educate their employees about the importance of the customer without giving similar consideration to their employees, without whom there would be no customers.

Companies are just not people oriented, although most companies will feign shock at this charge. The truth is that what they believe to be humanitarian practices are nothing more than compliance with social legislation and response to pressures of a competitive industrial society. How many companies really do more for their people than is actually required?

The motto is still, "What is good for business is good for people," whereas the opposite, "What is good for people is good for business," makes much more sense from a practical point of view.

MORALE

Employee morale is the attitude of an individual or group as related to work, co-workers, supervision, management, the company and the product or service that is provided.

It is generally assumed to be axiomatic that higher morale results in increased productivity. Hence there are serious efforts made to improve employee morale.

Good human relations builds good morale. This does not mean that a comprehensive personnel program, complete with techniques and scientific design, will automatically contribute to better morale. It may and it may not. It will if its application includes fairness, understanding and a respect for the dignity of man.

Communications also helps; employees appreciate being kept in the "know." They like to maintain their self-respect. They like also to respect their supervisor, not only as a boss but also as a person. They need to be reassured of their job security. They want, and should have, a voice in decisions that affect them.

Employees, as individuals, have their own hopes and ambitions. Morale is good when employees can use their jobs to fulfill their own personal aspirations. To the extent that these can be dovetailed into company objectives, both the employees and the company gain.

The key to better employee morale lies in good supervision. In supervisory training programs emphasis should be placed on dealing with employees as human beings and not as human machines. Their personal feelings and emotions must be considered as well as their work performance and production schedules.

"Whatever is good for people is good for business" would be an appropriate slogan or credo with which to inculcate the philosophy of supervisors and their attitude toward their responsibility. A department with high morale will get its work done easier and better.

Developing and maintaining good morale among workers is somewhat of an art. But it can be taught. With some supervisors this comes easy; others must work at it.

Good morale is difficult to define and explain. It is not hard to recognize. The evidence is in the payoff.

SUPERVISORS' RESPONSIBILITIES FOR MORALE*

Morale is one of the most precious elements in a business. What supervisors do with the good plans of the executive will make or mar the morale of the company.

People in supervisory positions are not doing their best for the company if they are content to administer rules. Fairness, consistency and demonstrated interest in employee problems are the backbone of supervisory morale building.

The supervisor is charged by management with taking a group of human beings, every one different in temperament, emotions and skills,

*Excerpted from The Royal Bank of Canada, Montreal, Monthly Letter Vol. 58, No. 7 and reprinted with permission.

and developing them into a satisfactory work unit. An important ingredient in that development is the reflection by the supervisor of the high principles of executive officers. Morale, it has been said, doesn't start at the bottom of an organization, but trickles down from the top.

Every supervisor has some job that is his special bit of the bigger job. He may set up a machine, lay out blue prints, check accuracy or prepare reports. But while he will do that part of his work well, it is not the part out of which he gets his greatest satisfaction.

The joy of leadership and the thrill of being in charge of men and women consists in spending the last ounce of your management talent so as to see the people under you fulfil their greatest abilities in their jobs and raise their stature as efficient workers.

It will pay every person who is in charge of workers, both for his own sake and for the sake of his firm, to make a personal inventory along these lines: Am I developing good human relations with my people, or am I content with casual daily contact? Have I some guiding principles in dealing with men and women in my department, or am I going along from day to day, doing the best I can according to how things look? Do I always seek the positive factor in a problem or a situation, or is my negative attitude putting a wet blanket on morale? Have I given thought to the fact that all these workers have the human instincts and emotions that I have, perhaps differently emphasized, or do I look upon them as "hands" hired to make the machinery run?

The supervisor who expects employees to be perfect is due for disappointment. No matter how carefully workers are selected, they bring to the workshop all their imperfections, peculiarities and limitations. You can't hire just the fine points about a person; you have to take all of him.

This, of course, gives the supervisors their great opportunity. There is little glory to be had in jotting down on charts the hour-by-hour performance of a smoothly-running machine, but to keep one operating that is given to breakdown, that needs gentling under load, that has to be carefully lubricated in particular places and at certain times, that is, indeed, a triumph and a satisfaction.

The supervisor's self-analysis should go further than merely listing things one should or should not do. Any man or woman in the shop could prepare a list like that: don't be arbitrary, don't discriminate, don't treat your workers as if they were parts of their machines, don't play favourites, don't give an order when a request will serve as well, don't brush off suggestions, don't say "no" as your first reaction to every request, don't put off decisions, don't pass the buck, don't be niggardly with your praise of a job well done.

The good supervisor will be aware of all these, but will wish to go behind them to seek the basic acts and attitudes that can be made to contribute to improving teamwork in the department, thereby enhancing his stature as a manager.

THE HUMAN WILL TO WORK

The era of leisure does grave violence to the spirit of work. Primitive life was ugly and full of danger, and with the discovery of work came beauty and reward.

The secret of satisfaction lies not in forced labor but in the human will to work. No country in this hemisphere has the natural resources of Brazil, but nowhere are the people more impoverished. They simply do not have the will to work. In Israel there is nothing in the way of natural resources, but it has the best economy in the Near East. The people there are willing to work.

Awakening within workers this "human will to work" is the challenge that awaits managements and that promises the greatest reward. This is our last frontier, in which every worker has a stake and in which every manager is a potential explorer.

INTERNAL vs. EXTERNAL

A manager's involvement with the human side of business leads me to a pet theory.

Most companies, in expanding and improving their personnel programs, dwell on the impersonal aspects of employee relations by building external benefits. In a welfare program, for instance, they concern themselves with putting together a good vacation policy, sick pay allowance, income protection, hospitalization/medical/surgical, life insurance, and retirement/pension, plus payment for holidays, jury duty, death and marriage leave. They spend endless hours in planning and thousands of dollars in administering these items. And yet, what are they doing?

They're worrying about an employee when he is *away* from work.

Look at these items: Sick pay applies only when a worker is absent because of illness; hospitalization protects him when he is flat on his back; retirement income helps him when he is too old to be of value to his employer; and how useful is he to you when life insurance pays off? Firms establish liberal vacation policies for a few weeks of the year —when the worker is *off* the job.

How about thinking more in terms of the worker when he is *on* the job?

While these external benefits are necessary increments of a good employee relations program, they only partially meet the needs of workers. The better programs recognize also the internal side of a person's job.

These internal considerations may be divided into four categories:

1. Physical: Make work comfortable and convenient.
2. Mental: Provide workers the chance to grow.
3. Psychological: Build up their prestige.
4. Spiritual: Help them put love in their hearts to push hate out.

EMPLOYEE RELATIONS	
Internal (on)	External (off)
1. Physical	Vacations Holidays Sick Pay
2. Mental	Income Protection Jury Duty Death in Family
3. Psychological	Marriage Leave Hospitalization/Medical Life Insurance
4. Spiritual	Retirement/Pension

It is gratifying to note that most offices and factories are making progress in improving the physical side of the workers' jobs. Adequate heat and light, air conditioning, and modern equipment and facilities are becoming more common every day.

As for the mental side of a job, it must be remembered that work which challenges the beginner only bores him after he has mastered it. A worker's growth must first be recognized and then rewarded, and a good practice is to promote from within in order to keep him interested.

Psychologically speaking, an employee must be made to feel that the work he is doing is worthwhile and useful so that he can feel good about it. It is not enough to tell a worker how to do something; he must also be told why.

On the spiritual side of a job, we must accept the fact that by nature the heart becomes a museum of ugly traits. By putting a healthy and wholesome construction on our day-to-day dealings with people, by treating co-workers with respect, and by being fair and understanding in our interpersonal relationships, we can keep these natural personality weaknesses from rising to the surface, and do our work in an atmosphere of harmony, trust and cooperation.

Motivating the employee to more and better productivity becomes easier when we consider the internal as well as the external aspects of his job needs.

ATTITUDE

We all know that attitude often makes the difference whether a job is performed well or not, or whether a person is successful in it. As managers or supervisors we're inclined to question the attitude of our workers. Our employees, on the other hand, must often wonder about the attitude of their bosses or of the company they work for. In actual practice there is something to be said on both sides.

Certainly we like the employee who has a good attitude toward his duties, his superior, and the company. As executives we do much toward that end, discussing the value of good attitude with workers generally, counseling with individuals who need correction or improvements, and as in the case of fringe benefits actually trying to buy better attitudes.

Attitude may be defined in different ways. In the dictionaries it reads: "A state of mind that is revealed by our behavior or conduct which demonstrates our opinion or purpose regarding some matter."

I like to think of it as putting a little of ourselves into our work, over and above the skill to perform it. We are already being compensated for what we do; it is this little extra that attracts attention, that pays off in recognition and inner satisfaction. How many times have we heard the truism that the more we put into our work the more we get out of it?

What distinguishes the professional from the amateur? Is it talent? I doubt it. More likely it is attitude. The professional writer, for instance, is a workman with a good attitude toward his work. Only in the movies does a person suddenly get an inspiration and then proceed to cash in on his brain child. In real life he schedules his work and then attacks it systematically.

The greatest musicians practice many hours every day. The first-rate artists are incessantly sketching or painting. The athlete never stops training. Greatness in any field is ability plus a right attitude to develop and use this ability.

PERSONNEL ADMINISTRATION HANDBOOK

Attitude is the Key

In this one word "attitude" lies the difference between having just another job and in being happy and successful in our life's work. A good attitude toward our duties will bring contentment in our place of employment which, in turn, will be reflected in our pattern of living.

In trying to explain attitude and its importance to workers I have used a very simple illustration. I try to draw a parallel between our working life and our happy school days. As school children, for example, we had recess; in the office or factory we call this "coffee break." We know about the three R's of our earlier school days. There are also three R's of adult life. And by that I don't mean: Romance at 25, Rent at 45, and Rheumatism at 65. The three R's of adult life are: Resources —training and other gifts we offer; Resolution—what we decide to do with these; and Responsibility—the sincerity of purpose we put into life.

Just as there are three R's of both our childhood and adult lives, so are there three A's of business life. These are: Ability, Ambition and Attitude.

Ability establishes what a worker does.
Ambition determines how much he does.
Attitude guarantees how well he does.

Ability will bring a worker a paycheck.
Ambition will get him a raise.
Attitude will lead to success.

Attitude is actually the "you" in the job. When ability and ambition in two persons are about equal, how does the supervisor select one over the other for promotion? Here is where attitude becomes the deciding factor. Attitude reflects a little plus—that something extra that is given willingly although not required.

But attitude, like arguments, contracts and many other aspects of everyday life, is no solo affair. One person has an attitude toward something, but others help create it. In fact, it represents a mutual relationship.

Look at the word itself. A-T-T-I-T-U-D-E. Is it a mere coincidence that "I" comes first and "U" later? If this has any significance, then in trying to understand the attitudes of people we should first examine ourselves in relation to those people. In cases of disappointment, perhaps we should wonder what we might have done to help bring about this negative attitude, or what we might have failed to do which could have prevented the development of a wrong attitude.

Who, Me?

Isn't it easy to criticize the other fellow and comment, "What's wrong with his attitude?" When two of us talk about a third person, all the blame is placed on him. But notice how much different the question sounds when just two are involved and we ask, "What's wrong with his attitude toward me?" About this time we begin to wonder about ourselves and our attitude, don't we?

It is well to understand that when we point an accusing finger at someone else, there are three other fingers of that hand that are turned inward and point back to us.

This is what I have tried to point out in the accompanying drawing of a double-intake and single-outlet faucet. The worker brings to the job his natural or acquired ability, previous training and experience, all of which are needed for effective performance. On the other side of the coin, he can expect the employer to provide quality materials, good equipment and understandable and workable methods. If any of these are lacking then obviously production suffers.

By the same logic it may be assumed that if all these requirements are fully present then production will be high. Here, however, is where attitude must be considered. A poor attitude will affect the output regardless of how qualified the worker may be or how good the working conditions are. For optimum results this attitude valve must be wide open.

Attitude is like a two-edged sword. Certainly it is important in the employees. But it is just as important, possibly even more so, in the employer. Or to put it more succinctly, managers and supervisors are largely responsible for the attitudes of their people since attitude is the product of the environment they provide.

Remember, attitudes are caught, not taught!

ATTITUDE TOWARD EXPENSE CONTROL

Attempts to influence attitude toward management problems, as for example, expense control, are made from different approaches. The following well-written poster on "Waste" is an excellent example on page 323.

ATTITUDE POSTERS

Posters, colorful and catchy, are used quite successfully by many firms to improve employee attitude. Rather than print and illustrate

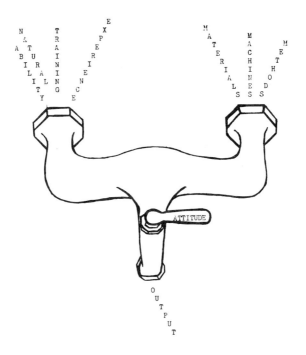

their own messages, companies purchase ready-made posters from suppliers who have, over the years, perfected them both as to content and design.

In general it is hoped attitude posters will help employees:

1. Build interest in better work habits.
2. Overcome negative attitudes with positive views.
3. Accept change in job content and methods.
4. Prepare for new ways of doing things.
5. Improve human relations skills.

It is a fact that the average employee will spend less than five seconds glancing at a poster message. These posters are intended to get the point across in that amount of time. These carefully-worded posters suggest, not shout; the low-pressure approach gives a laugh with each lecture.

The Economics Press, Inc. of Fairfield, New Jersey, offers a series of "Positive Attitude Posters" that deal with the attitudes of good work

WASTE...
You Can't Afford It

A successful business man was once asked the secret of his success. "I'll tell you," he replied. "It was a game I played with myself. I pretended that I owned the business. No matter where I worked, I pretended I owned the place . . . lock, stock and barrel."

Isn't it strange? At home, we worry if we leave one unnecessary light on all night, or if we waste food, or if someone we've hired to repair our property does a sloppy job. But in the office or at the plant, we'll waste light and power, equipment and material, time and workmanship and never bat an eye.

Why? Because we think of the business as "it", any profit and loss as "theirs". And we're inclined to say, "Oh well, the Company can stand the loss." On the other hand, at home we think of it as wasting "my" money, it's "my" loss.

They are one and the same, really. Loss for the Company must be absorbed by the profit, and each of us shares in the profit. So we, too, can play a game with ourselves. It goes something like this: "When I waste at the plant or the office, I am wasting 'my' time, 'my' job security, 'my' future."

Stop and consider how often a day we throw away pennies on the job. Each time a good paper clip is bent out of shape, a sheet of stationery with an easily erasable error is discarded, a rubber band, pencil or pen falls into the wastebasket, pennies are lost.

It's the same in plant operations. In our snack foods production, careful watch should be maintained at overflow cans located at conveyors; there is sometimes waste at the automatic weigher; machine operators should constantly determine that their machines are properly adjusted. Shipping areas, warehouse operations, maintenance departments, too, have particular areas where waste occurs through carelessness.

Carelessness which resulted in but 5¢ of material or service being wasted oftentimes seems insignificant to the man or woman involved. Suppose each of our employees works 245 days in a year. At an average of five cents a day, he will throw away ,$12.25 a year. Multiply this and the amount of loss or waste would be staggering.

It's the cumulative cost of fractional waste that adds up to big money. Each employee has a personal stake in keeping costs down. Remember, every nickel you save means just that much more opportunity for you.

Reprinted through the courtesy of
the Frito-Lay Bandwagon.

U. S. A.

The Hardest Part

Of Any Job

Is GETTING STARTED

Every Job Has

Some Unpleasant Duties

Grin and Bear 'Em!

in offices and factories. Their posters concentrate on the common sense fundamentals of doing a good job, things about which even the best employees may need an occasional reminder.

These posters are shipped subject to approval, a new one for display every two weeks. They come in two sizes, 14×22 inches and 22×34 inches. Walnut finished frames are available.

The above two illustrations were selected from the "Positive Attitude Posters" series. They are reprinted by the permission of the copyright owner, The Economics Press, Inc., Fairfield, New Jersey, 07006.

ATTITUDE SURVEYS

Who knows better than the employees themselves how working conditions are or what they ought to be? So why not ask them?

Done formally, this is known as an Attitude Survey. This is an industrial relations adaptation of opinion polls, used in political campaigns, market research and television ratings. In the employee relations program this becomes a "Morale Reading."

It is not easy for companies to conduct an Attitude Survey. Not that the procedure is difficult, but the idea of getting employees into the act is, to some managements, deliberately disturbing the calm. Why upset the *status quo?* Maybe conditions are not perfect, but when employees are given a chance to express their feelings, isn't some form of follow-up action called for? What if companies don't want to act? What then?

This is one of the problems of an Attitude Survey. The workers are closest to conditions which affect them and they have opinions of what is good, what is less-than-good, and what should be improved. To ask them and then ignore their well-intentioned advice is worse than not asking them at all.

The other problem of an Attitude Survey is that companies are afraid to face facts. In respect to some questions, they know what is wrong and have learned to live with the situation. In other cases, they don't know and actually don't want to know. Once the undesirable or unpleasant situation has been laid on the table, management loses its right to ignore it. The workers have spoken and this, in itself, demands they be given an answer.

Despite these obstacles, many companies have engaged in employee Attitude Surveys with excellent results. The program, to be successful, must be well planned, publicized to the employees, conducted carefully and openly, and the answers analyzed honestly, thoroughly and announced to the participants. Most important, corrective action that is called for must be taken promptly and directly.

This is where many Attitude Surveys break down; companies like to know what their employees are thinking, and once they learn this (too often chuckling privately over the answers) they procrastinate, or even worse, fail to take any action. In that case, they have done more harm than good.

Follow These Guidelines

Properly done, however, an Attitude Survey can be helpful to sincere managements. The procedure calls for:

1. Announcing the program to the employees.
2. Preparing a questionnaire.
3. Distributing the questionnaire.
4. Collecting the completed questionnaires by an announced deadline.
5. Reviewing the data.
6. Collating the answers.
7. Summarizing the results.
8. Publishing a report.
9. Taking any and all corrective actions that become necessary.

The usual method is to employ a multiple-choice-type questionnaire on which each employee is asked questions and directed to select the answer which seems most appropriate to him.

In designing the question-and-answer sheet:

1. Make it easy to complete.
2. Ask general questions.
3. Keep questions simple so they will not be easily misunderstood.
4. Don't slant questions toward desired answers.
5. Don't skirt the important issues.
6. Don't editorialize.

The questions should ask for personal opinions about:

1. The company in general.
2. Job satisfaction.
3. Working conditions.
4. Knowledge of company and its products.
5. Compensation.
6. Benefit program.
7. Personnel policies.
8. Co-workers.
9. Supervision and management.
10. Any special problems peculiar to the company, its location, its place in the community, its philosophy, etc.

The only identification seeks information about the employee's:

1. Sex.
2. Age (perhaps in 10-year brackets rather than specifically).
3. Job level.

In conducting the survey:

1. Get full participation.
2. Don't keep the survey secret—do it out in the open.
3. Keep it anonymous—don't require it be signed, otherwise you'll get a name and little else.
4. Don't try hidden codes or colors; people will become suspicious.
5. Take time to study the answers.
6. Announce and publish results.
7. Tell employees fast, while the project is still fresh in their minds.
8. Do something—this is not just a pet exercise for the amusement of executives. The findings must be translated into action.

Be Sincere

As mentioned earlier, conducting an employee Attitude Survey is not easy. There are certain pitfalls to guard against:

1. A clever questionnaire writer can phrase questions to fit preconceived answers.
2. Answers, summarized statistically, can be expressed to create misleading impressions.
3. A little gripe, such as a warm water drinking fountain which is constantly neglected, may cause an employee to fire full blast at management. Trivial complaints, not serious enough for formal grievances, can be blown out of proportion under the protection of anonymity.

It is also important to keep in mind the caution that opinions are expressed from the employees' point of view which could differ from those of management.

In summary, it should be mentioned that an Attitude Survey will point up *what* is wrong, not *why* it is wrong. Nor will it tell how to correct anything that needs attention, or for that matter whether the well-intentioned corrective action taken by management is what the employees expect and will accept.

An Attitude Survey, or morale reading, is a useful tool if properly planned and administered; it can become a "loaded" bomb if improperly used.

25 FACTORS THAT CAUSE EMPLOYEE UNREST

1. Poor supervision.
2. Lack of appreciation.
3. Supervisor "hogs" credit.
4. Favoritism, discrimination, unfairness.
5. Unexplained discipline.
6. Lack of someone to look up to.
7. Low salary
8. Inequitable salary system.
9. Insufficient fringe benefits.
10. Overwork.
11. Distasteful, disagreeable work.
12. Sunday and holiday work.

13. Split shifts.
14. Unpleasant environment.
15. Unsafe working conditions
16. No employee congeniality; personality conflicts.
17. Caste system or cliques.
18. Agitators or troublemakers uncontrolled.
19. Feeling of job insecurity.
20. Constipated communications.
21. Failure to understand how the organizational system functions.
22. Meaningless performance appraisal reviews.
23. Unavailability of any training.
24. No apparent chance for advancement.
25. No confidence; not trusted by supervisor.

BOREDOM AND OTHER INDUSTRIAL ILLS

As we make progress along technological lines we seem to fester problems in human relations. This sad fact is true in life as well as in business. In our eagerness to strive for innovation and sophistication, we often unintentionally distort existing values. For the answer to this dilemma we need to reevaluate our concept of a well-balanced life.

Relating this assessment to business, we need to reevaluate our concept of a well-balanced job to offset the inadvertent drift toward job deterioration. There are many situations in the office, shop, factory, store or service establishment that cause problems in human relations, and one of the big problems is that of boredom.

Work measurement and work simplification are accepted management tools, and their use can be justified on the basis of reducing operating costs by shortening training time and minimizing skill requirements. But if not properly understood and applied, either procedure can do more harm than good when emphasis is focused on the technique and away from people. Workers like to be thought of as human beings, not faceless cogs in a mechanistic routine.

The impact of this trend was aptly illustrated a few years ago when automobile assembly line workers in an Ohio facility received national attention with their well-publicized case of blue collar blues. But while factory work may be considered demeaning in today's more enlightened society, the work "blahs" are not a factory phenomenon. The same conditions exist in many large offices, which in reality have become nothing more than impersonal paperwork factories.

A steady diet of routine work in a paperwork factory is akin to eight hours a day on the assembly line in a plant. Tedium sets in and boredom results, and this combination triggers a host of problems that have little direct connection with the work itself.

This is what is known as "draining the resources of the human personality." According to this thesis, such workers try to remedy their situation and restore their own emotional equilibrium by resorting to unusual or unnatural outbursts. They will work quietly all day, then give vent to pent-up frustration by shouting themselves hoarse at sports events, or challenging other motorists on the homeward-bound expressway.

Sacrificing personal identification on the altar of efficiency is one of the underlying causes of boredom. When the personal satisfaction of job accomplishment is deemphasized through standardization (when the worker is required to work "for" the boss instead of "with" him), interest in the job wanes and boredom is the unwitting substitute. And this boredom goes beyond the job and back into life—with serious consequences.

The Impact

Just as jobs have been simplified to the point of unimaginative routine, so has life, in the name of progress, been made easier. With over half of the weekly food budget spent on convenience foods, it is more important to learn how to serve well-thawed-out meals than to prepare well-thought-out menus. In this day of pushbutton living, the housewife, surrounded by modern appliances, doesn't need a maid; she needs a mechanic.

The typewriter ruined handwriting, and television is ruining reading. The ten o'clock newscaster not only reads the news to us, he also selects what we should hear. Involvement has given way to passivity. No wonder the nation, particularly the business community, suffers from "creative sterility."

It is well known that surveys indicate the average family watches television six hours a day, seven days a week, but few families will admit this, because most everyone feels obscurely guilty about this modern form of addiction.

The explanation is boredom. It results from an unwillingness to learn, to grow in spiritual and emotional dimensions.

Boredom often masquerades in the passive forms of entertainment. Spectator sports provide an outlet for emotional release that is denied the worker on the job. This is also the reason our religious and national holidays have lost their higher meanings and are now observed by people "who couldn't care less" about their classic significance. It's only another day off with pay, away from the "old grind."

Boredom develops its own escapism—as addiction to alcohol, drugs, gambling, all the way to suicide. Boredom explains better than anything else the growing spread of juvenile delinquency—youngsters with no aims, no horizons, no values, no challenges to their abilities and energies. Students in high school, who display little interest in subjects their academic curriculum prescribes, account for the alarmingly high dropout rate.

In schools, in business, in life, things have been routinized to make them easy, in the mistaken notion that going in this direction makes things better. The disappointing results of this trend prove the old adage that "hard work never hurt anyone." Deaths from violence occur more frequently in countries that enjoy material wealth and have the most effective social legislation. The lowest rates exist in countries where life is harder and more uncertain.

Prince Philip, husband of Queen Elizabeth II of England, said in an interview published in an issue of *Director* magazine, that Great Britain is rotting. "In a great effort to make life easier for people, we have really, in many cases, removed the one thing that makes it interesting, which is a challenge and an opportunity, a risk both of loss and gain."

Stress

A boring job can also be a health hazard; it can literally make a person sick.

The University of Michigan conducted a survey for the National Institute of Occupational Safety and Health. The study, covering 23 occupations and involving 2,015 workers, found that men in boring, low-paid, simple, insecure jobs complained of illness three times more than workers in jobs with long hours, hard work loads and heavy responsibilities.

In its conclusion, the survey report showed that on the list of job stresses that can imperil a worker's health, work that is too easy and too simple appears nearer the top than work that is too complex or too hard. The social implications of such a study can be profound.

Job dissatisfaction turns to strain, which manifests itself in the form of anxiety, depression, irritation and worry. Such strain can elevate a person's blood pressure, raise blood cholesterol level, and cause the person to smoke, drink and eat too much. It can also cause low back pain, difficulty in sleeping, and can make the heart beat too fast.

Strain can also lead to psychomatic illnesses such as heart disease, high blood pressure and peptic ulcers.

Some medical authorities suspect that job stress may have a more detrimental effect on the overall quality of human life than any of the physical hazards workers face on the job, such as toxic chemicals, radiation, noise and other threats to health.

The problems of stress are found not only among the rank-and-file workers. The old saying, "Uneasy lies the head that wears the crown," applies also to business, as executives are under constant reaction to pressure, rivalry, defeat, disappointments and other strains. A change in status, relocation or organizational relationships often means the inevitable loss of power, and this results in fading prestige, less respect, ignored influence, challenges to leadership, and brings with it new social problems not only in business but also at home and in the community. The end result can be devastating.

Many of the disorders linked to job stresses could be prevented if jobs could be structured to provide more personal satisfaction. The key is job compatibility. A worker at any level with an undemanding job, who is unable to use his skills or make decisions, has more stress than one who works harder and longer but who likes what he is doing.

Tension

Tension is the body's reaction to threat. But that definition is too simple, too pat. What makes one person tense may not bother another person at all.

Tension rarely occurs by itself, as it is usually accompanied by anxiety (anxiety has been described as "fear spread out thin"). It is a painful uneasiness. Anxiety, of itself, isn't necessarily bad, since it keeps people alert. It is only when it causes overconcern that it can become harmful.

People suffering from tension and anxiety become irritable, angry, hypercritical and feel sorry for themselves. The symptoms are noticeable when people are too busy to eat, have trouble falling asleep, have trouble staying awake, are too tired to think, or turn into nonstop talkers.

Tension remains, grows and corrodes when it is bottled up. It is alleviated when released, when remedial action is taken. As far as workers are concerned, all these distresses are minimized as people move closer to finding jobs they like, are compatible with, and temperamentally suited for.

Management insight into the basic human needs is the discovery that work is not only an economic good but also a psychological necessity. Sigmund Freud called work "man's strongest tie to reality." It is the most effective way people have of relating themselves to the world, finding out what they can do and where they belong—of being somebody and meaning something to others and to themselves.

Work is also important to emotional health. To the degree that skills and abilities are utilized and ambitions realized, a worker's emotional needs are satisfied. It is, therefore, imperative not only to arrange for a worker to be happy on his present job but also to keep him interested in the prospects for promotion to more challenging assignments.

Ideally every worker ought to be in a job that is just a little "over his head" in order that he does not become complacent. It is unfortunate that the majority of workers, once they have reached their level of competency, are allowed to vegetate. After a worker has mastered a job he or she is ready to be moved to a higher level of responsibilities that demands greater concentration and thereby commands interst.

Expressed another way: "As long as we're green, we're growing; once we're ripe, we begin to rot."

Job Enrichment

One attempt to rekindle interest in the job is known as job enlargement or job enrichment. This is the antithesis of work simplification. Job enrichment is a program or rebuilding jobs to provide a greater variety of duties. It is intended to improve life at work.

Roy Walters, a consultant specializing in job enrichment, has studied many dead-end jobs and lists the following as the 10 most boring jobs:

1. Assembly line worker
2. Highway toll collector
3. Car watcher in a tunnel
4. Pool typist
5. Bank guard
6. Copy machine operator
7. Bogus typesetter (those who set type not to be used)
8. Computer tape librarian
9. Housewife (not to be confused with mother)
10. Automatic elevator operator

These and other boring jobs are in part a result of technological advancements. The damage done to workers is in terms of hostility, depression and nervous tension. Productivity and efficiency are affected and the opportunity to have people "turned on" is lacking.

The three characteristics of an enriched job are spelled out by Dr. Frederick Herzberg as follows:

1. It is a complete piece of work. It has an identifiable beginning and ending.

2. It is a job in which the employee has as much decision-making control as possible over how he or she carries out the work.

3. It is a job in which the individual worker receives frequent, direct feedback on his or her performance.

Efforts to restructure jobs to give people a sense of participating in the finished product or a feeling of contributing to the team effort is what job enrichment is all about. On the one hand, job enrichment is designed to put meaning back into jobs by counteracting the negative side effects of overspecialization; on the other hand, it dilutes the economic benefits of work simplification in operating procedures.

In concept, job enrichment and work simplification seem to present a dichotomy. Somewhere in between these extremes lies the solution for each job and each worker, with the most applicable features of both approaches considered. Just as jobs vary in their requirements and duties so also do workers differ in their reactions to job demands and challenges. There is no convenient back-of-the-book answer that fits every person or every circumstance.

The purpose of job enrichment are: (1) to provide the most interesting and fulfilling work possible, and (2) to make the greatest utilization of competence and talent.

The purposes of business are: (1) to produce more goods and better services, and (2) to continue to operate profitably.

A good manager tries to reconcile these two divergent, yet complementary, views.

Human Machines or Human Beings

The practitioners of behavioral science (a profession, ironically enough, coming into full maturity in the midst of the computer revolution) caution that we live in a depersonalized society. This development has dehumanized life and business.

In this society, making a living takes precedence over making a life. The dominant theme is "What's good for business is good for people," whereas the opposite theme, "What's good for people is good for business," seems more logical. Whom else are we trying to benefit with our technological progress than people?

Instead of enjoying their livelihood, workers in a cold, unfeeling industrial climate are uneasy over regimented job schedules and rigid mechanical work routines. Doing piecemeal work doesn't allow them to feel they have any significant part in a final, tangible product. At a time when people yearn for freedom, they become slaves to technology.

Consequently, too many people work for a paycheck and little else. Mortgage payments, family obligations or just plain apathy trap people into occupations that, at best, provide only economic security. They are actually imprisoned in their jobs and about as happy as other people who are confined and restricted.

The story is told of the violinist who frowned all through rehearsal. When asked if she didn't like the job she replied, "Oh, the job is fine. It's just that I hate music."

The United States Department of Labor Statistics maintains that 80% of the employed people in the nation are misemployed. They are working at the wrong jobs and doing things they are not most expert at doing. But they have no other choice.

A nation's greatest natural resource is locked up in "the human will to work." It will continue to be tragically wasted, however, as long as workers are denied their opportunity of expressing it.

Conclusion

In summary, workers require certain satisfactions from their jobs. Management that identifies these basic needs and makes sincere attempts to satisfy them is on solid ground. Management that is preoccupied with other matters will continue to muddle along wondering, "What's wrong with people today?" The opportunity to minimize problems is there for all. The landscape is the same; the difference is in the beholders.

The worker must see that his contribution flows into the common ocean of everyday human effort. The telephone lineman is not merely tying together two strands of wire; he is linking patient to doctor, and so forth. Similarly, the manager or supervisor in any business establishment is more than a skilled technician; he is engaged in a form of human engineering.

The manager who thinks people are working only for a paycheck is deluded. Only when he or she tries to understand that workers are flesh-and-blood human beings with individuality expressed in the way they act and respond, is that manager on the right track and going in the right direction—toward success for his workers, for his company and for himself.

In this connection it is important to recognize that the two most serious problems in offices and factories today are:

1. Pressure
2. Impersonality

and both are getting worse in the present conduct of business. No wonder there are emotional problems: workers race the clock and do it anonymously.

There is an overemphasis on productivity, achievement, speed and growth in the corporate, not personal, sense. There is an underemphasis on individuality and self-satisfaction. Truly, the industrial value system is debilitating from a personal point of view. High production is not enough unless with it comes a corresponding degree of innovation, imagination and creativity—factors that stir emotional juices.

The problem in human relations, a by-product of the technological revolution, may be said to be the price of bigness in business. Mass production methods, work simplification techniques, and other developments of the machine age have been big gains. But every gain has its price. The curse of bigness, which afflicts every level of society, not only dehumanizes us in our personal contacts, but also corrupts our sense of values.

People in business make a mistake when they think only of the work, and not the worker. Simplifying the duties, modernizing the environment, streamlining the equipment, mechanizing the operation—all these are merely more salad dressing on wilting lettuce unless we add understanding, compassion, tolerance and consideration.

Progress along scientific lines is to be encouraged, of course, but no such advance should be heralded unless at the same time there is a corresponding improvement somewhere in the human situation. Unfortunately, this is not always true today. Maybe someday wiser heads can explain how it is possible to improve the life of the work by destroying the soul of the worker.

STRESS

A study was conducted by the National Institute for Occupational Safety and Health, headquartered in Cincinnati, Ohio, to determine which occupations produce the most mental disorders.

This objective study attempted to provide occupational health professionals with an empirical basis for identifying and selecting specific occupations for further research into the relationship between job stress and worker health.

The list, provided by Michael J. Colligan, Ph. D., research psychologist, ranks 130 occupations from most stressful to least.

1. Health technicians
2. Waiters, waitresses
3. Practical nurses LPN
4. Inspectors
5. Musicians
6. Public relations
7. Clinical lab technicians
8. Dishwashers
9. Warehousemen
10. Nurses aides
11. Laborers
12. Dental assistants
13. Teacher aides
14. Research workers
15. Computer programmers
16. Photographers
17. Telephone operators
18. Hairdressers

19. Painters, sculptors
20. Health aides
21. Taxicab drivers
22. Chemists
23. Bank tellers
24. Social workers
25. Roofers, slaters
26. Secretaries
27. Nurses, registered
28. Operatives
29. Bakers
30. Struc. metal craftsmen
31. Upholsterers
32. Dressmakers
33. Machinists
34. Sales managers
35. Garagemen
36. Clergy
37. Designers
38. Mechanics
39. Clerical workers
40. Office machine operators
41. Guards-watchmen
42. Insurance adjusters
43. Barbers
44. Sales clerks
45. Office managers
46. Editors
47. Teachers
48. Sales representatives
49. Pressmen
50. Painters, construction
51. Cooks
52. Engineers, stationary
53. Draftsmen
54. Mine operators
55. Tool and diemakers
56. Bookkeepers
57. Food countermen
58. Lumbermen
59. Welders
60. Meat cutters
61. Engineers
62. Brick masons
63. Insurance agents
64. Furnacemen
65. Electricians
66. Radio-TV repairmen
67. Farm owners
68. Librarians
69. Mail carriers
70. Policemen
71. Shipping-receiving
72. Real estate
73. Carpenters
74. Dieticians
75. Gardeners
76. Pharmacists
77. Accountants
78. Janitors
79. Attendants
80. Truck drivers
81. Maids
82. Firemen
83. Laundrymen
84. Plumbers
85. Bank financial managers
86. Lawyers
87. Child care workers
88. Dentists
89. Garbage collectors
90. Sawers
91. Bus drivers
92. College, university personnel
93. Foresters
94. Cabinetmakers
95. Clerks, counter
96. Electronic technicians
97. Foremen
98. Farm laborers
99. Managers, administrators
100. Housekeepers
101. Vehicle washers
102. Managers-restaurant
103. Cement and concrete workers
104. School administrators
105. Railroad switchmen
106. Physicians

107. Craftsmen
108. Firemen, stationary
109. Sewer workers
110. Telephone linemen
111. Fork lift operators
112. Heavy equipment operators
113. Packers and wrappers
114. Officials and administrators (government)
115. Buyers
116. Electrical power linemen
117. Personnel-labor relations
118. Health administrators
119. Freight handlers
120. Decorators
121. Engineering science technicians
122. Surveyors
123. Checkers and examiners (quality control)
124. Professional technicians
125. Stock handlers
126. Ticket station agents
127. Chemical technicians
128. Tailors
129. Hucksters (auctioneers and salesmen)
130. Dyers

A study of this sort has limitations and the data should be used with caution. Personnel directors should be encouraged to note that they rank 117th on this list.

FATIGUE

The supervisor should recognize that signs of fatigue are not warnings of overwork but symptoms of something else.

There are three kinds of fatigue in the working world:

1. *Physical fatigue:* years ago men worked long hours at physical labor. They had to rest their bodies to be ready for the next day's work. Once refreshed, they were ready for another strenuous day's work. Where before, after a hard day's work, a man needed rest, today he needs exercise.

2. *Nervous fatigue:* fatigue in modern industry is nervous rather than physical. The worker may go home tired but still have plenty of energy for gardening, bowling or dancing. Nervous fatigue comes from strain and fear.

3. *Mental fatigue:* this is not tiredness but mind laziness. A worker may feel mentally drained from writing or figuring or making decisions of some kind. Just let a fire break out at that point and he is instantly as fresh and alert as ever. Better yet, watch a group of "mentally exhausted" men perk up when a pretty woman sweeps into the room. Psychologists claim that mental fatigue is chiefly loss of interest.

Employees who are fatigued are probably on wrong jobs, assigned to work for which they are not best suited, or simply not sufficiently challenged to keep them interested and keyed up. In such cases, don't treat the symptom; look for the cause.

BURNOUT

What the military refers to as "battle fatigue" business calls "burnout." In both cases it is a syndrome brought about by unrelieved stress.

It is more intense and more prolonged than stress. It can be devastating and life-threatening. It is a physiological and a psychological manifestation that individuals and corporations will be dealing with in the years ahead.

Just what causes burnout is debatable, but psychologists and consultants believe work stress is a major factor. Yet they do not advise trying to avoid stress. Some stress is healthy. The problem is finding the optimal amount.

Burnout is a demon rooted in the society and the times we live in and our ongoing struggle to fill our lives with meaning. It is born of good intentions by decent people who strive to reach a goal, don't admit limitations, and push themselves too hard too long. Exhaustion and despair set in.

The burnout phenomenon develops if the expectation level is dramatically opposed to reality, says Herbert J. Freudenberger, a pioneer researcher in the field. When such a person persists in trying to reach that expectation, trouble is on the way. It is a chronic condition contracted over time.

The symptoms of burnout are listed by Dr. Freudenberger in his book, *Burnout: The High Cost of High Achievement,* as:

1. Feeling of failure and frustration, a decline in self-esteem.
2. Flight or the compulsion to flee to another mode of life to escape.
3. Denial of the problem so obsessive it can have physical consequences.

People who experience burnout are ones who try to excel in their business and personal/family lives; there is no room in their philosophy for weakness. Their standards could be self-imposed or influenced by outside persuaders. As life settles into a routine, dullness and deadness take over. Energy turns to lethargy, enthusiasm to anger, and optimism to cynicism. They become detached, uninvolved, dissatisfied, empty, and unfulfilled.

Managers can fizzle out from burnout. Dealing daily with motivating many different personalities, facing increasing time demands, confronting operating pressures, and getting caught up in corporate complexities can overwhelm them. Their hope for a better life demands devotion to work and the frustration that ensues from failure to produce the expected reward leaves them drained.

Executives who are strongly motivated to control their work environments are especially susceptible to job burnout, warns Dr. Beverly Potter, author of *Beating Job Burnout*. At the first sign of stress, the direct causes should be pinpointed. Overpromotion, overextension of responsibilities, an overbearing boss or partner, or not enough to do—are possibilities. Don't be afraid to make drastic changes, if necessary. Dr. Potter advocates aiming for smaller, manageable goals instead of large, amorphous ones.

Burnout is like a disease, not a weakness. The effect it can have on employment, productivity, and society can be severe. It is worth noting.

JOB ENRICHMENT
(Using our Human Resources)

by ROY W. WALTERS, PRESIDENT
Roy W. Walters & Associates
Glen Rock, New Jersey 07452

Productivity is a national problem. Even though authorities can't agree on how to measure productivity, they do agree that the rate of productivity increase in the United States has been declining for a number of years. Economists do agree that this fact is contributing significantly to inflation.

What can be done about this? Many advocate that we had better utilize our financial resources, i.e., use dollars in different places and with greater wisdom. My own view is that organizations do a good job of utilizing their capital finances. I know of no organization that allows a nickel to lie around uninvested for five minutes. We really use money.

Others advocate better utilization of capital equipment—whether computers, typewriters, milling machines or steam shovels. I think American organizations are good at utilizing machinery. We really know how to get the most out of it. We probably can't improve here.

What's left? Only the people—workers, managers and executives. It's my position that most people in our working society are capable of doing far more than their jobs require or allow. This represents vast, untapped resources and is the major contributor to our productivity decline.

Now, why have we gotten to this position? I believe it is because we have failed to meet the human needs of people at work. Frederick Taylor, the alleged father of scientific management, fostered development of time standards, efficiency measures and simplified work processes. And they worked! Because they met the needs of a simple, agrarian society just beginning to move into the industrial era.

339

That type of management style served us very well for 50 years (1900–1950). But we began to see problems in the decade of the 50's. Reports of productivity slumps, worker dissatisfaction and organization trauma began to make daily reading pieces. Why?

Remember that post World War II made it possible for many to improve their education levels. When that happened it also raised their expectations of what they wanted out of life. Since to get what they wanted out of life could only be obtained through working, they focused their concern and ultimate dissatisfaction on their jobs. Why?

Because jobs were still "Taylorized" in concept and design; they no longer met the needs of the ever-increasingly educated working population. Study after study revealed increased job dissatisfaction. And dissatisfied workers have ways to strike back at organizations. They quit, are absent, habitually late, commit sabotage—overt and covert, increase grievances if unionized or beat the drums for unionization if not unionized, drown their pain in alcohol or dope. All manifestations of dissatisfaction with the work.

Management fails to understand this behavior because they constantly are aware of "how well we treat our people." They cite major efforts through the 50's and 60's of sending supervisors and managers to human relations training—teaching them how to treat workers like humans. They are cognizant of "communications programs" where millions were spent telling workers "how important they were" or "how good they have it." These programs began as one-way efforts—management telling its people through pamphlets, brochures, films, etc.

The response was minimal so we went to two-way communications. "Let's get them to tell us." This opened the way for attitude surveys. We're never quite certain what these responses really tell us but we continue to take them periodically. Eventually these die out because there is not much visible evidence to the workers of changes that affect their work lives.

Next we began to be concerned about the "whole individual." We wanted to make certain that we were doing all we could to improve his or her total life. This opened the way for recreational activities like bowling leagues, softball leagues, company picnics, Christmas parties, free turkeys at Thanksgiving, and the entire panoply of events intended to cater to the social needs of workers.

As worthy as these efforts are they do not appear to have solved the problems. Managers, at all levels, still state they they have productivity problems, quality problems and people problems. So what's causing these failures?

We've not looked at the real cause, i.e., what people *do* daily in their work lives. We've looked at all that surrounds what they do, but not at *what they do.* This adds an entire new dimension to management's set of responsibilities.

What makes people get turned on to their work? For workers who are really prospering in their jobs, work is likely to be a lot like play. Consider, for example, a golfer at a driving range, practicing to get rid of a hook. His activity is *meaningful* to him; he has chosen to do it because he gets a "kick" from testing his skills by playing the game. He knows that he alone is *responsible* for what happens when he hits the ball. And he has *knowledge of the results* within a few seconds.

Behavioral scientists have found that the three "psychological states" experienced by the golfer also are critical in determining a person's motivation and satisfaction on the job:

1. *Experienced meaningfulness:* the individual must perceive his or her work as worthwhile or important by some system of values he or she accepts—not those he's told by the organization to accept.
2. *Experienced responsibility:* the individual must believe that he or she personally is accountable for the outcomes of their efforts.
3. *Knowledge of results:* the individual must be able to determine, on some fairly regular basis, whether or not the outcomes of his work is satisfactory.

When these three conditions are present a person tends to feel very good about himself when he performs well. And those good feelings will prompt him to try to continue to do well—so he can continue to earn positive feelings in the future. That is what is meant by "internal motivation"—being turned on to one's work because of the positive internal feelings that are generated by doing well, rather than being dependent on external factors (such as incentive pay or compliments from the boss or company-sponsored recreational activities) for the motivation to work effectively.

Managers must begin to realize that the characteristics or construct of jobs are the only things that will produce these motivational benefits. Or the absence of these characteristics or constructs will prevent producing these motivational benefits.

So what job characteristics make it happen? Recent research has identified five "core" characteristics or constructs of jobs that elicit these psychological states. These five core job dimensions provide the key to objectively measuring jobs and changing them so that they have high potential for motivating people who do them.

1. *Toward Meaningful Work:* three of the five core dimensions contribute to a job's meaningfulness for the worker:

    a. *Skill Variety:* the degree to which a job requires the worker to perform activities that challenge his skills and abilities. When even a single skill is involved, there is at least a seed of potential meaningfulness. When several are involved, the job has the potential of appealing to more of the whole person, and also of avoiding the monotony of performing the same task repeatedly, no matter how much skill it may require.

    b. *Task Identity:* the degree to which the job requires completion of a "whole" and identifiable piece of work—doing a job from beginning to end with a visible outcome. For example, it is clearly more meaningful to an employee to build complete toasters than to attach electrical cord after electrical cord, especially if he never sees a completed toaster (note that the whole job, in this example, probably would involve greater skill variety as well as task identity).

    c. *Task Significance:* the degree to which the job has a substantial and perceivable impact on the lives of other people, whether in the immediate organization or the world at large. The worker who tightens nuts on aircraft brake assemblies is more likely to perceive his work as significant than the worker who fills small boxes with paper clips—even though the skill levels involved may be comparable.

Each of these three job dimensions represents an important route to experienced meaningfulness. If the job is high in all three, the worker is quite likely to experience his job as very meaningful. It is not necessary, however, for a job to be very high in all three dimensions. If the job is low in any one of them there will be a drop in overall meaningfulness. But even when two dimensions are low the worker may find the job meaningful if the third is high enough.

2. *Toward Personal Responsibility:* a fourth core dimension leads a worker to experience increased responsibility in his job. This is *autonomy,* the degree to which the job gives the worker freedom, independence and discretion in scheduling work and determining how he will carry it out. People in highly-autonomous jobs know that they are personally responsible for successes and failures. To the extent that their autonomy is high, then, how the work goes will be felt to depend more on the individual's own efforts and initiatives—rather than on detailed instructions from the boss or from a manual of job procedures.

3. *Toward Knowledge of Results:* the fifth and last core dimension is *feedback.* This is the degree to which a worker, in carrying out the work activities required by the job, gets information about the effectiveness of his efforts. Feedback is most powerful when it comes directly from the work itself—for example, when a worker has the responsibility for gauging and otherwise checking a component he has just finished, and

learns in the process that he has lowered the reject rate by meeting specifications more consistently.

These five core job dimensions are only conceptual in nature. They themselves mean nothing unless put into action. The managerial issue becomes one of making specific alterations to the design of jobs so that jobs do in fact provide for genuine feelings of *meaningfulness, responsibility* and *feedback*. Here is where we apply specific implementing action steps in order to make these alterations. This is the process commonly referred to as "Job Enrichment." Unless these changes are made there can be no enrichment.

These are the action steps:

1. *Forming natural units of work.* The notion of distributing work in some logical way may seem to be an obvious part of the design of any job. In many cases, however, the logic is one imposed by just about any consideration except jobholder satisfaction and motivation. Such considerations include technological dictates, level of worker training or experience, "efficiency" as defined by industrial engineering, and current workload. In many cases the cluster of tasks a worker faces during a typical day or week is natural to anyone *but* the worker. For example, suppose that a typing pool (consisting of one supervisor and ten typists) handles all work for one division of a company. Jobs are delivered in rough draft or dictated form to the supervisor, who distributes them as evenly as possible among the typists. In such circumstances the individual letters, reports and other tasks performed by a given typist in one day or week are randomly assigned. There is no basis for identifying with the work or the person or department for whom it is performed, or for placing any personal value upon it.

The principle underlying natural units of work, by contrast, is "ownership"—a worker's sense of continuing responsibility for an identifiable body of work. Two steps are involved in creating natural work units. The first is to identify the basic work items. In the typing pool, for example, the items might be "pages to be typed." The second step is to group the items in natural categories. For example, each typist might be assigned continuing responsibility for all jobs requested by one or several specific departments. The assignments should be made, of course, in such a way that workloads are about equal in the long run. (For example, one typist might end up with all the work from one busy department, while another handles jobs from several smaller units.)

At this point we can begin to see specifically how the job-design principles relate to the core dimensions. The ownership fostered by natural units of work can reduce or eliminate a feeling that they are irrelevant and boring. Natural units of work are directly related to two of the core dimensions: task identity and task significance.

A typist whose work is assigned naturally rather than randomly—say, by departments—has a much greater chance of performing a whole job

PERSONNEL ADMINISTRATION HANDBOOK

to completion. Instead of typing one section of a large report, the individual is likely to type the whole thing, with knowledge of exactly what the product of the work is (task identity). Furthermore, over time the typist will develop a growing sense of how the work affects co-workers in the department serviced (task significance).

2. *Combining tasks.* The very existence of a pool made up entirely of persons whose sole function is typing reflects a fractionalization of jobs that has been a basic precept of "scientific management." Most obvious in assembly-line work, fractionalization has been applied to non-manufacturing jobs as well. It is typically justified by efficiency, which is usually defined in terms of either low costs or some time-and-motion type of criteria.

It is hard to find fault with measuring efficiency ultimately in terms of cost-effectiveness. In doing so, however, a manager should be sure to consider *all* the costs involved. It is possible, for example, for highly-fractionalized jobs to meet all the time-and-motion criteria of efficiency, but if the resulting job is so unrewarding that performing it day after day leads to high turnover, absenteeism, drugs and alcohol, and strikes, then productivity is really lower (and costs higher) than data on efficiency might indicate.

The principle of combining tasks, then, suggests that whenever possible existing and fractionalized tasks should be put together to form new and larger modules of work. At the Medfield, Massachusetts plant of Corning Glass Works the assembly of a laboratory hot plate has been redesigned along the lines suggested here. Each hot plate now is assembled from start to finish by one operator, instead of going through several separate operations that are performed by different people.

Some tasks, if combined into a meaningfully large module of work, would be more than an individual could do by himself. In such cases, it is often useful to consider assigning the new, larger task to a small *team* of workers—who are given greater autonomy for its completion. At the Racine, Wisconsin plant of Emerson Electric, the assembly process for trash disposal appliances was restructured this way. Instead of a sequence of moving the appliance from station to station, the assembly now is done from start to finish by one team. Such teams include both men and women to permit switching off the heavier and more delicate aspects of the work. The team responsible is identified on the appliance. In case of customer complaints, the team often drafts the reply.

As a job-design principle, task combination, like natural units of work, expands the task identity of the job. For example, the hot-plate assembler can see and identify with a finished product ready for shipment, rather than a nearly invisible junction of solder. Moreover, the more tasks that are combined into a single worker's job, the greater the variety of skills he must call on in performing the job. So task combina-

344

tion also leads directly to greater skill variety—the third core dimension that contributes to the overall experienced meaningfulness of the work.

3. *Establishing client relationships.* One consequence of fractionalization is that the typical worker has little or no contact with (or even awareness of) the ultimate user of his product or service. By encouraging and enabling employees to establish direct relationships with the clients of their work, improvements often can be realized simultaneously on three of the core dimensions. Feedback increases because of additional opportunities for the individual to receive praise or criticism of his work outputs directly. Skill variety often increases because of the necessity to develop and exercise one's interpersonal skills in maintaining the client relationship. And autonomy can increase because the individual often is given personal responsibility for deciding how to manage his relationships with the clients of his work.

Creating client relationships is a three-step process. First, the client must be identified. Second, the most direct contact possible between the worker and the client must be established. Third, criteria must be set up by which the client can judge the quality of the product or service he receives. And whenever possible, the client should have a means of relaying his judgments directly back to the worker.

The contact between worker and client should be as great as possible and as frequent as necessary. Face-to-face contact is highly desirable, at least occasionally. Where that is impossible or impractical, telephone and mail can suffice. In any case, it is important that the performance criteria by which the worker will be rated by the client must be mutually understood and agreed upon.

4. *Vertical loading.* Typically the split between the "doing" of a job and the "planning" and "controlling" of the work has evolved along with horizontal fractionalization. Its rationale, once again, has been "efficiency through specialization." And once again, the excess of specialization that has emerged has resulted in unexpected but significant costs in motivation, morale and work quality. In vertical loading, the intent is to partially close the gap between the doing and the controlling parts of the job—and thereby reap some important motivational advantages.

Of all the job-design principles, vertical loading may be the single most crucial one. In some cases, where it has been impossible to implement any other changes, vertical loading alone has had significant motivational effects.

When a job is vertically loaded, responsibilities and controls that formerly were reserved for higher levels of management are added to the job. There are many ways to accomplish this:

a. Return to the job holder greater discretion in setting schedules, deciding on work methods, checking on quality, and advising or helping to train less experienced workers.

345

    b. Grant additional authority. The objective should be to advance a worker from a position of no authority or highly restricted authority to a position of reviewed, and eventually, near-total authority for his own work.

    c. Time management. The job holder should have the greatest possible freedom to decide when to start and stop work, when to break and how to assign priorities.

    d. Troubleshooting and crisis decisions. Workers should be encouraged to seek problem solutions on their own, rather than calling immediately for the supervisor.

    e. Financial controls. Some degree of knowledge and control over budget and other financial aspects of a job can often be highly motivating. However, access to this information frequently tends to be restricted. Workers can benefit from knowing something about the costs of their jobs, the potential effect upon profit, and various financial and budgetary alternatives.

When a job is vertically loaded it will inevitably increase in *autonomy.* This increase in objective personal control over the work will also lead to an increased feeling of personal responsibility for the work, and ultimately to higher internal work motivation.

5. *Opening feedback channels.* In virtually all jobs there are ways to open channels of feedback to individuals or teams to help them learn whether their performance is improving, deteriorating or remaining at a constant level. While there are numerous channels through which information about performance can be provided, it generally is better for a worker to learn about his performance *directly as he does his job*— rather than from management on an occasional basis.

Job-provided feedback usually is more immediate and private than supervisor-supplied feedback, and it increases the worker's feelings of personal control over his work in the bargain. Moreover, it avoids many of the potentially disruptive interpersonal problems that can develop when the only way a worker has to find out how he is doing is through direct messages or subtle cues from the boss.

Exactly what should be done to open channels for job-provided feedback will vary from job to job and organization to organization. Yet in many cases the changes involve simply removing existing blocks that isolate the worker from naturally-occurring data about performance—rather than generating entirely new feedback mechanisms.

For example:

    a. Establishing direct client relationships often removes blocks between the worker and natural external sources of data about his work.

b. Quality-control efforts in many organizations often eliminate a natural source of feedback. The quality check on a product or service is done by persons other than those responsible for the work. Feedback to the workers—if there is any—is belated and diluted. It often fosters a tendency to think of quality as "someone else's concern." By placing quality control close to the worker (perhaps even in his own hands), the quantity and quality of data about performance available to him can dramatically increase.

c. Tradition and established procedure in many organizations dictate that records about performance be kept by a supervisor and transmitted up (not down) in the organizational hierarchy. Sometimes supervisors even check the work and correct any errors themselves. The worker who made the error never knows it occurred—and is denied the very information that could enhance both his internal work motivation and the technical adequacy of his performance. In many cases it is possible to provide standard summaries of performance records directly to the worker (as well as to his superior), thereby giving him personally and regularly the data he needs to improve his performance.

d. Computers and other automated operations sometimes can be used to provide the individual with data now blocked from him. Many clerical operations, for example, are now performed on computer consoles. These consoles often can be programmed to provide the clerk with immediate feedback in the form of a CRT display or a printout indicating that an error has been made. Some systems even have been programmed to provide the operator with a positive feedback message when a period of error-free performance has been sustained.

Many organizations simply have not recognized the importance of feedback as a motivator. Data on quality and other aspects of performance are viewed as being of interest only to management. Worse still, the *standards* for acceptable performance often are kept from workers as well. As a result, workers who would be interested in following the daily or weekly ups and downs of their performance, and in trying accordingly to improve, are deprived of the very guidelines they need to do so.

These then are the concepts and the implementation action steps to increase the utilization of human resources *and* provide job satisfaction. Our choice of doing this or not doing it is no longer available. It's simply a question of, "When do we get started?"

CHAPTER V

TRAINING AND DEVELOPMENT

TRAINING: TEACHING or LEARNING

T RAINING is big business.

A speaker reports, "Already there are more trainers in business than there are business teachers in the schools."

An editor writes, "American business may soon spend more to train and reeducate its own personnel from the most marginal clerk to the most capable president than all our school and college systems combined spend to educate youth."

A consultant says, "The training budgets of industry add up to one-half the total budgets for all the colleges and universities."

On-the-job training has been going on since the first worker was hired. Someone shows the new employee what to do. This could be an individual designated to "break in" every new employee, a supervisor or leader who knows what the work entails, the outgoing employee who is vacating the position, or simply the handiest coworker who takes the new employee under his wing. This type of training is generally informal although lately, because of increasing turnover, much on-the-job training is structured.

Skill training has traditionally been delegated to the schools. Ideally, employees such as typists, secretaries, bookkeepers and laboratory technicians are qualified in their skills before they are employed. In the shop and factory preemployment skill training prepares printers, mechanics and draftsmen for work. This is also true of professions in the pretraining of chemists, auditors and architects.

The company normally does not teach the skill but does train a new worker in applying his previously-acquired skill to the business. With the shortage of skills in all categories, some of the burden for skill training has been absorbed by industry under the training function known as "upgrading skills."

The Approach Changes

When it comes to supervisory training or executive development, the picture changes. Formal education in college may qualify a graduate in his particular specialty, such as engineering, law or accounting, but does not ordinarily equip him for a general business career. True, most universities run extension courses, but these are attended by people already employed. This is precisely the point: Once employed, a person's education begins—from experience, from outside formal education, from internal development programs, from seminars, meetings, travel, coaching and so on.

Training in business is an unending process. The individual who feels he is through learning is through in his job also. Simply stated, jobs today grow faster than the people in them. Keeping up is the obligation of training.

But that isn't the problem. Companies have recognized the situation and have accepted the challenge. Facilities are available, if not in one form then surely in another. The problem lies in the motivation of the trainees. Managers, for example, do not need to be trained as much as they need to be stimulated.

The purpose of any training is to create within the individual the desire to learn. The best training program will be useless unless the trainees attend willingly and participate freely. This they will do more readily if the training program helps them and serves their purposes.

In discussing training it is not enough to consider it from a teaching viewpoint—with capable instructors, well-developed courses, good facilities and equipment, and company support. More important is the learning point of view. In the final analysis, self-development, utilizing whatever aids are available, is the best assurance that training will be successful. Abraham Lincoln proved that years ago.

ON-THE-JOB INSTRUCTION

It may be assumed, if selection techniques are effective, that the new worker possesses the ability to perform the job for which he was hired or to which he was promoted. Now he must learn the job itself. He must be taught how to apply his talent to his new duties. This is known as on-the-job training. Whether this job is in a factory, office, shop, hospital or store, the worker must learn how to perform it and perform it well.

The methods and techniques of job instruction are simple:

1. Telling: prepare the worker
2. Showing: present the operation

3. Testing: try out performance
4. Checking: follow up.

Most of this type of on-the-job training can best be handled by the supervisors in the departments where the workers are assigned. Often another worker on a similar job shows the new worker "the ropes." Occasionally, this training function can be centralized in one specific area within the department; someone or some group can be given the responsibility for training all new workers within a department or division.

Some aspects of on-the-job training can possibly be transplanted to a central training staff or delegated to other departments which are more specialized in a specific type of work. For example, supplementary training in telephone courtesy could easily be referred to the local telephone company which is glad to provide this assistance.

The responsibility for job instruction must always rest with the line manager or supervisor. Skill training, or the operation of a particular machine, may be learned on the outside, in school or elsewhere; but its application to the company's operations must be done by the line department.

RESPONSIBILITY FOR GOODWILL

In this era of technological change, work is shifting from manufacturing to service. The percentage of manufacturing jobs (blue collar) is going down and the percentage of service jobs (white collar) is going up. A few words to employees in service jobs may therefore be in order.

The major responsibility of each employee is service to the customer, the buyer of the company's products or its services. In your contact with the public you will have the opportunity for creating and maintaining goodwill. How can you do this? By observing the following 10 rules:

1. Always be courteous. The tone of your voice is as important as the actual words you use.
2. Recognize the fact that questions directed to you are based on understandable lack of knowledge—not on stupidity.
3. Remember that when a customer is irritated, his irritation is not aimed at you. In all likelihood he is perplexed or confused about some problem connected with the company's product or service. A calm and courteous response from you is the best remedy.
4. Answer only questions pertaining to your individual responsibility and on which you are thoroughly informed. Arrange

to refer questions which you cannot answer to the proper person.

5. Keep telephone referrals at a minimum to avoid having the customer repeat his story. If you are not sure where the call is to be transferred, ask for the caller's name, telephone and extension number, and follow up as quickly as possible.

6. See that correspondence is answered promptly and that all parts of a letter are covered. Never file a letter until all questions are answered.

7. If checking is necessary on your part, take name, telephone and extension number, and give assurance that you will call back, indicating whenever possible the time at which your call may be expected.

8. Always call back, if you said you would—even if it is to report that you do not yet have the answer.

9. If your work is with material or forms rather than directly with the public, see to it that information is correctly recorded and filed—to insure prompt handling of requests, bills or claims.

10. Hold the dealing of the company and its customers in confidence. Whatever information is shared by the customer is reported only to get an answer to his question or problem. No matter how interesting or unusual this may be, it is not intended for general publication and good ethics requires that it be treated as personal and confidential.

TELEPHONE COURTESY

As the good hosts we like to think we are, we enjoy welcoming guests into our homes. We add a warm handclasp to the greeting. We go out of our way to make our callers comfortable.

Our telephone visitors deserve the same hospitality. They are guests of the organizations we work with. Answering their calls puts us in the position of host or hostess. We should greet them with a smile in our voice.

Incoming Calls

1. Answer the telephone promptly, after the first ring whenever possible.

2. Never answer, "Hello," or "Yes." Always identify yourself. If you are the first person to answer the call, give your complete company name. If you work in a certain department,

give the department name and your own name; in all other cases use your own name.

3. Speak in a normal tone of voice, and hold the transmitter so it is about one-half inch away from your lips. Speak clearly for the telephone will emphasize any sloppiness or laziness in your speech.

4. Whenever leaving the caller, explain why he must wait for you. If you need someone else to take over the call say, "I'm sorry, but I do not handle that. If you will hold the line, I will call Mr. Brown, who will be glad to help you." Or if you have to get some information say, "Ill need to look that up. Will you hold the line, please?"

5. Don't keep the caller waiting all day; one or two minutes is the maximum. When you return to the line, say something to attract his attention: his name, "Hello" or "I'm sorry to have kept you waiting."

6. Be as helpful on every call as you can be. If the call is for another employee who for some reason is not available, do all you can to save the caller further inconvenience. For example, "Mr. Brown is out to lunch, but I expect him around two o'clock. May he call you then, or is there something I can do for you?"

7. If you do take a message, be sure it is accurate. A message should include the date, time, correctly-spelled name and correct telephone number.

8. Let the caller end the call. If he says, "Thank you," reply with "You're welcome," not, "Uh-huh," or, "Yes." If he has done your company a favor, say "Thank you for the order," or "Thank you for calling."

9. When appropriate, end the call with a friendly "Goodbye," not shortened to "Bye" or "Bye now."

10. Always allow the caller to hang up first. He originated the call, and he should have the privilege of ending it.

Outgoing Calls

1. Be sure you have the right number; don't trust your memory.

2. Dial carefully, so you won't get a wrong number, but if you do, be sure to apologize before hanging up.

3. Always announce yourself before going into the business of the call; to another office in your company: "This is Miss Smith in the Credit Department"; to another firm: "This is Miss Smith of the XYZ Company."

TELEMARKETING

Telemarketing, or selling by telephone, is becoming big business. The latest figures show that more than 300,000 people sell on the phone. Companies spend about $12 billion annually on telemarketing, and this figure is expected to keep on increasing.

Telemarketing has come a long way from the days when some anonymous individual in a boiler room came across as a crank caller trying to peddle storm windows in the middle of the night. Nowadays the efforts of telephone solicitors are programmed and monitored.

There are a number of easily-understood reasons for the recent boom in the new technique of telemarketing:

1. The high cost of in-person sales calls. The latest Dartnell survey, *Compensation of the Sales Force,* reports the cost of a business-to-business sales call is gradually approaching $200. In telemarketing, a company can reach 100 people for that price.
2. Sales resistance to prospecting. Sales people generally tend to shy away from and dislike making cold calls. In telemarketing, the rejection is not taken as personal and is therefore not discouraging.
3. The need to economically service low-volume accounts. Most companies have steady low-volume accounts that are geographically disbursed throughout the country. Telemarketing makes it financially feasible to service these low-volume accounts as well as accounts in difficult-to-reach locations.
4. The difficulty in finding capable salespeople. People who are naturally adept at selling are scarce. Telemarketing develops sales people who can make money for themselves and for their companies. Telemarketing controls:
   1. The quality of calls by listening-in auditing techniques.
   2. The types of prospects who get called.
   3. The time spent calling.

Proper recruiting, careful selection, and appropriate training will produce a staff of competent and responsible telephone sales people.

Selling over the telephone is different from selling face-to-face. When selling in person, a poor approach or a poor presentation might be overcome by personal appearance, by demonstrating the product, or by use of visual aids.

Selling by telephone is selling by voice alone. The sales presentation by telephone has only a voice to work with. The prospect cannot see

353

the sales person, and must form an impression through the personality of the voice. The product cannot be shown and the telephone voice must be able to paint an appealing and convincing picture in the prospect's mind.

The caller does not have much time to tell the story. So the sales pitch has to be planned and directed in order to:

1. Capture the prospect's attention quickly and hold it.
2. Create within the prospect a desire for the product or service.
3. Get the prospect to respond favorably and say "Yes."

An in-house telemarketing center, which is showing up on more and more company organization charts as part of the marketing division, can:

1. Find new prospects.
2. Reactivate inactive accounts.
3. Obtain solid telephone orders.
4. Service low-volume accounts.
5. Make appointments for salespeople.
6. Qualify advertising leads.
7. Do market research.

Telemarketing is the fastest-growing component in the marketing mix. The technique can be fitted into the regular marketing program to reverse the existing ratio of time—15% for selling and 85% for prospecting, waiting, and traveling.

CREATIVE BUSINESS LETTER WRITING

A cross-section of management personnel was asked how often they used the specific knowledge and training offered by each of 62 college courses. A summary of their replies showed that communications and human relations skills were by far the most frequently used. About 80% of the respondents put "skill in letter writing" at the top of their lists.

Maybe you don't consider yourself a writer. Does five average-length letters a day sound like a lot? Yet this means the annual output of written words reaches 300,000. When we consider that a professional writer is likely to turn out 150,000 words a year, we get an idea of the magnitude of the businessman's writing job.

Today we do much more communicating than ever before, squeeze this duty in between many other more pressing tasks, and dread the job so much that we produce ill-conceived and lifeless letters. The fact that the average businessman signs his dictated letters without looking them over indicates how much he wishes he could dispense with this unpleasant chore with as little fuss as possible.

This is a strange paradox. We are educated sufficiently to write good letters. We actually like to communicate; witness our desire to talk at the drop of a hat. But we fear the task, knowing that our efforts will forever be recorded on paper for possible second-guessing by ourselves and others.

Writing perfect letters may be impossible. Writing good letters does not come naturally to most people. With a little effort, patience and practice, however, anyone can learn to write better letters.

The History of Letter Writing

A study of business letter writing begins with a review of the history of business letters.

Most business letters today are assembled and not written. This comes about because the teachers of letter writing stressed the separate parts of a letter instead of the content. This is an unfortunate development, but understandable.

The early letter writers were the scholars, the educated few in each community who had somehow acquired a facility with words. Abraham Lincoln is known for his beautiful letters of condolence to next of kin. Just as people today go to professionals to have legal papers drawn up, so people in early days depended upon their learned neighbors for any serious writing that needed to be done.

Letters were originally prepared by heavy-bearded gentlemen in frock coats, written with a flourish at roll-top desks, with steel pen points dipped in messy ink. The process was conducive to thoughtfulness. The communications, at least those which were preserved, were classics in both substance and style.

There were no courses available for students of letter writing. The first books on the subject were merely collections of successful letters. Younger people learned by copying ideas from the older masters. Unfortunately what survived were the flowery phraseology and the stilted form.

As a result, 98% of today's business letters are not as effective as they could be. The criticism of business letters is that they are:

1. too long
2. too cold
3. too costly
4. too many
5. too widely distributed.

355

Mastery of the mechanics is not the answer to full letter writing achievement. The value of a business letter lies not in its form but in its content.

What's Wrong?

What's wrong with the archaic form? Many things. The inside address tells the reader where he lives. The uninspiring salutation is meaningless. The complimentary close is a useless formality. At the end is the writer's signature, his name typed, and his initials recorded as dictator, followed by other stenographic codes which add nothing to the letter as far as the reader is concerned.

All this paraphernalia is not the letter. This is but the framework used to build the communication. So far nothing has been created. The letter is a colorless patchwork of ready-made phrases which makes it impersonal. Somewhere in between all this ritualistic jargon there is supposed to be a message.

Even the body of the letter is stuffy, disjointed and often tactless. The opening paragraph is simply a rehash of the sender's letter, and the closing paragraph is an unimaginative escape into ennui. That leaves the center paragraph(s) of the body of the letter as the only one of nine parts in which originality may be exercised. But here most letter writers miss their golden opportunity by cluttering the letter with hackneyed stereotypes, overworked phrases, negative words, superfluous wordage and legalistic lingo.

Writers of business letters, to be effective, must "quit going to the Wax Museum and go instead to the Art Gallery."

Not Worth the Cost

Is it any wonder that business letters generally are ineffective and not worth the cost? The latest Dartnell survey shows the cost of a good business letter runs between four and five dollars each. An unfriendly, carelessly composed, ineffective letter costs infinitely more in further unnecessary correspondence and lost customers.

Contrasted with personal letters, which are usually written as a social exchange of correspondence, business letters always have a definite purpose. Each business letter is trying to produce a result or at least get a reaction. It should be a prudent investment in company funds.

Writing profitable letters is not easy. But like any other skill, this can be learned. A course in letter writing today devotes the first third to unlearning bad habits that have crept in over the years. Only after the old ground has been plowed over should the seeds of modern letter writing be planted.

With that background we now switch from learning how letters are written to how they should be written.

How to Write Better Letters

First, eliminate all the taboos. The things to avoid are flattery, condescension, preachiness, bragging, anger (cool off 24 hours), accusations, sarcasm, curtness, kowtowing, effusiveness, show-off words, pomposity, triteness, unflattering implications.

Superfluous wordage is an easy trap to fall into. These are mechanical fill-in words we drone out when we're not thinking. It would be better to pause in our dictation than to believe we must maintain a constant monotone of words to give the impression we're dictating fluently. A good way to correct this is to become consciously aware of our nonstop sentences and run-on paragraphs.

Here are 10 suggestions that should be helpful for those who are apprehensive about letter writing:

1. Don't be afraid to write letters or to dictate.
2. Get a good reference book as a guide.
3. Review the fundamentals of good English.
4. Practice letter writing; learn by doing.
5. Organize your thoughts before proceeding.
6. Get off to a fast, gracious start.
7. Make your letters easy to read.
8. End each letter with an appropriate close.
9. Add a goodwill gesture, even when saying "no."
10. You want action—ask for it.

It cannot be stressed too often that the value of a letter lies in its warmth. Your letter should be as warm as your handshake. A letter takes the place of a personal visit. It delivers the same message. Your letter is really you, calling by mail.

The Tone is Important

A very important characteristic of business letters is tone. Those who read your letters do not see you; many might not even know you. They judge you, therefore, entirely by the effect produced by your letters. This makes the tone of your letters very important.

The tone of a letter is like the flavor of coffee. We know that the flavor makes a cup of coffee good, but we can't really define or describe it. Just as the flavor of coffee is "brewed in" so also does a good letter contain "a little bit of yourself."

The tone of our letters depends upon the kind of hand we write. Is our hand:

1. Like a fist with brass knuckles: unfriendly, even threatening.
2. Like the smooth gestures of a sleight-of-hand artist: tricky and unbelievable.
3. Like a friendly handshake: genuine and sincere.

It's not always what we write as much as the way we write it. A good motto is to write unto others as we would have them write unto us.

The Message is Most Important

The normal flow of the message in a letter is from the opening through the body to the close. These are the three essential parts. Too many letters begin with mechanical openings and end with mechanical closes.

This three-part body of the letter is the only place where you can be creative. Don't waste the opening by repeating the obvious; energize it. Don't waste the close; this is the place for the "hook," the chance to ask for action. Use the opening to establish the mood, and use the close to build goodwill.

Between the opening and the closing statements is the message. This tells the story. Needless to say it should be friendly, not cold; honest, not insincere; helpful, not demanding; positive, not vague; specific, not general. Adapt to the reader and, whenever possible, write from a "you" viewpoint. Without resorting to undue familiarity, personalize the message. Above all, don't develop "I" trouble.

As one consultant expressed it, "The trouble with too many business letters is that they sound like an inanimate corporation speaking from the heights of Mount Olympus or the depths of a food freezer."

A good business letter should read as though a live, warm-blooded human being wrote it—just the same as a personal letter. After all, we don't answer letters, we answer people.

Parts of a Business Letter

In teaching letter writing the instruction calls attention to the nine parts of a standard business letter. They are explained below:

1. *Date line:* every written document or communication should bear a date; without a date it is worthless.
2. *Inside address:* this shows that the letter was properly directed; becomes an aid in filing.
3. *Attention or subject line:* the attention line is used to direct the letter to the person or department especially involved; it is

going out of style, the modern practice is to address letters to individuals; a subject line may be inserted instead.

4. *Salutation:* this was originally a form of greeting; it is now considered old-fashioned and superfluous by many companies; the salutation should be compatible with the name given in the inside address.

5. *Body:* this consists of three parts.
     a. the opening paragraph—this sets the tone and invites the reader's interest.
     b. the message—this tells the story.
     c. the close—this leaves the reader in the proper receptive frame of mind.

6. *Complimentary close:* this serves as an expression of farewell; it is eliminated today by many companies as useless; the complimentary close should be in keeping with the salutation in formality and familiarity.

7. *Signature:* this is used to personalize the letter and to fix authority and responsibility for it.

8. *Identification initials:* these identify the dictator and the secretary; omission of the first set of initials indicates that the stenographer wrote the letter for the boss' signature.

9. *Postscripts:* this is used to give added emphasis to some particular item; or to include something that may not necessarily relate to the message of the letter.

Suggestions

For the experienced letter writer, here are 10 suggestions for writing better letters:

1. Give your letters good appearance; first impressions count.
2. Insist on perfect typing and good grammar.
3. Impart life into the written word.
4. Let your personality show through.
5. Adopt a friendly "you" attitude.
6. Rewrite letters occasionally to see how they could be worded better.
7. Study incoming letters and borrow good ideas.
8. Put your letters on trial periodically.
9. Ask someone far removed from the situation to read your letters to see if he can understand or follow them.
10. Remember, you are dealing with situations and people—not just facts and figures.

Finally, we must write not so that we can be understood, but so that we cannot possibly be misunderstood. Of the really great letter writers it is said, "Their letters said exactly what they meant them to say. What's more, they meant exactly what their letters actually said."

MANAGEMENT OF CORRESPONDENCE

Letter writing is one of the most important activities in which an employee can be involved. Letters—whether form, guide or individually written—are a major means of communicating with customers and suppliers. In some cases letters are the only form of communication. All letters, whether written about products or services, should be clear and courteous, and should show concern for, and interest in, the person to whom we are writing.

Replies to correspondence should be mailed as promptly as possible. When this cannot be accomplished, an acknowledgement of the incoming correspondence or inquiry should be made, explaining the reasons for the delay and indicating when a reply can be expected.

Each management employee should understand, and make clear to those reporting to him, that the care and consideration given to written communications should be treated as a major responsibility. Frequency of correspondence, or familiarity with the recipient, does not change the intent of this policy.

THE SIMPLIFIED LETTER

It took a while, but finally business and personal travel was speeded up and modernized, high-rise buildings became more functional than ornamental, and dress is casual and colorful. Also at long last, house construction turned practical once grandfather's traditional models were discarded. In office procedures, too, change has gradually taken over and brought with it much-needed improvement.

But most of the letters that airlines carry between modern business offices and to new homes are still old-fashioned in format and appearance.

There is little concern about waste motion caused by antiquated style. The cost of old-style letters in time, money and goodwill is appreciable but not appreciated. Yet these letters could be made more practical in design without sacrificing appearance or effectiveness.

Much emphasis is placed upon other phases of office operations today. Work simplification, automatic machines and other technical advances are accepted as proper in modern business. Yet letter writing is generally neglected.

THE 12 C's of WRITTEN COMMUNICATION

clear : unambiguous; one reading should be sufficient to get the message.

correct : facts must be right; no excuse for incorrect grammar or spelling.

concise : message conveyed as briefly as consistent with effectiveness.

complete : all necessary data in logical order; no guesswork.

coherent : message should be syllogistically logical.

courteous : say "please" and "thanks"; courtesy is genuine, flattery is counterfeit.

considerate : write the kind of message you would like to receive.

confident : be the authority without acting it; assume the reader will do what he is asked.

cheerful : no one likes bad news; whatever the burden, give it graciously.

conversational : write as naturally as you talk; avoid offensive familiarity.

clever : there is little enough wit in the world so share yours; but don't try to be cute.

careful : written words can carry implications never intended by the writer; avoid emotionally charged overtones which can offend the sensibilities of the reader.

This is tragic since letters are the basic means of business communications. They serve as substitutes for personal contact, and as such ought to reflect the up-to-date, intelligent, businesslike company they represent.

Letters are also costly. Conservative estimates, as shown in the annual Dartnell letter writing survey, run between four and five dollars each. Any streamlining of letters that does not impair their effectiveness should be welcomed as a practical cost-saving measure. When such improvements can bring, in addition to cost reduction, a more impressive modern form, there would seem to be every reason for considering it.

Simplification

The conventional letter style is still influenced by outmoded tradition. It should be reviewed merely to keep pace with the concept of change which underlies all management principles in this scientific age.

To assist progressive managements with their letter writing problems, the Administrative Management Society has developed what is known as the Simplified Letter. Introduced some years ago, its popularity is increasing steadily as more and more companies adopt it.

Most present letter styles are modifications of what is called "block." The simplified form is really nothing but "pure" block style. Everything is lined up with the left margin—and the salutation and complimentary close are omitted while a subject is added.

Every line starts at the left margin—where the typewriter starts. This feature alone eliminates the time-consuming and tedious job of "positioning" the typewriter for each part of the letter. The typewriter follows its simplest mechanical course with the minimum use of space bar, tabulator set key and tabulator bar.

The first item at the top of the letter is the date. At least three spaces down the full name and address is entered in block style. This makes easy use of the window envelope.

The subject to be discussed is shown in capitals about three spaces below the address. Use of such title provides a provocative opening and also suggests a filing clue.

The body of the letter is prepared in block paragraphs. The useless indentation is ignored, which means no tabular delay.

After the closing paragraph the typewritten signature with title appears, usually in capitals. The initials of the typist, if used, are placed below the signature also at the left margin. If copies are directed elsewhere this information may be listed on the last line.

In this simplified style several customary items are omitted. The formal salutation, the complimentary close, the company name and the dictator's initials are not used.

The salutation is actually meaningless, and often poses a problem of correct usage as the dictator fumbles around not knowing how to address the reader. The complimentary close really adds nothing to the letter. The company name is shown at the top of the letterhead; hence, it is not necessary to repeat it. And since the writer's name appears both typewritten and signed, the dictator's initials are superfluous.

Modernization

The Simplified Letter is as modern as automation, cybernetics and other products of this advanced management era. Its use bespeaks efficiency and creates the favorable impression that the writer, up-to-

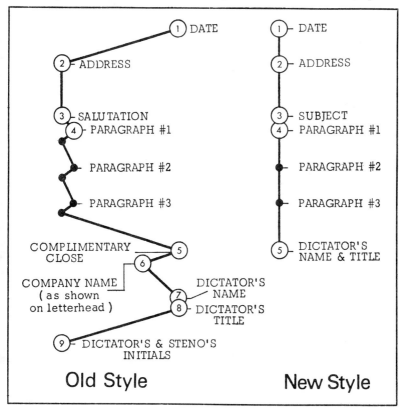

date in letter writing techniques, is also well informed on the subject of his letter.

Disadvantages are hard to find; everything is on the plus side of the ledger. The Simplified Letter is easier to read, easier to type and easier to file and find.

It has other benefits that can be measured in actual savings. Here are facts: a motion analysis of the typing alone on a 96-word letter proves a saving with the Simplified Letter of over 10.7 per cent. Multiplied by the number of letters written each day this saving can be sizable.

Declaring a title or subject at the outset requires the writer to organize his thinking as he begins. In so doing he immediately clarifies the point of his letter to the reader, putting him into the proper receptive frame of mind to understand what follows.

The simplified form will be the style of the future. It was not too many years ago that companies used salutations and complimentary closes in interoffice communications, but now that custom is practically obsolete with old-timers and unknown to new correspondents.

It's the Message That Counts

Letter writers must be cautioned, however, that changing the style, or simply adopting the Simplified Letter, will not automatically make them experts in business correspondence. It is not the inclusion or omission of the salutation and complimentary close that makes a letter courteous or effective; it is the message and the manner in which it is written that counts.

Users of this simplified form are urged to consider a few helpful instructions. The dictator must clarify his thinking in order to spell out the subject. Use of the title will immediately tell the reader what to expect.

He should dictate as though he were facing the reader, not his secretary. Really he should not dictate at all, but should speak in a natural manner, avoiding stock phrases as well as oversimplification. This will help to make the letter warm and friendly.

The message should then be presented in a straightforward and coherent manner.

No, adoption of the simplified form will not be a cure-all to a company's letter writing problems. It will not provide the creative thinking that is necessary in good letter writing.

But the philosophy behind the Simplified Letter formula seeks to reduce slow starting and the often stodgy results of conventional letter writing styles. With the Simplified Letter philosophy, a writer can stray the least from a normal, friendly, relaxed type of attitude such as is used in a successful conversation.

Instead of remembering a string of dusty clichés to link thoughts together, the dictator can seek the fresh, orderly flow of a clear mind, informed on the subject.

It may be well to remember the AMS slogan that there is much more to a truly Simplified Letter than simply dropping "Dear Sir" and "Yours Truly."

SECRETARY

Since the private secretary is such an important part of every company, and a good one is so hard to find, we felt a few words on her behalf might be appropriate.

Maybe we should begin with a definition of "secretary." The word "secretary" comes from the Latin word for secret and its original meaning was a confidant. Literally it means "keeper of secrets." In its original concept it has nothing whatever to do with the skills ascribed to the job today.

The secretarial occupation is 5,000 years old. The earliest secretaries were Babylonian scribes who took dictation on clay tablets. Considering the muscle that must have been required for "filing" away important documents, it's not too surprising that being a secretary was no job for a lady.

Filing was made easier by the ancient Egyptians, who invented paper by hammering the papyrus plant into long strips. The Egyptians wrote on this material as early as the third millennium B.C., and papyrus was used in the Greco-Roman world for a thousand years.

Shorthand is one secretarial skill almost as old as the profession itself. Historians have discovered traces of shorthand used by such people as the ancient Egyptians, Hebrews and Persians. But there was probably no true shorthand system before the one developed by Tiro, a Greek slave, who took down all the speeches of his boss, the Roman orator, Cicero, in shorthand as early as 63 B.C. Tiro's system gained widespread popularity in ancient Rome, where the people who used it were known as "notarii." Tiro's shorthand system was used by the early Christian church, and remained in use until the 9th century.

St. Luke used shorthand to record the Sermon on the Mount. St. Paul dictated his epistles to a stenographer. George Bernard Shaw wrote his plays in shorthand. Some of Shakespeare's plays were preserved in shorthand.

Early shorthand was for the educated few. It depended on memorizing thousands of symbols for individual words. It took the invention of phonetic shorthand, based on the sound of words, to make shorthand a widely useful tool.

The first practical system was invented in 1837 by Sir Isaac Pitman. But John Robert Gregg, a Chicagoan, in 1888 devised and promoted the system considered the easiest to learn, write and read. However, people who could take shorthand weren't in great demand until the typewriter came into general use.

The word "typewriter" originally referred not to the machine but to the operator—someone who writes with type. The first patent for a typewriting machine was granted in 1714 to Henry Mill, an English engineer, but the first practical typewriter wasn't patented until 1868. This early machine was mounted on a sewing machine stand with a foot pedal. Pressure on the pedal returned the carriage to the right and rolled the platen upward to space the lines.

The first U.S. patent was received by William Burt of Detroit in 1829. One problem was that any scrivener could write faster with a pen. In 1868 Christopher Sholes of Milwaukee patented his machine and in 1874 E. Remington & Sons, the arms manufacturer, agreed to make and market the machines under its own name.

There was quite an uproar when it was suggested that women might be able to work the complicated contraption. Nevertheless, the New York Young Women's Christian Association announced it would start a six-month course to train young women to be "typewriters." Eight young ladies were graduated without any problems developing, thereby opening a new field in which respectable women could earn a living. It was the typewriter that opened the door for women and gave them their start of joining and later competing with men in business.

Modern usage of the word "secretary" refers to a confidential employee having responsibilities to an executive—a clerical, administrative assistant to a busy boss.

The executive secretary is a manager. She must manage her time and often the time of her boss so that the necessary work gets out on schedule. The efficient secretary can attend to many demands with such ease that they seem to be part of a single activity.

She must demonstrate, in addition to the basic skills of typing and shorthand, the ability to take care of a multitude of details that fall in other fields. She must also possess a personality and a versatility such as is required by few other occupations.

A secretary becomes worthy of the title when she has assumed some of the responsibilities of an executive—responsibilities that call for the exercise of initiative, judgment, imagination and tact.

The best description of the secretary's job is simply, "My job is to make my boss's job easier."

THE CERTIFIED PROFESSIONAL SECRETARY

A Certified Professional Secretary is one who has successfully completed an examination developed and administered by the Institute for Certifying Secretaries, a department of The National Secretaries Association (International), and who has met the secretarial experience requirements.

The purposes of the CPS program are to:

1. Improve secretarial personnel by giving specific direction to an educational program and by providing a means of measuring the extent of professional development.
2. Provide secretaries with the assurance which comes from having attained a professional educational standard.
3. Promote the professional identify of the exceptional secretary.
4. Assist management in selecting qualified secretaries.
5. Plan and sponsor additional programs of continuing professional development for the Certified Professional Secretary.

Examination Content

The examination is based upon an analysis of secretarial work, with emphasis on judgment, understanding and administrative ability gained through education and work experience. It includes skills, techniques and knowledge in the following areas:

Part I—Environmental Relationships in Business. This part tests the principles of human relations and understanding of self, peers, subordinates and superiors. It focuses on the fundamentals of one's own needs and motivations, nature of conflict, problem-solving techniques, essentials of supervision and communication, leadership styles and understanding of the informal organization.

Part II—Business and Public Policy. This part examines knowledge of the major elements of business law involved in the secretary's daily life, particularly contracts and bailments, law of agency and sales, insurance, negotiable instruments and real property. Public policy in the form of government regulatory legislation is also examined.

Part III—Economics and Management. Three subject areas are included in this part: applied economics, principles of management and elements of business operation. The management of personnel, finances, production and marketing is examined.

Part IV—Financial Analysis and the Mathematics of Business. The principles of financial and managerial accounting are tested in this part. The candidate is also required to make the computations necessary for the analysis and interpretation of financial reports and statistical data.

Part V—Communications and Decision Making. This part is a performance test presented as an in-basket exercise. The candidate is asked to establish job priorities, describe actions to be taken, and specify how the work is to be completed. Dictation and typewriting abilities are necessary and skills are employed in editing, listening, composing, abstracting, judging work acceptability and follow-up.

Part VI—Office Procedures. This part tests the administrative know-how of the secretary. It concerns the basic concepts of current secretarial procedures and office and records management. The fundamentals of business data processing are also examined.

Time and Place

The examination is administered annually on the first Friday and Saturday in May at approved colleges and universities. A tentative list of institutions from which a candidate may make a choice is sent to qualified applicants.

Preparation

The examination is based on knowledges and skills which may be gained through education and work experience; however, every effort is made to develop an examination in which secretarial experience is an aid.

A variety of institutions offer courses designed to help candidates prepare for the examination. The Institute itself does not sponsor or offer any course.

The Examination May be Retaken

If one or more parts are passed on the first attempt, the candidate may use the next four consecutive examination periods to complete the remaining parts, taking one or all of the remaining parts at any one examination administration. All six parts must be passed within the next four years; otherwise, the candidate must repeat the entire examination sequence. No limit is set on the number of attempts on any part within this period.

New candidates and those retaking the entire examination must pass at least one part or they must retake the entire examination on their next attempt.

Certification

The Institute for Certifying Secretaries awards certification to successful candidates and will provide official notification. The Institute will, also, attest to certification when a valid inquiry is received.

A large number of colleges and universities automatically grant college credit for achievement of the CPS rating.

The terms "Certified Professional Secretary" and "CPS" are registered service marks of The National Secretaries Association (International), 2440 Pershing Road, Kansas City, Missouri 64108. Information about the program may be obtained by writing Lois J. Wilkinson, CPS, executive secretary.

SECRETARIES DAY

The last week in April is set aside as Secretaries Week, and Wednesday of that week is designated as Secretaries Day. This is the time when bosses are inspired to pay tribute to their secretaries for a year of faithful service.

The customary expression of appreciation is candy or flowers, but many executives take their secretaries to lunch. Some even have been known to let their secretaries go home early.

For anyone who thinks this arrangement is one-sided, mention should be made that National Bosses Day is October 16. It is always on the 16th even if this date falls on a weekend.

WHAT IS A SECRETARY

Secretaries are human . . . just like the rest of us. They come in both sexes, mostly female. They are available in a variety of shapes, sizes, ages and dispositions. Generally speaking, there are three kinds: prizes, surprises and consolation prizes.

They are found everywhere—in offices, on committees and in coffee shops. They are always on hand and never busy when we don't need them, and usually in the mailroom, print shop or stockroom when we're desperate. The best place to find them is in Pollyanna's Dress Shop. The hardest place to find them is in employment agencies.

Secretaries like three-day weekends, lunch invitations, sno-pake, single men, low-calorie salads, boss away at conventions, late TV movies and the typewritter-ribbon salesman. They don't like cigar-chewing dictators, corrections written on letters, filling desk pens, baby sitting in another boss' office, stale jokes and cleaning out files. They don't like bosses who boss.

They prepare letters, reports and cover-up excuses for their bosses. They are required to have the patience of Job, the wisdom of Solomon, the memory of an elephant, the disposition of a lamb, the experience of a travel agent, and the poise and personality of a Powers model. They are expected to produce, on a moment's notice, papers that were filed in brief cases, glove compartments and yesterday's coat pocket. Instinctively they are supposed to see things that never happen, and also to conveniently overlook other things that go on.

On television secretaries are glamorous women who save their bosses from one predicament after another. In real life they are women whose spelling, punctuation and paragraphing seldom agree with those of their bosses. Repairing a split infinitive is heresy.

When they do something good, that's their job. When they do something wrong, that's what we have to put up with these days. Secretaries dream about homes covered with ivy; the few who don't live in apartments have homes covered with mortgages. If they enjoy the luxury of driving cars to the company parking lots they're well fixed and don't need a raise, but if they ride the bus and arrive late they are part of the common herd and not worth promoting.

Because of their devoted dedication to duty, they deserve to be executaries in their own right. But until they realize this ambition they will continue to serve as their bosses' right arms. They will continue to make us look good, and we will go right on neglecting to tell them how important they are to us . . . a fact we discover, but never admit, every time they go on vacation.

May we forever bless that first day when some overworked boss invented that immortal labor-saving phrase, "Miss Smith, will you please bring in your book!"

EMPLOYEE EDUCATION

Employee education is not to be confused with employee training. Employee training equips the worker for better job performance; employee education equips the person for a better life.

INTERNATIONAL SALT COMPANY	CORPORATE INDUSTRIAL RELATIONS MANUAL	DATE EFFECTIVE
		APPROVED Administrative Committee

CORPORATE TUITION REFUND POLICY

I. PURPOSE

The company recognizes that educational development is becoming increasingly important and should be encouraged. For that reason, this policy has been established to provide an opportunity for the men and women of our company to obtain additional education or training in order to increase their competence in present jobs and to prepare for advancement in the future.

II. POLICY

Under this policy an employee will be reimbursed for tuition and laboratory fees up to $200 a term or $400 a year if the eligibility and procedural requirements are met. Participation in the plan is voluntary and in no case is to be made a condition of employment.

While it is the company's intention to continue the plan indefinitely, the company retains the right to amend or terminate the offering of reimbursement at any time.

III. ELIGIBILITY

A. Employees

1. The tuition refund is available to any full-time employee who has completed 13 weeks of continuous service prior to the date on which the course begins.

2. Tuition refund will not be given to an employee who qualifies for educational benefits under the G. I. bill. However, a veteran who is no longer eligible for government benefits may participate in the plan.

3. The lay-off or release of an employee after he has been enrolled in an approved course will not alter his eligibility for tuition refund benefits.

4. The resignation or discharge of an employee automatically terminates his eligibility for benefits under this policy.

B. Courses

1. Tuition refund will be given for courses by technical institutes, trade schools, correspondence schools or accredited colleges and universities.

2. The course must be related to the employee's present job.

3. There must be a probability that the course will contribute to the employee's development.

4. Course attendance must be on the employee's own time and should not interfere with his regular job.

International Salt Company's tuition refund policy

		DATE EFFECTIVE
INTERNATIONAL SALT COMPANY	**CORPORATE INDUSTRIAL RELATIONS MANUAL**	APPROVED Administrative Committee

C. Approval

    1. Approval for courses must be granted in advance of enrollment by the employee's district, plant or headquarters department manager and by the head of the division involved.

    2. Each subject must be approved individually.

    3. Blanket approval must not be given for all courses to be taken for a degree, unless the major course involved is judged to have a relation to the employee's job or future.

D. Reimbursement

Reimbursement for tuition and laboratory fees up to $200 a term or $400 a year may be obtained when the course is completed if, within 30 days of its completion, the employee submits to his district, plant or headquarters department manager:

    1. Evidence of his earning a passing grade for the course.

    2. A verified statement of his tuition and laboratory costs or adequate receipts.

IV. PROCEDURE

A. When an employee wants to participate in the tuition refund plan, he should complete a Tuition Refund Application which may be obtained from his personnel manager.

B. The employee should discuss his plans with his immediate superior to determine whether or not he is eligible to participate in the plan.

C. If eligibility is determined, the employee's immediate superior should forward the completed Tuition Refund Application to the district, plant or headquarters department manager for disposition.

D. If approved by the appropriate manager, the application should then be submitted to the head of the division involved for final approval.

E. The approved or rejected application should then be returned to the location personnel manager who will inform the employee of the action taken.

F. A new application must be completed and approved each semester.

G. When an eligible employee applies for reimbursement, a Reimbursement Authorization form is to be completed and sent to his payroll department.

H. Payments made to employees under this policy are considered wages and subject to the provisions of the Federal Income Tax Law. Therefore, the appropriate taxes will be deducted from the gross amount.

I. All records will become part of the employee's personnel file.

The motivation for employee education lies with the individual, although it is often encouraged by the company. Employee education can be provided by a teacher or be self-taught. It can be in-house or off the premises. It can be on released (company) time or on the employee's own time. It can be in classrooms or by correspondence. It can be degree-related or noncredit courses.

Employee education can be on any work level. Rank-and-file workers may want to broaden their educational backgrounds or executives may want to participate in nonjob-related development programs. Studying art or music may not make a person a better accountant, it's true, but this could be useful in rounding out his personality and making him more suitable for an executive position.

Every employee is hired initially for a specific job and it is the skill he possesses that makes him employable. The typist in the office and the machinist in the factory are put to work because of a single skill which is well developed. The same is true of upper echelon positions where an applicant is recruited because of his specialty—engineering, law, mathematics, marketing, etc. But as an individual moves up the ladder he broadens rather than deepens his qualifications.

It is easy for workers to enroll for vocational education programs that enhance their earnings potential. It is not as easy for workers to understand why they should want to participate in adult education which has no direct or noticeable bearing on their hopes of getting better jobs.

Likewise, it is easy for companies to conduct classes, or support workers, in the broad arena of training that enhances the employees' value to themselves and to their companies. It is not as easy for companies to accept the idea that any contribution, financial or otherwise, that they make to nonspecific education may, in the long run, even return a greater payback.

TUITION REFUND PLAN
of
International Salt Company

The "Tuition Refund Plan" of International Salt Company, Clarks Summit, Pennsylvania, for active employees, hourly and salaried, was introduced in 1962. It has since been liberalized to reimburse an employee 100% of the tuition and laboratory fees for up to six credit hours per school term.

"It has indeed been successful," says Arnold F. Campo, director of industrial relations. He reports excellent participation in all divisions of the company.

373

He adds that "one of the key points in our program is that participation is voluntary and in no case may it be made a condition of employment."

TUITION REIMBURSEMENT

It has often been said that the growth of any company is merely the sum total of the growth of its people. In the belief that it is in their best interest to do so, many companies pay part or all of the cost of education for their employees.

Aiding and encouraging employees to improve their educational background is considered good practice in the hope that this will:

1. Upgrade employees in their training, thus enhancing their value to the company.
2. Assure employees that the company is interested in their advancement and future security.

A policy of paying the cost of education is easy to implement when the courses are directly related to the industry. Sending insurance people to a school for underwriters, for example, is commonly done. Many trade associations conduct seminars and specialty schools to which member companies send employees.

The practice of paying for general education, more tailored to the individual than to his company, is a different matter. Companies ought not embark upon such a program without first thinking seriously upon some of the problems which might result. Once the program is underway it is almost impossible to backtrack and revise the rules. It is best that the terms and conditions be clearly spelled out.

Many companies, large and small, have a policy of "tuition refunds" for their employees. This means that under certain standards part or all of the cost of tuition, books and supplies will be paid back to the employee upon satisfactory completion of the course.

The rules are usually:

1. The course of study must be in line with the employee's work.
   a. Shorthand for a typist—yes.
   b. Sewing for a typist—no.
2. The course must be studied at an approved (not necessarily accredited) institution of learning.
   a. University night school—yes.
   b. Carnegie course—maybe.
   c. Dance studio—no.

3. The employee's enrollment must be approved by the company.
4. The employee must make a passing grade to receive the tuition refund.

Refunds vary from 50% to the entire bill. The refund includes tuition, registration, laboratory fees, books and supplies, but not insurance, recreation or travel.

In some companies the policy is quite restrictive and covers only those courses of study judged to be directly related to the employee's job. Example: sending a budget assistant to a finance school. Other companies take a liberal position and willingly pay for general education. Example: postgraduate study toward an LL.B degree for a salesman.

There is, of course, the other side of the picture. Many companies, in good conscience, feel that training is the responsibility of the individual. Workers such as typists, accountants, lawyers, nurses and others are already trained or they would not be hired. Since they have acquired this training at their own expense of time and money, is it fair to "give" others this kind of education? These companies, of course, are prepared to train their employees on the job and teach them the business. But they expect them to be already qualified in the basic skills needed to perform the duties of the job once these are learned.

The fact that the cost of an across-the-board policy of tuition refund can be charged off as a business expense makes the decision easier. Nevertheless, the decision is more generally one of principle, whether the education of its workers is a management or societal responsibility.

TUITION AID—A FRINGE BENEFIT THAT PAYS

Former Dean Paul H. Sheats of the University of California Extension Division tells of a friend who suggests that universities issue diplomas that disintegrate in 10 years. After the student updates his knowledge with further study, he would then be issued a replacement sheepskin.

Emeritus Professor Sheats believes that the effective period of the diploma might even be further reduced because "professional people now regard continuing education as a necessary career *process*—not as a step, or something which can be finished."

The California educator has made an equally interesting proposal: That America "move as rapidly as possible to build into the 40-hour week eight hours of paid time for voluntary participation in organized programs of continuing education. The paid time off for continuing education could be either on job-related or liberal arts oriented programs."

WILBERT E. SCHEER

presents his

personal formula for success, which he has recommended to thousands
of employed workers, applicants seeking work, and students preparing
for work. It applies to any person, on any job, any time, anywhere.
It will keep the person from being fired, get him a raise, bring him
the satisfaction of being appreciated. It can be stated in two words:

PERFORM

BEHAVE

This is the only advice he can offer workers which carries with it a
built-in guarantee for individual success. It simply can not fail.

This proposal, he says, is based on two results of the explosion of
knowledge. One is what Yale Professor Neil Chamberlain calls "the
steady downgrading of the occupational competence of all who are
employed." A second factor is "the changing requirements of the
work force as a result of automation and cybernetics."

No record exists as yet of "disintegrating diplomas." No union
contract as yet provides for 20% of a worker's paid time being devoted
to study.

But right now there are business-oriented programs that provide part
of that "necessary career process" of which Professor Sheats speaks.
These are the "tuition aid" plans devised to encourage employees, first,
to do something to avoid their own obsolescence and, second, to assist
them in a financial way thus to increase their capabilities and develop
their full potential.

ON-THE-JOB TRAINING SHOULD INCLUDE
CLASSES IN LITERACY

Illiteracy has become a growing worry and menace on the job as
increasing numbers of companies are finding that their employees
lack reading and writing skills necessary for the performance of
their work.

A foreman at one company, who was a good employee but illiterate, was not able to read the instruction manual for a new piece of machinery. As a result, he failed to set safety equipment properly, and a worker's hand was severed. After a hefty lawsuit had been filed, the corporate employer called in a consultant. The consultant was a professor of reading.

It has been estimated that about 20% of the adults in the United States are functionally illiterate and another 30% are getting by at what is regarded as only a marginal level. The country's educational system is shouldering the blame for failing to teach students the basic skills of reading, writing, and arithmetic, and for neglecting to provide them with the wherewithal they need in applying those skills to keep up with the new requirements of changing jobs.

There is a direct relationship between employment and skills. And it is not only the basic skills of reading, writing, and comprehension that matter. It also includes cognitive skills that are best developed in classrooms.

While many employees on entry-level jobs are sufficiently equipped with skills when requirements are minimal, they find themselves at a disadvantage as they move up and face greater challenges. Knowledge of spelling, grammar, and punctuation are needed by a competent secretary, but the broader skills of expression and communication are needed by those who do the dictating.

A study by The Conference Board found only 8% of companies provide basic education training, but this percentage appears to be increasing. Most of the in-house training programs are remedial as companies accept responsibility for aiding ill-equipped men and women to prepare for better earnings opportunities.

To get the disadvantaged and unemployable people ready for work they must first be taught the basic skills. A word-processing operator should certainly know English; a cashier or bank teller has to know mathematics. Learning how to push the right buttons is not enough. The mechanics of a job might change with technological progress but the fundamentals remain the same.

Company enthusiasm is dampened whenever the economy slows and produces a surplus of qualified workers. But company training can be more than refresher programs—such as brush-up courses in typing for homemakers whose skills are rusty—or improvement courses—such as shorthand for typists. Companies must also be ready to provide retraining for workers whose original jobs are taken over by machines. The country has enough unemployable men and women who are educationally deprived without adding yet another host of technologically unemployed simply because they lack the basic skills to readjust.

TRAINING FILMS

A very useful and effective component of company training programs is films—sound filmstrips or motion pictures.

For the most part these are seldom custom films designed and produced for each company. They are package offerings developed and sold by specialist firms. Each film or filmstrip is accompanied with a comprehensive guide for discussion leaders. Films can be purchased or rented, and preview examinations can be arranged.

Subject matter can be anything in office, factory or sales management. Supervisory training material leads to a stimulating and challenging interchange of ideas in the discussions that follow. Sales films are designed to put new sales personnel into action faster and to rekindle the spark in established salespersons.

Films can be effective in skill training, such as telephone courtesy, letter writing, interviewing and communication. They can also be used to train in techniques, including leadership, human relations, grievance handling, discipline, delegating and merit rating. Not to be overlooked is their value in explaining company policies and philosophy, as well as economics and the free enterprise system.

Particularly valuable in the management area is the series of films that The Dartnell Corporation makes called "On Target Supervision." These usually run around 15 minutes, are in full color and deal with such important problems as absenteeism, dealing with complaints, constructive discipline and common-sense orientation. Dartnell also has many films on training, inspiring and motivating salesmen of which the most famous is the one featuring Vince Lombardi entitled "Second Effort."

DARTNELL TRAINING FILMS

Dartnell has developed a library of outstanding sound motion picture and sound slide films. They cover salesmanship, supervisor and foreman training and some phases of management.

The catalog lists:

- Tough-Minded Salesmanship. This is a five-film series by Joe Batten
  — Ask for the Order . . . and Get It!

— Your Price Is Right . . . Sell It!
— Manage Your Time to Build Your Territory
— When You're Turned Down . . . Turn On!
— Sharpen Your Sales Presentation—Make It a Winner!

- **Stand Out,** a film that shows salespeople how to stand head-and-shoulders above their competition.

- **Salesman!** This is a story about a salesman who likes his job.

- **Wickersham,** shows sales people how to be better than their competition.

- **Prospecting for More Sales,** shows how to master the art of securing more customers.

- **Charge,** a motivation movie featuring Arnold Palmer.

- **Take Command,** featuring Wally Schirra, Command Pilot of Apollo VII.

- **Run Smart,** featuring Frank Sullivan, Master Salesman.

- **Who Cares?** Health-care film dealing with employee/patient relations.

- **A Gift From Mrs. Timm,** a delightful film for all employees who meet or work with the public.

- **A Call for Dr. Redd,** hospital fire safety film.

- **Second Effort,** featuring Vince Lombardi and his motivational principles.

- **Make It Happen,** featuring Julius Boros.

- **Put It All Together**

- **Second Effort II**

- **Introduction to 'Management by Objectives.'**

- Earl Nightingale's: **The Strangest Secret**

- **The Boss,** the truth about our free enterprise system by Earl Nightingale.

- **Gigo,** a film that takes the viewer into the world of the computer.

- **Wheelchair,** a safety program developed by the Rank Organisation of England.

- **Rx for Absenteeitis.**

- **Fair Warning,** the four steps to use in dealing with employee complaints.

- **This Matter of Motivation,** a series of behavioral science films based on the principles developed by Dr. Frederick Herzberg of the University of Utah.

- **Firm . . . But Fair,** supervision film dealing with constructive discipline.

- **A Good Start,** deals with getting new employees started off right.

- 11 Sales Training Films from England.
  - The Challenge of Objections
  - A Reason to Buy
  - Time Well Spent
  - Selling On The Telephone
  - A Matter of Confidence
  - Managing Salesmen
  - Learning From Experience
  - Starting The Interview
  - How to Close The Sale
  - The Art of Two-Way Communications
  - The Art of Negotiating

These films may be purchased or rented and they are available for preview. Write for free catalog.

TRAINING MACHINES

Industry has undergone tremendous change in the past half century. In the process, the unskilled worker and the labor foreman have virtually disappeared. The specialist, the technician and the manager have taken their place. Worker productivity and effective work management are vital to survival in the competitive business of today and tomorrow.

Change brings progress but it also brings the requirement for new knowledge and new skills to adjust for new tools and equipment, new processes and new procedures. The supervisor is therefore constantly confronted with the necessity for training and retraining to meet these changes.

The ability to train workers quickly and effectively is an increasingly important obligation for supervisors. The majority of supervisors, however, have neither the time nor the talent to train their people. The need for improving the ability of supervisors to train is so evident and the benefits so certain that special efforts to help them must be undertaken.

Teaching machines are one answer. An electronic multifunction projector provides a useful visual aid to training. The unit projects slides, motion pictures and artwork. The machine may be operated at variable speeds to allow precision in pacing a program to suit the learner.

Standard training programs can be obtained from the manufacturer. Included would be films, manuals, workbooks, tests and instructor guides. These standard programs cover common training needs in a wide variety of subjects.

The machine manufacturer can also assist in the preparation of custom training programs, similar in composition to standard packages, but tailored to the specific needs and circumstances of the particular user.

Typical programs easily adapted to the machines are:

- Typing—basic and refresher.
- Keypunching—numeric and alphabetical.
- Introduction to data automation.
- Fundamentals of computer programming.
- 10-key adding machine.
- Reading improvement.
- Methods improvement.
- Job attitudes.
- Safety.

Machine programs consist of carefully-designed instructional sequences (frames) planned to combine these features:

1. Step-by-step buildup: logical order.
2. Active response: recognized and acknowledged.
3. Feedback: confirmed or redirected.
4. Self-pacing: progress at own speed.

These four features form a repeating, learning cycle. As each succeeding frame is presented the program increases in complexity.

Programmed learning utilizing teaching machines is a process. It is a training method, a pedagogic strategy.

ADULT EDUCATION

Adult education is a vital necessity in our fast-moving modern life. Never has there been greater need for knowing more about ourselves and the world in which we live.

Education can no longer be regarded as completed with the preparation for vocations, whether at the close of the secondary-school period or at the completion of a professional course in a higher educational institution. Whether viewed from the standpoint of social need or of individual development, education is a process that continues through adult life.

This is the first generation in which our earlier training is no longer sufficient to carry us through life. A formal education received years ago is no guarantee that we can meet successfully the demands of modern living. New skills, ideas, facts and attitudes are required to cope with the rapid and continuous changes now going on.

Just as obsolescence occurs sooner in the material world, so also is it noticeably visible in the realm of knowledge. This is certainly understandable when we think of the outstanding advancements in the field of medicine; would we entrust the delicate operation on a loved one to a surgeon who had learned nothing new since he received his diploma years ago?

The need to keep apace of changing conditions is just as important, although not as dramatic, in other occupations.

Today much knowledge is out of date as fast as it is learned. More complete, extensive and reliable facts supplant earlier conclusions in all fields. More new knowledge has already been accumulated during the lifetime of the present adult population than the total amount that existed at the time of its birth.

Single-Skilled Worker is "Unskilled"

In the vital area of vocational skills, this obsolescence is even more apparent. Automation, electronics and other technological improvements dictate that adults adapt to new methods and learn new skills. Flexibility is the key word as employers prefer to move workers about instead of releasing them. Many jobs in offices, factories and shops are in a state of flux, and even if the number of jobs in a company or industry is not reduced, certainly the "mix" of jobs will be different.

The single-skill worker, the one who cannot adjust readily, becomes the victim of technological unemployment at the very time that skilled jobs go begging.

For survival and for progress, America needs all the experience, guidance and dependability of all available workers. But in an industrial

ADULT EDUCATION FACTORS

1. Adults must want to learn.

   a. Children may learn in response to compulsion.

   b. Adults must develop their own desire.

2. Adults will learn only what they feel a need to learn.

   a. Children learn many things for which they feel no need.

   b. Adults are more practical in what they study.

3. Adults learn by doing.

   a. Adults will forget within a year at least 50 percent of what they learn in a passive way; within two years they will forget 80 percent.

   b. Adults retain more of what they learn by practice.

4. Adult learning centers on problems, and the problems must be realistic.

   a. Adults expect more than rules, principles, and hypothetical illustrations.

   b. Problems should be based on experience and solutions should be practical in helping resolve these problems.

5. Adults learn best in an informal environment.

   a. Children may need to be regimented and controlled to get their attention and cooperation.

   b. Adults have progressed from school days and rebel against standardization.

6. Adults need a variety of learning methods.

   a. Information should reach the adult learner through more than one sensory channel.

   b. Movies, film strips, flipcharts, other visual aids can heighten the impact of a lecture or other verbal exposition.

7. Adults want guidance, not grades.

   a. They are not interested in competing or excelling.

   b. They resist tests and other devices for comparative evaluation; they fear embarrassment.

economy these commendable traits are useless without skill development. Adult education, therefore, can no longer be a marginal activity.

This emphasis on adult education should not be considered unusual. Organized education was originally devoted to the development of the mature, not child, mind. Plato and Aristotle taught men and women, not children. Even today, progress is founded on the ability of the adult mind to change by learning new things.

Since our society is controlled by adults, not children, it is foolish to pass over adults and concentrate on children in trying to develop a better world. Education can no longer be considered as the occupation of childhood but of a whole life. The full substance of education can be acquired only in adult life, when grownup men and women, stable in character and serious in purpose, bring varied backgrounds to the process of learning.

Yet in the truly American tradition of freedom, adult learning has always been optional. Beyond the formal education in youth, which is required, any additional learning was left heretofore to informal means, such as occasional books, mass communication media, and voluntary study groups, many of which were poorly planned, poorly executed, run more for social purposes, and with little resemblance to study in the school sense.

The curriculum of adult education originally consisted of an *a la carte* menu of miscellaneous subjects. It was concerned with remedying deficiencies in the education of youth, and in the areas of literacy, citizenship, vocational skills and better use of leisure time. It filled a limited need despite any ill-defined goal.

In more recent years adult education has been coming in for its share of attention and is getting assistance from government and social forces. During wartime, when Americans displayed an emotional antipathy for all things alien, the emphasis was on Americanization education. Later, the appeal of group dynamics had an impact on classroom discussion. More recently, education for the aged became popular.

The Horizon Broadens

Today the concern is for the common man. This is the era of the disadvantaged, the under-educated, the unemployed, the dropout. Welfare programs reveal there is a causal relationship between poverty of the mind and poverty of the body. A nation dedicated to human dignity is trying to help people who have never known that dignity.

Added together, nowadays the need is greater, more permanent and more demanding. Fortunately, adult education is no longer a hobby or pastime, a fifth wheel on the cart of learning. It attempts to expose the mind to a new body of knowledge that was unknown years ago, to train in new skills that were unheard of years ago, and to broaden the scope of living in a social world whose horizons are much wider.

Any definition of adult education includes these characteristics:

1. The persons concerned are beyond the compulsory school age.
2. They are engaged in an organized educational activity conducted by a responsible educational agency.
3. They are continuing their education on a part-time basis.
4. They are attending classes voluntarily.
5. There usually is a fee.

Most definitions will exclude incidental learning picked up by casual conversation, newspaper or magazine reading, or radio-television listening. This could be labeled "education of adults" as differentiated from adult education, which is better planned and directed.

Adult education is not recreation, nor a program of arts and crafts to provide busy work. Adult education does not have as its goal the primary purpose of providing worthy use of leisure time. Likewise, it is not exclusively a program to teach individuals how to make a living.

Adult education is as broad as life itself. The objective is to enable adults to function more efficiently as citizens, parents, home-makers, workers and human beings.

The aim of all education is to open the mind, not fill it as we would a bottle. The purpose of adult education is more than merely "to teach"; it is to reopen the mind and create within the individual the desire to learn. Adults need to be taught, yes, but even more so, they need to be stimulated. Once a person's mind has been set on fire, it will find a way to provide its own fuel.

But adult education is not an extension of previous formal classroom instruction. It is different. The adult has a few advantages and a few disadvantages as a learner.

The adult learner advantages:

1. Knows what he wants.
2. Recognizes an immediate need.
3. Expresses a definite purpose to learn.
4. Is self-motivated.
5. Feels his responsibility.
6. Brings with him a wide range of experience.
7. Is usually financially able.

Disadvantages:

1. Has limited time for education.
2. May be tired after working all day.

3. Struggles with preset ideas and habit patterns.
4. Most often has to "unlearn" before he can learn.
5. Could have a critical attitude.
6. May feel inadequate and need his confidence built up.
7. Expects too much and becomes easily discouraged.

There are two main reasons for grownups participating in adult education: (1) to equip themselves for better jobs; and (2) to make their lives more interesting and enjoyable.

The results of a national survey showed that the emphasis of adult education is on the practical rather than the academic subjects. Technical courses, business classes and other vocational subjects make up the largest segment. The humanities, religious and public-affairs categories which are more representative of the realm of ideas and values, run second. Television, a medium capable of attracting the largest audience ever, does not as yet loom up as a very significant force as a form of adult instruction.

The educational agencies in academic circles and in industry have recognized the obligation and the opportunity. The public has accepted the offer and has responded. One of five Americans pursues some kind of voluntary education each year. About three-fourths are high school or college graduates. In some respects the current boom in adult learning is gradually approaching the dimensions of a national craze.

JOB TRAINING PARTNERSHIP ACT

The Comprehensive Employment Training Act (CETA), enacted in 1973, is dead. In its place is the similar but different Job Training Partnership Act, enacted in 1983. It is very much alive.

The new law is intended to provide training and related assistance to economically disadvantaged individuals, dislocated workers, and others who are facing employment barriers. The ultimate goal of the act is to move trainees into permanent, self-sustaining employment. It relies on the area business, education, and community leaders to design programs that will meet local needs.

Title I establishes the job training partnership, the administrative structure for the delivery of job training services. The heart of the program lies in the 590 private industrial councils that are responsible for programs and policies. A majority of each council's membership must come from business and industry and the chairperson must be a business representative. The key is local representatives who have the best view of local job needs.

The philosophy of JTPA differs radically from the troubled CETA program. Local involvement was more advisory under CETA, which was administered by the federal government and often used to provide public service jobs instead of actual job training. CETA focused on short-term unemployment relief rather than long-term employment prospects.

The new act utilizes public policy as a way of focusing on retraining unemployed workers and making them employable again. The biggest challenge is to assist people during a job transition. Training is the primary goal, with 70% of the funding earmarked for training and limits imposed on administrative expenses. It is hoped to train one million Americans each year.

The trainees are economically disadvantaged (Title II) skilled and unskilled workers living at the poverty level. They could receive some remedial training before entering a job training program. But up to 10% of the participants can be nondisadvantaged individuals (Title III) who face other employment problems.

Attention is centered on future jobs in growth industries. Among these are electronics, food service, energy resources, health care, and information processing. Training for office work includes typing, grammar, punctuation, and communication. Jobs are filled to satisfy company needs, but the training is expected to develop individual skills and talents to enhance earnings potential.

Companies that employ these people could be reimbursed for up to 50% of a trainee's wages for a negotiated period of time, depending upon how complicated the training may be. The whole idea is to reimburse them for training expenses incurred, not to subsidize wages. They may also be eligible for future tax credits.

The program has attracted the attention of corporations, many of which donate personnel, money, and equipment to help get a program off the ground. Beyond this, companies cooperate by supplying qualified trainers for specific instruction.

On a national scale, it is important to deal with structural unemployment to reduce the number of people dependent upon welfare. Locally, the increased employment will translate into more revenue for community businesses.

RETRAINING

Training is a big problem that is getting bigger. But there is another aspect of this problem that is, or should be, of even greater concern. That is the immediate need for retraining programs.

Industry, which traditionally relied upon the schools and other outside agencies for much of the training needed by workers to qualify for jobs, has only in the last decade come out of its cocoon and accepted much of this training as its own responsibility. But this move may not have come in time.

The bigger problem today is not training, but retraining. Again industry is slow to face up to the problem it created. Token gestures in this direction have been made but collectively they do not even ripple the waters.

Retraining is necessary for many reasons. Technological progress has eliminated many jobs, rearranged others and created new opportunities. New products and new processes are affecting jobs. Complex and competitive business is obsolescing jobs faster than ever before. For the first time in our industrial history a person's earlier education and training are no longer sufficient to carry him through life.

So where do we look for a solution? Not to the schools which have proven to be inadequate even for original training so that more and more of that burden has fallen to industry. Not to industry, apparently, which seems to have its hands full at the moment trying to cope with the training needs it reluctantly accepted only lately. What then is left? The answer is easy—government.

The responsibility for retraining is going to government by default! And government, as usual, seems quite willing to move into the void. Already there are a host of programs in operation under federal acts. Businessmen who complain about unwelcome government interference should be reminded that leadership forsaken in one place will find expression elsewhere.

SUPERVISION

Every manager, department head or administrator is a supervisor. He supervises an activity or people—sometimes both.

A supervisor is engaged in supervision. The word "supervisor," if not by definition then at least by connotation, means someone possessed not with ordinary vision but with "super" vision. He must be capable of seeing over and beyond the obvious.

Ideally he ought to wear bifocal glasses: The short vision focused on the job to be done here and now, the distance vision adjusted to the impact this decision has on the future.

Look forward with wisdom and you'll look back with pride.

"Super" vision

HOW TO DISCIPLINE

Discussions with employees generally are in the nature of misunderstandings and dissatisfactions. But there is one more area of employer-employee relations and this must be handled with extreme care and utmost respect. This is corrective action.

Corrective action is a better term than disciplinary action. The word discipline connotes punishment to many people. Correction, on the other hand, implies an attempt to cure a fault in work production or attitude that an employee has developed.

In administering discipline, no matter what the cause, the following procedure is recommended for best results:

1. Identify the problem, get all the available facts, make certain there is common agreement on the specifics on both sides.
2. Get an explanation, evaluate the logic, consider the circumstances.
3. Discuss the situation, point out the problem it is creating, try to gain understanding.
4. Explore alternate solutions, select the most feasible one, obtain concurrence.
5. Explain the new course of action to all who are involved, proceed only when unanimity is reached, install the action, monitor its progress from the sidelines, check and follow up occasionally.
6. Commend the individual who provoked the problem when he responds to the correction, express appreciation to all who cooperated for their understanding in effecting the improvement.

Impartiality is of the utmost importance. A manager's sincerest efforts will boomerang if the workers feel he is showing favoritism, letting some employees get away with things that others are called on. The employee must not be allowed to feel that he is being picked on or that the boss has it in for him. In that case he becomes defensive and the reaction is often quite different from that expected. Once a strained relationship develops between people who should work together harmoniously, the lingering damage to *esprit de corps* could be considerably worse than the original offense.

Some Do's and Don'ts

As expected, disciplining an employee can run the gamut from a mild scolding to meting out punishment. To make this touchy chore easier on the manager and more palatable to the worker, there are a few Do's and Don'ts that might be helpful.

Do — Respect the dignity of the individual and talk with him privately.
Get all available facts before doing anything.
Listen to all sides of the story.
Give the employee a chance to be heard.
Be specific in any charges that are being made.
Be tactful, courteous, reasonable.
Make certain that a reprimand is deserved.
Be thorough in explaining the action you contemplate.
Make your decision promptly.
Be firm but fair.
Show how the situation can be prevented from reoccurring.

Don't — Humiliate the employee
Threaten.
Be sarcastic.
Lose your temper.
Use profanity.
Forfeit the initiative by procrastinating.
Fail to provide all the time it takes.
Be apologetic.
Pass the buck expecting someone else to do your dirty work.
Practice amateur psychology.

Take disciplinary action when this is called for. But make certain the action is necessary and appropriate for solving an employee problem. In order to make the right decision it is important to know the employee as well as the problem.

THE SUPERIOR SUPERVISOR*

What constitutes a "super" supervisor in the eyes of his subordinates? Fifty personnel executives were asked to research the question

---

*Reprinted with permission of United Parcel Service, 51 Weaver Street, Greenwich, Connecticut 06830

in their own firms recently. While none of the answers was particularly startling, they did reveal that the employees had very definite and concise ideas.

First, most employees stated they wanted to work for a boss who wants them to work for him. This feeling was revealed in their preference for working for the boss who hired them. In short, they wanted to be wanted.

The super boss, according to employees, is one who spends time helping new workers become acquainted with the job. But he doesn't stop there. He continues to work closely with them, pointing out their weak and strong points and making suggestions which help them carry out their assignments.

He always defines a job carefully, making sure the subordinate knows what is expected. At the same time, the supervisor listens to any suggestions offered by employees for performing various aspects of the job.

Their ideal supervisor is honest, sincere and has confidence in his workers, the employees told the personnel researchers.

Another of his personal traits is that he's a good communicator. Since they want to know what is happening in the company, the employees get this information straight from the boss.

TERMINOLOGY

Many of the problems in dealing with human relations lie in the confusion caused by conflicts in responsibility and authority. Some members of management formalize policy; others execute policy. To minimize these conflicts let's arrive at an understanding. Let's get the terms and definitions of *Supervisor, Manager* and *Administrator* straight.

The *supervisor* is the person who oversees a section of the whole; he is the one who gets things done.

The *manager* is the person who determines what should be done but not always specifically the methods to be used. He translates the several functions of subordinates to objectives and directs and reviews progress.

The *administrator* is the one who formulates the long-range objectives and the guidelines for their accomplishment. Administrative management is relatively removed in time and space from the "firing line" of business.

Let's illustrate these distinctions by switching to baseball which is appropriate and timely. The typical professional baseball club is an uncomplicated kind of organization which provides pretty clear examples of what we are talking about here.

In baseball there are usually several coaches on each team, each concerned with a single function, such as pitching, batting, etc. Each one is charged with his particular duty and held responsible for it. These are the supervisors.

The manager is the one who directs the total activity on the playing field. He determines tactics and integrates the various functions of pitching, batting, fielding, substitution, to produce the winningest combination. Winning each game is his immediate objective which must be harmonized with the longer-range goals of developing and improving the team. He is continually concerned with analyzing and appraising results, finding out what's wrong, and making sure it is corrected.

Above the field manager is the general manager, comparable to the administrator in business. While he is concerned about how the team plays, he doesn't or shouldn't try to mastermind the tactics and second-guess the manager. He is concerned with more than the day-to-day performance of the team, the manager and the personnel. His concern involves attendance, finances, physical facilities and long-range planning. The administrator is the mastermind behind the trades, the promotional activities, to stimulate attendance to pay for it all.

Whether in baseball or in business, too many of us in management are trying to play all the positions. In the area of human relations this confuses and confounds the individual player or worker who doesn't know who his boss is and to whom he is accountable. It even violates the Scriptures which tell us, in Matthew 6:24, "No man can serve two masters." For best results we'd better establish at the outset which job is ours and then stick to it and let the other job for the other person.

SUPERVISORY TRAINING*

Most of the discussion about supervisory training pertains to the instruction provided by management. But the subject should also include the training managers or supervisors provide for themselves.

The reasons for supervisory training are obvious. They may be stated in these two observations:

1. In today's fast-moving and competitive business operation, jobs grow faster than the people in them. Training attempts

*This updated outline is based on a speech, "Being Practical About Supervisory Training," delivered by the author before the Cedar Rapids, Iowa chapter of the Administrative Management Society, which won for the author first prize in the AMS International Speakers competition.

to help managers and supervisors grow into their expanded roles, which grow deeper as they grow broader.

2. A person's earlier training is no longer sufficient to carry him or her through life. This is easily understood when we relate it to medicine; we expect a doctor to keep up with advances made by medical science. In business and industry the changes might not be as dramatic but they are just as real.

The purpose of supervisory training is not to teach but to create within the individual the desire to learn. Managers and supervisors don't need to be taught as much as they need to be stimulated.

Simply said, a supervisor who rests . . . rusts. Remember, as long as we're green, we're growing; once we're ripe we begin to rot.

The subject is comprehensive but not complicated. A practical approach to this training can be developed from the following thoughts presented in outline form rather than in detail.

1. The two-fold need for supervisory training

   a. for effective performance now.
   b. for assurance of continued effectiveness as business expands or as qualified replacements are called for.

2. Supervisors need training

   a. to perform better on their present assignments.
   b. to keep apace of change.
   c. to prepare for greater opportunities in the future.
   d. to attain an attitude and philosophy of the real opportunities inherent in their jobs.

3. Supervisors must learn

   a. to manage things.
   b. to manage situations.
   c. to manage people.
   d. to manage themselves.

4. To accomplish this, management must

   a. provide training.
   b. give broadening experience.
   c. establish the climate for growth.

5. All training may be accomplished in five training procedures:

   a. training classes organized and led by training specialists within their own companies.
   b. training classes conducted by an expert brought in from the outside.

    c. attendance at seminars, lectures and conventions sponsored by various management associations.

    d. training classes run by universities as part of their adult night school or extension service.

    e. training activities planned and handled largely by the trainees themselves under the guidance of an experienced training counselor.

6. The four tests for measuring the usefulness of the several training practices:

    a. training objectives must be founded upon the expressed needs of the trainees.

    b. training programs and procedures must be built upon the experiences of the trainees.

    c. objectives, training procedures, evaluation methods must have flexibility and open-endedness; learning situations are dynamic.

    d. learning is achieved through activity—through the process of seeking truth and insight—and not by the collection of the wise conclusions of others.

Objectives:

1. To acquaint all levels and types of supervisors with company policies, practices and procedures which affect them and their people.

2. To review with supervisors the accepted practices of modern management, including planning and control.

3. To make available increased technical information and encourage the development of technical know-how.

4. To emphasize the fundamentals of human behavior in a manner that will help them to improve their skill in communications and in other human relations activities necessary for personal and for company progress.

5. To impress upon them the purpose, beliefs and philosophy of the company as it relates to stockholders, customers, workers and the community.

Areas:

1. *Presupervisory:* designed to prepare a steady stream of potentials by informing likely candidates of the requirements of supervisory jobs to which they aspire. This includes an appreciation of the scope of the supervisor's job, its many obligations, and the management viewpoint and attitudes that differentiate it from the job of production worker or clerk.

2. *Basic supervisory training:* begins with a comprehensive review of necessary technical and human relations skills. Also disseminates additional information as needed for satisfactory performance in a new activity. Included are orientation, methods of organizing work and work groups, motivation, morale, attitudes, grievance procedures and the like. Leadership is stressed.

3. *Advanced supervisory training:* proceeds from a review of fundamentals to a more comprehensive program of management skills. Included is training in how to lead and participate in conferences and meetings, as well as all other forms of appropriate communication.

4. *Executive development:* preparation for higher positions in management before or after promotion has been made. Advanced skill in management of things, situations, people and self to meet the changing and ever-increasing demands of executive positions. Includes training in organization structure, labor-management trends, costs and cost reduction, and other facets of this important work. Emphasis is on decision making and policy formation with the understanding that these are not made on authority, as is so often the case, but on logic, impartiality and judgment since there is seldom the opportunity for a second chance to correct mistakes at this level without a very high price.

CASE STUDIES FOR SUPERVISORY TRAINING

Supervisory training sessions, to be effective, should consider typical everyday problems based upon the experiences of the trainees, and offer solutions which help to meet their expressed needs.

The discussions should not be built around textbook problems whose answers are in the "back of the book." This type of classroom exercise may be suitable for students. But trainees in a business environment look upon theoretical learning as appropriate for night school bright boys. They welcome any chance to talk over their operating difficulties in the hope of getting useful ideas which they can apply in their work.

Training programs which the trainees attend reluctantly, and in which they participate passively, are those designed and conducted by outsiders who may know how to construct and lead classes but who are unfamiliar with the trainees' specific problems. On the other hand, training programs which the trainees are eager to attend, and in which they become enthusiastically involved, are those in which the trainees are encouraged to present and attempt to solve the problem situations in which they have a direct interest and in whose solutions they have a personal stake.

Just as it is impossible to deliver a gift-wrapped solution in advance, so it is unrealistic to present a set of canned problems which would lend themselves to supervisory training classes. The following 12 case studies are offered only as illustrations or "thought starters," used to stimulate lively discussions. The problems must be those they feel, and the ideas that are developed must be useful to them, in order to make the training program interesting and meaningful.

1. The central employment office uses a system of requisitions to fill job vacancies. Two applicants come in together. They are typical recent high school graduates with average typing abilities. The employment interviewer feels they should be separated in the company and the young women concur. One of them is hired promptly by an eager and not-too-experienced supervisor. The other one, about as well qualified and personable, is not hired by a more critical supervisor who is harder to please. Since they seem to be close friends influenced by each other, what is the next best thing to do?

2. A job is hard to fill. The worker must operate a Burroughs billing machine. In this community experienced operators are not available and training inexperienced workers on the machine has so far not worked out too well. Quite unexpectedly an applicant walks in one day to inquire about jobs. It turns out that she had been such an operator years ago and could very easily regain her former skill. References check out, salary is no problem, the applicant impresses with her sincerity. In fact, she is so straightforward that she mentions, without any prompting, that she is an epileptic albeit a controlled case. Should she be hired?

3. As a way of controlling costs, should offices insist on hiring 60-words-per-minute typists, even if it costs more to get them, or settle for less than 60 words per minute if the starting salary is not sufficient to attract better qualified applicants. What complications must be considered?

4. Secretaries are hard to get. A manager has been without one for some time. He interviewed a few prospects but none qualified. Finally a business college sends in a young man, well qualified, who applies for stenographic work. The company has never before employed male secretaries. Should the applicant be hired, and if so, will adjustments be required?

5. A secretary for a section manager is capable, busy, satisfied and adequately paid. A secretarial job for a higher executive opens up. She is recommended, interviewed and accepted. Now she has a higher-rated job, one with more prestige but with less work. When she was promoted she received a raise. Is it good to waste a capable secretary on a job that does not challenge her sufficiently, and is a higher salary fair when her contribution to the company is less? If this is not right, what can be done?

6. Many managers who require secretaries dictate very seldom and possibly not at all. Yet to accept an office typist who cannot take shorthand might lower their own jobs in the eyes of others. But to insist on shorthand is a waste of talent and could easily lead to making a skilled stenographer unhappy with the typing and clerical duties. What should be done?

7. Your company hired a correspondent for the customer service department. On her first day the personnel manager told her she would be trained until she became familiar with the work. He also said that she should "think big" and ask questions and offer suggestions for improving the job. Six months have gone by and the new employee feels she has mastered the job. The supervisor, however, will not permit her to use any of her ideas. He simply tells her to do the work his way because it is the right way. When she explains to him that his instructions to her do not coincide with the assurance she received from the personnel office, he tells her, "If you don't like it, go see personnel!" What should the employee do?

8. A typist works for a strict and unimaginative supervisor on a routine job. She is not unhappy, but one day she hears of an opening in another department, where she feels the employees have more fun. She requests a transfer. Because she is a good worker and no problem, the supervisor feels he cannot let her go; in fact, he says he cannot afford to lose her. For that reason he tells her she cannot be transferred because he would never approve her release. Should she be transferred or retained, and what about the supervisor?

9. You are a section supervisor over 10 employees in average clerical jobs. Susie is one of your best workers but is constantly tardy. She is a widow and has three school-age children whom she must care for each morning before she goes to work. Seven of your employees like Susie and realize her problem, but two others don't like her. They tell you that if Susie is permitted to come late so can they. Susie's tardiness problem seems to have no solution; until now you've decided to live with it. Now under pressure, if you release her you are heartless; however, if you continue to put up with it, you are spineless and can expect to have other challenges placed in your path. What should you do?

10. A new training film on "How to Handle People" has just been shown to the assistant managers. They are very much impressed and enthusiastic in their praise for the film and its message. Almost everyone in the group says, "I wish my boss could see this film; he's the one who needs it." What is the next step?

11. Your company and you try to comply willingly with antidiscrimination laws but the compliance inspectors never seem satisfied with the figures. Two female applicants are under consideration for a machine operator job in the plant. Both are married. One has an Anglo-Saxon

name and the other has a Spanish surname. Of course, the second woman may not be a minority applicant just because of her married last name. But with that last name she will most likely be checked off in the minority column on future reports which will make the percentages look better. Should she be given preferential treatment?

12. You are a newly-promoted section supervisor. You were promoted because of your ability and because management thinks you are a good potential. Your company has opened a new section in its operations. You have been asked to train the workers in new methods. The workers are long-time employees some of whom have been with the company for 20 years. They resent your youth and the fact that you were promoted over them. They are obviously reluctant to cooperate with you. How do you win their necessary cooperation?

THE IN-BASKET TRAINING METHOD

The In-Basket training method is designed to improve the managerial decision-making process.

It is a special case study tool which incorporates the best that the traditional case study has to offer, while embodying refinements to allow greater flexibility, realism and involvement.

A major problem of the traditional case is that it provides either too much or too little information, usually the former. Some cases run to astonishing lengths, the idea being to give the trainee in business or the student in the classroom as much background information as possible to make up for lack of actual experience with the particular situation.

The superabundance of information provided by the traditional case bears little resemblance to actual practice. No company burdens its executives with every minute bit of information that just might be relevant to a situation. After all, what a company requires of its managers is the ability to make sound decisions from the information they have.

The crucial difference is that the In-Basket provides only significant items of information with few extraneous facts. It is designed around typical business situations which allows the trainees to transfer and relate these study situations to their own experience. Here is where the organization and structure of the In-Basket distinguish it from the lecture, case or discussion method of training. It is situation oriented.

Using the In-Basket technique, the participant starts out by first working through the case by himself. Moreover, he has to do this within a specified time limit. There is no opportunity to review and discuss details of the case with the other managers. The participant is thoroughly involved because he takes the role of the person "owning" the in-basket and because he has a limited amount of time in which to arrive at his answers. Further, he must commit himself on paper. He applies his normal methods of making decisions and solving problems on the job.

Group Feedback

Subsequently, all the participants meet to discuss the In-Basket exercise. At this time, each participant gains individual feedback by comparing the discussion results with his earlier record of notes. It is in this phase that true learning (i.e., behavior change) occurs. And because the situation studied is a simulation of real business life—using his own company's background—what is learned is naturally transferable to the job. The participants analyze and discuss the who's, what's, where's, why's, and when's of each decision with an accent on understanding— an opportunity too rarely presented during busy working days. It is done in a permissive learning atmosphere, rather than within the confines of the boss-subordinate relationship.

For this feedback session to be fruitful, the discussion leader must be generally knowledgeable and well prepared. His job is to get the participants to thrash out the reasons for their proposed actions in terms of their own experience with company policies and philosophy. They should be able to justify their reasoning and appreciate the inherent assumptions on which it is based. They should also have some idea what the results of their decisions will be in both the long and short runs.

A manager can learn to come up with good solutions by gaining greater expertise through practicing with the tools at his disposal. The manager's tools are his company's policies and traditions, its channels of authority and communication, plus his skill at separating fact from opinion to identify the real issues involved. The manager who has never learned the systematic use of these tools relies on buck-passing and guesswork.

The strength of the In-Basket is that it is concerned not so much with solutions as with *how* and *why* they arose.

ASSESSMENT CENTER

A recent addition to the corporate toolbox is the assessment center. The assessment center is used to measure managerial potential by trying to discover and uncover a candidate's strengths and weaknesses. It is hoped that this technique makes it easier to identify and evaluate talent.

A small group of upcoming employees, the candidates, are transferred away from their regular work to individually, or in discussion groups, perform managerial exercises before a panel of peers who have been previously trained to act as judges.

399

One typical program used by a national food chain includes seven exercises spread over a four-day period. They try to bring out reactions rather than answers, since candidates are not expected to know the answers to situations they have not faced before.

The topic for each exercise is imaginary but the task of performing it is dead serious. Every trait is observed, from leadership, administrative ability, communications skills, mental alertness, tolerance of stress, problem analysis to decision making. The judges try to learn how a candidate's head works.

Each participant also takes an in-basket test, handling typical problems he may expect at his desk. Through all of this, the candidate gets a better insight into management problems, and his own ability to handle them. When a weakness, public speaking for example, is discovered, a definite training and development need is identified.

The technique has many proponents in the United States. It has really caught on in England. But it also has opponents.

The dissatisfaction is not with the technique, although this is rapidly becoming faddish, like a fraternity initiation. The concern is with the way the technique is used. Often it becomes a crutch. No one is promoted who has not survived the ordeal of being assessed. The device becomes a convenient substitute for managerial judgment. It is therefore embraced by inadequate management because it provides an acceptable way of getting "off the hook."

Nothing beats real experience for individual growth and development. The assessment center is built around practice sessions and these, of course, can be useful. The results of the program depend upon the validity of the evaluations of the panel of judges. Here again individuals hide behind group decisions.

The adroit manager will take advantage of every available assistance that will aid him in making his decision. But he will not let the technique make the decision for him. Entrepreneurial leadership is not cut from the synthetic fabric of industrial life.

SENSITIVITY TRAINING

Sensitivity training is an educational experience in which the goal is to help individuals work more harmoniously and responsibly together. To work toward such a goal, each person has to learn something about the many factors that interfere with or disrupt communications, decision making and active cooperation.

In formal education, the instructor explains how groups are formed and how they interact. This produces theoretical or abstract knowledge.

This knowledge is useful but not necessarily put to use by the individuals involved.

In sensitivity training, group members study their own behavior as they go through the process of forming a working group. They learn by doing and in the process of trying to do something, the group members begin to get feedback from other members in the group as to how they see what each is doing. Such feedback is a rich source of information about possible frustrations and conflicts which impede and disrupt the working of a group.

Members are encouraged to communicate with each other in a more open and honest manner than is typically done in the usual social or work situation. The idea is being used socially in cities as well as within company operations. There are church-and civic-sponsored groups which bring together people with diverse interests and ideas into one program. Results are being reported as excellent.

SUPERVISOR CAPABILITIES

What qualities of personality are of greatest assistance in gaining confidence, respect, obedience, cooperation and loyalty?

1. Integrity: don't lie.
2. Knowledge: know your job.
3. Empathy: understand your people.
4. Courage: take positive action.
5. Decisiveness: say what you mean and mean what you say.
6. Dependability: be known as someone who will get the job done.
7. Initiative: think and plan ahead.
8. Tact: approach others the way you like to be approached.
9. Justice: be firm but fair.
10. Enthusiasm: show it in everything you do.
11. Bearing: how do you look in the mirror of life?
12. Unselfishness: give credit where credit is due.
13. Judgment: don't make snap decisions.
14. Loyalty: be true to your company, your products and your people.

What supervisory practices lead to poor employee relations and adversely affect employee morale?

1. Showing favoritism.
2. Failing to keep promises.
3. Lacking interest in the individual.

4. Failing to give credit when earned.
5. Driving rather than leading.
6. Being tactless and blunt in dealing with employees.
7. Failing to take adequate disciplinary action.

What personal characteristics of the supervisor lead to effective employee relations?

1. A willingness to listen carefully.
2. An even disposition.
3. An interest in each employee as a person.
4. A sympathetic understanding of the employee's problems.
5. Enthusiasm and integrity.
6. Impartiality in dealing with employees.
7. Fairness.
8. A willingness to back up employees.
9. Willingness to assume responsibility.
10. Ability to make decisions.

What are the danger signals that should alert a supervisor to possible trouble ahead?

1. High turnover.
2. Absenteeism increasing.
3. Tardiness getting out of hand.
4. Lack of cooperation.
5. An attitude of indifference in the group.
6. Team spirit lacking.
7. Lack of employee suggestions.
8. Failure to meet deadlines.
9. Loafing on the job.
10. Requests for transfers without satisfactory reasons given.

TRANSACTIONAL ANALYSIS

More than a few companies are training employees in interpersonal relationships. One device they are using is transactional analysis. This is an approach to understanding human behavior by means of communicating between two or more people.

TA is based on how people interact by tracing the way a transaction is shaped by the ego state of each person. The ego states that determine behavior consist of three patterns: (1) parent, (2) adult and (3) child.

In some business situations we may act as parents and simply tell and talk down, feeling our right to criticize and admonish. As adults we deal more with factual information, logically and without emotion. As children we may respond to impulses both good and otherwise, displaying curiosity, rebelliousness and imagination.

One technique for stroking the ego is to use recognition, compliments and praise. Leading instead of ordering is recommended. The accurate exchange of meaning and intent among human beings is true communication. In all our communications, sincerity is a must.

There are four different life positions. They operate for the most part at a largely unconscious level of maturity, and are basic to all our behavior. These are:

1. I'm OK—you're OK. Supervisor and employees work well together; there are no hangups.

2. I'm OK—you're not OK. Supervisor feels smug and self-satisfied, superior to employees.

3. I'm not OK—you're OK. Supervisor is a loser and feels inferior; he needs approval from others.

4. I'm not OK—you're not OK. This is a negative situation when people are distrustful of each other.

Within one of these life positions, or in some circumstances possibly in combination, managers work with subordinates. In dealing with employees they tread on experiences and expectations. Their feelings and beliefs influence not only what they say but also what they hear.

This article is not an endorsement of TA which, as a technique, is still suspect. What is encouraging is that companies are beginning to appreciate the value of people in the success of their business.

EXECUTIVE EDUCATION

Business management is growing in importance and need. Yet its appeal as a career seems to be waning. This, despite the fact that in collegiate circles business administration is the nation's most popular major. Still, industry, eager heir to these graduates, is having increasing difficulty recruiting the next generation of managers.

The colleges and universities are careful not to acquire the image of trade schools. They are not guiding enough of their bright young prospects toward the executive suite. The students themselves are not responding to the corporate talent hunt, where jobs appear to be characterized by pressure, conformity and superficial values. Instead they prefer careers in government, social work, professions, research and academia.

Several large universities are phasing out undergraduate business programs. They are opting for business education at the graduate level. They are de-emphasizing business courses in favor of social science, humanities, physical science and mathematics. They argue that teaching specialized business subjects too early deprives the student of a broad background. These schools feel their role is to train people for top management.

But what about the other and greater need of business for managers and junior executives below top management? What about people with a good general knowledge of accounting, marketing, finance and economics? Can business education be developed without becoming vocational in nature? Whatever is offered should equip the student with a background that will stand up under technological and social change.

There are still many excellent opportunities for students interested in preparing for business careers. Fortunately, not all universities have abdicated their responsibility in this area. Some are still maintaining and expanding their curricula with well-qualified and properly-oriented professors.

Many good facilities are also available to the worker. Most universities conduct night schools where a worker may take a "how to" course in any subject where he recognizes a deficiency exists in his training or experience. Trade associations and industry groups operate schools and seminars for members.

EXECUTIVE TRAINING

The best executive training is a combination of:

1. In-house training sessions conducted by professional trainers assisted by senior officers: a problem encountered on the operational floor of business calls for results.
2. Off-the-job training in universities and in association seminars: a problem discussed or a trend revealed in the relaxed academic atmosphere permits thinking.
3. Work experience: this is, in the final analysis, the testing ground that teaches responsibility.

To build a program of executive training use:

1. Work within the company.
2. Job rotation.

3. Lectures and seminars.
4. Audiovisual equipment.
5. Meetings (away at hotels and resorts).
6. Outside study.
7. A number of observation points.

The key to success in executive training is guidance. This can be provided in the direction of thought by outside professors and seminar leaders. But probably the best training comes from guidance on the job by seasoned and successful older executives—if they can commit their experience and effectiveness to understandable training techniques. What is done is to assign the individual trainee to a "model boss" or trainer-coach.

Practical is Better than Theoretical

Work experience means more than simple routines, but does include routines. These teach responsibility for planning, coordinating and controlling—and for getting results. A trainee's knowledge, skills and abilities are deepened through experience. Ideally, the jobs he is assigned to should be over his head in order to challenge him. Once he masters these duties he should be moved on to more difficult assignments. In each case the trainer-coach should delegate the specific duty but not spell out how it should be done, and only keep the control to see that it comes to a good conclusion. In other words, he should give the trainee a destination and a green light, but not an old road map.

To be successful, allow for the expression of:

1. Ideas
2. Enthusiasm
3. Ingenuity
4. Imagination
5. Judgment
6. Decisions

Otherwise the executives, or potential executives, being given this special training will soon determine that it makes sense to play according to the established and accepted ground rules.

The trainer-coach must realize that the distinction in performance is not always between right and wrong ways. There may well be several right ways. He must expect that the trainee, unfettered by tradition and past practices, might come up with a different way which could be as good or better than the one which was expected.

When practical work experience, properly directed, is supplemented by other training, as it should be, the trainee will advance in position, prestige and compensation as fast as his increasing capabilities will take him and appropriate promotions and job vacancies open up for him.

INDIVIDUAL CAREER PATH CHARTING

For years, when a management position had to be filled, it was easy to go to the outside to hire somebody. Apparently it was felt that the regular work force consisted of drones and did not include many, if any, individuals of leadership stature.

As the source of qualified applicants began to dry up—and this has been and still is a critical shortage—companies tried to "home grow" their own managers through pre- and post-promotion training. This is today a common practice.

A third possibility exists. That is the discovery and identification of talent already "on board" and within reach. These are individuals who possess a native talent that is not being fully utilized on the job, or who through their own initiative have increased or broadened their capabilities and are getting prepared for greater challenges.

But in every organization there are still others who are not ready for bigger things but who can be helped to be made ready. Anyone who shows promise and demonstrates a sincere desire to make himself promotable is worthy of this attention. The procedure is to:

1. Find out what talents and abilities he possesses.
2. Point him toward the next logical higher position.
3. Take his personal aspirations into account.
4. Identify specifically what assistance he needs to qualify for the next position.
5. Chart a definite course that will guide and direct him toward the fulfillment of this objective.

This is called "Career Development." Companies have accepted the idea that operating procedures should be programmed. Should not a career also be programmed?

There Must Be a Better Way

Charting career paths is a technique recently introduced. In the past, bright, alert, well-educated young men and women were hired, dropped into the swim, and given catch-as-catch-can opportunities to work their way up. The approach to employee progress was simply to permit the individual to shift for himself. The responsibility for making good was on the struggling employee.

This method worked for some, and these were the success stories companies bragged about. There is no way of recounting the failures for companies kept no records of the ones who "couldn't cut the mustard." Some of the hopefuls who didn't make it settled for mediocre jobs in the company, but these were usually few. The majority dropped out and tried their luck elsewhere, possibly becoming successes in their own right where the new job demands were more compatible with their abilities or where the climate was more conducive to their own ambitions.

With human beings becoming recognized as the nation's last natural resource—and with people taking on added value as corporate assets—the earlier, indifferent approach to employee development is gradually being scuttled.

Something more formal is needed, although a formal program is not automatically the answer. A formalized procedure merely makes it easier for a manager to aid the development of each subordinate. The program, designed for him by outside consultants or in-house specialists, spells out the steps he should follow to arrive at a satisfying result. In the language of the day, it can be said that his selection, development and progress will be programmed.

The key is the manager's understanding of his new responsibility to his people. In a nutshell, he owes them every chance to make good. He hired them away from other employers, he painted a rosy picture which they obviously bought, he inferred that he would help them realize their personal aspirations—and a planned management development program, as espoused here, provides the assistance he needs to deliver on his implied promise—and at the same time help himself and his company. After all, the success of his company is merely the sum total of the success of his people.

A System is Needed

Without such a system his well-intentioned efforts become disorganized. He needs a device to help him analyze each subordinate's needs, capacities and ambitions. Then he needs guidelines on how to proceed to assist each subordinate, to get him to build on his strengths and overcome his weaknesses. Finally, he needs to work within a standard or uniform program with the corporation so that his efforts will blend into the overall picture.

In a company-wide program, all management members will aid their subordinates on all levels to:

1. Get to know themselves—their potential and limitations.
2. Increase their knowledge.
3. Develop a positive attitude.
4. Seek more responsibility in a favorable climate.
5. Improve themselves as workers and as persons.

While the general pattern can be standardized for all managers (so that everybody plays by the same rules), the success of the program depends upon individual applications. No two persons are alike, so no one program will work the same for everybody. Learning abilities vary, as do ambitions. Therefore, the development must be tailored to each individual and to his opportunities for fulfillment. Hence the term, individual career path charting.

It's All Predicated on the Appraisals

The appraisal of performance and the appraisal of potential, procedures that many companies are now using in one form or another, are not an end in themselves but only devices to accomplish the greater purpose. The importance of the entire appraisal concept does not lie in the form. The form should not be a report card. The form should be a road map to the objective; it should tell how well the person rated is on course and on time.

It should point up good accomplishments for which the individual may be properly recognized and rewarded. It should point up, without embarrassment, any weaknesses in performance and potential that require attention.

Any performance rating or appraisal system is useful when it answers the question of the ratee "How am I doing?" But in higher level positions it is also necessary to help the incumbent understand "Where am I headed?"

To do this the discussion, commonly referred to as the "Appraisal Interview," must be a two-way conversation between rater and ratee. It will not be effective if the rater does most of the talking and the ratee does most of the listening. Not until both parties to the discussion speak freely and get all their ideas across and their questions answered can the communication be considered complete.

Nor should the procedure become ritualistic. The rating should be done when appropriate, not solely by the calendar. The timetable serves only as a reminder that another rating is due, but it should not be allowed to become a deterrent.

Never, but never, confound the appraisal with any other personnel action, least of all a salary recommendation. In such uses it merely becomes window dressing to support the other action. The appraisal is intended to serve the individual's and the corporation's development needs. While it may also be used when other considerations come up, trying to serve too many purposes only clouds the main issue. If a worker's performance and potential are progressing, these other personnel actions will stand to benefit and become easier to administer.

Rating "Out in Front" is Difficult

It is always easier for a rater to look back, especially if he has good records, and document what he sees. But it is risky to look ahead and make a declaration of not "what was" but "what will be." In the event of a disappointment, the rater can always be second-guessed.

First, the rater has to know and know well, the person he is rating. Otherwise, how can he estimate future possibilities? To push an individual forward beyond his capabilities or interests does irreparable harm.

Second, the rater must know the direction in which he is encouraging the individual to move. This means he must have at least a working knowledge of the "jobs ahead" and their requirements. When he steers a man or woman along blindly, building false hopes, he does neither the person nor the corporation any good.

Third, he must have some way of identifying the gaps—those areas of deficiencies where guidance will be useful and appreciated. Here the needs and wishes of the ratee must also be taken into account.

All this places a tremendous responsibility upon the rater. He becomes much more than a scorekeeper whose reports, if accurate, are indisputable. Now he becomes an adviser, a counsellor, a designer, whose observations and recommendations are based on judgment. This is much more difficult to substantiate. These judgments can be dangerous or they can be helpful. They can be misleading. Needless to say, it is an ominous responsibility to assume involvement in another person's long-term welfare.

Each worker is not only trying to make a living; he is also trying to make a life. Amateur psychology, practiced by many managers, can be as lethal as a gun in the hands of a novice.

The best safeguard is to equip the manager with a carefully designed management development program. If it is not too complicated, he will understand it and apply it, not merely go through the motions. As long as it is practical and serves his interests, he will embrace it and give it his enthusiastic support.

It should be remembered, however, that the overall program is only a base or starting point. The program is objective in its design, but the individual applications of it are subjective. The success of the program depends more upon management's understanding of flesh-and-blood human beings than upon management's understanding of a lifeless set of forms, procedures and techniques.

The Fair Way is the Best

Whether a company has a system or not, the manager must still make the final decision on each action affecting an employee. But he no longer enjoys the luxury of making "his" decision; he actually has very little latitude really because he can make only right decisions. Unions, government and workers won't stand still any longer for "by gosh" selection. Final decisions must stand up if challenged.

Promotions must become more than routine rewards for good performance or a certain number of years of service. Employees should be groomed for greater responsibilities. Their potential should be recognized early, as well as the gaps in their knowledge and experience. When the promotion comes, the employee should be ready for it. And he or she should feel it was not his seniority but his contribution so far and potential contribution that helped him or her move up.

These decisions, of course, cannot be entirely neutral or impersonal. Transfers in national (and international) corporations, for example, must take into account the cost, inconvenience, reluctance and other problems of the employee and his family.

In the development of underlings, much can be said in favor of personal coaching. A leader's successful style gives strength and enthusiasm to his subordinates and reinforces their desire to do well.

But care must be exercised not to create the notion that the subordinate should imitate his boss and turn into a carbon copy of him. The age gap between them is enough to make them different. The assistant who eventually moves up and replaces his boss, or some other higher up, has to be smarter and better equipped than the man he replaces for the very simple reason that he begins where the other person leaves off.

Many companies are still making the man fit the suit, whereas in life the tailor alters the suit to fit the man. When an individual is thwarted in his sincere efforts to perform the best way he knows how, only because protocol or an unimaginative superior remains unreasonably fixed, he becomes frustrated.

Whereas in the past an organization often carried the imprint of its founder, it is more likely today to be influenced by the computer and other technology. Founder management and any other form of hardline management is rapidly being replaced by a different breed—a cadre of professionals.

What the textbooks refer to as "look see" management is now becoming management by information. This is an entirely new ballgame for many people and the boss and his subordinates may well be unable to communicate effectively.

Yet coaching can be helpful. The boss usually knows the business and also his technical specialty. Whatever he knows rubs off and becomes the springboard, not the blueprint, for his subordinate.

The Secret is Personalization

The key to career development is personalization. Career paths are designed for individuals. There can be no unilateral application. True, there are standard components but their arrangement and composition must be tailored to each person and to his particular set of circumstances.

This is not unlike the doctor's prescriptions that are written to improve the patient's well-being and health for the future. Again there are drugs in common usage and the same medical procedure can be applied to different persons. But the medication and treatment prescribed vary from one individual to another. No one should wear another person's eyeglasses.

The patent medicine day for curing "what ails ya" is over. Any tonic or pill that is good for everybody can't be of much specific value to any one individual. Similarly, the shotgun approach to training, on the theory that any training is better than none, may hit the target but miss the bull's-eye.

There are a number of canned training programs that have been established and refined over the years that do more for the aggrandizement of their promoters than they do for the participants. A few, like quack remedies, can actually do harm. The question should be "What does the patient need?" and not "What does the hustler have to offer?"

The physician does not prescribe until he knows the patient. He obtains a medical history, considers the past record, takes age and background into account, evaluates the environmental factors that may affect the future, and only then writes the prescription to fit the circumstances. In other words, he makes a complete diagnosis and then decides what the prescription should consist of.

Carrying this analogy further, the physician has considerable latitude in what he prescribes, once he has determined the appropriate remedy. The medicine can be liquid, pill, capsule or powder, and it can be a brand-name product or a drug sold by its generic term. Likewise, the patient has free choice of pharmacies or clinics in getting his prescription filled.

In a business career development program there is no one best route to follow once the course of action is established. Aids may include formal education, academic instruction, in-house training, coaching, self-development, job rotation, varied experiences, special project assignments, committee work or any of the many other avenues for growth that are open to the individual and to the company. What is required is to make the best use of the best sources that are available.

INDIVIDUAL CAREER PATH DATA

(supplement to Appraisal of Potential)

Name _____

Location _____

Question: What do you and he see as the logical advancement route within the organizational job family? Name the position(s) in the *job* career path.

_____

_____

How well does he meet the basic qualifications for entry into the next higher position?

    a.   Academically _____

    b.   Experience _____

    c.   Other _____

Question: What alternate route of advancement might be open to him? Name the
           position(s) compatible with his ambitions and interests that fit in with his
personal career path.

_____

_____

What qualifications does he possess that could entitle him to consideration in another
job field?

    a.   Education not presently fully utilized _____

    b.   Unique talent _____

    c.   Experience or training _____

    d.   Personal interest _____

Question: What do you and he agree are his needs for preparedness in extending his career?

a.   Skills development _____

b.   Specialized training _____

c.   Broadening experience, maybe job rotation _____

d.   Exposure outside the house _____

e.   Other _____

Question: At this time, how does he qualify for the next higher position?

a.   Is he ready now? Explain _____

b.   Can he be made ready soon? Explain _____

c.   Understands he has little chance for bigger assignments because

_____

Question: Are there any conditions or considerations which would have an effect on the employee's career plan or future (age, health, family circumstances, etc.)

_____

_____

_____

Date

Prepared by _____   _____
                        (manager)

In consultation with _____   _____
                           (employee)

Reviewed by _____   _____
                 (director of management development)

In both situations the important things are:

1. For the physician or the company to make the right diagnosis.
2. For the patient or the employee to heed the advice and follow instructions.

The next checkup in the doctor's office or the next performance and potential appraisal of the employee will tell at once the effectiveness of these two factors.

Is Potential Ever Reached?

The Peter Principle notwithstanding, it is a sad but undoubted fact that many people in business go through life only partially aware of the full range of possibilities that lie beyond their doorsteps. The great artists made it a point to place a doorway, or an arch, or an opening through trees in their pictures so that viewers would feel there is still more in the great beyond. Everyone needs to pass from the immediate scene to something wider so as to enjoy a largeness of view and a breadth of mental vision.

Every step up the ladder of success in business broadens the horizons and affords a wider perspective from this loftier point of view. Opportunities come into sight that were never noticed before because they could not be perceived. The higher the position the broader the outlook.

Individual growth and development is, and always will be, a personal matter. But career path charting can be a very useful and effective technique for aiding the individual in realizing the fulfillment of his potential—for the benefit of himself and his company.

SECOND CAREERS

Much has been written about "career planning." Career planning, in whatever form it is presented, defines some type of "internal management development." It suggests that companies have devised a way of identifying as well as aiding personnel on all levels who are promotable or who can become promotable.

In the absence of any formal company career planning program, individuals could set up their own personal career plans. Such plans have as their goal a position at a higher level within the same company, if the opportunity exists, or a shift to another company, possibly a competitor, where it is believed the experience accumulated to date can be utilized as a foundation for building on essentially the same type of job in the same general career field.

Career planning is a program broadly designed with the company in mind. In today's volatile employment market, especially for upper-echelon personnel, it is being superceded by "second-career planning" tailored to each individual. Here the planning *for* individuals becomes planning *by* individuals.

Career planning involves changing jobs. Second-career planning involves changing careers. It means totally removing oneself from the existing job environment and into an occupation that does not utilize prior expertise. It is a departure from the past and a move into a more personally-appealing future.

Reasons for second-career planning are both personal and technological. From the personal standpoint, someone might want to try to start over who:

1. Is going stale, is being bored, and is no longer challenged.
2. Dreams of increasing earnings by shifting to an alternate occupation.
3. Has fallen into a job out of economic necessity and is now entrapped.

From the technological standpoint, entire industries are disappearing and new ones created. Many long-established careers are dying out and new careers for which people are ill-prepared, are emerging. The traditional single-skill occupations don't last a lifetime anymore.

The security of job preparation (through education or experience) for a fixed occupation, which satisfied previous generations, is now gone. Making a shift to adjust to the present job opportunities is difficult, and designing a career path for the future is impossible. *The average college graduate these days can anticipate having five careers (not five jobs, but five careers) in his or her lifetime of work—three of which haven't even been invented yet!*

Second-career planning may be the answer for now inasmuch as the original career decision is being wiped out. But because of the speed of technological acceleration, even the second career will ultimately become perishable.

The answer, obviously, is to realize that resting on one's laurels means rusting on them. Planning must be ongoing because careers are so short-lived.

The "How to" of Second-Career Planning

Any employee arriving at a crossroad in life is in the ideal position of choosing whether to continue in the same career pattern, possibly making a job change, or "shucking the whole business" by abandoning

415

a well-worn rut, yielding to urges waiting to express themselves, and starting over on some entirely new and different career direction. Why an entirely new career?

There are many reasons, often a matter of necessity. Jobs are simply not perpetual. Careers are fragile. Single-skill talent or training is no longer sufficient to carry a man or woman through a lifetime of work. The industrial climate is fickle and job security is ephemeral, so unless people shift with the tide they run the risk of being left behind, victims of technological progress.

Making the change to another career direction can best be accomplished by revising the usual career planning procedure. The most effective approach for second-career planning consists of three phases:

1. The first step is to erase the normal built-in frustration. People who suffer the indignities of being "released" should be excused for harboring feelings of hostility. All workers, and particularly managers and executives, find the sudden need to reestablish themselves in new careers has caught them unready emotionally and psychologically. They are bitter about the unexpected turn of events which resulted not from any wrongdoing on their part but which nonetheless leaves them "out in the cold." They cannot think very clearly and "regroup" unless they first ventilate their feelings and purge their minds and hearts of any and all blame for the plight in which they find themselves.

2. The second step is to identify skills and inherent talents possessed by the individual to establish the new direction. This is accomplished with thorough and patient counseling (maybe including the family), in-depth interviewing (to gain insight), and appropriate testing (aptitude and personality). There are services and agencies available for this purpose.

3. The third step is to develop a self-marketing plan. This consists of instructions for writing the cover letter (not more than one page), preparing a "directed" resume (not a litany of meaningless data), developing a selective mailing list, and taking training on "How to sell yourself in the interview." The local library has books that could be helpful.

Most workers become locked into their jobs. They take jobs in the first place that are available and convenient. After a time these jobs might not be the kinds of work they want or are best qualified for. That is the reason the majority of workers are unhappy with their work. No, they might not register their discontent but neither do they exult great enthusiasm or delight.

Workers trapped in a field that satisfies their economic needs but little else must decide before it is too late whether to continue on the treadmill to ennui or take off in a new direction. For them a second career is the answer.

PERT

PERT (Program Evaluation and Review Technique) is a method for planning, controlling and monitoring the progress of complex projects. Originated to coordinate the work of a large number of subcontractors engaged in the development of the Navy's Polaris missile, PERT is credited with having cut two years off the time span of that project.

The emphasis on PERT is on time scheduling. A project is broken down into its component steps. These steps are represented graphically in a network to show the dependencies among them. The time required to complete each step is estimated and potential bottleneck steps are identified. A determination is made of the critical path (i.e., the sequence of events that will require the greatest expected time to accomplish). Having this information, management is able to reassign manpower and resources to speed up the steps that might cause the project to fall behind schedule.

To provide an additional dimension to PERT/time, the PERT/cost system has been developed for the specific purpose of integrating financial data with the associated time data of project accomplishment. In terms of control, the integration of PERT/time and PERT/cost provides substantial assistance in determining whether various levels of management are meeting schedule commitments, cost estimates and technical performance standards.

Because PERT incorporates a method for estimating the time it will take to do something which has never been done before—and for which, therefore, no time or cost standards exist—it is particularly useful with research and development projects.

PERT does have some limitations in its application. PERT seems to be too scientific and the results so definitive that management is often tempted to discount, or even disregard, the reliability of data fed into the system.

A second limitation is that estimates tend to be established as firm time and cost commitments, despite the fact that numerous revisions are generally anticipated. At the same time, cost estimates are not often easily identifiable in the normal activities of a department. As a result, the data are sometimes manipulated to make a specific aspect of the project look good at the expense of accuracy and reliability.

These limitations, however, are common to many control tools because of human behavioral considerations.

MANAGERIAL GROWTH

Much can be done by the company by creating a work environment which is conducive to the growth of people. The increasing complexity of their jobs will be the stimulation but the climate must be such that permits the self-development of people who respond to the challenge.

A company which wants its executives or managers to develop, should have

1. Clearly defined responsibilities.
2. Delegation of assignments.
3. Freedom to make decisions.
4. Arrangements to acquire needed additional knowledge.

In addition the company should

1. Have confidence in these people; give them a chance.
2. Provide coaching instead of criticism; every person who fails is a reflection on his boss.
3. Keep score; progress should be recognized and rewarded.

A baseball rookie going to bat in the big leagues is not left to his own devices. He is told what to do on every pitch—whether to bunt, hit away, take the pitch, etc. He draws upon the extensive backgrounds and varied experiences of seasoned veterans. In business we are inclined to hire an applicant or promote an employee into a management position and then, instead of oversupervising him we actually become guilty of undersupervising him. We have the feeling that once such a job is filled our problems are over and we retreat into our own busy world.

MANAGEMENT BY OBJECTIVES

Objectives of one sort or another have been used by managers for a long time. Dr. Peter Drucker, in his 1954 book, *The Practice of Management,* used objectives as the basis for a management system. He proposed that objectives serve as the vehicle for administering and directing a systems approach to managing an organization. With its gradual application in thousands of diverse companies, the concept was translated into practice.

Initially it was embraced as a device for improving performance by establishing goals to work toward. Evaluation techniques in the 1950's measured the degree to which managers were thought to possess, or to fail to possess, highly subjective character traits. Qualities commonly evaluated related to personality and behavior; factors were not keyed to results.

A decade later measurable goals replaced evaluation of traits. This was the beginning of Management by Objectives (MBO).

The definition of MBO, as expressed by its foremost proponent, Dr. George S. Odiorne, is: "Management by objectives is a process whereby the superior and subordinate managers of an organization jointly identify its common goals, define each individual's major areas of responsibility in terms of the results expected of him, and use these measures as guides for operating the unit and assessing the contribution of each of its members."

Management by objectives has many benefits since it:

1. Provides a way for measuring objectively (in preference to judging subjectively) the performance of subordinates.
2. Coordinates individual performance with company goals.
3. Clarifies the job to be done and defines expectations of job accomplishment.
4. Improves boss-subordinate relationships through the dialogue that takes place regularly.
5. Fosters increased competence and personal growth.
6. Aids in succession planning.
7. Supplies a basis for more equitable salary determination, especially incentive bonuses.
8. Develops factual data for promotion criteria.
9. Stimulates self-motivation, self-discipline and self-controls.
10. Serves as a device for integration of many management functions.

Don't Make It Complicated

What a company gets out of management by objectives depends on what a company expects from the program. Where multiple use is attempted this is justified on the theory that it is difficult to separate the many facets of management. Some programs have collapsed of their own weight because they were sold as the panacea for too many management ills. The majority of companies seem to prefer to keep their programs simple to understand and to operate. They are satisfied to develop single-purpose programs.

Whatever the purpose, the individual goals, upon which decisions relating to individual managers are based, are really smaller, personalized segments of larger, overall corporate objectives. Companies that practice management by objectives usually have:

419

1. Corporate goals—for overall achievement.
2. Group goals—for divisions and departments.
3. Individual goals—for personal direction.

Managers can participate in all three goals and may share in any or all rewards or payoffs.

The coordination between the hierarchy of goals is accomplished through what is known as "the pyramid." Each manager submits the drafts of his individual goals to his immediate superior for:

1. Coordination—to complement goals elsewhere.
2. Compatibility—with overall goals.
3. Approval—authority to proceed.

In funneling individual goals upward, the superior has the opportunity and the responsibility of making certain that the sum of all goals of people reporting to him is equal to his goals, for which he in turn is accountable to the next higher echelon.

Built-in Controls

One of the big reasons that management by objectives is effective is that it utilizes tight controls which are acceptable to managers since they are self-controls. Once the goals are agreed upon and the strategies set in motion, the manager need but follow the timetable to know how closely he is on time and on target.

In this respect, individual goal setting also encourages self-discipline and self-development. The manager is on his own, his superior having withdrawn to the position of coach, checking regularly and keeping himself readily available for counselling. He need not, indeed he should not, direct every bit of the action.

Once the program is underway the superior should step aside but not away. He can fulfill his obligation to watch over the progress of his subordinates by designing and utilizing a simple reporting procedure of automatic feedback.

Management by objectives, simple in theory, can be practical in its application if it is carefully designed, thoroughly communicated, thoughtfully implemented and genuinely supported.

INDIVIDUAL GOAL SETTING

Management by objectives is a concept that is growing in acceptance. It may be defined in different ways and it may mean different things. What it all comes down to, however, is a program of individual goal setting. Set goals, or objectives, for each individual in management, add them all together, and the company has a program of management by objectives.

Corporate objectives are not too difficult to establish. But to make corporate objectives serve any purpose, they must be brought down from the ivory tower to the individuals who are concerned and affected by them. When overall corporate objectives are broken down into smaller manageable proportions, i.e., individual goals, they become meaningful to managers. It is these individual goals which are close to managers, and not the overall objectives, which seem remote, that stimulate effort and provide a means of measuring the effectiveness of this effort.

Individual goals must interlock with corporate objectives, horizontally among departments, and vertically from the lowest position up through the organization to the very top.

The process is not complicated. The whole idea is simply to set measurable goals and try to meet them. Setting individual goals means declaring in advance performance expectations in understandable terms against which progress can later be determined. The steps are:

1. Establishing goals: reduce to writing the several goals each individual agrees to try to accomplish.
2. Writing programs: design separate programs for the fulfillment of these goals.
3. Developing strategies: spell out the procedures, responsibilities, priorities and timetable.
4. Gaining approval: obtain the endorsement and "go ahead" from the immediate superior.
5. Enlisting support: budget human and material resources that are necessary.
6. Communicating action: gain the understanding and cooperation of everyone who is involved or who stands to benefit.
7. Recognizing limitations: take cognizance of the constraints— legal, ethical, budgetary, policy—which affect the operation.
8. Evaluating results: monitor the progress regularly to determine how well each project is progressing on time and on target.

An important aspect of individual goal setting is the dialogue that takes place between a manager and his superior. Agreeing on goals requires that the two of them discuss their operation, define the needs, establish explicit goals and arrange the goals in priority order. These conversations result in a mutual understanding about the content of the subordinate's job and the responsibilities it includes. Further, understanding develops on what will constitute an acceptable level of performance and what needs to be done to improve performance.

There are two types of individual goals—operational and developmental. Operational goals define job expectancies and relate to performance improvements. Developmental goals recognize identifiable gaps in personal qualifications of self and staff for present and potential placements and strive to correct the deficiencies.

All goals have certain common characteristics. They should be:

1. Specific: something to aim toward.
2. Realistic: within reach.
3. Clear: to avoid misinterpretation.
4. Measurable: to permit objectivity.
5. Acceptable: not imposed upon someone.
6. Reasonable: within a manger's capabilities.
7. Flexible: revisable along the route.
8. Several: more than one but not too many.
9. Prioritied: lined up in order of importance.
10. Deadlined: with completion dates and interim targets.

And, of course, they should be useful and bespeak of worthwhileness. The manager who handily accomplishes five goals without improving the profit picture or customer service contributes nothing to the corporation except the useless perpetuation of his own job. On the other hand the manager, whose one objective is to become so efficient that he actually works himself out of a job, becomes the indispensable man.

Setting individual goals can serve many modern management purposes. Such a program can be used to:

1. Develop objectives.
2. Appraise performance.
3. Relate salaries to results.
4. Identify personal development needs
5. Assess promotability.
6. Contribute to succession planning.
7. Prepare feedback to the employee.

The aim of individual goal setting is as much to increase motivation and satisfaction as to increase operating efficiency and improve the organization.

25 WAYS AN EXECUTIVE CAN KEEP HIS DESK CLEARED FOR ACTION

A person's value to his company is measured not by what he has *on* his desk but by what passes *over* it.

The executive whose desk is piled high with work doesn't look impressive; he looks confused.

Some managers try to look important hiding behind a busy schedule. It isn't the amount of work they do that counts but rather the type of work.

Because an executive has to be prepared for action at all times, he cannot afford to be caught with a desk full of miscellaneous duties. The answer lies in learning how to organize his work, his day, his desk, his mind.

Since it is usually difficult or often impossible for him to avoid much of his work, it might be well for him to review some of the techniques available to him that can be useful in clearing a desk and keeping it ready for action.

Some of the following 25 suggestions may be considered:

1. Delegate some of your work to subordinates. This not only relieves you of much of the detail but it also helps to develop others who will then be better experienced to take some of the load from you.

2. Allow your secretary or assistant to do some of your work. Ofttimes they can actually do a job better because of fewer interruptions and closer acquaintanceship with other workers or departments that may be involved. Ideally, every duty should be performed by the lowest paid individual who is qualified to handle it. Anything else is a waste of company money and your valuable time.

3. Quit trying to keep your fingers in every detail. Don't become a slave of insecurity. It breeds incompetent "yes men" who complement the executive rather than challenge and stimulate him. Ultimately it discourages the ingenuity of subordinates by competing with them. Unless the executive can build up his staff so that he can trust them, he will wind up doing all the work whether he wants to or not. And who will get the nervous breakdown?

4. Schedule and evaluate your work. Get out of the woods and take a look at the trees occasionally. The usual executive rushes around doing 40 or 50 different and unrelated things. Too often when he goes home at night it is because he has run out of time, not work.

5. Arrange your work so as to dispose of those things that can be handled promptly. The few projects remaining are then not hard to cope with if the pile of work no longer looks like a hopeless task to tackle.

6. Attack the unpleasant or difficult jobs first and get them out of the way while you're fresh. Don't become attached to them by letting them accumulate.

7. On the other hand, stop wrestling with a problem that, for the moment at least, has you licked. Put it aside temporarily and come back to it when your mood and mind toward it have improved. Be careful, however, not to put it off indefinitely.

8. Develop organizational ability in your own work and that of your area of responsibility. The word "supervisor," if not by definition then at least by connotation, means someone possessed with "super" vision. Look over and beyond the obvious to determine what effect the action of the present may have on the future. Look forward with wisdom and you'll look back with pride.

9. Keep work on top of your desk where it will haunt you and thereby stand a better chance of getting done. Burying it in desk drawers keeps it out of sight and away from completion.

10. Check every single item that is on or in your desk at least once a month. Perhaps if it has had no attention for 30 days it could be filed or even discarded.

11. Put your many miscellaneous duties on trial periodically. By putting them to the test you may discover that some are habit and can no longer be defended as necessary. Habit and routine have an unbelievable power to waste and destroy your time and energy.

12. Develop short cuts wherever possible. For example: Writing your reply to a letter at the bottom of the page, instead of dictating a formal answer, saves both time and money.

13. Don't fall into the pattern of documenting everything. In some cases a telephone call may not only be quicker but actually better than some slower form of communication.

14. Don't file everything either. Much of the material placed carefully into file cabinets is never referred to again until years later when it is tossed out. Make certain there is a justifiable reason for filing something; don't do it routinely.

15. Stop vacillating. This wastes not only your time but also that of others who are depending upon you for sound direction. You should have firmness of conviction, based on sound moral standards. To be head and shoulders above the crowd you must be willing to stick your neck out. Humpty-Dumpty was a fence-straddling egghead, and when he fell there was no hope of reconstructing him.

16. Learn to make quicker decisions. It takes time to investigate a situation or listen to a problem. "I'll let you know later" only means that the scene must be recreated later when the decision is given. If the answer can be forthcoming when the problem is posed, the job is done.

17. Make decisions that are sound, fair and logical so that they will be acceptable. Decisions based on authority and unconcern can cause no end of repercussion. Making the decision is important, but making it right is essential. Unless the decision is the right one it will some day return to haunt you.

18. Take time to communicate with others who may be interested or involved with you in a project. A few minutes spent at the start explaining something can save endless hours afterwards should an unintentional mistake need correcting.

19. Discourage visitors and interruptions, however, especially when these do not pertain to your job and you are busy. An open door policy is fine, but remember that every-door still has hinges so that it can be closed when necessary.

20. Try to say "no" to some of the requests made of you. Everyone is flattered by being asked to serve on numerous committees and functions where he can share his talents, which he feels are valuable to the cause, and give advice, which is limitless. But these invitations are also cruel demands upon an executive's time and energy, which are certainly not limitless.

21. Concentrate more on your work and less on maintaining the symbols of status, many of them useless anyway. These visible appurtenances are not what gets the work done, you know.

22. Accept authority. Be big but don't act big. The unnecessary acting is what takes up the time.

23. Do not resist authority either. Many people who give orders cannot take orders. They can criticize freely but even well-intentioned suggestions upset them. This puts them in the wrong mood and prevents them from functioning at their best. Anyone given the right to command should first have learned to obey.

24. Accept responsibility. Don't run around looking for a crutch to lean on—either some item of company policy to protect you or a decision by a higher-up to hide behind. This approach not only builds weak managers but it is also time consuming.

25. Finally, don't let the briefcase become a grief case. Develop a balanced way of life. Outside interests and relaxations are needed to round out the whole personality. Work, play, love, worship—this is a good prescription for executive health. Unless the executive enjoys good health and peace of mind, he cannot be on the job and working well to keep his desk cleared for action.

Some years ago my first boss passed along bits of wisdom he had acquired in the school of hard knocks. One of his axioms made it clear that "the more important a person becomes the less work he does." This truism has been restated in an assortment of ways in later business textbooks and management courses. No matter how it is phrased, it suggests that the executive cannot afford to become bogged down in all the details of his job but that at all times he must keep his desk cleared for action.

TIME MANAGEMENT

The focus has always been on shortages—material, capital, skills, etc. But the most critical shortage is seldom mentioned. That is the shortage of time.

This seems surprising because in the business community it is recognized that "time is money." And business is always concerned about costs.

Managers cannot get all their work done because they spend too much time:

1. Attending meetings.
2. Reading published and printout material.
3. Putting out fires.
4. Handling special requests.
5. Meeting visitors.
6. Running into delays and confusion.
7. Preparing reports.
8. Procrastinating.

Employees cannot get all their work done because they keep too busy on:

1. Coasting along on easy work.
2. Functioning with insufficient information.
3. Proceeding on inadequate instruction.
4. Struggling with work that is beyond them.
5. Tackling too many things at the same time.
6. Reacting impulsively.
7. Yielding to interruptions.
8. Outguessing poor communications.

Some people feel they make the best use of their time when they are under the pressure of a deadline. It is true that a deadline is a good motivator for getting things done. But deadlining is not always enough. There should be milestones along the way toward the objective. The deadline is the goal, and the milestones are interim target checkpoints against which to monitor whether the work is progressing on time and on schedule.

Setting a deadline assumes that the individual has a sense of how much time specific tasks require. Unless workers know their own past performance records, they will misjudge the due dates. The deadline must be realistic and achievable. Scheduling must allow for unanticipated interruptions and unexpected events.

The reason some employees do not get their work done is that they are not well-organized in their personal work habits. Managers try to assist them by setting standards and then wonder why this does not help. Each individual has a personal work rhythm. Some people engage in fits-and-starts while others pace themselves with a steady and patient attack. Absolute rules cannot be imposed unilaterally. Individual uniqueness must be respected.

An employee's value is determined not on how hard the person works or the amount of time put in. The worth of any employee, upon which the salary and rewards should be figured, is measured in terms of work accomplished. It should not be based on how much time is spent but on how well that time is utilized. Unfortunately, most wage and salary programs are still related to time and not results.

Benjamin Franklin, America's first business philosopher, wrote, ". . . do not squander time, for that is the stuff life is made of."

TOASTMASTERS CLUBS

Communication sets the leadership pace in every organization and the level of communication ability among managers and employees vitally affects the organization's success. In today's business, and in the community, the effectiveness of communication depends upon how well people listen, think and speak.

Toastmasters International is a worldwide nonprofit volunteer organization devoted to improving its members' ability to communicate. The first Toastmasters Club was founded in Santa Ana, California, in 1924. From this unobtrusive beginning sprang forth an organization that has grown to over 3,300 clubs in 40 countries. More than a million men and women have benefited from membership in Toastmasters Clubs.

How a Club Works

A typical Toastmasters Club is made up of 20 to 40 people, either citizens drawn from the community at large or employees from within a specific company, government agency or other organization. Most clubs meet weekly, and in many localities there are morning, noon and evening clubs from which to choose.

Club meetings include "Table Topics," in which each member speaks extemporaneously on a topic assigned. This exercise gives members the opportunity to develop an on-the-spot speaking ability often needed to handle everyday business situations.

Prepared talks give members experience in organizing effective speeches to inform, persuade and entertain. These prepared speeches follow the Toastmasters Communication and Leadership manuals, a two-part program of 30 projects, beginning with an introductory "Ice Breaker" speech about oneself and leading to advanced communication projects. Even the business portion of the meeting serves a purpose —to build confidence in leadership situations and improve members' parliamentary skills. Constructive evaluation is also a vital part of Toast-

Official insignia of Toastmasters International.

masters training. This gives the speaker the audience's reaction and helps participants develop the ability to listen critically and analytically.

In addition to the Communication and Leadership Program, Toastmasters provides professionally-prepared resources on listening, discussion, parliamentary procedure, audiovisual techniques, and conference and meeting procedures, at member discounts. Every member receives *The Toastmaster,* a monthly magazine providing new insights on communication techniques, ideas and opinions.

Members also have the opportunity to compete in speech contests on the club, area, district and regional levels, culminating in the annual International Speech Contest, known as the "World's Championship of Public Speaking."

An Effective Corporate Tool

Because they are aware of the value of Toastmasters training, hundreds of firms, institutions, churches, fraternal organizations and national associations, as well as government and the armed services, have encouraged—and in many cases have sponsored—the formation of Toastmasters Clubs.

There are two ways to provide employees with communication and leadership training through Toastmasters: (1) by encouraging employees to join local community clubs, and (2) by establishing a club within the company. Many firms use both methods to provide this training to the widest number of employees.

Because Toastmasters is a nonprofit, volunteer organization, the cost of membership is low. Many firms reimburse employees for all or part of the cost of membership. International dues are less than $20.00 per year.

A directory of Toastmasters Clubs, and information about forming a new club, are available from Toastmasters International, 2200 North Grand Avenue, Santa Ana, California 92711. The telephone number is (714) 542 6793.

EXECUTIVE SUCCESS

Contrary to popular opinion, an executive is a specialist. He is a specialist who became a generalist. He used his particular specialty as the ladder upon which to climb to success. Even a chief executive is a specialist; he is a specialist at picking the brains of other specialists.

A discussion of executive success shifts the emphasis away from the specialist to that of the administrator. Let's use a few examples to make the point. To bake a pie and deliver it fresh, delicious and unbroken to a neighbor calls for technical know-how. To bake thousands of pies each day and deliver them unbroken, on time and acceptably priced to a series of outlets calls for management skills. Or, in our offices, much of the accounting is no longer done by bookkeepers but by data processing machine operators, many of whom do not know the difference between debits and credits. Or how about this—bread is no longer baked by bakers, but in today's modern automated bakeries bread is baked by machinists. The question is: How much of the work the executive finds himself doing is not the work for which he had trained himself? What skills does he need beyond the technical knowledge he acquired?

Shortage of Qualified Executives

Speaking within the framework of business and industry generally, let me say first that there is no shortage of people in executive positions. The jobs, for the most part, are filled, aren't they? But there is a very definite shortage of qualified executives. In fact, the scarcity of management skills is becoming a serious menace to industrial growth and expansion.

We see this disturbing situation all around us in business offices. It exists elsewhere too—in the fields of religion, education, science and government. It is also true in the professions. There is no problem with the technical skills; the problem is with the skills the technicians or specialists need for the executive or administrative part of their work.

In any program for the development of executives there are two sides to consider. First, what can the employer or the company do, and second, what can the individual do?

In our business offices we find the need for development of present and potential executives is caused by the simple fact that in today's complex competitive operations, jobs grow bigger first, ahead of people. Getting the people to grow to keep pace with their enlarged duties is the responsibility of management. It is a sad commentary that in many well-known companies management is content to fly in a jet age with nothing better than a broomstick.

To develop our people, three things are necessary:

1. Provide training.
2. Give broadening experience.
3. Establish the climate for growth.

Giving a man a title, a rug on the floor or a secretary to screen calls and callers won't make him an executive. Somehow we've got to equip him mentally, intellectually, emotionally, psychologically and spiritually—in addition to giving him physical facilities and visible appurtenances.

Neglecting our need to develop executives can be serious. But the fault may not lie entirely with management. No company can develop individuals who do not reach out for help on their own. Not everybody aspires to become an officer in the industrial army.

The key to executive development lies in self-betterment. Individuals must be awakened to the serious consequences of standing still, and to the realization that the world does not remain static. Those who do not move forward in effect fall behind.

The purpose of any training program is not primarily to teach but to create within the individual the desire to learn. The proper philosophy of training does not believe in spoon-feeding the trainees but encourages self-improvement, motivated from within.

Since in the case of training, the improvement depends more upon the patient than upon the doctor, let's concentrate on what the individual may do for himself in the development of necessary executive skills, especially as they relate to his dealings with others.

Executive Patterns

Executive ability does not come automatically. Many people who are promoted or who suddenly find themselves in positions of management wish it could come to them overnight. A man who is a good technician may have a genuine feeling of inadequacy as an administrator, with duties that call for skills which he has not had the chance to acquire.

Anyone who wants to become proficient in the administrative field should perhaps have some sort of model to pattern after. Let's look at some of the people who earn their living as business executives. No two executives are alike, but all fall into definite patterns. It is possible to group them into four types:

First we have the *originator*. This is the executive who thinks for himself. He can analyze his particular problem and arrive at an independent decision. He is not afraid to explore something new. He may make mistakes but he will contribute many useful ideas to the situation in which he is serving.

Then we have the *improvisor*. This is the executive who must first have the boundaries surveyed for him. Within these limits he operates with vision and imagination, understanding the problems and adapting accepted ideas.

Next we have the *follower*. This executive rarely designs any new programs or any part of a program. He observes what others in the field are doing to meet their problems, accepts what is common practice, then determines the minimum action necessary to keep abreast of competition.

Finally we have the *relaxer.* This is the satisfied executive who grew up with the system, is quite comfortable in it, and has no desire to change anything. He finally got where he is, feels it was hard work getting there, and now wants to sit back and enjoy the luxury of his position. He is willing to work hard but along the lines he understands, accepts and enjoys.

Everyone in management should ask himself, "What kind of executive am I?" It is difficult to change human nature and executives should be accepted for what they are. Each kind of executive can be effective, each in his own way. Since management positions, with their inherent challenges and opportunities, vary considerably, there is room for different kinds of executives. Best results are obtained when each executive is assigned to the type of job that best suits his personality and temperament.

In any case, the executive function is measured in terms of work goals. Increasing emphasis is on administrative ability, coupled with adroitness in human relations and communications skills.

Executive Qualities

There are certain broad and basic skills that the executive should possess, identified as technical, human and conceptual. All three skills can be developed by training, but conceptual skill is essentially a matter of raw intelligence and judgment, and is an indispensable element in top-level policymaking.

The executive job differs from the supervisory job in that it does not directly involve the control of people, but rather the control of ideas. While most executives would make good supervisors, good supervisors do not necessarily make good executives.

The qualities to look for in executives can be grouped into three categories:

Mental	*Personal*	*Physical*
verbal ability	self-confidence	vitality
reasoning ability	level of aspiration	endurance
memory, concentration	decisiveness	general health
judgment	work habits	feeling of well-being
flexibility	marital adjustment	balanced life
organization-mindedness	social, ethical standards	peace of mind

The executive should be made to realize that what he is learning or being taught along the lines of scientific management is new. But his trouble with the human element can be traced to conflicts as old as mankind. All human problems are rooted in a few basic weaknesses of

432

man. Theologians have long ago narrowed these failings to seven deadly sins, which the executive should try to avoid in the conduct of his work with others. These are:

Pride — all wrapped up in oneself.
Envy — inability to be objectively honest.
Laziness — not being industrious.
Anger — this betrays personal shortcomings.
Unchastity — lack of integrity and moral uprightness.
Greed — hunger for power.
Gloominess — fear and pessimism to cloud our thinking.

Great leaders are known for their great strengths, but what we forget is that they also may have great weaknesses. Executives must be convinced that their success depends upon their ability to build on their strengths and to recognize their weaknesses and keep these as far behind them as possible.

A man was trying to explain to another man why he had not spoken to his wife for six weeks. He said he had a violent temper and that if he pursued their difference of opinion he might say something in anger that would hurt her. "You probably can't understand this," he added, "because you don't have a temper." But the other man answered, "Yes, I too have a terrible temper, but knowing this, I've learned how to control it and never use it."

When we compare the successful executives with their less successful brethren we come up with the *positive* factors of success. Sometimes it is easier to make our point by turning the record over and emphasizing the *negative* side. Here are a few of the more common reasons for executive failure:

1. Limited viewpoint: cannot see the forest, too preoccupied with the trees.
2. Unwillingness to assume his share of the responsibility: looking for a crutch to lean on.
3. Using some other status, such as professional, to hide behind and to avoid facing up to executive duties.
4. Impatience in dealing with the slowness of others to grasp those things which may come easy to him; tolerance is the oil that takes the friction out of life.
5. Inability to participate in a free spirit of cooperation: insecurity.
6. Indifference to authority: dislike discipline. Anyone given the right to command should first have learned to obey.
7. Difficulty in supervising: cannot see the other person's side.
8. Prejudices which affect independent judgment: closed mind with cherished notions and fixed ideas. The trouble with

433

some of us is that we want to get to the promised land without leaving our own wilderness.

9. Overwork: unwilling to delegate.
10. Poor health which interferes with tending to business: simply cannot do justice to his responsibilities.

Now as to some of those positive skills that are necessary for executive success, a management survey might shed some light. Some 70 large corporations were asked what traits they considered most important to success. Of the answers, 70% said, "The ability to get along with people." They listed these requisites for getting along with others:

1. The ability to work cooperatively with others in a group.
2. The ability to communicate—to talk, teach, persuade.
3. Enthusiasm—initiative and drive. The executive who is not fired with enthusiasm should be . . . fired . . . with enthusiasm.
4. Appearance—not fashion plates but neatness and proper dress and manners.
5. Balance—especially emotional balance, personality balance.
6. Leadership—the kind of person others are impelled to follow, not compelled to follow.

The Carnegie Institute, after studying records of 10,000 employees, concluded that 15% of success is due to technical competence and 85% to personality development. Just as technical skills can be acquired, so also can personality traits be acquired and improved.

What we're saying is that the operation of business today is scientific, but success in business, as elsewhere, is still a personal matter. And while in technological achievements we are supermen, in human relations we are barbarians in dinner jackets.

Can You Communicate?

It must be obvious by now that whatever we bring up as necessary skills somehow gets us right back to this business of dealing with others. And in this part of our jobs that involves dealing with others, one important factor of success is the ability to communicate effectively at all levels.

There are three types of communications: verbal, written and nonverbal. It is the nonverbal which is the most effective if properly applied and the most dangerous if not properly applied—for this includes our attitudes, our expressions, our actions, our beliefs and our convictions.

Personal contacts in day-to-day procedures provide the most commonly used means of communication between people. In some situations this may involve dealing on the same level. In other situations it is downward, as a supervisor giving instructions to a subordinate, which is ordinarily not a consultation between equals but orders to be carried out unequivocally. Ofttimes this is from an executive to one of his peers, a person over whom he exercises no direct authority.

But levels should not enter into the consideration lest this complicate the method used. A good executive, no matter where he finds himself in the management hierarchy or where he appears on the company organization chart, never should rely upon his position or prestige for the accomplishment of his purpose. He cannot succeed, any more than others can, by imposing his will upon others. It is better to get results without resorting to the prerogatives of authority. The idea that is being promoted should stand on its own merits; it should not ride in on the coattails of executive authority or professional standing.

This is true especially of delegation, the passing of authority and responsibility to others. In dealing with others, and in this art of delegation to others, the usual procedure is to give orders or to command. There are five ways to accomplish this need to command:

1. Command through superior articulation: achieved through skill in persuading others to bring about acceptance of an idea or decision.
2. Command through technical competence: decisions rest with those who have the technical skills and knowledge that others do not possess.
3. Command through status: prestige and position in the organization have a bearing upon the right to decide issues.
4. Command through sanctions: a person not in a position to make the decision may exert influence upon another who, in turn, makes the decision.
5. Command by default: one person is left to make the decision in situations where someone else has taken no action either because of inability or willingness to pass the responsibility.

Rules Not Possible

When it comes to the full area of communicating with others, not just getting acceptance of orders and commands, we run into something else. It is difficult to give out any set of one-two-three rules to help an executive in his efforts to deal properly with people. What works with one person may not work with another because the two people are not alike, therefore do not react in the same way. One rule or principle that works in one situation may not work when transposed because circumstances may not be quite alike.

The point to make is that "just following the book" may not produce the desired result. The principles may be standard but their application must be tailored to the situation.

For example: it is often said, and often proved, that an executive will find the going easier if he consults with others before he makes his decision. This is the theory that says, "Put 'em in the boat with you and they'll not bore holes in it." So he embraces consultative decision making in the hope that it may be the mysterious key to unlock the door to success. He tries it only to find that while it seemed to make sense, and obviously worked elsewhere, it failed in his situation. Why? The employees were not properly conditioned for this sort of executive approach. They were reluctant to cooperate for any of several reasons:

1. They fear punishment if they are parties to a wrong decision.
2. Some people lose respect for the executive who, to them, should be the sole authority on a particular matter (a doctor, for instance, would not be expected to hold a conference with patients; he tells them and they accept).
3. They don't want to lend a flavor of participation to a decision that they feel has already been made.

What we're trying to emphasize is that any technique that is recommended carries with it the promise of success but may also have some built-in pitfalls or risks that must be recognized.

The issue of whether an executive should operate as a one-man show or, in the interests of better dealings with others, should occasionally bring them into the act, presents interesting observations. The industrial autocrat, the professional dictator, the strong individualist is, oftentimes, quite effective. When right he puts on quite a show of rapid-fire decision making. This may be very impressive for it does save a good deal of time for everybody.

But what is the percentage for a person's being right all the time? One authority says, "It is rare indeed for more than 25% of his decisions to be right." You make your own estimate if you don't like his. But it is doubtful if any of us would be foolish enough to claim that such a personality is 100% right all the time.

What happens when the decision is wrong? It is just as forceful and just as final as the right one. But others who are affected by it have little recourse. Chances are they know it is wrong and, when it is crammed down their throats, they give it only lip service. That may actually be the better of the two choices. The other is to fall in line with authority, be resigned to the ill-fated decision, go along with it and do things wrong.

We're not advocating that every decision should be referred to the group. What we would like to put across is that any group, through the exercise of teamwork, functions better than the hard-hitting executive who says in effect, "I'll do the thinking around here," as though he had a corner on brains. Whether the executive sits down to committee meeting with his staff, or whether he occasionally consults with them as individuals before he proceeds on his own, doesn't make much difference. In both cases he has the benefit of anything they might contribute to a sounder decision, plus the advantage of having pre-tested his idea on them before it becomes final. It is better, if an adverse reaction is coming, to be tipped off early enough to make a correction or an adjustment.

This business of dealing with others should not be taken lightly. On this skill rests our entire chance for success. This is true not only in our business but also in life generally. For after all is said and done, the great problems of the age—international, national and corporate—have to do with the relationships of people. We must be skilled in getting along with others. But this skill must rest upon some such foundation as this: technical competence in our chosen field, broad intellectual outlook, high sense of honor, moral and spiritual values, attention to the public interests, understanding and respect for the other fellow.

Five Keys to Success

In this presentation we've been all over the pea-patch of executive skills. As my personal contribution to you I should like to leave you with five factors that I believe are essential to executive success.

The first is *motivation.* An executive's value is in direct relation to his ability to motivate himself and his workers to more and better produc-tion. Since the other elements in business—materials, money, methods, machines, and markets—are usually fixed, or at least the same among all companies, the opportunity for improvement lies in the only vari-able element, the available workers.

The second factor is *vision.* Every executive is a supervisor; he super-vises people or an activity or both. The word "supervisor," if not by definition then at least by connotation, means someone possessed with "super" vision. Hence, a supervisor must be capable of seeing over and beyond the obvious. Look forward with wisdom and you'll look back with pride.

The third factor is *decision-making ability.* The person who can make decisions gets paid for it; the one who cannot must yield the authority and salary to the higher up who has to make the decisions for him. It's as simple as that! To be head and shoulders above the crowd a man must be willing to stick his neck out. The executive who wants to get some-where must be able to take a stand; he cannot ride both horses forever.

Humpty-Dumpty was a fence-straddling egghead, and when he fell there was no hope of reconstructing him.

The fourth factor is *good health.* To be on the job as needed, and to meet the demands of his increasingly heavy work load, an executive must be in sound physical condition. Much has been said and written about the broad subject of coddling employees, of benefits expanded and working conditions improved. But it is high time that management also take steps necessary to ease the tension, frustration, strain and effort of executives. Don't let the briefcase become a grief case.

But health is a many splendored thing. It embodies more than physical fitness. It may be likened to the Maltese cross. On each arm of the cross is a word representing a main element by which a normal human being lives. The words are: work, play, love, worship. When a person is short of one of these he should arrange to round out his life. Lopsided living is a common cause of ill health, and the four-sided cross comes close to the prescription for executive health.

The fifth factor is *humility.* As important as good health is, even more necessary for success is peace of mind. A true spirit of humility provides

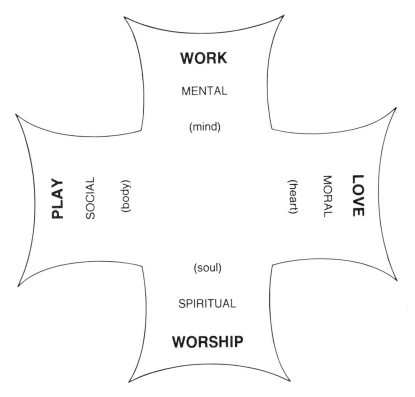

a source of executive strength that is greater than all others. It is a pattern of well-being and adjustment to life that has been found effective for centuries.

It is quite obvious that no one of us succeeds alone. We are all interdependent upon one another. It was Tennyson who said, "I am a part of all I have met." But there is more to success than that. Let me remind you that in life all of us have met more than each other.

The Unseen Helper

Throughout our lives there is an invisible means of support, which guides and directs our individual and national destinies. Whether or not we openly profess any religious affiliation, we are nevertheless living and prospering in the afterglow of a great Christian heritage.

That this climate is a factor in our personal success in dealing with others is evidenced by the fact that many problem situations in life, which may not conform to the obvious laws of nature or man, often find easy solution in the spiritual laws, which also exert an impelling force in the universe.

The unseen helper in our lives could well be the influence of a guiding philosophy that recognizes the shortcomings of self-sufficiency. For isn't it true that whenever we are carried away by our materialistic success we are given unmistakable warnings of our misplaced trust? How else do we account for the unpredictable earthquakes, the uncontrollable floods, the damaging droughts, the ravaging fires, the unseasonable frosts, and the many other unexpected upsets whenever Mother nature goes into one of her rampaging moods. These and other adversities have a purpose—to teach us the virtues of humility. These are painful lessons but necessary to prove to man that he can never tame the forces of nature. How then does he expect to rule his own destiny!

The lesson is a simple one, but by its very simplicity it leaves a profound message. If we want to be successful as executives, and successful in dealing with others, we must first come to a full and final realization that no one succeeds alone.

PERSONAL TRAITS OF AN EXECUTIVE

When discussing success for managers and executives, a question comes up. "What makes a good executive?"

We know what makes a good musician—if what he plays pleases us. Or a good artist—whose work wins the award. Or a good lawyer—who wins a difficult case. Or a good surgeon—who performs medical miracles. In executive performance, however, we can recognize competence only after long periods of observation and even then our opinions are subjective.

In describing what makes an executive good or bad, the personal traits of executives might offer a clue. These traits must first be divided into two categories—good and bad. By matching his performance against this list it is easy to determine whether an executive is effective or not.

Undesirable personal traits:

1. The inability to see the forest: bogged down in details.
2. Failure to accept responsibility: looking for a crutch—a written policy or higher boss.
3. The inability to lead: people must want to follow.
4. The inability to make room for other people: insecurity.
5. Unwillingness to communicate: afraid to share and build.
6. Resistance to authority: dislikes discipline.
7. Prejudices which interfere with judgment: closed mind with cherished notions and fixed ideas.

Desirable personal traits:

1. A desire for achievement: the pleasure of accomplishment.
2. An acceptance of authority: be big but don't act big.
3. A strong driving force: self-motivation.
4. Organizational ability: order out of chaos.
5. Decisiveness: decision-making ability.
6. Firmness of conviction: believes in something and lives it.
7. Activity and aggression: mentally and emotionally alert and alive.
8. A balanced way of life: outside interests and relaxations.

TYPES OF EXECUTIVES

Craftsman: He carries in his head the details of every job he's ever had. He is so concerned with minutiae that the big picture escapes him.

Head-stuffer: He prides himself on being a walking encyclopedia but is unable to make a distinction between what is worth remembering and what is trivia. His memory is phenomenal; his judgment childlike.

Accumulator: He is a paper freak. His files bulge, papers are stacked on every flat surface. His office needs a librarian, not a manager.

Talent-collector: He is obsessed with overskill; he has a college grad for a mailboy, an engineer for an elevator operator. He also has high turnover.

Technology buff: He uses a computer when an adding machine would do, a tape recorder when a memo would suffice. He could be wiped out by a power failure.

THE IDEAL MANAGER

The U.S. Department of Labor has compiled the following checklist of the qualities or attributes that a good manager should possess. A good manager:

1. Knows his own job thoroughly. Is a good worker as well as a good leader and understands all the jobs he supervises.
2. Has leadership ability rather than "drivership." Explains not only how but also why things should be done.
3. Gives orders clearly and in a friendly fashion. Doesn't shout or yell. Makes sure his instructions are understood.
4. Possesses the foresight to plan and delegate work in advance. Keeps subordinates busy without driving them. Assigns work fairly.
5. Maintains consistent standards of conduct, performance and quality.
6. Keeps up with each man's work. Judges him honestly and on merit only. Lets each one know "where he stands."
7. Appreciates and acknowledges honest effort and above-average work. Gives credit where credit is due. In case of bad work, investigates and holds the right person responsible.
8. Maintains discipline fairly and consistently. Does not discipline a worker in front of others. Makes his reprimand as impersonal as possible. Investigates and gives worker a chance to explain his side of the story. Doesn't lose temper while correcting him.
9. Believes in and practices safety. Provides full and proper safety instructions.
10. Makes sure that new or transferred employees know how to do their jobs correctly. Makes new workers feel at home.
11. Is liberal but consistent in his interpretation of plant rules and company policy. Does not appease the griper on complaints. Listens sympathetically to all grievances.
12. Takes a personal interest in his employees. Is loyal to the men above and below him. Is willing to take responsibility. Does not "pass the buck." Is willing to go all the way "up the line" for his men when necessary.

A READY GUIDE FOR EVALUATING EXECUTIVES

VISIBLE APPURTENANCES	TOP DOGS	V.I.P.s	BRASS	No. 2s	EAGER BEAVERS	HOI POLLOI
BRIEF CASES	None— they ask the questions	Use backs of envelopes	Someone goes along to carry theirs	Carry their own —empty	Carry their own filled with work	Too poor to own one
DESKS	Custom made (to order)	Executive Style (to order)	Type A "Director"	Type B "Manager"	Cast-offs from No. 2s	Metal
TABLES	Coffee tables	Decorative wall tables	Matching tables Type A	Matching tables Type B	Plain work table	None— lucky to have own desk
CARPETING	Nylon— 1 inch pile	Nylon— 1 inch pile	Wool Twist (with pad)	Wool Twist (without pad)	Used wool pieces— sewed	Asphalt tile
PLANT STANDS	Several— kept filled	Strange exotic plants	Two—repotted whenever they take a trip	One medium-sized repotted annually during vacation	Small— repotted when plant dies	Brings own from home
VACUUM WATER BOTTLES	Monogrammed	Silver	Chromium	Plain painted	Coke machine	Water fountain
LIBRARY	Private Collection	Autographed or complimentary books and reports	Selected references	Impressive titles on covers	Books Everywhere	Dictionary
SHOE SHINE SERVICE	Every morning at 10:00	Every morning at 10:15	Every day at 9:00 or 11:00	Every other day	Once a week	Shine their own
PARKING SPACE	Private in front of office	In plant garage	In company garage—if enough seniority	In company properties —somewhere	On the parking lot	Anywhere they can find space
LUNCHEON MENU	Cream cheese on whole wheat buttermilk and indigestion tablets	Cream of celery soup chicken sandwich (white meat) milk	Fruit cup spinach lamb chop ice cream tea	Tomato juice minute steak— fries salad—fruit cup coffee	Chicken croquettes mashed potatoes peas—rolls chocolate cream pie coffee	Clam chowder frankfurter and beans hot rolls—butter raisin pie ala mode two cups of coffee

13. Keeps his promises. Does not promise things he cannot deliver, and delivers as promptly as possible on all promises he does make.
14. Is open-minded. Welcomes suggestions and is willing to discuss them.

THE INDIVIDUALITY OF PEOPLE

We've become so accustomed to using mass techniques in education, advertising, manufacturing, marketing and even in bargaining agreements, that we also apply them to individuals. But these techniques do not always work in the same way because no two people are alike.

Let me explain it this way: Take a piece of wax, some meat, some sand, some clay, some wood shavings, and throw them all into a fire. One immediately melts, one starts frying, one dries up, one hardens, one blazes. They are all acted upon by the same force but they all react differently. Just so, under identical influences of circumstances and environment one person becomes weaker, one becomes stronger and one withers away.

Different people have different aspirations and different fears. They require different considerations.

Four centuries ago Charles V was emperor of the Holy Roman Empire, which then included most of Europe. Like other monarchs, he found the job of ruling people a troublous occupation. In his old age he retired to a monastery to rest his frazzled nerves. There he amused himself by tinkering with clocks. He had a house full of them. His pet ambition was to regulate them so that they would all strike at precisely the same time. But despite his most persistent painstaking efforts, he could not make them do it. Finally, he gave up. One day he philosophized: "I was a fool, trying to make my subjects think alike on everything. I cannot even make these helpless clocks strike alike."

Only as we are different do we become noticed in a world of conformity. The Tower of Pisa is just another landmark but it is distinguished because of a different slant.

In our social structure there is value to uniqueness. Imagine what a world we'd have if all people were alike. Differences are physical, mental and emotional. In our business structure it is better to build upon individuality than to try to impose sameness upon people who do not all respond in the same way to the same kind of treatment.

443

INDIVIDUALITY vs. CONFORMITY

There is both individuality and conformity in our makeup. On the one hand we have a tremendous compulsion to conform, and on the other hand we insist on expressing our individuality.

Driving my daughter and her girl friend home from high school one rainy evening, I commented about their habit of carrying textbooks and notebook paper in their open arms, something they did every day even in the rain. I offered them a choice of handsome, convenient briefcases. I was almost laughed right out of the car for being so antediluvian. All the kids did this and anyone who was sensible enough to use a handy carrying case was simply a "square."

The big thing was to conform, not be the oddball, not to defy the youthful tradition. Yet, in a period of a few short years these girls would have to go through a complete change of attitude and be willing, even eager, to assert their individuality. Would an employer select a new worker at random, eenie-meenie-minee-mo fashion, or would he want one who stood out from the group because of noticeable personal qualities? And how will a girl ever be that "one in a million" for somebody's wife if she insists on going through life as anonymous as "Brand X?"

When Henry Ford introduced his "flivver" he standardized on the model, style, color and power in order to provide a mass-produced automobile that the average wage earner could afford to buy. Every car was a black one-seater with one door on the right side (the side by the driver did not open). This mode of personal or family transportation, new to the nation and within reach of thousands, was very much appreciated, of course. But just as soon as this new car became commonplace, the individuality of man began to express itself. People wanted the car but now they wanted it to be different from that of their neighbors. This individuality has gone so far that today, if a Ford dealer were to display every different model, size, color and combination available from the manufacturer, he'd need a showroom larger than several airplane hangars.

In personnel administration we tend to develop programs and policies for the *masses* and not the *classes.* We think we're being fair by treating all employees alike. In one sense this works; giving them all annual vacations is acceptable. But expecting all employees to go at the same time, or to the same place, or for the same purpose is unrealistic.

Our regular working hours fit some people better than others. Some of us are early risers and do our best work in the mornings; others don't even think clearly until later in the day. Creative and scientific people are often oblivious to time and do not understand the regimen of fixed hours; they work by the challenge and not by the clock. That is the

444

reason many companies place their research and technical laboratories in out-of-the-way locations so that the idiosyncrasies of these specialized personnel do not come into conflict with the mundane nine-to-five routine of rank-and-file workers.

Similarities and Differences

There are similarities in people and there are differences. All people get hungry, but we don't all like the same food. Millions of people feel the need to worship, but they do not have the same beliefs. Not everyone depends on television for his entertainment; some participate in sports, recreation, movies, nightclubs, reading, card-playing and the like. The need for diversion is common but hobbies range all the way from gardening to chess.

Many young people go to college but their academic programs vary, they major in different subjects. Workers have a common need for training but their ability to learn is not the same.

But this differentiality is also true elsewhere in nature. No two animals are alike. Think what would happen if we tried to handle all animals the same way. What if we tried to teach every animal to swim, climb, run and fly? In the name of democracy and equality, all animals would be developed in the same skills. On that basis, ducks would be forced to waddle instead of swim, pelicans would flap their short wings in an attempt to fly, eagles would be required to run, and so forth. Some abnormal creature which could do all these things would become class valedictorian.

This is what psychologists call the "fetish of symmetrical development." It seemed easy enough to understand when we applied it to animals just now, didn't it? Why is it so hard to comprehend when we apply it to people? But this gets even more involved. Let's take a simple example.

There's a lot more to color than meets the eye. A given color does not look the same to everybody. We are not speaking of people who are color blind, but of average persons. Each sees a color a bit differently—some very differently. This may explain why a certain color combination may seem attractive to you but not to your spouse. You may be seeing different colors.

This same illustration can be made with food, which is not the same to all people. During World War II the American GI was sent into battle with rations that were nutritionally ideal in proteins, carbohydrates, fats, vitamins and minerals. They were packaged to meet all climatic conditions. They exceeded all standards of quality control.

But something was missing. Cans of discarded foods filled the gutters along the road to the front line. They piled up in storage dumps. A

445

reappraisal of the facts developed what was wrong, or what was overlooked in the planning. The missing factor centered about taste. The food, so carefully planned, was designed around the similarities of soldiers; but taste is an individual matter.

Few Monuments to Groups

In the military, in government, in business, in life—people are trying to maintain their individuality against growing odds. Society is being collectivized into a faceless mass and the big word is "conformity." And we wonder why so many of our industrial and political programs are in trouble.

Excepting identical twins, everybody is biologically, genetically different from everybody else. Diversity should not, however, be confused with inequality. Equality and inequality are sociological; identity and diversity are biological phenomena. Diversity is an observable fact; equality an ethical concept. Society may grant or withhold equality from its members; it could not make them genetically alike even if this were desirable.

In designing our programs it is not enough to understand the desire to conform brought on by the need for acceptance. Building on similarities is fine for groups, but the separate and varied aims and aspirations of the individuals within groups must also be taken into account. It is worth remembering that there are few monuments in parks to groups.

CREATIVE STERILITY

The danger is not in machines thinking like men but in men thinking like machines. Many managers are like machines—they can't think for themselves; they need a policy manual to tell them what to do, or a higher-up to whom they can go for an answer. The fact is many managers are unable to do any original thinking. Like the machine, once they master a routine they stick with it.

There is a reason for this. The way mass production and work simplification have set up jobs, we tend to make robots of our people. Then some day we want to promote one of these individuals and we wonder why they are lacking in ambition, initiative, and imagination. The trend toward simplified repetitive duties bores the creative employees into quitting and attracts mostly the type of workers who have temperaments that thrive on routine tasks. Overnight they are expected to reverse themselves and become different personalities—from loyal followers to capable leaders.

A simple illustration from business will make the point about creative sterility. A sign in a big chain store reads, "Please do not remove shopping carts from our parking lot." Across the street from the store lives an elderly couple. For years they had pushed the cart across the street, unloaded their groceries, and immediately returned the cart. They had been friends of the store manager for some time.

That manager was promoted and a new manager was appointed. The following week the new manager saw the couple pushing the cart filled with groceries out across the street to their home. He ordered a clerk to "go out there and tell those folks what the rules are." The clerk explained the situation, but the new manager responded in no uncertain terms, "I did not ask for an explanation of why rules are broken. As long as that sign is up there, carts do not leave the parking lot. Moreover, I don't want anyone who condones rule-breaking."

The clerk pleaded, "These people are good customers. They buy all their groceries here and they bring the cart back whenever they take their groceries home. If you want them to stop taking the cart off the premises, you'll have to tell them yourself; I haven't the heart to do it."

The manager hit the roof. He marched across the street and informed the couple of the rule. He pushed the cart back to the store. He lost a pair of good customers and he fired a good clerk. Rules were rules—in his narrow little mind. He proved he was a manager—a manager of things, not people.

You can have the manager; as for me, I'll take the clerk.

The use (actually, the misuse) of employment tests can contribute to the problem. A primary concern in developing a battery of tests, in today's nondiscrimination climate, is to design them so they become applicable to the job and not the individual. To further assure that the tests are appropriate for the company they are "validated" in-house by giving them to employees already on the job. This establishes a "profile" of a satisfactory worker and offers a standard against which the unknown applicant can be compared. The logic is that when the applicant resembles employees on the job, chances are good that the new employee will "fit in" and turn out to be a satisfactory worker too.

The weakness with this approach is that it merely perpetuates the present quality of workers. It brings in no fresh ideas because it shuts out all the candidates who do not fit the mold. I have always maintained that every firm with at least 100 employees can use one oddball, whose socks do not match, who forgets the time the office closes, someone who doesn't comprehend convention. This is the individual who reaches out for the untried programs that everybody else cautiously sidesteps for fear of failing. But this type of individual is considered a troublemaker by staid managements and stuck-in-the-mud companies.

This condition from which business suffers today I refer to as "creative sterility."

For some reason when employees are promoted they believe they are obliged to become clones of their predecessors. They do not look for the opportunity, or the challenge; they look for the established pattern, set out to master it, and then settle down to enjoy the protection of a very comfortable rut. These people find that looking ahead is obscure and risky; looking back is clear and understandable. This is the reason so many companies are "going nowhere" and are regularly bested by more productive competition. Making progress implies moving forward on the surface, not downward and deeper into a hole from which the business can never recover and in which it will ultimately be buried.

Not to reflect on past accomplishments, or to respect past successes, is heresy. To ignore the lessons of the past would be to deny a valuable source of strength. Aside from its sentimental value, however, the past is useful in providing not the blueprint upon which to continue operations but the springboard from which to proceed to new and better opportunities.

THE ILLUSION OF SECURITY vs. MAINTENANCE OF OPPORTUNITY

It is not the purpose of personnel administrators to make people happy. People must make themselves happy in their own way and at their own risk. The functions of personnel management lie entirely in the conditions or provinces under which the pursuit of happiness is carried on.

Management insight into the basic human needs is the discovery that work is not only an economic good but also a psychological necessity. Freud called work man's strongest tie to reality. It is our most effective way of relating ourselves to the world, finding out what we can do and where we belong—of being somebody and meaning something to others and to ourselves.

It is amazing how few personnel executives understand this. Consequently, they build employee relations programs on the wrong foundation, then wonder why they are not effective.

One of the weaknesses of personnel administration is that over the years it has acceded to social demands and has permitted itself to gravitate in the direction of least opposition. It has followed and not led.

In expanding personnel services most of the thought has been given to security measures—paralleling the similar trend in government. Perhaps this is good and possibly it is necessary, on the theory that building for security brings to the individual a steadiness of purpose. But that path in business tends to dull individual enterprise, something that business sorely needs.

Only lately are we coming around to understand that, more important than planning for security, is the need to stimulate personal incentive. Someone once wrote, "A ship in harbor is safe, but that is not what ships are built for." That same truism applies to personnel programs.

After all, there is really no such thing as security—as industry tries to guarantee it. A change in ownership, transfer of location, revised procedures or manufacturing processes, an individual's health, all affect security. But there is no curb on individual initiative.

Man's search for progress should be encouraged by the maintenance of opportunity, not hindered by illusions of security.

The only real security lies in permitting workers to grow, not in inserting clauses in policies or restrictions in procedures which serve only to hamper the free growth of people and companies.

COMMITMENT

Many people, particularly in the managerial ranks, are struggling with the problem of commitment to their employers, according to Dr. Harry Levinson, management psychologist, Cambridge, Massachusetts.

In his newsletter he writes that people used to put their trust in the organization saying, in effect, "You determine my career." But now, he says, organizations no longer can accept the responsibility for the length of a person's career, nor can a person trust an organization to do so.

That means people have to commit themselves to their own ego ideal. (An ego ideal is a picture one has in his own mind of himself at his future best.)

Once an individual has an idea of where he'd like to be in the future, he then must relate to the organization to the extent to which their values and their tasks help him in the realization of his goal.

Commitment arises out of one's own heart, and one can hardly be committed to an organization which does not fit with one's ego ideal.

Too often people stick with an employer because they hope their aspirations will be fulfilled. But when they aren't, these people are angry with themselves and their employing organizations. Such a person would have been better off making an earlier decision rather than having wasted part of his life in living with an illusion.

THE ART OF DELEGATION

A most important consideration in the efficiency of an executive is in knowing how to delegate. He should not try to lead the band and play all the instruments.

We have seen them—managers and supervisors who have no time for the concern of others. With others idle, they are hard at work at nights in empty offices. And we have heard them, too, complaining—

"This job is killing me."
"Route everything through me."
"Check with me before you proceed."
"I don't dare take a day off."

Their trouble lies in failure to appreciate that responsibility in a management position is far greater than the personal capacity to carry out all the details. No one expects the chief accountant to post all the ledger accounts. Certainly no one expects the president to personally service all the customers.

Dispersing authority and responsibility throughout an organization is achieved through delegation. According to the academicians, to delegate is to grant or confer authority and responsibility in equal measure from one executive or organizational unit to another in order to accomplish necessary assignments. By means of delegation one person extends his area of operations, for without delegation his actions are confined to what he, himself, can perform.

From a practical business standpoint, delegation may be defined as unburdening the boss for more profitable tasks. It also offers a basis for sounder and more acceptable decisions, development of subordinates and all-around better management.

The more delegation, assuming it is done effectively, the more time an executive has to fulfill his top managerial responsibilities. If his abilities, ambitions or authority keep him close to direct supervision of people or functions, his value to the company diminishes and his personal earnings potential becomes correspondingly less.

Customarily, delegation is considered as being from a higher to a lower level. However, delegation is also from a lower to a higher level, or between levels on the same plane. In other words, delegation can be downward, upward or sideways.

As examples, downward delegation of authority and responsibility is illustrated by a company president to one of his department managers, or from a doctor to a nurse; upward delegation by stockholders to their board of directors, or by workers to their employer as in the case of group life insurance purchases; sideways delegation by members of a professional or trade association to their committee chairman, as in the case of a conference in which they authorize fellow members to arrange and conduct a meeting in which they then willingly participate.

Delegator Remains Accountable

Actually neither authority nor responsibility can be delegated in the true sense. Authority can be shared and responsibility assigned. Delegation does not imply the permanent release from these obligations but rather the granting of rights and approval for others to operate within a prescribed framework. The delegator always remains accountable for what is or is not accomplished.

There are two types of delegation—general and specific. In both cases, vital to successful delegation are: (1) spelling out the instructions clearly, (2) fixing standards, (3) establishing limits and (4) keeping control.

General delegation of authority and responsibility is made possible by the establishment of company policies. These statements of acceptable company practices are devices to guide the manager in knowing what is expected of him and within what limits he may make decisions on general matters.

In the assignment of *specific* duties, or one-time jobs, delegation of sufficient authority and full responsibility should accompany the instructions. Some suggestions for specific assignments include:

1. Assign job to the person best suited to it.
2. Don't always use the same person, the handiest one.
3. Make clear the instructions, requirements and authority.
4. Don't make unreasonable demands.
5. Check up periodically.
6. Set a completion date and follow through on the project.
7. Keep the control.

The occasional job, which does not logically fall to any one employee, but which must be assigned specifically, provides an excellent opportunity to:

1. Uncover latent abilities.
2. Test the problem employee.
3. Train a worker in something unfamiliar.
4. Discover leaders.
5. Demonstrate confidence in workers.

Once a job is assigned, the manager should not change the signals but let the project run its course as planned. In his eagerness to get things done, he might have formed the habit, when asked a question by the person to whom he has assigned the job, of stepping in and personally doing the work because that is easier than explaining it again. In such case he'll soon find himself doing all the work while his people are standing by, willing to let him do it. And who will end up with the nervous breakdown?

The Point of Action

Although in many cases simple delegation may be all that is required, in practice both general and specific delegation usually involve more than two persons. The chief executive, with unlimited authority and full responsibility, extends these through his senior staff down the line of command into the work force. It is recommended that some measure of authority and responsibility be placed as close to the point of action as possible. This creates what is known as the "tapering concept" of delegation. In going downward the amount of authority and responsibility becomes smaller with each successive level.

Now the question naturally comes up, "What can or should the executive delegate and what must he be expected to do himself?"

Speaking generally, here are some of his duties divided into three broad categories:

Jobs the executive himself must do:

1. Assuming initiative and responsibility.
2. Planning the work.
3. Scheduling jobs.
4. Building the work force.
5. Establishing and maintaining good morale.
6. Helping employees grow.
7. Communicating at all levels.
8. Settling disputes.
9. Handling grievances.
10. Cooperating with other executives.

Jobs the executive might delegate part of:

1. Interviewing applicants.
2. Inducting, orienting and training workers.
3. Maintaining attendance and reducing tardiness.
4. Controlling production.
5. Improving methods.
6. Reducing costs.
7. Handling paper work.
8. Preventing accidents
9. Keeping equipment in repair.
10. Purchasing equipment, supplies, services.

Jobs normally delegated to others:

1. Opening the mail.
2. Answering telephone calls.
3. Providing proper reception of visitors and guests.
4. Running errands.
5. Making hotel and travel reservations.
6. Filing records.
7. Requisitioning supplies.
8. Caring for equipment.
9. Keeping the premises clean and in order.
10. Insuring company and employees against the unexpected.

It is easy to delegate responsibility. It is harder to delegate authority. There is still another aspect of delegation that is equally important but far more difficult. This is the delegation of decision making. Some executives find this impossible to do. The executive who operates as a one-man show can't see the wisdom of bringing others into the act.

Odds Against Autocrats

Beware of the person who says, "I'll do the thinking around here," as though he had a corner on brains. The executive who consults with others gets the benefit of anything they might contribute to a sounder decision, plus the advantage of having pretested his idea on them before it becomes final. It is better, if an adverse reaction is coming, to be tipped off early enough to make a correction or an adjustment. But even more important, if some of the decision making can be decentralized, chances are the on-the-spot decisions will better fit the problems and be more understandable to the individuals who are affected.

Perhaps the best reason for delegating authority, responsibility and decision making is that the executive who keeps his hand in the details of every job discourages the ingenuity of subordinates by competing with them. His responsibility to share with others, thereby helping to build them, is paramount; his reluctance to do so will cause him to inadvertently develop a group of inadequately trained or inexperienced workers, so that in the end he will have to do all the work whether he wants to or not.

Difficult but Necessary

The problem of delegation is a problem of personality. No one else can do the task as well as the owner or manager thinks he can . . . and he could be right. Nevertheless, because of time and pressure he should concern himself with the major factors of planning, directing and controlling, and let others do much of the work, even that of making some of the decisions. A good rule to follow is this: Every task should be done by the lowest paid employee who is capable of handling it; anything else is a waste of company money and talent.

In many instances it is difficult, often impossible, for an executive to comprehend just where he fits into the management picture insofar as delegation of company authority and responsibility are concerned. On the one hand he is encouraged to deserve and thereby acquire more authority, and to broaden his scope of responsibility; then when he has worked himself into a position of prominence and prestige he is asked to share his well-earned gains with subordinates. Yet this must be done in an enlightened industrial society because in building people we are building an organization.

More and more we're relying less and less upon the executive who depends solely upon his own judgment for decisions and his own accomplishments for results. We're moving away from the one-man type of operation to a more democratic form. It follows, therefore, that the more effective an executive, the more his own identity and personality blend into the background of his organization.

Take any well-known department store, manufacturing plant, service organization or office which enjoys an enviable position in the community. Most likely the individual who built the well-deserved reputation has long been forgotten. His influence is present, his identity is not.

It would be my hope that if I were privileged to visit your company, I should find not a number of prominent executives but rather an impressive program—to which all people in the company contribute and from which all benefit. The more we can conscientiously and confidently delegate some of our authority, responsibility and decision making to others, the closer we come to realizing this noble objective.

COMMITTEES

A committee might be aptly described as a "plural executive." As such it is a convenient device for hiding a decision.

Whenever committees meet it is like a bunch of ants riding a log down the river—they all think they are steering the log when in reality no one is.

If there is any complaint it is that companies and government suffer from too many committees. Many actions are the result of group decisions. What is worse is that many nondecisions are the result of group action.

Yet committees constitute an important part of organizational structures. They can function at any level, and are also effective at mixed levels. Mixed level committees would seem to be democratic, but rank tends to dominate, even over technicratic expertise.

The permanent ones are called "standing committees." The finance committee of the board of directors is an example. Another is the safety committee in the plant. While the membership may revolve, the activity is a continuing one.

There are also special or one-time committees. They are appointed for a particular purpose and disbanded when that purpose has been served. An example might be a committee of employees to plan and conduct the company picnic.

An ad hoc committee is an informal grouping of the logical people assigned, or permitted, to handle a special situation.

Committees can deal with a variety of subjects. Most have little more than advisory authority. But others are granted line authority and not only discuss and decide issues but also secure compliance of others with the decisions.

455

There are advantages to committees. Several organization members working together on the same activity is conducive to cooperation, coordination, and communication. People coming from different directions get to see the overall picture and offer ideas gleaned from their differing outlooks. The collective opinions tend to neutralize personal one-sidedness.

In contrast, there are subtle disadvantages. It is difficult to pinpoint responsibility. The decisions can easily be camouflaged and no one individual can be credited or blamed for the consequences. Much of the time the decisions are compromised and often shallow and watered down. Usually there is no follow-up.

Unless committee meetings are controlled—and most are not—they are costly time wasters. There is too much sparring, talking about trivialities, before the members get down to serious business. In government, particularly, they are handy burial grounds for proposals that opponents don't want to face.

Depending too much upon committees makes weak managers. An executive who is charged with the responsibility of a high position should not be allowed to cower behind a committee, letting the group take the action the executive is supposedly qualified for. Passing the buck to a committee is a cop-out.

TEMPORARY TASK FORCE

In every well-run company there are occasions when the existing organization does not lend itself to special assignment duties. A need arises to explore or develop new ideas or possibilities and the normal operations are not set up to routinely accommodate this need.

The type of situation that comes up might be advance preparation for a new line of business, selling off a product line, taking over some work formerly subcontracted out, automating at least part of the manufacturing process, consolidating branches, relocating into a new facility— anything that affects the overall company but is presently not part of regular operating procedures.

It is in these circumstances that the creation of a temporary task force, appointed from within the company, may be the best answer. A few employees from different departments or divisions are brought together for this purpose. For the duration of the assignment they are relieved of their regular duties, either full-time or part-time, and transferred to the temporary task force.

This arrangement entails a wholly different kind of delegation. For the development of the one-time project or program, the members are accountable to the leader of the task force who, in turn, reports in this instance to the president or some other high echelon officer. But since this task force is only temporary and not permanently added to the company's formal organization structure, the individual members of the temporary task force are, for administrative convenience, still tied to the former departments from which they were loaned and to which they expect to return again afterwards. It is always the expectation that the group will be disbanded when it finishes its work. Its members, therefore, will want to maintain their original relationship.

Membership in the group is determined by the number who are needed, their availability for special work, but most important because of their talents and interest in the project. Since there is generally no precedent to follow, one qualification is ingenuity or problem-solving ability. Unless the work is unchallenging, or in the nature of "clean up," the people assigned to the temporary task force should not be the leftovers who happen to be not busy at the time.

As a team, the group should expect to depart from traditional work habits as it attempts to understand its responsibility and work out a solution. The hours may be different. Some of the work may be done off the premises. Travel may be required. The nature of the assignment, not previous patterns, should govern.

There are by-products from the use of a temporary task force. This is an ideal proving ground to test "comers," to see how they function in a different setting, with full responsibility, less direction, and indirect authority.

For the members, the temporary task force presents a real challenge and a chance to display talents that might otherwise go unnoticed. For the company, it is an opportunity to use experienced in-house personnel to solve a problem.

OUTSIDE CONSULTANTS

There may be occasions when the personnel chief finds it advisable to bring in an outside consultant because the personnel staff lacks the expertise or time to solve a problem or install a procedure.

Once the necessity for outside consulting services has been established, the selection of the right consulting firm should be approached with care and deliberation, in much the same way an individual facing heart surgery selects a heart specialist. Factors to consider are:

1. Reputation: is the outside firm recognized in the consulting field?
2. Payback: is the estimated improvement or savings made convincingly clear?
3. Experience: how familiar is the consulting firm with the client's industry?
4. Staffing: does the consulting firm have an adequate number of competent talent to carry out the assignment thoroughly?
5. Proposal: has the consulting firm submitted a written outline of the approach to be used?
6. Credibility: in its initial presentation does the consulting firm inspire confidence?

The outside firm should have in-depth experience in a field of specialization or it doesn't qualify as a consultant. Just coming in from the outside with a novel perspective is not enough. The consultant should provide a point of view that is different, useful, and appropriate.

When it comes to personnel administration, it is better for the personnel people to request the assistance from the outside than to have it imposed upon them by top management. It is unfortunate when top management sees real or imagined shortcomings in the personnel staff and turns to outside professionals for ideas and guidance. It is unfair to expect the personnel people to administer someone else's program. The consultant must never be allowed to overwhelm the in-house staff.

One weakness of using outside consultants is that they don't have to live with the consequences of their recommendations. Often they engineer quite an overhaul, only to close out the contract once the change is accepted and implemented. If the change proves successful, the consultant gets the credit; if it fails, the personnel people are still around to get the blame.

There is a place for consultants in practically every area of management in today's complex industrial machinery. And this includes personnel management. But undue reliance upon consultants points up inadequacies in the present staff. The personnel executive who becomes the meal ticket for a consultant is not worthy of executive standing. There is no justification for having two high-priced specialists in one job.

The personnel executive who becomes too dependent upon outside assistance could be relegated to middle management mediocrity where the duties are tolerated but no counsel is sought. On the other hand, a personnel manager who grows into a personnel executive remains alert, accepts the challenge, and makes the use of consultants unnecessary by building a comprehensive program with a capable staff and delivering a convincing and measurable result.

THE USE OF DETAILED ORDERS

Advantages:

1. Dispels doubt as to meaning.
2. Standardizes procedure.
3. Tends to eliminate accidents.
4. Lessens chance to "pass the buck."
5. Eliminates bad operating practices.
6. Protects the supervisor and promotes "peace of mind."
7. Facilitates training.
8. Requires less follow-up.

Disadvantages:

1. Introduces an imagined insult to intelligence.
2. Often not flexible enough.
3. Puts damper on worker's initiative and ambition.
4. Often takes more time.
5. Hard to cover all situations.
6. Removes sense of responsibility from the worker.
7. Curtails suggestions and reduces job pride.
8. Makes operation appear complicated.

Use detailed orders:

1. Where standard procedure is essential.
2. When hazards exist.
3. On special or infrequent jobs.
4. For a worker with limited experience.
5. When methods and equipment change.
6. Where willingness is lacking.

HOW TO HANDLE CHANGE

There is a widespread notion that people resist change. This is not entirely true. What people resist is "being changed."

If people resisted change, why do car buyers prefer newer models, why do women's fashions differ from year to year, why are people willing to take unfamiliar jobs in completely new and strange surroundings?

When it comes to daily work procedures, however, people tend to resist change. This is especially true when the new method is rather drastic. Put a long-standing manual operation on the computer, for example, and a good share of the planning is concerned with presenting this conversion to the employees and getting their acceptance.

For some reason workers dislike having a regular routine, one which they have learned and mastered, disturbed. Yet in the name of progress, improvements in equipment and systems must be made. This means upsetting existing methods in favor of better ones. This would appear to be advantageous from a company point of view, but to the individual it means only adjusting his way of doing his job. Since he sees no direct personal gain, he cannot be expected to embrace the idea with the same enthusiasm as the company, which stands to profit.

No change, big or small, should be attempted unless and until the employees understand fully why it is necessary and how they fit into the picture. After all, the full cooperation of every involved worker is necessary for the accomplishment of its purpose.

When something big is being considered, such as the introduction of a computer system, the relocation of the plant or the merger with another firm, a complete communications program should be included in the overall scheme. Employees should be informed about the plans as soon as these can be announced, the program which is finally designed, and the progress as the changeover is being implemented.

Most modifications of office procedures or factory operations are not this dramatic. Usually they involve only a small part of the total organization, often occur in only one department, possibly are as small as one step in a worker's daily pattern. Nonetheless, these innovations are also important—to the company which would otherwise not make them, and to the workers who must adapt their ways to the new method. Therefore, no adjustments should be undertaken without careful thought, not only related to company cost-saving or productivity, but also to the consequences should the workers inadvertently resist. After all, the company can authorize the "go ahead" but it is the workers upon whom the ultimate success depends. As they say in sports, "It is the players who make the coach look good."

Wholesome Climate Needed

When changes are to be made, a manager or foreman should:

1. Study his group in order to understand how it operates and what feelings and ways of life make up its attitude; then
2. Introduce change in such a way as to cause the least upset and the shortest period of readjustment.

460

Thus, he will be able to influence and direct the thinking of the group so that it is in harmony with the objectives of the company.

The work climate has a direct bearing, too. Where the climate is uncooperative, upsetting an established procedure may trigger a whole new set of employee problems. Where employees and supervision work together in a climate of mutual respect and trust, a change is easier to make and could, in fact, be welcomed.

From a manager's or foreman's point of view, good human relations exist when workers are:

1. Voluntarily giving a little extra to their jobs.
2. Getting along with him and with each other.
3. Working not only for him but also with him.

The extent to which workers do these three things depends upon the degree to which they are getting satisfaction out of their jobs. It is the company's responsibility to blend the "satisfaction of wants" of the individual with the wants of the company.

The following is a list of the sort of satisfactions which people want from their jobs. Note there is nothing here that says they don't want change.

1. Job security: what is expected and how they stand.
2. Freedom from arbitrary action: no favoritism or discrimination.
3. Opportunity to advance: new challenges as they grow.
4. A meaningful task: its purpose and prestige.
5. Congenial associates: best part of day, week and life is spent at work; it should be pleasant.
6. Satisfactory working conditions: comfortable and convenient.
7. Fair wages: fair in community and fairly administered.
8. Adequate benefits: protection against the unexpected.
9. Recognition as an individual: not a number or robot.
10. A voice in matters affecting them personally: no feeling of being pushed around.
11. Competent leadership: bosses whom they can admire and respect as persons, not as bosses.

It is the last three factors of personal satisfaction that should be taken into account when changes are contemplated and introduced. If the worker can see value to himself in the company change he is more likely to understand, accept, and apply it. In the final analysis, this is the only way to look upon change, for whom are companies trying to benefit with technological improvements except people?

461

REPORTS

<u>Introduction:</u> Executives are busy people. They often do not have time to read the many reports, studies, proposals, and surveys that are placed before them. Yet we want them to read and understand the material we have so carefully gathered and arranged. How can we help make our reports read?

Presentation: Naturally, all reports should be well presented. They should be typewritten, neatly packaged, with flawless spelling and grammar. Any report that does not make a good first impression will be quickly discarded. A carelessly presented report is not worth the time and effort it took to prepare it.

<u>Style:</u> Many reports must, of necessity, be long. This makes them harder to read. A busy executive tends to skim over a long paper, trying in vain to pick out something of value in it. When a significant point is buried in a sea of endless words or long paragraphs it will very likely be overlooked. We cannot expect a busy person to pore over a tedious report the way he scrutinizes a legal document, insurance policy, or other paper where the fine print is important. For our report to be read it must be presented in a readable style.

Topic paragraphs: One innovation in report writing that has been found effective is that of setting up the lengthy report in a style—similar to the one used in this paper—which sets off the separate items in clearly identified paragraphs. At a glance the reader can glean an impression of what items are included in the report and, if he is busy, can pick out those which are of immediate interest and concentrate on them. The others of lesser importance can then be safely set aside for later reading.

This style makes the report easier to write, too. Each separate topic can be written individually and then the next topic taken up. There is no need for continuity of material with time and space taken up with unnecessary connectives. Just select the topics to be covered, write them one at a time, line them up in logical order, and the report is completed.

<u>Readability:</u> The real advantage, however, is the readability of the report by the the busy executive to whom it is directed. He can see at once that he need not wade through a maze of words to get your message. He can select the items he wants to read. Chances are the report will be so easy to read that he will go through it completely.

<u>Application:</u> This type of presentation has many applications. It can be used for the many reports we're required to submit . . . for summaries of surveys and other studies . . . for sales proposals. And, among other uses, it can be a handy data sheet enclosed with a letter of application for employment, with the separate categories of personal and other information clearly set up for easy reference.

MANAGEMENT MEETINGS

There are occasions when management has a report or announcement to make to officers, managers, foremen and supervisors. The news needs to be dramatized to emphasize its significance. This calls for more than a memo or president's letter. The occasion calls for a meeting.

Management meetings may be called as required or scheduled on a regular periodic basis. To add to their importance they may be arranged "after hours" in the evenings. Any gathering during the regular work day is usually referred to as a "staff meeting" whereas a special meeting with extra arrangements is a "management meeting."

Such a management meeting may be held on the premises if adequate facilities are available; otherwise in a local hotel or private club. In all these instances the formal meeting is preceded by a dinner with an excellent menu. Since this is a business meeting and not a party, pre-meeting cocktails may be considered inappropriate.

The atmosphere should be informal but businesslike. Any attempt at corny innovations should be avoided. The dinner should be "class," to set the proper tone for the rest of the evening. A head table is unnecessary unless the business session is held in the same room. If possible, the group should be transplanted to another location more suitable for meeting purposes. The business session should begin on time. It should not drag on endlessly.

Inasmuch as a management meeting has as its theme some timely and important topic of official concern, the presiding chairperson should be the president or other top officer who is in charge of the activity under discussion. The format will depend upon the nature of the subject that is being presented. An annual report meeting will be treated differently from a problem meeting. In all cases it is imperative that all levels of management who have been invited get an opportunity to be heard or ask questions. They should be 100% behind the program when the meeting is over.

For all intents and purposes this is a command performance. Although seldom expressed this way, attendance is mandatory. No one should let personal matters interfere although some excuses, such as illness in the family, would be acceptable. Being invited into the inner circles of top management is open recognition of status in the company. Who can afford to be conspicuous by his absence? It is not uncommon for some managers to return from vacation or out-of-town trips for the occasion.

If a management meeting doesn't merit that kind of response then it doesn't deserve to be called a management meeting.

HOW TO MAKE YOUR MEETINGS MORE EFFECTIVE

A meeting is a means by which information is communicated to or from or among a group of people.

There are two necessary parts to any meeting: (1) those who conduct it and (2) those who participate in it. Often this might be a speaker and the audience. In other meetings this could be the discussion leader and the members of the group.

For a meeting to be effective, both sides must be prepared. Those in charge should provide capable and informed leadership, adequate facilities and necessary equipment. Those for whom the meeting is conducted should show an interest by their faithful attendance, willing cooperation and active participation. Neither side alone can effect satisfactory results.

Kinds of Meetings

All meetings are not alike. Before a meeting is conducted a number of questions should be considered.

1. What is the purpose of the get-together?
2. What is the meeting intended to accomplish?
3. What should be discussed and what should be withheld?
4. Who should attend?
5. How should the presentation be planned?
6. What is the best method of conducting the meeting?
7. Who is best qualified to lead it?

In an informational meeting the leader dominates by presenting facts and other information which are new or unfamiliar to the audience. The group listens. There might be some time allowed toward the close for questions mainly to clarify points.

In a lecture-type meeting the leader dominates during the first part while he presents his subject in his own way. Then he opens the meeting to the group to discuss his topic and to ask questions for further elaboration on items of interest.

In a conference the members of the group confer with each other and the leader merely presides over the meeting making certain that the discussion does not stray or get out of hand. The leader will not dominate the discussion but he will keep control of the meeting, and at the close will summarize the discussion.

There are other kinds of meetings, such as conventions, banquets, after-dinner meetings, seminars, workshops, training sessions and the like. But essentially all meetings fall into these three categories.

The following graph illustrates these three kinds of meetings and shows how the parts played by the leader and the members of the group differ in each case.

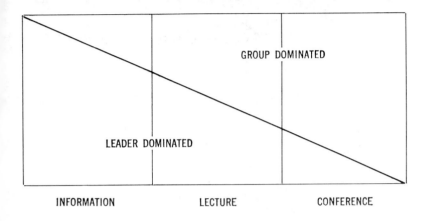

Arrangements

Before a meeting is conducted there are necessary arrangements that the person in charge should make.

1. Arrange for a room that is appropriate for the type and size of meeting. There is a difference between a lecture room, with its theater-style seating, and a conference room with chairs around the table. A room too small is obviously unsuited; but in a room that is too large, the meeting could appear to be poorly attended or the people might spread out too much.

2. Reserve the room for the date and time of the meeting or conference. This is understandable when the meeting is held in an outside hotel, but it is also important when the meeting is planned on company premises. Get confirmation in writing, if this seems advisable. This will avoid embarrassing confusion.

3. Send out a written notification to all participants, giving the date, time and place, as well as the purpose of the meeting. Remind them to bring along whatever data or material will be needed.

4. Have the room ready in advance with any necessary equipment. The leader may want a podium or table. If the room is large, have a turned-on microphone ready. Determine if

you need a stand for charts, screen, projector or other visual-aid props. If a blackboard is requested make certain that chalk and a clean eraser are there, too.

5. When outsiders are invited they should be given complete information about the name of the room, location, parking and other such details.

6. If a luncheon or dinner is part of the program, schedule it for a definite time, and make menu plans to fit the group.

Essentials

Certain essentials should be provided on the day of the meeting so that it will get underway promptly and proceed properly.

1. Individual tablets and plenty of sharpened pencils should be handy.

2. A pitcher of fresh ice-cooled water, with one or more glasses, should be placed at the speaker's or leader's position. Water and possibly paper cups should also be available for the members of the group.

3. A sufficient number of ash trays should be conveniently distributed.

4. The location of washrooms should be made known.

5. Cloak rooms or racks should be handy and indicated.

6. Arrival of any outsiders should be mentioned to the receptionist in order to have her ready to receive guests quickly and impressively.

7. An agenda of the meeting should be prepared for the leader and gone over with him.

8. Any and all supporting information, charts and exhibits should be ready for him.

Chairperson

To be effective, the chairperson of the meeting, the officer who is presiding, should follow certain rules acceptable to the group. The chair should:

1. Keep control of the meeting.
2. Try to maintain a good atmosphere.
3. Be firm, but fair, and stay "in charge."
4. Recognize members before they talk and then insist they stand and address the chair.
5. Give voice to both sides of a debate.
6. Restate the motion before the vote to make certain it is understood.

7. Call for the vote, giving everyone a chance to vote. Even when it appears the "ayes" have an overwhelming majority, he should still call for the "nay" votes.
8. Take a second vote, in case of doubt about the outcome, using a different method.
9. Respect members' wishes to abstain from voting and, upon their request, ask that this be noted in the minutes.
10. Announce the results of the vote.
11. Relinquish the chair when he wishes to speak on a motion or involve himself personally in a discussion.
12. Use good judgment in any conflict between the letter and the spirit of the law.

Agenda

The order of business should be prepared in advance of the meeting. It follows this fairly well standardized order of business:

1. Call to order by the presiding officer.
2. Roll call.
3. Reading of the minutes of the previous meeting
4. Reports
   a. Officers
   b. Standing committees
   c. Special committees
5. Unfinished business
6. New business
7. Announcements
8. Adjournment

Minutes

When meetings are run orderly or businesslike, a record of the proceedings is usually kept. In a formal organization the elected or appointed secretary will do this. For an occasional office meeting, the chairperson's secretary may take the minutes.

The secretary will take notes and make a documentary record of the meeting. The important action and decisions, not all the discussion, should be written into the report. The minutes should also include the name of the group, date, time and place of the meeting, the presiding officer, attendance and the time of adjournment. Any papers or reports that are read become part of the minutes.

Verbatim notes are not necessary, except for special occasions such as stockholders' meetings of large corporations, or board meetings when there is dissension among the directors. In such cases stenotypists or court reporters are brought in.

Ordinarily no attempt should be made to put everything down in full. Verbatim records should be made of important statements, resolutions or when someone asks that his views be made a part of the record. If in doubt, do not err on the side of brevity.

The minutes are a record of the meeting and a report of the proceedings. They are written for the minute book as the official record. Ordinarily there is only one copy made and it is ready to be read at the next meeting. Sometimes it might be advisable to distribute copies of the minutes of the last meeting to all who attended. This will give them a chance to agree with the report and especially their participation in it. At the next meeting it may then be possible to dispense with the reading of the minutes and merely accept them as submitted or with any necessary changes or corrections.

Parliamentary Procedure

In most cases it is enough to conduct meetings in a businesslike or orderly manner. When the occasion calls for a more formal method, the established rules of parliamentary procedure are applied. Parliamentary rules are as old as democratic legislative bodies. The rules followed by business or social organizations are usually adapted from these congressional and legislative rules. The most widely recognized authoritative source on parliamentary procedure is *Robert's Rules of Order.*

By following parliamentary procedure, or a satisfactory adaptation, it is easier to handle official matters in a businesslike manner and also maintain order during the meeting. But the real value lies in guaranteeing the will of the majority and in protecting the rights of the minorities.

Constitution

The purpose of the constitution is to identify the organization, explain its purpose, define the duties of the members, and set up the framework within which they operate. An organization drafts its own constitution which should be compatible with public policy and in conformity with any applicable laws.

A constitution consists of the fundamental provisions, written clearly and concisely. There are at least seven provisions which are usually expressed in separate articles. Each article, in turn, may be divided into sections.

Article I —the name of the organization
      II—the purpose and powers of the organization

III—the qualifications of the members

IV—the officers, their duties and length of term of office

V—the board of directors or any governing board of executive committee—and the method of selecting its members

VI—the time for regular meetings and provisions for special meetings

VII—the method of amending the constitution and the vote required

Drafting a constitution is the responsibility of a special committee appointed for this purpose.

Presenting the constitution is done by the committee chairperson. He makes his report and moves that the constitution be adopted. He or the secretary then reads the constitution, each article and section separately to make certain the members understand thoroughly the details involved and have a chance to ask questions and discuss anything that may not be clear. Following this procedure the entire constitution is then voted on as originally submitted or as amended.

Adopting the constitution is done by the members. A majority vote is sufficient. The constitution becomes effective immediately upon this vote.

Amending the constitution may be necessary from time to time. There is a provision in the constitution itself which spells out: (1) the type of notice to be given members (usually one or two readings at meetings preceding the one at which the vote is taken), and (2) the vote necessary to adopt amendments.

By-Laws

The by-laws delineate the details necessary to carry out the provisions of the constitution. Those dealing with the same general subject are grouped under one article, which may be divided into sections.

By-laws ordinarily cover the following:

1. Kinds of membership.
2. Membership qualifications
3. Procedure for admitting new members
4. Dues, method of payment, penalty for delinquents
5. Powers and duties of officers
6. Authority and responsibilities of committees
7. Election of officers and the vote needed
8. Appointment of standing and special committees
9. Provision for calling and conducting meetings
10. Parliamentary authority

11. Number constituting a quorum
12. Vote required for decisions
13. Procedure for amending by-laws.

Standing Rules

In addition to the necessary constitution and by-laws, organizations often set up standing rules. These standing rules are ordinarily not as rigid as the by-laws since they cover details of lesser importance.

Commonly included in standing rules are items such as these—

1. Order of business
2. Hour of meeting
3. Fines for minor infractions
4. Limitation on discussions
5. Regulations concerning guests
6. Special assessments
7. Entertainment of guest speaker

Standing rules are adopted by majority vote. No previous notice is necessary. Any part of these standing rules may be abolished this same way.

Introducing a Speaker

The chairperson of the meeting, or the individual who arranged for the program, should introduce the guest speaker. This should be impressive, and it will be, if done properly. When the moment arrives—

1. Address the audience, not the speaker.
2. Be brief!
3. Don't overdo the build-up.
4. Explain, but do not apologize, if the speaker is a substitute.
5. Mention those details only which qualify him for the meeting.
6. Give one or two reasons why listeners would want to hear him.
7. Avoid telling personal stories which might embarrass him.
8. Don't crab his style; let him tell the jokes.
9. Always close your introduction by giving the speaker's name *correctly* and the subject of his talk.
10. Remain standing until the speaker has taken his place on the platform; then sit down in the background.

After the talk, lead the applause for the speaker and thank him on behalf of the audience. If a question and answer period follows, let the speaker answer or clarify the questions. Avoid rehashing what the speaker said. If an honorarium or gift is given, present this to him privately.

Conclusion

Meetings are an effective means of communication, if run properly. They serve many useful purposes. They represent quite an investment in time, not only on the part of those who must plan and prepare for them, but also on the part of participants who are required to give up their own time for the meeting and possibly for travel. It doesn't take much thought to figure that the cost of a meeting can become sizeable.

Consequently, it is important that meetings be run right. A poorly run meeting can do more harm than good. A good meeting, on the other hand, can bring untold benefits to everyone who is involved.

WHY MOST SPEECHES FAIL

Our country has been called a public speaker's paradise. People in all sorts of organizations seem to be eager to listen to someone delineate on a popular topic. Subjects range from peaceful applications of atomic energy to the life and love of zebras in Africa.

The reason for so many speeches is difficult to explain. Why do busy men and women sit passively with their hands in their laps while someone else expounds his knowledge? Perhaps some of them are trying to get a night out, husband and wife together, with little cost. Others may be escaping from the monotony of a card-playing routine. Many undoubtedly are seeking satisfaction by participating in, or at least supporting, a worthwhile cause.

In our industrial society the occasions for some people to talk and for others to listen are certainly increasing. Associations and organizations of different types conduct regular or periodic business meetings or conventions that feature outside speakers. Ofttimes subjects are technical in nature and pertain to the objectives of the group. In other cases subjects are general and are justified on the theory that members should get away from their daily grind and broaden their intellectual outlook by exploring unfamiliar fields. In a few situations the subject matter makes little difference since the members of the group are merely enjoying a social night out with their companies quite willing to pick up the tab.

In all these situations, what are the audiences getting? Their attendance at the function implies that they want to be told what to do and how to do it. Yet advice from a speaker is usually futile. People in the audience accept those ideas of his which they agree with, and reject other ideas that run counter to their own personal prejudices.

As a result, a speaker tries to be careful not to offend his audience. In an effort to be amiable more than effective, he makes a mild attempt to entertain and then feeds the group, as eloquently as he can, a diet that may be nourishing but is as bland as pap. The members of the audience then applaud the speaker, politely and occasionally enthusiastically, and return to their homes and jobs doing precisely what they did before they heard the words of wisdom that they praised at the meeting.

This is the condition as it exists. Whether it is bad depends upon the views of each individual who is involved. Many people who attend meetings and conferences regularly may be quite content with the present pattern. Those, however, who seek improvement must ask where the fault lies and where changes should begin.

Three Areas of Speech

There are three component parts to each meeting, each of which contributes to the success or failure of the event. These are: (1) the audience, (2) the program planners, and (3) the speaker.

Not much needs to be said about the audience, except possibly that part which stays away, leaves early or in other respects is not present at the time of the speech. Usually the audience has little to say about the choice of speaker or his topic. For the most part, the audience remains faithful because of respect, loyalty or habit. This is certainly true when the speaker and his message fail to inspire. Still there are times when an audience does not do justice to a capable speaker, who has traveled far at great personal inconvenience, and who has labored long to prepare an adequate paper. Certainly he is entitled to a suitable listening group and it is indeed unfortunate when the audience is in a party mood, more concerned about libation than oration.

The audience is, of course, important. But more significant to the success or failure of a meeting is the program planning. Generally the planning is done by a committee and in many cases, because of the pressure of time or the diversity of interests, the program is thrown together.

The things which, in addition to martinis, impress the program committee members are big names in big companies. They will always be attracted to the president of the corporation, if he can be inveigled to appear, in preference to some lesser light, despite the fact that Mr. Big has not distinguished himself as a speaker. They hope to use the magic of a prominent name to swell the advance sale of registrations. The possibility of short-changing those who attend is secondary.

The usual practice for program committees is to hold regularly scheduled gatherings during which all sorts of names, titles and topics are bandied about—with no tangible results. Then with time running short, the program is "put together" with whatever talent is available and fits the limited budget. When the haze of meaningless conversation is lifted, the bald facts reveal why one speaker was selected in preference to others:

1. He has let it be known that he is available.
2. He is willing to participate.
3. He can be obtained because somebody knows someone who will intervene.
4. He comes well recommended by a vague third party.
5. In the interests of good public relations, his company is interested in having him cooperate with groups.
6. Like a salesman, he likes to talk.
7. He is a good story teller.
8. He has a selfish motive in behalf of a particular service or product being promoted.

Whether he has a message of particular interest to the sponsoring group is of minor importance. Often a program chairperson suggests to a speaker that he may choose his own topic. This is a dangerous practice because some speakers, having attained prominence on one limited subject cannot resist becoming self-styled experts on other far-flung topics. Even when the program committee spells out the subject or subjects in accordance with some loosely defined overall theme, the speakers are not necessarily chosen because they are the recognized authorities on the assigned subject. By their availability and willingness they happen to make the committee's thankless job easy and they also coincidentally just manage to fit the budget.

The Touchy Matter of Fee

This matter of budgets causes many program planners to be short-sighted in the fulfillment of their responsibilities to the people they represent. They do not hesitate to charge a registration fee or add a premium to the cost of the meal to cover expenses for the meeting. Yet they express amazement at a speaker's reasonable demand for a modest fee to compensate him, in part at least, for his services.

Chairpersons are completely unashamed in their requests for a free speaker. They even feel that a speaker should be grateful for their invitation to let him ventilate his views. The same people who would not give away their products, or render their services free, expect a speaker to give his talents, preparation, travel and time without change.

Although they sincerely believe they should not pay for a speech, nevertheless they do not want a speech that is worthless, but expect only the best. It may be that a speaker who works free is either a propagandist for a special interest, in which case he should be avoided, or he is not good enough to command even a modest fee, in which case he doesn't merit the collective time of his unsuspecting audience.

What the program chairperson considers a privilege a speaker thinks of as a chore, albeit a pleasant one. Like others who work, he too should be compensated in proportion to the contribution he makes. When he is paid nothing the listeners should not be surprised if they get nothing.

Why Speakers Fail

When it comes to explaining why most speeches fail, most of the fault can be laid right at the doorstep of the speaker himself. Where planning is adequate and audiences receptive, many meetings fail to serve their intended purpose because the speaker or discussion leader does not measure up to expectations. The plain truth is that few people know how to make a good speech.

Good speaking requires far more than an ability to use words, such as is necessary for good writing. A speaker needs a good voice and a certain quality that actors have of projecting the personality into a live audience. Some excellent writers have poor voices and little dramatic flair. Similarly, a speaker is lost who cannot utilize his personality to put his thoughts across.

To be effective, a speaker must

1. Be able to prepare his material.
2. Be able to present it.
3. Have something to say.

It is surprising how few men and women who ascend the platform know how to prepare their message. They use warmed-over ideas that proved successful last time and wonder why they did not meet with similar success the second time. This is because the conditions change but the speaker's preparation does not.

The message and manner of presentation must be tailored to each audience. The type of listening audience makes a difference. So does the time of day. The place on the agenda should be considered; an opening keynote address at a conference calls for a different approach from that of a late afternoon bread-and-butter technical session. A luncheon talk may be intended as a change of pace whereas an after-

474

dinner speech may be either humorous or serious on a topic of wide-spread general interest.

Audience Sets Style

The make-up of the listening audience also determines the way a talk is prepared. The same material, such as advice on how to succeed in business, must be rearranged depending upon whether the message is directed to executives, secretaries, technicians, machine operators, hospital administrators, students, scientists, professionals or others.

The mechanics of "packaging" the material must be understood. Some speakers start too soon. The playwright postpones any crucial line of the dialogue until he establishes the projectory of the "arc of attention" between the voices on the stage and the ears beyond the footlights. A speaker, likewise, should not get into the "meat and potatoes" of his message while his audience is still tuning in.

The style of presentation depends upon the amount of time available. For the usual half-hour address a lecture-type of delivery may be recommended. When the time slot is an hour or more, no speaker should expect his audience to sit still for any straight lecture. He should vary his format by using gimmicks, such as flannel boards or blackboards, handout material, demonstrations and exhibits. He might want to intersperse his lecture with questions from the floor. Where the group is small he may want to engage in a more intimate discussion-type presentation involving members of the group on a voluntary basis.

Upon the ability to organize his material to suit the type and size of his audience depends much of his chance for success. It is important to prejudge as accurately as possible what the people in the audience want. A speaker skilled in appealing to a group's feelings is like an organist playing upon the keys of human nature. If he inadvertently goes contrary to what people expect, his magnetism won't help much. The audience has to accept the speaker as a person before it will accept his message.

Therefore a speaker's ability to present his ideas is also vital. His platform manner should reflect sincerity for if the people cannot believe him they will not believe what he says. He must also display an air of authority but not superiority. He must be looked up to as someone worth hearing. A firm, smooth voice denotes confidence and poise. But an apologetic beginning will negate any good that may follow.

He should be able to speak . . . effectively. Here practice and more practice are essential. Critical self-analysis before a mirror or in listening to a tape recording can be very helpful. A spouse or disinterested observer can tell whether a speaker mumbles, slurs his words, cuts off sentences, stumbles over words or delivers in a monotone. An unpleasant voice irritates and distracts. A succession of "ahs" causes the listener to focus his attention upon the speaker's inadequacies. Starting every third sentence with "now" tells the audience how unprepared the speaker came. Reading a speech the way a professor reads a scientific paper is an imposition upon listeners who are supposed to be courteous enough to remain attentive. When the audience doesn't listen, it's the speaker's fault. When the audience falls asleep, it is time to wake the speaker.

No humor may be bad, but the misuse of humor is worse. No speaker should pretend to be a comedian until he becomes one, in which case he will forsake the podium for Saturday night television performance. A glib tongue and a fast line will tend to make a speaker appear fluent as he overburdens his listeners with his machine gun delivery. A good speaker, however, is one who has learned the drama of the emphatic pause. There are times, as we all know, when more can be said with silence than with any number of words.

While preparation and presentation are necessary, most important is that the speaker have something to say. Isn't it tragic how often a speaker sends his audience home empty-handed because he came empty-headed? A shallow message insults the intelligence of the audience.

The Importance of Something to Say

Some speakers rely upon their familiar name, or the reputation of their companies, to gain acceptance. A name may attract but only a message will impress. The chairman of the board who hopes to satisfy his audience by recalling the days gone by merely succeeds in making them wonder whether his personal success is due to his uncanny memory or his family's inherited wealth. The company president who refers vaguely to "the challenge before us" without ever identifying it or offering any solution, only encourages people to stay away from the meeting next month no matter how attractively the program committee bills it.

To hold the audience in the palm of his hand, a speaker needs more than an impressive title, personal charm or a big buildup by the master of ceremonies. He has to have something to say. He has to believe in something which he wants to share. This motivation may, or may not, be related to his regular job. His enthusiasm for it must be genuine, however. Only when he is fired up on something will he take enough interest to research the subject, enough time out of a busy schedule to develop his material, and enough spirit to present it convincingly. Actually, the only speaker worth listening to is the one who is crusading.

It is a tremendous responsibility that a speaker accepts when he agrees to participate in a meeting. Multiplying the number of people in attendance by the amount of time and money each one has expended, the obligation at once comes into proper perspective. The speaker who does not prepare his material, who has not learned how to present it, and who has no message worth listening to in the first place, must expect to be pointed out as the reason "Why Most Speeches Fail."

All this can be summarized in the following story. A man accepted the invitation of a friend and his family who were driving his way. First they stopped at a nearby service station to pick up the spare tire that had been left for repair.

The guest, trying to make conversation, asked the driver if he knew how much the tire weighed empty. He answered, "Fourteen pounds." Then the guest asked, "How much air did the service station put in?" And he was told, "Thirty pounds." So he asked again, "And how much did the tire weigh then?"

The driver said, "As long as our daughter is going to high school and learning such things, let's see what she answers." And immediately she said, "Forty-four pounds." The father commented, "See, their learning today doesn't teach them properly. She hasn't learned the difference between air pressure and air weight." And then the mother interposed, "I don't see what's wrong. If it weighed fourteen pounds empty and had thirty pounds added, why wouldn't it weigh forty-four pounds?"

The guest felt that the father should not make sport of his wife's and his daughter's error. "It's a common fallacy," he explained, "and I don't think they should be criticized."

Then he added, "The same thing is true with speeches. When a speaker tries to fill a specified time period, say a half hour, he often inflates his speech. Like the motorist, he too should realize that there is no weight to wind."

Yes, only when the audience is interested in listening, when the program planners are thorough in their selection, and the featured speaker prepares well, delivers well, and has something solid to say, will speeches no longer fail.

LEADERSHIP

Leadership is a quality whose true dimensions thinking people have always wanted to pinpoint and will continue to study. Social philosophers have attempted definition and have tried to capture its elusive nature in words.

In his book, *Office Management and Control,* Dr. George R. Terry explains that "Vital to motivation is the leadership present in the work

HOW TO MAKE A GOOD SPEECH

1. Acknowledge your introduction graciously. Recognize the chairperson and other dignitaries at the head table. Greet your audience.

2. Start off smoothly. Never begin apologetically. Try not to be clever lest you be corny. Don't try to "hook" your listeners before they are ready. Take a few sentences to warm up the speaker and the audience.

3. Don't "read" your speech as you follow the script. Be familiar enough with the contents of your paper so you can maintain occasional eye contact with different individuals.

4. Don't memorize your speech. This makes it sound canned and unreal. Rather select some persons in the audience and talk with them as individuals on a personal basis.

5. But don't talk "off the cuff" and expect to get any well-balanced presentation. At least use well-organized notes to avoid rambling and unnecessary wordage.

6. Use illustrations to make a point. It helps if these examples are funny or catchy, but don't tell jokes that are not pertinent to the topic.

7. A degree of nervousness, even for the "pro," can endear a speaker. The listeners respect a speaker who has obviously worked on his material and his presentation over one who appears cocky and lords it over them.

8. It doesn't hurt to jolt the audience occasionally. The speaker is working; the listener is sitting passively and may let his mind wander. Bring him back with a question, anecdote, quotation, poem or similar device.

9. Stay within the prescribed time limit and quit when you're through. A summarization of what you've discussed may be in order. A fast windup can be very effective.

10. Finally, don't follow any standard pattern, such as may be implied in the well-intentioned suggestions offered above. Accept them for what they are, nothing more than suggestions, and adapt them to your own personality, to the situation and to the audience. Like any formula for success, the rules for making a good speech must be individualized not only for the speaker but also for the occasion.

environment. People prefer to be with a successful leader. Being a part of victorious accomplishments, following a person who has demonstrated an ability to get things done, and having firsthand experience in observing successful management in action are in and of themselves highly motivating to an employee. Members of a group receive strong stimuli from effective leadership; and in turn, a strong leader acquires that position, in part, because of an ability to motivate members of the group."

Leadership Classified

The academicians have neatly classified leadership style into four kinds.

1. *Autocratic:* self-centered. This style has been historically effective. It is recognized as bossism.
2. *Technocratic:* work centered. The technical specialty influences actions and decisions. It is hard to argue with the expert.
3. *Idiocratic:* individual centered. The dealings are on a one-on-one basis. It gets results from respecting individuality and builds on differences rather than sameness.
4. *Democratic:* group centered. Actions encourage group participation. Decisions are based on consensus of opinion.

This is a convenient categorization of leadership styles and helpful in arriving at an understanding. But qualities of effective leadership defy quantification. Yet a floor of ingredients persists.

Leaders Classified

The following five classifications describe the leaders themselves. Each one exhibits a key element of leadership quality.

1. The *brain.* This is the individual who overwhelms others with his knowledge. He is bright, creative and possesses exceptional powers of recall.
2. The *dynamo.* His presence is felt everywhere and most of the time. By his own enthusiasm and exuberance he prods, cajoles, persuades, encourages and criticizes.
3. The *silver-tongue.* He can make people believe that the sun is shining at night. He is very persuasive. At the very least, he convinces others to do his bidding.
4. The *actor.* Although he may seem to be only entertaining his audience, his role goes beyond this. For he catches the mood of the public, synthesizes it and brings it toward a meaningful goal that coincides with his purpose.

5. The *puppeteer.* He manipulates his group like he plays his games. His moves represent an expedient and intricate system of gives and takes that puts his people in the barrel of a revolver aimed to the target he has selected.

These labels may aptly describe many leaders but they don't indicate success. To be effective any leader, no matter what type, must be the kind of individual the employees are impelled, not compelled, to follow. He must earn their respect not only as a boss but also as a person. It is not what he says, nor what he does, but what he believes that counts.

The Mystery of Leadership

The early studies of leadership hypothesized that the ingredient that made a leader effective was his personality. Proponents of this theory searched for traits common to successful leaders and came up with aggressiveness, self-control, independence, friendliness, optimism, etc. The mystery of leadership, however, is not that simplistic.

1. The *autocratic* leader has a source of authority from somewhere and he uses his power to reward and punish to get things done.
2. The *bureaucratic* leader relies on policies, procedures and rules and permits little deviation from the standard pattern.
3. The *diplomatic* leader lives by the art of personal persuasion, preferring to "sell" rather than "tell."
4. The *participative* leader invites his people to share in decisions, policies and practices, letting them advise or decide for him.
5. The *free-rein* leader sets the goals and terms and then lets his people free to operate as they deem best.

Whatever may be said of leaders and leadership, the traits and qualifications are easy to list from observing past behavior but hard to predict when assessing future performance.

Leadership Compromised

Like everything else in industry and in life, leadership too, is affected by changing conditions. The very concept is being reformulated. Traditionally the group has reflected its leader; in the future the leader will reflect the group.

As proof of this turnabout, the day of the entrepreneurial newspaper owner and editor, who swayed the mood and minds of the general public, is over. Today a faceless editorial staff tries to capture the tenor and purport of its market and then caters to the peccadillos and vagaries of this potential readership. The leadership obligation is no longer paramount.

Presidential candidates hope to gain acceptance and strength by riding in on the groundswell of popular opinion instead of assuming a positive stand that will stem the drift and guide the country out of its maelstrom of confused ideologies to more stable and prosperous times. Statesmanship is giving way to political expediency.

The story is told of the revolutionary in a Latin American country who was upstairs celebrating with visiting dignitaries. Outside on the street below there was quite a commotion which grew louder and more threatening as the multitude marched by. After a while the revolutionary asked his guests to excuse him, explaining, "I'd better go down there and join them. After all, I am their leader."

It used to be that people emerged as leaders by dedicating their talents and efforts, in fact risking their reputations, to causes in which they sincerely believed. They influenced opinion and guided followers in the direction they felt was best for the general good. The new breed of leaders in industry, government and education arrive on the scene of prominence not because of their beliefs but by virtue of privilege. They are not in the forefront espousing issues of their own but sitting back observing developments and following trends.

Leadership has been compromised. The lessons of the past are useless as new leadership qualities emerge. Leaders of the future will do less acting and more reacting.

AUTHORITY vs. POWER

There is a difference between authority and power. Authority can be defined; power is often not as clearly identified. Authority can be located on the organization chart; power can be illusory. Authority can be granted; power is inherent in certain people or circumstances.

Power does not necessarily parallel rank. Clearly described jobs may have their extent of authority clearly spelled out, but these jobs do not automatically have the power normally expected of the position.

The center of power may be anywhere in the organization and possibly not in the organization at all. Some vestiges of power may have been sacrificed to unions which, technically at least, have no management authority. The consuming public undoubtedly holds the balance of power in many cases. A key customer or industry may be calling the turns for the people in authority who sit in the driver's seat.

In its inception, a corporation will center its power with the organizers or with its source of financing. But as time goes on and the business becomes established, other forces will emerge and the power will shift around. It may be skewed toward engineering, research, packaging or some creative area. Once the product line is developed, power may well swing over to marketing.

Authority is clearly visible but the power behind the throne is often unrecognizable. Its presence is felt but its physiognomy may remain a mystery.

PRINCIPLES OF LEADERSHIP

Following are the principles of leadership expressed by The Dow Chemical Company, Midland, Michigan.

1. A leader must *lead,* not drive. People are unpredictable, different from one another, often irascible, frequently petty, sometimes vain, but always magnificent if they are properly motivated.

2. We must entertain a healthy respect for the ideas and opinions of others. A good leader will tolerate and in fact encourage diversity of opinions. The unfeeling leader—one unwilling to recognize other viewpoints—will wind up surrounded by sycophants. His descent from the road of creative leadership will then begin, perhaps slowly but always surely.

3. Many men and women live with a variety of fears, but fear of their leader should not be one of them. Neither must fear of failure overwhelm our will to meet new challenges. We must live with risk; that is what life is all about.

4. We must work to influence others by setting a worthy example and by candidly stating our own beliefs. Don't lecture others on their business or political or personal beliefs. We do business with a lot of different kinds of people. If many of them are not completely open minded, neither are we.

5. Informed employees are effective employees. We must communicate with them in the ways which best fit with our personal styles, of course. But we must also make certain that we are fully understood.

6. An informed public—our customers, shareholders, government officials, educators, opinion leaders and the proverbial man on the street—is a less suspicious public. As the world becomes more complicated, trust is harder to earn and to *keep.* Trust must be built upon day-to-day integrity and candor; one slip on this particular mountainside can plunge us into the abyss.

7. We must think of Dow everywhere while dealing with our specific

responsibilities. Dow is indivisible: what we do in one part of our organization affects every other part.

8. We must always think and build boldly, but spend with prudence. And don't take any pride in managing a large number of employees. Quite the contrary: fewer people can do more.

9. We must always remember the bottom line. It means everything: it imposes strong limitations on our abilities when it is not healthy, but it opens new worlds when it is right.

10. A successful manager must be his own man. He will consider any advice he receives in the spirit in which it is given. At the same time, however, he will use his own eyes and ears to keep watch on a changing world, and he will always work to broaden his vision. He will challenge, and he will accept challenge.

From these threads will come the fabric of the indispensable: the good manager.

A MANAGEMENT STYLE FOR THE EIGHTIES

by GEORGE S. ODIORNE
Professor of Management
University of Massachusetts in Amherst

In reviewing the last 30 years, it is apparent that the social and cultural climates of each decade were distinctive:

1. *The fifties:* From the viewpoint of the present, these were the Good Old Days. Eisenhower was a benevolent father figure; Korea and the Cold War still evoked patriotism; the space age struck man's mind; the emergence of the behavioral sciences elevated the role of highly-talented manpower, and the indulgent permissiveness of the schools reflected an era of peace, prosperity and complacency. But the era contained within it the seeds of a social explosion to follow.

2. *The sixties:* The revolt of the college-age students and nonstudents; the rise of the counterculture; the demands for power of alienated blocs of people, and the decline in respect for authority were typical of the sixties. A man on the moon contrasted with the rioter in the ghetto. The complacency of the fifties was uprooted by the realization that blacks were willing to work, organize and fight for opportunities to win jobs and complete under middle class values.

3. *The seventies:* Our present decade has created a managerial climate in which government becomes the partner of every executive. OSHA, ERISA, the environmental revolution, consumerism and

hundreds of other causes and regulations brought Washington intervention into the corporate decision-making process. The women's movement was sparked by changes in the law on equal employment opportunity. Due process in the work force, and the integration of the younger generation with its informal life style, attire, hair length and personal morality became the new order of the day. An energy crunch led to fundamental changes in the way business views growth and resource management.

This article seems quite modest to forecast what management styles will be required for the eighties since most of the influences which will shape the eighties are already present. It is impossible to predict cataclysmic events such as droughts, wars, terrorism, energy crises, scientific discoveries and similar major upheavals. But it is probably safe to bet that events of these proportions will occur and that we will not fully respond to them until the 1990's. Nevertheless, other events and developments are emerging that make it possible for management to prepare for the future.

To that end a bit of informed armchair prognostication isn't wholly without value. The purpose here is to increase future-mindedness and to prompt the reader to do his own futuristic speculating. For as Lincoln expressed it, if we know where we are, and something about how we got there, we might thereby see where we are trending. So alerted, we might then be able to avert through timely anticipation some of the less desirable outcomes which appear to lie naturally in our path or, alternatively, we might be able to exploit opportunities which might otherwise be missed.

There are 10 quite discernible elements of a management style for the coming decade.

1. *Less bureaucratic, more individualistic.* A very human and down-to-earth style will become the accepted manner of behaving and relating to people. Hortatory and inspirational speechifying is out. Listening carefully to others, responding with changes when confronted with opposition (without giving up basic strategies), and keeping pipelines open to the grass roots will be the executive way of the eighties. The president of the corporation may prefer fishing partners who were friends from his early days in the plant. Language will probably be more a "shucks" than the expletive-deleted style which followed the dirty speech movement on campus in the sixties into the Nixon administration in the seventies. In its most severe forms, this new "old-shoe" style might even be antiintellectual.

2. *More systematic.* It may seem paradoxical but at the same time the leader of the eighties is shuffling about in his old-shoe *modus operandi,* he or she will also be considerably more systematic than any generation

of managers before this decade. The systems approach will be ubiquitous. More computers, and especially more mini-computers and microcomputers will have a devastating effect upon many established practices.

3. *Development-centered management.* During the seventies, the training revolution and human resources development movement caught on and will become more pronounced in the eighties. Adult education which is so widely touted as their future growth area by the colleges and universities today probably may see its full flowering in the private sector rather than in the universities. Educational, training and development managers will undoubtedly rise in stature, rank and pay in business during the eighties, while some of the traditional personnel functions will decline proportionately, relegated to the bureaucratic chores of personnel administration.

4. *Situational management.* The manager of the eighties will probably be hearing and applying more situational management methods than ever before. The idea is to define goals and targets clearly, and then allow for more variety in the ways in which people get there. Orders are more apt to be of the kind which are situational. More attention to arranging situations so desired behavior is apt to occur is another facet of this rapidly growing style of management. The manager manages the entire situation, the physical environment, the group working teams, information flows, and opportunity for face-to-face discussions between people as well as the policies, rules and regulations to steer activity in the right direction. This will mean a corresponding decline in traditional charismatic and directive styles of leadership.

5. *Management by commitment.* If managers lose some personal control over people doing their work, managers must move people toward an even better form of control: self-control. Self-control requires that responsible employees make commitments in advance to their boss, perhaps their customers, their colleagues and even the government. They are then held accountable for delivering on the commitments which have been made. Getting people to internalize those commitments, of course, presumes that people have a thorough understanding and acceptance of the situation and the task. The most widely recognized way to win acceptance is to allow people to participate in decisions which affect them and for which their commitment is sought. The alternative is to overpay people and let their rewards be wholly monetary.

6. *Achievement motivation.* Studies by behavioral scientists show some tangible effects on output and growth where people have high achievement motivation. The major motivational influence in the workplace becomes the internal pressures to achieve. This is typical of successful organizations. Achievement motivation is encouraged by high goals;

485

the language of success rather than language of failure; systems which reward and reinforce the achievement of goals, and the building of teams of people jointly working toward these goals. There is good evidence that organizations, teams, companies and even nations whose leaders have a high level of achievement motivation become high-achiever organizations. There is also evidence that achievement motivation is amenable to training designed to produce it, and this new style of management predictably has an important effect on executive and supervisory development programs in all kinds of organizations.

7. *Group management processes.* Good group management starts with the board of directors, where outside directors, public interest representatives, audit committees and minority members will become more common. This emphasis upon team building will call for the more creative use of task forces, matrix management configurations of organization, and project management systems in research and development. It will mean a dimunition of traditional committees which go on and on without ever coming to a conclusion anyone can notice.

8. *Due process in personnel decisions.* Beginning with the campus rebellions of the sixties, flourishing in government and spreading rapidly to industry, the demand for due process has become "the" cause. Such properties or entitlements as a right to a job, a promotion, a benefit, a merit increase and the right to appeal decisions have followed a classic pattern of due process. People, under law, now have a right to be protected against anonymous statements about them in their personnel records, credit folders and governmental files. People are more ready to confront any accusers, insisting on a full hearing of their cases, and jealous of their rights under due process of law. While it will seem more difficult at first to fire people for incompetence during the eighties, it will merely mean that processes are being expanded to allow for the full working of due process. This calls for some revisions of clean-cut rules of employment, penalties for violation, and procedures for handling cases where penalties of any kind are to be assessed.

9. *Management by information.* It is especially appropriate for the eighties that management means "handling information." People in charge must know what is expected; how resources are employed; how well they are performing; how well they have done in the past compared with standards of performance, and what is impending. Insight into what lies ahead, based upon clear definition of the present situation, calls for more rapid and accurate information getting to the right place at the right time. Mini-computers, perhaps tied together in new kinds of networks, will dominate the eighties in response to these needs. Word processing, data retrieval, group sharing of information, and face-to-face dialogue between groups will expand. The skills of managers in the communication process will be essential. What used to

be called the "communication gap" in management will be subsumed under the new rubric of the "information revolution" which is already well underway.

10. *Physical aspects of the workplace.* The workplace will undergo some important changes to achieve the style changes under discussion. For one thing, the consideration of occupational health and safety will retain its new significance. Beyond this security-level physical factor, there will be more concern for the motivational effects of physical plant design and layout. The traditional concern for amenities will be supplemented by concern for the motivational influences at work. Work layouts will follow changes in planned work flows in order to give people control over their own work content, the sense of a client relationship with other people, better information about the results of their efforts, and more information about how others relate to their tasks.

Conclusion

There will be many changes in the next decade, and change will not always come quietly or politely. Some will require considerable management education. All will demand that managers change their behavior, either willingly or with considerable kicking and screaming.

Fortunately, when this occurs, there seems to be a fine placement corps of bright-eyed graduates who view all this change and the prospect of tough problems with considerable confidence and enthusiasm. For the first time in more than a decade they seem to be interested in working, assuming responsibility, earning money and living a good life. They will have until the year 2025 to show their stuff. If they don't solve all the problems during the eighties, there will be an opportunity to try harder in the nineties and beyond.

HEALTH AND SAFETY

EMPLOYMENT PHYSICAL EXAMINATIONS

IN ORDER to make the best decision, selection is based on many factors. These include the interviewer's subjective opinion supported by as much objective data as may be practical.

One of the many aids used in the selection process is that of the preemployment physical examination. Where a company is large enough to operate a full-scale clinic, a staff physician may give the examination. In smaller firms a local physician may come in one day a week or applicants may be sent to his office. In all these cases, the interviewer gets additional information about an applicant which serves as another bit of help in arriving at an appropriate decision.

The medical information provided in confidence to the doctor or nurse, and the results of the tests and examination are retained in medical files. Details are never divulged to others. Only the medical recommendation is offered, as the doctor classifies each applicant for certain types of work.

Typical classifications may be these:

A— in good health with no apparent health problem of any kind; fully employable.

B— in good health but with some correctable deficiency (Ex: bad teeth, less than 20/20 vision, overweight) which, if given proper attention, makes the applicant employable.

C— in good health but with some definite restriction (no lifting or very little standing, etc.) which, with the supervisor's understanding, makes the applicant employable but not for all jobs. (Ex: an emphysema victim wouldn't be given a dusty job.)

D— not employable, a poor health risk. The decision of who is placed into this category must rest with the physician. The supervisor should never ignore this advice and hire the applicant anyway.

The classification, but not the medical details, should remain in the employee's file so that it will be taken into account when the employee is being considered for a transfer or promotion to a different line of work.

In view of the success companies have experienced in hiring the handicapped, the tendency is to disqualify few applicants. Of greater concern is their proper placement in jobs for which they are suited. After all, very few people are in perfect health all their working lives. Yet almost everybody with a marketable skill is employable if properly placed.

EMPLOYEE PHYSICAL EXAMINATIONS (ongoing)

In addition to employment physicals, many companies give periodic physical examinations to employees. The practice is more common with executives and managers but by no means limited to the higher echelon groups.

Top level personnel may be given annual checkups. This is often done on the outside even if an employee clinic is operated. These people are sent to hospitals, sometimes overnight, or to recognized internal medicine specialists. Some corporations have been known to send their senior executives to such places as the Mayo Clinic.

Where a complete employee clinic is operated by the company, these checkups may be done on the premises, especially for middle and lesser management personnel. Some of the work may be done elsewhere, depending upon what is required, and some tests may be sent to laboratories.

As for rank-and-file employees, not as many firms give periodic physical exams and certainly not as frequently. These checkups may be offered, for example, once every three years. Much depends upon the size of the work force, the facilities of the company and, of course, the attitude toward this type of health program.

A company that offers and pays for such checkups does so on a voluntary basis. No employee, regardless of his job level, is required to participate. Few workers, as a rule, pass up the opportunity to avail themselves of this optional employee benefit.

One exception might be the compulsory periodic checkup in connection with a safety program. Employees in hazardous occupations may be asked to undergo examinations or tests at regular intervals to make certain that their work is not having any adverse effect on their health.

The results are discussed privately with the employee by the Medical Director or some other qualified professional in the Medical Division.

Any recommendations are made in the interest of the employee. The report and the action are kept confidential.

COMPANY DOCTOR

The company doctor is a practitioner of occupational medicine. He has regular hours and his practice is not nearly as tiring, or as burdensome, as private practice might be.

Patients don't come to him because of personal selection. His services are provided by the company and workers have no choice. This could raise the question of whom he serves.

Can he face the ethical issue while remaining objective? One Medical Director, in explaining his relationship to the corporation, told me, "Administratively, the company president can tell me what to do; professionally, he can not."

On the one hand, his role pits him against management as he eagerly complies with government health and safety regulations; on the other hand, his role seems to pit him against employees and unions who are suspicious that his interests lie with the corporation. For example, can he close down a plant that he considers a hazard?

The logical place, if he can maintain it, is to be neither a monkey of management nor a champion of the unions, but to give the best medical advice to fit individual situations.

CLINIC

An employee clinic may be established for a number of reasons.

This is where medical interviews or employment physical examinations are given to applicants being considered for jobs. Periodic check-ups for workers may also be done.

A clinic is also convenient for first-aid and medical services. An employee who becomes ill can receive medication and care here. The clinic may advise a manager or foreman whether such employee should remain in the clinic to rest a while, return to the job, be sent home, referred to the family physician or possibly taken to a hospital.

Workers injured on the job get immediate attention. These workers' compensation cases are ideally handled by the clinic. In addition to emergency treatment, and referral to appropriate medical facilities authorized by the insurance carriers, the clinic can process the paperwork that is involved.

Absences may also be better controlled where a clinic is operated.

PHYSICAL RECORD
(for physician's use)

TO BE COMPLETED
BY APPLICANT OR EMPLOYEE

Name _____ Soc. Sec. No. _____

Address _____ City _____

Age: _____ Birth Date _____

FAMILY HISTORY   Check if anyone in your family has or has had:

1. ☐ Tuberculosis   3. ☐ Epilepsy   5. ☐ Diabetes

2. ☐ Nervous or mental condition   4. ☐ Cancer   6. ☐ Heart trouble

OCCUPATIONAL HISTORY   (Explain further under Remarks if necessary)

7. Any particular hazards in previous occupations? _____

8. Ever compensated for occupational injury or disease? Describe disability, cause, duration, etc. _____

9. Now drawing disability benefits from Government or insurance company? If yes, explain __

10. Military Service.* From _____ To _____ If rejected, why? _____

MEDICAL HISTORY   Check if you have or have had: (Explain under Remarks)

11. ☐ Diabetes	24. ☐ Rheumatic fever	37. ☐ Ulcer
12. ☐ Tuberculosis	25. ☐ Hay fever	38. ☐ Frequent colds
13. ☐ Epilepsy	26. ☐ Cancer	39. ☐ High blood pressure
14. ☐ Heart trouble	27. ☐ Goiter	40. ☐ Dizziness
15. ☐ Venereal disease	28. ☐ Hemorrhoids	41. ☐ Paralysis
16. ☐ Rheumatism	29. ☐ Kidney trouble	42. ☐ Scarlet fever
17. ☐ Dermatitis	30. ☐ Chronic cough	43. ☐ Tumor
18. ☐ Asthma	31. ☐ Shortness of breath	44. ☐ Bleeding
19. ☐ Hernia	32. ☐ Stomach trouble	45. ☐ Discharges
20. ☐ Nervous breakdown	33. ☐ Backaches—strain	46. ☐ Other (indicate)
21. ☐ Arthritis	34. ☐ Fainting spells	
22. ☐ Pleurisy	35. ☐ Frequent headaches	
23. ☐ Pneumonia	36. ☐ Blood spitting	

*Not to be asked in New Jersey

Form No. PX-701

IF WOMAN: (Explain further under Remarks if necessary)

47. Periods regular?_____Lose time because of monthly cramps?_____

48. Have children?_____How many?_____Pregnant now?_____

49. Pregnancies and confinements free from accidents?_____

50. Any breast or female disorders?_____

SPECIAL HISTORY   (Explain the following in Remarks when necessary)

51. What injuries have you had?_____

52. What operations have you had?_____

53. What accidents have you had?_____

54. Ever in hospital, sanitarium, or institution?_____

55. Taking medicine regularly? Explain_____

56. Ever addicted to drugs or alcohol? Explain_____

57. Smoking habits_____

58. Days off from work because of illness in last 12 months_____

59. What do you consider to be the state of your health?_____

REMARKS   (If referring to specific item, please indicate by number)

(Use additional sheet if necessary)

I certify that the above statements are true and correctly recorded.

Date_____19____   _____
                                              Signature of Applicant or Employee

492

PHYSICAL EXAMINATION

TO BE COMPLETED
BY PHYSICIAN:

(Explain under Findings when necessary)

70. Height____ft.____in.   Present Weight_____   Usual Weight_____

71. Temperature_____   Pulse_____   Blood Pressure_____

72. General appearance: Good____ Fair____ Poor____

73. Development: Good____ Fair____ Poor____

74. Vision: Uncorrected: R 20/   L 20/   Near: R   L
              Corrected: R 20/   L 20/   Near: R   L

Color vision_____   Other data:_____

Pupils_____

Eyegrounds_____

75. Hearing: R_____   L_____   Hearing aid?_____

(Explain any abnormalities under Findings)

76. Skin   ☐ Nor ☐ Abn

77. Ears   ☐ Nor ☐ Abn

78. Nose   ☐ Nor ☐ Abn

79. Throat   ☐ Nor ☐ Abn

80. Tonsils   ☐ Nor ☐ Abn

81. Teeth   ☐ Nor ☐ Abn

82. Gums   ☐ Nor ☐ Abn

83. Neck: Glands ☐ Nor ☐ Abn
         Thyroid ☐ Nor ☐ Abn

84. Breasts   ☐ Nor ☐ Abn

85. Chest: Inspiration____inches
          Expiration____inches

86. Lungs   ☐ Nor ☐ Abn

87. Heart   ☐ Nor ☐ Abn

78. Abdomen (scars, tenderness, liver edge, etc.) ☐ Nor ☐ Abn
    Girth____inches

79. Hernia   ☐ No ☐ Yes

80. Inguinal rings ☐ Nor ☐ Abn

81. Genitalia   ☐ Nor ☐ Abn

82. Prostate   ☐ Nor ☐ Abn

83. Spine   ☐ Nor ☐ Abn

84. Rectum   ☐ Nor ☐ Abn

85. Extremities (deformities, limitations of motion, etc.)
    Upper   ☐ Nor ☐ Abn
    Lower   ☐ Nor ☐ Abn

86. Varicosities ☐ Nor ☐ Abn

87. Lymph nodes   ☐ Nor ☐ Abn

88. Venereal Disease ☐ No ☐ Yes

89. Reflexes: Patellar ☐ Nor ☐ Abn
              Romberg   ☐ Nor ☐ Abn

90. Other:

91. Vaccination history:

493

LABORATORY DATA

92. Urine: Specific Gravity_____ Albumin_____ Sugar_____

        Color_____ Reaction_____ Microscopic_____

93. Blood_____

94. X-Ray Chest_____

95. Other_____

_____

OTHER FINDINGS AND REMARKS   (If referring to specific item, indicate by number)

(Use additional sheet if necessary)

I have examined_____and would rate him/he

    A. ☐ Physically fit for any job.

    B. ☐ Having remediable defects, which temporarily limit employment to certain types of work.

    C. ☐ Having static defects, which permanently limit employment to certain types of work.

    D. ☐ So handicapped as to be hazard to self and/or others.

In regard to physical fitness for the position of_____

I would classify him/her as ☐ employable, or ☐ not employable.

Date_____19____   Address_____

Any employee who is absent because of illness may be asked to report back through the clinic where it can be determined whether the employee has recovered sufficiently to return to the job. By having to tell his story to a professional medical specialist instead of his supervisor, it is hoped that abuse of the sick-time-off-with-pay will be minimized.

Services may also be rendered in the form of flu shots and other immunizations. Health education programs may be initiated. One very important aspect of a clinic that should not be overlooked is the counselling that is provided. Employees are encouraged to come in to discuss their problems in an atmosphere of confidence and with some assurance of sincere personal interest and help.

Every action, from the initial physical examination to later clinic visits, should be made part of the official medical record. Any treatment given, any medications dispensed, any consultations with the family doctor, and any advice given should be documented.

Three cautions must be mentioned: (1) Medical and health information is personal and should be kept confidential, (2) the clinic must not be allowed to take the place of the family physician but should limit itself to emergency or on-the-spot treatment, and (3) the clinic is not to be used as a policeman to determine who is employable, who should be sent home, who should and should not be paid for absence blamed on illness and the like. Such decisions remain with the line organization which acts on the basis of sound advice and information provided by the clinic.

MEDICAL RECORDS

Where a preemployment physical, or at least a health interview, is done, certain basic questions about an applicant's general state of health are asked. The answers are documented on an individual medical record card which also lists the person's name, sex, date of birth, age, marital status and the date the interview takes place.

The initial medical history discussion will cover such ailments and illnesses as headaches, fainting spells, sore throat, hay fever, chronic coughs, blood spitting, backaches, stomach disorders, piles or fistula, skin trouble, childhood diseases, and in the case of females, menstrual disorders.

A more thorough health interview will include nervous breakdown, epilepsy, ear or eye disease, sinusitis, bronchitis, pneumonia, pleurisy, heart disease, rheumatic fever, rheumatism, kidney disease, diabetes, varicosities, tuberculosis, typhoid fever and venereal disease.

To complete the questioning a record of all previous illnesses, injuries and operations is made and discussed in sufficient detail to assure that placement is made in accordance with any health limitation that might exist.

A physical examination will include weight and height, pulse, an eye examination, hearing test, teeth, mouth and throat, heart and lungs, hernia, blood and urine analysis, blood pressure, possibly chest x-ray, and whatever else the examining physician deems appropriate for the applicant or for the position under consideration.

The data and results are recorded on the individual's medical record card. Any defects are noted in case correction is recommended. This kind of background information will prove helpful in any future health discussions.

Should it become necessary or advisable to discuss a health problem at some later date, or offer first-aid or emergency treatment, the visit is recorded on the medical record card. The date of the visit is entered, the complaint noted, the diagnosis recorded, as well as the treatment or advice that is given. The ultimate disposition and time lost are documented and the card initialed or signed before it is again filed.

Needless to say, medical information is personal and should be treated confidentially.

PHYSICAL FITNESS

A growing number of companies, at least 500, are offering physical fitness programs not only for executives but for rank-and-file workers as well. They see a correlation between physical fitness and efficiency.

These programs are designed to combat heart disease, obesity and hypertension. They provide workers a release from their emotions.

Individuals and groups can work out in exercise rooms complete with personal lockers. Indoor equipment could include stress test equipment, punching bags, treadmills, stationary bicycles. Off premises facilities may include tennis courts, jogging trails, racquetball courts, cycling and indoor/outdoor swimming.

A great outlay of money is not always necessary. The principle of good exercise is more important than expensive equipment.

Corporate interest in this employee service is in keeping with the President's Council on Physical Fitness and Sports which claims "physical fitness on the job reduces the cost and losses of long-term absences and premature death and disability due to back and heart problems."

HEALTH MANAGEMENT

In the comprehensive health management program of Kimberly-Clark Corporation, Neenah, Wisconsin, the accent is on wellness, not illness. The program, which is voluntary, is described by Darwin E. Smith, chairman and chief executive officer, as "one of the most extensive programs of illness prevention ever conducted in a company's own facilities for a large group of employees." The entire cost is borne by the firm.

The company hopes the program will improve productivity, reduce absenteeism, and hold the line on mounting costs of medical insurance for the 2,100 salaried men and women at its corporate offices and 15 other nearby facilities. The program may be extended to salaried employees across the country and offered to unionized production employees through collective bargaining.

Here is how the program works. First, an evaluation is made of the health risks of each employee through an extensive medical history (a 40-page questionnaire analyzed by computer and compared with standards for people of the same age and sex), a series of health tests (hemoglobin, blood sugar, cholesterol and triglycerides, liver function, urinalysis, chest X-ray, breathing, skin fold thickness and body density to determine percent of body fat, electrocardiogram, hearing, vision, blood pressure, and temperature), complete physical examination, and a treadmill test (which monitors heart action during exercise). The employee then receives an individual health prescription—such as supervised exercise, health education or counseling—to reduce, control or neutralize those risks. The program also is intended to motivate participants to accept the health prescription as an important part of their daily lives.

Dr. Robert E. Dedmon, staff vice-president—medical affairs, says, "We have to recognize that how we live can determine how long we live. This program is aimed at changing people's ingrained habits that are detrimental to their mental or physical well-being."

Supervised Exercise

The health prescription, prepared with the approval of the employee's personal physician, may call for supervised exercise, such as swimming, cycling, jogging or walking, in a new physical fitness building. This facility has a large pool, 100-meter track, exercise equipment, sauna and whirlpool, plus shower and locker rooms. Special exercise fitness programs are available for employees who have had heart problems or emphysema.

Besides exercise, the health prescription may recommend counseling

497

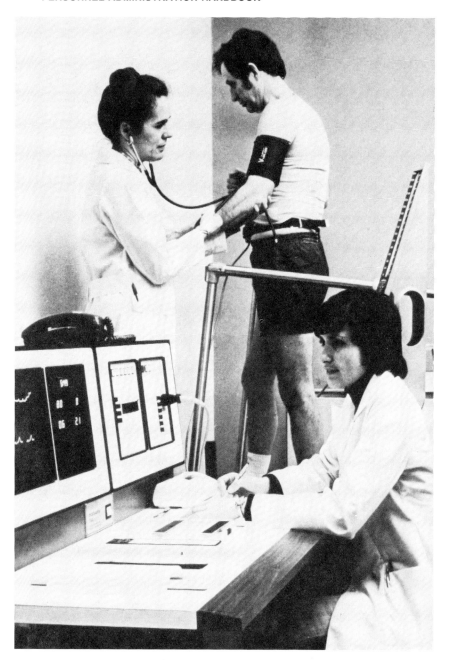

The treadmill test.

or attendance at after-work seminars on subjects such as obesity, nutrition, chemical intervention (alcohol and drug abuse), and stress.

Multiphasic screening will be offered annually to all eligible employees. Physical examinations will be offered every three years for employees under 40 years of age and every two years thereafter.

Medical histories and test results are maintained as confidential but, at the employee's request, the information is made available to the personal physician.

To sum it up, in the foreseeable future, nothing from the world of medicine is likely to improve the general status of health nearly as much as individual self-care in the form of wiser living.

FLU SHOTS

Most companies are insured against unforeseen losses, but what about the hazards of influenza? The costly effects of the flu virus are often ignored by even the most progressive business organizations.

Whether you call it flu, grippe or The Bug, a case of influenza is no laughing matter. It's an acute, infectious disease that begins suddenly with fever, chills and pains.

Flu is caused by a virus which is constantly changing. Most of the changes are minor, but every 10 years or so a major change occurs. When this happens, we may have a worldwide epidemic such as the Asian Flu in 1957, or the Hong Kong flu in 1968.

Oddly enough, you may be exposed to the flu virus but not get the disease. Or you may even get it and not know it; 25% of flu cases show no symptoms and can be detected only by blood test. However, for the remaining 75% symptoms occur within one to four days of exposure. The early symptoms may resemble a cold—except that your nose runs less, your body aches more, and you feel weaker.

Complications that sometimes result—pneumonia, bronchitis, sinus trouble and ear infections—are often more significant than the influenza itself. Many of these are caused by bacteria and can be treated with antibiotics.

Immunization Vaccine

A vaccine is used to produce immunity to influenza. It is especially valuable for:

1. Persons in whom influenza might represent an added health risk, such as individuals with cardiovascular or pulmonary conditions.
2. Persons over the age of 55 with chronic illness of any type.

3. Persons responsible for providing essential public services, such as law enforcement officers.
4. Industrial and other commercial organizations.

A transient stinging or aching sensation may occur at the injection site immediately after administration. Redness, induration and tenderness are common during the first 12 to 24 hours. The vaccine may cause fever, malaise and backache; the reactions tend to vary in severity with the amount injected.

Allergic reactions due to hypersensitivity to egg protein may occur. Such reactions have been rare, but they may be serious. Although they are uncommon, postvaccinal neurological disorders have been reported following the injection of almost all biological products.

In offices, factories and other places of employment "flu" immunization can:

1. Reduce absenteeism.
2. Eliminate the danger of a flu epidemic.
3. Avert postinfluenza fatigue.
4. Provide evidence of a company's interest in its employees' health.
5. Demonstrate leadership in public health and education.

HEALTH EDUCATION

Most companies are enough concerned about their employees that they are willing to cooperate in health education. This is true even where there is no clinic or other medical facility on the premises.

There is nothing wrong with displaying approved health posters. These may caution employees about coughs and colds, announce diabetes detection week, or stress good eating and sleeping habits. Material of this kind is readily available.

Booklets or pamphlets on artificial respiration, lifesaving, first-aid, exercise and diet can be placed at convenient counters or in reading racks. These tell employees how to look better, feel better, live better.

But companies may go further. When approached by the Cancer Society, for instance, they may agree to show the official film at employee meetings or in the cafeteria. This film points out the common danger signals of cancer.

Where a clinic serves the employees it is not uncommon to have the nurse speak during orientation classes or at other times on personal hygiene, cleanliness, body odor, overweight and other personnel matters.

None of this, of course, should be overdone. After all, personal

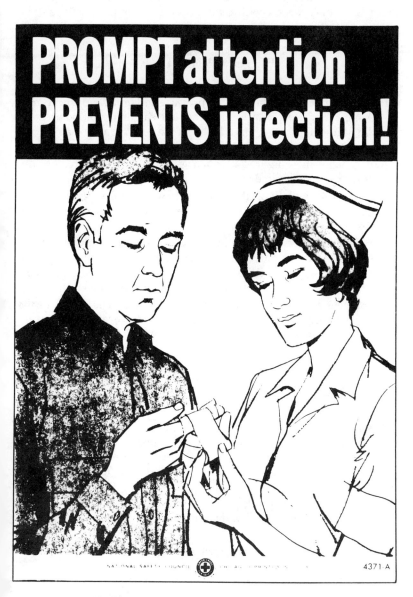

Health Poster courtesy of National Safety Council.

grooming and health care is the responsibility of each individual. But there is nothing wrong with offering an assist as long as it is done tactfully.

BLOOD PRESSURE

High blood pressure is a common and frightening problem. About 15% of Americans have high blood pressure and don't know it. Almost 100 Americans die each day as a result of untreated high blood pressure and the illnesses it causes. High blood pressure is the major risk factor in more than half the deaths in America each year.

What makes these figures alarming is that high blood pressure can be easily treated with daily medication.

Many companies believe that employees who suffer from high blood pressure should know about it, get the best possible treatment, and the support they need to take daily medication.

A free blood pressure screening program is not difficult to arrange. It is conducted in conjunction with the local chapter of the American Red Cross or a similar medical group. The agency provides volunteers to work with the company professional or nonprofessional staff.

Employees are scheduled for orderly processing. The results of the tests are held in strict confidence. Individuals with elevated readings are followed up to assure they are getting treatment.

BLOOD PRESSURE CHECKS

Blood pressure checks are becoming more common as an on-the-job health examination.

Because it is believed half of the 23 million Americans with high blood pressure don't know it, more companies are devising screening programs to test employees at work. In cases where treatment or further testing is indicated, the patients are referred to their personal physicians.

It is estimated that health problems related to high blood pressure cost industry 52 million work days a year.

BLOOD DONOR PROGRAM

by WILLIAM M. WALSH
President
Chicago Regional Blood Program

There are many companies that have established blood donor programs among their employees. Anyone in the workforce who qualifies may volunteer to donate blood. When 20% of the employees donate, all employees and their dependents are eligible to have blood replaced for them as the need arises.

The replacement plan is generally on a yearly basis. Arrangements are made with the local Blood Center or with a nearby hospital. Collection of blood at the work site is the most efficient way because of the volume, and the donor motivation of peer pressure is effectively utilized.

Whole blood has only a 21-day shelf life so an ongoing supply is essential. A donor may give blood every 10 weeks, or about five times a year.

The qualifications for blood donor usually go something like this. He or she should be between the ages of 17 and 65. Someone 17 to 21 may donate but the written consent or presence of parent or guardian is sometimes necessary.

A donor is rejected permanently if he has ever had: jaundice, malaria, diabetes or syphilis. A donor is rejected temporarily for any of the following reasons:

1. A cold or flu; wait one week after symptoms cease.
2. Childbirth; wait six months.
3. Tooth extraction; wait one week.
4. Appendectomy, tonsillectomy, hernia repair, hemorrhoids; wait two months.
5. Under doctor's care; a note from the doctor will allow donor to be accepted.
6. While taking antibiotics.
7. High or low blood pressure.
8. Certain inoculations (consult Blood Center).

As for diet, a donor is encouraged to eat during his regular scheduled mealtime; however, he should not eat any fatty foods such as butter, cheese, eggs, meats, milk, soups, etc., within 12 hours. He may have as much coffee or tea (without cream or milk), water, soft drinks, fruit juices and nonfatty foods as he likes.

Recipients of the benefits of the blood bank may be only those employees who contribute or may include all employees including those who do not or can not donate. In most such programs employee dependents or close relatives may also share in the benefits.

The arguments for a company blood donor program are obvious. Companies are in a unique position of providing an employee benefit and filling a community need. The arguments against such a program are simply that once a supply of blood is available, and easy to tap, employees will no longer respond to the individual needs of their

503

families and friends. Once blood becomes a commodity, the opponents feel, it loses its appeal as a health-saving "good Samaritan" act, and they ask, "Has anyone you know ever been denied the blood when he needed it?"

CANCER DETECTION

As a part of their health education efforts, companies are initiating cancer detection programs for both women and men. This is to encourage employees to practice good preventive health habits.

The American Cancer Society will cooperate. They are prepared to conduct teaching sessions on breast cancer self-examinations. Each half-hour meeting combines a lecture with a question and answer period and a film demonstrating self-examination techniques.

This service is offered to all female employees on a voluntary basis. Often wives of male employees and daughters of male and female employees are welcome to participate.

About 95% of breast cancers are first discovered by women themselves using this technique. If detected early, cure is possible for 85% of breast cancer patients. Education and self-examination are the best defenses.

Another service developed by the American Cancer Society is the colon and rectal cancer detection program.

Colon and rectal cancer strikes about 100,000 Americans a year and will kill almost half of them. Colon and rectal cancer strikes an equal number of men and women and is especially common in people over 40 years old. Most of the deaths can be prevented through early detection and treatment.

A detection kit costs very little (maybe 50 cents). It can be completed at home with very little inconvenience. It should be returned within five days to the designated place where it was obtained. An outside laboratory analysis will be made and the appropriate notification sent. Results are held in strictest confidence between the employee, the employee's doctor and the American Cancer Society.

CANCER DETECTION PROGRAM

A cancer education and screening program to protect employees from cancer was developed by Cannon Mills Company, Kannapolis, North Carolina, in conjunction with the Duke University Medical Center.

504

Present cancer work is: (1) diagnosis and treatment of the disease after it has developed, and (2) research in virology and immunology. This program added a third dimension, that of systematically and comprehensively educating an entire employed population in early cancer detection.

In less than 20 months, 18,000 men and women 20 years of age and older have been educated (each employee a full hour), and 12,000 have so far been screened (estimated another half hour per employee).

In addition to the 24,000 hours taken away from production time, the company's cost was approximately $10.00 per employee screened.

Each participating employee received personal information regarding tests and examination. Further, where results were not in the normal range, the employee was advised to see his private doctor to whom the results were made available.

CANCER SIGNALS AND SAFEGUARDS

The Seven Warning Signals:

1. Change in bowel or bladder habits.
2. A sore that does not heal.
3. Unusual bleeding or discharge.
4. Thickening or lump in breast or elsewhere.
5. Indigestion or difficulty in swallowing.
6. Obvious change in wart or mole.
7. Nagging cough or hoarseness.

The Seven Safeguards:

1. Lung: Reduction and ultimate elimination of cigarette smoking.
2. Colon-Rectum: Proctoscopic exam as routine in annual checkup for those over 40.
3. Breast: Self-examination as monthly female practice.
4. Uterus: Pap test for all adult and high-risk women.
5. Skin: Avoidance of excessive sun.
6. Oral: Wider practice of early detection measures.
7. Basic: Annual physical examination for all adults.

ALCOHOLISM

If, as the reports make unmistakably clear, alcoholism is a problem in life, to what extent does it spill over into business? Some of the statistics are disturbing.

505

A 138-page report prepared for Congress by the Department of Health, Education and Welfare delineates the bad news:

1. About 10 million adult Americans have drinking problems.
2. One in five high school students gets drunk at least once a month.
3. Heavy drinking is indisputably involved in causing cancer.

These figures are alarming. The seven to 10% of all employed people who are alcoholics account for twice as many work hours missed as other employees. Each adds an average cost of $2,500 annually to a company's payroll. Sickness and health benefits are at least twice as high for alcoholic employees as for those with no drinking problem.

Excessive consumption of alcohol takes a terrible toll on the health, safety and happiness of millions of Americans. More than 200,000 deaths each year may be associated with the misuse of alcohol, including half the traffic fatalities, half the homicides, and one-third of the suicides.

The human toll is frightening. Put simply, alcoholism is a progressive terminal illness. An alcoholic will lose many things in his life—his family, his friends, his car—before he loses his job.

That's because on the industrial scene there is good news. The National Institute of Alcohol and Alcoholism finds that Americans appear to be coming to grips with the problem of alcoholism.

Many companies, instead of being understanding in a passive sense, are beginning to take the initiative. In the past, corporate programs waited for a handful of obvious alcoholics to show up; now they're going out of their way to look for them.

Their bold strategy is putting teeth in their programs. They offer the same corrective measures but the difference is that they do two things: (1) detect alcoholism signs early, and (2) force workers to seek treatment. The signal is a drop in work efficiency. A common symptom of alcoholism is that the worker doesn't respond to ordinary reprimands.

The Job Offers Hope

The hope lies in relating the problem to job security. The desire to hold on to the job is a strong motive for heeding advice.

It is becoming increasingly evident that discharge is not the best answer to this difficult personnel problem. Larger companies have inaugurated programs to aid these troubled employees and the results justify this approach.

In addition to helping to rehabilitate the alcoholic, these programs also have an economic value. Studies indicate the alcoholic worker loses an average month of working days each year. Time lost by the production worker with a headache or hangover is easily measurable because he either stays home or his production goes down. The situation faced by the white-collar worker is not as quickly calculated because he may be in the office physically.

But what about the costs that are "more difficult to calculate?" Included are loss of experienced employees, friction in the work group, lowered morale and efficiency, waste of supervisory time, bad decisions, and damaged customer and public relations. Actually, a company never knows the full extent of the excessive costs created by the problem drinker.

The annual cost to business and industry nationally is conservatively estimated at $2 billion. Added in are lost time, absenteeism, accidents, insurance premiums, damaged equipment and ruined material. Mistakes caused by the alcohol-fogged mind are costly in this day of complex and expensive machines.

Considered as a Disease

The 200 or more companies that have established programs to help the alcoholic (and the company) are successful because they treat alcoholism, not as a personality problem, but as a disease. They consider it an illness, and a serious one. As such it gets medical attention.

An employee's drinking becomes a company problem when:

1. His work is reduced in efficiency and dependability.
2. The employee's drinking affects his health.
3. The employee's drinking affects his personal relations on the job.
4. He has alcohol on his breath during working hours.
5. He has an attendance problem.
6. There are complaints from other employees.
7. There are frequent on or off the job accidents.
8. There are unexplained disappearances from the work assignment.

Management representatives are in the best position to identify and help an employee with a drinking problem. The supervisor knows the person's job performance, attendance record, condition and appearance on the job, his habits, and very likely, something about his family and community relationships. The supervisor is one of the few people—perhaps the only one—who can motivate the problem drinker to seek treatment. A problem drinker who ignores the pleading of his friends or the urging of his family often will recognize his problem and seek treatment when he is faced with the possible loss of his job.

Help begins when the supervisor recognizes the symptoms. A person with a drinking problem will have certain behavior patterns such as:

1. Frequent Monday, Friday, post-holiday and post-payday absence and tardiness.
2. A variety of poor excuses for frequent absences for minor illnesses. Such people claim to be suffering from colds, gastritis, flu, stomach conditions, neuritis and a host of other ailments more often than do other employees.
3. Frequent on and off-the-job accidents.
4. Moodiness and unusual sensitivity leading to arguments or disinterest in the job.
5. Decreasing reliability evidenced by: an inclination to put things off; a tendency to neglect details formerly pursued; placing blame on other workers; a desire for different job assignments; obvious financial difficulties.
6. A marked change in appearance, such as swelling of the face, flushed face, red and bleary eyes. These changes are often accompanied by increasing carelessness in dress and appearance.
7. Hand tremor.
8. Memory blackouts.
9. Drinking habits that differ from those of companions (faster drinking, sneaking drinks, drinking for longer periods, or heavy spending on alcoholic drinks).
10. Evidence of domestic discord or increasing financial troubles.
11. Marked sensitivity to suggestions that alcohol is a problem.

What the Medical Department Does

When an employee accepts the referral to the medical department, the physician will make a medical judgment on the seriousness of the health problem. He will assess the underlying cause of excessive drinking.

Prior to the examination the supervisor should give the physician a complete written report of all the facts and personal interviews in the case. It is important to tell the employee that this information will be made available to the physician.

The physician will make a complete evaluation of the employee's physical and mental condition. Consultation with outside specialists will be obtained when necessary.

If the examination indicates that rehabilitation should be attempted, and if the employee agrees to cooperate, the medical director will then outline a program of therapy and follow-up for the employee. Basically, this program uses Alcoholics Anonymous, hospitalization when required, and regular counseling in the Medical Department. Other specialized care will be suggested when needed. The Medical Department welcomes, and seeks the cooperation of the employee's family, his personal physician, and his clergyman, and welcomes interviews with wife, supervisor and doctor present.

Documentation

Frequently in the administrative handling of an alcoholic case, the individual involved will deny that anyone has ever talked to him or her concerning the problem.

In handling an alcoholic case, it is very important to keep good records concerning each episode, interview or conference. Also include the facts relating to the supervisor's contacts with Alcoholics Anonymous, the company medical staff or other agencies. It may be advisable to include a second supervisor in these interviews if a witness will not jeopardize a good relationship which may have been established between the supervisor and the alcoholic employee.

All of a supervisor's records must be detailed, complete, dated and signed. It should be explained, for example, that the employee spoke incoherently, was unsteady in stance or walking, was untidy or shaky —rather than stating the simple conclusion that the employee was intoxicated. If disciplinary action is taken, there should be a written record of the reasons for such action. This record should describe the warnings given to the employee about his future with the company, as well as evidence indicating that the employee understood all of these warnings.

Self-Imposed Disease

Not everybody agrees that alcoholism is a disease. A newspaper item explaining that the state had decreed that the police should take alcoholics to hospitals for treatment rather than to jails brought this letter to the editor.

"If alcoholism is a disease, it is the only disease that is bottled and sold; and it is the only disease that is contracted by the will of man; it is the only disease that requires a license to propagate it; it is the only disease that requires outlets to spread it.

"If alcoholism is a disease, it is the only disease that produces revenue for the government; and it is the only disease that provokes crime; it is the only disease that is habit forming; it is the only disease that brings violent death on the highways; it is the only disease that is spread by advertising; and it is the only disease without a germ or virus cause.

"It just might be that it's not a disease at all."

PROBLEM DRINKERS

Today's enlightened managements treat employees who are problem drinkers as health problems.

The problem drinker is the employee whose consumption of alcohol either interfers with normal social adjustment at work or conflicts with satisfactory job performance.

A program of assistance is often available to help each person overcome his problem and regain his health. Any manager who suspects he may have such a case is asked to discuss the situation immediately with company medical personnel. This is to give the problem early attention, before it becomes more serious, and to protect the manager from drawing hasty conclusions.

The medical staff, after counselling with the employee, will develop a personalized rehabilitation program utilizing company and community sources. Management has the responsibility of encouraging strict adherence to the prescribed program. The employee must admit his problem and voluntarily request or accept help.

Recognizing the highly individualistic nature of these problems, the interpretation of each separate case should be closely coordinated between management and medical personnel. It is the responsibility of management, upon medical advice, to take any necessary administrative action, including transfer to another job when this is advisable to protect the individual and others, or termination when all efforts at correction fail.

DRUG USE AND ABUSE

People who take drugs and remain functional are users. When their use of drugs begins to interfere with performance, they become abusers.

Drug abuse is largely a problem peculiar to young people. There are many reasons young people resort to drugs. When it is all boiled down, the most prominent reason seems to be for "kicks."

Companies are dealing with the drug user or abuser, not the addict, most of whom are unemployable.

There are some parallels between alcoholism and drug abuse. Like all malignant dependencies, they both erode work performance, affect attendance and alter attitudes. Both the alcoholic and the drug abuser usually have serious problems in the physical, mental, social and economic areas. Like all progressive disorders, they degrade the employee and may lead to total and permanent disability or death.

MARIJUANA

How widespread is the use of marijuana in business and government? Nobody wants to admit anything, but a recent study reported that some 33.5 million Americans over the age of 18 probably used marijuana. Users are predominantly men under the age of 35.

Most users confine the practice to off-hours and off-premises. But it goes on to a lesser extent on the factory floor, in men's rooms and the parking lot. Marijuana is smoked in Friday afternoon brainstorming sessions, isolated private offices, second shifts and in cabs of long-haul trucks.

Smoking pot seems to be most prevalent in the so-called creative industries, such as movies, television, entertainment, advertising and fashion, but it also includes executives and professionals.

Users argue marijuana is less hazardous all the way around than drinking which, generally, is socially acceptable. Use is becoming more widespread because of declining penalties for use or possession and dwindling police interest in prosecuting cases. Companies do not openly condone the use of marijuana because it is illegal.

EMPLOYEE INCENTIVES

or
How to be Rich and Stay Healthy

For a person who smokes a pack of cigarettes a day, the cost is about $400 a year for cigarettes and accessories. A heavy smoker incurs a proportionally greater cost. Multiply this expense by the number of years a smoker indulges in the habit, and the cost runs up into thousands of dollars.

Besides, life span is reduced one minute for every minute smoked. A smoker who stops, will in 10 years increase the average life span by three years. This means three more years to collect social security and retirement benefits.

Recognizing these facts, James C. Miller, president of Intermatic, Inc. of Spring Grove, Illinois, decided to cooperate with employees who want to quit smoking. The difficulties of stopping smoking apparently are over-rated. Every year hundreds of thousands of people quit smoking, never to take it up again. The only way to stop is to decide to stop, then stop—cold!

In order to encourage employees to quit smoking, the company makes an offer. Anyone who signs up will, after one year of abstinence, receive a cash award.

511

Originally this cash payment was $50 per person. Later it became $1,000 annually, to be divided equally among those who signed up and survived the year. As an added inducement, anyone who enters can "bet" on himself for any amount up to $100; if he doesn't smoke, he gets as an extra payment the amount of his bet, and if he smokes during the year he contributes the amount he bet to the American Cancer Society. Names of winners and losers are listed in the company newsletter.

The latest available figures (1977) show 25 winners.

Because of the acceptance of this incentive, the idea was extended to include payment for reducing. In effect, the company buys excess fat.

Here again, overweight is a disease that kills. The overweight person is prone to a variety of ailments—high blood pressure, heart trouble, diabetes, kidney disease. There is no magic drug to cure this disease; only the victim can cure himself.

Enrollment is limited to employees who are at least 15 pounds over-weight. A year later they are weighed again and those who have lost a minimum of 15 pounds are paid $3.00 per pound of loss, without limit. In its first year, women accounted for 65 per cent of the 137 participants, but the men lost more weight. There were 43 winners who received checks from the minimum $45 to $150.

The winners receive cash rewards, they save money on out-of-pocket expenses and medical costs the rest of their lives, they enjoy better health and longer life expectancy, and they earn the respect of family, friends and co-workers.

GAMBLING ADDICTION

According to the last census, there are an estimated eight million compulsive gamblers in the United States. Many of them are employed in your company and mine.

Compulsive gambling is a progressive behavior disorder that psychiatrists look upon as they do any other very serious emotional illness. Compulsive gamblers have lost their ability to control the driving urge to gamble. Over any considerable period of time they get worse, never better.

The consequences of gambling could be financial losses, family emotional strain, divorce and broken home. It has often times led to pitiful and incomprehensible demoralization, sometimes to imprisonment and even suicide.

Compulsive gambling is an insidious illness, progressive in its nature. It can never be cured, but it can be arrested. The compulsive gambler is not necessarily a weak person or a bad person; he or she is really a sick person who needs help . . . and who can be helped.

Understanding, sympathy, patience and help are available through Gamblers Anonymous. This is a self-supporting fellowship of men and women who share their experience, strength and hope with each other that they may solve their common problem and help others to recover from a gambling problem.

At their meetings gambling is considered as a sickness and group therapy is the basis of treatment. It is here that any individual who admits gambling is a problem finds the surrounding influence and guidance for help.

In addition to free and open two-way discussion, sound advice is offered with difficulties that are legal (bad checks, fraudulent loans, etc.), financial (rent in arrears, past-due obligations, etc.), employment (out of work, dismissal warnings, etc.), and family (separation, strain, etc.).

The only requirement for membership is a desire to stop gambling. There are no membership fees or dues. It is not allied with any sect, denomination, politics, organization or institution; it does not wish to engage in any controversy; it neither endorses nor opposes any causes. The primary purpose is to help those who have found compulsive gambling a problem that has overpowered the manageability of their lives.

For the innocent victims of compulsive gambling there is Gam-Anon, a fellowship of men and women who are husbands, wives, family members, relatives or close friends who have been affected by the gambling problem. Its members learn to accept the spiritual values, such as patience, humility, honesty, and meet old situations with courage and confidence and new situations with strength and serenity.

Employers and employees seeking further information about the help that is available are urged to write Gamblers Anonymous, National Service Office, P.O. Box 17173, Los Angeles, California 90017.

ANNUAL PHYSICALS

Today's executive is sedentary, with a tendency to be overweight from lack of exercise. His main concern is his job, his concern about his health has a low priority unless, of course, illness has already manifested itself. It is the responsibility of management to safeguard one of its prime resources, the health of its key personnel.

Annual physical examinations should be required of such personnel. Under such a program each executive is allowed to select his own doctor or make a choice from a list of recommended physicians, subject to company approval. The cost to the corporation will run from $100 to $150 per examination, depending on the scope of the work done.

For the employee, the examination gives peace of mind and, in the event it turns up a problem, corrective action can be taken in time. For the corporation, there is the assurance that the key employees, or most of them, are in continuing good health. For those not in good health, the report will serve as a warning to take steps to change job responsibilities, ease pressure or relieve tension. In serious cases plans can be begun for the eventual replacement of any individual whose illness is a progressive one.

Coupled with the executive health policy may be a planned program of physical exercise. Most local physical culture studios will be happy to cooperate. A membership can be purchased for executives at a nearby health club or gymnasium or something like a weekly one-hour workout may be arranged on company premises.

MULTIPHASIC SCREENING

(A New Concept in Preventive Health Care)

One out of nearly every three Americans is a candidate for a heart attack. The American Heart Association notes that heart disease is the greatest single killer, responsible for more than a half million deaths annually. Among suggestions for lowering a person's danger of a heart problem is the advice to "get a physical checkup regularly."

The statistics on chronic bronchitis and pulmonary emphysema are also alarming. Over a million people in the United States are affected. The rate of deaths from bronchitis-emphysema, which rose 400% in one decade, exceeds that of lung cancer and tuberculosis combined. Again, the best defense is regular physical examinations.

But how many Americans see their doctors for annual checkups? Alarmingly, very few are receiving prevention attention. Industry spends millions of dollars and considerable effort to reduce industrial accidents. But for every worker killed by an industrial accident or an industrial disease there are more than 50 who die of cardiovascular disease.

If ever there was a challenging case for cost reduction in business, it is the early identification and treatment of employees with undetected diseases or abnormalities before they are handicapped or lost as effective workers. Aside from the dollars-and-cents benefits, a significant social and humanitarian contribution would accrue.

Mass health care at low cost is now available. The complex technology of modern medicine is within easy reach of every worker. This is made possible because of a development in mechanics with no change in *what* information is gathered but *how* it is gathered.

Automated Procedure

This new program is designed to do multiple tests of an individual's body functions and fluids, acquiring data that will help in determining his "state of health." Usually computer machinery is involved, which might explain why a series of relatively routine health tests have burgeoned into the mystical term "multiphasic screening."

The modern procedure, unavailable only a few years ago, makes it possible to carry out large-scale surveys on a systematic basis. The examination is simple, brief and inexpensive, yet thorough and conclusive.

A multiphasic screening system consists of three parts:

1. *Medical history:* the compilation of a complete medical history as supplied by the subject being examined, relative to general, family and personal history. The answers supplied by the individual are indicated through the simple expediency of making a printed history form which is, upon completion, directly compatible with data processing equipment and thereby computer compatible.
2. *Physiological profile:* height and weight, skinfold thickness, sight, pulmonary function, respiration rate, hearing, phonocardiogram, electrocardioanalyzer, electrocardiogram, blood pressure, pulse, temperature and tonometry.
3. *Laboratory profile:* hemotology, urinalysis, blood chemistry, fecal and serology.

The various physiological tests and the laboratory analyses measure and report on hearing and visual ability; obesity; metabolic, cardiac, urogenital, thoracic status; blood morphology, and pulmonary functions; symptoms of glaucoma, cervical and lung cancer, diabetes, internal bleeding; and, in addition to existing conditions, can alert one to any vulnerability to heart attack at a later date.

Routine periodic checkups lead to early detection, prompt treatment, better health and longer life expectancy. The employee may avoid long hospitalization and medical treatment, bills, discomfort and the unhappy fact of illness.

Three Types

Computer-based, automated health systems are already in use as a preventive medicine tool and a diagnostic aid. In broad terms, they can be divided into three types: permanent location, movable component units, and self-contained, portable module.

1. One type is in a fixed-site facility to which people go for their examinations. (This is not unlike taking an automobile to an electraac

515

or diagnostic testing center for a thorough going-over.) The health testing center makes appointments and schedules participants to avoid waiting. The individual processes himself through a series of connecting stations, moving at his own pace. He follows instructions and meets a technician only when the procedure, such as x-rays, calls for personal service. At each step he presents the I.D. card which was prepared for him by the receptionist when he first entered. Men and women use the same general facilities up to a point when procedures not common to both sexes, such as cytology and mammography, require they go their separate ways, only to return to common stations toward the end.

2. In the second type, one or more components may be transported by truck to a temporary location, such as a factory or office. The testing center brings in whatever units of equipment are required and the technologists to operate them. The company provides the space and electric power.

3. The third type is the same as the others except that the entire health testing center is portable and can be easily "moved in." This is similar to the familiar mobile x-ray unit which is operated by a technician, and which runs through a large number of employees on a schedule that causes a minimum of work disruption, and prints out an objective report. The similarity ends with the realization that instead of one procedure, such as x-rays, the portable health testing module performs a complete series of physiological tests. At the same time, blood urine, and fecal samples are collected for processing in an automated laboratory.

Data accumulated by the system includes the aforementioned medical history, physiological tests and a laboratory analysis. The components incorporated in the console are standard medical instruments whose accuracy and reliability have already been proven in hospitals, clinics and physicians' offices.

A New Concept

In all multiphasic screening systems the procedure does not replace the physician but is a supplement to his work. The system prepares a printout of information and data similar to that usually collected and assimilated by allied health personnel. This is made available to the family or company physician within 24 to 48 hours and supplies him with much information so that he may evaluate findings, detect symptoms, and begin treatment.

A multiphasic screening program is intended to make use of regular periodic examinations. Annual checkups are recommended. Utilized sequentially, the screening can not only detect apparent abnormalities on the first examination, but also the development of subtle changes

Multiphasic Screening

Test	Determines presence of
Blood: hemoglobin	anemia
blood sugar	diabetes
cholesterol and triglycerides	heart disease risk
Liver function	hepatitis, cirrhosis
Urinalysis	bladder infection, diabetes
Chest X ray	heart and lung abnormality
Pulmonary function	asthma, emphysema
Skin fold thickness and body density	excess percentage of body fat
Resting electro-cardiogram	heart malfunction
Audiometry	hearing impairment
Vision	vision impairment
Tonometry	glaucoma
Blood pressure	hypertension — stroke risk
Temperature	infections

Multiphasic Screening tests to determine presence, progression, or potential of ill health.

over a period of time. Progression of damage may be arrested, and in some instances reversed so that impending disability may be averted.

The whole concept of preventive medicine is a departure from the customary illness care. Companies have provided coverage for illness insurance but not for health insurance. People generally do everything to cure illness but little to prevent it.

Hospital care and medical treatment are generally oriented toward curative treatment of established disease at an advanced or critical stage. The shift in emphasis from sickness care to health care means not only trying to restore health but also to protect it.

HEALTH CARE vs. ILLNESS CARE

The trend of health care in the future may be away from health services and toward individual self-care in the form of wiser living.

Americans today are getting more and better health care but the picture remains unchanged. The life span is not being extended and the killers—cancer and heart disease—are still at the top of the list.

The answer apparently is not more doctors, bigger hospitals, sophisticated equipment for diagnosis and treatment, or new drugs and vaccines. Perpetuation of this after-the-fact medicine only results in higher costs and more frustration.

The country's health bill is already 8.3% of the gross national product. Reduction in mortality rates and extension of life expectancy are not resulting.

There is a whole school of thought that what is needed is prevention —avoid getting sick in the first place. Too many people are condemning themselves at an early age to a serious and fatal illness later in life.

Dr. John H. Knowles, president of the Rockefeller Foundation, says: "Americans have come to look on sloth, gluttony, alcoholic intemperance, reckless driving, sexual frenzy and smoking as constitutional rights, and they've come to expect government-financed cures for all the unhappy consequences."

One person's freedom is another person's shackles in taxes and insurance premiums. Money won't solve the nation's health problems which get progressively more costly.

CARE OF THE HEART

Many known factors increase the risk of a heart attack before age 60. The well-publicized risk factors are: (1) hypertension, (2) obesity, (3) high blood cholesterol, and (4) cigarette smoking.

Personality can also contribute risk factors. Among these factors are: (1) impatience, (2) excessive ambition, (3) overwhelming aggression, and (4) fast walking and talking. These people work too hard, worry too much, and are slaves to the driving force that keeps them going. They should spend more time in recreation and relaxation. Apparently it pays to be easygoing.

EMERGENCY

An emergency is defined as anything that disrupts the normal, orderly operation or endangers lives and/or property.

1. Fire, bomb threat or any disaster which necessitates evacuation of all or part of the premises.

2. Serious injury, fight or any bizarre behavior that could lead to injury.

What to do in case of a bomb threat:

1. Keep the caller on the line as long as possible to determine:

    a. time the bomb is to go off.
    b. location of bomb.
    c. voice peculiarities—accent, pitch.
    d. background noises.

2. Inform the caller that the building is full and that many people will be hurt.

3. If possible, have someone else listen in on the line.

4. Notify your security officer immediately.

EMERGENCY OFF-HOUR PROTECTION

Most offices and plants have some first-aid program for their workers. This service may run all the way from a full-time clinic, staffed with one or more registered nurses with possibly a doctor on the premises or on call, down to a minimal facility in which one person is trained in Red Cross or first-aid work.

But what about people who are working when or where such service is not available? This could include:

1. Workers in smaller locations away from the headquarters building.

2. Workers in any location who are on overtime or irregular-hour schedules when the official first-aid room is closed.

These people are entitled to the same protection as the other employees receive. From a company viewpoint it is dangerous to neglect these people.

To meet any such contingency, arrangements should be made in advance so that every employee is covered at every location and every possible working hour. And every employee, particularly the supervisors, should be adequately instructed what to do in case of emergency.

Usually it is sufficient to have a working agreement with a physician in the locality. He should know what he may expect. The employees should have his name, address and telephone number for quick reference. His office hours should also be posted.

It may be advisable to make special arrangements for services that are not performed by the general practitioner. For injury to the eye, for example, the emergency patient should not be taken to one doctor only to be referred elsewhere. Delay or unnecessary double transport could be dangerous and costly.

Arrangements should also be made with the nearest hospital. It may be necessary to go there after the doctor's office hours, in cases when he cannot be reached, on orders from the doctor or in emergencies or accidents.

In making all these advance preparations include also ambulance service. It is advisable to have a second, or backstop, ambulance service available—just in case. The fire department may also be called for emergency service, so this telephone number as well as that of the police, should be handy.

All this information should, of course, be posted where every worker will see it.

These off-hour workers, or employees in outlying areas, are generally supervised. The supervisor should not panic but do the best he can under the circumstances. In those cases where the employee may be alone, it is hoped he or she will be resourceful enough to know what to do, particularly if he or she has been properly briefed and the needed information is at his fingertips.

In all cases, the incident must be reported at the first opportunity so that care is not neglected. Someone ought to call the boss at home or at headquarters as soon as possible to give him a chance to take any further action that may be necessary. Certainly the incident should be reported to the clinic or other appropriate first-aid facility first thing in the morning. This gives the company a chance to make a proper record for official purposes, such as Worker's Compensation. But more important, it allows the proper medical authority to investigate and review the case, either by calling in the employee for a checkup, or even visiting him at home or in a hospital, in order to ensure that all possible medical attention is being given.

HEALTH ON SECOND SHIFTS

Management, workers and unions are interested in whether shift work, night work or interrupting a normal pattern of working influences health, sleep, digestion and longevity.

Medical research has very little objective evidence that shift work continued for any length of time significantly affects health in terms of sickness, absence or mortality. Temporary changes in sleep or eating routines may occur when starting a new shift, especially when the worker is unable to adapt to the changed rhythm of life imposed by shift work.

Considerable research is being done on circadian rhythms. One conclusion reached as a result of these studies is that it takes time to adapt biochemically to night work even though the body adjusts to changes in temperature and sleep patterns within a few days.

SAFETY PROGRAM

A company safety program is a well-defined effort to organize and direct all activities to prevent incidents. A successful safety program is:

1. Planned: to fit the needs of operations.
2. Organized: to encourage willing participation.
3. Administered: with support and dedication.
4. Stimulated: to perpetuate interest and enthusiasm.
5. Evaluated: to encompass new ideas and methods.

Department heads and supervisors are key persons in the success of any safety program. As part of their duties they must stimulate employee interest and participation in safety. They must recognize hazards and eliminate all unsafe conditions and unsafe acts. They must also investigate promptly incidents in the department.

Safety Rules. A safety program includes a set of safety rules. Specific rules are made in order to protect employees from possible hazardous conditions. The six basic requirements when developing safety rules are:

1. All safety rules should be written.
2. A rule should be practical.
3. A rule should reflect an unsafe act or condition.
4. Safety rules should be limited to safety matters only.

5. Employees should assist in the development of operating safety rules.
6. Rules should be adopted and enforced.

Safety Meetings. Safety meetings differ little from other department meetings. Each meeting will consist of a review of past incidents, discussion of preventive measures and suggestions for improvements. Communication is important and employees should be encouraged to participate in the overall safety program, discuss problems and contribute ideas that promote safe work conditions and practices.

Safety Training. Safety training is no one-time or occasional shot in the arm. To be effective it must be continuous. Safety training should start on the employee's first day on the job and should never let up throughout his employment. General orientation sessions for new employees will introduce them to the safety program and its purpose. Constant reminders in the form of message posters help to keep employees safety conscious.

Accident Prevention. The causes of accidents and injuries are:

1. Mechanical. (Ex: poor equipment; safety features ignored).
2. Physiological. (Ex: poor eyesight or hearing; improper lifting).
3. Psychological. (Ex: taking chances; horseplay).

A good prevention program is the Triple E:

1. *E*ngineering. (Ex: safety guards, cutoff switches; technically safe design).
2. *E*ducation. (Ex: rules and instructions; posters about work habits; safety practices).
3. *E*nforcement. (Ex: posted warnings; follow through on infractions).

Safety Inspections. Periodic inspections should be made both on a regular schedule and occasionally as a surprise. A walk-around visit is a means of checking equipment, operations, facilities, storage and practices to see how they conform to prescribed standards. Unsafe conditions or acts can be easily spotted by the trained eye and these should be cited and reported so that maintenance, repairs and other corrective action can be taken. Warnings on violations should be issued and penalties imposed when citations are ignored.

Safety Records. There are two types of safety records and reports that, if conscientiously completed, will help in understanding and improving the safety situation:

1. Frequency: the number of occurrences, no matter whether time lost or not.

2. Severity: the length of the inconvenience caused; the amount of time off; the cost in terms of worker suffering and pain.

Safety Committee. While department heads are responsible for conditions in local areas, a company safety committee can be helpful in overseeing the entire program. This committee can consist of a revolving membership, so that all areas of company operations are represented. It is best, however, to designate an appropriate permanent chairman so that continuity can be maintained. This committee establishes policies, sets the rules, reviews reports and looks after enforcement.

SAFETY PRECAUTIONS FOR NIGHT WORKERS

There is a danger inherent in asking employees, particularly women, to work late into the night. Even though nothing happens in most cases, the women are scared when they are alone in the night waiting for public transportation in a neighborhood that is dark and frightening.

Usually nothing is done by the employer until some tragic incident gets the company and the community alarmed. But why wait until too late? Why not take some precautions?

Here are safety measures formulated by police authorities:

1. Notify the local police precinct, which can assign a radio patrol car to accompany employees as they leave the building.
2. Report all incidents, no matter how minor.
3. Ask female workers to walk in groups to transportation facilities.
4. Light office building lobbies and ground floors adequately to discourage loitering.
5. Report any action of a suspicious nature immediately by telephone to the police.

Some companies are using specially-hired taxis to pick up employees at prearranged times, to take them either all the way home or to the nearest transportation. Other firms merely allow their women on overtime work or night shifts to take taxicabs home and then reimburse them for the cab fare.

FIRE and EVACUATION DRILLS

In schools we had occasional fire drills. Why not in offices and plants?

A fire or other sudden incident could be disastrous if employees are not prepared to evacuate the premises quickly and orderly.

An evacuation program should not be any one-time practice. It should be covered by a management policy and the policy should be known.

The policy, preferably written, should spell out where the authority lies, both during a real emergency and also for the practice sessions. Who sets the evacuation in motion? Who sounds the alarm and who calls the fire department? What responsibility do supervisors have in a mass exodus? Who has final responsibility for the safety of people and the safeguarding of property? Who can and will make on-the-spot decisions? Unless all this is clear, chaos could result.

To get ready for the real thing, periodic drills should be conducted. These need not be surprise drills; they could be announced in advance. For example: "Next Tuesday morning, between 9 and 10:30 o'clock, we will hold a practice evacuation." Employees should learn what the "clear out" signal is, from whom to take orders, where to find the nearest "open" exit (leaving elevators and inside stairwells for firemen and rescue workers), how to "walk, not run," how to fend for themselves in the event leadership is cut off. Even in a practice drill some rules need to be worked out in advance and explained. These include cutting off telephone conversations without panicking the caller, how to shut off machines, power and automatic equipment, who should pull down the fire doors, whether to lock up or leave unguarded any cash and whether to remove or abandon other valuables, where the emergency first-aid station is located and what services are available. Finally, they should recognize the "all clear" signal and understand how to return to their desks and machines and resume work.

After each drill management would do well to review the procedure. What lessons can be learned? What was the time it took to empty the building? How can this be improved? Did the employees understand what they're expected to do? Were managers and supervisors "on alert" and ready to move into action? What violations were observed, and how will violators be dealt with?

The evacuation procedure should be discussed with managers and foremen regularly. It should also be included in supervisory training classes. A tour showing location of fire extinguishers and hoses and demonstrating their use would be appropriate.

As for new employees, they should have this evacuation procedure explained to them as part of their original indoctrination. Be careful not to leave the impression that the premises are unsafe, but rather take credit for having established a well-thought-out safety precaution program. Don't just talk about it; walk them over to the nearest exit.

This is something that is easily neglected. One tragic experience will make the point unmistakably clear. This is known as "learning by accident." Avoid that possibility by developing a sound policy and safe practice.

CAUSES OF FIRES

In one year approximately 12,000 Americans perish and 300,000 are seriously injured in nearly three million fires. In Canada, there are nearly 900 deaths caused by approximately 79,000 fires.

The chief causes of fires, in order of the toll taken, are:

1. Smoking.
2. Electrical wiring.
3. Heating and cooking equipment.
4. Children playing with matches.
5. Open flames and sparks.
6. Flammable liquids.
7. Suspected arson.
8. Chimneys and flues.
9. Lightning.
10. Spontaneous ignition.

The total loss that is due to fire in one year is estimated at $3 billion in the United States and $250 million in Canada.

SAFETY EDUCATION

When safety problems arise, the best source of information is the National Safety Council, 444 North Michigan Avenue, Chicago, Illinois 60611. This nonprofit, nongovernmental, public service organization operates solely on membership fees and is interested and helpful in all areas of safety. It is dedicated to reducing the number and severity of all types of accidents and occupational illnesses.

It had its origin in 1913 in industry, specifically the steel industry. Because of its usefulness, it soon spread to other industry. From there it was only logical to move to offices. Today its specific areas of interest are: farm, home, industrial, labor, motor transportation, public safety, religious leaders, school and college, state and local safety, traffic, women and youth. A catalog is available listing NSC publications, posters and training aids.

While safety measures are usually associated with the factory or plant, the need for safety education and precautions is just as great in the office. The biggest office hazard is the belief that there is no hazard. The

NSC calls attention to the danger of coffee spills on floors, fracture traps such as lower file drawer left open for someone to trip over, or a loose paper clip on a waxed floor for a women in spike heels to slip on. Open desk drawers, telephone or electric cords, misplaced wastebaskets are all potential danger spots.

The NSC advises holding on to handrails on stairs and using a ladder to reach high shelves. Of course any defective electrical equipment can give an unsuspecting employee the shock treatment. Such electric machines should never be cleaned with flammable fluid.

Razor blades, thumbtacks and pins can bite if not stored in containers. Paper cuts hurt and can become infected. Keep fingers clear when using paper cutters, and pick up broken glass with a paper towel. Lifting can be harmful and overloaded files, with the top drawer opened, can fall forward.

Over 15,000 business firms, schools, public agencies and private individuals are members. The NSC staff, working closely with members and a vast support network of volunteers, generates programs that reach more than 170 million people.

The NSC welcomes inquiries from companies and individuals concerned with the problems of safety, both on and off the job.

BODY MECHANICS

The manner in which an individual stoops, reaches, lifts, carries equipment, sits or stands may increase or lessen fatigue. The worker who understands the normal use of the body and applies this knowledge to his own posture, will be less vulnerable to strain and injury.

Stooping.

1. Stand close to object.
2. Place feet apart with one foot in front of the other so you have firm footing for the task to be done.
3. Bend your hips and knees, lower your body, keep your back in good alignment, and bring your hands down to the object.

Lifting.

1. Grasp the object firmly and as close to the center as possible.
2. Get set for lifting load, have good timing.
3. Lift by pushing with the legs. Straighten the ankles, knees and hips to an upright position.
4. Keep the load as close to the body as possible while lifting.

5. Do not twist the body.
6. Change your direction while lifting by moving your feet.

Carrying.

1. Keep your back as straight as possible.
2. Keep weight load close to the body and centered over your pelvis.
3. Counterbalance your load by shifting part of your body in the opposite direction from the load so your load will be in balance.
4. Put your load down by bending the hips and knees with your back straight and load close to the body.
5. If the load is too heavy—get help.
6. When the load is carried by more than one person, let one be the leader so you have good timing and coordination. This will prevent injury to the lifter or person being lifted.

Pushing.

1. Stand close to the object to be moved.
2. Crouch down with feet apart.
3. Bend your elbows and put your hands on the load at chest level.
4. Lean forward with chest or shoulder against the object. Do not push with arms or shoulder.
5. Keep your back straight. Crouch and push with your legs.

Pulling.

1. Place your feet apart, one foot in back of the other keeping close to the object to be moved. Allow enough room so the forward foot will not be injured.
2. Grasp object firmly as close to its center of gravity as possible.
3. Crouch, lean away from the object, counterbalance weight of the body with the resistance of the load.
4. Pull by straightening your legs. Keep your back straight.
5. Walk backward with crouching strides so the legs do all the work.

Reaching.

1. Use a footstool whenever possible.
2. Stand close to object. Keep center of gravity over the base of support.
3. Place your feet wide apart, one in front of the other so you

have freedom of movement forward and backward as arms are raised and lowered.

4. Keep good body alignment. Move close to object. Do not reach outward to the point of straining.

5. When reaching for an object which is above the head, grip it with palms up and lower it. Keep it close to the body on the way down.

SAFETY RECORDS

To attain high safety it is necessary to know what accidents happened, where, when and type of injuries incurred, and the conditions that caused them. Without good records to study, corrective action cannot be taken.

There are two widely used indexes in safety statistics:

1. The *frequency* rate: the number of occurrences.
2. The *severity* rate: the seriousness of each case.

One accident resulting in 10 days off from work is considered more serious than 10 minor accidents causing no lost time.

SAFETY PAY

As an example of how effective incentives can become, here is the case of Parsons Pine Products, Inc., Ashland, Oregon, as it relates to safety improvement.

Mr. James W. Parsons, president, explains: "Our accident rate was our largest problem. With an experience rate of 160% of base rate— base being $10.36 for our particular operation—we are paying over $100,000 per year to the state accident insurance fund. In late 1976 we went on what is called a 'Retro Plan,' whereby we would be returned premium money not used for accident and some administrative charges. At the start of the Retro Plan we promised our people we would give half of the premium return to them, so it was up to them to work safely.

"Our cost for the whole year was only $2,500. This means we would receive back $89,000 in returned SAIF premiums. The SAIF people are astounded at the change and our employees are ecstatic. Everyone monitors safety now."

The company pays an extra two hours' pay per month to every employee who has not sustained an accident during the quarter.

Factory Safety Poster courtesy of National Safety Council.

529

Office Safety Poster courtesy of National Safety Council.

The Claims Administrator in the Employee Benefits Department of Alcan Smelters & Chemicals, Ltd., in Kitimat, British Columbis, Canada, wrote a letter to be sent to all supervisors, which her employer decided should have broader coverage.

SAFETY

From the Woman's Point of View
by Winnie Gray

It's a so-called, well-known "fact" that a woman is a natural born worrywart and completely illogical. However, if perhaps a few distaff thoughts were correlated, some logic may appear, and I'm thinking particularly about safety. For instance:

As a wife, I used to worry about my husband at work. This was especially true when he worked underground. I would hear horrendous stories of miners sustaining crushing injuries, amputations or becoming a fatality. In every case, there was a cause. The victim didn't treat his dynamite and blasting caps with respect, or didn't hose down before commencing work. I would worry at the thought of trying to raise a family on compensation or, probably worst of all, watching an otherwise strong, healthy man propelling himself around in a wheel chair. When he left for work each day, the worrywart in me would ask, "Will he be next?"

As a mother, I worried about my children and how to prevent them from harming themselves by their immature attitudes and actions. My teen-aged son and his chemistry set were a troublesome combination plus the fact that he liked to experiment with gadgets. One day I brought home a vegetable cutter, and in a matter of minutes, he had scooped a ball of flesh out of his index finger when the gadget's platform suddenly dropped, simply because he was not "expecting the unexpected." On another occasion, I bought a new carving knife and, because he failed to treat it with respect, the back of his hand required four stitches. I couldn't help worrying, "Will his next injury maim him for life?"

When I first wrote this article in 1969, I was a clerk in the Alcan Safety Department. Many changes have taken place since then in both plant operations and my own life. However, as Claims Administrator, I still read all the First Aid Reports and *they* haven't changed. Noting the careless acts, the disregard for safety rules and regulations, and the late reporting of injuries, I become deeply concerned. A woman has difficulty understanding a man's love of danger. Is it because he can no longer find a dragon to slay, or don a suit of armour and tilt a lance at an opponent, that he must find excitement elsewhere?

531

I can sympathize with a man's enthusiasm for fast cars, snowmobiles, boats, planes and hunting, or anything else in which there is an element of risk. But I can't comprehend the reason why he sometimes appears to deliberately expose himself to known hazards in his normal, workaday life. And as I note the injuries for the day, week, month and year, the worrywart in me says, "It's just about time for the next big one. I wonder who it will be?"

OFFICE HAZARDS

The office is considered to be a safer place to work than the factory. It has less heavy equipment and no dangerous raw materials. Yet accidents can and do happen in the office.

Office accidents include:

1. Fires: burns, electric shock, careless smoking.
2. Falls: tripping over objects or down stairways, slipping.
3. Injuries: cuts, punctures, infection.

The causes of office accidents are:

1. Mechanical: dilapidated equipment, machine safety features ignored.
2. Physiological: poor eyesight or hearing, improper lifting.
3. Psychological: taking chances, horseplay.

Accidents can be prevented if the hazards are identified, located and removed.

SMOKE HAZARD AT MEETINGS

"Smoke-filled conference rooms may be a hazard to your health." This warning ought to be posted.

Smoke from an idling cigarette is about twice as toxic as the actual smoke inhaled by the smoker.

Cigarette smoke-filled rooms with poor ventilation build up concentrations of carbon monoxide to the level of several hundred parts per million, exposing both smokers and nonsmokers to toxic hazards. To comprehend what a number like this means, bear in mind that carbon monoxide concentrations of 100 parts per million often occur in garages, tunnels and behind idling automobiles.

Maybe offices should follow the example of the airlines and restaurants and divide rooms into smoking and nonsmoking sections.

Sign of the times: More establishments are banning smoking.

OCCUPATIONAL HEALTH

Never before has the potential threat to the health of the American worker been greater than it is today.

The United States Public Health Service points out that rapid-fire, technological advances are creating a whole new crop of health hazards and a stack of deadly serious statistics.

More than 14,500 U.S. workers died and another 2,200,000 were temporarily or permanently disabled in one year as a result of industrial accidents, according to a National Safety Council report.

Other studies reveal that the average American worker loses at least five days of work annually because of illness or accident, a major percentage of which is due to occupational causes.

Over and beyond these startling statistics is the fundamental challenge of the new occupational health hazards emerging in our new world. Here, for example, are some of the questions being raised:

1. What are the effects of new work environments such as nuclear submarines, submersible oceanographic research vessels and laboratory "clean rooms" on physical and mental health?
2. What is the effect on human health of continuous exposure

to infrared and ultraviolet light and beams of the whole new family of lasers and masers?

3. What is the effect on the human ear—and on the body as a whole—of exposure to sonic booms and ultrasonic sound waves beyond the range of the human ear?

4. Are exotic new chemicals and space-age fuels toxic to humans working with them—and are powerful new pesticides harmful to agricultural workers?

These questions are asked at a time when American corporations are making unprecedented efforts to protect employees against on-the-job health hazards, and tremendous strides have been made in providing in-plant medical and first-aid facilities and protective clothing and devices for workers dealing with dangerous equipment or substances.

The U.S. Public Health Service is concentrating funds on research in the area of occupational health. If the results of this assault could reduce the rate of sick absence from work by only 20%, it would add more than $11 billion to national production. But as the surgeon general's study group points out, far more important than any financial benefits to the nation, would be the elimination of any factor that makes the worker pay with his health or his life for the privilege of having a job.

It is true, of course, that the occupation of a man or woman may adversely affect health especially when the office or plant is dusty, dirty, noisy, risky or generally unpleasant. On-the-job hazards may create physical or emotional ailments.

As serious as the situation is, there may be times when the blame is misplaced. Many ills are blamed on a person's occupation even though he spends only about one-fourth of the week on the job. Very little is said about what he does at home or while traveling to and from his place of business. All too often he may be safer at work than at home.

It is easier for employees to blame the company for injuries, bronchitis, heart attacks and hernias. The source of the trouble is seldom questioned among those who develop disabilities known to be caused by hazards associated with certain working conditions.

OSHA

Companies have generally been concerned about the safety and welfare of their employees. This is the unwritten record over countless years. Now the U.S. Department of Labor, charged with administering OSHA, makes management's concern a requirement of law.

OSHA is the Williams-Steiger Occupational Safety and Health Act of 1970.

Job safety probably got its first big shot in the arm from labor unions. In the 19th century when coal mining was at its peak, so were job death rates because of "Black Lung" disease, a major cause of death. Labor unions in those days fought hard to provide compensation and improve working conditions.

OSHA was devised to totally protect all workers. OSHA is expected to do what no other safety program has been able to do—eliminate or drastically reduce the illnesses and injuries in today's industry.

OSHA does not provide rules and regulations for individual companies to follow. Rather it provides general requirements applicable to all phases of industry.

The Act

OSHA was passed "to assure so far as possible every working man and woman in the nation safe and healthful working conditions and to preserve our human resources."

Its purpose is to:

1. Encourage employers and employees to reduce hazards in the workplace and to implement new or improve existing safety and health programs;
2. Establish "separate but dependent responsibilities and rights" for employers and employees for the achievement of better safety and health conditions;
3. Establish reporting and recordkeeping procedures to monitor job-related injuries and illnesses;
4. Develop mandatory job safety and health standards and enforce them effectively; and
5. Encourage the States to assume the fullest responsibility for establishing and administering their own occupational safety and health programs, which must be "at least as effective as" the Federal program.

While OSHA continually reviews and redefines specific standards and practices, its basic purposes remain constant. OSHA strives to implement its Congressional mandate fully and firmly with fairness to all concerned. In all of its procedures, from standards development through implementation and enforcement, OSHA guarantees employers and employees the right to be fully informed, to participate actively and to appeal its actions.

Standards. The general duty clause of the Act states that each employer "shall furnish to each of his employees employment and a place of employment which are free from recognized hazards that are causing or are likely to cause death or serious physical harm to his employees."

In carrying out its duties under the Act, OSHA is responsible for promulgating legally enforceable standards. OSHA standards may require conditions, or the adoption or use of one or more practices, means, methods or processes reasonably necessary or appropriate to protect workers on the job. It is the employers' responsibility to become familiar with the standards applicable to their establishments and to assure that employees have and use personal protective gear and equipment required for safety. Even in cases where OSHA has not promulgated specific standards, employers are responsible for following the intent of the Act's general duty clause.

OSHA standards fall into three major categories—General Industry, Maritime and Construction. Free single copies of each category may be obtained from the nearest OSHA office.

Inspection. In order to enforce its standards and regulations, OSHA is authorized under the Act to conduct workplace inspections. Every establishment covered by the Act is subject to inspection by OSHA compliance safety and health officers, who are chosen for their knowledge and experience in the occupational safety and health fields, and trained rigorously in OSHA standards and in recognition of the hazards they cover.

With rare exceptions, inspections are conducted without advance notice. In fact, alerting an employer in advance of an OSHA inspection can bring a fine of up to $1,000 and/or a six-month jail term.

If an employer refuses to admit an OSHA compliance officer, or if an employer attempts to interfere with the inspection, the Act allows for appropriate legal action.

Priorities. Obviously, not all five million workplaces covered by the Act can be inspected immediately. The worst situations need attention first. Therefore, OSHA has established a system of inspection priorities.

Imminent danger situations are given top priority. An imminent danger is any condition where there is reasonable certainty that a danger exists that can be expected to cause death or serious physical harm immediately or before the danger can be eliminated through normal enforcement procedures.

Serious physical harm is any type of harm that could cause permanent or prolonged damage to the body; or which, while not damaging the body on a prolonged basis, could cause such temporary disability as to require in-patient hospital treatment.

Temporary disability requiring in-patient hospital treatment includes injuries such as simple fractures, concussions, burns or wounds involving substantial loss of blood and requiring extensive suturing or other healing aids.

Injuries or illnesses that are difficult to observe are classified as serious if they inhibit the bodily system in the performance of its normal functions, cause reduction in physical or mental efficiency or shorten one's life.

Health hazards are included among imminent danger situations, for they also may constitute a serious threat to life. For a health hazard to be considered an imminent danger, there must be a reasonable expectation (1) that toxic substances or dangerous fumes, dusts or gases are present, and (2) that exposure to them will cause irreversible harm to such a degree as to shorten life or cause reduction in physical or mental efficiency, even though the resulting harm is not immediately apparent.

Random inspections are conducted in establishments of all sizes and types, in all parts of the nation.

Citations. After the compliance officer reports to his or her OSHA office, the area director determines what citations, if any, will be issued, and what penalties, if any, will be proposed

Citations inform the employer and employees of the regulations and standards which have been violated, and of the time set for their abatement. The employer will receive citations and notices of proposed penalties by certified mail. The employer must post a copy of each citation at or near the place the violation occurred, for three days or until the violation is abated, whichever is longer.

To assure that protection is offered to employees in the shortest possible time, the compliance officer has authority to issue citations on the worksite, following the closing conference. To do so, the compliance officer must first discuss each apparent violation with his or her area director by telephone and receive approval to issue citations.

Penalties. These are the types of violations which may be cited, and the penalties which may be proposed:

De Minimis: A violation that has no direct or immediate relationship to job safety and health. A notice is issued but citations and proposed penalties are not.

Nonserious Violation: A violation that has a direct relationship to job safety and health, but probably would not cause death or serious physical harm. A proposed penalty of up to $1,000 is discretionary.

Serious Violation: A violation where there is substantial probability that death or serious physical harm could result, and that the employer knew, or should have known, of the hazard. A proposed penalty of up to $1,000 is mandatory.

Imminent Danger: A violation where there is reasonable certainty that a danger exists that can be expected to cause death or serious physical harm immediately or before the danger can be eliminated through normal enforcement procedures.

Other violations for which citations and proposed penalties may be issued are as follows:

- Falsifying records, reports or applications can bring a fine of $10,000 and six months in jail.

- Violations of posting requirements can bring a civil penalty of $1,000.

- Assaulting a compliance officer, or otherwise resisting, opposing, intimidating or interfering with a compliance officer in the performance of his or her duties is a criminal offense, subject to a fine of not more than $5,000 and imprisonment for not more than three years.

In addition, for any employer who willfully or repeatedly violates the Act, penalties of up to $10,000 for each such violation will be assessed. If an employer is convicted of a willful violation that has resulted in the death of an employee, the offense is punishable by a fine of not more than $10,000 or by imprisonment up to six months, or both. A second conviction doubles these maximum penalties.

Employer Responsibilities. As an employer, you must:

1. Meet your general duty responsibility to provide a hazard-free workplace and comply with the occupational safety and health standards, rules and regulations issued under the Act.
2. Be familiar with mandatory OSHA standards and make copies available to employees for review upon request.
3. Inform all employees about OSHA.
4. Examine workplace conditions to make sure they conform to applicable safety and health standards.
5. Remove or guard hazards.
6. Make sure employees have and use safe tools and equipment (including personal protective equipment) and that such equipment is properly maintained.
7. Use color codes, posters, labels or signs to warn employees of potential hazards.
8. Establish or update operating procedures and communicate them so that employees follow safety and health requirements for their own protection.
9. Provide medical examinations when required by OSHA standards.
10. Report to the nearest OSHA office, within 48 hours, the occurrence of any employment accident which is fatal to one

538

or more employees or which results in the hospitalization of five or more employees.

11. Keep OSHA-required records of work-related injuries and illnesses, and post the annual summary during the entire month of February each year.

12. Post at a prominent location within the workplace the OSHA poster informing employees of their rights and responsibilities.

13. Cooperate with the OSHA compliance officer by furnishing names of authorized employee representatives who may be asked to accompany the compliance officer during the inspection. (If none, the compliance officer will consult with a reasonable number of employees concerning safety and health in the workplace.)

14. Not discriminate against employees who properly exercise their rights under the Act.

15. Post OSHA citations of apparent violations of standards or of the general duty clause at or near the worksite involved. Each citation, or copy thereof, shall remain posted until the violation has been abated, or for three working days, whichever is longer.

16. Abate cited violations within the prescribed period.

Employer Rights. As an employer, you have the right to:

1. Seek advice and off-site consultation as needed by writing, calling or visiting the nearest OSHA office.

2. Be active in your industry association's involvement in job safety and health.

3. Request and receive proper identification of the OSHA compliance officer prior to inspection of the workplace.

4. Be advised by the compliance officer of the reason for an inspection.

5. Have an opening and closing conference with the compliance officer.

6. File a Notice of Contest with the nearest OSHA area director within 15 working days of receipt of a notice of citation and proposed penalty.

7. Apply to OSHA for a temporary variance from a standard if unable to comply because of the unavailability of materials, equipment or personnel to make necessary changes within the required time.

8. Apply to OSHA for a permanent variance from a standard if you can furnish proof that your facilities or method of operation provide employee protection that is at least as effective as that required by the standard.

9. Take an active role in developing job safety and health standards through participation in OSHA Standards Advisory Committees, through nationally recognized standards setting organizations, and through evidence and views presented in writing or at hearings.
10. Avail yourself, if you are a small business employer, of long-term loans through the Small Business Administration (SBA) to help bring your establishment into compliance, either before or after an OSHA inspection.
11. Be assured of the confidentiality of any trade secrets observed by an OSHA compliance officer during an inspection.

Employee Responsibilities. As an employee, you should:

1. Read the OSHA poster at the jobsite.
2. Comply with all applicable OSHA standards.
3. Follow all employer safety and health rules and regulations, and wear or use prescribed protective equipment while engaged in work.
4. Report hazardous conditions to the supervisor.
5. Report any job-related injury or illness to the employer and seek treatment promptly.
6. Cooperate with the OSHA compliance officer conducting an inspection if he or she inquires about safety and health conditions in your workplace.
7. Exercise your rights under the Act in a responsible manner.

Employee Rights. As an employee, you have the right to:

1. Review copies of any of the OSHA standards, rules, regulations and requirements that the employer should have available at the workplace.
2. Request information from your employer on safety and health hazards in the area, on precautions that may be taken, and on procedures to be followed if an employee is involved in an accident or exposed to toxic substances.
3. Request (in writing) the OSHA area director to conduct an inspection if you believe hazardous conditions or violations of standards exist in your workplace.
4. Have your name withheld from your employer, upon request to OSHA, if you file a written and signed complaint.
5. Be advised of OSHA actions regarding your complaint and have an informal review, if requested, of any decision not to make an inspection or not to issue a citation.
6. File a complaint to OSHA within 30 days if you believe you have been discriminated against, discharged, demoted or

otherwise penalized because of asserting an employee right under the Act, and be notified by OSHA of its determination within 90 days of filing.

7. Have the authorized employee representative where you work accompany the OSHA compliance officer during the inspection tour.

8. Respond to questions from the OSHA compliance officer, particularly if there is no authorized employee representative accompanying the compliance officer.

9. Observe any monitoring or measuring of hazardous materials and have the right of access to records on those materials, as specified under the Act.

10. Request a closing discussion with the compliance officer following an inspection.

11. Submit a written request to the National Institute for Occupational Safety and Health (NIOSH) for information on whether any substance in your workplace has potential toxic effects in the concentrations being used, and have your name withheld from your employer if you so request.

12. Object to the abatement period set in the citation issued to your employer by writing to the OSHA area director within 15 working days of the issuance of the citation.

13. Be notified by your employer if he or she applies for a variance from an OSHA standard, testify at a variance hearing, and appeal the final decision if you disagree with it.

14. Submit information or comment to OSHA on the issuance, modification or revocation of OSHA standards, and request a public hearing.

To both employers and employees OSHA says, "You are encouraged to learn all you can about OSHA, its aims, policies, programs and practices, because you are the reason for them. And the more you know about OSHA, the better you can contribute to its pursuit of safer and more healthful working conditions for all Americans.

Posters

Under the Act, employers are responsible for posting a notice of employee rights and obligations. OSHA is now printing these required posters in Spanish for companies with a high percentage of Spanish-speaking employees. They are supplied at no cost to the employer.

While the law does not require posters in Spanish, no matter what percentage of Spanish-speaking employees, it is advisable to display them. Not only will these employees appreciate it, but it might help relations with OSHA inspectors. In case anyone wonders, Spanish posters cannot be used instead of English ones if the employees do not speak Spanish.

Apprehension

At the time the law was passed there was a feeling, not yet substantiated, that OSHA is a dangerous fraud. Under the guise of promoting industrial safety and health, it is a convenient tool for harassment, another attempt by the mushrooming bureaucracy to weaken the free enterprise system so fundamental to the nation.

As an arm of growing federal power, OSHA has produced a myriad of standards, regulations and edicts which are being enforced by an army of compliance officers. Their visits have resulted in an enormous number of fines, citations and costly demands. The OSHA standards, some of which are looked upon as ridiculous and some as impossible, have the effect of giving the government the power to control and even destroy business.

CHAPTER VII

EMPLOYEE SERVICES

COMPANY–SPONSORED EMPLOYEE ACTIVITIES

THERE ARE two kinds of employee activities going on in practically all companies. Some are sponsored by the company and others are promoted by employees.

Common among company-sponsored employee activities are Service Recognition Dinner, Holiday Party, Picnic and the like. Of course, many companies go much further. Much depends on the location, size of organization and the nature of the business.

Company-sponsored events are generally organized and promoted by the company. This is usually done through an official committee appointed for the occasion. This committee is often composed of high-level management personnel and, unfortunately, does not always have employee representation.

Where employees are not included in the planning, it is not surprising if the results are disappointing. The block booking for a musical show or ice carnival may excite the personnel director but few others. The summertime excursion to a place of historic interest may find no takers. Some experiences show employees to be apathetic toward the company junket, preferring to arrange their own social life, apart from work.

Some companies question the time, effort and money expended. The headaches and problems connected with outings, picnics and parties may not be worth the trouble.

Companies should not promote events just for the sake of promoting. Employee activities should be sponsored in answer to a need. In a Service Recognition Dinner the company may logically expect most eligible employees, particularly the honored guests, to attend. At other functions, such as the Christmas Party, it may be unrealistic to hope to reach everyone. For dances or special attractions that appeal to limited numbers, a break-even attendance should satisfy. Not everybody enjoys going out to a night baseball game, or a concert, or an opera, or a circus.

The best way to appeal to the greatest possible number is to conduct the affair with dignity in a first-class location, with a good menu, first-run entertainment and quality prizes. If an employee activity is worth doing, it is worth doing well.

EMPLOYEE-PROMOTED ACTIVITIES

In addition to company-sponsored employee activities there are usually other activities promoted by the employees themselves. These are generally more limited in scope than a program planned by the company for all employees. These employee-promoted activities are offered company-wide but they appeal to special interest groups.

They are often built by and around one certain individual who has a personal interest in some project. He talks it up among his friends, develops enough enthusiasm to bring it to company attention, gets official sanction and possibly some measure of financial support, and the program is underway. Some of these programs fall by the wayside when the spearhead leaves or loses interest.

This is how many bowling leagues start. Someone, usually not from management, gets the idea, sells it all around, and makes it run. Softball teams, basketball teams, volleyball teams, men or women, get their impetus and development this way. Some of these activities continue year after year, under rotating leadership, while others run their course and die.

Less common than athletic or recreational programs are projects which appeal to only certain individuals. A few employees who share a common hobby might want to meet once a month on convenient company premises. These could be stamp or coin clubs, poetry clubs, foreign travel groups, home movie fans and the like. Many choral groups are conducted on just this type of informal basis.

The company gets involved by granting official endorsement, some form of financial assistance, publicity and use of company facilities such as meeting rooms, printing, telephone and house organ. There is no rule of thumb on how much financial support to give since these activities vary so much. A bowling league involves regulars and substitutes for 35 weeks plus possibly an awards banquet, whereas a golf-driving exhibition is a one-time occurrence. Without any guide then, most companies are willing to pay entrance fees, league costs, perhaps uniforms, and something toward the group's treasury to be used for prizes or a dinner.

Since the company is not sponsoring these informal employee activities, it should not attempt to run them. It must, however, keep a watchful eye to prevent an unrestrained eager-beaver from going too far at the risk of possibly embarrassing the company.

SERVICE RECOGNITION

It is customary, in large companies especially, to recognize long-service employees in a special way.

The most common form of recognition is a service pin. It is usually issued every five years beginning with the fifth year. For the men it is a lapel pin and for the women, an identical service button with a clasp instead of a pin. There are variations. Men may get theirs on a tie clasp or with cuff links, and women possibly as a charm for a bracelet or a dress pin.

The same style pin is awarded each time except that the number of years is different. Sometimes a small gem is added to the longer service pins.

In addition to the pin, gifts are sometimes given to recognize length of service. A five-year employee, for example, may get a desk calendar suitably inscribed with his name and the number of years. His ten-year gift could well be a desk pen set. Companies prefer to give a gift that the employee can and will use and display proudly at his desk. The problem is that such gift ideas are almost impossible to apply to factory workers. This leads to giving personal gifts, preferably something the employee and his family can use every day at home.

It is not uncommon to award United States Savings Bonds. The face amount of these bonds increases with the length of service. Gift certificates or some other type of monetary award may be substituted.

The traditional service gift is a good "name" watch for 25 years of service. The only problem here is "how to top this" at 30 years and beyond. It is best to have an established policy in effect.

Gifts, pins and other awards may be presented ceremoniously or without fanfare. A five-year employee may get his service pin in the manager's office and be given a ticket for a free lunch in the cafeteria at the same time. A 20-year employee may be escorted up front to the vice-president's office and possibly even taken out to lunch to dignify the occasion.

The Annual Party

Most companies that have some recognition program plan a dinner once a year, off the premises generally, in some hotel or country club.

This is a gala event to which all honored guests, as well as those previously honored, are invited. The program includes flowers and music and possibly entertainment. It may feature a speaker, usually the president of the firm, who takes this opportunity to thank his loyal, long-service group of employees, and who may also reminisce a bit about "the struggle of the early days." Once a year he is entitled to get sentimental.

Some firms use this annual dinner also to distribute pins and awards. The disadvantage is that an employee could well be months beyond his anniversary date before he receives his recognition. Also, an employee who terminates between his anniversary date and the party will no longer be around to receive the award he earned.

The author prefers to recognize each individual on his anniversary date, the day which is significant to him. This is the day, like his birthday, which is personal to him, when he is unlike co-workers. It is his big day! Putting 25 red roses on the desk of an employee the day of his 25th employment anniversary makes much more sense than handing him a watch after he's been with the company 25 years, eight months, and seven days.

Just when to begin a recognition program can be a problem, not at the start but years later when the earlier pattern cannot be undone. Small or young firms may be tempted to invite everyone with five years of service out to dinner. After the firm gets older and the eligible group larger, this arrangement may no longer be practical. But how can it be stopped?

The large banks and utilities, with their record of employee seniority, usually have "25-year clubs." This does not mean that employees with less than 25 years of service are ignored, but it does mean that the "quarter century group" are feted in grand style. One large utility has 25% of its workers in its 25-year club, a record of seniority which in today's fluid employment market is truly amazing.

Do It Up Right

Seniority and length of service are important to a stable company. Any form of recognition, therefore, deserves to be a quality program. Do it up well, or don't do it at all. Above all, be sincere in your appreciation of loyalty and long service. If a dinner is planned, schedule it in a "big" location (where at least some employees may ordinarily never get), have a good dinner, preceded by a reception and possibly a receiving line of corporate officers, and do the party up in style. Don't make it too formal, however, or some rank-and-file workers may be scared away. Give them an event that they can look forward to and remember afterwards.

The recognition must always be personal, not automatic. Don't arrange to have a clerk in the personnel office, where records are convenient, send out a standard, official, preprinted card or free lunch ticket routinely. This defeats the purpose. Whatever you give, even a pin or a wallet service card, should be delivered and presented personally, properly gift wrapped, and climaxed with a warm hand clasp or other congratulations.

Any anniversary is important to the individual. But it is just as important to the company, isn't it?

STOCK SERVICE AWARDS

Recognition of long service by employees of Levi Strauss & Company, San Francisco, California, takes on a new dimension. Service pins and similar awards for multiples of five years' service are accompanied by shares of Levi's stock.

All of Levi's nearly 35,000 employees, with the exception of officers, directors and division presidents, are eligible to receive one share of the company's stock for each year of service. The shares are awarded to an employee at five-year intervals.

The 127-year-old diversified apparel company estimates that at present employment levels the awards annually will involve about 10,000 shares to 2,000 employees. The company will pay the employees' withholding tax on the stock awards.

The brochure highlighting this policy explains the program was installed "because of its recognition that the continuing success of Levi Strauss & Company is largely based upon the dedicated service of its employees."

SERVICE RECOGNITION AWARD

The Pennsylvania State University, University Park, Pennsylvania, values the service of long tenure employees, faculty and staff alike.

Those who complete 25 years of regular full-time service (the last 10 years of which are continuous) are awarded an official Penn State captain's chair or rocking chair. An engraved brass plate is included with the chair, as well as a certificate mounted under glass on a walnut plaque.

This beautiful piece of furniture, usually displayed by the recipient at home, serves as an act of goodwill, and the cost to the university is nominal. The chair seems to be an especially good award because it is sufficiently utilitarian so as to enter the daily life of the employee.

RESPONSIBILITY FOR JOB-RELATED OUTSIDE EVENTS

How much responsibility does a company have when an employee gets hurt or encounters some other problem outside the regular job but at an employee function that is job-related?

Maybe the first thing to do is separate the functions into two groups: (1) those that are directed by the company, and (2) those that are run by the employees.

Certainly if a company sends a group of employees out officially, say to a convention, the measure of responsibility is great. These people are, in effect, engaging in company business even though they are away from the office or plant and involved beyond work in pleasure activities. The fact remains that they were directed to go, under company sponsorship, for the good of the firm.

The measure of responsibility is less at a company social event, such as a Christmas party or picnic. True, the activity is company sponsored and employees attend because of loyalty. If a softball player gets hurt, is the company liable for medical bills and wage payments for subsequent time off? It all depends. Possibly the regular group insurance program will cover the situation so there may be no problem from that end. But what about pay for any time off?

There are many questions to be answered first. Actually, the employee was not ordered to play ball; he could have watched as a spectator. Did he play at his own risk possibly because his age was beyond that of his teammates? If the company feels responsibility toward an employee in such circumstances, does this sense of responsibility carry over to guests, such as member of his family?

The chances are an employee or guest who suffered injury at a company function would be hard-pressed to make a case unless he could prove negligence on the part of the employer.

If a car is dented on the approved parking lot, a coat stolen from the authorized checkroom, a watch or ring picked up in the washroom, time lost because of excessive sunburn, etc.—these can hardly be blamed on the sponsoring company although in many cases the employer may want to make good.

The measure of responsibility becomes least for sports events and other activities which are conducted by the employees themselves and not run by the company. This is true even when the company makes a contribution, say for bowling shirts carrying the firm's name. Bowling, to continue with that example, in the name of the company does not officially represent the firm. This is more of a group of fellow workers bowling for their personal enjoyment.

When 10 women want to celebrate a birthday by going to dinner and a show, is the employer involved in any way simply because these women work together in his company? What about a group of employees on a weekend excursion to Las Vegas whose return flight is delayed for some unexpected reason. Will they be paid if they miss a day's work?

When 20 or 30 men and women working in the same company want to form a chorus because they enjoy singing, is the employer liable for what may happen to or from rehearsals anymore than a church is legally responsible for the members of its choir?

It is hard to generalize. In some cases, a company may be legally liable. In others the company, although not responsible, may wish to help. In still other cases, the employees should be made to understand they are entirely on their own should anything happen.

What it really boils down to is that this is not a legal matter as much as it is a personnel problem. Legally a company may easily be absolved, but it must still live with its employees. Therefore, it may want to do the right thing, whatever is appropriate under the circumstances.

CREDIT UNION

A credit union is an independent financial cooperative organized for the purpose of promoting thrift among its members and providing loans for virtually any worthwhile purpose.

Participation in a credit union is entirely voluntary, but members must have a common bond of association. Examples of common bonds include working for the same company or belonging to the same church, fraternal group, labor union or closely knit community.

Credit unions are chartered by the state, provincial or federal government, and are incorporated under credit union law. The government that issues the charter supervises the credit union operation.

Under most laws, a credit union charter is granted to seven or more persons, and to a field of membership of 200 or more.

The governing body is a board of directors, whose members generally serve one-year terms. Expirations and vacancies are filled by the election of members at the annual meeting. The officers are president, vice-president, treasurer, and secretary. They are elected by and from the board.

The board of directors appoints a credit union manager. Depending on the size of the credit union, the manager might be the only paid employee. However, a trend has developed in past years for credit unions to hire additional personnel trained to serve as financial counselors, tellers, and loan officers.

This trend is due in part to the need for qualified personnel to handle the new and better services credit unions provide their members. The "professionalism of credit union personnel" also stems from the dramatic growth credit unions have experienced individually and collectively in recent years.

There are now more than 22,000 credit unions in the United States. More than 37 million Americans belong, with new members joining at the rate of 2.5 million a year, or about five every minute. Between 1970 and 1977, credit unions' total assets tripled to more than $54 billion.

Credit unions are best known as America's consumer lenders. Between 1970 and 1977 credit union share of the consumer installment loan market jumped from 12.7% to 17.2%. At the end of 1977, loans outstanding totalled more than $35 billion.

The largest single portion (43.7%) of the overall credit union loan portfolio in mid-1978 was the $20.5 billion held in automobile loans, accounting for 23.1% of the total auto lending market as of June 30, 1978.

Loans for other durable goods—such as boats, furniture and home furnishings—comprise about 13% of the credit unions' loan portfolio. Residential and home improvement loans account for about 10.5%. Personal loans for such things as vacations, education, medical expenses, tax payment and debt consolidations account for about 35%. This personal loan category is where credit unions most visibly continue to fill a void left by other lenders who either are not willing to offer such loans, or offer them only at very high interest rates.

Low Rates Attract

One of the main reasons Americans are turning to credit unions is their low interest rates. Each of the nation's more than 13,000 federally-chartered credit unions is prohibited by law from charging more than 12% annual percentage rate (APR) on any loan. And, although a number of the 9,000 state-chartered credit unions are permitted by their state regulators to charge higher interest rates, few have exceeded the traditional 12% limit. Many charge even less on certain loans, particularly for automobiles.

"Even if a credit union doesn't charge the lowest interest rate on a loan in a particular area, it still has a positive effect on the consumer," says Herb Wegner, president of the Credit Union National Association, Inc. (CUNA), the national trade association for U.S. credit unions. "You can be sure that the institution that beats our rate wouldn't be offering such a deal if we weren't in there competing," he explained.

On the savings side, nearly two-thirds of all credit unions return better than 5½% on member savings accounts—compared with legal ceilings of 5% for regular commercial bank savings accounts and 5¼% at savings and loans. Credit unions are permitted to offer members the higher return since they are cooperatives, operated on a not-for-profit basis. Extra earnings, after operating expenses and reserves, are returned to the member owners in the form of dividends or new and better services.

In 1966, total credit union savings deposits were $10.1 billion. By 1976, they had almost quadrupled to $39.1 billion. Today, they exceed $45 billion.

Saving at a credit union is becoming even more attractive as federal credit unions can now join the many state-chartered credit unions in offering share certificates that pay up to 7¾% on $500 or more for periods ranging from 90 days to six years, as well as three new types of savings accounts, each with a different twist to give savers more flexibility. Notice accounts require members to give at least 90 days written notice of intent to withdraw funds from higher yield accounts; minimum balance accounts require a specified amount to be kept in for an entire dividend period; split-rate accounts pay one rate for a minimum balance and a higher rate on funds in excess of that balance. Each of these accounts allows members to decide which method of savings is in their best financial interest for their own lifestyle.

More than Loans and Savings

While loans and savings accounts remain the primary credit union focus, many credit unions are expanding their value to members by using modern technology to implement services that will provide for *all* their consumer financial needs.

Together, credit unions are in the process of developing a national financial and support system to facilitate liquidity management and the clearing and settlement of transactions. This system will enable credit unions to efficiently offer such modern services as share drafts, credit cards, 30-year mortgage loans and funds transfer services.

Credit union progress in harnessing the new technology to benefit consumers has been impressive. A good example of this is the share draft—a payable-through draft which may be used by a credit union member in a manner as convenient as checking to obtain funds from his or her transaction account without going to the credit union office.

The share draft program enables some 500,000 members of more than 1,000 credit unions to receive earnings on funds that can be conveniently withdrawn while making purchases or paying bills. After the member writes a draft to make a purchase, pay a bill or receive cash, the draft clears through the bank clearing system like any other cash item such as a personal check, money order or travelers check.

Convenient access to low cost credit makes the fledgling credit union credit card program an important consumer service. Members can use credit-union-issued credit cards at any of the thousands of retail and service outlets that accept them. Most of the credit unions presently issuing credit cards are charging 12% APR on card charges, computed from the date of posting. Where state law requires a grace period, a higher interest rate may be charged. Other card issuers generally charge up to 18%.

More Americans will now have another access to residential mortgage loans at less cost as new powers granted by Congress and the state legislatures enable credit unions to significantly increase their share of the home mortgage market. Many will begin offering mortgages for the first time. Credit union mortgage loans are competitively priced, but generally do not include prepayment penalties, and have lower closing costs in comparison to most other lenders. Credit unions also tend to finance ordinary rather than luxury homes, and try harder to accommodate the riskier borrower. As a result, the availability of another source of housing funds should provide a needed boost to the home-building industry. Credit unions are also stepping up their home improvement and mobile home loan activity as a result of liberalized maturity periods.

By operating on a pro-consumer, pro-competitive basis, rather than from a profit motive, credit unions are continuing to be a valuable part of the nation's economic system. Many credit union services, such as share drafts, are not particularly cost-efficient from an institutional standpoint, but are provided because members need and want the service.

The basic intent to encourage thrift and to provide personalized financial service to American consumers will remain unchanged even as credit union operations become more sophisticated and take advantage of new technology. The technological advancements will simply make it easier for consumers to have access to these services and their money.

UNDERSTANDING THE C/U MOVEMENT

In San Francisco's Chinatown a credit union exists solely for members of the Lee family.

American sailors and marines around the world can join the $500 million Navy credit union.

Arabian horse owners have their own group in California.

There are credit unions for ex-drug addicts, high school students, labor union members, government employees, teachers and prison inmates.

Thousands of companies have credit unions for employees. Churches have them for members. Some communities have them for local residents.

The concept was devised as a community pool in the 1850's by Friedrich Raiffeisen, mayor of a small German town, to help farmers avoid usurious rates. Alphonse Desjardins started the movement on the North American continent in 1900 in Levis, Quebec to fight 1200% interest charged by loan sharks. In 1909, the first credit union in the United States was organized in New Hampshire. The first state law was in Massachusetts, and in 1934 a federal law was passed permitting credit unions anywhere in the United States.

The credit union movement began as the place a person went for a small loan he intended to pay back quickly. Originally credit unions provided small loans to people with a "common bond" of association who pooled their savings to help each other. Their good record on loan repayments supports their slogan, "A person's character is his best collateral."

The reason for credit union popularity and success is easy to understand. The credit union pays good dividends, and at the same time extends credit far more freely and at lower true cost in the long run than most other sources of consumer financing.

The explanation is simple. A credit union requires no heavy capital, no elaborate space, no competitive location. Generally its officers serve without pay. The borrowers are dependable, and losses are few. And don't forget its exemption from taxes.

It is, in actual fact, an organization of common bond membership, run by the members themselves, for the benefit of the members. Therein lies the story of its successful history over the past many years.

Once a group of people obtain a charter, this is what they do:

1. put their money (shares) into a common fund,
2. elect some of their members (as directors) to manage the fund,
3. lend money to each other from the fund,
4. charge interest for the use of that money,
5. and with the interest (credit union income)
6. pay the cost of running the credit union, and then
7. distribute the rest of the earnings to shareholders (as dividends).

But credit unions are no longer that simple. They have progressed to the point where they are now invading the turf of commercial banks. They are the nation's fastest growing financial institution.

Banks, savings and loans, and currency exchanges are becoming concerned about the competition.

Its growth is spurred by more professional management, federal deposit insurance and looser definition by regulatory authorities of "common bond."

UNITED STATES SAVINGS BONDS

The United States Treasury Department encourages employers to aid employees in the systematic purchase of United States Savings Bonds, usually through payroll deduction. Those employees who participate on a voluntary basis agree to have a specified amount deducted from each paycheck which is then applied toward the purchase of a bond. As soon as the full purchase price has been accumulated the bond is issued.

A representative of the government may call to request the company to conduct a campaign to promote the sale of bonds to employees. Many companies go all out to support such a patriotic program. Even those who do not actively promote the drive, nevertheless do cooperate as a courtesy to employees who may wish to use the convenience of payroll deduction for their purchase of bonds.

The representative will emphasize that a payroll savings plan:

1. Provides a valuable employee benefit: it is a foolproof way to establish a habit of saving money regularly.
2. Boosts employee morale: it contributes to team spirit through a company-wide activity.
3. Supplements retirement plans: augments company pensions.
4. Contributes to a healthier business climate: nearly one-fifth of the privately-held portion of the federal debt is represented by Savings Bonds.

There are a few things that should be done to get a drive underway:

1. Make a personal commitment: the chief executive should give visible support.
2. Endorse the effort: set goals and timetables.
3. Announce the plan: use letters and company publications.
4. Select good leadership: pick a top, promotion-minded colleague to serve as chairperson.

5. Build a representative team: name canvassers carefully—one for each 12 to 15 employees.
6. Take advantage of available assistance: requisition free promotional material and let the local representative advise.
7. Generate interest and enthusiasm: train leaders and instruct canvassers.
8. Conduct the campaign: move quickly to take advantage of momentum.
9. Give credit where it is due: upon completion, recognize workers with personal appreciation, possibly awards.

The steps to a successful payroll savings campaign are:

1. Establish timetable for a person-to-person solicitation.
2. Inform all levels of management about the campaign.
3. Prepare letter to all employees urging participation.
4. Appoint canvassers to contact employees individually; present bond buyers make good salespersons.
5. Personalize authorization cards by inserting names of employees.
6. Publicize campaign with posters and in employee publication.
7. Indoctrinate canvassers in sales techniques.
8. Invite every employee, by personal contact, either to join or to increase the amount of present bond allotment.
9. Prepare final report for senior executive and bond representative.
10. Recognize work of canvassers with note of thanks.
11. Request citation from Savings Bonds Division after reaching campaign goal.
12. Install a sustaining program through which new employees can enroll.

In any type of employee drive—and the campaign for U.S. Savings Bonds is no exception—the employees should not be coerced into signing up. The company sponsorship should not be construed as pressure. Employee participation should be voluntary.

Some employees want to buy these bonds and appreciate the convenience of obtaining them the easy way through the company. Others, and there is nothing wrong with this approach, need encouragement in making up their minds to support a program which is in their own interest as well as that of the nation. Those, however, who are forced or embarrassed into buying bonds against their will, most likely will cash them in as soon as the minimum waiting time has passed. This accomplishes nothing except needless work and employee resentment.

CAPITAL ACCUMULATION PLANS

Many companies provide their employees with an opportunity to save money in capital accumulation plans. These plans take on a variety of forms.

The first thought of an employee savings program is the thrift plan. Employees are given a chance to set aside part of their earnings in company-encouraged savings accounts. The employers then match part or all of the sum the employees invest.

With employee consent, payroll makes regular deductions in whatever amount the employee designates and authorizes. The employee receives credit for all interest earned. The combined funds are invested by the company in bank accounts, in company shares, or in government or corporate securities. Withdrawals are possible, subject to rules. Upon termination the employee is paid off.

Thrift or savings plans of this type usually continue uninterrupted during the period of employment. But there are variations that are designed for shorter duration.

One innovation is the vacation club savings program. It functions on the same principle as a regular thrift program except it lasts for only one year at a time. Every year, probably the first week in May (or possibly January 1) the employees are reminded about the vacation club program for the following term and invited to sign up if interested. Checks are distributed (or made available) at the end of the twelve months.

Another similar plan is the Christmas club. This is a 50-week deduction program that pays off automatically in time for holiday shopping. An employee who terminates may request a refund or may continue by making deposits direct.

In both the vacation club and the Christmas club plans arrangements are made with a nearby bank which maintains a separate account for every employee who elects to participate. The bank pays interest on all accounts in full, and the bank also issues individual pay-out checks in the employees' names. The checks are generally distributed through the company, not mailed to the employees' homes.

More and more companies are offering another type of contribution vehicle which is usually a supplement to the company's regular pension plan. It looks like the typical savings program but is modified to take advantage of Section 401(k), one of the tax-law provisions that grew out of amendments to the federal tax code of 1978. It allows employees to contribute a portion of their earnings on a pre-tax rather than after-tax basis.

It should be pointed out that the appeal of these newer plans is that they are tax dodgers and therein lies an element of risk. The tax implications are complex and uncertain. The changes have produced an unintended windfall, and many advisers believe the amendments were never designed to let employees shelter large sums of their income. The final interpretation could someday produce rules by the Internal Revenue Service that could establish a tax liability for either the company or the employee. Apart from any tax monies that might then be due, untangling the resulting payroll mess would pose a horrendous task.

A company thrift program is intended to establish in employees the habit of saving money systematically. With the cooperation of their employers, they develop thrift and increase their independence. It gives them a "nest egg" to fall back on in time of necessity. As time goes on, the number of participants and the dollar volume tend to increase.

SUGGESTION SYSTEM

A suggestion system is a formalized procedure for getting ideas out of the heads of employees on to paper, evaluated and then into the hands of someone who can implement them. These formalized suggestion systems can be either successful or not so successful depending upon how well they are planned and executed.

In order for a suggestion to be considered eligible under a formal suggestion system, all five of the following elements must be present:

1. The suggestion must pose a problem, potential problem or opportunity to improve an existing process or situation.
2. The suggestion must present a solution to the problem posed. (Therefore, ideas which merely complain about an existing situation but offer no solution are not suggestions within the terms of a suggestion program.)
3. The suggestion is written on a prescribed form or blank.
4. The suggestion is signed by the suggester.
5. The suggestion form has been received and date/time stamped in the suggestion office.

There are several different types of suggestion systems. The most popular is the fully-identified system in which the suggester is known to the evaluator and all members of the suggestion office as well as to his fellow employees. At the other end of the scale is the anonymous system, which used to be quite popular but which has subsequently lost favor, in which the identity of the suggester remains secret. Very few anonymous systems are in existence today; these are the systems which employ a number with the suggester retaining a matching numbered stub. In between these two extremes lie the other types of systems which are: partially identified and signature optional.

Essentials for Administration

A suggestion system should not be taken lightly; it will require time and effort to make it work properly. There are five essentials of a successful suggestion system program. These are:

1. The suggestion must be written and the idea must be adequately described. The rules of the suggestion plan must have been communicated to the individual suggester, preferably right on the back of the suggestion form.
2. The supervisor must be part of the suggestion chain because, sooner or later, that supervisor will likely be called upon to evaluate the suggestion. Properly-motivated supervisors are essential to the stimulation of flow of good suggestions.
3. The awards must be commensurate with the value of the savings to be expected from the implementation of the suggestion.
4. Management must be involved with the system from the top down because if insufficient personnel or money is allocated to the operation of the system, it will die a swift death from bottlenecks or disinterest.
5. Evaluation and reward for adopted suggestions must be made in a timely manner. Interest in the program will soon be lost if recognition and reward are too far distant from the inception of the idea in the first place.

There need to be three separate publications guiding the administration of a successful system.

The first is a rule book wherein all questions concerning eligibility, both of suggestions and suggesters are spelled out. Procedures for the calculation of awards, both tangible and intangible, are also in this book. (A tangible award is one with which it is possible to calculate actual dollar savings. An intangible award is one in which this calculation is not possible; safety awards, energy conservation awards and environmental improvement suggestions are in this category since it is difficult to quantify the dollar savings on awards of this type.)

The second book is one which guides the supervisor. This is the individual who stimulates the flow of suggestions and who must have a positive attitude toward the program. Frequently, this will be the person contacted for the evaluation of the suggestion submitted by a subordinate. The supervisor, ordinarily, is in the best position to recognize the value or the pitfalls of a given suggestion.

The third is a brochure which is distributed to the employee himself.

It solicits his ideas, provides the award formula and instructs him in the mechanisms for making a proper submission.

All three of these brochures or manuals must be published and available to all members of the plan.

Eligibility Limitations

All members of a company, agency or manufacturing entity should be eligible to participate in a plan. Many companies, however, limit eligibility to employees below the management level; where the management level begins varies from company to company, of course. Suggestions which could be considered part of a person's normal job are very often not eligible for suggestion award consideration. However, when a person makes a suggestion out of his normal area of competence, he or she should certainly be considered for proper reward.

Certain areas are, of course, "off limits" with regard to suggestions. Suggestions which come in the field of corporate policy, legal problems (which can include patentable ideas, and union management relations) are usually excluded from suggestion eligibility.

Suggestions are accepted on a "first in" basis, that is, when duplicate suggestions come in, the earlier one is recognized as having priority for award. When two or more individuals originate a suggestion (and all of their names are signed on the suggestion blank) they are eligible to divide the award among themselves. This is known as a "joint" award.

Suggestion forms are normally available in the suggestion office or at selected suggestion information distribution points throughout the company. Provisions for the collection of suggestions may be made at these distribution points, or the suggesters may be directed to send them through the mail. The suggestion information distribution points also afford an area for display of promotional material relating to the system.

Many companies use a suggestion committee to evaluate suggestions. The members of this committee should come from all departments of the firm because, in many cases, it will be necessary to review not only production but also cost accounting, personnel impact and sales reaction to proposed changes. Also, an award decided upon by a committee is more apt to be accepted by the suggester than one which is perhaps decreed by a single individual. Management needs to be prepared to staff such a working committee with management personnel who are available, knowledgeable and interested. The decision of the suggestion committee is the final one and this needs to be specified somewhere in the company rules.

A good publicity program is essential to maintain interest in the suggestion system. Included may be posters, handbills, letters from management, honor rolls of successful suggestions, and stories about winners and their winning ideas. If the company has a house organ, stories of this nature will find a ready place in it.

The Payoff is Important

The courts have decided that a contract exists between the suggester and management once a suggestion is made and accepted. Part of the terms of this contract is adequate reward for the suggester. Many firms select 10% of the net first year's savings as a proper amount. Any suggestion adopted must be rewarded in some fashion.

Most companies favor cash awards although there are others who use merchandise or savings bonds. Frequently, it may be necessary to stimulate interest in the program through use of special, short-time savings thoughts, for instance, energy savings suggestions for which a special, incentive-type award will be made.

One of the biggest benefits of a suggestion system is that it focuses the thinking of the employees on doing things better and developing creativity. The constant stimulation employees get when a suggestion plan is in operation, assuming, of course, that it is being properly operated, is that it keeps them alert and sparks their interest in their jobs. Although employee suggestion systems are intended to provide solid, bottom-line results, they also provide a very effective two-way channel of communication between employees and management. Knowledge that the front office wants their ideas, will consider them seriously, and will share the savings with them makes the employees feel they belong to the operation and are important to the success of the business. Recognition extended to the employee at award time or when a suggestion is implemented gives management an opportunity to be present on the scene in the employee's environment.

An employee who submits good suggestions over a period of years and has a high adoption rate—the national average being 25%—will enjoy substantial benefits to his paycheck. The record at the present time is held by a General Motors employee who had earned over $100,000 in extra recognition payments over a period of 14 years. Maximum awards as high as $75,000 have been made for one single, adoptable idea which, of course, generated many times that amount in savings. The experience with the operation of suggestion systems has shown that they will return just about $5 in savings for every dollar invested in them.

In Summary

The management of a business enterprise, either the president and other officers of a large corporation or the owner of a small business, cannot watch constantly over every detail of what goes on. Alone, no one can find all the "bugs" that are eating into profits or affecting service. But there is a staff of specialists whose talents can be enlisted —a staff as large as the payroll list.

Each worker is a specialist in his own particular job and a valuable source of information and ideas on how to improve it. A suggestion system is a device for capitalizing on the use of the brain power and imagination of workers.

A suggestion system benefits all. For the management it cuts costs, increases efficiency and builds better employer-employee relations. For employees it offers the chance to earn extra money and the realization that they and their ideas are appreciated. For customers it means better products and service.

IMP—IDEAS MEAN PROGRESS

Nationwide Insurance Companies, Columbus, Ohio, has had a successful suggestion system for a long time.

In the early days of suggestion systems, Nationwide paid $5 for each approved suggestion. From these the best of the week, month, quarter and year were selected with small additional payments added each time for the best suggestion in the period.

Then in 1959 they went to their present program called the Improved Methods Plan, and from this developed the IMP which represents the suggestion program to the employees. Under the new policy payments range from a minimum $10 to a maximum award of $1,000 based on 10% of estimated first-year savings. IMP has resulted in increased participation company-wide with an average of more than $100,000 in savings annually for the company.

The objectives of IMP are:

1. To provide concrete recognition by the companies of the importance of broadened participation on the part of employees in developing ideas which will improve our service to the policyholder.
2. To provide the means by which the inherent creative ability of employees can be made more effective.
3. To offer stimulation by recognition of individual achievement and by making financial awards commensurate with the value of the individual's contribution.

What is Eligible

In order to determine awards for IMP suggestions, the benefits of the suggestion are classified as "tangible" or "intangible."

Tangible suggestions are those that provide a monetary savings.

Intangible suggestions relate to improvements in work quality, schedules, safety, service, public relations and working conditions. They provide benefits other than monetary savings. Approved suggestions may earn awards up to $75 based on an evaluation chart.

An acceptable suggestion, eligible for an award, may be defined as a practical idea which contains the identification of a problem or condition and a proposed solution or improvement that, for example, may:

1. *Improve* product quality, service production methods, equipment, communications, employee morale or working conditions anywhere in our offices.
2. *Reduce* costs, waste, production operations or employee fatigue.
3. *Eliminate* duplication, "bottlenecks" or safety hazards.
4. *Increase* sales, productivity or operating efficiency.
5. *Save* time, material, power.
6. *Provide* better service to our customers, or a better way of doing a job.

All ideas submitted and approved through the IMP system automatically become the sole property of the company.

Everybody Benefits

Good suggestions benefit everyone.

The *employee* receives extra cash for each award-qualifying suggestion adopted, earns recognition for his cooperation and capability, and increases his opportunity within the company.

The *supervisor* receives credit for promoting creative thinking among employees, helps establish a better working team, and increases departmental efficiency.

The *company* upgrades product quality, increases productivity, reduces costs, improves operating efficiency and promotes safety and good housekeeping.

The *customers* receive better service, greater satisfaction and more confidence in Nationwide Insurance.

NATIONAL ASSOCIATION OF SUGGESTION SYSTEMS

The National Association of Suggestion Systems is located at 435 North Michigan Avenue, Chicago, Illinois 60611.

NASS is a nonprofit organization founded in 1942 to encourage the

EMPLOYEE SERVICES

Press Firmly	Print, Type, or Write Legibly	Use Extra Sheets if Necessary	Supply Samples or Sketches	Be As Thorough As Possible

Present Method, Procedure or Situation: What is done now? When is this method or procedure used? How often? Where used? What employees or agents are involved? What forms? What is the cost of the method? (Salary, Forms, Supplies, Equipment, Space, Postage, Time, Etc.)

Proposed IMProvement: What change are you proposing? When would the proposed method or procedure be used? How often? Where used? What employees or agents are involved? What forms? How much money will this method or procedure cost? (Salary, Forms, Supplies, Equipment, Space, Postage, Time, Etc.)

Compute Savings: (Labor, Forms, Supplies, Equipment, Space, Postage, Time, Etc.)

Other Benefits: (Convenience, good housekeeping, morale, safety, sales, losses.)
Is there an expense involved in starting this suggestion? What is it?.............................
Estimate cost $........................ Approximately how many people are affected?........................
How frequently or for what period will the benefits result?........................

For Employee or Agent Use	FOR OFFICE USE ONLY	
Name .... No.	REGION	HOME OFFICE
Region .... Disbursement Code	Date suggestion rec'd	....
Dept./Div./Sect.	Suggestion Number	
Suggestion Subject		
Supervisor ☐ YES ☐ NO Salary Grade	Category Number	....
	Committee Action ☐ ACP ☐ REJT	☐ ACP ☐ REJT
	Savings: $..................	
	Award Amount $..................	....

The official suggestion form used by employees in the IMP program.

adoption of suggestion systems and to exchange ideas relating to the administration of such programs. It has grown from the original group of 35 members to a membership of nearly 700 diversified companies and government agencies, reaching over 10 million employees. Membership is open only to employers, not individuals.

The national association has several publications. The most comprehensive is the Key Program, a 500+ page, loose-leaf compendium of information on all aspects of suggestion system operation. For information on this publication, or on the Association itself, contact the Chicago headquarters office.

WHAT MAKES A GOOD SUGGESTION?

The Board of Advisors for Dartnell's bi-monthly Foremanship Bulletin say that the following are points that good suggestions should have:

- cut costs
- save time
- reduce errors
- improve customer satisfaction
- increase repeat business
- improve employee morale
- improve department appearance
- decrease processing time
- help avoid misunderstanding over work
- distribute work more evenly
- cause greater pride in the organization
- help attract better employees
- promote greater uniformity
- lessen accidents
- lower absenteeism
- lessen accidents
- eliminate waste
- utilize equipment more fully

- utilize manpower to better advantage
- prevent unnecessary wear and tear on equipment
- be easy to put into operation
- result in enough advantage to pay people for the trouble of changing
- be of long-range advantage or result in significant savings now
- be better than similar suggested improvements
- be simpler than the present method

EMPLOYEE LOUNGE

Not all employees eat or drink on their breaks. Most of them, however, take their scheduled rest periods. For many employees just having a comfortable place to sit and visit is all they ask. It gives them a change in the work routine and a different environment.

An employee lounge need not be fancy although it should be as pleasant as circumstances permit. The location should be nearby, yet away from the work stations. The atmosphere should be unlike that of the work area so a feeling of being transplanted results. The chairs and sofas should be comfortable and inviting, similar to living-room furniture. Tables should be available for writing and card playing. Lamps, rugs and pictures can be used to good advantage. Music helps.

It is customary to equip a lounge with current popular magazines and other reading material. Some people read to pass the time; others come in to keep abreast of current events. Put the magazines into binders so that no one will be tempted to walk off with a copy.

An employee lounge should be a pleasant place to go so that employees will use it. Someone described a typical office, with its neat rows of identical desks, as looking like "a box of aspirins—filled." Similarly, too many employee lounges resemble bus stations, with a miscellaneous assortment of odd, leftover chairs lined up along the walls.

Someone in your organization has a bit of the interior decorator's flare. Let such a person or persons rearrange the furniture into groupings to simulate rooms. Display trophies of employee events, safety awards or United Fund contributions. Add an innovative touch here and there and the lounge will come alive and serve as the hub of employee activity.

565

EMPLOYEE CAFETERIAS

Company cafeterias, which received their greatest impetus during World War II, are by no means a war-born frill. Many progressive firms had feeding facilities for years, all the way from free soup and coffee to lunch wagons and cafeterias. The basis for any such food service is the contention that there is a correlation between proper diet and production, although this is difficult to prove statistically.

Employee cafeterias or food vending service are referred to in the industry as "in-plant feeding." Today, installations run all the way from automatic vending machines dispensing packaged, ready-prepared meals to caterers bringing in hot foods cooked in a central kitchen, to elaborate cafeterias and dining facilities with complete kitchens and trained personnel. All together this adds up to big business. In one year, 41,000 companies serve 23,000,000 meals each day to their employees.

Employee feeding has come a long way from competing with the lunch bucket in the factory or the brown bag in the office when anything was better than pot luck from yesterday. In many offices and factories of medium and larger sizes, employees today have available full-scale cafeteria operations complete with food service staffs with all food purchased, stored, prepared and merchandised on location. Cafeterias in companies are operated on a break-even basis, a cost-plus-fee arrangement, or as is usually the case subsidized, with management contributing toward the cost of food and labor in addition to buying the equipment and providing space rent free.

Well Planned

The design of the cafeteria is no longer left to chance—utilizing whatever leftover space is convenient—but is well planned, quite often with the help of restaurant consultants. Kitchens in the newer installations are models of efficiency with modern, stainless equipment. The serving area is moving away from the familiar tray-slide line to the faster "break in" or shopping center concept of separate stations for different departments. Dining areas are no longer graduated by rank; insulating executives from the rank and file is a practice democratic personnel directors frown upon. Modern employee cafeterias are air-conditioned, pleasantly decorated and feature piped-in music and live plants. They are intended to make workers feel transplanted into a nonwork environment. A successful employee cafeteria brings the company "a little closer to home" for the workers.

Many companies look upon employee cafeterias and dining rooms as a necessary function of the employee relations program, like work conditions and fringe benefits. Sometimes the provision of a cafeteria is a necessity, especially when firms move to outlying areas, or where crowded and expensive downtown locations make for poor and hurried eating.

Other companies shy away from this responsibility, saying to themselves that a worker's eating is his own concern, just as is transportation. Lunch programs, they assert, are paternalistic. They waste space and capital. Besides, they cause problems, and management has enough headaches without inviting more. They claim it is better when employees get away during the day for a change.

Companies with cafeterias defend their decision by explaining that workers can eat in less time by staying on the premises—usually a relaxed half-hour instead of a hurried one hour. This results in better work hours for the entire day. It also cuts down fatigue. In mills and factories, feeding workers in the plant cuts into the nearby saloon trade.

Outside Management

A number of organizations, notably banks, insurance firms, colleges, hospitals and the military, which formerly preferred to operate their own feeding facilities, now seem to be moving toward concessionaires. Other companies have already assigned this responsibility to outside food management firms, content to retain control over scheduling, hours, prices, portions, quality and cost, but eager to be relieved of the day-to-day work and operational problems in a field in which they feel less qualified than the professional specialists.

In selecting an outside food service management firm, it is well to recognize that all who bid for the job or submit proposals are not alike. Some gained their experience and built their reputations on campuses, in hospitals, with vending operations or in public restaurants. Their objectives and approaches vary all over the map and the results a client gets may not be what was expected or promised.

There is a difference between customers on the street and employees in a company . . . also between college students and employees . . . and between hospital patients and employees. If this assumption is valid, then experience in restaurants, campus feeding and hospital food service cannot be applied routinely to business feeding. In-plant feeding in offices and factories, while similar in many respects to other food services, also has its own uniqueness which must be understood.

One difference is where to place the emphasis. In campus feeding, the important thing is quantity; big portions are served to youngsters who want to get as much for their money as they can. In hospitals, the meals must be balanced; special diets and calorie-controlled meals are designed individually for patients. In restaurants,

567

the idea is to make money; meals must be substantial, well presented and cost-priced.

By contrast, the employee in industry has money and can afford to spend it on quality. He is used to eating regularly and well, and expects similar quality in his company cafeteria. But while quality is his most important consideration, the real criteria by which employees evaluate and patronize their cafeteria are service and attention.

Some purveyors attempt to replace manually-run cafeterias with partially- or fully-automated food service. This idea is proposed more to managements, who hear the arguments for cost reduction, than it is to employees who still prefer the personal touch. A company cafeteria is much like a moderately-priced restaurant in certain respects, but there the similarity ends. Because of self-service, the prices are lower; because of its location in the same building, it is more convenient and time for eating is less (a half hour for lunch makes an earlier quitting time possible). For these and similar considerations, the employees are willing to make concessions. But they take for granted—and expect—high quality, varied menu, good service, cleanliness, courteous attention, pleasant surroundings and a friendly atmosphere.

If any of these suffer, the employees react. No, maybe they don't quit because of a bad cafeteria, but the converse is surely true: When the cafeteria is good, they have one more reason for not quitting. Since they don't usually react by quitting—and that way take their gripes with them—how do they react? They become vocal. And today employees assert themselves at the least provocation and managements become concerned. Companies know all too well that most reaction these days is negative and should be avoided at all costs.

The Subsidy Angle

From a company point of view, the operation of an employee cafeteria must always have a selfish motive. Any subsidy is considered an investment. Management expects its cafeteria to "pay off" by contributing to better employee relations. It is one of the few fringe benefits that has universal application—everybody uses it and benefits from it. And the cost, when averaged out among all employees is much less than other big items in the fringe benefits package—vacations, for example. Or compare its cost with that of rest periods. If a company works a 37½-hour week and gives 15-minute morning and afternoon rest periods, the cost is $1/15$ of payroll, far more than even the most liberal cafeteria subsidy.

Not all companies, of course, believe in subsidizing their cafeteria operations. On the other hand, many firms are quite willing to put money into their cafeterias beyond paying for equipment and space. For example, they contribute toward the cost of food and labor. They know from experience that fringe benefits are part of the cost of doing business. But don't get the impression that companies are not cost conscious. The comptroller may be a very difficult person to deal with as he observes the increases in cost and subsidy, but his concern is with one side of the picture and his views must not be permitted to dominate. Nor should the personnel executive be granted blank-check authority without restraints. The quantitative factors, which are easy to read and analyze, must be balanced with the qualitative factors, which are more difficult to evaluate.

Company officials are willing to listen to reason when the facts are broached. Ask them if they are ready to sacrifice quality to cut costs. Ask them if they will accept less service. Try to get them to approve more secondary menu choices or smaller portions. The answer is usually "No." Apparently it is easier to placate a watchdog comptroller than run the risk of disturbing a trained work force in today's restless employment climate.

Control Remains

Whether subsidized or not, the responsibility for food service is often delegated to an outside food management firm because its people are experienced and knowledgeable in this line of activity and should be expected to do a better job. Clients are satisfied to give the professionals a free hand in the purchasing, preparing, merchandising and serving of food and expendable supplies. But they do not relinquish control.

Turning employee feeding over to others does not mean that management is absolved of its responsibility. To be effective, an outside food management firm cannot operate as an outsider. The manager and his staff are, in effect, working for the client company, although their paychecks and direction come from a third party. When cafeteria problems come up, such as that of exceeding the budget, the cafeteria manager must consider these from the company point of view, as well as his own, and must work with the company in solving them.

Not all dealings with cafeteria management relate to problems. In fact, in a good working relationship the problems are averted; that way they don't become troublesome. The company and the cafeteria resident manager meet often, regularly perhaps, to discuss the entire gamut of requirements—operations, changes, special events and the like. In such get-togethers the client hopes to tap the expertise of the professional, but does not abdicate his decision-making responsibilities. The food management firm reports, investigates, analyzes and recommends. The right to implement or change anything remains with the client company.

Such duties as menu planning, purchasing decisions, recipe choices, food preparation, technical production and safety education are left entirely to the cafeteria manager. The company wants to have confidence in the operating statements and looks for straightforward reporting with easily-identified benchmarks or guides, and few variations. In a mutually beneficial arrangement such as this, the manager and his staff must realize that the cafeteria is often a safety valve and that gripes or complaints—against Monday morning coffee, for example—don't always represent a true criticism of the cafeteria.

Additional Benefits

Most of the discussion about company cafeterias is concerned with the obvious benefits which certainly cannot be over-emphasized. These are convenience, lower prices, less time, good quality food and better balanced meals. But the cafeteria can also be used for innovations; special menus can offer dishes for people of foreign descent or ethnic background, others on restricted diets or low-calorie meals. Steak on payday, for instance, is well accepted. The company may reward employees with an occasional free meal, or bargain dinner, on a holiday or special occasion. Free coffee can be furnished as an attention getter for a new product or a significant official or personal anniversary. There are all sorts of possibilities.

But there are other advantages, not quite as obvious, but just as real. For the convenience of early arrivals, the cafeteria can be opened before work so employees may come in for breakfasts of one sort or another. These people are on their own time and they come down for reasons that are important to them personally, not the least of which is the conviviality at a table of friends which certainly beats eating toast and coffee alone at home or at a lunch counter.

The employee cafeteria can be used for morning and afternoon 15-minute breaks. When this is done, food and beverages are kept out of the work areas and this rule helps keep the premises clean and orderly.

There is yet another benefit. People don't sit in two's or small groups ordinarily, as do customers in a public restaurant. As members of formal and informal teams wherein friendships develop, they gather in groups at the larger tables and many times crowd in extra chairs.

Employees Can Participate

Employees use the cafeteria; hence, employees know the cafeteria. It is easy to get the feeling that it would be advisable to have employees assist in designing and operating the cafeteria. They know more about what is wanted since they patronize it several times a day. Management can run into problems and expensive revisions by letting the architects influence the layout and letting company officers make the decisions when these people seldom use the facility, preferring to go out for business luncheons in a hotel or social luncheons at the club.

It's the rank and file employees who use the cafeteria. Here, at coffee breaks and during lunch periods, friends gather to discuss their common interests. The group often consists of employees who work together; mailroom clerks might sit with each other, or keypunch operators might be in the same spot day after day. More often than not, the make-up of the group consists of people who do not come from any one department, who normally would have no contact with each other, but who somehow enjoy these daily get-togethers with friends in the same circle. Here they visit about all sorts of things, telling about vacation plans or reporting on trips completed, discussing last night's television program or the late show, second-guessing yesterday's ballgame, commenting on the latest developments in the news, or just talking about personal or family happenings. Supervisors and managers join in at tables with employees, not necessarily their own, and the conversations which often relate to business cross divisional lines.

The freedom to meet, talk, listen, and expound has many benefits. It is good for individual and group morale. It is an excellent communications medium since word of a personal or official nature really gets around. It is an ideal opportunity for management to plant a well-placed rumor or to listen to reaction of some official policy or decision. Not to be overlooked is the almost total elimination of the nuisance of employees wasting time while visiting at desks, work stations or water coolers.

Military campaigns have been told, "An army marches on its stomach," and many a hopeful young lassie in love has been given maternal advice that "The way to a man's heart is through his stomach." So also have the sloganists among the food purveyors advised managements that they can "get to a worker's heart through his stomach." This is naiveté at its worst. Not even the best employee cafeteria can be used as a substitute for an employee relations program that does not place emphasis on recognition, opportunity, challenges and rewards. But a good in-plant feeding facility can make the best personnel program even better.

IN-PLANT FEEDING CHECKLIST

What is the *Objective?*

Is the company need clearly defined?
How is the feeding facility related to the overall employee program?

What is the intended effect upon morale?
What direct and indirect benefits are to be achieved?
What is the extent of company financial support?

How about the *Operations*?

Should it be operated by company?
Is it better to contract with an outside professional caterer?

Who is included in the *Coverage*:

Are top executives separated from rank-and-file employees?
Will managers be privileged people?
Will office personnel be scheduled or allowed choice of time?
Will factory workers eat at different times or in different locations?

Which *Type of Service* should be provided?

Should table service with waitresses be available in certain areas?
If a cafeteria, would tray slide be preferred or the shopping center?
Would a modified manual system be workable?
Can vending or automatic service do the job?

Has the *Layout and Design* been adequately planned?

Is square footage adequate?
Are kitchen and dining areas properly equipped?
Can capital investment be justified?
Has use of consultants been considered?

Is *Merchandising* deserving of attention?

Who determines variety and breadth of menu?
Would employee participation and response stimulation be helpful?

Are *Controls* being established?

Who does the purchasing?
Is maintenance separate or part of company services?
Are sanitation and inspection provided for?
Will cost and portions be watched?
What safeguards are there to keep quality high?
Are cash handling and accounting procedures set up?
Will periodic audits be made?
Will the personnel office oversee the operation?

The "break in" or shopping center concept of food service in a typical company cafeteria.

HOSPITAL FEEDING

Hospital food service, the hub of hospital social life, is different from public or industrial feeding. There are three hospital communities to consider. These are: (1) patients, (2) staff and (3) visitors.

1. Meals for patients are prepared in accordance with standard and approved formulae in cyclically varied menu selections. Many of these meals are specially handled to meet a specific dietetic regimen. Here food is important, for in no other area (except therapy) does the hospital have the opportunity to create as favorable an image for itself and its staff.

2. Hospital staff workers are captive employees on continuous duty, seven days a week, 24 hours a day. Their cafeteria is an exclusive "eating club" where they go for meals, but also for a change of pace,

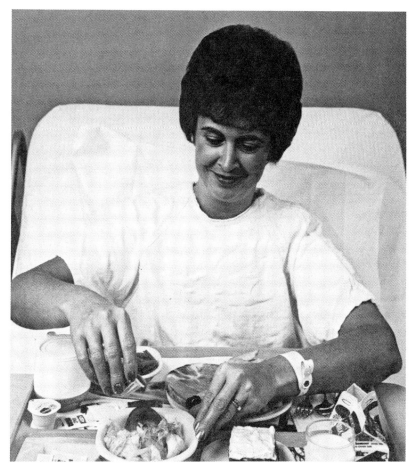

Imaginative and professional patient food services (within the limitations of prescribed diets) play a role in the ultimate impression of a hospital.

a moment of relaxation and conversational fellowship. The food, service and surroundings should be the best.

3. In addition to patients and people who see to their care, hospitals must also be prepared to feed visitors. Whether they are concerned friends or expectant fathers, their visits are far more pleasant if snacks and refreshments are easily and inexpensively available. These may be provided in coffee shops operated from generous contributions of time and effort by guilds and auxiliaries, or by sharing space in the employee cafeteria, or by conveniently located modern vending machines dispensing hospital-sanctioned food and beverages.

Most hospitals operate their own food service, but many today engage professional food management firms. A caterer provides the personnel, including back-up staff, plans for regular meals as well as special functions, does the purchasing, sanitation and accounting, maintains controlled production and quality, and can assist in layout of kitchen, serving, dishwashing, storage and dining areas.

Use of an outside food service relieves the dietitian of niggling daily chores and personnel emergencies that arise in the dietary department and enables her to concentrate on the therapeutic responsibilities of the position. The hospital administrator can feel he is free of the day-to-day problems associated with food, while yet continuing to retain complete control of every phase of the operation.

VENDING MACHINES

Vending by machine has proved completely acceptable in thousands of locations, sometimes in place of a company-operated cafeteria, other times as a supplementary service to it.

Vending, of course, is not new to industry. Candy, gum and peanut machines began to appear in factories as early as the 1920's, and eventually became as common as the drinking fountain. The cigarette machine soon followed, as did the soft drink vendor. Rather than resulting in wasted time on the job, management soon found that the ready availability of such products made it unnecessary for workers to leave the premises.

World War II gave impetus to the coffee break. The fresh-brew coffee vending machine appeared shortly afterward and met the need for a fast, convenient, economical means of providing hot coffee on the job. In more recent years, as younger workers preferred cold soft drinks over coffee, the multidrink dispenser took its place in the battery of vending machines.

Strategically located throughout a plant, these vending machines require no additions to personnel to serve any or all shifts. They eliminate long walks to and from central cafeterias, and end the morning and afternoon exodus of people in search of refreshments. Not the least of the machines' benefits is that they provide a drink whose quality is completely satisfying, yet whose price requires no subsidy.

With the widespread popularity and continuing rapid growth of food and beverage vending, it is difficult to realize that this modern means of in-plant feeding is relatively new. Some pieces of food vending equipment antedate the 1960's, such as the hot canned food vendor and the "buy on faith" sandwich machine which concealed the product until it had been paid for and delivered. The concealment was not deliberate, to be sure, but reflected an unprepossessing stage in the development of a business which was new to the operator and new to the personnel director as well. If food at first appeared to have little potential for growth, in common with most pioneering efforts, it was also productive of little income. But it did open the way and things happened fast thereafter to bring food vending to the relatively sophisticated level it holds today.

The Automatic Cafeteria

Manufacturers of vending machines, taking a lesson from merchandisers in other retail lines, began to provide for display areas where foods behind glass could be plainly seen and exert their appetite appeal upon the prospective patron.

Almost overnight it seems, although designers and engineers would deny it, vending equipment became available in attractively matched units. Gleaming glass and bright metal trims took the place of drably-painted surfaces. Machines were illuminated to give showcase display to products.

Coin mechanisms became more versatile. They returned proper change and permitted the vending of a far greater variety of products at price levels based on fair values. Under- or over-pricing to adapt to the limited versatility of early coin changers was eliminated.

No mere mechanical revolution, however, enabled the vending operator to expand his services as a robot restaurateur. Food packers and processors and packaging people saw the future in food vending and prepared to serve it in such a way as to secure their share of its ultimate rewards.

There is, for example, no special knowledge needed to prepare a combination salad, although the aesthetic disposition of its crisp, fresh ingredients adds to attractiveness and salability and helps motivate a customer to better balance his nutritional intake. But what of the container for an individual portion of the salad that can be displayed within the refrigerated vending machine to best advantage, eaten from and easily disposed of? Such a container was not available in quantity at first, nor at a cost compatible with retail prices. Initially, the cost of a plastic salad bowl represented some 25% of the selling price which, with ingredient costs, labor, overhead, taxes and all the rest, was prohibitive. But the plastics converters saw the opportunity, gambled on the future, and began producing vending salad bowls in volume sufficient to permit cost reductions and take salads out of the "loss leader" category.

Improvements in clear sandwich wrappings and the creation of special machinery to reduce handling and labor costs have greatly facilitated production, attractiveness of display and labelling. Research carried on with packers has resulted in hot canned food products which, with no loss of taste, texture or wholesomeness, stand up for many hours under heat and are table ready when vended. The benefit of this research extends beyond vending and is shared by the housewife buying similar products at the grocery store.

Instant Meals

The introduction of the electronic oven has done much to speed service as well as to expand menus. Within but eight or nine seconds, the vending machine patron can bring a casserole, sandwich or entree and vegetable dish from a refrigerated state to table temperature.

There is today scarcely any selection of food for which the customer is willing to pay that cannot be vended. Even gourmet meals offer no problem except one of arithmetic, and that because the vending machine and the customer are not yet psychologically adjusted to the vending of "high ticket" items.

With the equipment available these days, any company regardless of size can provide "cafeteria service" for employees. All it takes is a refrigerated unit to store prepackaged, dietetically balanced, nutritious and tasty meals, and a microwave oven to heat them almost instantly. There are regular restaurants that operate on this principle and customers never know the difference.

Although personnel directors in general turned to vending enthusiastically, some may be reluctant to abandon entirely the cafeteria concept of in-plant feeding, even when this change is economically or otherwise advisable. They are concerned that employees, having had things pretty much their own way at the company cafeteria, might tend to find fault with automatic food service. It is suggested that a combination of vending machines and an attended cafeteria counter would bridge the gap between the one and the other, particularly at the noonday meal.

This can be accomplished by using hot and cold self-service cabinets, a short-order preparation area with an attendant, along with vending machines. The employee patron finds he can order special items, varied from day to day, that are not on display in the cabinets or the machines. Perhaps more important to him, he retains the opportunity to exchange a little banter with the lady behind the counter. Interestingly enough, it has been found that, given greater freedom of choice than is provided through vending machines alone, the customer tends to select the vended item which is immediately ready and waiting for him.

The aim of the vending industry is to provide the company with facilities that will best meet the particular requirements for in-plant food service, not to replace the manual cafeteria and dining room which will still prevail as the best food service for years to come in those instances where economics or policy permit.

The combination of vending and limited service may be preferred by some companies. Others may find complete vending ideally suited to their needs. Still others may want the full manual cafeteria or dining room, or both.

This bank of vending machines, supplied and maintained by Canteen Corporation, Chicago, Illinois, becomes a self-service cafeteria.

COFFEE VENDING

A typical coffee vending machine brews 10 cups of coffee at a time and begins a new brew cycle when the batch falls below a certain level. If the coffee stands for some time, the machine automatically dumps the standing batch and brews another.

It's really quite a device. The amount of ground coffee used for the batch can be varied according to the strength of brew most liked in a particular location. In addition, the machine permits the customer to select his cup of coffee in nine options: (1) black, (2) black and sugar, (3) black and extra sugar, (4) black with cream, (5) black with extra cream, (6) black with cream and sugar, (7) black with extra sugar and cream, (8) black with extra cream and sugar, (9) black with extra cream and extra sugar. Since the machine must keep its cream supplies fresh and cold, and yet brew hot coffee, it contains both a refrigerator and a heater.

With all this, the machine makes change for the customer—but does so only after its coin reading assembly determines that it is working on bona fide money and not slugs.

PURCHASE DISCOUNTS

In a personnel handbook we spend considerable time on wage administration programs and their separate component parts—such as job evaluation, performance rating, incentives, government regulations and the like. And this would seem to be in order. Yet there is a whole area of jobs that is unaffected by any system of wages. These are the thousands of jobs performed everyday by volunteers and others who donate their services.

Similarly, in a retail merchandising handbook all aspects of selling, costing, price protection and the like are covered. Yet there are sales made every day which ignore all the bases of a sound pricing program. Since many of these exceptions are available to employees, they are mentioned here.

Many firms sell company products to their employees at a discount. The usual procedure calls for placing orders for personal and family use only. These orders are entered maybe once a week and are filled and packed for pickup at the exit gate. Payment is made in cash at the company store or through deduction from payroll.

A common practice is for department stores to sell all sorts of merchandise at less than the listed prices. A store employee may purchase anything at a regular sales counter. By showing his employee identification card to the sales clerk, the bill is reduced by an employee discount, probably 20%. In addition, employees are often given advance notification of bargains before they are opened to the general public.

Manufacturers of hard goods sell their products to employees at dealer's cost. The order may even be delivered by company truck and serviced by a franchised distributor. They may offer inventory surplus, demonstrators, floor models, samples and returned goods at clearance prices.

In all these instances where employees may get purchase discounts, the retired employees usually enjoy the same privilege.

For that matter, many products and services are often free to certain people—own employees or even outsiders. Some doctors do not bill clergymen, nurses and teachers. Doctors don't charge other doctors.

Airline employees get free air transportation and railraod employees get passes. Police and firemen in uniform are not charged for rides on buses or subways. Telephone employees get some free phone service depending upon position and length of service.

Free beer is available at most breweries for on-the-premises consumption.

Automobile manufacturers allow their executives free use of new cars, and automobile dealers do the same for their salesmen because they want them to appear in presentable cars. The auto manufacturers offer discounts to some people, such as prominent executives, politicians and newspapermen.

The clergy is often favored with gifts or passes to ballgames and such. One pastor has a habit each year of acknowledging publicly from the pulpit the gifts he receives from congregation members. But there's always one wise guy in every group, and this particular clown gave the pastor a bottle of wine for Christmas. Next Sunday he was sitting in church just waiting to see how the preacher would handle this one. But the clergyman was not about to refuse the bottle of wine so he merely announced, "I appreciate receiving the fruit of the vine, and especially the spirit in which it was given."

EMPLOYEE DISCOUNTS

Employees of Montgomery Ward are entitled to "Employee Discount," described in their handbook as follows:

An employee discount of 10% which is available to all employees and members of their immediate families (defined as a member of the family with whom the employee lives) is authorized on most merchandise, repair parts, service contracts and repair and auto services performed by Wards employees. If a special discount is offered to the general public, the employee discount will be allowed in addition.

Discount is allowed at the retail store or from the catalog upon presentation of your Employee Discount Card.

In addition, at certain times of the year, discounts of 15% are provided on select merchandise.

DISCOUNT PROGRAMS

by GEORGE S. THOMPSON
Executive Director
Virginia Governmental Employees Association, Inc.

A very effective yet inexpensive way for management to improve employee morale is available to all firms and businesses.

Initiate a program of employee discounts. Amusement theme parks, such as Disney World, Sea World and other nationally known attractions, as well as local theaters, parks, stores, auto firms and others welcome the opportunity on a formal basis of offering discounts to company employees.

As a rule these discounts range from 10% to 20%. They represent a considerable savings for employees.

Contact the theme parks in your area as well as the big ones in Florida and California. You will be pleasantly surprised to find how eager they will be to work with you.

EMPLOYEE SERVICES

The employee service program of Grumman Aerospace Corporation, Bethpage, New York, is unique. Mr. Charles J. Fuschillo, director of employee services, graciously agreed to share the policy and programs with our readers.

The following is reprinted from their "At Your Service" brochure:

Did you ever wish you had an "extra pair of hands" so you could get things done? Do you wish there was someone to help you when everything seems to go wrong? Well, there is. Grumman Employee Services department is at your service.

For example, suppose some morning your faithful alarm clock doesn't ring. As a result, you're late and miss your car pool. You have to drive your own car to work, a little too fast according to the officer who presents you with a traffic ticket. That's when you realize your auto registration expires in three days. Also, you remember that tomorrow is your spouse's birthday and you haven't had a chance to buy a present. When you finally get to work, you discover that your medicine is still at home. Far fetched? Possibly, but it could happen! If it happened to you, what would you do?

Well, rather than go back home or worry all day, you can solve all of these problems by making one telephone call. Really? Sure!

When big or little problems plague you, the number to call is the Grumman Employee Services department. Yes, unique in industry, this department and its reliable representatives exist solely to serve you. They will gladly help you with life's daily problems. They provide a wide range of free services, and will even save you time and money. Incredible? No, it's true!

Let's take a look at how Employee Services can clear up the problems which began when your alarm clock failed to ring. First, that traffic ticket. An Employee Services representative will save you from standing in line at the traffic court. All you need to do is provide a check or money order for the amount of the fine and the matter will be taken care of for you. Second, that auto registration that's due to expire. Just hand over the necessary renewal forms and a check or money order. Your Employee Service representative will do the rest. What! You don't have a checking account? Well, Employee Services will get you a money order!

Now, about your medicine. If it's essential that you take it before you would normally return home from work, arrangements can be made for an Employee Services representative to go to your home and bring your medicine to you. That's three of your major worries taken care of. Now what's left? Oh yes, the birthday present for your spouse. Quite possibly you could find something suitable at one of the Employee Services "Flight Shops" and save money, too, since the merchandise is sold at a discount. And while you're there, you can even buy a new alarm clock or clock radio! That takes care of all of today's problems—thanks to Employee Services. Impressed? That's just a sample of the multitude of problems which Employee Services helps to solve.

Would you be interested in "what else" Employee Services can do for you? Fine, just keep reading.

Some of the services which are available to you as a Grumman employee include:

1. The Flight Shop which sells such items as:

   - Newspapers, candy and snacks

   - Grumman glasses, jackets, pens and jewelry

   - Watches, radios and smoke detectors

- Discount tickets to shows, special events, the Circus and other entertainment features

- Stamps, money orders, stationery and postcards

- Grumman canoes and "The Grumman Story"

- Cosmetics, sunglasses, cameras and film

- And lots of other things—come take a look.

2. The Flight Shop also offers:

- Notary Public service

- Lost and Found service

- Film processing service

- Company benefit plan or income tax forms

- Applications for Job Opportunity or Supervisory Promotion vacancies

- A complete discount buying service.

3. The following types of Emergency Services are also rendered:

- Transportation of a sick or injured employee to a doctor's or dentist's office or to a hospital for treatment (after first aid is given by company personnel).

- Driving the disabled employee (and his/her car) home.

- Running of special errands (medicine, etc.).

4. The following types of Regular Services are offered:

- Discussion of a problem and direct assistance or referral to other company departments or outside agencies.

- Assistance in cutting "red tape" in regard to many different matters at work or off the job.

- Obtaining auto, boat or trailer licenses or registrations for employees.

- Payment of traffic tickets for employees.

5. Employee Services representatives also bring a ray of sunshine by:

- Visiting sick employees at home or in the hospital on a regular basis.

- Sending flowers or a basket of fruit to hospitalized employees.

- Delivering salary or benefit checks.
- Counseling and assisting employees with the complexity of medical claims, disability insurance, etc.
- Visiting the spouse of a deceased employee to assist with funeral arrangements.
- Providing assistance to widows/widowers in such matters as appraisal and sale of a house, life insurance claims, Social Security, etc.

6. The Employee Services department also performs such occasional duties as:

- Coordinating the annual "Family Picnic."
- Distributing turkeys to employees at Christmas.
- Sending flowers to the family of a deceased employee.
- Assisting with the annual "Twenty-five Year" luncheon and the Stockholders Meeting, United Way and Bond Drive.
- Lending sick room supplies, crutches, canes, wheelchairs, etc. to employees.
- Supporting the Grumman Garden Forum.
- Coordinating the Company Blood Program.

By now you should have a better idea of the many ways in which the Employee Services department can serve you. Perhaps you feel there are other things which Employee Services should do. If so, we'd certainly like to hear from you.

In case you're wondering why Grumman goes to all this trouble and expense, let's just say that top management—from 1942 to the present day—considers the Employee Services idea an excellent investment and a tangible way to demonstrate to employees that the company really cares about them. It's the Grumman tradition.

Of course, aside from tradition and the "human relations" aspects, there's also a good business reason for having such an extensive Employee Services program—greater productivity. An employee who is worried about a problem can't be productive. Psychologists tell us that problems not only affect employees' productivity, but their safety and health as well. If the company can alleviate or eliminate employees' problems, there will be a corresponding improvement in attitude, safety, health and productivity and a decrease in waste, accidents, medical costs and absenteeism. Our experience in World War II—when Grumman achieved the highest production rate of any aircraft manufacturer in the world—further attests to the value of the Employee Services function.

Now that you know some of the why's and wherefore's of Employee Services, we sincerely hope you'll leave your worries on our doorstep and let us help you walk on the sunny side of the street.

RECREATION

One of the fastest growing fringe benefits is company recreation programs. These range from company-encouraged ballgames, parties or clubs, to company-supported bowling leagues and golf outings, to company-sponsored picnics and choirs, to company-owned swimming pools and country clubs. These leisure time activities are for employees and often extend to "family fun." In many cases, retirees may continue to participate.

Small cities may have inadequate facilities for sports, games and pastime. Companies provide their own in order to attract and hold workers. Some company properties, such as golf links, swimming pools, auditoriums, may also be made available to the townspeople under certain conditions.

The use of outdoor areas, such as wooded groves for family outings, skating ponds and baseball diamonds, is greater with companies located in small or medium-sized cities, where community facilities are often limited. In the large cities, when open spaces are not available or too far out to be practical, the diversionary needs of employees are met with social clubs, indoor play courts, and bowling leagues using public establishments.

Many activities are provided free; others, such as clubs, are covered by dues. Some charge membership fees. Proceeds also may come from vending machines. Typically, company support is indirect and channeled through self-governed employee clubs that plan and conduct many of the activities.

Body building exercises or calisthenics provided in gymnasiums, with the aid of physical director and a masseur, are for executives and managers to reduce waistlines, help blood circulation, and "prevent weekend heart attacks." Most programs, however, aim for wide participation and are open to all employees, white collar salaried personnel as well as the increasingly affluent blue collar workers.

Companies usually hesitate to reveal how much they spend on recreation since, in the words of one executive, "a lot of stockholders still look on such things as pork barrels." But surveys show that companies and employee groups spend a minimum of $10 per capita to build, maintain and staff these facilities. Companies claim these programs lead

Basketball, tennis (in rear), and shuffleboard—three of many sports enjoyed by employees of Prairie State Screw and Bolt Corporation, Northbrook, Illinois.

to a reduction in absenteeism and turnover, and aid in recruiting the people they need and want.

Since companies are involved in some measure in these employee activities, they buy insurance as a backstop against the unexpected. Worker's Compensation covers after-work involvements which are supervised, sponsored, subsidized or identified with the company, such as an advertisement on bowling shirts or softball uniforms. There is, however, a gray area between what is compensable and what is not. No clear line has yet been drawn by state industrial commissions.

How effective are company recreation programs? Some fail, but others continue year after year, and grow. The A. E. Staley Manufacturing Company of Decatur, Illinois sponsored an employee football team. Until the 1920's one of its principal rivals was Wisconsin's Acme Packing Company. Sponsorship has since changed hands, and the two teams are now competing professionally as the Chicago Bears and the Green Bay Packers of the National Football League.

RECREATION PROGRAMS

Time changes the definition of "leisure."

A classical definition of leisure says that it requires little or no expenditure and the only prerequisite is time. The connotation is that this is idle time.

But people have decided to use leisure time not merely consume it. They work hard at leisure, spending billions of dollars on recreational leisure time activities.

As an employee service, many companies cooperate with employees by offering recreation programs. A list of some of the employee recreational activities in United States and Canadian firms follows:

archery
art classes
auditorium, for theater and music groups
baseball
basketball
billiards
boating
bowling, duckpins
cabins, on a lake
camera club, darkroom on company premises
camping sites
card playing, bridge

chess
choir or choral groups
Christmas parties
coin club
country club
curling
dance lessons
fishing
flag football
golf driving range
golf, 18 hole, championship course
golf outing
golf putting green
health clubs, calisthenics
hiking
hockey
horseback riding
horseshoes
instructional groups
knitting and sewing, needlework, macrame
miniature golf
model airplanes and railroads
motorcycling
physical fitness
picnics
ping pong, badminton
pistol range, rifle range
playgrounds, kiddie-rides
pony rides for children
racquetball
running, jogging
scouting
self-defense, karate
shuffleboard, boccie
skating
skeet shooting, trapshooting
ski clubs, tobogganing
soccer
softball

squash courts
steam baths
surfboard riding
swimming
talent shows
tennis
theater or ice follies parties
tournaments
travel club, to take advantage of group rates, show films
vacation areas, usually for outdoorsmen
volleyball
water skiing, including instruction
weekend excursions
weight lifting
yacht club

NIRA AND CIRA

The National Industrial Recreation Association (NIRA) is located at 20 North Wacker Drive, Chicago, Illinois 60606. It is a membership association and the international clearing house of information on employee recreation programs.

NIRA offers a professional certification program, dedicated to the continued improvement of its members. The successful completion of the Certified Industrial Recreation Administrator requirements is recognized with the CIRA award.

VETERANS' CLUB

The following example of an employee club is taken from *The Dofasco Way,* employee handbook of the Dominion Foundries and Steel, Limited, of Hamilton, Ontario, Canada.

War veterans of Dofasco have an organization known as the Dominion Foundries and Steel Veterans' Association. The Vets' Club is located in the Sherman Centre at 1047 Barton Street East.

Active membership in the Association is open to any Dofasco employee with three or more months of Company service, who volunteered for military service with the Allied Forces.

BARBER SHOP

Here is an unusual service provided by Woodward Governor Company, Rockford, Illinois, as described in its employee handbook.

A service greatly appreciated by most of the male members of the company is the Barber Shop. Members are contacted by the barbers for haircuts which are offered approximately bi-weekly to those desiring them. This service is also available to women members, but it is limited to hair cutting.

CHARITY DRIVES—ONE OR MANY?

Charity drives and fund-raising campaigns run throughout the year. How many should a company participate in? How often can employees be approached? Which of the programs, all worthwhile, should be recognized?

In most communities there is now a United Fund organization which consolidates most of the major fund-raising activities into one annual drive. By cooperating wholeheartedly with this community-endorsed activity, both the company and its employees feel they fulfill their responsibility to the welfare agencies operating locally and nationally in their behalf.

When a company takes the position that supporting one all-out campaign is the extent to which it can afford to solicit funds from employees, what about the separate programs that come up at other times? One suggestion is that the company may want to cooperate with any additional drive that it feels worthy of supporting, but let employee participation entirely up to each individual. Contributions might even be made directly.

Posters may be placed on bulletin boards, collection cannisters may be located at strategic stations, literature and mail-in envelopes may be kept handy. In this way an employee who is moved by the agency's story may donate without any pressure being implied.

It is customary to clear any such appeal for funds through the person-

590

nel office. Otherwise a rash of "little pockets of giving" may spring up throughout the office or plant, for causes which may not be understood and could possibly be questionable. Clearing requests for contributions through personnel would also serve as a control over the sale of raffle tickets, sympathy donations and similar solicitations.

Companies generally prefer one combined annual fund-raising campaign in which the major agencies share as against a series of many separate smaller donation requests. Obviously the line must be drawn somewhere, and this arrangement seems to be acceptable to companies and employees.

UNITED FUND APPEALS

Chances are very good that your company participates in some way in the annual United Fund or Community Chest drive in your community. Normally, a business leader is chosen to head the fund drive and all businesses are asked to cooperate.

On the prescribed day or week of the month, pledge cards are handed out to employees. The company contributes time and effort by gathering the pledges and, in some cases, making deductions from the employees' paychecks or wages.

The responsibility for collecting more money, by inspiring employees to give more, is falling on corporate shoulders. Organization is the key word.

The business community is gradually coming around to recognizing that the corporation, serving in the community, has social responsibilities. As one executive explained, "There is no longer anything to reconcile between the social conscience and the profit motive." Expressed another way, business should account for its stewardship on the corporate balance sheet.

For a campaign to accomplish its purpose there are many things a company can do to encourage employees to contribute to a worthwhile welfare cause:

1. Give the drive an official endorsement. Let the announcement go out over the president's signature, as a personal appeal from him for understanding and cooperation.
2. Have senior officers take a personal interest by addressing meetings of employees.
3. Set up a committee with members drawn from the higher echelons of management.
4. Assign captains (ratio: one captain for each 10 employees) to distribute and collect pledge cards.

5. Take time to explain the need and the program to a meeting of captains. Have a representative from fund headquarters present.
6. Let fund headquarters schedule a tour to a welfare agency for the committee and, if the captains can be spared for a half day, include them.
7. Show the official motion picture to employees.
8. Display banners and posters, prepare a payroll insert, and use other media to publicize the campaign.
9. Carry the story in the employee house organ.
10. Post the progress being made and the final results on conveniently located "thermometers."
11. Issue pins, stickers and other items of evidence to employees who contribute, and have some form of recognition for workers, such as a group photo in a magazine, individual "thank you" letters, desk Oscars, etc.
12. Make it a concentrated drive. Hit hard and hit fast. Don't let the campaign drag out over weeks, except for employees who are absent.

Do But Don't Overdo

Sometimes companies get carried away in their enthusiasm and turn the drive into a competitive fun game, with prizes to individuals, awards to departments which get 100% participation or meet or exceed pre-established quotas. This practice is frowned upon and the preferred program calls for an educational approach designed to appeal to the heart. The employees should be made to feel they "want" to give to help their less fortunate brethren.

Companies that are sincerely interested in cooperating in a drive for welfare funds should understand that pledges are better than cash. Further, the giving on the part of employees can be almost painless, and more productive, if the amount of individual pledges is spread over a period of time and handled through payroll deduction. Ideally, many fund drives prefer continuous payroll deduction every payday throughout the year. This steady flow of money into the fund treasury obviously produces the best results. But any arrangement of sustained giving is better than "passing the hat" or even a one-time payroll deduction. Different arrangements that have worked well are: five or six successive deductions, once-a-month deductions, etc. While some firms require a specified percentage, such as one day's pay or 1% of annual salary, particularly of managerial personnel, most companies are reluctant to dictate the amount of giving, or to make welfare contributions a condition of employment.

Remember when charity was a virtue and not a business.

OFFICE COLLECTIONS

The custom of taking up office collections, or "passing the hat," gets different reactions, depending upon size of organization, makeup of the work force and circumstances.

Admittedly, direct collecting for a gift for a person who is well-known and well-liked, is easy to accept. But even then the married woman who is contributing regularly to wedding gifts for new brides in her department is in about the same position as the single man who is asked to "chip in" for a baby gift every time one of his associates becomes a father. They soon lose enthusiasm since there can be no reciprocal arrangement and the one-way giving becomes a demand request instead of a voluntary donation.

If collections remain localized the requests can be kept under control. What happens too often is that a personable prômoter in one department gets carried away and goes elsewhere in the office or plant where perhaps he is known and respected but where the individual for whom he is taking up the collection may actually be a stranger. This happens quite regularly in hardship cases when an employee is made to feel like a heel if he doesn't willingly agree to help out an unfortunate co-worker. No matter how worthy the cause, when the practice gets out of hand it becomes distasteful and annoying.

There are always certain individuals who delight in arranging something. Champagne parties for employees who become grandmothers for the first time, or "fun gifts" for expectant fathers, are the latest innovations in celebrations. Fellow workers who have other demands on their time, or are noticeably less enthusiastic than the promoters, are nevertheless expected to "shell out" to share in the cost.

Managers and employees who are in favor of collections argue that they are an effective means of promoting cooperation. They further claim that this type of spontaneous employee activity contributes to the kind of climate that offers stimulation to the work group. They state simply that people seem to enjoy office collections which are earmarked for remembrances and unofficial parties.

Some companies encourage get-togethers when employees leave or are transferred and they knowingly allow extra time at lunch for such occasions. Sometimes a manager allows his workers 15 or 20 minutes during the day for the presentation of gifts; more often than not, such informal parties take place at the work desk, or on extended pass periods in the cafeteria without the supervisor even being consulted.

Many firms "frown on" office collections. They try not to encourage them, but at the same time they recognize that some get-togethers and gift exchanges are aids to morale. Usually they ask that these activities

stay within a department or other work are in order to keep them from getting out of bounds. When six women work together every day it is almost inevitable that they will remember each other at birthdays or with a grab bag at Christmas.

Writing rules is impossible because the conditions in no two cases are alike. Last year the men in the paint shop took old Joe to the tavern across the street and presented him with 25 silver dollars on his 25th wedding anniversary. It was a great idea and everybody enjoyed participating in it. Today they have a man who started work six months ago who is also observing his silver wedding anniversary. What do they do now that a precedent has been established? Will the new man be offended if his anniversary is ignored? Will the old-timer be insulted if the new employee, who may not be well liked, is accorded equal treatment? Who will take the responsibility next morning when an irate foreman finds bad morale is affecting the spirit of teamwork?

Attempts to do something about too many collections, inconveniently scheduled, and benefiting an assortment of people and causes, have resulted in employees forming "flower and gift funds." Under such arrangement, each employee who elects to participate contributes a fixed amount, perhaps $5 or $10 a year, or 10¢ or 25¢ per week, which is then used by fund leaders to administer standard benefits to fund members under specified conditions. This takes care of flowers in cases of illness to an employee or death of an employee's close relative, and may also include wedding and baby presents and possibly termination gifts. Obviously it does not cover everything but it does make the whole problem easier to live with and more acceptable to everyone involved.

GIFT OR FLOWER FUND

To avoid passing the hat . . .

Companies have established, or allowed their employees to develop, informal Gift or Flower Fund organizations. These are generally simple but effective plans administered by employees for employees.

There is something nice about being remembered on special occasions. But there is something unpleasant about taking up collections, or being asked repeatedly to chip in for some worthy cause. For these reasons a Gift or Flower Fund is formed. It provides an easy and automatic way of giving a nominal amount each payday for remembrances for various occasions, without the necessity of individual solicitations.

It also has another advantage. It equalizes the giving and the receiving. All members get the same benefits and contribute the same amount. Without a plan it is likely that employees in some areas might get more and better gifts, or employees in large departments could be asked to contribute oftener than others.

A typical voluntary plan calls for a contribution of a nominal amount each week for the employee, handled through payroll deduction. The company may or may not match the employee contribution in full or in part. When it does contribute, this could be on a formula basis (so much per member per week) or whenever the club treasury needs a little financial boost.

For this the members receive these benefits—

Deaths   : $20.00 spiritual or floral remembrance for the death of a member, immediate family of a member (husband, wife, children, father, mother, brother, sister, or any other relative residing in the same household as the member).

Illness   : One $10.00 floral piece, plant, book or other gift in any calendar year for an illness serious enough to warrant a member being absent from work for 10 or more working days.

Wedding   : A $10.00 gift or merchandise certificate, if the employee is not terminating at the time of marriage.

Terminations: The value of the termination gift will be based on $5.00 for each full year of membership. This could be a check.

A Gift or Flower Fund is popular with employees because it costs so little and eliminates the nuisance of collections. Companies like it since it solves a delicate problem and requires a minimum of time and effort to operate.

The administration of an Employee Gift or Flower Fund calls for a president, treasurer and a few representatives from throughout the workforce. These local representatives learn of the need for a remembrance or gift, and they do the gift buying for their co-workers.

Every employee who joins the Employee Gift or Flower Fund shares in both gift giving and gift receiving.

OFFICE AND PLANT POOLS

Many firms are beginning to clamp down on employee betting. This practice not only disrupts work schedules, but often establishes a plant "bookie" who spends a part of his time collecting and paying off bets.

Sports pools aren't the only problem, although football bowl games and the World Series baseball are common occasions for wagering. One company found its employees paying $1 a week for 13 weeks for a "drawing." Another turned up a lottery based on paycheck digits.

Some supervisors throw up their hands in despair, saying "There isn't much that can be done with so many people involved." What makes the problem difficult is that managers and supervisors, who should control or curb the practice, often participate and are the biggest offenders.

In companies where the custom of conducting an occasional "company pool" is considered little more than employee fun, keep an eye on the goings-on to prevent a harmless practice from developing into a problem situation.

GIFT ACCEPTANCE

It is the policy in many companies to not permit employees to accept gifts and favors proffered by individuals, groups, suppliers and others with whom the company does business.

The company's services, benefits and purchases are rendered solely on the basis of merit and value received. Wherever practical, services and purchases are awarded on competitive bidding. Employees, therefore, are not permitted to accept gifts, favors or unusual hospitality from business contacts that might tend to influence them in the performance of their duties.

Minor business attention such as luncheons or sporting events tickets may be accepted as long as they are not accepted on a continuing basis and do not reflect negatively on the efficiency or integrity of the company.

LOST AND FOUND

In any medium or large company it is likely that items of intrinsic or sentimental value will be lost or found. Once the employee group grows larger than a close-knit, family-type unit, the workers will not know each other too well, which will keep them from readily recognizing each other's personal belongings.

Umbrellas might be left in the lobby, sweaters in cloakrooms, purses in the cafeteria, rings or watches in the washrooms, pens in conference rooms. It is amazing what items are forgotten or misplaced—eyeglasses, gloves, scarves, train tickets and other miscellany. These items are usually found by other employees, supervisors or the night cleaners.

There should be some convenient central place where lost items may be turned in by those who find them, and reclaimed by those who lost them. This "lost and found" location should be well known to all. Quite often, as in the case of a wallet, it is important that the loser recover the lost item quickly.

Care should be taken when returning items to people who claim them. Some attempt should be made to have the claimant describe what he is looking for before it is shown. The recovered item should go only to its rightful owner.

Some items will never be claimed. Employees may not realize where they lost things. Once in a while the collection should be cleaned out. Some things, such as soiled or wornout clothing, may be discarded. Other items may be placed on a table in some public place, such as the cafeteria, urging employees to take anything they recognize as their own. After a reasonable time, unclaimed items may be disposed of in any manner that seems suitable.

EMPLOYEE COMPLAINTS

Complaints by employees are an irritation whereas they should be a source of deep concern. It is human nature to take offense at a complaint especially when management's sincere intention is to keep the welfare of employees constantly in the forefront.

Employees, by complaining, are trying to tell their bosses something. Instead of being annoyed, managers should welcome the opportunity to listen.

Complaints, which are an expression of discontent, should not be taken lightly. Sometimes their apparent smallness, from the official point of view, may cause a company to deal with them in an offhand way. The grievance which may be almost invisible to the supervisor looms large in the eyes of the complainant, or he or she would never have bothered to express it.

Nine times out of ten the situation is exaggerated. Often it is imaginary. Sometimes it is fabricated. Nevertheless, it deserves to be handled in a spirit of attentive interest. Every complaint, even the smallest one, is a signpost along the road to trouble.

The discreet and skillful handling of an employee complaint is a constructive action in the company's interest. The principal points to practice are:

1. Acknowledge the complaint at once.
2. Indicate a genuine interest in it.
3. Make a speedy investigation.

4. Resolve it objectively.
5. Give the decision without delay.

There are two ways of solving any problem: management can do something or the employee can do something. Management might not even be expected to resolve the difficulty; it could be enough just to show interest and hear the employee out. When this is not done, the employee can hardly be blamed for acting alone. The easiest way for the employee to be relieved of the problem in the company is to walk away from it by quitting the job. That way the employee is free of the annoying situation; the employee leaves but the problem remains behind where it could well continue to plague the company.

The Value of Complaints

Beyond the importance of saving an employee for the company, there is something else to consider. That is, the value of complaints.

A case can be made as to why a company would want to be concerned about the occasional complaint when the great majority of workers say nothing. Just as nine-tenths of an iceberg lies beneath the surface of the sea, so the complaint may be a signal of something worse that lurks behind the scene.

The ideal way to avoid trouble with complaints, of course, is to prevent things from happening that give rise to grievances, to be careful to give no grounds for a justifiable cause of distress. Thinking of the interests of employees is the best way of safeguarding the interests of the firm.

If no complaints were ever voiced, how would companies know where improvements are needed? Accept it as a basic law of business life that there is always room for improvement. Complaints are valuable because they direct attention to possible areas of improvement in operating efficiency and employee relations.

Companies might go one step further and seek to uncover grievances. When not given expression, irritations will build up to the point of explosion. The principle of stepping out to meet trouble rather than allowing it to fester unnoticed, is a sound one. When someone sees that the company is making efforts to discover and rectify conditions that displease employees, especially when nothing has been reported, the action impresses employees and makes them more appreciative of management's concern for its workers.

In summary, employee complaints should be looked upon as something more than gripes. Somewhere in the background there is a message and management should consider the reason for the complaint as telling them more than the complaint itself. In this context, companies should not only treat the symptoms but also look for the cause.

EMPLOYEE GRIEVANCES

While a certain amount of employee griping is considered normal, a good grievance system can prevent small seeds of discontent from growing into a jungle of dissatisfaction. The importance of this was underscored by the Greater Boston Hospital Council, which included grievance machinery among 15 recommendations to members.

The following description outlining the grievance procedure that has worked well at the New England Medical Center Hospitals was made available through the courtesy of Francis Matthews, personnel director.

Intent. It is the intent of the hospital to provide a framework for the resolution of employee problems which arise from interpretation of policies and procedures. This should be accomplished in an atmosphere of fairness, mutual respect and frank discussion of differences. The procedures described below should be used freely by employees. They are designed to provide a workable means of presenting such differences in a frank and open manner to obtain for the employee a prompt and fair decision.

Employee assistance. Any employee is entitled to assistance in preparing and/or presenting an appeal at any level. It is suggested that the employee contact either the Employee Service Representative or any member of the Personnel Department staff for advice or assistance. However, the employee does have the right to ask any other hospital employee for assistance. Such assistance may include aid in preparing and/or presenting the appeal in writing, appearing with the employee at any level of the appeal, and speaking on the employee's behalf.

Appeal coordinator. A member of the Personnel Department staff will be designated as the "Appeal Coordinator." This person is responsible for ensuring that the appeal is accomplished in a timely manner and that the provisions of the policy are communicated to all parties through the appeal process.

Informal Procedure

When a problem arises for an employee, the immediate supervisor is normally in the best position to help solve it. Often, a frank discussion between the employee and the supervisor, while the problem is still fresh, may be all that is needed. An employee should always be encouraged to first seek resolution of a problem at this informal level and may choose to have assistance, as previously defined, at this informal level.

Formal Procedure

If a satisfactory solution is not obtained at the informal level or if for any reason the employee is not able to discuss the problem with the supervisor, the employee is encouraged to use the formal procedure outlined below. For the purpose of this policy, workdays are defined as Monday through Friday, excluding scheduled hospital holidays.

Step 1 (Department Head). The employee's first step of the formal appeal is a written request to the Director of Personnel that the department head hear the appeal. The request should be made within two workdays after the discussion, if any, with the supervisor or within five workdays of the problem which has caused the appeal.

The department head will review the facts and, within four workdays of the request, give a written response to the employee and will provide a copy of that response to Personnel.

In the event of an adverse response, the employee will be made aware of the right to move the appeal to the next step. If the department head is not available within the time limits provided, the appeal will automatically move to Step 2.

Step 2 (Division Director). If a satisfactory solution is not obtained at Step 1, the employee may request in writing to the Director of Personnel that the appropriate division director hear the appeal. This request must be made within two workdays of the response given at Step 1.

The division director will call on all interested parties to meet and to review the facts of the appeal and, within four workdays of the request, will give a written response to the employee and will provide a copy of that response to Personnel.

In the event of an adverse response, the employee will be made aware of the right to move the appeal to the next step. If the division director is not available within the time limits provided, the appeal will automatically move to Step 3.

Step 3 (Appeal Review Committee). If a satisfactory solution is not obtained at Step 2, the employee may request in writing to the Director of Personnel that the appeal be presented before an Appeal Review Committee, appointed for the specific purpose of hearing that appeal. The request must be made within two workdays of the response given at Step 2.

The Appeal Review Committee will convene within five workdays of the written request to review the facts and previous responses. The Committee may ask to have interested parties appear before them to present facts pertinent to the appeal.

Within three workdays of convening, the Committee will make a written recommendation to the Executive Director, based on its examination of the appeal. Within five workdays of receiving the recommendation of the Appeal Review Committee, the Executive Director will make a final decision, based on that recommendation and all other available information.

Appeal Review Committee. The Executive Director will appoint, on an ad hoc basis, an Appeal Review Committee of seven hospital employees, selected for their fairness and objectivity. In no instance shall any member of the Committee be from the same department or work area as the employee requesting the appeal.

The employee, requesting the appeal, has the right to disqualify without prejudice up to two of the appointed members of the Committee, if desired. Disqualification must take place prior to the presentation of the appeal to the Committee.

WORK WEEK	MONDAY WORKDAY 1	TUESDAY WORKDAY 2	WEDNESDAY WORKDAY 3	THURSDAY WORKDAY 4	FRIDAY WORKDAY 5
1	Incident Occurs	Talk with Supervisor			Appeal to Step 1 (2 workdays)
2				Department Head's Response (4 workdays)	
3	Appeal to Step 2 (2 workdays)				Division Administrator's Response (4 workdays)
4		Appeal to Step 3 (2 workdays)			
5		Convene Appeals Review Committee (5 workdays)			Committee Makes Recommendation to Executive Director (3 workdays)
6					Executive Director Makes Final Decision (5 workdays)

Procedural notes.

1. In the case of a suspended or terminated employee, the Appeal Procedure will be expedited as much as reasonable without harming the employee's right to a complete and fair hearing.
2. Time limits provided in this policy may be waived or amended only by mutual agreement.
3. For the purpose of clarity, the following outline illustrates the progression of steps and time limits provided in the appeal procedure:

OPEN DOOR POLICY

Dominion Foundries and Steel, Limited, Hamilton, Ontario, Canada, has an established procedure for hearing employee complaints. Here is the way it is described in *The Dofasco Way,* the employee handbook.

If you feel dissatisfied about the treatment you are getting as a Dofasco employee, first talk to your foreman about your problem or complaint. If he does not give you a satisfactory answer within a reasonable time, you are then entitled to see higher levels of the management. If you feel that it is necessary, it is your right to see the following persons, in the order listed below:

1. Your Foreman.
2. The Superintendent of your department.
3. The Vice-President to whom your Superintendent reports.
4. The Director of Personnel.
5. The President.

It is your right, as a member of the Dofasco family, to use this procedure with the assurance that nothing will be held against you for doing so. As a matter of courtesy, you should, of course, tell your foreman or others to whom you go for interviews, if it is your intention to carry your problem higher. They will help you in completing the arrangements.

COUNSELLING

Employees have two kinds of problems: (1) personal and (2) job-related. The need to discuss their problems is a real one. Employees should be given an opportunity to resolve their problems.

Employee personal problems relate to money, financing, wage assignments, mortgages, income tax, other tax rulings, court judgments, legal matters, moving, age verification, social security or medicare for self or parent, personal or family health, and a host of other items.

Employee job-related problems relate to supervision, opportunities for advancement, transfer, relocation, wages, lost paycheck, benefits, schools, maternity furloughs, military orders, insurance coverage for self and/or dependents, insurance claims, retirement planning, vested rights and many other similar items.

The above examples are specific and clearly-defined needs. In addition, employees have concerns about their jobs, the company and their future.

They feel *inadequate.* They are not clear on just what is expected and how their work is judged. They don't understand other departments and feel sometimes that another department keeps them from doing their best. They want to do quality work but the supervisors keep emphasizing production.

They feel *unappreciated.* They often suspect favoritism in promotions and salaries. Some employees, frankly, are afraid to open their mouths; complainers, they find, don't last long.

They feel *neglected.* Their friends in other companies get two more holidays, better vacations or benefits, more privileges. Management never comes around unless there is trouble brewing.

They feel *insecure.* The company is standing still. Sales are dropping. Deliveries are late. No new products are in evidence. The firm is planning to sell out, merge or move. The government is taking over.

Not all employees, of course, have all these problems all the time. But there is enough discontent, misunderstanding, confusion, bad feeling and other problems that their existence should be recognized. No employee can do his best as long as he is plagued with doubt, fear and similar distracting forces.

Every employee should have an outlet for his problems. In a small place this might well be the boss himself. In larger offices and plants this could be someone in the personnel office. In all cases, the person who is trying to counsel should resist the temptation to say, "I'll tell you what to do." No one can tell another person what he must do. All the person who is doing the counselling can do is help the other employee work out his own solution. This is enough of a responsibility.

Guidelines to Follow

Here are some suggestions for making the counselling discussion between manager and worker effective:

1. Make the employee feel welcome and comfortable. Provide privacy to make the interview confidential.
2. Let him talk. He has a need to express himself and tell about his trouble. Get the conversation going and then hear him out.
3. Hear the problem. Listen, get the full background, find out his attitude toward the problem. Do not assume after a few opening statements that you recognize his situation.
4. Get the pertinent facts. He may be emotionally upset, contradict himself and confuse you. Keep probing until all relevant facts are clear and fall into place.
5. Don't take sides. Accept what is said but express no judgment of his opinions or actions. Nor be sentimental or sympathetic with his side. Never lecture or moralize.
6. Help him gain insight into his problem. Once he has unburdened himself he may see the situation in a broader perspective. It is not uncommon to find him solving his own problem. Usually he knows what to do but wants first to "go on record" with it and then get some understanding to help him overcome it.
7. Let him suggest the solution. If his plan is satisfactory and you foresee no other involvement which could lead to trouble elsewhere, let him proceed. But you owe it to him to keep him from doing something that might only make the situation worse or lead to more serious consequences.
8. Conclude the visit; arrange for follow-up if necessary. Unless you are involved in the solution, get out of it and let the employee work it out on his own. You might casually check at a later date to see if things worked out as planned.

Getting involved in someone else's problems or troubles is serious business. Try to be helpful; that's the reason he came to you. But don't pretend to know all the answers.

COUNSELLING TECHNIQUES

Counselling is a means of getting people to do the right things: (1) in their jobs, and/or (2) in their personal lives.

There are two techniques that are used in counselling—the directive and the nondirective. In the directive counselling approach someone gives advice and guidance. In the nondirective counselling approach the counselor gives neither advice nor guidance but assists the other persons to work out solutions to their own problems.

The directive counselor controls the interview and moves the individual toward a counselor-chosen goal. The nondirective counselor stresses means by which the individual becomes more conscious of his own attitudes and feelings, with a consequent increase in insight and self-understanding.

In directive counselling the interviewer should explain the purpose to gain worker acceptance, have all facts thoroughly in mind, not take understanding for granted, control impatience, never talk down, and be absolutely certain the advice given is best for the other person, considering all circumstances and options. In nondirective counselling the interviewer should encourage the person to talk out his problem, not pretend to have the answer, listen patiently, be friendly, display no authority, give no moral admonition, never argue, try to relieve fears or anxieties, praise the person for opening up and revealing his feelings, and help him bring out the solution he can handle.

PROBLEM SOLVING

The steps in logically solving a problem are the following in the order shown:

1. Identify the problem.
2. Determine the objective.
3. Get the facts.
4. Analyze all possibilities.
5. Establish possible corrective courses.
6. Select the most appropriate one.
7. Explain the solution decided upon.
8. Obtain concurrence to proceed.
9. Take the action.
10. Check results.

General approaches are simply based on experience, observation, chance, quoting the book, consulting the boss, reading policy manual and the like. The above planned objective approach produces better results.

CHAPLAINS

Chaplains in industry have had enough success during the past decade to dispel the old notion that religion and business do not mix. Both church leaders and businessmen have been impressed.

What does an industrial chaplain do? Very little of his work is directly related to religion. Most of the time he serves as friend and confidant, a man to whom workers—and executives—can go with their troubles. A growing percentage of the ministers entering industry are also trained as psychologists, and their day-to-day work is far more involved with counseling than with preaching.

What do workers discuss? Mostly they bring up personal problems —marital and family troubles, alcoholism, and personality difficulties. Only about 10% of the visits are concerned with job-related problems.

Regardless of his denomination, the man of the cloth works with men and women of every religion, and also with those of no religion. A bulletin board announced his presence by saying simply he is here "to listen and help if he can."

To be effective, he must be left alone, not directed by the company. Otherwise he may be regarded suspiciously as a new gimmick to improve employee relations, or worse, a company spy. But once the workers discover for themselves that he is operating independently his acceptance is assured and his usefulness begins.

Flick-Reedy's Chapel of the Workers is dedicated to all of its deceased employees. This meditation room contains an excellent wood carving of St. Joseph the Worker. The main altar piece is a glass sculpture of "Christ on the Mount" by world renowned Pascal, the only person in the world who sculptures in glass.

CHAPEL

One of the many unique facilities available to employees of the Flick-Reedy Corporation, Bensenville, Illinois, is The Chapel of the Workers. Here employees of all faiths can come before or after their workshift, or during their lunch hour or coffee breaks, for a few moments of contemplation or prayer, or to read a passage from the Bible.

They also conduct religious services in the company auditorium on Holy Days; present programs of inspirational music; make up theatre parties to see idealistic and spiritually-oriented shows; and when a troubled employee seeks personal counsel, they ask if he would like to talk with his own clergyman.

A WILL

A good citizen demands the same careful planning for the disposition of property after death as for its use during life. For this he needs a will. A revocable trust may also be used; the same guidelines apply.

What is a Will?

In simple terms it is a legal document, signed and witnessed, by which a person directs the distribution of his property upon his death.

Why Make a Will?

There are dozens of valid reasons that could be advanced for making a will. They vary with the priorities and values a person lives by, as well as concern for loved ones left behind. A will enables a person to preserve the maximum amount of his estate for the support of spouse and children through the elimination of unnecessary estate taxes and court costs.

It lets a person choose the guardian for his children as well as the executor of his estate. It permits a person to designate what percentage, if any, is to be left to favorite philanthropic or charitable purposes. It may help to keep peace among survivors by removing any doubt as to how possessions are to be divided.

Why Should You Have a Will?

Practically everyone needs a will. It is not necessary that a person own a substantial amount of property. In fact, a will can be most valuable when the estate is small and assets must be conserved for the benefit of the surviving family.

In the case of married persons, both husband and wife should have wills. Of course, if a husband and wife own all their property jointly, the will of the first to die will not have to be probated and the property will pass automatically to the survivor. But if both die at the same time—in an accident, for instance—or under circumstances that make it difficult to determine which one died first, then it can be very important that each has a will. In any event, the survivor will eventually die and will need a will to control the disposition of property at that time.

When Should a Will be Made?

For anyone of legal age who doesn't already have one, the first rule in making a will is: "Don't put it off." No one knows, even young people, when tomorrow may be too late. Besides, when a person waits until he is advanced in age or seriously ill, the chances are greater that the will may be contested on grounds of incompetence or undue influence.

A will can be changed at any time during the lifetime. In fact, it should be reviewed and probably revised whenever a person's family or financial situation change.

What Should be Included in a Will?

A person should decide first what he would like to do. He should discuss the matter with his spouse and perhaps others in whom he has special confidence. As far as possible his will should provide for dependents—spouse, children, parents, others. It might be well for him to list the vital statistics of each beneficiary named, as well as the assets and liabilities of his estate. He may also wish to name institutions or organizations he would like to remember.

How may a Person Write his Will?

Don't try to write it—get a lawyer. Many wills have failed because they were not properly prepared. A will is a legal document, the preparation of which requires special knowledge. Legal requirements vary depending on where a person lives. The fee for a lawyer's service is small in comparison to the potential benefits to the beneficiaries. By having a qualified lawyer prepare a will, the chances are minimized that it will fail or be misinterpreted. Furthermore, a competent lawyer is able to advise on the best way to achieve the results desired.

What happens if . . .

You Leave no Will?

- Your property will be distributed in a manner prescribed by law, which may be inconsistent with your wishes and the needs of your family.

- The administrator of your estate will be appointed by the court and may not be familiar with your family's situation.

- Transfer of real estate may be delayed, especially if you are survived by minor children.

- Your spouse may not be allowed to administer property for minor children without the consent and supervision of the court.

- At a legally-fixed age, usually 21, children's shares will be distributed outright.

- Taxes and expenses may be incurred, including the cost of a bond, which might have been reduced or eliminated.

- No distribution will be made to your church or other organizations or institutions.

You Have a Will ?

- You are assured that your property will be distributed according to your wishes and with consideration for any special needs of your family.

- You will name the person who will administer your estate.

- Delays in transfer of real estate, as well as other problems, can be avoided by proper provisions in the will.

- You can leave your entire estate to your spouse if you wish. You can create trusts for minor children, naming your own trustee, to whom you can give broad, flexible administrative power.

- You can specify that children's shares be distributed at the age or ages at which you feel they will have attained adequate maturity and judgment.

- You may be able to reduce taxes and expenses. Usually you can provide that your executor serve without bond.

- You can make bequests to your church and other organizations or institutions.

INCOME TAX AID

Employees who seek assistance in filling out their income tax returns may get help from the Internal Revenue Service either by telephone or personal visit to one of the IRS offices.

A special telephone number is designated for telephone inquiries. This service is available each year from January 1 until April 15. The telephone number is publicized to make it known generally, or companies that wish to announce this to their employees may get this special number from the local IRS office. Qualified personnel are on hand to answer telephone inquires.

People may also visit their nearest district office where IRS agents are available to assist them in filling out their returns. Extra agents are transferred to the neighborhood office locations during the first few months of each year to handle the volume of inquiries.

COMPANY LIABILITY FOR ADVICE

Just as there is an inborn tendency for a son to listen to his father, so also do many employees automatically accept the advice of their employers, especially when it is favorable.

People are flattered when asked for advice. When the boss' opinion or counsel is sought, there is a temptation on the part of the manager or supervisor to say, "Now I'll tell you what to do." What happens if the well-intentioned advice goes awry? Who is to blame? Who has the responsibility?

An employee assumes, and rightfully so, that his boss knows what he is talking about. After all, he is in a higher position which requires more know-how, he probably helped build the business, he has had more experience in problem situations. But is this really true?

A person may be well educated in mathematics, or experienced in metal fabrication, to the point of impressing those who work for him with his thorough knowledge of his job. But does that automatically qualify him to counsel a co-worker on marital or financial matters?

The same also holds for companies. When a firm offers its employees accommodation discounts at a so-called wholesale furniture dealer, have the quality of the merchandise and the ethics of the seller, especially on financing arrangements, been thoroughly checked out so they can be endorsed by the company? When a company permits an out-of-state land promoter to show his films and make his presentation to a group of employees, even if they attend the meeting voluntarily, what happens later if some of the employees (who purchased land because they trusted their employer) feel they've been duped?

The safest course to follow is to offer no advice. This, of course, is not possible since many employees actually seek counsel from the boss they have come to know and respect. When asked, don't tell someone what he ought to do. Tell him instead, "Here is what I might do" in similar circumstances.

A company clinic should not tell an employee what to do or which doctor to see for treatment. It should point out the need for attention and let the employee choose from a list of several doctors. But let the employee make his own selection.

The same is true for lawyers. A company may suggest certain specialty attorneys for specific situations and let the employee know where he may go for help. A counsellor in the personnel office can point out the Legal Aid Society in the community for someone who cannot afford to engage a private lawyer. Again, let the employee be responsible for his own course of action.

A company, through its supervisors, should always be willing to help employees, particularly those who ask for help. But no one should tell another person what to do unless he is willing to assume full responsibility for any consequences. After all, what one person wants or likes may not fit the other person. As they say in sales, "If we want to know what John Smith buys, we've got to look through John Smith's eyes."

NOTARY PUBLIC

A notary public is a public officer or other person authorized to authenticate certain papers and take affidavits. In companies this often is a member of the legal, financial or personnel staff.

What does the notary seal mean? Many people believe that this seal is a guarantee of the truth, that the signer promised to purchase something or pay someone. This is not so.

The notary's seal is only a guarantee of the fact that one or more persons appeared before the notary and signed the document in his presence. The notary seal confirms only that the signer showed proof of identity, not that what is stated on the document is the truth.

PROBLEM EMPLOYEES or EMPLOYEES WITH PROBLEMS

Problem employees quite often are simply employees with problems. These are not employees who are disloyal, unproductive or untrained. Their problems are such that the employees usually have little or no control over the situation.

These are the people in the workforce who have developed physical, mental, emotional or psychological ills. Their problems may be tempo-·rary or permanent. Generally the condition shows up after they have been with the company a while. Because their work record is usually good, they have the benefit of job security although they may no longer be able to carry their fair share of the load.

Included in this broad category are all sorts of workers who are no longer performing up to previous standards. And there are no similarities between the many types, except that they have become less-than-good workers. The list is long and includes white collar workers and blue collar workers and cuts across all strata of society.

Many employees develop mental, nervous and emotional ills which may not be job related. Aside from the popular occupational diseases —caused by tension, pressure, worry and the like—there is an almost endless list of conditions that change an otherwise good worker into a problem employee. A worker's marital or family situation, financial status, health and such concerns may so disturb him that he can no longer concentrate on his job. Quite often he keeps his troubles locked up inside his heart, ashamed to admit them and fearful of his job.

The supervisor, not knowing the real reason, may jump to an erroneous conclusion, and take action that aggravates the situation. But even when the cause of a worker's changed attitude or performance is known, many times the temptation to dispense discipline rather than understanding is too inviting for the self-righteous supervisor to ignore. No supervisor has been endowed with the divine right to pass judgment over a fellow human being. Nor is this advisable from a purely selfish viewpoint. A good employee gone wrong becomes a better employee if faith in him is maintained and he is helped over the rough spot in his life.

A big area of problem employees involves those who develop physical limitations. Through no fault of their own they are no longer adequate for their regular work although still useful under new terms. These are the people who are recovering from heart attacks, who suffer amputations, who develop chronic illnesses, and so on. Is it fair to shelve them when their former value declines? On the other hand, is it fair to other good employees to give all workers equal consideration when it is obvious some of them are unable to compete? Maybe the answer is to transfer these physically-limited workers, temporarily or permanently, to jobs that are within their capabilities and to continue to compensate them, as much as is practical, in accordance with their length of service and other previous contribution.

In all these cases, and others like them, it may be well to remember that loyalty works equally well both ways. Companies expect loyalty from their workers. When the shoe is on the other foot, is it asking too much for the company to show its loyalty to the employees? An employee who has given the best years of his life to a company may have no other place to turn for help and understanding.

It might be hard to prove, but it shouldn't be hard to believe, that a company that builds people also builds loyalty, dedication, understanding, appreciation and character—all of which help to build profits.

WAGE ASSIGNMENTS

When an employee becomes delinquent in paying a debt, it is customary for his creditor to attempt to collect the debt from the compensation due the employee. This places the employer in the unpleasant position of an innocent stakeholder between his employees and their creditors.

The two major creditor remedies are wage assignments and garnishments. Both are regulated by state laws which vary from one state to another.

Collection of a delinquent debt by means of a wage assignment is a convenient procedure available to creditors. Like the wage deduction process, the source of the collection is the compensation payable by an employer to the debtor-employee. Unlike the wage deduction process, the wage assignment process may be begun without first obtaining a judgment against the debtor.

There is varied company reaction to this unwelcome intrusion, making the employer a legally-constituted collection and remitting agency for an unknown, and often questionable, creditor or finance office. Some employers cooperate willingly in an effort to be helpful to their workers, disregarding the cost in time and effort. Other employers want no part of bad debt involvement and automatically discharge an employee when he gets into money trouble.

Some companies officially frown upon the bad habit of employees using unsound financing practices. Companies may encourage employees with money problems to visit the personnel office for counsel and advice, and may recommend them to the Credit Union as one possibility for a solution. They reason it is better to seek help before trouble starts rather than afterwards when embarrassment may result.

Many companies simply hold an employee's paycheck as a weapon to move the employee toward taking action to resolve his problem. They do not give him his paycheck until a written release is obtained from the creditor. Whether this practice is legally permissible is debatable.

In a large number of companies, wage garnishments are simply not tolerated. An employee is subject to automatic discharge upon receipt of a wage assignment. As one handbook says, "If you stick your neck out for more installment purchases than you can afford, you may lose your job." These companies take the position that they don't want to assume any measure of involvement for their fiscally-irresponsible employees, and they hope their announcement of a firm stand will serve as a deterrent to indifferent employees.

Generally, an employer does not have to put up with garnishments and may fire an employee for having one filed against his salary. However, before doing so, it would be wise to check with a lawyer to see whether there might be a state law which forbids discharge. At any rate, a company should not take any hasty dismissal action because a creditor might have filed wrongfully, or the employee, by taking prompt positive action, might succeed in having the garnishment withdrawn.

Wage assignments, garnishments, levies, judgments, assessments, and other forms of attachments should be filed in the employee individual file folder since they do tell something about the person away from his job. It is not recommended, however, that these papers be filed when the assignment is readily resolved by the employee, or if the claim was submitted erroneously. Why retain for possible future reference any information which might reflect adversely upon the employee, especially when the employee is really not at fault and his record is good?

WAGE ATTACHMENTS

A typical company policy on "Garnishments and Wage Attachments" might read as follows:

It is company policy to comply with applicable wage assignments and garnishment laws while at the same time understanding and cooperating with employees who are experiencing financial difficulties.

When an employee's earnings become the subject of a garnishment or other legal process served on the company requiring it to withhold earnings, the following action is to be taken:

1. The employee is to be immediately advised that the company has received the garnishment or wage assignment requiring deductions from his earnings, and the amount which is to be legally withheld.
2. The employee is to be given every chance to clear up any possible misunderstanding and, if he succeeds, to bring in a release from the creditor or his agency.
3. When this fails, the employee is to be strongly urged to satisfy the debt or make other arrangements for payment before payroll deductions begin.
4. If the employee is unable to have the garnishment or attachment removed, the company is required by law to deduct from the employee's earnings the amount specified in the process.

It is recognized that each garnishment must be considered in light of the individual's circumstances and his control over the situation which

615

prompted the action. As a rule, however, an employee who repeatedly becomes involved in salary attachment proceedings may be considered a personnel problem, but any action that is taken must be consistent with state laws.

BANKRUPTCY

Under Chapter XIII of the federal Bankruptcy Law, a company must fulfill its legal responsibilities if an employee of the company is declared to be bankrupt. The company forwards the employee's paychecks in their entirety to a named trustee, who makes the required deductions under power of attorney and releases the balance of the check or checks to the employee.

TRANSPORTATION PROVIDED BY COMPANY

One of the problems that develops when a company relocates into an outlying area is that some employees may have difficulty getting to work. Whatever means of transportation they had been using is no longer appropriate and comparable substitute arrangements may not be available.

As a result, a company may find itself in the transportation business. The company involvement may be in any one or a combination of the following three forms:

1. Company buses.
2. Company-sponsored vanpooling.
3. Company-encouraged private carpooling.

One nationally-known manufacturing concern moved from a convenient downtown location to an inconvenient suburban location. True, the company could have fulfilled its employee needs by drawing from the local community. But management felt an obligation to the many loyal old-timers, many of whom were now stranded. So for years the company operated several buses to transport workers between the former address and the new one.

Vanpooling is becoming useful. Zenith Radio Corporation gets almost a hundred nonexempt and exempt employees to and from their jobs in the new plant in Glenview, Illinois this way. The company leases the vans, which are really sports club wagons. Each van holds 12 passengers (11 with the driver). The passengers on each route all pay the same nominal monthly rate which is deducted from paychecks. The driver rides free and also receives the fares of the 10th and 11th passengers. The fare of the first nine passengers is used to defray operating and maintenance costs.

The volunteer drivers, to whom the company assigns the vehicles, are selected on the basis of: (1) geographic location, (2) driving history, and (3) regular 8:30 to 5:00 work schedule. There is a small charge for the personal use of the vans by the drivers on weekends or evenings.

Company-encouraged carpooling is popular because of: (1) savings in gasoline, (2) reduction of highway traffic, and (3) fewer company-provided parking spaces (estimated at $1,000 each per year). Employees residing in the same neighborhood are put in touch with each other. They make their own arrangements including sharing the driving or paying a share of the cost. Instead of providing company buses or vans, some employers may prefer to offer a financial incentive to drivers who bring in other workers.

In these cases of employees riding to work in groups, each member has the telephone numbers of other members. A chain call system is used in emergencies and for last minute substitute driver arrangements. One big benefit companies see in group riding is that members tend to police each other in getting to work on time.

CAR POOLING

Togetherness is five members of a car pool riding 30 miles to work in a compact car. The original idea of a car pool was to spare each member having to buy a second car to drive to work. Now that second cars in families are taken for granted, car pools continue for another reason—saving gas and money.

To make a car pool work, rules must be established and followed. Each member is assigned a day of the week to drive. They can trade with each other, of course, if the car is needed at home on a particular day. But everyone takes his turn regardless of weather.

Upon arriving at a member's house, the driver waits only a certain length of time before taking off. The same is true at the place of work for the return trip. The penalty for lateness might not only be missing the ride but may also cost the offender the price of a drink the next evening.

Anyone who misses his turn to drive during the week must pay the driver who fills in for him. The rules can be whatever the group decides is best in their situation. But the rules should be explicit.

There could be minor problems and aggravations. One car may not be air-conditioned. Another car's heater may be out of order. Or a car could be too small. A car could be so old as to be dangerous or unreliable. These things have to be resolved.

Company Sponsorship

Quite a few companies encourage car pools or even sponsor them. Reducing the number of single-driver automobiles on the expressways during rush hours helps reduce congestion and, of course, saves precious energy. But aside from any egalitarian motivation, there is sometimes a very practical side that causes companies to get into the transportation business.

A company that moves from its downtown location, which was adequately served by public transportation, may find itself and its employees out in the boondocks. To get employees to and from work special arrangements are made.

One arrangement is to put employees in the same locality in touch with each other. One employee may agree to have another employee pick him up at a convenient location and drive him to work and back home again afterwards. Paying the driver a modest amount for this courtesy, perhaps the equivalent of bus fare, would seem appropriate. With a few such paying passengers each day, the driver eases considerably the financial cost of his own transportation.

Instead of providing buses to transport workers to a plant in an outlying location, a company may prefer to pay car drivers for bringing in other workers.

Carrying this idea one step further, a company may purchase cablike vehicles which carry nine passengers. If the passengers pay for their rides, the driver rides free; if the passengers ride free, the driver is paid for hauling them around.

There is expense for the company, but in certain circumstances this cost can be justified. On the plus side, it keeps employees from quitting, promotes better attendance, is a tangible morale builder, and fosters good community relations.

VANPOOLING

In 1973 the 3M Company, St. Paul, Minnesota, experimented with its "Commute-A-Van" idea to help alleviate mounting traffic and parking problems. The original six-van, pilot program was an instant success with employees and has been expanded to 100 vans.

In one year this vanpooling program will save 2.5 million vehicle miles and more than 200,000 gallons of gasoline. In addition, it will remove nearly 400 tons of pollutants from the air in reduced auto exhaust emissions. It has also helped the corporate headquarters loca-

Employees from the 3 M Company of St. Paul, Minnesota do their share toward energy conservation by boarding their "Commute-A-Van" for their commute home.

tion eliminate 650 parking stalls at an estimated capital savings of $2.5 million.

More than 900 company employees in the Twin Cities ride the vans to and from work. Average occupancy per van is 11 passengers and the average daily round trip mileage is 49. Rider surveys show that 80% said the vanpool is more convenient than their former mode of travel, and 97% intend to stay with the program permanently.

The advantages of vanpooling and 3M's emergence as the acknowledged leader in the field led to the publication of a handbook, now updated, that most of the 100 vanpooling companies and agencies in the United States used to begin similar programs. Information may be obtained by writing 3M Company, Building 220-13E, St. Paul, Minnesota 55101.

PUBLIC TRANSPORTATION USE

Two innovative plans designed to encourage employees to use public transportation and thereby conserve energy were introduced by American Hospital Supply Corporation of Evanston, Illinois, a company with more than 25,000 employees worldwide.

First, to cut the use of downtown parking, the AHSC made a pay adjustment to all headquarters employees, regardless of whether or not they drive to work, equivalent after taxes to the annual cost of leasing a parking space. This amounted to $554 annually before taxes and $360 after taxes. The employee decides whether to spend the money on parking or on other things.

Second, in cooperation with the Chicago Transit Authority, the company sells monthly unlimited CTA passes to home office employees. The AHSC buys the bus and rapid transit train passes for $25.00 each and sells them to employees at a 25% discount for $18.75.

The company is trying to work out similar arrangements with other transit companies and commuter railroads servicing the areas in which most employees live.

According to Mr. Karl D. Bays, chairman and chief executive officer, the company is trying "to find solutions to the many problems associated with massive individual use of automobiles for transportation —the congestion, pollution and over-consumption of energy."

AUTOMOBILE ALLOWANCE or LEASED CARS

When automobiles are used in business some form of tax-free compensation is made. A company could offer an allowance or expense reimbursement for use of private automobiles. Or it could provide free use of company-owned or commercially-leased cars.

A monthly automobile allowance is usually based upon a percentage of the car's cost or the maximum allowed towards the purchase of a car —such as 80% of the retail price of a car up to $6,000. Some companies will advance this amount as an interest-free loan. The monthly allowance is then used to reduce the outstanding amount of the loan.

As to providing a leased car, the Internal Revenue Service will rule that there is additional income unless there is a charge made for personal use of the car. Some organizations charge a flat dollar amount per month for personal use, such as $50 per month. This charge, being so obvious to the employee, could result in a negative reaction. Another approach might be to furnish a leased car, requiring the employee to keep it washed and garaged, and to provide the gasoline.

Automobiles can be leased under several arrangements. One of these is a maintenance lease where the leasing company assumes all the risks. Another is a finance lease where the lessee takes the risk. With the warrantees in effect today, it would seem financially advantageous for the corporation to take this risk, particularly if the fleet of cars is substantial. Further, with the cost of money at an all-time high, it might be advisable to consider prepaying the leases rather than paying the high interest that the leasing company would have to charge for the use of its money. If this is done, involve legal counsel so that such cars remain unencumbered on the books of the lessor.

PARKING

The company parking lot is rapidly becoming a requirement as firms move to outlying areas away from public transportation and as more and more employees rely upon their private automobiles to get to work.

A parking lot is included as a normal cost of operation. It is used by customers, visitors and employees.

The location of the company facilities determines whether a parking lot is provided. Firms in outlying neighborhoods have little choice; the convenience is necessary, regardless of cost. In the metropolitan district the expense may be prohibitive and public transportation may suffice.

In most cases the parking lot adjoins the office or factory building, or is next door or across the street. Seldom is it more than one block away.

For convenience and comfort, such a lot is lighted and surfaced. Blacktop is popular for spacious areas, concrete is sometimes found in downtown, congested locations, and occasionally the lot is gravel.

Weather is a factor. Overhead walkways may lead to the building as protection from rain or sun. Use of snow removal equipment is part of maintenance, as is oil and grease cleanup.

For safety, the lot is patrolled, walled or fenced. One-way traffic patterns avoid congestion. Speed limits are posted and attempts made at control. Cross-lane humps are built into the paved surface, or barricades are erected to prevent speeding. Painted guide marks aid the flow of traffic and signs identify special areas and reserved spaces.

There are no services, such as car washing. But in below-zero weather some on-the-spot help may be made available for starting stalled vehicles.

Detailed instructions on the use of the company parking lot are given to new employees. Individual employees are assigned to a reserved lot or section but not to a specific space. Drivers use the lot on a first-come, first-served basis, which aids to encourage employees to come early. All companies, however, have individual spaces reserved and marked for executives and for others, such as in-and-out salesmen, plant nurse, etc., as a necessity.

Smaller spaces are marked off for foreign and compact cars, and a small corner set aside for motorcycles and bicycles.

One difficulty is spotting trespassers. A parking sticker on a window or bumper is an attempt to meet this problem by identifying those who are authorized to use the lot. Violators of common sense speed regulations, safety precautions and other rules lose their parking lot rights, usually after a first warning.

There is a problem when the company grows and the parking lot doesn't. In such cases there is usually a waiting list to "get in" and replacements may be selected by seniority or job level. One plan that has been used where the parking facility is inadequate to serve everybody is to assign spaces for car pools in preference to solo drivers.

From an employee viewpoint, users take the parking lot for granted just as they do other fringe benefits. From an employer viewpoint, the day of the automobile makes the parking lot as necessary as the washroom.

PARKING LOT REGULATIONS

As one example of the rules governing the use of company parking lots, here are the Parking Lot Regulations taken from the Member Manual of the Woodward Governor Company, 5001 North Second Street, Rockford, Illinois 61101.

Although these rules apply specifically to the main parking lot behind the (Rockford) plant, the emphasis on courtesy and safety applies to driving and parking anywhere on company property.

Assigned Spaces. Approximately 250 parking spaces are assigned. These spaces are assigned to the first 250 on the seniority list who drive regularly. Members who have assigned parking spaces must drive their cars regularly or drive their cars as a part of a riding pool. Only one member of a riding pool is entitled to an assigned space. Members should not ask for a reserved space when they drive infrequently.

After 8:00 A.M., unoccupied, assigned spaces may be used by any member unless a marker on the space indicates otherwise.

Unassigned Spaces. Members who do not have an assigned parking space may park in the open parking area on the basis of first come first choice, in the area assigned to the particular exit and entrance used. The dividing line between the assigned and unassigned areas is clearly indicated.

Be Careful of Your Neighbor's Car. Please park in the center of your parking space. Use care in opening your car doors. You don't want your car dented or scratched, so give the same consideration to the other fellow. It is required that all drivers back into parking spaces.

Special Parking Area for Waiting Cars. The parking area north of the regular parking lot and parallel to the cement drive is for cars and drivers who come to pick up members after they leave work. This area is not to be used for regular parking while the driver is at work. Cars parked here must leave by the North Gate.

Ten-Mile Speed Limit on Company Property. Drive at a safe speed in the parking lot and on the drive leading out to the highway.

Do Not Pick Up Riders After Leaving Individual Parking Spaces. Riding groups should all get in the car where it is parked. When a car stops to pick up riders in the drive near the gate house, it is hazardous and annoying to the occupants of following cars.

Exit Gate. The parking lot to the rear of the main building is divided into three areas, one for each gate. Cars *must* leave by the gate corresponding to the area in which they are parked.

Additional parking, convenient for general office and engineering departments' use, is located to the south of the main building. The same rules of courtesy and safety apply to members using these lots.

FREE ADVERTISEMENTS

Ever notice the "news tree" on college campuses, used by students to make announcements, inquire about rides home, or offer articles for sale? This convenient clearing house of information is popular because it is an effective means of direct communication.

In business the need for employees to reach fellow workers also exists. Many companies, as an accommodation to their employees, provide for such a medium of exchange. It may take the form of a handy bulletin board, to which workers may attach notices. Where there is a "house organ" magazine, a space is often devoted to this purpose.

Many employee publications offer free advertisements. Here employees may offer cars and other items for sale or exchange, may express a desire to purchase something, and may even seek or offer apartments or homes for rent or sale.

MUSIC

Programmed music is the prearranged use of melody and rhythm to provide a specific end result. This definition immediately brings to mind the concept of background music for industrial and commercial application.

The origins of music programmed to achieve a specific result date back to the religious dances of early man, the pounding drums aboard Roman warships, the work songs of prison chain gangs. It has permeated our cultural traditions and can serve as a stimulating force, a form of entertainment, a relaxing influence, a means of setting an atmosphere, or a masking influence to overcome the effect of noise pollution. Music is a powerful emotional tool.

Since music affects the sense of hearing, its emotional impact is understandable. Sound can bring pleasure or can be deeply disturbing. It can lift the spirits of people or leave them emotionally drained. To some extent people can be influenced without their consent or knowledge.

Stimulation, or the increase in worker productivity, has always been claimed to be one of the prime reasons for the installation of a background music system. Yet, in studying field reports on this utilization there are widely-varying statistics relative to its effectiveness. For every study indicating improved productivity there is another with negative results. It appears that the common mistake is to think of music itself as establishing a specific rhythm to "pace" the work pattern. Rather, the value of the music lies in its ability to relieve monotony—serving as a positive force to eliminate worker fatigue and reduce errors—a means to create a pleasant working condition.

There are some applications, however, where the stimulus effect can block certain types of activity. It has been found, for example, that people involved in highly-intensive thought processes, often object strenuously to all forms of music while they are working, claiming that they cannot concentrate "with all that noise."

Music can also have a masking effect, useful both in overcoming objectionable ambient noise and in establishing an aura of privacy.

The effect is applied by raising the level of background music in an office to overcome the annoying sounds of the typewriter, keypunch machines or nearby conversations. In a more positive way, it can provide privacy in areas of confidentiality where it overcomes the lack of effective acoustical isolation. In both of these instances, the background music must not be too loud lest it become an annoyance on its own.

Many and Varied Applications

Not directly related to any of the above categories are the somewhat more unique applications. "Music on hold" is becoming quite common in business telephone systems. Mood music for contented cows (no pun intended) has been shown to increase milk production. Experimentation relating the effects of music on plant growth has been reported in several scientific journals. Mentally disturbed patients have been found to react favorably to specially programmed music. There seem to be no limitations to the beneficial effects of music when properly applied.

Programmed music, when used in business and industrial applications, does have certain requirements which are important for most effective utilization. The music should be familiar and with definite rhythm. It should be melodic in nature, and with little or no introduction to the main theme. Also, the volume level must be fairly constant with a minimum of peaks and valleys.

Beyond these few basic rules, the main criterion appears to be one of providing music to which the listener can readily relate. It must also be appropriate to the type of activity involved. Bach and Beethoven do not lend themselves to the production assembly line; neither does hard rock. Age, education and ethnic background are but a few of the factors which influence the desires of the listener. Other variables are more subtle. There is no single music program that will please all people.

Background music has become just as important a factor for business and industry as proper color on the walls, carpets on the floor and suitable lighting. It is an accepted, almost expected, aid to the effective operation of any business office, industrial plant or commercial establishment.

Music hath charms and when properly programmed for a specific purpose can be an effective aid to increase productivity—through stimulation, through creation of a pleasant atmosphere, through masking of objectionable noise. Its utilization can be extremely varied, but when properly applied to the task at hand its emotional appeal is almost universal.

Telex Music Machine. The Telex TMS is an automatic 8-track cartridge changer. The unit plays standard stereo tapes, and with practically every type of music now prerecorded with new titles released weekly, the choice of program material is as flexible as a company wants.
The Telex TMS is suitable for any size installation. It can serve as a self-contained system in small shops or offices or can be connected to existing public address or sound distribution systems in larger places.

CHECK CASHING

A check cashing service can be more than a convenience. Plants which are located away from a handy bank or currency exchange might find it necessary to arrange for cashing paychecks on the premises. But there are also other reasons.

If a company pays its employees by check, and an employee is injured on the way to the bank to cash the paycheck, is the company liable? A New York State court held that the employee was "working for the company" at the time of the injury and that the company was responsible.

The employee was struck by a pushcart while returning from cashing her paycheck during the noon hour, and she sustained injuries. The court concluded that the injuries arose out of, and in the course of, employment.

In some plants employees will turn over their paychecks to one of their number to go to the bank to cash them before closing time. There have been numerous instances of these messengers being held-up and often injured. Hold-up men often frequent public check cashing establishments where they can select their victims. Not only is this type of messenger service hazardous, but it also allows the earnings of individual employees to become a matter of general knowledge. This can cause personnel problems.

One solution to problems such as these might be to bring in a mobile check cashing service. There are three types of service.

1. Person-to-person. Bonded cashiers wheel money carts directly to each individual at his work station.
2. Central plant location. The cashier sets up a portable service in some central location inside the plant, in the cafeteria, for example, where checks may be cashed during the lunch hour or relief periods, or at some other location easily accessible.
3. Outside plant. Cashiers work directly from armored truck parked at plant gate or in parking lot serving employees as they leave at the end of the shift.

Check cashing service has these advantages. It

1. Discourages tavern check cashing. This eliminates the problems of absenteeism, tardiness, inefficiency, accidents, late home arrivals and such which are associated with drinking.
2. Cuts unexcused errands. This solves the problem of employees sneaking time, extra at lunch or early at quitting time, to cash checks on the outside.
3. Gives psychological boost. The convenience and consideration of management does, in many cases, result in an increase in production.

As a by-product, the service usually has insurance coverage:

1. For the employer. Each account served is fully covered by liability insurance against any damage, physical or otherwise, for which their trucks or cashiers are responsible.
2. For the employee. The employee who cashes his paycheck is protected against loss of his earnings by force while en route to his home.

A pioneer in this field is Thillens Checashers of Chicago, a service recognized and regulated by the State of Illinois. Established in 1932, its fleet of 20 armored trucks serve more than 125,000 wage earners each week. Their check cashing service is always "free" to the firm. Only the employees who wish to cash their checks pay a nominal fee, usually two or three times less than a currency exchange charge.

A Thillens Checashers truck parked at plant gate waits to serve employees at the end of their shift.

There are similar check cashing operations in a number of other states around the country.

DIRECT PAYROLL DEPOSIT

Every employee looks forward to payday, but not to the prospect of waiting in a long line at the bank to cash or deposit a check.

In the past several years a number of companies have set up direct payroll deposit systems with their primary banks. For the company this arrangement reduces paperwork, and for the employees who elect to participate it eliminates the hassle of changing checks into cash.

It is now possible for a company to arrange for salary disbursals to be deposited in numerous banks, savings and loan associations, credit unions and other savings institutions at the same time. A clearing-house splits up the lump sum deposit and dispatches the proper amounts to designated savings institutions.

Computers at the savings institutions separate the deposits to be credited to individual accounts.

CASHLESS SOCIETY

Imagine a day when no one has a dime in his pocket. Instead of cash, a checkbook and a fistful of credit cards, a person may need only one card to handle money transactions.

If the idea sounds far-fetched, consider that money is only a social means of exchange representing an agreement that a certain item is worth so much of another item. Since the days when man swapped pelts for arrowheads, money has become more and more abstract. The next step may be giving up paper cash and paper checks for a set of electronically recorded numbers.

If this does come to pass, it won't happen overnight. Some experts in fund transfers feel that people will never completely stop using checks and cash. But people probably will use less cash and fewer checks because the financial institutions will be able to handle electronic impulses more efficiently and economically than paper items.

Buying and savings habits will undoubtedly be affected by these changes.

Volume Will Dictate

There are signs that the cashless society is coming but it is evolving slowly because it is difficult to change old and comfortable habit patterns. That it will ultimately happen is inevitable because banks are inundated with the increasing volume of bills, checks and other paperwork that are spewed out from today's consumer transactions.

American money transactions generate billions of checks and other pieces of paper a year (estimated at 85 billion by 1980). The system of processing and controlling the work is approaching a point of complete breakdown.

The change that is coming will do away with paper. But it will do more. It will also change the way money is handled.

A favorite phrase within the cashless society is "instantaneous transfer of funds." When a purchase is made the customer's account will be reduced the instant the clerk presses a button on his computer terminal to record the sale. No more waiting for payments, no more unpaid bills.

Not every bank can be connected with every store. Shared facilities or a common clearing house may be required.

Some cash for small items, such as bus fare, tips and the like may still be carried. It may not be feasible to process small transactions through an expensive computer system.

EFT Already Here

A new automatic, money-handling procedure is already in use. Under this system of electronic banking, common financial transactions are being completed by computer.

All of us have seen "automated tellers" that are placed in bank lobbies, projecting through the bank building wall, or at a bank drive-in facility. This 24-hour-a-day service will be expanded.

These are actuated by a customer's plastic identification card placed in a slot. A magnetic strip on the card identifies the customer. As a further safeguard, most machines also require the user to punch a secret number on a keyboard. The customer is then free to make deposits, withdraw cash, transfer funds from one account to another, or authorize payment of bills. A printed receipt is issued for each transaction.

This part of electronic banking is known as electronic funds transfer (EFT). This system:

1. Brings banking services to customers in bank and nonbank areas such as supermarkets, shopping centers, railroad stations, airline terminals and other convenient locations.

2. Provides instant access to deposited cash—or credit—at any time of the day or night.
3. Relieves customers of handling and depositing any regular income items such as paychecks and Social Security, while making the proceeds instantly available to their accounts.
4. Handles payment of routine expenditures, such as mortgage payments, insurance premiums, utility bills, without the necessity of writing and mailing checks.

Outlying Locations

When units are installed in locations away from a bank they become CBCT's—customer bank communication terminals.

This raises the controversy of whether these CBCT's are branch banking, something forbidden by law in some states. The savings-and-loan industry, not subject to the same branch limitations, is going ahead with its own version of the CBCT.

Technologically all this represents quite an advance in banking convenience. But the idea is not embraced by all people. Reasons for reluctancy are:

1. A hesitancy to give up checks as proof of payment.
2. Loss of right to stop payment on a check.
3. Frustrations of dealing with computers to correct errors.
4. Loss of "float" time. The electronic network works too fast: a typical EFT transaction takes 20 seconds. Customer's don't like losing the "float," the use of money between the time a check is written and cashed, or between the time a purchase is charged and the bill arrives.

The Ultimate

Banks and stores are already quite willing to cooperate in electronic funds transfer programs which would eliminate cash and checks from the economy. An identification card inserted in a machine would automatically transfer a purchase amount from the customer's checking account.

Ultimately, EFT could lead to automatic (not customer-activated) transfer of funds to pay many charges and bills, even including a person's annual income tax.

The two objections would be:

1. Loss of control over one's money.
2. Loss of privacy.

A firm step in this direction has already been taken by the Social Security Administration in its direct deposit (to banks or savings and loans) program. In Canada, a committee has been formed to write the rules for a computer system that could merge the use of check cashing with the credit card systems so that purchases could be automatically deducted from a customer's checking account without paper checks.

It is not too early to prepare yourself, your employees and your company for this development. It's no longer a question of whether it will happen but rather how soon people will be ready to accept it.

CHECKLESS PAYROLL

Service-minded banks are eager to put their new, sophisticated data processing equipment to full-time use—with an eye toward increasing business and adding customers in wholesale lots. The result is that banks have developed and are promoting the "checkless payroll" program. The concept has been around for some years. The earliest systems used mechanical calculators. Today computerization and magnetic ink character recognition devices simplify the job and make it profitable.

A key point is that many banks are capable of tailoring a system to fit the specific needs of a company. The type or amount of service has a broad base. For this reason, the checkless payroll idea is enjoying a steady growth throughout the country. An impressive number of business and industrial operations are already in the fold.

Under this arrangement a company's entire payroll is deposited with the cooperating bank. Each individual employee's "take home" pay is credited to his personal checking account. Instead of a paycheck he receives an "earnings statement" which is, in effect, a receipt for the amount deposited in his name.

The employee gets a checking account with a specified number of free, imprinted checks each month and there is no service charge. He does not have to take time off to cash his paycheck, nor pay any check-cashing fee, and he does not carry a large sum of cash on payday. He does not have to go out to buy money orders.

How It Works

Here is how the system works. The employer turns over a computer tape to the bank where it keeps its payroll account. The tape is the same one that would be used in preparing the usual paychecks, except that it includes some additional information, mainly the name and code number of the bank where each of the employees has an account.

The host bank strips from the tape the necessary data on all company employees with accounts in that bank. Then it sends the tape over to a central clearing house whose computers prepare tapes for each bank where the remainder of the employees have accounts. These tapes can be delivered or transmitted between interconnected bank computers.

Ultimately this system could lead to automatic deductions from individual paychecks, such as is presently done for Social Security and employee benefits, to include utility bills, mortgage payments, insurance premiums and even credit card charges.

Benefits For All

Under this program the employer is relieved of the cost of making out and distributing paychecks. The employee is relieved of the bother of getting to the bank to deposit the check or of mailing it in. The bank is relieved of considerable paperwork costs and perhaps an irritated customer waiting in line at the teller's window.

The employer does not have to allow employees time off to go out to cash their paychecks, nor buy a mobile check-cashing service to come to his premises, nor leave a large amount of money on deposit at a nearby bank where employees may go to cash their paychecks free. More important, by turning over the entire payroll function to the bank, the company is spared all necessary details of check writing, reconciling, protecting, filing government reports and making payments. The bank automatically prepares all federal W-2 statements as well as the required state withholding information forms, and either transmits them to the employer for distribution or mails them directly to the respective employees.

The union is agreeable since collection of dues can be arranged by the deduction of union dues from the checks on an individual basis, with the total receipts turned over directly to the union. Each union member signs a statement authorizing this deduction, and the collection of dues becomes a matter between the union, the employees and the bank.

The bank, of course, is happy to get fuller utilization of its data processing facilities and in the process win new customers and to service them in all of their banking needs.

ADVANTAGES OF THE CHECKLESS PAYROLL PLAN

Direct cost savings to the employer:

1. Except for the submission of source documents and reporting of changes, payroll accounting costs are virtually eliminated.

2. There is no longer any investment in payroll checks.
3. There is no preparation of Social Security reports.
4. Nor is there preparation of federal W-2 forms and State information returns.
5. No preparation of Depositary Receipt and monthly deposit of Withheld Taxes.
6. No longer needed is an internal control-laden paycheck distribution system.
7. Time-consuming paycheck signing is eliminated.
8. Time-consuming payroll account reconciliation is no more.
9. Other benefits inherent in a payroll system (i.e., payroll distribution reports, cost accounting data, etc.) can be realized without a heavy investment in equipment.
10. Eliminated also is the need for a separate payroll checking account maintained by the company.

Indirect benefits:

1. Strengthens internal control over payroll operation.
2. Reduced embezzlement possibilities.
3. Reduces error incidence.
4. Eliminates "payday absenteeism"; employees no longer need an extended lunch period in which to rush to the bank to cash checks and buy expensive money orders.
5. Improves employee morale by furnishing free checking accounts.
6. Encourages greater financial responsibility on the part of employees.
7. Insures confidential payroll handling by transferring out payroll accounting function to the bank.
8. Reduces petty jealousies resulting from too-wide knowledge of salary data.

Payroll accounting is not difficult. However, because of the confidential nature of payroll, many companies require that the work be done by one of their higher-level (and higher-paid) employees. Transfer of this function frees that employee for more difficult and profitable tasks.

CHAPTER VIII

WAGE AND SALARY ADMINISTRATION

EVOLUTION OF COMPENSATION

DO COMPANIES pay for the job or for the person? That is the question which underscores the kind of wage administration that is used as the basis of determining compensation.

Carl F. Lutz, senior vice-president of The Jacobs Company, says, "From the scientific management revolution, whose articles of faith were so well articulated by F. W. Taylor, Henry Laurence Gantt and the Gilbreths, came the idea—unique in human history—that compensation, job titles and personal advancement depended upon the value of the work a person performed. Past social and economic station, seniority and other nonwork-related factors had nothing to do with this fundamental concept. It was a peculiarly American idea, growing out of the American frontier and the much-maligned Protestant Ethic. In the annals of history there is no comparable idea, and in developing countries (and some European countries) it is a novel idea today."

Compensation based on work that is related to the job—an impersonal collection of duties and responsibilities—is a creature of management. Compensation based on the person is related to the qualifications and characteristics of the incumbent.

EMPLOYEE COMPENSATION

Employee compensation is a cost to the company just as rent or purchases. As a cost of production, direct and indirect wages must be accurately planned and intelligently controlled. The cost of manpower services should be kept in line with other operating costs.

Employee compensation, however, is more than just another cost of operation. Properly administered it becomes an incentive for expended efforts, cooperation and attitude toward the job and the company. It is a potent influence over the nature of the manpower services.

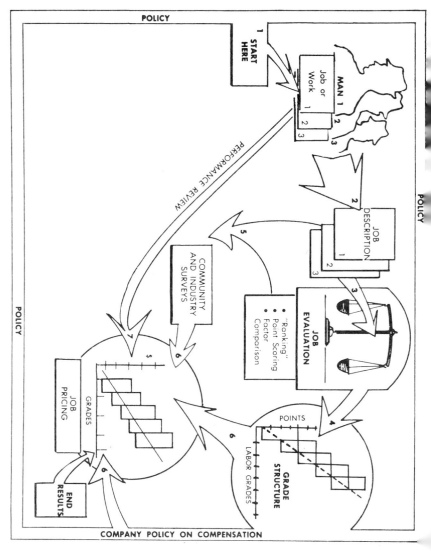

Bureau of Industrial Relations, Graduate School of Business, University of Michigan.

Two factors are inherent in a good wage program: (1) rates should be internally consistent; they should be based on an objective evaluation of each job as related to all other jobs, and (2) they should also be externally consistent, comparing favorably with community averages.

Three factors make up the individual wage of each employee:

1. The rate for his job in comparison with other jobs. Examples: The hourly rate for a carpenter is higher than that of a gardener. A bookkeeper is paid more than a messenger.
2. Recognition of individual effort. The jobs of two typists may be identical, but since no two individuals are quite alike their output on the job will most likely vary. When the better worker is paid the same salary as the poorer performer, the incentive to give more and better production disappears.
3. The wages will reflect labor market conditions. A realistic wage program recognizes the influence of outside competitive conditions.

To management wages are another administrative function; they will be fair if properly established and administered. To workers wages are a very personal thing; they will be fair only if they are considered adequate.

THE SALARY CASTE SYSTEM

For a country that prides itself on having no social classes, the United States has put up for a long time with a wage structure that epitomizes the caste system.

1. Factory and plant workers, and labor and service personnel, are paid by the hour.
2. Office clerical workers and technicians are paid by the week.
3. Professional and managerial personnel are paid by the month, often on annual terms.
4. Chairmen and chief executives, as well as celebrated sports and entertainment personalities, are given long-term contracts with liberal perquisities and individualized concessions.

WAGE and SALARY RELATIONSHIPS

Salary administrators in the personnel office are inclined to rely upon job evaluation or some similar system to establish the worth of a wage-

and-hour job or a salaried position. This is an objective method, and acceptable to many, as long as it is related to the job and not the incumbent.

A chief executive often has a different way of determining how much to pay an individual, particularly someone in a management, professional, or executive position. Whether this is recognized or not, the decision is based on three determinants: (1) job value, (2) market influence, and (3) personal value to the company.

The personnel executive can advise the president of the value of the job in relation to all other jobs in the organization. This is where a job rating or evaluation system provides objective data. But this is only the starting point for the chief executive. Nevertheless, it is a sound base without which any other considerations would likely be erroneous.

Some jobs are in such scarce supply that the "going rate" reflects market influence more than job value. A physician on the company payroll is paid more for knowledge than for duties, especially when assigned to paperwork or other nonprofessional tasks. Computer analysts, fire prevention engineers, actuaries, are scarce in the employment market. A company has to be willing to pay whatever it takes to "buy" a qualified applicant away from another firm, or to keep its present employee from accepting a tempting offer from a competitor.

Finally, there is many an individual with a background, experience, training, or talent that is not required in the job but which the chief executive recognizes is always available. Clerical or factory employees who can speak a foreign language, direct an employee chorus, or coach a softball team are examples. A personnel director who can write speeches for the president is a handy person to have around and this convenient talent could well be worth extra money.

This is not to say that a chief executive should ignore the guidance provided by a systematic salary program and go off on unrealistic salary tangents. This is to say the personnel executive should not look upon any salary system as a straightjacket, but must accept that there could well be circumstances for going beyond it. There are reasons for making exceptions which are understood, but often not explained, by the chief executive who, in the last analysis, has the final responsibility.

METHODS OF PAY

Originally workers were paid off in cash. At the end of each week, the manager would hand each employee a little brown envelope with the bills and coins carefully counted out. Cartoonists still use the "pay envelope" in their jokes.

But all that has changed. Government demands upon the wage earner and taxes imposed on the employer require accurate record keeping. The use of paychecks serves these purposes.

Hourly employees are customarily paid by the week for the number of hours worked. This is in keeping with the Fair Labor Standards Act which calls for an overtime rate after a certain number of hours in each work week. Since it takes a day or more to complete the computations, there is often "lag time"—a period of a day or more following the close of the work week or work period before the employees get their money. Firms that prefer to pay "on time" have to anticipate the last day or two as they prepare checks in advance. They make any necessary adjustments in the next check, and this can be confusing.

Exempt employees, those not subject to wage-and-hour regulations, are generally paid on a monthly basis, usually getting paychecks on or about the 15th of the month and again at the end of the month. These checks are distributed "on time," not later, since fewer last-minute deductions or adjustments are made. Some firms, in the name of convenience, pay all their employees, exempt and nonexempt, on a common payday. To do this requires the monthly or annual rate of the exempt personnel to be converted into a weekly amount, most likely some odd figure.

To avoid payroll tampering, many auditors recommend that the people who do the calculating and prepare the entire payroll should not be permitted to distribute individual paychecks. Paychecks of terminating employees should be referred to the personnel office where they will be delivered as part of the exit interview.

Deductions from paychecks are of two kinds: those (1) required by law and (2) authorized by the employee. Those required by law are withholding tax and social security tax, and those authorized by the employee cover group insurance premiums, savings bond purchases, United Fund contributions, credit union shares or loan repayments, etc. The check stub should show each specific deduction, properly identified, and possibly in the case of taxes, the amount accumulated to date.

INCENTIVE METHODS OF PAY

How to get equitable wages to better workers is always a problem. On a one-rate job, such as is often the case in a union agreement, all workers on that job get the same wages regardless of their individual differences in production. In many wage programs, both union and nonunion, jobs have a spread or range of pay (minimum to maximum) and this allows for variations in wages paid. The weakness in the administration of too many of these plans is that merit raises, granted periodically, are related more to time (another year went by) than to productivity.

The danger in any poorly-designed and routinely-administered wage plan is that the good worker, who knows he or she is out-producing others, will become unhappy if the less-than-good worker, or worse yet the goof-off, gets equal salary consideration.

A policy that pays "a fair day's pay for a fair day's work" is not enough. There must also be a provision for "better pay for better work" or the program won't work.

Some companies, recognizing that pay is a good motivator for more and better production, have gone to incentive methods of pay. Any such arrangement is based upon the concept of results and not upon time put in. A salesperson's commission is an excellent example; the more sold, the more earned.

To make any incentive system effective it is necessary that the company have a continuous supply of work and that equipment always be in running order. Incentives are easiest to install in factories where units of work can be measured. Lately, however, incentives have been used with success in offices.

An incentive can be applied best on work that is readily counted or measured. In the factory this would be such tasks as cutting, drilling, stamping, polishing, inspecting, wrapping, etc. In the office, letters typed, keypunch strokes, telephone calls, orders priced or footed, etc. First, standards of performance must be set: how much work is required for base pay and how much extra will be paid to those who exceed the normal or standard output.

One of the oldest pay incentives is piecework. A worker is paid so much for each "piece" turned out. There are many variations and the usual piece rate system includes some form of guaranteed pay. Many are combination plans which pay for both results and time.

Use Suitable Plan

Where individual incentives are not feasible, some form of group incentive may be developed. There is much indirect labor, work which is necessary to the total result but which cannot be measured or reduced to a standard "so much per hour" output. Supporting jobs in the factory, such as timekeeping, or creative work in the office, are examples. Whenever an activity of this nature meets or exceeds its predetermined quota or goal, it may be rewarded with a group incentive based on overall results. There is logic to the argument that incentives or bonuses should not be segmented but that all who have a part in the end result, direct and indirect labor, should share.

There are many types of incentives. Bonus or sharing programs are a method of returning to workers some of the benefits they helped accomplish. Supplementary pay plans are a delayed payoff if results are good. Profit sharing is a form of incentive but not always appreciated by workers if they do not benefit immediately.

A proper base salary schedule will accommodate age, seniority, past and present performance. Such salaries are relatively stable and dependable. Incentive awards, on the other hand, are transient and fluctuating. The base salary is built for durability and constancy, and the incentive provides the excitement and the motivation.

The textbooks are full of incentive plans. Many involve intricate mathematical formulas which could be difficult to explain, hard for workers to understand and therefore embrace, and complicated to administer. To avoid pitfalls a company would be wise to get the assistance of experts in establishing an incentive program.

BONUS

A bonus is considered a form of incentive, but actually it is different. A bonus is something given in addition to the customary or required amount. An incentive is defined by Webster as something that influences action.

An incentive is a "before the fact" challenge. If the program is fair and logical, and the rules clearly stated and published, each individual will understand the criteria for measuring his efforts and the rewards for results above and beyond normal expectations.

Bonus plans are generally after-the-fact disbursements of money awards, which often do not recognize individual differences in production or performance. They are "share the wealth" arrangements which distribute a portion of the company's good fortune resulting from many factors, irrespective of the separate contribution of each participant.

The players of professional sports teams all share alike in the extra money derived from post-season playoff games, regardless of their different base salaries or the part they played in the series.

While some bonus programs attempt varying payout schedules, by applying a percentage formula to base pay instead of lump sum, it can be said that bonus payments are given to groups and incentive awards are earned by individuals.

PEOPLE, PERFORMANCE and PRIZES

As an incentive to achieve goals—sales increases, cost reduction, attendance, increased product knowledge or other performance improvements—cash is the popular management choice because it requires very little imagination or effort to install a program. But if results are wanted, cash may not be the most effective or economical.

Performance Incentives Corporation, a division of the Carlson Companies headquartered in Minneapolis, Minnesota, one of the three biggest firms in the incentive and motivation field, makes a good case for the noncash award. "The truly effective award is one that has identifiable and lasting trophy value. Cash immediately loses identity and becomes co-mingled with other monies," they explain.

Merchandise and travel awards are best suited to provide the needed motivation in any performance improvement program. Awards are used to motivate employees to sell more merchandise or services, control absenteeism, reduce accidents, cut waste, encourage recruitment, stimulate suggestions and the like.

Merchandise awards have utility and can be proudly and repeatedly displayed to family, friends and neighbors. Thus, the impact of the program is retained long after the completion date. Further, permitting the participant to choose his own award from a wide range of choices displayed and described in a Book of Awards has a decided advantage over a committee's preselected item. And, merchandise is highly promotable.

Travel awards also motivate people. The jet age makes it easy to move large groups of participants to any place in the world in just a few hours. Carefully planned, well promoted, efficiently executed travel programs provide the winning participants with an experience that is unlikely they would enjoy on their own.

Cash, on the other hand, is extremely difficult to promote. Cash must be translated into a need or want to be a motivator. Most participants translate cash to "bill paying" so the trophy value, the value to members of the household, the lasting impact is lost. Frequently, cash is viewed as deserved income rather than as a special award for achievement. Resentment is felt when this opportunity is withdrawn. And, it is gauche to brag to friends and neighbors about a cash award.

Points to Consider

Based upon proven psychological factors and years of experience, Performance Incentives Corporation has found that:

1. Merchandise and travel awards stimulate the involvement of the entire family. This enhances the efforts of the participant and gets the family support of the sponsor during and after the campaign period.
2. Participants who select their own awards will invariably se-

lect harder-to-achieve goals for themselves than would have been set by the sponsor's management.

3. The need for individual identity, for recognition and acclaim, to be unique among the masses, is more powerful today than ever before in history. Properly structured incentive programs provide the vehicle, the means and the direction to satisfy this overwhelming but many times subdued need.

4. The incentive program rules should be carefully prepared to include: (a) realistic goals, (b) competition within the peer group, (c) fair measurement of progress and results, and (d) simple, easy-to-understand direction.

The incentive business has become a highly sophisticated, professional operation. Warehouses stacked with millions of dollars worth of merchandise support the entire effort. A client services department handles the program administration on behalf of the client.

Incentive programs, more accurately described as performance programs, are big business. U.S. companies spend about $1 billion annually to achieve improved performance from dealers and distributors, from salesmen and other employees.

Any company considering a performance improvement program might examine the advantages of a professionally prepared and executed merchandise and travel awards campaign as opposed to a cash incentive.

DEFERRED COMPENSATION

Companies today look for ways to keep valued key executives. Money is seldom the answer. Taxes dilute the value of salary increases and cash bonuses.

Deferred compensation is one solution. Deferred compensation is an agreement, not insurance in itself. The company arranges to pay a portion of the salary beginning at a specified future date. This guarantees a better income after retirement when the income tax bite is most likely not as severe.

In return a retired employee may offer to make himself available as an advisor or consultant. He usually agrees not to work for any competitor or divulge trade secrets.

Deferred compensation simply means the company maintains a reserve and pays it either on termination of employment or at retirement, in a lump sum or monthly installments, for a period of time or maybe even for life, to the former employee or his estate. A typical deferred payment arrangement combines retirement and death benefits.

643

To provide money for deferred compensation agreements, the employer may buy, own or be beneficiary of a certain amount of insurance on the life of the employee. The usual policy is a "life paid-up at age 65." After the employee retires, the policy remains in force without payment of additional premiums. Proceeds received at the time of death reimburse the company for payments made to the employee. The insurance proceeds the company receives are tax-free. Payments made to the retiree are deductible from current company income, just as though they were normal salary payments. Payments received by the retired employee are taxable as personal income during the year received, but they are usually taxed less because the employee gets an extra deduction for being over 65 and his taxable income is generally less than it was when he was working.

When installing a deferred compensation program, it is necessary to consult an attorney, an accountant and a qualified life insurance agent.

TIME OFF
(PAID AND UNPAID)

There are occasions when employees need time off from work, other than vacations and holidays. Companies recognize these needs and provide for them.

Illness

For the infrequent, short period of illness absence a company usually has a practice of allowing a specified number of "sick days" per calendar or employment year. This means simply that when an employee is absent for a few days because of illness or accident, he will still be paid his regular salary. When the number of sick days is used up, he will no longer be paid for illness time off during that year. These sick days are not a right but a protection; hence, the employee is ordinarily not paid for any sick days left unused at the close of the year.

For the long-term illness or accident, when the time off exceeds a few days, provisions are often made for a definitely spelled-out salary continuation program or a Health and Accident insurance policy, which provides weekly income for a certain period of time. In both cases the allowances are designed to pay less than regular salary as an incentive for the employee to return to work.

Personal

There are circumstances when an employee needs time off for personal reasons. These could be emergencies at home, illness or problems in the family, personal affairs or any of many similar situations. He tries to work out a solution without disrupting his work, but when this is impossible he will want to be excused from work for a while. Such time off, granted as a favor, is not paid for. Care must be taken to keep some people from taking too much time off—the housewife who wants to stay home for a week at a time every few months, or the wife who wants to travel with her husband several times a year. Such on-and-off workers should not be placed on regular full-time jobs, but should be hired, if at all, under a different set of terms.

Military

Quite a few young men still have military obligations to fulfill after they are employed. Their once-a-week duties are usually in the evenings or on weekends and do not interfere with work. But many are required to go to camp two weeks in summer. Companies do not require them to use their vacations for this purpose, and nowadays companies are paying these employees the difference between their regular salary and their military pay.

Jury Duty

When employees are called for jury duty or to serve as witnesses, they have no choice but to take time off. Companies encourage their employees to fulfill their civic responsibilities and most of them pay either full salary or the difference between regular salary and jury pay.

Voting

Companies also encourage their workers to vote, and those who need extra time are permitted to arrive late or leave early, generally with no loss in pay. Many states have laws which make it mandatory for employers to allow employees time off for voting, say up to two hours, but they do not insist that the employee must be paid.

Taking off all day to work at the polls is another matter. This is considered personal time and the employee is not paid since he is paid by the election board.

Marriage

Some companies have a practice of giving an employee an extra week off with pay at the time of marriage. While this policy is appreciated by those who profit from it, it may not be appreciated by employees who were already married at time of hire. To get universal acceptance, a policy should have universal appeal and not benefit only a limited group.

Death

Paid time off at time of death in the immediate family is allowed by most companies. A typical policy provides up to three days off for funerals in the local community and up to five days off if out-of-town travel is involved. The immediate family is defined as parents, spouse, brothers and sisters, children, and any other relatives who had been living in the same household. This policy would seem fair since it covers all employees.

Religious observances

The standard six to 12 holidays recognized by companies are considered national holidays although some, such as Christmas, are religious in origin. There are some employees who observe other religious holidays and who request additional time off. This presents a delicate problem. Denying them the days off is not the answer, and yet giving them more paid holidays than other employees is not the best solution either. Some companies include in their list of holidays a personal day which then can be used by these people. Other firms may have other arrangements such as trading holidays in cases where a few employees may be required to be on the premises or man the switchboard during regular holidays. Otherwise the safest procedure to follow is to grant them the days off without pay.

A ruling of the Equal Employment Opportunities Commission requires that an employer must give his workers time off for religious holidays unless he can prove it causes an undue hardship in his business. But it does not say he must pay them for the time off. The EEOC guidelines impose upon employers the obligation of accommodating employees who do not wish to work on Saturdays because of their religion unless there is an undue hardship on the company.

Others

There are, of course, many other occasions for time off. These include furloughs for further education, such as the registered nurse who studies for her academic degree. Short periods of time off for educational purposes include an actuarial employee taking the next exam toward a fellowship, or an accountant sitting for his CPA examination.

There are many requests for extra time to extend vacations. During the height of the summer vacation season it is impractical to have too many employees away at the same time. Granting one or more employees extra time usually means that others have to delay their vacations and it might well be unfair to expect them to do this.

Companies generally are not inclined to dock an employee for an occasional day off, especially if the work record is good and the request is reasonable. Extended time off, however, usually means the employee's income stops, unless an insurance program or definite company policy provides for some degree of salary continuation.

GENERAL INCREASE

While most wage and salary increases are given on an individual basis, many companies give "general" or across-the-board wage increases. In some companies these general (or all-at-one-time) wage increases are given instead of individual consideration. In other cases the general increase is in addition to any program of individual merit raises.

Companies review their wage scales periodically, perhaps annually. When they find their rates are no longer competitive, they take steps to make the necessary upward adjustment. This can be done by either of two approaches.

1. *General wage increase.* All employees (with the possible exception of managers or others who may be on a different program) receive the same raise at the same time. This is either a percentage increase or a flat cents-per-hour increase. A combination of these two ideas may be a specified dollars-per-week up to a certain salary, a slightly higher dollar increase for the next higher earnings group, and a still larger dollar increase for the highest-paid workers.

Companies feel such an automatic adjustment is justified when

   a. present salaries, especially hiring rates, are no longer adequate.
   b. the company has had a good year and wants to share the profit with employees.
   c. the wage scales are geared to the cost-of-living index.

2. *Revised wage structure.* The company raises the entire wage structure but does not make immediate individual adjustments except in those minimum number of cases where this cannot be avoided.

   a. Since starting rates are now higher, present employees below the new minimum are reviewed and, if performance warrants, are brought up to at least minimum as soon as practicable (one ground rule might to be space raises 90 days apart).
   b. Where this action "bumps" other new employees, at present salaries slightly above minimum, their rates must be reviewed and adjusted where performance warrants this.
   c. The idea is to give the least number of "corrective" adjustments in order to eliminate the notion of any widespread general increase.
   d. Wage adjustments continue to be given on a merit basis on the employee's regular review date. With a higher wage structure to work with, the increase may be more than the normal increment.

Pros and Cons

Both methods have advantages and disadvantages. Advocates of a general increase point to its ease of administration, the elimination of individual application, and the impact on morale when the announcement is made. They point out that when the wage structure is raised, without any significant number of individual adjustments, the company muffs a real opportunity to give employee morale a "shot in the arm." In addition, assimilating the new wage scale into the existing pay pattern puts a prolonged strain on managerial judgment which, at best, could still be fallible.

On the other hand, giving employees a raise that is not related to performance violates a basic concept of wage administration; it is believed that individuals appreciate a raise in pay that is deserved more than one which is granted because of some other or abstract reason. Also, a general increase rewards all employees alike, the less-than-good workers get the same benefit that the good and the outstanding workers receive. Finally, letting managers decide each case on its own merits at the regular review date, and granting raises based on individual merit, gives them an excellent chance of correcting any inequities that are bound to creep into even the best wage program. Undeserving employees may get no raise, average workers may get a normal increment, and the "big" money awarded to the better performers.

Ideally, in any wage administration program better salaries should be paid to better workers. When the better workers are not paid proportionately more than the less-than-good employees, there is the danger that they will either lose some of their incentive to do good work (since it is not rewarded anyway) or quit and take their chances elsewhere. Meanwhile, the less-than-good workers, whose wages are increased despite their low production or poor attitude, soon find themselves getting more money than they are worth . . . and they cannot afford to quit.

What is the result? The company loses some of its better workers and finds itself with more than its share of less-than-good workers. Efficiency and production suffer because the workforce is no longer up to par. When this happens, companies should not complain about the caliber of workers; they have only themselves to blame.

COST-OF-LIVING WAGE INCREASES

Many so-called merit increases are really not pay raises in the literal interpretation. At best they are adjustments for keeping up with inflation. They are not rewards for better production or improved performance.

A few companies are recognizing this misconception and are trying to do something to correct it. Periodically they adjust their wage schedules without disturbing their established wage administration program of reviewing individual wages regularly on a calendar basis.

Blue Cross of Southwest Ohio, headquartered in Cincinnati, gives employees a cost of living allowance each year and pays it quarterly. The cutoff, or maximum annual salary to which the adjustment is applied is based upon the government index for a family of four living at the intermediate level in the Cincinnati area. They make the same percentage allowance to pensioners on the amount of retirement income for a couple to maintain an adequate standard of living in that area.

The percentage of the cost of living payment is determined by the rise in the consumer price index from one year to the next.

Rise in Consumer Price Index One Year to the Next	Cost of Living Percentage to be Paid
8.0 and above	5.0%
7.5 to 7.9	4.8%
7.0 to 7.4	4.6%
6.5 to 6.9	4.4%
6.0 to 6.4	4.2%
5.5 to 5.9	4.0%
5.0 to 5.4	3.8%
4.5 to 4.9	3.6%
4.0 to 4.4	3.4%
3.5 to 3.9	3.2%
3.0 to 3.4	3.0%
2.0 to 2.9	Actual Percentage
Below 2%	Nothing

PAYROLL DEDUCTIONS

Certain deductions from the employee's salary are required by law. Among these are federal, state and city income taxes. The company must also deduct Social Security tax on the annual income up to a specified limit; the company matches the amount paid by the employee.

Employees may authorize the company to make other deductions from their paychecks when they choose to participate in programs offered by the company. These could be group health and life insurance, pension contributions, U.S. Savings Bonds, thrift or savings plans, United Fund pledges, credit union savings or loan repayments, and possibly other commitments.

MONTHLY SALARY DEDUCTIONS

Exempt employees (and sometimes other workers) are paid on a monthly basis rather than hourly. The theory is that these people are paid to do a job, not paid for hours put in performing the job. They are theoretically on duty full time, all hours of the day and weekends.

Ordinarily, an employee on a salaried (monthly) payroll is not docked for time off because of illness absence or for personal reasons. But there are occasions when deductions are necessary. The question is how to figure the salary for less than the full period, as in the case of:

1. Personal time off (not job related).
2. Start of employment (after the first of the month).
3. Termination of employment (before the last of the month).

The Fair Labor Standards Act, as well as an applicable union contract or other form of agreement, spells out those absences for which it is permissible to dock a salaried employee for time not worked. In those instances when the employer and employee agree that two days of a semi-monthly pay period need not be paid for, how is the deduction calculated? If there are 10 work days but 15 calendar days in one half of the month, should the employee be docked 2/10 or 2/15 of his regular semimonthly salary? Or should the monthly salary be converted to an annual rate and should the deduction possibly be 2/365 of the annual rate?

February has less work days than May, and 2/28 would be a larger deduction than 2/31 of one month's pay.

What about an employee who starts on an exempt position on the first of the month, but actually the first day worked is Monday, the 3rd? Or the employee on an exempt position who terminates at the end of the month when the last work day is Friday, the 29th? Should these people be paid for a full month? Possibly yes.

But how about the one who starts on the 10th? Or the one who leaves on the 20th? In both cases, salary for a full pay period is not required nor expected.

One equitable method is to figure the deductions on an annual basis. To illustrate: multiply the semimonthly salary by 24 or the monthly salary by 12 to get an annual rate. Divide this annual rate by 52 to get the weekly rate. Divide this weekly rate by 5, if the normal week consists of 5 work days. Then deduct the daily rate for each work day the employee was not on the job.

There are other methods, of course. Some companies calculate deductions for time not worked on a monthly basis, subtracting from the semimonthly or monthly check that fraction of the month the employee was not working. This can lead to misunderstanding since an employee who leaves on the 20th of February gets 20/28 of his monthly check, whereas the one who leaves on the 20th of May gets only 20/31 of the same monthly rate. The employee who feels the system shortchanged him will squawk.

Since the implications fall more into the employee relations area than they do in the mechanics of payroll preparation, the decision on the formula to be used should preferably be made by the personnel executive and not by the accountant.

Once the formula is established, it is best to stick with it. Otherwise the amount of the "short" check, if questioned by the recipient, will hardly be defensible.

GUARANTEED WAGE

The guaranteed annual wage is being advocated by some unions. This is an attempt to assure income security for hourly workers. Their earnings presently are subject to fluctuations.

Arguments in favor—

1. The workers' living expenses continue all year long.
2. People need to know what income they can expect.
3. They need the security of steady income.
4. In a time of rising prices, it takes money to live.
5. A continuous payroll eliminates layoffs.
6. Working steady should reduce strikes.

Arguments against—

1. People should not be paid when they're not working and earning their pay.
2. Wages means remuneration for services performed.
3. If it is started in one industry it will spread to others.
4. It will contribute to higher costs of manufactured goods.
5. It could wreck a company.
6. It restricts company freedom to operate.

It boils down to the battle between security and free enterprise. The idea of a guaranteed wage runs counter to the best traditions of American business where every worker is proud of his work and happy with the reward. Nevertheless, proponents of a guaranteed wage point out that a person without an income, or with periodic interruptions in his income, is a drag on the up-cycle economy and either government or industry has to help him and his family over the rough spots.

651

CHRISTMAS GIFT OR BONUS?

Is giving Christmas gifts a fading practice? Apparently many employees look at a Christmas gift from their employers as an affront. Time and again, companies participating in the Dartnell Survey on Christmas Gift and Bonus Practices stated that the program was dropped because employees thought the gifts were "cheap," or "insufficient" or "unfair."

While the slight majority of responses indicates the practice is still in existence, there is an underlying current which reveals a potential discontent. Perhaps the "family" concept of the work force is giving way to a colder, more formal employer-employee relationship.

From comments in the survey, it is evident that employees feel they earn everything they get, including a gift or bonus at Christmas. They want it spelled out, in advance, and they want it guaranteed.

Somehow this takes a little of the shine from a company's attempt to show appreciation. It's also a reflection of today's actual family gift-giving—where the children expect (and receive) many presents which are all but ordered in advance.

The problem? It goes back to communication. Does the employee know and understand *why* the company *wants* to give him a gift at Christmas time? If the employees think or feel that the gift is due them, then it would be the better idea to incorporate the gift into annual salary or wages and forget it. On the other hand, does the company make the Christmas gift an actual extra? Is it given in the spirit of the season? Does it have strings attached (or even threads)?

The Bonus. The year-end or Christmas bonus is a different matter. In most cases, today, this is paid on the basis of profits, merit and perhaps service. Here it is perhaps unfortunate that Christmas falls at the end of the year. Many companies have changed to a fiscal year plan which brings the bonus in February, May or even July.

An employee today is normally told in the initial interview that the company "has a generous bonus program." This is either explained in detail or vaguely described. At any rate, comes Christmas time, he expects his money. He feels it is ludicrous if the president, the treasurer or the supervisor comes up on Christmas Eve and slides him a check and a Ho-Ho-Ho.

In some cases, the Christmas bonus is just that, and it should be clearly indicated that it is a Christmas present from the company—even with Social Security and income tax removed. The answer here is a definite policy, a clearly-stated and easily-understood statement.

652

PATENTS

Employees often come up with new ideas which are patentable. Companies are always in search of new or improved methods or products, and many corporations have large staffs of engineers, scientists and other technical specialists whose assignment is to find, create or invent better things to produce and market.

What happens when an employee discovers a new technique, succeeds in fusing a better alloy, creates a new design, or invents a new product? To whom does it belong? Who should hold the patent rights?

Much, of course, depends upon the nature of the business. An isolated discovery in an office or nonmanufacturing plant poses no serious problem. If a person were to come up with a better ink pen while working at his desk job, or a better label brush while working in the shipping room, most likely the idea would be his and any benefits would then accrue to him. But what about the person who discovers a new formula while working in the company laboratory, or invents a test model while working in the company shop? Then who has the rights?

To avoid confusion, misunderstanding and possibly a lawsuit, it would be best to have an established policy and get the employees in agreement with it. There could be situations when the decision may favor the employee and other situations when the employee would willingly consider his innovation as part of his job. A written statement or even a contract would be protection for all who are involved.

Ideas processed through a suggestion system become the property of the company. By accepting a suggestion system award, and signing a receipt and a release, the employee signs away his rights.

Where there is no suggestion system or other established procedure, each invention must be considered individually. One question that must be answered is whether the invention was accomplished during a worker's research for the company. In other words, is it job related? What about post-employment inventions, begun while with the company?

Employers may feel the invention belongs more to the worker than to the company. If they can use it in their business they may purchase it outright. Or the inventor may receive a share or royalties when the company sells or licenses his invention.

Some Questions

The following questions and answers published by the United States Department of Commerce may be of interest.

INVENTION AND SECRECY AGREEMENT

TO:

I, _____, as part consideration for my employment hereafter by _____ or by one of its subsidiaries or successors in business (hereinafter called the "Company") and for the wages or salary now or hereafter to be paid to me during the continuance of such employment, agree as follows:

(1) I will disclose fully to the Company all inventions, discoveries, improvements or developments (hereinafter called "inventions") which during the term of my employment were or were caused to be conceived or developed or reduced to practice by me, either solely or jointly with others, either (a) during my working hours, or (b) at the Company's expense, or (c) using the Company's material or facilities, or (d) otherwise, but relating to the Company's business. All such inventions shall belong to the Company, whether or not patent applications are filed thereon and whether or not the inventions are patentable.

(2) I will assign to the Company the inventions and all patent applications and patents which may issue thereon in any and all countries during and subsequent to my employment, and I will assist the Company during and subsequent to my employment in every proper way in obtaining, at its expense, patent protection covering the inventions, and I will execute any and all documents desired or required by the Company to achieve that end.

(3) I will hold in strictest confidence and will not disclose directly or indirectly any unauthorized person and will not myself use for any unauthorized purpose, without the Company's prior writ~~ten~~ ~~permission~~ion, at any time during or subsequent to my employment, any knowledge not already available to the public ~~ac~~quire respecting the inventions or respecting designs, methods, systems, improvements, trade secrets, manufact~~uring~~ ~~techn~~iques and processes, sales promotions and ideas, customers lists or other private or confidential matters of the C~~ompany~~

(4) I have set out below a complete list of invention~~s covered~~ by patents or patent applications, including the numbers thereof, which I had made prior to my employment ~~by the Co~~mpany and which are to be excluded from the scope of this agreement. I agree that any patentable improvem~~ent mad~~e upon the listed inventions subsequent to my employment by the Company are to be the property of the Company i~~f withi~~n the scope of Paragraph (1) hereof.

(5) At the time of leaving the employment of the Company, I will deliver to the Company and will not keep in my possession or deliver to anyone else any and all drawings, blue prints, notes, memoranda, specifications, devices, documents or any other material containing or disclosing any of the matters referred to herein.

(6) This agreement supersedes all earlier invention and secrecy agreements between us, if any, and may not be modified except by an agreement in writing signed by me and by an officer or other authorized executive of the Company.

(7) The provisions of this agreement shall inure to the benefit of and shall be binding upon the heirs, personal representatives, successors and assigns of the parties.

_____   _____
Witness   Employee

ACCEPTED:

By_____

Dated: _____, 19_____

Q. What is a patent?
A. A patent is a grant issued by the United States Government giving an inventor the right to exclude all others from making, using or selling his invention within the United States, its territories and possessions.
Q. For how long a term of years is a patent granted?
A. Seventeen years from the date on which it is issued; except for patents on ornamental designs, which are granted for terms of 3½, 7 or 14 years.
Q. May the term of a patent be extended?

A. Only by special act of Congress, and this occurs very rarely and only in most exceptional circumstances.

Q. On what subject matter may a patent be granted?

A. A patent may be granted to the inventor or discoverer of any new and useful process, machine, manufacture or composition of matter, or any new and useful improvement thereof, or on any distinct and new variety of plant, other than a tuber-propagated plant which is asexually reproduced, or on any new, original and ornamental design for an article of manufacture.

Q. On what subject matter may a patent not be granted?

A. A patent may not be granted on a useless device, on printed matter, on a method of doing business, on an improvement in a device which would be obvious to a person skilled in the art, or on a machine which will not operate, particularly on an alleged perpetual motion machine.

Q. What do the terms "patent pending" and "patent applied for" mean?

A. They are used by a manufacturer or seller of an article to inform the public that an application for patent on that article is on file in the Patent and Trademark Office. The law imposes a fine on those who use these terms falsely to deceive the public.

Q. How does one apply for a patent?

A. By making the proper application to the Commissioner of Patents and Trademarks, Washington, D.C., 20231.

Q. Can the Patent and Trademark Office give advice as to whether an inventor should apply for a patent?

A. No. It can only consider the patentability of an invention when this question comes regularly before it in the form of a patent application.

Q. Will the Patent and Trademark Office help me to prosecute others if they infringe the rights granted to me by my patent?

A. No. The Patent and Trademark Office has no jurisdiction over questions relating to the infringement of patent rights. If your patent is infringed you may sue the infringer in the appropriate United States court at your own expense.

Q. How does one obtain information as to patent applications, fees and other details concerning patents?

A. By ordering a pamphlet entitled *General Information Concerning Patents* from the Superintendent of Documents, Washington, D.C., 20402, or through any District Office of the United States Department of Commerce.

655

PSYCHIC INCOME

Man does not live by bread alone. While money is necessary, it is not the only form of wealth, nor in the final analysis the most important. In addition to material wealth, employees need to add to their cultural wealth, social wealth and spiritual wealth.

An awareness of these needs is important in trying to learn how to motivate people. But efforts at understanding what motivates employees should not be limited to rank-and-file workers. The same logic applies to managerial and executive personnel.

Here we are not referring to the trappings of the office, nor to the exemption from rules which the privileged are often apt to accept as rights that go with rank. Any extras they enjoy are the intangibles that belong to the position.

By psychic income we mean tangibles. These are hard-and-fast substantial dollar value wages that are not reflected in the paycheck. They are over and beyond the intangibles and are used, frankly, to "buy" executives. They serve as incentives to coax an attractive candidate into joining the firm, and they are also used to keep a good man or woman from being easily lured away.

The list is long and includes such standard provisions as stock options, free life insurance, air-conditioned leased cars and the like. Country club memberships for prestige are common. Innovations are such items as a toupee for a bald executive.

Many senior executives are today placed under contract. The security such an arrangement offers is often enough to help him make the decision to change. At least he has a guaranteed period of time in which to prove himself, or to effect changes in organization or operations. At least he is protected in the event that, through no fault of his own, he is not successful. Psychic income is used to accentuate his importance on the inside and enhance his value on the outside.

The big attraction, however, is that psychic income cannot be taxed away. Therein lies its practical appeal.

NO-PAY WORK

Despite the general policy of the United States Department of Labor of refusing to allow workers to waive their rights to wages, there are many thousands upon thousands of men and women who give away their time and talent.

A good illustration is the unnumbered volunteers in hospitals. They even provide their own uniforms (the cost of which is deductible from income tax) and they furnish their own transportation and buy their own meals.

There are other workers who give faithful service to a cause for which they are not paid. Some examples that come to mind are church workers, officers and committee members of community organizations, Scout leaders, school boards, charity and welfare workers, United Fund door-to-door canvassers, tag day collectors, youth workers, counsellors in YMCA, Boys Clubs and the like, volunteer firefighters, business and trade association members, hostesses in such places as Travelers Aid and USO, all the way to one-dollar-a-year people in government. Legally these people need not be paid regardless of the kind of work they do.

This is really big business. There are 1,200 benevolent organizations in New York alone. There are activities of this nature in every state and every community, and they penetrate deep into the very fabric of everyday life.

The success of these programs is accomplished through voluntary effort, which for some reason has never been converted to a cold dollars-and-cents basis. Therein lies the secret. It takes an unusual mind to see the obvious. The most obvious thing we overlook is the enormous amount of good in everyday, plain people. Putting a price on their personal contribution to better living would destroy the incentive.

OVERTIME

Overtime is one of the perennial problems of business. Despite the best efforts to eliminate it, the problem persists. Many companies are unable to control it. Some managers are resigned to it and accept the inconvenience as part of their jobs. Employees generally resist overtime work, but not always. To some it is an easy and lucrative way of enhancing the value of their jobs.

Some overtime work is, of course, to be expected. It results from help shortages when the workers must extend themselves to offset vacancies in the department. Overtime occurs during peakload periods, such as end-of-month closings in the bookkeeping areas, or inventory counting or pricing done after hours. The reasons are many and easily understood; the solutions are not as easy to come by.

Under the Fair Labor Standards Act of 1938, there is no limit to the number of hours an employee may be required to work, but the employer must pay time and one-half at the employee's regular rate of pay for all hours worked in any one week in excess of 40. There are exceptions. Bona fide executives, administrative, professional, and outside sales personnel do not have to be paid overtime (see Exempt Positions).

Employers operating under government contracts of $10,000 or more must also meet the requirements of the Walsh-Healey Act, which differs in some respects from the Fair Labor Standards Act. The Walsh-Healey Act requires the payment of overtime for all hours over eight worked in one day.

In plants or offices that are organized, the overtime terms may yet be different depending upon the provisions of the agreement with the union. Quite often the union will bargain for overtime on a daily basis rather than weekly, i.e., for time worked in excess of eight hours in any one day. It may insist also that workers be paid at overtime rates for all hours worked on Saturdays, regardless of time worked during the rest of the week; this has the effect of premium pay for Saturday work. Double time for Sunday is not uncommon, and employees who work on a holiday, when fellow workers are off from work and still being paid, often get overtime pay in addition to holiday straight-time pay.

Control is Vital

Since overtime becomes expensive, attempts to control it are made. In most companies there is a policy about overtime, or at least a rule of thumb, which sets guidelines within which managers may authorize overtime work. As one example, a company may not question overtime in any department which is less than two percent of all hours worked. This says, in effect, that some overtime is considered normal. But when overtime exceeds the permissible two percent, the problem must be brought to top management's attention, explained, analyzed and special authorization granted.

There are employers who feel that overtime is a disease. Employees get into the overtime habit, find the overtime pay more than offsets the overtime inconvenience, and gradually find themselves enjoying, even seeking, overtime. Then when work slacks off they cleverly manipulate their daily workloads to allow for overtime work. Some employees have actually been accused of deliberately stalling during the regular day, or stretching their work, to make overtime necessary. At any rate, there are managements who believe that workers, accustomed to an eight-hour day, cannot maintain their level of productivity or efficiency consistently over a prolonged period of 12-hour days and that they purposely or otherwise taper off during the day, thereby actually making overtime necessary. In these cases the best way to cure the disease is to eliminate, by decree, all overtime and see what happens. More likely than not, the overtime necessity will disappear.

What to Watch For

When overtime seems excessive and threatens to develop into a major problem, here are some signs to look for:

1. Is the amount of overtime increasing?
2. Is the amount excessive; example, does it go beyond the guidelines established by management as reasonable?
3. Is overtime general throughout the company or is it localized?
4. Is it becoming a habit with a certain few?
5. Are people doing overtime work willingly, even eagerly?
6. Is the manager or foreman beginning to schedule overtime as a regular practice instead of the exception?
7. Is top management indifferent to overtime and its cost?
8. Has the problem been studied lately?

Another Side

There is another side to the overtime picture. Some employees do not want to work overtime. Many workers are no longer receptive toward overtime. The added taxable money from overtime is not an effective incentive despite complaints about insufficient wages.

There are a number of possible explanations, among them:

1. Disinterest in their work. The report of HEW concerning work attitudes showed that more than half of the work force may be suffering from serious and debilitating job satisfaction. All day on the job is all they can stand without staying overtime.
2. Outside activities. Since their jobs are monotonous they seek personal fulfillment outside of work in fraternal, community, social and athletic endeavors. The unscheduled overtime demands interfere with their scheduled hobbies.
3. Disruption of family life. Wives and children are expressing an unwillingness to continue a second-rate existence as overtime widows and orphans.
4. Women at higher levels. Many women are already working full time as housewives and mothers and eight hours away from home is all they can afford.

As one illustration of how attitude toward overtime is changing, here is the situation with a Canadian manufacturer. His labor contract originally included a clause which read:

> "Employees with the most seniority have the first chance at overtime work."

659

This provision has, over the years, been revised until today it reads:

> "Employees with the most seniority have the first chance at refusing overtime work."

SUPPER MONEY

When employees work overtime, some companies pay meal allowances. This is particularly true for supervisors and managers who are exempt employees and not subject to overtime compensation. This way they are at least reimbursed for their expenses.

But such supper money is not limited to exempt employees. Often it is also paid to wage-and-hour employees who leave the premises to eat evening meals and who do not include the time away in their report of overtime hours.

The conditions are usually clearly spelled out. Employees must work a specified number of hours beyond their regular work day to be entitled to supper money. And they must interrupt their work, i.e., take a supper break, not merely collect the money whether they eat or not.

Similar arrangements may also be in effect for employees who work overtime on a nonworking day, such as Saturday, Sunday or holiday. Companies may give them a lunch or supper allowance if they put in a required number of hours. This practice, however, is not as prevalent as that of paying for supper on a regular workday.

During a crisis or emergency all sorts of concessions are made but these are not considered the same as the supper money policy related to ordinary overtime.

In the majority of instances these meal allowances are fixed amounts. A few firms prefer actual expense account or petty cash reimbursements for the cost of the meals and tips.

SHIFT DIFFERENTIAL

It is customary in most industries to pay somewhat higher wages to employees on a second or third shift. This is known as a "shift differential"—the amount over and above the regular scale.

Premium pay is offered simply because the hours, and possibly other working conditions, are not as attractive as those on the day shift. Transportation during the late evening is not as good as during rush hours, eating facilities not as available, and surely concern for personal safety is a consideration. Besides, the facilities within the company itself may be more limited; the clinic is likely not open for just these few workers, the cafeteria closed, personnel counselling unavailable, and so on. To offset these inconveniences companies offer the better wages.

Shift differentials have been common in factories and plants for years. Most union contracts provide for a difference in pay scales for different shifts. The rule is generally 10% although lately the trend seems to be moving to "cents per hour." What this means is that workers on a second or third shift get the same pay that is listed for that same job on the regular shift, *plus* a premium for the night work.

In office operations there is no universal rule, possibly because the problem does not exist in the same measure. Fewer offices than factories operate more than one shift. The night workers in offices are usually key punch, tabulating machine, teletype and computer operators. Where this is happening some extra consideration is given.

A shift differential should be applied to a true second or third shift and not extended to employees who are on odd-hour or short-hour jobs. In offices, for example, most key punch operators are not on a second shift but are, rather, working a few hours in the evening. These may be housewives who cannot work until the husbands come home to watch the children, or they could be employees from other companies who are moonlighting.

Employees who start earlier, or work later, than the regular workforce are not on a second shift. They are considered to be on the regular shift but with their hours changed. Early morning mail openers, engineers who get the building ready, and those employees who close the office, such as outgoing mail clerks, cashiers who see that the money and books are put away, truck dispatchers, are examples. Nor is any wage differential applied to janitors and maintenance people whose regular duties are performed after the office or factory is closed.

Wage differentials are not only applied to the pay scales of regular workers but are also added to starting rates. Recruiting literature will list the beginning rate for a job, such as bus driver, and spell out the extra cents per hour paid for second and third shifts.

A wage differential is intended for workers who do the same work as their counterparts on the regular daytime shift. It is added to the "going rate" to compensate for the less attractive hours and working conditions.

NIGHT SHIFT

Many of the 20 million Americans who work the night shift have problems, both personal and intimate and impersonal and threatening, a group of medical researchers reported to a House of Representatives subcommittee.

"Throughout the years of human evolution the Earth has been rotating once every 24 hours, subjecting all its inhabitants to a highly predictable cycle of day and night." In response, humans developed timepieces that "beautifully equipped us for the environment of our origins," they explained.

There is no solution except for the handful of workers who, for whatever reasons, take a liking to an odd shift all the time and opt to stay on it long enough for their own body clocks to get the new message. For the majority who prefer shifting back and forth, about all employers can do is keep them on the schedule long enough for them to adapt.

MINIMUM WAGE

To assure America's lowest paid workers a livable wage, Congress in 1977 raised the minimum wage in four stages, the last of which sets the wage at $3.35 per hour, effective January 1, 1981.

There are business people and economists who argue that the federal minimum wage law looks better on paper than it does in practice. There is a difference between intent and impact.

Some people may get more money, to be sure, but others may lose their jobs and get no money. Labor can demand higher wages for workers but business might feel some jobs are not worth the higher rate. The consequence is that some people may be deprived of employment because their services become uneconomically expensive. This makes it more difficult for the unskilled and the young to get beginning jobs.

A few members of Congress try to strike a compromise. They propose that teenagers be paid 85 per cent of the rate for a period of time. So far the suggestion for a sub-minimum pay has always been voted down.

JOB EVALUATION

Just as the job analysis becomes the basis for the job description, so the job description becomes the basis for job evaluation.

Job evaluation is a systematic (not scientific) method for objective determination of the relative worth of jobs within a company. It is a procedure for measuring the relative contribution of each job and for ranking these jobs in accordance with these measurements.

Actually the lineup of jobs, that is, the arrangement of jobs by importance, may be accomplished by a number of different means. This can be done by classifying jobs through agreement, by collective bargaining or by personal judgment of management (which suffers from all the frailties of human nature). Most companies prefer to use the point system for the study and comparison of jobs because it is objective. Employees, including unions, find it acceptable because it is fair.

Under the point system the job evaluation administrator, working through a job evaluation committee, breaks each position down by understandable factors that are common to all jobs. These component factors are considered separately, not the job as a whole.

Factors of Each Job

The factors upon which each job is rated fall into four categories. These are:

1. Skill (job knowledge, experience, education, training).
2. Effort (physical, mental, concentration).
3. Responsibility (for equipment, money, safety, public relations, employees).
4. Job conditions (working conditions, hazards, annoyances).

Since these factors are not equal in all jobs, each overall factor is divided into its logical subfactors (the attributes shown in parentheses above) and these subfactors in turn are broken down into degrees. The separate levels of each factor are defined, weighted and points assigned.

Example: a complex job that is beyond the scope of a high school graduate and calls for additional specialized training or formal education would get extra points for this higher skill requirement. An outside painter's job, subject to unpleasant weather and hazards, would get more points under working conditions than the inside painter's job.

The degree to which each of the factors or subfactors is required by the job is estimated and points expressed accordingly. The sum of the points of all factors of the job determines the total point value for the job.

After this analytical process has been accomplished for all the jobs, the jobs are then lined up in point order, from low to high.

Ultimately, points become dollars. The more points, the higher the job and the rate for it. Rates are not applied to individual jobs but are established for groups of jobs that are evaluated about the same number of points. This is what is known as labor grades or salary grades.

Useful and Acceptable Tool

The reason the point system is an effective management tool and acceptable to employees is that it takes advantage of the fact that all jobs possess certain elements in common. This makes it possible to compare unrelated jobs. Without a factor breakdown, it would be quite impossible, for instance, to compare such jobs as porter and stenographer. What job evaluation attempts to do is establish the relative value of jobs in the company in order that the people in these jobs are equitably paid.

It should be pointed out that job evaluation is dynamic in nature. This is no one-time project but must be maintained on an ongoing basis. Jobs change and it is imperative that when this happens the job description and the evaluation of the job be reviewed and amended, if necessary, to reflect the change.

It should also be mentioned that job evaluation is a concept, not any locked-in-system that can be automatically transplanted from one company to another. The factors that are considered must be applicable to the industry and to the particular company. Even within each company variations of the concept may be adapted for different groups—such as clerical, sales and management.

Since wages paid depend on the classification of jobs, it is of the utmost importance that job evaluation be done conscientiously and administered judiciously.

JOB ANALYSIS

Job evaluation begins with job descriptions. A job description begins with a job analysis.

The procedure for writing a job description need not be complicated. The manager of the job has the responsibility of getting each job description in the area completed properly, but certainly may enlist the cooperation of assistants and even the individual workers themselves. After all, who knows more about the jobs than the people who are actually performing them?

The assignment begins with gathering data. In many cases the manager may already know everything about a job. More often than not, however, specific details of job duties, as well as helpful ideas on how the job should be performed may be obtained by soliciting the advice of others. This may be done informally or by use of a simple questionnaire.

The process of gathering the facts, sorting them out, eliminating the chaff, and organizing all of this is known as job analysis. A typical job analysis inquiry form, to be filled out by the manager or in some cases by the employee, asks questions such as:

1. What is a good title for the job?
2. Where is the job located (in what department or area)?
3. To whom does the employee in the job report (what is the next higher job)?

4. Is this an existing job or a new one?
5. What does the job consist of (what does it do)?
6. What else might be included in the job on an incidental or occasional basis?
7. How much supervision is readily available?
8. Does this job supervise any other jobs?
9. What are the minimum qualifications for performing the work satisfactorily?
10. How best can these qualifications be acquired?

The collection of this basic information may take many shapes, depending upon the type of job under consideration and the kinds of workers assigned to it. Out of it all there is essentially the necessary information that must be assembled for a comprehensive job description.

To consolidate all this information from many sources into a cohesive program, the overall responsibility is delegated to the personnel staff. These specialists have been officially appointed and charged by management to establish and maintain the company-wide program. They become the catalyst to see that the work gets done correctly and on schedule.

The personnel staff issues the instructions, sets up the completion timetable with interim target dates, and writes the guidelines. They generally design a standard questionnaire to aid managers in gathering data, and this also lends uniformity to the effort. Naturally, personnel stands ready to give counsel and assistance as needed.

There is sometimes the temptation to let the personnel staff do all the work, but the program will be more effective if the responsibility is shared by all who are involved. Analyzing jobs serves many purposes beyond that of providing a data base for job descriptions. The list of side benefits includes reviewing each job, studying its effectiveness, discovering overlapping, clarifying authority, pinpointing responsibilities and other details. Engaging in a long overdue analysis of each job is of itself a beneficial exercise for the company and the employees.

JOB DESCRIPTION

Having completed a job analysis to determine what a job consists of, the next step is to prepare a job description.

A good job description aids in the functions of hiring, instructing, training, promoting and wage administration. One description should serve all these purposes. For all its uses, the job description should be inclusive enough to be useful and simple enough to be used.

POSITION ANALYSIS

Title of position _____

General Division of the Organization: □ Executive   □ Finance and Accounting   □ Engineering   □ Sales   □ Transportation

□ Purchasing   □ Personnel   □ Other _____

Organization nature of the position: □ Line   □ Staff   □ Combined

Will report to: _____ Title _____ Age _____

Will be located at: Plant _____ City _____ State _____

The position is: □ A new one   □ An established one   □ Established but has new factors

For what functions in the organization will the person in this position be responsible? _____

_____
_____
_____

Describe any responsibilities associated with the position such as: Travel, community activities, association activities, public speaking, etc.

_____

Rate Range for this position: $ _____ to $ _____   Expected hiring rate $ _____

Describe nature of pay incentive _____

To what positions would next promotion normally lead? 1. _____

2. _____ 3. _____

Which of these should be considered in the appraisal?   □ 1   □ 2   □ 3

If accepted candidate does his/her job well, how soon could he/she reasonably expect promotion? _____

_____

After initial training, how closely will employee be supervised?   □ Hourly   □ Daily   □ Weekly   □ Monthly   Describe _____

_____

How much of the person's work will be checked by others? _____

Which of these qualities should the person have to a high degree? □ Flexibility; accepting changes   □ Resourcefulness   □ Creativity

□ Empathy   Explain _____

What kinds of problems, immediate or long range, are inherent in this position? _____

Form No. JA-601

666

SUPERVISORY RESPONSIBILITY

How many employees will report directly to this person? _____ Indirectly? _____

Titles of all supervisors who will report to this person and number of employees reporting to each:

1. _____   7. _____

2. _____   8. _____

3. _____   9. _____

4. _____   10. _____

5. _____   11. _____

6. _____   12. _____

WHAT AUTHORITY WILL APPLICANT HAVE:	TO RECOMMEND		TO DECIDE AND ACT	
1. Allocation of budget	☐ Yes	☐ No	☐ Yes	☐ No
2. Organization of own section (split or combine sections).	☐ Yes	☐ No	☐ Yes	☐ No
3. Increase or decrease number of employees under his/her supervision	☐ Yes	☐ No	☐ Yes	☐ No
4. Release or demote an employee	☐ Yes	☐ No	☐ Yes	☐ No
5. Revise standards of quality or quantity of product or service	☐ Yes	☐ No	☐ Yes	☐ No
6. Revise work flow	☐ Yes	☐ No	☐ Yes	☐ No
7. Revise operating policies	☐ Yes	☐ No	☐ Yes	☐ No
8. Establish own itinerary	☐ Yes	☐ No	☐ Yes	☐ No
9. Establish itinerary of those reporting to him/her	☐ Yes	☐ No	☐ Yes	☐ No
10. Expenditures outside of budget	☐ $50 ☐ $250 ☐ $1,000	☐ $100 ☐ $500 ☐ $10,000	☐ $50 ☐ $250 ☐ $1,000	☐ $100 ☐ $500 ☐ $10,000

11. _____

12. _____

13. _____

Analysis developed by _____ Date _____

First approval _____ Date _____ Approved _____ Date _____

In general, the long-accepted form for a job description lists:

1. A summary statement
2. Relationships
3. Specific duties
4. Responsibilities
5. Authority
6. Qualifications

More specifically, the job description goes into detail on all of the following:

1. Job title (a functional title, hopefully)
2. Location of job in the organization
3. To what higher position the job is tied
4. How much direction is given to the job
5. Job's basic function
6. Specific duties performed:
   a. regularly, such as daily
   b. less frequently, but regularly
   c. occasionally
7. Unrelated tasks that could be assigned (emergency, fill-in, relief, etc.)
8. Extent of job authority (if any)

By way of instruction, here are guidelines for the writing of job descriptions:

1. Show what is required in a job in terms of performance and results.
2. Focus on two basic elements:
   a. principal duties and responsibilities
   b. accountability and relationships
3. Include minimum qualifications for the adequate performance of the job, after a reasonable period of training; the skills, if properly described, will make the qualifications apparent.
4. Begin with a short one-paragraph summary.
5. Follow this with a listing of specific duties and responsibilities, mentioning only major aspects of the job while ignoring the incidental or nonrecurring duties.
6. List the most important part of the job first, then work down, using the inverted pyramid principle.
7. Use simple, direct statements and avoid ambiguous terms (the popular style is to begin each statement with a verb form —as is done in this outline).

668

8. Indicate the chain of command and spell out the delegation of authority.
9. Keep in mind that the job description is a statement of duties assigned, not a measure of employee performance.
10. Review job descriptions periodically, because jobs change; the descriptions should at all times reflect accurately the nature and content of the jobs.

The role of the personnel staff should be clarified at the outset. In some companies the personnel technician may write all the job descriptions based on the job analysis forms he receives from managers. Generally it is preferred to involve managers in writing the descriptions of the jobs in their departments.

Under this latter arrangement, the personnel office distributes samples of typical job descriptions so that managers have a pattern to follow. The personnel specialist may find it necessary to rewrite some of the descriptions in order to standardize the format.

No matter who does the actual writing, once the manager approves each final job description he should sign it indicating thereby that it represents his view of the job. Keep in mind that the personnel technician merely asks questions about each job; he does not dictate job content.

Do not make the job description complex and cumbersome, to flatter the incumbent, to impress an applicant, or to influence the salary analyst. It isn't the length of the job description, but rather the substance that determines the value of the job. Don't, therefore, include every little detail. But don't make it too skimpy or skeletal either. One page is the acceptable size for an average job.

In a meaningful job description the duties of the job are clearly set forth; this avoids misunderstanding. The lines of authority and accountability are carefully drawn; this eliminates confusion. The necessary qualifications for performing the job are outlined; this results in better placements.

A symphony orchestra is a good example in a microcosm of how to put an organization together. Valid job descriptions are as vital to the successful management of a company as musical scores are to a successful orchestra.

MANAGEMENT JOB DESCRIPTION

Every member of management is expected and required, as an essential part of his responsibilities, to promote the interests of his industry generally and those of his company specifically; to conduct his activities within the framework of corporate policies; and to facilitate the work of others which his actions affect.

In order that he may know what is expected of him, it is well to have an understanding. This can be accomplished by describing his job, preferably in writing.

While the specific duties of jobs vary all over the industrial map, there are many standard provisions, or boiler plate, common to all management positions. Among these are:

1. Planning for long-range objectives and shorter range goals, including the means for achieving them.
2. Understanding and complying with corporate policies.
3. Developing and administering realistic budgets.
4. Directing methods improvements in operating procedures.
5. Initiating revisions in the organization structure to make it more efficient.
6. Managing the staff—selecting carefully, training, motivating, appraising and compensating personnel.
7. Distributing work judiciously and assigning responsibilities clearly.
8. Instituting safety measures in work practices and equipment.
9. Establishing and maintaining effective two-way communications on subjects of company and employee concern and interest.
10. Cooperating actively with associates, both line and staff, to foster productive teamwork.
11. Keeping informed on developments affecting the service or area of specialization involved.
12. Creating an atmosphere conducive to growth and development of employees by encouraging and praising initiative, creativity and resourcefulness, and by advice and example in the exercise of judgment.

The specific duties and responsibilities assigned to each position, in addition to the basic responsibilities enumerated above, are detailed out in the respective job descriptions.

The long-accepted job description is a listing of a summary statement, specific duties, relationships, responsibilities, authority and qualifications arranged into a standard format. This is the approach that has been followed over the past several decades. There is nothing wrong with this procedure, and its successful application in an endless variety of situations attests to its effectiveness. But like everything else that is changing, job descriptions are also being refined and improved. Innovation is encouraged.

Some of the recent attempts to make management job descriptions more meaningful concentrate on results, ends and accomplishments—

performance unique to the position. What is done daily or periodically, or what talents or training are required, are incidental to the objective. What does it matter whether the salesman is a college graduate or not as long as he makes his quota? Is a lathe operator paid in relation to his responsibility for keeping his machine in good order, or is he paid for turning out finished products which he would be unable to do if he neglected his machine? In the past, descriptions have standardized on specifications and results have varied. It might be more sensible to agree on results first and let the methods and qualifications follow.

One consequence of writing a job description around a list of specific duties instead of results is that the incumbent feels he is performing well and deserving of monetary rewards and other considerations because he keeps busy with the string of duties detailed on paper. How much better if he reached a goal through adequate planning and its execution without being overwhelmed in all sorts of tasks. The question: Should he be rewarded for working or for getting a job done?

Detailed job descriptions itemizing duties down to the finest minutiae, are hardly encouraging to an individual who craves responsibilities and who wants an opportunity to capitalize on his own initiative and imagination.

This newer outlook on the practicality of job descriptions, while applicable to all jobs, has a particular value for management positions where the duties are not always prescribed.

INTRODUCING A JOB EVALUATION PROGRAM

The following steps are essential in preparing for a Job Evaluation installation. The company must:

1. Recognize the need and decide to install an easily understood system.
2. Assign an individual to administer the program.
3. After he has become knowledgeable on the subject of Job Evaluation, have him explain in detail to the top executives exactly what is involved.

The chief executive should:

1. Call an executive meeting of his management staff to explain the total program, but only after he has fully understood and accepted what is involved.

In this meeting he will:

a. Give his endorsement.
b. Outline the objectives.

    c. Announce the appointment of the designated individual who will administer the program.

    d. Ask the Job Evaluation Administrator to give a step-by-step explanation of what the program entails to arrive at a clear-cut understanding of

       (1) the cooperation required of each manager, and

       (2) the assistance provided by the administrator.

    e. Discuss the details, such as the amount of work involved in both the installation and maintenance, the value and benefits to be gained, the limitations to be faced, and the authority to make the program serve its purpose.

2. Repeat the above type of conference if necessary to include everybody who will be *working* on the program.

3. Let employees know what is going on, being careful to

    a. Stress the significance of an objective procedure which will emphasize fairness in paying wages, and

    b. Assure all employees that no one will get hurt in the process.

Implementing the Program

Evaluation of jobs consists of four steps:

1. Preparing job descriptions (following an analysis of each job).
2. Evaluating and grading jobs.
3. Establishing a salary structure.
4. Providing a plan for administering the program.

The separate parts of a comprehensive Job Evaluation program are discussed under individual headings in this section.

THE MECHANICS OF A POINT SYSTEM

The point system, which is the most popular plan used in job evaluation programs, is applied by using the following procedure:

1. Using a committee of top managment people, decide upon a set of factors. These should be factors that are common to all jobs.

2. Break each factor down into several degrees. It is very important when assigning degrees of factors to various jobs that the levels be identified only by a letter designation. Use of numbers colors the thinking.

3. Against this yardstick, each individual job can be evaluated by the administrator in combination with the committee. In

this evaluation procedure it is advisable to have the manager or foreman whose jobs are being considered sit in to contribute to the discussion.

4. After all jobs are evaluated they should be cross-checked on each factor separately. Reexamine conflicts and make corrections. This purifies the evaluation.

5. Assign point values to each of the factors. Assuming 100% for the sum of all factors, establish the relative weight of each factor to the whole.

6. The percentage is then converted to points. A factor which is 15% of the total is 150 points if the total of all points is 1,000.

7. The points assigned to each factor represent the *maximum* points for that factor. Assign corresponding lesser numerical values to each degree of each factor.

8. Do not merely adopt the point values which have proven satisfactory in another installation. Establish the relative importance of factors and degrees to fit your specific situation.

9. Once point values are agreed upon, it is merely a clerical job to change letter assignments to their corresponding numerical values. Add the point values for each job and arrange jobs in ascending or descending point order.

10. At this time it is well to cross-check all jobs again, considering them not on the basis of separate factors but in total against all other jobs. Jobs which appear out of line in this final evaluation should obviously be restudied.

Grading of Jobs

Jobs are divided into grades so that when rates are established they are not applied to individual jobs but rather to groups of jobs that are rated about the same number of points.

To break the total list of jobs into grades, an even-point distribution is recommended, recognizing acceptable natural divisions between jobs. The point spread within each class determines the number of grades.

Use a constant point spread to establish grades. Example: beginning with the lowest job or just below, start grades with a 60 or some other constant point interval (60, 120, 180, etc.).

Pricing the Jobs

It follows that ultimately points become dollars. A salary structure has to be designed. To establish realistic rates for job grades:

1. Take regularly-recognized representative jobs in each grade (called benchmark jobs) and obtain community rates. Inquiries may be made to companies directly or wage surveys of associations and trade groups may be helpful. Be careful to compare like jobs. Do not compare jobs by titles; this can be misleading. Compare duties.
2. Enter present wages of employees alongside each job in each grade. This can be done visually by plotting existing wages on a graph or scatterdiagram.
3. Show the community comparisons in the same way, using perhaps another color. If wages are shown graphically, plot the community wage comparisons on the same graph.
4. Establish minimum and maximum rates for each grade (the grouping of jobs with about the same point totals) based on prevailing rates and consistent with company policy. The minimum rates for grades should be separated by a constant percentage. Examples: 6% or 8%. These should become a pattern of even uphill steps. The percent difference between minimum and maximum should be the same in all grades. Examples: 40% or 50%.

Writing a Wage Policy

Finally, it is necessary to write a procedure spelling out the rules covering administration of wages. These tell how to move between minimum and maximum ranges of any one grade, and also how to move between grades. The procedure should cover:

1. Review dates and their frequency.
2. Method of review.
3. Suggested progression showing increment which should be realistic in consideration of the base rate.
4. Rules for hiring:
   a. Below minimum.
   b. At minimum.
   c. Above minimum.
5. Promotions and transfers, also demotions.
6. Jobs out of line when program is put into effect.
7. Authority and control for making wage rate changes
   a. On individual adjustments.
   b. For wage program as a whole.

Employees are paid within the ranges depending upon their performance and possibly length of service. Unfortunately, seniority somehow seems to sneak in as an influence on wages paid. The frequency of when wages are reviewed, the increment available each time, and the procedure to be followed are covered separately under the subject of Wage Administration.

PUTTING THE WAGE PROGRAM INTO OPERATION

After a wage program has been decided upon, jobs described and evaluated, and the workers appraised, how is the program put into operation?

It is important that the top level or levels of management understand and thoroughly approve of the program. Without full understanding and support the very inequities between departments or divisions that the program guards against will be fostered.

Others will want to know about the program, too. There is probably no area in which the grapevine present in any organization will be more active than on matters pertaining to the employee's pocketbook and status with the company. It is likely that everyone will know that a wage program has been undertaken.

Usually it is agreed at the beginning of the program that no wage cuts will result from it and that those found to be below the minimum will be brought up to at least the minimum rate if their appraisal shows them to be adequate for the job. This policy must be explained.

Upon completion, the fact of the program is often published and each individual is told the grade and wage range for his own job. In addition, he is sometimes told of the range of the job immediately higher in the scale than his own. Of course, it is not advisable to reveal the actual pay received by other employees. In some cases it may be decided to publish to all hands the grades and ranges of all jobs within the scope of the study. This is often included in a union contract that is published and distributed to members.

A copy of the complete wage program, including the Job Evaluation Manual, with all the job descriptions company-wide, should be distributed to each manager. This serves as a constant check on all managers and upon the neutrality of the administrator. It also helps extend the manager's horizons beyond the scope of his own activities.

Subjectivity Enters

A program of the sort described here is purely objective in its considerations and aims to provide a method of paying employees fairly in relation to their skill, responsibility and effort. There are other factors of a more subjective nature that enter into wage determination. Each company will, of course, decide for itself how much additional weight these factors should have.

Reference is often made to longevity, for example. A long-service employee provides some stability to the work force which has value to the company and should be recognized; but when a worker has attained his peak efficiency on the job, additional time on the same job does not increase his productivity or demonstrable worth to the company. Any payment above that point in his job range that is indicated by the employee evaluation is in fact a bonus and not pay for work performed. A wage program brings this into focus so that the company can recognize it and form its own policy in this regard.

Maintaining the Wage Program

A wage program must be dynamic, not static.

Job evaluation should be kept current. Job descriptions must be kept up-to-date, new jobs added, old jobs deleted. The simplest procedure calls for the administrator as a neutral agency to work out any changes or additions with the manager. Where agreement is reached, the revision is put into the Job Evaluation Manual; where the two cannot conscientiously agree, the dispute can be referred to the standing Job Evaluation Committee.

In like manner, the wage structure must be kept up-to-date. Community wage surveys must be participated in at regular intervals. Published reports of wage trends and the cost-of-living index should be studied. Adherence to the basic wage policy is assured by promptly making changes in the wage structure when indicated.

Outside Participation

It should not be assumed that the introduction of a Job Evaluation system and a Wage Administration policy is always the total responsibility of the company. There could be willing or unwilling outside participation.

The installation of a new Job Evaluation program, or the revision of an existing one, provide tailor-made opportunities for the use of consultants or professional job evaluation specialists. As outsiders they bring with them an unbiased viewpoint and can quickly discern abnormalities in jobs and job rates peculiar to the company. Since they are more objective they can serve as arbiters to resolve disagreements which might otherwise be influenced by rank or other unrelated effect.

Their programs are usually well-tested in industry, and in a minimum of time they can install a system that will develop few "bugs" afterwards. Caution should be exercised, however, to avoid selecting experts who offer a "gimmick" method in order to emphasize their different or unique approach to job evaluation. They don't train in-house people to run the program once it is installed; rather, they succeed in perpetuating themselves in the program since nobody else comprehends their strange approach.

Companies whose employees are organized may be required, or even offer to include union representation in the planning, development and operation of of any job evaluation program which affects the earnings of union members. This is accomplished by adding one or more union members to the Job Evaluation Committee so that the union will understand the system used, know why jobs rate as they do, and have an opportunity to contribute to decisions which are acceptable. This is the old concept of "put them in the boat with you and they won't bore holes in it later."

JOB EVALUATION FOR OTHER THAN WAGE-AND-HOUR JOBS

Job evaluation systems are in widespread use for the jobs of plant workers and office personnel. There is then a noticeable drop in programs covering engineering and technical positions. There are few job evaluation systems used for salesmen. Exempt positions are considered more difficult to evaluate; hence not many supervisory, staff, managerial and executive positions are included. Systems covering wage-and-hour (or repetitive) jobs cannot be utilized because the factors for evaluating these jobs do not apply to the higher positions.

Here are thoughts on job evaluation systems that might be considered for management positions:

In the preparation of job descriptions the procedure calls for individual detailed questionnaires followed by personal interviews. The job descriptions should contain the purpose, duties, scope, accountability, authority (including limits) and standards of performance of the position.

The system should use factors which are useful in measuring the distinctive differences between jobs. Enough factors should be included to enable all significant aspects of each job to receive consideration. The factors must, of course, be tailored to the specific industry.

In management position evaluations it is important that points give equal weight to staff jobs. Many systems in existence tend to favor line jobs. Staff positions are more intangible; hence they are more difficult to measure.

A sample set of factors might contain the following:

1. Necessary job knowledge.
2. Amount of planning.
3. Opportunity for creative work or innovation.

677

4. Administration (authority and supervision).
5. Contacts with others—subordinates, peers, superiors.
6. Relationships with persons not employed by company.
7. Degree of influence position has on programs of the company.

In selecting benchmark jobs against which to price all positions, care should be taken to select jobs which are fairly well understood, stable and not subject to fluctuation.

The use of a committee is very important, and the involvement of outside consultants helpful, in the evaluation of management positions. This brings a broader base of knowledge of jobs, it tends to reduce bias, and creates more thorough understanding of the program and its objectives, and will, therefore, get it acceptance.

The pricing of exempt jobs reflects different criteria from those used on the wage-and-hour level. For officer positions: the relative value of the job, the size of the company, and the nature of the industry. For middle management jobs: labor market influence and demand. For lower management jobs: pay relationship with subordinate jobs, geographic location and size of community.

Often an executive or manager is paid for what he is, not only for the job he holds. An administrative physician in an insurance office is paid for what he knows more than for what he does.

The three forces governing an executive's salary are: (1) his job in relation to other jobs, (2) his market value, and (3) his personal or uniquely individual worth to the company. These complicating factors make job evaluation of executive positions difficult and in some cases actually impractical.

NEMA/NMTA JOB EVALUATION

Most of the standard (nongimmick) job evaluation systems in use are based on a concept established in the 1930's. It would seem appropriate, therefore, to look at the initial idea.

In 1937, the National Electrical Manufacturers Association developed the NEMA Job Rating Plan for hourly-rated jobs. The plan, the first of its kind in existence, was not copyrighted. It was adopted by the National Metal Trades Association and known as NMTA Job Engineering. In 1949 the original concept was expanded to cover clerical, supervisory and technical jobs.

After an adequate job description has been agreed upon for each of the covered jobs, an evaluation is made for the degree of requirement for adequate performance for each of the following factors, common to all jobs.

Each of these factors has at least five degrees of importance (some more) to each of which has been assigned a time-tested point value. The factor-point totals determine a grade number and place each job on a scale relative to other similarly-rated jobs. The job rating plan determines the relative value of jobs within a given industrial establishment.

In postwar years, when job evaluation came into widespread use, efforts were concentrated on shop and clerical jobs. In recent years, business has become increasingly aware of the need for a systematic objective approach to setting the value of each management position in relation to others within a company management group, and to similar management positions within a geographic area or an industry. The difference is that shop and clerical plans evaluate *duties* while a management plan evaluates *responsibilities.*

Information about this plan, now offered as the MIMA/NMTA plan, is available from the Midwest Industrial Management Association, 9845 West Roosevelt Road, Westchester, Illinois 60153.

AMS CLERICAL JOB DESCRIPTIONS

The following job titles and descriptions for office positions were developed by the Administrative Management Society for use in the AMS annual office salary survey:

Mail Clerk—File Clerk

Circulates office mail, delivers messages and supplies. May process incoming or outgoing mail and operate related machines and perform other routine duties. Performs routine filing and sorting operations according to an established system. Locates and removes material upon requests and keeps records of its disposition. May perform related clerical duties.

General Clerk B

Performs clerical duties in accordance with established procedures. Maintains records and may prepare reports from basic data which does not require the development of secondary data. Job requires considerable supervision.

General Clerk A

Performs complex and responsible clerical duties requiring independent analysis, exercise of judgment and a detailed knowledge of department or company policies and procedures. Minimum supervision required.

NEMA/NMTA JOB EVALUATION

Shop	*Office*
Production, Maintenance and Service Jobs	Office, Clerical, Engineering, Administrative, Professional, Sales and Supervisory Jobs

Skill	Training
1. Education	1. Education
2. Experience	2. Experience
3. Initiative and Ingenuity	

Effort	Initiative
4. Physical Demand	3. Complexity of Duties
5. Mental or Visual Demand	4. Supervision Received

Responsibility	Responsibility
6. Equipment or Process	5. Effect of Errors
7. Material or Product	6. Contacts with Others
8. Safety of Others	7. Confidential Data
9. Work of Others	

Job Conditions	Job Conditions
10. Working Conditions	8. Mental and/or Visual Demand
11. Hazards	9. Working Conditions

	Supervision
	10. Type of Supervision
	11. Extent of Supervision

FACTORS AND DEGREES

JOB FACTORS	DEGREES						
	1ST	2ND	3RD	4TH	5TH	6TH	7TH
1. Education	15	30	45	60	75	100	
2. Experience	20	40	60	80	100	125	150
3. Complexity of Duties	15	30	45	60	75	100	
4. Supervision Necessary	5	10	20	40	60		
5. Effect of Errors	5	10	20	40	60	80	
6. Contact with Others	5	10	20	40	60	80	
7. Confidential Data	5	10	15	20	25		
8. Mental and/or Visual Demand	5	10	15	20	25		
9. Working Conditions	5	10	15	20	25		
Add for Supervisory Jobs Only							
10. Type of Supervision	5	10	20	40	60	80	
11. Extent of Supervision	5	10	20	40	60	80	100

GRADE RANGES

Score Range	Grades
100 and under	1
101-130	2
131-160	3
161-190	4
191-220	5
221-250	6
251-280	7
281-310	8
311-340	9
341-370	10
371-400	11
401-430	12
431-460	13
461-490	14
491-520	15
521-550	16

The Job Factors and Degrees used by the NEMA Job Evaluation Plan showing also how the score range places jobs into appropriate salary grades.

Accounting Clerk B

Checks, verifies and posts journal vouchers, accounts payable vouchers or other simple accounting data of a recurring or standard nature.

Accounting Clerk A

Keeps a complete set of accounting records in a small office, or handles one phase of accounting in a larger unit which requires the accounting training needed to determine proper accounting entries, prepare accounting reports, analyze accounting records, etc. May direct work of junior clerks or bookkeepers. (Excludes supervisors).

Bookkeeping Machine Operator

Operates a bookkeeping machine to record business transations of a recurring and standardized nature, where proper posting has been indicated or is readily identifiable. May balance to control figures.

Offset Duplicating Machine Operator

Sets up and operates offset duplicating machines. Cleans and adjusts equipment but does not make repairs. May prepare own plates and operate auxiliary equipment, and may keep records of kind and amount of work done.

Telephone Switchboard Operator

Operates a single or multiple position PBX telephone switchboard. May keep records of calls and toll charges, and may operate a paging system and perform duties of receptionist.

Typist—Clerk

Types letters, reports, tabulations and other material in which setups and terms are generally clear and follow a standard pattern. May prepare stencils or offset masters. Performs clerical duties of moderate difficulty.

Stenographer

Transcribes from dictating equipment, or records and transcribes shorthand dictation involving a normal range of business vocabulary. May perform copy typing or clerical work of moderate difficulty incidental to primary stenographic duties. May operate as a member of a centralized stenographic area. May perform the secretarial function for a small group.

Secretary B

Performs secretarial duties for a member of middle management. General requirements are the same as Secretary A, but limited to the area of responsibility of the principal.

Secretary A

Performs secretarial duties for a top level executive or a person responsible for a major function or geographic operation. Does work of a confidential nature and relieves principal of designated administrative details. Requires initiative, judgment, knowledge of company practices, policy and organization.

Correspondence Secretary

Operates all types of automated equipment in a word processing center, is responsible for transcribing and copy typing the many types of work handled in the center.

Key Punch Operator B

Operates an alphabetic or numeric keypunch machine to record precoded or readily usable data following generally standardized procedures. May verify the work of others, using a verifying machine.

Key Punch Operator A

Operates an alphabetic or numerical key punch or verifier to record or verify complex or uncoded data working from source material which may not be arranged for key punching. Selects appropriate number and kinds of cards. Follows a pattern of operations generally standardized but frequently including rules, exceptions and special instructions which demand operator's close attention.

Tabulating Machine Operator

Sets up, operates and wires a variety of punched card equipment, including tabulators and multipliers. Wires boards from diagrams prepared by others for routine jobs, uses prewired boards on complex or repetitive jobs. May locate and correct job difficulties and assist in training less experienced operators.

Computer Operator B

Operates computers utilizing established programs or programs under development. Loads computer and manipulates control switch on console in accordance with programmed instructions. Observes functioning of equipment. Detects nature of errors or equipment failure and makes normal console adjustments. Maintains necessary operating records.

Computer Operator A

Operates computer utilizing established programs or programs under development. Oversees loading of computer and manipulation of controls. Detects nature of errors or equipment failure. May instruct or give limited directions to less experienced operators.

Programmer

With general supervision, analyzes and defines programs for electronic data processing equipment. Is generally competent in most phases of programming to work on his own, and only requires general guidance for the balance of the activities. Conducts analyses of sufficient detail of all defined systems' specifications and develops block diagrams and machine logic flow charts, codes, prepares test data, tests and debugs programs. Revises and refines programs as required and documents all procedures used throughout the computer program when it is formally established. Evaluates and modifies existing programs to take into account changes in systems requirements. May give technical assistance to lower level classifications. Normally progresses from this classification to a lead programmer.

Systems Analyst

Under close supervision, assists in devising computer system specifications and record layouts. Is qualified to work on several phases of systems analysis, but requires guidance and direction for other phases. Conducts studies and analyses of existing and proposed operations. Prepares all levels of computer block diagram and may assist in the preparation of machine logic flow charting.

THE DICTIONARY OF OCCUPATIONAL TITLES

The Dictionary of Occupational Titles (or the D.O.T. as it is referred to) is a book published by the U.S. Department of Labor's Employment and Training Administration.

This single-volume, five-pound dictionary contains job titles and comprehensive job descriptions for more than 20,000 occupations. It focuses on occupational classifications and definitions. It is designed to provide a standardized and systematically organized body of occupational information to assist in matching jobs and workers.

The first edition was issued in 1939. The fourth edition, published in 1977, is a complete revision of the 1965 book. It reflects the impact of changing technology on the occupational structure of industry.

As one notable change, 3,000 job titles that include allusions to sex and age have been altered. For example, baseball's "bat boys" are now listed as "bat handlers." Over 2,000 new occupations (Examples: credit-card clerk and photocomposition keyboard operator) have been added, and other titles (Example: load-control agent) have been deleted.

Nonsexist Job Titles

The latest edition eliminates all sexism from job titles.

Foreman becomes supervisor, salesman is salesperson, repairman is repairer, assemblyman is assembler, draftsman is drafter, and all references to workman change to worker.

Deleted are such titles as cameraman, congressman, anchorman, publicity man. Also hatcheck girl, cameragirl (nightclubs), 26 girl, cigarette girl, charwoman, scrubwoman, restroom matron.

Added are public-relations representative, public information officer, sales-service promoter, sales clerk, sales agent, sales engineer. Also, photographer, scrubber, restroom attendant, fountain server, gambling dealer.

The new titles are descriptive of the work and not the worker.

WAGE ADMINISTRATION

The last of the four steps in implementing a job evaluation system is to devise a plan for administering the program. This becomes a policy decision. Knowing what to pay, based on the evaluation of jobs and the salary survey in the competitive community, it now becomes necessary to establish a guide so managers can make ongoing wage and salary decisions that are consistent with the plan and, more importantly, reward workers equitably for their performance.

In some companies wage administration is still little more than annual review of salaries done at a time when top management is reviewing the past year and making estimates for the coming year. Depending upon how they appraise the situation at the time, they agree on both the amount of money available for raises and the formula for distributing it. No individual, for example, may get more than a certain percentage or no department may be allowed more than a given amount.

Perhaps a better method would be to issue guidelines for managers that permit them to make adjustments throughout the year as the occasions and the opportunities arise. Managers feel more comfortable and less subject to being second-guessed when they have instructions to follow. But these instructions should not be rigid so as to make raises automatic; they should allow for judgment and decision making, both as to timing and amount.

A wage administration policy includes the following:

1. Starting rates for all grades, hopefully at or near minimum of the range.
2. Instructions on when and how to hire above the normal starting rate.
3. Frequency of wage reviews, and whether these are geared to employment year (individual consideration) or calendar year (group consideration).
4. Pattern of reviews, whether reviews are more frequent for employees in lower-rated jobs than higher-rated technicians and specialists, and whether reviews come oftener in the early days of employment (Ex: after first 90 days but certainly not every 90 days thereafter).
5. Increment, whether this should be a recommended dollar amount or a percentage and how much leeway a manager has in making individual applications.
6. Promotion raises, what the amount or percentage should be, how soon they become effective, and what these off-cycle raises do to the regular review process.
7. Types of raises, whether they are automatic (as the first one often is), when they are truly merit (rewards for performance), or related to time (because another six months rolled by).
8. Handling special raises such as those given for longevity, irrespective of performance (long and faithful service is appreciated).
9. Cost-of-living adjustments or general increases and how these tie into the regular program.
10. Authorization and how far this extends in levels of management, at what point is a higher-up's approval necessary, and which raises get committee review (exceptions, shortened time interval, double jumps, etc.).

A policy and the procedure for implementing it help govern decision making and result in greater consistency and equity in wage distribution. The policy translates corporate philosophy into management action.

While managers need and appreciate the procedure guidelines, it is not suggested that they be deprived of their own interpretation of the policy in specific cases. Because it makes their job of administration easier, they will be tempted to "go by the book." But they must learn to recognize when blind adherence to the rules may be an ill-advised course to follow. The official policy must leave them an "out" and a chance to plead their case.

A typical company policy on

WAGE ADMINISTRATION PROGRAM

1. Purpose: The purpose of the Wage Administration Program is to set the standard for administering wages of employees on jobs covered by the Job Evaluation system. It is the policy of the company:

   1.1 To provide a wage that will attract and hold above-average employees.

   1.2 To pay employees equitably for performance.

   1.3 To provide financial incentive for sustained meritorious performance of work.

2. Program: Minimum and maximum rates are established for all grades. The progression schedules are attached to this policy, and include the rates and a brief explanation of administration.

3. Administration: Wise use of the salary dollar dictates that the emphasis be on the performance of the individual being considered in terms of the specific job to which he is assigned.

   3.1 New Employee: New employees should, whenever possible, be hired at the minimum rate. An employee may be hired at a rate lower than the minimum if he is hired as a trainee for that particular job. He will be increased to minimum as soon as he obtains those qualifications necessary, but in no case longer than the time specified in the job description.

   3.2 An employee may be hired at a rate higher than the minimum, provided he has special training and/or experience, in which case he may be paid a starting rate corresponding to his ability, experience and training. But only in exceptional cases, with the approval of the divisional Vice-President and the concurrence of the Director of Personnel, should an applicant be hired above the minimum. In these cases the time for the first wage review will be on the 9-month anniversary for employees in grades I through V, who are hired below the salary indicated under 9 MOS. Merit Review. In all other cases the first wage review will be on the 12-month anniversary. The amount of the increase will be the normal next step on the rate progressional table.

4. Automatic Increases: An automatic increase will be granted in 90 days or less to full-time employees in grades I through V:

4.1 To new employees hired at minimum.

4.2 To promoted employees whose Promotional increase bring them to minimum.

4.3 To trainees when they reach minimum.

5. Merit Increases: All increases (including Promotional, but not including Automatic and Longevity) will be based on merit. These merit increases may be granted at intervals and in amounts in accordance with the attached schedules and the terms of this policy. The qualifications necessary for merit increases are spelled out on these same schedules. The decision should not be based on subjective opinion but must be backed up by objective records of performance.

6. Promotions: When an employee is promoted he will be given an increase within 30 days effective on the beginning of the next regular payroll period. The normal amount of the increase will be approximately the amount of the next step on the schedule.

7. Transfers: No wage action will be taken when an employee is given a lateral transfer between jobs in the same grade. The employee will be considered on his next scheduled review date.

8. Demotions: In the event of demotion, the wage rate will be altered to coincide with wages paid for comparable performance on jobs in the same grades, unless—

8.1 The existing wage does not disrupt harmony or cause conflict.

8.2 The demotion is made for the convenience of the company.

9. Longevity Increases: The company recognizes that an employee with long and faithful service may be entitled to special consideration. Accordingly, a seniority raise may be granted to an employee who has completed 10 years of continuous service and who has not had any raise in the past 3 years. A second and final seniority raise may be granted to an employee with 15 years of service who has not had any raise in 3 years. These may be granted even after an employee has reached the maximum for his grade. The increment will be as follows:

Amount of Weekly Raise	When Present Weekly Salary Is
$ 5.00	$ .00 or less
$ 7.50	between $ .50 and $ .00
$10.00	$ .50 or above.

10. <u>Leave of Absence and Furlough:</u> An employee who has returned from a Leave of Absence may be considered for a wage increase on his regular review date.

In the case where a Disability Absence has been extended beyond 30 days, the wage review date may be properly adjusted accordingly.

An employee who has returned from a Furlough may be given consideration for the time worked prior to the Furlough, but, of course, will receive no wage consideration for the Furlough period.

11. <u>Less-Than-Full-Time-Employees:</u> Less-than-full-time employees will be paid on an hourly rate with the first increase consideration 6 months after the start of employment. Subsequent increases will be considered at 12-month or 24-month intervals in conformance with the schedule for hourly employees.

12. <u>Procedure:</u> Raise increase recommendations will be handled according to the procedure outlined below:

12.1 The Division will be notified by Personnel approximately one month in advance, when an employee is due for wage review. It will be the Manager's responsibility to recommend the appropriate action to his Assistant Vice-President.

12.11 When an increase is indicated the appropriate Personnel Changes reporting form (RB-11) will be submitted.

12.12 When an increase is not indicated the reason for the rejection, and the employee's reaction to the explanation, should be entered on the reminder notice and returned by the Vice-President or Assistant Vice-President to Personnel to be filed in the employee's folder for future reference.

12.13 In either case, whatever action is taken, it is the responsibility of the Manager to discuss this action with the employee in private.

12.2 Each increase will be initiated by the Manager and referred to the Assistant Vice-President for action.

12.21 Below review point—if acceptable, the Assistant

Vice-President will approve it and refer it to Personnel where it will be audited to avoid any unintentional violation of policy.

12.22 Above review point—(and this is defined as any amount above that shown in last column before review point) recommendation will be referred to the Salary Review Committee through the wage and salary administrator in Personnel following endorsement by the Assistant Vice-President, in cases below the executive review point, and by the Vice-President beyond that point.

12.221 In preparing each case for committee review any additional data, such as salary history, will be provided.

12.222 The committee (see item 13) meeting regularly will review the cases before it and make its recommendations for approval or disapproval.

12.223 Cases below the executive review point will be referred to the Vice-President for his consideration to approve or disapprove, and cases beyond this point (and this is defined as any amount above that shown in last column before executive review point) will be referred to the Chief Executive Officer for his consideration to approve or disapprove.

12.2231 Approvals will be referred to Personnel for processing.

12.2232 Disapprovals will be returned to the originator through Personnel, with one copy retained in the individual employee's folder.

12.224 In those cases where the Vice-President and the Salary Review Committee are not in agreement, the Vice-President has the right of appeal to the Chief Executive Officer.

12.3 Exceptional merit cases, where the increase is more than one step in the rate progression table and/or less than the prescribed waiting period, will also be referred to the Salary Review Committee.

12.4 Except for automatic increases, the reason for recommending a wage increase should be adequately explained under "Comments."

12.5 No increase will become effective nor should any announcement be made to the employee until all necessary approvals and audits are received.

12.6 All details relating to wage increases should be completed before the effective date entered on form RB-11. It is especially important that sufficient time be allowed in cases where the recommendations require committee action. Otherwise, when the normal routine processing procedure cannot be completed before payroll is closed, the increase will not be retroactive but will have to become effective on the first payroll period following approval.

13. Committee: The Salary Review Committee shall consist of three members appointed by the Chief Executive Officer: A Vice-President, who will act as chairman (and serve for not more than one year when he will be replaced by another Vice-President), the Systems Director, and the Director of Personnel. The wage and salary administrator will be the nonvoting secretary. In the absence of the Vice-President another Vice-President will be asked to serve as alternate.

14. Exceptions: Any exceptions to this policy require the approval of the Chief Executive Officer.

Examples of work done in each of the 18 Federal Civil Service labor grades.

GS- 1   Messenger

GS- 2   File clerk

GS- 3   Typist

GS- 4   Senior stenographer

GS- 5   Engineering technician

GS- 6   Secretary

GS- 7   Computer operator

GS- 8   Computer operator

GS- 9   Buyer

GS-10   (Not used very much)

GS-11   Job analyst

GS-12   Attorney

GS-13   Chief accountant

Civil Service pay scale

Rank	Years of service									
	1	2	3	4	5	6	7	8	9	10
GS-1	$6,219	$6,426	$6,633	$6,840	$7,047	$7,254	$7,461	$7,668	$7,875	$8,082
GS-2	7,035	7,270	7,505	7,740	7,975	8,210	8,445	8,680	8,915	9,150
GS-3	7,930	8,194	8,458	8,722	8,986	9,250	9,514	9,778	10,042	10,306
GS-4	8,902	9,199	9,496	9,793	10,090	10,387	10,684	10,981	11,278	11,575
GS-5	9,959	10,291	10,623	10,955	11,287	11,619	11,951	12,283	12,615	12,947
GS-6	11,101	11,471	11,841	12,211	12,581	12,951	13,321	13,691	14,061	14,431
GS-7	12,336	12,747	13,158	13,569	13,980	14,391	14,802	15,213	15,624	16,035
GS-8	13,662	14,117	14,572	15,027	15,482	15,937	16,392	16,847	17,302	17,757
GS-9	15,090	15,593	16,096	16,599	17,102	17,605	18,108	18,611	19,114	19,617
GS-10	16,618	17,172	17,726	18,280	18,834	19,388	19,942	20,496	21,050	21,604
GS-11	18,258	18,867	19,476	20,085	20,694	21,303	21,912	22,521	23,130	23,739
GS-12	21,883	22,612	23,341	24,070	24,799	25,528	26,257	26,986	27,715	28,444
GS-13	26,022	26,889	27,756	28,623	29,490	30,357	31,224	32,091	32,958	33,825
GS-14	30,750	31,775	32,800	33,825	34,850	35,875	36,900	37,925	38,950	39,975
GS-15	36,171	37,377	38,583	39,789	40,995	42,201	43,407	44,613	45,819	47,025
GS-16	42,423	43,837	45,251	46,665	48,079	49,493	50,907	52,321	53,735	
GS-17	49,696	51,353	53,010	54,667	56,324					
GS-18	58,245									

Source: Civil Service Commission

This Civil Service pay scale is shown only to illustrate how wages in different labor grades progress in relation to time.

GS-14   Personnel director

GS-15   Personnel director

GS-16   Supergrades—

GS-17   Supervisors,

GS-18   Directors of bureaus

SALARY INCREASES

There was a time when merit increases (salary raises as a reward for good performance) were viable and meaningful to employees. But rapid inflation and federal guidelines are changing that. In order to keep up with inflation and also reward performance, salary hikes would have to be large indeed, and this would either violate government guidelines or be out of the question economically for most companies.

There is still some relationship between performance and pay, but it is mostly other factors that decide the matter:

1. The profit position of the company.
2. The combination of fringe benefits offered.
3. Salaries paid in the same job field or geographic area.
4. The employee's starting (buying-in) salary.
5. The employee's length of service.

SALARY SURVEYS

Companies want to know how they stand in the community salary-wise. Are wages paid still competitive? Are wages adequate so the company is still able to attract applicants and hold employees? To find out, they participate in salary surveys.

These studies are sponsored by a trade association to which the company belongs, by a prominent corporation against which it competes for applicants, by an industry of which it is a member, by government, or by a group of good neighbor firms who are willing to share and compare data.

Salary surveys are conducted periodically and regularly, perhaps annually. This gives the program continuity and a note of standardization since after a while the participating firms get to know and understand each other. A better comparison results.

Key jobs are reviewed. These are benchmark jobs, identical or at least very similar in all companies. They are the common, easily-defined

CONFIDENTIAL

WAGE SCHEDULE
(Suggested Steps)

SALARY GRADE	TRAINEE	MINIMUM	AUTOMATIC 90 DAYS OR LESS	MERIT REVIEW 6 MOS. AFTER STARTING DATE	9 MOS.	12 MOS.	MERIT REVIEW NOT LESS THAN 12 MONTHS AFTER LAST RAISE	MERIT REVIEW NOT LESS THAN 12 MONTHS AFTER LAST RAISE				MERIT REVIEW NOT LESS THAN 24 MONTHS AFTER LAST RAISE	
I	—	xxx.xx	xxx.xx	—	xxx.xx	—	xxx.xx	xxx.xx	xxx.xx	xxx.xx	xxx.xx	xxx.xx	xxx.xx
II	xxx.xx	xxx.xx	xxx.xx	—	xxx.xx	—	xxx.xx	xxx.xx	xxx.xx	xxx.xx	xxx.xx	xxx.xx	xxx.xx
III	xxx.xx	xxx.xx	xxx.xx	—	xxx.xx	—	xxx.xx	xxx.xx	xxx.xx	xxx.xx	xxx.xx	xxx.xx	xxx.xx
IV	xxx.xx	xxx.xx	xxx.xx	—	xxx.xx	—	xxx.xx	xxx.xx	xxx.xx	xxx.xx	xxx.xx	xxx.xx	xxx.xx
V	xxx.xx	xxx.xx	xxx.xx	—	xxx.xx	—	xxx.xx	xxx.xx	xxx.xx	xxx.xx	xxx.xx	xxx.xx	xxx.xx
VI	xxx.xx	xxx.xx	—	xxx.xx	—	—	xxx.xx	xxx.xx	xxx.xx	xxx.xx	xxx.xx	xxx.xx	xxx.xx
VII	xxx.xx	xxx.xx	—	xxx.xx	—	—	xxx.xx	xxx.xx	xxx.xx	xxx.xx	xxx.xx	xxx.xx	xxx.xx
VIII	xxx.xx	xxx.xx	—	xxx.xx	—	—	xxx.xx	xxx.xx	xxx.xx	xxx.xx	xxx.xx	xxx.xx	xxx.xx
IX	xxx.xx	xxx.xx	—	xxx.xx	—	—	xxx.xx	xxx.xx	xxx.xx	xxx.xx	xxx.xx	xxx.xx	xxx.xx
X	xxx.xx	xxx.xx	—	—	—	xxx.xx	xxx.xx	xxx.xx	xxx.xx	xxx.xx	xxx.xx	xxx.xx	xxx.xx
XI	xxx.xx	xxx.xx	—	—	—	xxx.xx	xxx.xx	xxx.xx	xxx.xx	xxx.xx	xxx.xx	xxx.xx	xxx.xx
XII	xxx.xx	xxx.xx	—	—	—	xxx.xx	xxx.xx	xxx.xx	xxx.xx	xxx.xx	xxx.xx	xxx.xx	xxx.xx

(Vertical annotation over the "12 MONTHS AFTER LAST RAISE" columns: REVIEW EVERY 12 MONTH POINT)

(Vertical annotation over the "24 MONTHS AFTER LAST RAISE" columns: EXCEPTIONAL DEVELOPMENT POINT)

FAIR DAY'S PAY FOR A FAIR DAY'S WORK

An increase is proper during this period providing an employee is developing in reasonable degree, or provided an employee who started at satisfactory level of performance has maintained it.

BETTER PAY FOR BETTER WORK

The basis for consideration should be very satisfactory work performed consistently.

TOP PAY FOR TOP PERFORMANCE

For superior exemplary performance which must be adequately explained and supported under "Comments."

CONFIDENTIAL

WAGE SCHEDULE
Hourly Employees

WAGE AND SALARY ADMINISTRATION

SALARY GRADE	STARTING RATE	6 MONTHS	12 MONTHS	12 MONTHS	12 MONTHS	24 MONTHS
I	x.xx	x.xx	x.xx	x.xx	x.xx	x.xx
II	x.xx	x.xx	x.xx	x.xx	x.xx	x.xx
III	x.xx	x.xx	x.xx	x.xx	x.xx	x.xx
IV	x.xx	x.xx	x.xx	x.xx	x.xx	x.xx
V	x.xx	x.xx	x.xx	x.xx	x.xx	x.xx
VI	x.xx	x.xx	x.xx	x.xx	x.xx	x.xx
VII	x.xx	x.xx	x.xx	x.xx	x.xx	x.xx
VIII	x.xx	x.xx	x.xx	x.xx	x.xx	x.xx
IX	x.xx	x.xx	x.xx	x.xx	x.xx	x.xx
			AVERAGE	REVIEW POINT	EXCELLENT	REVIEW POINT SUPERIOR

Hourly employee's rates are figured at the regular weekly rate divided by 37½ hours and raised to the nearest 5 cents.

All increases are given on a merit basis for work performed. Wages shall be reviewed at regular intervals as indicated above.

Regular less-than-full-time jobs are paid on an hourly basis with full employee benefits granted.

Temporary less-than-full-time or full-time jobs are paid on an hourly basis without employee benefits.

This illustration shows how salary grades in a job evaluation system can be structured.

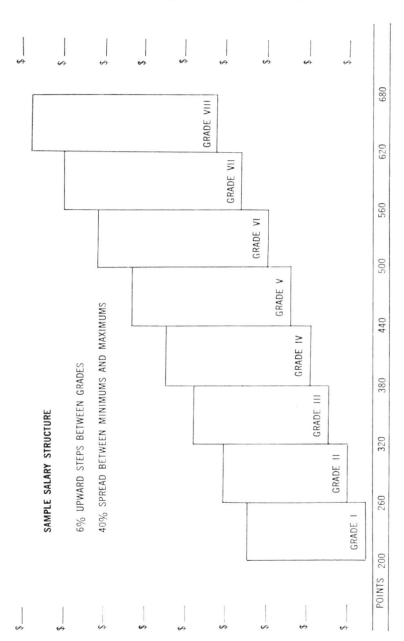

SAMPLE SALARY STRUCTURE

6% UPWARD STEPS BETWEEN GRADES

40% SPREAD BETWEEN MINIMUMS AND MAXIMUMS

GRADE I GRADE II GRADE III GRADE IV GRADE V GRADE VI GRADE VII GRADE VIII

POINTS 200 260 320 380 440 500 560 620 680

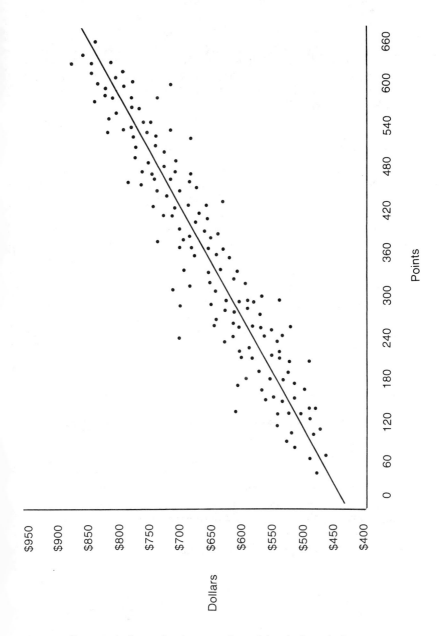

A scatter diagram, similar to the above, may be used for plotting salaries.

jobs, with sizable numbers of employees. Good examples are: key-punch operator, typist, computer programmer, janitor, drill press operator, switchboard operator, tool and die maker, etc.

Specialty jobs are avoided since they are less standardized and more uniquely individualized. Titles alone are not enough; a comptroller in one company will be different from his counterpart in another firm. It is best to use a few lines to describe the duties and then include the job in the study (regardless of title) only if the duties are comparable.

A study of salaries may often include fringe items such as hours worked, vacations, sick pay policies, lunch periods, insurance benefits, etc. It seems easy to gather extra data at the same time.

The method calls for sending out a questionnaire to eligible, participating companies. A separate page is used for each job under consideration. It calls for minimum and maximum of the range plus the actual wages paid different incumbents. If time permits, a personal call is preferable to a mailing since it assures better data. All respondents receive copies of the final report.

If medians and quartiles are calculated, the method is explained. The finished report also contains copies of all data used, such as the capsule job descriptions, ranges, number of incumbents, etc.

Individual companies are identified on the index of participating firms so all will know which companies cooperated. But in the details company identification is represented by a code number, known only to the survey team and the company so marked.

PAY: PERFORMANCE vs. SENIORITY

There are several types of pay raises. These indicate the reason for an upward adjustment in an employee's rate of pay.

Examples are:

Automatic—Given after a beginning period of time, such as probationary or qualifying period, irrespective of performance.

General—A fixed or percentage amount given across-the-board to all employees (or all members of a designated group) as a cost-of-living or similar adjustment with no relationship to individual differences.

Merit—Given periodically to recognize satisfactory, or preferably, meritorious work.

Promotion—Given at the time (or shortly thereafter) that a worker is transferred to a higher-rated job with its higher pay scale.

Longevity—Given to old-timers who have reached their production peak but who are nevertheless deserving of consideration because of long experience.

At least these are the labels used in the textbooks to describe wage increases. And this is also the way personnel practitioners refer to salary adjustments when they talk to each other. But what happens in actual practice?

If the truth were ever admitted, most pay raises are granted, pure and simple, on a seniority basis. Another six months or 12 months have passed, salaries are reviewed, and adjustments made, hopefully, to deserving workers. But the reason for the action is "time" more than "merit."

Some companies review all salaries at one time, say around the first of the year. The better programs consider wages individually, the review date related to start of employment, transfer or promotion, or most recent wage increase. In all cases a specified period of time has elapsed since the last salary action and another review is called for by the schedule. Again it is the calendar that dictates the action.

It is unfortunate that so many raises in so many companies are granted because of seniority. This kind of wage administration gives the better wages to employees with the longer service. While some consideration should be given to length of service, the most important factor should be job performance. Anything else will discourage the good worker, the very employee that companies can least afford to lose.

PERFORMANCE (MERIT) RATING

Once the jobs are evaluated, the other half of the wage program calls for an evaluation of the performance of the employees in those jobs. This is commonly called Merit Rating, although Performance Rating would appear to be more easily understood and applied.

Performance rating is defined as an orderly, systematic method of appraising an employee's performance in the job in terms of the requirements of the job. It is a method of obtaining opinions about an employee; it is not a method of "measuring" productivity or personality traits.

The manager or supervisor (the rater) expresses opinions, usually by asking standard questions that appear on a preprinted form, and checking the most applicable of a series of possible answers. There are any number of forms that can be used: short answer checklists, chart systems, narrative descriptions, forced distribution, linear, etc. The most popular is the graphic form because it is easy to understand and simple to use. On all such forms, the answers are subjective.

The rating is done periodically and regularly. The most popular frequency seems to be semi-annually for wage-and-hour employees and annually for exempt personnel. The timing of the rating is best related to each individual employee's employment date, or the date of his latest promotion; if done on a calendar basis the manager finds himself burdened with ratings for all his employees at one time and possibly cannot be as thorough as when the ratings are spread out and completed one or two at a time.

Performance rating is useful in any personnel action, but should be done independent of the action taken. To be effective it should be done when nothing is at stake, then referred to when some action is called for. To be fair and impartial, and thereby meaningful, it should not be done in connection with a salary increase, promotion, discharge and the like. Done at a time when the employee is under consideration for some action, the rating becomes window dressing to support the recommendation.

The factors upon which a worker is rated fall into three general groupings—what the worker

1. *is*: intelligence, ambition, dependability, initiative
2. *knows*: job knowledge, present activity, related procedures
3. *does*: cooperation, quality of work, responsibility, quantity of work, diligence, housekeeping.

The factors used should be common to all jobs, otherwise uneven ratings will result. Do not include "attendance" since rating an employee presupposes he is on the job. If he fails to meet minimum attendance standards he should not even be rated. Dependability is a much better factor than attendance since it embodies arriving on time, not leaving ahead of time, staying within prescribed pass and lunch periods without being policed, and in general being on the job as needed. Avoid personal characteristics such as judgment, personality and the like because it is impossible to support opinions about these.

For uniform understanding and interpretation, each factor is adequately defined. The factor, in turn, is subdivided into degrees which are clearly spelled out on the scale—usually four to five degrees or levels are set forth. A range of points is thereby assigned to the factors, and a total score or quantitative value arrived at by summing up the points for each separate rating. Where each trait is rated on a numerical scale, there is usually an effort made to weight each trait in proportion to all others; all factors of estimating job performance are not of equal value.

Different sets of factors, and therefore different forms, are used for wage-and-hour employees and exempt personnel. A worker is rated

PERFORMANCE RATING

NAME:_____   DATE of RATING:_____

DEPARTMENT:_____   JOB CLASSIFICATION:_____

	How Well Does This Employee Understand The Requirements Of Job To Which Assigned:				
JOB KNOWLEDGE	Thoroughly understands all aspects of job.	More than adequate knowledge of job.	Has sufficient knowledge to do job.	Insufficient knowledge of some phases.	Continually needs instruction.
	How Accurate, Neat And Complete Is The Work:				
QUALITY OF WORK	Consistently neat, accurate and thorough.	Careful worker seldom needs correction.	Work is acceptable.	Occasionally Careless —needs checking.	Inaccurate and careless.
	Does This Employee Work Harmoniously And Effectively With Co-Workers And Supervision:				
CO-OPERATION	Exceptionally willing and successful as a team worker.	Usually tactful and offers to assist others.	Gets along well enough, no problem.	Cooperation must be solicited, seldom volunteers.	Tends to be a troublemaker.
	How Does This Employee Accept All The Responsibilities Of The Job:				
RESPONSIBILITY	Accepts all responsibilities fully and meets Emergencies.	Conscientiously tries to fulfill job responsibilities.	Accepts but does not seek responsibility.	Does some assigned tasks reluctantly.	Indifferent—avoids responsibilities.
	How Well Does This Employee Begin An Assignment Without Direction And Recognize The Best Way Of Doing It:				
INITIATIVE	Self starter, makes practical suggestions	Proceeds on assigned work voluntarily and readily accepts suggestions.	Does regular work without prompting.	Relies on others, needs help getting started.	Must usually be told exactly what to do.
	How Much Satisfactory Work Is Consistently Turned Out By This Employee:				
QUANTITY OF WORK	Maintains unusually high out-put.	Usually does more than expected.	Does sufficient amount of work.	Inclined to be slow.	Inadequate turn-out of work.
	How Faithful Is This Employee In Reporting To Work And Staying On The Job:				
DEPEND-ABILITY	Places company interests ahead of personal conveniences.	Punctual and does not waste company time.	Generally on the job as needed.	Some abuses — occasionally needs to be admonished.	Chronic abuses of working schedules.

COMMENTS:_____

_____

_____

Rated By:_____   Discussed With Employee: By_____

Is any action being taken to help this employee improve his performance? ☐ No ☐ Yes—Specify_____

_____

_____ Dept. Manager_____

RB—9-7-59

701

only on present performance. Where a worker's potential is considered a separate system must be used. In the case of rank-and-file workers, the function of the manager as he rates his people is that of a repairman. Where supervisors or potential managers are rated, the rater also serves as a talent scout.

The significance of performance rating lies not in the form or the way it is filled out. The real value is in the counseling interview, or face-to-face discussion that follows. Every employee wants to know "How am I doing?" The performance rating then becomes a device to give the manager and the employee the opportunity to sit down together to talk over the employee's progress and find areas for improvement.

There are many advantages to a performance rating program.

For employees, it improves job performance; serves as an aid in promotions, transfers and layoffs; contributes to better decisions on wage increases; identifies needs for training; improves morale; gets employees closer to their supervisors; earmarks candidates for development and other considerations.

For managers, it brings them closer to their employees; improves their analytical ability; and gives them practical experience in learning and administering the personnel program.

Always keep in mind: Performance rating never fails; the people who use it sometimes do.

INTRODUCING PERFORMANCE RATING

Suggested memo introducing the new Performance Rating program to employees:

No matter where you are or what you are doing, your actions are being judged by other people. On the job the manager continually rates the performance of the people working with him so that he knows, for instance, whom to promote or give an increase in salary.

To make this rating procedure in our company orderly and equitable, a formalized system of Performance Rating has been established which will help the manager in this necessary and continuous task.

Performance Rating has been in use in most progressive companies for many years. It is a proven systematic approach to the management of a business which, if used properly, increases the effectiveness of the administration of fair salaries and work opportunities.

The reason for Performance Rating is to provide those people who are responsible for evaluating the performance of others with a uniform guide. In this way your performance is the sole determining factor in the whole evaluation process.

Since we believe that you would like to know how well you are doing, twice each year your manager or supervisor will visit with you to discuss your performance on the job. This will give both of you an opportunity to discuss your progress on the job, and a chance to do something about the little things which might spoil an otherwise good performance.

With your cooperation and understanding this will be a mutually beneficial program.

Suggested company policy covering the subject of

PERFORMANCE RATING

Definition: Performance rating is an orderly, systematic, method of appraising an employee's performance on the job in terms of the requirements of the job. It is a method of obtaining opinions about an employee's work performance and work habits; it is not a method of measuring productivity or personality traits.

Frequency: The rating of wage-and-hour employees is to be accomplished three months after each salary review; however, in no case should more than six months elapse without a rating.

Any employee may be rated at any time that the Department Manager decides the previous rating is no longer applicable.

Orientation: The Department Manager will be responsible for rating the employees of his department. He may enlist the cooperation of such assistants who can help him arrive at the most valid rating. Technically, the rating should be made by the immediate supervisor, the person closest to the employee. The Department Manager, however, will be held accountable and responsible for the ratings of his employees.

No one will rate, or assist in the rating of, an employee without adequate preliminary instruction. Semi-annually, a meeting will be held during which Performance Rating and its objectives will be discussed, the procedure explained, and questions answered.

Employee Review: Each employee's Performance Rating will be discussed privately with the employee by the rater.

The rater will discuss both the employee's strong and weak points as revealed by the rating, without reference to point value of factors or total score. This can best be accomplished by conducting a conversation between the rater and the employee in such a way as to give the employee a feeling of individual worth and foster a sense of pride in himself and his work.

Anything significant mentioned by the employee during the conversation may be recorded under "Comments," and the form then forwarded to Personnel.

Scoring: The factors will be scored as follows:

	Degrees	1st	2nd	3rd	4th	5th
1.	Job Knowledge	20	16	12	8	4
2.	Quality	20	16	12	8	4
3.	Cooperation	15	12	9	6	3
4.	Responsibility	15	12	9	6	3
5.	Initiative	10	8	6	4	2
6.	Quantity	10	8	6	4	2
7.	Dependability	10	8	6	4	2

Filing: The score of the rating will be recorded on the employee's individual progress card in Personnel, and the rating sheet will be placed in the individual employee's file.

MANAGER EFFECTIVENESS RATING

A company does, or should, review the performance of each manager or department head, usually on an annual basis. In so doing, the manager's superior will take into account not only how well or how poorly the individual manager handles his specific responsibilities but also the less definitive, intangible aspects upon which subjective opinions must be expressed and defended.

The specific items to be considered in judging his effectiveness will include his ability to:

1. Get good results from planning.
2. Select and develop good people.
3. Organize his own work.
4. Cooperate with others.
5. Exercise the proper judgment at propitious times.
6. Perform under pressure.
7. Create goodwill outside the company.

8. Demonstrate the way in which his unit benefits the company through increased profits, improved service or any other measure of progress that may be applicable to his operation.

APPRAISAL BY RESULTS

Appraisal by results, as differentiated from the more formal Management by Objectives, is a performance appraisal at the management level measured against previously-established goals.

It involves these steps:

1. An individual manager determines the results he expects to reach during the period ahead, usually one year.
2. He and his boss confer about his proposed targets. Adjustments are made to coordinate his goals with those of other managers and blend all of them into unified corporate planning objectives. The manager and his boss reach an agreement on his challenging but attainable goals.
3. The manager goes to work doing his job all the while keeping his goals and target dates in mind.
4. At the end of the year, when salaries are reviewed, the manager's performance is appraised in terms of how well he met the goals he himself set earlier with the guidance and concurrence of his superior. Salary consideration or other action may be taken on the basis of this results-oriented appraisal.
5. Based on the previous year's experience, new goals are drafted for the coming year.

This type of appraisal is useful for exempt positions where results count more than the fulfillment of a string of miscellaneous duties as outlined on the written job description.

PERFORMANCE RATING INTERVIEWS

It should be noted that the significance of performance rating lies not in the form that is used, or the way it is filled out, scored, and then recorded. The real value is in the counselling interview, or face-to-face discussion, that follows.

The most important step in the entire rating procedure is this manager/employee talk session. This is the time when confidence and morale can be considerably strengthened and poor behavior and work patterns that may have developed with or without the employee's knowledge can be corrected.

Every employee wants to know "How am I doing?" The performance rating then becomes a device to give the manager and the worker the opportunity to sit down together to talk over the worker's job performance and to point up areas for improvement.

Without some kind of system, complete with "come up" reminder dates, a manager might be inclined to overlook the opportunity of discussing job progress with each employee. The unrelenting press of everyday work easily devours a manager's good intentions. But let an error cause trouble, or confusion louse up the schedule, and the fur starts flying immediately.

The result of overreacting only in crisis situations is that all the discussions are negative. Overlooked is the plain fact that even in the case of a serious mistake, not everything the employee does is bad. But the continued good performance day after day is taken for granted while the problem is blown out of proportion.

A performance rating form covers all aspects of a job. When a manager discusses the employee's performance on a particular job, both the good and less-than-good points are brought up, and at a neutral time unrelated to any specific incident—good or bad.

The Interview Procedure

The following are general comments which should be used as a guide in performance rating interviews:

1. An interview means two-way communications. The employee is closest to the job and may suggest improvements if encouraged to "open up."
2. Make the individual feel at ease. Provide an informal attitude and atmosphere—come out from behind the desk. Pass the time of day for a minute or two.
3. Explain to the person what the interview is for and relate the general factors used in the rating, using your own terminology.
4. It is an insult if you do not come prepared. Have your notes in order. Familiarize yourself with the requirements of the job.
5. Start the critique with those items that are praiseworthy. Remember, this person is an individual with an ego, who likes acknowledgement for things done well.
6. Do not read the performance rating form to the employee, or mention anything about numerical scores. The performance should be explained in your own words—words the employee will understand.

7. In discussing a person's shortcomings, resist the temptation to do any preaching. State the facts and then ask the person if there is some reason why—get the other side of the story and evolve from it the solution to the problem.
8. The solution to a problem should come from the employee with some guidance on your part. In this way the solution will be understandable and acceptable.
9. Provide at least 15 minutes for each interview—really get to know the employee.
10. The interviewer should finish the meeting. Don't leave the employee hanging in mid-air; put a conclusion to the meeting with a statement of confidence in the employee.

Summary

In conducting these all-important performance rating interviews it is well to remember that:

1. Where workers are rated on the results of their work, and where an attempt is made to orient the discussion to the job, the relationship between superior and subordinate is healthy.
2. Where rating forms focus on personality traits, appraisal interviews are carried out half-heartedly, in an atmosphere of mutual embarrassment, and with little wholesome effect.

Keep in mind that in a performance rating interview the manager is not discussing the employee but rather the employee's performance. This is a distinction that must be made.

PERFORMANCE STANDARDS

Standards have been used in the factory for a long time. Efforts are being made to apply standards to office work. While progress has been minimal, the promise is great.

In any business situation, standards can be set only after the work has been standardized, i.e., made uniformally applicable. Standards then become points of reference from which measurements of quantity, quality and performance are made. In practice they are objects of comparison we invent or adopt to facilitate both our minute-by-minute judgments and our longer range decision making. Their importance to managers derives from their function in feedback; by their means a manager can tell how he is doing, how his operation is doing.

A standard may be a metal bar in a Paris museum or the wavelength of light emitted by an excited atom. In office management it is ideally a numerically exact entity or a precisely described circumstance, like 30 purchase orders processed, zero steps taken, same-day coding of all stock deletions. Sometimes, however, it is difficult or impractical to apply standards in ways which yield precise measurements or descriptions. The standard in letter-writing, for example, may be comprehensibility to the layman; degrees of compliance with this standard may be measured by taking surveys and giving comprehension tests to naive subjects, but to most firms the cost of such tests would cancel out any benefits.

Nevertheless, wherever possible, standards should be constructed in such ways that their effectiveness may be gauged precisely, and that means mathematically. Quantity, quality and performance are bound to vary even in controlled environments. It is important to know how to measure these variations and to know when the variations are significant. This means that the manager must know enough math to compute his own mathematical interpretations, or enough to understand someone else's if his firm employs statisticians. The day of the man who could drive an office by intuition probably never was.

What a manager does in using standards is to compare reality with a concept. Unlike the metal bar in a museum vault or radiation at the point of a needle, standards in office management most often exist only in the minds of the persons using them. To be sure, standards exist for the size and weight of paper, the inkiness of nylon ribbons, the durability of file folders, and the aesthetics of desk trays, but concern with these is usually peripheral to a manager's thinking. His job is the collecting, processing, storing and distributing of information, and his concern with standards reflects these primary activities. For this purpose he forms mental models of these activities, and uses them as measuring sticks in judging the real work going on around him.

But while they are not real in the sense of being physical objects, standards must be realistic. They are not imaginings of what ought to be, but are based on actual processes and things. A standard is a criterion of acceptable performance. A standard may be established by custom or authority on the basis of:

1. past performance (what was)
2. future estimate (hopefully, what will be)
3. scientific analysis (what can and should be)

In constructing standards the manager has recourse to past performance in his own office, his memory, the experiences of his acquaintances, and accounts in trade journals. But standards are really guideposts to future means and ways of accomplishing work. Projections into the future based on available data will only be as valid as the data are reliable. This is another argument for recording measurements in numbers which, because of their universality and lack of ambiguity, form the most precise language possible.

The application of standards lends itself well to office management. These standards should be carefully established and developed to the point that practicality permits. Their judicious use is one of the best tools in the planning and control of office work, and aids immeasurably in the rating of individual performance upon which many personnel actions are based.

This is more than enough reason for the personnel executive to involve himself in the establishment, understanding and application of work standards.

WORK MEASUREMENT

Merit rating, or what is better referred to as performance rating, calls for subjective opinions. A supervisor expresses judgments about various aspects of an employee's work.

Anything in the job that is measurable should not be included as a factor on the rating form. Thus, "Attendance" is not appropriate because time sheets can tell precisely how many times an employee is late or absent. A better factor would be "Dependability" which means broadly "being on the job as needed" and embodies, besides starting promptly, such things as not overstaying pass and lunch periods, not leaving ahead of time, and generally being on the job and tending to business. There are no accurate records kept on these elements of dependability; hence, a supervisor's personal opinion about them is the best expression upon which to base an action or make a decision.

But on the factor of volume or production some measurement is possible. Certain jobs lend themselves to measurement better than others. Output on a machine is easier to measure than work of a more general nature. To lend itself to measurement, work should be repetitious, continuous and unchanging. It is easy to measure manual work, impossible to measure mental work. For this reason work measurement is more common in factories than in offices. But lately considerable progress in this area has been made in clerical work.

Measuring work, however, is meaningless unless we measure time also. Then we relate the two. How many punches per minute, how many pieces per hour, or how many calls per day. This results in a standard.

A personnel handbook is not the place to discuss how to set standards against which performance is gauged. They may be established by custom or authority, or they may be set by observation, stopwatch or other study. They may be stated in written specifications, shown as a model or sample, expressed as an accepted rule or regulation, become unwritten customary practice (habitual usage), or simply presented in verbal communication. A standard does not imply perfection; a standard means average or typical performance and output.

Suffice it to say that where reasonable standards are set, an individual's performance may be measured against the standard and it can be determined whether the worker's production is below, on a par with, or above the accepted standard—and by how much.

Understand, this record of volume does not take into consideration any thought of accuracy. But standards can also be set for reliable work and the number of deviations from the standard, i.e., the errors or scrap that will be tolerated can be expressed. A worker's quality of work can be measured against this type of standard.

Standards help a manager distribute work loads fairly, define job success in tangible units, analyze performance and highlight where remedial help is needed.

EXEMPT PERFORMANCE APPRAISAL

As an integral part of measuring the performance of the total company, or any of its divisions or departments, it is necessary first to measure the performance of individuals within the company. In the parlance of the trade, this is known as Merit Rating for clerical employees and shop workers and Performance Appraisal for higher level personnel.

The principles are the same but the application varies. The chief distinction between rating performance in nonexempt jobs and exempt positions is that the former is subjective and the latter is objective—or at least it should be.

When a manager rates his clerical employees he expresses subjective opinions about loosely-defined traits. He comments on such soft factors as job knowledge, quality, quantity, cooperation, responsibility and dependability. He tells each employee, first on paper and then in an interview, how well he thinks the employee is performing the duties and meeting the responsibilities of the job. Actually, the device is really not all that important; the value of performance rating lies in the face-to-face conversation that follows.

In exempt performance appraisal, on the other hand, the rating should not be trait-oriented but should center on results. At this level it is virtually impossible, for example, to develop a set of traits that can be ascribed to the ideal manager. There are just too many cases on record, not only in business but also in other aspects of life, of people who possess all the desirable personality traits but who are not productive. To be sure, there is nothing wrong with being a "nice guy" but that is not what a manager is paid for. He is paid, or should be paid, in proportion to the results he delivers. This is the only fair basis for differentiating salary-wise between a good salesman and a mediocre one, isn't it? The same logic holds true for line and staff managers.

The work of technicians, supervisors, managers and professionals should not be judged in the same way as assembly-line work. These people are not compensated for what they do, in the sense of a string of specific duties, but rather for what they accomplish, in the sense of making the company better and more profitable.

The performance of their functions should be evaluated against standards that are appropriate for measuring results, not effort. The concept is simple enough, and consists of establishing in advance mutually-acceptable expectations and then determining afterwards how well the anticipated results compare with actual results. What this becomes is a simplified version of management by objectives. It breaks down overall company objectives into functional specifics and expresses these in terms of individual goals.

Sound complicated? Really, it isn't. Like any other management tool, there are systematic procedures to follow that make this technique understandable and effective, without becoming burdensome. Individual Goal Setting, discussed separately, is one possibility.

This type of performance appraisal, suitable for exempt positions, utilizes objectivity since it measures performance against results instead of merely expressing opinions, many of them debatable. It is somewhat like a game. As an activity it is well structured. The rules are clear and easily acceptable. The score (feedback) is instantaneous.

Once the goals are agreed upon between each manager and his superior, and the strategy set in motion, the rating becomes unnecessary. The manager will know at all times that by meeting the requirements of his position, which he helped declare earlier, he will be satisfying the demands placed upon him. Nor will it be necessary to set up any outside control mechanism since self-controls are built into the system. Each manager need but follow the timetable to know how closely he is on time and on target. In the process of fulfilling the responsibilities of his position, the manager will display that elusive ingredient for success, self-motivation, by bringing his talent, training, resourcefulness and personal improvement to bear.

Could anything in the management tool kit be more practical?

APPRAISAL OF POTENTIAL

Evaluating the job and evaluating the employee's performance in that job are accepted techniques for determining equitable wages. But what about an employee's value beyond the job to which he is presently assigned? What promise does the future hold for the individual who is, or can become, overqualified for his current responsibilities? Rather than run the risk of losing someone whose potential goes unnoticed and unrecognized, can the company identify this potential and take measures to capitalize on it.

The additional worth of certain employees, over and above the satisfactory performance of their current duties, falls into two categories: (1) readiness to handle an emergency or unexpected activity for which no preparation was possible, and (2) promotability that makes them eligible for greater responsibilities. These people possess a talent or potential that makes them invaluable; no company can afford to lose them.

There are different ways in which people of this type can be located. Generally, top management knows from prior involvements whom they can count on and who is capable. This is perhaps not the best way for it can lead to "favorite son" allegations. People of this caliber must be "discovered" objectively and a practical device for accomplishing this is the Appraisal of Potential.

In contrast to the Performance Appraisal, which concentrates on how well an employee is doing, the Appraisal of Potential attempts to learn: (1) what other types of work, or what greater responsibilities, is the employee capable of, and (2) in what direction are his personal interests leading him.

The easiest way to know something about an individual is to ask him. His work history and his record of accomplishments should also be examined. All the facts should be gathered and studied. No hasty judgment should be permitted. The Appraisal of Potential attempts to be neutral and greatly reduces the danger of bias, prejudice, bad blood, long memories, personality conflicts and other unfounded reasons for negative decisions.

Where the procedure is formalized this becomes a Manpower Inventory. Through the use of an initial questionnaire followed by annual updatings, an individual's official record at all times catalogs his entire range of qualifications and interests. The complete information is recorded, manually or mechanically, for ready reference. Unless everything is known about everybody how can a company possibly find the ideal candidate for a special assignment or promotion?

APPRAISAL OF POTENTIAL
(sample form)

Name _____

Location _____

Type of Appraisal of Potential

_____In conjunction with periodic Appraisal of Performance

_____Special. Reason _____

_____

Date of last Appraisal of Performance

Summary of rating _____

_____

_____

Date of last Appraisal of Potential

Summary of rating _____

_____

_____

Employee's advancement potential at this time

Promotable to position _____

now_____or how soon _____

and/or to position _____

now_____or how soon

This two-page Appraisal of Potential form is taken from the Dartnell Management Guide. **Corporate Growth Through Internal Management Development.**

_____ Meets or exceeds requirements of current position but should remain in this job for now. Reason _____

_____

_____ Not performing satisfactorily in current position for one of the following reasons:

      _____ portions of job unsatisfactory but should remain in job and should improve

      _____ skills and interest better utilized in another occupational field at same or lower level

      _____ will probably be terminated unless level of performance improves considerably

_____ In current position only_____months and not long enough for judgment.

Comments _____

_____

_____

                                                          Date

Prepared by _____ _____
                    (manager)

In consultation with _____ _____
                    (employee)

Reviewed by _____ _____
                  (director of management development)

Development Needs

NAME	POSITION	DATE

IN YOUR OPINION WHAT SKILLS, KNOWLEDGE, TALENT, QUALITIES SHOULD BE DEVELOPED OR STRENGTHENED? **BE SPECIFIC.**

WHAT IS HE PERSONALLY DOING TO BECOME MORE PROFICIENT IN HIS PRESENT ASSIGNMENT, AND TO PREPARE HIMSELF FOR A MORE RESPONSIBLE POSITION?

WHAT DOES HE THINK THE COMPANY COULD DO TO ASSIST HIM IN BECOMING A MORE VALUABLE EMPLOYEE?

WHAT ARE YOUR PLANS AND RECOMMENDATIONS FOR A DEVELOPMENT PROGRAM FOR THIS EMPLOYEE? **BE SPECIFIC.**

WHAT DO YOU SEE AS THIS MAN'S NEXT STEP POSITION(S)?

HOW SOON WILL HE BE READY FOR THIS?   Now _____ ,   1-2 years _____ ,   3-5 years _____ ,   over 5 years _____ .

_____   _____
SUPERVISOR'S SIGNATURE   EMPLOYEE SIGNATURE

The Appraisal of Potential is a rating resulting from a discussion between a superior and a subordinate. The employee's abilities and ambitions are evaluated as his future is discussed and he is then earmarked for possible promotion in the same job field, for transfer to a job more to his liking, for remaining where he seems happy, or for training where this is called for.

Companies that are going nowhere have managers who may be reasonably well qualified for their present positions but who suffer career arrest. Not every employee, of course, aspires to become an officer in the industrial army. The developable people, however, must be identified and encouraged to grow. Otherwise there is no potential for either the people or the company.

EXEMPT POSITIONS

Purpose: In order that the company will comply with federal laws, this policy is prepared to define and delimit the terms under which a position in the company may properly be considered exempt from wage-and-hour regulations.

Classification: The following types of positions are exempt provided they meet all legal requirements:

> Executive
> Administrative
> Professional
> Outside Salesmen

Definition: According to the Fair Labor Standards Act of 1938, as amended, the above positions are defined in summary (full text available upon request) as follows—

Executive: An "employee employed in a bona fide executive capacity" must

(a) have as his primary duty the management of an establishment, department or subdivision; and

(b) regularly direct the work of at least two other employees; and

(c) have the authority to hire or fire, or his recommendations on this are given particular weight; and

(d) regularly exercise discretionary powers; and

(e) devote not more than 20% of his workweek to nonexecutive duties; and

(f) be compensated for his services at not less than $155 per week.

Note: An employee who is compensated at not less than $250 per week is exempt provided he meets requirements (a) and (b) above.

Administrative: An "employee employed in a bona fide administrative capacity" must

(a) as his primary duty do nonmanual work in the office or field directly related to management policies; and

(b) regularly exercise discretion and independent judgment; and

(c) (1) assist an exempt executive or administrative employee, or

(2) do special or technical work under general supervision, or

(3) do special tasks under general supervision; and

(d) devote not more than 20% of his workweek to nonadministrative duties; and

(e) be compensated at not less than $155 per week.

Note: An employee who is compensated at not less than $250 per week is exempt provided he meets requirements (a) and (b) above.

Professional: An "employee employed in a bona fide professional capacity" must

(a) primarily do work

(1) requiring advanced knowledge in science or learning acquired by long study, or

(2) original and creative in character in a recognized field of artistic endeavor, and the result of which depends primarily on the employee's talent; and

(b) exercise discretion and judgment; and

(c) do intellectual and varied work, the output of which cannot be standardized; and

(d) devote not more than 20% of his workweek to nonprofessional duties; and

(e) be compensated at not less then $170 per week.

Note: An employee who is compensated at not less than $250 per week is exempt provided he meets requirements (a) and (b) above.

Outside Salesmen: An "employee employed in the capacity of outside salesman" must

    (a) be working away from the employer's place of business for the purpose of—making sales or obtaining orders or contracts for services; and

    (b) devote not more than 20% of time worked by nonexempt employees to nonsales work.

Observations:

1. Content of job and not title determines whether the job is exempt or nonexempt.

2. Trainees for exempt positions are not exempt until all requirements for exemption are met.

3. Hiring or firing includes direct action by the executive employee or recommendations to those to whom hiring and firing functions are delegated. Recommendations as to promotion, pay increases and the like must also be given weight.

4. Exercise of discretion and judgment must be performed customarily and regularly, not necessarily constantly, but oftener than occasionally. This test concerns the decision-making authority in significant matters, and without immediate supervision, as opposed to determining merely whether certain standards are met.

5. Nonexecutive duties are those not directly and closely related to executive work, usually that which is performed by subordinates.

6. Administrative work is of three kinds—

    a. executive and administrative assistants who take over many duties of their superiors;

    b. staff employees who are usually advisory specialists to management;

    c. special assignment employees who take up and complete special jobs, only under general supervision.

Approval: Any position will be reviewed when necessary, and all existing exempt jobs will be audited annually by the senior officer in charge, together with the personnel director to guarantee that legal requirements are being met. The responsibility for exempting a new position, or for continuing to exempt an existing position, lies with the line organization.

EQUAL PAY FOR EQUAL WORK

Elimination of different pay scales between men and women employees doing basically the same work has been a long-sought goal.

The first proposal to enact the equal pay principle into Federal law was introduced in the 79th Congress in 1945. On June 10, 1963, success was finally achieved when the 88th Congress passed the Equal Pay Act to prohibit discrimination in wages on the basis of sex.

The Equal Pay Act of 1963

The Equal Pay Act covers most private and public employees subject to the Fair Labor Standards Act, including executive, administrative, professional and outside sales employees who are otherwise exempt from its minimum wage and overtime provisions. The 1974 amendments to the Fair Labor Standards Act extended coverage to large numbers of employees including most federal, state, and local government employees, as well as employees of certain small chain stores, telegraph agency employees, and employees of large motion picture theaters, among others. (Military personnel are not subject to the Equal Pay Act requirements).

Men and women performing work in the same establishment under similar conditions must receive the same pay if their jobs require:

1. Equal skill
2. Equal effort
3. Equal responsibility

"Equal" does not mean "identical" but jobs to be compared under the Equal Pay law must involve the same primary job function and must require substantially equal skill, effort and responsibility.

The Four Tests

Equal skill includes such factors as experience, training, education and ability. Skill applies to the performance requirements of the jobs under consideration, and not to the skills which employees may possess but which are not needed to perform the job.

Equal effort is the measurement of the physical or mental exertion needed for the performance of a job. Two jobs may require equal effort, even though the effort may be exerted in different ways. The occasional or sporadic performance of an activity which may require extra physical or mental exertion is not alone sufficient to justify a finding of unequal effort. Of course, if substantial differences exist in the amount or degree of effort required in the performance of jobs, the equal pay standard would not apply even though the jobs may be equal in all other respects.

Equal responsibility deals with the extent to which an employer depends on the employee to perform the job as expected, with emphasis on the importance of the job obligation. If jobs are otherwise equal, a minor or insignificant difference in the responsibility exercised by the employees does not justify a finding of inequality.

719

Similar working conditions generally assumes that employees performing jobs in an establishment that require equal skill, effort and responsibility are likely to be performing them under similar working conditions. Slight or inconsequential dissimilarities or the fact that the jobs are in different departments do not establish dissimilarity of working conditions.

It should also be noted that an employer may not reduce the wage of an employee in order to comply with the law.

Also, it is illegal for a labor organization or its agents to cause or attempt to cause an employer to pay lower wages to an employee because of sex.

Exceptions

There may be reasons other than sex for paying different wages to employees performing equal work. Such differences in pay, which are in fact shown to be based on some factor other than sex, are not prohibited by the Equal Pay Act.

Exceptions are accepted if it can be shown that the wage differential is based on a seniority or merit system, a system measuring earnings by quantity or quality of production, or on any other factor other than sex.

Any system of payments based on an exception to the equal pay standard must be applied equally to employees of both sexes. Thus, when applied without distinction to employees of both sexes, shift differentials, incentive payments, production bonuses, performance and longevity raises, and similar things will not result in violations.

Administration and Enforcement

The Wage and Hour Division of the Employment Standards Administration has responsibility for the administration and enforcement of the Equal Pay Act for private, state and local government employees and for employees of the Library of Congress, the U.S. Postal Service, the Postal Rate Commission and the TVA by agreement with the agencies. The U.S. Civil Service Commission is responsible for administering the law as it applied to all other federal employees.

Authorized representatives may enter establishments, inspect records, interview employees and investigate any facts necessary to determine whether any provision of the law has been violated. They advise employers of any change which will aid in achieving and maintaining compliance with the law. Names of complainants, records and other information obtained from employees and employers are treated confidentially.

While most employers comply with the law once they are informed about a violation, some do not. In such instances, the Department of Labor often will seek enforcement action through the Federal District Court.

Beneficial Effects

The law helps both men and women. It provides no special advantage or treatment for women workers. The Equal Pay Act provides only that there be equal pay for equal work regardless of the sex of the employee performing the work.

The law when uniformly applied can have many beneficial effects. It

1. Contributes to higher worker morale.
2. Helps eliminate the age-old myth that the economic value of women's work is less than that of men.
3. Increases efficiency.
4. Reduces turnover.
5. Provides for the optimum utilization of the nation's available resources.
6. Improves purchasing power and helps maintain an adequate standard of living for workers and their families.
7. Helps reduce welfare costs by encouraging low income workers to remain employees—particularly women who are supporting families.
8. Reduces an unfair method of competition.

Employed men and women should be treated alike on pay day when their work is equal. That one sex should be given pay preference over another under such circumstances is both immoral and illegal. Work performance should be judged on the basis of individual achievement, regardless of the sex of the employee.

CHAPTER IX

BENEFITS

COMPENSATING THROUGH FRINGE BENEFITS

THE COMPENSATION package consists of direct and indirect pay. The indirect wages are the fringe benefits. They cost the company money and they are worth money to the employee.

Fringe benefits are sometimes referred to as the "salary with the fringe on top." This is an apt label. While not paid in cash to the workers, the fringes nonetheless represent a substantial cost-expense to the employer and a sizeable cost-saving to the employee.

In many respects the fringe benefits may be the only difference between earnings in one company compared with those of another. Many factors, such as the tendency toward local and national wage increases, industry-wide policies, the proliferation of compensation surveys, and the practice of tandem adjustments, have contributed to near-equalization of job rates. Fringes, therefore, often make the difference.

Applicants and employees realize full well that there exists only slight variations in wages during days of full employment. Hence, they shop around for the best total compensation package which consists of tangible and intangible components.

Fringe benefits is a relatively new term. The earlier usage referred to "welfare work." But because this was, and still is, an unpopular phrase in the lexicon of business, the textbooks tried to promote such substitutes as "service activities" or "employee services." This service work, according to one definition, included "all those activities which are not directly concerned with production, but which make the plant personnel a healthier, sounder-thinking, more forward-looking group." The notion prevailed that those services would better the "condition" of the workers.

Today such features as individual lockers and clean washrooms are considered facilities of employment by companies and as a right of employment by workers. The fact that they are not under the supervision of the personnel executive indicates that they have passed from being employee benefits to being operating necessities. The personnel office maintains an interest in their adequacy for safety and sanitation but exercises no direct control over their function.

By contrast, industrial health and in-plant feeding have not only remained under the direction of the personnel officer but have also grown in importance. The medical services in many firms have gone from a small first-aid station to a complete clinic offering free flu shots and annual physical checkups. Cafeterias provide more than convenient, well-planned, low-cost meals; just as important is the change-of-pace atmosphere available during rest periods and lunch hours which permits employees to relax, meet their friends, and engage in personal conversations which are discouraged at their work places.

The percentage of increase in fringe benefits costs during post-war years has been twice that of the rise in wages. The U.S. Chamber of Commerce surveys show that in 1965 they ran 28% of payroll, in 1971 34%, and in 1975 40%. Much of what is included in the fringe benefit package is the result of government programs and is nothing more than the cost of social legislation passed on to employers.

What is the Purpose?

In analyzing fringe benefits emphasis must be placed on the cash wages to which the fringes are added. If the base pay is not right the fringes will not be effective. Fringes are "plus" and cannot be expected to offset inadequate wage scales. Fringe benefits will not accomplish their purpose where starting salaries are below going rates and therefore do not attract workers in the first place. Where fringes are used to replace rather than augment salary, they are a misrepresentation of an employee benefit program as well as an unsound compensation practice.

But because the dollar amount on the paycheck does not have as much meaning as before, there is increasing interest in nonmonetary compensation items. Most fringe benefits have the advantage of being tax free, whereas salary in cash is subject to taxes.

Both union settlements and management adjustments in nonunion factories and offices have placed considerable emphasis on fringe benefits, since these do not sound as inflationary as direct wages. The value of fringe benefits to the employee is now rising at an average rate of nearly 10% a year.

The reasons for the establishment and expansion of benefit programs are many: tax consideration, legal requirements, increase in leisure time through shorter hours, preoccupation with security, questions of public and employer responsibility. In addition there are the social considerations: maintenance of a modest living standard in times of adversity, avoiding depletion of savings in case of illness, and sustaining purchasing power during old age.

Many benefits are for the corporation and not for the employees, according to one point of view. The corporation objectives may be to:

1. Meet competition; they help attract and hold workers.
2. Provide for the employees' security—a social objective.
3. Secure more profit; higher employee morale may increase productivity.
4. Expand total compensation—especially when it does not cost the corporation anything.
5. Satisfy government regulations.
6. Fill the life span gap with financial support from age 65 to death; the family is the target of fringe benefits the employee earns.

Generally, the purpose of fringe benefits is to help attract applicants and to hold workers. Specifically, each type of benefit has its own objective. If, for example, the aim is to increase skills, then a form of tuition refund or off-the-job training is recommended. If the labor market is to be widened then flexible working hours or company-operated transportation should be considered. Attendance rewards may be tried in an attempt to reduce absenteeism. To maintain workers on the job and keep production going are the reasons that convenient health facilities are available. In a cost-conscious climate the reason is selfish, no longer paternalistic, and never corporate benevolence.

The "cradle to grave" school of thought has had its day and today fringes are expected to pay their way in order to justify their existence. A true fringe benefit should show a value to both the employee and the employer. Social and humane considerations might appear to be unprofitable to companies, but they are of tremendous worth if they help to prevent strikes, reduce turnover and the like.

Which Way To Go

In looking at trends there is little chance of regression. What companies would dare take anything away that employees have come to accept for granted? Before the program is altered it might be advisable to consider how to justify the change or addition, not only to the comptroller but also to the employees.

The basic question is whether to *liberalize* present benefits or *enlarge the scope* of benefits by adding new ones or even possibly *experimenting with innovations.* The upcoming changes fall into three classifications:

1. *New dimensions* to existing benefits, such as expanded medical coverage.

2. *New benefits,* as for example, free travel for long-service employees.

3. *New approaches,* tailored to individuals *vs.* generalized for administrative convenience. (Ex: flexible benefits or the "Smorgasbord" concept).

Some fringes, although available to all employees, are geared to special groups. When this is obvious the workers who see themselves at a disadvantage might react negatively and the fringe might actually do more harm than good. A retirement program has little appeal to the young married woman whose immediate ambition is the establishment of her home. Other examples here are: company-paid memberships for management or professional people, personal time off for office employees, income tax help for hourly-paid plant workers, wedding gifts for newlyweds, remembrances when babies are born, and wedding anniversary gifts for old-timers.

It is not good practice to copy fringe benefits from other companies. Some fringes are suitable to one company and not applicable to others, such as selling "own goods" at wholesale. Many are peculiar to one locality, as evidenced by the wide variance in number and dates of holidays across the country.

The benefits made available to retired employees are usually in the health and service categories. A number of employers pay the Medicare medical premium for retirees (and sometimes spouses) or offer free or low-cost complementary health insurance. Some permit discount purchases of company products, free telephone use, secretarial assistance, cafeteria privileges, income tax guidance and the like.

For high-level positions the fringe benefits are influenced by the complexities of modern tax laws, changing personal values, and the undaunted continuation of inflation. Executives are interested in tax-sheltered forms of compensation.

Cost of Doing Business

Nonwage benefits are here to stay. While some of our more pedantic colleagues prefer to speak of "payments other than wages and salaries" or "indirect compensation," the terms "fringe benefits" or "employee benefits" have obtained a fairly clear identity and ready acceptance in management circles. But like many other such terms, while they are convenient to employers, they are not necessarily clear to employees.

"Employee benefits" is perhaps a better description than "fringe benefits." The miscellaneous benefits could possibly be classified as "fringes" but other major or even minor items in the total package are anything but fringes. Such things as free parking, libraries, purchase discounts, notary public services, and the like are the fringe items. They are not universal and depend upon the type of company and its location.

But practically all firms all over the country offer certain standard benefits which certainly cannot be classified as fringes. These substantial items are the wage replacement plans, such as sick pay allowances, income continuation policies and disability insurance. They also include the other insurance programs such as hospitalization, life insurance and pension plans, which employers know employees need and which can be purchased more conveniently and advantageously in group arrangements than individually.

Anyway, these nonwage extras can hardly be called fringes anymore. But by whatever term these benefits are known, it is well to recognize their existence in the total scheme of managerial operations. Any discussion on this subject takes into account not only the effect of a benefit program but also its cost, which today is larger than most companies realize. Managements should itemize their fringe benefit bill, just as they make other cost analyses; the results will open their eyes.

Before any meaningful study of costs can be made, however, a definition must be established in order to know what should be included and what should be excluded. Fringe or employee benefits are defined by one company as: "Anything which benefits the employee directly or indirectly in the form of extra income or services in excess of established straight-line earnings, whether required by law or not."

Employee benefits have these characteristics:

1. They increase the cost to the employer of a production work-hour.
2. Add to employees' take-home pay in the form of benefits they would otherwise have to pay for.
3. Are available to all employees, or most of them.
4. Vary in total cost as the workforce changes in size.

Under this definition benefits which generally contribute more to the well-being of the company than to the welfare of its employees, and are designed and developed for that purpose, should not be considered fringe benefits. Such things as safety clothing, first-aid rooms, personnel counselling, physical examinations for applicants, music at work, house organ and training material are excluded. The salary of the plant nurse and the cost of medications should not be included under this rule; but the cost of polio shots or other personal accommodation services are employee fringe benefits.

Any study of cost should include a complete inventory of the many separate fringe benefit items and a realistic analysis of the net cost to the employer. As shown in the following outline, everything besides direct wages that is intended to benefit the worker and which costs money to provide should be counted. However, the cost of overtime, shift differentials and premium pay for Sunday and holiday work should not be included; such items compensate employees for working at certain times and under certain conditions.

Logical and Systematic

One of the best studies of fringe benefit costs is the biennial survey by the Economic Research Department of the Chamber of Commerce of the United States. A breakdown of the major types of fringe benefits covered in their studies shows the following categories:

1. Legally-required payments (employer's share only)—old age, survivors and disability insurance; unemployment compensation (federal and state); worker's compensation; railroad retirement tax and unemployment insurance; state sickness benefits insurance.
2. Pension and other agreed-upon payments (employer's share only)—pension premiums; life insurance premiums, death benefits, sickness, accident and medical care insurance premiums, hospitalization insurance; contributions to privately financed unemployment benefit funds; separation and termination pay allowances (accumulated severance pay but not "two weeks' pay in lieu of notice"); discounts on goods and services purchased from company by employees, miscellaneous benefits (free meals or subsidized part of cafeteria operation, compensation payments in excess of legal requirements, payments to needy employees, clinic services, cost of credit union, parties, picnics, and recreational activities, tuition refunds, savings and stock purchase plans, etc.).
3. Time away from job but not deducted from pay—paid rest periods, paid lunch periods, wash-up time, check cashing time, travel time, clothes-changing time, get-ready time.
4. Payments for time not worked—paid vacations and payment in lieu of vacations; payment for holidays not worked; paid sick leave; paid leave for national guard or reserve duty, jury, witness or voting pay allowances, paid funeral leave; marriage leave; personal paid leaves of absence.
5. Other items—profit sharing payments; Christmas bonuses or other supplemental compensation; suggestion awards; special wage payments ordered by courts, payments to union stewards, etc.

To compute the cost—

Total the cost of all fringe benefits paid out in a year, using the foregoing outline as the basis. Divide this total cost by the annual payroll for a percentage of how fringe benefits relate, or add to, the direct payroll cost. When the total fringe benefit cost is divided by the number of employees on the payroll during the year, the dollar value to each employee will be averaged out.

The number of employees on the payroll at any one day, such as December 31, or the day the study is made, will very likely not be the average for the year. For a more accurate figure it is better to add the end-of-month totals for all twelve months of the calendar or fiscal year and divide this total by twelve to arrive at the average for the year.

The annual payroll should be the total actual wages including overtime.

Communicating Their Cost and Value

Because of the growing cost of fringe benefits, more and more companies take steps to inform employees of the cost and extent of the fringes provided for them. Various media are used, including booklets, house organs, bulletin boards, letters and meetings. Charts, pictograms and special forms are used to dramatize the message for greater impact. One company sends out the "invisible check" which brings employee "security, recreation and peace of mind."

Despite this emphasis on "telling the story" it is generally agreed that employees do not fully appreciate fringe benefits except in those cases where they might have personally experienced or felt this value. If there is any truth to this charge, then managements, not employees, are to blame. While the cost of fringe benefits continues to mount, the communications effort has not kept pace, nor has it been properly directed in most companies. Those firms which report these benefits to workers usually follow the traditional "accounting method" approach of itemizing the cost and in effect telling workers, "Look how much we're spending in addition to your salary." This type of presentation undoubtedly has merit, but it has limited appeal to the individual.

Averaging of benefits provides an interesting statistic relating to the amount spent by the company "on the average" for each employee. This is a favorite topic for discussion during contract negotiations. But an employee who doesn't bowl or golf, or who is located away from the subsidized cafeteria in the home office, or who isn't enrolled in night school, might feel cheated since these expenditures bring him no return. Given a choice, such employees would rather have employers put additional money into base pay than into fringes, on the theory that they see little prospect of "cashing in" on many of the broad benefits.

With the availability of the versatile computer, either in-house or at a service bureau, it is now possible to develop an individual, personalized annual statement for each employee, reporting the specifics of his benefits and their estimated dollar value. This "benefit facts" statement is by far the most effective communications device, especially when mailed to the home for the family to read.

Of the three methods used: (1) averaging-out is meaningless to the individual employee, he is unimpressed; (2) hidden payroll or non-negotiable check is dramatic but ineffective; (3) the individualized, personal annual statement is the best.

Companies that want to drive the point home would be better, it seems, to stress the benefit and not the cost. They could take a lesson from the automobile salesman, who in his sales pitch hardly mentions the price but does emphasize the innovations, features and advantages. The cost does not impress the workers who expect managements to provide benefits just as they furnish desks, leased cars, space, supplies and the like without any reference to their cost. But if a benefit can be brought home to the employees as a personal gain or advantage, it will be easier for them to understand it and grasp its significance. A typical case history covering a well-known fellow worker will tell the story with greater psychological impact than the best set of statistical graphs or the best-worded letter.

What Lies Ahead?

Although some spokesmen feel that fringe benefits have already gone way out of hand, the record shows that they keep on growing. And the outlook is for this trend to continue.

Unemployment payments will continue to be extended during every declared emergency. Health and welfare benefits are expected to expand, particularly in comprehensive and major medical coverage. In some cases new ideas, such as dental needs and home nursing care, will be considered. It is also probable that the employer will pay a larger proportion of the cost and eventually may pay all of it.

In retirement plans, the changes to look for are in such areas as lowering the compulsory retirement age, more guaranteed vesting rights, portable pensions, paid-up life insurance, provisions for survivors and automatic escalator clauses.

The number of paid holidays will not decrease. Any increase in the number of holidays will see such innovations as floating holidays to make long weekends. Don't be surprised to see the introduction of a "personal" holiday that the employee may use at his convenience, either on his birthday or anniversary, Friday after Thanksgiving, for Christmas shopping, for an extra religious observance or otherwise.

Attempts will be made to reduce the number of years needed to qualify for a three-week vacation from 15 to 10 or from 10 to five years. For long-service employees more firms will be offering four weeks vacation per year. And the notion of granting sabbatical or extended leave, with full pay, to 25-year employees is already being tried in a few companies.

Fringe benefits are increasing in number, size, diversity, complexity and cost. While employers can do little or nothing to stem the tide, they don't really try, being satisfied to influence the direction these benefits take. Like the employees who take the fringe benefits for granted management, too, has resigned itself to the inevitable—more and costlier fringe benefits.

While managements may express disappointment that their employees do not understand or appreciate the value of fringe benefits, it is disturbing to note that many companies do not understand the purpose of their fringe benefit programs. Firms that consider fringe benefit programs as motivation devices are no longer in tune with the facts of industrial life. Managements who comment "What's wrong with people today?" also postulate, "and look at all we're doing for them!" But the sad fact is that just as fear is no longer effective in motivating employees to better productivity, neither are fringe benefits. Upping paid-up life insurance, say from $1,000 to $2,000, will not show any corresponding increase in individual output.

Over the years fringe benefits have become so commonplace that to workers they are conditions of employment. In a broader sense, fringe benefits in our industrial society are properly defined as "productivity's contribution to social development."

That, in itself, is a full-sized obligation and a noble one.

CAFETERIA FRINGE BENEFITS

The cafeteria approach to fringe benefits—whereby employees may select benefits that best suit their personal circumstances—received an unexpected boost from the government. New tax-law provisions that grew out of amendments to the federal tax code in 1978 make it possible for employers to introduce a whole new series of more attractive innovations.

Until lately employee benefits were offered in a rigid benefit structure. Benefit plans were designed in the 1950's for a family where the father worked while the wife stayed home with the children. The new flexible benefit plans let employees select from a menu of options instead of having to accept whatever the company serves up. They are intended to accommodate the needs of a changing work force which includes single parents and two-career families.

Under the new tax law bonanza, tax-free wages can be used to pay for such costs as child care, live-in housekeeper, elderly parents' care, legal advice, orthodontic work, even home and auto insurance. An employee can buy insurance for dependents, increase or decrease disability coverage, take additional paid vacation days, or convert allocated vacation time into credits or cash. There is almost no limit on types of benefits offered or the way they are arranged.

To administer benefits tailored to individual needs, the firm takes money from the employee's pretax wages and puts this into a "reimbursement account." The funds are not reported on the employee's W-2 annual statement or earnings. Yet the worker can withdraw the money, tax-free, to pay for agreed-upon benefits.

The employee not interested in these optional benefits may want to trade any or all of them for cash. But any cash payments would be subject to income tax as regular earnings. Or the employee has the option of putting the money into a tax-deferred retirement account.

But there is a caution that makes some companies wary. The reimbursement accounts come under the law's section 125. Because the tax implications are complex and uncertain, the Internal Revenue Service has been slow writing even the preliminary rules and release of final rules is uncertain.

Flexible Compensation

Nevertheless, the 1980's may be the decade when flexible compensation programs flourish. Their popularity arises from the cafeteria, or smorgasbord, approach to fringe benefits. The number of "choicemaking" programs is increasing because of their appeal.

From a relatively unknown concept, the flexible compensation programs are rapidly achieving widespread growth and acceptance. Such plans are recognized by a variety of labels—reimbursement accounts, flexible spending accounts, employee spending accounts, benefits banks, or flex funds.

Under the typical program, a specified number of dollars are allocated to each employee's account. Providing each employee with a flat-dollar amount ensures that all employees receive equal value—not more for high users nor less for low users. Whenever an employee incurs certain types of tax-favored expenses, that employee can then request reimbursement from the fund for these expenses. This reimbursement has no effect on the employee's taxable income, any more than payment for other fringe benefits does, such as health insurance, legal services, etc. From a tax perspective, the reimbursement account is viewed as employer money and, therefore, nontaxable when used in specified ways.

At the end of the year, common practice is to return any unused funds to the employee by either transferring the money to a capital accumulation plan or to pay out the funds in cash. Returning unused funds to the employee is a feature that tends to encourage frugal expenditures of account funds.

The first consideration in designing a plan is the source of the money to fund the account. The principal alternatives are: (1) new company money, (2) all or a portion of the money saved through reductions in other benefits, and (3) voluntary reduction of an employee's salary in exchange for a contribution by the company to the flexible reimbursement account.

The second major consideration is the broad category of benefits allowed under the account. The primary types of eligible expenses include health care (medical, dental, hearing, vision), personal legal bills, and dependent care.

The third major consideration relates to the disposition of unspent funds at year-end. Unused funds are usually paid in cash (which then becomes income tax liable), transferred to a 401(k) plan, or rolled over to the next year.

Employers have three reasons for adopting flexible reimbursement plans:

1. To appeal to the needs of a diverse workforce.
2. To control the escalating costs of employee benefits.
3. To minimize the tax bite for employees.

In some cases, flexible reimbursement accounts are often the only element of flexibility in the company's fringe benefit package. In other cases, it is part of a broader flexible program. The rapidly growing interest in flexible reimbursement accounts cannot be fully separated from the growing interest in flexible compensation generally. They are a subset of flexibility.

While many companies may be tempted to take advantage of the tax dodges, conservative employers are taking a wait-and-see attitude, hesitant to grab at the unintended windfall. They believe that the changes in the law were never intended to let employees shelter large sums of their income. They are afraid that the final rules could establish a tax liability for either the company or the employees. Apart from any tax monies that might then be due, untangling the resulting payroll mess would pose an horrendous task.

Those companies that have decided to proceed with the benefit innovations that are permissible apparently do not consider the risk to be insurmountable. They like the opportunity of upgrading benefits, giving fringe benefits high visibility—all without adding costs.

PERQUISITES

A new word has crept into the business vocabulary. It is "Perquisites"—those special privileges for upper-echelon management members. They could be aptly described as status symbols.

These prerogatives or supernumerary benefits have progressed a long way from "the key to the executive washroom" which is still a closed preserve, widely kept off-limits to all but corporate officers.

Webster defines perquisites as "a privilege, gain or profit incidental to regular salary or wages." Some compensation specialists include perquisites in the same class as regular employee benefits. This concept is not correct because employee benefits are an indirect part of the basic compensation package. Perquisites are above and beyond the established compensation program.

Among the popular "perks" are better office decor, country club dues, luncheon club memberships, separate dining room facilities, liberal expense accounts, company cars for personal use, privileged parking, choice office locations with luxurious furnishings, free medical exams and first-class travel tickets.

Free legal advice, personal use of planes, boats, chauffeurs, subsidized homes, company-paid resort facilities and spouse's expenses on business trips are less common.

Some Examples

Here are a few examples of perquisites offered by companies for their executives. These may be provided on the basis of job level, annual salary or employment contract.

Financial counseling: More companies are providing outside financial counseling services. Busy executives often do not have the time to determine the most effective use of their incomes. To assist them, companies retain outside financial advisors from consulting firms, law firms, public accounting firms and banks. Usually financial counseling programs include investment management, estate planning, insurance planning, compensation planning and income tax preparation.

Executive loans: Many companies provide loans to executives at low or no interest for the purpose of exercising stock options, purchasing homes, paying for children's college costs, etc. Employers do not have to notify anyone on loans to nonofficers, but if the loan is made to an officer, the Securities Exchange Commission requires disclosure in the proxy statement of publicly held companies. It is important to define the repayment terms in an executive loan arrangement because the Internal Revenue Service could claim the loan was a salary advance, and tax it accordingly.

Company car: A company car is considered a prestige item and is well received by most executives. The car is usually leased from an agency on a fleet basis, with the company paying the monthly rental. The executive usually pays for the fuel and has no restrictions on the use of the car. Where the executive normally drives to work, the use of the company car is worth anywhere from $4,000 to $6,000 in addition to the status value. The Internal Revenue Service is keeping a close watch on this perquisite.

Company apartment/suite: More and more companies are maintaining apartments or permanent hotel suites in key cities for the convenience of their top executives and their business contacts. In areas where lengthy commutes are common, executives can stay in the accommodation after a late evening meeting. There is significant status attached to being permitted to use a company apartment or suite.

Special vacation arrangements: Executives are usually granted a minimum of four weeks paid vacation. The stress of working in today's business world is generally considered so hectic that executives are being granted more liberal vacation arrangements. A number of major corporations grant their executives six weeks annual paid vacation.

Sabbatical leave: Sabbatical leaves are starting to become popular. Executives in technical capacities especially find these leaves very beneficial to their work. Other executives who are 15 to 20 years past their undergraduate studies find that returning to school helps them qualify for promotion to top management.

Executive physicals: Executive physical examinations are really more of an employer benefit than an employee benefit. By providing executives with preventive medical care, the employer protects his human assets investment, and reduces future disability insurance costs.

Tempting Tax Target

In European countries these untaxed extras are a prominent part of the total compensation package. In Britain an executive's salary may be small, but he doesn't mind because this is the portion on which he pays income taxes that are among the highest in the world. He may get a company car, upkeep on his house, free gardener, unlimited expense allowance, paid telephone service and the like. Some get free apartments, cheap mortgages, interest-free loans and overseas bank accounts.

Perquisites used for personal pleasure are actually subject to tax but it is not too difficult to camouflage them in Europe as business expense. Accepted for years as a normal way of conducting business in foreign countries, perquisites are gaining in popularity in the United States.

A caution should be noted. Of late, these executive trappings are getting increasing attention from a spoilsport federal government.

The Securities and Exchange Commission wants companies to disclose more about the extent and cost of executive benefits. The Internal Revenue Service would like to make recipients of corporate largesse pay taxes for some of these pleasures. Accountants warn that it isn't unreasonable for executives to fear being socked for back taxes and penalties.

HISTORY OF GROUP INSURANCE

Group health insurance was among the first of the fringe benefits. In both Europe and the United States, associations of individuals "helped" each other during times of personal misfortune. These were often associated with family groups, clubs or craft guilds. One early example is the Manchester Unity Friendly Society, which was sufficiently organized to publish a book in 1907 with detailed data from their experiences.

As some of the key dates shown below illustrate, early plans developed from the need for them combined with society's need for certain services. For example, if the country wanted merchant seamen or firemen, it had to do something to take care of them during illness or injury.

Typical key dates include:

1798— U.S. Marine Hospital Service established by the United States Congress. Compulsory deductions for hospital service were made from the wages of seamen.

1880— A contract written by the Traveler's Insurance Company for the Board of Fire Commissioners of Baltimore to insure the members of the city's fire-fighting force.

1884— First Compensation Act in Germany.

1910— First group accident and sickness policy issued.

1911— Workmen's Compensation Act. By 1920 all states were covered.

1928— Development of hospital, surgical and medical coverage for employees and dependents.

1932— First city-wide Blue Cross Plan tried out with a group of hospitals in Sacramento, California. In the early 1930's during the "Great Depression," hospitals had a considerable problem collecting their bills. To prevent the hospitals from becoming insolvent, local societies were formed for the prepayment of hospital-type bills. These groups were the forerunners of the present Blue Cross plans.

1939— First Blue-Shield type plan formed.

1942— World War II "wage freeze" led employers to offer increased types and amounts of welfare or fringe benefits in lieu of prohibited wage increases. Employees became more dependent upon employers, who assumed responsibilities for workers beyond the payment of wages. Fringe benefits became a competitive necessity. Employers felt that group plans would help attract workers, reduce turnover and lead to greater productivity.

1949— First major medical-insurance contract issued by Liberty Mutual Insurance Company to the management personnel of General Electric Company.

1949— This year was of major importance to the field of group insurance. In the Inland Steel decision of that year, the U.S. Supreme Court ruled that group insurance was an appropriate subject for collective bargaining. After this decision numerous insurance plans were incorporated into labor contracts as a result of union negotiations, even in firms where such programs had been in effect before unionization.

In the years before unionized labor insisted on being heard, company management decided questions of insurance according to its own criterion, "The best possible coverage for the least amount of money," and it was the company's prerogative to determine what this was. When the situation changed so that managements had to negotiate with unions or keep up with the pattern set by unionized plans, these prerogatives were wiped out.

Since the Inland Steel case, labor unions have taken an increasingly larger share of the decisions away from company managers and placed them on the bargaining table. Even if there is no union present, management has to be aware now of what the competition is granting in fringe benefits as a result of union pressures.

The unions, of course, have kept their demands for group insurance and pensions moving toward ever-increasing coverage. Fringe benefit bargaining is often balanced against increases in wages or improvements in physical working conditions. Cost data and conclusions on benefits should be in the hands of the employer to enable management to effectively evaluate union demands. It is better to know the strong points of your programs and their inadequacies, if any, from your own estimates than to be told about them in the heat of collective bargaining sessions.

Other agencies besides the unions, including the government, have been drawn into the administration of insured employee benefits. The federal and state governments have conducted numerous studies and investigations of group plans, all of which must be registered with the U.S. Department of Labor. Organizations such as the Foundation on Employee Health, Medical Care and Welfare offer advice to companies and unions on good practices in buying group insurance.

EMPLOYEE HEALTH INSURANCE PROGRAM

Five major forms of health insurance are common in a company's health program for its employees. These are:

1. Hospital insurance
2. Surgical insurance
3. Regular medical insurance
4. Major medical insurance
5. Loss-of-income protection.

Hospital insurance covers the usual hospital expenses, room and board, nursing care, drugs, operating room and equipment, laboratory and x-ray. About 82% of Americans have some form of hospital insurance. There are many policies available. A low premium policy naturally pays low benefits. How much of the hospital bill does your coverage pay? Does your program pay a specific daily amount or does it pay all reasonable hospital costs up to a high maximum? Make a study. Your program may have fallen behind the tremendous progress made by medical science and may no longer provide the protection your employees are lead to believe they carry.

Surgical insurance covers surgeon's fees, usually with dollar limits, including some preoperative and postoperative services. This kind of insurance also covers anesthesiologists' fees. About 76% have this type of coverage at present. But does your plan pay the physician's customary charge or is it limited by a fixed fee schedule? Check some time to see how much of the bill your employees are still required to pay out-of-pocket.

Regular medical insurance pays for nonsurgical care and, in some cases, includes procedures in the doctor's office. There is a tendency to expand this kind of insurance to pay for diagnostic services. About 72% of employee health plans include regular medical insurance.

Major medical, as a rule, pays over and above medical and surgical costs. It supplements basic insurance and comes into effect after other benefits are exhausted. It also includes benefits beyond the scope of basic insurance, such as private duty nursing, prescription drugs at home, office and house calls, psychiatric care. The typical major medical policy has a deductible (Example: the employee pays the first $100 each year), a co-insurance arrangement (Example: the employee pays 20% of the amount over $100, the carrier pays 80%), and an outside limit on expenses for a single illness or injury (Example: $10,000). About $33^{1}/_{3}\%$ of employee programs now include major medical protection.

Loss-of-income protection provides regular weekly income for a specified period of time to partially replace the income an employee loses during a period of illness or disability. How good is your program? Are payments related to earnings? Are they limited to a period of time, say 26 weeks? What then? Have you a Disability Insurance program for those employees whose illness or injury leaves them permanently disabled?

Check Your Company Program

How long since you've taken inventory of your employee welfare program? What does it include? How good is the coverage? How well does it meet employee needs?

Are you aware of the trends in this field? The tendency is for the company to pay more or all of the premium costs. Unions are asking for annual physical checkups, dental care, eye care, prenatal and postnatal care, and psychiatric care is high on their priority list. Nursing home care is coming in for its share of attention. Finally, employees look for paid-in-full benefits.

The big industrial firms—like automobiles and steel—are the pattern setters. Medicare is now a benchmark for other coverages, and labor and management will feel pressure to eliminate differences between what employees get and what oldsters are legally entitled to.

Through Medicare and Social Security all five of the major forms of health insurance are available, to a degree, to retired or disabled workers and their families. Unless companies move to provide at least comparable benefits to workers, the government may take the initiative.

Medicare is a blessing in disguise in another respect. Companies no longer have to provide and pay for the full benefit cost for workers and retirees after age 65. These savings can be diverted into buying better programs for regular employees and their dependents.

HEALTH CARE or ILLNESS CARE

People talk about health care when what they ask for and get is sickness care. More attention is given to restoring health than to protecting it.

What companies provide in fringe benefit programs is not health insurance but illness insurance. Hospital care and medical services are oriented toward curative treatment of established disease at an advanced or critical stage.

Claims are paid when the employees are ill and receive medical attention. Except in a few isolated cases, there is no payout to the employee who remains well. Companies help their employees cure illness but do little to prevent it.

Some firms have seen the wisdom of offering annual physical examinations. But these are limited to people in upper echelon positions. The logic is that today's executive is sedentary and is prone to overweight from steady business dining and lack of exercise. Their main concern is their job responsibilities and their health suffers. By providing these free annual physicals, a company is trying to safeguard one of its prime resources, the health of key personnel.

Coupled with the health policy providing exams might be a planned program of physical exercise. The exercise facilities, once installed, could be made available to all employees on a voluntary basis. Employees on all levels may spend their rest periods doing supervised exercises instead of indulging themselves in caffeine-laced coffee or cola, junk food snacks, and the unnecessary cigarette. Companies that sponsor exercise programs see less absenteeism from work because of illness. As a supplement, the company could offer nutritional or dietary advice and guidance in the form of lectures or pamphlets.

A new concept in preventive health care is multiphasic screening. Annual physical checkups provide for early identification and treatment of employees with undetected diseases or abnormalities before they are handicapped or lost as effective workers. Because this is a big-scale procedure that is performed systematically, the cost per individual is surprisingly nominal.

Using computer equipment, multiphasic screening tests body functions and fluids. It provides a medical history, physiological profile, and laboratory readings. The results, especially when negative in any respect, are forwarded to the employee's personal physician for follow-up. More important than the results of any one-time test are the comparisons of tests from year to year.

The argument against preventive care is that money, time, and pro-

739

fessional talent are wasted on well, or near well, people who need no medical services. The essence is that the few positive results do not justify the overall costs.

On the other hand, if but one abnormality is uncovered in time to prevent the onset of a disease, or arrest progressive damage, or reverse an impending disability, what is this effort worth? How can medical economists assess the estimated value of a human life?

GROUP INSURANCE

A company group insurance package includes many or all of the following separate components:

- Hospitalization insurance
  Blue Cross
  commercial insurance
  self-insurance

- Medical-Surgical insurance
  Blue Shield
  commercial insurance
  self-insurance

- Major Medical insurance

- Drug coverage

- Dental coverage
  checkups, cleaning, X-rays
  restorations, bridges, inlays
  dentures, orthodontic work

- Vision care
  examinations
  eyeglasses
  contact lenses

- Hearing aids

- Group legal insurance

- Group auto insurance

- Health and Accident insurance
  (temporary disability) Some states now have laws requiring disability protection for workers. This is insurance for benefit payments while unable to work.

THE GROUP INSURANCE PACKAGE

A company group insurance package includes many of the following separate components, with the costs paid in full or in part by the employer.

- Hospitalization insurance

  (free choice of hospital)
  Blue Cross
  commercial carriers
  self-insurance

- Medical/surgical insurance

  (free choice of doctor)
  Blue Shield
  commercial carriers
  self-insurance

- Health Maintenance organizations

  monthly service fee
  covers health care (exams)
  and all treatment

- Major medical insurance

  corridor deductible
  then 80% reimbursement

- Drug coverage (prescription)

- Dental coverage

  checkups, cleaning, X-rays
  restorations, bridges, inlays
  dentures, orthodontic work

- Vision care

  examinations
  eyeglasses
  contact lenses

- Hearing aids

- Group legal insurance

- Group auto insurance

- Health and accident insurance

  weekly percentage payments
  during temporary disability

- Disability insurance

  regular monthly payments when
  permanently/totally disabled
  and unable to work

- Travel accident insurance

- Life insurance

  basic (burial) insurance
  supplemental (optional)
  key-man

- Pension

  regular payments after
  stated years of service
  irrespective of age

- Retirement income

  regular payments after
  stated age irrespective
  of length of service

- plus mandatory

  Workers' compensation
  Unemployment compensation
  Social Security

Employees need insurance but do not buy enough protection themselves. So employers accept the responsibility. Group insurance is not eleemosynary, and can be best defined as industry's contribution to social development.

- Travel Accident insurance
  This may be offered by the company at group rates or paid for in full or in part by the company. It is usually 24-hour coverage, on the job and away.

- Life insurance
  The most common is term insurance, only in effect while employed by the company, no paid-up or cash surrender value.

- Pension or Retirement income plan
  This provides a lifetime monthly income after the established retirement age. It may also include provisions for a beneficiary or survivor (spouse). It may be contributory or noncontributory on the part of the employee.

- Other programs
  thrift or savings plan
  profit-sharing plan
  stock option ownership plan

Group insurance programs have been defined as industry's contribution to social development. There are many good reasons for companies to accept this social responsibility.

1. Employees need insurance but do not buy enough protection themselves.
2. No physical examination is required; an insurer accepts all risks in the group. People who cannot pass an insurance physical are still eligible for coverage. In some cases this may be the only insurance they carry.
3. Companies can purchase insurance for employees in group plans at more favorable rates than the individuals would be required to pay.
4. For a low cost, companies try to get increased employee morale and lower turnover.
5. Company cost is further decreased by a tax deduction. The cost can be charged off as a legitimate business expense.

Some characteristics of group insurance are:
1. Premiums are collected or paid for by the employer.
2. One contract is signed but individual certificates are issued.
3. Coverage is the same for all employees, but the amount of coverage may vary with salary, occupation and/or length of service.
4. There is usually a waiting period which may be to qualify participants or for administrative convenience.

5. An employee who elects not to participate is asked to sign a waiver or rejection card.
6. The company handles the necessary clerical work—

- application cards
- waiver cards
- rosters and records
- name changes
- status changes (single to family)
- beneficiary designation and changes
- claims
- terminations and drop from billing
- payroll deduction authorization
- announcements
- distribution of statements, etc.
- selling and counselling.

Some considerations are:
1. Should employer pay the full cost or is there something to be said in favor of having employees share in the cost? Do they appreciate it more? Where employees contribute to the cost, their monthly payments can be arranged through convenient payroll deduction.
2. What about a waiting period? Should this be only to meet administrative requirements (first day of the month following a full month of employment, for example) or should employees wait six months or a year for some of the coverage just as they wait a prescribed time for some retirement programs to include them.
3. How about including dependents? In a hospitalization and medical-surgical program spouses and dependent children are usually included. In other coverage, such as life insurance, they are not normally covered but named as beneficiaries.

The cost of a group insurance program is governed by: (1) kind of insurance included, (2) amount of coverage, (3) number of participants, and (4) their ages. The trend is up and will continue upward. The cost of benefit plans to employers has risen almost twice as fast as wages and salaries in the past decade.

GROUP INSURANCE TRENDS

If one word could be used to summarize current trends in employee group insurance plans it would be "more!"

What is happening now, and what is indicated for the future, for *employers* is:

1. Higher costs.
2. More record-keeping.
3. More work to stay well informed and in control of how much more of everything is involved.

As a result of these factors, *employees* will gain:

1. More personal coverage in terms of dollar benefits.
2. More coverage for dependents and widows.
3. More mobility (under certain job conditions).
4. More of a certain kind of "protection" through government regulation or participation in more phases of various plans.

Employees must also anticipate certain negative possibilities, such as:

1. More dollar contributions to be required of them in company, union-sponsored or "association" plans.
2. Inevitable increases in taxes because of increased government activity in this area.
3. Erosion of purchasing power because of added inflationary pressures.
4. Some loss of freedom and related intangibles in return for probable increases in material comforts and improved services to be gained by accelerated institutionalism (private and governmental) of medical care, nursing homes, mental-health facilities, large-scale retirement housing centers and other geriatric projects.

As everybody moves in these directions together, employers who adapt themselves to the best possible combination of "give and take" may expect to improve and reinforce their practical framework of good industrial relations policies and practices.

SICK PAY

The practice of the United States Government in allowing civil service employees "sick" pay has spread to business. It has long been the practice of most companies to take care of salaried employees when they are away from work because of illness. Now policies are in effect which cover all employees, office and factory, on the same or similar terms.

At first there was a reluctance to pay people when they were not at work lest this practice encourage some to stay home every time they had runny noses. But that viewpoint is changing. Now companies prefer to have ill employees stay home to avoid spreading sickness to co-workers and at the same time endangering their own health.

For the occasional one-day or two-day absences firms are willing to write a policy which is fair to all. Many companies simply pay up to a certain number of days, say 10, for each employment- or calendar-year. Other firms allow so many paid days for each separate illness.

The amount of sick pay is usually related to seniority. A typical program might provide 10 days per year and then increase this to 15 days after 5 or 10 years. Once the allowance is used up, the employee is no longer paid, unless he is covered by some other income-protection program.

It is not uncommon for companies to have a waiting period, especially during a worker's early years of employment. This might be a waiting period of two days during the first year, one day during the second year, and no waiting period thereafter. The reasoning (which many managers feel is fallacious) is that a longer-service employee can more likely be trusted not to abuse the sick pay privilege.

And abuses there are. For an absence of several days an employer could rightfully ask an employee to bring in some report from the doctor who attended him. But most employees do not see a doctor when they are unable to come to work for a day or two because of a cold, fever, upset stomach, headache and the like. They merely call in sick and return a day or two later, mentioning the reason for the absence. Even with a clinic checking them back in, some of their stories can easily be doubted.

The best control is to check the pattern of absences. An employee who is absent six times a year, all on Mondays or Fridays, might well be suspected of taking long weekends. Supervisors who know their people can usually spot the phony stories and may want to remember these absences when an employee comes up afterwards for salary review or other consideration.

The theory of sick pay protection is like fire insurance—it is intended for the employee who has need of it. This is an assurance that his wages will not suffer if, through no fault of his own, his work is interrupted. This is not a right. Some employees feel that if they do not use their sick leave they should be paid extra for this.

Since the ill employee (and especially the one who stays away for personal reasons but calls in sick) gets paid, the loyal and dedicated worker who never or seldom lets his employer down may feel, with some justification, that the policy of sick pay favors the less-than-honest worker. Therefore some companies, against the advice of principled personnel administrators, do pay extra for unused sick time. Other plans which do not "pay off" at the end of the year allow unused sick days to accrue and be used later in case of a long term or catastrophic illness absence.

SICK PAY POLICIES

Although absence from work is discouraged, companies recognize that employees may have urgent reasons to absent themselves from their jobs at certain times. The most frequent and logical reason is that they are ill and unable to work.

The Administrative Management Society surveyed its chapter members to determine the company policies in dealing with illness absences. A total of 235 AMS members responded.

1. *What is the average number of days an employee is absent because of illness during a year?*

Respondents indicated that men were absent from work for illness on an average of four days per year; women were absent from work for illness on an average of six days per year.

2. *Are employees paid when absent for illness?*

Of those responding to this question, 98% indicated that employees do receive their pay when absent for illness.

3. *If so, how long does pay continue?*

Responses are as follows:

At Full Pay		*At Partial Pay*	
1 week or less (5 days or less)	20.1%	1 week (5 days or less)	5.5%
2 weeks (6–10 days)	28.3%	2 weeks (6–10 days)	5.5%
3 weeks (11–15 days)	6.5%	3 weeks (11–15 days)	16.6%
4 weeks (16–30 days)	10.2%	4 weeks (16–30 days)	5.5%
2 months (8 weeks)	15.5%	2 months (8 weeks)	5.5%
3 months or more	20.1%	3 months or more	61.1%

Other Absences

4.*What is the average number of days an employee is absent for personal reasons during the year?*

The majority of the respondents reported that 3 days is the average number of days employees are absent for personal reasons.

Death in the Family

5. *Is this absence excused with pay?*

Ninety percent of respondents reported "yes" to this question; 10 percent reported no set policy or the policy varies.

6. *How many days are allowed*

Most of the companies reporting said employees are permitted to take 3 days off for a death in the family.

7. *Is the excused absence restricted to the death of a member of the immediate family?*

Of those repsonding to this question, 80 percent said "yes"; 20 percent said "no."

COMPANY POLICY ON SICK PAY ALLOWANCE

The Company shall provide regular payment to employees during absences due to illness or nonoccupational accidents in accordance with the following schedule:

	Sick Pay Allowance		Waiting Time (each illness)	
Qualifying Period	Wage-Hour	Exempt	Wage-Hour	Exempt
First 3 months of employment	none			
Next 9 months	7 work days		3 full days	
First 12 months of employment		10 work days		none
Second year of employment	10 work days	10 work days	2 full days	none
Third, fourth, and fifth years of employment	10 work days each year	10 work days each year	none	none
After five years of employment	15 work days each year	15 days each year	none	none

After 6 months of employment, an employee on a wage-and-hour job shall not be charged with the 3 or 2 days' waiting time for any absence of 10 or more work days . . . providing the employee presents a doctor's statement upon return to work and the Clinic concurs.

An employee who, on recommendation of the Clinic, is excused from work shall be paid in full for the day . . . and this absence shall not be charged against sick pay allowance.

An exempt employee, who is absent because of illness, will in accordance with federal law be paid for a full week, even after sick allowance has expired, for any week in which he is eligible to be paid for time worked and/or paid under some provision of company policy.

An employee who has been absent because of illness or accident will not be considered "back on the job" until the Clinic has given written approval to return. It is necessary to furnish a certificate from the attending physician, which must be presented to our Clinic for concurrence. Such certificates may be waived in short stays upon the recommendation of the Clinic.

Unused sick pay allowance may not be accumulated from one year to another.

SALARY CONTINUATION

In addition to sick pay allowances, to cover the occasional short term illness absence, many companies also have a policy to cover the long term illness absence by continuing salary, on a full or partial pay basis, for a specified period of time.

Where no formal policy spells out the terms, it is not unusual that an employee, particularly a salaried worker, be kept on the payroll under some informal or undeclared arrangement. This is especially true for executives and managers, or for long service employees.

A typical formal program might be:

Term of Employment	Full Pay	Half Pay
6 months to 1 year	None	6 weeks
1 to 2 years	None	9 weeks
2 to 5 years	4 weeks	9 weeks
5 to 10 years	13 weeks	13 weeks
10 to 15 years	13 weeks	39 weeks
15 to 20 years	26 weeks	26 weeks
20 to 25 years	39 weeks	13 weeks
25 years or more	52 weeks	None

Any such special consideration would begin after sick pay allowances are used up. If, for example, an employee is entitled to 10 paid sick days per year and had seven left, the special program would be applied starting from the eighth day. Some companies permit unused sick leave from one year to be accumulated and applied later. Under such plan an employee with 20 or 30 unused sick days to his credit would, of course, be paid in full until all this accrued sick time had been used.

As an alternative, companies may purchase Health and Accident Insurance which would pay an employee benefits for a certain number of weeks while he is absent from work because of illness or nonoccupational accident.

GROUP DISABILITY INCOME INSURANCE

Employees wonder what would happen to their paychecks if they were injured at home or away from work and unable to perform their jobs. Or what if they were to become suddenly ill and in bed or confined to the house for days or weeks at a time.

Most companies have a sick-pay allowance program which is intended to cover short-term illness. Generally companies allow a specified number of paid "sick days" per calendar or employment year. But what protection is there for the longer-term illness? The rent and other expenses continue after the paychecks stop.

One way to meet this problem is to purchase group disability insurance, sometimes called health and accident insurance. This type of insurance provides employees with income protection payable weekly, which replaces in part income lost during periods of disability. Disability in this case means the employee is prevented from performing his job as a result of sustaining accidental bodily injury or sickness.

The day benefits begin, the amount (or percentage) of weekly benefits, and the maximum benefit period for each disability, are negotiable. Usually payments are designed to start when sick pay runs out, and they continue until the employee returns to work or goes on some type of permanent disability program.

All employees are automatically covered in the group policy after a short waiting period—say, six months. There are no pre-existing sickness conditions.

The amount of the weekly benefit payment is related to salary. It is less than full salary, otherwise it would wipe out any incentive to return to work. A benefit schedule showing weekly payments is part of the policy that is purchased.

Coverage is for nonoccupational disabilities only and should not be confused with workmen's compensation, which covers on-the-job accidents.

PERSONAL ACCIDENT INSURANCE

Employees, especially managers and executives, often are extended an opportunity to buy personal accident insurance through the company at group rates. This is supplemental insurance, separate and apart from other protection provided by, and paid for in full or in part by, the company. The employee pays the premium, usually through payroll deduction. Enrollment is voluntary.

The coverage is Personal Accidental Death and Dismemberment Insurance. A typical rate might be 70¢ per $1,000. As with other group plans, the rate is the same for everybody. It is customarily paid annually. The amount of coverage is independent of salary but is offered in increments of, say, $25,000. Renewal is usually not automatic because needs change.

Using the above-mentioned rates, a schedule would be:

Total Coverage	Total Annual Premium
$ 25,000	$17.50
50,000	$35.00
75,000	$52.50
100,000	$70.00

The coverage provides 24-hour protection. It pays the principal amount to the designated beneficiary in case of accidental death, and lesser amounts to the insured for accidental dismemberment. It also provides full benefits in case of total and permanent disability resulting from an accident.

This accident insurance is generally offered once a year and eligible employees may sign up at that time. There is ordinarily no other waiting period. Under some plans coverage, probably not for the full amount taken by the employee, is also available to spouses and dependent children.

HOSPITALIZATION INSURANCE

Hospitalization insurance is protection in the form of financial assistance limited to a specified number of days and certain definite contract provisions. It pays for (or toward) the cost of room and board in accredited hospitals plus related miscellaneous services performed there by the hospital staff. The coverage ordinarily does not include the services of doctors or private duty nurses.

Most frequently the miscellaneous or necessary charges cover drugs, use of operating rooms, preparation for surgery and similar expenses. The following explanation is representative of the term "other hospital charges"—"Whenever the term 'other hospital services and supplies' is used, it means the actual charges made by the hospital, on its own behalf, for services and supplies rendered to the individual, and required for treatment of such person, other than charges for room and board. It does not include the professional services of any physician, and any private-duty or special-nursing service, regardless of whether such services are rendered under the direction of the hospital or otherwise."

It is a well-known fact that the cost of hospital services has increased steadily over the years, and seems to be continually increasing. This means that the cost of hospitalization insurance has a corresponding increase. It also means that most people today cannot afford to be without such form of group or individual protection.

The cost in a group plan may be borne entirely by the individual employee, or paid for by the company, or a combination of the two. The trend in both union and nonunion firms is to move toward increasing the employer's share. Some companies even pay the full amount, not only for the employee but also for his family.

Most plans, regardless how they are financed, cover the employee after a brief (one or two months) waiting period. For a higher premium rate the employee may also include the spouse plus dependent unmarried children under a certain age, say 19. The worker's share of the cost is usually handled through monthly payroll deduction.

Nonprofit vs. Commercial Plans

The main difference between the voluntary nonprofit plans, such as the Blue Cross Plans, and the programs of the commercial insurance carriers is that the former, as a rule, pay "service in full" benefits while the insurance companies allow fixed benefits—so much per day plus so much for extras. Example: the nonprofit plan may pay the entire cost of a semiprivate two-bed room (or the common semiprivate rate toward a private room), whereas the insurance company often pays dollars-per-day toward the cost of the room. The same is true of hospital services. The former may pay in full for all ancillary services that are required, whereas the latter may have a lump sum allowance to be applied toward these extra services. The Blue Cross Plans contract with the hospital and pay the hospital directly.

Not only are hospital costs increasing, as medical science advances and new techniques are introduced, but the average working man or woman is also becoming more sophisticated in the use of hospital care. Now that insurance coverage is so readily provided, and much of the financial sting removed, it is human nature for people to want to take advantage of the benefits for which they have been paying. Consequently, utilization is also increasing. More people are willing to go into the hospital where personal care is available, especially when this costs them very little in the way of out-of-pocket expense. Controls are being applied in hospitals and by the medical staffs, and educational programs are, or should be, initiated by companies to avoid abuses. Such benefits as home care, preadmission testing, one-day surgery and second opinion on elective surgery are aimed at cutting down inpatient hospitalization.

One recent development in the control of costs is the "coordination of benefits" provision which keeps two insurance companies from paying for the same basic benefits. The prime carrier, i.e., the one covering the employee, will pay for his spouse who is covered under another program only after the other carrier pays its share to the limits of that contract. Then the prime carrier will make differential payments if its contract is better and pays greater benefits or covers more services.

Hospitalization coverage is so widespread today that practically every permanent employee who wants to be covered can arrange for group hospitalization benefits under one type or another. Most people in business for themselves, seasonal or temporary employees, can obtain nongroup coverage on a direct-pay basis. Some union workers have access to union welfare clinics. Some companies prefer self-insurance. Over-age 65 people on Medicare can purchase coverage to supplement their Medicare coverage.

Hospitalization insurance, in one form or another, is available today through voluntary nonprofit group plans, private insurance carriers, and government programs, often in combination of two or more of these services.

MEDICAL-SURGICAL INSURANCE

Medical-surgical insurance plans available for groups of workers cover the doctor bills that accompany a stay in a qualified hospital. Some plans cover medical care and surgery no matter where performed within the limits of the specific plan.

Companies that provide hospitalization insurance for employees usually have a companion medical-surgical program. The two are generally administered together, with the same waiting periods (if any), dependency coverage, cost-sharing (if any), and payroll deduction applicable to both.

Some plans, such as Blue Shield Plans in certain areas, provide coverage on the basis of "usual, customary or reasonable" physician charges, which means payment in full to participating physicians. Other programs pay other amounts, and a few Blue Shield Plan programs are based on the employee's income level.

Most plans, including almost all offered by commercial insurance companies, are indemnity programs which pay flat amounts according to an established fee schedule.

What started as surgical insurance has been expanded to embrace medical coverage also. The medical coverage usually means payment to the insured for doctors' services in or out of the hospital.

Some of the more liberal plans provide benefits for diagnostic services, dental care, office and home calls, home health care, visiting nurses and nursing homes. There apparently is no limit. Insurance companies are prepared to write almost any kind of contract that employers and employees want and will pay for.

BLUE CROSS AND BLUE SHIELD PLANS

Blue Cross and Blue Shield Plans are the pioneer, prepaid health care organizations in this country. They provide protection to millions of Americans. The names are household words and stand today, as they always have, for nonprofit, community-oriented, voluntary health care prepayment Plans and the services they offer in the health care field. Their benefit programs range from local to national in scope.

In addition to their basic and most widely-recognized responsibility to pay for health care services, they are leaders in area-wide health care planning; they maintain unique relationships with physicians, hospitals and other health care professionals and institutions; and work with physicians and hospitals to help contain the cost of health care. Overall, they are dedicated to broadening the availability, increasing the quality and containing the cost of health care.

There are 69 Blue Cross Plans in the United States and Puerto Rico, plus five affiliated Plans in Canada and one in Jamaica. U.S. enrollment was 83.5 million in 1978. Blue Cross Plans serve another 26 million people through their administration of federal programs such as Medicare and Medicaid. The Blue Cross Association is a prime contractor to the Department of Health, Education and Welfare for Medicare Part A: hospitalization plus certain extended care and home care services. Blue Cross Plans serve Medicare recipients as subcontractors of the association. In private business and government programs, Blue Cross Plans serve 110 million people, almost half of the nation's population. Canadian enrollment is five million.

There are 71 Blue Shield Plans in the United States and Puerto Rico, with four affiliated Plans in Canada and one in England. U.S. enrollment in 1978 was 70.9 million and Blue Shield Plans served another 20 million through federal programs, principally as intermediaries for Part B of Medicare: physician and other professional services.

Local, Yet National

Many activities of the Plans are coordinated through the Blue Cross Association and Blue Shield Association in Chicago. Among other things, the national associations help member Plans maintain quality operations to meet approval standards that relate to high benefit performance and associated levels of responsibility. Altogether, the Blue Cross and Blue Shield Plans and Associations have 85,000 employees.

Plans operate under state not-for-profit, enabling legislation. Each Plan is governed by a board of trustees elected from the area served by the Plan, a total of some 2,000 public-spirited persons from business, industry, labor and the professions. Except where board composition is mandated by law, Plans have—or are moving toward—consumer majorities on their boards. Blue Cross Plans have contracts with nearly 7,000 hospitals and about 80% of all practicing physicians participate in Blue Shield Plans.

Blue Cross and Blue Shield Plans specialize in health care benefits and are the most experienced in the field. They write basic hospital, surgical and medical benefits, extended benefits and major medical programs. Included in the extended or major medical categories are such benefits as skilled nursing home care, outpatient psychiatric care, home care, prescription drugs, intensive care, second surgical opinion for surgery, dental care, outpatient x-ray and laboratory services, and home and office calls.

Basic benefits—hospital, surgical and medical—generally are covered on the basis of "service benefits," which means the Plan pays the physician or hospital directly. Instead of receiving an amount of money, the subscriber actually receives the services needed and covered. More than half of all Blue Shield subscribers are now covered by "usual, customary or reasonable" (UCR) programs which pay in full for medical/surgical services. Plans have elaborate auditing systems to assure that hospital and/or physician services for which claims are submitted were medically necessary and were actually received by the subscriber.

Individuals and Groups—Small and Interstate

All Plans enroll both individuals and groups. All subscribers receive identification cards. Because of the agreements between Plans and providers of care, Blue Cross Plan subscribers may enter any member hospital without advance deposit and the bill will be sent directly to the Plan, eliminating the need for the patient to pay and then recover his benefits. Blue Shield Plans offer the same arrangements through their participating physicians.

Subscribers have free choice of doctor or hospital, and special benefits apply when the provider of service is not a participant with the Plan. Special telecommunications arrangements among Plans make it possible for a subscriber to receive any of his covered benefits wherever he is. When a person leaves a covered group, he or she is also privileged to convert to individual (nongroup) coverage without interruption of protection.

Blue Cross and Blue Shield Plans cover groups of almost every description. Some are as small as five or 10 members. The largest voluntary health care group in the world is the Federal Employees Health Benefits Program, in which more than five million federal employees and their families have chosen Blue Cross and Blue Shield coverage. Of the five largest corporations in the U.S., Blue Cross and Blue Shield Plans cover four.

Plans write both local and national benefit programs. Groups with members in the areas of two or more Plans can get uniform benefits and rates under the Plans' "national accounts" programs.

On the average, including group and individual subscribers, Blue Cross and Blue Shield Plans pay out approximately 95 cents of each income dollar in benefits. Of course, there are variations among Plans in different locations.

Any employer interested in Blue Cross and Blue Shield coverage should call or write the local Plan.

HEALTH MAINTENANCE ORGANIZATIONS

It is the feeling of many leaders of the professional community that employers have their best chance of cutting runaway health insurance costs by enrolling their employees in a Health Maintenance Organization (HMO) instead of buying health insurance for them.

Under the traditional fee-for-service arrangement, the patient or the patient's insurer pays for medical services as they are provided by the doctor or hospital of his choice.

By contrast, the member of the HMO pays a flat monthly fee in

755

advance and agrees to use the staff and facilities affiliated with the HMO. The membership fee covers in full the medical service or treatment no matter how serious the condition or how many visits may be necessary.

The backers of HMO cite two reasons in favor of their system to provide better care at lower cost:

1. HMO members are encouraged to come in for medical checkups, innoculations and other preventive care.
2. The flat-fee formula gives doctors an incentive to avoid needless hospitalization.

Individuals acting alone generally cannot join an HMO. The employer signs a contract for his group and is required to pay a share of the fee. The employer does not process claims.

MAJOR MEDICAL INSURANCE

Major medical insurance pays the big medical bills. It pays where other programs leave off. In addition, it covers services that are not included in the basic programs.

The usual major medical plan has a ceiling, say $10,000 or $50,000 per person for a lifetime. Within this limit, it will pay toward the excess portion of hospital, surgical and medical expenses that are not paid in full by the basic coverage. If, for example, a surgeon charges $1,500 for an operation, against which the surgical insurance pays $1,000, a claim for the difference of $500 may be filed with the major medical program. Or if a hospitalization plan pays 30, 60 or 120 days, the major medical plan will pick up any excess days of the long-stay case.

But there are other services which may be collectible only from the major medical plan. These include nursing services, prescription drugs, laboratory fees, home and office calls, and the like.

The design of a major medical plan usually calls for a deductible and a co-insurance feature. A typical plan will not pay for the first $100, and then pay 80% of all eligible costs above this first $100 in any one year. The theory is that the insured should share a reasonable amount of his medical bills but that the insurance will protect him against any medical catastrophe.

People who have been through the tragedy of a complicated illness or accident, or a dread disease, appreciate and approve the security provided by major medical coverage. As an employee fringe benefit, it is gaining in popularity.

A NEW APPROACH TO CONTROL HEALTH CARE INSURANCE COSTS

Health care costs have been, and still are, escalating faster than the cost of living. Companies, through their insurance carriers, traditionally pay whatever health care providers charge. Overcharges and abuses are seldom challenged. This has led to cost increases of 20% annually.

Efforts by companies to try to control their health insurance costs have been centered on cost-sharing by employees. They increase the deductible or the co-insurance amounts. The theory is that when employees have to absorb more of the cost they will be inclined to demand less care.

That logic is flawed. The fallacy is that when an employee (or dependent) gets sick, the necessary care must be provided. All that happens is that more of the burden is transferred to the employee. The question of health care costs being "out of line" is not addressed. This arrangement results in "cost shifting" instead of cost cutting.

Some companies are now trying another approach. They are developing incentives to encourage employees to shop for less expensive care. They want employees to assume financial responsibility for managing their medical affairs.

These employers have "pre-certification programs." Based on current medical data, these plans have guidelines for the cost of different procedures and services and on the length of time for hospital stays. Within these guidelines the company will pay most or all of the costs. Beyond the guidelines, the employee is not reimbursed.

Here's how the plan works. Employees are required to get formal approval before embarking on elective surgery or entering a hospital. The doctor informs the company's coordinator of the diagnosis and treatment, who then declares how many hospital days the plan will cover. (If the doctor objects to the hospital-stay guidelines, another doctor will be brought in to consult on the case.) Should complications develop, the doctor can apply for a longer stay. If these terms can be met, the employee will be reimbursed up to the plan's limits.

For full coverage of elective surgical costs, employees must get a second opinion before surgery. Necessary pre-surgery tests must be performed before entering the hospital. And the typical plan will not cover admissions to the hospital on the weekend unless they are medically necessary. Emergency treatment needs no advance approval.

Certain procedures are expected to be performed outside the hospital, such as hemorrhoid removals, tubal ligations, and tonsillectomies. Outpatient surgery is usually covered 100%.

The companies still are willing to pay the health care costs for their

757

employees (and dependents) but they can't continue to allow runaway costs to continue unchecked. In effect they are serving notice on the medical community that since doctors and hospitals seem unable (or unwilling) to "get a handle" on costs, the companies will take over the management of health care costs for their employees.

This idea of trying to hold costs down may seem novel but it is really not new. It uses the same principle that has always been applied where insurance pays only for semi-private room accommodations but the patient is free to request a private room and pay the difference. What was limited to one isolated item, hospital room charges, is now extended across the entire spectrum of health care costs. Employees are still free to agree to longer hospital stays or higher physicians' fees, but they will know in advance that they will have to absorb the excess charges.

Employers who have introduced the pre-certification programs are optimistic that these plans will result in lower cost while maintaining quality health care.

DENTAL INSURANCE

One of the fastest moving trends in the group insurance industry is prepaid dental care coverage.

It all started with the longshoremen. Teachers took up the idea next. Before long the United Auto Workers and steel and aluminum union members were also in the vanguard.

Called dental insurance, plans are really a budgetary system for prepaying an expected expense, rather than a method of insurance against risk.

There are a variety of programs. They are offered by national Delta Plan, Blue Cross-Blue Shield, and commercial insurance carriers. To hold down costs, deductibles, co-payments, waiting periods and yearly maximums can be written into the contracts.

Benefits emphasize preventive care, including regular checkups, cleaning, x-rays and fluoride treatments. A building block approach adds restorations, crowns, caps, bridges and inlays to basic programs, and could go as far as dentures and orthodontic work.

Dental insurance works on a group basis, usually through employers who may pay all or part of the premiums. In the 1980's it is estimated 60 million dental patients will have some form of coverage.

The Need

The need is widespread and generally overlooked. Dr. Roger Egeberg, head of federal medical agencies, said in an interview, "One quarter of the people in this country have no teeth. Another quarter have only half their teeth." Statistics show that less than one-half of the people in the United States saw a dentist during the past year. The average 16-year-old has a mouthful of 10 untreated, decayed teeth.

Part of the reason is fear; people delay going for dental checkups fearful of what may be found. Another reason is cost; dental fees go up an average of 12% a year.

Companies that want to stay in tune with employee needs are looking into dental insurance. Comprehensive dental coverage plans for greater segments of the population looms large.

One Example

American Airlines has an excellent group dental insurance plan. It provides comprehensive dental coverage for the employee and family. The company pays the entire premium cost.

In general, the plan pays 80% of covered dental expenses that exceed the $50 calendar-year deductible. It pays 50% for inlays, gold fillings, crowns and fixed bridgework. The maximum payable during any calendar year for each covered person is $1,000.

The plan covers reasonable and customary charges made by a dentist or physician for the services and supplies that are required for the dental treatment of disease, defect or accidental bodily injury. In addition it also covers the preventive treatment such as cleaning every six months, fluoride treatment for children and space maintainers.

Specifically covered are oral examinations, x-rays, and laboratory tests; extractions and oral surgery, including fractures and dislocations; fillings and crowns; treatment of gum disease; root canal therapy; false teeth—full dentures, partial dentures and fixed bridgework.

PRESCRIPTION DRUG INSURANCE

Group drug insurance, apart from its inclusion in most major medical coverage, is also available as a separate program. It is offered to employers and unions and the individual's ID card may bear the identity of the sponsoring group as well as the name of the agency or insurance company that administers it.

In most cases payment for the cost of prescription drugs is a "copay" arrangement with the member paying a deductible, commonly $1.00 to $3.00, and the carrier paying the rest. The pharmacist is reimbursed for either the average wholesale price (AWP) of the drug (as listed in the Red Book) or the net acquisition cost, plus a professional dispensing fee.

Plans vary, but in general they cover federal legend drugs (any medicinal substance which bears the legend "Caution: Federal Law prohibits dispensing without a prescription"), compounded medications (any medicinal substance of which at least one ingredient is a federal legend drug in a therapeutic amount), injectables and insulin (with or without a prescription).

Not covered, usually, are over-the-counter products, contraceptive medications, therapeutic devices or appliances (hypodermic needles, support garments, etc.).

Some plans cover spouses, families, dependent children under a specified age, disabled at any age, and retirees. The ID card indicates who is covered, the copay deductible, the expiration date and the claim-filing instructions.

VISION CARE

Most regular group insurance plans do not cover eyeglasses, examinations or prescriptions. This is strange because studies conducted by various government and industrial groups show that half of the employees in office and factory work have visual deficiencies needing attention.

Managements are becoming interested in eye care for their employees. Poor or bad eyesight has been known to cause abnormal fatigue, headache, vague feelings of illness, increasing errors and lowered efficiency. Indirectly it also has some effect on absenteeism and turnover.

Students of the problem remind us that for thousands of years man used his eyes as nature intended—for distance seeing, out-of-doors. Then, as he became an indoor creature and began using his eyes for prolonged close work, the change in his seeing habits put a heavy burden upon his eyes.

Until the development of artificial lighting, practically everybody worked only during daylight hours and slept during the darkness. Today most men and women work indoors much of the time, with their eyes performing difficult tasks far different from the simpler ones before. Reading, writing, drawing, sewing and operating intricate machinery are only a few of the eye-fatiguing jobs now being performed.

Gone are the days when applicants were required to have 20/20 vision. Job applicants with substandard vision are hired today because they possess skills or other qualifications needed by the company.

Vision care, as part of the group insurance plan or separate, is still relatively unknown. But the trends toward new programs will be worth watching. Eye care may very well emerge as a popular fringe benefit.

As the well-trained, competent employee becomes more and more valuable to the employer, it seems to be good sense to take constructive steps to keep him in good health, aid him in poor health, and thus keep him on the job—in production—as much as possible.

MEDICARE

With the passage of Public Law 89-97 (effective July 1, 1966) commonly referred to as Medicare, the hospitalization and medical-surgical portions of company benefit programs have had to be rearranged. This change affects coverage for:

1. Employees 65 years and older, and their dependents.
2. Retirees 65 years and older, and their dependents.

Medicare is a federal health insurance program run by the Social Security Administration. There are two parts: A—hospital, and B—medical. A quick review of the provisions will highlight the intent and the letter of the law.

Part A

Part A—hospital insurance. This helps pay for medically necessary inpatient hospital care, and, after a hospital stay, for inpatient care in a skilled nursing facility and for care at home by a home health agency.

From the 1st day through the 60th day in each benefit period, Part A pays for all covered services except the first day deductible (originally $40 in 1966 and gradually increased to $356 by 1984).

From the 61st day through the 90th day in a benefit period, it pays for all covered services over a specified amount (originally $10 in 1966 and gradually increased to $89 by 1984). The beneficiary has to assume responsibility for this basic specified amount.

Major services covered for the hospital inpatient are:

1. A semiprivate room (2 to 4 beds in a room).
2. All meals, including special diets.
3. Regular nursing services.
4. Costs of special care units, such as an intensive care unit, coronary care unit, etc.
5. Drugs furnished by the hospital during the stay.
6. Lab tests included in the hospital bill.
7. X-rays and other radiology services, including radiation therapy, billed by the hospital.

8. Medical supplies such as casts, surgical dressings, and splints.
9. Use of appliances, such as a wheelchair.
10. Operating and recovery room costs.
11. Rehabilitation services, such as physical therapy, occupational therapy, and speech pathology services.

Some services not covered are:

1. Personal convenience items such as a television, radio, or telephone in the room.
2. Private duty nurses.
3. Any extra charges for a private room, unless it is needed for medical reasons.
4. The first three pints of blood.

Part B

Part B—medical insurance. This helps pay for medically necessary doctors' services, outpatient hospital services, outpatient physical therapy and speech pathology services, and a number of other medical services and supplies not covered by Part A.

There is a basic payment rule that applies. After a deductible (originally $50 in 1966 and increased to $75 in 1982), Part B pays 80% of the reasonable charges for covered services during the calendar year. Reasonable charges are determined by the *customary* charge (generally the charge most frequently made) and the *prevailing* charge (high enough to cover the customary charges in three out of every four bills submitted). Increases are limited from year to year by an "economic index" formula. This formula does not limit the amount a doctor may charge a patient; it only limits the amount Medicare will pay.

There are two ways payments are made under Part B: (1) to the doctor or supplier, or (2) as reimbursement to the patient. When a doctor or supplier agrees to "an assignment" of the payment, it means he or she will accept the reasonable charge approved by Medicare as the total charge.

Major doctors' services covered are:

1. Medical and surgical services.
2. Diagnostic tests and procedures that are part of the treatment.
3. Other services which are ordinarily furnished in the doctor's office and included in the bill, such as:

- X-rays received as part of treatment

- Services of the doctor's office nurse

- Drugs and biologicals that cannot be self-administered
- Medical supplies
- Physical therapy and speech pathology services

Some doctors' services not covered are:

1. Routine physical examinations and tests directly related to such examinations.
2. Routine foot care.
3. Eye or hearing examinations for prescribing or fitting eyeglasses or hearing aids.
4. Immunizations (unless required because of an injury or immediate risk of infection).
5. Cosmetic surgery unless it is needed because of accidental injury or to improve the functioning of a malformed part of the body.

Major outpatient hospital services covered by Part B are:

1. Services in an emergency room or outpatient clinic.
2. Laboratory tests billed by the hospital.
3. X-rays and other radiology services billed by the hospital.
4. Medical supplies such as splints and casts.
5. Drugs and biologicals which cannot be self-administered.

Whereas coverage for Part A is practically automatic, Part B is voluntary. Part A (hospital) insurance is provided at no cost to beneficiaries, but there is a 50/50 shared cost for Part B. Originally the cost per person was $3.00 per month, and this has gradually been increased to $14.60 by 1984.

Third Party Administration

Under the law, Medicare does not cover care that is not "reasonable and necessary" for the treatment of an illness or injury. Nor does Medicare cover care that is "custodial."

Medicare payments are handled by private insurance organizations under contract with the government. Organizations handling claims from hospitals, skilled nursing facilities, and home health agencies are called *intermediaries.* Organizations handling claims from doctors and other suppliers of service covered under Part B are called *carriers.*

This is a very complex piece of legislation which cannot be discussed in detail here—nor should it be. Suffice it to say that the above Medicare coverage comes under Title XVIII of the 1965 Social Security Amendments. Title XIX covers hospital and medical benefits for state welfare recipients regardless of age, including over-65 medically indigent, dependent children, blind, and totally disabled.

Health Insurance for Active Employees 65–69

Companies that have active employees between the ages of 65 and 69 must consider the impact of the "Employer Health Plan Primacy to Medicare for Active Employees 65–69," by Amendments to the Age Discrimination in Employment Act and the Social Security (Medicare) Act brought about by the Tax Equity and Fiscal Responsibility Act of 1982 (TEFRA).

These revisions have required the Health Care Financing Administration to issue regulations under which Medicare will operate. The Equal Employment Opportunity Commission has also approved regulations covering the age discrimination portion of these new requirements. The equal cost provision (a requirement that employers must expend the same amount of health care dollars for older employees electing to take Medicare as primary coverage as for employees electing to remain with the employer's plan as primary coverage) has been eliminated.

The highlights of these regulations are:

1. Employers must offer employees age 65 through age 69 the same health care plans offered younger employees, at no extra cost.
2. The employer must give each eligible employee an opportunity to elect, in writing, either to have primary health coverage under the employer's health plan *or* to reject the employer's plan and take Medicare as primary coverage.
3. Employers are not permitted to offer employees age 65 through age 69 any type of coverage that supplements the benefits covered by Medicare (i.e., where Medicare would be the primary payor and the employer's plan would be the secondary) or that encourages employees to elect Medicare as primary coverage.

It should be noted that an employer can offer supplemental plans covering health care services not covered at all by Medicare (outpatient prescription drugs, dental services, eye exams and glasses, hearing exams and aids, routine physical exams), as long as the plans are offered to all employees through age 69 on an equal basis. Nor need an employer pay Medicare Part B premiums.

The spouse of an employee age 65–69 must be provided coverage under the same conditions that coverage is provided to the spouse of a younger employee, regardless of the spouse's age. But if that employer does not provide health care for the spouse of any employee, the employer is not required to do so now.

The underlying intent is to shift the costs of providing any health care coverage for the older active employee (65–69) from Medicare to the employers.

Health Insurance for over-65 Retirees

Companies may be tempted to take a generous attitude toward their former employees who are retired. They may feel that the government program, which was designed to pay 50% of the total cost (but no longer does), might not be adequate, especially in comparison with what had previously been provided. They may, therefore, wish to protect their retirees with some form of supplemental insurance. In those programs where companies had also been covering the retiree's spouse and any under-age dependents, they may want to work out some arrangement with the insurance carrier to provide them with more complete protection.

This attitude is noble and noteworthy, but there is one note of caution that should be expressed here. Companies unthinkingly take the position of providing their over-65 retirees with "the same protection they had before Medicare." In other words, they will give them everything they had before but carve out Medicare benefits, since they are now getting these benefits from the government. This they reason keeps their coverage intact; it means they have the same protection as before, only that it comes from two different sources.

What these companies overlook is that under this policy the over-65 retirees actually have more coverage than before. They have everything they originally had *plus* many new and additional benefits which are in the Medicare package but which were not in their previous employee program. The upshot is that these over-65 retirees have *better* coverage than the employees.

Once this advantage dawns on the employees, the door will be open for increasing their basic benefits to bring them up, or at least closer, to the level of benefits which the over-65 retirees enjoy. Hence, employers who take this generous attitude toward their retirees may find themselves unwittingly contributing to the escalation of benefits for all of their employees, and facing the prospect of increasing their costs accordingly.

WORKERS' COMPENSATION

States have Workers' Compensation laws whose purpose is to promote the general welfare of the people by providing compensation for accidental injuries or death suffered in the course of employment.

These laws are designed to provide protection to workers suffering occupational disabilities:

1. Accidents arising out of and in the course of employment.
2. Occupational diseases for illnesses resulting from exposure to hazards peculiar to particular employment.

Employers are also liable for injuries during nonwork activities if they are a company promotion, or for the good will and companionship of the employees, or the company stands to gain. Compensation payments have been made:

- For a broken arm suffered in an after-hours softball game sponsored by an employer.

- For injuries sustained during a crap game on company premises.

- To a flight attendant because she developed an allergy from cigarette smoke in plane cabins.

- To a widow whose husband was killed while returning from a company golf outing.

The laws in most states are now a half-century old. They were enacted to counteract employer abuses. Prior to the enactment of Workers' Compensation laws, injured workers could sue under "common law" but it was necessary for them to prove negligence on the part of the employer. Today, the concepts of blame and negligence have been eliminated and compensation is paid regardless of fault.

The amount of compensation differs in the states, but this is clearly spelled out in each law. Benefits cover payments for:

1. Medical expenses
2. Time loss
3. Disfigurement or dismemberment
4. Death

Generally, lump sum payments are made in case of death, the amount varying by number and type of dependent survivors. Burial expense allowance may be added.

In nonfatal cases the compensation usually includes a fixed schedule of reimbursement for medical services and specified weekly payments during the period of incapacity. The amount again is related to the number of dependents. In cases of long-term permanent disability, settlements are often worked out.

Schedules of benefits are established by law. Circumstances concerning accidents and extent of disability are often disputed.

Insurance rates reflect claims paid (usage). Employers may elect to self-insure or may prefer to transfer their entire liability to pay such compensation to an authorized insurance company.

UNEMPLOYMENT COMPENSATION

Unemployment Compensation is a part of the social security philosophy. It had its origin in countries other than the United States.

Germany set up social security programs to cover old age and sickness in the 1880's, but unemployment insurance was not introduced there until 1927.

In 1935, when the U.S. Congress passed Social Security legislation, it required each state to establish basic unemployment compensation laws. These benefits were designed as a cushion against a cessation of spending when factories cut back work forces. On the whole, the net effect of labor and security laws has been beneficial to the national welfare.

The program is a Federal-State partnership. The U.S. Department of Labor provides guidelines and Federal grants for operating costs; and State employment security agencies pay unemployed workers out of State unemployment insurance funds. The sources of both Federal and State funds are employer taxes; workers contribute to UI funds in only three states—Alabama, Alaska, and New Jersey.

Unemployment insurance is a weekly benefit paid for a limited time to eligible workers to tide them over between jobs when they are involuntarily unemployed. It protects workers against the personal catastrophe of being out of work and having nothing to live on.

To be eligible for benefits a person must: (1) have worked long enough in covered employment to meet the State's requirements, (2) be involuntarily unemployed, (3) be available for and seeking work, and (4) not refuse a suitable job offer.

To apply for payments, jobless workers must file a claim and register for work at the nearest public employment or unemployment insurance service office. While drawing benefits, they must be available for jobs.

767

Each State specifies its eligibility requirements and amounts of weekly and total benefit payments. The general rule is that the jobless worker receives 50% of the average weekly wage formerly received. Most States limit payments to a maximum of 26 weeks. A federal program provides that, during times of high unemployment, individuals who have exhausted their benefits under State law may continue to receive payments for half as long as their regular entitlement.

Each State sets penalties for disqualifying acts such as voluntary quit without good cause. Penalties can range from postponement to denial of benefits for the duration of the current period of unemployment. Since 1978, States cannot deny benefits solely on the basis of pregnancy or recency of pregnancy (pregnant individuals do, however, have to meet generally applicable requirements of seeking work and being available for and able to work).

Unemployment benefits are a right and are not based on need. Hence, income unrelated to former jobs does not affect benefits. But since the program is designed to compensate workers for their wage loss, payments related to wages—such as severance pay, workers' compensation, and pension benefits—are considered disqualifying in some States.

Almost all workers are now covered under unemployment insurance. In 1978 coverage was extended to: (1) state and local government employees (with some exceptions, such as elected officials, members of the legislature or judiciary, and persons in part-time advisory positions); (2) household workers whose employers pay at least $1,000 a calendar quarter for such workers; and (3) workers on farms where the operator has a payroll of at least $20,000 in a calendar quarter or has 10 or more employees in 20 weeks.

Keeping Costs Down

The amount of tax each company pays depends upon the number of former workers claiming compensation and the unemployment situation in the particular State.

The following suggestions may help a company reduce its unemployment insurance tax rate:

1. Keep good personnel records. It is better to rely upon facts than to trust memory.
2. Hold exit interviews and record the reason for leaving.
3. Keep improving hiring and indoctrination procedures. Try to reduce the number of misfits who have to be fired.
4. Stabilize employment. Avoid seasonal work as much as possible.

5. Check figures supplied by the State. Make certain the base earnings period is stated correctly and the amount agrees with payroll records. Make sure the tax rate is right.
6. Charge each operation with its own payments. In multi-plant operations, recalculate the rate each establishment should have.
7. Get the tax manager and the personnel manager to cooperate. The two can make a good team.
8. Rehire ex-employees whenever possible. If the former employee's work record is clear, and suitable work is available, it is better to put the former employee back to work than to permit the person to continue to receive compensation for not working.
9. Make direct testimony at hearings. This takes time but it is worth it, since it shows the company is sincerely interested in good administration of the law.
10. Watch legislation. Be familiar with the statute and keep an eye on developments. Support the legislators who give evidence of keeping the law within reason.

Other Unemployment Allowances

The *Disaster Relief Act* helps people in major disaster areas get restarted. In addition to benefits for corporations and communities, it provides disaster unemployment allowances in the form of weekly benefits for eligible individuals whose jobs or earnings are affected by the disaster. Sometimes other emergency legislation is enacted to liberalize benefits temporarily.

Under the *Trade Act of 1974,* special help is provided to American workers who are totally or partially unemployed or underemployed because of import competition. In addition to trade readjustment allowances to supplement State unemployment insurance payments, available assistance includes counseling, testing, referral to training and jobs, job search assistance, job relocation assistance, and supportive services. Separated workers who are unable to find suitable jobs comparable to their previous employment within their commuting area are entitled to training in another occupation, along with transportation and subsistence allowances. They are also entitled to job search assistance and allowances, not to exceed $500, and job relocation assistance and allowances of 80% of "reasonable and necessary" expenses incurred in moving to another location, plus a lump-sum payment equivalent to three times the worker's average weekly wage, up to a maximum of $500.

DISABILITY INSURANCE

There are two types of retirement programs. The one commonly thought of is age retirement; workers reach a designated age, say 65 or 70, and are retired from the company.

But there are other workers who are retired from the company, who have to leave the workforce before they reach normal retirement. These are the people who through accidental bodily injury or illness become totally disabled and are unable to continue working.

It is fortunate for them if they have been associated with a company that provides an income when they are no longer able to work. The safest way to handle this is through Disability Insurance.

Disability insurance, or a disability retirement program, provides a worker with a reduced weekly or monthly income when he becomes totally and permanently disabled.

Benefits are based on salary and length of continuous service. One example might be 50% of the first $650 of monthly salary plus $33^1/_3\%$ of that portion in excess of $650. Usually there is a maximum benefit, say $1,000 per month.

This amount is payable monthly for a prescribed period of time. An example here might be five years of benefit payments for five years of employment, increasing gradually to 15 years of benefit payments for 10 years of employment, with benefits payable for life for all employees with more than 10 years of service.

If the disabled employee is also eligible, or later becomes eligible, for payments under the federal Social Security system, the amount of these payments will very likely be deducted from the benefits paid by the company's disability insurance.

Usually there is a considerable waiting period before an employee is covered. This insurance is intended to help protect the earning power of the longtime faithful employee who would have built his career with the company were he not incapacitated.

Other exclusions might be service in the armed forces, intentionally self-inflicted injury, chronic alcoholism, wrongful use of narcotics, or participation in a felonious or criminal act.

Payments do not begin immediately, but usually start six months after the disability has existed. A medical committee will rule on each case to determine whether the employee is entitled to receive benefits. Further, the disabled employee will likely be required to submit to medical examination or to furnish continued proof of his disability periodically.

An employee is declared disabled when he is forever prevented from engaging in any occupation comparable to that which he had held.

770

GROUP AUTOMOBILE INSURANCE

There's a new wrinkle in automobile insurance. Casualty insurance companies have introduced automobile insurance on a group basis, much the same as hospitalization coverage has been offered over the years.

The procedure calls for an agent or broker to approach a company with the idea of selling individual insurance policies to interested employees and collecting the premiums through regular payroll deductions. They claim the rates are lower if the insurance is handled this way.

Unlike other group insurance, there is no percentage of employees who must participate. The company takes whatever business it can get. Nor is there any uniform rate or uniform benefits for all. Instead there are individual underwriting and separate insurance policies. Claims are handled individually through regular company claims adjusters. Changes and cancellations are between the insured employee and the insurance carrier; the employer is not involved, nor has he any voice in the dealings between the two parties.

To begin a program of group automobile insurance in a company, a letter announcing the availability of this insurance is sent to all employees. For those who are interested, individual interviews are arranged with the insurance company salesmen. Any employee who buys the insurance signs a payroll card authorizing the regular deductions to be made by the employer to cover his premiums.

Then as an ongoing activity, an insurance company salesman visits the employer's office at specified times, say once a week, to talk with new employees, to answer questions, to change the coverage and to discuss problems.

The selling point is that this is an employee benefit with the company's involvement kept at a minimum. This is fine as long as everybody is satisfied. But it is doubtful that an employer can stand by idly if one of his employees becomes unhappy with the rate, the service or the treatment. In such a case, the employee is likely to blame his company for letting this happen to him.

PREPAID GROUP LEGAL SERVICES

Prepaid group medical insurance is the rule in employee benefit plans and group dental coverage is becoming standard. Prepaid group legal service is similar to these plans but in a new field.

Prepaid legal services means a plan in which the cost of possible legal services needed in the future is prepaid in advance by, or on behalf of, the client who receives such services. The plan is usually offered to a group of clients (Ex: a company-sponsored employee group) so that the combined payments are pooled, and the principle of spreading the risk between users and nonusers is achieved.

For the payment of sums deducted weekly or monthly, a set amount of legal services is provided either in terms of gross dollar amounts for specified work functions of lawyers (counselling, negotiation, litigation) or for maximum amounts payable for a set of specified legal work tasks (adoption, divorce, bankruptcy or drawing a will, et cetera).

Within the organized bar, the term "prepaid legal services" has usually meant that the individual group member may have a free choice of participating lawyers. Also, the range of services that the individual group member may enjoy is usually broader than job-related matters.

There are four basic administration methods:

1. By the sponsoring group, i.e., the employer or a hired third party.

2. Through lawyers or a law firm.

3. Through an insurance company.

4. Through a joint trust (employer and employee) which may, in turn, hire a third-party administrator.

Typically legal plans offer such services as preparation of wills, adoption proceedings, sale or purchase of property, divorce or annulment, and consumer complaints. In most of the programs, 98% of the problems fall into three categories: domestic relations, property, and wills and probate.

The U.S. Department of Labor reports that 3,500 prepaid legal plans have filed annual reports under ERISA (Employee Retirement Income Security Act). Total national coverage is estimated at more than three million employees, mostly blue-collar and middle-income workers.

The real impetus for prepaid legal plans has been the Tax Reform Act of 1976. The act says the "employer-paid legal services can't be counted as taxable income for the employee."

These plans are emerging slowly but steadily. In the litigious United States future legal disputes are as inevitable as medical problems. "These plans are definitely the next big employee benefit but we may be into the 1980's before things really get rolling," says James T. Goodman, executive director of the American Pre-Paid Legal Services Institute, an affiliate of the American Bar Association.

GROUP LIFE INSURANCE

One of the earliest elements in the employee group insurance program was life insurance. As offered today, the most common form is term insurance, in effect only as long as the insured is employed by the company. It contains no paid-up or cash surrender value.

This all began when an employee died and co-workers learned there was no money for burial. So they passed the hat. To avoid any future embarrassment, companies began to provide a modest amount of insurance free to assure decent burials.

Most companies today provide some basic life insurance. This may be only a nominal amount, say $1,000, equivalent to burial insurance. This coverage is related to time; it is given after a period of service, say six months or a year.

In addition, the employee may purchase additional insurance at group rates. There is one rate for everyone in the employee group, regardless of age. The amount available is geared to annual salary. As salary increases the employee becomes eligible for more insurance. The company pays the difference in cost; the company also keeps any rebate or credit.

Each employee names a beneficiary. Claims are payable on death from any cause.

There are many reasons for companies to accept the social responsibility:

1. Employees need insurance but do not buy enough protection themselves.
2. There is no physical exam; people otherwise uninsurable can buy it.
3. The company charges off its share of the cost as a business expense.

Some of the characteristics of employee group life insurance are:

1. Premiums are collected or paid for by the employer.
2. One contract is signed but individual certificates are issued.
3. Coverage is the same for all employees but the amounts may vary.
4. There is a waiting period; this is for company administrative convenience.
5. An employee who elects not to participate is asked to sign a waiver.

The employer handles all the necessary clerical work: application cards; waivers; rosters of eligibles; records; changes in name, status, beneficiary; claims; terminations and drops from billing; payroll deduction authorizations; announcements; distribution of statements; selling and counselling.

The cost of the basic life insurance is paid by the company. Since there is no payout unless an employee dies, the cost is nominal; most of the premium is rebated at year end. The supplemental insurance is customarily provided to employees at a below-cost rate with the company absorbing the difference.

A good feature of group life insurance is that no medical examination is required if the employee enrolls when eligible for the initial amount or later increases. They may be all the life insurance some people can get. If an employee who originally turned down all or part of this insurance decides during a subsequent re-enrollment to make application, the employee will be required to provide proof of insurability.

Accidental Death and Dismemberment

Life insurance policies for employees usually include an Accidental Death and Dismemberment provision. This is a double indemnity in case of accidental death. Payments are also made for the loss of limbs or eyesight.

As one company explains, "The prudent person finds that accidental death and dismemberment insurance is of prime importance in a well-rounded insurance program. It gives one's family a financial bridge over the gap that occurs when the breadwinner meets unexpected death. Or, for the tragedy of accidents resulting in loss of sight or dismemberment, it provides a sum that may be needed to train one for a new career in keeping with the handicap."

A D & D insurance pays extra for accidental death, usually double indemnity, or twice the amount of the schedule of ordinary life insurance carried. There is also a fixed set of benefits payable in case of accidental loss of one or both eyes or limbs.

The benefits are usually geared to the earnings of the employee. As a rule dependents of employees are not included.

When an employee leaves the firm for whatever reason, the total package of life insurance coverage remains in force for 31 days. During this grace period the employee may convert to an individual policy, without a physical examination or health statement, but at a rate based on the employee's age at time of termination.

Excerpts from a typical company policy on

GROUP LIFE INSURANCE

Your beneficiary will receive the full amount of your life insurance in the case of your death due to any cause. There are no exceptions or exclusions.

When death results from an accident, your beneficiary will receive payment from both Life Insurance and Accidental Death and Dismemberment. This is double indemnity for an accidental death.

The Accidental Death and Dismemberment Insurance also pays when a dismemberment results from a nonfatal accident judged to be involuntary. For instance: the full amount of insurance would be paid for the loss of both hands or for the loss of one hand and one foot. One half the amount of the insurance would be paid for the loss of one limb or the loss of the sight of one eye. The complete schedule is in the certificate.

Your beneficiary may be any person or persons you name. You may change your beneficiary at any time by signing the appropriate change form in the personnel office.

If your employment is terminated because of total disability before you reach the age of 60, your Group Life Insurance will be continued without cost to you during such disability. You will, of course, be required to submit evidence of your continued disability from time to time.

Should you leave the company, your Life Insurance coverage remains in force for the next 31 days. During this 31-day period you have an opportunity to buy from the Insurance Company an individual policy at the prevailing rates at that time without a physical examination or health statement.

KEY-MAN INSURANCE PLANS

Key-man insurance is often called "profit protection" insurance, a term that describes its basic function. While most other insurance protects employees, this type of coverage is designed to protect the employer on the following points:

1. The cost of hiring and training a new person, usually an executive.
2. The value of sales, production or profits which might be lost because of the "key man's" absence.

This type of insurance is highest among the smaller companies, those employing fewer than 100 people. This reflects the serious need for such protection on the part of smaller companies, where the "first team" of executives often includes executives without understudies or immediate replacements.

As would be expected, larger companies are usually in a better position to replace a key executive. They are also apparently less vulnerable to suffering a loss when one man dies or becomes disabled.

In carrying this type of coverage, the key man must be identified and a dollar value given to him. Just as manpower programs and replacement plans should be updated annually, so should key man insurance. An executive whose replacement was correctly stated at $100,000 two years ago could easily be worth $200,000 or more today.

It is also important never to cut this insurance even when the person covered is no longer indispensable. The insurance value built up over the years represents a considerable investment. It is also possible that the former key man may again become important to the company or one of its projects sometime in the future.

One element of this type of insurance has a vital bearing on the welfare of all employees. This is the case—usually in smaller companies—when the death of the principal owner could mean the forced sale or liquidation of the enterprise to settle the estate.

The benefits work both ways—for the employees and those sharing the estate—when insurance is set up to provide funds for one or more of the persons experienced in the business, but lacking capital to buy the controlling interest from the heirs of the principal owner. This is often arranged with the understanding that such a purchase is for the purpose of continuing the enterprise in a form closely resembling the aims and policies of the original management.

With a combination of insurance and replacement planning, it is possible for most companies to arrive at the desirable goal of reasonable security in this area.

RETIREMENT INCOME AND PENSION

Retirement from active employment is intended to permit older workers to enjoy their twilight years without the everyday pressures of working. In this context there is a fine line distinction between retirement income and pension.

A *retirement income* is a form of monthly income after a person's working days are over. A company retires a worker in accordance with the terms of an established program. The mandatory age in private industry has been raised from 65 to 70, although earlier retirement is not uncommon.

It is debatable whether a person retires voluntarily or is retired by the company according to policy. Workers who have no company affiliation—such as farmers, shopkeepers, professionals, legislators, judges, and other elected and appointed officials—do not arbitrarily stop working at a prescribed age but often continue in a productive capacity as long as their health allows.

A company asks an otherwise capable worker to vacate the job and accept, in return, a retirement income. This regular monthly income check, mailed out from a trust, is less than the regular salary. It is less because the worker:

1. Has reduced living expenses in leisure years.
2. Is usually in a settled financial situation.
3. Becomes subject, for the first time, to a third-party income (Social Security).

The amount of the retirement income is calculated on: (1) average career earnings during time of employment with the company or pegged to higher earnings in later years, and (2) the length of employment. Such retirement income is guaranteed for life. Many programs offer options to cover joint pensioners (spouses) or other beneficiaries.

A *pension,* on the other hand, is related to earnings and length of service but not to age. Usually an employee who has worked a required number of years is eligible to leave the job and still continue to receive part—or possibly all—of the salary, irrespective of what the age may be at the time.

One of the best examples is the military pension program. A man or woman may choose the armed forces for a career. Then after 20 years of service, the pensioner receives 50% of "base" pay; after 30 years, 75%—for life. Since military personnel embark upon their careers early in life, they are still relatively young when they are pensioned off and many of them enter the civilian work force. This is what the term "double dippers" refers to—employees who receive benefits from two programs.

Retirement or pension programs need the approval of the Treasury Department since their cost is charged off as a company operating expense. It is well, therefore, to deal with a recognized insurance company or a reputable consultant when setting up a program. There is too much at stake, considering the amount of money that is invested and the number of people who are affected.

EARLY RETIREMENT BUYOUT

Faced with increasing operating costs and decreasing profits, many companies are trying to thin out their work forces. As an alternative to layoffs, early retirement incentives are being examined.

Such programs take many forms but typically involve partial salary spread over several years along with extended benefits. To qualify for consideration, employees must usually combine a specified minimum age (Example: 40 years) with a minimum number of years of service (Example: 25) to reach or exceed the qualifying number (Example: 65). All levels of employees must be included.

In return, employees who accept the early retirement incentive are terminated from employment and receive reduced wages (Example: 50%) for a period of time (Example: 2 years) after which regular retirement income begins. As an inducement, the number of years an employee may remain on the reduced payroll will perhaps be lengthened for young eligibles (Example: 3 years for under age 55).

Any losses in pension resulting from early retirement are usually offset by other enticements. Some offerings are health, dental, and vision coverage, life and accident insurance, employee discounts, and the like. But once these employees are permanently removed from the payroll, they then become eligible for regular fringe benefits as they apply to under-65 and over-65 retirees.

The cost to the employer must be carefully weighed. Payroll costs will be reduced and benefit costs could be increased temporarily. In the long run, savings will result as the supplements expire. The lifetime income of these retirees will most likely be less because their total number of years of service (one of the multiples in the retirement income formula) will be down.

The employees should be made to understand that the compelling reason for the program is as an alternative to inevitable layoffs. In presenting this offer to employees, the voluntary aspect should be stressed so that they can accept the assurance that those in the eligible group are not being pushed out as failures but rewarded for long service. It is also important to mention that this is a one-time program so that nobody is tempted to hold out for a better deal.

One problem is that early retirement is "offered" and not made mandatory. Eligible employees may accept or reject the offer without repercussions. As in any volunteer program, there is no way to control the results. True, the total number of employees in the overall is reduced, especially if their jobs are abolished or filled by others whose jobs, in turn, are absorbed. There is, however, no guarantee that expendable employees will be the ones who leave and key employees will be the ones who remain. Often quite the opposite happens.

Attractions to eligible employees are not only monetary. There are other concerns, among them personal and family health, opportunity to move elsewhere earlier than anticipated, likelihood of other employment, and the chance to try something else while there is still time.

Besides being a humanitarian method of reducing payroll costs, early retirement incentive programs provide: (1) a means of rewarding long-tenured employees who are prepared to leave, (2) promotional opportunities for younger staffers, and (3) an easing of affirmative action plans as goals are more easily met.

FOCUS ON THE RETIRED EMPLOYEE

The company press has commenced to pay more attention to the retired employee, and the trend is a sound one. For many years, in too many companies, the retiree has been shunted into industrial oblivion with only a watch to consult and a few handshakes to remember.

The mounting national concern about and interest in the aged has helped shape this newer viewpoint. However, there are other considerations; entirely apart from the fact that it is simply good, old-fashioned human decency to remember the retired employee, it is good business to do so. More and more companies are finding this out.

The retired employee is one of the best ambassadors in the community, provided he is satisfied and not a disgruntled retiree; provided he terminated his employment with good feeling about the company and did not come away from the plant soured on it and its management. The retired employee can influence favorably a local recruitment drive. The retired employee can contribute to the firmness and the soundness of the company's image within the community. As a participant in his company's retirement plan, he is a figure in a growing and important aspect of our national economy.

Surveys of employee attitude constantly expose employee ignorance of retirement benefits. It may be argued—and it generally is—that information is as close as the personnel office, that a handbook on retirement "explains everything." The fact remains that many employees, even on the brink of retirement, have hazy notions about what their retirement holds.

Into this breach the company publications appear to be moving, somewhat hesitantly, but with some good early effects. The range of coverage is wide and impressive. It is more than explaining the details of the retirement program; the better articles grasp the opportunity to knit the company and retired employee more closely together.

Enterprising communications people look upon their retiree "coverage" not simply as a vehicle to extol the virtues of long and faithful service, not to publish the names and addresses of retired employees. They view coverage as a much-needed investment in corporate goodwill; they view retirement itself as something all employees might reflect upon from time to time.

LUMP SUM VS. MONTHLY PENSION PAYMENTS

The purpose of pensions is to secure lifetime incomes for employees when they retire. In the past few years, however, increasing numbers of retiring corporate employees are asking for, and getting, lump sum pensions instead of the usual monthly fixed amount of retirement income. The demand is becoming so persistent that most pension plans will soon have to offer this option.

Lump sum pensions are desirable whenever inflation and interest rates are high. Retirees become convinced that by investing their accrued pension funds themselves they can receive a better rate of return and thus have better protection against the spiraling cost of living. At the same time, they can still handle another enemy—the tax collector.

The Employee Retirement and Security Act (ERISA) stipulates that a single sum received from a company pension plan can escape taxes by being "rolled over" within 60 days into an Individual Retirement Account (IRA). Moreover, the money in an IRA continues to compound and becomes taxable only when the retiree begins to withdraw it, which is not mandatory until the age of 70 1/2 years.

This trend toward lump sum payouts worries pension experts. It defeats the original purpose of pension plans which is to assure a lifetime income. Do individuals have enough experience or understanding in investments to know how to handle a sudden windfall. Are they prey to the advice of fast-talking investment counsellors?

The idea itself may contribute to discrimination if payouts are too large and may constitute forfeiture of pension benefits if they are too small. If the lump sum offer is available to only some eligible pensioners, based on status, salary, or other concern, is this likely to be considered discriminatory at some point? Too many lump sum payments, particularly big ones to high earners, can seriously drain the fund and adversely affect its future earning power.

Actuaries warn that many companies use a formula for calculating the lump sum that may result in excessive payouts. The formula involves two assumptions—life expectancy and interest rates. The calculation is the amount that the retiree would get in an annuity less a deduction for the interest this amount would earn over the years of life expectancy; using the customary conservative interest rate discounts the payment too little. The Internal Revenue Service rule now requires each company to spell out the interest rate it uses.

What is the company obligation to a retired employee who invests a lump sum unwisely? For that matter, what is the company obligation to all retirees who check out of the company forever by taking lump sum? Employers customarily maintain contact with former employees who remain affiliated by virtue of a continuing stream of company pension checks. Companies may provide services, such as legal and financial advice, mail them the company publications, invite them to lunches or reunion dinners, and display a genuine interest in them in a variety of ways. Most important, they retain them in their employee group insurance plan, for hospitalization, medical/surgical, and major medical coverage (possibly even full coverage for under-age-65 dependents), and often provide this protection at no cost. Are lump sum payments treated as severance pay and are these employees cut off not only from regular monthly income but also from fringe benefits? How does a company maintain contact with former employees who have elected to become disassociated from the company?

A growing number of companies periodically adjust the pensions of retired employees to help them cope with inflation. These are seldom automatic cost-of-living increases, but are usually ad hoc arrangements. Retirees who request lump sum settlements do not participate in these adjustments; their separation from the company is considered a once-in-a-lifetime decision which precludes any follow-up attention.

This whole notion is not a dollars-and-cents issue for either the company or the employees. It is a true test of human relations for both.

INDIVIDUAL RETIREMENT ACCOUNT (IRA)

An individual may set up a tax-sheltered retirement program. A worker may set aside a portion of pay, before taxes, in an Individual Retirement Account and pay no taxes on that income or on the interest it will earn until the funds are taken at retirement or earlier.

There is no need to be a member of a group or to have the employer's approval. The worker can arrange for everything—with the help of his banker or savings and loan counsellor.

Under the Tax Equity and Fiscal Responsibility Act of 1982 (TEFRA), any working person under age 70½, who is employed or self-employed, can qualify and begin any time.

There are several types of IRA accounts in which a worker may participate. The "regular" IRA allows contributions up to $2,000 a year; if both spouses are working, each is eligible to contribute $2,000 of earned income in separate accounts. In the "spousal" IRA, for a worker with a nonworking spouse, the maximum annual contribution is $2,250. The IRA for "self-employed" covers the worker but does not require including any employees. Lump-sum funds from a company pention plan may be "rolled over" into a personal IRA with the same tax deferment benefits if the transaction is completed within 60 days.

It is important to distinguish terms. IRA is tax-sheltered, not tax-free. Tax-shelter is a delay in a tax obligation until the funds are actually distributed. In IRA, the principal and interest are tax-sheltered. There is a day of reckoning for taxes. But the advantage is that distribution of funds may be expected to take a lower rate after retirement.

Distribution of funds may begin as early as age 59½ and must start by age 70½.

There are options for taking distribution of funds. One may take funds in a lump sum, for which there is a special "averaging" to reduce taxes. Or one may take funds on a regular payout basis over a period of years.

In case of death of the participant, funds would be distributed to the designated beneficiary without penalty by IRS. In case of total disability of the participant, funds would be paid out, also without penalty by IRS. There would, of course, be a tax obligation at the time of payout under either circumstance.

THE KEOGH PLAN

Retirement plans for corporation employees are an accepted feature of contemporary life. For some time corporations have been able to set aside tax-free dollars to provide retirement income for their employees. Until recently, however, the self-employed business and professional person had no such plan available.

In 1962 Congress passed the Keogh Act or the Self-Employed Individuals Tax Retirement Act. Since that date the law has been amended to broaden the tax benefits, and a later revision allows the self-employed individual to contribute each year up to $15,000 or 15% of earned income, whichever is less. "Earned income" is basically compensation for personal services. In general, it is computed after deducting business expenses.

Owners of nonincorporated business, self-employed business or professional practitioners, sole proprietors and partners in a partnership may use the Keogh plan. An employer with a 10% interest must include all full-time employees who have three years or more of service in the business and who work at least 1,000 hours per year.

Here's how the Keogh plan works. During each year the self-employed individual may invest up to 15% or $15,000 of earned income, whichever is less. During the years the plan is in force, earned interest is added. No federal income tax is paid on either contributions or interest until funds are paid out at retirement. An equal percentage of an eligible employee's earned income must be contributed by the employer.

The employer determines the percentage to be contributed at the time the plan is initiated. A contribution formula may be chosen which, if compensation should exceed available net profit, would reduce contributions to reflect available profit.

Additional voluntary contributions may be made by each participant —employer and employee—up to 10% of earned income (maximum $2,500). Voluntary additions may be withdrawn at any time without penalty although earnings thereon can only be taken out when normal retirement benefits commence. Voluntary additions are not tax deductible but the earnings are free from tax until retirement.

Benefits are paid upon retirement, but not before age 59½ or later than age 70½. Benefits are also paid upon permanent disability or to a named beneficiary upon death.

In case of termination of employment of an employee, funds in the employee's account will be left untouched while continuing to accrue interest and remain tax-sheltered until the employee's normal retirement date.

Contributions made by the employer on behalf of participants may not be attached or garnished. Neither the employer nor the employee may borrow from his retirement account. Payments at time of retirement may be in annuity form, lump sum or monthly checks.

PIGGYBACK PENSIONS

Many private pension plans ride piggyback on top of Social Security payments. A company with a typical plan looks at the percentage of income replaced by Social Security benefits when setting private pension levels.

What this means is that when a company applies its formula for figuring retirement income it includes the amount of Social Security payments. As Social Security payments increase, the company pension amount decreases, while the combined total remains constant.

Retirees feel this is unfair treatment. It's bad enough when company pensions remain fixed and are not responsive to inflation. But a policy of tying company pensions to Social Security deprives them of the cost-of-living benefit built into the Social Security system.

PENSION OPTIONS

The traditional, defined employee retirement income plans usually allow the employee to specify how the money accumulated on behalf of the employee is to be paid out after retirement. Some time before retirement (usually two years) the employee is asked to select the option considered to be best suited to the individual's circumstances. The choice of options is unlimited, but 98% fall into these four "pension payment options."

1. Single life annuity: the retiree receives a regular monthly amount until death.
2. Joint and survivors annuity: the retiree and a named beneficiary receive a lesser monthly amount (since two lives are covered) and payments continue until the survivor dies. This type of arrangement can be structured so that the amount is larger while both are living and reduced for the one survivor.
3. Guaranteed certain annuity: monthly income is assured for a specified period of time (Example: 10 years) and payments are made: (a) until death of the retiree, even one who outlives the guaranteed period, and (b) to the beneficiary for the remainder of the guaranteed period if the retiree dies before the guaranteed time.
4. Lump sum: this method is used to eliminate small monthly payments (Example: $25 per month) but is not recommended in most other cases. It defeats the intent of the program which was designed to provide monthly income and not a once-in-a-lifetime windfall. Lately, however, some employees have opted for lump-sum settlements which they then "rollover" (to avoid immediate income taxes) into insurance company annuity policies, hoping to gain financially in the long run. Employees who choose the lump sum option should recognize they are forfeiting any right to future cost-of-living increases.

PORTABLE PENSIONS

When pensions are not transferable, it often becomes necessary for an employee to turn down another job opportunity because of the requirement to abandon accrued pension rights in one company and reestablish eligibility from scratch in another company. Upon termination of employment, a person can obtain a refund of the portion he paid into the fund, but he cannot cash in on the contribution paid by his employer. This problem is serious enough to have spawned a raft of proposed legislation in Congress.

The idea of portable pensions does not sound complicated, but fund managers see it as an actuarial and bookkeeping nightmare of hopeless proportions.

From a bookkeeping standpoint, the U.S. Social Security program would indicate that portability is practical as long as revenues are co-mingled and as long as payouts are fairly standardized. And as long as an omnipotent Uncle Sam administers it.

DOUBLE-DIPPERS

The administration in Washington keeps focusing attention on double-dippers. This is a term describing retired military personnel who draw pensions while working for the government. The House Appropriations Committee learned there are 150,000 double-dippers on the federal payroll.

In 1978 there were 33 members of Congress receiving military pensions or Veterans Administration Disability payments. Some of the double-dippers do not keep their pensions. Rep. Charles E. Bennett (D., Fla.) does not accept his $1,040 monthly disability payment. He feels if he is able enough to be a Congressman, he is not disabled.

Military pensions are protected against inflation by cost-of-living increases. On the other hand, widows on veterans' pensions have their checks decreased each time their Social Security benefits increase.

ERISA
EMPLOYEE RETIREMENT INCOME SECURITY ACT

by JOHN W. ANNAS
Vice President Management Counsel
Doherty Associates, Inc.

The Employee Retirement Income Security Act (ERISA), which was enacted September 2, 1974, affects the design, communication and administration of every covered pension or profit-sharing plan. When first introduced, ERISA was an administrative nightmare. As a result, The Department of Labor in December 1976, issued revised rules and regulations regarding minimum standards for participation and vesting under pension plans.

Key points to remember include:

Hours of Service

The basic unit for determining credited service for participation, vesting and benefit accrual is the hour of service, which is defined in the regulations as each hour for which an employee is paid or entitled to payment (including back-pay)

- for the performance of duties, or

- on account of a period of time during which no duties are performed.

Nevertheless, not more than 501 hours of service are required to be credited for any single continuous period during which no duties are performed (regardless of how long that period runs). For example, an employee on long term disability from June 1, 1977 to December 1, 1984 need only be given 501 hours of credit for this 7½-year period.

Under the regulations, payments made from a trust fund or insurer to which the employer contributes are considered payments by the employer. However, payments that just reimburse an employee for medical expenses are not considered payments requiring an hour of service to be credited.

Equivalencies

The regulations permit plans to employ different methods of crediting service using records that do not reflect the actual number of hours of an employee. A plan may use different methods for different classes of employees, provided the classes are reasonable and consistent. If any of these methods is used, the plan must credit hours of service using the following equivalencies:

Equivalencies based on working time:

> 870 hours worked = 1,000 hours of service
> 750 regular time hours = 1,000 hours of service, where regular
> time hours exclude overtime or other hours in excess of the
> standard workweek or workday.

Equivalencies based on periods of employment:

> 1 day   = 10 hours
> 1 week   = 45 hours
> ½ month = 95 hours
> 1 month   = 190 hours
> 1 shift   = number of hours in shift

In using these equivalencies, the number of hours shown (on the right side) must be credited for each period (on the left side) for which the employee is entitled to at least one hour of service.

Equivalencies based on earnings:

If an employee is paid on the basis of an hourly rate, a plan may determine his or her hours by dividing his or her earnings during the year by either—

- his or her hourly rates in effect from time to time in the year

- his or her lowest hourly rate during the year, or

- the lowest hourly rate payable to an employee in a similar job.

A plan using this approach must credit 1,000 hours of service for each 870 hours determined under this method.

A similar approach may be used for employees who are not paid on the basis of an hourly rate if 1,000 hours of service are credited for each 750 hours determined under the method.

Elapsed Time

Before ERISA, most plans used the elapsed time method of counting service. However, since this method was not mentioned in ERISA while the 1,000-hour rule was, the original regulations did not permit elapsed time. The Department of Labor received many protests about this omission and finally, on June 30, 1976, issued a technical release permitting an elapsed time alternative to the 1,000-hour rule. The new regulations contain an elapsed time alternative.

Elapsed time: Elapsed time may be defined as the length of time during which the employee is employed by the employer or employers maintaining the plan, regardless of the actual number of hours worked. Under this method, service is required to be taken into account from the date the employee first performs an hour of service until the employee's severance from service date. When an employee has several periods of service that must be added together, a single adjusted employment commencement date may be used.

Severance from service: The severance from service date is the earlier of the date the employee quits, is discharged, retires or dies, or one year from the date the employee is continuously absent from service for any other reason. This one year period is required to be taken into account as service.

Service spanning: If an employee returns to work within one year after a quit, discharge or retirement, the intervening period must be taken into account for eligibility and vesting purposes, but not for benefit accruals.

Use of elapsed time and 1,000-hour rules: The regulations do not require a plan that uses elapsed time to use it for all purposes. For example, a plan may use elapsed time for vesting and accrual service and the 1,000-hour rule for eligibility service. Similarly, a plan can use elapsed time for certain classes of employees (e.g., full-time) and the 1,000-hour rule for other classes (e.g., part-time), so long as prohibited discrimination does not result. The different rules may not be used to prevent employees from becoming legally entitled to coverage. A plan could possibly use the 1,000-hour rule for employees who work the standard week. On the other hand, a plan could not define part-time employees as employees who have less than 1,000 hours of service and apply the 1,000-hour rule to these employees and elapsed time to the others.

Transfers between methods: Since different methods of counting service may be used for different classes of employees, a problem exists when an employee transfers from a class using the 1,000-hour rule or vice versa. The regulations cover this contingency. In general when the transfer is within the same plan, credit must be given up to the date of transfer on the basis of credit under the original method plus, for the computation period including the date of transfer, credit must be given in such a manner that the employee is no worse off than if he hadn't transferred.

When an employee transfers between two plans of the employer that use different methods, all service under the plan he or she transfers to must be redetermined using the method applicable to the plan to which the employee transfers.

Break in service: An employee incurs a one-year period of severance under elapsed time if he or she does not perform an hour of service in the year following his or her severance from service date. If the period of severance of a nonvested employee is at least as long as his or her service prior to severance, he or she may lose credit for all service before the break. This is similar to the rule of parity under the 1,000-hour rule with one important distinction: under the 1,000-hour rule, service and breaks in service are measured only in full years; under elapsed time they are measured in years and fractions of a year.

A plan may not disregard a period of service of less than one year until an employee has incurred a period of severance of at least one year.

Eligibility Computation Period

An eligible employee must be allowed to participate in a plan if he or she is 25 years old and has completed one year of service. If the plan provides for full and immediate vesting, the plan may require three years of service and age 25 before the employee is eligible to participate. A plan of a tax-exempt educational organization which provides full and immediate vesting for all participants may require participants to be age 30 and have one year of service.

The eligibility computation period, which establishes initial eligibility to participate, is the 12-consecutive-month period beginning on the day the employee completes his or her first day of service. An employee who completes 1,000 hours of service during this period is credited with one year of service for eligibility purposes.

If an employee does not complete 1,000 hours of service between his or her employment commencement date and the first anniversary of employment, the 12-consecutive-month period begins again. The 1,000 hours of service must then be completed between the first and second anniversary dates of employment, and so on.

An alternative to this method is to shift the eligibility computation period to coincide with the plan year after the first 12-month period. A plan may designate plan years beginning with the plan year that includes the first anniversary of an employee's employment commencement date. For example, assume the plan year is the calendar year and an employee is hired on September 5, 1977. The first period to be tested would be September 5, 1977 to September 4, 1978. If the employee has 1,000 hours in either the employment or the calendar year, he or she must be credited with at least one year of eligibility service. If he or she has 1,000 hours in both periods, he or she may be credited with two years of eligibility service.

Vesting Computation Period

The vesting computation period may be any 12-consecutive-month period designated by the plan. It must apply uniformly to all employees.

If the vesting computation period is changed to a different 12-consecutive-month period, the last day of the first computation period must be included in the new vesting computation period. In addition, no employee's vested percentage may be less on any date after such change than it would be if the change were not made.

After an employee has completed the eligibility requirements, all years of service are counted toward vesting, except for service forfeited under break-in-service rules. However, a plan does not have to count service toward vesting during the following periods—

- when an employee elected not to make a mandatory a contribution

- when the employer did not have a plan

- during years of service before age 22 (but years of service as a plan participant before age 22 must count under the rule of 45)

- during service before January 1971, unless the employee has at least 3 years of service after December 31, 1970.

If an employee does not complete more than 500 hours of service during the vesting computation period, a break in service may occur. Service before a break is nonforfeitable if the participant has some vested rights before the break in service. If a vested employee completes a year of service following the break, the years before the break will be counted for vesting purposes. An employee must complete 1,000 hours of service during his or her reemployment vesting computation period in order to have completed a year of service.

Rule of parity: A rule of parity is applied to an employee who has no vested rights and who incurs a break in service. This rule states that an employee forfeits the service before his or her break if the number of consecutive one-year breaks equals or exceeds the years of service before the break.

Accrual Computation Period

The accrual computation period may be any 12-consecutive-month period designated by the plan. It must apply uniformly to all employees.

The plan sets the number of hours of service required for full accrual of benefits for a year of participation. Although the plan must credit a year of service for eligibility and vesting purposes after 1,000 hours of service, it may require, say, 2,000 hours of service to accrue a full year's benefit. However, if an employee completes 1,000 hours of service during the accrual computation period, the plan must credit him or her with a proportionate part of a year for benefit accrual.

Special rules apply if an employee begins participation in a plan on a date other than the first day of an accrual computation period.

Many defined benefit plans prorate accruals where the employee has less than a full year of service. Either the benefit or the service may be prorated, but not both.

For example, assume a plan provides a benefit of $6 per month for each year of service, and 1,800 hours are required to get the full benefit. If an employee works 1,200 hours, the plan can compute the benefit in one of two ways:

- the plan can consider 1,200 hours as $2/3$ of a year and accrue a benefit of $\$6 \times 2/3 = \$4$, or

- the plan can prorate the $6 for $2/3$ of a year but give a year of service. In this case also $\$6 \times 2/3 = \$4$.

In this example the plan cannot use a benefit of $4 and $2/3$ of a year of service to get a benefit of $\$4 \times 2/3 = \$2.67$. This would be a prohibited double proration. Similar rules apply for benefits based on earnings.

Break in Service

A one-year break in service may occur if an employee does not complete more than 500 hours of service in a computation period. The eligibility computation period is used to determine breaks in service for eligibility to participate, while the vesting computation period is used to determine breaks in service for vesting. The vesting computation period also is used to measure completion of a year of service for vesting after a break. If an employee reenters the plan after a break in service, he or she may be treated as a new employee and have a new eligibility computation period. The new eligibility computation period is the 12-consecutive-month period following the first date on which the employee completes an hour of service after a break in service.

The 500 hours of service for a break represent one-half of the 1,000 hours required for a year of service. Similarly, under methods where 870 or 750 hours are equivalent to a year of service, half of these, or 435 and 375 hours, respectively, are the criteria for determining breaks.

Controlled Groups

Rules on coverage under multiple employer plans, plans maintained by controlled groups of corporations and commonly controlled trades or businesses, and multi-employer plans are also found in these regulations.

Participants of a plan maintained by more than one employer will be treated as though there is a single employer if they maintain continuity of either employment or plan coverage. Credit must be given for participation, vesting and accrual purposes if the participant moves from covered service with one employer to covered service with another.

Multiple employer plans: When an employee moves from uncovered service with one employer participating in the plan to covered service with another, he or she need not be credited for uncovered service since neither continuity of employment nor plan coverage is maintained. This kind of move is called noncontiguous noncovered service in the regulations.

Controlled groups: Similarly, all employees of corporations that are members of a controlled group of corporations or trades or businesses that are commonly controlled will be treated as if they have one employer. All service with any member that maintains a plan will be credited for eligibility and vesting purposes.

Final Thought

ERISA rules now offer more flexibility than at first, and further change may be in the picture. Before deciding whether to make changes in the company plan, an actuary should be retained to ensure that the latest interpretations are considered and employed. According to Murphy's law, anything that can change will.

PRERETIREMENT COUNSELING

A satisfactory definition of retirement is difficult to formulate because of the many variables associated with the concept of retirement.

In many cases it means the complete breaking away from useful and productive employment. For some people it is a change to another occupation, full time or part time, generally for lower earnings. To others it is little more than working on "make do" activities on a reduced time basis. It can also be the beginning of a new career at an age when adapting to change is fraught with uncertainty.

For all it is a reliance on resources other than wages.

All of this can be very traumatic to the employee nearing retirement. Individuals should be encouraged to plan for retirement and companies should help prepare them for this last big step in their lives.

Most people, rich and poor alike, share deep-seated anxieties about retirement and aging which cause them to avoid thinking seriously about these two realities. Then because of this shortsightedness, they find themselves overwhelmed by a sudden large amount of free time, trapped by idleness, poverty and loneliness.

To reduce the impact of this sad situation, preretirement counseling is proposed. There are compelling reasons for establishing such a program, beyond the expected increase in morale and the value of improved public relations.

A person who is retiring should be prepared for it emotionally, psychologically as well as economically. He should be given the opportunities to learn how to use his time, skills and experience constructively so that he can continue to contribute to and participate in both the nation's economy and society. He should be able to hold his head high instead of feeling that he has been discarded.

The latest Dartnell survey on this subject shows that 40% of the 250 companies contacted offer some form of preretirement counseling and 13% more expect to begin soon.

In these companies, counseling takes the form of classes, seminars, private consultations, films and publications. The formats differ but the subject matter does not.

Topics include eligibility requirements for medicare and social security, living on a reduced income, tax and estate planning, housing and relocation, use of leisure time, stress and other health-related issues, legal affairs, and making the adjustment from worker to retiree.

Perhaps the philosophy behind such programs is best summarized in a "Retirement Awareness" statement issued by Brandon Mental Health Centre, Brandon, Manitoba. It reads:

"As management is becoming aware of retirement as more than a gift-giving, farewell speech party for the faithful old employee, so too is the feeling of responsibility growing to provide employees with 'planning material' to meet the challenge of the retirement years."

While a growing number of companies feels a responsibility for preretirement counseling, it is noteworthy to point out that very few companies keep in touch with these former loyal employees and offer post-retirement programs. This sorry state of affairs can be expected to draw attention in the future.

AIM PRERETIREMENT COUNSELING

Action for Independent Maturity (AIM) conducts retirement planning seminars for companies. The topics discussed are:

1. *Challenge of Retirement.* What changes you'll want to make. How challenges can create opportunities. Adding more years to your life. New life to those years. Scaling new peaks of knowledge.

2. *Health and Safety.* How retirement will affect your health. The value of medical checkups. The best forms of exercise. Prevention of major medical problems. How to anticipate potential accident-causing conditions. Suggested safety precautions. Proper nutrition in the later years. Where to get medical information and help.

3. *Housing and Location.* Where do most people retire? Is there a perfect climate? What about the cost of living? How to stay put. Do you want to move? Your choices of housing. How to get housing you need, want and can afford.

4. *Legal Affairs.* Your legal obligations in everyday transactions. Special situations of retirement. When you may need a lawyer and how to choose one. Special legal considerations of contracts; buying, selling and renting. Types of ownership. How a will shows you care and saves you money. Problems of probate. Estate planning. Other legal rights and obligations.

5. *Attitude and Role Adjustments.* Changes as a way of life. Humor is happiness. Shifting roles in retirement. Retirement: Danger time

for marriage? How to be a happy grandparent. Keep your friendships in repair. What about the single older person? Late or second marriages. If you are widowed? Steps to happier living at any age or state.

6. *Meaningful Use of Time.* What is leisure? Factors that mold our concept of leisure. What we want from the time we spend. Activities for self-expression, "fun and games," participation, recognition, adventure, learning, physical fitness or income.

7. *Sources of Income.* Where will the money come from? Emergency money, guaranteed money, investment money and extra money. How much will you have? Where can you get more? How adequate will it be?

8. *Financial Planning.* How much money will you need? What will you spend it on? How to budget your money. Practical tips on cutting expenses on housing, food, medical care, clothing, transportation, taxes, personal and miscellaneous items. Should you take early retirement?

POST-RETIREMENT SERVICES

The notion that once employees retire the company has no further obligation is no longer valid. Retirees are not outcasts. It is downright inhuman to abandon them and ignore their plight. This neglect merely reinforces their feeling of being "the forgotten employees."

There are many services a company could provide for employees after they've retired. If they are still carried in the employee group insurance plan, with medicare benefits carved out, it is important to update the coverage when necessary, by increasing major medical ceiling, adding drug or dental, and assisting them in claims filing. Legal and financial questions could be answered and advice by company specialists could be offered. In some cases possibly secretarial services and copying machines could be made available. Helpful mailing can be subscribed to.

Mostly companies should keep abreast of money concerns. The predicament of retirees as they stand helplessly watching their fixed incomes being eroded as management and labor fuel the fires of inflation is changing from concern to worry. Protection against cost-of-living rises through automatic escalator clauses is already built into 10% of private retirement plans. What are the other 90% doing?

All military and federal pensions are automatically adjusted. The Social Security Administration recognized the fairness of this policy and since 1972 Social Security payments are increased proportionally when the Consumer Price Index rises by as much as three percent.

The reason for active interest in retirees is not altogether altruistic. This change in policy benefitting retired employees is also a morale booster for current employees. In today's competitive labor market for key personnel and scarce talent that consideration could be a big plus for a company trying to develop or maintain a good image.

SOCIAL SECURITY

The Social Security Administration administers the federal programs of retirement, survivors, disability insurance benefits and health insurance for people 65 and over (Medicare).

The basic idea of Social Security is simple. During working years employees, their employers and self-employed people pay Social Security contributions, which go into special funds. When earnings stop or are reduced because the worker retires, dies or becomes disabled, monthly cash benefits are paid from the funds to replace part of the earnings the family has lost.

Part of the contributions go into a separate hospital insurance trust fund so that when workers and their dependents reach 65 they will have help in paying their hospital bills (this is Medicare Part A). Voluntary medical insurance (Medicare Part B), also available to people 65 and over, helps pay doctor bills and other medical expenses. The Part B program is financed out of premiums shared half-and-half by the older people who sign up and the federal government.

Apart from Medicare, basic Social Security is the nation's method of providing a continuing income when family earnings stop or are reduced because of retirement, disability or death.

Nine out of 10 workers in the United States are earning protection under Social Security. Nearly one out of every seven persons in the country receives monthly Social Security checks.

Through the years since Social Security was enacted in 1935, there have been many changes to improve the protection it gives to workers and their families. At first, Social Security covered only the worker upon retirement. In 1939 the law was changed to pay survivors when the worker died, as well as certain dependents when the worker retired.

Social Security covered only workers in industry and commerce when the program began. But in the 1950's, coverage was extended to include most self-employed persons, most state and local employees, household and farm employees, members of the Armed Forces, and members of the clergy.

Disability insurance was added in 1954 to give workers protection against loss of earnings due to total disability.

795

As a result of legislation enacted in 1972, Social Security benefits will increase automatically in the future as the cost of living goes up. Legislation passed in 1977 restored the financial soundness of the program.

Retirement Payments

The amount of a worker's retirement payment is figured from his average earnings under Social Security. A worker can start receiving benefits as early as age 62. But, if he starts benefits before he reaches 65, the amount of his benefit will be permanently reduced. If a person works after he starts getting benefits, and his added income will result in higher benefits, his benefit will be automatically refigured at the end of the year.

Disability Payments

A worker who becomes disabled before 65 may be eligible for benefits. A person is considered disabled only if he has a mental or physical condition which prevents him from doing any substantial, gainful work and is expected to last or has lasted for at least 12 months or is expected to result in death.

Family Payments

Monthly payments can be made to certain of the worker's dependents when the worker gets retirement or disability benefits, or when the worker dies. These dependents are:

- Unmarried children under 18, or 22 if they are full-time students. Unmarried children 18 or over who were severely disabled before 22 and continue to be disabled.

- A wife or husband 62 or over.

- A widow or widower 60 or older.

- A wife, widow, widower or surviving divorced mother if caring for a worker's child under 18 or disabled and the child gets payments based on the worker's record.

- A wife 62 or older, or widow or widower 60 or older, even if there are no children receiving payments.

Payments may also be made under certain conditions to a divorced wife. After a worker dies, monthly payments may be made to his dependent parents at 62.

A wife who chooses to receive benefits before she is 65 and a widow who chooses to receive benefits before she is 60 will receive permanently reduced benefits.

Tax Exemption

Social Security payments are not subject to federal (and probably in most states) income tax.

Financing

Federal retirement, survivors and disability benefits, and hospital insurance are paid by contributions based on covered earnings. Employed persons and their employers share the responsibility of paying contributions. Self-employed people pay contributions for retirement, survivors and disability insurance at a slightly lower rate than the combined rate for an employee and his employer. The hospital insurance contribution rate is the same for the employee, employer and self-employed person.

Contributions are deducted from an employee's wages each payday. His employer sends them, with an equal contribution as his own share, to the District Director of Internal Revenue.

A self-employed person reports his earnings and pays his contributions when he files his individual federal income tax return each year.

Keeping income and payouts in balance is a delicate problem. The deficit is well publicized. The two factors contributing to the revenue imbalance are:

1. Inflation, which automatically triggers increases in benefits that must be paid.
2. Recession, which cuts into payroll tax revenues as more workers lose their jobs or retire early.

A person's earnings are entered on his own record by the Social Security Administration. This record of earnings is used to determine a person's eligibility for benefits and the amount of cash benefits he will receive.

Individual Verification

With the Social Security tax climbing, the amount of tax withheld each year adds up to a substantial amount. Workers can and should check on the accuracy of the earnings credited to their individual accounts every few years to make certain they are getting all the benefits they are entitled to.

To get the complete picture, a worker should complete and mail post card form OAR-7004, available at local Social Security offices.

The government's statement will show the number of quarters of coverage which have been credited to a worker's account, the total earnings for all the years worked under the Social Security system, and the earnings credited for each of the past three complete calendar years.

A worker should compare this statement with the yearly W-2 forms provided by his employer. Since the last three years are the only complete listings, it is best to check the Social Security statement at least every three years for accuracy.

If an error is found, it must be reported within three years, three months and fifteen days after the period covered by the report or correction may not be possible. It would be a good idea to inform employees of this fact as they, too, have an interest in what they have accrued.

Identification Cards

Every person must have a Social Security number if his work is covered by the Social Security law or if he receives certain kinds of taxable income. A Social Security card can be obtained at any Social Security office.

Social Security Offices

There are over 1,300 Social Security offices located conveniently throughout the United States. These offices have representatives who go regularly to other communities.

The people in these offices will be glad to answer questions about Social Security. The address of the nearest Social Security office can be found by looking in a telephone directory under Social Security Administration or asking at the nearest post office.

For more information about Social Security, ask for a free copy of the booklet "Your Social Security."

SOCIAL SECURITY TRENDS

In a speech sponsored by The Conference Board, A. Haeworth Robertson, chief actuary of the Social Security Administration, listed seven points as reasonable expectations of Social Security trends. These are the kinds of changes that can be expected in the present law and in the behavior of the population covered by that law.

1. Taxpayers must become accustomed to paying higher taxes for social security benefits unless benefits are reduced below current levels. It is just not possible to pay for the current social security benefit levels with the taxes now being collected.

2. The automatic adjustment provisions must be revised so that replacement ratios will not continue to rise.

3. Beginning about 25 to 35 years from now employees will probably be working longer and retiring at higher ages. For this to be feasible, the present socioeconomic arrangements must be revised to

YOUR SOCIAL SECURITY RECORD

If you want a statement of your social security earnings, please fill in the other side of this card.

In the space marked "Social Security Number," show your number *exactly* as it is shown on your social security card. We need your correct number to identify your record. If you have more than one social security number, give all of them.

You do not need to pay anyone to help you get a statement of your earnings. There is no charge for this service.

Be sure to put a stamp on this card before mailing it.

FORM OAR-7004 (3-74)

POSTAGE REQUIRED

SOCIAL SECURITY ADMINISTRATION

P.O. BOX 57

BALTIMORE, MARYLAND 21203

REQUEST FOR STATEMENT OF EARNINGS

SOCIAL SECURITY NUMBER →

DATE OF BIRTH →

MONTH	DAY	YEAR

Please send a statement of my social security earnings to:

NAME _____

STREET & NUMBER _____

CITY & STATE _____ ZIP CODE _____

Print Name and Address In Ink Or Use Typewriter

SIGN YOUR NAME HERE (DO NOT PRINT) _____

Sign your own name only. Under the law, information in your social security record is confidential and anyone who signs another person's name can be prosecuted. If you have changed your name from that shown on your social security card, please copy your name below exactly as it appears on your card.

"Request for Statement of Earnings" postcard, mailed to the Social Security Administration in Baltimore, Maryland, to verify an individual's Social Security record.

SOCIAL SECURITY

The tax rate for 1985 and later years is as follows:

In	Rate
1985	7.05%
1986–87	7.15%
1988–89	7.51%
1990 and later	7.65%

When Congress passed an amendment in 1977, establishing the above rates, the "parity tradition" was preserved. This means that employers and employees will continue to pay equal amounts.

The wage base (amount subject to tax) is adjusted automatically each year on the basis of the annual increase in average wage levels in covered employment.

make it easier for persons to continue working until advanced ages, perhaps in less strenuous jobs, part-time employment, etc. This development could lessen the financial problems of the social security program during the next century. A later effective retirement age is tantamount to a reduction in benefits.

4. It seems unlikely that the traditional financing methods will continue to be the sole source of tax revenue for the program. This will probably result in the use of some form of nonpayroll tax for at least one-third of total social security expenditures sometime after the turn of the century.

5. Social and economic changes in the nation will result in a substantial revision of the program. The changing role of the family unit and of women; changing patterns in the incidence of work, education and leisure throughout a person's lifetime; lengthening life expectancy and improved health in old age; an increased (or reduced) need to work in order to maintain the desired standard of living; all of these changes and more will require that drastic revisions be made in the benefit structure if the evolving economic security needs are to be satisfied appropriately.

6. If the nation experiences sustained inflation at relatively high levels, it is likely that the portion of an individual's economic security needs which can be met by the private sector will decrease over time; the needs must somehow be met; and the Federal government will be left as the only entity with the audacity to make unqualified promises to pay benefits 75 to 100 years in the future based upon indeterminable, cost-of-living increases.

7. Some way will be found to make participation compulsory for all State and local employees. Alternatively, if and when nonpayroll taxes are used to a significant degree to finance social security, State and local employees may insist on being covered by social security in order to receive their money's worth from their general taxes. Full participation by all State and local employees and Federal civil servants would reduce the long-range cost of the social security program by about two percent (i.e., less than ½ per cent of taxable payroll).

In the future, public understanding or misunderstanding will play a much more critical role in determining the shape of the program than it has in the past when the payroll tax was relatively low and when the taxpayer was in a less-questioning frame of mind.

THE ORIGIN OF SOCIAL SECURITY

The Social Security system had its origin in Germany in the 19th century. Chancellor Otto von Bismarck pioneered the program, not out of humanitarian concern, but for political advantage.

It was a way to produce revenue. Ten years after his death in 1898, his pension scheme recorded a $26 million profit for the government.

Bismarck engineered compulsory retirement for workers at age 65 in order to undermine the opposition which appealed to workers with proposals for social reforms. "Why should not the labor soldier receive a pension, just as much as the man who has been disabled or grown old in the army of civil service?" he argued.

His idea had popular appeal. But the cunning Bismarck knew that 98% of industrial workers of the day died before age 65.

In 1883, the German Parliament approved Bismarck's plan for mandatory insurance against sickness. The next year it enacted his bill for state-regulated insurance against accidents. The capstone of his welfare program became law in 1889 when he prevented a nationwide strike by the railroad, and walkouts in other key industries, by offering compulsory, pensioned retirement at age 65.

Later amendments provided for contributions by workers, employers and government to a pension fund administered by government.

The crafty Bismarck reasoned that money spent on pensions was a good investment since it kept people content and easier to manage.

RAILROAD RETIREMENT

The Railroad Retirement Board administers a federal retirement-survivor and unemployment-sickness benefit system for railroad workers and their families. The retirement-survivor program is a two-tier plan in which the first tier benefits are the equivalent of social security benefits and the second tier benefits are comparable to industrial pensions paid over and above social security benefits. The unemployment and sickness benefits can be compared with some of the more liberal state programs. Coverage is confined to employees in, or closely affiliated with, the railroad industry.

Retirement and Survivor Benefits

Regular Retirement Annuities

The following paragraphs refer to annuities applied for since January 1, 1975, when certain eligibility requirements were liberalized.

The minimum work requirement for regular retirement annuities is 10 years (120 months) of service. An employee receives credit for a month of service for every calendar month in which he (she) worked for a covered employer. All railroad service after 1936 is creditable. Railroad service before 1937 and time spent in military service are creditable under certain conditions.

With 10 years of service, an employee may begin to draw a full annuity at age 65 or a reduced annuity at ages 62–64. With 30 years of service, the employee can retire on a full annuity at age 60 (called a 60/30 retirement).

An employee with 10 years' service who is permanently disabled for all regular employment can receive a disability annuity at any age. If an employee is permanently disabled for work in his (her) regular railroad job, he (she) may start drawing a disability annuity at any age after 20 years of service or at age 60 after 10 years of service. To be eligible for this occupational disability annuity, the employee must have had a prescribed pattern of recent employment in the railroad industry (called a "current connection").

The spouse of a 60/30 retiree may qualify for a full annuity at age 60, or at any age if caring for a minor or disabled child. The spouse of a railroader 62 or over retired since 1974 with less than 30 years of service may qualify for a full annuity at age 65 (or at any age if caring for a minor or disabled child) or a reduced annuity as early as age 62.

Supplemental Retirement Annuities

In addition to a regular retirement annuity, the employee may receive a supplemental annuity. To qualify, the employee must be 65 or older (60 or older for 60/30 retirees) and have at least 25 years of railroad service and a "current connection." Supplemental annuities are payable only to employees who were awarded regular annuities after June 1966.

Survivor Insurance Benefits

Survivors of railroad workers may receive monthly and lump-sum benefits. The eligibility of an employee's family for monthly benefits depends on whether the employee was "insured" at the time of his death. To be insured, the deceased employee must have had at least 10 years of railroad service and a "current connection." Otherwise the social security system has jurisdiction over the case.

If the employee leaves a widow(er), she (he) is eligible for an annuity at age 60 if she (he) does not remarry. The widow(er)'s annuity may begin before she (he) is 60 if she (he) is caring for a child who is under 18 or disabled, or if the widow(er) is at least age 50 and disabled.

Each of the employee's unmarried children under 18 can receive an annuity. An older child can also receive an annuity if he (she) became permanently disabled before 18 or if he (she) is a full-time student under 22.

If the employee leaves no widow(er) or child eligible for an annuity, his (her) dependent, unremarried parents can receive annuities at age 60.

An insurance, lump-sum benefit is payable when a survivor annuity is not immediately payable. The payment is made to the widow(er) if there is one; otherwise it can be used to reimburse the person who pays the employee's funeral expenses.

Residual Payments

There is one type of death benefit for which an insured status is not required. This benefit, called the residual payment, is payable if the total of the retirement benefits paid on the basis of the employee's railroad earnings and all survivor benefits paid by the Board or Social Security amount to less than the total retirement taxes the employee paid before 1975.

Amounts of Benefits

The amounts of the retirement benefits paid to an employee and spouse are generally related to the employee's railroad earnings and the length of railroad service. Benefits are based on the employee's combined railroad retirement and social security earnings and are subject to a reduction when social security benefits are also payable. Under the retirement program, railroad employees and their families are guaranteed that their monthly benefits will be at least equal to the amount social security would pay in a similar case. Survivors receive benefits roughly 30% higher than their social security equivalents.

Transfer of Credits

The railroad credits of employees who have less than 10 years of service when they retire or die are transferred by the RRB to the Social Security Administration. Railroad credits are also transferred if the employee is not insured at the time of death. In any event, survivor insurance benefits are based on combined railroad and social security earnings and are paid by only one agency.

Filing for Benefits

The best way to apply for retirement or survivor benefits is to visit an RRB field office. When a benefit is awarded, the Board will explain how working affects benefits and other conditions governing the payment of benefits.

Financing

The regular retirement and survivor programs are supported by taxes paid on employee earnings by the worker and the employer. Railroad employers deduct the employee's share of the taxes from his (her) paychecks. The employee's taxes are, in effect, equal to social security taxes; employers pay the social security rate plus an additional 9.5%.

The supplemental annuity program is financed separately by a special tax on railroad employers. Employees do not contribute to the plan.

Health Insurance Benefits

Railroad workers and family members have the same Medicare protection as workers covered by social security. The Medicare hospital insurance plan pays most of the costs of hospital and related care. It is supported by payroll taxes paid by employees and their employers. The Medicare supplemental medical insurance plan, which is voluntary, helps to pay doctor bills and charges for other medical expenses. Persons who enroll in the medical insurance plan pay a small monthly premium for the additional coverage. The Federal Government makes at least a matching contribution.

Unemployment and Sickness Benefits

Railroad employees may receive unemployment benefits when they are out of work, provided they are able to work and available for work. They can also receive sickness benefits when they are unable to work because of sickness or injury (including pregnancy, miscarriage and childbirth).

A new benefit year for unemployment and sickness benefits begins every July 1st. To be qualified in a benefit year, the employee must have earned at least $1,000 in railroad work in the preceding calendar year (base year), counting no more than $400 in any month. Also, if the employee had newly entered the railroad industry in the base year, he (she) must have worked for a railroad in at least five months of that year.

The amount an employee receives depends on how long he (she) is unemployed or sick and on his (her) railroad earnings in the base year. Unemployment and sickness benefits can each be paid for up to 26 weeks in a benefit year. Extended unemployment and sickness benefits are available for long-service employees who exhaust their normal benefits. Extended unemployment benefits are also available to new employees during periods of high unemployment in the nation or the industry.

To claim unemployment benefits, a railroad worker should call in person at a railroad unemployment claim agent's office. Sickness benefits can be claimed by mail. The necessary application forms for sickness benefits can be obtained at any RRB office.

The funds to pay unemployment and sickness benefits are provided by a payroll tax paid only by railroad employers.

Service and Earnings Records

The Railroad Retirement Board maintains records of the service and earnings of railroad employees after 1936. This information is recorded under employee social security account numbers.

Each year, the Board issues statements of service months and compensation (form BA-6) to individual employees working in the railroad industry. The form gives each employee a record of his (her) cumulative service and earnings since 1936 and of his (her) service and earnings in the most recent calendar year.

Railroad Retirement Board Offices

The headquarters office of the Railroad Retirement Board is in Chicago, Illinois, at 844 Rush Street, 60611. There are about 100 field offices in localities easily accessible to a large number of railroad workers. In addition, the Board maintains part-time service in outlying areas. The address of the nearest Board office can be obtained at any post office.

For more detailed information on the Board's program, ask for booklet IB-2, *Railroad Retirement and Survivor Benefits;* booklet UB-9, *Unemployment and Sickness Benefits for Railroad Workers;* or booklet RB-20, *Medicare for Railroad Workers and Their Families.*

PROFIT SHARING

In Profit Sharing Research Foundation literature, profit sharing is defined as "any method of raising output and lowering costs through human cooperation which is brought about through the direct participation of the employees (in addition to their regular wage) in the total results of the enterprise as measured by profits."

Some people feel that a definition such as the one above tends to beg the question. That is, raising output and lowering costs is a hoped-for result of profit sharing, not really a part of its definition.

In the constitution and by-laws of the Profit Sharing Council of America, profit sharing is defined as "any procedure under which an employer pays or makes available to regular employees subject to reasonable eligibility rules, in addition to prevailing rates of pay, special current or deferred sums based on the profits of the business."

The essential distinguishing mark of a profit sharing plan is that company contributions to the plan fluctuate with current profit levels. Profit sharing programs are thereby differentiated from individual incentive plans, group production plans, Christmas bonuses (not tied to profits), thrift plans, pensions and stock purchase plans. Plans

There are two fundamental approaches to profit sharing:

1. *Current Distribution Plans,* often called *Cash Plans,* where cash is paid to an employee as soon as profits are determined—monthly, quarterly, semiannually, but most often yearly.

2. *Deferred Distribution Plans,* where the employee's share is put into a fund to be distributed to him at some later time, such as retirement, or other dates or stated circumstances, such as disability, death, severance or under withdrawal provisions during employment.

All profit sharing plans stem from these two basic types, but can branch into almost endless variations. For instance, plans may have combination cash and deferred elements side by side, be contributory or noncontributory on the part of employees, have broad coverage with all or almost all employees included, or have limited coverage with only specified groups participating.

Further, the percentage of profits distributed, rules of eligibility and participation, methods of payment, and other considerations differ from company to company. Plans may have many features in common and other elements that are as unlike as fingerprints. Profit sharing is an incentive system and productivity booster whose design, application and approach vary from one company to another, according to the needs and problems of the individual firm.

Objectives

Among the objectives of profit sharing plans are inspiring a sense of partnership, incentive, security, attracting and retaining capable people, rewarding employees, economic education and flexibility of compensation.

Many executives feel that profit sharing satisfies a deficiency in modern corporations by restoring to individual employees the traditional vital element of personal involvement in the fortunes of the enterprise. They claim profit sharing both demonstrates and encourages partnership in industry. In that sense profit sharing is not donating a part of the profits to workers but rather sharing with them the earnings resulting from greater efficiency.

The final test of profit sharing must always be, "Can a company get greater profits by giving some profit away?"

Tax Treatment

There are many benefits derived from favorable tax treatment accorded deferred profit sharing plans. Once a deferred plan has been qualified by the Internal Revenue Service, company and participants enjoy these major advantages:

1. The amounts contributed by an employer are tax deductible up to 15% of the compensation paid to participants. What's more, the 15% limit has credit and contribution "carryover" features for flexibility during good and poor profit years. The fund member does not pay a

A quick look at profit sharing's two major plans:

	Current Distribution	Deferred Distribution
Distribution of profits	Monthly, quarterly, semiannually, but most often yearly	On retirement, disability, death or severance or some financial emergency
Chief advantages	Strong incentive—employee sees "immediate" results in cash	Earned security—employee sees comfortable, dignified retirement ahead
Service required for eligibility	3 months to a year	Longer periods, usually 12–18 months
Permit employee savings or contributions	None	⅓ to ½ plans do
Allocation most influenced by	Pay scale and individual performance	Compensation and years of employment
Employee ability to borrow against share	None	1 in 4 plans
Employee ability to withdraw part of his account	Employee receives everything in cash	1 in 2 plans
Vesting rights	Immediate	Usually graduated at approximately 10% per year
Administration	Relatively simple	More complicated—usually with some employee representatives
Trustees	None	Corporate trustees (banks) or individual trustees
Investments	None	Common stocks, bonds, guaranteed principal plus interest contract, or combination
Median annual distribution per participant	11% of pay	9% of pay
Tax-free limits	No tax-free provision for employees	Up to 15% of total compensation of participants, with carryover features

BENEFITS

tax on his share of the company's contribution when it is allocated to his account.

2. Profit sharing trust funds enjoy compound growth year after year without taxation. No taxes are paid until distributions are made.

3. Participants may enjoy lower taxes. If they receive their share in installments, it is taxed at ordinary rates, but often this is at retirement when they are in lower tax brackets. If they receive their share as a lump distribution, a combination of capital gains tax and favorable 10-year averaging usually apply.

4. The amount in a participant's account contributed by the employer can pass to a named beneficiary free of estate tax if paid in installments or as an annuity, but not if paid in a lump sum.

5. There is also a $5,000 death benefit exclusion from the deceased member's estate.

Advantages

In addition to tax advantages, deferred plans have these benefits:

1. Profits go into a flexible fund capable of meeting contingencies of retirement, severance, disability or death, and even financial emergencies of employees (i.e., downpayment on home, major home improvement, college education of children, major medical problem).

2. Workers are quick to see how their accounts benefit both from earnings and appreciation on investments.

3. As the individual account grows, it builds an increasing long-term incentive on the part of the employee.

Deferred profit sharing plans, however, are not the only types that have advantages. Cash plans have these advantages:

1. Immediate incentive to better productivity and reduced costs.

2. A tangible reward on a regular basis.

3. Acceptable to all employees—money talks.

4. Female and younger members of the firm tend to prefer it.

5. Direct relationship between profits and distribution is easy for employees to see.

6. Simple to explain to everyone.

7. Easy to administer.

Disadvantages

But cash plans have their weaknesses, too:

1. There are no tax advantages. The distribution is taxable as ordinary income.

2. No security funds are built up for layoff times, for retirement, separation, disability, financial emergencies or death.

3. Employees rarely gain company stock ownership through cash programs.

4. Employees are more apt to consider sharing as their due, with possible adverse effects during years of no or little sharing.

Advice

So challenging is profit sharing that those who have entered into it temper their advice with almost as many "Don'ts" as "Do's." Some of their recommendations are:

1. Don't expect profit sharing to substitute for competent management; profit sharing is no panacea. It cannot produce profits, even in normal times, if management can't.

2. Don't go into profit sharing unless you are willing to accept the worker as your "partner in business"—with whom you will share appropriate responsibility and information as well as profits.

3. Don't expect profit sharing to work unless you contribute enough to motivate your employees.

4. Don't just copy another firm's plan, even in your own industry. Your objectives, your size, your potential differ from other companies.

5. Don't go into profit sharing unless you are willing to expend time and energy communicating the philosophy of profit sharing to employees, stockholders and management at all levels.

On the brighter side, they suggest:

1. Do consider profit sharing if you want to create a unity of purpose, a cohesive team spirit in your company.

2. Do consider profit sharing if you want to give each employee a direct stake in cost reduction and profit improvement, if you want to motivate him to superior performance.

3. Do consider profit sharing if you want to broaden capital property ownership among your employees.

PROFIT SHARING RESEARCH FOUNDATION

The Profit Sharing Research Foundation is a nonprofit, publicly-supported educational foundation, dedicated to discovering and publishing facts about the experiences of companies with profit sharing, employee stock ownership and participative programs:

1. As a practical guide to those designing/operating such programs;

Perpetual Calendar

1786	1781 1787 1798	1782	1777 1783	1778	1779	1785	1792 1804	1776	1788	1812	1784	1796	1780
1797	1810 1821 1827 1838 1849 1855 1866	1793 1799 1805 1811 1822 1833 1839 1850	1794 1800 1806 1817 1823 1834	1789 1795 1801 1807 1818	1790 1802	1791 1803	1832	1816	1828	1840	1824	1808	1820
1809 1815 1826	1877 1883	1861 1867 1878	1845 1851 1862 1873 1879	1829 1835 1846 1857 1863 1874	1813 1819 1830 1841 1847 1858	1814 1825 1831 1842	1860	1844	1856	1868	1852	1836	1848
1837 1843 1854 1865 1871	1894 1900 1906 1917 1923 1934	1889 1895 1901 1907 1918	1890	1885 1891	1869 1875	1853 1859 1870	1888	1872	1884	1896	1880	1864	1876
1882	1945 1951 1962 1973 1979 1990	1929 1935 1946 1957 1963 1974	1902	1903	1886 1897	1881 1887 1898	1928	1912	1924	1908	1920	1892	1916
1893 1899 1905 1911 1922 1933 1939 1950		1985 1991	1913 1919 1930 1941 1947 1958	1914 1925 1931 1942	1909 1915 1926	1910	1956	1940	1952	1936	1948	1904	1944
1961 1967 1978 1989 1995			1969 1975 1986 1997	1953 1959 1970 1981 1987 1998	1937 1943 1954 1965 1971 1982	1921 1927 1938 1949 1955 1966	1984	1968	1980	1964	1976	1932	1972
					1993 1999	1977 1983 1994		1996		1992		1960	2000
												1988	

2. To reveal the role these programs can play in resolving critical socio-economic problems afflicting industrial societies today.

A participative philosophy of management seeks to improve relationships between employees and management, to create a cohesive, cooperative team working toward mutually rewarding goals. This involves:

1. *Information-sharing:* communication, plans and progress, economic education.
2. *Responsibility-sharing:* task redesign, delegation, decentralization, multiple management.
3. *Gain-sharing:* financial participation in productivity/profit gains and/or in corporate ownership.

These programs reinforce and strengthen each other. Together they form a hierarchy of psychic and financial incentives.

PSRF's primary job is to do the research which business, labor, government and academic communities need on sharing/participative programs as they bear upon motivation, productivity, inflation, employment security, labor-management relations, quality of life and retirement income.

For information write to Profit Sharing Research Foundation, 1718 Sherman Avenue, Evanston, Illinois 60201.

PERPETUAL CALENDAR

In personnel administration the occasion to go back, or to look ahead, to establish what day a certain date falls on, comes up often. Old or future calendars are usually not available.

To solve this problem, the perpetual calendar has been designed. To find the day of the week of a past or future year, refer to the previous table that shows how the annual calendars repeat themselves. The years in each column have the same calendar dates.

CHAPTER X

LABOR RELATIONS

LABOR UNIONS

L ABOR, as we know, means work. It is the way people make a living and provide for food, clothing and shelter for themselves and their families.

Usually, when we say people are laboring we associate this with hard work. But this is not necessarily true in today's offices and factories. In the 1800's, however, it really meant hard work. Not only that, but the early employers often ignored the welfare and safety of their employees. Alone the workers were at the mercy of their employers. So they organized unions and sought to better their wages and working conditions.

Any company that gets a union deserves it. Leadership is like water. Companies don't realize until too late that leadership forsaken in one place will find expression in another. An enlightened management could make unionization unnecessary if it wanted to. Many prominent, well-known corporations have proved that.

But a union is not the answer for all employees either. Workers join for various reasons. Very often the objectives an employee is looking for do not materialize after the union gets in.

The strongest unions today are in the fields of construction, entertainment, manufacturing, mining, transportation, printing and publishing. Agricultural workers and white collar employees in such fields as banking, finance and insurance have little union organization.

According to the U.S. Department of Labor, union membership, although gaining in numbers, has not kept pace with employment. While total employment increased, union membership slipped to a smaller percentage. Unions represent a smaller proportion of the American work force than they did a decade ago.

The biggest gains were in the white collar field. Sizeable gains were reported among government workers and women.

Union membership is concentrated in certain geographic areas.

Nearly two-thirds of organized labor is in 10 states. New York, California and Pennsylvania combined contain roughly one-third of the nation's total union membership.

Union Structure

There are two kinds of unions: craft unions and industrial unions. The members of a craft union may work in many different companies; examples are electricians, airplane pilots, barbers, etc. Industrial unions represent diverse workers in certain industries; for example, automobile workers, mine workers and steelworkers have industrial unions.

There are three levels of union organization: (1) the local union, (2) the national or international union, and (3) the federation.

Local unions usually represent groups of workers in a geographic area, such as a city or county. For example, there is the Amalgamated Meat Cutters and Butcher Workmen of North America. Most of the packinghouse workers in the Chicago area are members of this union.

The national or international unions are local unions in a craft or industry joined together. Many of these unions are called international because they have locals outside the United States. The national union supervises the most important union job, collective bargaining. The national union also handles getting new members, promoting laws favorable to labor and welfare.

The American Federation of Labor and Congress of Industrial Organizations (AFL-CIO) are a federation of national and international unions. Of the 16,500,000 union members in the United States about 13,700,000 belong to unions affiliated with the AFL-CIO. Not all national unions belong to the AFL-CIO. The Teamsters and the United Auto Workers are the largest independent unions.

The AFL-CIO has five major activities:

1. To work for laws favorable to labor and general welfare.
2. To help organize workers who are not in unions.
3. To settle disputes and encourage friendly relations among member unions.
4. To take part in the world labor movement through the International Confederation of Free Trade Union.
5. To help educate union members and the general public on the aims of organized labor.

How They Operate

To support his union, every union member pays dues that at one time averaged from $3.00 to $4.00 per month. Today each union member pays from $7.00 to $8.00 dues each month. In addition, there are initiation fees ranging from $5.00 to $25.00 although some unions charge considerably more.

Most union contracts include checkoff agreements requiring employers to withhold fees, dues and assessments from members' paychecks and transfer the money to the union.

Union stewards are elected by fellow employees to assure that all terms and conditions of the contract are given to the employees. The union trains them as to labor history, what contract means, what grievance procedure is, and what they can and what they cannot do. Their big usefulness to employees is that they are easily accessible, will listen to them, and will go to bat for them.

Bargaining between unions and employers is chiefly "bread-and-butter" issues such as pay, overtime, hours and leaves of absence; fringe benefits including sick pay, health insurance, pensions, paid holidays, vacations; promotion policies and work assignments; layoff and recall policies, severance pay and other job security matters.

Strikes get a lot of publicity. Actually, lost time because of strikes totals less than one-third of one percent of all available work time. About 98% of all contract negotiations are concluded without a strike.

Some unions maintain strike funds so that strikers may receive income. Payments often range from $20.00 to $50.00 a week per striker, usually a week or two into the strike. Strike funds are maintained by dues or assessments. Some states allow strikers to draw unemployment compensation.

Shifting Demands

Traditionally, unions have been known to press for higher wages, direct and indirect pay. But with wages getting so high in some industries that jobs are being priced out of the market, union demands change.

Another big factor is the changing demands of the state of the economy. Here a good lesson was learned from the recession of the mid-1970's. When the auto business was booming, the union negotiators were preoccupied with the right of a weary auto worker to refuse to work overtime. After striking Chrysler Corporation, the UAW won at least limited right for its members to turn down extra work.

Three short years later they played the other side of the record. With one-third of their 700,000 Big Three members out of work in 1974, the demands switched to job security. The issue was assuring there is enough work to go around, or failing that, protecting workers' incomes when there isn't.

Shorter work weeks or occasional hours off will spread the work, of course. But the unions still want a full week's pay and no docking for the time off. Their view is the equivalent of an extra paid holiday or extended paid relief period. What it all boils down to is the same or increased payroll costs and less production time.

What Does the Future Hold?

Is greed ruining the union cause? After all, there is a limit on wages, and unrestricted union demands are already doing more damage than good in certain industries.

The trade union is a product of capitalism. It came into being against powerful and cruel capitalist forces at a time when much good needed to be done. But the conditions today are different. Modern managements are more responsive and human resources are gaining the same respect that financial resources have always received. The ruthless capitalist force has been disarmed and the labor union movement can claim much of the credit.

What then is the role of the union after abuses of wages and working conditions are corrected? The original purpose of unions was to bargain for better wages and unfortunately most unions can't bring themselves around to admit they may have achieved that objective. There is a practical limit on how high they can drive wages before they price certain trades right out of the competitive market. Higher wages are not absorbed but are passed on in the form of higher prices until ultimately the consumer does without or is satisfied to accept a cheaper substitute.

The continuing upcycle union wage demands contribute to inflation and thus unionism becomes an agent of national misery. Nobody gains, least of all the working man and woman who pay the higher prices for the union-made products they buy.

Wage inflation punishes those with a social conscience and plays into the hands of the selfish and unscrupulous. It hurts the poor, the aged, the sick and helpless, and the handicapped. These groups are the casualties because they have no way of organizing and are therefore powerless.

Meanwhile, a minority of people and a minority of workers—and organized labor is a minority, albeit a vocal one—look out for their own interests, no matter the consequences of their actions on others. Their smug leadership thinks in terms of greater demands, not sensible constraints. Their pressure is based on power, not logic. One has to wonder, "Where will it all end?"

What the labor movement lacks is statesmanship. It would be appropriate to remind everybody that the main objectives of unions are (or should be) to: (1) help workers get fair and just wages, (2) promote a harmonious relationship between employer and employee, for the benefit of both, and (3) contribute unselfishly to a better society in which to work and live.

THE TRADE UNION MOVEMENT

When talking about unions in general, reference is made to "the trade union movement." And in one sense at least, the word "movement" takes on a different connotation.

There is some serious question whether the unions are moving at all and whether they are moving with the nation's labor force. Are they keeping pace with changes in the economy that has undergone several revolutions?

A labor force that was once—

> manual,
> production-based,
> located in the North and Midwest, and
> contained few women,

has now become—

> mental,
> service-based,
> moving into the South and West, and
> heavily female.

Are the unions moving with the body of labor or is their influence dwindling in the role they've taken for themselves? That is a good question.

THE ORIGIN OF LABOR UNIONS IN THE UNITED STATES

Although labor disputes and movements can be traced as far back as the Middle Ages, this section deals only with their origin in the United States. The establishment of labor unions in this country was solely the result of a growing "new country" and the rise of merchant capitalists prior, during and after the Industrial Revolution. The labor movement in Europe had no visible effect on the birth of unions in this country.

One of the first recorded labor disputes occurred in colonial America around the year 1636. It was over the withholding of wages from a group of fishermen employed by a Robert Trelawney on Richmond Island off the coast of Maine.

The labor movement began in this country after it was sufficiently populated enough to produce settlers with surplus income. When these wealthier settlers needed a home built, furniture made, etc., they would gain the services of what may be called a "master builder." This man soon evolved into a strong employer who gathered together various types of journeymen to accomplish whatever task he had been commissioned to complete. After this master received his pay from the wealthy settler, he would in turn pay the journeymen (withholding, of course, a handsome profit for himself). In these colonial days it may be said then there existed no employer-employee relationship. All prices were set and agreed to verbally, a strong contrast from labor today which must have everything in writing.

As America began to grow, it began to push westward. With this push the number of masters grew and the labor movement began. The movement began to cause labor disputes. The second American labor dispute was recorded in 1676. It appears the city of New York ordered its licensed cartmen to remove dirt from the streets for threepence a load. The cartmen felt this was too low and they banded together in protest and refused to comply. This then was the origin of workers getting together in various trades to protest an alleged injustice by a master craftsman. Many incidents of early labor disputes have been recorded between 1676 and 1792. It should be noted, however, these disputes were not organized protests. They were gatherings of groups of workers to protest verbally an injustice.

Trade Societies Led the Way

During the latter half of the 18th century many trade societies were established. These societies later became the original unions. They were at that time, however, only social organizations formed by various trades for philanthropic purposes such as death benefits, sickness insurance and social activity. Economics fell out of their scope. By the 1790's almost every trade had established a society. In the year 1794 the Federal Society of Journeymen Cordwainers came into existence in Philadelphia. It is considered to be the first real trade union in America. This society was formed for shoemakers only and existed for about 12 years. They conducted their first strike in 1799 and picketed a master's shop for the first time in American history. A few months later in New York a group of journeymen printers established another society, and thus began a long line of societies for all the trades. With the beginning of the 19th century there came into existence societies for artisans and mechanics. Prior to the turn of the century the only societies formed were for printers and shoemakers.

The push of society and civilization toward the West opened up new horizons for the employer. The demand for goods increased and large factories to accommodate these demands began to develop. With the expansion of factories came the competitive markets of employers. In order to meet costs under highly-competitive conditions in the 1880's and 1890's, employers sought to hold down wages. They lengthened the working day to meet production requirements and they looked for cheap labor markets. The search for cheap labor led to the employment of children and foreign immigrants looking for a promised land with no money in their pockets. The employer began to exploit the worker.

With the development of production lines and hiring of unskilled labor there arose a new problem, the discontent of the skilled artisan. He saw this move by the employer as a move to lower the living standard and as a loss of his status. He began to look to the new West for employment. New towns springing up in the West were offering higher wages to the worker. Skilled and unskilled laborers began to move out of the factories in the East, but the employer still ruled the roost. The skilled artisans began to militate and trade societies began to gain new prominence and take a more active part in economics.

Employers Develop Resistance

The employer in the face of stiff competition and the militation of the artisans started to fight back. Employers grouped together to help prevent closed shops caused by strikers belonging to these new trade societies. In most cases they were unsuccessful, and they turned to the courts when they could not cope. They attacked the workers as being conspirators to the restraint of trade. The first such court action occurred in 1806 and the second in 1815. In both cases the employer won. He won because the workers could not defend themselves in court. The judges ruled not against the workers' rights but their methods.

In 1819 a severe depression swept the country and because of the scarcity of jobs most of the trade societies which were taking a more active interest in economics ceased to exist. During most of the 19th century these societies thrived during prosperous periods and died away during depressions. The only trade society which has been recorded as even partially existing during a depression in the 19th century existed during the 1890's. Some of the early leaders of trade societies during those days were Thomas Skidmore, George Henry Evans, Robert Dale Owen and Francis Wright.

Union organization and strong leadership gained a foothold in 1870. There was a depression during this year and as a result a great deal of worker exploitation. Workers began to strike and there was intervention by the police which eventually led to bloodshed and killing for the first time in the history of the American labor movement. Trade societies began to unite and increase. In the year prior to the 1870 strike a new society titled the Knights of Labor was formed. After the strike and bloodshed the society began to grow and amalgamate with other societies and so arose the first "one big union."

Interunion Struggles Arise

With the forming of the big union there came a power struggle within the union. Opposition rose in its ranks. There were many voices of opposition to what the big union interpreted as the "workers interest." One of the loudest voices heard was that of a man named Samuel Gompers. He banded together a strong group of workers and opposed the Knights of Labor. Out of this opposition came the American Federation of Labor (AFL) under the direction of Mr. Gompers. Out of this opposition also came the demise of the Knights of Labor. The day of the American unions had arrived and the day of the small trade society was part of history.

Although Mr. Gompers gained fame after 1896, he had already been an active participator in the moves of various trade societies which had by this time become small individual trade unions. He was born in England but came to America when just a boy. He was a journeyman cigarmaker and joined the cigarmakers union in 1863. He became such an active member that he participated in its reorganization in 1877 and later became president. He became chairman of a committee of a newly-created Federation of Organized Trades and Labor Unions in 1881. It was this organization that grew into the American Federation of Labor and opposed the Knights of Labor. He was president of the AFL from 1886 to 1924 with the exception of the year 1895. He was chiefly responsible for its nurturing and developing. Although unions did not start with Mr. Gompers, it can be said he was the father of the American unions as we know them today. Under his leadership trade societies became local unions, and local unions later became the AFL.

Volume upon volume can be found on labor unions during and after Samuel Gompers. Our discussion concludes with his emergence on the American labor scene since we are concerned here only with its origin. To summarize the history of unions it can be said its history falls into six categories:

1. 1792 to 1827— This was the period of the formation of local trade societies or craft unions.

2. 1827 to 1850— A period of political and social agitation for the craft unions.

3. 1850 to 1866— A period in which the local craft unions began to emerge into a national organization.

4. 1866 to 1886— A period of amalgamation of national craft unions.

5. 1886 to 1935— A period of federation. It was during this period the AFL was formed.

6. 1935 to ____ — A period of industrial unionism. This period has seen the forming of the Congress of Industrial Organizations (CIO) and the merging of the AFL-CIO into a giant voice in the American labor movement.

The time from 1786 to 1886 was the first century of growth and development for the American unions. During most of this century there was no labor movement worthy of the name, although there were several events of the utmost importance to the future of organized labor. Among these events was the first labor dispute court case, establishment of white manhood suffrage, etc. In 1886 the national labor union was formed.

For fifty years (from 1886 to 1936) the American Federation of Labor dominated union history. It was during this period the labor movement took root, established itself, worked out its philosophy and methodology, and became a permanent and accepted part of American life. Today the numbers and history of labor after Samuel Gompers are too great to be treated even generally in one paper. It does suffice to say, however, their influence for good or bad has been greatly felt in the developing of our country and the building of its industry.

MIDDLE MANAGEMENT UNIONIZATION

Discontent is growing among middle management. They're caught in the squeeze between top management's ever-increasing pressure and employee independence and indifference. As organizations expand, and as more staff specialists move into influential positions, the line managers feel left out. What's more, they stand alone trying to maintain morale while their companies become more impersonal toward personnel.

These neglected managers have noted a definite trend toward unionization of professionals and technicians. Class distinction has been wiped out. In many respects, their employees fare better than they do because of protective legislation and group organization. More and more middle managers are looking toward unions for their rightful share of wages, more appropriate fringe benefits, salvageable retirement credits, as well as security in the face of mergers, reorganization and relocations, and especially for a voice in company affairs which affect them.

To counter this development, companies should not take middle management for granted. They too should be given consideration that rank-and-file workers get. Not the least of these considerations is psychic income in the form of status. The communications base should be broadened to include them and they should be encouraged to share in participative management.

COLLECTIVE BARGAINING

Collective bargaining is an American institution of long standing. Employers and employees sit down together to work out their differences and agree upon mutually-acceptable terms for the period of the next contract.

They're in this thing *together*. That is the key word. One cannot exist without the other. Workers need a company to hire them, and the company needs workers to provide the service or manufacture the product. But what is happening in too many cases is that

Labor *and* Management

has become

Labor *vs.* Management

and this situation is detrimental to both. Negotiations are not between friendly enemies. They're more like a grudge match.

The two sides have conflicting goals, and the outcome of bargaining is influenced by the skill of the bargainers. But the common interests are far weightier and far more important to both sides than their differences. They have a common interest in protecting and enhancing the competitive position of the company and industry. And they have a common interest in a healthy, growing economy.

A company, in order to fulfill its part of the bargain, should provide realistic wages, adequate benefits and proper working conditions to meet the reasonable demands and complaints of its employees, in order to build and maintain a capable, industrious and cooperative work force. Management, despite noticeable advances in the field of human relations, still leaves much to be desired in too many cases.

Workers, in return for their demands, should give loyal, dependable and dedicated service. In most large industries and many small companies, too, they are now highly paid and coddled, yet indifferent and indolent.

Management, employees and labor leaders agree on their common interests but they view them from different vantage points. This is where the disagreements come in. When they meet in a bargaining session these disagreements are placed on the table and an attempt made to work out adjustments that are acceptable to both sides.

Differing Viewpoints Need Not Conflict

This process of reconciling conflicting views in order to serve common interests is not a unique feature of labor negotiations. Almost all business relationships and most personal relationships involve some differences in viewpoint between parties who nevertheless share mutual aims.

Generally speaking, such relationships are conducted reasonably, with good will on both sides. The one thing that is unique about bargaining for a new labor-management contract is that reason, composure and mutual respect are often put aside for the duration of the negotiations. Over the years little progress has been made toward reducing the atmosphere of militancy and crisis that surrounds all too many negotiations.

This unpleasant atmosphere is a dangerous anachronism, an obsolete carry-over from the bitter labor-management conflicts of a generation or more back. It survives primarily because the image of management, portrayed as the exploiter of the worker, has become deeply imbedded in union folklore.

Actual bargaining sessions are usually preceded by announced demands. Much of what is demanded in the prenegotiating period may be discounted, although a lot can be learned from the volume, the tone and the content of the union's preliminary barrage.

Present trends are making the problem worse instead of better. In too many situations, particularly those of a big scale which attract national attention, labor and management work *against* each other instead of *with* each other. When they are at loggerheads with each other and the national interest is endangered, public sympathy is alienated, and third party intervention results. Unless new private procedures are devised to assure the settlement of crippling strikes in critical industries, public pressure may bring about compulsory arbitration of labor disputes.

Respect Brings Understanding

To curb this unwelcome development both workers and management must accept that their progress can come only from willing cooperation with each other. To get full cooperation there must be a radical departure from the present relationship between labor and management. Such a change will be difficult to get because of past habits.

Management must regain and retain its logical position as the leader of cooperating workers. The wage-payer still can boss the wage-earner, although in the interests of both some aspects of this authority can be shared with labor unions.

This is not what is happening now. Labor and management too often are at opposite poles, fighting each other instead of fighting together against the common problems that accompany progress. The worker has had to go to the union to get his due. Management's benighted attitude toward the worker has been largely responsible for the situation that exists.

The need is for understanding. The worker is not interested in increasing efficiency of operation when such increased efficiency will result in his losing his job. But neither must the rights of the workers be forced on management by the union. Cooperation is essential to bring a unified effort to the "division of labor" that we call modern industry.

To create this mutually beneficial and constructive climate the habits and conceptions of labor-management relations must be reexamined.

THIRD-PARTY BARGAINING

Something new has been added to collective bargaining in past decades. This is the entrance of a third party to the negotiations.

Outside help in negotiations is of three kinds:

1. Volunteer—requested to participate in bargaining or to set the bargaining policy.
2. Paternal—for guidelines but not participation.
3. Intruding—when the President, the Secretary of Labor or an appointed committee moves in to avoid a stalemate.

Third party intervention is somehow justified by government under the guise of "the national interest"—"the public welfare"—"a national emergency"—"the interest of national defense."

A third party is unwelcome unless it is

1. Requested by both interested parties in the bargaining process, or
2. Required by contract as in the case of arbitrable matters, or
3. Called for by law as in the case of the NLRB and the courts.

Finally, in order to give a flavor of legality and sanctity to all types of intervention, there is now the possibility of Congressional action through the so-called "arsenal of weapons" approach. In this arsenal there are:

1. Fact finding without recommendations.
2. Fact finding with recommendations.
3. Compulsory arbitration.
4. Labor courts.

These weapons might well be used for the actual settlement of labor disputes. Another group, which would include injunction and various forms of seizure, might be proposed to deal with crippling strikes without actually effecting a settlement.

The rising incidence of third-party intervention and the "arsenal of weapons" indicates an increasing vote of no confidence in free collective bargaining. To preserve a sound American institution, both labor and management must rededicate themselves to making two-party, free collective bargaining work. Otherwise they will face legislation which really comes to grips with the basic problem, namely, monopoly power.

WHITHER WHITE-COLLAR UNIONS

Make no mistake about it, the major union forces are out to organize the white-collar workers at all levels. This is nothing more than a battle for survival. The number of blue-collar workers, where unions have centered most of their strength, is decreasing; the number of white-collar workers, which unions have long neglected, is increasing. To maintain their position, unions must follow the trend.

The first step is to convince the white-collar worker that joining a labor union is not unprofessional. The notion that professional workers —the so-called snobs of the white-collar sector—do not join unions is evaporating. Almost half of all salaried nonmanagement professionals are now protected by collective bargaining.

The ranks include teachers, clerical workers, draftsmen, technicians, salesmen, retail clerks, journalists and broadcasters, telephone operators, claims adjusters, social workers, entertainers, doctors, nurses and athletes.

The receptiveness of these hitherto untouchables has three major sides:

1. The attitude of management: indifference has taken over.
2. Public policy: labor laws and court decisions make it easier.
3. Economic gains: group pressure accomplishes results.

In its original context, a white-collar worker was an employee in an occupation that did not require special work clothes. Through usage, the term came to denote work performed in an office rather than a factory. This work was primarily mental rather than physical. It tended to favor formal preemployment education over vocational skills learned from experience or apprenticeship.

The unions, recognizing limitations to their organizing efforts by concentrating on office workers, broadened the term to include professional personnel as well. This move also added stature and removed the stigma that unions were good only for workers in dirty jobs, unable to look after their own welfare.

The term "white-collar worker" now covers office and professional workers, both of whom work for companies or institutions and not for themselves. Like factory workers before them, they also may need protection from unscrupulous employers. The myth that office workers, by virtue of proximity, are close to management, and thereby share some of management's attitudes and advantages, has largely been exploded.

The reasons white-collar workers join unions are:

1. Job security (safety in numbers).

2. Substandard wages.

3. Wage inequities.

4. Inadequate employee benefits

5. No respect for loyalty and length of service.

6. Little personal recognition or appreciation.

7. Favoritism.

8. Unfair and harsh treatment by supervisors (their chance to get even).

9. Failure of company to put policies in writing.

10. A chance to achieve status and social recognition.

If it is true that unions increased their membership by representing faceless workers in sweat-shop factories then it is understandable that they may someday make similar gains in offices. Large offices today, with their work simplification, scheduling and mechanization are really nothing but paperwork factories, guilty of the same inexcusable sins—impersonality and pressure. Office workers are suffering from white collar fever. With no other cure forthcoming, they may be easy to convince that unionization is the best remedy.

WHY OFFICE EMPLOYEES DO OR DO NOT JOIN A UNION

Office employees do not join a union for any number of many reasons, including these:

1. Satisfactory work conditions. Office work is considered better than factory work. It is quieter, cleaner, safer and less tiring. The need to improve work conditions in the office is usually not critical.

2. Loss of status. Office employees, more than shop workers, are identified with management. To them it is generally more important to be associated with those "in the know" than with union co-workers.

3. Loss of individuality. The office offers the worker the last vestige of individuality, the opportunity to be himself. In the factory the rate and conditions fit the job; in the office these are more likely to fit the person.

4. Automatic union benefits. Office employees often get the advantages of unionism without becoming members. As benefits are negotiated for the factory workers in the company, the office employees usually get a "free ride" as the new terms are also made applicable to office employees.

5. Characteristics of office workers. People who are cut out for office work tend to be conservative. They are less eager to change the status quo and less likely to be moved by the appeals of union organizers. Many are women or secondary wage earners whose main interest in life is not centered in a lifetime career with long-term benefits.

What are some of the reasons that office employees join a union? Here are a few:

1. Need to improve conditions. When the work condition, or some part of it, is unsatisfactory, and going through channels fails to bring any results, employees cannot be blamed if they listen to the voice of an outsider who promises to intercede in their behalf.

2. Discontent with wages. If wages are below the community average (and workers know) and the problem is not recognized or its solution is not communicated, employees may actually seek someone to champion their cause. This is especially true where factory workers earn more than office employees, which is so often the case.

3. Inadequate benefits. Fringe benefits are expected to be comprehensive. They should be known and understood by workers. When a situation arises in their personal or family lives for which the

benefits seemed inadequate, workers may feel that management has shortchanged them.

4. No feeling of justice. To whom do they go with their grievances when there is no formal grievance procedure established? They will look for someone to listen to their gripes.

5. Insecurity. The fear of automation, procedural changes, management reorganization and similar changes, if left unanswered, will send employees scurrying for job security measures, such as the protective umbrella of seniority.

6. Poor supervision. Employees want supervisors whom they can look up to and respect. If management leadership is missing, don't be surprised if employees go elsewhere for the guidance they need.

7. Lack of communication. Companies talk about an "open door" policy. But who walks in? In a union representation there is always a steward handy and eager to listen to employees. What's more, he can get a quick answer from management to the employee's question or problem.

More likely than not, employees join a union or do not join a union because of little things. The big problem situations are either well known or soon become evident, and management generally responds with dramatic and prompt action. It's the little things, ordinarily unrecognized and therefore left unattended, which cause the problem. It doesn't take any talent to spot the obvious, but it does call for real managerial acumen to locate the potential trouble spots that are not apparent on the surface.

ORGANIZING EFFORTS

Some day representatives of the millions of organized workers may knock on the door of your company and ask to be admitted. The purpose of this report is to briefly analyze the position you may take as to possible union organization.

The report is divided into four sections:

1. Methods of approach used by union organizers.
2. Possible promises the organizers will make to employees.
3. Company's position in reference to the law.
4. Recommendations as how to deal with the problem.

1. *Methods of approach.* The organizers' first appeal may be made to management in hopes of winning both company approval and endorse-

ment. Typical requests which may be made of management by the organizers could be these:

    a. To make speeches on company time and on company premises.

    b. To distribute leaflets and booklets regarding unions on company time and premises.

    c. For the names and addresses of all employees.

    d. For a desk on company premises to use as a base of operations.

The organizers in appealing to employees will probably use one or a combination of approaches. When they appeal to the employees they might try to win the sympathy and help of key clerical personnel within the company to aid them in their drive. These individuals will be promised positions of importance in the labor union if it wins the election. Another approach could be the use of professional union organizers. The professional organizer knows all the tricks of the trade in "how to win friends and influence people."

The professional organizers commonly use several methods of appeal when they approach workers. The organizers may attempt to get the workers to give up their "vain delusions" of Horatio Alger success. They will tell the workers that the mail clerk can no longer rise to become president and the only way that the clerk will ever rise is through his alliance with the union. This method of appeal has not proven too successful and it will probably be dropped in favor of an appeal to the "middle class group."

White collar workers usually come from the vast "middle class" of American society. This group is generally known as the "great joining group" and it attempts to develop feelings of security and prestige through participation in group activities. White collar work has become increasingly routine. Opportunities for promotion have declined, and in many cases wages have dropped below factory level. Thus, the white collar workers feel a sense of frustration and a feeling of insecurity in their attempts to gain increased monetary rewards, greater security and more prestige. The organizers will play upon these emotions and will try to convince the workers that the union will give their jobs more of a "professional status" and that union affiliation will provide a group activity like the Rotary or Professional Club for managers and the afternoon bridge or social service club for women.

In their attempts to dispel the negative feeling that white collar workers have toward "unions and blue collar workers," the organizers may even hold teas and cocktail parties in downtown hotels. Such parties give the unions an opportunity to have the organized and unorganized meet and mingle. These meetings convey the idea that organized employees are not "blue collar workers" but that they are the same as office people. During these meetings, and by other methods of communication, the unions will make strong claims as to what it can do for the workers in terms of wages and benefits.

2. *Possible Promises the Organizers will make.* Unions in our present day society think big, act big and above all talk big. Management can expect the union to make great claims as to what it will do if elected. Listed below are some of the points upon which the union may build its case.

   a. Wages. Increased wages are one of the most common of all union demands. In recent years, fringe benefits have become increasingly important, but they are usually in addition to an increase in wages. A company's wage scale may be below the community average, particularly in the eyes of the union. This item will then be one of the biggest talking points used by the union.

   b. Favoritism regarding promotion. The union organizers will claim that they will eliminate favoritism promotion. They will appeal to the older workers by claiming to install a system of promotion through seniority. Seniority will also be enforced in the event of job displacements, layoffs and possibly even overtime. Every employee who was disappointed in the past, who felt he was shortchanged in promotions or transfer considerations, will be a likely audience for this type of promise.

   c. Hours. The shorter work week is a future objective of the union movement. Regardless of what present work hours are, the union will likely ask for a reduction. If the starting and quitting time cannot be changed, they may try to lengthen the half-hour lunch period to an hour on the basis that the young women in the workforce need more time to shop at noon.

   d. Formal grievance procedure. In its very first contract, the union will install a formal grievance procedure. Because of the routine nature of their jobs, employees in lower pay grades tend to feel insecure and frustrated. In many cases they are hesitant about bringing grievances to the attention of their supervisors for fear of reprisal. The union will guarantee that all grievances will be brought to the attention of management, no longer through the supervisor, but through the shop steward. Very few nonunion companies have effective grievance mechanisms established and this shortcoming makes them vulnerable.

   e. Fear of automation. The unions have used the word "automation" as a scare word and have set themselves up as the guardian of the worker against the evils of automation. True, unions are not opposed to technological change, for this spells progress; but they don't want to see any workers get hurt in the changeover. Automation, or rather its effect upon the individual employee, could very well be an important plank in the union organizing platform.

f. Additional benefits. In addition to the possible claims listed above, the union will try to win support on smaller but more tangible items. No matter how good working conditions and fringe benefits may be, look for possible promises such as these:
   (1) Free lunches
   (2) More paid holidays
   (3) Longer vacations
   (4) Severance pay
   (5) Cost of living clause in a wage contract.

3. *The company's position in reference to the Taft-Hartley Law.* The prime purpose of the Taft-Hartley Law is to protect the rights of the individual worker—to join a union or not to join. The law has set down unfair labor practices for both employers and unions.

   a. It shall be deemed an unfair practice for an employer to:
      (1) Interfere with, restrain or cause employees (in the exercise of their rights) to join or not to join a union.
      (2) Dominate or interfere with the formation or administration of any labor organization or contribute financial or other support.
      (3) Discriminate in regard to hire or tenure of employment or to encourage employment or discourage membership in any labor organization.
      (4) Discharge or otherwise discriminate against an employee because he has filed charges or given testimony under this Act.
      (5) Refuse to bargain collectively with representatives of his employees.

   b. It shall be an unfair labor practice for a labor organization to:
      (1) Restrain or coerce employees from joining or not joining a union.
      (2) Cause or attempt to cause an employer to fire an employee because of any act other than nonpayment of dues.
      (3) Refuse to bargain collectively with an employer.
      (4) Cause or effect a secondary boycott on a third party to bring economic pressure on the original employer.

    c. In addition to the above unfair labor practices the law states
that:
The expressing of any views, arguments or opinion or the
dissemination thereof, whether that is written, printed,
graphic or visual form, shall not constitute or be evidence of
an unfair practice under any of the provisions of this Act, if
such expression contains no threat of reprisal or force or
promise of benefit.

4. *Recommendations.*

    a. Be friendly but do not formally endorse the unions or comply
with any requests such as those listed in Section 1 for fear of
causing an unfair labor practice or creating a biased opinion
for employees.

    b. Call a meeting of all management and supervisory personnel
to inform them of the problems. Tell them not to say anything which might be construed as condemning the union.

    c. Publicly state that due to the law and in fairness to the em-
ployees, the company will maintain a neutral attitude.

    d. Take any action to improve wages or benefits prior to an
organizational drive to avoid charges of an unfair labor practice.

    e. Expect an acute problem in communication to develop. Em-
ployees are going to look for advice but officially the company must remain silent. It is recommended that a study be
made of the "informal group" and an attempt to locate its key
members. Once these key members are located, the grapevine can be used to pass along information to the employees.

    f. A counter propaganda campaign can be waged through the
grapevine to let every individual employee know that he or
she is an important and integral part of the company. If this
idea can be instilled in the minds of the employees, the union
will be considered an outsider trying to invade the family
circle and will be rejected.

Facts.

The union wants to deal with the Highest Man, who has power to
make decisions.

According to the T/H Act, the union has a right to organize employees who so desire; employees have the right to join or not join.

Your company deals with the public which includes union members.

You can . . .

1. Express opinions if they can be supported and are not antiunion.

2. Continue to enforce established company rules against solicitation.

3. Keep union organizers off the premises, and out of the cafeteria since this is not open to the public and to outside solicitors.

4. Warn supervisors to maintain a strictly neutral attitude.

5. Answer false and misleading charges made by the union.

6. Debunk every rumor; answer without being obvious.

7. Use the grapevine system to get management's views across. Feed into the grapevine; use it also to get reactions.

8. Discuss advantages and disadvantages of union membership.

9. Prevent any employee from being intimidated.

10. Deny any request for a list of employees, office space or bulletin board privileges.

You cannot . . .

1. Interfere with employees' right to organize.

2. Threaten reprisal.

3. Promise reward.

4. Make new rules against union organizers.

5. Spread false information about the union.

6. Start writing employees now if not in the habit of doing so regularly (this is legally proper but not good policy).

7. Put anything in writing (legally, yes, but this is loaded).

Your company does not discriminate. As individuals you do not discriminate against unions. Nevertheless, you do not want anyone coerced into joining anything he does not want to join.

Any employee as an individual has a right to join almost any organization . . . without being discriminated against by your company. But in any other organization it is possible to drop out. But different from other organizations, once an employee joins the union he cannot drop out.

There will be dues, assessments, etc., to get the benefits claimed.

Before an employee says everything is going to be rosy, he should ask himself if joining a union means he can get everything he will want.

ORGANIZING ATTEMPTS

The following is taken from the revised edition of *When Labor Problems Confront You* published by the Illinois State Chamber of Commerce.

The first union move is a demand for recognition.

Ordinarily you will receive very little warning of the union effort to organize your employees.

Union organizers are expert in their field. Not only do they have the benefit of years of experience, but enlightened unions train their personnel through various workshops and seminars in the practical applications of labor laws, contracts, negotiations, strikes, unemployment compensation, safety regulations, fair employment practices and other similar laws applicable to labor relations. They are ready to exploit any weakness that may exist.

They are prepared, as employers should be, for any situation which might arise!

Your warning of union activity may come from the plant grapevine. Or you may hear of picnics, open meetings, visits to homes of employees or beer busts sponsored by the union. You may see leaflets or handbills distributed at the entrance to your business.

On the other hand, you may have no warning. Instead, you may receive a telephone call, a personal visit or a registered letter in which recognition is demanded by the union organizer claiming that his union represents a majority of your employees. In fact, a picket line may be posted without any advance warning.

What should you do? Remember these two primary reactions:

> Do not panic!
> Obtain competent advice!

Here are some further suggestions for detailed planning in particular situations:

In the rumor stage—

Separate the wheat from the chaff. Keep your ears and the ears of your supervisors open, but do not interrogate employees. Evaluate what you hear carefully.

Go over your personnel checklist carefully to see what practices and procedures have been ignored or not followed up. Is there some source of discontent which you have overlooked?

Check with your legal adviser to determine whether you may at this time correct any bad situations which exist pertaining to wages, working conditions, etc.

Consult other employers in the area to determine if the activity is general or localized. If general, it may be desirable to provide a means of keeping each other abreast of all the facts.

Solicit the active cooperation of your supervisors. Be certain their attitudes and actions are consistent with company policy. Have them keep careful records of any unusual situations. Keep your supervisors carefully instructed and fully informed. But be sure the supervisors whose cooperation you are soliciting are "supervisors" as defined in the NLRA. Check with your labor attorney for guidance on this issue.

Foremen should watch out for slowdowns.

Improve communications among personnel, particularly from top to bottom, and encourage contact from bottom to top.

Improve and step up personal contacts.

Note presence of strangers. Keep copies of leaflets you find.

During union contacts with your employees—

Remember that the organizer has certain legal rights, too. He can distribute handbills on public property. He can call on your employees at their homes. He can call meetings of your employees in public places or in such places as he may obtain.

You need not let a nonemployee organizer talk to your employees on company property under most circumstances. An exception may occur if you (1) are covered by the "lack of access to employees rule," or (2) are enforcing an unlawful broad no-solicitation rule and are making "captive audience" speeches to employees. These are complex areas. This is a changing and developing field and care is warranted.

You need not let a nonemployee organizer distribute handbills in your plant (subject to the above limitations), but your own employees have somewhat wider latitude in this connection.

The governing rule remains: Working time is for work. Conversely, during nonworking time (lunch breaks, etc.) your employees are free to solicit memberships and discuss unions (except in department store selling areas) and, in nonworking areas, distribute union literature.

Perhaps you have already concluded—as you should have—just what your response to the organizer will be.

During a telephone call or personal visit from a union organizer—

Be courteous

Be extremely careful. (Keep in mind that usually the reason for this contact is a request for recognition on the basis of signed authorization cards.)

Be calm! Do not jump to conclusions or be pressed into ill-considered actions! Take enough time both during and after your talk to consider carefully the next step to take.

Be as brief as you can. Obtain but do not give information until you have had a chance to talk to your adviser. The organizer is a "pro" in his field. Most of them are well-trained in just this sort of thing. Think about how much, or rather how little experience you have had and act accordingly.

Ask the union representative to send you a letter stating his position.

On receipt of a letter from the union—

Be certain to seek guidance as to appropriate response.

Be mindful of the cautions on authorization cards.

Be certain that the letter is answered in a reasonable period of time.

During an organizational strike or recognition picketing—

Alert the chief of the law enforcement body in the jurisdiction in which your place of business is situated. Maintain close liaison.

Ask your labor attorney to advise you and to consult with the law enforcement officers concerning the rights of those who wish to work.

Consult with your attorney as to whether the strike or picketing is illegal recognition picketing. Consult with him, also, as to the advantages and disadvantages of filing an Employer's Petition for an NLRB election under these circumstances. Ask what information he will need if he is to take legal action.

Alert your supervisors, office personnel and other people who are not affected by the strike. Advise them of the facts and your policy regarding the strike.

Instruct all personnel to avoid loitering near the picket line. In general, avoid exchange of conversation with pickets to minimize the danger of unwanted incidents.

When considering voluntary recognition:

Some employers are willing to accept union demands for recognition without an election. There can be many reasons for such a decision, particularly among employers associated with the building trades and construction industries, where 80% of the employees are organized— compared to five percent in the retail trade. They may believe sincerely that the benefits, such as a ready source of employees, the union label and an anticipated attitude of cooperation, outweigh the disadvantages of organization. These have been persuasive considerations under proper circumstances.

This is your decision. We suggest only that you consider carefully the long-term nature of any such relationship; your future financial position and the effect on it and your employees of quick recognition and agreement with the union. Temporary expediency, such as the hope— or promise—of an "easy" first contract, should not be allowed to blind you to the long-term effects of your decision.

And remember, although *you* may be willing to recognize the union as the representative of your employees, it is nearly impossible to tell how *your employees* really feel without an election.

The Labor Management Relations Act says, in Section 7:

> "Employees shall have the right to self-organization, to form, join or assist labor organizations, to bargain collectively through representatives OF THEIR OWN CHOOSING, and to engage in other concerted activities, for the purpose of collective bargaining or other mutual aid or protection, AND SHALL ALSO HAVE THE RIGHT TO REFRAIN FROM ANY OR ALL OF SUCH ACTIVITIES except to the extent that such right may be affected by an agreement requiring membership in a labor organization as a condition of employment as authorized in Section 8 (a) (3)."
> (Emphasis supplied.)

You must be adequately sure that the union does represent a majority of your employees before you may recognize the union. And even if you are sure, there may be legal dangers involved if a second union is also trying to organize your employees. Consult your attorney on the legality of recognizing a union without an election!

If you do recognize the union, nothing in the law gives the union the right to dictate the terms of your collective bargaining agreement. This is a matter for bargaining which is discussed elsewhere in this section.

When the demand for recognition is based on a claim of authorization cards signed by a majority of your employees—

Be wary because a request that you check the cards is loaded with legal implications which may result in your being required to recognize the union without benefit of an election.

Authorization cards are ofttimes unreliable indicators as even the

NLRB and the courts have had occasion to observe. Social pressures, fear, uncertainty or misrepresentations might have played a part in the signing—you aren't really in a position to know—and the employees' actual views might be diametrically opposed.

If you do not wish to consider union recognition on a card-check basis—

You should suggest the proper forum for deciding any question of representation has been statutorily determined to be the NLRB.

You should state the need for consulting with your labor relations adviser before you can take any position.

You should not discuss, look at, review or accept the cards.

You should not interview your people to ascertain whether or not they signed (although interrogation is legally permissible in some circumstances, the limitations are many and technical).

You should not agree to a "quickie" election by an impartial third party. It may be just as poor a test of real employee sentiment as the cards. In general, you should regard an NLRB election as the *only* really reliable and legally sound means of determining employee desires.

You should not engage in objectionable conduct, stalling and the like.

You should not give the impression you are against unions categorically.

After discussing the union demand with your labor relations adviser you may wish to promptly raise any question you may have concerning the appropriateness of the bargaining unit requested. It is imperative that you act affirmatively and at once if you intend to contest the union claim!

Can an Employer Campaign, Too?

Yes! First of all, we suggest again that you refer regularly to the checklist under "Preparedness." These are always items of concern. In addition, the law allows you considerable leeway in taking an active part in a campaign, if you desire to do so.

Employer campaigns have many times proved successful. Even though a substantial majority of your employees may have signed union authorization cards initially, this does not mean that the union will win a secret election. Employees sometimes sign membership cards much in the same fashion that many of us sign petitions, without reading carefully or fully understanding exactly what they have signed.

But the election conducted by the NLRB will be by secret ballot. Both you and the union will have full opportunity to carry your message to the employees, who then exercise their choice in the privacy and secrecy of the voting booth.

The result of the election will be determined in many cases by whether the company or the union has done the most effective selling job during the campaign.

Some general suggestions and a caution.

Do not overestimate the loyalty of your employees:

Your employees may be bored, broke, aggrieved, hurt or bitter. The union organizer knows the score. He can exploit the weak spots, the holes in the fence you failed to mend.

It is a good idea to have your supervisors prepare a private and conservative analysis of probable election sympathies on an individual employee basis. If the analyses are critical in fact and not colored by wishful thinking and if you count all doubtfuls in the union column, you will have a reasonably accurate indicator. Repeat the process during the election campaign, of course. Another rule of thumb, if you insist on predictions—the union polling maximum will approximate 2½ times the number of people who attended their last preelection meeting. (Not as reliable as well-informed supervisory opinion, but a guideline.)

Your employees have their own image of you, based on what they observe, not necessarily on what you say.

Keep in mind that the union will have inside help. The alert organizer will look for those employees who have a feel for leadership, a need for prestige or an axe to grind.

Take a positive and realistic approach:

There is no time to wallow in self-pity, resentment or anger either at the union or the employees you thought would never do such a thing to you.

Recognize your weak points, but capitalize on your strengths! An effective employer campaign should communicate to employees a proper blend of the company's strengths and the union's weaknesses. Before an effective campaign can be conducted, you must endeavor to learn everything there is to know about the union. Your adviser can provide you with much specific information about the union's history, background and practices.

You must win votes in the same way a candidate for office wins them —do not assume that your employees will vote for you just because they may have known you longer than the union organizer.

Your supervisors are on the front line and will carry a heavy portion of your campaign burden. But don't forget they need indoctrinating, too. All too many will hesitate or feel uncomfortable in talking to their people about unions. There are also those who will feel on the defensive, who will consider it slightly sinful to acknowledge that the company is making money, and intends to continue to make it. In other words, you have to sell your supervisors before you can sell your other employees.

Sincere identification with your employees through your common background may cause them to identify with you on election day. (Particularly in smaller communities, your common interests are often many—your children may play in the same Little League, you may belong to the same church, the same PTA, the same lodges.)

Remember, this will not be an easy campaign, but unions don't always win, either! True, on the surface at least, it would appear the union has a strong head start since there must be a "showing of interest" in the unit (signed authorization cards) from a minimum of 30% of the employees. But, according to a survey reported by the NLRB Chairman, unions which had signed up from 30% to 50% in advance won only 19% of the time while companies, on the other hand, won 26% of the elections involving units in which more than 70% of the employees had originally signed union cards.

Do not stray from the limits of the law in your words and actions:

Avoid any statements or actions by members of management which could be construed either as a threat or a promise.

Plan your campaign carefully; review your plans and the text of your letters or speeches with your labor relations attorney.

Be alert to your rights as well as your limitations!

You can talk to your employees.

The Constitution and law itself provide you with freedom of speech, limited only to the extent that you cannot directly or indirectly threaten, promise or intimidate your employees by the words that you speak or by the manner or background in which you say the words. Your professional adviser will caution you about the practical and legal effects of talking to your employees, as well as where and when such talks may be made.

There is, however, a wide choice of things you may say freely, including the following:

You may emphasize your belief and your opinion that the people do not need a union; you may talk about the loss of their independence. You may emphasize that an outsider will come between the employee and you. You may state that without a union your door is always open.

You may refer to the cost of union initiation fees, dues and assessments.

You may state your personal opinion concerning the union organizers, providing you do not exceed the legal bounds of libel and slander.

You may express openly the hope that your employees vote against this or any union.

You may remind the employees that they have a right either to join or refrain from joining the union.

You may remind your employees that they do not have to vote for the union because they have signed a membership card.

You may describe the good features of working for you—job opportunities, longevity, job security, steady work—your strong points.

You may state that the union cannot guarantee additional pay. Only the employer meets the payroll.

You may state that the union cannot guarantee the security and success of the business, only customers can do that.

You may discuss the possibility of strikes and serving in picket lines, and you may review the history of the particular union as to such matters.

You may describe the experiences which other employers have had with this or other unions, including those in your own community.

You may urge all employees to vote.

You may call attention to any union falsehoods.

You may explain the meaning of check-off and union shop and the effect they may have on all employees.

This is not a catalogue of what you should say. It is a list of statements that are accepted as a proper exercise of free speech. You will have to decide from your own situation whether it is appropriate to say any or all of these things to your employees.

In addition, if you have never talked to your employees before the union appeared, remember to weigh carefully the impact of a new and dramatic gesture of this kind against possible criticism that you are insincere or "buying good will."

Letters to employees.

Letters to employees should be short, plainly worded, factual, dignified. They are most effective when limited to one topic. Other suggestions which employers have found useful are:

Plan your campaign so that your letters will be well spaced. Consider the use of letters as follow-ups to talks to employees.

Have a series of envelopes prepared in advance of mailing, personally addressed. Have at least an outline of letters prepared in advance.

Mailing letters to employees' homes may give them more time and privacy to review them, and will give their families an opportunity to hear your side of the argument.

Remember that the same prohibitions apply to the written word as to the spoken word—you must not promise, threaten, coerce or intimidate, or in any way interfere with the employees' freedom of choice.

Your written or spoken word is usually considered in light of your actions to determine if there is any violation of employees' rights. Review your letters with your labor relations attorney!

Do not misrepresent. Be truthful.

Use the NLRB—It's your agency too!

Do not be afraid to avail yourself of the services of the NLRB in a proper case. Union coercion of employees is prohibited by law, and certain types of strikes, picketing and boycotts are also prohibited.

Be alert to union statements which are substantially untruthful or activity such as threats, following your employees, or other evidence of interference which may be grounds for setting aside an election.

Use your supervisors to keep a record of all that transpires in this connection.

If the union has demanded recognition, but has not asked the Board to hold an election, consider filing an employer petition for an election.

Avoid the following pitfalls:

Do not offer wage increases or other inducements during this particular period unless the increases are a part of an established pattern, or can be justified by clear evidence of business necessity. Any such evidence should be carefully evaluated by your labor attorney before you decide to rely on it.

You may and should continue to operate your plant in its established pattern. This is not only proper but vital to you.

Do not threaten to fire, suspend or otherwise discriminate against anyone because he joined the union, or because he is prounion. By discriminate, we mean a failure to treat both union and nonunion employees alike in making assignments of preferred work, overtime and the like. Be certain to enforce plant rules impartially.

Do nothing which can be construed in light of all the circumstances as an effort to undermine the union.

Do not threaten to shut down or move the plant if the union gets in.

Do not lay off or discharge an employee for union activity.

Do not prohibit solicitation of union membership during nonworking hours.

Do not ask your employees to name other employees who have attended meetings.

Do not interrogate employees about meetings that the union has held, or the number of persons or identity of persons who have signed cards or attended meetings.

Do not promise employees promotions, raises or other benefits if they get out of the union.

Do not have straw votes.

Do not violate the NLRB limitations on captive audience speeches during the 24-hour period immediately preceding the election. It's a hard and fast rule. For example, answering questions following a last-minute speech will void a result favorable to the Company if the answers run into the proscribed period, even though the speech itself was concluded in time.

Consult your attorney about any question you have in this area!

HOW TO KEEP THE UNION OUT

The following is taken from the revised edition of *When Labor Problems Confront You* published by the Illinois State Chamber of Commerce.

Preparedness/Self-Analysis

The human relationship is an integral part of every business. There are countless reasons why employers become the objects of union effort, but usually it results from the breakdown of some aspect of that relationship.

Problems involving manufacturing, sales, marketing and research constantly demand and receive priority in management time and attention. Yet employee morale problems can be and frequently are more important.

It is just plain bad business to permit the inefficiency and lack of ambition such problems provoke, to grow and flourish. To put it another way, the inability to assign a precise dollars and cents effect on the balance sheet may be a reason for slighting human relations problems, but it is no excuse.

Accordingly, you as an employer must be constantly vigilant for any factor which could disrupt a good relationship between you and your employees.

Now is the time to take a look at your own human relations picture!

Employee attitudes are developed in day-to-day work experience and in reaction to employer communications, company policies, personnel practices and management motives. Once the union has appeared on the scene and committed its forces to battle, it may be too late to take positive and constructive steps. Last-minute, patchwork corrections cannot normally effect any change in employee attitudes in the short time available. Moreover, such efforts frequently will be condemned as illegal or seized by the organizer as proof of his claims.

You have an image which your employees see. What is that image?

Are you aware of yourself as others see you? Are you alert to that image?

There are numerous critical areas in which you can destroy a good image. This is a partial list you should check regularly:

Morale

Paternalism is not the key to good morale nor does aloofness bar the door to it. Employee attitudes, whether favorable or unfavorable, are more often the product of a number of separate and on the surface relatively unimportant items. Consider these—

Do you treat all of your employees fairly and without favoritism?

Are you consistent in your actions?

Do you show an interest in your employees? Do you keep them informed, in advance if possible?

Do you recognize and respect your employees as human beings, ones who hear, see, talk and feel? Do you acknowledge shortcomings in your management and correct accordingly?

Do you afford an opportunity for your employees to advance before hiring others to fill the job?

Do you attempt to orient new employees? Do you give your employees a sense of belonging?

Do you regularly and consistently survey the needs of your employees? Do you provide a forum by which they can be heard without fear of recrimination?

Do you follow up programs which you start?

Do you reduce confusion by proper planning and organization?

Do you exhibit your loyalty to your employees?

Do you promote your common interests?

Do you practice merit employment and adhere strictly to the policy of no discrimination on the basis of race, color, national origin, sex or religion?

Written policy

Employees should know about the company and where they fit into its plans.

Informing employees where they fit into the company picture is the purpose of the personnel policy. It should tell employees about the company's plans and about matters directly affecting the employee-employer relationship. A personnel policy is, in short, the link between your objectives and the duties of your employees. It lets employees and prospective employees know what you expect from them and what they can expect from you.

Employees who are familiar with your policies, who know where the company is going, how it's doing and what part they are expected to play will feel they are a part of the company team. This aids in building morale.

Wages

Contrary to popular belief, earnings represent only one of several reasons why employees elect to seek union help in dealing with their employer. Review your position objectively, but don't permit satisfactory answers to lull you into feeling they insulate you from organizational activity. Ask yourself—

Are your wages and fringe benefits, such as insurance, vacations and paid holidays, in line with those of others similarly engaged in your area? Are you keeping pace? Do your employees know it?

Are these wages and other benefits fair and reasonable?

Do the same rates apply to all who do the same work?

Do you carefully plot the natural progression of new employees in your overall wage structure?

Grievances

Generally, union organizational leaflets will give grievance procedures equal billing with wages and fringe benefits. Unions know that the small worry, stifled by fear of reprisal (whether or not warranted) or the simple lack of a good listener, very often grows into the large antagonism that is grist for the organizational mill. Only an open and free line of communication will do the job for the employer.

Do your employees need a spokesman? Do they need to invite a union organizer to talk for them?

Do you have an effective process for prompt handling of employee complaints, either real or fancied?

Do you keep your office door open—or is this a myth for public consumption only?

Do you follow up your decisions based on complaints to ascertain their effect on morale?

Supervision

The competence of the person directing your employees is not measurable by reference only to production reports or the frequency with which schedules are met. His performance evaluation should depend as much on what he knows about his workers and their reaction to the company.

Do your supervisors effectively represent you to your employees?

Do they know they speak and act for you—that you are responsible for what they do and say?

Do you train your supervisors? Do you keep your supervisors informed?

Do your supervisors have an ability to teach and to communicate with your employees? Do they assist employees in understanding their duties and privileges?

Do your supervisors treat all employees fairly and without favoritism?

Do they react properly to criticism?

Do your supervisors promptly and effectively correct problems as they arise?

Do your supervisors nurture and maintain a close relationship between employer and employee? Do they have the respect of your employees?

Do they understand what they can and cannot do about union activities?

Marginal employees

Retention of people who cannot carry their share of the load is no favor to them or to the company. It's also a hardship on those who may have to help hold up their end.

Remember, too, it is not at all uncommon to find such people in the forefront of an organizing drive. Dissatisfaction is usually the trigger to action and no one is more apt to be unhappy and frustrated than the employee who has reached a promotional and economic dead-end.

Do you carefully select and properly place your new employees?

Do you regularly and consistently weed out marginal employees?

Do you regularly and at frequent intervals dismiss those employees who do not conform to the standard of workmanship required?

Education

Opportunity and recognition are basic requirements for all employees. There are limits to what an employer can do but whatever he does should be "sold" to his employees.

Do you give your employees an opportunity to improve their skills? Both in-plant and out?

Do you communicate with your employees regularly to explain company policies and their relationship to the economic facts of life; various changes in policies and reasons for them, and plans for the future?

Do you explain to your employees the necessity for maintaining production schedules, the effect on themselves and others when they are not met?

Do you keep tabs on additional training and education your employees may have acquired since they were hired? Do you attempt to utilize new skills and knowledge?

Physical plant and working conditions

The favorable effect of good physical environment on employee morale is fairly obvious. It need not be equated, however, with the amount of money expended. A little attention to detail may suffice. As a starter—

Do you have adequate lighting, heating and ventilation?

Do you require good housekeeping in your plant?

Do you have adequate toilet and cleanup facilities?

Do you have proper provision for first aid?

Does your equipment have proper safety features?

Do you have provision for recreation and/or facilities for eating during lunch hours and break periods?

Remember—unions don't just "happen" to come to your door. There is usually a good reason. Find it . . . and correct it!

THE UNION POINT OF VIEW
FROM OPEIU SPOKESMAN

Caught between low salaries and spiraling prices, more and more office and clerical workers today seek collective bargaining to better their lot. The best-known union in the white-collar field is the Office & Professional Employees International Union, AFL-CIO/CLC. Although this union has been in existence since 1904, it began its real expansion toward the end of World War II when it received its international charter from the American Federation of Labor. Office workers employed under OPEIU contracts generally earn $1,000 a year more than nonunion employees. They are an elite group, many in the lowest office grade now earning $10,000 a year.

Since establishment of the International Union in 1945, its membership has grown from 22,500 to more than 100,000 in some 300 locals in the United States, Canada and Puerto Rico. In giving due consideration to the unusual problems inherent in organizing white-collar workers, the OPEIU has rendered exceptional performance in its field of unionism. Its progress is described each month in its official publication, *White Collar,* mailed to each member.

In Many Industries

OPEIU members today include office, clerical, technical and professional workers in every conceivable type of private industry. These number, among others, the pulp and paper industry in the United States and Canada; thousands of Blue Cross and Blue Shield employees in both countries and Puerto Rico; stock exchanges on Wall Street; the petroleum industry in Texas; motion picture, television, and the radio broadcasting industries in Hollywood; steamship, shipbuilding and repair yards; the Tennessee Valley Authority; public utilities of all types —including atomic power and aerospace projects—the retail, wholesale, and distributing trades, with strong representation in industrial establishments.

This white-collar union's most recent organizing breakthrough has been the unionization of some 3,000 clerical workers and tellers in several large commercial and savings banks in the United States and Canada, in addition to another 1,500 in more than 60 credit unions. Throwing off traditional attitudes, young bank workers today are showing an increasing interest in white-collar unionism, according to OPEIU President Howard Coughlin. He attributes this to low pay of bank staffs, compared with high bank profits, resulting in a loss of social status and economic prestige that bank workers formerly enjoyed in their communities.

From the beginning, organized labor in the United States and Canada has been concerned, above all, with improvement in wages and working conditions. In collective bargaining relationships with employers, labor unions still concentrate on these fundamentals. Their primary service to members is to improve their economic position.

But labor unions also serve their members in another important way. They give to the individual worker a feeling of belonging, of strength in united action, of membership in a group with a common objective. Where the individual is weak, the union gives him a sense of security. In a world of atomic change, it gives him some assurance of permanence and continuity.

Through the OPEIU an office worker asserts his freedom and expresses his wishes as a member of our economic society, growing ever more complex and perplexing for the individual in this technological age. Finally, through his elected union representative has a voice in the determination of his wages and conditions of employment—something the nonunion worker does not enjoy.

The Glamour Unions

Most young people today don't realize that every actor and actress they see on television or in a movie belongs to a union. It is also true that every Broadway performer, every musician in the orchestra, those familiar radio voices, the screen writers—even cameramen and directors—all belong to some union.

Why do all these prominent individuals belong to a union? Why will a performing artist never set foot on a stage or a movie set without a written contract? Why do airline pilots, who earn as high as $60,000 a year, teachers, and civilian aerospace technicians belong to unions? For the same reason that every American or Canadian or Puerto Rican should belong to a union. It makes good business sense. Besides, citizens of the United States, Canada and Puerto Rico have legal rights to belong to a union—guaranteed by law and court decisions.

If you ask why a typical OPEIU member belongs to the union, he will reply something like this: "Because I'm proud of my job; it makes me a better employee in a better job. Our white-collar union puts things on a businesslike basis. I like that. We put everything down in a written contract which we, ourselves, negotiate. My employer, who is a businessman, wouldn't think of doing business without a signed contract. It's just as good business for an employee to have a signed union contract. We've found that our union contract benefits all of us, and makes our office a better office to work in."

Of course, unions are changing with the times to keep abreast of modern developments but they haven't changed as much as business has. And the rapid changes in business provide some very strong reasons why a union like the OPEIU is necessary for the office worker. Here are a few:

1. Business has grown larger, more impersonal. The bigger the company, the more likely you are to be just a number, a work station or simply part of the "bunch downstairs." People are hired and fired in groups. Where do you stand in that setup?

2. Companies are changing, managements are merging and consolidating; they're transferring people, whole departments and entire plants. What kind of person-to-person relationship can you have with an employer when that happens?

3. Jobs are growing more specialized with training and skills that often leave an employee with only two choices: Do it their way or quit. Even general skills have become so specialized that all you know is how they want the job done where you work. Where does that leave you if that particular job is eliminated?

4. Modern management techniques often result in more and more rules, regulations and restrictions. When that happens where you work, do you have a voice in the changes?

5. Perhaps more alarming, technology and automation are being applied to more and more jobs. Science brings some

great advances to help our lives in many ways. The computer and electronic data processing may have helped to create your job. But what happens the day somebody brings in a machine to replace you completely?

ORGANIZED LABOR AND THE HANDICAPPED

In a booklet published by the AFL-CIO, President George Meany says: "We look upon the handicapped worker just as we look upon any group that suffers from prejudice, discrimination and inadequate opportunity. We want to help them win their full status as productive citizens."

This booklet, "Working Together—The Key to Jobs for the Handicapped," quotes the following key statements of the AFL-CIO policy toward hiring handicapped persons:

1. It is the policy of the American Federation of Labor and Congress of Industrial Organizations that every practical means shall be used to insure equal opportunity in employment of all qualified handicapped workers—both mentally and physically handicapped.

2. The Federation strives to increase employment opportunities for the handicapped through collective bargaining and union-management cooperation.

3. The use of preemployment physical examinations for any other purpose than to determine physical or mental ability for a suitable job is unsound.

4. The Federation recognizes the wisdom of active participation in community programs for the handicapped and encourages its state and city central bodies to take an active part in the state and local committees for the employment of the handicapped.

THE ELECTION

The following is taken from the revised edition of *When Labor Problems Confront You* published by the Illinois State Chamber of Commerce.

In this section, we address ourselves to a subject of interest only to employers who are within the jurisdiction of the NLRB. Those who are not under the Labor Management Relations Act are considerably less inhibited in what they can do during a fight to keep a union out—but the same holds true for union efforts to get in.

Early in the game—sometimes even simultaneously with receipt of the demand for recognition—you will be served with a copy of a representation petition, filed with the NLRB by the union. The petition seeks an election in a designated employee unit. The exact timing of the filing of the petition will depend upon appraisal of its own vote-getting position.

Occasionally, of course, the union may not file at all. All you will see is a picket line while the union is working to obtain support. However, the Landrum-Griffin Act amendments fix a time limit of 30 days on organizational as well as recognition picketing and give you some relief in this area. You are entitled to seek an election if the union does not, providing there is a demand for recognition.

There is almost an infinite variety of strategic and tactical approaches which can be pursued at this stage. Choice will vary as the facts change. But since eventually all petitions are processed by the Board, you should have a general idea of what is likely to occur when union.

Once a petition has been filed with the NLRB

- by the union
- by the employees, or
- by the employer

there is an investigation by the Board to determine:

- if the employer is "in commerce" and
- if a question of representation exists
- if there is sufficient showing of interest (in the case of petitions filed by the union or the employees, 30% of your employees must have indicated a desire for an election before the Board will proceed further)
- if there is another labor contract which might bar an election
- if there has been an election or certification within the previous year.

If the petition has not been disposed of following the investigation

- by dismissal by the Regional Director
- by withdrawal of petitioner
- by the parties in a consent adjustment

either a consent proceeding or a formal hearing ensues.

Consent Proceedings

There are two types: Type one—agreement for consent election, and type two—stipulation for certification on consent election.

Under both types:

1. You agree that

- you are engaged in commerce
- the petitioner is a labor organization
- the unit requested (as may be modified by the mutual agreement of the company and the union) is appropriate
- an election should be held at a set time and place
- a specific payroll date will be used as a cut-off date for determining voter eligibility.

2. You waive a preelection hearing.

Although these two types of consent proceedings are essentially the same, they differ in the following aspects:

Under type one, post-election issues, certifications and their amendments are finally determined by the Regional Director, whereas under type two these matters may be taken by the parties to the Board in Washington, D.C.

Unless one of the two types of Consent Proceedings is adopted, you will have:

Formal Proceedings

A hearing is set before an NLRB representative to determine one or more of those issues which are agreed to under consent proceedings. You may examine and cross-examine witnesses, present testimony on any relevant point including jurisdiction, existence of a labor organization and appropriate unit. You may file briefs and/or argue orally. The hearing officer summarizes the evidence, analyzes the issues and submits his report to the Regional Director for decision.

As a result of this proceeding an election will be scheduled or the petition will be dismissed. Unless this petition is dismissed, an election will be directed to be held within 30 days thereafter.

Election can be held before hearing under Landrum-Griffin amendments where the union has engaged in organizational or recognition picketing.

Conduct of Election

1. Whether the election is the result of a consent or formal proceeding, you will have to provide the Regional Director with a list of names and addresses of employees in the election unit within seven days of the date the election is approved or ordered. The Regional Director will in turn make this list available to all parties in the case.

2. The Board will require that you post an official "Notice of Election." The Board will also request that you post additional notices advising employees of certain rights they have under the statute. You are not required by law to post this latter type of notice, but you are required to post the former one. Consult your labor attorney as to which notices you must post and which ones you need not post.

3. You may campaign during the interim.

4. A preelection conference will be scheduled to determine eligible voters (the employer is required to furnish the payroll list for the period immediately preceding the Board's direction of election or approval of the consent agreement), and time and place of election, the number of observers for each party, and the places for posting notices of election.

Questions of eligibility may include the right of temporary, part-time, laid-off, absent, vacationing and striking employee to vote.

5. Your observers must be instructed to challenge all voters you do not consider eligible. A challenged ballot is separately sealed and not opened unless it can affect the result of the election. Challenges must be made at the time the voter is given the ballot.

This is a highly technical area. Provide your labor relations adviser with the applicable facts so he can properly advise you and your observers.

After the election an opportunity exists to file objections to the conduct of the election or the conduct of the other party which allegedly constituted interference with the election process.

If either the company or the union violates the applicable law and regulations in their election campaigns, the election may be set aside.

Be a graceful as well as grateful winner. Holding grudges against employees who disagreed with you does nothing but encourage resentment against you.

Mend your fences! Do not give your employees further reason to seek out a spokesman!

WARNING—Under both consent and formal proceedings, careful attention to the unit is essential. Consider carefully whether to include or exclude employees who, under Board law, may be found to be office clerical, professional, technical, supervisory, plant protection employees or who, on other grounds, may not clearly be part of the requested group. Once in the unit, they will be there a long time. Any decision to include borderline employees in the unit with the hope of thereby affecting the result of the election should be adopted only after a careful evaluation.

BARGAINING

The following is taken from the revised edition of *When Labor Problems Confront You* published by the Illinois State Chamber of Commerce.

If you have lost the election and exhausted all review procedures, your job is cut out for you—both by law and by economic necessity.

Perhaps your preelection campaign was hard fought and emotional, with hard feelings generated on both sides. These are not uncommon by-products of the election procedure. In addition, if this is the first time you have been obliged to sit down and bargain with a union, your mind is filled with foreboding and some fear at the prospect. Further, you may be angry because your employees have "turned against" you. Nevertheless, you cannot permit your emotions to govern your thinking. Normally, there is nothing to be afraid of or angry at. You are faced with contract negotiations which will determine the impact which the union will have on the future operation of your business and you cannot allow yourself the luxury of permitting emotions to govern your behavior.

Your first contract negotiations may be your most important, since the manner in which they are conducted and carried to conclusion will, in large measure, determine future relationships.

Certification of the union as the representative of your employees will follow soon after the election (unless you file objections) and a union request to meet and begin contract talks will normally follow on the heels of the certification. Your prompt, courteous response is recommended.

Duty to Bargain

You are obligated by law to bargain in good faith with the union. "Good faith" is a frequently-used expression in labor relations. By and large, it means having honest and substantial reasons for your actions and positions. The statute does not mean that you are required to agree to a union proposal nor are you required to make a concession. The Act does not require an employer acting in good faith to surrender his rights at the negotiating table—you may and should insist on retaining those rights which you feel are necessary for the successful operation of your business. If the question of your good faith is raised by a charge filed with the NLRB, there are standards which determine whether you have complied with this requirement.

We wish to emphasize the existence of these standards or rules of bargaining conduct because employers frequently overlook the fact that the issue of good faith bargaining is resolved not only by examining the employer's attitude during negotiations, but by an investigation of his conduct from the time the union made its initial demand for recognition.

Accordingly, the Board will examine many factors. Some of these are:

Your general attitude in reacting to each of the events which led up to the election; the manner in which you have accepted the results of the election; your response to the union request to meet to begin negotiations; the frequency of your negotiating meetings; your bargaining positions, whether changing or unchanging; the overall atmosphere or climate you have created by your statements and actions.

In other words, you will be judged in the context of all of your activities.

Undue delay in scheduling meetings, unreasonable demands, refusal to discuss or to give your position on issues, and antagonistic attitudes or responses to union requests are but a few of the factors which may go into the formulation of an "anti union motivation" and ultimately undermine an otherwise legitimate strategy.

A word of caution: Unions frequently present a "form" contract at the opening negotiating session. You are not required to agree to such a contract in whole or in part. Unfortunately, some employers have done so in the mistaken belief that all other employers had the same contract or that the union had the legal right to insist on specific language.

Bargaining—General

Your first contract not only establishes the dollar cost of a union, but will in large measure set the tone and pattern for your future negotiations and relationships with the union. Even if a second election is held a year later and the union loses, your labor agreement has established your economic base.

Another, very important point—anything which goes into a labor agreement giving the union an opportunity to speak and be heard on your business operations and procedures, is a relinquishment of a management right—this includes so-called "mutual consent" clauses which provide that before management can act, the consent of the union must be obtained.

Once you have given up any management right, you will have a hard time getting it back. Accordingly, the watchwords are deliberation and forethought in negotiating all contract matters.

Issues

You probably will be asked by the union to bargain on the following subjects:

Economic

- Wages
- Overtime—daily and weekly
- Shift starting times
- Premium pay for Saturday and Sunday work
- Shift premiums
- Paid holidays
- Vacations
- Insurance
- Other fringe benefits

Union Security

- Union shop
- Check off of dues and fees
- In-plant union representation (the number of stewards, their rights, privileges, superseniority)
- Grievance procedures
- Seniority during layoff and recall and in promotions and transfers

Job Security

- Job bidding
- Job classification and jurisdictional work limitations prohibition on foremen working

The above represent typical union demands. You may be asked to negotiate on other subjects in addition, such as leaves of absence, safety, pensions, supplemental unemployment benefits, termination pay and a variety of special fringe benefits.

You will want to examine each one of these demands from the standpoint of how it affects your operation, bearing in mind that any concession will be with you for a long time. Remember, the test of a good contract is the absence of restrictions which hamper you unreasonably in the effective discharge of your management responsibilities.

In addition, you will want to present to the union the strongest possible management rights clause—one which will reserve to you the right to operate your business efficiently and productively. For example, if subcontracting is an essential aspect, you will want to protect it. If the size and makeup of your business dictates that supervisors be permitted to work in the shop, be certain that you do not limit that right. If flexibility in assigning employees is an essential, cover it. New products, new equipment, new processes and new methods are constantly being developed; maintain the flexibility necessary to incorporate such changes in your operation. If additional facilities are ever contemplated, limit your recognition clause to the specific address of the location involved in the current negotiations and provide for the management prerogative of determining the number and location of your plants.

Seek competent, professional advice. Remember, your opponent on the other side of the bargaining table will be a skilled and experienced negotiator.

Checklist

Here is a checklist of some of the items on which decisions will have to be made before negotiations start:

Negotiating strategy

Often, employers are poor negotiators, leaving themselves to the mercy of union demands simply because they have no goal and plan of action established for negotiations. As a result, their position is a purely defensive one.

Accordingly, before negotiations begin, set down in writing what you want to accomplish. Make decisions as to objectives:

- Which cannot be compromised.

- Which can be compromised to some degree in exchange for what.

- Which are included to combat unreasonable union demands and which can be discarded as the union shows willingness to retract from its unreasonable position.

- Determine what you can and cannot do economically.

Keep your strategy flexible to effectively contend with unexpected developments during the course of negotiations.

Time and length of meetings

Decide whether to meet during or after working hours.

- Can management afford the time during the day? Will the loss of production of absent union committee employees be significant? Will you pay the union committee employees if you meet during working hours? (You have no legal obligation to do so).

Agree on how long your meetings will last before they start. Marathon sessions make good headlines but bad contracts.

Meeting place

Select a comfortable location.

Consider the effect of meeting:

- At your place of business Will it encourage union showboating for its new members? Will it interfere with customer relations? Will it cause a problem during recesses?

- At a neutral location Will it be available when you want it? Will it be costly? Will the union share in the costs?

The management team

Determine the number.

Select your chief spokesman and stick to him throughout the entire negotiations.

Post your spokesman on his exact authority.

Assign one of your team (not the spokesman) to the job of taking notes—particularly of the union position on all subjects discussed.

Management must, at all times, present a united front. Any disagreements within the management group must be resolved in recess—not before the union.

Profanity and personal abuse are out. Should they appear, recess the meeting automatically. (If you are able to make this rule stick, company demeanor must be above reproach.)

- Sometimes, letting off steam is necessary, but orderly negotiations are the most productive.

Make it clear whether your agreement on a specific provision is tentative and subject to agreement on the entire contract, or whether it is final on a piecemeal basis. Strategy will, of course, vary depending on the circumstances, but it must be made clear, whichever way it goes.

- Settle all noneconomic issues first. Save your money to buy final agreement on disputed issues.

Union demands

Obtain as many contracts as you can to which your union is a party. Particularly, try to find some contracts with newly-organized employers.

- Check with your local Chamber of Commerce. They can help.

Make a survey of wage rates and benefits in your area and industry so you can determine the kinds of costs you may need to consider.

- Check with your local Chamber of Commerce.
- Check with your trade association.

Know your opposition

The union will have its problems, too. You can spot them and adjust your approach accordingly.

- Does the representative rule with an iron hand or is he still trying to win the committee's confidence—by acting tough with the company—by reciting long experience—by threatening a strike?
- Is he catering to any particular committee members or views?
- What are the reactions on the union committee employees? Where are the strengths and weaknesses?

At some point in negotiations you will have to evaluate the representative's positions, demands and final goals and the only way to do so, with any degree of accuracy, is to assess them without being influenced by meeting room theatrics.

Discussion of proposals

Get control of negotiations. Review the union demands first with the union and explore, without argumentation, the exact extent and nature of each proposal.

Prepare and present a complete counter-proposal which will balance the union demands. At this point you should attempt to move all further discussions away from the union's original demands, to a thorough analysis of management's proposed contract, placing the emphasis on the company's demands.

- You are not limited in your counter-proposal to issues raised by the union.
- Avoid a contract termination date during your busiest season.

- You are not obligated to grant any benefits retroactively.

- Consider communications with your employees if you reach a stalemate.

Warnings

Avoid "inability to pay" as an argument, or the next thing to it—according to the Board—"refusal of an increase in order to stay competitive."

- You might be obligated to open your books to the union.

Avoid flat rejections.

- Deliberate consideration of proposals is a requisite of good faith bargaining.

Avoid misunderstandings as to what has been agreed upon.

- Have union and company officials initial and date copies of provisions agreed upon.

Ascertain union authority to negotiate.

If the union membership must ratify the committee's agreement, strive for a commitment from the committee that they will recommend ratification of the agreement.

Arbitration clauses

The union may ask you to agree to an arbitration clause should you request a no-strike clause.

Such a clause, of course, gives a third party the right to decide what the contract means in case of a dispute that cannot be resolved between the employer and the union.

You must, therefore, decide at the outset whether the security of a no-strike clause outweighs the hazard of having a third party, a stranger, interpret your labor-management agreement.

Should you decide to include an arbitration clause in your contract, be sure you define or provide for:

- The exact method of selecting an arbitrator.

- The time limits for this selection.

- The powers he shall have when selected.

- The limitations on his authority (that is, subject matters which cannot be considered, such as wages, rates of pay, the right of subcontracting, etc.).

Of course, it is essential that you know as much as possible about prospective arbitrators before you are called upon to make a choice. An arbitrator skilled in wage rate cases, for example, may have little or no experience in disputes involving discharge or discipline.

Your selection should be as educated as possible.

CONTENT OF A LABOR CONTRACT

The legal framework of collective bargaining is a labor contract which usually covers these items:

1. Union recognition: the exclusive right to represent employees.
2. Extent of bargaining unit: who is, and is not, included.
3. Management rights: guarantee of noninterference in operations.
4. Union security and status: good faith partnership.
5. Strikes and lockout: the rules of conduct.
6. Union activities and responsibilities: ability to function.
7. Wage determination: pay scales (single rate for grades or ranges), job evaluation, shift differentials.
8. Wage administration: raises (calendar or merit), premium pay, incentives, bonus.
9. Overtime: at what rate and when applicable.
10. Benefits: insurance, pension, unemployment.
11. Security and protection: job bidding, transfers, promotions, layoffs, recalls.
12. Seniority: regulations to be followed.
13. Health and safety: concern for employee welfare.
14. Working conditions: hours, schedules, services, conveniences.
15. Time not worked but paid: vacations, holidays, rest periods.
16. Discipline and discharge: warnings, penalties, suspension.
17. Grievances: procedure for handling.

GIVEBACKS—AN UNEXPECTED DEVELOPMENT

A quiet revolution in labor relations was spawned by the economic recession of the early 1980's. As this emerged, it became evident that unions were no longer writing the rules.

Unlike industry-wide wage reductions or freezes, which have high visibility, work-rule revisions were being negotiated at the grass roots level by plant managers and union locals.

Factory workers surrendered seniority rules governing the rehiring of laid-off workers. Craft rules that limited management's flexibility to assign workers to different jobs were eased. Airline pilots extended their hours which made carrying a third pilot unnecessary. Long-haul truck drivers eliminated costly rehandling of certain freight.

Unions are understandably hesitant to discuss work-rule concessions since these changes result in job losses. But many work rules, easily negotiated in a period of upcycle prosperity, are outdated and wasteful and cannot be defended.

Unions are belatedly realizing that by their insatiable appetite for more and more they have allowed wages to rise above free-market levels, which contributes to unemployment. Some labor leaders are credited with becoming enlightened and are applauded for being reasonable and consenting to concessions.

These concessions of hard-fought earlier gains are known as "givebacks" of wages and benefits. Whether agreed to reluctantly or willingly, they do attract public attention and earn "Brownie" points for the unions. But in reality, most givebacks aren't actually giving anything back.

While the rate of hourly wages has slowed, profitability has not been fully restored. The result is that despite cutbacks, the index of "real" wages continues to rise and the imbalance between the cost of producing goods and their market value remains unaffected.

The emphasis has, however, shifted from increasing wages to increasing productivity and efficiency. And that's a sign of a long-overdue move in the right direction. As one union leader admitted, "It's pure economics."

STRIKES

The following is taken from the revised edition of *When Labor Problems Confront You* published by the Illinois State Chamber of Commerce.

A strike is a test of economic strength between the union and its members on the one hand and the employer on the other. Regardless of the basis for the strike, the result is economic warfare.

When a union calls its members out on strike its action is always calculated and deliberate. Most unions have internal constitutional requirements to follow in advance of strike, including a vote of the membership involved. But don't be fooled! Only an inept or insecure union will fail to obtain a strike authorization from its members. (Ordinarily an affirmative vote can be obtained simply on the representation to the membership by the international representative that a strike authorization is an essential bargaining tool.) Another thing—experience demonstrates that it is relatively easy to get the employees to walk out—and once out, to stay out for a reasonable period. There are exceptions, but in the absence of concrete and positive evidence to the contrary, planning should be predicated upon this general rule.

Reasons for Strikes

A multitude of reasons can be cited as to why a strike will be called by a union. Here are some:

- To compel recognition of the union.
- To exert pressure on the company during bargaining.
- To protest layoffs, discharges or other actions taken.
- To demonstrate sympathy with another union or local.
- To teach the company a "lesson" and soften it up for future demands.
- To challenge the right of another union to perform work.
- To induce the company to cease doing business with another employer.

If the purpose of the strike is illegal it is unprotected by the Labor Management Relations Act. Otherwise, it is protected activity and your conduct is regulated more fully.

Generally, protected strikes can be divided into two categories—economic and unfair labor practice. In the former case, you have a greater opportunity to respond with economic measures of your own, including permanent replacement of the striking employees. In the latter, you are responsible if an unfair labor practice is proved for your conduct and for reinstatement of the employees.

An economic strike can be turned into an unfair labor practice strike almost any time the company commits an unfair labor practice.

Considerations Checklist

Here are some of the things you will have to think about before your employees walk out:

Your ability to meet your customer or contractual commitments; the effect of any inability on your present as well as future business.

Your employees' ability to secure—

Employment in nearby areas (in farm communities, is it a busy agricultural season with plenty of work? Would your farmer employees just as soon have time off to work their farms?)

Moratorium on time payments at banks, building and loan and small loan houses.

Public assistance or public aid—such as food stamps and aid to families with dependent children of unemployed fathers.

The rights of any of your employees who can or will work during the strike.

Your limitations with respect to obtaining striker replacements.

The tactical means of minimizing union threats if you cannot take a strike. (Offset any appearance of weakness by positive steps; if possible seize the initiative.)

Preparation

Of course, just as in every other phase of your relations with a union, preparation is an essential. You should:

Consult

Your attorney, because again this is a most technical field where following the proper statutory approach will make a substantial difference in dollars and cents.

Inform

Your employees concerning their rights, the status of negotiations or other circumstances involved.

Review

Your commitments and plan carefully how you can meet them as far as possible.

Your other sources to help you meet commitments.

Your inventory (stockpile in advance).

Your security measures.

Your maintenance problems.

Decide

How and where nonstriking personnel will perform their functions. (Be sure you have taken adequate measures to guarantee your continuing access to necessary records.)

How you will distribute pay which you owe to strikers.

864

Whether and how you will pay group insurance premiums.

How you will handle unemployment compensation claims. Be certain to notify your UC office at once!

How you will handle inbound shipments from common carriers—demurrage, etc.

How you will ship outbound goods—deliver to docks of carriers away from your premises, etc. Note: Consider availability of carriers. Not all carriers will cease making pickups or deliveries during a strike. A contract or common carrier operating under an Interstate Commerce Commission certificate of authority has service responsibility even in the face of a strike or picket line.

How you will record all incidents during strike—alert office employees, supervisors and others who work to report untoward acts. Record these incidents and document with sworn statements while they are still fresh in everyone's mind. Such evidence may prove essential to the success of an injunction proceeding or one before the NLRB.

How you will solidify community relations and utilize—

Radio, newspaper and TV releases or ads.
Local chamber of commerce.
Other local organizations.

How you will handle—

Vendors who want to come to your place of business.

How you will maintain customer relations—

Keep them informed.
Ask their help.

What action you will take with respect to violence or other misconduct by striking employees or others. (Disciplinary action, criminal prosecution, etc., present both legal and practical problems.)

There are almost as many approaches which can be followed during a strike as there are strikes. Each one is different from every other, but there are common threads to all. Remember these points:

You have a duty to continue to negotiate with the union certified as representative of your employees during the course of a legal strike.

Even if the strike started as an economic one, almost any conduct considered to be an unfair labor practice may convert it into an unfair labor practice strike.

The law enforcement agencies must be consulted and considered. You have two "strikes" against you if you cannot rely upon law enforcement or have not made adequate provision for it.

Every strike ends sooner or later and you then will have to face up to the conflicts in interest between replacements and returning strikers.

You cannot grant replacements superseniority under the law but you probably will have offered them regular employment.

The union will be in the position of having to insist upon reinstatement of all strikers. Unless you are careful, you will end up with twice as many employees as there are jobs.

Don't make promises to replacements that you may not be able to keep.

There are also various legal strategems which may be employed in connection with resistance to a strike. Under certain circumstances you may have a damage action against the union. If there is mass picketing or violence you may be in a position to obtain an injunction. You have remedies under the federal law against certain types of union activity and you may be in a position to file charges with the NLRB. The board in turn has the right, and in some cases the obligation, to seek an injunction against any such union conduct.

The Aftermath

Complete plans for return to full operation.

Plan carefully the method of recall of your employees. Notify them when and how they should report.

Be concerned with seniority, whether some have been replaced, etc.

Consider the use of local press, radio and TV to recall.

Be sure you have covered how the employees' period of absence during the strike will be treated for such items as vacation eligibility, pension service credit and the like.

Discuss with your supervisors and other nonstriking personnel how to treat returning employees to avoid further ill will.

Follow-up letter to all employees, relating that the strike is over, that there is no ill will, etc. This also may be accomplished by a general meeting of all employees.

Complete and fulfill both the letter and spirit of all agreements.

WHAT TO DO WHEN A STRIKE OCCURS

Unforeseen strikes can be nasty and disruptive, but by being prepared a company can minimize the chances of serious trouble. Develop a security plan to maintain control as soon as a strike begins. According to *Occupational Hazards*, the following steps are sound practice:

1. Alert police and fire departments, public utilities, and the mayor's office.
2. Compile a list of names, addresses, and home telephone numbers of all management personnel, local and international union officials, and all employees, whether union or nonunion.
3. Establish a temporary headquarters outside your place of business.
4. Check offices and telephones for possible wiretapping.
5. Have a photographer on hand to take pictures of unusual picketing activities or any overt hostilities that may arise.
6. Keep duplicates of vital records and computer tapes in a safe place outside the plant.
7. Check to see that fences, gates, and lighting systems are secure and insure that parked cars are kept away from perimeter fences.
8. Protect any windows and lights that may be within rock-throwing distance.
9. Arrange for temporary 24-hour security guards.
10. Check fire protection systems and remove flammables from exposed areas.
11. Have mail picked up at the post office rather than having it delivered to the plant.

STRIKES NO LONGER USEFUL

The news is not good for unions these days. The percentage of membership is declining. Representation elections are being lost in increasing numbers. Givebacks more than offset gains.

The union image is tarnished. The labor movement has little vigor. Organized labor has lost its political clout.

For many union workers this is their first brush with reality. Workers are tempering their demands. There is less militancy. Some union locals are conceding on work-rule changes, giving up marginal fringes, and forfeiting concessions already won. It has finally dawned on them that a job is not guaranteed in the Constitution. Job security comes only from a financially strong employer/company.

Under these conditions, maybe the time has come for organized labor to set aside its chief weapon—belligerency. This may be the time for an examination of the strike as the ultimate weapon of organized labor. It seems appropriate to question whether strikes are producing the same result as they did originally. Have they become counter-productive? Is there a better approach?

In today's economy, strikes are costing more in real terms than they are worth. Locked in battle to the death, strikers seem oblivious to the fact that they are being sucked into a quagmire from which they will not emerge unscathed. Nobody gains anymore. In a prolonged walk-out, workers do not recoup lost wages. In all cases where strikes, or the threat of strikes, obtains an increase in pay scales, the additional labor costs are simply passed on to the consumers, including union members and their families, and things gradually even out, only at an inflated level. Where is the gain in this standoff?

The ripple effect of a shutdown is disrupting. Pushed beyond the point of no return, many employers are dealt a staggering blow jeopardizing their ability to maintain existing jobs. In desperation, staff is cut, jobs are eliminated, plants are closed. How gratifying is it to be the highest rated claimant in the unemployment compensation line?

Allied industries (the suppliers) also suffer when a major business (the buyer) is shut down. Innocent victims with nothing to gain from the strike are deprived of their rights. Tenuous financial support for these and kindred industries is strained. Things may never again be the same.

Over the years union negotiations have concentrated on better wages but not better production. The delicate balance, so vital to a vigorous economy, has been eroded. This trend, obviously, must not only be stemmed but actually reversed. It is not unreasonable to suggest that the legitimate needs of workers must be coalesced with the realities of economic life.

The union movement is ailing, but its demise is not imminent. This is no time for managements to be thinking about dancing on the grave of unionism. Rather, it presents an opportunity to improve the relationship between management and labor instead of continuing the pattern of lopsided encounters.

Management and labor share many mutually beneficial objectives, the most important of which is the revitalization of our industrial base. There are many common goals both sides can identify with, such as more jobs and better workmanship. They don't always have to agree on methods, but they should rise above selfish interests and agree to resolve their disagreements for the common good. There must be a commitment to cooperation rather than antagonism. Maybe strikes should give way to conciliation or arbitration so as not to disrupt production.

The deterioration of industrial output makes it imperative for management and labor to establish rapprochement. The economic advantages enjoyed after World War II have disappeared in part because of persistent problems to which union hostility has contributed.

Union relations have not matured. Union leadership still wears blinders. Insistence upon the obsolete strike, union's iron fist, is evidence of that. In the strike by the nation's air traffic controllers, for example, the PATCO president, leading his 12,000 minions astray, made a regrettable and irreversible decision.

It is time for 19th century union attitudes to adjust to 20th century enlightenment. Unions look back and want to perpetuate programs that proved to be successful. Managements have to look ahead in order to survive and prosper. Progress implies moving forward, and progress made while standing still is really nothing more than digging the hole deeper.

Organized labor can regain its position of usefulness by abandoning practices of the past that don't work anymore and by adopting a better attitude, one of cooperation in a climate where workers are smarter and the current mentality of modern managements outshines the animosity of the proponents of the traditional adversarial approach to collective bargaining.

INCENTIVE AGREEMENT

Faced with a "no job situation," the United Rubber, Cork, Linoleum and Plastic Workers of America union worked out an unusual productivity pact with the management of Pennsylvania Tire and Rubber Company of Mississippi, Inc.

Plagued by losses, the plant in Tupelo, Mississippi closed its doors, throwing 800 employees out of jobs. The supplemental agreement was negotiated in an effort to re-open the facility on a more productive basis.

The contract calls for workers to get 70% of their pay hikes if plant output reaches 75 pounds of tires per man hour, up from 72 pounds when the plant closed. They get 100% when hourly output hits 85 pounds.

The arrangement was an immediate success for both sides. The first month's results indicate production exceeded the 85 pounds per manhour.

SETTLEMENT OF DISPUTES

The customary way to settle disputes between management and the union is to keep on bargaining until the issue(s) is settled. When this fails, there are ways of bringing in an outsider.

1. Mediation: a third party sits in and tries to guide the discussions.
2. Conciliation: a third party tries to help the disputants reach a settlement.
3. Arbitration: an impartial umpire hears the arguments on both sides and renders a binding decision.

GRIEVANCE PROCEDURES

by WALTER E. BAER
Industrial Relations Consultant and Labor Arbitrator

In many companies, the first-line supervisor is given responsibility and authority to deal with the problems and grievances of his employees—and to resolve them by application of the proper remedy. In these companies, the job of administering the labor contract falls squarely on the supervisor's shoulders.

In most cases, the supervisor had no hand in negotiating the contract, nor did he share in drafting its provisions. Nevertheless, he is the one who deals most frequently with employees and with the union—and he must be equipped to represent management's interests and preserve management's rights, or they will quickly go down the drain.

The following list of "Do's and Don'ts" pinpoints the principal practices and pitfalls that the supervisor should be familiar with in handling the grievance machinery. Naturally, all these points are not applicable to every case, but if the supervisor is familiar with all of them —and observes them in his handling of grievances—he will be prepared for almost any kind of case that may arise.

1. Do investigate and handle each and every case as though it may eventually result in an arbitration hearing.
2. Do talk with the employee about his grievance; give him a good and full hearing.
3. Do enforce the contractual time limits.
4. Do comply with contractual time limits on the company for handling the grievance.
5. Don't argue the merits of the grievance first if the grievance is untimely.

6. Don't make agreements with individuals that are inconsistent with the labor agreement.
7. Don't hold back the remedy if the company is wrong.
8. Do visit the work area of the grievant.
9. Do determine if there were any witnesses.
10. Do examine the relevant contract provisions.
11. Do determine if the company has been consistent.
12. Do examine the total agreement and make interpretations based on the whole.
13. Don't admit to the binding effect of a past practice.
14. Do examine prior grievance records.
15. Do produce all available evidence.
16. Do permit a full hearing of the issues.
17. Do identify the relief the union is seeking.
18. Do treat the union representative as your equal.
19. Don't relinquish your authority to the union.
20. Do admit your errors and take corrective action.
21. Don't settle grievances on the basis of what is fair.
22. Do bear burden of proof in discipline and discharge cases.
23. Do treat union representatives and employees as people.
24. Don't argue grievance issues off work premises.
25. Don't give away your copy of the written grievance.
26. Don't discuss grievances of striking employees during an illegal work stoppage.
27. Do satisfy the union's right to relevant information.
28. Don't file management grievances.
29. Don't overlook the precedent value of prior grievance settlements.
30. Don't give long-written grievance answers.
31. Don't trade a grievance settlement for a grievance withdrawal.
32. Do handle cases involving discipline or discharge of union representatives with extra caution and consideration.
33. Don't deny grievances on the premise that your hands have been tied by management.
34. Do control your emotions, your remarks and your behavior.
35. Don't withhold grievance information.
36. Do maintain records of matters relevant to your labor relations situations.
37. Do fully inform your own supervisor of grievance matters.
38. Do remember the union is the moving party.
39. Do determine if there has been equal treatment of employees.
40. Do command respect from employees and union representatives.

41. Do hold your grievance discussions privately.
42. Don't make mutual-consent agreements regarding future management action.
43. Do use the grievance meeting as another avenue of communication.
44. Do know your employees as individuals.
45. Do demonstrate qualities of leadership to your subordinates.

Before entering this discussion and review of the qualities of leadership referred to, here are a few suggestions to supervisors that may enable them to better serve their employer by achieving the greatest degree of cooperation and effectiveness from the workers. Although these are relatively few in number and brief in description, each is important.

Suggestions for Supervisors

1. The foreman should recognize at all times and under all stances that he is supervising people. Nothing in the department should ever become more important in his mind than the people.
2. When he thinks in terms of people, he must always remember that the whole man is his concern. You are not dealing with a workman or a mechanic, but with a human being whose emotions, purposes, prejudices, sympathies, feelings and ideals are part of his life—both on and off the job.
3. Therefore, do not by your words or acts contribute unnecessarily to employee dissatisfaction in your department. Employee dissatisfaction is unnecessary when it is caused by a supervisor's carelessness, sharp tongue, bad temper, poor planning or lack of fairness.
4. You must recognize that there are two sides to every situation and that you do not know the story until you have heard the other side. Do not assume that your story, or the story you know, is always the right story or the whole story. In every situation, keep your mind open until all the facts are in.
5. You should take the initiative yourself when something that affects an employee is wrong or unfair. Let your people see that they can depend on you to go to bat for them. If employees run to the union steward with everything, if they make a grievance of everything, the supervisor is partly to blame because he is not on the job.
6. You should always recognize the importance of time and place in dealing with people. Be a good stage manager. Whenever you have a choice, pick the most favorable time

and the most favorable place for giving employees good news or bad news, for giving them criticism or a pat on the back, for granting a request or denying it.

7. As a mature supervisor, you must be willing to accept responsibility for your own mistakes. People like a man who is "big enough" to admit when he is wrong, and if they cannot like him, they at least respect him. Never underestimate the real importance of your personal relationship with your workers. It will work for you or against you, but it will never be neutral in the long run.

8. And always remember that when you are on the job you live in a glass house. People see more than you realize and then measure you by your actions rather than your words.

What a Follower Looks for in a Leader.

1. He or she wants to follow a leader who is not afraid—not afraid of his/her position, not afraid of his boss, not afraid of a tough job, not afraid of the people who work for him, not afraid of honest mistakes, either theirs or his/hers.

2. He wants a leader who believes the work is important and all those who are in it with him.

3. He wants a leader who will fight for him irrespective of the odds and the circumstances, if he believes him to be right.

4. He wants a leader who will tell him what's what when he knows himself it's coming to him, and without losing his temper.

5. He wants a leader who recognizes him as a person, regardless of his experience, school or training, and regardless of his religion, race, station in life or any organization he may belong to.

6. He wants a leader who knows most of the answers, but who will admit it when he doesn't know and will obtain the answer.

7. He wants a leader who is predictable; that is, one he can depend on being the same all the time.

8. He wants a leader he can't put anything over on, but one who is human enough to look the other way when he occasionally makes a foolish mistake of small consequence.

9. He wants a leader he knows understands him, to whom he is not afraid to go when he has been a fool, when he's ashamed, or when he's proud and satisfied.

10. He wants a leader who is as square as a die, who can't be bribed by anyone, and being square himself, can see through crookedness in any form, regardless of how much or how little crookedness there is.
11. He wants a leader he can get to when he really needs him, and one he can get away from when he's through with him.
12. He wants a leader who will listen when he has something to say, but will terminate the conversation gracefully when he does not.
13. He wants a leader who knows all that's going on first-hand and turns a deaf ear to gossip.
14. He wants a leader who, when he can't be loyal to his company or supervisors, nevertheless does not malign them or undermine them—and, if necessary, may consequently terminate his position.

NOTE: Interested readers who may want further elaboration on any of the above points are encouraged to write directly to Mr. Walter E. Baer, 400 Mansion House, St. Louis, Missouri 63102.

UNION TRENDS

Union growth depends upon its ability to come to grips with at least three main issues:

1. Internal union administration.
2. Union responsibility.
3. Union organizing.

1. *Internal union administration.* A popular criticism is that labor has lost the crusading spirit of a social movement. Apathy of union members "who never had it so good" has replaced the zeal of the 1930's. The rank-and-file union member is content that his membership provides protection against the absolute rule of management over wages, hours and working conditions. He does not participate in the activities of the union except in a crisis when he comes to the aid of the union cause.

The direction is left to professionals who can comprehend the legal and political aspects of unionism. Policy decisions, industry economics and internal union administration are alien to the average member who, it seems, couldn't care less. His personal interest, so necessary for growth, can best be stimulated through involvement and opportunities for up-from-the-ranks leadership.

2. *Union responsibility.* Union responsibility means more than living

up to agreements and concern with the employment effects of union policies. The common characteristic of the union responsibility theme in all periods is self-denial on the part of union leadership. The labor organizations, in formulating their wage and price policies and other demands, must look beyond the counsel of their tradition and out into the broad field of modern economic realities. A union exists for the benefit of its members but its concern over their immediate welfare should not endanger their jobs over the long range.

The issues of labor management are far too complex, far too potent and far too influential on the rest of society to be resolved in the small arena of one group and on the old testing ground of force and power.

3. *Union organizing.* The "no union" vote measured by NLRB representative elections or by valid votes cast has been higher within the past few years than it has ever been; or conversely, the union vote is lower than it has ever been. Therefore the union batting average is lower. The union attitude toward organizing is one of pessimism, defeatism and complacency.

There are three reasons for this:

1. The difficulty in organizing small companies.
2. The indifference of the white-collar worker.
3. Interunion rivalry.

Recognizing these difficulties, attributed to a change in the industrial community, the unions are revising their tactics. The traditional appeals which worked in the evangelical days of unionism are not effective in reaching potential members working in a much more affluent society. The classic blitz campaign must be replaced by a long-run educational program.

Unions in a Different Light

Is the day of the "outside" organizer over? Have employees learned to trust their company leadership more than some stranger with exaggerated promises? Is the antibusiness propaganda of unions actually alienating recruits who work for modern, progressive companies that have come a long way from the early days of worker oppression?

In the past, union leadership could function from a sense of outrage against injustice and be supported by a sympathetic federal administration and by a sympathetic, intellectual middle class. The temper of the times has now changed. The union is no longer regarded as the underdog. Its excesses are not forgiven as readily. The economic atmosphere is uneven. The net effect is that outrage as the dominant mood of the union thrust must be modified to include analysis and reflection.

The public generally accepts the function of the union, but it is a grudging, complaining acceptance. Someday perhaps, we may talk not only of the union's responsibility to the public but also about the public's responsibility to the union, as an indispensable adjunct to our free society.

GOVERNMENT EMPLOYEES UNIONS

Until recent years, unions in private industry have dominated the labor scene. Now public employees have been joining unions in increasing numbers.

Latest figures reveal that 74% of full-time firemen and 55% of police now are members of unions. Of the nation's 9.2 million state and local government employees, 51% belong to unions.

The organizing has been going on quietly, unlike the labor-management confrontations in the early days of trade unionism. Within five years public employees unions are expected to comprise a force rivaling private sector unions in size and in clout.

Not including the military, there are 15 million public employees in the United States. About 6 million are represented by unions. Some of these groups are affiliated with organized labor; the teachers are part of the AFL-CIO. Some aggressive public employees unions have banded together in the Coalition of American Public Employees.

Public employees unions have grown despite a handicap that doesn't afflict private labor unions. The Taft-Hartley Act of 1947 forces private management to negotiate with any union or agent selected by a majority of his employees. However, the Act specifically exempts units of government and most nonprofit organizations from compliance.

GOVERNMENT UNIONS vs. PRIVATE UNIONS

by KARL H. METTKE
Forest Service Personnel Officer
United States Department of Agriculture
Duluth, Minnesota

In private industry and government there are a number of unions and employee organizations. A comparison of the two points up their differences.

Unions in both sectors (private and public) are covered by different legal requirements and laws. The two major laws governing private sector employers and unions are the Wagner Act (1935) and the Taft-

Hartley Act (1947). Government employees are not covered under either law.

Prior to 1962, when government employees didn't have the right to bargain or negotiate with their employers, unions were striving to increase their membership. In 1962, President Kennedy signed Executive Order 10988, Employee-Management Cooperation in the Federal Service, giving government employees encouragement to bargain collectively. This Executive Order stimulated the unionization drives of state, local, and municipal employees. In 1969, President Nixon amended 10988 and issued Executive Order 11491, Labor-Management Relations in the Federal Service, the most powerful Executive Order to ever affect federal employees. Executive Order 11491 enlarged the scope of collective bargaining for federal employees and further enhanced the role of the union.

One of the major impacts which evolved from 11491 concerned the criteria governing unfair labor practices by management or the union. These unfair labor practices are similar in scope to the ones covering private sector employers and unions. Also in importance was the section dealing with discrimination against employees by labor organizations. In 1975, President Ford had a further impact upon federal labor organizations by signing Executive Order 11838, amending 11491, Labor-Management Relations in the Federal Service, which significantly expanded the scope of collective bargaining. The new Executive Order allows labor organizations to negotiate on personnel policies and practices and matters affecting working conditions similar to previous Executive Orders, but in addition permits negotiations on all agency regulations except those for which there is a "compelling need."

As already mentioned, federal employees are not covered under any statute as are private sector employees. Only through Executive Orders are government employees protected. With one stroke of a pen, a President may eliminate any Executive Order. To right this inequity, federal labor organizations are fighting through Congress continuously for Federal Labor-Management laws. Without the passage of a fair Labor-Management law, government employees will never have the same rights as employees in the private sector of the economy.

Denial of Rights

Government employees are also restricted from participating in politics under the Hatch Act. This Act in particular disturbs many government labor organizations. In the private sector, labor organizations may participate actively in politics, whereas in the public sector employees are limited in their participation. Many private labor organizations will back politicians publicly, yet government organizations representing

American citizens who also vote, are restricted in voicing their opinions. Also, while private labor organizations are contributing money for campaigns and elections, government labor organizations cannot provide any money because they would be in violation of the law. In this area, federal employees are denied the basic freedom of choice as expressed in the Constitution. The idea of freedom of speech is unequivocally the right of every American citizen, yet federal employees are denied this right.

An important right currently being denied federal employees is the right to strike. The reason government employees are denied this right is that many jobs are of a critical nature. Yet, in private industry employees in critical industries have the right to strike. Possibly Congress could pass legislation in accordance with Title II of the Taft-Hartley Act, allowing an 80-day cooling-off period prior to any strikes. Another solution to the problem could be worked out through binding arbitration such as with the United Steelworkers of America. Without this right government employees will never have fair and equitable rights.

The major point of difference between government employee organizations and private industry unions concerns legislation. Before equality can be achieved between both private and government labor organizations, Congress must enact needed legislation. Through this legislation labor organizations will be able to communicate freely and openly with management officials. Lacking this, government employees continue to trail behind workers in industry.

The federal sector is just one small area which needs protection under legislation. Within state, local and municipal governments employees are organizing at a faster pace than any group of employees in the United States. These employees also need protection under a Labor-Management law. Many critics fail to recognize these injustices occurring. With the many cities, towns and villages failing to recognize employee labor organizations, much strife has developed. Because of the withholding of recognition, many employees become disenchanted and actually disrupt the orderly flow of work. The evidence can clearly be seen in the Postal Service strike of 1970. By not granting the postal employees exclusive collective bargaining rights, the employees walked out on an illegal strike, disrupting mail service throughout the Northeast. After the walkout, Congress passed legislation granting postal unions collective bargaining rights. Through these rights postal employees were able to negotiate an ironclad contract with the United States Postal Service. Without the legislation, postal employees may never have achieved exclusive recognition. Although strikes are still illegal, postal employee unions still threaten management with wildcat strikes. Until management and the unions realize the necessity and advisability of binding arbitration, mail service may again be disrupted.

Legislation Needed

In the near future other government employee organizations could conduct similar illegal strikes and wildcats, unless Congress passes legislation giving federal employees exclusive collective bargaining rights under the Labor-Management law. Without the passage of laws guaranteeing government employees equal rights, the services they perform for the public will become inefficient and costly from the standpoint of the American taxpayer.

For the past 40 years, while private unions were granted exclusive rights to bargain collectively with their employers, government unions were denied this right until 1962. And even with the Executive Orders, federal employees are still being denied the right to strike. Until Congress reaches an equitable solution, government employees continue to be discriminated against.

Federal employees should not be held responsible for the free spending policies of politicians. Yet, when the government tries to cut back spending programs, the first employees affected are federal employees. In order to protect their constituents, government labor organizations need laws governing their rights in order to protect their membership. Presently, without any legislation, government labor organizations cannot defend their membership effectively. To further complicate matters, the government hierarchy fails to realize the importance of this needed legislation. Until its passage, government employees and their organizations will continue to lobby Congress for the passage of government Labor-Management laws.

The only answer for government employees to attain equitable rights is an illegal strike or wildcat strike. This would be the only way that Congress could respond to the needs of government employees. Through a strike Congress could be made aware of the inequities which are presently inflicted upon government employees. Until the enactment of a fair labor relations law, federal employees will continue to be treated as second-class citizens.

In summary, the main difference between government labor organizations and unions in the private sector is the lack of coverage under a Public Employee Labor Relations law similar to, but not the same as, the Taft-Hartley Act. Today, in some states it is illegal for public employees to join a union or to strike, whereas other states have enacted laws for collective bargaining of public employees. Until a federal law is enacted, public employee unions will be restricted to negotiate on matters and policies which management allows them to negotiate.

NATIONAL LABOR RELATIONS ACT

It is in the national interest of the United States to maintain full production in its economy. Industrial strife among employees, employers and labor organizations interferes with full production and is contrary to our national interest. Experience has shown that labor disputes can be lessened if the parties involved recognize the legitimate rights of each in their relations with one another. To establish these rights under law, Congress enacted the National Labor Relations Act. Its purpose is to define and protect the rights of employees and employers, to encourage collective bargaining, and to eliminate certain practices on the part of labor and management that are harmful to the general welfare.

The National Labor Relations Act states and defines the rights of employees to organize and to bargain collectively with their employers through representatives of their own choosing. To ensure that employees can freely choose their own representatives for the purpose of collective bargaining, the Act establishes a procedure by which they can exercise their choice at a secret ballot election conducted by the National Labor Relations Board. Further, to protect the rights of employees and employers, and to prevent labor disputes that would adversely affect the rights of the public, Congress has defined certain practices of employers and unions as unfair labor practices.

The law is administered and enforced principally by the National Labor Relations Board and the General Counsel acting through more than 45 regional and other field offices located in major cities in various sections of the country. The General Counsel and his staff in the regional offices investigate and prosecute unfair labor practice cases and conduct elections to determine employee representatives. The five-member Board decides cases involving charges of unfair labor practices and determines representation election questions that come to it from the regional offices.

The Rights of Employees

The rights of employees are set forth principally in Section 7 of the Act, which provides as follows:

> Sec. 7. Employees shall have the right to self-organization, to form, join or assist labor organizations, to bargain collectively through repre-

sentatives of their own choosing, and to engage in other concerted activities for the purpose of collective bargaining or other mutual aid or protection, and shall also have the right to refrain from any or all of such activities except to the extent that such right may be affected by an agreement requiring membership in a labor organization as a condition of employment as authorized in section 8(a)(3).

The Union Shop

The Act permits, under certain conditions, a union and an employer to make an agreement (called a union-security agreement) requiring all employees to join the union in order to retain their jobs (Section 8(a)(3)). However, the Act does not authorize such agreements in States where they are forbidden by State law (Section 14(b)).

A union-security agreement cannot require that applicants for employment be members of the union in order to be hired. The most that can be required is that all employees in the group covered by the agreement become members of the union within a certain period of time after the contract takes effect. This "grace period" cannot be less than 30 days except in the building and construction industry. New employees may be required to join the union at the end of a 30-day grace period after they are hired. The Act allows a shorter grace period of 7 days in the building and construction industry (Section 8(f)).

The Right to Strike

Section 7 of the Act states in part, "Employees shall have the right . . . to engage in other concerted activities for the purpose of collective bargaining or other mutual aid or protection." Strikes are included among the concerted activities protected for employees by this section. Section 13 also concerns the right to strike. It reads as follows:

> Nothing in this Act, except as specifically provided for herein, shall be construed so as either to interfere with or impede or diminish in any way the right to strike, or to affect the limitations or qualifications on that right.

It is clear from a reading of these two provisions that the law not only guarantees the right of employees to strike, but also places limitations and qualifications on the exercise of that right.

The lawfulness of a strike may depend on the object or purpose of the strike, on its timing, or on the conduct of the strikers. The object or objects of a strike and whether the objects are lawful are matters that are not always easy to determine. Such issues often have to be decided by the National Labor Relations Board. The consequences can be severe to striking employees and struck employers, involving as they do questions of reinstatement and back pay.

The Right to Picket

The right to picket likewise is subject to limitations and qualifications. As with the right to strike; picketing can be prohibited because of its object or its timing, or misconduct on the picket line. In addition, Section 8(b)(7) declares it to be an unfair labor practice for a union to picket for certain objects whether the picketing accompanies a strike or not.

Collective Bargaining and Representation of Employees

Collective bargaining is one of the keystones of the Act. Section 1 of the Act declares that the policy of the United States is to be carried out "by encouraging the practice and procedure of collective bargaining and by protecting the exercise by workers of full freedom of association, self-organization, and designation of representatives of their own choosing, for the purpose of negotiating the terms and conditions of their employment or other mutual aid or protection."

Collective bargaining is defined in the Act. Section 8(d) requires an employer and the representative of his employees to meet at reasonable times, to confer in good faith about certain matters, and to put into writing any agreement reached if requested by either party. The parties must confer in good faith with respect to wages, hours and other terms or conditions of employment, the negotiation of an agreement, or any question arising under an agreement.

These obligations are imposed equally on the employer and the representative of his employees. It is an unfair labor practice for either party to refuse to bargain collectively with the other. The obligation does not, however, compel either party to agree to a proposal by the other, nor does it require either party to make a concession to the other.

The Employee Representative

Section 9(a) provides that the employee representatives that have been "designated or selected for the purposes of collective bargaining by the majority of the employees in a unit appropriate for such purposes, shall be the exclusive representatives of all the employees in such unit for the purposes of collective bargaining."

A unit of employees is a group of two or more employees who share common employment interests and conditions and may reasonably be grouped together for purposes of collective bargaining. The determination of what is an appropriate unit for such purposes is, under the Act, left to the discretion of the NLRB. Section 9(b) states that the Board shall decide in each representation case whether, "in order to assure to employees the fullest freedom in exercising the rights guaranteed by this Act, the unit appropriate for the purposes of collective bargaining shall be the employer unit, craft unit, plant unit or subdivision thereof."

Generally, the appropriateness of a bargaining unit is determined on the basis of the common employment interests of the employees involved. Those who have the same or substantially similar interests concerning wages, hours and working conditions are grouped together in a bargaining unit.

How a Bargaining Representative is Selected

Although the Act requires that an employer bargain with the representative selected by his employees, it does not require that the representative be selected by any particular procedure so long as the representative is clearly the choice of a majority of the employees. As one of the methods by which employees can select a bargaining representative the Act provides for the NLRB to conduct representation elections by secret ballot.

The NLRB can conduct such an election only when a petition has been filed requesting one. A petition for certification of representatives can be filed by an employee or a group of employees or any individual or labor organization acting on their behalf, or it can be filed by an employer. If filed by or on behalf of employees, the petition must be supported by a substantial number of employees who wish to be represented for collective bargaining and must state that their employer declines to recognize their representative. If filed by an employer, the petition must allege that one or more individuals or organizations have made a claim for recognition as the exclusive representative of the same group of employees.

The Act also contains a provision whereby employees or someone acting on their behalf can file a petition seeking an election to determine whether or not the employees wish to retain the individual or labor organization currently acting as their bargaining representative, whether the representative has been certified or voluntarily recognized by the employer. This is called a decertification election.

Provision is also made for the Board to determine by secret ballot whether the employees covered by a union-shop agreement desire to withdraw the authority of their representative to continue the agreement. This is called a union-shop deauthorization election and can be brought about by the filing of a petition signed by 30% or more of the employees covered by the agreement.

Section 9(c)(1) provides that if a question of representation exists, the NLRB must make its determination by means of a secret ballot election. In a representation election employees are given a choice of one or more bargaining representatives or no representative at all. To be certified as the bargaining representative, an individual or a labor organization must receive a majority of the valid votes cast.

Unfair Labor Practices of Employers

The unfair labor practices of employers are listed in Section 8(a) of the Act; those of labor organizations in Section 8(b). Section 8(e) lists an unfair labor practice that can be committed only by an employer and a labor organization acting together.

Section 8(a)(1) forbids an employer "to interfere with, restrain or coerce employees in the exercise of the rights guaranteed in section 7." Any prohibited interference by an employer with the rights of employees to organize, to form, join or assist a labor organization, to bargain collectively, or to refrain from any of these activities, constitutes a violation of this section. This is a broad prohibition on employer interference, and an employer violates this section whenever he commits any of the other employer unfair labor practices. In consequence, whenever a violation of Section 8(a)(2), (3), (4) or (5) is committed, a violation of Section 8(a)(1) is also found. This is called a "derivative violation" of Section 8(a)(1).

Section 8(a)(2) makes it unlawful for an employer "to dominate or interfere with the formation or administration of any labor organization or contribute financial or other support to it." This section not only outlaws "company unions" that are dominated by the employer, it also forbids an employer to contribute money to a union he favors or to give it advantages that are denied to rival unions.

Section 8(a)(3) makes it an unfair labor practice for an employer to discriminate against employees "in regard to hire or tenure of employment or any term or condition of employment" for the purpose of encouraging or discouraging membership in a labor organization.

Section 8(a)(4) makes it an unfair labor practice for an employer "to discharge or otherwise discriminate against an employee because he has filed charges or given testimony under this Act."

Section 8(a)(5) makes it illegal for an employer to refuse to bargain in good faith about wages, hours and other conditions of employment with the representative selected by a majority of the employees in a unit appropriate for collective bargaining.

Unfair Labor Practices of Labor Organizations

Section 8(b)(1)(A) forbids a labor organization or its agents "to restrain or coerce employees in the exercise of the rights guaranteed in section 7." The section also provides that it is not intended to "impair the right of a labor organization to prescribe its own rules" concerning membership in the labor organization.

Section 8(b)(1)(B) prohibits a labor organization from restraining or coercing an employer in the selection of a bargaining representative. The prohibition applies regardless of whether the labor organization is the majority representative of the employees in the bargaining unit.

Section 8(b)(2) makes it an unfair labor practice for a labor organization to cause an employer to discriminate against an employee in violation of Section 8(a)(3).

Section 8(b)(3) makes it illegal for a labor organization to refuse to bargain in good faith with an employer about wages, hours and other conditions of employment if it is the representative of his employees.

Section 8(b)(4) prohibits a labor organization from engaging in strikes or boycotts or taking other specified actions to accomplish certain purposes or "objects" as they are called in the Act.

Section 8(b)(5) makes it illegal for a union to charge employees who are covered by an authorized union-security agreement a membership fee "in an amount which the Board finds excessive or discriminatory under all the circumstances."

Section 8(b)(6) forbids a labor organization "to cause or attempt to cause an employer to pay or deliver or agree to pay or deliver any money or other thing of value, in the nature of an exaction, for services which are not performed or not to be performed."

Section 8(b)(7), added to the Act by Congressional amendment in 1959, prohibits a labor organization that is not currently certified as the employees' representative from picketing or threatening to picket with an object of obtaining recognition by the employer (recognitional picketing) or acceptance by his employees as their representative (organizational picketing).

Conclusion

The objective of the National Labor Relations Act, to avoid or reduce industrial strife and protect the public health, safety and interest, can best be achieved by the parties or those who may become parties to an industrial dispute. Voluntary adjustment of differences at the community and local level is almost invariably the speediest, most satisfactory and longest lasting way of carrying out the objective of the Act.

Long experience has taught that when the parties fully understand their rights and obligations, they are more ready and able to adjust their differences voluntarily.

NATIONAL LABOR RELATIONS BOARD

The rights of employees declared by Congress in the National Labor Relations Act are not self-enforcing. To ensure that employees may exercise these rights, and to protect them and the public from unfair labor practices, Congress in 1935 established the National Labor Relations Board to administer the Act.

The purpose of the National Labor Relations Act is to serve the public interest by reducing interruptions in commerce caused by industrial strife. It seeks to do this by providing orderly processes for protecting and implementing the respective rights of employees, employers and unions in their relations with one another. The achievement of this aim through evenhanded administration and judicious interpretation and enforcement of the Act is the overall job of the National Labor Relations Board.

In its statutory assignment, the NLRB has two primary functions:

1. To determine and implement, through secret ballot elections, the free democratic choice by employees as to whether they wish to be represented by a union and, if so, by which one; and
2. To prevent and remedy unlawful acts, called unfair labor practices, by either employers or unions.

The NLRB does not act on its own motion in either function. It processes only those charges of unfair labor practices and petitions for employee elections which may be filed with it at one of its regional offices, or other smaller field offices.

History of the Law

The present National Labor Relations Act has developed from three congressional enactments. The 1935 Act, often called "The Wagner Act," outlawed only employer unfair labor practices—such as interference with employees' freedom to organize and bargain collectively, domination of unions, antiunion discrimination and refusal to bargain.

In 1947, the Taft-Hartley Act, formally titled the Labor Management Relations Act, added prohibitions against certain types of union conduct—such as intimidation of employees, restraint or coercion of employers, refusal to bargain collectively, and engaging in certain types of strikes and picketing such as jurisdictional disputes, so-called secondary boycotts, and the like.

In 1959, the Landrum-Griffin Act, titled the Labor-Management Reporting and Disclosure Act, again amended the basic labor relations statute. Much of this Act was designed to provide safeguards for union members, in terms of ensuring the protection of individual members' rights against possible abuse by their union. Portions of the Act are enforced by the Department of Labor and other portions are enforceable by district courts on civil actions brought by union members. But the 1959 Act also modified the National Labor Relations Act in certain respects: Restrictions were placed on organizational and recognitional picketing, secondary boycott provisions were tightened, hot cargo contracts were outlawed, and steps were taken to eliminate the "no man's land" between federal and state jurisdiction in labor relations disputes.

Whatever the changes in the Act itself, the NLRB is now and has been for several decades, dedicated to the efficient and impartial administration of the law entrusted to it.

Structure of the Board

The NLRB has five board members and a General Counsel, each appointed by the President with Senate consent. The board members are appointed to five-year terms, the term of one member expiring each year. The statute specifies that the President shall designate one member to serve as Chairman of the Board. The General Counsel is appointed to a four-year term. Reappointments may be made.

Headquartered in Washington, the NLRB has 32 regional offices and 16 smaller field offices throughout the country. Total Washington and field staffs number approximately 2,700.

The NLRB's judicial functions are separate, by law, from its prosecuting functions. The five-member Board acts primarily as a quasi-judicial body in deciding cases upon formal records, generally upon review from Regional Directors' or Administrative Law Judges' decisions. The General Counsel is responsible for the investigation and prosecution of charges of violations of the Act, and he has general supervision of the regional offices.

The NLRB has no statutory independent power of enforcement of its orders, but it may seek enforcement in the U.S. Courts of Appeals. Similarly, parties aggrieved by its orders may seek judicial review in the courts.

Annually, the U.S. Courts of Appeals hand down some 350 decisions related to enforcement and/or review of Board orders in unfair labor practice proceedings. Of these, about 85% affirm the Board in whole or in part.

NLRB Procedures

Upon the filing of an unfair labor practice charge with an NLRB regional office, members of the professional staff of that office investigate circumstances from which the charge arises, in order to determine whether formal proceedings are warranted. Approximately one-third of the unfair labor practice allegations are found, after investigation, to require legal disposition. In such cases, the regional office works with the parties in an attempt to achieve a voluntary settlement adequate to remedy the alleged violation. A very substantial number of cases are settled at this stage. If a case cannot be settled, then a formal complaint is issued, and the case is tried before an Administrative Law Judge.

NLRB Administrative Law Judges conduct formal hearings and issue decisions, which may be appealed to the five-member Board; if they are not appealed, the Administrative Law Judges' recommended orders become orders of the Board.

The NLRB's traditional emphasis on voluntary disposition of cases at all stages means that only about five percent of the unfair labor practice charges originally filed with the regional offices are litigated all the way through to a decision of the Board. Yet, despite the small percentage, the Board is still called on to decide more than 1,000 unfair labor practice cases and some 600 representation cases each year—an extraordinarily demanding case load for a five-member tribunal.

In representation election cases, the 32 Regional Directors have the authority to process all petitions, rule on contested issues, and direct elections or dismiss the requests, subject to review by the Board on limited grounds. The NLRB, through its regional offices, conducts some 9,000 representation elections a year in which more than half a million employees exercise their free choice by secret ballot.

A Busy Board

Each fiscal year the NLRB receives more than 50,000 cases of all kinds. Some two-thirds are unfair labor practice charges. Over the years charges filed against employers have outnumbered those filed against unions by about two to one. Charges are filed by individual workers, employers and unions. The total flow of cases of all types filed with the NLRB has sharply increased in the past decade.

Since its establishment, the NLRB has processed more than 300,000 cases alleging violation of the Act's prohibitions against unfair labor practices. And it has conducted more than 250,000 secret ballot, employee self-determination elections in appropriate worker groups. Millions of employees have cast ballots in these elections—the 30 millionth voter entered the polling place in 1976.

THE RAILWAY LABOR ACT

The Railway Labor Act of May 20, 1926, as amended, governs the labor relations of railroads and airlines and their employees. The act makes it the mutual duty of carriers and employees to make and maintain agreements, guarantees and provides for the exercise of labor's collective bargaining rights, and prescribes methods for the settlement of various types of disputes.

The act applies to all railroads, express companies and sleeping-car companies engaged in interstate commerce and their subsidiaries (such as refrigerator car companies, bridge companies, and others engaged in transport, transfer or storage services) and to airlines engaged in interstate and foreign commerce and transportation of mail.

Two agencies administer the act:

The National Mediation Board in Washington, D.C., composed of three members appointed by the President, with the advice and consent of the Senate, handles disputes concerning

1. designation of representatives for collective bargaining purposes,
2. negotiation of changes in rates of pay and new or revised collective bargaining agreements, and
3. interpretatation of agreements reached through mediation.

The National Railroad Adjustment Board in Chicago, Illinois, is composed of 34 members, 17 of whom represent and are paid by the carriers, and 17 who represent the national railway labor organizations. Unlike the National Mediation Board, it has jurisdiction only over railway carriers and employees. It makes final and binding decisions in disputes growing out of grievances or the application and interpretation of existing agreements.

Rights of Employees

Section 2 of the Act states that: Employees shall have the right to organize and bargain collectively through representatives of their own choosing. Section 2 (3), (4), and (5) of the Act, outlined below, which protect this right, are made a part of every collective agreement.

In order to protect workers in exercising this right, carriers are forbidden to do any of the following acts:

1. To deny or question the right of their employees to organize or to interfere with their organization (sec. 2(4)).
2. To use funds of the carrier in maintaining any labor organization or to pay any employee representative (sec. 2(4)).

3. To influence employees to join or not to join any labor organization (sec. 2(4)).
4. To require employees to sign any agreement promising to join or not to join any labor organization (sec. 2(5)).

Determination of Collective Bargaining Representatives

Section 2(3) of the Act states that collective bargaining representatives shall be designated by the respective parties without interference, influence or coercion by either party over the designation of representatives by the other; and neither party shall in any way interfere with, influence or coerce the other in its choice of representatives.

It is specifically provided that employee representatives for collective bargaining shall not be required to be employees of the employer.

The Act states that the majority of any craft or class of employees shall have the right to determine who shall be the representative of the class or craft (sec. 2(4)). While the Board has no power to establish crafts or classes of employees, it may designate who may participate in representation elections. Such determinations are usually made in the light of accepted practice in employee self-organization over a period of years.

Where any labor organization, committee or employee representative asserts that a dispute exists concerning representation of employees for the purposes of the Act, it is the duty of the National Mediation Board to investigate such a dispute and conduct an election by secret ballot or any other suitable method to determine who is the collective bargaining representative of the employees (sec. 2(9)). If a majority of the employees in a craft or class chooses an individual or a labor organization, the Board then issues a certification of that fact to the parties and the carrier.

The Act was amended in 1951 to specifically provide (sec. 2(11)) that carriers and labor organizations may negotiate union shop and checkoff agreements.

Interference by carriers in the designation of employee representatives is a misdemeanor. Employees may also appeal to the federal courts for an injunction to restrain the carrier from violating the act.

Duties of Carriers and Employees to Bargain Collectively

Section 2(1) states: It shall be the duty of all carriers, their officers, agents and employees to exert every reasonable effort to make and maintain agreements concerning rates of pay, rules and working conditions, and to settle all disputes, whether arising out of the application of such agreements or otherwise, in order to avoid any interruption to commerce or to the operation of any carrier growing out of any dispute between the carrier and the employees thereof.

Every carrier is required to file with the National Mediation Board a copy of every contract with its employees, as well as all changes when made.

Procedure in Making and Revising Agreements

The Act provides for the following procedure in making and revising agreements:

1. *Notice*—Carriers and employees alike are required to give at least 30 days' notice of any intended change in their collective bargaining agreements regarding rates of pay, rules or working conditions, and within 10 days the time and place for a conference shall be agreed upon.

2. *Mediation*—In case of a dispute not settled in conference, either party may request the mediation services of the National Mediation Board. The Board, at its discretion, may also proffer its services without a request.

3. *Arbitration*—If mediation is unsuccessful, the Board shall endeavor to induce the parties to submit their controversy to arbitration. However, the Act does not compel the parties to arbitrate. Arbitration boards, when agreed upon, may consist of three or six members, one-third of the number being appointed by each party to the dispute, who must then choose the remaining members. If they fail to do so within a time limit specified in the Act, the Board appoints the neutral members. At the request of either or both parties, any arbitration board so established shall also have authority to pass on any dispute over the meaning or application of its award.

4. *Emergency Boards*—Should arbitration be refused by either party and the dispute remain unsettled, and should it, in the judgment of the National Mediation Board, threaten substantially to interrupt interstate commerce to a degree such as to deprive any section of the country of essential transportation service (sec. 10), the National Mediation Board is required to notify the President. The President may then, at his discretion, appoint an Emergency Board to investigate and report within 30 days. During this period, and for 30 days after the Board has made its report to the President, no change may be made in the conditions which gave rise to the dispute except by mutual agreement of the parties.

Procedure in Disputes

The National Mediation Board, on request of either party, will give interpretations of agreements reached through mediation. The following procedure is prescribed for all other instances of disputes arising out of agreements.

1. When disputes arise growing out of grievances or out of the interpretation or application of agreements, they shall be handled through the regular grievance procedure in the contract up to and including the chief operating officer of the carrier.
2. If no adjustment is reached, either or both parties may petition the appropriate division of the National Railroad Adjustment Board, submitting a full statement of the facts and supporting data. The Board is divided into four divisions, each representing the carriers and the labor organizations equally.

   Divisional jurisdictions are:

   > First Division   —train, engine and yard service employees.
   > Second Division—shop crafts.
   > Third Division   —station, tower, telegraph, dispatching, clerical, store, maintenance-of-way, sleeping car and dining car employees and signalmen.
   > Fourth Division —Marine service employees, and all other employees not included in the first three divisions.

3. The appropriate division may hold hearings if requested by either party and make an award.
4. If the division fails to agree and cannot itself agree on a referee, the National Mediation Board is required to appoint a referee to sit with the division and make an award.
5. Awards of the Adjustment Board are final and binding. If a carrier fails to comply with a money award, such as the payment of back pay, the employee or labor organization in whose favor it is made may apply to a U.S. district court for enforcement.

Procedure in Disputes—Airlines

Airline carriers and their employees are required by the Act to establish machinery for the adjustment of grievances as a part of their collective agreements.

Maintenance of the Status Quo

While conferences on making or revising agreements are being held and while the National Mediation Board is acting in any dispute, the carrier may not alter rates of pay, rules or working conditions.

Posting Notices

All carriers covered by the Act are required to post notices specified by the National Mediation Board stating that all disputes will be handled in accordance with the Act, and reprinting sections of the Act relating to the rights of employees.

Penalties

Violation by a carrier of the provisions outlined above regarding rights of employees, determination of collective bargaining representatives, giving notice of intended change of agreements, and posting notices, is a misdemeanor punishable by a fine up to $20,000, imprisonment or both. Claims of violations should be filed with the U.S. district attorney in the area where the violation occurred.

EMERGENCY PROVISIONS OF THE TAFT-HARTLEY LAW

These are the prescribed steps the President of the United States takes when he invokes the emergency provisions of the 1947 Taft-Hartley Act:

1. Finding that a strike or lockout threatens to imperil the public health or safety, the President names a fact-finding panel and fixes an early deadline for it to report. Usually the panel has three members. The deadline has ranged from less than one day to 24 days.
2. After receiving the report, the President may direct the attorney general to obtain a U.S. District Court injunction sending the strikers back to their jobs and requiring that bargaining be resumed with the help of federal mediators.
3. Within 60 days after the issuance of the court order, the fact-finding panel must file a second public report that includes a statement of the employer's last offer.
4. Within another 15 days, the National Labor Relations Board must complete a secret ballot among the workers on the last offer. The voting results are reported to the attorney general.

5. Within five more days the attorney general must ask the court to discharge the injunction.

This completes the 80-day "cooling off" and bargaining period. If the last offer from the employer has been rejected and no agreement reached by bargaining, the union is free to resume its strike.

Failure to obey the injunction against striking can result in charges of contempt of court and a fine. Strikers who had been receiving unemployment compensation, food stamps or welfare payments would no longer be eligible for such benefits if they ignored a back-to-work order.

RIGHT-TO-WORK LAWS

State right-to-work laws provide that no one shall be forced against his will to belong to a union in order to hold a job. Such laws now apply to private sector workers in 20 states and to public employees in 32 states. Right-to-work laws are permitted under a section of the federal Taft-Hartley Act which the labor unions have been trying to persuade Congress to repeal.

Right-to-work laws guarantee the right of employees to voluntarily form, join or assist lawful labor organizations. They also guarantee the right of workers not to join or support unions. These laws are based on the premise that no American should be compelled to join a union.

Union opposition refers to proponents of state right-to-work proposals as "labor haters, labor baiters and labor traitors." But right-to-work laws are not advanced by labor haters. They are proposed and supported by people who want to preserve liberty.

At one time the other side of this proposition required job applicants to agree never to join a labor union. Such a requirement by employers was banned years ago in a statute prohibiting what even the law books call "yellow-dog contracts." There was no complaint from the unions when this change was enacted. Now the unions are yelling "unfair" because these state right-to-work laws make it illegal to require anyone to belong to a labor union as a prerequisite for holding a job.

Compulsory unionism that denies employment to nonmembers is more unfair than when companies deny employment to union members because, shielded against antitrust laws, unions are monopolies while companies are not.

Two terms should be defined. "Union shop" means forced membership. "Agency shop" means forced dues payment whether member or not.

In a free society the argument that those employees who pay dues

894

provide benefits to the "freeloaders" cannot justify forced membership or financial support by those who disapprove of a union's position or tactics. A union is a private organization and if it cannot sell membership on its merits, should government be expected to legislate its membership for it?

The father of trade unionism in America, Samuel Gompers, opposed compulsory unionism.

Modern day union spokesmen, however, castigate nonunion employees as "free riders" who receive the benefits of collective bargaining without paying their share of the cost of bargaining. Unions, they complain, are unfairly obligated by law to represent both members and nonmembers.

Industry likes right-to-work laws and, other things being equal, often moves where it can have their protection against compulsory unionism in its plants. The 20 states with right-to-work laws continue to create more manufacturing jobs than the remaining 30 states. According to an analysis by the U.S. Labor Department's Bureau of Labor Statistics, a net gain of 928,000 manufacturing jobs was achieved by the 20 right-to-work states, collectively, between 1966 and 1976, and during that same period a net loss of 1,237,500 such jobs was suffered by the non-right-to-work states, collectively. It may be argued that these laws stimulate economic growth by attracting job-creating investments.

The debate will go on. There are divergent viewpoints. Industrial leaders, the labor movement, the politicians and the individual workers all have their own interests and opinions. The fundamental issue, however, is the freedom of an individual to earn a living without being compelled to obey and pay tribute to an organization that may be actively opposing his personal interest and conviction.

Right-to-work is really several rights:

1. The right to join a union.
2. The right not to have to join a union.
3. The right to pay union dues if not a union member.
4. The right not to pay union dues if not a union member.

In short, right-to-work laws reflect a climate in which union officials are accorded fair, but not special, treatment. For the workers the right-to-work laws mean only that every person shall have access to a job regardless of his union membership or nonmembership.

Excerpts from the
IOWA RIGHT-TO-WORK LAW

Section 736A.1. Right to Join Union.—It is declared to be the policy of the State of Iowa that no person within its boundaries

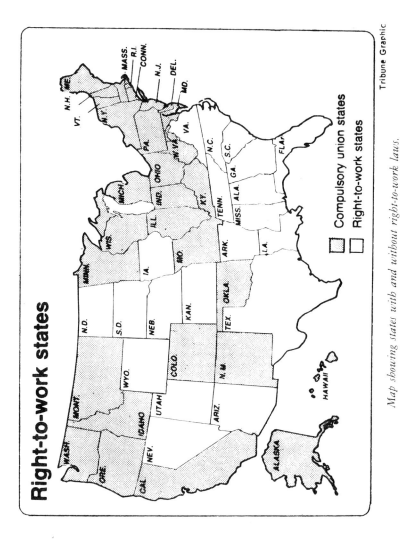

Map showing states with and without right-to-work laws.

Tribune Graphic

shall be deprived of the right to work at his chosen occupation for any employer because of membership in, affiliation with, withdrawal or expulsion from, or refusal to join, any labor union, organization or association, and any contract which contravenes this policy is illegal and void.

Section 736A.2. Refusal to employ prohibited.—It shall be unlawful for any person, firm, association or corporation to refuse or deny employment to any person because of membership in, or affiliation with,

STATES WITH RIGHT-TO-WORK LAWS

Private sector employees are shielded from compulsory unionism by laws or constitutional provisions adopted by the following 20 states:

Alabama	Nevada
Arizona	North Carolina
Arkansas	North Dakota
Florida	South Carolina
Georgia	South Dakota
Iowa	Tennessee
Kansas	Texas
Louisiana	Utah
Mississippi	Virginia
Nebraska	Wyoming

The forced unionization of public sector employees is forbidden by the following 32 states:

Alabama	New Jersey
Arizona	New Mexico
Arkansas	New York
California	North Carolina
Connecticut	North Dakota
Delaware	Ohio
Florida	Oklahoma
Illinois	Pennsylvania
Iowa	South Carolina
Kansas	South Dakota
Louisiana	Texas
Maryland	Utah
Mississippi	Vermont
Missouri	Virginia
Nebraska	Washington
Nevada	Wyoming

or resignation or withdrawal from, a labor union, organization or association, or because of refusal to join or affiliate with a labor union, organization or association.

Section 736A.3. Contracts to exclude unlawful.—It shall be unlawful for any person, firm, association, corporation or labor organization to enter into any understanding, contract or agreement, whether written or oral, to exclude from employment members of a labor union, organization or association, or persons who do not belong to, or who refuse to join, a labor union, organization or association, or because of resignation or withdrawal therefrom.

Section 736A.4. Union dues as prerequisite to employment prohibited.—It shall be unlawful for any person, firm, association, labor organization or corporation, or political subdivision, either directly or indirectly, or in any manner or by any means as a prerequisite to or a condition of employment to require any person to pay dues, charges, fees, contributions, fines or assessments to any labor union, labor association or labor organization.

Section 736A.8. Exception.—The provisions of this chapter shall not apply to employers or employees covered by the federal Railroad Labor Act.

CHAPTER XI

ADMINISTRATION

PERSONNEL RECORDS

PERSONNEL records have always been necessary for good personnel administration. Now they take on added importance because of
federal and state labor and antidiscrimination laws. These records
should be accurate, complete and convenient.

It is necessary that certain information be retained and made readily
available for managers and supervisors, union committee, government
inspectors, reference inquiries, as well as personnel staff.

Most personnel offices maintain an individual file folder for each
employee. The papers collected in this folder are kept in date order.
Into this file folder are placed the original application blank, the test
profile, replies to reference inquiries, and any other helpful information gathered at time of hire. To these basic data are added all performance ratings, salary increases and rejections, transfer notices, leaves of
absence, and finally the termination notice and exit interview report.
At this time the file is closed and stored for handy reference for a period
of time (say five years) after which it is destroyed.

There are other records important to personnel administration.
These could be emergency notification, skill listing, educational
achievement, military history, work background and the like. This type
of information, if on loose sheets, may be filed in each employee's
folder, or recorded on a personal history card either in full or coded,
notched or punched.

Since these file folders can become cumbersome, especially for a long
service employee for whom many sheets of paper are accumulated, it
is advisable to post the data each time the sheet is processed on a handy
employee Progress Record Card for instant reference. This 5 x 8 card
is kept in alphabetical or department order in a convenient visual file
tray or cabinet. In addition to minimum summary information, such as
name, address, telephone number, Social Security number, marital status, birth date, seniority date, and payroll or clock number, it also
carries condensed information about education, tests, dependents and

899

so on. To this is posted in chronological order the progress the employee makes in jobs, salary, performance ratings, etc.

Separate records are kept for insurance and retirement information. In addition, personnel clerks may develop their own systems for salary review and performance rating reminders. Seniority lists for service recognition may also be maintained. When these manual methods become burdensome the time is at hand to consider putting records on IBM or other form of mechanization.

Personnel is also required to retain the application forms of all applicants who are rejected or otherwise not hired. Government compliance inspectors make it necessary for Personnel to keep some kind of unofficial inventory of minority group members and the progress they make.

Besides the official company records maintained in Personnel, it is customary for department managers to keep their own records. This is not a Personnel function or concern and therefore managers may abstract any information they feel might be useful to them as the personnel papers come to their desks for signature.

As a company grows larger, or a personnel program becomes more comprehensive, it may require a more sophisticated system of personnel record-keeping. When a manual method is no longer adequate, the personnel executive is directed to refer to the section on "Computerization of Personnel Records and Reports" page 953.

LIVING RECORDS

Just as in life we have too much government by law and not enough government by men, so do we in business have too much automation, not in the machines and procedures, but in the minds of men. The real danger is not in machines thinking like men but in men thinking like machines.

This sad state of affairs is all the more deplorable when it affects the employee program. In a materialistic age we substitute impersonal procedures for personal considerations. We worry about automation, then try to apply automation principles to human values.

In too many personnel offices the staff is concerned more with paperwork than with people. The clerks, particularly, busy themselves with records, reports and statistics, keeping track of all sorts of information, which of itself does nothing to contribute to a better organization.

The papers, and the figures on these papers, are lifeless. But behind each piece of paper is a human being. Viewed in this light, each record, each posting, each statistic takes on real significance.

Any clerk who cannot recognize this distinction does not belong in the personnel office.

UPDATING PERSONAL DATA

At time of employment, personal data about each employee are recorded. Much of this comes from the application blank, resumé, interview results, tests, insurance application cards and the like. Once the new employee is "processed on the payroll" the information is recorded and filed.

A file may be reviewed at a later date when an employee is up for consideration or possibly in trouble. It is surprising how many employee file folders or record cards are never looked at, except possibly to add salary or status changes to the progress card or a paper of some kind to the file folder.

The personal information is seldom, if ever, changed. It makes one wonder what value personal data that was obtained 10 years ago may have. Surely an employee at age 30 is noticeably different from what he was when he first came out of school.

To meet the problem, some companies make an effort to keep personal data current. Probably the most common approach is to verify addresses and telephone numbers annually, or to get a statement once a year about whom to notify in case of emergency. But there are other things personnel offices may do to keep their employee records current and, hence, of more worth.

Changes in marital or family status may be asked for. Additional education acquired or new skills should be noted. Outside activities, particularly offices held or honors received, would certainly enhance an employee's data in the file. Depending upon the nature of the business, or the type of workforce, other personal data may be updated.

This is really not too difficult when employee records are processed mechanically. Each employee may be given a print-out of his own record of personal data, with the request that if any of the recorded information is not current he may wish to have changes or corrections made. When records are handled manually, the updating is done by contacting each employee by written memo or in person, with the same invitation to keep his record up-to-date in order to reflect him at his best.

If people change, then the records and reports about them should also be changed. Otherwise they lose some of their value as time goes on.

PRIVACY PROTECTION

Public policy issues such as individual privacy do not suddenly spring up fully developed. They creep silently into people's lives, often not being perceived until considerable damage is done. The early implementation of information privacy protection initiatives helps assure that the potential threats to freedom, through continuing erosion of individual private rights, are being directly addressed.

Gone are the days when companies regulated the personal, off-the-job lifestyles of their employees. Going are the many forms, interview techniques, and testing devices which are seen as intrusive and unwarranted questionings about workers' personal lives. Today the emphasis is on discontinuing the gathering of unnecessary personal information and guarding against the improper use of personal data in the files.

Companies have always invaded people's privacy with routine questioning and steel file cabinet storage. But computer systems with their expansive facilities for collecting data, their unlimited capacity for retaining data, and the ease with which the information can be readily retrieved and instantaneously disseminated, even to remote outlets, have intensified the problem.

In 1966 the Freedom of Information Act responded to a growing concern among workers about government records kept on their private lives. The Privacy Act of 1974 gave access and permitted review of this information by citizens.

Both these pieces of legislation apply only to government files but wider-ranging legislation continues to find support on national and state levels. Seven states—California, Connecticut, Maine, Michigan, Ohio, Oregon, and Pennsylvania—have already enacted laws protecting employees against intrusive or mistaken information in personnel files. Bills numbering in the hundreds on private sector privacy protection have been presented to the Congress. The lawmakers seem to be responding to a strong concern throughout the general population for limiting information gathered on individuals and opening those files to them.

There is a strong concern for privacy protection among the industrial democracies of Europe. Sweden, France, West Germany, Austria, and Belgium have enacted omnibus bills. The United Kingdom has a privacy commission studying possible legislation.

Employer reaction to the privacy issue shows they might be more sensitive to the ways privacy might be invaded than the data subjects themselves. Personnel people recognize that other ways than direct personal questions must be found to determine whether an applicant is a good prospect for employment.

Much of the information in personnel files is gathered and kept to comply with government regulations or to protect the employer against possible discrimination proceedings. There seems to be a conflict between the strong movement toward confidentiality in record-keeping and the employer's need to collect enough information to assure that the company is in compliance with state and federal demands.

The Equal Employment Opportunity Commission regulations demand updated forms and procedures for initial hirings. The Occupational Safety and Health Administration and the Office of Federal Contract Compliance Programs require records for their own purposes. Performance appraisals must be adapted and firmed up in the light of recent interpretations of the Age Discrimination in Employment Act amendments regarding mandatory retirement. These and many other changes are necessary if employers are to avoid costly grievance suits. Many personnel offices feel obliged to amass data on workers to defend the company against possible charges of discrimination.

In a sense, companies may feel they are caught up in a "no-win" situation.

Consider All Personal Data

In addition to the basic information—such as name, Social Security number, and the like—that personnel files start out with in initial employment, there is a continuing accumulation of data relating to the employment record. The following personal information must also be taken into account when privacy protection policies are formulated:

Pre-employment testing: Skill tests determine a candidate's suitability for the position applied for and because they must be directly related to the job, they take their place in the pre-employment process. Personality and psychological tests should be directly job-related, if they are to be used at all. Any widespread use of polygraphs or other instruments whose effectiveness is under question is incompatible with privacy protection.

Medical: Companies collect medical data on employees—the pre-employment physical, subsequent reports of physical examinations, work restrictions, etc. This information is of a highly personal nature and should be kept separate from the general personnel file and certainly from any circulating file. If medical files are examined, a designated physician should be present.

Benefit: If a company receives and processes benefit claims in-house, those claims forms should be protected by stringent privacy safeguards. Those claims filings and their ultimate disposition should be kept separate from personnel files. It is an invasion of employee privacy to make promotion or termination decisions on the basis of the number and cost of benefit claims.

Arrests and convictions: In the light of recent state laws and federal regulations, employers no longer verify arrest records. Arrests without conviction cast an aura of guilt over a person who has not been legally convicted of any crime. There have been enough stories of innocent people, especially among minorities, who have been arrested unfairly. Conviction records may be sought for certain jobs and there are valid reasons for conviction searches by reputable firms.

Credit: Only about 10% of companies run credit checks on applicants. Apparently such checks are useful for only a small number of sensitive jobs. The position for which the applicant applies should determine whether or not a credit check is run on the individual.

10 Principles

Personnel records are legally the property of employers. The rights have as yet no basis in federal law. Any privacy protection policy must carefully consider the following 10 underlying principles since they find a place in most of the state legislation passed, or in pending state and federal laws.

1. *Mutuality* means that the data keeper and the data subject both have an interest in proper and accurate record-keeping.

2. *Consent* says that employees have some decision-making power over the content, use, and disclosure of the contents of their individual files.

3. *Relevance* requires that only job-related information be demanded.

4. *Fiduciary duty* means that the employer has the responsibility that the data collected are kept securely and passed through proper hands.

5. *Notice* demands that there be no data system on a person whose existence is kept secret, even though access is not given to some files.

6. *Access* means that employees are allowed to see their files, and permitted to correct mistaken information in the record.

7. *Confidentiality* means that information is only given to third parties, whether within or outside the company, on a strict need-to-know basis.

8. *Warranty* determines that information be used only for those purposes for which it was obtained.

9. *Accuracy* is self-explanatory; records should undergo a periodic review and all obsolete material be reclassified, sealed, or destroyed.

10. *Remedy* means that legal protection (or in the case of voluntary compliance, grievance procedures spelled out in the policy books) guards the rights of both workers and management in the whole area of record-keeping.

To translate these principles into practice, the following procedures have been found workable:

1. Employees are informed of all files kept on them, using the handbook and other normal modes of communication.
2. Only relevant information is collected and stored, depending on jobs involved.
3. Managers of personnel files have reasonable assurance that the records they keep are accurate, complete, and up-to-date, therefore useful in decision-making.
4. Access on the basis of a clear need-to-know underlies all internal (within the company) communication of data.
5. Disclosure of personal data outside the organization requires the individual's consent unless valid legal cause can be shown.
6. The employees do have the right to see and copy their own records.

There is quite a difference between notice and access. Certain information of a business-sensitive nature might be kept separate and the employees, while given notice of it, might be denied access to it. Manpower planning charts, succession planning lists, promotability and salary or bonus increase data, supervisor's personal notes in preparation for performance review appraisals, need not be given open access.

Case Study

Companies stand to gain many peripheral benefits from policies which safeguard personnel record confidentiality. Morale gets a boost as employees perceive the company's efforts at fairness. Wasted space in data gathering and storage systems is eliminated as records are streamlined. The files on individuals become more useful as irrelevant information is purged. Cause for employee or union grievance is lessened. And a practice is put in place which might become the focus of an internal or external public relations theme.

International Business Machines Corporation took a stance on fair information practices before the emergence of privacy became an issue with government, civil liberties groups, and activists. It established a privacy code that could become a prototype for other organizations.

Their practices, published for the guidance of managers and communicated to employees, are:

1. Collect, use, and retain only personal information that is required for business or legal reasons.
2. Provide employees with a means of ensuring that their personal information in IBM personnel records is correct.
3. Limit the internal availability of personal information about others to those with a business need to know.

4. Release personal information outside IBM only with employee approval, except to verify employment or to satisfy legitimate investigatory or legal needs.

If an outsider wants to verify that a person works for IBM, the company will release the individual's latest job title, the most recent place of work, and the dates of employment—without contacting the employee. Such information as a person's salary or five-year job chronology is given out only after written approval from the employee.

As for creditors, attorneys, private agencies, and others desiring non-job-related information, nothing is given out without the employee's consent, unless the law requires disclosure. Legitimate requests from government agencies are honored, though the investigators are required to furnish proper identification, prove their legal authority, and demonstrate that the information sought is needed.

Another company, Sentry Insurance, has stated, "Americans are concerned about how much information is gathered about them and why. They want to know how it is gathered, whether it is accurate, and how it is used. They want access to it, and the right to correct, amend, or answer it. They also want to know who else has access to it and under what conditions."

Increased legislative interest on both federal and state levels might well mean that some regulatory action is on the horizon. In that event, companies that have not anticipated this could be caught with only a short preparation time to comply with record-keeping practices that have been publicly discussed for two decades. The principles and general policy statements are already well-defined and have achieved strong consensus. Further, the experience of companies that have already implemented such policies has shown that they are workable.

MICROFILM

Definition of microfilm: *photographic miniaturization.*

History records the concept of microfilm as early as 1829 when John Danzer of Manchester, England, successfully produced a reduced-document-image photograph through the use of a microscope camera lens. It appears again in 1870/71 during the Franco-Prussian War when messages were reduced to small film frames and carried over enemy lines into Paris attached to the legs of homing pigeons.

The development of roll filming, whereby paper and film travel together, was achieved almost simultaneously in the late 1920's by George McCarthy (later to become president of Eastman Kodak's Recordak Division) and Raymond Hessert, both of the United States.

Roll filming proved to be an economically feasible tool as a safety device against the loss of original documents for banks, insurance companies and similar institutions.

Vigorous growth of another microfilm tool, the aperture card, was forced by World War II. After Pearl Harbor, an appeal to the nation brought forth a deluge of topographical material (maps, pictures, etc.) of enemy territory which threatened to inundate government personnel responsible for classifying, sorting, filing and retrieving the various documents. Material was photographed and reduced to a uniform-size, film frame, and mounted on cut-out cards that could be easily sorted, indexed and retrieved as necessary. The prototype cards were laboriously cut by hand, using a razor blade. Today, key-punched aperture cards can be machine-sorted at speeds of 60,000 an hour.

Microfilm adaptations have advanced to the stage where they provide a feasible and economical medium for a multitude of end uses. Technology continues to bring forth smaller and smaller reproductions. While the ultra-micro reductions tend to be limited for specialized use, they are interesting to note. The "microdot" (photochromic microimaging), for instance, actually exists and is not the sole product of science-fiction scriptwriters. The creation of a photograph on film involves a chemical change of various crystals to produce an image. Scientists in the field today are striving to attain an image reproduction within the single crystal—reduction 10 to the 28th power.

Equipment and Microforms

1. Cameras—3 types.
    a. Planetary—the most common for finest clarity.
    b. Rotary—high-speed, low quality mass documentation.
    c. Step and repeat—grid pattern for microfiche.
2. Processor—for film development.
3. Reader—for enlarged visual reading on screen.
4. Reader-Printer—to produce original-size, hard copy.
5. Forms
    a. Roll or reel (for storage).
    b. Magazine or cartridge (for retrieval).
    c. Microthin jacket, aperture or tab card, film strips.
    d. Microfiche (1 3″×5″ sheet holds 98 8½″×11″ pages).
    e. Ultrafiche (1 3″×5″ sheet holds 1,000 8½″×11″ pages).

Microfilming has many advantages:

1. Saves space: the contents of 160 standard file cabinets equals one microfilm cabinet, a total of over 3 million 8½″×11″ documents.
2. Avoids copying errors.

3. Protects records from wear and tear.
4. Reduces fire hazard.

PAPER SHREDDERS

Personnel records are confidential. Their confidentiality is safeguarded while the information is in the active files. But when files are purged, or old files discarded, how is this confidential information destroyed? Haphazard disposal can be more than merely careless; it could be dangerous.

A paper shredder, or electric wastebasket, is one answer. This preserves the confidential aspects of records even after they have outlived their usefulness. It prevents information falling into unauthorized hands. It thwarts forgery of signatures.

Some throat-feed models have flat tables across which the operators pass each item manually. Other flat-table units have conveyor belts to feed material into the shredder gradually. Still other models have sloping tables and papers enter the cutting apparatus by gravity. Most paper shredders turn out strips between $5/_{16}''$ and $1/_{32}''$ wide.

Shredding is faster and cleaner than incinerating records.

REPORTS

What can be said about personnel reports? All personnel offices issue reports, possibly more than they realize. But there is no standard pattern that applies to all companies. Some firms are report happy, others are quite the opposite.

If the boss wants a weekly report of job openings, or involuntary terminations, or new workers hired above minimum, or whatever—he gets it. Some personnel executives send out reports as evidence that they are working. "Look how busy we've been," they say as they list all the things they did last week while they were not writing reports.

Mechanizing personnel records is conducive to the production of all sorts of reports. These might not be the most useful reports; they are the most automatic to grind out. People to whom they are distributed find them interesting perhaps, but what do they do with them?

Some reports, of course, are very necessary. The report of an accident is part of the worker's compensation claim. Reports should be made of committee actions and decisions. Reports for control purposes, such as acquisition cost or turnover, can certainly be justified. Reports cost time and money and an attempt should be made to determine whether they serve enough of a purpose to offset their cost.

There are reports which are simply protective, which in itself is a good enough reason for their preparation. Unions make it necessary to record and publish certain activities in the employee program. Government demands reports to assure that companies comply with laws and executive orders. This area of government compliance is growing rapidly and causing increasing work.

Personnel reports are of two classifications: (1) those which are for its own use, i.e., documentation, and (2) those which are sent to others for information.

Many actions in personnel administration should be recorded. These include disciplinary cases, warnings, grievances, complaints, requests and the like.

Reports for the dissemination of information tell about training programs, wage developments, policy changes, employment trends, safety progress, and so on.

Will They Hold Up If Tested?

Personnel reports, like all other reports in a company, should be put on trial occasionally. It is safe to say that many reports have outlived their usefulness and many others could well be simplified. Let me cite an example from personal experience.

For years we published a monthly turnover report in my personnel office. It showed turnover for the month and for the year by various breakdowns. Originally intended for officers, its distribution was widened steadily as more and more people asked for copies.

What began as a simple report became over the years a much more involved and complicated one as the breakdowns were refined, smaller work units identified, male and female indicated, work groups compared with one year ago, interdivisional transfers listed, temporary help first included and later excluded. Many of the other divisions in the company were relying on the "people data" which we in personnel were providing—or so at least it appeared. The budget administrator in particular seemed to be making good use of our report and came in each month to balance the figures.

When I woke up one day to the realization that my senior personnel clerk was devoting two full days each month to the preparation of this report, I felt an evaluation was in order. Others in management apparently liked to receive the report; it made interesting reading and occasionally they could spot a discrepancy and bring it gleefully to our attention. But we discovered that the miscellaneous data that had crept into the report actually served no useful purpose, or was available from their own sources.

I made up my mind that our responsibility was not to supply others with data but to observe turnover trends and locate trouble spots. So we streamlined the report to bare essential details. On one page we showed the monthly and yearly turnover percentages of the seven divisions as well as the company in total. That's all. And know what? To this day there has been nary a squawk.

When I was hired I asked my new employer what reports he wanted. I was coming from a company where everything I did in personnel had to be recorded. We had reports of number of applicants per week, number of placements, turndowns, terminations, clinic visits, etc.—all broken down into detail and reasons spelled out. "Document everything—and send me a copy," was the standing order from my superior. So I was pleasantly surprised with the answer I received during that final employment interview. "Reports," said my new boss, "I don't want any reports. All I want is a favorable reaction about personnel from the other division heads."

TIME OFF REPORTS

Some personnel offices find it necessary or desirable to issue regular time-off reports. Following the completion of a time interval, possibly a payroll period or calendar week or month, a report is prepared showing the extent of time off.

Depending upon its use, this report might indicate the names of the employees who were absent and the days each one was away, or it may simply be a comparison of the total amount of time off in each department.

Information of this sort is helpful since it pinpoints where the absentee problem exists. However, it is useful only if someone does something about it.

If this type of information can be prepared automatically by machine, it is difficult to criticize the idea. But where the data are gathered, summarized and typed manually, it doesn't take much to question whether the value is worth the cost. Unfortunately, there are personnel offices full of clerks who spend time on such unproductive duties.

Actually it shouldn't be necessary for the personnel office to report this information to departments. The managers or supervisors ought to know which of their employees are abusing privileges. The personnel office should work with managers, not in reporting the problem, but in solving it.

TIME RECORDS AND TIME CLOCKS

A fundamental, inescapable factor of payroll accounting is the need under federal and state laws to keep adequate records of attendance time and hours worked for all nonexempt employees. They must be paid according to the time worked, and at an overtime rate for all time over scheduled hours.

Time records can be accomplished either manually or mechanically. Individual or group (department) time reports may be done by hand or recorded on individual cards by mechanical time clocks.

Manually, this basic information can be obtained in three ways:

1. Each employee writes in or reports his own time.
2. A supervisor (or his designate) writes in and reports the time of subordinates.
3. A timekeeper checks employees "in" and "out."

Regardless of the efficiency or cost of these methods, they are all dependent upon human nature with its vagaries. When an employee enters his own time, his record cannot be questioned without questioning his honesty and integrity. When a supervisor or timekeeper writes in the time, the problems are those of one person checking another. Disagreements relating to favoritism, friendship, partiality and personal differences could arise.

On the other side are the mechanical time recorders. They are completely impersonal and accurate. They can operate only when operated and will show only the exact time. They cannot discriminate nor show favoritism. Each employee has the same opportunity to make his own record fairly, accurately and impartially.

Since it was first invented in 1884 by a young engineer in a southern furniture factory, the time clock has increased in usefulness until today some 600,000 recorders are providing indisputable time data.

The advantages of mechanical time recording are summarized by the Cincinnati Time Recorder Company, Cincinnati, Ohio as follows:

1. An impartially-made record is furnished.
2. Disputes are precluded because of the impersonal record.
3. Neither the employee nor the employer can question the completely accurate record showing the exact day or date, hour and minute of arrival and departure.
4. Automatically-printed cards are proof to employees they are being credited with precisely the hours they have worked.
5. Employees have the opportunity to audit and verify their time records without consulting supervision.
6. Employees can record their time faster, easier and more accurately.
7. Employees have a greater time consciousness of the scheduled work hours.
8. A "partnership in time" is established between employee and employer. The employee is responsible for arrival in the morning and return from lunch. The employer is responsible

A typical time clock, courtesy of Cincinnati Time Recorder Company, Cincinnati, Ohio.

for the time between arrival and lunch and after lunch until departure.

Some managers believe a mechanical device for attendance time-keeping should not be introduced since this could become a symbol identifying a low strata of employees. In the United States we maintain "all men are created equal" and a time clock, some feel, is detrimental to this belief.

Either way, working time must be documented. Records must be legible, acceptable for audit and conform to laws. Exempt as well as wage-and-hour employees should be accounted for. All employees benefit when the method is efficient, simple, fair, impartial and accurate.

One caution: If the supervisors cannot get the workers to report on time, no clocks or other system will work either. Even the best device cannot be expected to accomplish what direct supervision cannot do.

TIME AND PAY RECORDS UNDER THE FAIR LABOR STANDARDS ACT

Employers must keep certain records about each worker who is entitled to a minimum wage and overtime pay under the Fair Labor Standards Act. The law requires no particular form for the records. All it requires is that the records include certain *identifying information* about the employee and data about the *hours* he or she works and the *wages* he or she earns. And, the law says, the information must be *accurate.*

Here is a breakdown of the basic information that must be recorded:
Identifying Information:

1. Employee's full name.
2. Address.
3. Birthdate, if under 19 years of age.
4. Sex and occupation in which employed.

Hours:

1. Time of day and day of week when employee's workweek begins.
2. Hours worked each day.
3. Total hours worked each workweek.

Wages:

1. Basis on which wages are paid (by the hour, by the week, piecework).
2. Regular hourly pay rate for any week when overtime is worked.
3. Amount and nature of each payment excluded from the "regular rate."
4. Total daily or weekly straight-time earnings.
5. Total overtime earnings for the workweek.
6. All additions to or deductions from the employee's wages for each pay period.
7. Total wages paid each pay period.
8. Dates of payment and of the pay period covered by the payment.

At first glance, this may seem like a lot of information to keep track of. But most of the information required by law would be kept by any company that observes good business practices.

Records with somewhat different and, in some cases, with more limited information are required for workers with uncommon pay arrangements, homeworkers, certain hospital employees, tipped employees, employees who are paid with board, lodging or other facilities, and those who are exempt from the minimum wage and overtime requirements.

What About Timekeeping?

The employer must keep track of the hours worked each day and workweek by every employee entitled to the minimum wage. This is true whether or not the worker also is subject to the law's overtime requirements. It is also true regardless of whether the worker is paid by the piece, the hour, week, month, tips, commissions or on any other basis.

The employer may use any timekeeping method he wants. He may use a timeclock, or have a timekeeper keep track of hours for all workers, or tell the workers to write their own time on the records, or use any other method that suits his needs. Any timekeeping plan is acceptable as long as it is *complete* and *accurate.*

If you use a timeclock, the number of work hours credited every day and every workweek must be recorded. These figures may be kept on the timecard itself or on another record.

Here is a sample form you may but are not required to follow:

Day	Date	In	Out	Total hours
Sunday	Apr. 6			
Monday	Apr. 7	8:00	12:02	8
		1:03	5:03	
Tuesday	Apr. 8	7:57	11:58	8
		1:00	5:00	
Wednesday	Apr. 9	8:02	12:10	8
		1:08	5:05	
Thursday	Apr. 10	7:58	12:00	8
		12:59	5:01	
Friday	Apr. 11	7:58	11:35	8
		12:34	5:02	
Saturday	Apr. 12	8:00	12:01	4
			Total _____	44

Sometimes workers will be credited with more or fewer hours of work than the time punches show. When there's a discrepancy of more than a few minutes, a brief note should be made on the timecard to explain the difference. This will avoid disputes about the time actually worked.

When the worker is credited with fewer work hours than the time punches indicate, explanatory notes may say: "Stayed late for personal reasons," or "Punched in early but started work at 8:00." Similarly, when the worker gets credit for more work hours than the punches show, the explanation may be: "Excused for 3 hours jury duty," or "Machine breakdown." Of course, these explanations are only examples of reasons for discrepancies. There may be differences between hours punched and hours credited for many other reasons.

Explanations of such discrepancies also should be noted on the records in plants where methods of timekeeping other than timeclocks are used. In your plant, the worker himself may enter starting and stopping times on timeslips or in a timebook, or a timekeeper may fill in the working hours. If so, the differences between "in" and "out" times and hours credited should be explained just the same.

Pay Period Ending October 15, 19___			
Date	Day	Hours Worked	Total
1	Saturday	4	4
2	Sunday		
3	Monday	8	
4	Tuesday	8	
5	Wednesday	8	
6	Thursday	8	
7	Friday	9	
8	Saturday	4	45
9	Sunday		
10	Monday	8	
11	Tuesday	9	
12	Wednesday	9	
13	Thursday	8	
14	Friday	8	
15	Saturday	4	46

When the Pay Period is Longer Than a Week

In some plants the worker is paid every two weeks, twice a month, once a month, or for some other period that doesn't coincide with one workweek. As far as the law is concerned, workers don't have to be paid weekly.

But, because of the law's pay provisions, the employer must keep track of the total hours worked each workweek. That is why it is important that the employer decide the time and day of the week when the worker's workweek starts.

A workweek is a regularly recurring period of 168 hours in the form of seven consecutive 24-hour periods. The workweek need not coincide with the calendar week; it may begin any day of the week and any hour of the day. Coverage and the application of most exemptions are determined on a workweek basis.

The above timesheet is only a sample. It might be a useful form to follow, but it is not required.

Note that in the third column ("Hours Worked") the total of work-credits for each day is listed. The fourth column ("Total") lists total hours worked for the workweek, when the whole workweek falls within the pay period. Also, it lists total work-hour credits for that part of the workweek that falls within the pay period—in this example, four hours' credit for work on Saturday, October 1.

Remember, you must keep track of work hours on a *weekly* basis, even when the workweek and the pay period don't coincide. It is easier to keep track of the total hours worked each week if your records clearly separate the number of hours worked each week.

Office Employees

Many employees, for example office employees, are on a fixed working schedule from which they seldom vary. In these cases, the employer may keep a record showing the exact schedule of daily and weekly work hours that the worker is expected to follow and merely indicate that he did follow the schedule. When the worker is on the job for a longer or shorter time than the schedule shows, the employer should record the exact number of hours the worker actually worked.

How Long Should Records be Retained?

Keep all records containing the information required by the regulations for three years.

Keep all records on which wage and hour computations are based for two years. Records that must be kept for two years are employment and earnings records such as timecards and piecework tickets, wage-rate tables, worktime schedules and records of additions to and deductions from wages. Other records which must be kept for two years are order, shipping and billing records; also records which the employer makes which explain the basis for payment of any wage differential to employees of the opposite sex in the same establishment.

All of these records always should be open for inspection by the Wage and Hour Division's representatives, who may request the employer to make extensions, recomputations or transcriptions. Microfilm copies of records may be kept if the employer is willing to provide facilities for viewing them. The records may be kept at the place of employment or in a central records office.

Complete information about the Fair Labor Standards Act is available at the nearest office of the United States Labor Department's Wage and Hour Division.

VERIFICATION OF AGE

Records are becoming increasingly important. But records are of value only if they are correct.

Employee records should be right. This is especially necessary when it comes to age. A certain percentage of employees will falsify their age for any of many reasons. At some later date, perhaps when retirement vested rights or income payment are at stake, one of these employees will try to have his personnel records altered to reflect a more favorable situation.

What happens when the traditional records are unavailable or unobtainable—birth certificate, baptismal record, earlier school record, etc. When attempting to establish a valid birth record, great care must be exercised in examining the supporting evidence. On a Certificate of Naturalization, for example, if the birth date recorded on the papers was self-serving, it cannot be accepted; if it was obtained by the Court through proper legal channels, then it may be submitted as evidence.

Other evidence than an actual (not delayed) birth certificate or a baptismal certificate, which is considered sound, is a

1. Notarized statement, by two witnesses who are older than the person involved, and who have known the person since childhood.
2. Permanent grammar school or high school records.

As a last resort, the records of the Bureau of the Census of the United States Department of Commerce, may provide an answer. While it is

917

true that the census taker is merely "told" a person's age, and asks for no proof, doesn't it seem likely that an age of 17, during a given year when there apparently was no occasion to "doctor" the birth date, could be used as a reliable data base for an employee now nearing retirement age?

One Billion Names!

Since its beginning in 1790 the U.S. Census has recorded identifying data for close to one billion names, including of course, those duplicated from census to census. It has handed copies of these records back to several million of the counted as legal proof of age, place of birth, citizenship or kinship.

When the Founding Fathers made constitutional provision for a decennial count of the population to determine allocation of representatives in Congress, they could not have foreseen how the Census would yield a by-product of such direct benefit to many of the people it would count. Requests for personal census records range from the routine—persons who realize they are without legal proof of birth or age and want to be prepared "if anything comes up"—to those of desperation—citizens with plans made for a trip abroad who are suddenly faced with a no-birth-certificate, no-passport situation; old people unable to obtain Social Security and Medicare and other needed assistance without proof of age; persons unable to claim their rightful shares of estates because of inability to prove relationship.

The Personal Census Service Branch maintains the data from federal censuses beginning with 1900 for searching purposes. These records are confidential under Title 13 of the United States Code. Information furnished is the personal data recorded for the individual which includes name, relationship to the head of the household, age, place of birth, and if foreign-born, citizenship data.

Regular birth certificates are not issued by the Bureau of the Census, but by the Office of Vital Statistics or similar agency in the state in which the birth occurred. However, since it was 1920 before the last state adopted compulsory birth registration, many persons born before that time did not have their births recorded. Even persons who keep orderly records—with or without governmental urging—sometimes find themselves without necessary credentials of existence. Fire and flood and fate in various other forms have a destructive way with even the best-kept records.

Verification Procedure

Assuming the birth was not registered, and that acceptable proofs, such as affidavits from the doctor or midwife who attended the birth, family Bible records or baptismal certificate, cannot be offered for a delayed certificate, census records may be the only recourse.

Here is the procedure:

1. Ask the Personal Census Service Branch, Bureau of the Census, Pittsburg, Kansas, 66762, for an Application For Search of Census Records form.
2. Read the instructions printed on the form, then fill it out and sign.
3. Send the completed form with remittance—$8.50 for a search conducted in order of receipt of the requests.

The personal information in the records of the 1900 and later Censuses is confidential and may be furnished only upon the written request of the person to whom it relates or, for a proper purpose, a legal representative such as guardian or administrator of estate. Employers who want this information must therefore get written permission from the employee.

Logically, the job of the Census record searcher is one which will eventually work itself out of existence, since birth registration has now been compulsory in all states since 1920. However, with millions of Americans still without legal proof of birth, and thousands more each year who for many reasons find they cannot obtain birth certificates, there are no plans to terminate this searching service for a number of years. Requests for personal census records have been averaging over 200,000 a year.

PROOF OF AGE

What does the Social Security Administration accept for proof of age when no birth or baptismal record is available?

If a public or religious record of birth established before age 5 does not exist, other evidence of age may be used. The following are among the better types:

1. A school record recorded before age 21.
2. The 1910, 1920 or 1930 Federal Census Record.
3. A domestic or Canadian delayed birth record established before age 55.
4. Insurance policies taken out before age 21.
5. Immigration records recorded before age 31.
6. Religious records recorded before age 18.

One or two of these documents are usually enough evidence for Social Security claims. If these types of records do not exist, other types of evidence may be used, but the issue can become more complex and can take longer to process.

It is recommended that an individual seek evidence of age six months to a year before it will be needed. Some records are available immediately but some custodians of records cannot respond immediately because of the large number of requests.

Social Security offices have the forms that may be used to request some types of documents. These include the census record, school record, and marriage and birth certificates.

MISSING PERSONS

An employee may seek advice and counsel in locating a missing person—a family member, other relative or friend. Here are some suggestions:

1. Send a letter to the person's last known address, even when this has been done before and failed.
2. Write the postmaster (enclosing $1) for any change of address the person may have left behind.
3. Use the telephone book, or long-distance information (area code plus 555-1212), or out-of-town phone books at the public library.
4. Under certain conditions, Social Security, the Veterans Administration, and the Railroad Retirement Board are authorized to forward letters.
5. Put a want-ad in the newspaper for the person or his friends.
6. Check unions, clubs, churches or associations to which the person may belong.
7. Libraries have books that cross-index phone numbers and addresses. Maybe an old neighbor knows where your friend or relative went.
8. Check person's last employer or fellow workers.
9. The local Salvation Army has a missing person's service with contacts even private detective agencies don't have.
10. If the missing person is a young runaway, ask the telephone operator for the federal runaway hotline.

REFERENCE REPLIES

Just as the personnel office sends out reference inquiries to former employers, on applicants being considered or already hired, so also does the personnel office receive reference inquiries from other companies to whom former employees may be applying for work.

These inquiries take on many forms. Some are telephone calls and an exchange of information takes place immediately. The majority are mail requests, usually form letters, in which the prospective employers ask about dates of employment, work records, outstanding good and bad traits, and the like.

Most of the time a personnel clerk tries to provide answers to questions asked, abstracting such data from the terminated employee's file. It is easy to verify or provide dates of hire and termination, nature of the work, a general comment about the work performance, last salary earned (if willing to divulge this), reasons for leaving, and whether the record is clear to permit rehire.

Some of the incoming questionnaires are anything but simple. A few are idiotic. Using a standardized form asking about a former employee's personal integrity, honesty, loyalty or dependability when the person worked as a summer temporary during a school vacation 10 years ago, for a supervisor who left long ago, is not only meaningless but downright dangerous. Such a form may be beautifully designed, expensively produced and carry the seal of approval of a superior, but it is practically worthless as a tool in the placement process. The best suggestion is to answer those questions which are routine and to ignore those which are impossible and unreasonable. It is better to give no information than to guess.

Some inquiry forms ask for information which may be interesting but of doubtful value. Certainly it is not worth the effort clerks must exert to obtain answers. A school system in a large city established a committee of school guidance counsellors and businessmen to discuss the variety of such questionnaires received by the school and to endeavor to standardize on a form which would provide useful information to companies and still be easy for schools to complete, using recorded data readily available in the administration offices.

It turned out that certain questions asked previously, which conscientious school clerical personnel tried to answer, made it necessary for clerks to spend endless hours searching through the archives in the basement, only to have the businessmen who were asking the questions admit that the information didn't help them after they received it. On the other hand, there was information readily available in the offices which the companies were not asking for which would have been far more helpful.

Therefore, personnel offices have fulfilled their obligation when they reply to reference inquiries by giving only such information which is convenient, factual and current. No inquirer has the right to ask thoughtless questions which put the company to a lot of unnecessary trouble. In those few exceptional cases, when the inquirer is checking on certain details for a specific reason (example, lawyer or FBI agent), he will find companies more than willing to cooperate.

As a protection to employees, it is advisable never to give out any confidential information without the consent of the employee. Releasing salaries, for example, should not be made to mortgage houses without the employees knowing about it and authorizing it. Extreme care must be exercised in giving out any information over the telephone, unless the caller is known. When in doubt or suspicious, ask the caller for his telephone number and offer to call back. Employees of a company have the right to expect the personnel office to guard carefully the information to which they have access, which is given in confidence.

CREDIT VERIFICATION

With the proliferation of charge cards, and for the purpose of establishing identity for check cashing services, or to develop a good credit rating in the community, applicants are required to give their place of employment as a reference. The credit bureau where the application is made then checks with the named employer to verify certain information.

The information requested depends upon the credit agency and the extent of the risk. For check cashing purposes possibly "verification of employment" (does the person work there?) may suffice. For a first mortgage on a home purchase considerably more questions are asked about length of employment, prospects of permanency and income.

Since information is given to the employing company by an applicant or worker voluntarily as part of his employment record, the details should be considered personal and treated confidentially. Discretion must be exercised as to the amount of data that can safely be divulged and to whom such information may be released.

Addresses should not be given out lest this confidential information get into the wrong hands—peddlers, collection agencies, lawyers, union organizers or such people as jealous suitors, former husbands or possibly even the syndicate. Keep in mind that this type of information belongs to the person and not to the company and that actually the employer has no right to betray an employee and give away his information.

Sometimes the inquiry comes from a representative of the Internal Revenue Service or the FBI. Upon presentation of credentials, it is appropriate to cooperate with any reasonable request.

Over the telephone it is easy to be trapped into revealing confidential or useful details to an unauthorized caller. If in doubt, or if this becomes a problem, make it a point not to reply directly. Ask for the caller's name, his company and telephone number, and let him tell his reason for wanting the information. Then offer to call back. This cautious approach will cull out the nuisance requests and the unscrupulous inquirers.

Never, but never, give out confidential or personal data without first getting the approval of the employee involved. Whose business is it how much salary or bonus a person receives? If he needs to supply this information to a mortgage house, for instance, he will permit his employer to release this. But when a lawyer asks how much money a man makes he may be trying to settle an accident claim against him. This is between the lawyer and his client and the company has no part in the transaction. Similarly, an insurance salesman checking salary data as a procedure for underwriting a policy has no right to expect the employer to give out salary information. Collection agencies, particularly, look for any kind of assistance in forcing settlement of bad debts but there is no reason for the employer to get mixed up in delinquent accounts which are an employee's personal problem and normally not related to his job.

A safe rule to follow is that the employer should work in the interests of his employees and should protect personal data that they furnished routinely and in confidence. A company expects loyalty from its employees; it should also expect to be loyal to them. The employer does not owe the same consideration to strangers, many of whom undoubtedly have legitimate and reasonable requests; others, and it is difficult to distinguish the difference, may actually be conniving cleverly to use the information for the aggrandizement of their own selfish aims and against the employees.

ONE FORM FOR ALL PERSONNEL CHANGES

In his last two places of employment, the author developed and used a personnel changes reporting form that allows reporting on one form all changes that affect an employee from the time he is added to the payroll until he is removed. It replaces sundry individual notices and memos which were previously used.

A separate form is used for each action. It is prepared in triplicate: the original is for the payroll section with instructions to change the record; the second copy is retained in the personnel office which audits and records the change; and the third copy is returned to the originator as his notification that the action has been completed.

The top third is the identification section, with space for personal items such as name, address, social security number, employee number, seniority date, job classification and grade, date the form is prepared, date action is to become effective. The middle third reports the action,

PERSONNEL CHANGE
(Fill in applicable section only)

To: Payroll Section

Date:_____

Effective Date:_____

NAME:_____ Soc. Sec. No.:_____

ADDRESS:_____ Emp. No.:_____

TELEPHONE:_____ DEPARTMENT:_____

SENIORITY DATE:_____ JOB CLASSIFICATION & GRADE:_____

_____ ADD TO PAYROLL   Salary: $_____ per week $_____ per hour $_____ per month _____temporary / regular

_____ TRANSFER OR PROMOTION   from Department_____ Job Classification & Grade_____
to Department_____ Job Classification & Grade_____

_____ SALARY CHANGE   from $_____ to $_____ _____Automatic _____Merit _____Promotion _____Longevity
LAST INCREASE $_____ DATE OF LAST INCREASE_____

_____ LEAVE OF ABSENCE OR FURLOUGH   from_____ to_____
Reason:_____

_____ DROP FROM PAYROLL   _____VOLUNTARY   _____INVOLUNTARY   Would you rehire _____Yes _____No
Reason:_____

COMMENTS:_____

SALARY REVIEW COMMITTEE

_____Recommended   _____Not Recommended

_____ RECOMMENDED
_____ APPROVED
_____ PRESIDENT
_____ AUDITED

DISTRIBUTION:
White — Payroll
Green — Personnel
Yellow — Division File

DATE   CHAIRMAN

v.i.p. PAYROLL CHANGE NOTICE

PLEASE ENTER THE FOLLOWING CHANGE(S) IN YOUR RECORDS TO TAKE

EFFECT _____
(DATE & TIME)

EMPLOYEE _____

SOCIAL SECURITY NO. _____ CLOCK NO. _____

THE CHANGE(S)

✔CHECK ALL APPLICABLE BOXES	FROM	TO
☐ DEPARTMENT		
☐ JOB		
☐ SHIFT		
☐ RATE		
☐		

REASON FOR THE CHANGE(S)

☐ HIRED   ☐ PROBATIONARY PERIOD COMPLETED

☐ RE-HIRED   ☐ LENGTH OF SERVICE INCREASE

☐ PROMOTION   ☐ RE-EVALUATION OF EXISTING JOB

☐ DEMOTION   ☐ RESIGNATION

☐ TRANSFER   ☐ RETIREMENT

☐ MERIT INCREASE   ☐ LAYOFF

☐ UNION SCALE   ☐ DISCHARGE

☐ LEAVE OF ABSENCE FROM _____ UNTIL _____
(DATE)   (DATE)

☐ OTHER   (EXPLAIN) _____

_____

_____

_____

CHANGE AUTHORIZED BY _____ DATE _____

CHANGE APPROVED BY _____ DATE _____

FORM # 08320   AMSTERDAM PRINTING AND LITHO CORP, Amsterdam, N.Y. 12010

925

such as add (or reinstate) to payroll and on what basis, change in salary, transfer or promotion within or between departments, leave of absence or furlough, and termination. Necessary supporting data and reasons are asked for. This portion is also used for reporting, under Comments, changes in address and telephone number, as well as any exceptions to policy that should be documented. The lower third is for the authentication, providing for the signatures or initials of the manager making the recommendation, the official authorized to approve it, the personnel director who checks it against policy to spare the line organization from inadvertently doing something that might not be in its best interest. The concurrence or approval of the salary review committee and/ or the president, when required, is also provided for.

There are many advantages. With one form no one has to wonder about the proper form to use, or to invent an acceptable one for the occasion. Those to whom the change is directed recognize only one form. The management and clerical personnel who must see it for consideration, approval, checking and recording get it in turn since all forms follow a processing procedure which, once learned, becomes the normally accepted pattern. Distribution of copies is clearly indicated, which means information is not easily sidetracked into the wrong office. It makes filing neater and easier since all reports are a uniform 8½ x 11 inches. Since reasons and comments are required as supporting data, the frequent use of this form builds up a rather extensive file of recorded objective opinions about an employee and his performance which is available for future reference.

The form, with one-time-carbon, has received immediate acceptance and is serving its purpose well. The idea of using one composite form for all personnel changes is apparently unique. Quite a number of other companies have reviewed it and adopted or adapted it to their needs. The form is not copyrighted and there are no restrictions on its use.

PERSONNEL FORMS

Dealing with the human element in business should be personal. Yet the administration of the personnel program involves paperwork. Despite the personal application, which is paramount, the amount of paperwork is increasing steadily.

In the area of personnel forms, here is a list of some of the more common ones already in use:

Application Blank
Employment Requisition
Induction Papers (W4, Bonding, Flower Fund, etc.)
Add-to-payroll Authorization

Termination Notice
Exit Interview
Salary Change
Promotion or Transfer
Status Changes
Job Classification Change
Change of Address and/or Telephone Number
Age Correction
Notification and Instruction pertaining to Leave
of Absence or Furlough
Payroll Deduction Authorization
Telephone Reference Check
Mail Reference Inquiry
Reference Reply
Progress Record Card
Medical History
Medical Record
Performance (Merit) Rating
Performance and/or Potential Appraisal
Grievance Statement and Settlement
Warning Report
Probation Notice
Overtime Slip
Suggestion System Entry
Accident Report
Questionnaires
Meeting Announcements
Employment and Promotion Tests
Test Profile
Agreement (patent, conflict of interest, etc.)
Tuition Refund Application
Job Rating Specifications
Job Evaluation Factor Breakdown
Job Description
Insurance Application
Insurance Waiver
Insurance Claim Form
Retirement Application
Retirement Option Request
etc.

In addition there are many different report forms to be completed periodically. Included may be:

Turnover
Compliance Data

Illness Absence
Fringe Benefit Costs
Manpower Inventory
Acquisition Results Study
Layoffs
Seniority Lists
Surveys and Analyses
etc.

Not all of these forms are in use in every company. On the other hand, some companies may have other forms necessary for their particular purposes. The use of forms simplifies the procedures. Imagine, for example, what might happen if employment data were not standardized on a handy application blank. At the same time, care should be taken not to become "form happy" since too much paperwork can shift the emphasis in personnel from a personal program to an impersonal system. In any personnel program the important ingredient is people, not paper.

PERSONNEL BUDGETS

Personnel, like all segments of the business, should have its budget. This spells out for the personnel staff the amount of money allocated for its operations. It also permits personnel expenses to be charged properly for accurate cost accounting.

Academically, a budget is a forecast of income and costs for the period ahead—most generally one year. A personnel budget, obviously, focuses on costs alone; but these costs are, nevertheless, related to income.

The forecast is based on assumptions of future trends developed from historical cost patterns. It lists expected future events and their estimated costs.

Some budgets simply set aside sums of money that are earmarked for use during the year for specified programs. In a personnel budget the total amount may likely be broken down by functions, such as acquisition costs, operating expenses, salaries and the like.

Other budgets may be on an "Object of Expenditure" basis with itemized charges provided for the specific times when they are expected to occur. Thus, the amount budgeted for help-wanted advertising may be more in winter months than in June when applicants may be easier to get as schools let out.

Items in the budget include acquisition costs—advertising, agency fees, employee referral bonds, applicant travel, relocation reimbursements; expenses—differentiating between expenses of individual personnel staff members and those of employee groups; memberships—annual dues and participation in activities; equipment, stationery, printing, supplies, tests, etc.; payroll and overtime of personnel staff; operating costs—postage, telephone, telegrams.

The above budget covers the activities and expenses of the people in the personnel office. There may be similar budgets for the entire employee group: company official functions—parties, dinners, picnics; employee relations—handbook, music, recreation, sports programs; training—materials, equipment, reprints; benefits—insurance, payroll taxes, etc.; cafeteria.

All of these can be periodic budgets (annual), progressive (revised as they go along), or moving (12 months with new month added and same month a year ago dropped).

A good budget is a guide, not an inviolate limitation. Personnel activities must never be put into a straightjacket. Provisions should be made for "shifting gears" as the year unfolds, for a personnel program, to be effective, must be viable and dynamic.

Budgetary Control

The personnel director is concerned with the details of the budget. His superior is usually content to look at the bottom line. He gets into specifics when the totals seem out of line.

Budgets are used to:

1. Support operational activities with necessary financial resources.
2. Commit moneys for the satisfactory completion of planned programs and projects.
3. Control and keep track of moneys spent.
4. Measure one aspect of the personnel director's effectiveness by verifying how closely he stayed within limits.

In measuring this effectiveness there are two kinds of costs to consider:

1. Committed costs—those which are beyond his control.
2. Management costs—those subject to his judicious use.

More important than going over or under the budget on certain items is the reason for the unexpected deviation.

Zero-base Budgets

Mention should be made about zero-base budgeting because of the attention it has been getting lately.

Zero-base budgeting is offered as a new way of preparing annual budgets. It contrasts with the current way, known as incremental budgeting.

Incremental budgeting takes a certain level of expenses as a starting point and focuses on the proposed increment above that level. Zero-base budgeting begins with zero and requires that every dollar must be justified.

Zero-base budgeting calls for preparing and analyzing a budget from scratch each time. Every component must be broken down anew into a decision package. There is no carryover.

Most of the units in a budget are not really totally manageable in the zero-base context since they are continuational operations from one period to the next and don't have to be reinvented all the time. The incremental budgeting is more like fine tuning the financial plan that is already in motion.

Zero-base budgeting is a prestigious term. It has caught on as a new concept. But it may be too overburdening to really be useful.

Nonmonetary Budgets

The customary budgets, and the ones described above, are money budgets. But budgets do not necessarily have to be expressed in dollars. There are other types of budgets and some lend themselves to good personnel use. Here are two examples:

Manpower budget—the present number of employees, listed by number, grade and location, is a starting point. For the period of the budget, say one year, manpower needs are anticipated. The total number may go up or down, and fluctuate from month to month. The expected changes are entered for the month in which they should be made. The accountant will, of course, relate this to labor cost, but the personnel staff uses it as a guide to know when to expect to hire or transfer (or layoff) workers by grade and department.

Performance budget—the goals of a department or an individual manager are agreed upon a year in advance. Adjustments may be made during the year if changing conditions warrant and management concurs. At the end of the year the department's or the manager's results are measured against the stated objectives. Group bonus or individual salary increases may be based on how well the objectives were met.

In any event, the personnel activity is too big to be run by "the seat of the pants" anymore. The use of budgets makes the administration of the personnel program more orderly.

OPEN HOUSE

There are many benefits to be derived from an Open House. But to get any good out of one, it must be carefully planned and executed. Thorough planning is the key to its success.

A booklet on open house programs, put out by The Northern Trust Company, covers some points which might be considered:

In order to have a successful open house, you must plan every step in detail. Set up committees to work on various phases and appoint a coordinator to keep a close watch on the overall picture. And start early —time slips by quickly.

First block out the broad theme of your celebration, then refine your outline. Remember, close attention to details can make the difference between a smoothly-run open house and utter confusion.

If there are outside suppliers to be engaged, such as florists, photographers, caterers, display designers, etc., make arrangements early.

And if you plan to give mementos to those who attend, order the gifts early and make sure they arrive on time.

Printing of tickets, invitations and souvenir brochures should be arranged far in advance.

Reasons for conducting an open house include:

1. Opening a new building.
2. Observing an anniversary.
3. Cooperating in a civic endeavor.

The purposes can be many: to introduce new facilities, recruiting aid, employee morale, get-acquainted between families and company officers, pride in company and jobs, product announcement, demonstrations, community relations.

The best time seems to be late spring or early summer when weather is good and people are in a visiting mood. The most popular hours seem to be nonworking time, such as Sunday afternoon; otherwise after hours—late afternoon or evening.

The question of whom to invite depends upon the occasion:

1. Employees' families and friends
2. Retirees
3. Board members
4. Shareholders
5. Customers
6. Suppliers
7. Students and teachers
8. Neighborhood people
9. Service organizations and trade associations

The guests may be invited through the employee house organ magazine, bulletin board announcements, public address system, paid advertisements in local newspapers, radio and television spot announcements, newspaper stories and mailing inserts with invoices and checks.

Guest tickets can be used to get an even flow of traffic by specifying different hours. They can also be used to get messages across, such as "Smoking in Cafeteria only," or "Sorry, no cameras." Return coupons will indicate the amount of activity to plan for.

Many things are "musts" in the planning of such an ambitious undertaking:

1. Greeters or reception committee.
2. Commemorative program, with floor plan and directions.
3. Tour guides or hostesses wearing name badges.
4. Route markers on floors and walls.
5. Identification signs.
6. Ribbon-rope for "off limits" areas.
7. Handout circulars with appropriate "welcome" message.
8. Equipment demonstrators.
9. Parking (mechanic to help with flat tires or motor trouble).
10. Buses for transportation from parking lot if distance is great.
11. Guards or police protection.
12. First-aid room with registered nurse in attendance.
13. Rest rooms clearly marked, and lounges.
14. Souvenirs (playing cards w/ building picture, sample of product).
15. Refreshments—coffee, milk, tea, cokes, finger sandwiches, ice cream, cookies, hot dogs, etc. (if served outdoors, make provision in case of rain).

Other items that might be included in the planning:

1. Flowers for decoration.
2. Corsages for hostesses.
3. Music (organ, strollers or piped-in Muzak).
4. Guest book.
5. Pictures (by company or press photographer).
6. Press coverage (prepare a press kit).
7. Entertainment (clown for kids).
8. Movies, especially about company product or service.
9. Door prize drawings.
10. In-receiving line at entrance.
11. Out-receiving line at exits.

A few final reminders. Give the entire plant and office a thorough housecleaning. Have the parking lot swept down. The premises should get the "white glove" inspection (a la Army).

Arrange to have a dry run. Experiment a time or two in advance.

Plan to pay people overtime for all hours beyond their regular work schedule.

Keep the United States flag flying all day.

EXECUTIVE SECURITY

While there has been a general increase in the world's crime rate over the past decade, there has been a particularly sharp and well-publicized increase in the number of kidnappings reported. In many countries the victims have been corporate executives or managers, and in a significant number of cases were employees of American companies.

Such an incident poses a most acute problem for a firm's directors and managers. There can be no question that a corporation has a moral obligation to its employees; but opening the company's treasury to criminal elements may in later, calmer moments be viewed as much an abdication of managerial responsibility as an exercise of it.

Developing reliable numbers on kidnappings and on ransoms paid is extremely difficult. The Federal Bureau of Investigation puts the number of worldwide kidnapping attempts in 1974 at better than 3,500, about three times greater than the figure had been just three years before. Some 80% of these attempts were successful, and nearly half were directed at businessmen. Out of these, one in five was directed against an American businessman. Ransom demands for somewhat over 30% of all kidnappings in 1974 involved approximately $146 million. One source estimates that since 1974 more than 4,000 businessmen have been kidnapped and hundreds of millions of dollars paid in ransom to political terrorists as well as common criminals, who have been quick to return to kidnapping as a lucrative venture.

Most kidnapping of business executives happens abroad, and the risk is greatest in those countries where it has become an announced tactic of political terrorists. For these groups, kidnapping a businessman provides an exceptional opportunity for propaganda, as well as a means to extort large sums of cash to finance the group's activities—including other kidnappings. While local businessmen are, of course, subject to this threat, overseas employees of U.S.-based companies are often prime targets, both because of terrorists' common hostility to American business and because U.S. companies are presumed to have unlimited wealth.

The victim need not be a prominent American executive, particularly

933

if the goal is ransom rather than propaganda. A relatively obscure employee can be as vulnerable to kidnapping as the managing director of a subsidiary, since the kidnapper is likely to assume that the company will pay for the release of any employee because, regardless of position, he represents the company, especially to the American public. In that sense, it is not the employee but the company and its worldwide reputation that is being held hostage for ransom; the individual is the victim solely because of his association with the company.

Kidnap attempts on corporate executives are causing growing concern in the U.S. In a report on terrorism issued by the Law Enforcement Assistance Administration in 1976, there was concern for the future. "Terrorism is contagious; success and new developments in one part of the world are likely to attract ready imitators in another." The fact that there were, during the past three years, a total of 775 kidnappings in the U.S.—with ransom demands of at least $28 million—may be some indication about the accuracy of that viewpoint.

A Personal Strategy

There is no iron-clad method an executive can employ against the threat of kidnapping. For example, one of America's most prominent jewelers has for years steadfastly refused to be photographed. He gives almost no interviews, avoids celebrity gatherings, and maintains a very discreet private life. As a result, though his name is immediately recognizable, very few people know him on sight—which is precisely what he wants.

For many business executives, avoiding the limelight to that degree is not practical or desirable; on the other hand, it is likely that focusing a great deal of attention on oneself and one's family could bring an executive to the attention of criminal elements as well. Many executives, for this reason, have chosen to live very unobtrusively, shunning personal or family publicity with the usual, published photographs. A number have given up using conspicuous limousines or cars with easily-identified, special license plates, and many corporate planes now carry only the legally-required identification. Their corporate logos or names have been removed.

It is usually a good defensive measure for corporate executives to avoid publicizing their travel plans, particularly if they plan on going abroad. At home, many deliberately vary the route they take to work each morning; the time they leave the office each day; and, in general, any fixed and predictable public schedule. For example, they make it a point not to have dinner in the same restaurant on the same day each week.

A Corporate Strategy

In addition to recommending personal defensive measures to their executives, a number of corporations are developing management strategies they can put into operation in the event they are faced with an actual kidnapping.

One of these strategies is the creation of a crisis management team composed of company executives from different parts of the country and possibly from abroad. Their initial task is to study and familiarize themselves with all aspects of kidnapping and terrorist attacks, including legal, financial, security, personnel and public relations. Once this is accomplished, they are then able to map out a tentative corporate plan for responding to a kidnapping, and put it into action should one occur. The aim, of course, is to treat the threat of kidnapping as simply another corporate contingency which must be prepared for, rather than force management to react to an emotionally-charged situation without adequate information or preparation.

One measure usually recommended to relieve management of the financial burden of kidnapping is the discreet purchase of appropriate comprehensive insurance coverage. Policies can be written to cover all directors and employees of any company, as well as their immediate families, in the event they are abducted and held for ransom, or if a threat to their personal safety is received and extortion money demanded. Coverage which is worldwide is not restricted to key persons. It is written to indemnify a company, within limits, if it is forced to make payments, under either circumstance, to secure the safety of any of its people.

For obvious reasons, one condition of the policy is strict confidentiality, and most insurers take exceptional precautions to keep the purchase of such a policy secret. All correspondence relating to it is considered confidential and kept secure. A second condition is that the insured must cooperate with the police in the event a kidnapping occurs.

Insurance Company of North America (which supplied the above information) is among the companies which provide kidnap and ransom coverage and counsel to businessmen. For information, write to: Insurance Company of North America, 1600 Arch Street, Philadelphia, Pennsylvania 19101.

INDUSTRIAL ESPIONAGE

The free world faces a powerful enemy whose avowed purpose is world domination. Espionage and subversion are among his primary weapons. Much of his technological advancement has been accomplished through information obtained by his espionage and intelligence apparatus.

Companies with government defense contracts are prime targets because of the weapons they produce and the information they possess. Their security responsibilities are real. In each employee there is placed a trust that is vital to the defense of the nation, the citizens and the American way of life. Employees must not, through ignorance, negligence or carelessness betray that trust.

A government contractor is contractually, legally and morally obligated to comply with government laws and regulations that protect the nation's defense secrets. Employees, in turn, must be responsible for protecting and safeguarding classified information, both on and off the job, even after employment is terminated. Unauthorized disclosure or failure to properly safeguard classified information is punishable under federal law. Violation of company security regulations is cause for disciplinary action and discharge and under government clearance criteria is cause for denial or revocation of security clearance.

Private information is defined as records, data, information, documents and the like that require controlled distribution and access.

Proprietary information is defined as trade secrets, "know-how" data or designs developed by the company but not covered by a patent.

The loss of private or proprietary information can be very costly, can result in the loss of important contracts, earnings and employee jobs, and has in some cases put a company out of business.

Industrial espionage, which is sometimes called competitive intelligence, is usually motivated by competition or individual personal gain.

PILFERAGE

In a typical year more than $3 billion in cash and merchandise are stolen from American businesses by employees. That averages out to about $10 million a day.

Who are these thieves? According to Michael H. Kluever of Employers Insurance of Wausau, most are family men and women more at home teaching Sunday school or supervising a Scout group than patronizing a corner bar or a bookie joint. Their income is average or above. Very few have ever had any prior difficulty with the law. They are neither psychotic nor possessed with a "get rich" urge. Many are the most trusted employees in their firms.

When the scheme is uncovered, the employer's response is invariably, "I just can't believe it. He was like a member of the family. He would have been the last one I would have ever suspected."

Why, then, do these employees steal? There are a variety of reasons. Some never steal; they just "borrow" because it is so easy and they expect to put it back. Some want a few extras in life. Revenge is sometimes the reason. Others finance a private venture. The thrill compels many. It may be the handiest way to meet a financial crisis or pay off debts. Some need extra money to support an expensive indulgence, such as drinking, women or gambling.

Some employees merely emulate their own company's questionable business practices, such as price fixing, shady contracts, tax evasion, false advertising, misrepresentation of products, misadventures in overseas sales, payoffs and payola, and illegal political campaign contributions. They don't feel any guilt at all.

Whatever the reason for stealing, all losses share several similar characteristics. First, the employees are highly trusted by their employers, usually having access to large sums of money. Second, in each employee, an overwhelming need exists or develops requiring more money than he has or can legally obtain. Finally, because of the employer's blind faith and/or poor controls, the employee is provided with a golden opportunity to take whatever amounts he needs. Lack of dual control over transactions, no periodic examination of the books or surprise audits provide temptations to an employee in need that is almost impossible to resist. Many employers create the very conditions which allow employees to steal.

LIE DETECTOR

For centuries men and women tried to establish methods for determining truth and deception. However, not until Lombroso's work in the late 19th Century has there been any hope that this could be accomplished with any degree of accuracy.

After Lombroso's crude beginning, other people continued work in this area. The late Leonard Keeler helped develop an initial technique known as the relevant and irrelevant form of questioning. He also helped to commercialize the polygraph. At the time of Keeler's death in 1949, there was very little written about the so-called "lie detector," and only a brief course of training in its use existed.

John E. Reid, formerly the chief polygraph examiner at the Chicago Police Scientific Crime Detection Laboratory, in 1947 established John E. Reid and Associates, which has become the nation's leading firm in the polygraph field.

Their services include:

1. *Honesty screening programs.* This is a combination of a paper and pencil honesty test and the polygraph.

937

The control question technique improves the examiner's ability to interpret truth and deception from the charts produced on the polygraph.

Behavior symptoms of polygraph subjects are recognized as an important element in evaluating subjects.

a. *Pre-employment polygraph examinations.* A validated psychological questionnaire gives an insight into the applicant's attitude toward honesty, and a polygraph examination covers specific areas of interest.

b. *Specific applicants.* This is an extension of the regular pre-employment program, but with special concern for specific positions or responsibilities, e.g., police officers, firemen, security directors, guards, administrators, etc.

2. *Honesty evaluation programs.* This is a program directed at present employees.

a. *Routine or periodic polygraph testing.* This is a polygraph examination administered to individual employees to investigate whether or not they have been involved in specific acts of dishonesty, such as thefts of money or merchandise.

b. *Group questionnaire.* A specifically-designed pencil and paper questionnaire is used to accurately evaluate large groups of employees. Those employees with poor attitudes toward honesty are identified, and concentration can then be made upon those whose attitudes are less than average.

3. *Investigation of specific problems.* The majority of cases handled is in regards to individuals who have been accused, suspected, involved or just associated with a particular crime, misdemeanor or incident about which someone, if not the individual himself, desires to find out or substantiate the truth.

a. *Specific polygraph examinations.* Numerous studies on reliability and validity dramatically support the contention that in the hands of a professional examiner, the polygraph is an invaluable investigative aid.

b. *Interrogation.* The purpose of the skilled interrogation is primarily geared towards obtaining a valid and corroborated confession or admission of guilt or to identify and eliminate those innocent suspects from suspicion.

c. *Interviewing.* When the above methods are premature because of the large number of potential suspects, interviewing and observation of behavior symptoms can narrow the large group down to a select few. The process is done in a manner as to not forewarn or unduly alarm the guilty nor upset or demoralize the innocent.

Inquiries about the practical use of the lie detector in personnel work may be directed to John E. Reid and Associates, 215 North Dearborn Street, Chicago, Illinois 60601.

939

THEFTS

There are figures and statistics available for almost every kind of business loss. But there is no way of knowing how much money is lost each year because of employee thefts, inventory manipulation, juggled books and other forms of "inside" dishonesty.

The estimate is that American businesses are losing $1 billion a year because of employee thefts, plus some $3 billion because of embezzlement of company funds. The amount of industrial thefts is escalating about 20% a year.

The reason no factual data are available is that little is said about this problem because it is unglamorous. Companies don't like the public to think their employees are dishonest. Nor do they want to admit they operate so inefficiently that thievery goes on unchecked.

Company stationery and office supplies that are taken home may seem like a minor item, but if the practice becomes widespread it can add up to an expensive problem. Stolen equipment is less frequent but because of its greater value adds considerably to the amount of office or plant thievery.

In the office, employees pilfer pens, pencils and envelopes for home use. In the plant, workers walk away with tools, copper or steel to peddle for beer money.

After a while some of these inside thieves come up with rather ingenious schemes. In one case, two new IBM electric typewriters were missing from the storeroom where they had been stockpiled. Everyone was baffled about their sudden disappearance. It turned out that two mailroom clerks had boxed them as outgoing parcel post, complete with fake labels and postage-meter tapes. When the after hours mail truck arrived for its pickup, these typewriters were wheeled out unnoticed and handed to a buddy.

In another instance, a number of $800 calculators were disappearing mysteriously. Here it was discovered that the night cleaners were taking them down to the loading platform buried under the trash.

Sometimes there is collusion between office and shop employees. A corporate vice-president and a shipping superintendent headed up a team of employees that stole by the truckload. Blue collar workers did the legwork and white collar workers did the bookkeeping coverup.

The biggest reason for stealing is temptation. Place temptation in front of an employee and he may weaken and yield to the chance of getting something. Other reasons include sex, liquor, drugs, gambling and extravagant living. In these cases the thief connives to steal because he needs money to maintain his habit.

Behind the surge of employee dishonesty are the growing use of part-time workers, the extension of working hours with early or late jobs or overtime workers inadequately supervised, the absence of any specific company policy covering petty thievery, and a reluctance to crack down on dishonest employees suspected or caught in the act.

Who Is Vulnerable?

To some people, "inside" crime conjures up visions of company spies armed with miniature cameras, stealing secret plans for a new product or proposed merger. The attitude seems to be, "This does not affect me." What they read and hear they apply to large offices and industrial plants, especially those working on confidential government contracts.

A little larceny lurks in the hearts of many people. According to Daniel Reid, who administers honesty tests for employers, only 30% of the general population in the United States is trustworthy. Another 40% is trustworthy but likely to give in to temptations. The remaining 30% is not trustworthy.

The paper-and-pencil tests he administers are handled by the office of his uncle, John E. Reid, the man who pioneered in the use of the polygraph, known as the lie detector. It is frightening to learn that the average thief is an average citizen, not a desperate villain.

What should a company do to reduce these losses? If there is no written policy, then draw up one. Make it unmistakably clear how serious the company considers the problem and what the consequences are for any employee caught stealing. Take a position, then stick to it.

If a case is discovered—act promptly and in accordance with the announced policy. Word will get around. Never, however, divulge the details, especially how the deed was perpetrated. This might give someone else ideas.

Look into any suspicious situations, such as some items being consumed too rapidly or in unreasonable quantities. Watch for high concentration of certain purchases or other evidence of merchandise transactions that are difficult to follow or explain. There are plenty of signposts along the crooked road and a manager can be alerted to recognize and observe them.

Any form of thievery adds to the cost of goods or services, reduces profits and ultimately is passed on to the customer. Most of all, dishonesty on the part of a few employees is an insult to the majority who are honest, not because of any company rule but by virtue of personal integrity.

DAYLIGHT THEFTS PLAGUE OFFICE BUILDINGS

A Wall Street Journal article tells about the following crimes committed in a typical month in one single block of New York City: 50 or so burglaries or thefts, a dozen instances of robbery, assault or other crimes against persons, and an assortment of narcotics violations, bomb threats and arson tries.

The block in question is occupied by the World Trade Center, the twin 110-story towers and adjoining buildings that dominate New York's busy downtown financial district. The figures come from the center's own statistics.

Actually, this block isn't a special hot-bed of crime. Considering the density of occupation, this is still an average neighborhood.

It illustrates a trend: the movement of a variety of crimes off the streets and into urban office buildings. Major cities have experienced a rise in offenses in their central business districts over the past few years.

Thefts range from personal items—coats, purses left on desks—to expensive machines—photocopiers, calculators. Electric typewriters seem to be in demand because they are easily fenced. Grand larcenies (thefts of $250 or more) and robberies (thefts involving physical force) are on the increase, and take place in washrooms, stairwells, elevators and small offices.

The reasons for the increase in crime are varied: expensive machines, portability of equipment, lax security, absence of trained guards and workers' carelessness. Thieves blend in easily, they wander around and nobody wonders about a strange face.

Disguises include a mail bag slung over one shoulder, a waiter's white jacket, a repairman's coveralls and simply a neat coat and tie. When challenged they claim to be making a delivery or looking for the employment office.

INDUSTRIAL SECURITY

Not all thefts in business are "internal" crimes, committed by employees or people on the inside. This is also big business for outsiders. Security measures have to be taken against both possibilities.

Recent news reports reveal that office building thefts are on a sharp rise in some cities. These thefts occur during business hours. Thieves enter the building on legitimate business or on the pretext of business. Articles from purses to office machines are removed with surprising frequency.

942

The opportunities are all over. Unauthorized persons wander around unchallenged. Valuables are left on desktops, and petty cash boxes are clearly in sight. Offices remain unattended and windows and doors, especially restroom doors, are unlocked. Anyone in a service uniform can walk out with an office machine in broad daylight. No one should assume that a thief does not have the nerve to walk into an office and then walk out with stolen property.

Companies are responding to the mounting threats to industrial security. Approaches to the problem include:

1. Posting guards.
2. Changing locks.
3. Installing closed-circuit television systems.

These security measures are mechanical safeguards and are meant to deter criminals more than catch them in the act. They are moves in the right direction but they are not the whole answer. They may keep a company only half safe.

Policies, action programs, communications and reporting procedures are also necessary. Does a telephone operator know what to do with a call about a bomb threat? Who reports a prowler on the premises, and to whom is the report made? What is done about strangers roaming about without visitor badges? Can anybody enter the building, or proceed to any floor, or ask questions in any department? What are the rules and who is responsible for enforcing them?

THEFTS—PERSONAL PROPERTY

What should a company do when an employee reports, "My coat has been stolen." The theft of personal property poses a problem for which few companies have found a satisfactory solution.

The problem is twofold: (1) how to prevent the theft of personal property, and (2) how to make restitution for losses incurred.

The problem is concerned with three types of property—clothing, personal items and money. Most of the complaints are about stolen clothing.

In an attempt to keep the problem within containment, a company will provide facilities and a statement of what these facilities are intended to protect. Usually a company assumes no responsibility for lost money, advising its employees never to leave wallets or purses lying around but to carry them at all times. Similarly, employees are cautioned not to be careless with their personal property, such as watches, gold pencils and even tools, but to take care of them and guard them carefully.

But in the matter of clothing, where the problem often crops up, what can a company do and what should employees be expected to do? Large firms provide cloak rooms where employees hang their hats and coats, leave galoshes and umbrellas. Employees should be careful not to leave valuables in pockets, although they customarily slip scarves into coat sleeves.

But what happens when a sweater or topcoat is reported missing? What measure of responsibility does the company feel when an employee follows the rules, uses the designated public cloakroom and loses something? Certainly the employee is not at fault. But the willingness of a company to make good in such cases could easily lead to a still bigger problem, that of false claims.

What about the value of a missing item? If it is no longer in evidence, how can it be appraised? Will the claimant overstate its value? What is a fair settlement?

An employer's policy for reimbursing workers for reported money losses is an even greater risk. This could soon become a simple way of picking up easy money similar to that of buying a woman a new pair of hose if she says hers were snagged on a desk or file. A company leaves itself open.

In schools, the students are provided individual lockers. This is also done in many factories. Under these conditions the individual assumes total responsibility for apparel and personal items. A company can absolve itself of responsibility. But when a company provides something less than optimum protection, it does not follow that the company can avoid some coresponding degree of the consequences should a theft occur.

EMPLOYEE SECURITY

Because of the danger of break-ins in hotel and motel rooms of guests, companies are distributing portable, foolproof door locks to employees sent on overnight business trips.

The Midlock Company, 2211 North Cicero Avenue, Chicago, Illinois 60639, is distributor for "Port-A-Lock," a new concept in personal privacy and security. It is completely portable and requires no installation.

This lock can be easily carried in pocket or purse. It fits all doors that have a strike plate and open inward. It locks the door from the inside and prevents entry even if intruder has a key or picks the lock.

Slide locking head forward against door. Door now may be opened only from the inside. To release, depress locking buttons and slide locking head back. Not a hazard in case of emergency.

KICKBACKS

Kickbacks for favors done or anticipated are not always paid in cash. That is too obvious. Other methods cited by authorities on white collar crime include:

1. Paying for auto rentals by recipients of kickbacks.
2. Providing paid vacations.

945

3. Unlimited use of credit cards and charge accounts by recipients.
4. Paying rents on homes away from home.
5. Providing unsecured loans.
6. Opening up brokerage accounts under aliases.
7. Providing free goods in the form of samples.
8. Buying from businesses run by relatives of recipients.
9. Putting relatives on company payroll as consultants.
10. Giving scholarships to children.
11. Offering gift certificates.
12. Paying for country club dues.
13. Furnishing company aircraft.
14. Permitting special discounts at donor's sales outlets.
15. Rigging company contest so recipient is sure to win a prize.

COMMUNITY RELATIONS

In many companies, especially the small or medium-sized ones, community relations comes under the personnel director. Since he deals with the community in surveys and information exchanges, he is a logical company representative for other community relations activities.

He keeps in close contact with the schools for the referral of graduates. This relationship can easily overflow to the extent that he may be expected to cooperate with the schools on committees, dedications, honor assemblies and other programs. He may serve on boards or be a speaker before classes.

By participating in surveys he becomes familiar with other firms and acquainted with their key personnel. He should join a trade association or service club to gain access to other companies. This could well lead him to an active membership involving work for the association which, of course, broadens his connections.

More than likely he is the company chairman in community money-raising campaigns such as the United Fund. He may also be the executive selected to receive awards that are granted to the company for outstanding service. The nature of his work makes him a logical choice to work beyond the company on behalf of the company.

This does not mean that others in the company should not participate in community work. They should, in fact, be encouraged to do so. Members of the sales force should join the local service group to expand their contacts. The specialists, such as the computer staff, accountants, statisticians and professional people, should be the proper individuals to represent the firm by memberships in trade associations in their particular fields. But here again, the personnel officer may be the likely choice for coordinating all these outside activities.

With the personnel director playing a leading role in community relations, both as a participant and a coordinator, it may be that the job of public relations may also fall to him. He knows what is going on in the company, and he is known in the community. If he is good with words, as he ought to be, the job of public relations could well be his.

The size of the company, its relation to community life, the nature of the business, all have a bearing on the extent and depth of the community relations program. The ability and willingness of the personnel director determine whether or not he directs the activity. In many situations he is the logical choice.

MASLOW HAS A MESSAGE

by JOHN KING BRUUN
Professional Consultant in Personnel
Teacher, Lecturer, Writer—and Volunteer

The personnel director who conscientiously encourages the development of corporate executives for their own long-term benefit, as well as to strengthen the organization, often overlooks the most important executive of all.

Himself!

Like the shoemaker's children who go without shoes, the personnel director frequently becomes so involved in the development of others that he tends to neglect his own growth. Many a highly-competent personnel administrator, daring to take time out for reflection, is dismayed to see that he stopped growing as a person 10 years before. Oh, he still does an A-1 job on what he is paid for—but then he always did. And he is well regarded within the organization. From a myopic standpoint all is well.

There is another viewpoint, though. The one that says, "You have espoused the theory of need fulfillment, of recognizing Maslow's hierarchy of needs, and the importance to the individual of esteem, self-respect, self-realization. What about yourself?

Esteem. Self-respect. Self-realization.

An answer for many personnel executives has been to participate actively in community organizations as a means of self-development while providing invaluable aid as a volunteer executive.

Richard H. Brown, vice-president of personnel for the Household Finance Corporation, puts it this way. "Each of us cannot help but obtain a great deal of personal satisfaction by making a contribution to the betterment of our community by giving of our time and personal expertise to governmental or charitable organizations."

That "personal satisfaction" is hard to define. For one person it is the opportunity to put knowledge to work in making child care efforts more effective in a local agency. For another, it is training social service workers in the techniques of employee development. And for still another, it is the opportunity to provide personnel budget assistance and review to an agency forced to stretch its dollars to the last thin dime, and yet have a quality program.

The Opportunity is There

There is no end of ways. The need for the competent personnel executive's expertise is almost limitless with understaffed and overburdened service agencies, usually neck-deep in day-to-day problems which leave little time for the refinement of personnel policies and procedures.

John Baker, vice-president of personnel, Combined Insurance Companies of America, feels an obligation to support such agencies financially. But giving money isn't the whole answer or, perhaps, even the most effective.

He says, "I saw how much good social agencies such as the United Way, the Chicago Boys Club and others were doing. Our communities would be chaos without them. When I found that I couldn't give enough dollars, I decided to offer my time and my knowledge so that agency funds might be spent more effectively."

Altruistic? Yes, but almost every volunteer agrees that he receives more than he gives when his horizons expand.

As Mr. Brown reflects, "Working for a corporation, your rewards come primarily through compensation. Working outside your company in your community, the reward you receive is the knowledge that perhaps you have done something to help make your community a better place to live. Obviously, the professional contacts you make are worthwhile; and the problems you encounter are typically of a different nature than the problems you encounter within your company."

Mr. Baker concurs. "Take budgets, for example. I prepare a budget for my department; then I present it and justify it to my superiors. But at the Chicago Boys Club it is the other way around. The officers of the Club prepare their budgets and they review them with me. I become the reviewing executive and, believe me, sitting on that side of the desk is an eye-opening experience. I feel I have a considerably improved perspective and better understanding of my own role as a result of my experience with the Chicago Boys Clubs.

948

"I think that those of us who participate in volunteer activities do so without thought of reward. But the reward is there. It is inescapable."

Donald E. Nordstrom, vice-president of personnel, F. W. Means and Company, Chicago, phrased it this way.

"Someone has said that when buying a yacht, you are not ready if you need to know the price. Using that analogy, an individual should not enter into community and industry volunteer activities with the thought of 'What's in it for me?' Rather, one should start with the intent of 'What can I contribute?' "

Among the satisfactions which Mr. Nordstrom receives from his active participation is the opportunity to share with his family some experiences that they would be unlikely to have on their own. His own eyes have been opened and—but let Don Nordstrom tell it in his own words.

"One pleasant fringe benefit of my volunteer activity has been the opportunity to tell my wife and children of the needs of less fortunate families being served by community agencies. Things I have seen firsthand. It makes a difference. And I stress the many wonderful and dedicated people I have met who are helping to solve community problems. I think it helps the children, especially, to begin developing a sense of social responsibility."

Contacts Broadened

Many personnel executives have enriched their circle of friends through contact with other volunteers. By and large, community organizations seem to attract leaders and "doers" in business and industry whose interests exceed the scope of a single organization. One personnel director who recently became actively involved disclosed that he could phone 10 or 12 highly-placed executives in as many firms for a chat or a luncheon—people he hadn't even known a year ago. "I made more new friends in the last year," he said, "than I did in four or five years before."

That expanding circle of friends and contacts is a source of new knowledge stemming from informal conversations and observations of how other top executives perform.

"Mr. L_____ is a chief corporate officer and this past year has served as chairman of our service organization. He is the most competent, skillful discussion leader I have ever seen. His ability to draw people out, depersonalize emotional situations, keep discussion moving toward a solution is unbelievable. He is a true professional. Being part of that group has been, for me, a post-graduate course in human relations. I wouldn't trade what I have learned from that one man for a dozen courses at a university."

The personnel director who made that observation is with a large midwestern manufacturer. "The funny part of it is," he added, "when our president suggested that I volunteer with this service organization I had a 'why me?' reaction. It wasn't until I really became involved that I found the answer.

"Up until then I thought our little world was 'it.' Now I realize there's a bigger world right outside. Volunteering opened the door for my own personal growth and development."

Corporations encourage their executives to take an active role in voluntary organizations. Being a good corporate citizen means participation in community programs not only with money but also with people. Good people. Those who will enhance the corporate image as they render a major service.

The president of a national chain added one more reason. "Why do I encourage my personnel director to work with community agencies? Very simply, because it gives him an opportunity to gain experience we could never provide through his job alone. He is gaining poise, maturity and recognition for his good ideas in some pretty complex situations. One day very soon it's going to pay off for him in a major step up the ladder here."

CONSUMER AFFAIRS

Consumerism seeks to give representation to all interests, especially to the individual buyer, consumer and citizen. Ordinarily these people have no adequate voice in the power structure.

The four ingredients of consumerism are:

1. Government—more legislation coming.
2. Activists—calmer but still pushing.
3. Public—skeptical, getting involved.
4. Business—changing and becoming more concerned.

If business does what it should and can, then government will be depended upon less, activists will see progress within the system, and the public will find that even if this can't be a perfect world, it can be run well.

Customer complaints are some indication of how well a company is serving the consumers and also how well it is being accepted in the community. It doesn't really matter why a given consumer is seeking to register a complaint. To the consumer—rightly or wrongly—the complaint is a legitimate one. The handling of complaints should be prompt, efficient, courteous, personalized and as effectively managed as any other function of prime importance.

EMPLOYEES IN POLITICS

Believing that everyone has a stake in politics, Exxon Company, U.S.A., Houston, Texas, a division of Exxon Corporation, encourages employees to be active in public affairs. The emphasis has been placed largely upon registering, voting and local party participation.

The official company policy, "Employee Participation in Public Affairs," is as follows:

Our Company believes in the participation by all citizens in local, state and national political affairs. In order to encourage such participation by Company employees, the following Company policy relative thereto has been adopted:

1. An employee engaging in political activity does so as a private citizen and not as a representative of the Company. The Company will not discriminate against an employee because of his identification with any lawful political party or activity.

2. The Company considers that qualifying oneself to vote, serving in civic bodies, and keeping informed on political matters are all highly important rights and responsibilities of the citizens of a democracy and therefore are to be encouraged. The right of an individual to contribute financially to the party of his choice is an important element of our political system. Campaigning for public office and the holding of such office by employees are also recognized as being a part of their rights as citizens, although there may be instances when the position of the Company and the individual employee with relation to a particular office is such that the exercise of these rights might not be advisable.

3. An employee should consult with his supervisor before making himself available for public office, the holding of which might detract from his ability to perform his work assignments.

4. In many cases an employee seeking public office or participation in political party activities will be able to carry out such activity without interfering with his job responsibilities. If, however, this is not possible, he must request the appropriate, regular leave of absence.

5. If an employee is elected or appointed to a public office which will demand all or a substantial part of his productive time over an extended period, or which will otherwise substantially detract from his ability to perform his Company assignments, or which may create a conflict of interest which could be eliminated by a special leave of absence, the Company may grant the employee a special leave of absence without pay. Such a special leave of absence will not normally exceed two years. This leave may be extended at the Company's discretion on request by the employee.

6. This policy is applicable to all employees of the Company in the

United States, whether they are covered or exempt under the Fair Labor Standards Act.

GOOD CITIZENSHIP

Many companies, recognizing that good citizenship is important to the country, also believe it is important to the company.

They encourage employees to get into civic and political activities. Further, they cooperate and support them. As a result, in many corporations it is not uncommon to find mayors, township committeemen, school board members, city aldermen and village trustees, and others holding public office in their communities.

One Canadian company, for example, encourages political participation by offering employees a month's paid leave of absence to campaign for federal or provincial office. If elected, an employee can go on unpaid leave for one full term of office up to five years. But if re-elected, the worker is expected to quit the company in favor of his new career.

EMPLOYEE INFORMATION SYSTEM

Some type of employee information system, whether manual or computerized, is essential for the operation of a comprehensive personnel program.

An employee information system is a storage, manipulation and retrieval system for one or more kinds of employee data. It may gather the data through manual procedures or mechanization programs. It makes any or all of the data immediately available and thereby provides faster and better ways of access to information about employees for decision-making purposes.

For placement and planning purposes it would include a skills bank that would yield information about each employee's background, experience, training, specialties, interests and job preferences. In addition it would show progress in the company, with job progression, wage history and appraisal scores.

The employee information system will merely produce data as valuable and accurate in its output as it was carefully collected and entered into the system. It will make selection preferences, matching its answers to the questions it is asked, but it will not make decisions. These must still be made subjectively by management on the basis of information supplied.

COMPUTERIZATION of PERSONNEL RECORDS and REPORTS

by LEWIS A. MELTZER
Senior Human Resource Systems Consultant
Information Science, Inc.
Montvale, New Jersey 07645

For several decades, computers have been effectively utilized in varying forms of inventory control. This inventory has taken on forms of dollars, parts, etc. Computers are able to perform repetitive routine clerical functions with phenomenal speed and accuracy, thus allowing additional effort to be devoted to the managing aspect of business.

Why not apply this principle to people resources?

Wages and benefits are the two largest continuing expenditures of most businesses. It seems reasonable and entirely feasible to take advantage of a proven, cost-effective method of managing people inventory. The concept of automating human resources has been accomplished by many large organizations during the past several years. Now, with the advent of minicomputers, smaller businesses are able to take advantage of this same concept on a smaller scale.

This automation process can typically take between several months upwards to several years depending upon the degree of sophistication desired and the availability of manpower and financial backing. So as not to re-invent the wheel, software firms, whose major goal is to provide programming and installation expertise, have been able to develop and market prepackaged human resource systems.

There are several obvious and not-so-obvious benefits of purchasing such a system. When shopping for a human resource system, please keep in mind that not all vendors are equal. The following benefits may be stressed with some software firms more than others.

1. The system has been developed by specialists with considerable experience in the combined areas of Personnel and Data Processing.
2. A great amount of research has been done to identify the professional needs of personnel managers. Enhancements to the systems are an ongoing process as needs change and regulatory measures evolve.
3. The system is expandable and flexible even though it is a package.
4. Any one of several personnel-related modules (which will be described) can be "plugged in" to the basic human resource system, thereby synchronizing the needs of an organization to a well-tailored, efficient and effective personnel system.

953

5. It is certainly an advantage to know how much time and money a project will require to successfully install. Software firms can give a fixed price and implementation schedule so that you will be able to better budget your resources. They have considerable experience in forecasting the amount of effort involved to get a system going. On the other hand, a company which has no experience with personnel systems, can only guess the amount of programming and computer testing necessary to implement a system which is developed in-house.

6. Most software firms provide a user-oriented information retrieval language to obtain comprehensive analysis and reporting capability which does not require the services of a programmer. Simple reports can be formatted easily, and depending on computer turnaround time, a report can be available within minutes of its request.

The typical human resource system will store information on several thousand employees (although there are minisystems which can efficiently power a system involving less than one thousand employees). It will take between six to 12 months to install, depending on what modules are purchased and manpower availability of both client and software house.

Considerable on-site training will be given to the client project team to prepare them to manage the system after it is installed on the client's hardware. The data stored (depending on modules) will be able to generate extremely useful management reports.

In addition to a variety of routine reports, modules can generate Benefit Statements, EEO reports, ERISA Pension Projections, Skills Inventory, Career Planning, Attendance Reports and many more.

The basic form used by the human resource system is a multicopy, computer-produced report called the Employee Profile. It displays substantial amounts of data for each employee stored on the system. This profile serves as a turnaround document in which changes are made by crossing through the old information and writing the new information above it. The new data will be input to the system which will generate an updated profile to be distributed to management, replacing the obsolete profile.

As changes are made to significant fields of data such as salary, job, location, etc., an historical master file is retained for each event. This historical file expands (as information is added to each employee), thus allowing reports which are date sensitive such as those for EEO or ERISA purposes to be generated historically.

954

Detailed Affirmative Action reports showing movement of protected classes can be listed using the EEO module. This system determines and displays all relevant labor pools and automatically computes and prints statistics for participation, distribution percentages and parity indices.

There are several other modules available which, when used with the correct mix of software, can add power to a human resource system, helping it to become an effective tool to assist management in the day-to-day operations of a personnel function.

The InSci Human Resource System is a computerized data system which provides management with maximum information about employees at minimum costs.

Effective use of this information lessens the ever-increasing burdens of the personnel staff—mainly, compliance with government legislation —helps define and solve current problems, and aids management in planning for the future.

An overall view of the InSci HRS shows how the handling of employee information by the computer, with its inherent speed and accuracy, can increase the availability of information, resulting in greater benefits to both management and employees.

1. *Personnel record and employee profile.* As the nucleus of the system, the personnel record accepts and maintains employee data. The employee profile, a document produced automatically from personnel record transactions, displays key employee data. Features:

- full salary administration capability.

- generates chronological work history automatically.

- maintains education and training information.

- processes for multicompany/divisions.

- automatic error-checks and editing.

- calculates salary percent and equivalents.

- full series of user-defined table files.

- provides Equal Employment Opportunity (EEO) compliance data.

- records prior-employment information.

- maintains job/position control data.

- calculates benefits coverage/participation.

Personnel record and employee profile can be interfaced with a payroll system.

employee profile

YOUR COMPANY NAME and LOGO

InSci
Information Science Incorporated

NOTICE OF TERMINATION/RESIGNATION

Instructions: 1 - Complete appropriate sections. 2 - If possible conduct exit interview. 3 - Forward completed form directly to personnel.

MANAGER

Name

Date of Resignation | Date Gave Notice | Last Day of Work

Employee's Forwarding Address (include Zip Code)

Eff. Date of Address | Vacation Pay Due | Other Pay Due

Employee's Reason for Leaving - Check appropriate reason and give further explanation under comments (attach Letter of Resignation if applicable)

INVOLUNTARY

- ☐ Insubordination (350)
- ☐ Fighting on job (351)
- ☐ Profanity
- ☐ Refusal to carry out orders (353)
- ☐ Lying (354)
- ☐ Theft of money or property (355)
- ☐ Damaging property (356)
- ☐ Damaging business reputation (357)

- ☐ Violating company rules (358)
- ☐ Inefficiency (359)
- ☐ Excessive absenteeism (360)
- ☐ Inability to keep financial affairs in order (361)
- ☐ Discontinuation of function (365)
- ☐ Reduction in force (366)
- ☐ Temporary lay off (367)

VOLUNTARY

- ☐ Personal reasons (300)
- ☐ Maternity (301)
- ☐ Marriage and moving (302)
- ☐ Return to school (303)
- ☐ Relocation (304)
- ☐ Health reasons (305)
- ☐ Military service (306)
- ☐ Other employment (307)

- ☐ Failure to return from leave (308)
- ☐ Dissatisfaction with
  - ☐ Working conditions (310)
  - ☐ Type of work (311)
  - ☐ Promotional opportunity (312)
  - ☐ Compensation (313)
  - ☐ Hours (314)
  - ☐ Supervision (315)

Rehire Eligibility: Yes No Enter Y or N on Line 1 (Block 028)

Secure From Employee: ☐ I.D. Card ☐ Charge Cards ☐ Other

EXIT INTERVIEWER

Information Covered with Employee
- ☐ Hospitalization (conversion)
- ☐ Group Life Insurance (conversion)
- ☐ Retirement (vesting)

- ☐ Loans
- ☐ Educational Aid
- ☐ Vacation Pay Due

- ☐ Unemployment
- ☐ Other (describe)

Is employee or any member of family presently hospitalized or under doctor's care? Yes No

If Yes explain

EMPLOYEE PROFILE AND AUTHORIZATION

Date Change Made

Month Day Year (enter on top of reverse side)

For detailed instructions see Manager's Manual
PLEASE PRINT ALL ENTRIES CLEARLY.

☐ **CHANGE IN CONTROL INFORMATION** route to personnel through appropriate levels of supervision for approval.
- ☐ Leave of Absence – enter expected return date from leave on line 1 (Block 001). Reason (Check one) ☐ illness ☐ education ☐ maternity ☐ military ☐ personal ☐ other
- ☐ Return from Leave – forward employee profile to personnel. Indicate date of return under comments.
- ☐ Location Transfer – enter new location code and date on line 11 (Block 025). Explain under comments.
- ☐ Termination – complete notice of Termination/Resignation and send directly to personnel.
- ☐ Position – enter new job code and date on line 2 (Block 029). Explain under comments
- ☐ Other Changes – cross out old data and enter

☐ **CHANGE IN SALARY INFORMATION** route to
Enter type, amount of change, eff. date and

☐ **CHANGE IN PERFORMANCE REVIEW** –
Enter type, date and rating on line 5 (Block

☐ **CHANGE IN PERSONAL INFORMATION** –
- ☐ Name – change on line 10 (Block 002)
- ☐ Marital Status – change or enter on line 10
- ☐ If Applicable – Spouse's first name enter on
- ☐ If Applicable – Spouse's date of birth enter
- ☐ Address/Telephone – change entire address
- ☐ Other Changes – cross out old data, and en

You may want to use this side of the Profile as your employee performance appraisal form, salary or promotion review form, or to implement your management-by-objectives programs. Some of the space can be used for special instructions, notations, or codes, as desired by the user.

☐ **CHANGE IN BENEFITS INFORMATION** –
- ☐ Beneficiary – change entire beneficiary designation on line 16 (Block 040).
- ☐ Benefits Participation – change participation code and effective date on line 14 or 15. Use appropriate participation/plan codes.

☐ **CHANGE IN OTHER INFORMATION** – cross out old data on reverse side, enter new. Route to personnel.

☐ **CHANGE IN FORMAL EDUCATION** – cross out old data on reverse side, enter new below. Refer to Manager's Manual.

Level Code	Level Name	Yr Att	Subject Code	Subject Name	School Code	School Name			Credits Obtain	Credits Need
0 2							Highest Level			
0 2							Add'l Level 1			
0 2							Add'l Level 2			

☐ **CHANGE IN CERTIFICATION AND TRAINING COURSES** – cross out old data on reverse side, enter new below. Refer to Manager's Manual.

Course Code	Date	Description/Location	Duration	Grade	1	2	3

Company Name	From	To	Job Title/Duties

The computerized "Employee Profile" is the heart of the InSci Human Resource System developed by Information Science, Inc., Montvale, New Jersey. The document is produced automatically from personnel transactions and displays key employee data.

The upper half is for the manager's use and gives the employment progress and present status of the employee. The lower half is given to the employee so he will know what information about him is in file, and whether it is current or in need of correction.

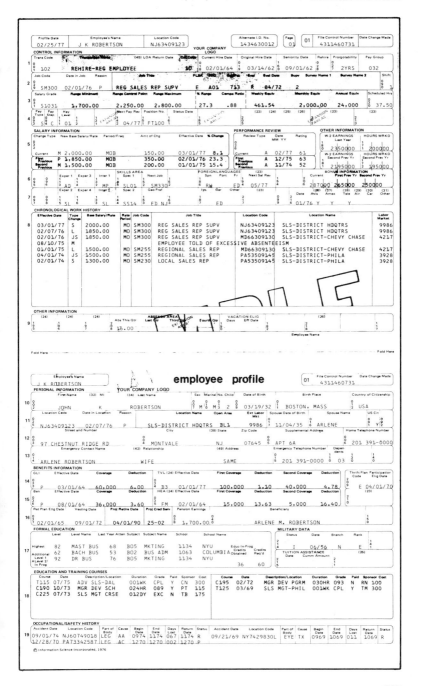

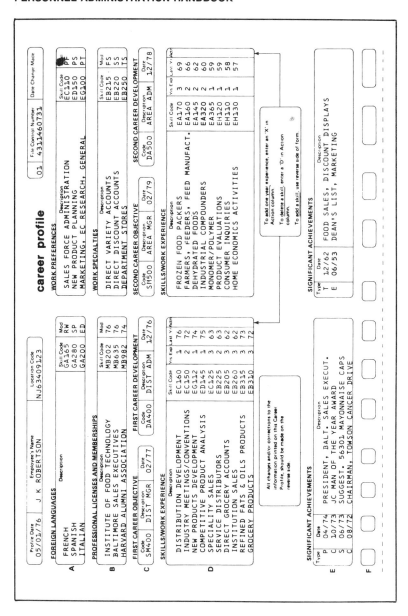

The individual Career Profile developed by Information Science, Inc., Montvale, New Jersey. This automatic, computerized printout system is a talent directory, or skills inventory, showing qualifications and career capabilities of every employee.

IMPORTANT · PLEASE REFER TO YOUR CAREER PROFILE

BOOKLET BEFORE COMPLETING THIS FORM.

Foreign Languages · Description	Skill Code	Mod
1	045	
2	046	
3	047	

Work Preferences · Description	Skill Code	Mod
1.	048	F P
2.	049	S P
3.	050	T P

Open Vocabulary · Description	Skill Code	Mod
1.	051	
2.	052	
3.	053	

Open Vocabulary · Description	Skill Code	Mod
4.	054	
5.	055	
6.	056	

156 | 164 | 146

158 | 221 | 148

157 | 220 | 147

159 | 222 | 149

Skills/Work Experience · Description	Skill Code		
1.	057		A
2.	057		A
3.	057		A
4.	057		A
5.	057		A
6.	057		A
7.	057		A
8.	057		A
9.	057		A
10.	057		A

Skills/Work Experience · Description	Skill Code		
11.	057		A
12.	057		A
13.	057		A
14.	057		A
15.	057		A
16.	057		A
17.	057		A
18.	057		A
19.	057		A
20.	057		A

	Type	Date	Achievements · Description
1.	058		
2.	058		
3.	058		
4.	058		
5.	058		
6.	058		
7.	058		
8.	058		

After completing change(s), please sign on reverse and forward to your supervisor.

106 | 107 | 108 | 109 | 126 | 127 | 128 | 129 | 138 | 139 | 168 | 169

959

InSci Human Resource System

Expanded EEO Compliance System	Benefits Statement System ERISA	Expanded OSHA System	Expanded Career Profiling System	Expanded Benefits/ERISA Administration System

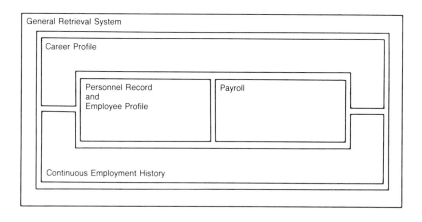

General Retrieval System

Career Profile

Personnel Record and Employee Profile

Payroll

Continuous Employment History

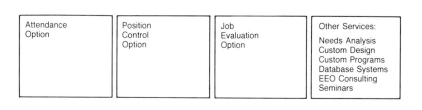

Attendance Option	Position Control Option	Job Evaluation Option	Other Services: Needs Analysis Custom Design Custom Programs Database Systems EEO Consulting Seminars

The InSci Human Resource System is a computerized data system which provides management with maximum information about employees at minimum costs. It lessens the ever increasing burdens of personnel staff in dealing with various problems—one of which is compliance with government regulations.

2. *Payroll.* The most advanced, flexible, user-controlled payroll system on the market. The payroll design is based upon proven computer techniques and user requirements. Features:

- processes for multicompany/division, hourly/salaried pays.
- prestored data tables and processing rules for minimum data entry.
- labor-distribution module.
- standard and optional reports controlled by the user.
- up to 999 different types of earnings, taxes and deductions.
- full tax-routine update and support.
- complete personnel system interface.

3. *Continuous employment history.* Collections of data can be maintained for Equal Employment Opportunity (EEO) and Employee Retirement Income Security Act (ERISA) compliance. Manpower planning requirements, historic and demographic statistics are also readily available. Features:

- records all significant changes in employee status, including salary, job/title, Fair Labor Standards Act (FLSA) and EEO categories, education, insurance coverage, performance/potential, disciplinary actions, accidents, etc.
- maintains historical benefits administration data.
- monitors applicant flow.
- calculates "from and to" dates for monitoring work histories.
- provides job/position tracking and career pathing data.
- additional information available in "archive files."

4. *Career profile or expanded career profiling system.* Management can have a detailed breakdown of the skills, talents, work experience and career preferences of every employee. Features:

- 32 categories of career/talent/qualifications information with the career profile.
- unlimited categories of career/talent information with the expanded career profiling system.
- supports "promotion from within" policies.
- supports affirmative action plans.

- prints out a talent directory.
- identifies training program needs.
- provides "career-pathing" capability.
- monitors employee objectives.

5. *EEO compliance system.* Developed under the EEO Commission guidelines, legislative reporting requirements of Executive Order 11246, 11375, Revised Orders 4 and 14, are specifically addressed, and a full workforce analysis can be performed. Features:

- maintains data on recruitment, placement, transfers, promotions, etc.
- reports distribution and population statistics.
- determines and displays relevant labor pools.
- compares current and historical employee data to labor market statistics.
- compares actual employee data to affirmative action goals.
- generates parity indices.
- monitors and reports on applicant flow.
- supports all statistical tabulations with detailed data listings.
- can be linked to a personnel system or operated alone.

6. *Expanded benefits/ERISA administration system.* Information necessary to comply with the Employee Retirement Income Security Act (ERISA) is maintained, along with other benefits administration data. Features:

- maintains data to meet ERISA requirements.
- maintains data for pension, profit sharing, thrift and stock purchase plans, life, sickness and accident insurance.
- handles group insurance administration.
- generates actuarial reports.
- calculates accrued and vested benefits.
- monitors eligibility, suspension, reinstatement, contribution, withdrawal dates.
- generates employee benefits profiles.
- projects costs of benefit programs.

962

7. *Benefits statement system-ERISA.* A statement showing any or all benefits coverage can be produced for each employee. Features:

- lowers cost with full text processing capability.
- defines and formats text according to specific needs.
- prints out ERISA data.
- maintains data to calculate accrued and vested benefits.
- can be generated from a personnel system.

8. *Expanded OSHA system.* Designed specifically for the reporting and data maintenance requirements of the Occupational Safety and Health Act (OSHA), it encompasses many of the features of the personnel record with the legal requirements of OSHA. Features:

- maintains log of OSHA-reportable cases.
- estimated injury/illness costs automatically.
- prints out OSHA Forms 100 and 102 automatically.
- produces environmental exposure histories.
- maintains and produces complete injury/illness histories.
- calculates measures of injury experience, including frequency and severity rates.
- compares actual vs. estimated incident costs.
- schedules employee physical examinations.
- monitors working conditions by health/ safety standards.

9. *Attendance option.* Designed to provide managers with more accurate and timely information about salaried and/or hourly-employee absenteeism. Features:

- analyzes cost by division and/or group.
- determines absence causes by occurrence, date, reason.
- formatted and user-defined reports.
- records full seven-day, 53-week attendance.
- determines paid or nonpaid absence.
- maintains year-to-date accumulations.
- maintains career-to-date accumulations.
- monitors vacation eligibility.

963

10. *Position control option.* The ability to monitor and control all positions within the company on an individual basis, assures management that the addition of positions is regulated according to salary scales and budgets. Features:

- produces manpower tables.
- controls and reports projected and actual salaries.
- controls and reports projected and actual assignments.
- processes independently from personnel system.

11. *Job evaluation option.* Records of data are maintained for companies who wish to efficiently measure the relative status of jobs. Features:

- calculates salary ranges.
- analyzes job points and related salary ranges.
- updates mass changes for recalculated ranges when job evaluation formulas change.

12. *General retrieval system.* Executives, managers and other authorized personnel are provided with the ability to search computer files without requiring the aid of a programmer. Features:

- searches, selects, analyzes, calculates and displays information from any file or data base.
- report requests are made in simple English language statements.
- performs as many as 99 searches simultaneously.
- runs most searches at maximum computer speed.
- accumulates numeric data.
- displays as many as six levels of totals.
- calculates averages and percentages at detail or summary levels.
- dictionary of search terms custom-tailored for any data base.
- perpetual system maintenance guaranteed.

Complete EDP documentation, users' manuals, managers' manuals, and customized input/output forms are provided. All InSci products include the General Retrieval System for comprehensive analysis and reporting capability as well as full software warranty.

CHAPTER XII

POLICY

POLICY

POLICY is merely the outgrowth of practice. We have policies whether we realize this or not. Our job is to make policies understandable, fair and acceptable. Reducing them to writing usually helps accomplish this.

Policies are *formulated* at the worker level; they are *formalized* by the executive group.

In any operation there is a customary way of doing things. This is the practice. When the performance of a single task is standardized, a method is established. A series of interrelated steps performed in sequence becomes a procedure. A system is a network of related procedures. All of these activities are accomplished within the framework of company policy, whether written or unwritten.

A written policy is a commonly accepted statement of understanding or formula. It facilitates delegation of decision making. It assures fairness and consistency in decision-making criteria. It saves time in reaching the decisions since the answer is determined in advance.

Companies that boast they have no established policies are actually admitting that they have a confusing array of policies. Whether this plethora of policies is a problem depends upon other factors, such as size of the company, complexity of its operation, and the like.

Resistance to written policies suggests an unwillingness to conform. The argument that "we're different" is usually more in the mind than in reality.

Guide—Not a Bible

Yet no set of written policies should become a straitjacket on management thinking. Two of the most elastic terms in the vocabulary of industry are "company policy" and "corporate objectives." The first is often a cloak to hide behind; the second is a managerial haven for generalities.

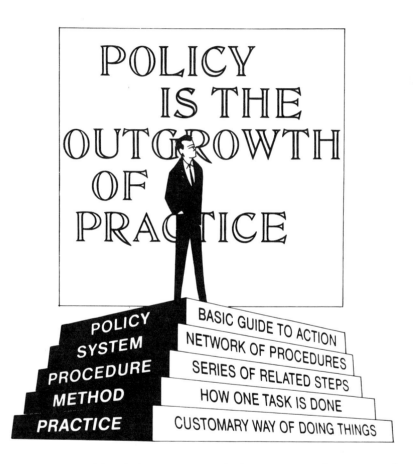

Policy is not copied from books, it is an outgrowth of practice. Our "Policy Man" stands firmly on a platform built by the practice, method, procedure, system and policy of his company.

A policy manual should help a manager solve a problem, not limit him. A book on grammar is useful, not for people who know how to express themselves, but precisely for those who don't. The artist Da Vinci certainly did not need a numbered paint set. Queen Marie of Romania once remarked, "Etiquette is for people without breeding, just as fashion is for people without taste." Any set of rules is at best a substitute for natural talent.

The purpose of any set of standards is to see that everybody is playing the game by the same rules. Following the established practices makes for fewer arguments and less confusion. But people of overwhelming talent make their own rules, guided by some inner ear, by some pulse of the heart, that makes their decisions instinctively right and acceptable. To this type of manager a policy manual is useful as a guide, not as a Bible.

POLICY MANUAL

A policy manual is a very useful tool for managers and supervisors. It tells them what the official position is on most of the policy questions they may expect to encounter in dealing with workers.

Employee handbooks cover the more common practices for the convenience of employees. But these handy books are written in general terms, the policies stated briefly, and the information aimed at *selling* the policies rather than *administering* them. The managers need more specific instructions on how to handle a particular situation when it comes up.

Policy information is disseminated to supervisory personnel in many different ways. Often this may be in memo form from a superior officer to a supervisor telling him how to meet a problem. Unless other supervisors get copies, there is little likelihood that the next situation arising elsewhere will be similarly handled. And unless policy instructions are numbered, or issued under some pattern, it may well be that the instructions, issued earlier, may not be found when needed.

One good solution is to issue a policy manual to each executive, manager and supervisor—those who have authority over other workers. Such a manual should be looseleaf so it can be kept current simply by adding or replacing pages.

Each policy item in a policy manual is on a separate page or pages. Thus, the Vacation policy will be separate from the Life Insurance policy. These policy items, mimeographed or printed on 8½ x 11 punched paper, are filed in alphabetical order in a ring binder, separated by dividers for easy lookup. Jury Duty is under "J", Blood Banks under "B", and so on.

POLICY FORMALIZATION

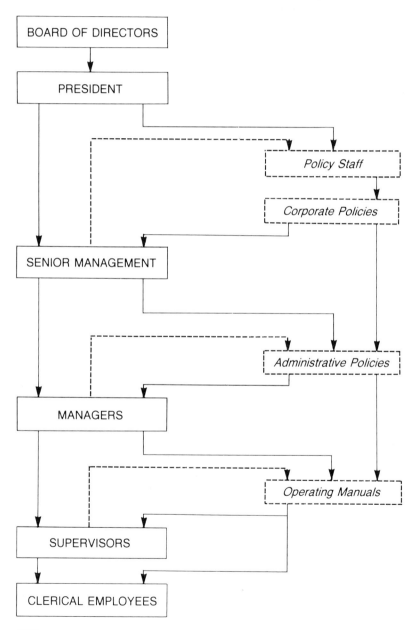

Each policy should be clearly spelled out in enough detail to enable the supervisor with the question to proceed toward a satisfactory solution. It should not be so detailed, however, that it becomes a straightjacket, but should allow the supervisor some leeway. By staying within the framework of established policy, the supervisor knows that any decision he makes will not conflict with similar decisions made by other supervisors. Everybody, this way, is playing by the same rules.

Policies should not be copied from a book nor borrowed from other companies. They should be written and included in the policy manual only as they are needed to resolve problems. There should be no hesitancy to revise any policy when it is no longer adequate to meet a new or changed situation.

The preparation and maintenance of the policy manual should rest in one location, and the personnel office is the most likely first choice. The personnel staff is charged with the implementation, accountability and continuing conformance to policies by supervisors throughout the company. Who then is more logical to originate and update policies as they relate to the employee program? This does not mean that the personnel officer has sole authority for initiating or changing company policies; but he has the responsibility for getting the policy-making group, such as senior staff, to listen to and act upon his recommendations and for getting the president to give each policy the approval it needs to be put into effect.

A policy manual is a confidential reference guide to aid supervisors and should be issued to all who need it, but not indiscriminately to others. A good control over the use of these policy manuals is to include in the binder the list of management personnel to whom the original binders, and later changes or added pages, are distributed.

CORPORATE POLICIES

The need for clear, well-thought-out corporate policies has never been greater than it is now. Policies that express the philosophy, principles and purpose of an organization help each executive conceptualize with the corporation as a whole instead of identifying only with his own specialty or assignment. Realistic policies stating the corporation's position become the natural bridge of communication between decentralized or segmented operations.

Policy setting is largely the private domain of the chief executive of the corporation. Policy statements provide a means whereby he can communicate his intentions and directions to his executives. Similarly, the senior officers of divisions of the corporation, taking their cue from the chief executive, shape divisional policy statements to communicate

Putting Corporate Philosophy Into Action

PHILOSOPHY

the thinking of the various influences on the organization molded into a common synthesis

PRINCIPLES

accepted truths used by the organization, and the individuals in it, as guides or rules of conduct

PURPOSE

the mission or role of the organization in a changing society, or its reason for being established and maintained

CREED

beliefs and standards that determine the character of the business and justifies its existence

ASSUMPTION

temporary hypothesis regarding a very important future development or state of conditions accepted as a basis for establishing objectives in support of purpose

OBJECTIVES

definite commitments to action to be carried out within specified parameters

GOALS

time-related targets for achieving the various elements of the objectives

POLICIES

the idealistic interpretation of corporate goals, in terms of direction and guidance, from which precise application plans are formulated

5-YEAR PLANS

statements of time-phased steps for realizing long-range goals within policies

ANNUAL PLANS

statements of quantified first phase of the 5-year plans with interim checkpoints for monitoring the progress toward immediate goals

PROGRAMS

systematic subdivisions of plans into component tasks with assignments of resources, priorities, and schedules

PROCEDURES

series of related methods giving detailed instructions at the individual level to accomplish the desired result

CONTROLS

the procedures, including budgets, by which activities are regulated, restrained, directed, or verified to assure conformance to goals, policies, programs and standards

OPERATIONS

actual performance necessary to fulfill responsibilities

REPORTS

oral, visual, or written communications between organizations, organizational subdivisions, or individuals regarding the progress or results of one or more activities

EVALUATION

the analysis and assessment of results to determine whether deviations from expected results have accrued, the reasons, alternative actions for correction, and the optimum course of action

their intentions to other divisions and their direction to subordinates.

The terms that are used have fine line distinctions. There is confusion about the terms because they are often used carelessly. For clarification, a glossary is included in a corporate policy manual. The major distinctions are that a purpose tells why a company is in business; a philosophy is what it believes in; the principles are the code of conduct; objectives tell what it wants to accomplish; and the policies explain how it carries out its activities in order to fulfill its purpose and achieve its objectives.

A policy is a guide for action and decision making. A policy is also a declaration of intent about an organization's obligations and responsibilities. Policies are flexible guidelines and as such are more effective than the earlier rigid rules of managerial conduct. They accommodate better the continual prospect of change and they make allowance for the growing humanistic approach to management.

This need for corporate policies is paramount today since the corporate environment is changing, too. Objectives, which have caught on lately, give an executive a better perspective about his role in the company, but policies provide him with an insight into the company's role in society.

The Complexion of Management

Companies that felt they had to reach two kinds of customers—those who buy their products and those who buy their jobs—now recognize the importance of also gaining acceptance from other groups: suppliers, unions, competitors, communities and government. Businessmen have always felt a measure of responsibility to the community in which they were privileged to serve. They formerly discharged this responsibility by supporting community activities and contributing to charitable funds and worthy institutions. Where tokenism satisfied before, the new climate calls for involvement. With the changes in socioeconomic conditions, business leaders are becoming increasingly aware of a kind of trusteeship for groups and programs identified more closely with the pluralistic characteristics of society than the singularly selfish motives of industry.

Legal constraints and environmental demands are altering the complexion of management. Executives must be capable of dealing with problems at a combined economic-political-cultural level. They are discovering that to gain acceptance and obtain results they have to operate less in the harsh context of authoritarian leadership and more in the soft breeze of managerial freedom.

In this enlightened era of modern management, the board of directors and the president often take a stand on issues that confront their business activities. Their understanding of what is best for the company is clear enough in its intent, but in the press of day-to-day administration, the best intentions can easily be compromised as the official position is filtered down through the organization and brought into direct contact with realistic operational pressures. To avoid the painful consequences of misunderstanding, the corporate posture on all important considerations should be carefully documented in written corporate policy statements.

The Purpose

The reason for establishing and maintaining the official corporate policy manual of any company is to:

1. Express the basic philosophies of the corporation and its divisions.
2. Establish the boundaries within which the management of the corporation operates.
3. Provide management with direction and thereby minimize the vulnerability to inconsistent decision making.

It is this last point which epitomizes the real need for a policy manual and which places a value on the total effort.

To serve their useful purpose, corporate policies need not be complicated and involved. There are four simple rules that apply. Corporate policies should be:

1. Comprehensive enough to cover most situations that arise in the normal course of events.
2. Simple to avoid misinterpretation.
3. Stable, changing only when the nature of the business changes.
4. Flexible so as not to choke a dynamic business.

The establishment and documentation of corporate policies, understood to be flexible directions, help to:

1. Perpetuate the continuity and stability of management.
2. Integrate functions and activities and encourage teamwork.
3. Improve internal operating relations through the resultant consistency of management decisions.
4. Permit executives to handle problems more quickly and with greater freedom.
5. Enable executives to fulfill their responsibilities by defining constraints within which they must perform.

The basic philosophy of a business should be sacrosanct, once it has proved sound. Nothing short of official (board) action should change its principles. Its policies should be revised to fit changing times and needs albeit only after prudent deliberation. The procedures for carrying out the policies, however, should be revised or discarded whenever they become obsolete or better ones can be devised.

The creation of a corporate policy manual must not be a "make work" project for an enterprising staff assistant or for a leftover executive suffering career arrest. Nor can it be a management exercise culminating in futility on every executive's private bookshelf. Properly established and used, an official corporate policy manual becomes a viable instrument of good management. Its usefulness, however, must be apparent.

CORPORATE POLICIES

Community Service
(Sample)

Purpose: The purpose of this policy is to demonstrate the company's genuine interest in the community by encouraging and supporting employees who serve in community activities.

Scope: All employees.

Summary: It is the policy of the corporation to meet some of its responsi-

bility to the community by actively encouraging employees to participate in community affairs, especially as these relate to the free enterprise system.

1. The company hopefully expects executives and managerial
   personnel to establish and maintain rapport with business and
   trade associations, service clubs, labor groups, religious organizations, professional societies and government agencies.
   Should their involvement call for company time, facilities
   and expenses, it should be done with the knowledge and
   approval of the appropriate senior officer, with any costs
   charged to the budget of the department to which the individual is assigned.
2. Management will encourage employees at all levels to volunteer for community service work on their own time and in
   programs of their own choosing. Employees who "donate
   themselves" to worthy causes should be made to feel that
   management is interested in the programs and proud of the
   employees.

In all cases, it is assumed that any outside activity will be such that
avoids any possible conflict of interest with the company's business.

Accountability: The office of the Vice-President, Public Relations will
serve as the clearing house for community activities of company employees. This office will make available to Personnel a report of individual accomplishments and experience for the employee record, and will
publicize appropriate activities in the company house organ as recognition for the individual and encouragement to others.

Authority: Minutes of the Board of Directors' Meeting, February 15,
19__.

ADMINISTRATIVE POLICIES

Administrative or operating policies are written within the framework of corporate policies. If this sounds confusing, let's back up a bit.

A corporate policy is an official position statement taken by the
corporation. For example, Blue Cross does not pay for blood. This is
a stand taken by the board of directors who feel that blood is not a
commodity. Having thus taken this position, the sales people and the
claims administrators act accordingly.

The president or chief executive officer, taking his direction from the
board of directors, is responsible for corporate policies. Within these
corporate policy guidelines, the president then delegates authority and

ADMINISTRATIVE POLICY

sample

CREDIT CARDS

Summary: It is company policy to minimize employees' financial outlays for travel expenses. Normal travel costs are reimbursed promptly on submission of expense statements. Abnormal cash outlays are avoided generally by providing before departure airline tickets and cash in the form of an "advance" to the employee. This procedure goes a long way toward eliminating the need for a profusion of credit cards.

Specifics: For good control, the number of credit cards outstanding in the company's name should be kept to a minimum. The following credit cards may be issued to individuals or positions as designated:

1. Airline Travel Card.

2. Telephone Credit Card.

3. Gasoline Credit Card— issued only to individuals to whom leased vehicles have been assigned or loaned to authorized personnel when they use company pool cars.

4. Auto Rental Credit Card.

5. American Express Credit Card (or substitute).

6. Other (specify).

The individual to whom a credit card(s) is issued is primarily responsible for safeguarding credit cards and avoiding their misuse by others. When a credit card is lost or stolen the department which provided the card must be notified immediately.

The Comptroller's office is responsible for authorizing the issuance and controlling the use of company credit cards.

assigns responsibilities downward to division vice-presidents to write their respective administrative policies.

The marketing vice-president writes sales policies, the controller writes financial policies, the production superintendent writes manufacturing policies, the administrative vice-president writes operating policies, the medical director writes professional policies, the personnel director writes employee policies, and so forth—all consistent with corporate policies as delineated by the president.

These administrative policies are the detailed instructions division heads issue to subordinate managers to guide them in making company-acceptable operating and employee-relations decisions. When published they communicate their intentions to other divisions.

Carrying this one step further, managers issue companion procedure manuals for the guidance of employees in specific departments and jobs. This is the OST concept—objectives, strategies, tactics.

Policies and procedures help govern decision making and result in greater consistency and equity in making decisions at all levels. The policies translate management's philosophy into managerial action.

EMPLOYMENT POLICIES

Every company should have a clear understanding of its employment policies. The terms should, preferably, be in writing. They pertain to the attitude and conditions related to:

1. Hiring workers.

   a. Full time: full employee benefits.
   b. Part time: what benefits do they get?
   c. Temporary: usually get no benefits.

2. Re-employment of former workers: do they start over as new employees or are they given credit for past seniority and earned rights?

3. Employment of relatives: if husband and wife may both be hired, must they be in different departments?

4. Under age.

   a. 18 years and older: no limitation.
   b. 17-year-olds: verification of age certificate.
   c. 16-year-olds: work permits; may be employed for any number of hours and during any period of time, except in occupations declared hazardous by the U.S. Secretary of Labor.
   d. 14- and 15-year-olds: limited to certain occupations outside school hours and under specified conditions of work.

5. Age limit: usually cannot be hired over 70 years of age as regular employees where a retirement program exists.

6. Education minimum: is it general (no one below high school graduate; which may be difficult to substantiate) or specific by job?

7. Nondiscrimination by:

    a. race, color, creed, national origin.

    b. sex.

    c. age.

EMPLOYMENT POLICY
(sample)

In the employment of workers, the aim is to hire, from among available applicants, the person best qualified for each job and who also shows potential for development. At the same time it is hoped to give each worker the type of job he wants which he is able to perform.

The continuing policy of the company shall be to use employment and promotion practices based on factors other than age, sex, race, creed, color or national origin. In the interview procedure as well as in later promotions, appropriate tests, validated for the specific jobs, are utilized in order to give every candidate an equal chance.

Men and women get equal pay for equal work which means equal skill, equal effort, equal responsibility, performed under similar working conditions. Any wage differentials are based on seniority, merit, performance and other criteria of the wage administration program, but not on sex.

EMPLOYMENT OF RELATIVES

Civil rights experts say that companies can develop specific policies for couples without fear of successful litigation as long as they enforce the regulations equitably. The "Employment of Relatives" policy of Blue Cross-Blue Shield of Georgia/Columbus, Inc. stood the test.

The policy reads as follows:

> The Plans will not employ a person who has a relative employed by the Plans. This includes spouse, mother, father, child, brother, sister, grandparents, aunts, uncles, mother-in-law, father-in-law, sister-in-law or brother-in-law.
>
> Employees who already have relatives employed by the Plans may continue to work but should an

977

employee with a relative leave employment, the former employee would not be eligible for rehire. If two employees are married while employed with the Plans, both may continue to work.

It is (also) the policy not to employ or retain in our employ, a worker either male or female, whose spouse is employed by an insurance company competing with the Plans in the sale of health care protection.

The second part of the policy, relating to employment by competitors, does not extend to blood relatives. A secretary challenged the rule after she was fired because neither she nor her husband, a salesman for a commercial insurance company, would resign. She lost her sex-discrimination suit in a U.S. appeals court. She contended that Blue Cross had failed to take any action against a male employee in a similar predicament. Blue Cross said it had been unaware of that situation; when it found out, it reminded the male employee of its rule, and his wife quit her job with a competitor.

EMPLOYMENT POLICY

The following is the "Hiring Policy" of Montgomery Ward & Company, Inc.

The continued growth and health of our society depends to a large extent on the ability to provide a good life for all of our citizens. American industry has a vital stake in a healthy society, and we must do everything possible to enhance and promote the elements which contribute to progress and stability. One of these elements is full employment and the opportunities of growth for all. This can only be achieved when as a nation we are able to provide continuous and *meaningful* employment and opportunities for growth and development for *all* members of the labor force.

Montgomery Ward has a policy of nondiscrimination and is fully committed to the principles of equality in employment and opportunity for all and expects all Ward employees to actively adhere to these principles. In the administration of this policy, all Company personnel charged with the responsibility for hiring, training, supervising, transferring and promoting employees will take affirmative action to assure that job applicants as well as employees are considered without regard to their race, creed, color, sex, national origin or age. This places on each member of management, and especially those with hiring and promotion responsibilities, the obligation to hire and upgrade all qualified people, and to implement this policy in the interest of assisting the Company in providing equal employment and promotion opportunities.

MOONLIGHTING

At a time when millions of workers are unemployed, it might seem unfair that untold numbers of other people have two jobs. These are the moonlighters.

At any given time, approximately five per cent of workers are moonlighting. On their own time they take on additional jobs, usually not in their regular line of work. Moonlighting dates back to medieval days when farmers labored in the fields and also served in the army of the lord of the manor.

Moonlighters take second jobs for different reasons. While some are hobbyists turning a pastime into a second income, most are family men and women who use the extra money to help meet regular expenses and to pay off debts. They find the extra money makes it easier for paying off the mortgage or a loan, for putting children through school, or building a nestegg for retirement. *They are thus trading time for money.*

Some occupations, by the very nature of work schedules, allow time that can easily be converted into money. Examples are firefighters, teachers, airline pilots.

Beyond the money incentives, many who moonlight are engaging in an outside activity in order to give expression to a special skill or unique talent. The second job serves as a kind of apprenticeship for a new career. *They are thus trading time for experience and opportunity.*

Many of the moonlighters in this second category are self-employed in their second jobs which makes it easier to set the hours. The additional employment, such as writing, painting, or entertaining, is often a profitable excursion into fantasy land.

Moonlighting can be a way to:

1. Pick up needed money to meet bills or pay off debts.
2. Obtain extra income for "mad money" activities.
3. Let off steam from the pressures of the regular job.
4. Get pleasure if present job is monotonous or restrictive.
5. Prepare for part-time retirement work.
6. Indulge in a hobby and make it pay off.
7. Try out a new career without giving up present job.

While companies may frown on the idea of moonlighting, for the most part they look away realizing there isn't really very much they can

979

do about it anyway. What employees do on their own time is their own business, they rationalize. As long as the extracurricular activities do not interfere with the regular performance of their jobs, or conflict with or cause embarrassment to the company, they see no problem.

A typical company policy on

OUTSIDE ACTIVITIES

You may engage in outside activities such as part-time employment, community affairs, school attendance, etc., as long as they do not adversely affect your performance on the job, cause embarrassment to the company, or result in a conflict of interest. Normally, it is not possible to rearrange work schedules to facilitate your participation in these outside activities.

GAMBLING

Gambling in offices and factories is widespread. Most managements look upon it as a harmless pastime. In some situations it borders on a fringe benefit.

Managers themselves conduct and/or participate in baseball and football pools. They wager openly at the local racetrack. They "donate" to charity through the Irish Sweepstakes.

Is this to be tolerated? What about shooting dice in the locker room? Is an employee permitted to run a little numbers game on the side?

Most "No Gambling" signs are dust covered. Rules can be enforced by progressive discipline:

1. verbal warning
2. written warning
3. suspension
4. layoff
5. discharge

Gambling can lead to thievery—to recoup losses. It can affect productivity if gambling takes on a higher priority. Like a cancer, it can spread until it is uncontrollable. It is best to nip it in the bud.

RULES AND REGULATIONS

A fundamental of military leadership is that no order should be given which cannot be enforced. A good business rule, like a good law, should be in the general interest, and not merely in the company's interest. It should appeal to the employee as a sensible requirement of employment.

Rules and regulations should be known. This is often done in the form of an employee handbook. What is not as well published are the consequences for disregarding or violating these necessary rules.

Company regulations pertain to safety (personal and property) and to conduct on the job. Wearing a hard hat in the foundry is a typical rule. Safety rules govern machines, apparel and behavior. It is obvious that such regulations must be observed.

In the factory and office it is important that employees demonstrate business sense toward their job responsibilities. Much of this is self-understood and little more than common sense or good social graces. But because employees forget, become indifferent or deliberately try to see how far they can go without being reprimanded, they must often be told. In such cases employees need to be reminded of the customs, spelled out as house rules.

While companies like to be lenient and make things pleasant for their employees, they cannot let people go off in different directions. So they make rules. Employees are expected to comply willingly.

What happens when rules are not followed? An employee who is habitually tardy is counselled in hopes of helping him overcome the bad practice. An employee who starts a fight may be fired. An employee who steals may be apprehended.

If discipline is to be meted out to offenders, the procedure should be clearly spelled out, publicized and enforced. Rules and regulations should be reasonable so they can be accepted, and they should be respected so that infractions and penalties will be minimized.

PENALTIES

The following is taken from *The Dofasco Way*, the employee handbook of Dominion Foundries and Steel, Limited, Hamilton, Ontario, Canada.

We feel that you will find little difficulty in adapting to our rules. Yet, we must warn you that you may be reprimanded or penalized by suspension or dismissal, depending upon the frequency or seriousness of your offences. In general, disciplinary action will be applied as follows:

Infractions of a Minor Nature

An employee committing a minor infraction is subject to:

1st offence—written warning.
2nd offence—up to 3-day suspension.
3rd offence—see No. 10—Major infractions.

Minor infractions consist of conduct which could reduce the employee's ability to perform his tasks, or could reduce his fellow workers' effectiveness, or could affect morale, including:

1. Absence without notification or permission.
2. Tardiness.
3. Loafing.
4. Sleeping on the job (while on duty).
5. Improper use of company property.
6. Minor violation of safety rules.
7. Failure to punch, improper punching or punching another employee's time card.

Infractions of a Major Nature

Employees are subject to immediate dismissal for wilful misconduct or disobedience or for wilful neglect of duty that is not condoned, including:

1. Absenteeism.
2. Theft.
3. Disorderly conduct, including fighting, threatening another employee.
4. Being on the company's premises while under the influence of alcohol or drugs.
5. Bringing, having or consuming intoxicating beverages or drugs in the plant.
6. Smoking in prohibited areas.
7. Wilful damage to company property or property of others.
8. Walking off the job (leaving the work station), or leaving the job before quitting time.
9. Major violation of safety rules.
10. A minor infraction which, after warning and a suspension is repeated.

The company reserves the right to add to, to delete from or to revise this partial list of violations and probable penalties.

An employee who loses time through a suspension will lose the option of working in lieu of vacation during that vacation year.

ACCEPTANCE OF GIFTS AND FAVORS

Following is a statement of Inland Steel Company's policy with respect to acceptance of gifts and favors by employees:

> "No employee of the company or any of its sub-
> sidiaries, or members of the employee's immedi-
> ate family, shall accept any gift, services, special
> accommodations or other favors from any sup-
> plier or from any other party with which the com-
> pany or any of its subsidiaries does business."

This policy does not preclude normal ethical business practices, such as luncheons, token gifts or entertainment of nominal value. The basic criterion is whether acceptance of these gratuities would cause a critical third party to suspect an attempt to influence one's independence of judgment. In making such an assessment, if there is any doubt as to the propriety of a gift or favor, it should be rejected. Obviously, the policy forbids gifts in the form of cash or gift certificates. The solicitation of gifts of any kind or amount is absolutely forbidden and will be the basis for severe disciplinary action.

Inland Steel Company expects its employees to maintain the highest ethical standards in their conduct of company affairs. Throughout the company and its subsidiaries, the true value of a supplier is measured by his business performance. The rating of such performances must not be encumbered by other influences.

WORKING CONDITIONS

In the early days, working conditions and other human considerations were secondary to production and profit. The employees were there to serve the interests of the business, not vice versa.

During the past several decades, however, the picture has changed. In a tightening labor market, workers were expecting and getting a better work environment. No longer were they content to spend the better part of each day in dismal surroundings.

The influx of women into factories and offices has also had a marked effect. Their contribution has been more than chintz curtains and periodic rest periods. They brightened up the place in more ways than one, they introduced new concepts of cleanliness, they required quieter and safer equipment. Oddly enough, as women caused improvements, men did not object.

Adequate heat is now taken for granted. Air-conditioning is becoming commonplace in older buildings as well as standard in new construction. Acousticon ceiling treatment abates machine noise. Tile floors, which are waxed regularly, have replaced the old wood floor which was scrubbed infrequently. Carpeting is used freely, even in high traffic areas. Fluorescent light is used in place of the former inadequate incandescent fixtures. Liberal use of glass in walls lets in an abundance

983

of natural light. Bright pastel colors have made even old-timers forget the dingy tan walls of the office and the unpainted brick surfaces of the factory.

Sanitation and health facilities are better and maintenance is done on a daily basis. Good housekeeping is part of everybody's job. Noise, odors, dirt, fumes and hazards are well controlled and minimized as much as possible through modern methods. Piped-in music is designed to make the day pleasant.

All the while these changes were taking place, managements went along willingly to provide the better working conditions. They liked the improvements themselves and began taking pride in the physical facilities and work environment. More important, they found the new approach was better for business since it contributed to increased production from employees who felt appreciated because their employers demonstrated "we care."

The old notion of "whatever is good for business is good for people" has, over the years, been turned about and managements today understand and accept that "whatever is good for people is good for business."

WORKING CONDITIONS AND WORK RULES

Workers who think back to "the good old days" might be interested in a comparison.

The rules for nurses published in 1880 are enlightening. Nurses were told they must:

1. Bring a scuttle of coal each day.
2. Report every day at 7 A.M. and leave at 8 P.M., except on the Sabbath "on which day you will be off from noon until 2 P.M."
3. Graduate nurses in good standing will be given an evening off each week for church services.
4. Any nurse who smokes, uses liquour, goes to a beauty shop, or frequents dance halls will give the director a good reason to suspect her worth, her intentions and integrity.
5. The nurse who performs faithfully and without fault for five years will be given an increase of five cents a day, providing there are no hospital debts outstanding.

In the field of merchandising, a list of "Work Rules and Conduct" carrying a date in the 1800's, reads:

1. Store must be open from 6 A.M. to 9 P.M.
2. Store must be swept, counters and base shelves dusted, lamps

trimmed, filled, and chimneys cleaned, a pail of water, also a bucket of coal, brought in before breakfast, and attend to customer who calls.

3. Store must not be open on the Sabbath Day unless necessary, and then only for a few minutes.

4. The employee who is in the habit of smoking Spanish cigars, being shaved at the barber shop, going to dances, and other places of amusement, will surely give his employer reason to be suspicious of his honesty and integrity.

5. Each employee must not pay less than $5.00 per year to the church and must attend Sunday School regularly.

6. Men employees are given one evening a week for courting and two if they go to prayer meeting.

7. After 14 hours of work in the store the leisure time should be spent mostly in reading.

Have we made progress in the past 100 years?

FLEXTIME

For years companies adhered to rigid work hours. All employees worked the same standard hours. Then Flextime was tried. And in many cases it proved to be a successful innovation.

Flextime gives employees optional working hours that coincide with their personal preferences. The hours selected by each employee still serve the company purposes and fit personal circumstances. Employees choose from a range of fixed or flexible hours. They work during a specified "core time" and accumulate a set number of hours each day or each week. Within these limits they come and go pretty much as they choose.

Typically, a company on Flextime opens its doors at 7:00 A.M. and closes them at 6:00 P.M. All employees must be present during predetermined peak hours (core time)—say, 10:00 A.M. until 12:00 noon and 1:00 P.M. until 3:00 P.M. Beyond that they determine for themselves when to arrive and when to leave. They are required to put in their eight hours each day.

Most companies require that employees maintain a similar schedule from day to day. But some companies tolerate erratic patterns in which employees can work uneven hours during the week—nine hours one day and seven on another, as one example. This is known as gliding time. Here they are required only to put in their forty hours each week.

The Germans, renowned for Prussian punctuality and considered the inventors of the work ethic, conceived and introduced Flextime. It had its roots in West Germany's economic miracle of the 1950's and

1960's. There were more jobs than applicants and attempts were made to lure housewives and mothers into industry to alleviate the labor shortage. Flexible starting and quitting times were offered to help them cope with their household chores and child-rearing duties.

Proponents of the idea claim advantages for both the employees and for management.

For employees (clear and immediate):

1. Hours are scheduled to keep drivers out of rush hour traffic.
2. Hours permit commuters using public transportation to avoid congestion.
3. Hours can suit the needs of their personal lives.
4. Hours can be set for personal convenience.
5. Hours can be adjusted to accommodate family situations.
6. Hours can be arranged to meet child care requirements.

Because they're trusted to behave as responsible adults, employees feel better about the company and their jobs.

For management:

1. Lateness virtually disappears (a tardy worker simply makes up for lost time by staying later).
2. Absences decline (employees can adjust hours instead of staying away all day).
3. It boosts morale and enthusiasm (less guilt feeling).
4. Hiring is easier (hours fit applicant too, not only company).
5. It spreads democracy among employees.
6. Telephones are manned more hours of the day.
7. Customer service is spread out longer.
8. Under a flexible schedule, an employee can finish a job which under a fixed schedule would be left unfinished.

There could be disadvantages. It might create scheduling conflicts. Some functions go uncovered during parts of the day when other people in the company depend on them. Supervisors could lose a measure of control over subordinates who arrive before or leave after the boss does.

Flextime breaks the boss-employee working relationship which always made it seem necessary that both be present at the same time. Under Flextime employees have to be more responsible and be trusted to work without direct supervision part of the day.

Flextime should not be confused with staggered hours. Under Flextime, the employee decides what hours to work; under staggered hours, the employer dictates the terms, and workers are told to come in earlier or later.

Flextime is not suitable for all business operations. The variable working schedules are easier to implement in service industries, such as banks, insurance, or case work, than in industrial production or retail stores with set customer hours. It does not work in operations that are continually interdependent; it would, for example, not work on the assembly line.

Flextime is available to half the white-collar labor force in Germany and Switzerland, and is growing in use in the United States and Canada. According to a study by the University of California's Institute of Governmental Studies at Berkeley, it was found that Flextime reduced absenteeism (from 1,100 worker-days a year to fewer than 100), reduced turnover, increased morale, and raised production.

Acceptance of the concept of Flextime apparently will spread.

FOUR-DAY WEEK

Interest in the four-day work week was high in the early 1970's. It lagged during the 1974 recession. Now interest is being revived.

It is estimated that 1.2 million employees, or about one percent of the full-time work force, are on a four-day work week. About 10,000 companies, mostly small nonunion operations, have experimented with the idea. The results are a mixed bag—from less absenteeism and higher morale to worker fatigue and safety problems.

The objectives of the four-day week are to:

1. Create more jobs.
2. Increase leisure time.

The idea is appealing to organized labor. They support it as a solution to rampant unemployment through a sharing of available work. It is also appealing to workers as evidenced by the trend toward long holiday weekends.

The four-day week won't take hold as four ten-hour days. It will really grab when unions get the standard 32-hour work week they are driving toward.

But the unions are realistic and not pushing for it at this time. They don't feel the economy is ready for a 32-hour work week at 40 hours' pay. So they bargain for some of its advantages through more paid time off. In its latest contract the United Auto Workers won 13 additional days off over a two-year period. Steelworkers are entitled to 13 weeks off with pay every five years in addition to normal vacation time.

One reason the idea hasn't caught on is that many people don't know what to do with three-day weekends on a regular schedule. So they moonlight, which defeats the whole idea of spreading the work to help the jobless.

If the four-day work week someday becomes a reality it will be through either union collective bargaining or government legislation. The trend has been toward a shorter work week.

In 1840 President Van Buren issued an executive order establishing a 10-hour work day for federal employees. New Hampshire in 1847 became the first state to fix 10 hours as a legal work day. The Fair Labor Standards Act of 1938 set the 40-hour week as the standard. At that time industry generally was on work weeks of 45 hours or longer.

As the trend continues, four eight-hour days makes more sense than five days of six and a fraction hours each. Working four days out of seven is a distinct possibility with the spread of service jobs in customer-oriented establishments that already remain open more than 40 hours each week.

The most innovative concept is to scrap the downward trend of hours altogether in favor of a three-day work week. An employee would work three longer days and then have four uninterrupted days off.

A family could live in unspoiled "hinterlurbia" where schools are better, community life easier and taxes less. Commuting by modern travel would make it possible for the worker to spend four days and five nights at home. On his work days he could live in nearby company-operated dormitories shared with other split-week workers.

WORK AT HOME

More and more companies are developing an informal policy of letting some employees do certain work at home instead of at the office.

Typical jobholders who can perform at least some of their work from a home base are authors, architects, photographers, salespersons, and creative people. Typical jobs that can be performed at home are research, planning special projects, speechwriting, reports, proofreading, program develoment, budgeting.

This arrangement has advantages such as less distractions, no telephones jangling, saving commuting time, and relaxation of rules which make possible casual clothes, flexible working hours, shortened Fridays (in summer). Among disadvantages are children running about, laxity because of no supervision, and being out of touch with co-workers.

Working at home is not conducive to jobs that require on-site presence such as secretaries, bank tellers, machinists, keypunch operators.

There is a trend developing to provide communication linkups making coming to the office unnecessary for some workers. There is one big problem, however. Under present in-office practices workers are paid for time they put in. This new development calls for some way to pay for work produced irrespective of time.

Then there are other people who can not work at all except at home. Physical handicaps that make traveling difficult, or a necessity of caring for children, elderly, or sick family members can prevent otherwise capable and qualified people from joining the outside labor force.

A few companies are trying what is called "cottage keyer" programs whereby workers at home have computer terminals connected to the central computer at the main office. These workers usually pay a fixed fee that covers terminal, telephone, and paper costs. They are paid a flat rate for units of work completed.

Other companies that have picked up on this cottage keyer idea provide compensation by conventional payroll practices. These at-home workers are added to the employee roster and are treated much the same as employees who work on the premises. They are covered by all state and federal mandated protection and become eligible for other company sponsored benefits as dictated by personnel policy, such as health insurance, salary continuation, vacation, pension, holidays, and sick pay. The salary is figured the same as for other employees performing the same functions and is subject to overtime, state and federal withholding taxes, and Social Security. Time to pick up or to deliver basic work materials is considered as time worked.

Performance and production are observed and are expected to be comparable to the work of employees on similar jobs in the main office. Equipment installation, maintenance, and general care are provided for. The risk factor for loss of data caused by neglect or fire in a residential dwelling is covered by insurance. The confidential nature of the work is also addressed.

Most companies that have a work-at-home program consider it as a means of obtaining a service to supplement in-house productivity in a labor market that does not yield adequate numbers of employees with the required skills. This additional work force is not readily available under conventional approaches.

But there are other concerns that could offset these expected advantages. The planning and controlling of productivity present problems more difficult to resolve than when the work is performed under direct supervision. Supervision by remote control is a new experience for managers.

A work-at-home program is a combined effort that is considered by line managers, designed by the personnel staff, and approved by legal advisers.

ATTENDANCE VS. ABSENTEEISM
(sample statement)

You were hired because you were needed; your presence on the job is therefore necessary. Absences should be kept to a minimum since they disrupt the work flow and inconvenience other employees who have to fill in.

Should it be necessary for you to be away from work, common courtesy expects you to notify your supervisor as soon as possible so that the necessary adjustments can be made.

ATTENDANCE BONUS

Many companies with nagging tardiness or uncontrollable absences try to reduce these problems by offering bonuses to employees. Payoffs are made only to employees with perfect attendance, but it is hoped others will be moved by the incentive to try to improve their records.

Payoffs are sometimes made in the form of cash but more generally with additional time off. In my first place of employment, a small wholesale drug jobber, it was important to telephone the retail drug store customer for his order before the larger wholesalers did. Therefore, anyone who was present and on time every day of the week found an extra one dollar in his pay envelope.

Some programs add points or credits for perfect attendance to the employee scorecard, which gives credit toward merchandise for many other aspects as well, such as employee referrals, suggestions, etc. There are bonus plans that pay off in trading stamps.

The most common reward comes in additional time off. Each employee who has a perfect record for 30 or 90 days, for example, might get an extra one-half or one day off from work, or added to his vacation. Immediately one has to wonder about the logic of such approach since the company could easily give away more time than it gains.

A typical time-off program might be—

Beginning immediately, something new has been added to our employee program which will make this an even better place to work.

Many employees have through the years of their employment maintained a perfect record of attendance. We have adopted a plan to recognize this perfect attendance by granting free time off from work, in addition to the regular vacation time already provided.

All programs need rules to operate by, and the rules for our Bonus Time Off Plan are as easy as we can make them. It is our hope that before long all eligible employees will have free time to their credit.

The rules:

1. One half day will be given to each eligible employee for each 30 consecutive work days of perfect attendance.

2. The 30-day period may begin on any work day of the month.

3. a. Bonus Time may be accumulated to a total of one full day.

   b. The Bonus Time off must be taken within 30 days after it is earned.

   c. Holidays, vacation or Bonus Time Off, falling within a work period, do not count against perfect attendance.

4. Perfect attendance is understood to mean:

   a. Being on time in the morning and when returning from lunch.

   b. Remaining on the job until the beginning of the lunch hour and until quitting time.

   c. Observing the time of the 15-minute pass period.

   d. Employees will be considered late if not in their department and ready for work at the established time each day.

   e. An employee sick, tardy or on leave without pay, begins a new 30-day work period the work day following the break in his or her record.

Any program, such as the one above, saddles the manager or foreman with additional administrative detail. It is almost necessary for the supervisor or someone he designates, to make separate entries on individual employee record cards several times each day.

A recent survey reveals that many firms are rewarding good attendance rather than punishing poor attendance. Here are some of the arrangements used:

1. Day off for perfect attendance. Many variations of this, such as a day off for every 60 days of perfect attendance. Perfect attendance also includes not being late to work as well as not being absent from work.

2. Bonus for employees who don't use up sick days. The bonus is prorated on the basis of unused days.

3. An extra week's vacation for perfect attendance. Illness of the one-day variety has been cut by 50% at one firm where an extra week's vacation was added for a year's perfect attendance.

4. Use of trading stamps. One company gives 100 trading stamps for each week of perfect attendance. In this case, wives literally push husbands out the door to work.

The whole notion of an attendance bonus is not well accepted by many managements, however, because of two very basic reasons:

1. These firms have serious misgivings about paying any employee *twice* for part of his job. He is already being adequately compensated for being there and doing his work.

991

Why pay him extra for only doing what is rightfully expected of him?

2. This is just another instance of a management using a "device" to do what supervision obviously is incapable of doing. To them the introduction of such a plan is an admission of weak supervision.

WELL PAY

Not only to curb absenteeism and lateness but also to reward dependability, Parsons Pine Products, Inc., Ashland, Oregon, introduced its "Well Pay" program which has attracted national interest.

Every employee who is neither absent nor late—no exceptions—is given eight hours extra pay per month. The company explains "The extra money we pay into this program does not hurt us at all since we have the (semi-annual) bonus plan. It maybe makes the bonus a little less, but at least it is rewarding our good people."

The plan has cut late arrivals to almost zero and absenteeism is down 30%.

TARDINESS

There are two basic approaches that are used in dealing with the problem of tardiness:

1. Attempts at control through
   a. Punishment
   b. Reward
2. Acceptance

Occasional tardiness is easier to tolerate than habitual latecoming. Both are easier to justify when the employment market is unfavorable and when the employees involved are key workers or good performers.

The chronic latecomer presents a problem few companies can handle or want to become involved in. The usual method is to warn the offender a few times that if he doesn't or can't "shape up," he will be terminated. Some companies make a more intensive effort to help employees correct the problem and thereby retain their jobs.

A reward and punishment method simply means that offenders are punished by being docked, or the nonoffenders are rewarded in some way over and above their usual pay.

A typical punishment plan consists of perhaps three steps:

1. Face the employee with the facts. Go over time sheets. Point out the extent or frequency of tardiness. Ask about causes.

POLICY

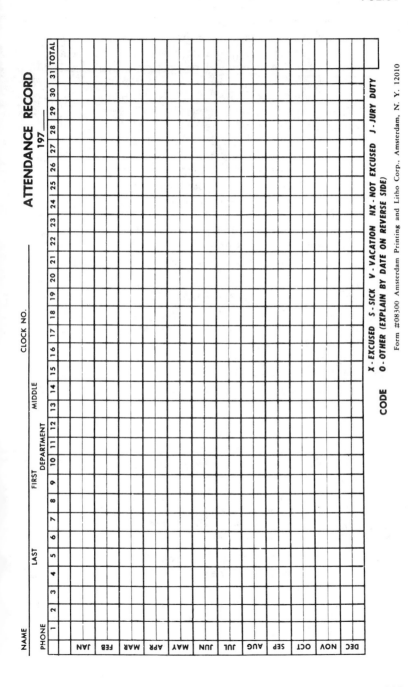

993

Some employees, when they see that the company is genuinely interested in helping them, will try to do better.

2. If the situation does not improve, it is time for a second interview. This might well be a performance review in which all aspects of the job are discussed. If work performance is good, this is mentioned, and it is also pointed out that the work record would otherwise qualify the employee for a raise, say a normal increment of $25, but because of the uncorrected tardiness, the raise will be only $15. Now the employee understands that he, and not only the company, is being penalized by tardiness.

3. If this doesn't work, and other attempts at reasoning fail, most companies feel they have no choice. They terminate the offender because they cannot ignore the problem any longer and disturb team morale, nor can they permit the bad habit to spread and upset production.

In these meetings with tardy employees the companies are satisfied to point up the problem. They don't preach to the employees or advise them how to overcome some of the basic reasons for their inability to conform to the standard starting time of the entire work group. To do so would be practicing "amateur psychology" for which they and their supervisors are not equipped.

The exception to this approach is the creative type person, who feels he must be a nonconformist in order to retain his individuality. Good engineers, scientists, physicists and others are in high demand and short supply. To keep these people working at full efficiency is the big opportunity, and companies are reluctant to annoy these people with restrictive rules and regulations which actually do not contribute to the creative or inventive process. If their tardiness causes embarrassment, it may be advisable to isolate them from the rest of the workforce so their irregular work habits go unnoticed.

What can be done about tardiness? First of all, the supervisor has to set a good example by being on time himself. His employees expect to see him there when they arrive. If he is indifferent toward starting on time, his employees will soon follow the leader.

Every employee has to be handled on an individual basis. The problem of tardiness is common but the reasons for it are many and varied. The employee who is late knows what he is doing. He might not know why. Criticism won't help, and the supervisor who picks on the tardy employee because he has him at a disadvantage, makes the employee defensive instead of cooperative.

The best way to work toward a solution is with understanding, not of the problem but of the individual. The company responsibility is to help employees develop to their finest potential and the key is leadership.

PROMPTNESS vs. TARDINESS
(sample statement)

Accepting a job includes accepting the responsibility that goes with it. One of these responsibilities is arriving at work on time without being prompted. You should arrange your travel to work so that tardiness does not spoil the picture of an otherwise good performance.

DEPENDABILITY
(sample statement)

For good job performance, which is the basis upon which you are recognized and rewarded, it is important that you stick to the job. This means returning from pass periods on time, not overstaying lunch periods, not leaving ahead of time, and in general not abusing privileges.

Good workers are those who can discipline themselves.

HOW TO REDUCE ABSENTEEISM

The problem of absenteeism from work goes back a long way. In early Egypt, absenteeism was attributed to one of three reasons: the missing person was sick, out appeasing the gods, or just plain lazy.

In modern business the problem is not much different. Half of the reasons are legitimate, but in the other half of the cases, the employee simply would rather be somewhere else.

Some employees who don't feel "up to it" in the morning when they arise, stay home and call in sick, while others, similarly disposed, drive themselves to work. Why? Some people are more conscientious than others, yes, possibly more honest than others. Some employees like their jobs and prefer going to work instead of staying home even for an excuse that would be quite acceptable.

In a full employment market, offices and factories are hiring more secondary wage earners, men and women who are not the sole breadwinners for their families. A missing day's pay is not enough to offset the temptation to stay home to look after the house, go shopping, wait for a delivery, or to prepare for a party dinner (Example: Wednesday before Thanksgiving). Even married men and women whose spouses are working, or for that matter any worker who has another income as a cushion against being docked, is more likely to take a day off occasionally than the worker who lives from one paycheck to another.

Don't overlook the very distinct possibility of an employee taking a day off to look for another job. Most jobs are filled during regular working hours.

There are, of course, many reasons. Everybody probably has a list. And the reasons are not all bad.

Solutions Not Easy

Just as there are many reasons for absenteeism, so also are there many attempts to solve or at least reduce the problem. Most of them do not have much effect.

Docking an employee for taking a day off works against the conscientious employee; it actually gives the secondary wage earner a clean conscience to say, "Why complain when I take a day off? You're not paying me for it." Rewarding the employees who do not have absenteeism by giving them extra money or time, seems to be one way of circumventing the problem but not solving it.

The consensus of most companies is that the supervisor is the main line of defense in combating absenteeism. This is just another way top management absolves itself of responsibility by shifting the burden to the supervisor who has neither the time nor the authority to do anything about it. This also explains why the problem is not being solved: today's breed of "instant" supervisors just isn't that good. They are work-pushers, not problem-solvers.

Most companies keep records of the "causes" of absences. Few keep records of the periods of time off. There is a difference between an employee who is absent five days in a row and one who is absent five separate days in a year.

Also worth watching is the type of day. Some employees have a pattern of time off which can easily be pinpointed. Some are off mostly on Mondays or Fridays (to give them long weekends). Some stay away before or after holidays or on heavy workload days. One married woman got an extra week vacation (unpaid) three years in a row simply by telephoning in long distance on the last Friday to report she was under doctor's care in her relative's home town.

Control Measures

When absenteeism gets out of hand and becomes serious, managers should look for the cause and try to find a cure. In order of frequency, here are the usual causes and some suggestions for remedies.

1. Illness
   a. colds
   b. headaches
   c. aches and pains
   d. run-down condition

To combat illness absences consider
    a. preemployment physicals
    b. periodic physical exams
    c. general health care education

2. Unexplained
   a. boredom
   b. doesn't get along with supervisors or co-workers
   c. too much overtime
   d. just doesn't like job
   e. feeling of little importance or responsibility
   f. dead-ended—sees no chance for advancement
   g. distance to travel to work
   h. group pressures

The situation could be improved by
    a. more suitable job placement
    b. some variety in the work
    c. reassignment to new environment
    d. strong disciplinary policies
    e. good supervision
    f. overtime kept reasonable

3. Personal
   a. death in the family
   b. doctor or dentist appointment
   c. taking care of personal business

Solutions might include
    a. granting permission to take off time and make it up later
    b. scheduling outside appointments for first or last hours of the day so the whole day is not lost
    c. flextime (so employees can arrange their days)

4. Industrial injuries
   a. on-the-job accidents
   b. occupational diseases

In the interests of safety and health
    a. implement a comprehensive safety program
    b. train employees in proper use of machines
    c. educate employees to all potential hazards
    d. identify and remove, or at least reduce, all dangers and hazards

In general, to control absenteeism, or to eliminate the abuses, here are recommendations that will be helpful:

1. Gather the facts. The frequency, the length, the pattern, the status of the employee, the job—all these are quite easily documented.
2. Set up standards of what would normally be acceptable.
3. Determine the accountability for absenteeism. Hold the supervisor accountable for that is where the problem and the inconvenience are. If it is conveniently "dumped" into the personnel office, who are far removed from the immediate problem, it merely becomes a record-keeping and automatic reporting function.
4. Set up controls and give the supervisor the authority and backing needed to act.

    One thing is certain. Rules and regulations won't solve the problem of absenteeism. Good supervisors, supported by management, represent the best hope of bringing the problem down to manageable proportions.

ABSENTEEISM

An analysis of absenteeism reported that:

- 54.8 percent of one- and two-day absences follow or precede legitimate time off for holidays or weekends.

- Absenteeism rises as jobs become more plentiful.

- An "incredible" correlation exists between employee "illness" and major sports events.

- Companies without "sick-pay" plans frequently have a record of fewer absences than those who have such plans.

REST PERIODS

"Breaks" are generally referred to by the people who take them as "coffee breaks." But this is a misnomer. Not everybody can afford coffee anymore, and the younger generation is hooked on cold soft drinks.

Calling breaks "rest periods" is also misleading. Very few people in offices and modern factories work hard enough to actually need a rest.

This typically American custom has become more of a habit than a justified need. The worker of today, using labor-saving equipment and performing pleasant duties in ideal surroundings, is hardly in need of rest after an hour or two of work. Diversion, possibly; rest, hardly.

Whatever they are called, they are here to stay. They provide a change-of-pace, in the case of strenuous mental or physical work, and a relief from monotony, in the case of routine, work-simplified tasks.

Can the break be abolished? Should it be? Companies that try to eliminate breaks meet with considerable opposition. Other firms agree they are helpless, and the reason is real: breaks became popular back in the 1950's when offices allowed their employees to break for coffee. In 10 years, 94% of office and factory workers enjoyed at least one break a day. Now it's a rare company that doesn't include breaks as an established part of their employee relations program. Most employees get scheduled breaks but thousands of others simply break when they choose.

Breaks for factory and office workers are generally of 15-minute duration and one is granted each forenoon and in the majority of cases, a second one is granted during the afternoon. There are some 10-minute and some 20-minute pass periods, but 15 minutes is by far the most popular.

Like recess in school, it is customary to grant these breaks during the middle of the morning and again during the middle of the afternoon. It is argued that employees should not get a rest period first thing in the morning since they should not be in need of any rest before they actually begin working. Where this is allowed it is little more than an excuse for starting work late. Likewise, no employee should be permitted to skip his afternoon pass period in order to leave work 15 minutes ahead of time. An employee who manages to go all afternoon without one doesn't need a rest period.

Advantages Claimed

In favor of breaks are arguments such as these:

- Higher production and accuracy make up for any loss of time.

- People seem to work better when they get their second wind.

- The boost to morale makes the cost insignificant.

- It's like getting their batteries recharged.

It is hard to detail the advantages or disadvantages of breaks. Companies don't even try. They are resigned to the practice as a condition of employment. They rationalize, "Employees take the time off anyway. If there were no authorized breaks, they'd duck into the washrooms to exchange the latest gossip or visit more at desks or work benches."

Contrary to the popular notion, there are no federal or state laws requiring companies to give employees a period of rest for every four hours worked. Some states have statutes specifying relief periods in certain industries or under certain conditions, and union contracts often spell out the terms.

In any case, breaks are "paid time." They are the single biggest cost item in the fringe benefits package. A company that works a 7½-hour day and gives 15-minute breaks in the forenoon and afternoon knows that $\frac{1}{15}$th of its payroll cost goes for time not worked. The cost is even higher, considerably higher, when rest periods are not carefully policed and employees abuse the privilege.

Take Charge and Control

When this happens, and breaks become a problem, what can be done? Here are a few suggestions:

1. Don't allow all employees to take their breaks at the same time. In a large office this means wasted time waiting in long lines; in small offices there is a complete work shutdown.
2. Time limit all breaks. Each employee should know what the duration is. If it's 15 minutes, don't let it drag into 20 minutes. When a group breaks at once, a timing bell might be sounded.
3. Schedule break times sensibly. According to the National Safety Council, disabling injuries occur most frequently between 10:00 to 11:00 A.M. and 3:00 to 4:00 P.M. This is just before weariness reaches its peak, and weariness results in errors in mental work also. Breaks should not be scheduled close to starting time, lunch or closing time.
4. For employees who want coffee, keep it convenient. It isn't handy when a restaurant across the street is patronized and an hour of one worker's time is wasted taking orders, making the purchase and distributing the coffee, or worse yet, when each employee fetches for himself. When a restaurant won't deliver telephoned orders, experiment with other means. Some firms keep community hot water pots boiling so that workers can utilize their own concentrated coffee, tea and nondairy creamer. Many have installed commercial vending machines in convenient locations. A company cafeteria is perhaps the best unless the service is slow or the atmosphere lends itself too easily to leisured and lengthy drinking.

1000

5. Consider the "unlimited" and untimed coffee break. This means the worker can take as many breaks as he or she likes whenever he or she chooses, but is expected to take these at the desk. This works out well with office employees who are under pressure to complete specific jobs at a stated time. Now they find themselves working while they are "break-ing," and they take refreshment when they really need it.
6. Discourage cliques. These are the workers who pal around together and who can't wait for the break so they may enjoy long visits with each other. One good way to dissolve such groups is to assign different break times to each member.
7. Don't hesitate to reprimand the flagrant offender. Returning late from breaks is no different from being late to work or extending the lunch period.
8. Don't be afraid to take charge of the break. Employees are hired to work, say, eight hours, and now they are excused from work 30 minutes each day but still being paid. The time really belongs to the company, not the employees, and they should understand this.
9. Consider giving a little to get more. Some companies have free coffee and soft drinks available to workers. This makes many workers feel morally obligated to get right back to the job at the allotted time.
10. Let management set a good example. If executives and super-visors parade their rights by taking their breaks at privileged times, or by going oftener than their workers, or by ignoring the time limit—then employees will soon pick up these bad habits and the situation will get out of control.

PERSONAL TELEPHONE CALLS

Personal telephone calls can be costly in more ways than one. Every company has only a limited number of trunk lines. When a personal call is made during business hours, it ties up the line, interferes with the firm's business, interrupts the employee's work, and creates extra work for the switchboard operator and sometimes for management employees.

Personal phone calls can also be annoying and could cause a conflict between the supervisor and the employee. Few supervisors relish the idea of acting as "personal secretary" to the workers, by being required to relay personal messages, or seek an employee who is absent from the desk when a personal call comes in.

It isn't easy to attempt to control personal phone calls and, at the same time, try to maintain a policy of a democratic working atmo-sphere. It is impractical to set rules governing personal phone calls which would be acceptable or enforceable among the company's many different types of employees. Even the conscientious worker resents "restrictions."

One of the few places where a "no calls" is strictly enforced is the school. Parents are not permitted to call their children at school; classes are not interrupted. Emergency messages may be left with the office, and because of this stringent rule, only a minimum number of personal calls are made to the school.

If personal calls, incoming and outgoing, can be controlled in schools, why not in business? The answer is simply that companies do not want to be that restrictive. They prefer to treat their employees as adults and hope they will be sensible and conscientious about the privilege.

The problem comes about because some employees cannot resist the convenience of a free telephone. They not only get messages, which would be understandable, but they often engage in lengthy conversa-tions. They know full well they are taking unfair advantage of an easy-going supervisor.

In spite of all efforts at control, personal telephone calls continue to be a major source of irritation, loss of work hours, and added costs to large and small businesses. The best approach seems to be sincere efforts to gain employee understanding of the company's side of the problem, followed by sympathetic and effective supervision.

PERSONAL APPEARANCE

An employer has the right to expect employees to be suitably attired and groomed during working hours or when representing the com-pany.

Since styles change and work situations vary, employees are usually left to use their own judgment for determining what is proper. The best look is whatever is appropriate and practical for each job.

When a supervisor feels an employee's attire is out of place, immedi-ate counselling is called for.

DRESS CODE

Until recently everybody subscribed to the idea that men in business wore business suits. This meant their clothes were of a standard style and cut and of similar colors. When women entered upon the business scene they adopted the conservative look with dresses, or blouse and skirt combinations, that were severe and plain.

What to wear didn't require much imagination. People were expected to look presentable but the focus was on work performance, not on worker appearance. Instructions on manner of dress and grooming were unnecessary. Common sense prevailed.

All that has now changed. Oh, how it has changed in some cases!

Because of this newly-discovered freedom to dress more casually, there is considerable conversation about the desirability (perhaps necessity) of establishing a carefully-spelled-out company policy, commonly referred to as a dress code. A business is judged by not only its products or services but also by its people. They are supposed to act and look businesslike.

The dress code practically all companies have today is one they let happen rather than planned. No company can say it has no dress code; this simply means that anything goes. Managements may be unhappy with what they've got, which is usually a combination of desirable and undesirable male and female attire created by default because the company had neither the foresight nor the courage to take the initiative by setting standards.

Establishing a fair dress code would seem to be one of management's prerogatives. There should be some sort of standard on dress just as there are other standards on conduct and performance that employees are expected to respect. Informal work standards are giving way to more formalized measurement programs. In telephone calls and customer correspondence, employees are expected to exercise discretion. They can't come and go as they please. They ought not dress as they please, either.

Although most rules and regulations relating to employees have generally been relaxed, they have not been totally abandoned. Some effort is still being made to get employees to report on time and not leave early. Rest periods and lunch hours are policed to avoid abuses. A degree of control is maintained over personal telephone calls, company postage and office supplies. Without supervision, the result would be chaos.

Guidelines Could Be Expressed

The majority of men and women are aware of what constitutes proper dress and good grooming in a business environment. But some people who do not know, or do not care, need to be reminded.

A rigid set of rules and regulations is not the answer. As a practical measure, an inflexible code for men and women in business would never work. How a person dresses or wears his hair is really a personal right. But a company does have a license—and indeed an obligation—to suggest proper attire for office workers, especially when a lack of instructions results in carelessness and indifference.

The idea of changes in business attire is generally accepted. In most offices it is pleasing to see men wearing colored shirts and ties because these add an air of friendliness. On the other hand, some companies feel the sedate dark suits and white shirts are the uniform of professionalism.

Many businesses have intentionally or unintentionally relaxed their rules on what is considered proper dress. A certain amount of flexibility in dress is a good thing for it allows a person some individuality and freedom of expression. So long as the exercise of independence remains within reasonable bounds there is no problem.

Uniforms Are One Answer

Some public service type organizations advocate uniforms to present a more businesslike appearance among workers. The organizations which require their employees to wear uniforms seem to meet little resistance with the specifications they prescribe. Modifications have been made, of course, and this is appropriate in a world of change. But the wearing of a standard uniform is still being imposed upon employees with no serious repercussions.

Imagine a baseball team in the World Series, or a football team in the Super Bowl, or a hockey team in the Stanley Cup playoffs, with one player appearing in blue jeans. The standard uniform is still reflective of the needs of the particular sport and makes no allowance for the peculiar whims of individuals.

No matter how the uniforms may be altered or modernized, a medical technician still looks like a medical technician, a nurse still looks like a nurse, an usher still looks like an usher, and so on. But today not every office worker looks as if he or she belongs in an office.

Standard attire is also used to identify an occupation. Only members of the clergy wear turn-around collars. In commercial airplane travel the flight attendants have dress-alike outfits; some have more than one type of uniform and on certain flights the uniform is replaced with dress apparel befitting the destination, e.g., a sarong on a trip to Hawaii, or a kimono on a flight to Japan.

In the Playboy Clubs the hostesses wear bunny costumes. In hotels and airline terminals the luggage handlers wear bellboy outfits. In restaurants the captains, waiters, waitresses and bus boys all have distinctive clothing.

Concessions have, of course, been made. In most uniformed work groups the spirit of individuality arises as people glory in the opportunity of breaking away from the pattern of conformity. Savings and loans associations, for example, have "dress up" day once a month when tellers and clerks may wear whatever they please. Even in the armed services, military personnel are authorized to be out of uniform when not on duty.

More Than Identification

Dress is also used for distinction. In a department store the floorwalker wears a flower in his lapel to distinguish him from the customers. For the same reason clerks in large stores wear smocks and many workers in supermarkets wear name tags.

A business suit in an office is a badge of status. Clothes not only reveal the "inner you" but they also give others an impression.

Clothes are worn for more than looks and comfort. They serve also as a means of communication. For example: a police officer's uniform indicates authority. Cowboys don't really need boots, do they? They wear them as a symbol of virility.

While a dress code is usually unofficial, companies tend to promote executives who wear the corporate gear. This means conservative clothes, not high fashion nor casual attire.

As for women, they should look like business people, not visiting housewives. At a business luncheon they should look like equal members of the group, not as guests invited along.

Who Decides?

Have people the right to expect the same freedom as workers that they enjoy as citizens? This is really the question.

An employee should always remember that when he works for a company he has a responsibility to that company to maintain a good image for the general public. Slovenly and indifferent work reflects not only on the individual who is guilty but also on the company he represents. So does improper and inappropriate dress and grooming.

It cannot be emphasized too strongly that this should not be considered more of a concern for one sex than the other. Companies must accept the idea that is is an ethical abrogation of a person's rights to regulate dress and grooming for women when no equivalent standards exist for men, and vice versa.

Nor does rank or level exempt anyone. Improper attire is not related to economics. The offenders are not necessarily at the lower end of the scale but also among the affluent. A professional man or a senior executive in a "rah rah" suit demeans himself and his position in the eyes of his people. To them he looks as ridiculous as his workers whose sweat-shirt-and-jeans and make-shift outfits he criticizes. The wrong attire has nothing to do with money, or lack of it; it has to do with taste, or lack of it.

Companies must expect to back away from their outmoded Victorian outlook, but they should not capitulate completely. They should draw the line somewhere.

Establishing standards that reflect the current ethos while at the same time conform to a businesslike acceptance isn't easy. Managements have learned that. Discarding rules of conduct and dress altogether isn't the answer either. Managements have learned that, too. What managements apparently have not learned is the obvious fact that while most people know instinctively what is appropriate for business wear, others would gain from having guidelines spelled out for them.

This is where a "soft sell" dress code for men and women comes in.

CAREER APPAREL

Suitable dress is important in the business office or the industrial plant. The well-dressed office woman chooses suits and dresses of neat and conservative design. Too casual and ultra-extreme costumes should be saved for other occasions.

The well-dressed man customarily wears a coat to the office although he may not be required to keep it on all day. If his jacket and trousers do not have an identical match, as in a suit, they should be at least be in good taste and complement each other. He should wear a clean shirt, not necessarily white, and also a matching necktie. Sport shirts, particularly the gaudy type, are taboo in most offices.

For both women and men, propriety and conventionality are of foremost importance.

In the plant, personal safety is of as much consideration as is comfort. Women performing production-type jobs are usually required to wear slacks or jeans, blouses or shirts, and sturdy oxford-type shoes. Shorts are not acceptable attire.

Men may wear work clothes or coveralls, depending upon their duties, and open-collar shirts are appropriate. Safety shoes, of course, are vitally important for some jobs.

In both the office and the factory, clothing should be appropriate to the jobs. These are places where work is performed, not opportunities for competitive, style shows. Off-beat casual wear, latest mod street clothes, and cocktail and party outfits have no place on the industrial scene.

Uniforms

Originally, uniforms were used for identification in such professions as military, law enforcement and nursing, and such trades as mechanics, deliverymen and waitresses.

They are now used for sales clerks, bank tellers, secretaries and even funeral directors.

The wider use of uniforms was developed as a corporate response to the liberated dress styles of a few years ago. Companies didn't like their employees coming to work looking like trolls, sharecroppers and hootchie kootchie dancers. The soft sell approach was to offer workers free clothes, thereby controlling the styles. In large measure this solves the dress code problem.

In jobs that serve the public directly, most uniforms run to the airline and car rental look: slacks and blazers for men, and smocks, pantsuits and cheerleader outfits for women.

Custom-designed work clothes are part of a company's public relations program. It aids in creating a desirable corporate image. The uniform becomes the company trademark.

But distinctions must be recognized. The waitresses in a family-type restaurant do not want to carry the "burger and fries" or the "drive-in" appearance. The outfits each type wears complement the atmosphere and decor.

Uniforms are highly styled by fashionable designers. The intent is to bring out the concept of efficiency, attractiveness, quality and professionalism. Most standard uniforms come in mix-and-match combinations to allow the employee some flexibility.

Most organizations absorb the cost of the clothes, others split the cost down the middle with employees. Upkeep is usually the employee's responsibility but maintenance, such as cleaning on a scheduled basis, may be done by the company to assure that the uniforms are always presentable.

The biggest complaint is loss of individuality. Harmonizing styles and colors are sometimes offered so that employees are not dressed identically. Accessories lend a personal touch. There are companies that have a once-a-month "dress up day" when the rule for wearing the standard uniform is waived.

Some employees may resist or react negatively. For example, they may have to lug extra clothing along on days they go out after work. As a rule, however, the response is favorable from both employees and customers. For the company it sets a new fashion in fringe benefits.

DRESS AND CONDUCT CODES

The MidAmerica Commodity Exchange, Chicago, Illinois, has attracted national attention with its dress and conduct codes (Regulation No. 917(2.0)010378).

By way of introduction, this exchange is a federally-licensed commodity exchange under the jurisdiction of the Commodity Futures Trading Commission. It was founded in 1868, and in 1880 incorporated as the Chicago Open Board of Trade. The name was changed to MidAmerica Commodity Exchange in 1973. Present membership is over 1,200. Commodities traded are live hogs; wheat, corn, soybeans and oats; silver bullion; U.S. silver coins and gold bullion.

Dress and conduct codes in the Exchange Hall. All persons present in the Exchange Hall will appear and conduct themselves therein in a manner befitting the serious nature of the marketplace and the dignity of the Exchange and its good name. Without limiting the generality of the foregoing, the following dress and conduct codes apply to all members, employees of members, guests of members and employees of the Exchange.

A. The Doorkeeper shall have the authority to deny access to the Exchange Hall to any persons not in compliance with the following dress codes:

1. All persons are required to wear a trading jacket, suit jacket, blazer or sport coat.
2. All males are required to wear either a turtle neck sweater or a collared shirt with properly knotted tie. String ties are not an acceptable substitute.
3. All persons are required to wear appropriate socks or stockings and conventional business footwear. Athletic shoes (e.g., gym shoes, sneakers) are prohibited.
4. All persons are required to wear an identification badge as provided by the Exchange.
5. Blue jeans, denim pants, tee-shirts, tie-dyes, clothes which are torn or wrinkled, or clothing which is revealing or detracts from a business atmosphere (shorts, halters or midriff blouses) are prohibited.
6. All males are prohibited from wearing hats, head scarfs, bandanas and other headcover which is not a part of a religious habit.

B. The following conduct is considered to be disruptive to the orderly transaction of business in the Exchange Hall and is, therefore, prohibited:

1. Smoking in the Exchange Hall.
2. Eating and drinking in the Exchange Hall.

3. Leaving or throwing refuse on Exchange furniture or floor.
4. Using profanity, vulgarity or speech which intimidates others.
5. Any conduct or appearance which is demeaning to the Exchange or which endangers the personal safety of others on the floor.

C. Except by special permission of the Chairman, Vice-Chairman, President, Secretary or Treasurer, the following equipment will not be permitted to be brought into the Exchange Hall by any person: cameras; typewriters; radios; televisions; communication equipment (except that which is subject to formal agreement between a member or member firm and the Exchange) or any other equipment that, in the judgment of authorized Exchange personnel, appears to be inappropriate in the Exchange Hall.

The aforementioned dress and conduct codes are effective during regular trading hours. Any member of the Floor Conduct Committee or any of its duly authorized designees, upon such evidence as may be deemed sufficient, are empowered to levy a summary fine of $25.00 for any violation of this regulation, the payment and collection of which shall be pursuant to Rule 316.

CLEAN-UP TIME

Employees are expected to perform their assigned tasks from the official starting time until the official closing time. In factories and plants this means working from the starting bell until the signal ending the shift.

There are, however, some jobs on which it is the policy to allow a reasonable amount of time for the employee to clean up, and for cleaning machines, work benches, etc., or for returning tools and equipment to the tool cribs.

The supervisor is usually more familiar than anyone else with the requirements of each job for which clean-up time may be necessary, and he is relied upon to apply the policy in a fair and equitable manner in his area of operation.

TOOLS and EQUIPMENT

Employees working in certain jobs are required to maintain an adequate supply of personal hand tools necessary for their own use in performing their assigned work. In the interest of safety and good workmanship, these tools should be kept in good condition. They should also be kept locked in the employee's personal tool box when not in use.

1009

Tools and equipment furnished by the company and dispensed from various tool cribs are not to be considered personal. Nor should tools of this nature be brought from home lest they be confused with company issues. These tools should not be abused and must be returned in good order after they have been loaned out. Any tool found to be damaged, defective or worn out, should be returned to the crib and the attendant told about it. No employee should attempt to alter, repair or correct any company-issued tool. A tool that is no longer needed should be returned promptly so it will be available for someone else.

An employee will be charged at cost for any company tool assigned out to him which is not returned.

COMPANY AND PERSONAL PROPERTY

The following policy on company property is taken from the employee handbook, *The Dofasco Way,* of Dominion Foundries and Steel, Limited, of Hamilton, Ontario, Canada.

You are expected to safeguard Company property which is used or controlled by you, as well as the property of other employees, against improper usage, loss or damage.

The gate guards will not permit you to remove Company property from the premises or to take articles into the plant unless you have obtained written authorization. If you have parcels with you when you come to work, they should be left at the gate office until you leave. Of course, these rules do not apply to your wearing apparel, lunch box or to your safety hat.

If you are allowed to bring your vehicle into the plant, you should declare any tools, tool boxes, electrical equipment, etc. you may be carrying in your vehicle as well as any personal appliances, etc. being brought in for repairs. The guard will complete a form when such items are brought in and declared so you will not have any trouble if your vehicle is stopped for a spot check when leaving the plant.

The gate guards have been instructed to examine any packages being carried into or out of the plant. You can avoid embarrassment by voluntarily showing the contents of a package to the guard.

WORK CLOTHES

Certain jobs require, or make good use of, special work clothes. These can be uniforms to identify the profession, or protective clothing to safeguard the worker.

The first illustration that comes to mind is the professional athlete.

His attire is described as functional. Imagine a lifeguard working in street clothes!

Hospital personnel, except those in the business office, have uniforms which are suitable for the performance of their work and which readily identify their jobs. Besides surgical and floor nurses, there are nurses aids, dietitians, technicians, housekeepers, service people and candy-stripers, all wearing distinctive clothing.

A nurse in a company clinic will wear a uniform, but a nurse doing clerical work in a claims department will don regular clothing. Cafeteria employees will put on laundry-supplied uniforms or large white aprons, possibly chef's hats. Waitresses have a variety of styles and colors to choose from. Mailroom girls and file clerks may wear smocks over, or instead of, regular dresses.

In the factory or plant there are many jobs that require special clothing. Specialists, such as electricians, plumbers, painters and carpenters are easily recognizable because of their outfits. Maintenance men and engineers usually change to coveralls.

Plant guards wear uniforms resembling the garb of policemen. Doormen are equipped with special uniforms, often gaudy, depending upon the nature of the business. Chauffeurs can be spotted in their black caps and dark suits. Railroad conductors have their own uniforms and we've all become accustomed to airline flight attendants in their specially designed outfits.

There are a host of jobs that require protective clothing or equipment, all the way from bullet-proof vests to lead shields in x-ray rooms. Examples are the welder with goggles and the acid worker with gloves. Safety shoes are needed for many types of work.

In many cases, but not in all, these uniforms or special clothes are furnished free by the company. In other instances, such as safety shoes, the necessary protective equipment may be purchased conveniently, and for a nominal charge, through the company. Many firms feel that if the special work clothes are required on the job they should be provided as are desks, machines, and company cars.

A typical company policy on

LOCKERS

Policy: Lockers are provided for employees who are required to wear uniforms during their work period.

Procedure:

1. Locks and key for employee lockers will be issued by Personnel.
2. A deposit charge is required at the time the lock or key is

Some jobs require the use of protective clothing and equipment, as illustrated by this poster, courtesy of National Safety Council.

issued and the deposit will be refunded at the time of termination if the lock and/or key is returned in acceptable condition.

3. A charge will be made for replacement of locks or keys lost by employees.

PERSONAL CONDUCT

A company tries to make as few rules as possible but there are certain ones that cannot be avoided. An employee guilty of any of the following acts (this is a typical list) could be subject to discipline, up to and including discharge.

1. Dishonesty.
2. Refusal to comply with instructions from authorized supervisors.
3. Submitting false or misleading information for the purpose of securing employment.
4. The punching or marking of a time card, clock card or time ticket other than his own.
5. Gambling on company property.
6. Consumption, distribution or being under the influence of intoxicants or drugs while on company property.
7. Theft.
8. Attempting to cause bodily injury to another employee on company property.
9. Committing or attempting to commit damage to company property by act or neglect.
10. Possession of dangerous weapons on company property.

Other situations to be dealt with might be:

1. Falsifying reports.
2. Flagrant disregard of safety instructions.
3. Smoking in unauthorized places.
4. Failure to report an accident involving an employee or company property.
5. Refusal to cooperate in an investigation.
6. Falsely claiming sick pay.
7. Sleeping on the job.
8. Padding expense accounts.
9. Refusal to work overtime in emergency.
10. Spreading malicious gossip about the company, its management, its products or any of its personnel.

Some companies take action against employees who engage in unauthorized distribution of literature or handbills of any kind, or in any solicitation of membership, subscriptions, petitions, or signatures, or like matters during work time or on work premises.

SMOKING AT WORK

Smoking in the office and plant became more widespread as permissiveness in general spread. Now that antismokers are waging, and have won, vigorous campaigns to restrict smoking, thought is being given to control the practice and reduce the annoyance.

A recent Dartnell survey showed that 30% of the respondent companies have a policy on smoking at work and many of these programs were implemented in the past five years. In some cases smoking is restricted to designated areas and forbidden where fire and safety hazards exist (laboratories, flammable materials, records storage, etc.).

Where there is no stated policy, clerical and supervisory personnel in offices are still allowed to smoke at their open desks, and executives may smoke in the privacy of their offices. Smoking is permitted in washrooms, locker rooms, lounges and cafeterias.

Smoking is generally *verboten* in jobs where employees meet the public. This means receptionists, information clerks, ticket sellers, tellers, cashiers and interviewers are expected not to smoke on the job. It is also "off limits" in departments with sensitive electronic instrumentation.

It is against the law to smoke in elevators. The "traveling cigarettes" —carried by people smoking as they walk about from one location to another, or in aisles or corridors—is frowned upon in many companies. Pipe smoking or cigar smoking is usually limited to private offices or at least semiprivate areas.

In factories, plants or shops the regulations must, of necessity, be more stringent. Smoking is forbidden in manufacturing areas as a safeguard to people and property. If the fire hazard is great, the insurance carriers will insist on the bans being enforced. Production workers have areas of the plant designated for smoking, with safety ashtrays and other precautions in effect.

Arguments in favor of letting employees smoke on the job include:

1. Improves production.
2. Lessens the time wasted on smoke breaks.
3. Builds better morale.
4. Eases complaints against restrictions.

Arguments against include:

1. Offends customers.
2. Annoys nonsmokers.
3. Creates an unbusinesslike atmosphere.
4. Gives conference room a pool hall air.
5. Increases the fire and safety hazard.

There can be no distinction in the rules for men and women anymore. Smoking has become such a habit with many people that companies accept this practice in the offices and plants.

Nonsmokers do not really get equal rights and generally have no recourse where their privacy is invaded. This is particularly noticeable in group meetings where the smokers show complete disdain for the rights of others who are annoyed or allergic to second-hand smoke.

About the only control most companies exercise is concerned with safety. In other companies the concern is financial liability. But now a new element has entered the picture. Employees have won awards in Worker's Compensation cases where they felt their rights have been violated. Out of it all managements are beginning to realize that nonsmokers are also entitled to courtesy and consideration.

PERSONAL MAIL

Because of the large volume of official or business mail, companies request that employees arrange not to receive personal mail at work. They don't want to be responsible for letters, bills or other mail addressed to individuals in care of the company. Where an employee is not identified with his department or location, it means mailroom clerks must take time to learn where such employee works so his mail can be brought to him. Most mail sent to a company is opened in the mailroom to catch cash, checks and other payments, or to determine where the mail should be routed. Routinely opening personal mail would violate its privacy.

Nor should personal mail be placed in the "out" box handled by the mailroon, and dispatched with company metered mail.

The same rules apply to personal packages delivered by mail, express or parcel service. They should not be sent to an employee at work. This is certainly true of C.O.D. packages. It follows that company time, materials, facilities and delivery services should not be used to send our personal parcels.

As much as possible, personal business should not be mixed in with company business.

ROBOT MAIL DELIVERY

Employment offices that experience difficulty in hiring and holding mailroom employees for the distribution and pickup of in-house mail, might be interested in the "Mailmobile" manufactured, sold, and serviced by Lear Siegler, Inc., Zeeland, Michigan.

The Mailmobile is a self-propelled, automatically-guided office delivery vehicle. Travelling to and from a mailroom or other central facility, it covers a fixed "messenger route" throughout an entire floor.

In making its rounds it automatically stops at designated stations for pick-up and drop-off of mail (both interoffice and outside), packages, copy work, requisitions, computer materials, blueprints, word processing material and miscellaneous office supplies.

At each stop, incoming mail is removed from trays. Outgoing mail is placed into rear drop boxes. Interoffice mail is placed into appropriate trays and travels directly to the recipient, eliminating further sorting.

The unit moves at a safe speed of about one mile an hour, slower than the average person walks. Soft, pressure-sensitive bumpers stop it when obstacles block its path.

Mailmobile is driven by rechargeable batteries and utilizes a patented guidance system that follows an invisible guidepath. This guidepath requires no structural alterations in the facility, and is compatible with all floor surfaces. While it cannot be seen or felt, it can be removed and rerouted. It is literally a harmless fluorescent chemical that is painted on the floor. It can be chemically erased and can be coded at any number of points to actuate timed-interval stops. It is applied and maintained by trained service personnel using equipment developed by the manufacturer.

HOUSEKEEPING*

The physical facilities of the Woodward Governor Company represent to the community, our customers, our vendors and our fellow workers the pride we feel in our corporate partnership association. Clean, attractive and orderly facilities convey to the general public the quality of our people, our organization and our product.

It is the responsibility of the membership, both individually and collectively, to contribute to the maintenance of clean, safe and attractive facilities.

Each member is directly responsible for keeping his own work area neat and orderly at all times and to notify his supervisor of any general

*Taken from the employee handbook of Woodward Governor Company, Rockford, Illinois.

The Mail-mobile, an automatic, self-propelled delivery vehicle for offices.

Mailmobile's invisible guidepath is applied and maintained by trained service personnel using equipment developed by the manufacturer.

1017

area in need of attention. Adequate receptacles have been provided for the safe and efficient disposal of refuse.

Only by a cooperative effort of all the members will we be enabled to maintain the pride of association that has characterized Woodward members in the past.

NAME PLATES

Desk name plates have a practical value in identifying workers at their work stations. There is also the psychological importance of making the identified individual feel he or she is a recognized part of the organization. In addition, there is a matter of being able to exert more competent supervision in an office situation when employees seated at desks are more readily identifiable by name.

BADGES

Individual, custom, pin-back buttons can be produced inexpensively with Badge-A-Minit. Any slogan, emblem, design or photo can be placed on a badge.

The personnel office will find this system ideal for identification, visitor passes and security. This could also be a basic tool for meetings and conventions.

Quality, permanent badges are made with a hand-held die press and color-coded dies. Information may be obtained from Badge-A-Minit, Ltd., Civic Industrial Park, La Salle, Illinois 61301.

IDENTIFICATION

Employee identification badges are issued where security is involved. They are worn to show at a glance that the individual is an employee and allowed on the premises, and by color code permitted access to restricted areas, such as the confidential computer room or the private cafeteria.

Badges are worn on the upper left quarter of the body in plain view of guards when entering the plant and at all times while in the plant. An employee is required to submit his identification for inspection at any time when requested by a member of the security force or by any supervisor.

Badges and identification cards issued to employees must, of course, be surrendered upon termination of employment.

Visitors, salesmen and other outsiders may obtain temporary badges or passes at the security gate of the plant or from the receptionist in the office. A pass signed by the supervisor is also required for the removal of material or machines in connection with company business.

WASHROOMS

Washrooms in office and factory buildings often present a problem. It isn't enough to have them on a regular maintenance schedule, such as night cleanup and occasional daytime inspection. Nor is it feasible to keep an attendant on duty in each washroom full time.

For some reason men and women using public washroom facilities are often not as considerate as they would expect to be at home. Sinks and mirrors are untidy, floor cluttered with thrown paper, drains clogged and other careless or unintentional indiscretions.

What happens when employees complain about the condition of the washrooms they are assigned to use? The clinic nurse says that while sanitation may be within her domain, the inconsiderate sloppiness of employees is not. The janitor says he cannot stand guard to prevent the deliberate plugging of plumbing. The personnel office says its responsibility is to see that adequate facilities are provided but not to police them.

So where does this leave us? Managers and foremen have little control over their people after they leave their work area. Employees should not be asked to spy or report on each other. The matron, when she happens to be present, has no authority to reprimand offenders.

The best solution calls for clean and comfortable restrooms to begin with, in the hopes that most people will cooperate with management that shows concern. Some regular during-the-day service might be provided as a normal part of maintenance. Should the problem grow beyond reasonable limits, signs or notices might call attention to the need for cleanliness and neatness. If the problem gets out of hand, group meetings addressed by a "health or sanitation specialist" rather than authoritative management, would not be improper. In such a gathering the educational approach should be stressed.

HOLIDAY DECORATIONS AND CHRISTMAS TREES

What should be done at Christmastime about holiday decorations and trees? This poses an annual problem in many offices and factories.

In stores, banks, restaurants and similar places of business which serve the public directly, this is no problem. It just seems appropriate to establish a festive atmosphere and charge off the expense as a cost of normal operations.

But what about those areas in offices and plants which are occupied only by employees? From a strictly business standpoint, something as personal as a Christmas mood may not belong. Yet, employees do not leave their personal beliefs and Christmas excitement at home; much of the spirit of the holidays pervades their place of work. Many employees, in fact, get carried away in their efforts to share their Christmas joy with fellow workers.

How many trees should a place allow? Should every department have its own? Should these trees be supplied by the company or does this make Christmas impersonal and hence detract from the enthusiasm?

What about decorations? Aside from regular restrictions about what may be attached to painted walls or suspended from celing fixtures, how much latitude should employees be permitted as they attempt to "deck the halls" to spread cheer?

What's more, should this be done on company time or after hours?

There is no hard-and-fast rule, of course. Much depends upon the size of the company, its many separate locations, the nature of the business, the company attitude and many other factors. Some firms encourage the practice of letting employees enjoy some measure of the holiday spirit at work; others take a firm position against this, arguing that it causes too much interference with work.

In any case, it might be wise to establish certain ground rules. Trees may be permitted for every specified number of workers. They should not be so tall that they cannot be trimmed by employees while standing on the floor. Decorations should not be so elaborate as to appear gaudy. While Christmas is a Christian holy day, it is observed by many as a national holiday and therefore the motif of the decorations might have to be somewhat restrained so as not to appear "preachy" to some people. As a general rule, liquor in the office on Christmas Eve is *verboten.*

Much can be gained in the way of employee morale if the spirit of Christmas is allowed to permeate the work climate. But if no common sense restrictions or cautions are exercised, departmental competition for attention could run rampant and hurt feelings might result. This whole subject need not be a delicate one so long as it does not get out of hand.

PRIVATE OFFICES vs. GENERAL OFFICES

No one has ever explained why generals sit in private offices and privates sit in the general office.

Officers in the industrial army also set themselves apart from rank-and-file workers by sitting in separate enclosures. There is no pattern, of course. In some business firms, such as advertising agencies, there are many private work areas to accommodate the amount of creative effort. In banks, most all the officers sit out in the open to facilitate easy direct dealings with customers.

Private offices are decided on rank in some firms and on functions in others. Executives, department heads, managers, as well as professional, research and personnel people usually have private offices. The four factors to consider are: (1) prestige, (2) function, (3) concentration, and (4) confidential work. Alternatives to private offices are enclosed or semi-enclosed work areas made of movable partitions.

Should there be uniformity in private offices or should there be variations? The trend is toward flexibility. Companies try to standardize private offices in such matters as size and location, and allow them to be personalized in the choice of pictures, lamps and colors. A private office should express the executive's personality.

It is accepted that a private office adds weight, influence and respect to jobs in the eyes of employees and visitors.

RELIGION AT WORK

Religion is becoming more common in the workplace. The idea of spirituality entering into corporate affairs is gaining in popularity. Divine guidance has caught on.

Religion colors many facets of the business day, with important decisions preceded by prayer and with God regarded, not at all facetiously, as a sort of senior partner. Participants pray for guidance, not profits.

The prevailing philosophy is a fundamentalist Christianity. Religious beliefs are fostered either through providing facilities such as private chapels for prayer and meditation or through a series of religious rites and theological discussions.

Companies are sponsoring early morning devotionals, midmorning inspirational breaks with coffee, Bible study sessions on company time, lunch hour services, three-day retreats with spouses—all on a voluntary basis.

An excellent example is the National Prayer Breakfast, an annual Washington gathering of politicians, including the President, businessmen and others.

Practitioners regard this trend as the practical application of the Golden Rule.

QUIET HOUR

There is an old proverb that reads, "As the first hour of the day goes, so goes the day."

The Michigan Millers Mutual Insurance Company of Lansing, Michigan, has introduced the "Quiet Hour" to promote good work habits.

All employees, including department managers and top management, were asked to adopt this resolution:

THE FIRST HOUR OF EACH DAY (8 to 9 A.M.) IS THE "QUIET HOUR." DURING THIS PERIOD WE REQUEST THAT NONESSENTIAL CONVERSATIONS BE AVOIDED.

They were instructed to please:

- Hold outgoing calls and the gathering of materials necessary to complete these calls until after 9 A.M.

- Avoid contacting other departments on routine matters until after 9 A.M.

Exceptions to the rules are, of course, recognized. These are:

1. When it is necessary for new employees under training to talk with their supervisors, this should be done as quietly as possible.
2. Field personnel, who need assistance before leaving on assignments, may obtain this help.
3. Incoming business calls may, of course, be taken.
4. Matters pertaining to other departments of an urgent nature are excepted from the "quiet hour" rule.

When discussion is necessary during the "quiet hour," employees are asked to be considerate of others.

"The 'quiet hour' continues to be an important part of our program," says Duane Bower, personnel director. "I'm certain all of our employees look forward to the opportunity to handle important matters, relatively free of interruptions, during this period."

NOISE

Factories and offices are getting noisier, jeopardizing the hearing of millions of employees who work in them.

This point is made in a training manual, *Industrial Noise—A Guide to Its Evaluation and Control.* The text is published by the United States Public Health Service, the national center for urban and industrial health in Cincinnati.

"An estimated seven to eight million workers may be exposed to noise conditions hazardous to hearing in our increasingly technological society," it says. The manual lists two kinds of hearing loss among workers: temporary loss, caused by initial brief exposure to intense industrial-type noise, or permanent loss, caused by prolonged exposure to the same noise.

Noise abuses affect more people than any form of environmental pollution. The noise level of a rock band is 115 decibels, for a drop hammer 125 decibels. In the United States the maximum legal limit for noise pressure is 90 decibels for an eight-hour day.

Noise can be defined as an unwanted, painful sound. Sound is a vibration or form of energy which is transmitted through the air as waves that enter the ear and create a sensation, which is called hearing. Like all forms of energy, sound can be measured as to its pressure, intensity, frequency, pitch and duration.

Of these properties, pressure and time duration are the most relevant ones concerning the harmful effects of industrial noise. If sound waves hit the ear drum hard enough and/or often enough they could break it or vibrate it hard enough to cause irreparable damage to other sensitive parts of the ear.

Besides this auditory damage, other adverse effects are interference with speech, loss of efficiency in performance because of the distraction, and the psychological factor of annoyance.

Ear muffs or ear plugs are not the answer because they also shut out the shouted warnings of "Watch Out" in times of danger. The answer is in reducing the noise level as much as possible.

HOLIDAYS

Paid holidays are granted nowadays to all regular employees—plant or hourly as well as salaried or office. The minimum number of such paid holidays is six—New Year's Day, Memorial Day, Independence Day, Labor Day, Thanksgiving and Christmas. Of these six days, Christmas is the superstar because in addition to a day off, it may also mean parties, bonuses and corporate gifts.

When one of these six holidays falls on a nonworking day, such as Saturday or Sunday, the day before or following is often recognized as the day on which the factory and office shall be closed and employees paid. Apparently few firms want to be accused of giving less than six holidays a year.

The most popular holiday after the "basic six" appears to be the Friday after Thanksgiving. This seems like an unlikely choice because it is difficult to commercialize in good taste, and it is impossible to secularize it the way Christmas and Easter have been.

Quite often extra holidays slip into a firm's work calendar. When Christmas falls on a Thursday some firms close on Friday too. Or if Independence Day falls on a Tuesday some firms close on Monday too.

The trend is toward more holidays. The latest Dartnell Holiday Survey reports 61% observe eight to 10 holidays, and 13% have 11 to 13 holidays; in other words, three-fourths of the companies have eight or more holidays. Generally, in eastern and northeastern states more holidays are observed, and in southern states and possibly elsewhere there are local holidays which are observed.

A not uncommon practice is to recognize the regular six standard holidays plus two "floating days," the selection depending upon the calendar each year. Thus a Friday after Thanksgiving may be a holiday one year but not the next.

The author likes adding one personal holiday to the list. This would give each employee "one day in the bank" to use as he chooses—possibly for a special religious observance, extra day of travel, shopping, birthday or whatever is useful to him.

It is easier to close on a "national" holiday than on a "church" holy day. In this context, Christmas is considered a national holiday since Christians and nonChristians alike observe it.

Full-time employees are paid for holidays; part-time workers are not paid as a rule. When an employee works on a holiday he gets time-and-a-half (overtime) or possibly double-time, in addition to regular pay for the holiday.

THE CASE FOR MONDAY HOLIDAYS

The movement to celebrate most holidays on specified days rather than calendar dates has finally been recognized. In altering the dates, the trend moves toward weekend holidays.

For years many companies and some state legislators have been trying to have holidays observed on Mondays. The Monday observances of national holidays—an idea adopted in England and other countries—creates three-day weekends for workers.

The U.S. Chamber of Commerce reported the results of a poll in which 85% of its 10,000 members favored Monday holidays. This, incidentally, was the second biggest positive response the chamber ever received to any survey.

The bill passed by Congress and signed into law by President Johnson in 1968 assured five three-day holiday weekends each year. The measure made Columbus Day a federal holiday and provided for it, Washington's Birthday, Memorial Day, and Veterans Day to be observed on Monday each year. Labor Day already falls on a Monday. Ten years later, however, Veterans Day was rescheduled to its original November 11 date because the public demanded it.

Washington's Birthday is now observed on the third Monday in February, Memorial Day on the last Monday in May, and Columbus Day on the second Monday in October. The bill is limited to observance of holidays by employees of the federal government and the District of Columbia. But most states tend to follow suit, with Memorial Day still running into resistance.

There is nothing sacred about the days on which certain holidays have been celebrated anyway. Many of these days were arbitrarily selected in the first place and there is no rational reason for keeping the same dates.

Washington's Birthday does not truly fall on February 22. He was actually born on February 11, 1732. Twenty years later, the new calendar style was adopted by the American colonies, 11 days were struck off the calendar, and his birth was celebrated on February 22.

Memorial Day has no particular meaning in terms of any specific date.

Independence Day, which we observe on July 4, commemorates an event that was actually realized on July 2—the date on which the resolution of independence was adopted.

Before Thanksgiving was settled on Thursday by President Lincoln in 1862, it had been celebrated on various days of the week.

As for Christmas, it has been celebrated on a half-dozen different dates during the Christian era, since no one knows on what date Jesus was born, but the most educated guess is around August. In our society it falls on December 25 only because we say it does. But there would probably be too much emotional resistance to changing the date.

Proponents of "Threekends," as the three-day holiday weekends have been dubbed, claim these advantages: better work production, greater opportunity for family relaxation, fewer requests for extra days off, and easier planning ahead both for business and for travel.

One of the main objections against three-day holidays is the greater number of highway accidents simply because there are more cars on the road.

VETERANS DAY

When the "Monday holiday" law was passed by Congress in 1968, Veterans Day was set for the fourth Monday in October. This change didn't make sense to most people. Although states and localities accepted changing three other holidays to Mondays to provide more long weekends, 46 of the 50 states resisted the Veterans Day change.

Legislative bodies, all major veterans' organizations, and countless individuals attached historic and patriotic significance to the original date. It began as Armistice Day—commemorating the end of World War I officially on the 11th hour of the 11th day of the 11th month. In 1954 the day of observance was broadened as a time for tribute to veterans of all wars. It was at this time that the name was changed.

So in 1975 Veterans Day was rescheduled by Congressional action for November 11. Because of calendar changes and other problems, the bill's effective date was set for 1978, ten years after the day was switched.

VACATIONS

The policy of granting vacations in business stems from the long-standing practice of giving vacations to school children. But the motivation and reward are changed.

School vacations are a product of a rural economy. The children were excused from classes during the summer months in order to help their parents with the crops. Had ours been an urban society it is questionable whether youngsters would have been given this free time, or at least so much free time, during the hot summer. Whereas farm children had work to do, their city cousins often do not know how to keep occupied. They become bored and in too many cases their idleness leads to trouble.

Workers in business get vacations, not because they are needed elsewhere at certain times, but rather as a change of pace from their regular work routines. For years office employees were given the same vacation privileges as the management people they served, but factory workers, who were paid only for the hours they worked, were not given paid time off for vacation purposes. Since World War II the practice became universal and the same vacation policies are applied to all workers in a company.

A declining number of companies still do as the schools do, close down for a period of time when everyone, or almost everyone, goes on vacation. The reasons, however, are such concerns as plant cleanup, equipment repair, inventories, etc. A typical example is a plant that shuts down during the first two weeks in July every year. Practically all employees go on vacation at that time. Those who remain carry on the necessary office work and such plant work as repainting, cleaning, and repair and replacement of equipment.

Most firms, however, now remain open year round and let their employees spread their vacations over a period of time. Even this vacation period, which originally was synonymous with summertime, say May through September, has been extended in many companies so that employees may take their vacations any time during the calendar year.

Other practices are changing, too. Few companies require that an employee take his entire vacation, say two weeks, at one time. Split vacations are popular, especially since policies have been liberalized and many workers today qualify for three or four weeks. It is not uncommon for employees to take both winter and summer vacations. Jet travel has made this possible; it is no longer necessary for a vacationer to spend a good share of his time traveling to and from his destination.

There are, naturally, many variations. The practice of taking a vacation a day at a time is frowned upon. This defeats the purpose of the vacation which is intended to get a worker away from his work long enough so he will come back refreshed and renewed.

A typical company policy on

VACATIONS

Employees (except temporary) shall be granted vacation with pay depending upon length of continuous employment as of January 1 of each year.

Qualifications:

Employment for 12 months or more but less than 10 years	2 calendar weeks
Employment for 10 years but less than 25 years	3 calendar weeks
Employment for 25 years or more	4 calendar weeks
President and Vice-Presidents	1 month
Others on Management Payroll	3 calendar weeks

New Employees: Employees hired during the first 6 months of the year . . . 1 week vacation after 6 months of employment, provided it can be taken in the same calendar year. Two weeks' vacation in the following calendar year after 12 months of employment.

Other New Employees: Two weeks' vacation in the following calendar year, after 12 months of employment, with option of taking one of these weeks after 6 months of employment.

Carry-Over: Employees shall not be authorized to carry over any unused vacation time from one calendar year to another. Any unused vacation will be forfeited unless such vacation remains unused at the company's request, in which case disposition will be made by the president.

Vacation Pay:

    a. *Wage-and-Hour:* Unless otherwise directed by the employee, and approved by the manager, a payroll check will be issued on the last workday preceding start of vacation, for time worked plus vacation allowance.

    b. *Exempt:* Prior to leaving on vacation an employee will receive any check or checks which normally would have been distributed during the period of his vacation.

Payment in Lieu of Vacation: Since vacations are intended to provide rest and diversion from the regular work routine, payment in lieu of time off will not be granted.

Holidays During Vacation: When a recognized holiday falls during a scheduled vacation period, an additional day off, mutually agreed upon by the employee and the manager will be granted. This additional day may be taken in advance, if it is contiguous to the vacation. It need not be contiguous if taken afterwards.

Scheduling: Vacations shall be taken at a time mutually agreed upon by the employee and the manager. All other factors being equal, schedules will be arranged on the basis of the work load and employee (companywide) seniority.

Vacation time will be taken in units of not less than one full calendar week, and shall begin on the first day of the week. Vacations will not be scheduled to begin on the last Monday of December when it becomes impossible to complete a 5-day vacation period within the same calendar year.

Reporting: Immediately after January 1 of each year Personnel will furnish each division with a list of employees and their seniority dates. A supplementary list will be submitted on July 1, covering employees hired after January 1.

Vacation schedules will be reported in writing to payroll not later than May 1 of each year. Earlier vacations, cancellations or other last minute changes will be reported in writing as soon as they are authorized.

Additional Time Off: Because of the heavy vacation schedules during the summer, no extra time for extended vacations may be granted between June 1 and September 15. The approval of the president is required for any exceptions (exceptions most likely to receive approval are for marriage or overseas travel). Extended vacation time at the employee's own expense may be granted during the rest of the year, when in the judgment of the manager, such time off does not cause undue hardship to the department operations and so long as it does not result in any unfairness or inconvenience to other employees.

Terminations: Any employee who has been employed for 12 months or more shall be paid at time of termination for any unused vacation. In such cases, the effective date of termination will still be the last day worked.

Employees on Less-Than-Full-Time or Temporary Jobs:

   a. Employees on regular less-than-full-time jobs shall receive vacation time proportionate to the average number of hours worked.

b. Employees working on temporary jobs, either full time or less-than-full-time, shall not be entitled to any vacation rights.

Exceptions: Any exceptions to this vacation policy, or to any of its provisions, shall be reported in writing to Personnel and must carry the approval of the president.

VACATIONS—ANNUAL SHUTDOWN

In the early days of manufacturing it was common practice to grant vacations to all factory workers at the same time, usually two weeks in July when the plant was shut down for repairs. While production was halted, the maintenance crew repaired and replaced equipment, cleaned and painted the premises, and made other alterations and improvements.

Fewer and fewer companies are continuing the practice because it is no longer necessary in many cases. Changes in operating procedures and servicing of machines can now be accomplished without any serious interruption in the flow of production.

Advantages could be cited for the standard vacation policy. All vacations were taken at once and for the rest of the year a full staff of workers was on the job. But it also created problems. Nobody had a vacation choice. This was acceptable generations ago when the head of the household was the only worker; the family planned its vacation accordingly. Today there are primary and secondary wage earners in many families and conflicts develop when they cannot schedule vacations together. Also, a new employee, not yet eligible for two weeks' vacation, was required to take time off without pay or have fill-in work created for him. And today, longer service employees get more than two weeks of vacation and have to take the other weeks off anyway.

Systems improvement and automation machinery have contributed to the elimination of a practice once considered necessary. This progress has also removed a sticky employee relations situation.

PAYMENT FOR TIME NOT WORKED

There is more truth than poetry to the saying that when we hire a worker we are actually buying a share of his time. In return for the production he turns out during this time he is paid his wages. This would seem to be a fair exchange were it not for the fact that for some of the time we pay for we get no production.

This is what is listed in a fringe benefit survey as "payment for time not worked."

First we must differentiate between direct and indirect wages. Indirect wages cover: (1) taxes—social security, railroad retirement, worker's compensation, unemployment compensation, state sickness programs, etc., and (2) insurance—hospitalization, medical-surgical, health and accident, disability, life insurance, death benefits, pension and retirement plans. These are among the fringe benefits which add substantially to the cost of labor.

We're thinking here only of direct labor costs. Something like "a fair day's pay for a fair day's work." No extras. Included are the base rate plus any overtime, premium pay, shift differential, earned incentive and production bonus.

But it's not that simple or clear cut. Whereas we assume we pay for time worked, in reality we pay for other time, too.

Take rest periods, for instance. Wherever these are granted no one expects the worker to punch "in" and "out" and not be paid for this time. This cost is sizeable. A company that works a $37\frac{1}{2}$-hour week and grants 15-minute morning and afternoon passes, has $\frac{1}{15}$ of its payroll going for "time not worked" on this one item alone.

Another big item is vacations. Here an employee is paid yet not expected to work. How big is this item? If an average of two weeks' vacation is given per employee, then another $\frac{1}{26}$ of the payroll is for time not worked. This cost increases when vacation allowances are liberalized, as is the trend these days. And it increases further when double wages are paid to employees who "sell back" all or part of their vacation.

The cost of holidays also adds up. The minimum number of national and religious holidays is six, and this number is double or more in certain sections of the country. Holidays are not just days off from work; in our culture it is taken for granted that these are paid holidays.

These are the big items. These are the obvious costs. But these are not the only ones. There are all sorts of other company policies that provide for pay for time not worked.

It is customary for most firms to "not dock" workers who stay home ill for a day or so. The argument is that the employee's living expenses continue so his income should not be interrupted. Quite a few companies have salary continuation programs, on a full or partial basis, for the long-term illness absence.

It is not uncommon for employers to pay for an occasional personal day off. Companies generally pay a worker who is serving on a jury or as a court witness, or while he is voting. Lately more firms are making up any difference in pay for employees on temporary military leave or national guard duty.

There are other items. It is the policy of most firms to pay employees who are absent because of death in the family. Some companies have a marriage leave policy which allows an employee an extra week off with pay. In cases of involuntary terminations or discharges, companies pay two weeks' salary in lieu of notice.

Then there are the special arrangements peculiar to certain companies, types of work or union agreements. These include paid lunch periods, get-ready time, clothes-changing time, wash-up time and sometimes travel time. And there are some payments that are required under guaranteed work week or work year.

Wages and salaries are charged against the cost of production. But a growing percentage of the annual payroll never finds its way into finished goods or services. It ought rightfully be considered as a contribution to social customs that have crept into the industrial fabric of our everyday lives.

DEATH IN THE FAMILY

In the event of *death in the employee's family* . . .

It seems to be customary for companies to give paid funeral leave to employees in case of death in the immediate family. Usually they allow up to three days for local funerals and up to five days if the funeral is out of town and requires travel.

Family members include mother, father, brothers, sisters, husband, wife, sons, daughters, and usually any other close relative living in the same household. Some policies include grandparents and in-laws with possible fewer days off.

In the event of *death of an employee* . . .

When an employee dies, the shock waves stir up feelings of sympathy within the company. While conversations and arrangements disrupt to some extent the normal conduct of business, there are a few very practical personnel actions that must, of necessity, intrude upon the traumatic scene.

Whatever has to be done, there are two basic considerations to observe:

1. Proceed into the inner circle of the bereaved with diplomacy and tact. Minimize the bother this involvement calls for, extend comforting condolences, and make a genuine offer of personal and company support and assistance.
2. Act promptly, particularly if money is to be paid, for the survivors will likely be frustrated and frightened about bills and debts and unfamiliar with benefits and payments due them.

As for *life insurance,* the company should request the beneficiary whom the employee had named to present a death certificate as soon as possible, and in a case involving accidental death, a coroner's report. The beneficiary should also be asked to fill out the necessary life insurance forms.

As for *accumulated wages,* the deceased employee's earnings since the last payday are remitted to the surviving spouse, children, or parents.

As for *unused benefits,* any unused vacation (maybe accrued sick days), and all other benefits or monetary rights due, are also paid to the estate.

While co-workers and friends will show up at the wake or attend the funeral, somebody from management should officially represent the company. This individual delivers the specially prepared check for monies the deceased employee had earned and also for insurance payments the beneficiaries have coming. The check should be presented in a sealed envelope with quiet dignity to the appropriate person (the details can be spelled out in a statement enclosed). At a later date the less urgent details and loose ends can be discussed and cleaned up.

Section 101 of the Tax Code permits an employer to pay a "widow's bonus" up to $5,000 of tax-free income to the widow or the beneficiary of a deceased employee. The employer can deduct such payment and there is no tax liability to the widow if the following conditions are met:

1. Payment must be made to the spouse of the deceased employee.
2. Payment can not be made to the employee's estate.
3. Company can have *no obligation* to make the payment.
4. Payment must be out of affection, respect, admiration, or charity.
5. Company can derive *no economic benefit* from the payment.
6. Spouse performed no services for which compensation was anticipated.
7. Services of the deceased employee must have been fully compensated.
8. The gift in no way represents accrued vacation or sick pay.

If the Internal Revenue Service deems the payment is a "bonus agreement" rather than a gift, the amount is taxable as part of the employee's estate.

A typical company policy on

JURY DUTY

The company at all times tries to be a good corporate citizen. It encourages employees to be good private citizens.

Accordingly, the company has adopted a liberal attitude when an employee is called to serve on the jury, or is required to appear as a witness in court.

Any employee summoned to jury duty or subpoened as a witness will, upon presentation of notice, be considered "on-the-job" and will be paid at the regular rate of salary for the period required to serve. In addition, he will be permitted to retain whatever jury pay he receives.

While on jury duty an employee will be expected to return to work during those hours when he is not required to be in court or on call. Exception to this provision can be made when an entire jury is under protection of the court.

Absences for jury or witness duty will be recorded on the time sheets with the letter "J" in black.

VOTING TIME OFF

There is no federal law that requires employers to give their workers time off for voting. But 30 of the 50 states have laws which set the rules. The terms vary. Companies must give time off, under certain conditions, usually upon request. In 20 of the 30 states companies are required to pay for the time but need not count the hours as time worked.

Most companies encourage their employees to take their civic responsibilities seriously. They urge their employees to vote. Many gladly give them time off, either by allowing them to arrive later in the morning or leave earlier in the afternoon, whichever is more convenient to both the worker's personal voting arrangements and the company's work schedules. In cases such as these, companies usually are more than willing to "not dock" the workers for the time away from work. This is not the problem. The problem is that workers are *entitled* to time off in some states and employers should acquaint themselves with the law in their state.

Some firms have been known to open up an hour or two later than usual, particularly on national election days. This not only takes the pressure off workers, who then have more time to fulfill their voting obligations, but it also allows the younger employees, those below the voting age, to stay home a while with their younger brothers and sisters, while their parents vote.

Occasionally a worker asks for the entire day off. He may have volunteered to serve at the polls either as an unpaid watcher or a paid election clerk. Granting this time off is up to the company. The usual practice is to permit the employee to take the day off but not pay him, since he very likely may be paid by the election commission for working at the polls.

LEAVES OF ABSENCE AND FURLOUGHS

Companies try to avoid the "on again, off again" employees—those who do not work steady. But even regular employees sometimes need to take time off for various reasons. Reasons include:

1. Illness or accident
2. Pregnancy
3. Personal or family affairs
4. Military duty
5. Travel

A leave of absence is granted for a short period away from work. In the case of prolonged illness this leave may be extended upon medical advice.

A leave of absence implies that employee benefits are uninterrupted, seniority continues, vacation rights accrue, and his job is saved for him. Wages stop although some form of insurance coverage or welfare policy may provide a type of compensation.

When an employee wants to be away for a longer period of time a furlough may be considered. A furlough is like a termination except it carries with it certain rehire rights. Employee benefits are discontinued, seniority does not accrue during the absence, and the job is not guaranteed to be saved. Wages, of course, stop.

Benefits and seniority are, however, held in abeyance. Upon return to work, to a position of like status and pay (if available), full employee benefits are immediately reinstated where they left off at the time the furlough began, and seniority (like a rewound clock) is accumulated to the previous record.

A typical company policy on

LEAVES, ABSENCES AND FURLOUGHS

Purpose: It is the purpose of this policy to assure employees of certain job rights or considerations pertaining to their employment status in accordance with the conditions and privileges stated herein.

1035

Procedure: Upon the written recommendation of the manager, the division director in charge may grant an employee time off without pay under one of the following arrangements:

1. Personal Leave of Absence

Conditions:

1. Should be requested by employee.
2. Must be for employee's personal convenience, unrelated to the job.
3. Cannot exceed 30 days or one month.
4. Cannot be extended beyond 30 days or one month.
5. When an employee is absent for personal reasons for one week or more, even when the period includes a holiday, a Personal Leave of Absence should be initiated.

Rights:

1. Seniority continues to accrue.
2. Employee benefits are uninterrupted.
3. Employee maintains the right to his particular job.

2. Disability Absence

Conditions:

1. Should be requested by employee or initiated by the manager on behalf of the employee who is absent because of illness or accident. (Separate policy for Worker's Compensation cases.)
2. Must be supported by written advice of the employee's physician to our Clinic.
3. Must have concurrence of the Clinic.
4. Begins when sick pay runs out.
5. Cannot exceed 30 days or one month.
6. With the approval of the Chief Executive Officer, extension may be granted for not more than 30 days or one month at any time. In no case should the disability absence plus extensions run more than 6 months.

Rights:

1. Seniority continues to accrue.
2. Employee benefits are uninterrupted.
3. Employee maintains the right to his job (even when it has been filled temporarily by another person).

3. Disability Furlough

Conditions:

1. At the expiration of a disability absence, and/or its extensions, an employee who, in the opinion of our Clinic, is still medically unable to return to work will automatically be placed on a Disability Furlough.
2. The length of the Disability Furlough will be for any known or at least reasonable period of time, subject to periodic verification that the employee is medically unable to return to work as determined by our Clinic.
3. In no case will the Disability Furlough including any Disability Absence immediately prior thereto, extend more than one year from the date Sick Pay expired.
4. At the end of this one year, employee will be terminated subject to reemployment rights as outlined below.

Rights:

1. While absent from work:
   a. Group Life Insurance (both basic and supplementary).
      (1) Waiver of premium (retroactive to date of disability) becomes effective subject to approval of carrier.
      (2) If later return to work, life insurance coverage and payments can be resumed in company group.
   b. Health & Accident insurance claim once established will run its normal course, but employee will be dropped from our group.
   c. Disability insurance, where applicable, will pay regular benefits according to the contract.
   d. Group Hospitalization and Medical-Surgical insurance, single or family coverage may be
      (1) Continued in group with employee making arrangements to pay the total cost while on Disability Furlough.
      (2) When Disability Furlough ends before employee returns to work, employee transferred to Individual Membership, with employee making payments direct to carrier.
2. In the event of return to work:
   a. During period of Disability Furlough.
      (1) Full credit toward seniority for previous service, with seniority date amended to reflect time off.
      (2) Prompt reinstatement of all employee benefits, with the next scheduled vacation allowance prorated.

(3) Every possible consideration for a job of like status and pay provided one is open.

b. After employee has been terminated.

(1) Seniority rights and benefits will be decided at time of reinstatement on payroll and will be based on length of previous service, prior position, etc.

(2) Job and salary to be offered will depend upon qualifications of the returning worker and availability of suitable job opening.

4. Military Leave of Absence

Conditions:

1. Should be requested by employee as a result of his military duty orders.
2. For temporary service in the National Guard or Reserve.
3. For a period not to exceed 15 calendar days.

Rights:

1. Seniority continues to accrue.
2. Employee benefits are uninterrupted.
3. Employee maintains the right to his particular job.

5. Extended Military Service Furlough

Conditions:

1. For any employee who enlists or is recalled to extended military duty.
2. Furlough to coincide with his military orders.

Rights:

1. Upon evidence of his acceptance into military service the employee will receive:
   a. Pay for one extra week, if he has at least one year of continuous service.
   b. Pay for two extra weeks, if he has at least two years of continuous service.
2. Following his military service, he must, under the Selective Service Act of 1948, be reemployed to a position of like status and pay unless the employer's circumstances have so changed as to make it impossible or unreasonable to reemploy him if:
   a. He has an honorable discharge.
   b. He applied within 90 days after discharge (or within 90

days from hospitalization following discharge for a period of not more than one year).

c. He is still qualified to perform the duties of the position he left.

To qualify for full reinstatement the employee will be asked to present his discharge certificate (a photostat copy may be made for Personnel records) and to provide such information about his military record as may be considered advisable to bring his personal history up-to-date.

6. Personal Furlough

Conditions:

1. When it is necessary for an employee to take time off from work for a longer period than provided under Personal Leave of Absence.
2. Or for a reason not covered in any of the preceding arrangements.
3. May be used by the manager in preference to an outright release in the case of an employee who leaves (except to try another job) for whom we want to keep the "return to the company" door open.
4. Cannot be extended and in no case can it be granted for more than 12 months.

Rights:

1. Full credit toward seniority for previous service, with seniority date amended to reflect time off.
2. Prompt reinstatement of all employee benefits, with the next scheduled vacation allowance prorated.
3. Consideration for a job of like status and pay provided one is open.

Furloughs: An employee on Furlough will be considered as having terminated, as far as records and payroll listing are concerned. Benefits will also end except that an employee on a Disability Furlough may continue in the Group Hospitalization and Medical-Surgical insurance portion of the benefit program as described earlier. Like any other termination he will be paid for unused vacation, reported as a termination to the Employee Gift Fund Committee, replaced on the job (unless the job is abolished), etc. Upon return to work he will be subject to "Rights" as explained above.

Benefits Continuation: An employee on a Personal Leave of Absence or a Disability Absence has the right as explained earlier to continue under the company's benefit program. If he is paying part of the cost as in the case of Group Hospitalization and Medical-Surgical insurance family coverage and/or contributory Life Insurance, he can cooperate to continue these additional benefits. He may authorize a deduction from his final paycheck to cover his share of the cost of the benefits during his leave period or he may make arrangements for payment monthly, in advance, by sending his check to Personnel. If payments should lapse, his benefits will revert to employee only protection.

Reports: Notification of Leave of Absence or Furlough must be reported individually to Personnel and should be sent whenever possible prior to the effective date. When a furloughed employee is rehired an "add notice" will be completed to reinstate him on Payroll.

MATERNITY AND CHILD CARE LEAVES

The following is the policy of The Procter & Gamble Company of Cincinnati, Ohio, pertaining to leaves of absence granted for maternity and child care reasons.

Maternity

Maternity leaves shall be offered in all cases of normal pregnancy.

Maternity leaves will normally begin four weeks before the expected date of birth, as verified by the employee's physician, in the case of nonphysically strenuous jobs such as office or secretarial work. Guidelines will be issued by the company's medical staff to determine the normal duration of leave from more physically strenuous jobs. Any lengthening or shortening of these normal periods by the company will be based on the opinion of the employee's physician and the company's medical staff regarding the employee's medical fitness to perform her normal duties or other available work. If the employee for personal reasons requests that a leave be granted prior to the start of maternity leave, the company will give consideration to granting her request.

Maternity leave will normally end six weeks after delivery. Any extension of the leave by the company following normal delivery will be based on the opinion of the employee's physician and the company's medical staff that the employee is not yet able to perform her duties or other available work. If the employee for personal reasons requests that a child care leave be granted following the maternity leave, the company will give every consideration to granting her request. However, the child care leave may extend no longer than the first work day six months after the date of delivery.

During any one pregnancy involving personal, maternity and/or child care leaves for an employee, the leaves shall be considered as one for purposes of approval and contributions to company plans. Once approved, a maternity leave may be extended by the Plant Manager or Division Head if delivery is delayed.

Child Care

A child care leave may be granted at company discretion to *either parent* but only to permit one of the parents to be with the child until age six months. The parents will decide which of the two will be with the child.

The leave, which extends the usual maternity leave period and grants the privilege to fathers for the first time, was instituted because local infant care facilities are scarce.

ADOPTION BENEFITS

Adoption benefits are the latest fringe benefit. Companies equate the new benefits, which help defray costs of adopting children, with pregnancy expenses for other employees.

Adoption assistance, intended to parallel existing maternity benefits, reimburses employees of International Business Machines Corporation up to 80% of adoption costs, up to $800 per child. Eligible expenses include adoption agency and legal fees, temporary foster care, and benefits for the natural mother.

PATERNITY LEAVES

The trend toward equality of wages and benefits for women and men means a move toward paternity leaves.

The U.S. Labor Department (no pun intended) was the first federal agency to grant paternity leaves. Male employees, under a new collective bargaining agreement, are allowed up to 30 days' leave when their child is born. The time off—which cannot begin more than 30 days before the expected delivery date, nor be extended more than 30 days afterwards—can be charged to annual leave or taken without pay.

One of the more innovative features of the new Bell maternity plan permits a father to take up to six month's unpaid leave to care for a newborn child and still get his old job back.

The leave, which extends the usual maternity leave period and grants the privilege to fathers for the first time, was instituted because local infant care facilities are scarce.

If an infant is adopted, a leave for this purpose will be treated as a child care leave. Adoption of an older child will be treated as any other leave for personal reasons.

MILITARY LEAVE

A military leave of absence is generally granted to an employee who enlists in the Armed Forces or to a member of the National Guard when called for active duty, summer training and emergency duty.

A typical policy to cover this situation could be something like the following:

When you enlist for active duty, you will be terminated but you have reemployment rights as long as you:

1. were employed in a nontemporary position prior to your entry,
2. left your job to enter military service,
3. receive a certificate of satisfactory completion of military service, and
4. apply for reemployment within 90 days of your discharge from military service or from hospitalization continuing after discharge for a period of not more than one year.

When you go on active duty as a Reservist or National Guardsman, you will have reemployment rights as long as you:

1. were an employee in a nontemporary position prior to induction,
2. left your job to enter military service,
3. satisfactorily completed your training duty, and
4. apply for reinstatement within 31 days after your release from training duty.

When you return to work, you will be placed in the nearest comparable job (that you are able to perform) to your former job with like seniority, status and pay. Your seniority will be reinstated (including time spent in military service), and benefits will be restored. Any benefits maturing during leave will be offered to you upon rehire.

As for summer training, you will be granted military reserve training leave for a maximum period of 10 working days if you are a full-time or regular part-time employee who has been employed at the company for one year or more. The company will *pay the difference* between your military pay and base salary, without overtime, that you normally would have received during this time period. If you have been employed for less than one year, you will be granted a maximum of 10 working days leave without pay.

If you are a full-time or regular part-time employee and you are a Reservist called to active duty in regard to civil disturbances, you will be granted leave with pay, regardless of length of employment. You will receive the difference between your military pay and your base salary.

CHAPTER XIII

PERSONNEL STATESMANSHIP

PERSONNEL SHOULD NOT BE A DEPARTMENT

I N MANY organizations the central headquarters for the employee
program is referred to as the personnel department. This is done
whether or not the chief personnel executive is considered to be the
equivalent of a department manager in authority, responsibility and
influence.

This unintentional classification is unfortunate from two viewpoints.
First, the personnel officer conducts himself much the same as a department head, even while his opportunity is greater. Second, others in
management look upon the personnel activity as a service function
about on a par with other departments.

Use of the word "department" unwittingly introduces the unnecessary concept of levels, which adds nothing to the status of the activity,
or to the acceptance of an idea, or to the administration of the program.
It can only confound the issue since in this case "level" has nothing
whatever to do with effectiveness. Each separate aspect of the employee
program should stand on its own merits and not be accepted or rejected
on the basis of any superficial consideration such as the prestige or
position of the individual who is proposing it.

Higher ups who have a natural tendency to look down upon their
own subordinate departments cannot be blamed if they then look down
upon personnel, if it is tagged as another of many departments. Conversely, assistants who look up to department managers for leadership
and direction may be predisposed to accept carte blanche any guidance
and suggestions which the personnel director proffers.

What Not Who

In any situation involving the establishment or application of policy,
the introduction of a new procedure, the evaluation of an applicant's
qualifications, the interpretation of placement tests, the granting or
rejection of a wage increase or promotion, or any other aspect of

personnel administration, any discussion between parties should be objective or neutral, not affected by personalities or organization rank. When an idea is good, it doesn't become better because a vice-president, instead of an assistant manager, proposes or supports it.

Personnel decisions should not be made on the basis of majority vote but only on what is right or wrong in the particular circumstance under consideration. An employee program, to be effective, must reflect the attitudes of the work force, not the peculiar whims of unprofessional personnel advisers no matter how well-intentioned they are or how high they rank in the organization.

A personnel executive who is content to be a department manager will soon find himself administering other people's ideas, many of them untried. Then when the stew, because of too many cooks, is unpalatable who will be blamed? He will. And he should be—for letting it happen. Too many corporate officers want to be relieved of the dirty work while still maintaining control.

No one, when promoted to an executive or management position, acquires overnight the skill and insight that the trained personnel executive has acquired over the years and which he is continually testing and challenging. Topside should lend support and authority to personnel programs considered to be sound, practical and in the company's interest, but should be careful not to use its authority to dictate in a field which is potent and volatile and not responsive to the logic of managerial rationale.

The personnel officer should also be careful not to degrade or upgrade himself and his program in relation to other facets of management. What does it matter whether he is, or thinks he is, more or less important than the purchasing agent, or the comptroller, or the production superintendent? His value lies not in prestige nor in the place he occupies on the company organization chart. Just as he should not be expected to let others dictate his program, simply because they outrank him, so also should he not be permitted to impose his ideas and his program upon others.

Authority Not Needed

Ideally, the personnel administrator should have no authority. If he needs position or rank to put his program across, then there is something wrong with it. A comprehensive personnel program, well designed and properly communicated to all concerned, will be accepted by employees, by managers, and by the company for the reason that it works.

The easiest way to foul up an otherwise good program is for the personnel officer and the line executives he serves to get all tangled up in needless controversy about rank. Instead of lining up against each other they would be better advised to line up alongside each other to face their common problem and try to arrive at a mutually beneficial solution.

I will never forget a discussion I had some years ago with a vice-president of the company for which I was personnel director. I had been there one year when he called me in.

"Something bothers me," he began, "and I would like to get it off my mind. We had a personnel program before you joined us, and I'll be the first to admit we now have a better one.

"But as you build your program, and expand your influence, all with our approval and blessing, I have to wonder where you get your additional authority.

"As I picture it, there is only 100% in the management pie. I have my share, and for purposes of this discussion it doesn't matter whether it is larger or smaller than that of the other fellow. What does matter is that I worked hard for my share and I don't relish the idea of relinquishing even a small part of it to anyone, including you, regardless how effective you are."

So he concluded with the question, "Where do you fit in?"

I explained, by way of oversimplification, that his was a line function and mine was staff. The management pie, as he described it, was the operations end of the business. In effect, I was not part of that pie at all. The responsibility for running the company belonged to him and the other line operators. My sole purpose for being there was simply to make their jobs easier.

"Think of yourself, and the other line executives, as the operating pie," I suggested. "Then think of me as the whipped cream over the entire pie, not as part of the pie itself. The pie, with its several unevenly cut slices, was probably good to begin with. If I am successful, as you admitted earlier, then the entire pie should be better because of the addition of my effectiveness."

This explanation seemed to satisfy him. There never again was any conflict between us. We understood our respective roles in the company and he knew my program was intended to complement his activity, not compete with him.

PERSONNEL ADMINISTRATION IS A WAY OF LIFE

Personnel management is many things to many people. The confusion results from misunderstanding.

If top management is confused, this is to be expected. No two personnel practitioners, it seems, can agree on the scope of their responsibilities or the challenge of their opportunities. They might have identical titles, but that's where the similarity ends. Their programs vary all over the map from centralized employment to service functions to management development to organization planning.

The reason is that most personnel managers have jobs, albeit good jobs. The truly dedicated personnel executive does not have a job; he has a vocation. Expressed another way, only one man in a thousand plays the drum; the others beat it.

Thousands of personnel administrators strive for lifetime careers in this relatively new but rapidly growing facet of management. Depending upon external influences over which they have little control, such as the economic climate and the stability of company operations, many of these personnel executives enjoy a fair measure of personal prosperity. How many, however, are making any notable contribution to better management?

Personnel managers could bring service to their companies, benefit to the employees who depend upon them, and credit to themselves, if they could just be made to realize that personnel administration is much more than day-to-day performance of necessary administrative duties.

Personnel administration is a science that can be learned, an art that can be acquired, and a profession wherein stature can be attained.

Science is knowing what and how to do; it is accumulated knowledge systemized and formulated. Art is the way the job is done: the application of natural talents. Profession is the manner of performance: conforming to ethical and moral standards of conduct.

Know-Why is More Important Than Know-How

Many personnel practitioners have the know-how, but not the know-why—they are scientists but not artists. Some possess a superficial knowledge of many procedures without the depth of understanding. Others work hard at the methods, and become quite adept too. They are the recognized technicians, the master mechanics, learned in all the "tools of the trade" but not the purpose behind them.

All of these people miss the whole point of their opportunity: Where they leave off is where personnel administration first begins!

Personnel administration is an area of management that is changing faster than most others. It is no longer safe to learn the techniques, either from books or experience, and then expect to go out and practice them. Personnel administration cannot be run by the book. Neither is it a trade that can be performed with cold efficiency the way a mechanic uses his hands as he follows a blueprint. Nor can it be governed by the head, with emotion or sentiment or tradition dictating the actions.

To be effective, personnel administration must be personal, not in its procedures necessarily, but in its effect or meaning to the individual whom it is intended to benefit. It should deal in human values. What the soul is to the body is what human relations is to personnel administration. Employee programs that are made up of techniques but not understanding have a shell for a body and an ache for a soul.

The field is gradually coming of age. Personnel management is maturing because the growth of companies carries with it a complexity of new duties involving people. And in the total management picture personnel is no longer in the periphery, but closer to the center of activity where the hard decisions are made. In the process the breed of successful personnel practitioners has changed from professional do-gooders to technical specialists, and finally to practical philosophers as the emphasis shifted from making employees happy to making them productive.

Forms and Procedures are Not the Job

Fortunately there are personnel executives who are growing as their reservoir of functions is being deepened as well as widened. They are the leaders who are making progress in their profession and in their companies. No company can give recognition to people it feels unworthy of the award; on the other hand, no company can deny recognition earned by the consistent day-to-day performance of the dedicated personnel executive who works from the heart.

The personnel directors who are making a contribution to the field are those who are developing a philosophy of what the work is all about. The forms, procedures and devices used are not the job; these are merely the paraphernalia of the personnel administrator. In short, personnel management is not something they do, but something they believe in.

To them personnel administration is not a job; it is a calling. It is not a way of making a living. Personnel administration is a Way of Life.

WHAT IS THE PERSONALITY OF YOUR PERSONNEL PROGRAM?

In many companies there is a tendency to discount the significance of personnel management. Where this attitude prevails one or both of two factors may be involved: (1) the company has not yet felt the need for putting all elements of management into proper focus, or (2) the personnel executive has not learned to appreciate fully his responsibility and opportunity.

In either case the impression exists that to be effective in employee relations requires little more than common sense and good intentions. Of course, common sense is necessary if for no other reason than that the employee program be logical and orderly. And good intentions can certainly be helpful in the administration of any program. There is, however, much more to a personnel program—much more.

Take a careful look at some of the personnel programs in your particular locality or industry. What does such a study reveal? It is disheartening to note that many companies still have no clear idea of the nature of personnel work. Often they confuse it with welfare activities and various paternalistic practices.

Many Born of Emergency

Then ask yourself how many personnel programs were established because some farsighted executive recognized the wisdom of treating employees with the same consideration generally accorded customers. Most personnel programs were emergency-created, and their present status is merely the gradual outgrowth of some earlier problem situations. Some are still considered a luxury or expense, not expected to contribute much to the firms' cost-cutting or operating efficiency.

Consequently the field is cluttered with many personnel managers who have not taken the trouble or time to become acquainted with the fundamental challenges inherent in their jobs. These misguided individuals include former supervisors, foremen and others who came up through the ranks, some rewarded with promotions because of loyal performance elsewhere in the organization, others actually "demoted upstairs" in order to get them out of the way.

Is that what is meant by personnel leadership and personnel administration? What about scientific principles? A few actually become adept and turn into master mechanics in the field of personnel. But operating professionally in the techniques of personnel administration is not sufficient if they remain amateurs in the area of humanism.

Especially where scientific procedures have been developed to a high degree, the thought of humanizing the personnel activity is considered secondary if it is considered at all. These people fear that such an approach would vitiate what they believe is essentially an impersonal piece of scientific management.

It would be a mistake not to pay attention to the engineering aspects of the personnel program. But it would be an even bigger mistake to imagine that an engineering plan would be the solution to the employee program. Undue reliance upon scientific methods would create more problems than it would solve.

These scientific programs cannot become straitjackets, precluding all flexibility, initiative and spontaneity; they can not be iron case regulations covering every action, telling exactly what must be done, and how, on every occasion. The best plans are no more than frameworks into which living people must be fitted.

That "Extra Something"

However personnel administration is defined, it is not only techniques and procedures. The significance of employee relations goes much deeper to embody the motives and methods of dealing with and organizing people of all levels at their places of work in order to get them to give and accomplish the best that is in them while at the same time getting the maximum degree of personal satisfaction.

The best way to bridge the wide gap between intent and accomplishment is by developing, in addition to common sense practices and scientific procedures, that extra something that gives substance to the program, namely, the personnel personality. In a sense, every personnel program already has some sort of personality, just as every dog, even a mongrel, has some sort of pedigree. The opportunity facing every personnel administrator is to shape the personality of his program so that it will be a favorable one.

Generally the personality of the employee program is not created—it just happens. Like hash, it accumulates. Usually it mirrors the personality of the chief executive, or the person or persons who influence its operations. It is well, therefore, to analyze some impacts of personality on the employee program. There are a number of characteristics about the leaders that may have a vital influence on the company. They include the basic beliefs of the chief executive and his advisory staff of senior assistants. Their administrative practices, their particular specialty and management experience, their history with the company, and their effect on organizational pressures are all factors to consider.

When Management Overpowers

In these types of situations personnel programs are often a hodge-podge of centralized activity, reflecting the fancies of top management executives who complain about the ineffectiveness of personnel functions yet unwittingly dominate the personnel personality.

Personnel program developers should recognize that their responsibility goes beyond trying to impress officials in whose hands their personal job destiny is centered. To fulfill their obligations they cannot be just the administrators of everybody else's ideas. They would be wiser to develop a program that reflects the character and personality of the work force.

Nor should a personnel personality be built by using some other company's blueprint. Too often a business, in its personnel program, will try to duplicate or adapt the successful features of another company's program. Just as managers yield to some terrible compulsion to conform in dress and appearance, even in their thinking, they likewise like to copy personnel ideas from other firms. This does not build a company personality. When a personnel program adopts a little item from this company, another from a second company, and so on, it is more nearly to develop a program that is characteristic of chop suey.

Difference is Important

Why copy another company's program? In that case, why should people want to work for one employer in preference to another? Stepping out of character to imitate others is forfeiture of individual personality.

In referring to the personalities of individuals or business the attention is not on their similarities, but rather on the subtle differences that distinguish one from the other. Actually, there is very little difference between one person and another. But that little difference is tremendously important. This also applies to personnel programs. In many respects they are all alike—in their functions and in their responsibilities. So it is not in their similarities that they are distinctive but in their distinguishable differences. These are very significant.

The difference may not be very obvious, but that degree of difference is what determines the personality.

Every personnel program is composed of various elements in varying proportions. What makes one product different from another are not only the elements that go into it but also the proportions of every element used. Take a cake recipe, for example. Different ingredients will result in different kinds of cakes. But even the same ingredients will turn out cakes that are not alike if the amount of the ingredients varies.

With the same 88 notes on the keyboard, why does one person's music sound better or worse than that of another? It is the skill used in arranging the notes, the tempo with which they are played, and especially the touch or feeling that is put into the playing that accounts for the difference. When a musician goes flat on one note he spoils the entire effect.

A personnel program of 88 component parts will likewise not be the same in one company as in another even if the identical 88 components are used. Expressed another way, just putting notes together won't make music; it is more likely to produce noise. Putting separate personnel procedures together will not, of itself, result in an effective program.

The elements that go into creating a personnel personality must all be present in sufficient quantity to assure having a personality at all. But the degree of emphasis placed on each of the component elements will make the difference between one personality and another.

Look for Meaning

The combinations and permutations of these component elements is what makes one personnel personality distinctive from another. What these elements are and what degree of emphasis each element should receive is the decision of the personnel executive as he strives to fashion the type of personnel personality that best suits the needs of the company and its work force.

Conscientious personnel administrators who seek guidance in this matter are reminded that there are basic functions of all personnel programs. The day-to-day personnel activities, and the scientific or systematic methods used to perform them, tend to make all employee programs alike. But personnel executives must be concerned not only with the functions but also with their meaning. The extent to which these functions are humanized determines the meaningful difference between programs.

A good personnel executive knows at all times how closely the program matches the personality of the work force. He studies not only the efficiency but also the behavior and cultural pattern of people available for employment. He builds his program by building people.

Business, you see, does not exist merely to produce more goods or better services, though that is no small part of its task. Business also, especially in today's enlightened era, affords the principal means whereby individuals may gain the satisfaction of accomplishing something more than merely sustaining their own lives.

A personnel program built around procedures, even though each separate instrument is a technical masterpiece, is lifeless. A program built around people is warmly effective because it has a personality. The administrator of a coldly efficient program is an ordinary personnel manager. The administrator of a personality plus program is an extraordinary personnel executive.

The question then becomes: Is your personnel program thing oriented or people oriented? The answer can be found in another question: What is the personality of your personnel program?

WHAT IS THE PHILOSOPHY OF YOUR PERSONNEL PROGRAM?

Before we can begin any kind of employee program, we should have a philosophy of what we are trying to accomplish. What is such a philosophy as it applies to the personnel program? Maybe it can be explained with an illustration.

Many young pine trees were planted in their particular forest. A few have already disappeared but most are struggling valiantly. Here is one almost covered over with dead weeds. We must let in the sun to give it a new chance. Here is another that is being choked by large vines. Again we must come to the rescue. Some are lifting their tiny arms into the sunlight free from hindrance. All are trying. This is the glory of creation—all are trying. Mankind's function here is to help bring order and overall progress out of aimless growth and blind competition.

The human garden is in very much the same condition. Most employees either want to grow and don't quite know how, or they are struggling with a handicap, real or imagined, which they themselves don't know how to eliminate or live with. This is where we come in.

Employee development is a living thing, and like any living thing needs constant attention. Workers need more than working space, materials and methods. In order to grow they need the sound cultivation of good work environs, the sunshine of warm-hearted interest, the nourishment of other people's knowledge and experience, the fresh air of inspiring and patient guidance, the good climate of mutual respect, and the deep roots of security and permanence.

Managements must be loyal to the fundamental faith in the very personal quality of the individuals who want to grow with the company. It takes unselfish executive leadership to build others. Yet, unless workers profit, management cannot profit.

As its workers grow, so a company prospers. For the growth of any organization is merely the sum total of the growth of the individuals constituting it.

WHAT IS PERSONNEL EVOLVING INTO?

Life is changing. So is business. But more important than the changes themselves—over which we may have little control—is the way we react to change—over which we have total control.

The world is changing and most of us would not want to go back. International diplomacy is changing. Medical science is always changing, and each breakthrough creates a new excitement. Surely the business community has changed by developing a corporate social conscience.

In the industrial society one of the areas most affected is personnel administration. We're caught up in this fast-moving change, too. The question is: *Are we changing or are we being changed?*

From where I sit I get the impression that we're running hither and yon, grasping at all sorts of straws, bending in all directions—trying to make it appear that our programs are viable instruments and the whole field of personnel is alive and dynamic.

But is this true? With the introduction of the behavioral science approach, the addition of consultant-proposed sophistication, and the proliferation of staff functions, haven't we in personnel management merely put on a full dress suit but retained our dirty shoes?

I go into companies and find a disturbing expansion of personnel activities. Candidates for promotion are no longer tested; they are psychoanalyzed. Programs are no longer developed to fit a need; they are bought lock-stock-and-barrel from the university laboratory. Executives sit in lonely ivory towers and try to communicate with impersonal words written by technicians.

I say "Take off the personnel formal attire and put on an informal shop apron."

In its willingness to change, personnel should not move toward any new, untried and inappropriate mystique, but should return to old principles, oft proved but inadvertently overlooked in our eagerness to appear scientific.

In trying to improve our personnel program, or any part of it, we concentrate our efforts on techniques. Important as these are, we cannot stop there. The effectiveness of employee relations does not rest in the central staff office—where the bright boys are—but in the departments—where the troops are.

We need more field generals and less Pentagon generals.

THE HUMAN ELEMENT IN BUSINESS

Let me philosophize a bit about the human element in business. This is not the type of technical discussion that is intended to put ideas into your notebook. In this kind of presentation we're not trying to move the pen; we are trying to move the spirit.

The really dedicated personnel practitioner, whether this be a staff specialist in the personnel office or a manager or supervisor in the line organization, believes there is a right place in this world for everyone. The difficulty is that we may not always know where to find it. It's just that some folks are easier to help than others; usually these people need our help the least. But all people, including those who pose more of a problem, are entitlted to our interest and fairness in our consideration.

Look at this selfishly if you want to. It's a case of "employ 'em or support 'em." Our job is to place people where they are best suited.

But in that regard we must never for one moment lose sight of the plain fact that there is good in everyone. If we don't believe that then we're debasing the glory of creation. Because people are not biological accidents; they are created. And things and people are created for a purpose.

Emerson described a weed as "a plant whose virtues have not yet been discovered." Not long ago medical science found in the venom of the deadly cobra a possible cure for polio. The center of your football team is just as valuable as the quarterback—even though he does see half of the game upside down and backwards.

Whose Standards are Used?

Yes, there is good in everyone, although we may not always understand it. That's because we insist upon measuring everybody by the same standards—our standards. I heard an award-winning news commentator say that "the only reason some of us are down here while other folks are in the stone institution atop the hill is that for the moment we outnumber them." That's quite a profound statement—worth pondering.

Talents vary, but they are all God-given. Don't we believe that people are created in the image of God? Who is there among us who will suggest that possibly in a few instances the Divine Planner might have made a mistake?

Perhaps it is just that we have not yet learned the proper place for some people—the spot for which they are intended. They don't fit as well into the standard pattern of life which the rest of us have established as socially and industrially acceptable.

For example: There are many jobs that outstandingly mature and well-educated individuals would be appalled by, at which individuals with certain exaggerated personality traits fare better. Some neurotics are submissive persons who are glad to do extra hours of work that others reject; some are extreme perfectionists who turn out accurate and reliable work because anything less makes them uncomfortable. These people have a built-in quality control that others acquire only under heavy discipline. But don't confuse these useful neurotics with the troublesome types.

Every personality has a hidden switch. It is up to us to keep trying until we find it—even if we blow a few fuses occasionally.

So we may conclude that when people are misplaced in our work situation the fault may be more ours than theirs. Those who don't learn as well as others may be learning wrong things.

In World War II, I saw conditions 8,000 miles away where natives, God's creatures, lived and existed in primitive surroundings where no one of us would have remained sane very long. Even under army conditions, which meant that a part of the familiar and comfortable U.S. had been transplanted temporarily to a tropical isle, I watched well-educated men gradually go berserk. One of my former tentmates, who was sent back to the states with a boatload of carefully guarded mental degenerates, was later quite normal and again working as an industrial sociologist.

Proper Placement is the Key

Take him, and some of us perhaps, out of our environment, and we become the misfits. Likewise, take the individual who seems out of place in our office or shop, find a more suitable niche for him in society, and he becomes better adjusted.

There are three kinds of workers in the labor force: the Fits, the Misfits, and the Counterfeits. The Fits are no problem, and these are the one we usually brag about as our success stories. But we have little or no right to boast because they are naturally Grade A material and we can't claim much of the credit. The Misfits obviously need help and there is a conscientious effort in most companies to shift them around and to work with them to fit them better into the organization. But it is the Counterfeits who test our talents, patience and ingenuity as we strive to increase the efficiency of our work force.

Getting all people placed where they do the best for themselves, for their companies, and for society is the obligation that awaits all of us who are privileged to serve humanity.

THE DOW CHEMICAL COMPANY OBJECTIVES

Following are the objectives of The Dow Chemical Company, Midland, Michigan. Says Zoltan Merszei, president and chief executive officer, "The new objectives are not just a restatement of our aims and aspirations. Instead, they are a realization on our part that society has changed over the years. If it is to continue to make its valuable contributions, our company must change along with it."

In explaining why his company has a set of written objectives, he emphasized that their objectives "are more than printed words. They are the measure of everything we do. They put us on record about our values and our attitudes toward business and society. And that's of interest to a lot of people. This is particularly true at a time when there are increasing demands for ever more precise definitions of corporate accountability."

THE DOW CHEMICAL COMPANY OBJECTIVES

To seek maximum long-term profit growth as the primary means to ensure the prosperity of our employees and stockholders, the well-being of our customers, and the improvement of people's lives everywhere

To attract and hire talented, competent people, and pay them well for their performance

To provide our employees with equal opportunity for career growth and personal fulfillment

To give our employees greater opportunity to participate in decision making

To strengthen our commitment to individual freedom and self-renewal

To be scrupulously ethical in the means to our ends and in the ends themselves

To be responsible citizens of the different societies in which we operate

To grow through continuous innovation of our products and processes

To make price a measure of true market value for our products and services

To practice stewardship in the manufacture, marketing, use and disposal of our products

To share in the responsibility of all peoples for protection of the environment

To make wise and efficient use of the earth's energy and natural resources

To make this world a better place for our having been in business

Zoltan Merszei
August, 1977

JOHNSON WAX "THIS WE BELIEVE"

The following is taken from the document titled, "This We Believe," a statement of corporate philosophy of S. C. Johnson & Son, Inc., Racine, Wisconsin.

The world environment in which we work and live is changing more rapidly today than ever before, leading to confusion, uncertainty and lack of confidence. Therefore it is important for us all to restate and reaffirm the principles which have guided us since the founding of the company.

These principles have been summarized before, in the memorable words of H. F. Johnson, Sr., during a Profit Sharing speech given on Christmas Eve, 1927:

"The goodwill of the people is the only enduring thing in any business. It is the sole substance. The rest is shadow."

The sincerity of this belief encourages us to act with integrity at all times, to respect the dignity of each person as an individual human being, to assume moral and social responsibilities early as a matter of conscience, to make an extra effort to use our skills and resources where they are most needed, and to strive for excellence in everything we do.

These principles are translated into practice through a set of basic beliefs, which relate to five groups of people to whom we are responsible, and whose trust we have to earn:

Employees: We believe that the fundamental vitality and strength of our company lies in our people.

Consumers: We believe in earning the enduring goodwill of consumers.

General Public: We believe in being a responsible leader within the free market economy.

Neighbors and Hosts: We believe in contributing to the well-being of the countries and communities where we conduct business.

World Community: We believe in improving international understanding.

These are our principles and beliefs. Our way of safeguarding them is to remain a privately held company. And our way of reinforcing them is to make profits through growth and development, profits which allow us to do more for all the people on whom we depend.

Employees

. . . and we commit ourselves to:

- **Maintain good relations among all employees based on a sense of participation, mutual respect and an understanding of common objectives, by:**

Creating a climate whereby all employees freely air their concerns and express opinions with the assurance that these will be fairly considered.

Attentively responding to employees' suggestions and problems.

Fostering open two-way communications between management and employees.

Providing employees with opportunities to participate in the process of decision-making.

Encouraging employees at all levels and in all disciplines to work as a team.

Respecting the dignity and rights of privacy of every employee.

- **Manage our business in such a way that we can provide security for regular employees and retirees, by:**

  Retaining the permanent employees, if at all possible, as economic conditions fluctuate.

  Pursuing a long-term policy of planned orderly growth.

- **Provide equal opportunities in employment and advancement, by:**

  Hiring and promoting employees without discrimination, using qualifications, performance and experience as the principal criteria.

- **Remunerate employees at levels that fully reward their performance and recognize their contribution to the success of the company, by:**

  Maintaining pay and benefit programs that are fully competitive with those prevailing within our industry and within the marketplace.

  Maintaining, in addition to our fully competitive pay and benefit programs, our long-standing tradition of sharing profits with employees.

- **Protect the health and safety of all employees, by:**

  Providing a clean and safe work environment.

  Providing appropriate occupational health services.

- Develop the skills and abilities of our people, by:

  Providing on-the-job training and professional development programs.

  Helping employees qualify for advancement opportunities in the company through educational and self-development programs in related fields of interest.

- Create environments which are conducive to self-expression and personal well-being, by:

  Fostering and supporting leisure time programs for employees and retirees.

  Developing job enrichment programs.

  Maintaining the long tradition of high quality and good design in our offices and plants.

CORPORATE PARTNERSHIP

The business philosophy of the Woodward Governor Company, 5001 North Second Street, Rockford, Illinois 61101, is unique. It is based upon implied constitutional concepts in our free enterprise system: That each human being has the right to develop a living standard for himself and his family commensurate with the relative value of his capability and output; that the purpose of an industrial organization is to provide a medium through which he may, in cooperation with others, promote his legitimate aims; that he has the right to individual freedom, dignity, justice and opportunity; and that the sanctity of these rights is contingent upon his individual and our (the company's) collective determination to defend them.

Although the company is legally a corporation, internally it operates as if it were a partnership subject, of course, to the legal restrictions applicable to corporations. The system is best described in the *Constitution* of the Woodward Governor Company, from which the following, through the courtesy of Mr. Bruce M. Livingston, president, was excerpted.

Woodward Business Philosophy

The purpose of the Woodward Governor Company is to provide the opportunity, environment and protective legal framework in which its shareholders and workers may cooperatively and harmoniously combine their capital, time, talents, energy, loyalty and will-to-do, in the profitable production of goods and services.

The success of the Woodward Governor Company will depend upon the quality, capability, will-to-do, efficiency, loyalty and teamwork of its membership; the suitability of its facilities and the extent to which they are efficiently utilized; the timeliness, quality and fair value of its products and services; a sincere and cooperative relationship with its customers; and the honesty of its relationship with all those with whom the company deals.

The obligations of the Woodward Governor Company to itself and to its customers shall be to design and build quality products within the prime mover control field, provide expert engineering and product services, establish fair prices for such products and services, and deal honorably and forthrightly. The company shall honor its legitimate obligations to society in general, and specifically to the communities in which it is located.

The obligations of the Woodward Governor Company to its membership shall be, within its capabilities, to: (1) encourage, preserve, improve and protect the moral, mental, physical and financial welfare and legitimate rights of its workers; and (2) preserve, improve and protect the assets and legitimate rights of its shareholders.

The fulfillment of these obligations is best accomplished by a cooperative relationship of the workers and shareholders as "members" of a successful partnership, there being no "employees" in the usual application of the term.

The Woodward philosophy of industrial association, "Corporate Partnership" (CorPar), is a simulated liability, limited partnership between Woodward Governor Company shareholders and Woodward Governor Company workers within the legal framework of the corporate laws of the State of Delaware, U.S.A. The workers' contribution —time, talent, *esprit de corps* and a will-to-do—is relatively mobile and transferable to other endeavors without significant loss of asset value. The shareholders' contribution—land, specialized facilities and working capital—is relatively immobile and is generally transferable to other endeavors, only at a loss in asset value.

In any organized effort by two or more individuals or entities, authority and final decision must be vested in one individual or entity. In CorPar legal authority and final decision are vested in the shareholder entity or its elected representatives. Participation of the worker member group in company control and direction shall be in a consulting and advisory capacity.

The duty and privilege of the worker membership, because of its intimate involvement in operations, shall be to sincerely and continually protect and promote the political, moral and economic welfare of the company.

The duty and privilege of the shareholder membership, through the Board of Directors, shall be to support the political, moral and economic welfare of the company, to provide needed facilities and to sincerely and effectively direct the management.

The duty and privilege of the management personnel shall be to protect and promote with firmness and fairness the welfare and the continuity of the company and the investments of both its shareholder and worker members.

Guiding Concepts

Membership in the Woodward Governor Company shall be open to all who have the necessary qualifications regardless of race, color, religion, sex or national origin. The company is entitled to each member's individual and collective loyalty and sincere concern for its welfare. An individual who cannot honestly and conscientiously accept these premises should not become or remain a member.

Individuals aspiring to regular worker membership in the Woodward Governor Company shall serve a probationary period of two years, during which time the company shall decide whether the probationary member has the necessary ambition, self-discipline and other qualifications to maintain essential harmony and teamwork with the regular members. At the same time, the probationary member shall decide if he can in good conscience accept the responsibilities of membership, and if the future the company has to offer is commensurate with his aspirations. Formal induction into regular membership shall be solemnized in the presence of a company chaplain by an exchange of pledges of loyalty, integrity and devotion to the mutual welfare between the inductee and the regular membership as represented by an official of the company.

It is expected that membership in the Woodward Governor Company will require full and conscientious application of each member's time, talent, energy and will-to-do. Since efficiency is directly affected by physical and mental health, each member is obligated to maintain (insofar as possible) a mental, moral and physical fitness essential to his most efficient contribution to the company endeavor.

Loyalty and continuity of service (seniority) are assets valuable to the company's welfare and shall be recognized appropriately.

The main differential between worker members shall be in base salary established annually from the member evaluation process. Benefits shall be allocated among all members on an equitable basis. All members under similar circumstances shall be treated alike.

All job openings will be filled from within the organization if qualified personnel are available, or if members may be trained to the job requirements within available time. Job rotation shall be utilized as extensively as practicable.

Corporate Partnership (CorPar)

In the United States there are three principal legal business frameworks—sole proprietorship, partnership and corporation. Legally, the Woodward Governor Company is a corporation, incorporated in 1901, under the laws of the State of Illinois, and under the laws of the State of Delaware in 1977. However, to enjoy the simplicity, flexibility, harmony and efficiency of a partnership framework, while retaining the protective features of the corporation, the Board of Directors has conceived a fourth framework known as "Corporate Partnership" (CorPar). The philosophy of Corporate Partnership, a simulated partnership between shareholders and workers, is based on corporate operation externally and partnership operation internally.

Gross company revenues shall be divided into three categories: (1) basic business costs including a fair return on the contributions of the worker members and the investment of the shareholder members, (2) justifiable costs to preserve the work force and income producing facilities, and (3) profit.

CorPar requires that profits shall be determined at the end of each fiscal year and distributed to the shareholder and worker member partners in proportion to the relative value of the contribution of each to the combined endeavor.

In our CorPar concept, each member receives a base compensation plus earned extras. Each worker member's total compensation is a summation of his base compensation, his proportional share of work force preservation, and his portion of sharable profits. Each shareholder member's total compensation is a summation of the base compensation on his investment, his proportional share of facilities preservation, and his portion of sharable profits.

Basic business costs include all costs of materials and services, insurance, taxes, compensation for the workers, and compensation for the shareholders. Base salaries for each worker member shall be determined yearly as a result of the member evaluation process.

Preservation costs are the expenses of providing those services which contribute to the well-being of the worker membership and to the maintenance of adequate facilities and capital. These expenses shall be varied according to economic circumstances. Included in preservation costs are provisions for seniority recognition, personnel maintenance, development and retirement.

Sharable profits are determined by subtracting the basic business and preservation costs from gross revenues. Sharable profits, if any, are to be divided annually between the worker and shareholder members in a ratio determined by the proportional capital values of each to the total. The net worth of the company and the total base salaries of the worker members will be used to determine the relative capital values.

Member Evaluation

The company attempts to evaluate the contribution of each worker member fairly and impartially and base any wage adjustments upon the results of this evaluation.

Evaluation of New Members: The new member's performance on the job is reviewed and his rate considered at periodic intervals during the first two years of his employment. If his work merits an increase, the supervisor recommends a rate change. Rate changes are approved by the next in line of authority over the supervisor at the first and second periods, and by the Member Evaluation Committee at the third and fourth rating periods. These evaluation periods are as follows:

1. Between 60 and 90 days after starting date.
2. Nine months after starting date.
3. Fifteen months after starting date.
4. Twenty-four months after starting date.

First Evaluation: Approximately 60 days after the starting date of a new member, the Personnel Department furnishes the supervisor with a progress report form for the new member. The supervisor reviews the performance of the new member and makes any recommendation for a change of rate. Any rate changes are approved by the next in line of authority over the supervisor.

Second Evaluation (9 months after starting date): The same as first rating.

Third Evaluation (15 months after starting date): Same procedure as in the first and second ratings with respect to progress report. However, after the supervisor has made out the progress report, he places the member on his current department ranking list. This rating is reviewed by the Member Evaluation Committee. The hourly rate is set according to the rates of the adjacent members on the list; usually the same as the next member below, or if there is no member lower in the list, the rate will be equivalent to or less than that of the next member above.

Fourth Evaluation (24 months after starting date): Same procedure is followed as in the third evaluation. In addition, the Evaluation Committee places the member on the master ranking list. This is accomplished by placing the member somewhere on the master list between the names of the two members on the department list above and below the member being ranked. Regular meetings of the Evaluation Committee are held monthly for the purpose of considering the members who have received the third or fourth evaluations.

Rate changes approved at these meetings become effective at the start of the pay period immediately following the evaluation.

Annual Evaluation of Regular Members: After successful completion of the two-year probationary period, every regular member of the organization is included in the annual member evaluation program. This program takes place during the months just prior to October 1st, as any wage changes developing from the evaluation program become effective the first pay period following October 1st (fiscal year). The evaluation program concludes with a list of the entire regular membership of the company in numerical order according to the overall value of the individual to the company. This listing of members, in order of value, is accomplished through a series of coworker evaluations in which each member of the organization participates, and through supervisor and Member Evaluation Committee review. This Member Evaluation Committee is composed of company officials, executives and supervisors with extensive backgrounds.

The worker is also obligated to evaluate his supervisor. The final evaluation of the supervisors is provided by the supervisors themselves and by the Member Evaluation Committee whose job it is to know intimately the qualifications of each. The supervisors rate the executives and vice versa. This rating procedure, including a final review of executive ratings by the head of the company, progresses in a final and confirmed listing of every worker in the company—including company officials.

The final step is dividing the master list into pay blocks. Each worker is allotted a base wage commensurate with the relative value of his contribution to the total team effort and, therefore this determines his position on the list. Changes in his individual position on the list, either up or down, can result only from a change in the relative value of his contribution to the company.

Facilities

People are the most important ingredient in any enterprise. Adequate facilities are necessary, however, to provide the means with which the people can do their work most efficiently and effectively. The company facilities include the home plant at Rockford, Illinois, which houses the Aircraft and Hydraulic Turbine Divisions as well as Corporate Headquarters, and the Engine and Turbine Division, which is located at Fort Collins, Colorado. There are assembly plants in Slough, England; Hoofddorp, The Netherlands; and Tomisato, Japan. There is also an international sales office at Zurich, Switzerland.

The home plant is located on 32 acres of ground about five miles northeast of downtown Rockford. The main building is of buff-colored brick, with a Lannon stone front and Bedford stone trim. The manufacturing areas are on one floor and nonmanufacturing functions are on two floors. The building is windowless. It is completely air-conditioned and all incoming and recirculated air is electrically cleaned of all smoke, dust, pollen, etc.

Year-round temperature is held in the 70-degree range and the relative humidity at approximately 50%. The ceilings of the manufacturing and office areas are made of soundproofing metal squares. The fluorescent lighting fixtures are flush and the dimensions are such that the lighting and soundproofing units are interchangeable. The lighting intensity may be increased to a maximum of 150 foot-candles if desired.

The machine and service connections are all introduced from below the floor. The manufacturing area has ceramic tile walls and a terrazzo floor. The office has painted walls and carpeted floors. A paging system of broadcast quality covers the entire building. In addition to paging and time signals, music and news are broadcast at stated intervals.

The basement area contains many nonmanufacturing service departments: a cafeteria, which is the source of plain but excellent food; a complete medical department, including x-ray rooms; a dental clinic; a library; tiled locker room with air-conditioned lockers; a barber shop; and a rest area containing reading tables and game tables. Above and at the front of the building is an auditorium with a seating capacity of 500.

Also included at the home plant are research and development facilities, an environmental test building, a product test building, storage facilities, a building for storage and maintenance of grounds-care machinery, and a large greenhouse. The greenhouse provides seedlings for the plantings which surround the building. It also provides cut flowers and plants during the winter months throughout all buildings.

Our tools and machinery, with the exception of some special equipment used in research and development and certain specialized production machines, are general purpose machine tools. Due to the extreme accuracy and cleanliness essential in our specialized business, however, our depreciation and obsolescence rate is quite high. The maintenance cost to minimize machine downtime is well above average.

The branch plants consist, at present, of some purchased and some rented properties. These branches are being brought up to a status comparable to the Rockford facilities as each plant's assets expand. In recent years new plants have been constructed in Fort Collins, Colorado; Hoofddorp, The Netherlands; and Tomisato, Japan.

Summary

In conclusion, let us note that the "corporate partnership" plan has operated efficiently and fairly. It provides the flexibility necessary to properly accommodate the fluctuation in production resulting from varying customer requirements. The plan also results in more stable employment. It permits the worker members, for instance, to work long hours in the winter and short hours in the summer without penalizing the stockholder members. It assures maximum quality, the best delivery and the lowest justifiable prices to our customers. Our volume of business, like that of most others, is determined by quality, delivery and finally, by price. Our total net income and our individual incomes are dependent upon our individual and collective performance. The "corporate partnership" plan is the only plan of which we have any knowledge that tends to preclude suspicion and misunderstanding and, at the same time, provides an honest incentive for economy, efficiency and teamwork.

Our formula for determining base incomes and the sharing of additional income has proved quite satisfactory. It has provided a foundation on which the worker members and stockholder members can move up and down the income scale together in harmony and understanding, if not at all times in complete enjoyment. No one likes to have his income reduced but, if it is necessary, there will be far less discord if everyone concerned receives proportional treatment. Such mutual accord encourages liberality on the part of the stockholder in the purchase and maintenance of facilities that will permit the worker to use his aptitudes and energy most effectively. It encourages the worker to strive for the ultimate in efficiency since his income is directly affected. The whole plan pays both partners proportionately a premium for harmony and efficiency and a penalty for discord and indolence.

The worker has sufficient personal power and prestige within the organization to get immediate redress if his personal prerogatives are infringed. He can also get immediate action if he feels that conditions exist or are imminent that will adversely affect the welfare of the company. The full power and prestige of the company are solidly back of him as long as his motivation and conduct are a credit to the organization.

Probably the principal reason our company has had reasonable success and no personnel difficulties in over 100 years of existence is because it is operated *as a means to a satisfactory life* rather than just as a means to money making. Its philosophy takes into consideration that all people have basic economic aspirations; that in a corporate or corporate partnership endeavor both the stockholders and the workers are necessary; that each group has a definite contribution to make; that the relative value of the contribution of each can be determined with reasonable accuracy by people anxious to be fair; that each is entitled to his fair share.

QUO VADIS—WHICH WAY?

by JACK C. STAEHLE
Distinguished Industrial Relations Authority

Two people look down their career roads and choose a course of action. Quo Vadis—which way? It is a free choice. One will go down the one-mile road and end up in a soft chair. One will travel the two-mile road and will find that there is no end, only more challenges. Personnel is a two-mile road and each person who would start down that road must decide whether he will go one or two miles. He and he alone must make that decision.

The measure of the decision will be his depth of proficiency in the technical, legal, operational and yes, the art of the personnel discipline. Although most personnel people are competent in these areas, some must certainly wonder why they are never promoted to middle management or above. They fail to comprehend that to go that second mile additional abilities, techniques and philosophies are needed. They must look further than just the basic "form."

Today, as never before, business, politics and government are needful for those "second milers." The "high and the mighty," whether it be in government or business, have been swept from their positions because they did not know, or they failed to follow, what personnel professionals must know to complete that second mile.

Personnel professionals who go that second mile have found opportunity for advancement and continuing self-fulfillment. On the other hand, those who depend on basic "form" and rigidly follow only day-to-day meeting of routine problems are heading up blind alleys. The second milers, however, are finding compensation limited only by their accomplishments and abilities.

These second milers are, in many instances, taking over the helm of the business because of their wide as well as deep insight into company personnel, policies and organizational structure. They know that today most companies are so large that no two executives have the same opportunities. They also often find complete satisfaction in becoming the power behind the throne. The opportunity to motivate, to understand, and to thus participate in full decision making is complete fulfillment for many of these multitalented individuals.

Nothing Changes Except Attitude

Second milers realize that today's employees have the same work standards they have always had. The only change is in the attitude of management. This new breed of managers insists that there are no inefficient employees; there are only incompetent managers. There is an old saying that "A good workman never blames his tools." A manager who blames high costs, union activity and inefficient production on his employees, is reflecting his own incompetence in the results he is getting from his employees. This is a self-fulfilling prophecy.

We all too often hear today that jobs are "too routine and boring to interest the employee." The fact is that most people like routine jobs. If you don't believe that, just go out and change some part of the office routine and listen to the people say, "But we have always done it that way!" Strikes have resulted when the routine has been changed. One only has to study the Hawthorne experiment to realize that it isn't the routine people find frustrating, but the lack of good personal communications with their supervisor of foreman. Employees need the satisfaction of knowing that when they help to increase the profitability of their company, that in turn makes it possible to pay good wages and to ensure their long-term security. Employees yearn for the opportunity to be heard, to give management sound advice, and to recommend needed action which will improve employee relations. Many new or revised policies have been adopted as a result of this kind of communication.

Second milers are well aware that the factors which lead to the top are anything but new. Some are over 5,000 years old and were used by the Egyptian civilization for 3,000 years. It is not pure coincidence that their civilization lasted 10 times longer than any other civilization. It was they who developed Management by Objectives and we thought this was a new and modern technique. We even see evidence that the Egyptians were familiar with organization levels and job evaluations. The selection and training of administrators by not only the Egyptians but also the early Incas have been brought to light by studies of their civilizations. We have only to open our Bibles to the Book of Genesis to read how Moses' father-in-law, Jethro, advised him how to develop the delegation of authority and chain-of-command techniques. Inspection of goods, auditing of personnel, inventories, money and methods all were developed through these ancient civilizations and are spread out in history for those who have the interest and insight to comprehend the full scope of management.

One needs only to look at the downfall of many proud and one-time, prestigious organizations to realize that years before the walls began to crumble, the basic foundations had begun to weaken. This weakening process can be traced, if one has the patience to pursue the history of the organization, to the departure of the ancient truths of basic management.

Basic Factors

Here then, are some of the factors that the second milers have learned to apply to maintain a strong, vibrant and ever-growing organization, whether it be in business, religion, politics or social structures:

1. Understand that an organization must have a positive attitude directed toward a specific set of long-term as well as short-term goals. This is sometimes characterized as a philosophy of management but whatever name it is given, it will be traceable to some visionary individual who realizes its importance as the lifeblood of the organization.
2. Realize that personnel management does not live on tests, routines, forms, instruction books alone, but it must have spirit, a philosophy of life neither rigid nor soft, with a knowledge of facts and then pursuing the right path leaning neither toward the employee, the union nor management.
3. Maintain daily contact with employees at all levels. This contact can only be gained by a face-to-face contact as a result of daily trips through the office and plant. It means talking to employees and listening to employees. It means using the grapevine as the most efficient form of communication. Feed it, nurture it and pay heed to what you hear; but don't jump to conclusions at the first whispers. Many times the grapevine is telling you something far more subtle and important than mere words can convey.
4. Keep notes, letters, bulletins, carbon copies (in and out), and phone calls to a minimum. Lay the pencil down, get out of your chair and see the person face-to-face. Your demeanor, expression, even your eyes, do far more to convey your message. Remember, a memo has no ears and even a phone call cannot always transmit a smile, a twinkle of the eye or a frown.
5. Be human. After all, you are dealing with other humans. Follow some of the old proverbs and sayings; they have their roots in ages of truth.
6. Look ahead. Devote at least 20% of your time planning for next year and 30% of your time in the five-to ten-year projection. Yet, as these plans develop, allow them to be as viable as needs require.
7. Become your own public relations manager. Keep your name in "soft lights." Let others blow your horn while you

allow the harp strings of your of your personality to play the background music of your soul.

8. Reach your middle management people as well as those above. Remember that the middle management group are on the firing line. They are taking the daily heat. They are the ones who are closest to the people and the operation. They are tomorrow's top management. Teach them that self-motivation can be learned. These are the people who are yet young enough in your organization to become self-motivated.

9. Be self-renewing. You can do this by setting for yourself goals for a day, week, month, year and beyond. You must constantly check on the attainment of these goals, analyzing why you fall short when that happens, and deciding whether your attainment was too short or your goal was misjudged.

Self-Renewal

You become self-renewing through proper delegation of your responsibilities. Thus, you permit growth in others and the opportunity to judge the progress of those individuals to whom you have delegated.

In the process of self-renewal, one must realize that every negative condition or problem is a golden nugget of opportunity. Without the negative aspects of your job, there would be no challenge, no new opportunities and life would be pallid indeed.

Self-renewal requires one to be future and action oriented. Only by assessing one's accomplishments in the cold light of facts can you determine whether you are making progress toward your goals. Certainly one must fully identify with the goals of his organization. No matter what opinion you have of your personal accomplishments, if your organization hasn't achieved its goals, you have failed to make proper progress in your own goal achievement.

One of the most important measuring devices in assessing the self-renewal process is the activity of those channels which permit feedback on your own ideas and acts. It is in this area that we find the truth in the statement that "What you are speaks so loudly I cannot hear what you say!" Many people so sell themselves on what great guys they are that they fail to acknowledge what their peers and others really think of them. One of the most difficult things any of us has to do is to gulp down the bitter gall of criticism or failure.

Finally, continually finding new interests in people, places, things and above all, new ideas keeps the wellsprings open in the whole self-renewal process. When Franklin Roosevelt was sworn into office, Chief Justice Oliver Wendell Holmes was too infirm and ill to go through the ceremony. One of the other senior justices was pressed into service to handle the ceremony. However, Roosevelt wanted history to show that he was sworn in by the Chief Justice. So, family Bible in hand, he was driven to the home of Mr. Holmes. He found him, at the age of 92, studying the Greek language. If such an individual as Justice Holmes felt that it was important to learn something new at the age of 92, then we can take a page from his philosophy to continue to renew our educational process. He indeed is a prime example of the second miler.

There will always be the first and second milers. The beautiful part of our heritage is that the choice is ours.

IS PERSONNEL MANAGEMENT A PROFESSION?

Personnel management is here to stay. Very few people will disagree on that point. But as to the purpose of Personnel, and the place of Personnel in different organizations, there apparently is considerable misunderstanding.

Some years back this newest member moved in on the management family. At that time, and since then, it received varying degrees of welcome from other members of the family. For the most part this new addition, which gradually became known by the name of Personnel, was tolerated and accepted because it was too small to get into anybody's way.

But now it is growing up—and beginning to command attention. Some members of the family are accepting it as an equal, others still seem to look down upon it as a stepchild. What complicates matters further is that this youngster Personnel has a tendency to confound the others by its behavior. Sometimes it gets into trouble; at other times it actually shows signs of having outgrown the pecadillos of its mixed-up youth.

A factual appraisal of the situation reveals that Personnel has not yet attained the position it deserves. Personnel practitioners can dream about equal status with other segments of management. Planners can place Personnel high on the charts on drawing boards. Professors can theorize in the classroom. But the fact remains that in most companies Personnel has not yet been recognized as it could or should be.

And this is for only one reason: Personnel generally is not yet making the kind of contribution to general management which merits a place for it topside.

There is an opportunity for Personnel to grow up and eventually approach the bigness that the others have already attained. There is also a need for this.

One way might be to grow up professionally.

The Pattern of Professions

Before accepting the thesis that professionalization of the personnel activity is the solution to Personnel growing up, it might be well to consider whether the pattern of the established professions is adaptable to the cause of personnel administration.

In the professions are individuals who by their choice of lifetime work and their specialized training have set themselves apart from other workers in the community. Because of their practice they are different from others, better in their particular respect, and therefore to be looked up to. This is the attraction which appeals to the advocates of professionalization of the personnel activity. There is a serious danger for personnel people who follow this path to professionalization for it tends to isolate the personnel practitioner from the people he serves. While all the evidence points to the fact that top executives come from the ranks of line managers, personnel people move away from the role of manager toward the staff titles which imply consultative work. Instead of joining the ranks of management people they are inclined to set themselves apart. They have even developed a lingo of their own designed to mystify and impress others with their singular importance.

To be effective the personnel administrator must move more in the direction of generalization, toward a well-balanced personnel service which is integrated into every other aspect of management. Ideally, he should strive for relative anonymity, with his own identity blended into the background of his company. He cannot serve the purpose of personnel by setting himself up as a professional specialist. Only by involving himself in everybody's else's business can he hope to earn a place in the everyday councils of management where the hard decisions are made.

The one type of approach builds the individual who grows in stature by being different from those he serves. The other type of approach minimizes self as a separate entity and gets its strength from general integration. While these are opposite approaches, they both can lead to professional stature.

The Standard

On this basis, what can be learned by looking at the established professions such as medicine, law and the ministry? What distinguishes them from other respected vocations? A quick analysis points up these distinct characteristics: (1) their qualifications, usually an isolated body of knowledge, (2) their progress or relentless drive for improvement, and (3) their standard of ethics, which motivates and guides them toward desired goals.

A profession . . .

1. Develops a code of ethics, not only in writing but branded into the conscience and conduct of its practitioners.

2. Possesses a vast body of organized knowledge developed by predecessors over the years, and available to newcomers, who in turn perpetuate, refine and add to it for the next generation.

3. Calls for specific skills unlike those of other professions.

4. Requires that its members receive a certain defined formal instruction, preferably leading to a degree from a recognized institution of higher learning.

5. Provides for certification of proficiency before a member can achieve professional status.

6. Follows an orderly process in the fulfillment of responsibilities.

7. Offers opportunity for the promulgation and interchange of ideas among its members.

8. Demands an acceptance of the disciplines of the profession, realizing that the price of failure or malpractice is "out" of the profession.

To qualify in other professions members must first meet definite academic requirements. No one is entitled to use "M.D." until he has completed prescribed courses of study and passed necessary examinations. A lawyer must first pass the bar before he can practice. This is certainly not the case in Personnel. Although there are many courses of study available to personnel administrators, it is not necessary to complete even one of these in order to hold down a personnel job. Personnel management has been considered more a process of osmosis and rote than specialized preparation for a profession; education and practice have been highly fragmentized.

When the company doctor leaves the firm who would think of promoting his successor from the ranks? Yet this is often the way personnel vacancies are filled. The same companies that hire a trained accountant to do cost analyses, or a certified actuary to figure insurance rates, seem to feel that any pleasant, understanding sort of fellow can do personnel work. Getting along well with people seems to be the main requisite. While these are fine traits, they do not compensate for knowledge of systematic personnel procedures nor for professional expertness in personnel administration.

Too often the personnel manager is a former supervisor or manager who came up through the ranks, whose loyal performance was rewarded by promotion because he knows the customs, traditions, policies and personalities of the company. And, of course, he is a friendly and pleasant person.

Unskilled Application

One danger of such a practice is that these personnel practitioners, while they are capable of following orders from higher up, and are capable of keeping the employee relations program from running into the ground, they do not have the depth of understanding to distinguish right from wrong in various personnel techniques. They are suckers for all sorts of personnel gimmicks which they embrace in an attempt to look good but which they really don't comprehend. They will buy a "pig in a poke" because they cannot appraise its potential value or possible harm. They will adopt another's successful procedure or device, then wonder why they do not get comparable results. They are like the church organist who knows music but cannot get the congregation to sing; he plays with his hands, not his heart.

Being relatively unskilled in their jobs it is not surprising to find these personnel people using outdated or discredited programs. They rely upon their special ability to "size up people." They work on hunches because they don't know how to be objective with facts. They tune in on official thinking before they stick their own necks out, and when they do make a decision they rely upon authority more than judgment. Usually they limp along, concerned mostly with keeping their own noses clean.

Possibly some may argue that it is preferable to advance in the personnel field by building upon work experience rather than "book learning"—and in view of the many so-called successful people operating in the field of Personnel this is a strong argument. Yet even in these situations there is nothing to prevent sincere personnel managers, who have come up through the ranks, from determining their understanding of this field by measuring their capabilities against prevailing standards.

Many people in management, including many personnel people themselves, somehow feel that personnel work does not call for any specialized training other than that which can be acquired as they go along. Yet, can anyone practice medicine or law or teach?

Outmoded Techniques

Perhaps another notable feature of the established professions is their eternal struggle to keep abreast of the times. Truth does not change but the ways of propagating it certainly do. Outmoded teaching methods must be abandoned. In medical science the vast accumulation of knowledge is as nothing compared with what it will be 10 years from now. Unfortunately, in personnel work research is by no means as important as practice.

Personnel administrators are still depending upon the old standbys of recruiting, methods which are rapidly reaching the point of no return. In hiring they still pretend to go through a process of selection when actually the selection procedure has become a series of rejections. The tests they use, developed decades ago and validated under conditions existing then, could be losing their usefulness and leading to erroneous conclusions. Their concern over the shortage of skills usually does not go beyond that of typists and secretaries in the office, or tool and die makers in the shop, when the real serious shortage of available skills is higher up, among executives. Companies still devote time and money to training, when the big problem, brought about by technological change, is retraining, which they ignore and thereby let the door of opportunity wide open for more government intervention. Not enough personnel practitioners recognize their responsibility to the field which has provided them with a livelihood.

But a still more significant distinction between professional people and personnel administrators is something more vital than either of these other two factors. This is the standard of performance. In the conduct of their work true professional people are moved by a belief or a creed which goes beyond their day-to-day work, one which gives meaning to their actions. The clergy is the best example; theirs is a guiding philosophy which does not permit compromise. The medics have their Hippocratic oath which leads them to unbelievable heights of accomplishments. A reputable lawyer would much prefer to utilize his powers of persuasion to bring a broken family together than make an extra dollar handling a divorce case.

Master Mechanics

Before personnel administrators can even think of becoming professional they must develop a philosophy to guide them in all their actions. Too many personnel administrators are still concentrating on techniques, their goal being that of becoming master mechanics.

Some personnel directors are as blind as a lawyer who is so deep in books he can't see the people who are affected; or as neglectful as an architect who designs houses to impress other architects rather than the tenants. The dehumanizing process of life in the modern world is caused in part by the bureaucratic mazes of vast impersonality which clog the system within which the professionals perform their service. The professions become ingrown and self-serving.

On the road to professionalization a technique cannot be a destination in itself but merely a way of travel. A doctor does not practice medicine; he treats patients. A teacher does not teach a particular subject; he teaches students. A dedicated personnel administrator does not perform personnel duties; he deals with factors which affect not only a worker's living but also his life. Professionalism in any field should be a means of serving the people's deepest needs, not an abstract exercise in virtuosity.

That personnel administrator is on his way to executive status who concerns himself not only with the function of things but also with their meaning. He attains bigness when he goes beyond personnel administration and begins to practice personnel statesmanship. As soon as he learns to conduct himself in a professional manner the desire to professionalize his activity ceases to be important.

Certification by Decree

The desire for professional status is manifest in the many attempts to upgrade the position of the personnel administrator, not by performance but merely by changing the title to a more impressive one.

Personnel management calls for the use of scientific techniques and to some people this makes it a profession. It will be a long time, however, before any educational institution or professional society will accept the responsibility of certification of personnel executives as professional people. Meanwhile some trade groups, such as personnel associations, are toying with the idea, but it seems inadvisable to certify personnel administrators by decree.

Yet there are similarities between personnel management and the professions, especially in their formative years. The early professions surrounded themselves with mystery and paraphernalia. They used a special jargon—some still do. They claimed uniqueness and expected special privileges. They created bizarre titles for themselves. These descriptions fit many personnel executives.

Not all professional people, of course, are worthy of the cloak of respectability that shields them from criticism or suspicion. Some are mountebanks and others are out-and-out fakes. Many personnel practitioners are phonies, too, impressing no one but themselves, as they surround themselves with specialized terms and incomprehensible language, involved procedures, trappings of the office and other outward appurtenances to confuse the laity. They forget that it is not through position or prestige that the personnel executive accomplishes his mission.

Socrates remarked that the only man who deserves to be given power is the man who doesn't want it—for he is the man most likely to treat his office as a trust and not as a trough.

A certificate on the wall does not make a person a professional. It merely gives him a label in a particular field. There could be, and sometimes is, a marked difference between professional identification and professional conduct.

Professionalization Through Performance

The central theme of any profession is unselfish service to mankind, not service to self. The motivation should never be money. The legal definition of a professional worker is different from the one in common usage. In everyday language, being professional merely means accepting money for service. A professional baseball player is paid. The difference between professional golfers and amateur golfers is that the first get paid, not that they are any better or even different. This merely adds dignity to the job but not much else.

Dedication to duty should be ahead of every other consideration. This service, humbly rendered, is associated with guidance, extended with pride and authority. But in performing this service there is no turning away from the ways of the world. The profession is a part of the society in which it acts.

Professional people strive to get respect in their field, to be recognized by their peers, to accomplish their purpose, often against struggle and misunderstanding, and always because they are dedicated individuals and believe in what they are doing. But always they try to serve mankind rather than run mankind.

To be in a profession means to *profess,* to take a vow of service, to live one's career by a higher standard than is expected of others. This, in turn, means that common sense about helping people is the keystone, not merely the polished capstone.

Instead of talking up professionalization, personnel executives would do better to raise the level of their performance. If they would work toward developing a philosophy of what personnel administration is all about, they will increase their effectiveness and thereby enhance their stature. Then the struggle for professional status will no longer exist— for they will have arrived there.

CAREER OPPORTUNITIES BEYOND PERSONNEL

Personnel activities of many companies are expanding and at the same time opportunities for advancement from personnel posts to high-level management positions seem to be rising.

Arnold R. Deutsch, Chairman, Deutsch, Shea & Evans, Inc., a human resources communications and consulting firm based in New York, comments: "Management now realizes that the personnel department is a profit center. There is a much greater awareness of the importance of human resources in relation to a corporation's success."

He explains that years ago personnel departments at many companies were quite small and headed often by a reluctant manager assigned to the task. Now top management has begun to realize that its own people are real assets and hence the personnel function has gained new recognition.

There has also been what he calls "Government intrusion," which has made personnel functions more complex. Companies must cope with new government safety standards, pension rules and antidiscrimination laws. A recent survey he conducted showed such problems accounted for about 40% of some corporate personnel departments' man-hours.

Personnel, out of necessity, has become a highly-professional occupation, involving a diversified roster of specializations.

The prospects for personnel people look bright because they have great visibility. According to Mr. Deutsch, more top-level management jobs will in the future be filled by personnel managers, taking their place along with financial, legal and marketing experts.

PERSONNEL ADMINISTRATION—A LOOK INTO THE IMMEDIATE FUTURE

During the Industrial Revolution the emphasis was on technological progress. Human resources did not get into consideration; it was not in the thinking of the day. There were dire consequences to this neglect, which managements realized too late. One example was the widespread unionization of defenseless workers who responded to the leadership from outside when their own companies failed them.

The past several decades have produced unprecedented progress in the fields of automation and electronics. But again the advances have all been one way; no corresponding improvement has been made in human relations. People, as usual, have been taken for granted and are once again beginning to assert themselves. The pendulum is swinging back to people. Only this time they're getting their encouragement and assistance from government.

Government intervention in the affairs of business is, of course, not new. We've long had government regulating hours, working conditions, overtime rates, minimum pay and th elike, and we've learned how to build our personnel programs around these requirements. Business has come to accept these controls against exploitation of employees by employers. In addition, pensions, insurance and welfare payments are established and administered by government, and industry has no choice but to fall in step. Business, largely, is in sympathy with the motives.

The new intrusion on the part of government, which we are discussing here, is however, something entirely different. The socialistic trend so evident in government planning during the last 40 years has produced a geometric patchwork of social programs designed to extirpate all social evils from poverty to rheumatism. These schemes have been so varied and so all-encompassing that government is finding it necessary to form "government-industry partnerships" to carry them out.

A New Burden

In short, business is expected to implement government social legislation. And government is no longer subtle in its efforts to saddle business with this responsibility. The forced cooperation that results does nothing to help business operate more effectively; in fact, it impedes operating efficiency much as a millstone around the neck hampers the swimmer.

Government has all sorts of ways to "influence" business to come around to its way of thinking. It holds all the trumps. There is hardly a business enterprise, no matter how small, that is not involved in some way with government business, if not as a prime contractor then at least as a subcontractor. The contract says in effect that the contractor agrees to do business with government on government terms. This can mean anything from corporate subservience to the laws to willing compliance with executive orders. As the nation's largest direct and indirect employer, government is now setting the standards.

Industry has already been directed to revalidate employment tests, even discontinue the use of some tests, since they work a hardship upon applicants who have little or no chance of passing them. Compliance investigators have "suggested" that nothing detrimental should be included in an employee's file, that negative responses to reference inquiries, prison records, unemployment claims, wage assignments and the like serve only to prejudice a manager against an individual who may be under consideration for employment or promotion.

Already new words are coming into the industrial vocabulary. First we heard of the *disadvantaged,* then the *unemployed* and *underemployed,* and now we're getting pressure to help the *unprepared.* Industry is told to put them on the payroll, with some measure of reimbursement toward the costs of recruiting, counseling, on-the-job training, remedial education, and supportive services such as minor medical care and possible transportation. The idea seems to be "employ 'em or support 'em" with employment the preferred choice, since this supposedly will reduce the skyrocketing tax burden. Whether industry gets its fair share of productivity from these substandard workers, and all the red tape that is necessary, seems to be of little concern to the social planners.

Big Brother is Watching

And red tape there will be. It is not sufficient to submit obediently to the laws and carry out the provisions of the contract, but a company is always suspect to the burgeoning, faceless army of government auditors and investigators. Charges against a firm are easily made, and even a routine inspection can call for endless and detailed records and reports just to prove a company is innocent of any alleged or implied wrongdoing.

The penalties for passivity in meeting the government's terms, instead of enthusiasm for embracing a positive program, are in such devices as prolonged investigations of complaints, public hearings and always the threat of contract cancellation. Lately there has come the hint of "negative" penalties in the form of assurances that firms which meet the government's terms willingly with an announced program of cooperation may be rewarded with extra consideration in the awarding of government contracts and more definite profit guarantees.

How serious is all this? A Washington spokesman addressing 300 top executives of companies which are prime contractors said existing personnel procedures are no longer adequate. He advised these companies to "throw away the book and start over."

In summary, personnel administration as we learned and practiced it is a thing of the past. The gradual encroachment of government upon the industrial scene has bent the established and proven concepts out of shape. As a result, we will revise forms, records, reports, tests and test norms, recruiting sources, hiring standards, promotion sequences, training qualifications, grievance procedures, dismissal practices and other personnel techniques which have served business so well. From now on our primary purpose will be to promote the government's social legislation aims.

PERSONNEL ADMINISTRATION—
YESTERDAY, TODAY, TOMORROW

What is personnel administration? How do people in the field of personnel view their management responsibility? What do line managers and foremen consider is their involvement insofar as personnel administration is concerned?

At the outset, let's understand that personnel administration is not some responsibility "up front," or the job of one person or one staff, but is the obligation of all who work with people. Whether hiring, training, promoting, disciplining, rating or whatever, these are all part and parcel of the same activity, commonly lumped together under the catch-all name of personnel administration.

Neither is personnel administration an accumulation of various clerical tasks. Many personnel offices consist of clerks who spend unproductive hours keeping all sorts of records and reports which nobody does much about and which do not change the picture anyhow. Keeping track of tardiness and absences, for example, may be better handled in payroll where the time sheets are available. What is done with the information such records reveal is, of course, a responsibility of personnel.

Nor is personnel a central service organization. This concept started with centralized employment and then began to embrace all sorts of odd jobs in an effort to build a staff and to justify its existence.

Let's get something else straight, too. Personnel administration is not to be thought of as a job. It is not an occupation that young people are encouraged to enter for a good livelihood. This is not a series of scientific or systematic procedures that can be learned in the university or on the job. It is rather a vocation, something to believe in. Then it becomes a business of arts and crafts instead of science and technology.

To make my point, let me take you back to your military experience. If you're crawling up on a pillbox you'd much prefer to be covered by a guy who thrilled to joining a fighting outfit than some kid who signed up looking for "benefits." Similarly, I'd hate to entrust the ideals and attitudes of our workers to people who went into personnel work because this was better than driving a truck.

In an attempt to understand what personnel administration is, or should be, it is necessary to erase from our minds the picture we see today and go back to its start, see how it came about, how it developed, and where it is heading.

The Early Days

Before World War II, company management was concerned mostly with only five of the six M's of management—Money, Markets, Material, Methods and Machines. No money or time was appropriated for the other M—Manpower. It was not in the thinking of that day.

Until the early 1930's, the personnel activity was pretty much restricted to employment, to see that every position in the organization was kept filled with men and women. Then as the employment market gradually tightened, managers found that the chore of finding suitable new workers was becoming more time consuming and that it interfered with their many other duties which were also becoming more complex and involved. That made them willing, in fact eager, to let some other person worry about the problems of locating applicants, sorting out the undesirables, and referring the acceptable ones for their consideration.

In its modest and unobtrusive beginning certain unwanted tasks related to employment were relegated to this central office. In addition to the actual recruiting and screening, the details associated with keeping adequate records, conforming to company policy and government regulations, were permitted to drift into this central office. Nothing of fundamental importance beyond arranging the annual picnic was entrusted to them. It is significant to note, that while management was willing to share some of the work, there was no thought of relinquishing any of the control. Personnel was an orphaned box on the organization chart.

Since this new office was given no authority of its own, it attracted the type of person who expected to be bossed by higher-ups. From the outside came school teachers who were lured away from the classrooms by the prospect of better earnings. Welfare workers came to do good in business where certainly much good needed to be done. A wave of idealism attracted do-gooders of high principles and great naiveté. Often when the personnel jobs were filled from within the organization they were given to former supervisors, foremen and others who came up through the ranks, some rewarded with promotions because of loyal performance in unrelated work elsewhere in the company. Many were actually demoted uphill to get them out of the way; personnel became a dumping ground for burned-out executives. The personnel people came to their new and undefined jobs from sales, from production, from accounting, depending on who could be spared. In the history of personnel development it is sad to reflect that many people arrived by accident.

There was no precedent to go by and this indeciveness as it concerned qualifications resulted in personnel making only halting progress. The many different practitioners, using various job titles, had no guidance either. Literature was sparse and few schools had courses that offered proper training in this new field. The bosses didn't know what they wanted either; they knew only what they didn't want—trouble from unions and government, and release from the nuisance of hiring.

The first personnel administrators were hired as a defensive measure. Management had an attitude that the job was a necessary, but unwelcome, bother.

Uneven Growth

From this meager start the personnel activity began to grow. But its growth was uneven and unsteady. In some companies it grew very little; in some places it died out as an activity of its own and its several duties were again absorbed by others. Wherever it failed to make progress the fault lay with lack of encouragement on the part of management or lack of leadership on the part of the personnel people. But there were some companies that were ready to recognize the contribution a sound employee relations program was prepared to make toward more efficient operation. And fortunately there were some personnel executives who were able to grow with their programs.

The big growth came after World War II. There were three contributing factors. First, employment was no longer hit or miss. With the rapid industrial development that followed war's end, personnel programs began to become necessary to cope with the hiring and placing of men and women. Adequate help was getting harder to find and the entire complexion of the nation's workforce was changing. New applicants, such as housewives, came into the employment picture. Conditions and circumstances surrounding work were considerably affected.

Second, management no longer had the unqualified upper hand. Somewhere along the line new forces had come into play. For instance, new motivations had to be established when such things as fear no longer proved effective. Workers, including those not organized, were being heard and had to be reckoned with.

Third, something new entered the picture in the development of third party influences. First the arrival of New Deal legislation involved companies in legal responsibilities which logically centered in the personnel office. At about the same time labor unions had grown in size and strength and this focused management's attention on the practical necessity of getting its house in order. The personnel administrator was destined to become the person to deal with these increasingly important and militant forces.

As business operations, especially in the areas of dealing with employees, became more involved, companies began to attach new significance to their personnel programs. The personnel reservoir of functions was being deepened as well as widened. Personnel, which originally only added more services to its sphere of activities, now began to add influence also. Jobs like training, wage administration and benefit counseling, which began as minor functions because they received little attention, were, in the process of development, expanded with the expansion of industry, the growth of labor unions, and the increasing complexity of legislation.

Better qualified administrators, most of them technically minded, began to be attracted to the field. They introduced and developed techniques and procedures which, after years of painful trial and error, have become refined and formalized. In the present picture, personnel is attracting a higher level of academically trained "successor prospects" which give the entire activity a fresh and vigorous balance of experience, training and ability.

Earning Recognition

All this indicates that there are signs that personnel management, which was originally marked by mediocrity, is now emerging from stepchild status in the corporate community. It has gone so far that some large organizations, having experienced the contribution personnel can and does make, have created vice-presidential positions for their top personnel executives. While it is true that not every program has succeeded this well, it is just as true that throughout all companies the personnel activity has been upgraded in the eyes of management and the workers. For the qualified and dedicated personnel executive the door of opportunity is open wider.

No longer is personnel staffed with do-gooders or industrial misfits, but with practitioners who approach their responsibilities and their opportunities from both technical and philosophical standpoints. The old myth that every management man had, namely that he knows all about how a company personnel program should be set up and run, has long ago been exploded. Many company presidents have said that they go out to hire the best personnel executive available because they realize that in our enlightened era "business is people" and the conditions of employment and development of manpower lie within the province and purview of the personnel executive. The company president is no longer the sum total of all management functions and he and his senior staff know that they are not expected to understand and direct the employee program effectively with all its ramifications. This is the job for the personnel executive who has the necessary skill, training, background and outlook to understand not only the personnel functions but also their purpose.

The field is slowly coming of age. Personnel management is maturing because the growth of companies carries with it a complexity of new duties involving people. And in the total management activity personnel is no longer in the periphery but closer to the center where the hard decisions are made. We've gone a long way from making people happy to making them productive. The stardust has been shaken out, and in the process personnel executives have learned for themselves, and demonstrated to others, that personnel administration is much more than day-to-day performance of necessary administrative techniques.

Personnel management is still beset with handicaps, real and imagined. How fast it grows and what kind of progress it makes depends upon the personnel practitioners more than upon the management of the company. No company can give recognition to people it feels unworthy of the award; but on the other hand, no company can deny recognition that is earned by the good, consistent performance being done every day by personnel people.

Better Outlook

What I've said so far is that the field of personnel management is growing up. Naturally I cannot speak for you as an individual and whether you too are growing up. We'll come back to that later.

Personnel programs have come a long way from the early days when garbage-can tasks were dumped into their convenient central office. No longer is personnel a storage place for unwanted duties. No longer do personnel staffs lose more men and women to other divisions than they obtain from those divisions.

Where once the personnel man symbolized weaknesses in company operations, he now symbolizes strength, for the strangth of any company lies not in its products but in its people who design, make, sell and distribute those products.

Top management may still be disillusioned by visions of holding control and direction, but the personnel director is beginning to make his mark, namely that it is in the best interest of the company to design its employee relations program to fit the workers' needs, not the personal whims of management, and to conduct its personnel programs accordingly.

After experiencing the peccadillos of adolescent youth, there is now some hope that personnel management is growing up. In many places it is taking its rightful place as a full-fledged member of the management team.

To prove that this is not wishful thinking, let me give you three unrelated illustrations from everyday business life to show how personnel management is growing up.

In the first place, personnel practices are being improved. For example, in the employment of workers there is less discrimination than before. The problem has not been completely solved, nor will it be despite well-intentioned legislation, for bias is buried in the heart where no law reaches. But simply as a matter of economics, qualified members of various minority groups are having less difficulty finding suitable jobs. Companies are realizing that ability knows no restrictions and that unfounded prejudices create artificial barriers to success which are too costly to tolerate.

There is still discrimination in the hiring of older workers, although this situation is coming in for its share of attention. By ignoring this problem managements have left the door open for still more unwanted government intervention. Companies need qualified workers; skills cannot be arbitrarily cast aside because of an unrealistic age barrier.

Women, too, are gaining in acceptance. Long ago established as a vital part of the nation's workforce, they are now moving into positions of responsibility and authority. Here again, no one sex has a corner on brains.

In a democratic society these moves spell progress. In our industrial society they indicate that personnel management is growing up.

Better Practitioners

Secondly, the field of personnel management is attracting better caliber men and women to be the practitioners. It is true that the field is cluttered with all sorts of personnel administrators operating under various titles and with varying degrees of effectiveness. But as the demands for a really professional-type service increase, the misfit with the title is being replaced by the more competent technician, better trained in the skills and better equipped in the understanding of human relations.

The colleges are turning out hundreds of graduates who are well schooled in personnel precepts. These technicians, trained in the laboratories of the campus, are bound to have a wholesome impact on personnel work as they acquire practical experience in the laboratory of life. More and more their influence will be felt. This also is a sign of personnel management's growing up.

In the third place, some of the personnel executives, those who are making a contribution to the field, are beginning to develop a philosophy of what the work is all about.

Better Attitude

For the first century and a half of this nation of ours the emphasis was on the development of physical resources—technological progress.

Without any slackening in attention to technical improvement, during the past several decades there has been far greater attention paid to human values than ever before—from physical resources to human resources. This is no shift from things to people; it is just bringing both into proper perspective and balance.

There are indications that managements are becoming aware of the importance of emphasizing the human side of progress. Technologically we have found the key to plenty. Yet the world that technology can build is only a half-world. For a complete world we must look beyond the slide rule and be concerned with the meaning of things, not merely their function. In the final analysis people, not science or technology, will determine the kind of world we live in.

When the history of the industrial revolution is written in its entirety, the closing chapters will record four stages in the evolution of personnel management.

In 1925 personnel administration was in its infancy, and was usually emergency-created. It took on many forms, but amounted to little more than centralized employment and record-keeping.

HISTORY OF PERSONNEL ADMINISTRATION

DATES BACK TO	DEVELOPMENT	OUTLOOK	EMPHASIS	STATUS
1925	BEGINNING INAUSPICIOUSLY	PRACTICAL	CENTRALIZED RECRUITING and RECORD-KEEPING	CLERICAL
1945	STRUGGLING FOR RECOGNITION	TECHNICAL	INTRODUCTION OF TECHNIQUES	MANAGER
1965	IMPRESSING WITH SOPHISTICATION	IMPERSONAL	COMPUTERIZED PROGRAMS and REGULATED CONFORMANCE	JUNIOR EXECUTIVE
1980's	PROMISING FULFILLMENT	PHILOSOPHICAL	HUMAN VALUES: SOMETHING TO BELIEVE IN	EXECUTIVE

Approximately in 1945 it began struggling for recognition with the introduction of techniques which emphasized necessary specialized training. At this point it generally acquired departmental standing.

By 1965 it had emerged as an adolescent with its computerized programs and government-regulated conformance. Unfortunately, this impressive sophistication caused a very human activity to become impersonal.

For its future, it is expected to move into the grown-up stage, with the development of a philosophy, something to believe in, not just something to do. Once this is accomplished it will have attained executive status.

Realizing Fulfillment

Before we conclude this recital, it might be well to ask ourselves what our personal future in this field will be. We've heard where the field of personnel management is destined to go. How about you?

Perhaps many personnel administrators might be satisfied with the progress they have made. After all, it is a good way of making a living. As jobs go, there are many, many other jobs that are less attractive.

To me this sounds like the attitude of people who are going nowhere. When they leave to go elsewhere or into retirement the field of personnel will not miss them. People who are content to stand still in effect fall behind, for the world around us is not static. I firmly believe that those of us who make our living in personnel work have a responsibility to the field which provides us our good fortune. But in order to progress beyond our present position we must do more than build a greater central service activity or introduce more techniques.

The forms, procedures and devices we use are not the job; they are merely the paraphernalia of the personnel administrator. On the way to personnel success such techniques are not a destination in themselves but only a means of travel. They are the scaffold used to erect a sound employee relations program.

As long as you're content to be a department manager then concentrate on your personnel procedures, all the while administering in your central office other people's ideas and policies, many of them unsound. However, if you aspire to become a company executive, then rise above these necessary techniques and concentrate on their meaning, while training and developing the line managers to perform the personnel functions. Don't think of yourself as dealing with people but rather dealing with the factors that affect people.

There is quite a distinction here. The landscape is the same; the difference is in beholders.

Just as there are hucksters in advertising, quacks in medicine, shysters in law and scoundrels in religion, so also do we have miscreants in personnel. The doctor's mistakes are in the cemetery; the lawyer's mistakes are in jail; the preacher's mistakes may be in hell; and the casualties of misguided personnel practitioners are strewn along the tobacco road of frustration.

The architects can cover their mistakes with ivy, and brides theirs with mayonnaise. But you and I can't do that. We cannot afford to make mistakes. Not as long as we're dealing with something as mysterious and potent as the human personality.

Once we understand, accept and apply that philosophy to our everyday administrative duties, then personnel management will serve its useful purpose. Then the past will have taught its lessons, the present will offer the proving ground, and the future will be assured.

DO WE THROW AWAY THE BOOK AND START OVER?

It was not many years ago that I heard a member of the President's cabinet in Washington address a meeting of 300 prime government contractors on the subject of hiring practices. He made many accusations of existing bad practices and a number of bold suggestions for correcting them.

His closing statement—and I shall never forget it—was that in the light of the present employment market, social climate and rights legislation, it would be best for companies to "throw away the book and start over."

That directive might be hard for successful, hard-line personnel executives to swallow. Yet it contains a basic truth, namely that change is upon us. For the title of this article, you will notice, we took the liberty of rephrasing that statement into a question, "Do we throw away the book and start over?" This, you see, gives us the opportunity of going both ways. I firmly believe that in some respects we must start over, but in others we should maintain procedures we've developed and refined over the years.

The following, then, is my list of 24 discussion topics we might want to consider as we decide which personnel practices we should preserve, abandon and introduce.

PRESERVE	ABANDON	INTRODUCE
1. historical records and records of progress	manual record keeping	mechanized records
2. simple forms	needless questions on employment application blanks	few direct questions for straightforward answers
3. recruitment	selective sources	open recruiting
4. exempt recruitment	stalemate practices	worldwide recruiting
5. employment procedure	hiring overqualified applicants	hiring for the job
6. job write-ups	overstating requirements	better utilization of talent
7. position identification	job flattering titles	functional titles
8. testing	test and norms that favor bias	revalidations that hold up when challenged
9. decision making	"by gosh" selection	match applicants to jobs via computer
10. promotions	sentimental considerations	objectivity
11. upgrading employees	going on the outside	continuous training
12. wage administration	raises based on time	raises related to performance or productivity
13. turnover	taking employees for granted	grievance procedure
14. holidays	minimum 6 notion	innovate with personal or floating holidays
15. group insurance	sickness alone coverage	preventive health care
16. pensions	stringent vesting	portable pensions
17. retirement programs	ignoring retirees	escalating income

PERSONNEL ADMINISTRATION HANDBOOK

PRESERVE	ABANDON	INTRODUCE
18. communications	pap and drivel	adult level fact data
19. company day and week	standfast hours and terms	adaptable working conditions
20. written policies	rigid policies	policies to fit workforce
21. employment continuity	security concept	opportunity concept
22. personal aspects	all mechanistic employee recognition	a handshake, a pat on the back, a dozen roses, a recognition lunch with the boss
23. personnel uniqueness	using the personnel office as a haven for leftovers	qualified and experienced personnel specialists
24. personnel practitioners	personnel committees of nonpersonnel members	authority in personnel position and responsibility to "deliver or move out"

What the foregoing list indicates is that the day of "business as usual" is over. Many of our time-worn concepts of personnel management are due for a trip to the laundry. Past practices that are no longer workable should be abandoned. A new outlook is needed, although this does not imply a complete reversal from old values. In fact, the old values should be preserved and applied in a new climate.

The main problems for business are social and political ones, problems of living with other organizations in the society. As contrasted with its employee group, over which it has life and death authority, business will have to deal with many diverse groups over whom it exerts very little direct influence.

As I remind you of the question, "Do we throw away the book and start over?" I would hope to direct your thoughts away from the drift toward impersonal technical procedures back to the human consideration. In the final analysis it is people, not technology, that will determine how useful and effective our personnel programs are.

PERSONNEL AS A MAJOR MANAGEMENT FUNCTION

It is often said, "Personnel has come of age." It may be more accurate to intone, "Personnel is over the hill."

The growing up refers to more and more sophisticated management tools added by the theoreticians to the personnel practitioner's mixed bag of duties. But that very development may be its undoing.

Many observers believe that "Going, going, gone," better describes the fate of the personnel director and his job. After raising the level of the personnel director's position through more sophisticated techniques, academically-trained practitioners, and better all-around performances, the cause may already be all but lost.

The sad commentary is that the personnel directors themselves believe they are emerging as professionals when in fact they are only becoming master mechanics, applying impersonal techniques to the personal side of business.

There are sinister forces working against the personnel director, no matter how dedicated he may be. These are:

1. Top management: looking for more sophistication than they expect to get from the run-of-the-mill personnel programs.
2. Outside consultants: moving like predatory opportunists into a void they help create in order to keep their high-priced staffs busy.
3. The personnel director himself: too complacent with the present level of his position.

The question is: what can personnel management do to gain the recognition it needs to develop properly, and how can the personnel leadership conduct itself to earn its rightful place in the management hierarchy?

The Struggle for Recognition

To illustrate the point let me tell this story. A sales manager died and went to heaven (it's possible!). When he arrived at the Pearly Gates he shook hands with St. Peter very enthusiastically and, of course, began to talk.

"Where," he asked, "do all the good sales managers go?"

"Do you see that nice row of cottages just to the right of the Golden Stairs? Well, that section is reserved for sales managers."

That was fine, thought the sales executive, a location right in front befitting the position.

"And where," he continued, "are some of the other company officials?"

"The comptrollers are in the row next to the sales managers. And behind them are the treasurers."

"Aha," he broke in, "glad to see that divine providence recognizes true executive rank.

St. Peter went on. "Works managers are in the row of cottages immediately to the left of the Golden Stairs. In the second row are the advertising directors, and behind them are the legal advisers."

By this time the sales manager was really wearing his best look of self-satisfaction. Everybody was in prominent places—and properly so —but nowhere in this management row had the personnel social climbers been mentioned.

He wondered how heaven ranked them, so he asked.

"Oh, see that mountain away off in the distance—you can hardly see it."

"Yes," he said, after finally sighting it. "What about it?"

"Well, at the foot of that distant hill is a row of cottages. Those are for the personnel people," he was told.

That did it. And so he commended the divine planning by commenting, "And that's where you think personnel directors belong?"

"No, not exactly," explained St. Peter. "It's just that personnel people are the only ones we can trust out of our sight."

So maybe we'll get our due someday in heaven. But the immediate question is what can we do here on earth?

The Precedent Has Been Set

As a starter, let me suggest that we step back from our daily routine long enough to identify and define the responsibilities of a comprehensive personnel program. Further, we must remain alert to the opportunity that is ours; otherwise, our chances of fulfilling our obligation will erode as certain functions—usually high-level ones—are delegated elsewhere or are usurped by others. This trend will leave the personnel director with more administrative duties and less authority, more detail and less influence, and more doing and less thinking. If we're not careful, the personnel director could go off the organization chart and into industrial oblivion.

By way of corollary, let's analyze the job of the office manager. Years ago every well-run company had an office manager who looked after the nonproductive aspects of business operations, the office duties referred to in accounting courses as "burden." Essentially he was trusted to keep the office running smoothly at the lowest cost. He hired the clerical help he needed, purchased supplies and equipment, distributed work and shifted people around, doing whatever was necessary to make workers productive, thereby keeping overhead down. He supervised order billing, mail, files, switchboard, payroll, credit, accounts receivable and payable, claims, housekeeping and other services that supported the main functions of manufacturing and selling.

It was a good job. The office manager held his head high and wore his suit coat. He was hired by the owners, but he had no financial stake in the enterprise. One thing was clear: as far as the office force was concerned, he was the boss. He was looked up to and respected, and he enjoyed the prestige of his lofty position.

As the office became bigger and more complicated, he had to struggle to keep apace of progress. Unfortunately, the office manager usually did not grow as fast as his job. In some cases, he was content with his managerial position and had neither the talent nor the inclination to rise further. In most cases, however, he simply got himself so bogged down in details, trying to respond to accelerating pressures from all directions, that he had to be rescued. His duties were divided and several specialized managers moved into his territory. He was so busy "doing" that he no longer had time to reflect on what was happening.

While all this was going on a new corporate officer began emerging on the management scene. This was the comptroller who, two generations ago, did not even exist. He filled the void created by the office manager. Because he was unencumbered with day-to-day duties of supervising the details, he moved fast and high. Almost from the start he was a top executive, sitting in top management councils. Today the comptroller is firmly ensconced in the executive ranks.

As further proof of this development, it can be noted that some years ago the National Office Management Association, a very worthwhile organization, changed its name to the Administrative Management Society because of a gradually dwindling membership. There just were not enough executives around anymore with the title of office manager. Dr. George R. Terry has just completed the seventh revision of his very popular and successful textbook, *Office Management and Control.* But he is quick to point out in the introduction that he is no longer aiming at the office manager but rather anyone who manages a section, group or function in the office.

Personnel is Falling Into the Same Pit

Now the same kind of job deterioration is affecting the personnel director and endangering his position in the organization. Overburdened in a rapidly worsening climate, he finds himself inundated with a flood of paperwork until he finally directs a coldly-impersonal personnel program. His own difficulties increase in number and scope, employees become more vocal on issues affecting them, the company becomes concerned with its people problems, and impatience and criticism from internal and external sources cause him to react until he is too preoccupied to act.

In this confusing situation, when the hustle-and-bustle of everyday personnel activities gives the impression of falling short of expectations, everybody tries to be helpful. First the personnel director goes to the outside for assistance, not necessarily because he lacks the ability but simply because he does not have the horses to please everybody.

Next, his company tries to assist and, through the appointment of high-level committees, whose nonpersonnel members rely more upon their authority and selfish interests than their understanding and objectivity, institutes or revises employee programs for the personnel director to administer. Finally, top management executives, recognizing their own shortcomings in a potent and volatile field, turn to the professional consultants for ideas and guidance.

With the invasion of the outside consultants comes a new approach to personnel relations—the application of prepackaged ideas, gimmick projects and costly perpetuation of their involvement. When this happens, the average personnel director is doomed because he is overwhelmed.

There is a place for consultants in practically every area of management in today's complex industrial machinery. But something is out of kilter when a company has more faith in strangers with their paper credentials (who, incidentally, need no license or certification) than it does in its own familiar personnel leadership, against whom a whole list of shortcomings can be imagined. It will always remain a mystery how a specialist from a consulting firm can rearrange an organization or redesign a system better than the executives who not only know the problem but who also have a stake in resolving it successfully.

The beauty of the consultant's involvement is that it does not require him to live with the results of his recommendations. In all too many instances the one who engineered the dramatic overhaul with its subsequent impact is often not around a year later to face the consequences. Sometimes he is even out of the consulting field altogether.

Who is Responsible?

The reason the consultants are in the picture is that the personnel director has made this necessary. If the personnel director and his staff were doing their jobs, the need for outside assistance would not exist. If the employment manager were doing his job, the search firm would not be called upon. If the salary administrator were doing his job, the wage specialist would not be engaged to design an incentive plan. If the job analyst were doing his job, no outsider would be brought in to install a job evaluation system. If the counsellor really understood the needs of the workforce, he would not have to step aside and let the company's lawyers take over during a union-organizing drive. If the training director were doing more than acting as a classroom instructor, he would set up the career path charting that established meaningful training opportunities. If the personnel program were effective, it would not take a sociologist to conduct the morale survey to tell management what it already knows, or should know.

In short, when the vice-president of personnel becomes the meal ticket for a consultant, then he is inadequate in his position and unworthy of his executive standing. There is absolutely no justification for having two high-salaried people in one job; one or the other is unnecessary.

The big reason for the overuse of consultants is the necessity to perpetuate themselves in their client's affairs in order to keep their high-priced staffs working. They give a "yes" answer to any problem that is posed and make a project out of each assignment.

Because of the significance they attach to their work, the unprecedented latitude they are accorded, and the prices they charge, they get acceptance. As the president of a billion-dollar corporation explained, "I don't pay that kind of money and then disregard their recommendations." Their whole approach is dogmatic. The consultants enjoy a built-in advantage.

The consultants start off with the personal endorsement of top management (which the personnel director never sought nor received openly). They get a busy executive to accommodate them during prime time (because while they are on the premises the meter is running). They are able to introduce new programs or change existing programs simply because they are accepted as experts, something seldom questioned. One may wonder whether some of their staff specialists become better qualified because they are on the payroll of a consulting firm instead of that of a client company.

There is Yet a Bigger Threat

As though the consultants having a field day with company personnel programs were not enough, there is an even more sinister danger. And it is more insidious. That is the encroachment into company personnel leadership positions by the behavioral scientists.

Top management, which has never really understood the personnel director or the role he tries to fulfill in applying human relations to business, is impressed with the behavioral science perspective. This creates a new excitement for them. Throughout the history of personnel administration, top management has delegated to the central personnel office all sorts of unwanted tasks, such as recruiting, record keeping and report filing, but has been unwilling to relinquish control. It has viewed the personnel activity as only a bookkeeping service to higher management.

Like other departmental activities, personnel has become lackluster and lost its allure as conditions and topside indifference reduced it to a mundane operation. To the top management policy planners it is tired, stale, uneventful and in need of a shot in the arm.

In this context, top management gives orders and direction to the personnel people, but does not consult with them as equals or as experts in their field. Here is where the behavioral scientists come in. Top management is captivated by the mystique, which they do not comprehend, but which they support rather than reveal their ignorance.

When top management and the behavioral scientists talk to each other they discuss the present personnel program, its shortcomings, the unimaginative staff and the lack of sophistication. They don't talk about filling jobs or raising the wage level; those conversations are too plebeian. The discussions deal in abstractions, heavily "interfaced" with other technical buzzwords. Motivation, which nobody ever defines in everyday language, is a popular topic.

The New Order of Things

The president enjoys the attention he is getting and giving (in an area where he gave little attention before), he likes what he calls action (without evaluating it), and he decides this is the new order of things. He envisions a progressive, dynamic, sophisticated employee program to reinforce the steady, methodical, sensible personnel program that for years has somehow been keeping jobs filled, wages current, production rewarded, benefits administered, and records and reports straight.

With that kind of blessing, the behavioral scientists have muscled in. This is the new order in many prominent companies today. Let the practical personnel department struggle along with its activities (someone has to do the daily work) and let the experts do the thinking. What's wrong with that combination? It covers all aspects of the employee program—those elements that are being done and additional ones that should be. It satisfies all the interests of management—the planners and the doers. Conceivably it may result in some degree of improvement for employees.

This is a good theory. In actual practice it doesn't seem to be working out that way. Technical expertise in the field of personnel relations has evolved and expanded but attitudes and conduct of the practitioners have not improved. The same signs of ossification that are evident in our governments, our churches, our school system, our courts and our penal system are very noticeable in personnel administration. More devices are invented but results get worse. In industry as in life, the more progress we make along scientific and technological lines the more we seem to fester problems in human relations.

The behavioral scientists have been making inroads with their mysterious theories while letting human relations deteriorate into a collection of unrelated, impersonal procedures. The new breed of personnel people like to research, study, survey, quantify and distill human conduct, overlooking the fact that there is work to be done. With their graphs and flip charts they impress management and are rewarded with the titles, prestige, privileges and higher salaries.

Their acceptance by management is merely another manifestation of top management weakness in which the senior officers labor under the mistaken notion that their positions of authority automatically carry with them the corresponding necessary wisdom when, in fact, very few can actually distinguish between good and bad advice. But at their level they don't have to make this distinction; all they have to do is make the decisions.

So Now What?

Where does this leave the personnel director and his thankless job? He is relegated to middle management mediocrity where his duties are tolerated but his counsel not sought. He can take his place alongside the office manager, another vanishing breed.

Alongside the comptroller and other corporate officers now sits the behavioral scientist who took over the leadership of the personnel program, dolled up with the fancy label of human resources. Think of it—a cold, calculating scientist heading the one company function that is least adaptable to logic and reason.

This is the picture as it already exists in many companies. Other companies in which this has not yet happened are cautioned: this may be the direction in which personnel administration in general is heading. The outsider is trying to get inside.

Whether the personnel director brings in the consultant or top management does, it will follow that the consultant will play on the inadequacies of the personnel program that make his services necessary. Then to justify his continued involvement he will stress the abstract behavioral science approach, which is like hitting below the belt because this is where the average "good guy" personnel director is vulnerable and the easiest place to discredit him in the eyes of top management.

Is it too late to stem the tide and reverse the trend? Personnel directors who are beginning to see the handwriting on the wall and want to try to redirect their efforts should take stock of the situation in which they find themselves.

There are two contributing factors to this shift in direction, both of which reveal the complacency of the personnel director who is letting this happen. First, the company top executives don't look to him beyond a certain point, and second, he has failed to deliver a total package of personnel management, being comfortable with his day-to-day routine. He is so busy putting out endless little fires, so eager to please everybody, and so protective of the importance of his position, that he has grown smug. He has no time to innovate or add programs that today's circumstances require.

The Personnel Director Must Re-establish Himself

Anyone who recognizes the situation as described here must conclude that the personnel director has slotted himself and his function somewhere in the middle of the organization, short of the higher-level position that the responsibility and opportunity call for. Unless he can re-establish himself as a corporate executive, fully accountable for the total area of employee utilization, he will be asked to move over and yield the importance of the position to other forces.

It can be avoided, and in the best interest of all—companies, personnel directors and employees—it should be avoided. To accomplish this, however, requires abandoning the status quo and sincere rededication on the part of three facets of the present problem.

1. A company should give its personnel director a chance to deliver by giving him the recognition, authority and support he needs, by relinquishing control that rightfully belongs to his position, and by holding him accountable for developing and maintaining a comprehensive program for the best utilization of the firm's human resources.

2. The consultants, if their services are needed, should be contracted for by the personnel officer and do his bidding, not theirs, to avoid working at cross purposes and embarking on a collision course, since working together in one common cause is the only course that will produce the desired result.

3. The personnel director, who lacks the outsider's advantage of dramatic impact, should build a complete and well-balanced employee program that fits the personal needs of the workforce and the objectives of the company, that changes with the changing climate, and that demonstrates an irrefutable effectiveness by quality performance.

This is a large order and will not be accomplished overnight. But every right move is a step in the right direction. The momentum will develop as the results prove their value.

There is Hope

We have always liked to believe that somewhere up yonder, beyond the moon's purple dust, there is a special Heaven, a cosmic corner set aside for personnel executives who have fought the good fight and kept the faith.

In the corporate hereafter there will be no problems, at least no insurmountable problems—only the final fulfillment of all the solutions we tried so hard to promote on earth. It will be a paradise of no turnover, built-in recruitment, no strikes over wages and working conditions, no petty grievances or complaints, no special interest groups, no misguided or selfish motivations. We'll have our own Gabriel, (perhaps in the person of Dartnell), and in a prominent place on this hallowed ground will be a Hall of Fame for all the unrecognized, but deserving, personnel practitioners who labored so faithfully in the cause of human dignity.

Inside the emerald ark will rest a sacred document whose title, lettered in gold, reads: *"Personnel Administration Handbook."*

It's a lovely dream. I relate it not from a spiritual dedication to our profession but rather to emphasize that the perfect personnel executive and the perfect personnel program are not to be found on earth. Many personnel directors and many companies may feel they have reached perfection, but the hidden imperfections have a way of rising to the surface to penetrate this wholly unrealistic belief.

To get back to our original question: what can we do here on earth? Let's not strive for perfection; that is a totally unrealistic goal. Let's be satisfied to make progress toward that goal; that in itself would be quite a noble achievement.

INDEX

INDEX

INDEX

INDEX

INDEX

INDEX

INDEX

INDEX

INDEX

INDEX

INDEX

INDEX

INDEX

INDEX

INDEX

INDEX

INDEX

INDEX

INDEX

INDEX

INDEX

INDEX